Volumes 1·2·3

Natsumi Ando

**Translated and adapted by
Andria Cheng**

**Lettered by
North Market Street Graphics**

Ballantine Books ∗ New York

A Del Rey Manga/Kodansha Trade Paperback Original

Published in the United States by Del Rey, an imprint of The Random House Publishing Group, a division of Random House, Inc., New York.

DEY REY is a registered trademark and the Del Rey colophon is a trademark of Random House, Inc.

Publication rights arranged through Kodansha Ltd.

First published in Japan in 2003 and 2004 by Kodansha Ltd., Tokyo

ISBN 978-0-345-51577-3

Printed in the United States of America

www.delreymanga.com

2 4 6 8 9 7 5 3 1

Translator/Adapter: Andria Cheng
Lettering: North Market Street Graphics

Honorifics Explained

Throughout the Del Rey Manga books, you will find Japanese honorifics left intact in the translations. For those not familiar with how the Japanese use honorifics and, more important, how they differ from American honorifics, we present this brief overview.

Politeness has always been a critical facet of Japanese culture. Ever since the feudal era, when Japan was a highly stratified society, use of honorifics—which can be defined as polite speech that indicates relationship or status—has played an essential role in the Japanese language. When addressing someone in Japanese, an honorific usually takes the form of a suffix attached to one's name (example: "Asuna-san"), is used as a title at the end of one's name, or appears in place of the name itself (example: "Negi-sensei," or simply "Sensei").

Honorifics can be expressions of respect or endearment. In the context of manga and anime, honorifics give insight into the nature of the relationship between characters. Many English translations leave out these important honorifics and therefore distort the feel of the original Japanese. Because Japanese honorifics contain nuances that English honorifics lack, it is our policy at Del Rey not to translate them. Here, instead, is a guide to some of the honorifics you may encounter in Del Rey Manga.

-*san*:   This is the most common honorific and is equivalent to Mr., Miss, Ms., or Mrs. It is the all-purpose honorific and can be used in any situation where politeness is required.

-*sama*: This is one level higher than "-san" and is used to confer great respect.

-*dono*: This comes from the word "tono," which means "lord." It is an even higher level than "-sama" and confers utmost respect.

-kun: This suffix is used at the end of boys' names to express familiarity or endearment. It is also sometimes used by men among friends, or when addressing someone younger or of a lower station.

-chan: This is used to express endearment, mostly toward girls. It is also used for little boys, pets, and even among lovers. It gives a sense of childish cuteness.

Bozu: This is an informal way to refer to a boy, similar to the English terms "kid" and "squirt."

Sempai/
Senpai: This title suggests that the addressee is one's senior in a group or organization. It is most often used in a school setting, where underclassmen refer to their upperclassmen as "sempai." It can also be used in the workplace, such as when a newer employee addresses an employee who has seniority in the company.

Kohai: This is the opposite of "sempai" and is used toward underclassmen in school or newcomers in the workplace. It connotes that the addressee is of a lower station.

Sensei: Literally meaning "one who has come before," this title is used for teachers, doctors, or masters of any profession or art.

-[blank]: This is usually forgotten in these lists, but it is perhaps the most significant difference between Japanese and English. The lack of honorific means that the speaker has permission to address the person in a very intimate way. Usually, only family, spouses, or very close friends have this kind of permission. Known as *yobisute*, it can be gratifying when someone who has earned the intimacy starts to call one by one's name without an honorific. But when that intimacy hasn't been earned, it can be very insulting.

WILD @ Heart

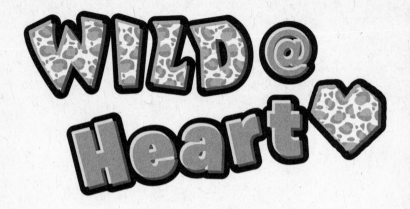

Volume 1

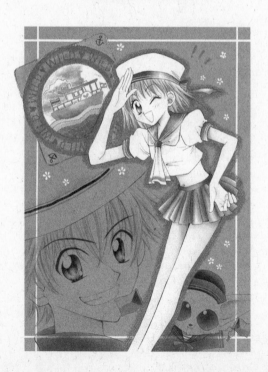

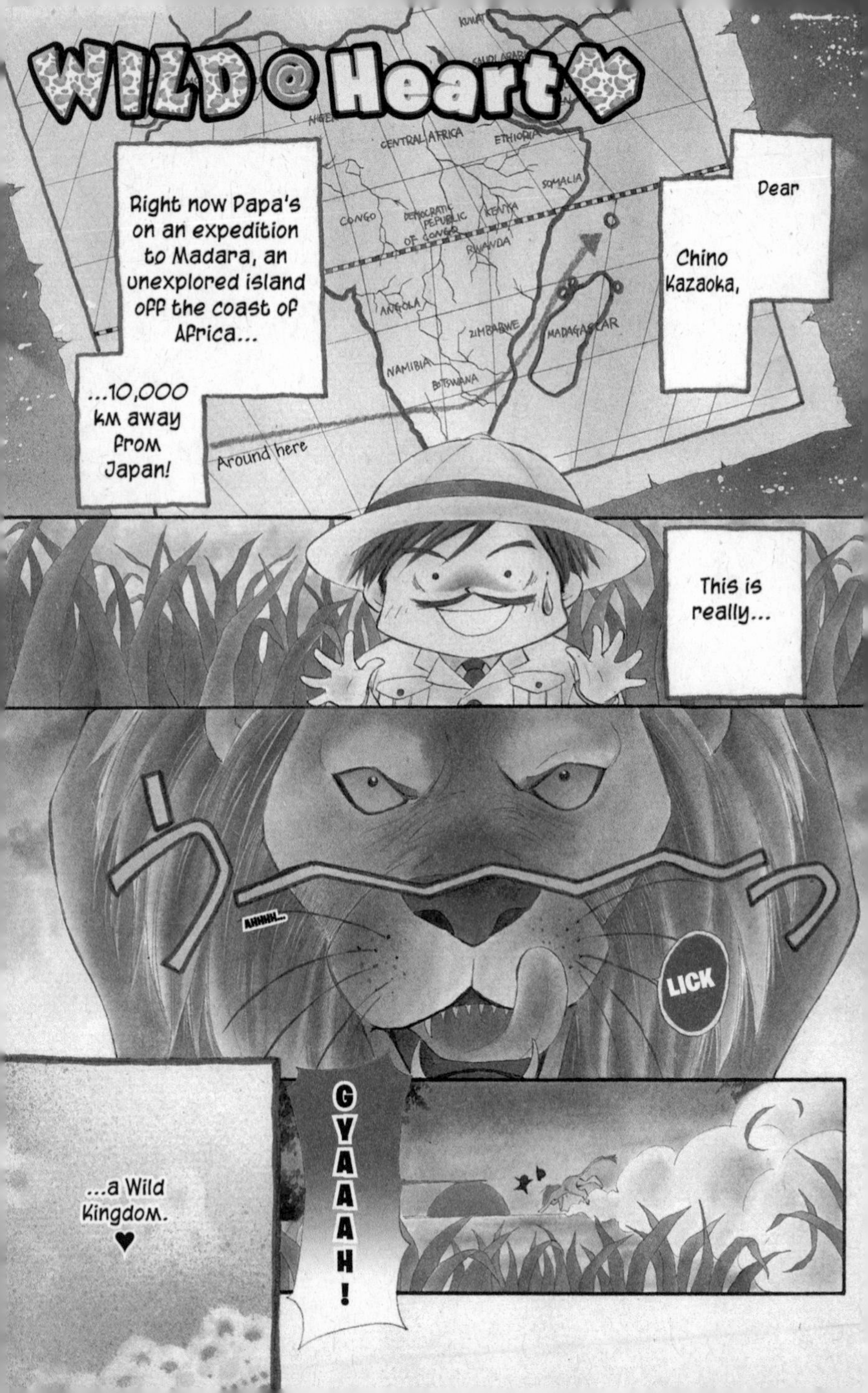
WILD @ Heart ♥
Dear Chino Kazaoka,
Right now Papa's on an expedition to Madara, an unexplored island off the coast of Africa...
...10,000 km away from Japan!
CENTRAL AFRICA
ETHIOPIA
SOMALIA
CONGO
DEMOCRATIC REPUBLIC OF CONGO
KENYA
RWANDA
ANGOLA
ZIMBABWE
MADAGASCAR
NAMIBIA
BOTSWANA
Around here
This is really...
AHHHH...
LICK
GYAAAAH!
...a Wild Kingdom. ♥

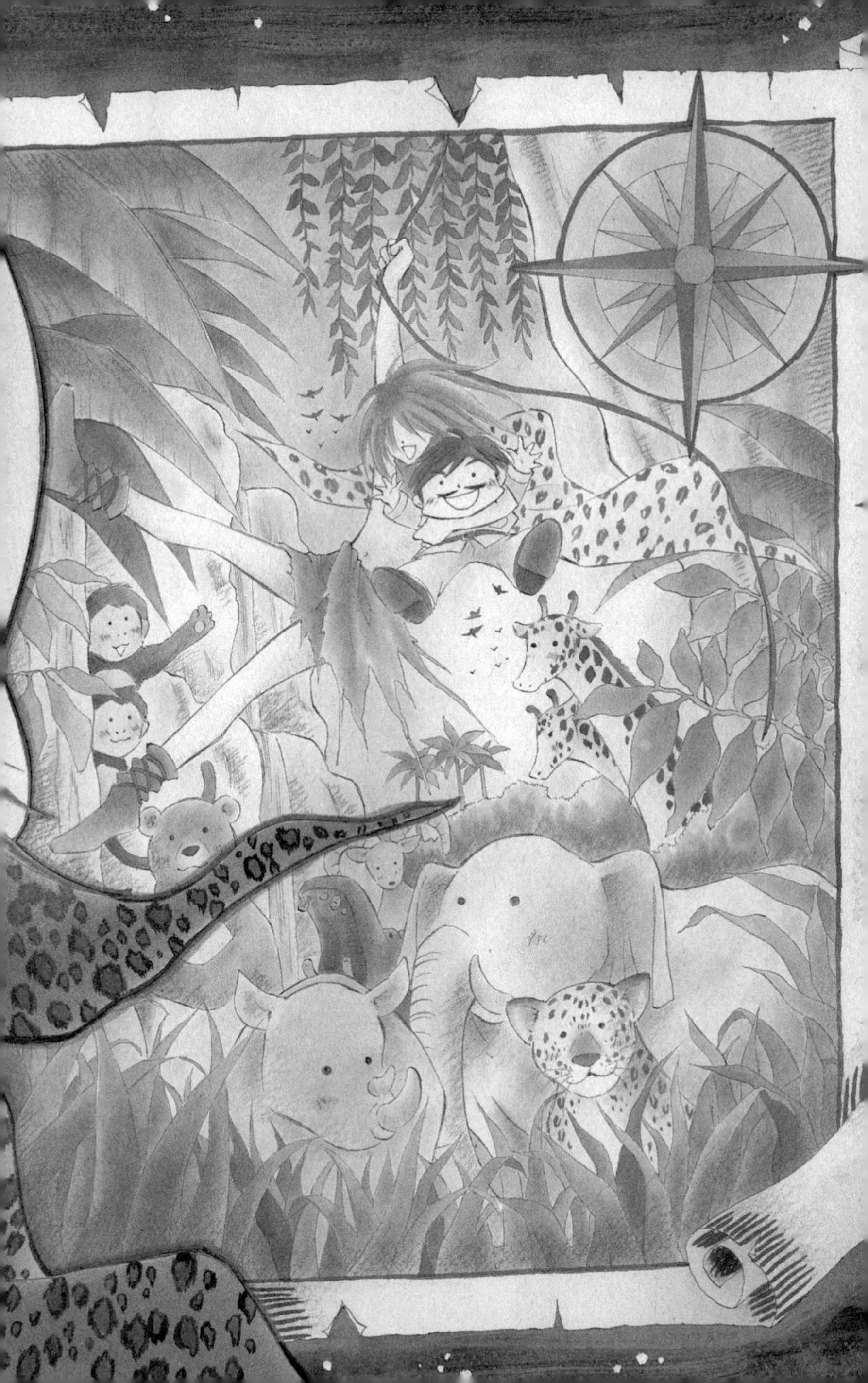

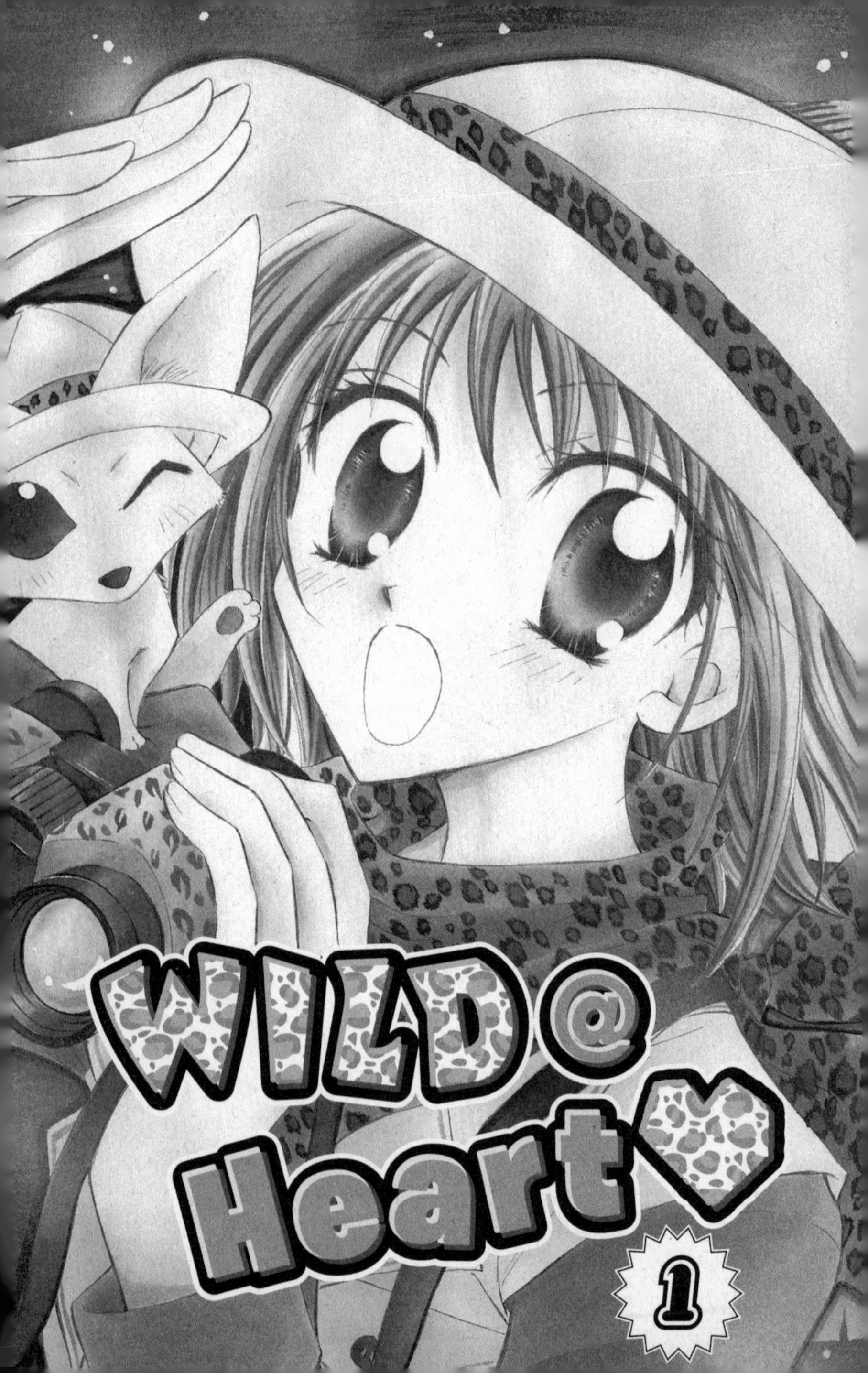
WILD @ Heart
1

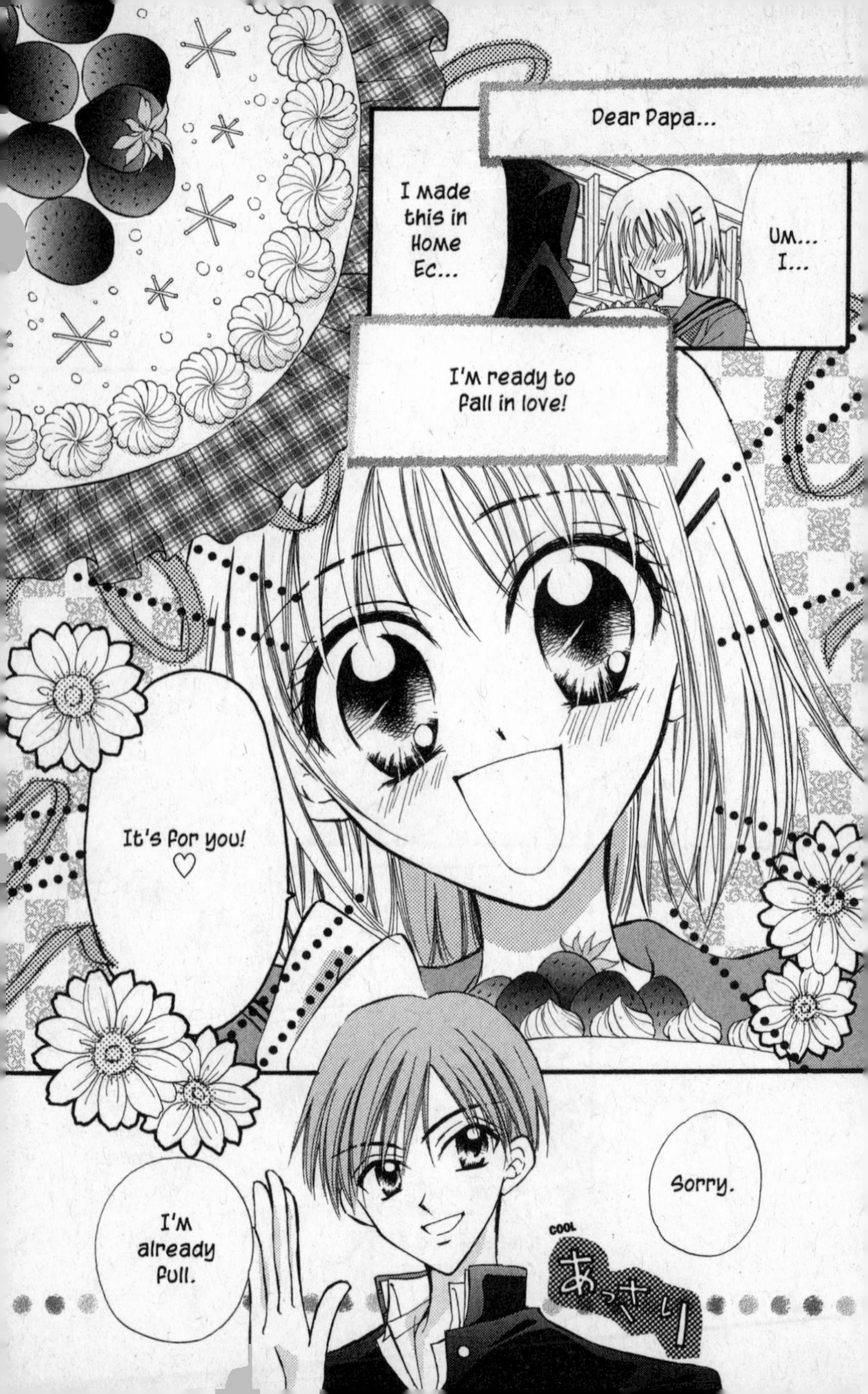
Dear Papa...
Um... I...
I made this in Home Ec...
I'm ready to fall in love!
It's for you! ♡
Sorry.
COOL
あっさり
I'm already full.

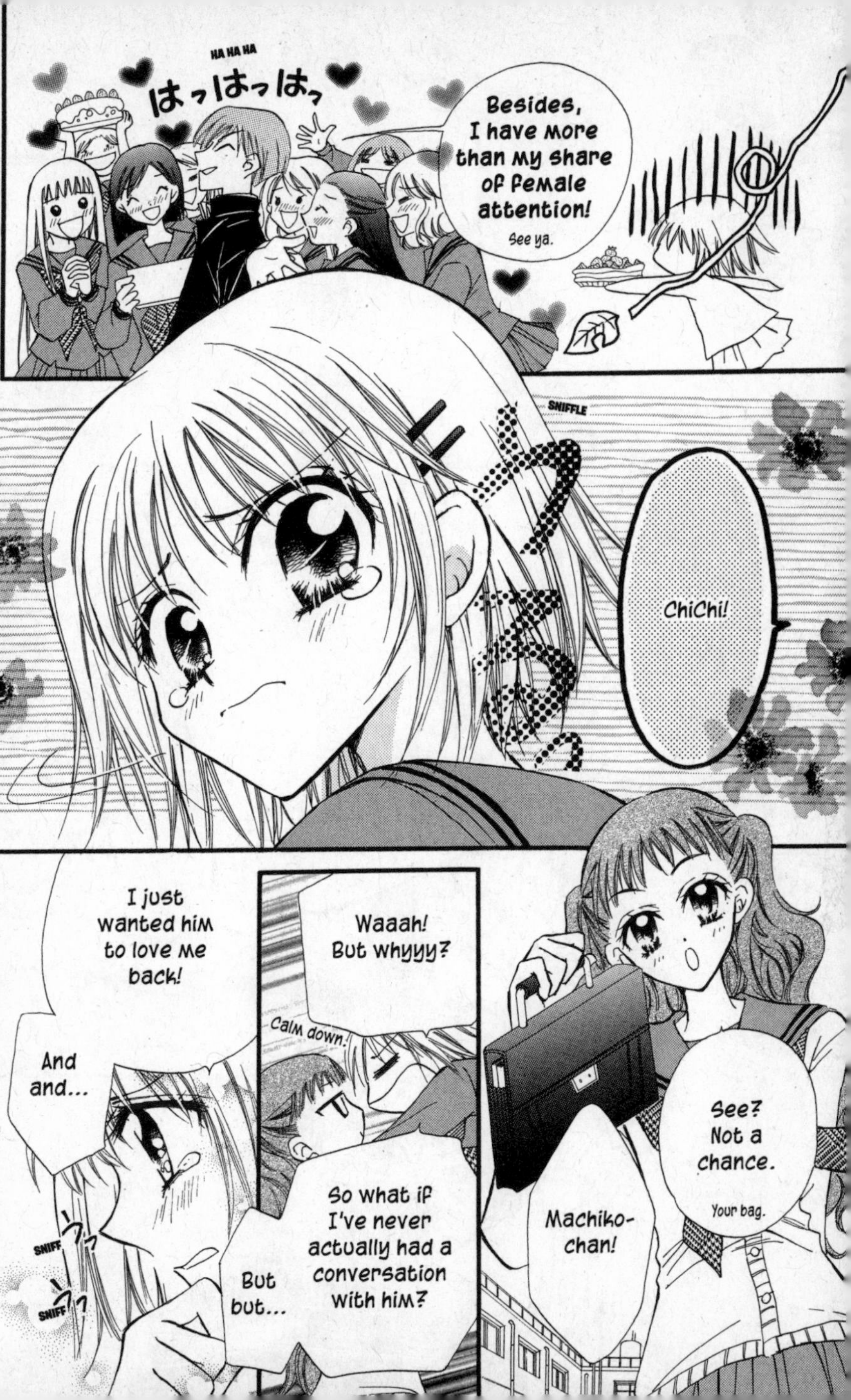
HA HA HA
はっはっはっ
Besides, I have more than my share of female attention!
See ya.
SNIFFLE
ChiChi!
See? Not a chance.
Your bag.
Machiko-chan!
Waaah! But whyyy?
Calm down.
So what if I've never actually had a conversation with him?
But but...
I just wanted him to love me back!
And and...
SNIFF
SNIFF

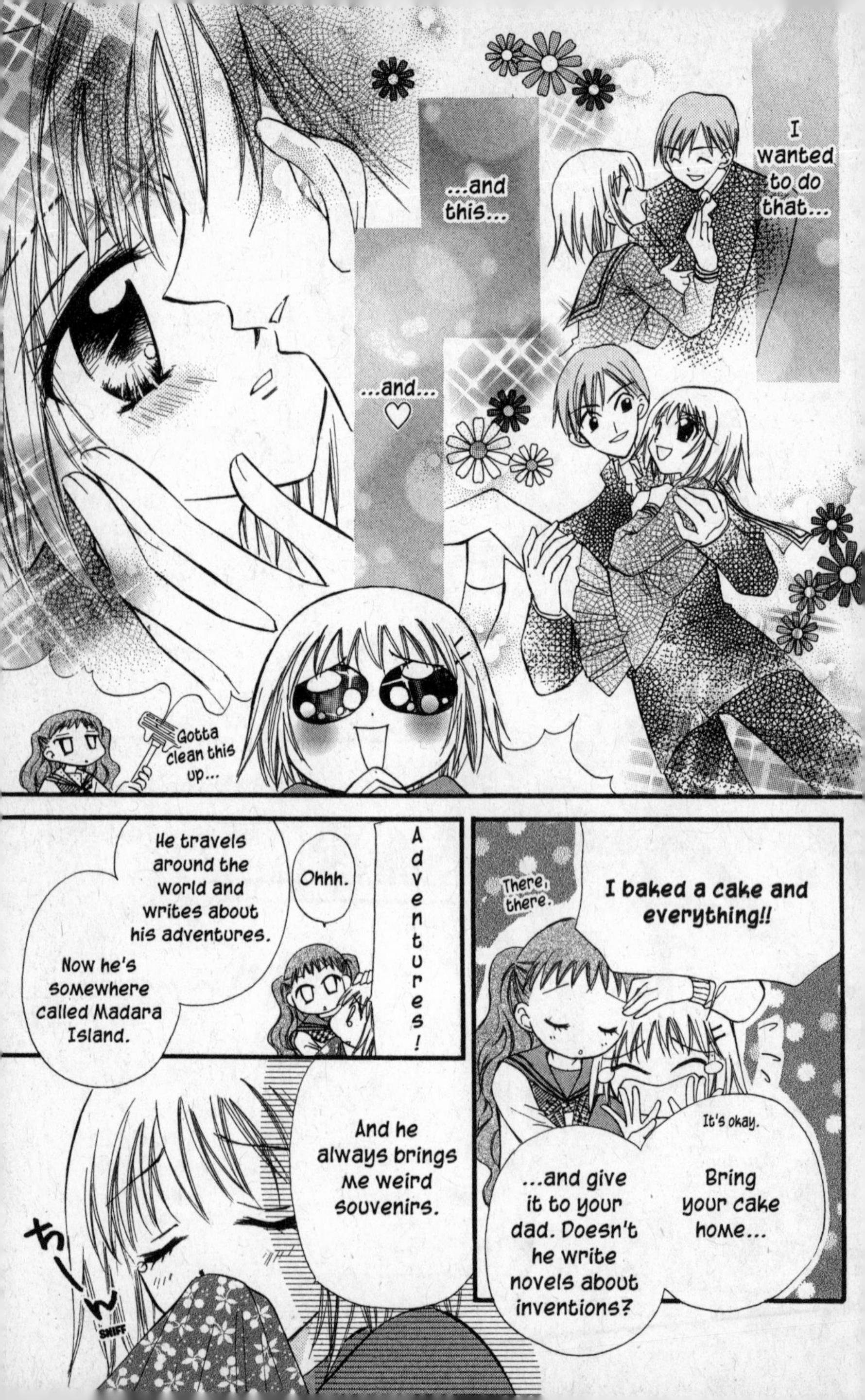

I wanted to do that...
...and this...
...and... ♡
Gotta clean this up...
I baked a cake and everything!!
There, there.
It's okay.
Bring your cake home...
...and give it to your dad. Doesn't he write novels about inventions?
Adventures!
Ohhh.
He travels around the world and writes about his adventures.
Now he's somewhere called Madara Island.
And he always brings me weird souvenirs.
ち～ん
SNIFF

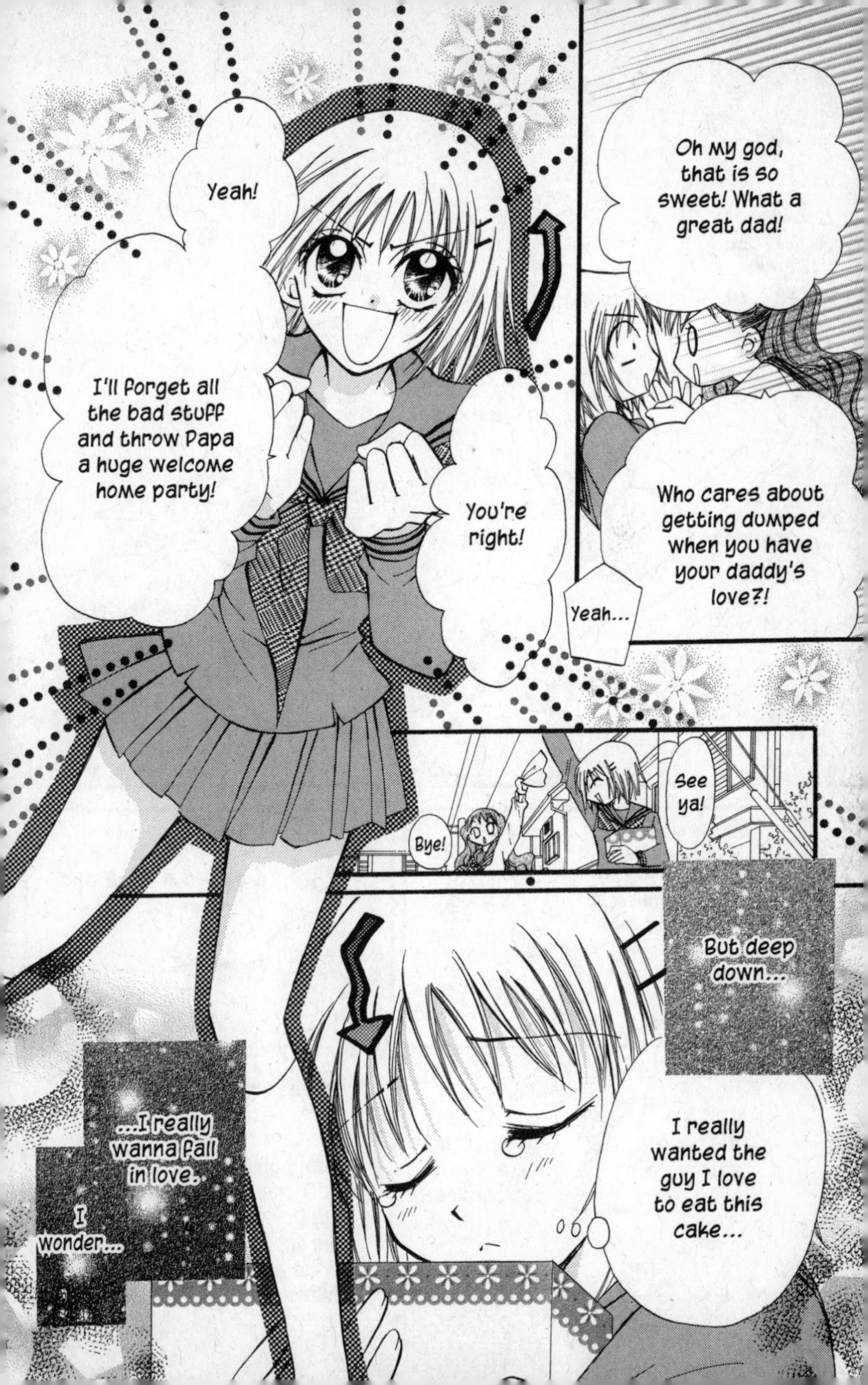
Oh my god, that is so sweet! What a great dad!
Who cares about getting dumped when you have your daddy's love?!
Yeah...
You're right!
Yeah!
I'll forget all the bad stuff and throw Papa a huge welcome home party!
See ya!
Bye!
But deep down...
I really wanted the guy I love to eat this cake...
...I really wanna fall in love.
I wonder...

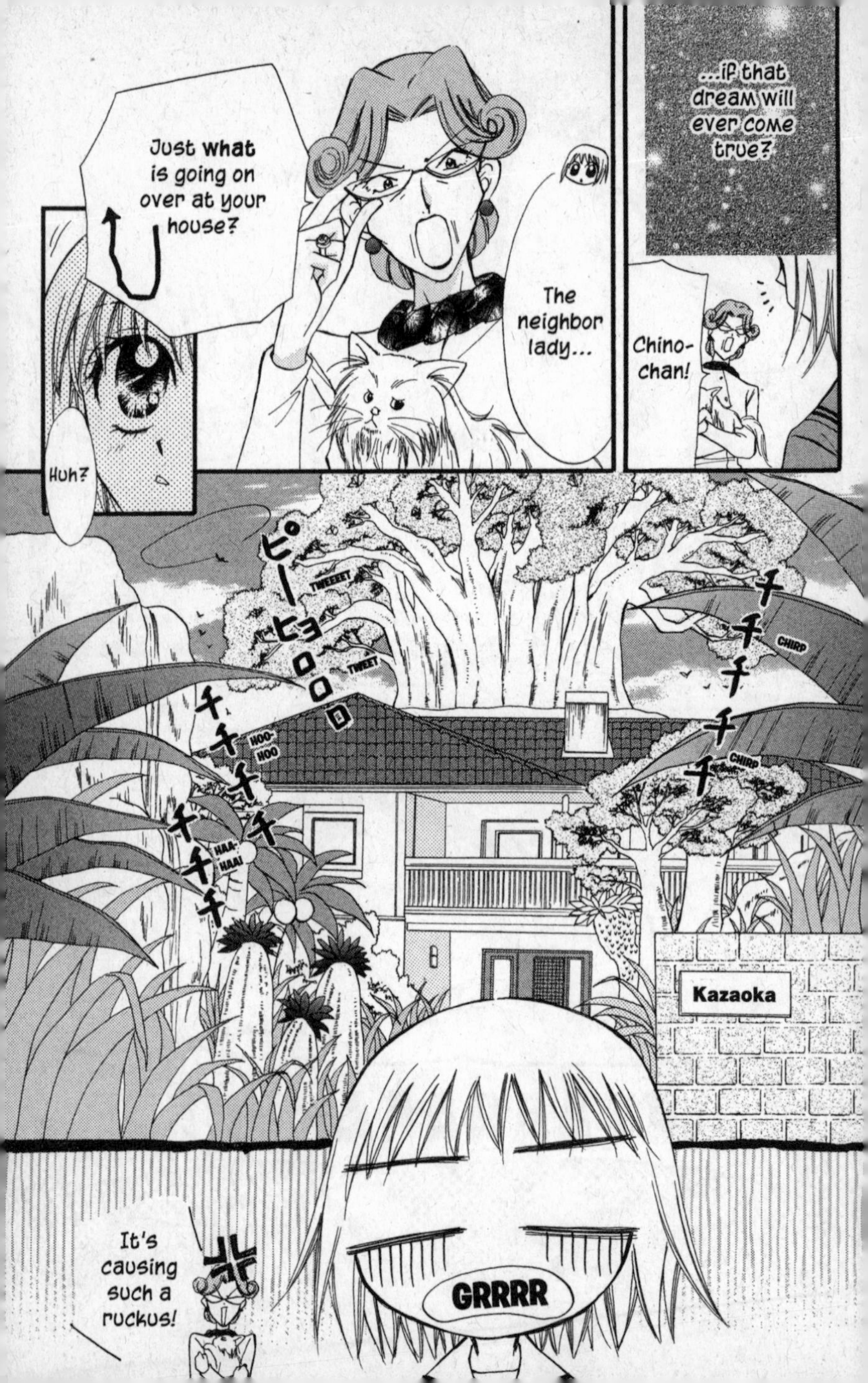
...if that dream will ever come true?
Chino-chan!
The neighbor lady...
Just what is going on over at your house?
Huh?
チチチチチ
CHIRP
CHIRP
ピーヒョロロロ
TWEEEET
TWEET
チチチチチチチ
HOO-HOO
HAA-HAA
Kazaoka
GRRRR
It's causing such a ruckus!

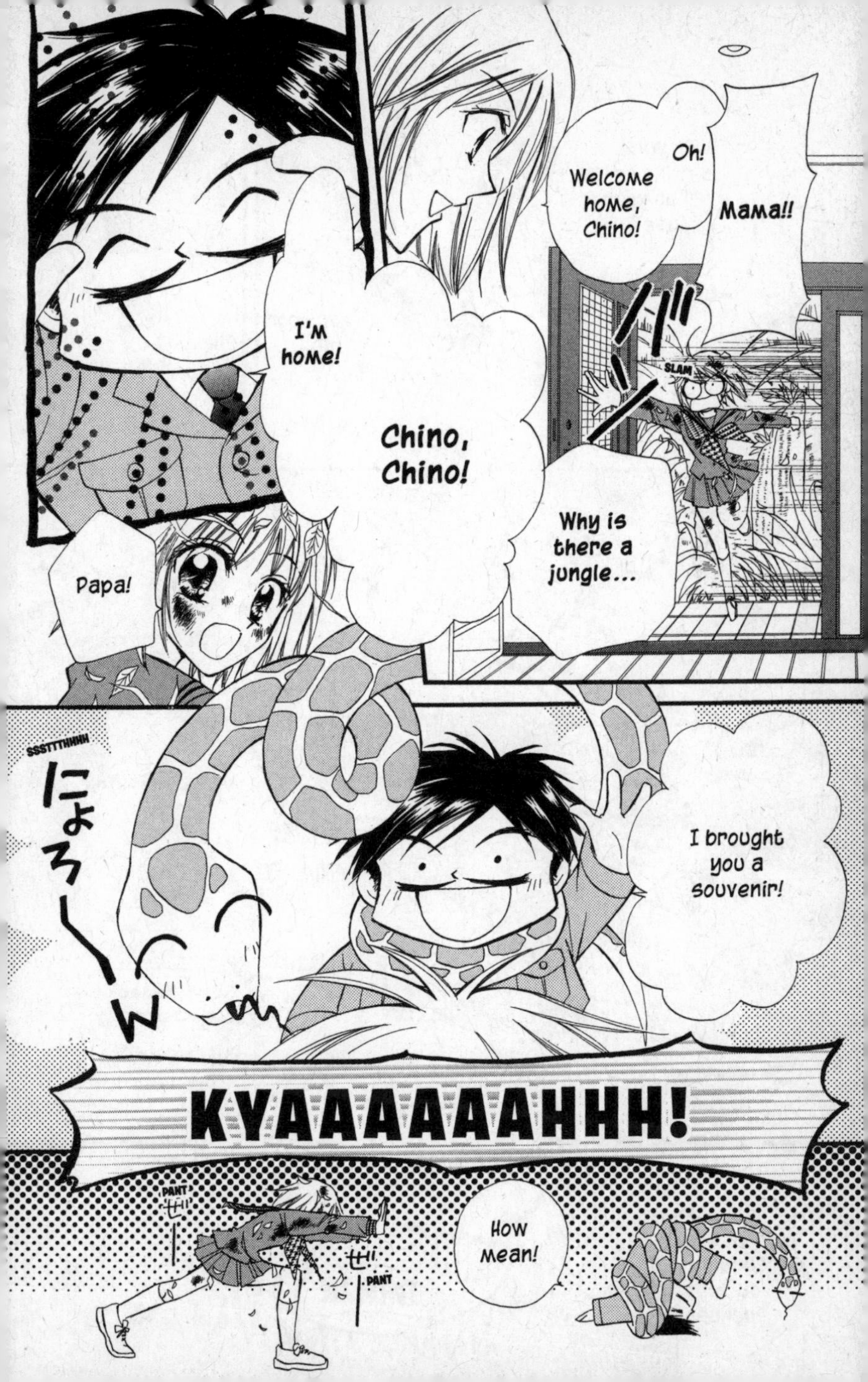
Mama!!
Oh!
Welcome home, Chino!
SLAM
Why is there a jungle...
I'm home!
Chino, Chino!
Papa!
I brought you a souvenir!
SSSTTTHHHH
にょろ〜
KYAAAAAAHHH!
How mean!
PANT
PANT

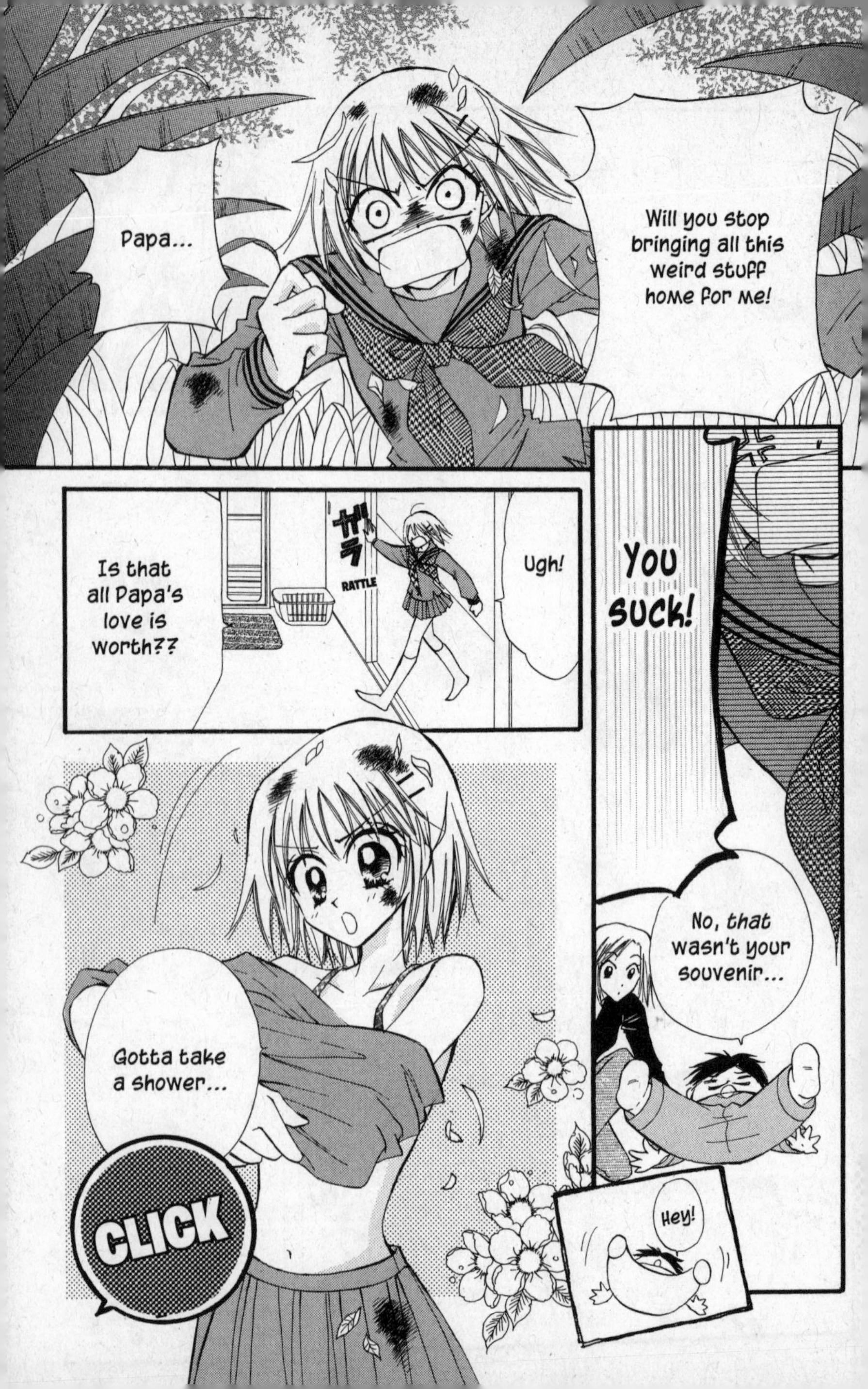

Will you stop bringing all this weird stuff home for me!
Papa...
YOU SUCK!
No, that wasn't your souvenir...
Hey!
Ugh!
ガラ
RATTLE
Is that all Papa's love is worth??
Gotta take a shower...
CLICK

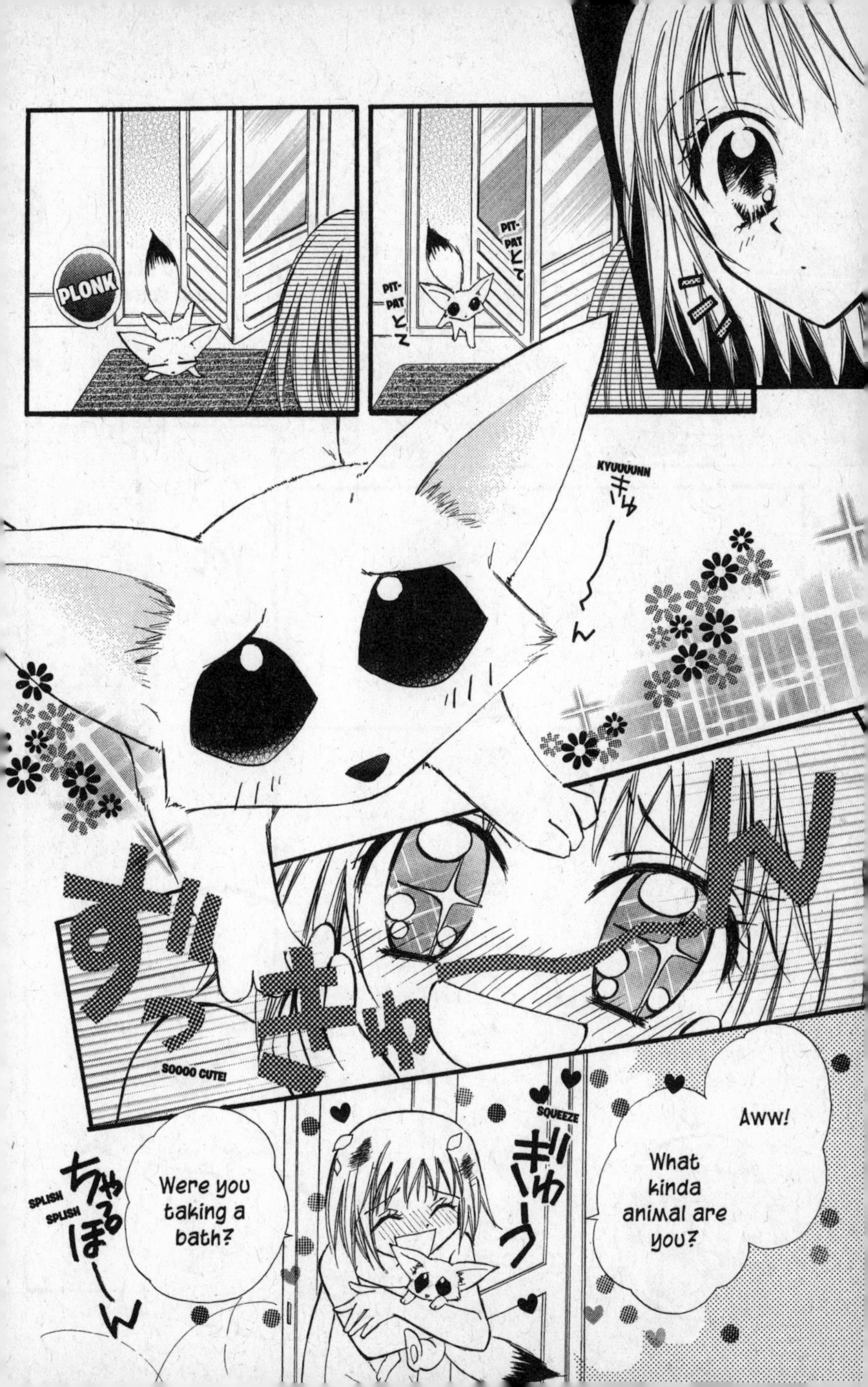
PIT-PAT
PIT-PAT
PLONK
KYUUUUNN
SOOOO CUTE!
Aww!
What kinda animal are you?
SQUEEZE
Were you taking a bath?
SPLISH SPLISH

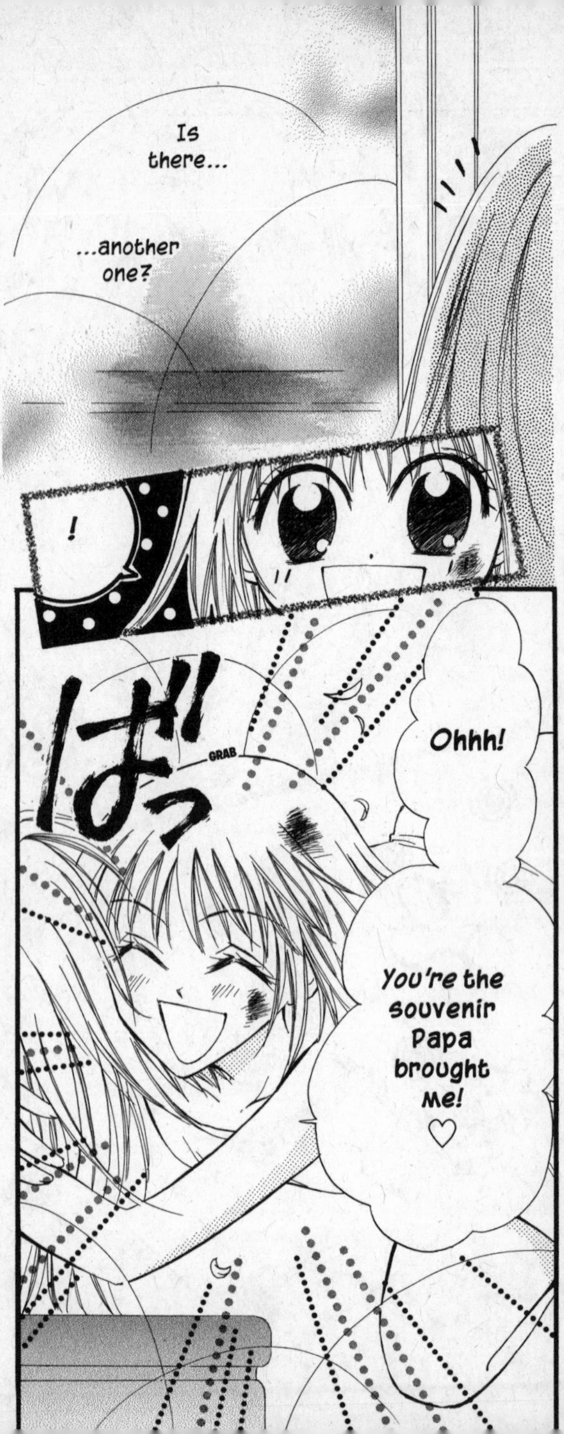
Is there...
...another one?
!
ばっ
GRAB
Ohhh!
You're the souvenir Papa brought me! ♡

1.

Nice to meet you, I'm Natsumi Ando! Thanks for picking up a copy of *Wild @ Heart*! ♥

Mwah ♥

HEHE

I drew the cover a bit differently than I usually do. The protagonist takes up a smaller portion of it. I haven't seen the finished product yet so I hope the balance is okay. I made the hearts from ribbons, so I hope that turned out great, too. It looked good on the color copy. I love looking at wrapping paper. I always think, "Oh, this is so cute, why can't I make something like this?" I don't think I'd make very good wrapping paper, though.

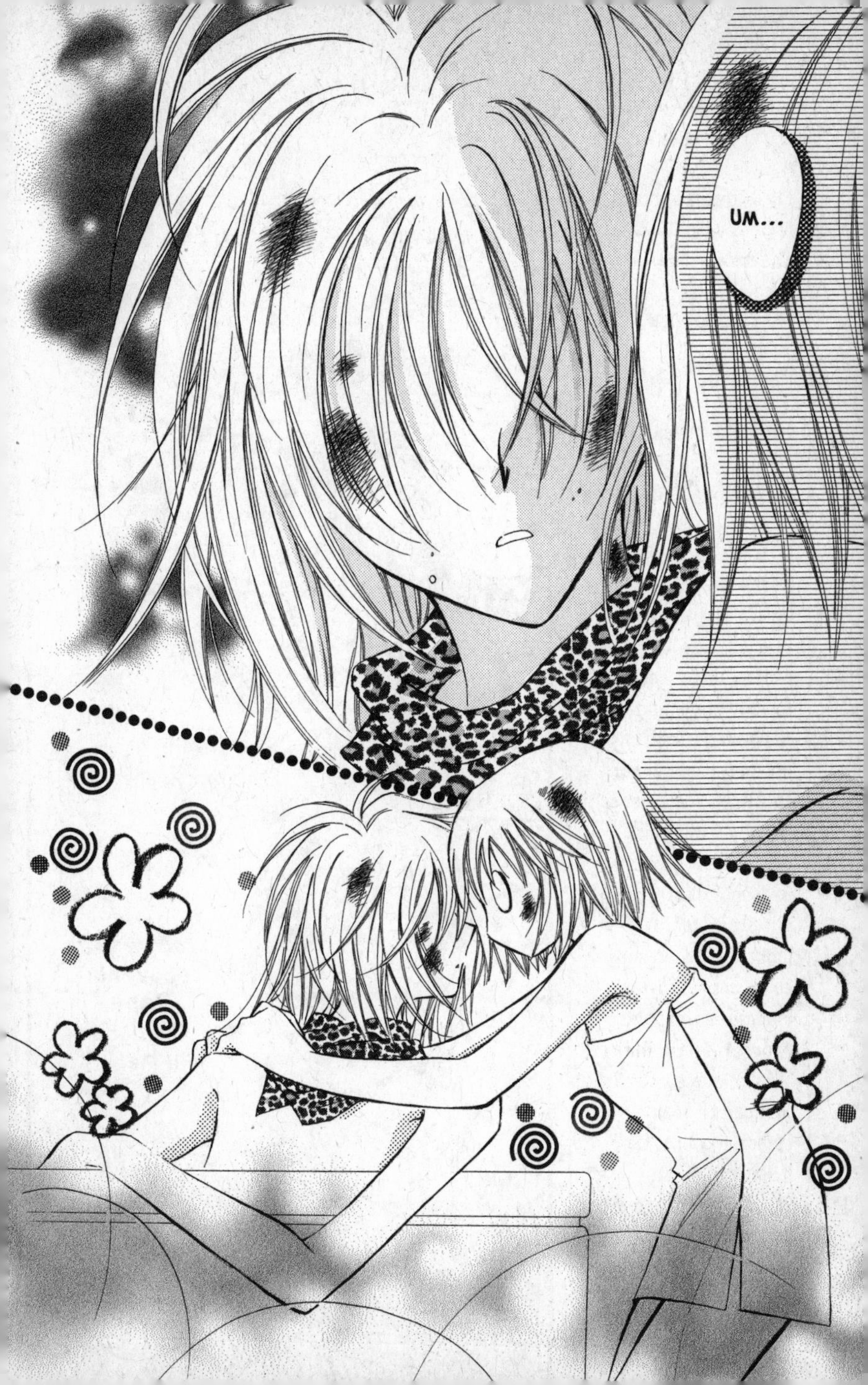
UM...

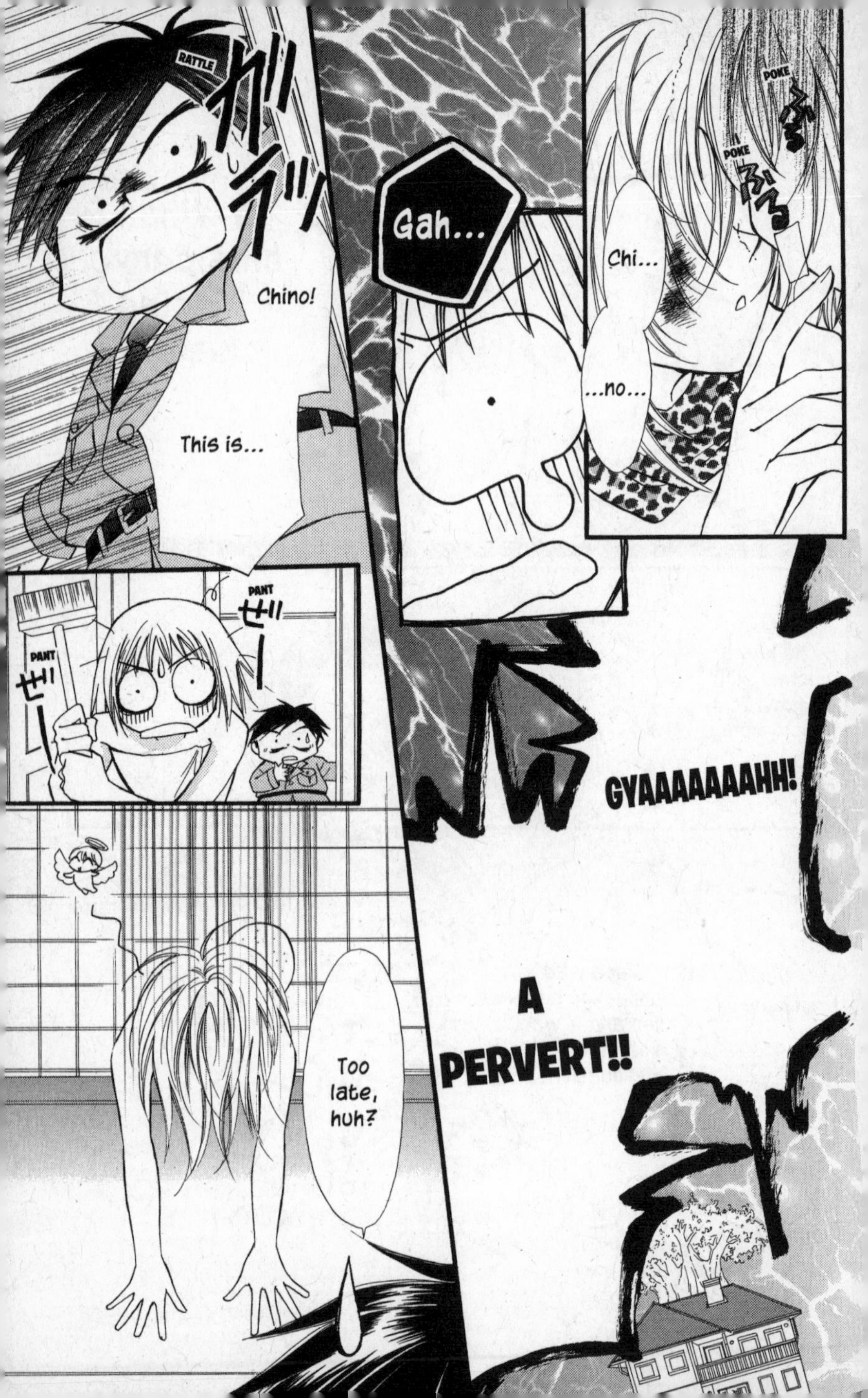

POKE
POKE
Chi...
...no...
Gah...
RATTLE
Chino!
This is...
GYAAAAAAAHH!
A
PERVERT!!
PANT
PANT
Too late, huh?

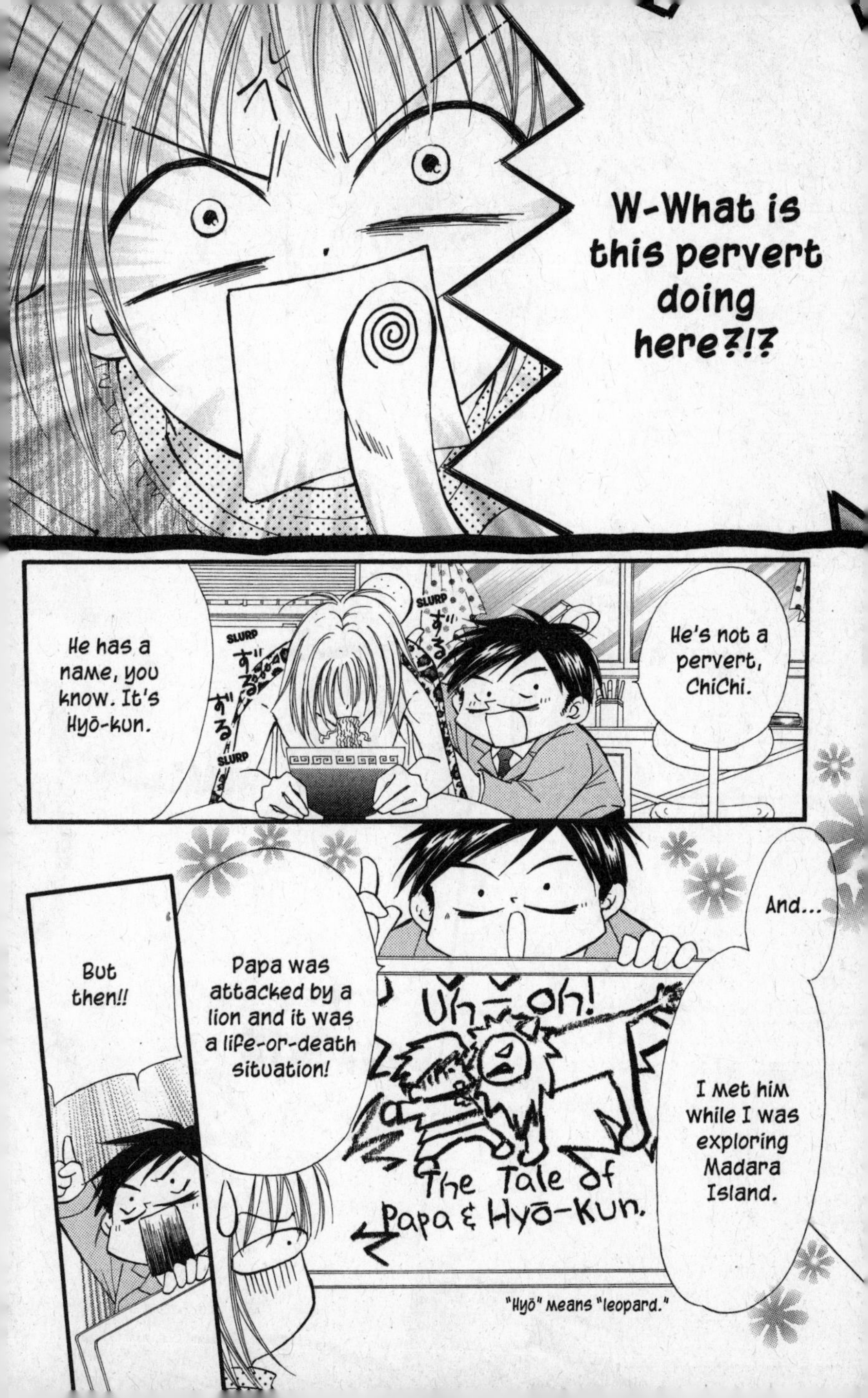
W-What is this pervert doing here?!?
He's not a pervert, ChiChi.
SLURP
SLURP
SLURP
He has a name, you know. It's Hyō-kun.
And...
I met him while I was exploring Madara Island.
Uh-oh!
The Tale of Papa & Hyō-Kun.
Papa was attacked by a lion and it was a life-or-death situation!
But then!!
"Hyō" means "leopard."

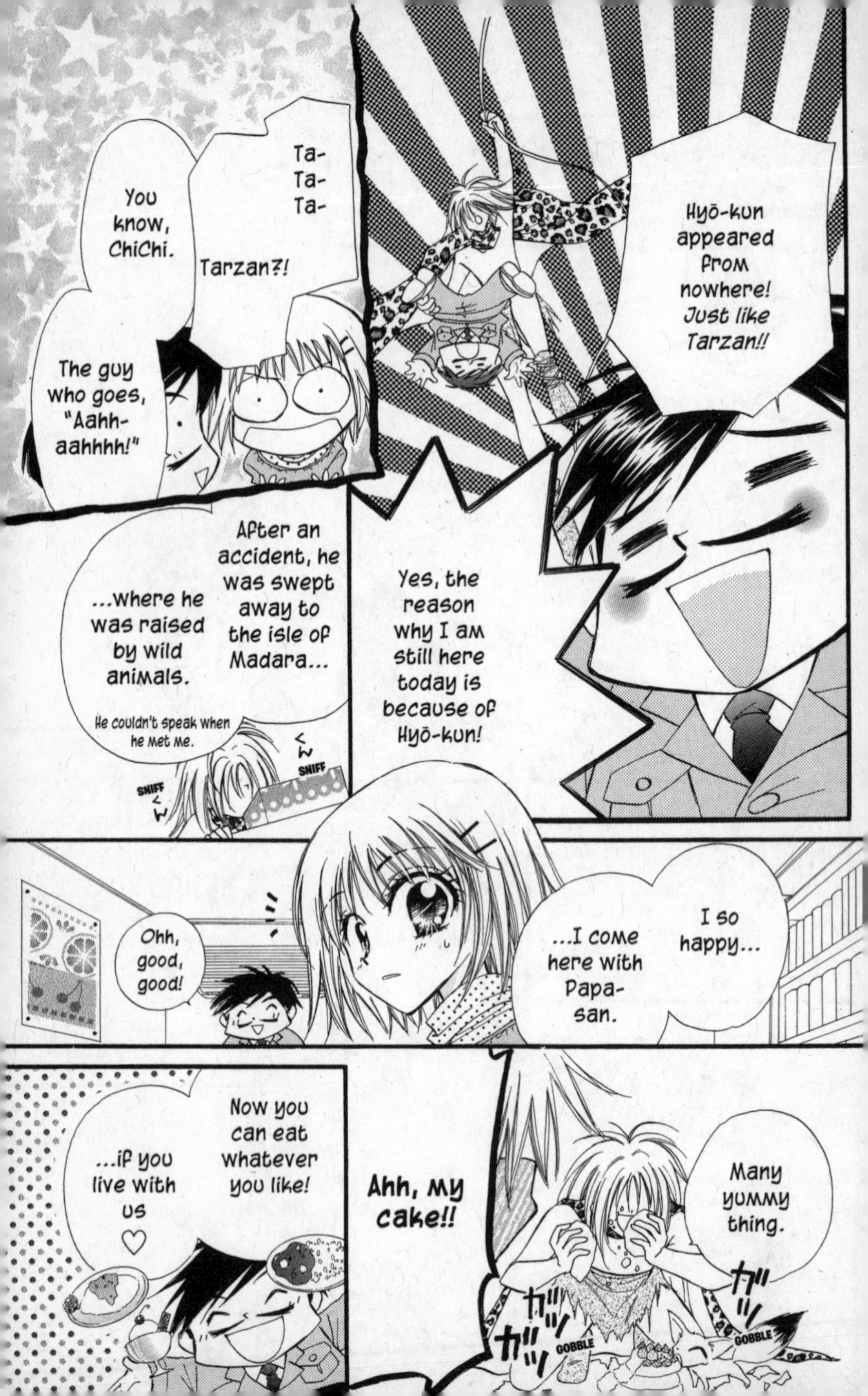

Hyō-kun appeared from nowhere! Just like Tarzan!!
Ta- Ta- Ta-
Tarzan?!
You know, ChiChi.
The guy who goes, "Aahh-aahhhh!"
Yes, the reason why I am still here today is because of Hyō-kun!
After an accident, he was swept away to the isle of Madara...
...where he was raised by wild animals.
He couldn't speak when he met me.
SNIFF
SNIFF
I so happy...
...I come here with Papa-san.
Ohh, good, good!
Many yummy thing.
GOBBLE
GOBBLE
Ahh, my cake!!
Now you can eat whatever you like!
...if you live with us ♡

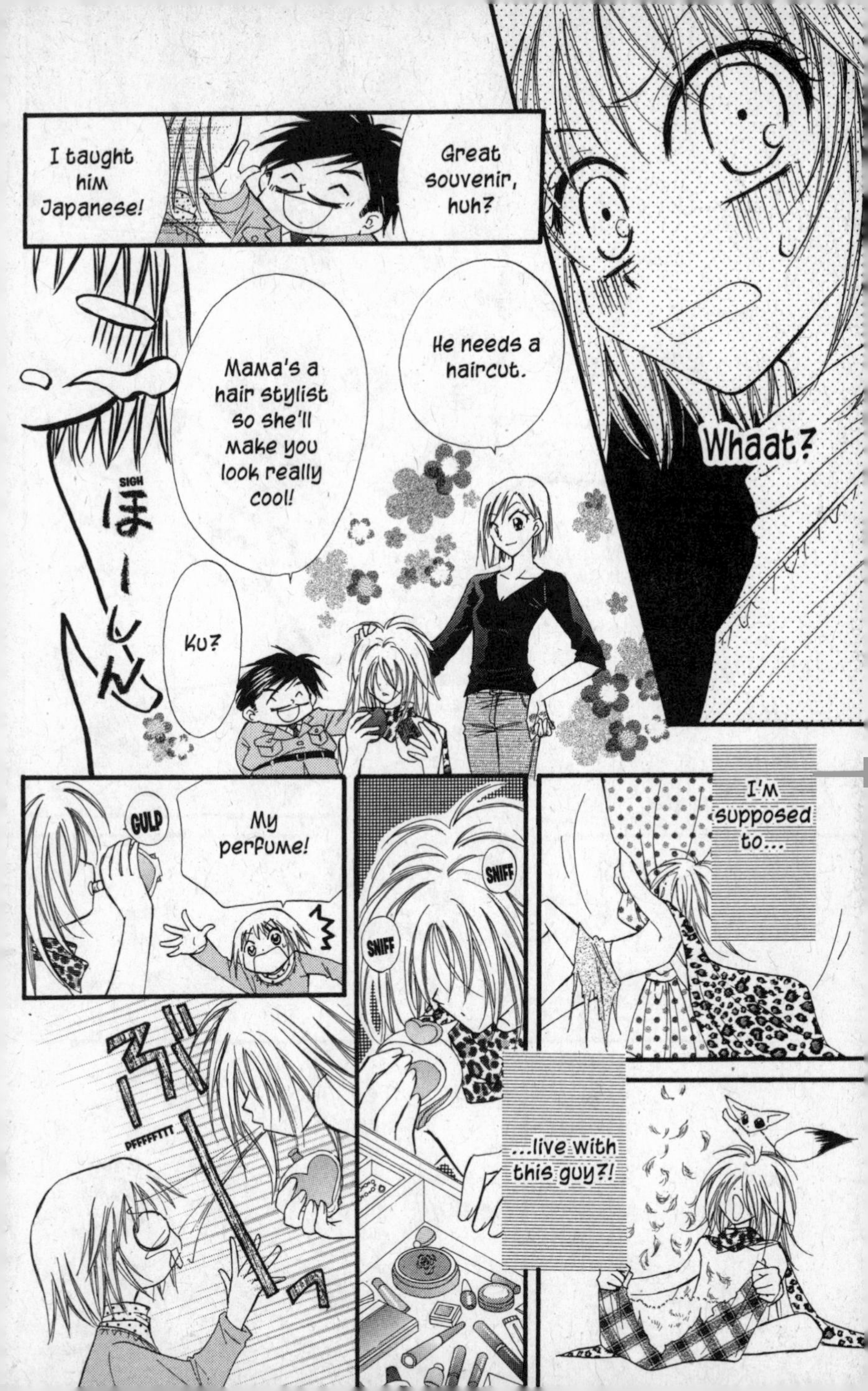
Whaat?
Great souvenir, huh?
I taught him Japanese!
He needs a haircut.
Mama's a hair stylist so she'll make you look really cool!
SIGH
ほーしん
Ku?
I'm supposed to...
...live with this guy?!
SNIFF
SNIFF
My perfume!
GULP
PFFFFTTT

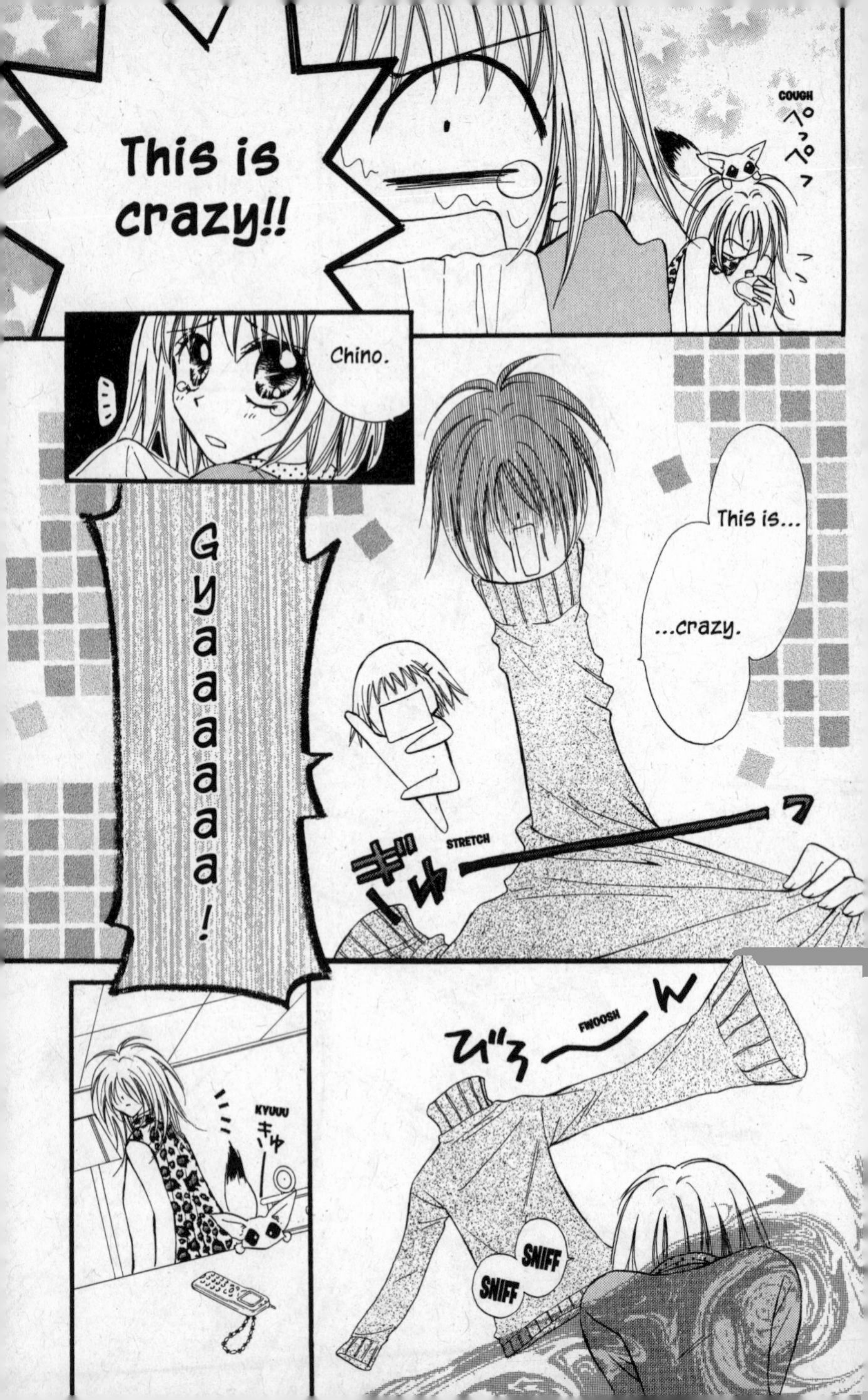
COUGH
ぺっぺっ
This is crazy!!
This is...
...crazy.
STRETCH
ぎゅーっ
Chino.
...
Gyaaaaaaa!
FWOOSH
びろ〜〜ん
SNIFF
SNIFF
KYUUU
キャー

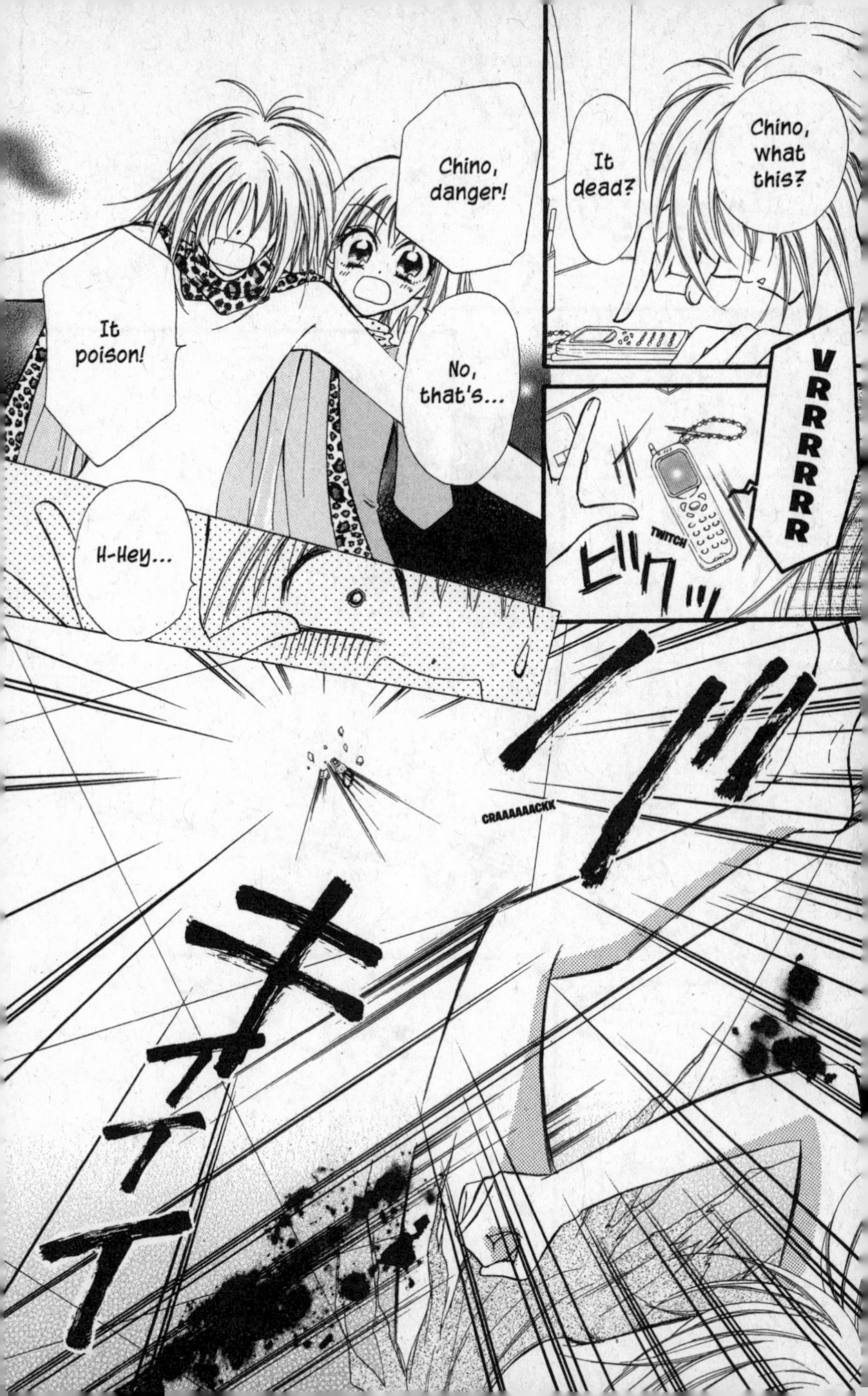
Chino, what this?
It dead?
VRRRRRR
TWITCH
ビクッ
Chino, danger!
It poison!
No, that's...
H-Hey...
CRAAAAAACKK

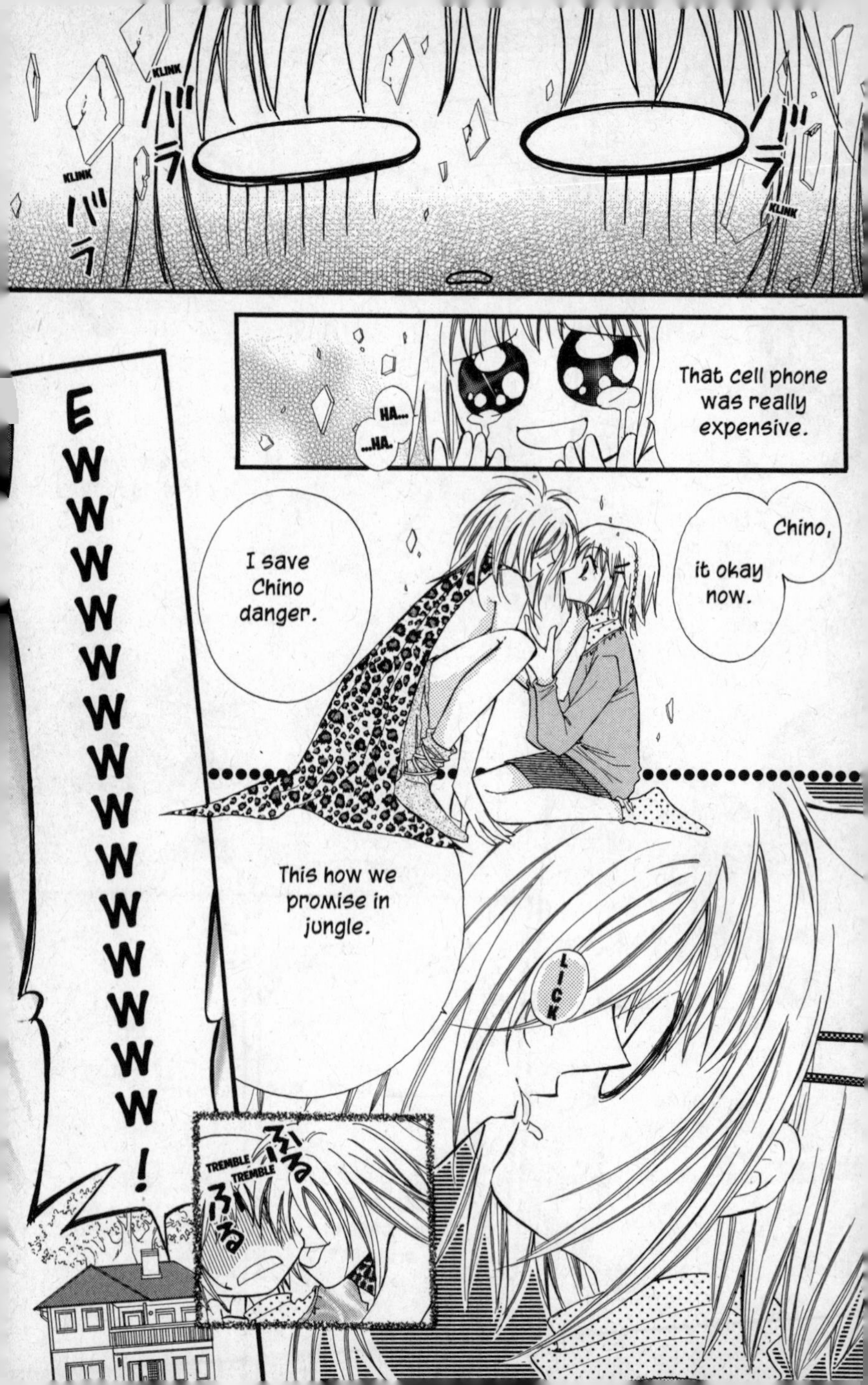
KLINK
バラ
KLINK
バラ
KLINK
バラ
That cell phone was really expensive.
HA...
...HA.
Chino, it okay now.
I save Chino danger.
This how we promise in jungle.
LICK
TREMBLE TREMBLE
ふるふる
EWWWWWWWWWWWWWWW!

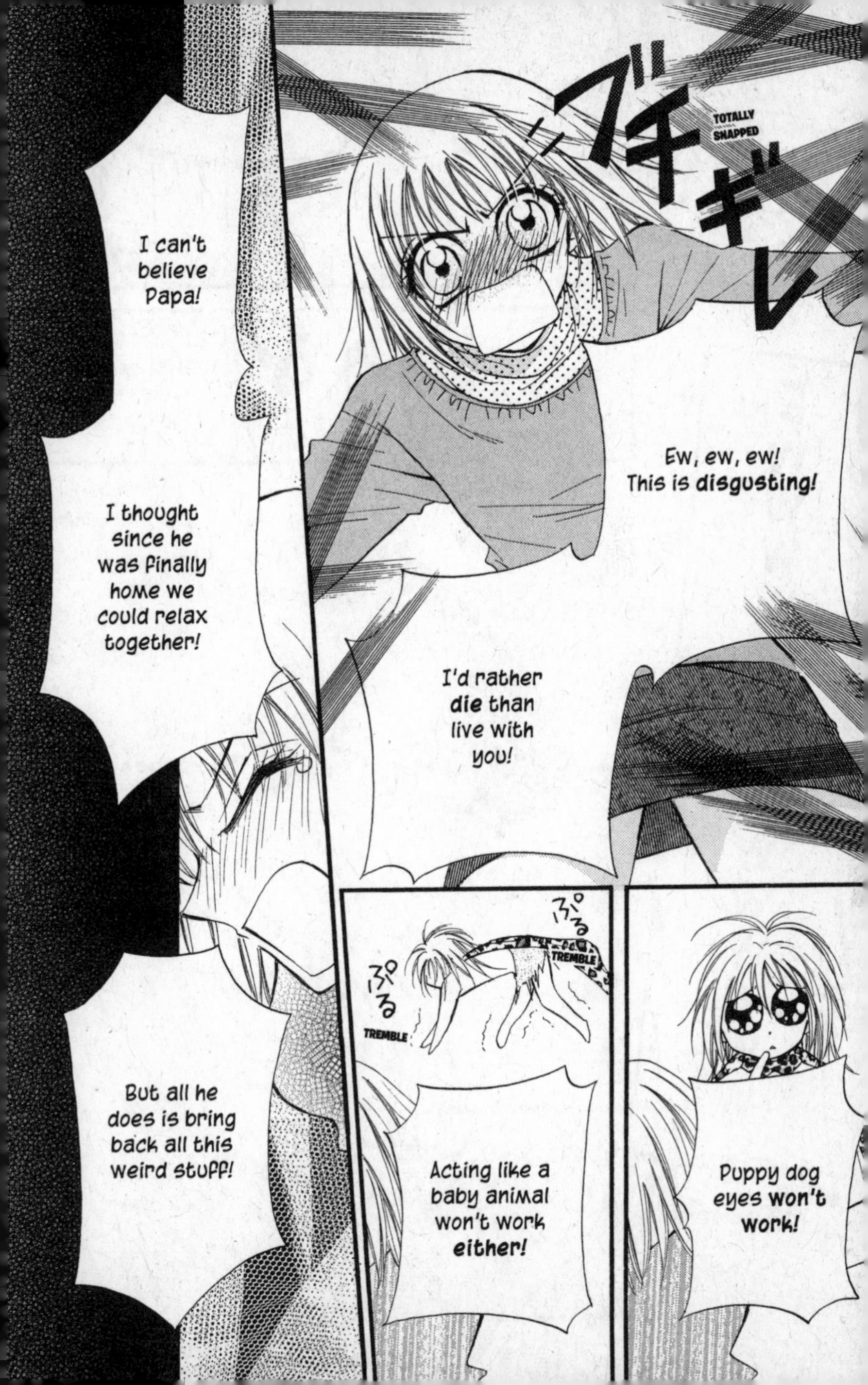
ブチギレ
TOTALLY SNAPPED
Ew, ew, ew! This is **disgusting!**
I'd rather **die** than live with you!
ぷる
TREMBLE
ぷる
TREMBLE
Puppy dog eyes **won't** work!
Acting like a baby animal won't work **either!**
I can't believe Papa!
I thought since he was finally home we could relax together!
But all he does is bring back all this weird stuff!

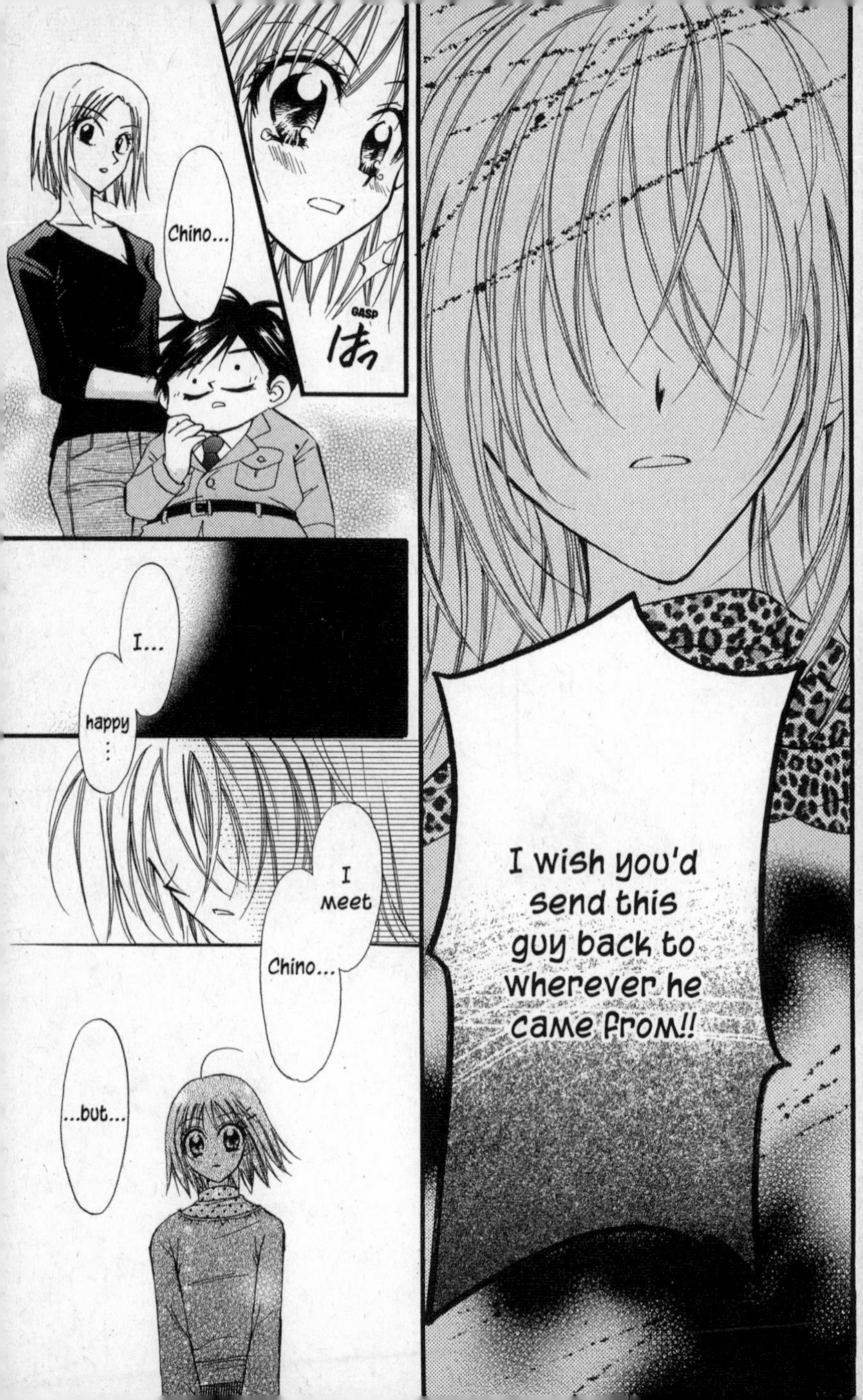

I wish you'd send this guy back to wherever he came from!!
GASP
はっ
Chino...
I... happy...
I meet Chino...
...but...

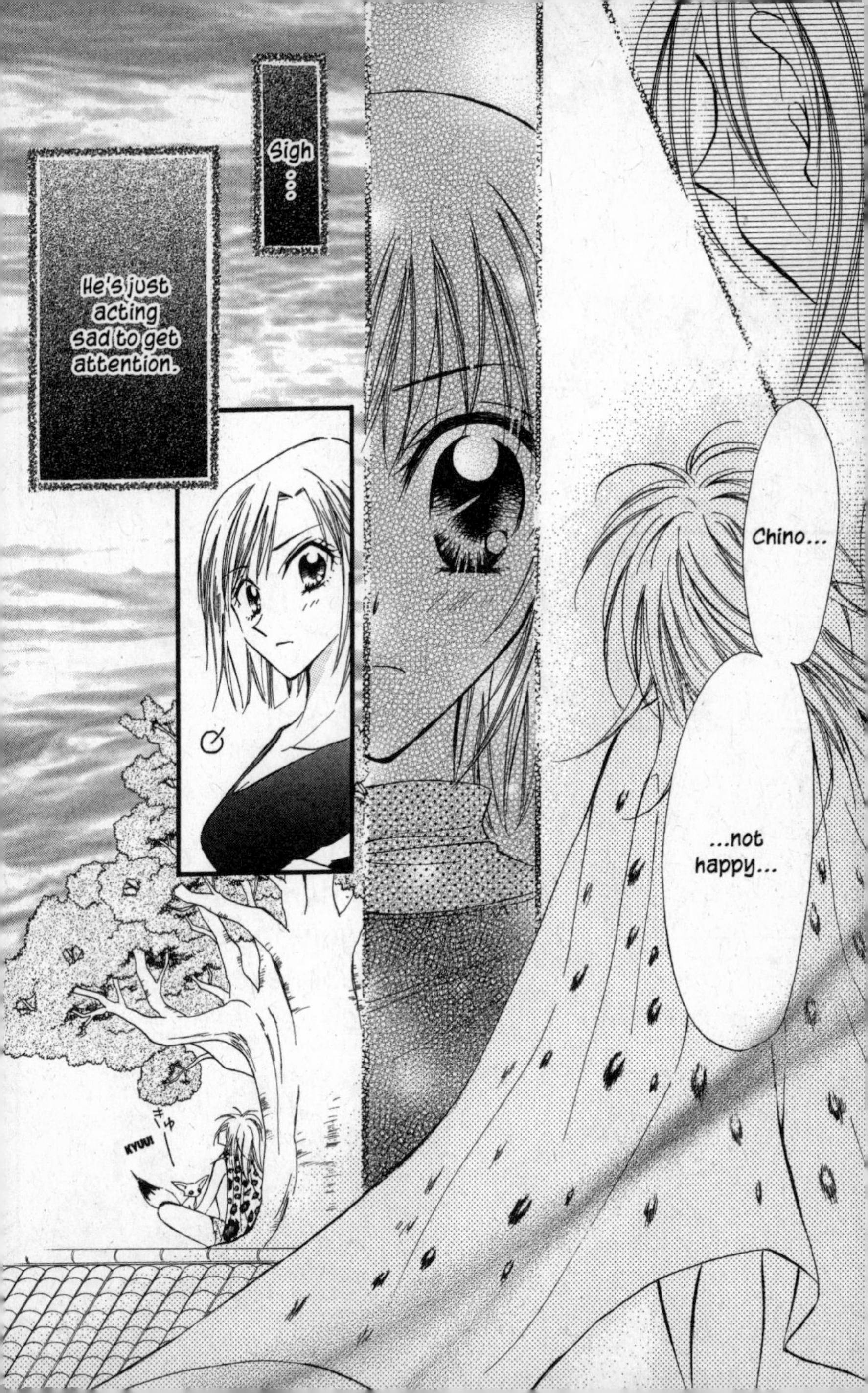
Chino...
...not happy...
Sigh...
He's just acting sad to get attention.
きゅー
KYUU!

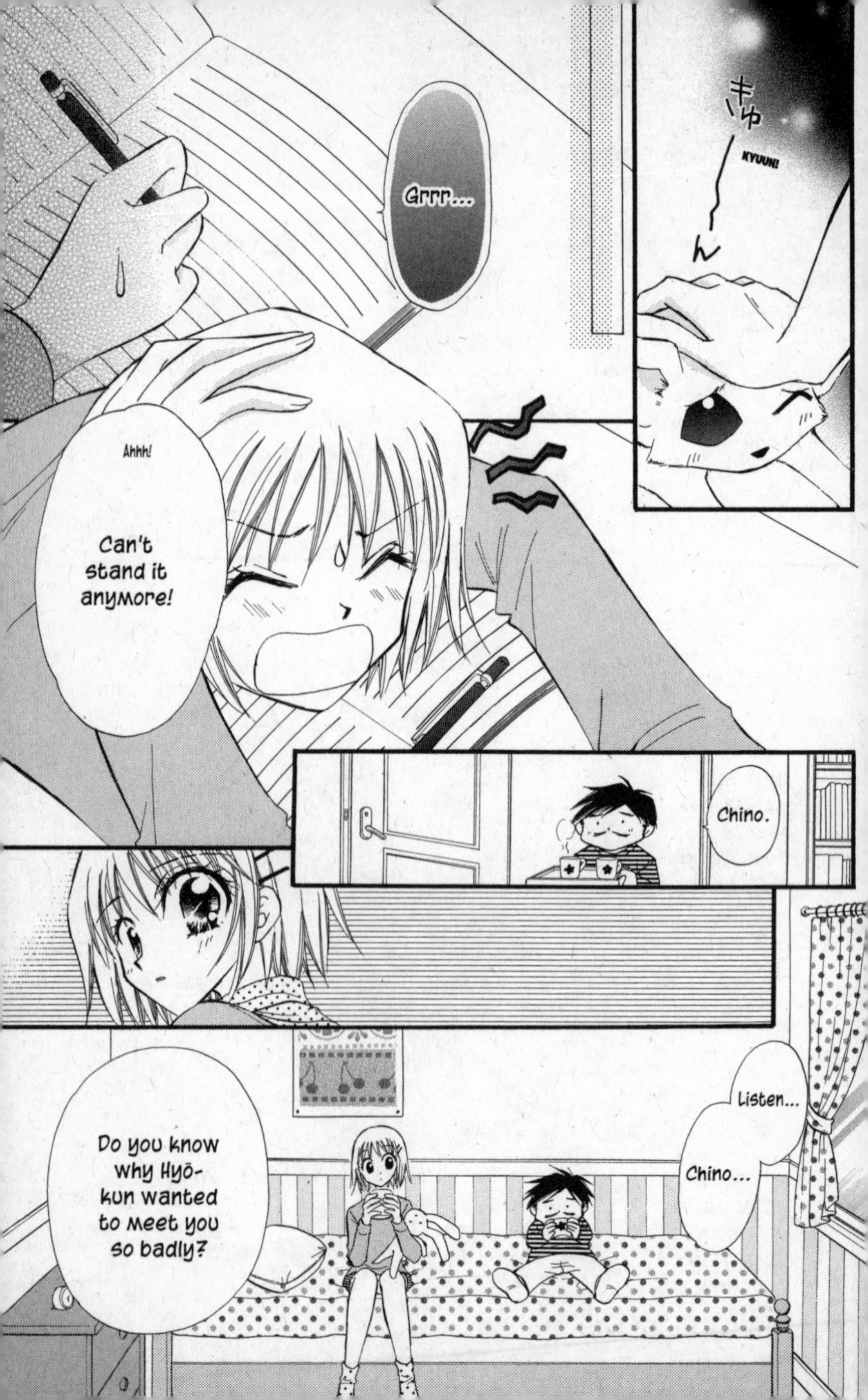
きゅ〜ん
KYUUN!
Grrr...
Ahhh!
Can't stand it anymore!
Chino.
Listen... Chino...
Do you know why Hyō-kun wanted to meet you so badly?

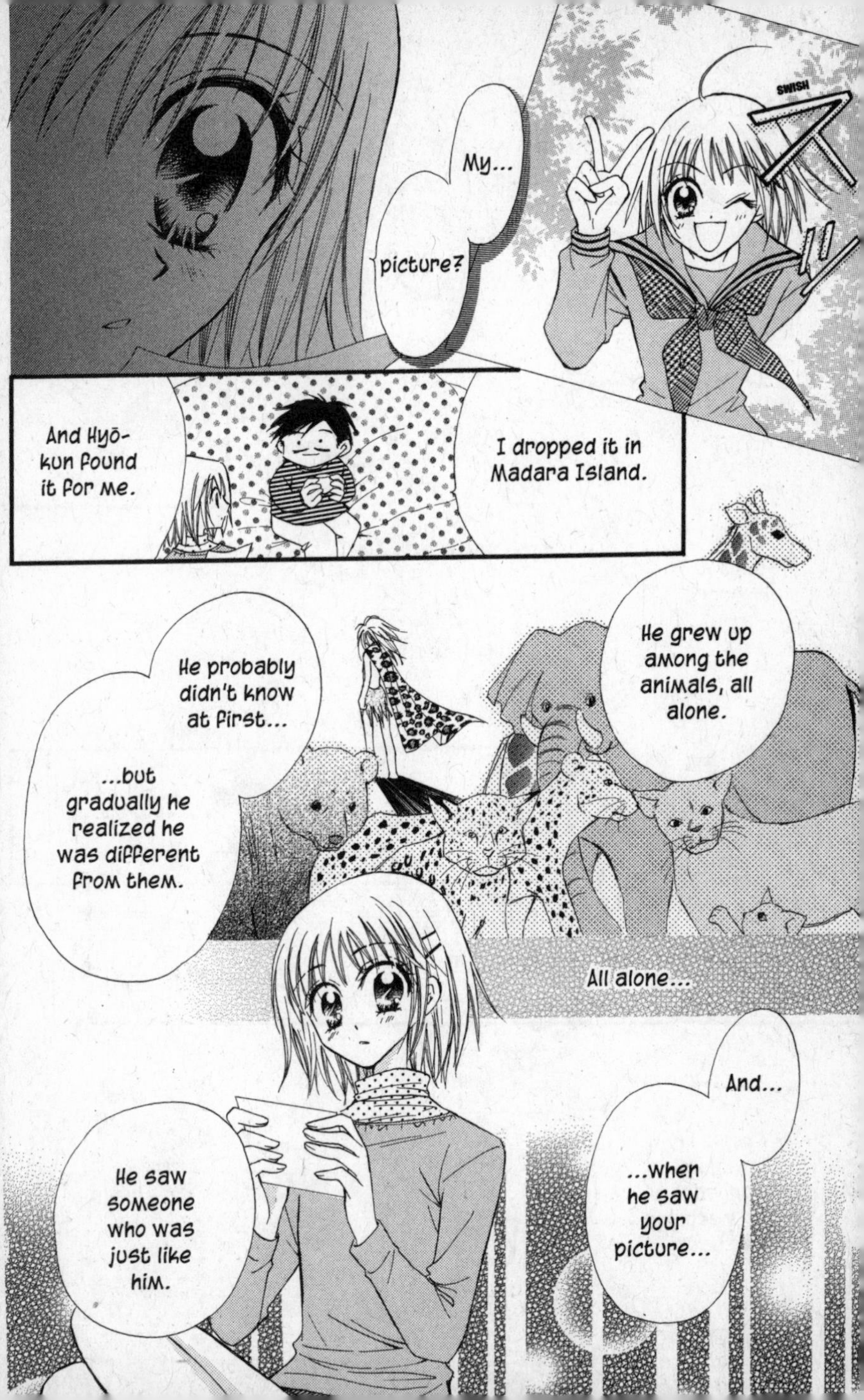
SWISH
My...
picture?
I dropped it in Madara Island.
And Hyō-kun found it for me.
He grew up among the animals, all alone.
He probably didn't know at first...
...but gradually he realized he was different from them.
All alone...
And...
...when he saw your picture...
He saw someone who was just like him.

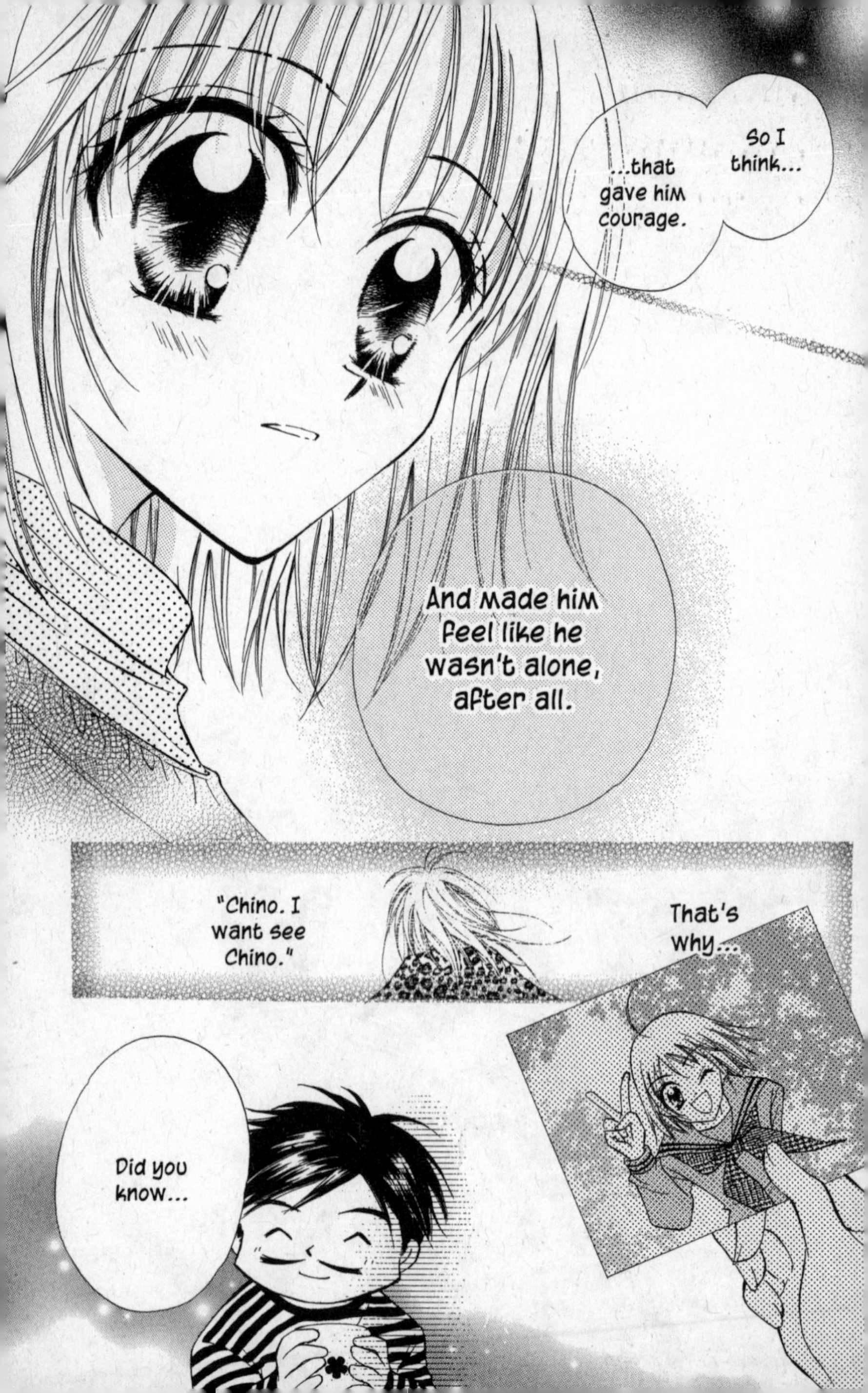
So I think...
...that gave him courage.
And made him feel like he wasn't alone, after all.
"Chino. I want see Chino."
That's why...
Did you know...

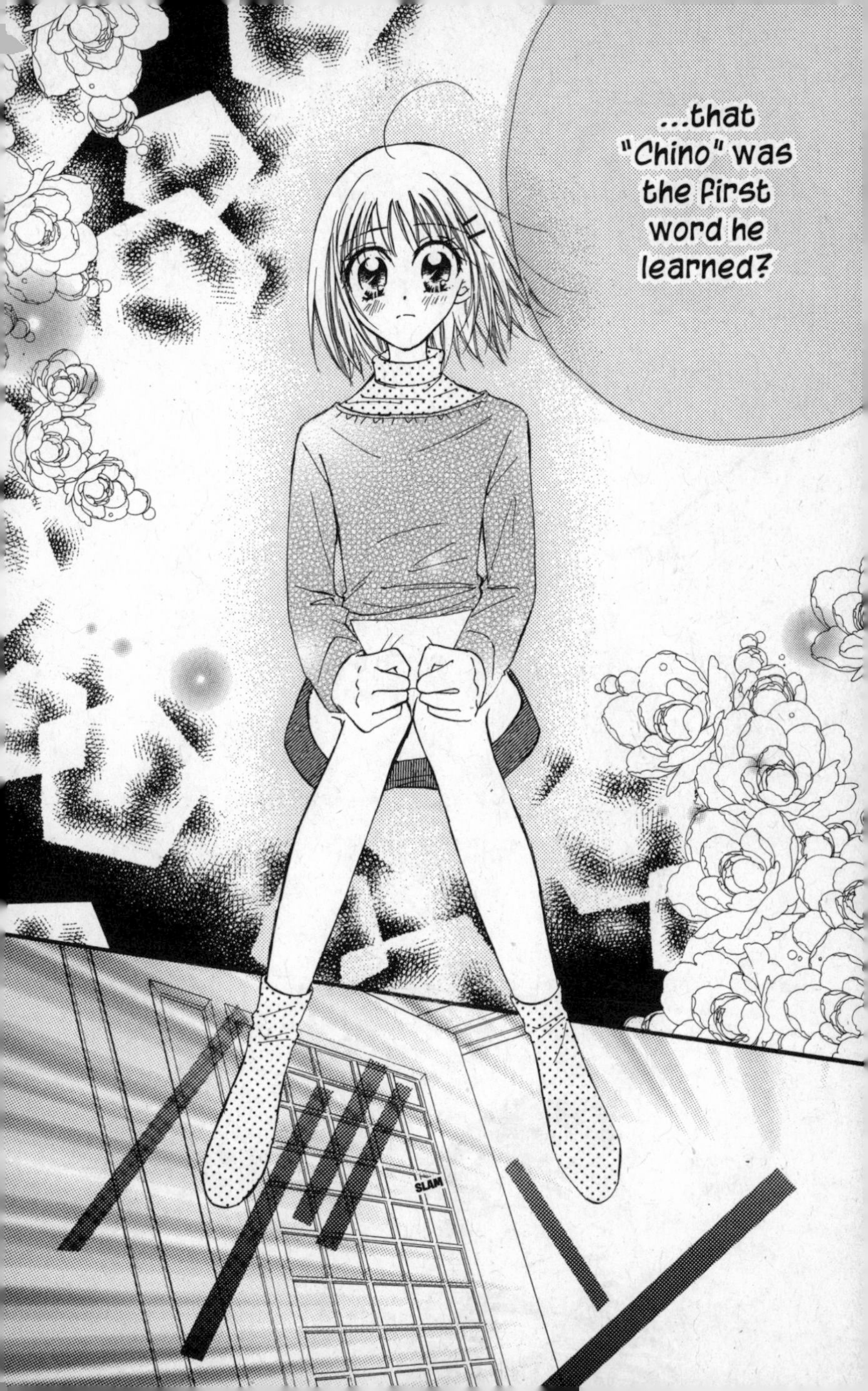
...that "Chino" was the first word he learned?
SLAM

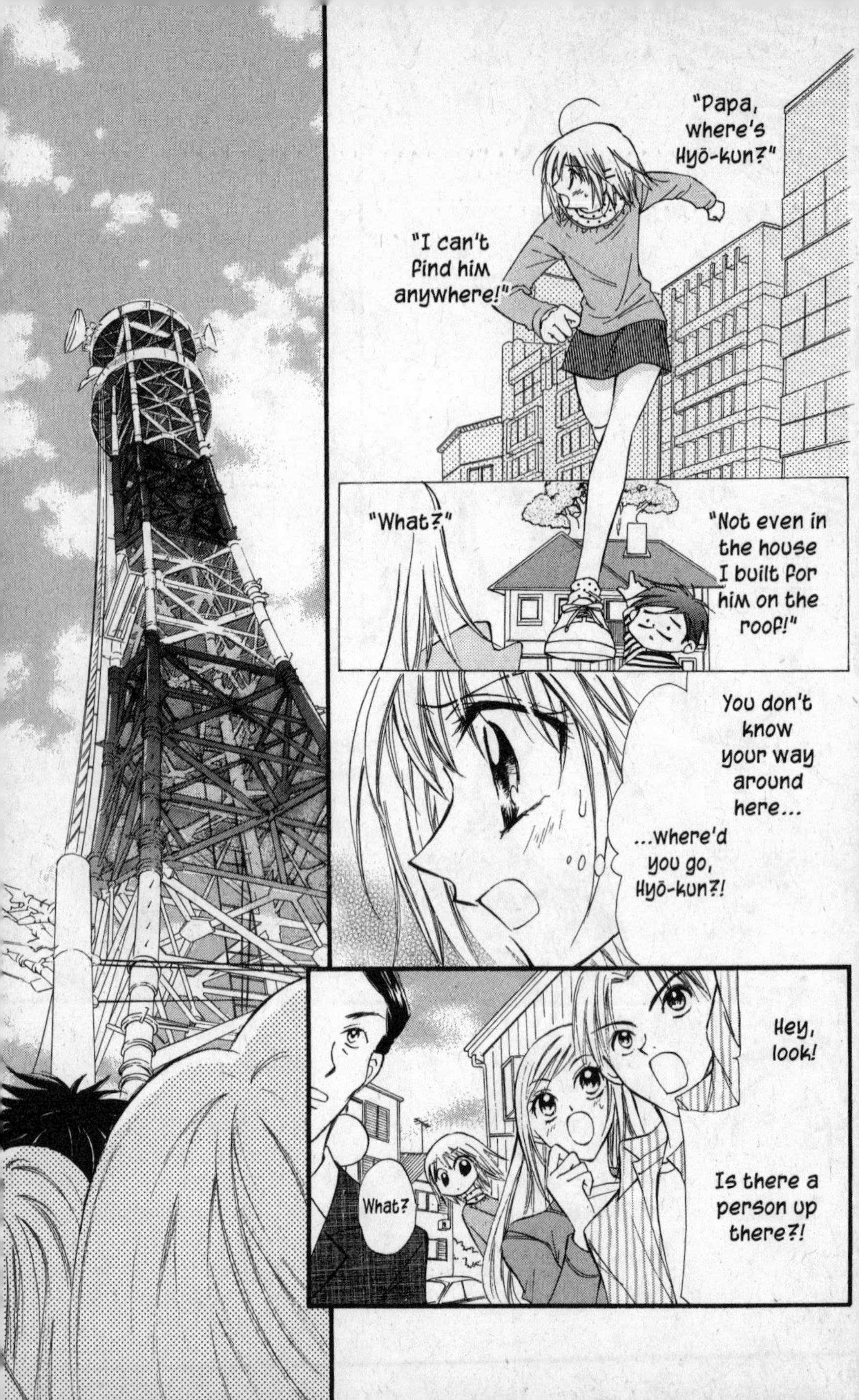
"Papa, where's Hyō-kun?"
"I can't find him anywhere!"
"Not even in the house I built for him on the roof!"
"What?"
You don't know your way around here...
...where'd you go, Hyō-kun?!
Hey, look!
Is there a person up there?!
What?

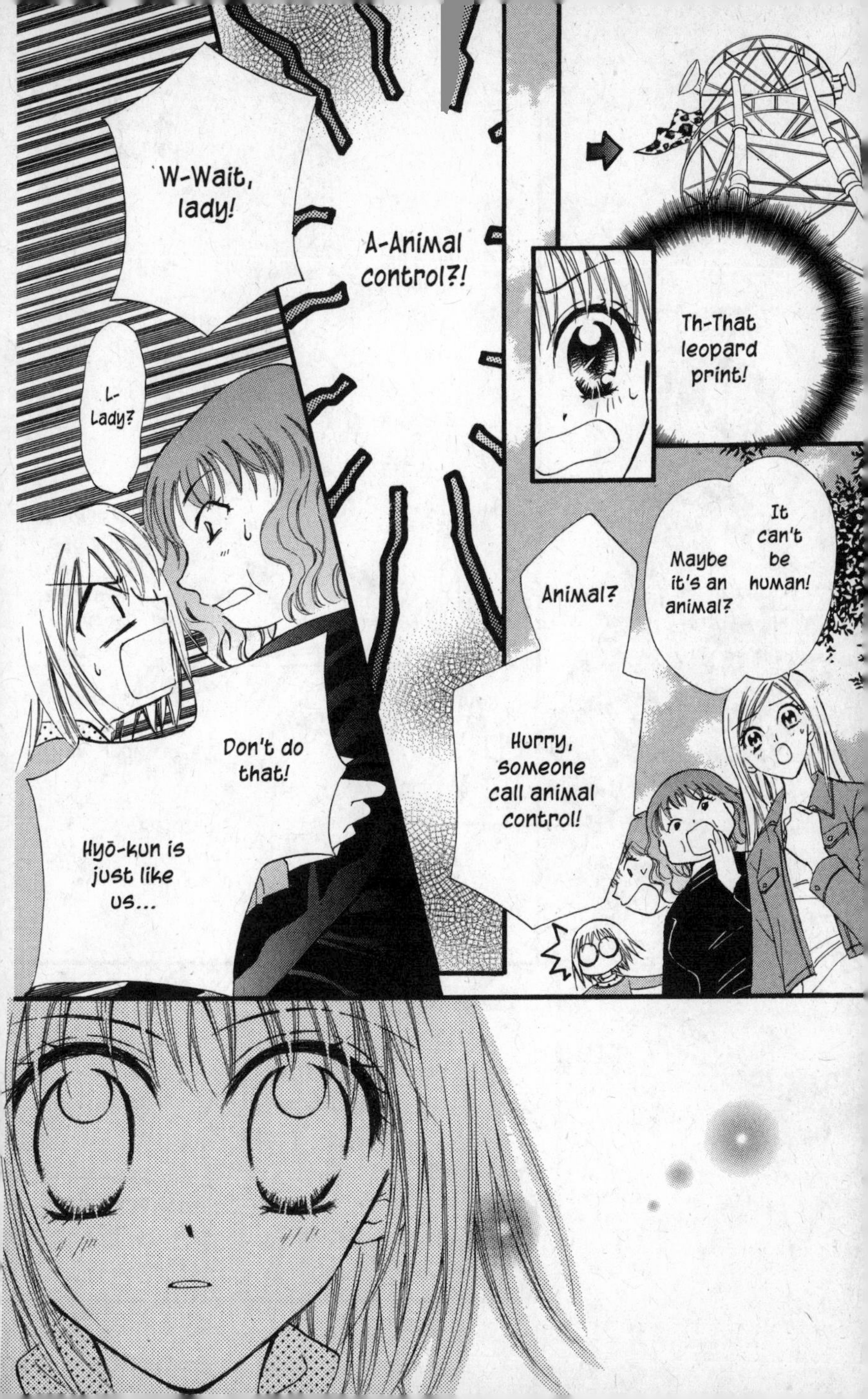
Th-That leopard print!
It can't be human!
Maybe it's an animal?
Animal?
Hurry, someone call animal control!
A-Animal control?!
W-Wait, lady!
L-Lady?
Don't do that!
Hyō-kun is just like us...

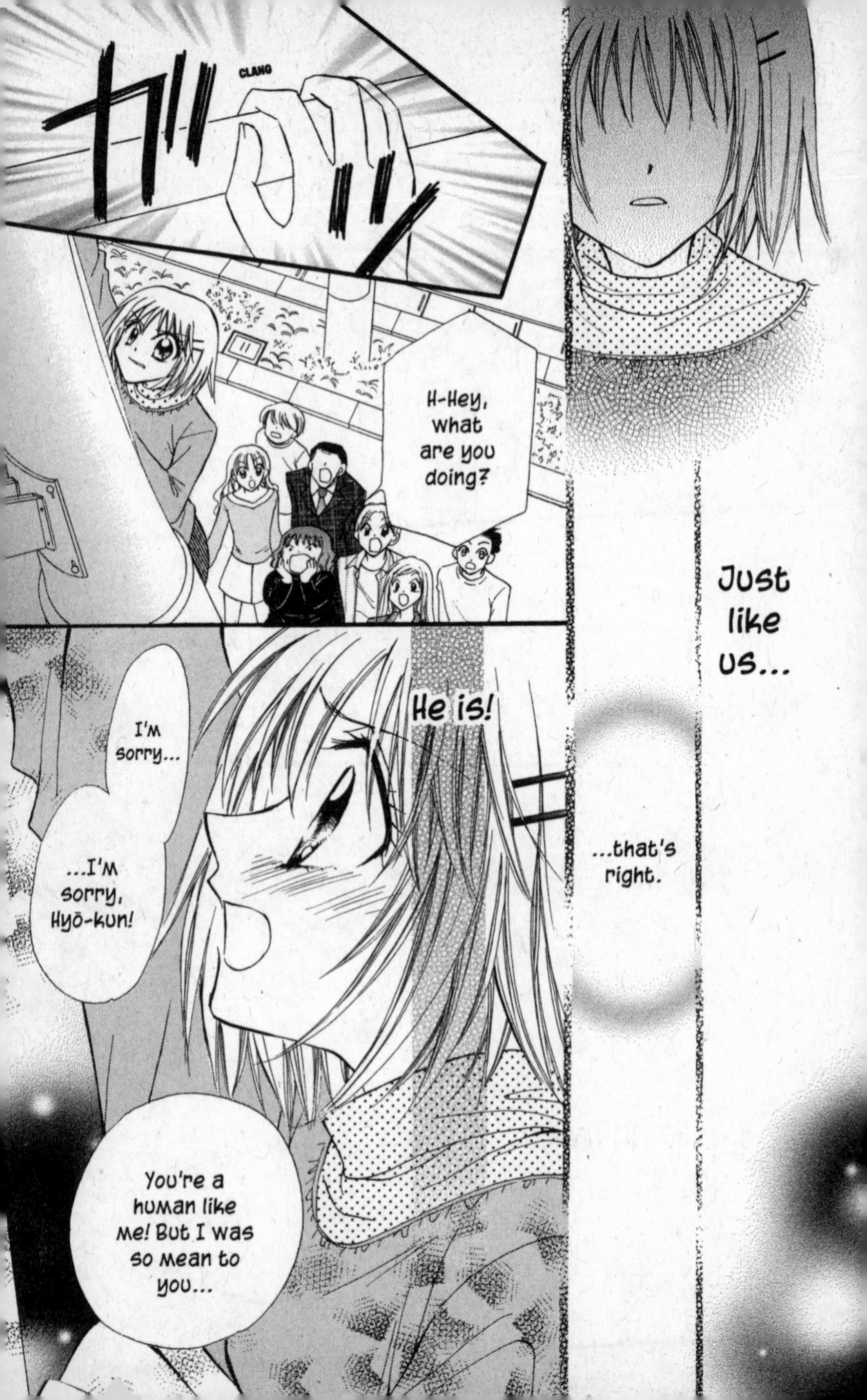

Just like us...
...that's right.
CLANG
H-Hey, what are you doing?
He is!
I'm sorry...
...I'm sorry, Hyō-kun!
You're a human like me! But I was so mean to you...

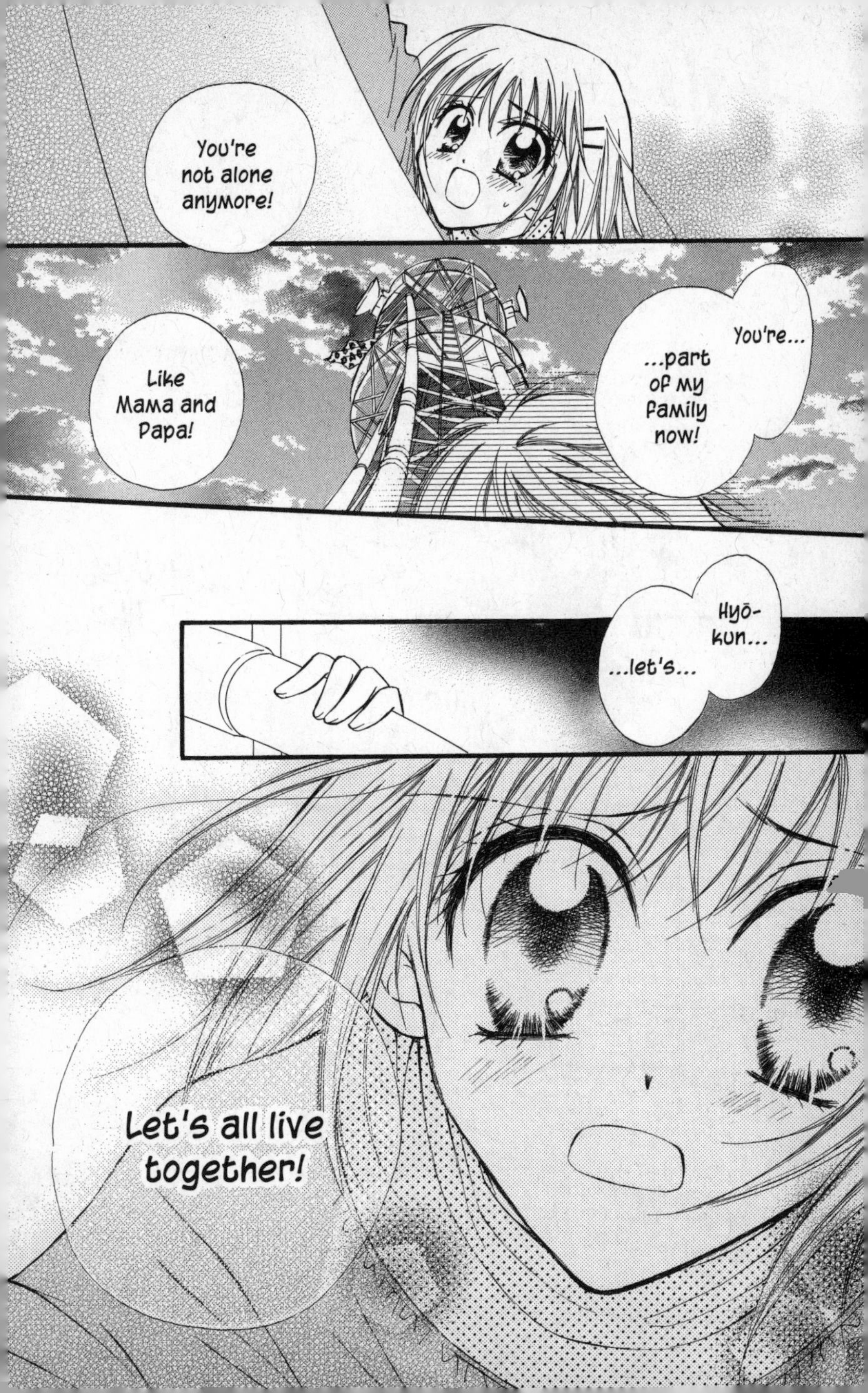
You're not alone anymore!
You're... ...part of my family now!
Like Mama and Papa!
Hyō-kun... ...let's...
Let's all live together!

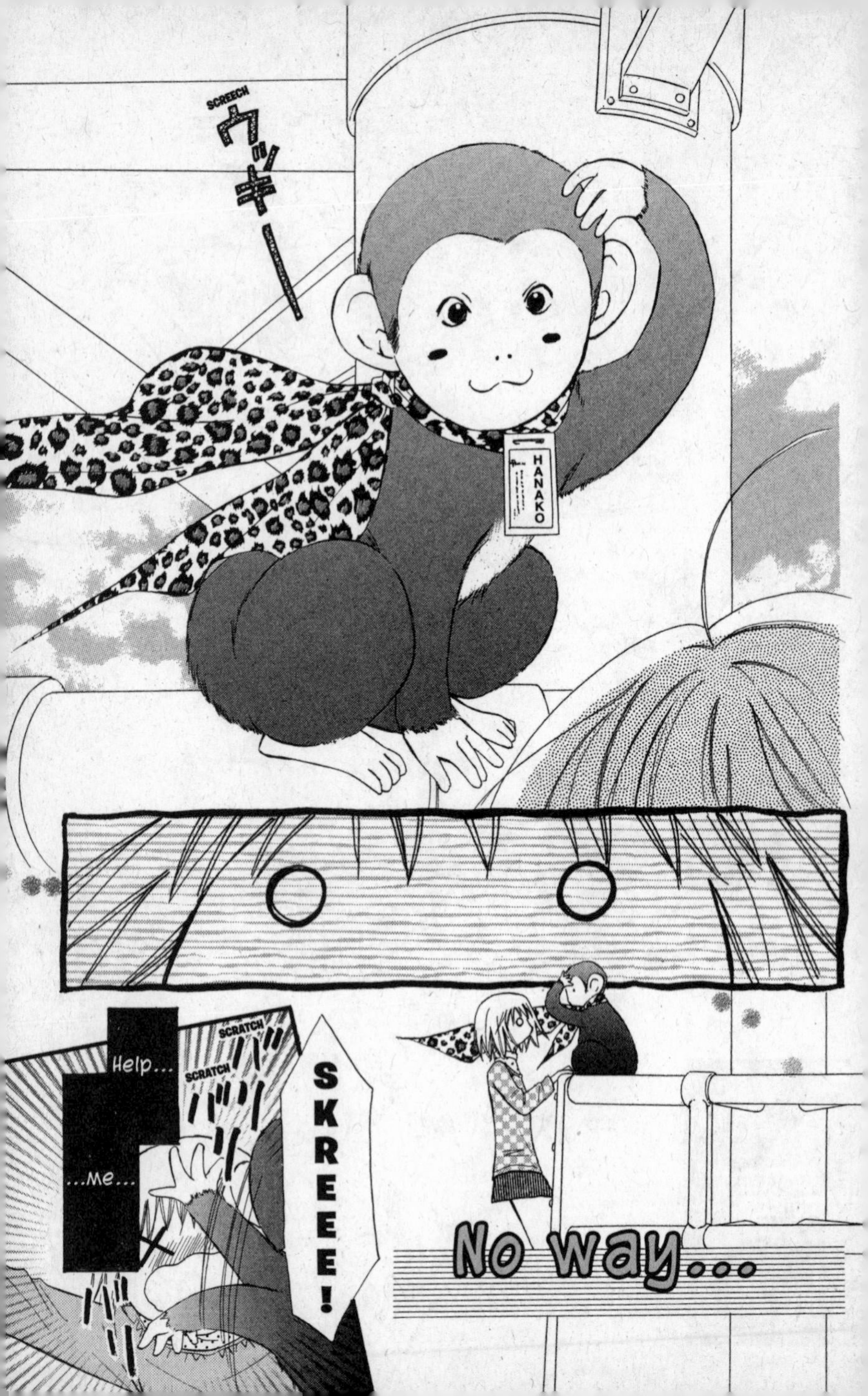
SCREECH
ウッキー
HANAKO
No way...
SKREEE!
SCRATCH
SCRATCH
Help...
...me...

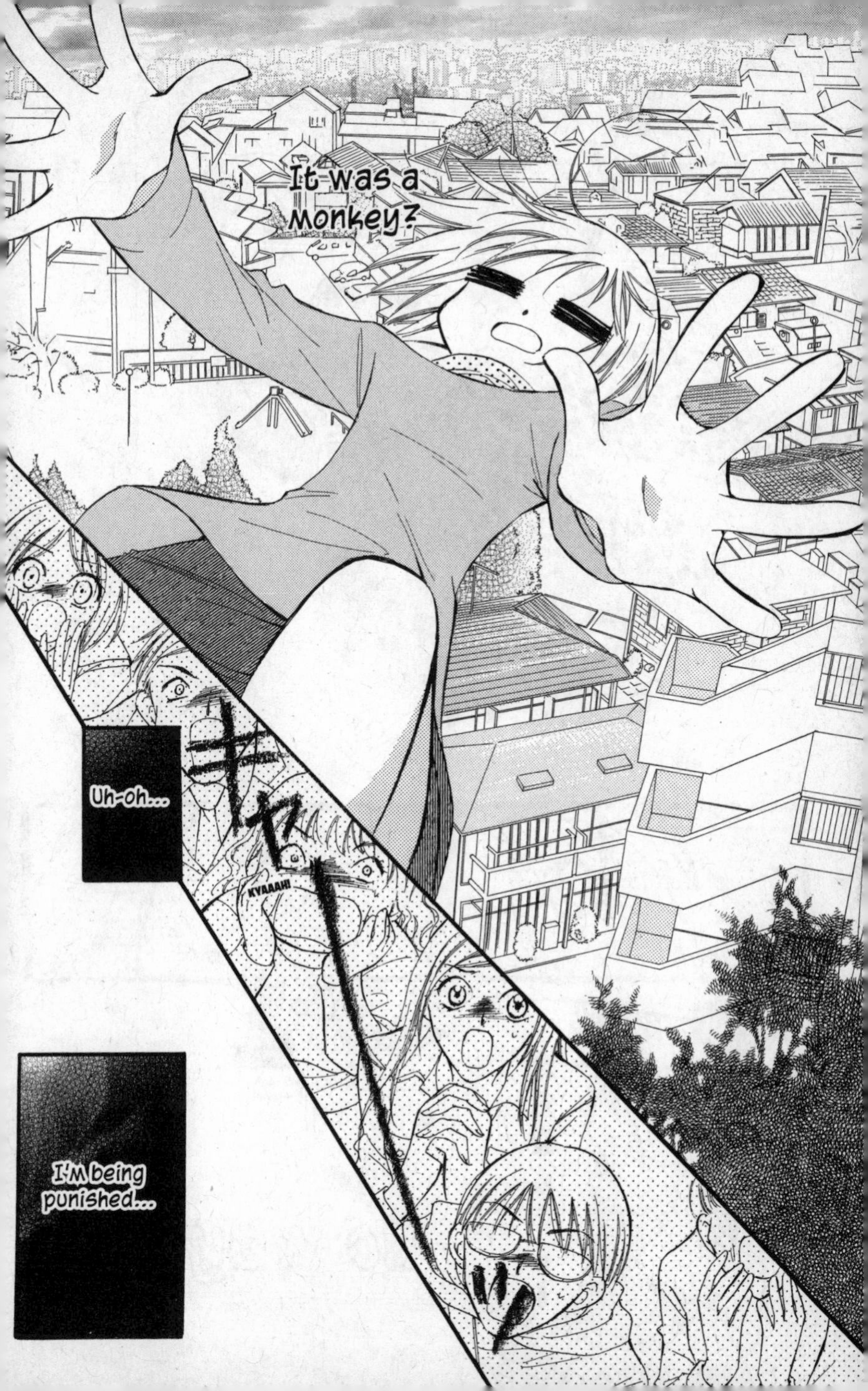
It was a monkey?
Uh-oh...
KYAAAH!
I'm being punished...

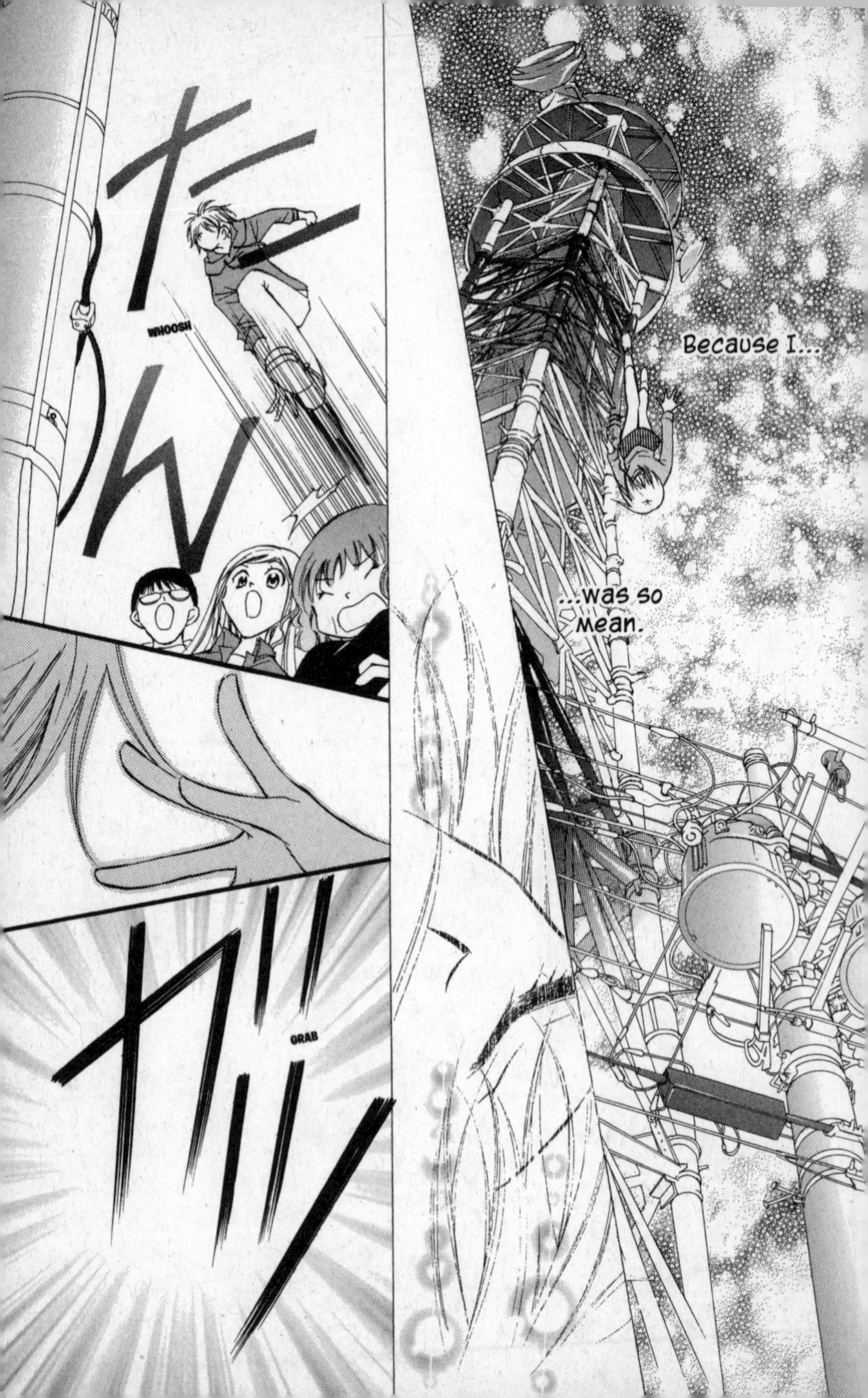
Because I...
...was so mean.
WHOOSH
GRAB

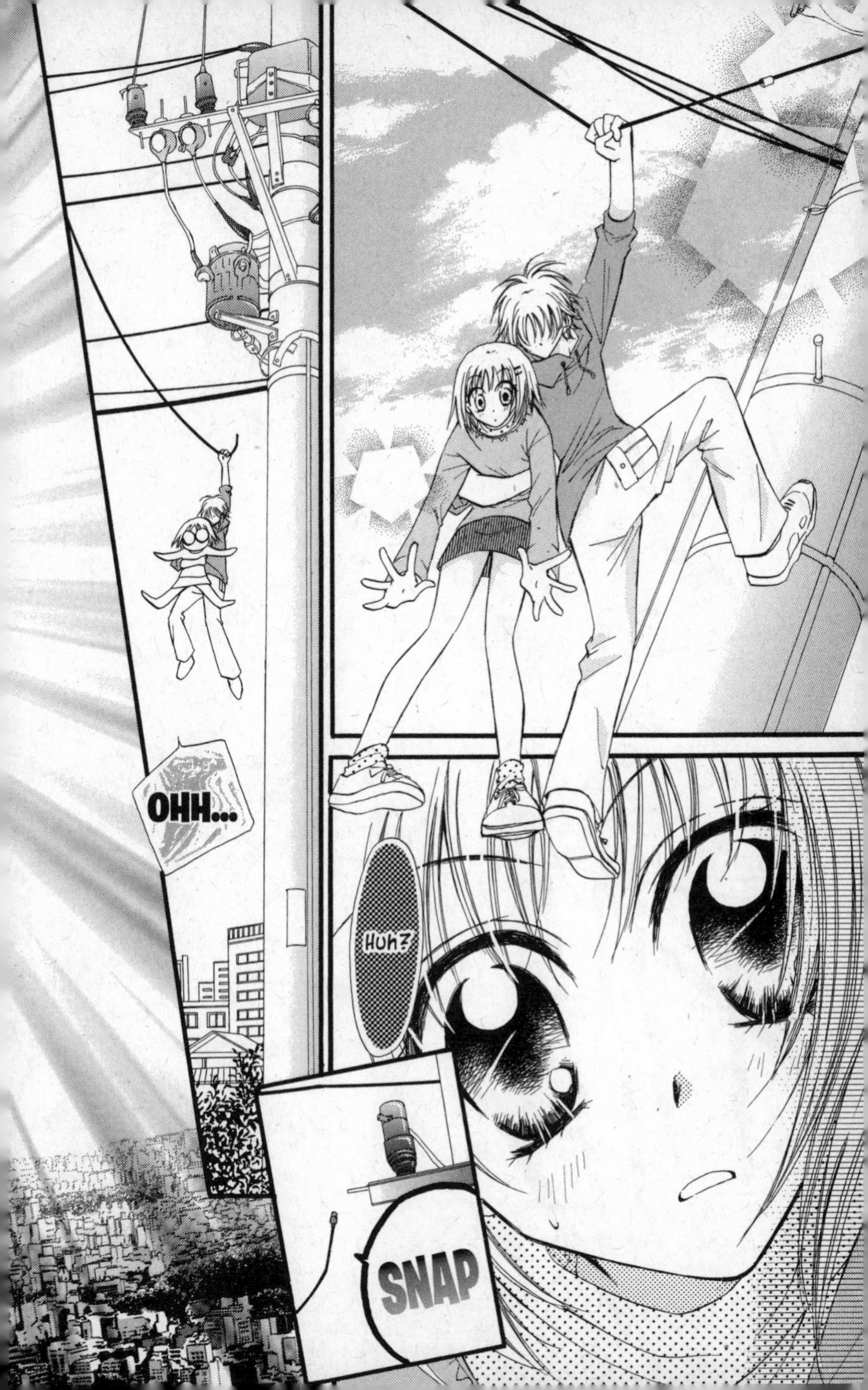
HUH?
SNAP
OHH...

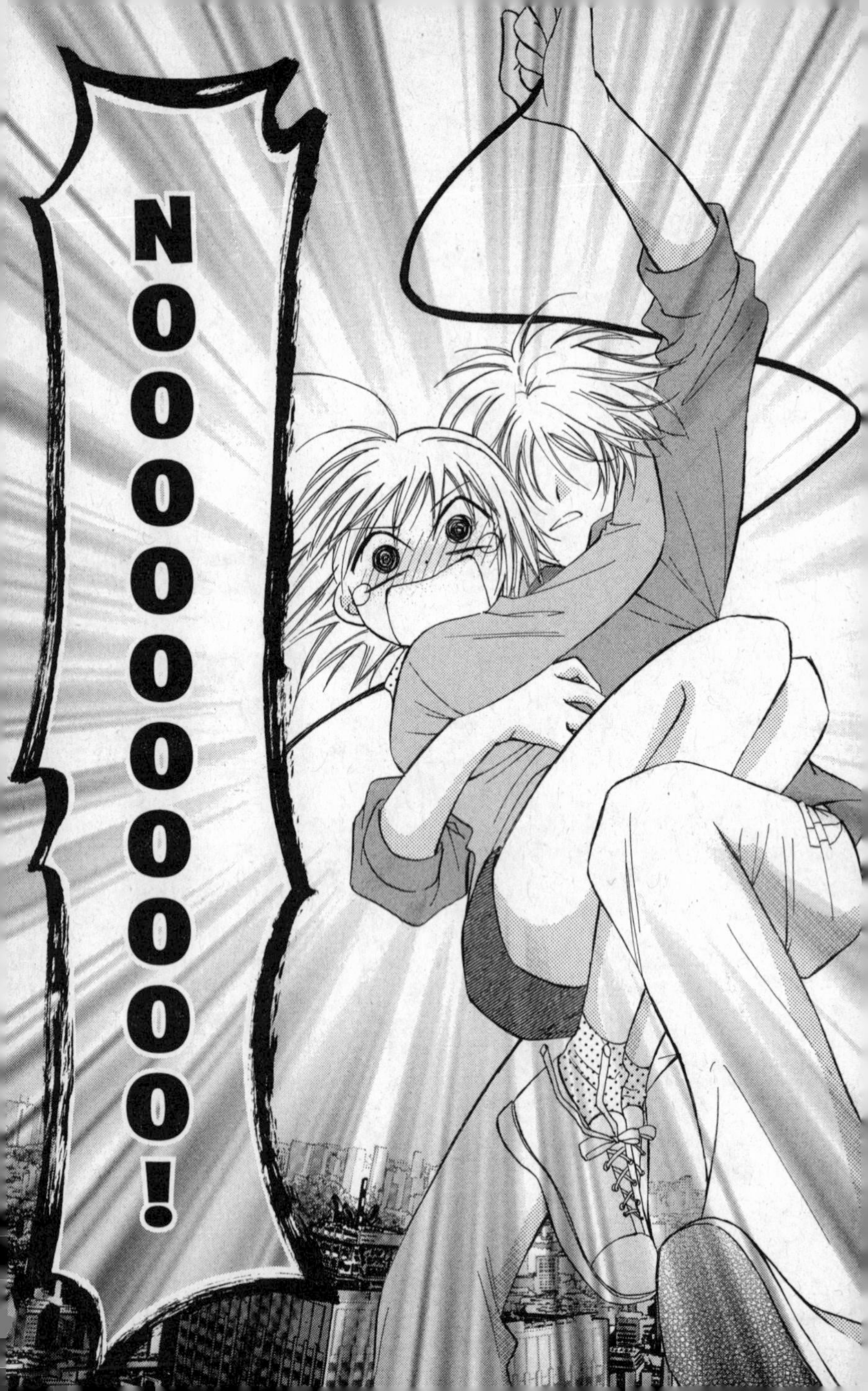
NOOOOOOOOOO!

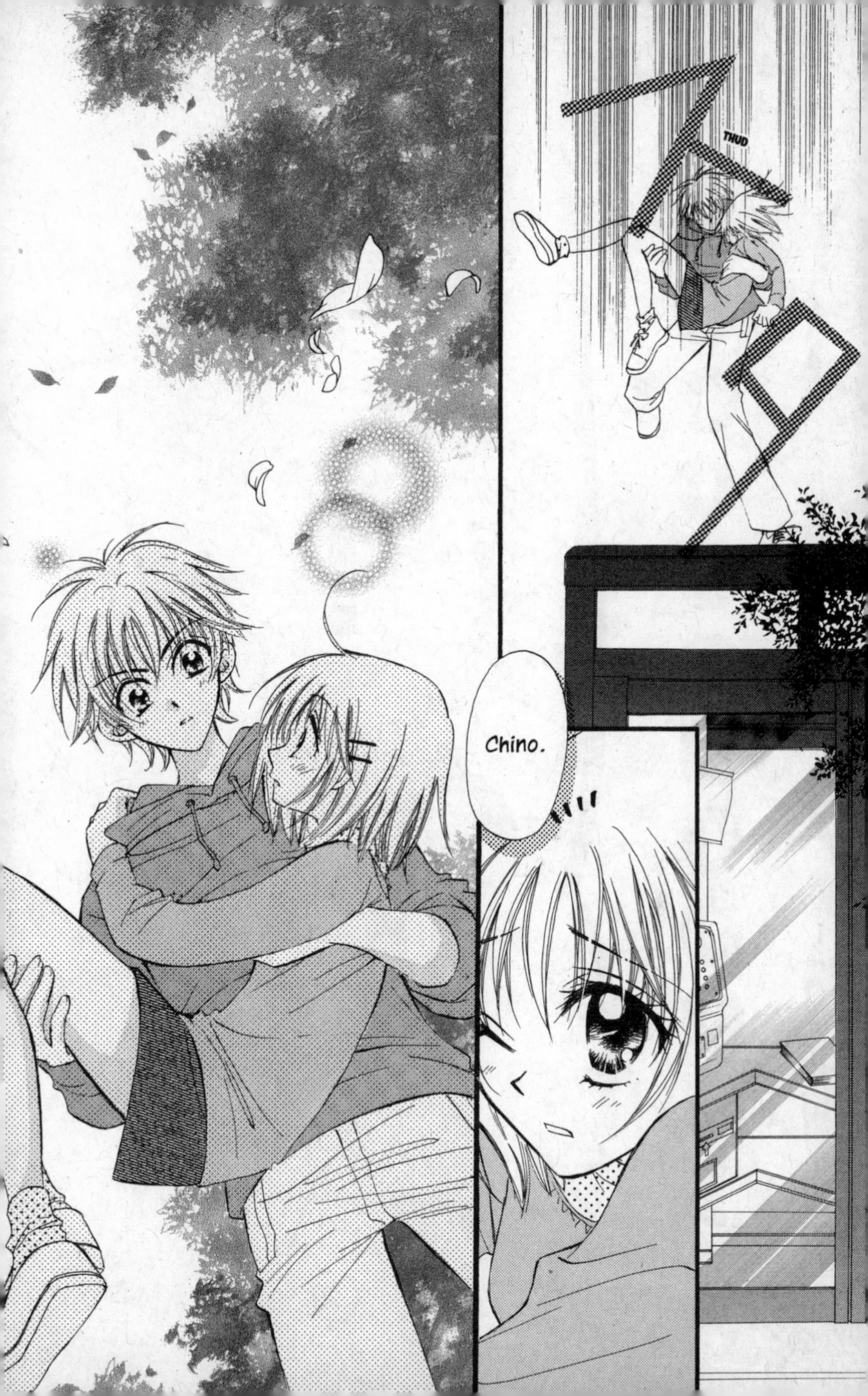
THUD
Chino.

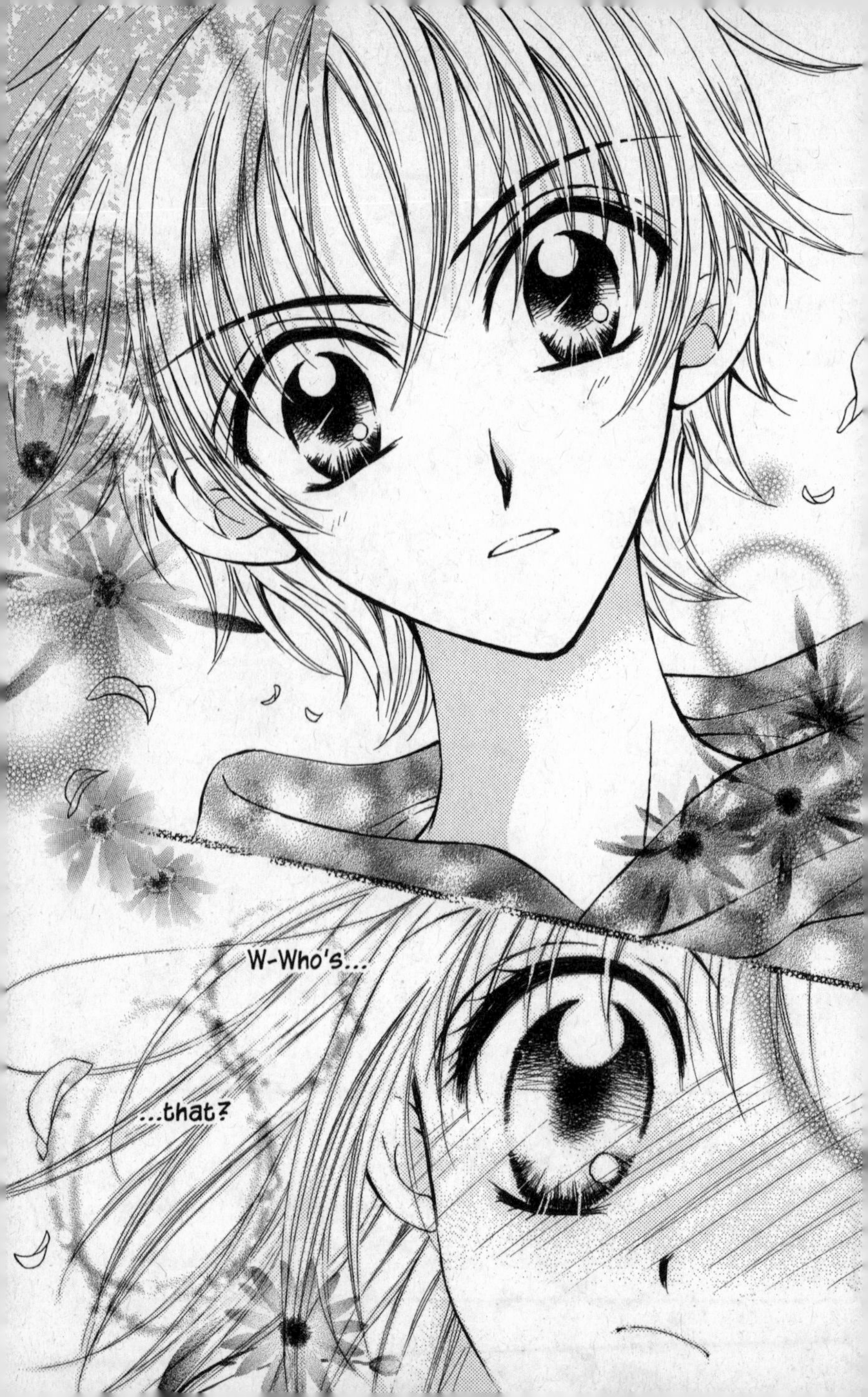
W-Who's...
...that?

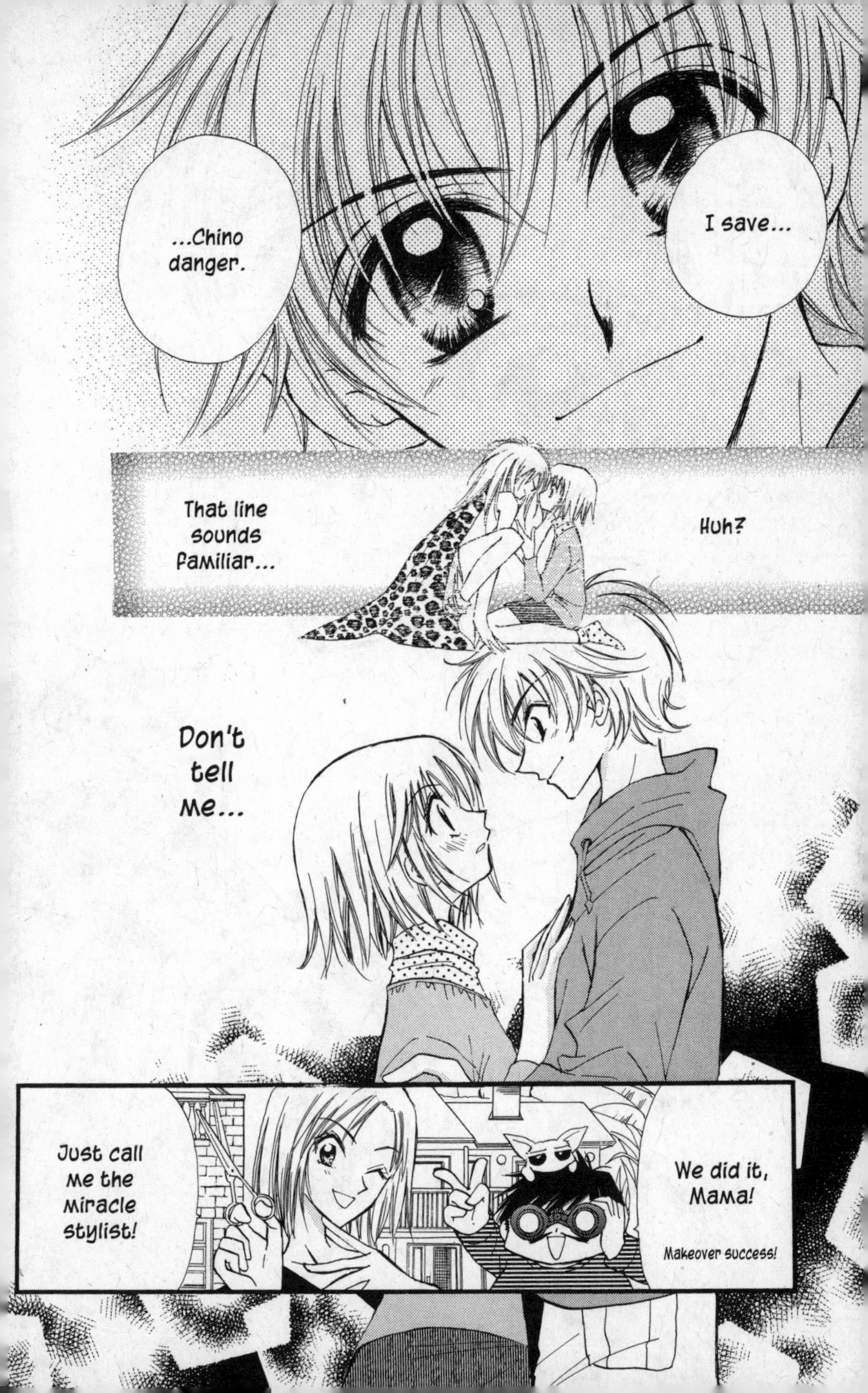
I save...
...Chino danger.
Huh?
That line sounds familiar...
Don't tell me...
We did it, Mama!
Makeover success!
Just call me the miracle stylist!

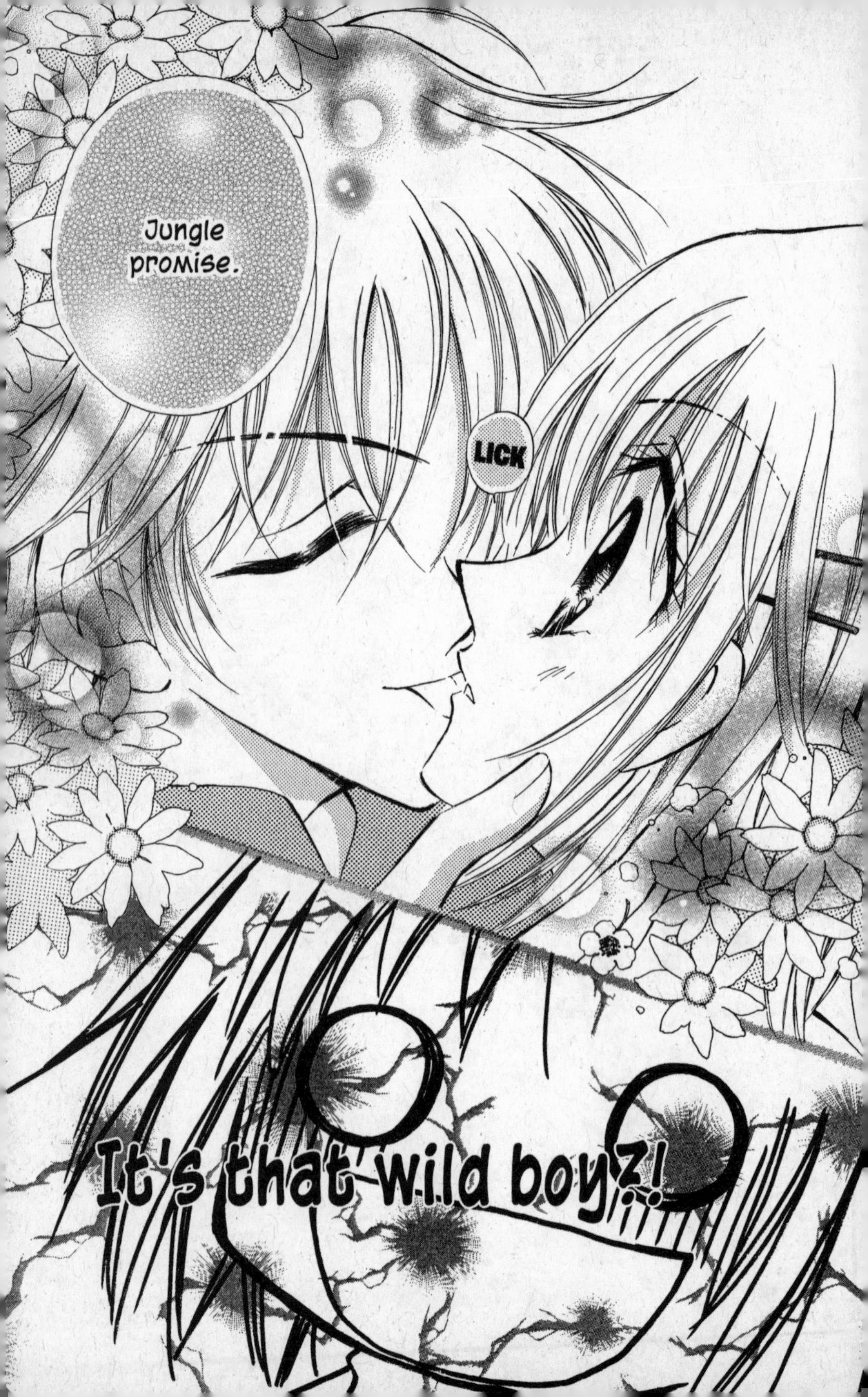
Jungle promise.
LICK
It's that wild boyz!

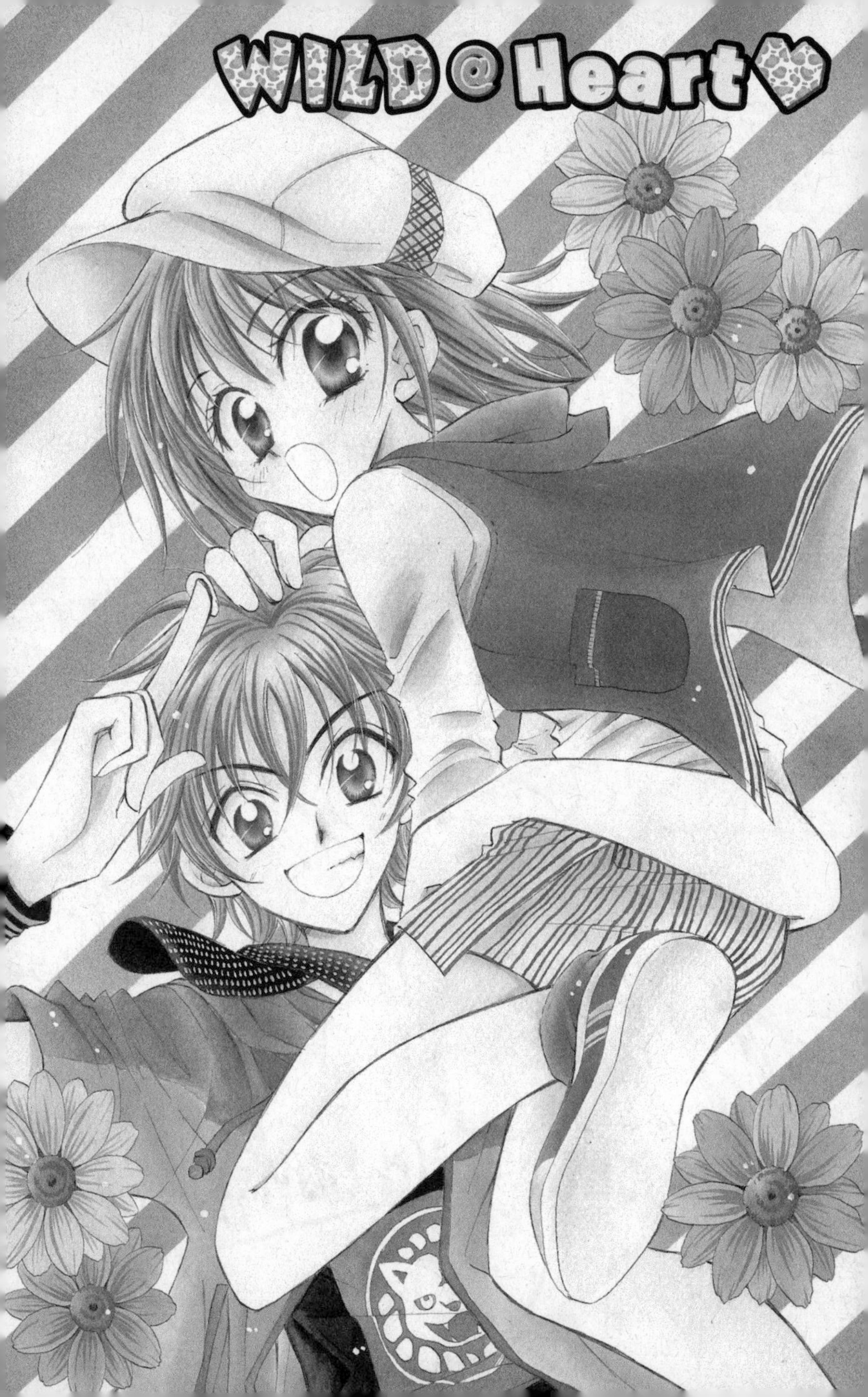
WILD @ Heart

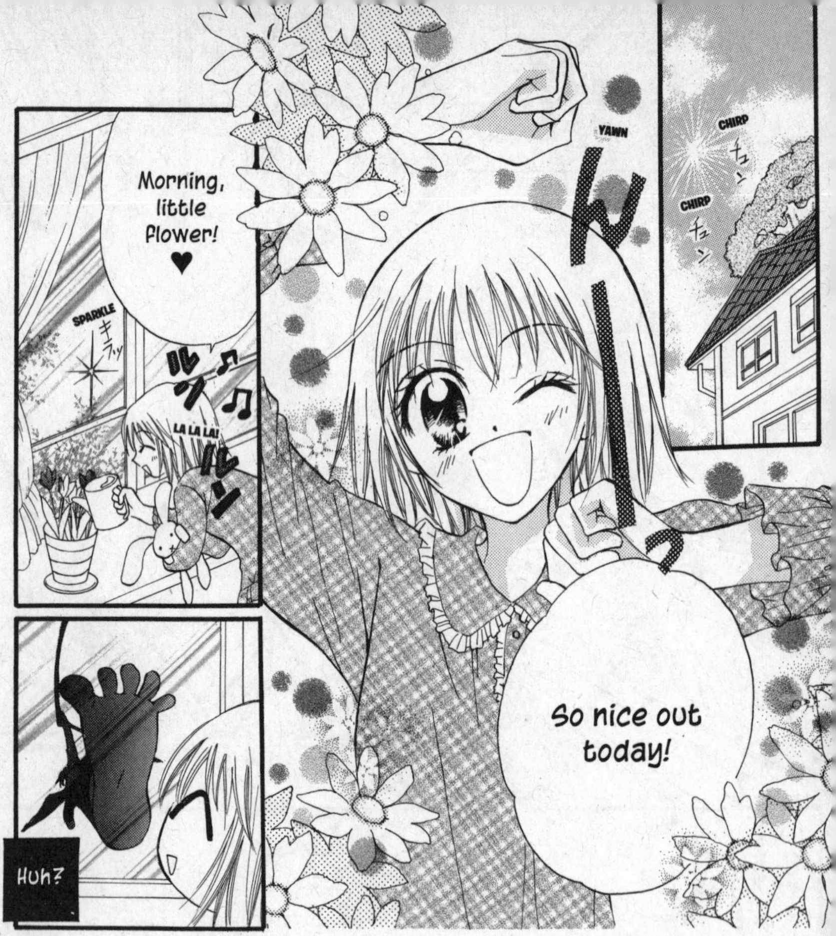
CHIRP
チュン
CHIRP
チュン
YAWN
So nice out today!
Morning, little flower! ♥
SPARKLE
キラッ
LA LA LA!
Huh?

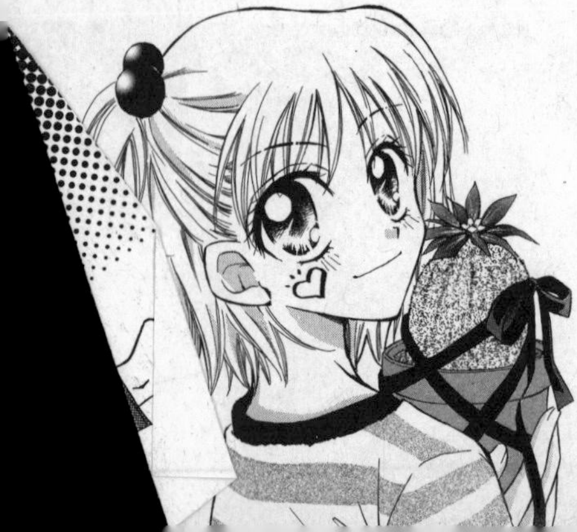

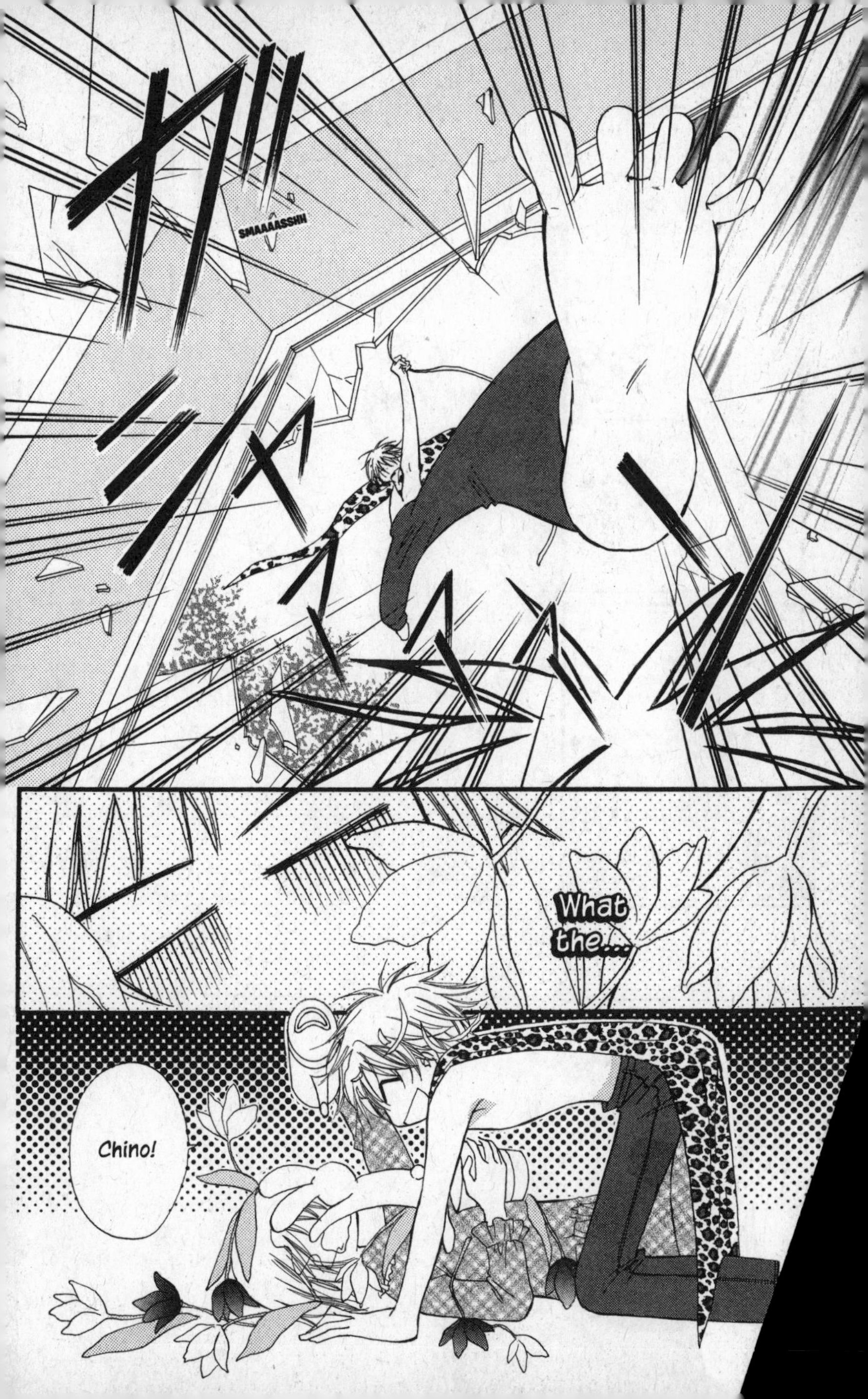
SMAAAASSHH
What the...
Chino!

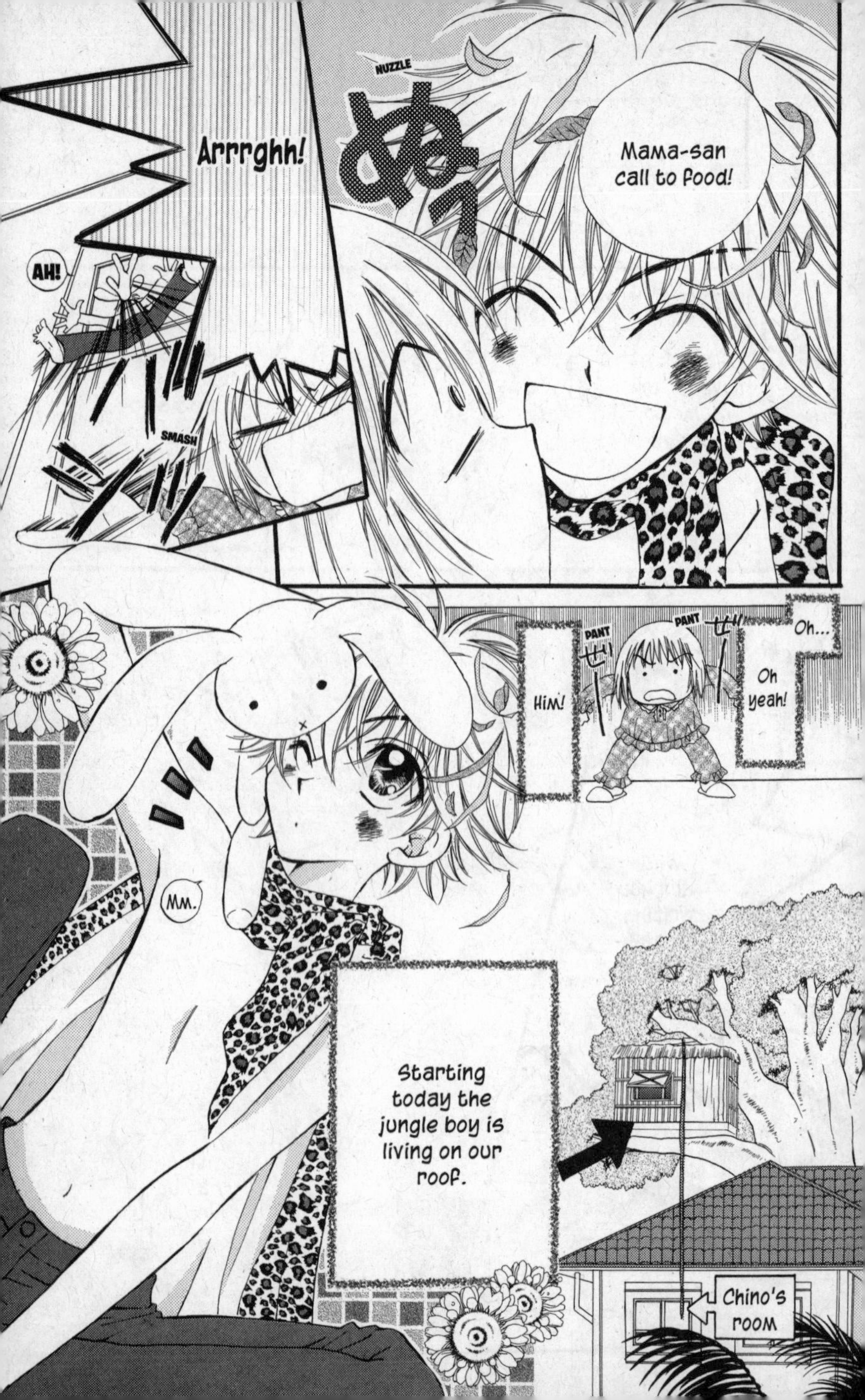
NUZZLE
ぬっ
Mama-san call to food!
Arrrghh!
AH!
SMASH
Oh...
Oh yeah!
PANT
PANT
Him!
Mm.
Starting today the jungle boy is living on our roof.
Chino's room

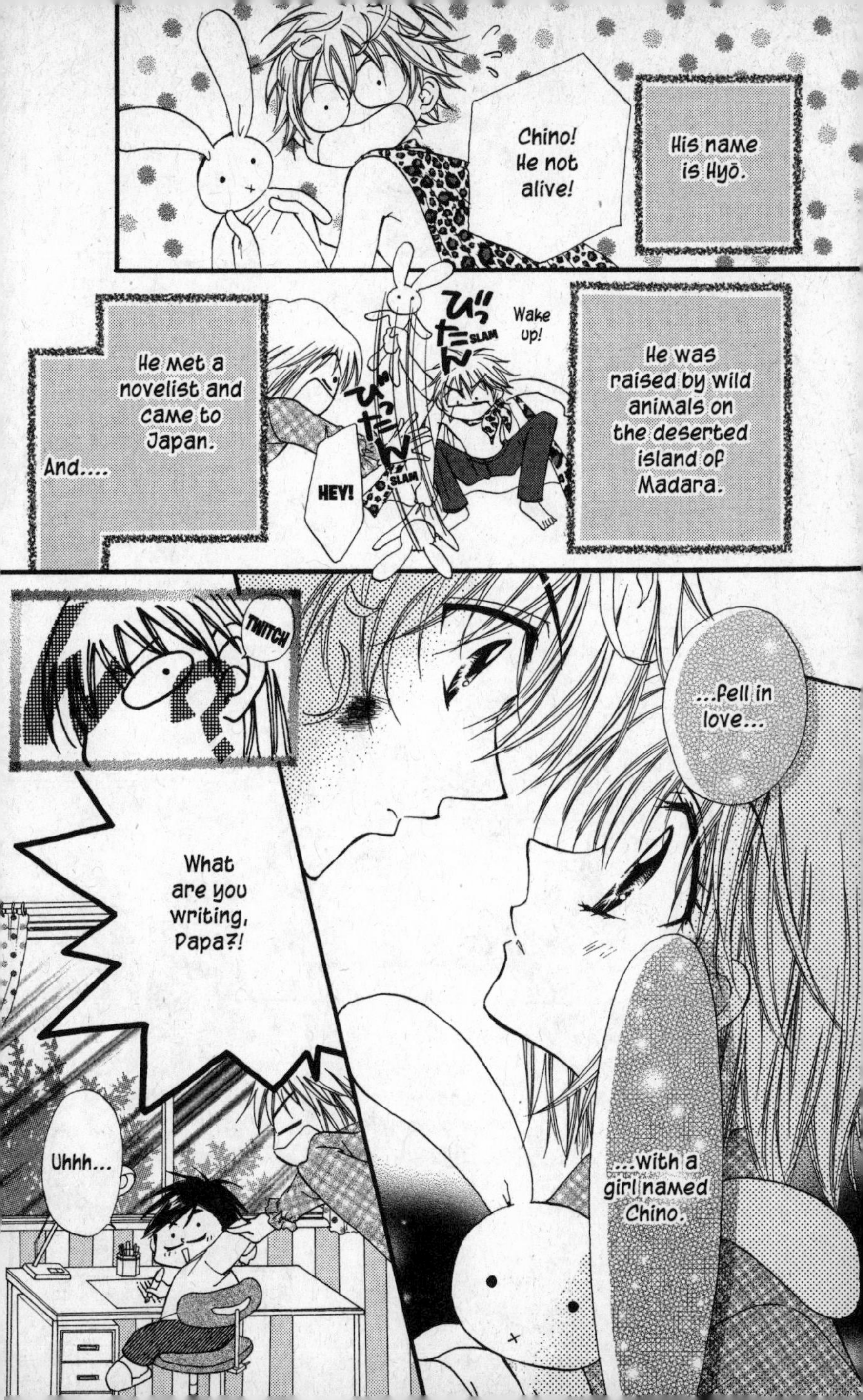
His name is Hyō.
Chino! He not alive!
He was raised by wild animals on the deserted island of Madara.
Wake up!
びったん SLAM
びったん SLAM
HEY!
He met a novelist and came to Japan.
And....
...fell in love...
...with a girl named Chino.
TWITCH
What are you writing, Papa?!
Uhhh...

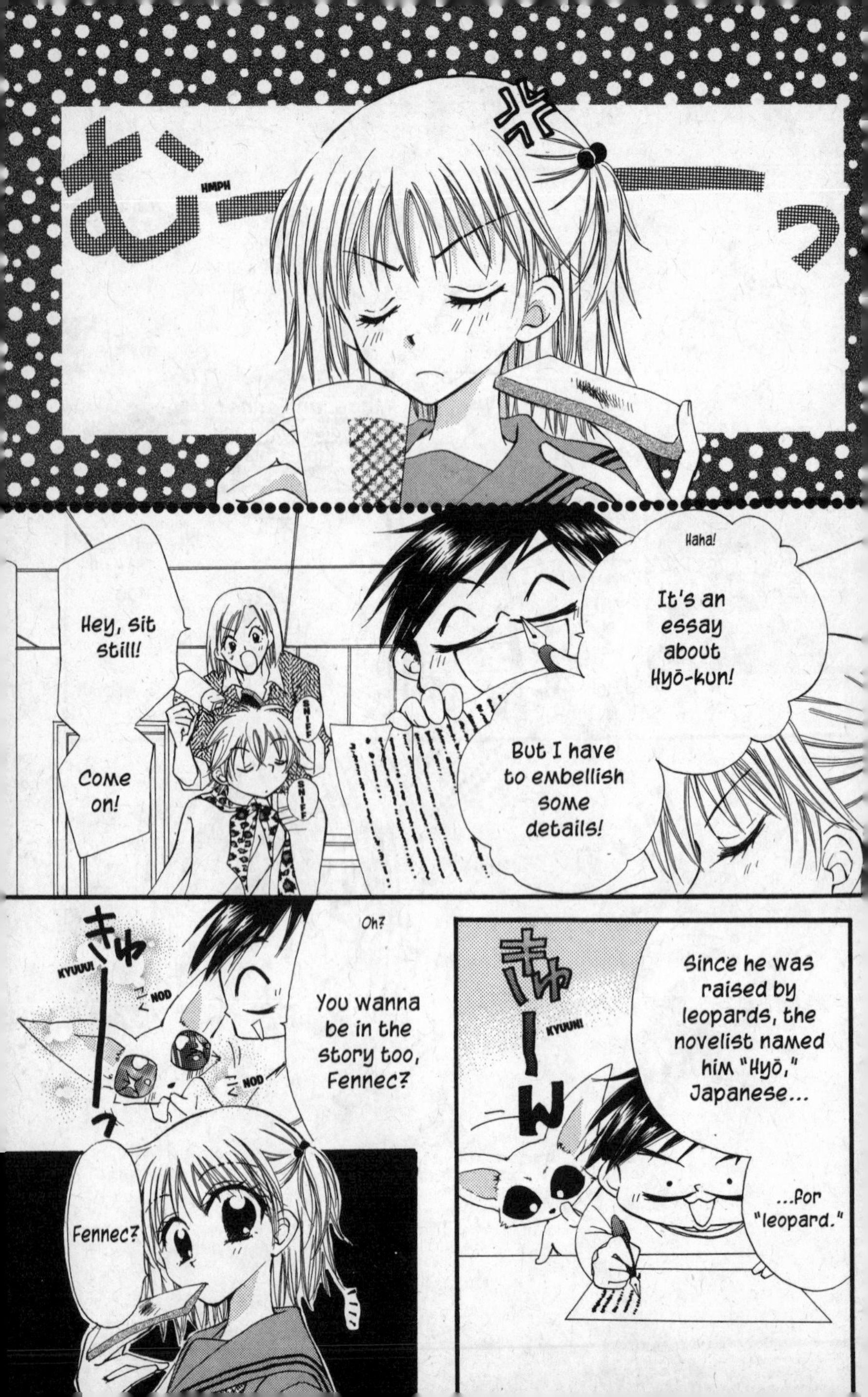
むーっ
HMPH
Haha!
It's an essay about Hyō-kun!
But I have to embellish some details!
Hey, sit still!
Come on!
SNIFF
SNIFF
きゅーん
KYUUN!
Since he was raised by leopards, the novelist named him "Hyō," Japanese...
...for "leopard."
Oh?
You wanna be in the story too, Fennec?
きゅーっ
KYUUU!
NOD
NOD
Fennec?

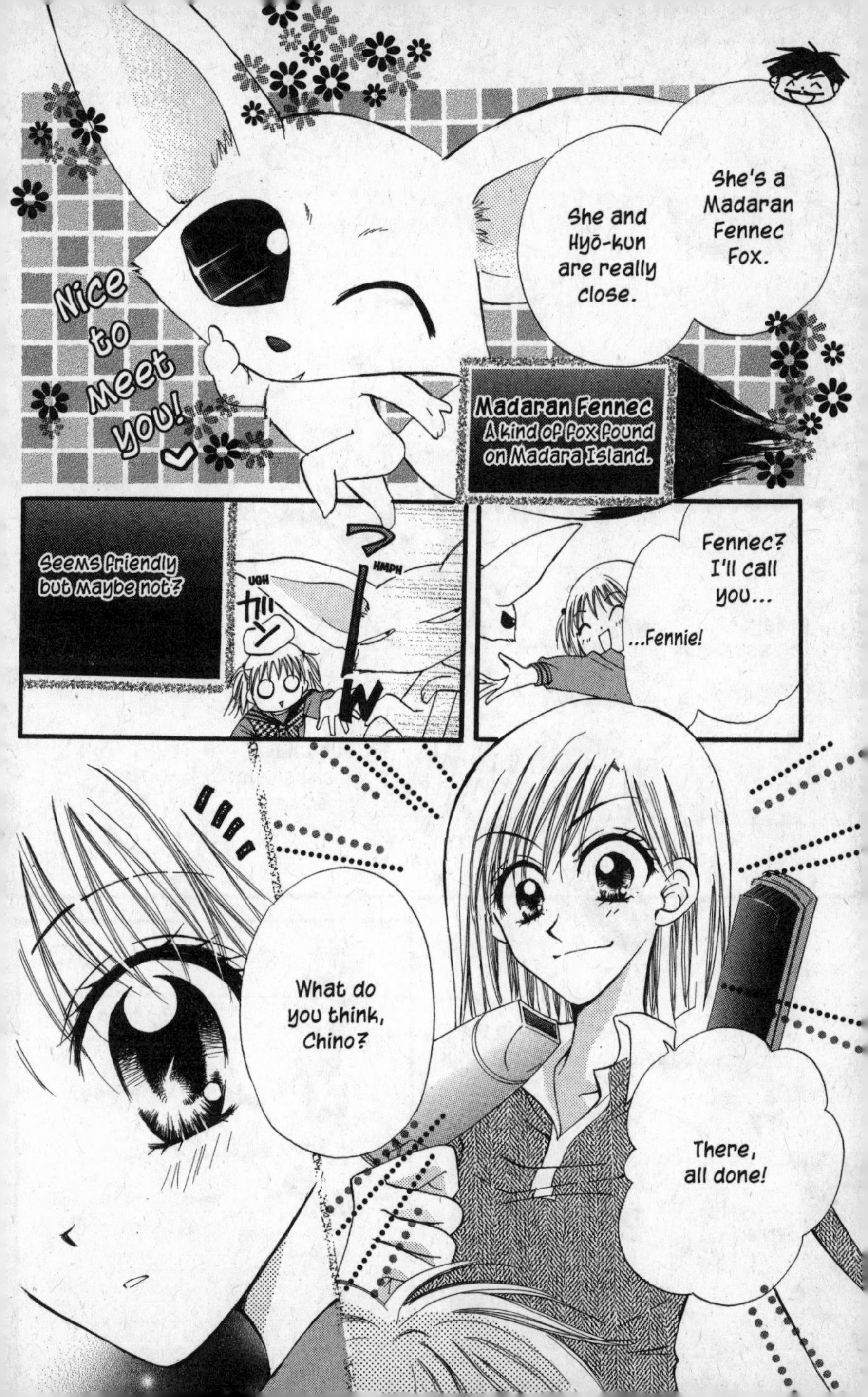
She's a Madaran Fennec Fox.
She and Hyō-kun are really close.
Nice to meet you!
Madaran Fennec
A kind of fox found on Madara Island.
Fennec? I'll call you...
...Fennie!
HMPH
UGH
Seems friendly but maybe not?
There, all done!
What do you think, Chino?

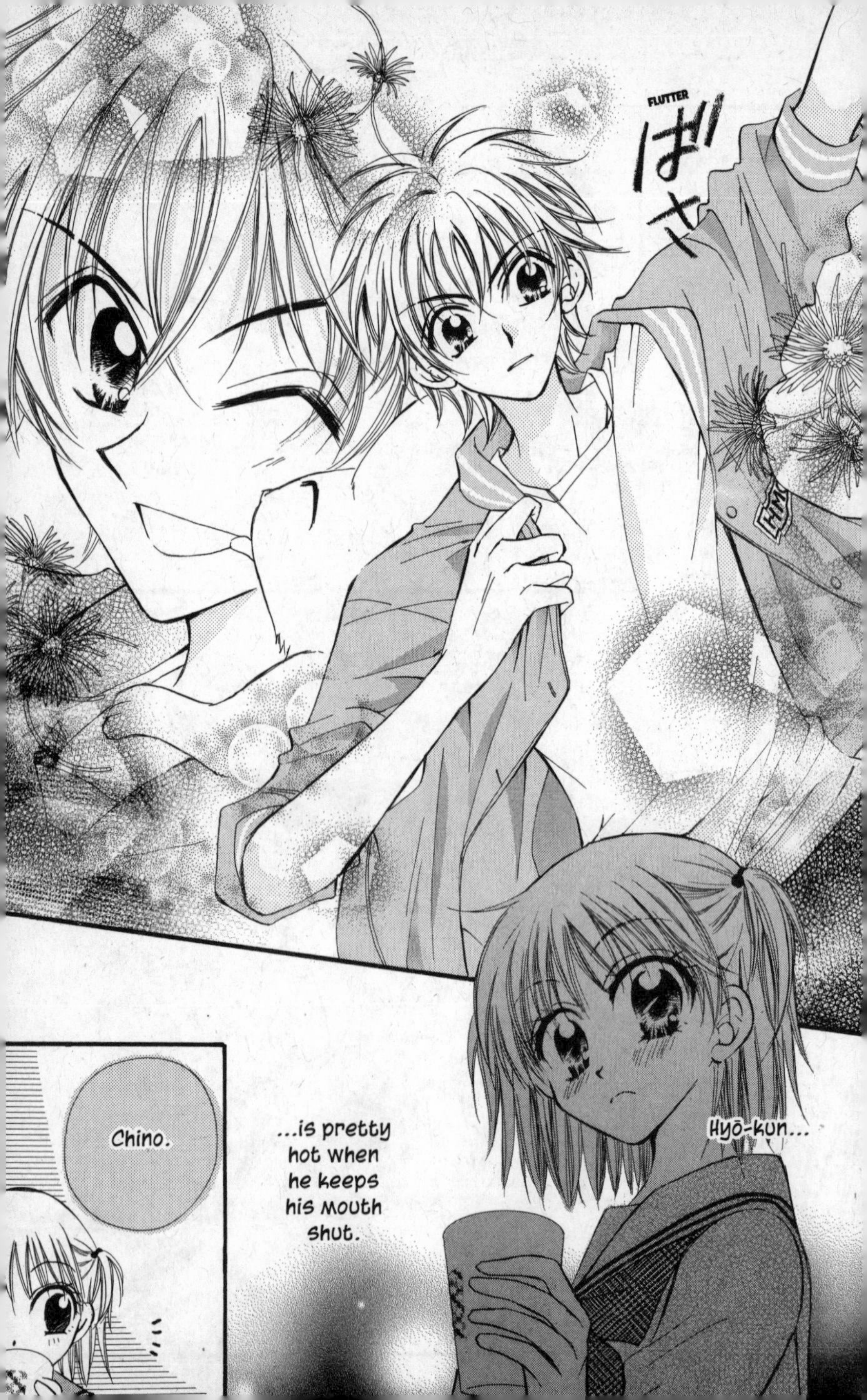
FLUTTER
ばさ
Hyō-kun...
...is pretty hot when he keeps his mouth shut.
Chino.

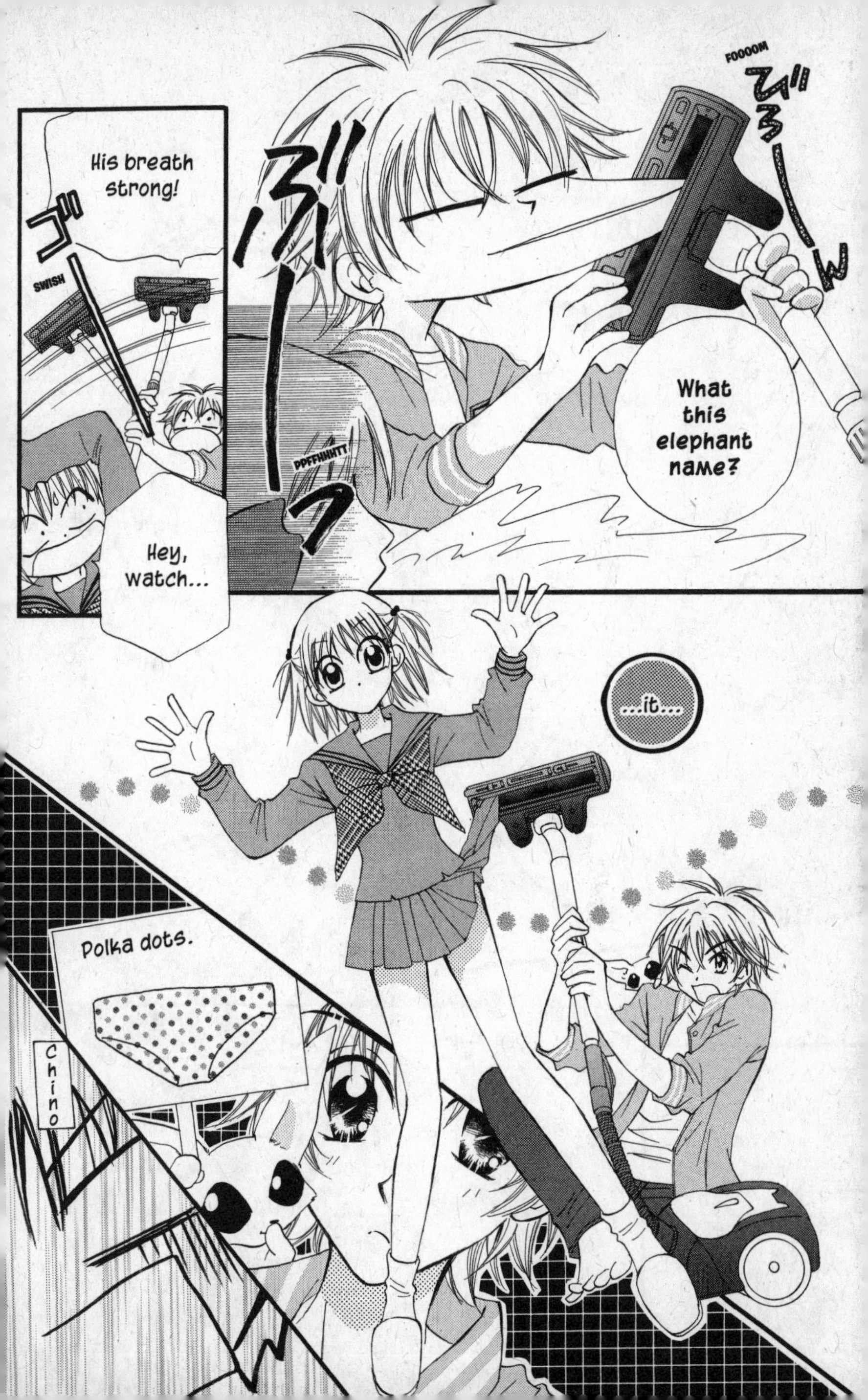
FOOOOM
What this elephant name?
PPFFHHHTT!
His breath strong!
SWISH
Hey, watch...
...it...
Polka dots.
Chino

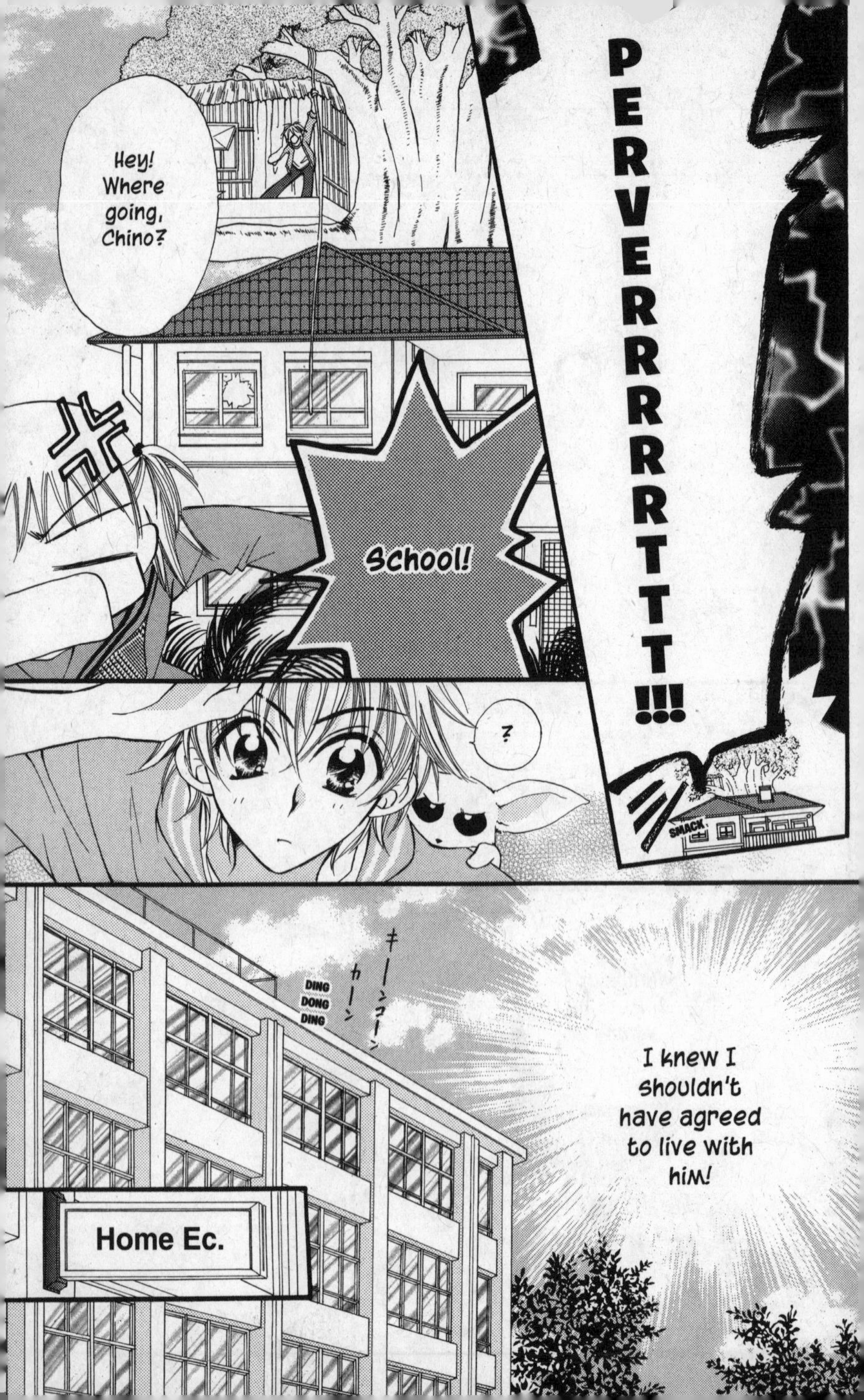
PERVERRRRTTT!!!
SMACK
Hey! Where going, Chino?
School!
?
I knew I shouldn't have agreed to live with him!
キーンコーン
カーン
DING DONG DING
Home Ec.

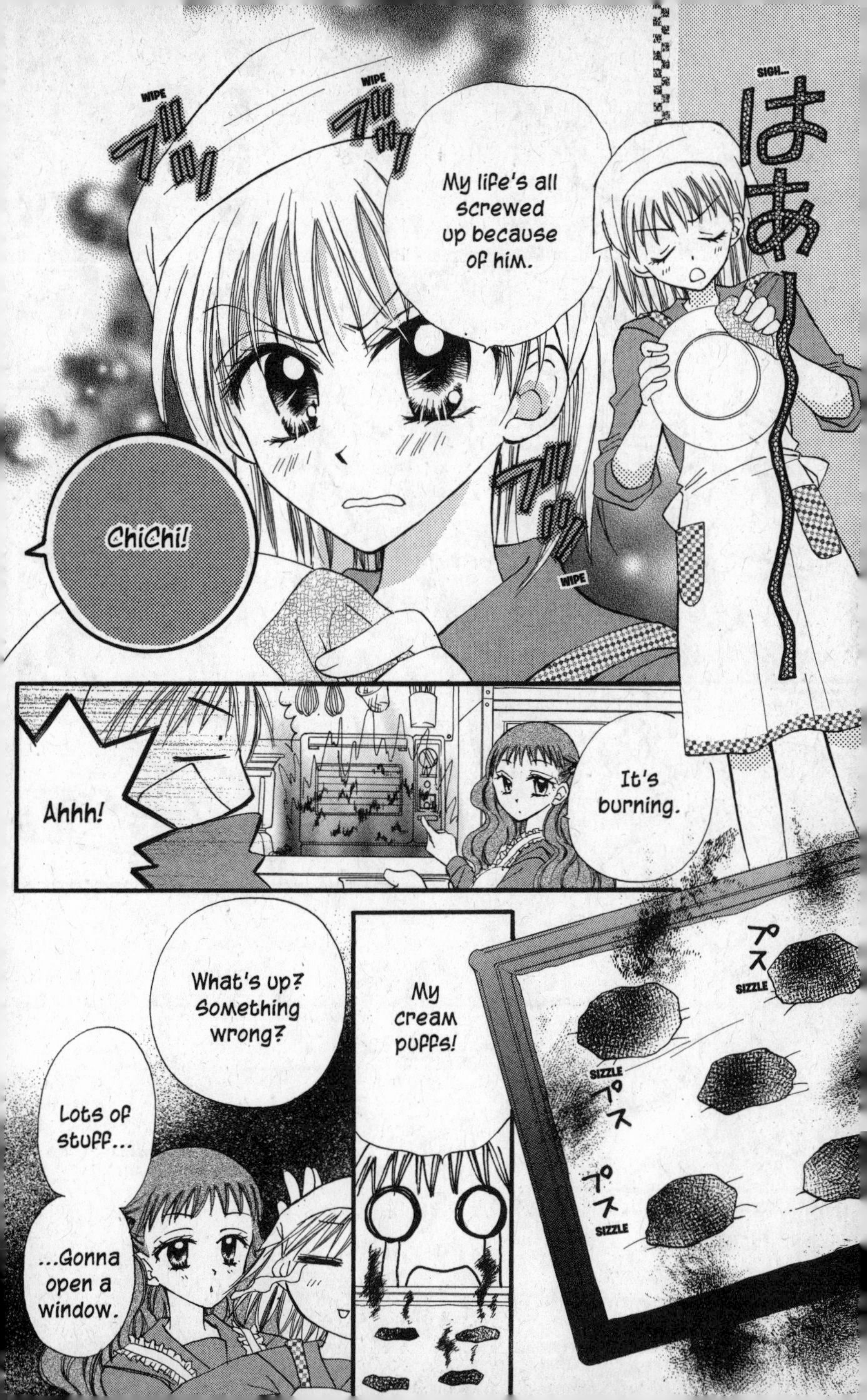
SIGH...
はあ
WIPE
WIPE
My life's all screwed up because of him.
WIPE
ChiChi!
It's burning.
Ahhh!
プス
SIZZLE
SIZZLE
プス
プス
SIZZLE
My cream puffs!
What's up? Something wrong?
Lots of stuff...
...Gonna open a window.

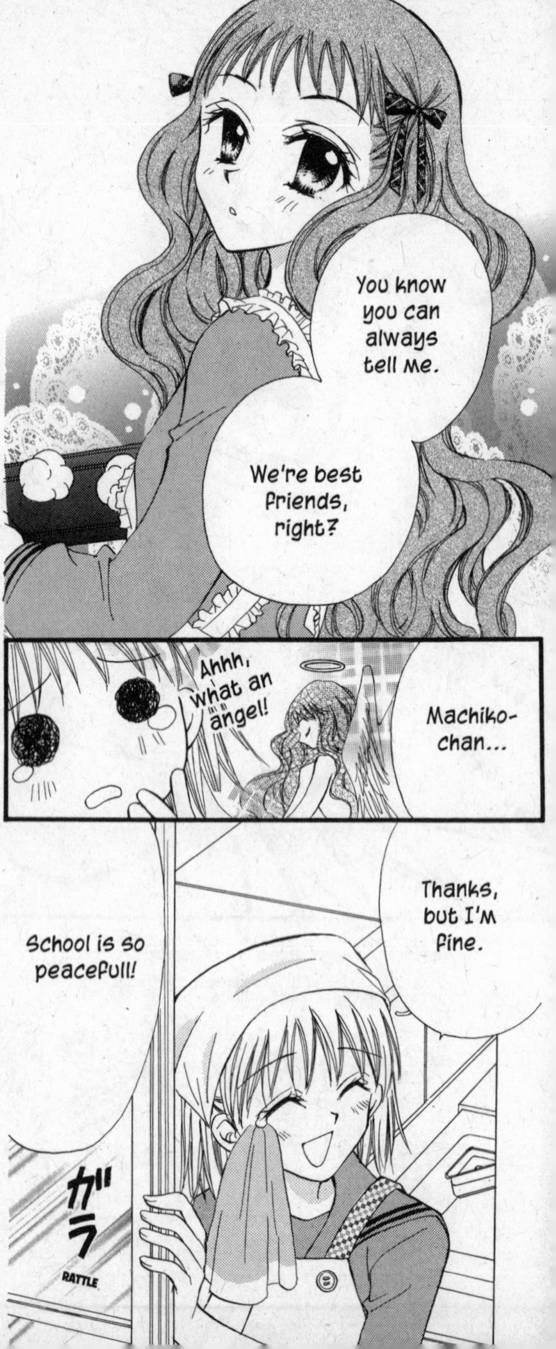
You know you can always tell me.
We're best friends, right?
Machiko-chan...
Ahhh, what an angel!
Thanks, but I'm fine.
School is so peacefull!
ガラ
RATTLE

2.

Before I started *Wild @ Heart* I visited a safari park. It was the first time I'd ever been to one. It was just like Africa with its vast fields and animals running around everywhere... at least that's what I imagined, but it was actually just kind of like a big zoo. Oh well. I did get pretty close to the animals though (we were in a Jeep), so that was pretty exciting. At one point I had the chance to feed some grass to a giraffe but it walked away before I could do it. I was so disappointed!

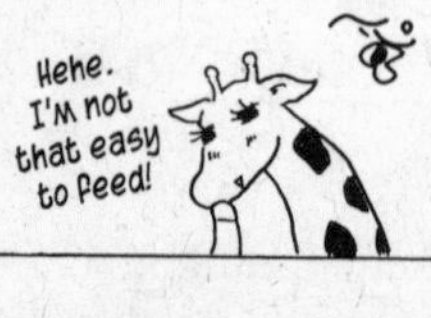
Hehe. I'm not that easy to feed!

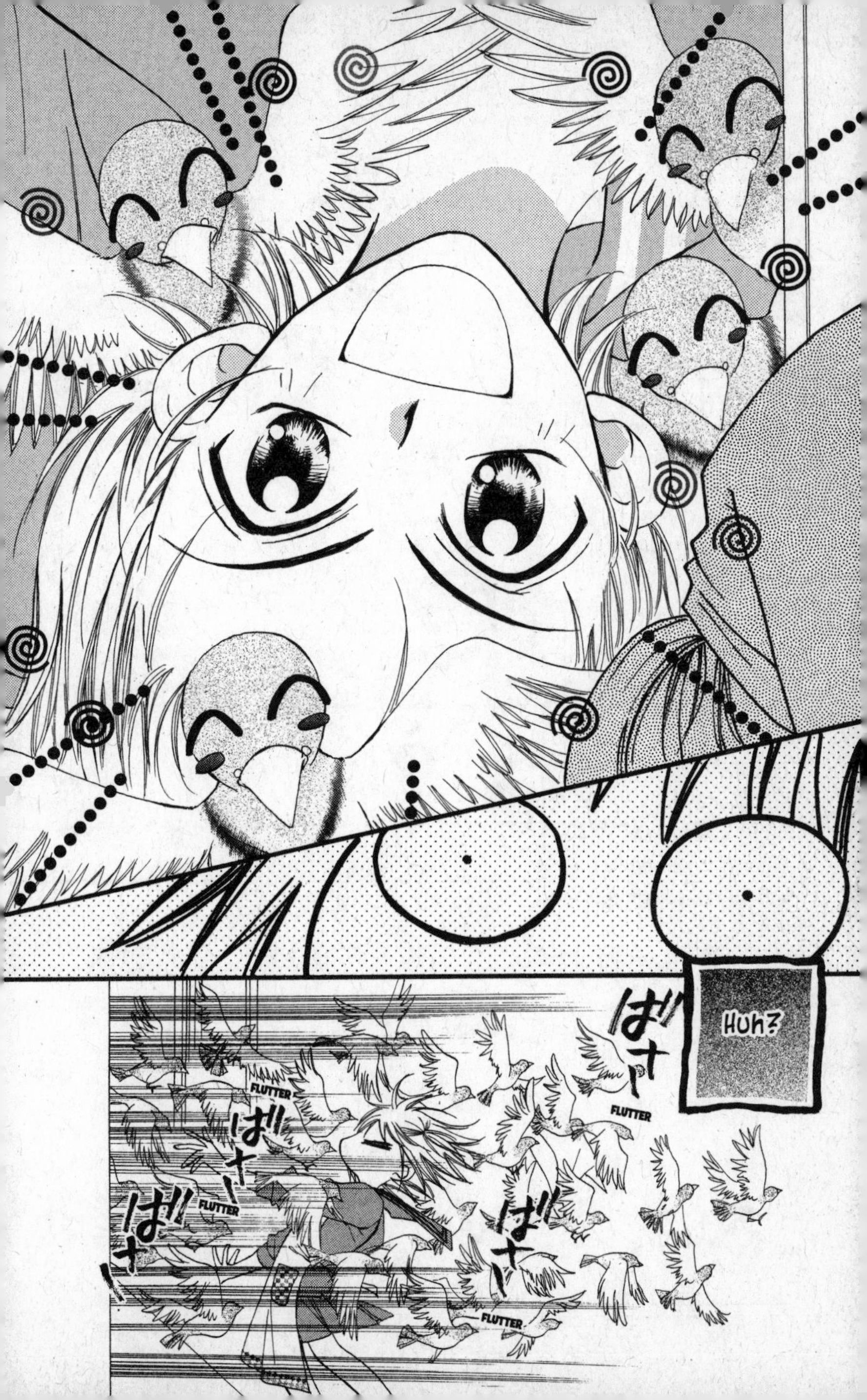
Huh?
FLUTTER
FLUTTER
FLUTTER
FLUTTER

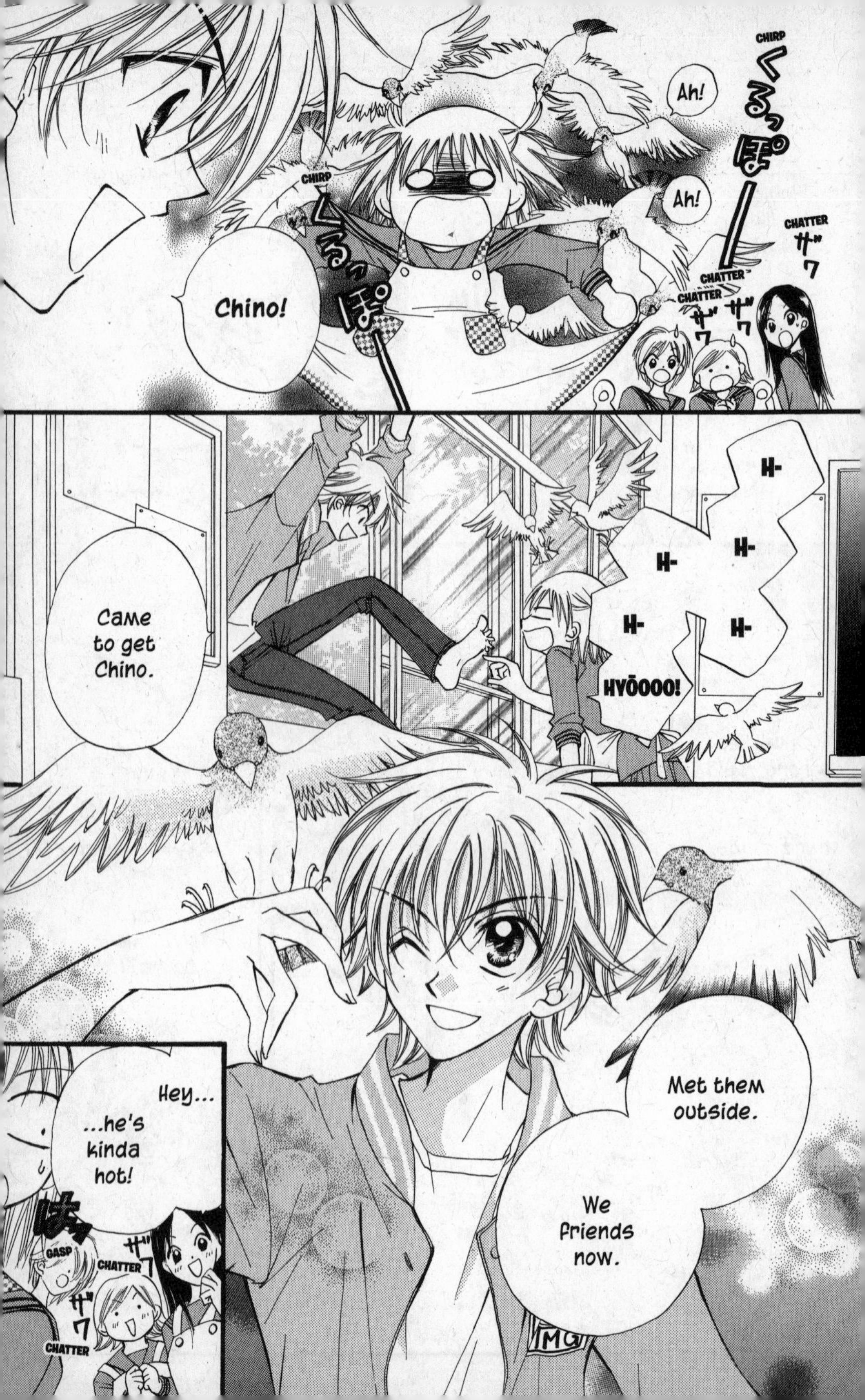
CHIRP
くるっぽー
Ah!
Ah!
CHATTER
ザワ
CHATTER
ザワ
CHATTER
ザワ
CHIRP
くるっぽ
Chino!
H- H- H- H- H-
HYŌOOO!
Came to get Chino.
Met them outside.
We friends now.
Hey...
...he's kinda hot!
はっ
GASP
CHATTER
ザワ
ザワ
CHATTER

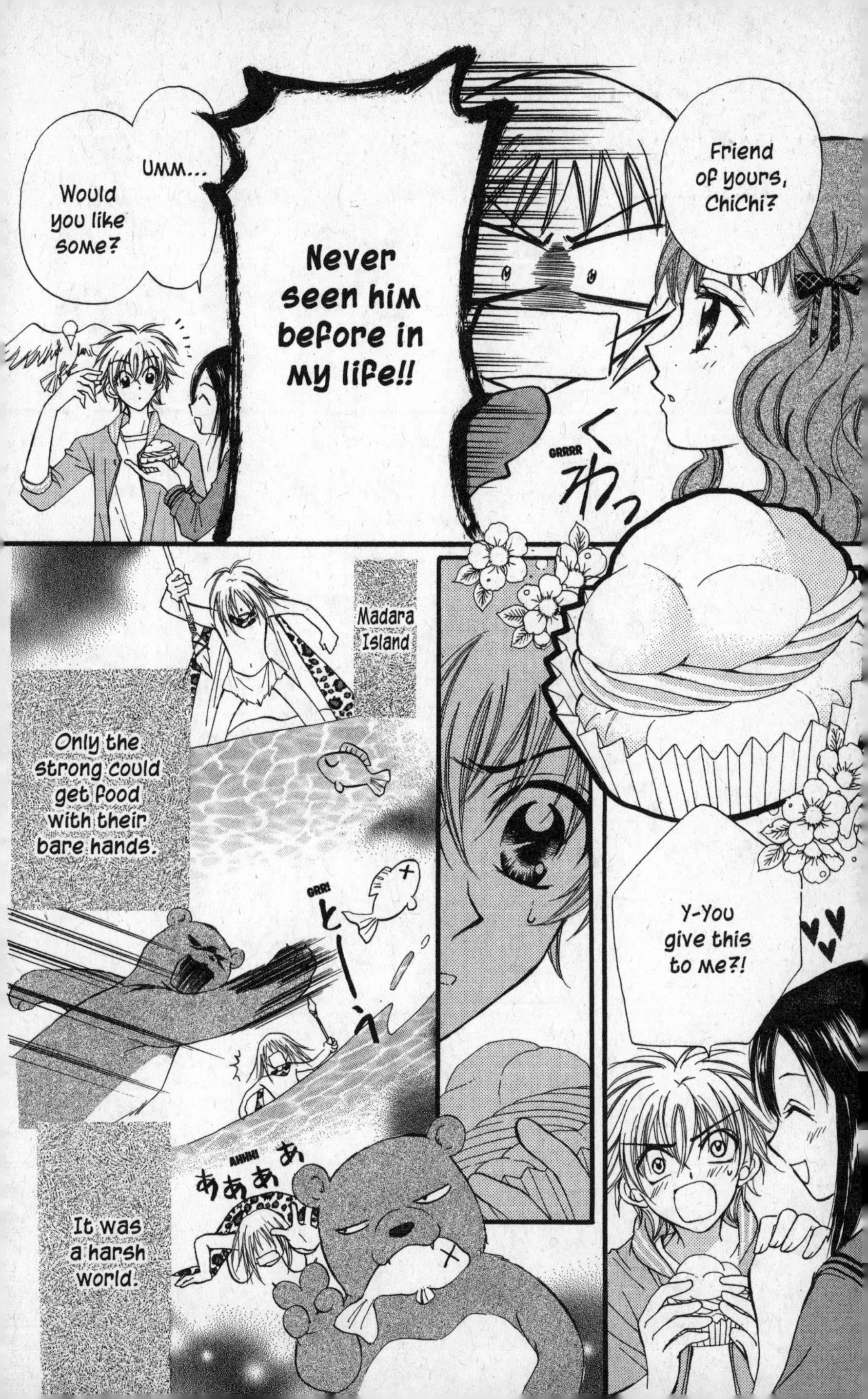
Friend of yours, ChiChi?
Never seen him before in my life!!
GRRRR
Umm...
Would you like some?
Y-You give this to me?!
Madara Island
Only the strong could get food with their bare hands.
GRR!
AHHH!
It was a harsh world.

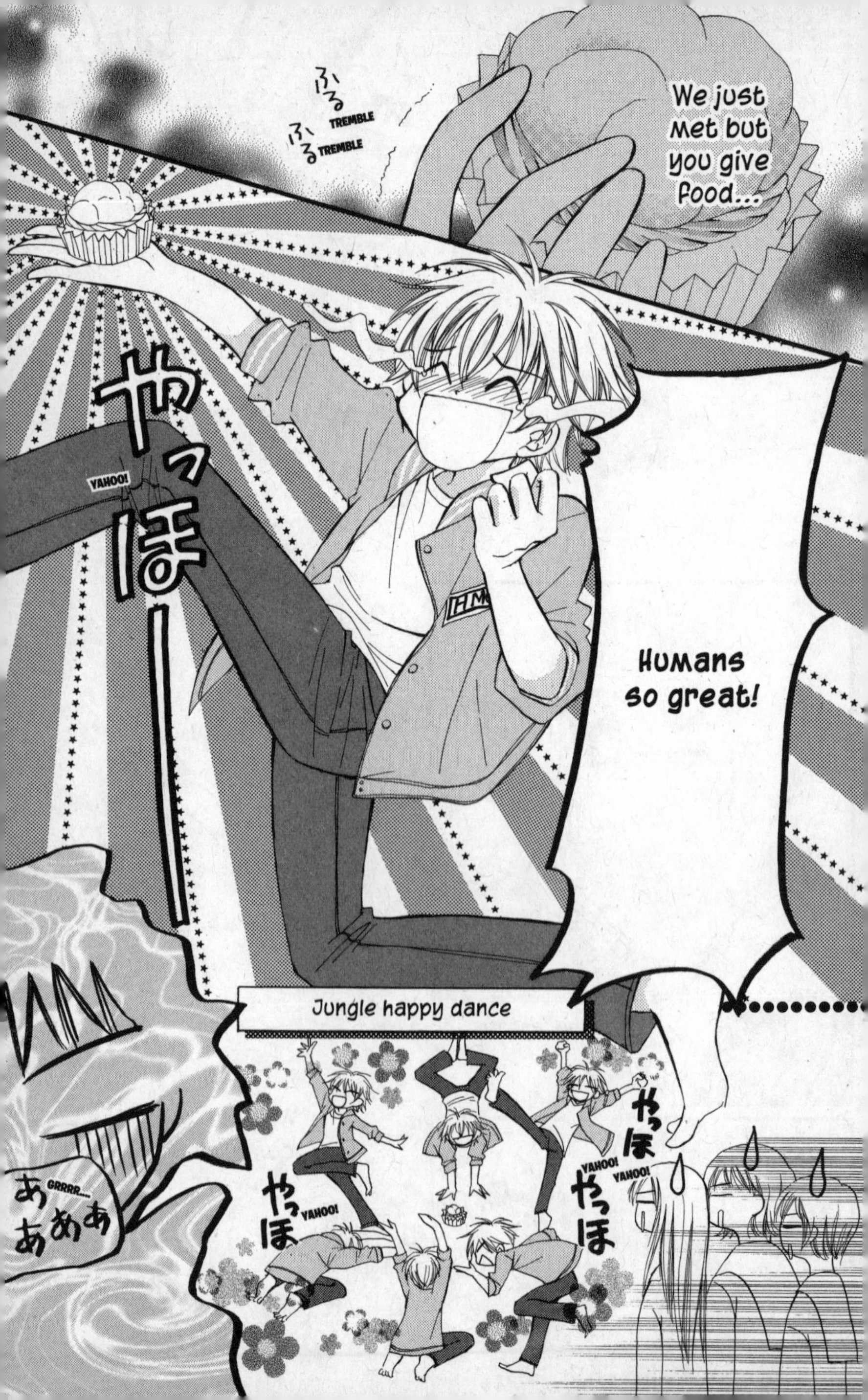
We just met but you give food...
ふるTREMBLE
ふるTREMBLE
Humans so great!
やっほー
YAHOO!
Jungle happy dance
やっほ
YAHOO!
やっほ
YAHOO!
やっほ
YAHOO!
ああああ
GRRRR...

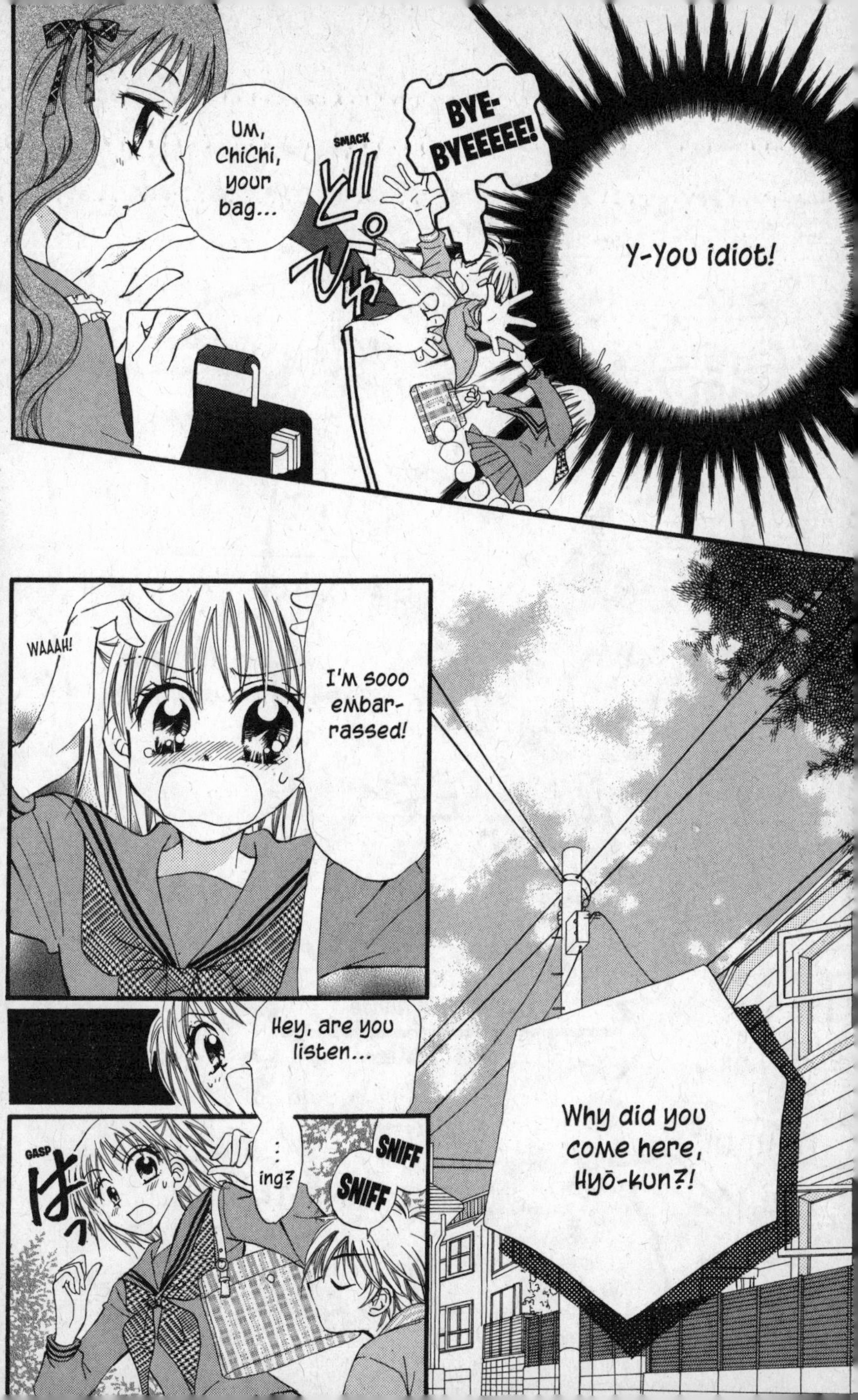
Y-You idiot!
BYE-BYEEEEE!
SMACK
Um, ChiChi, your bag...
Why did you come here, Hyō-kun?!
I'm sooo embarrassed!
WAAAH!
Hey, are you listen...
...ing?
SNIFF
SNIFF
GASP
はっ

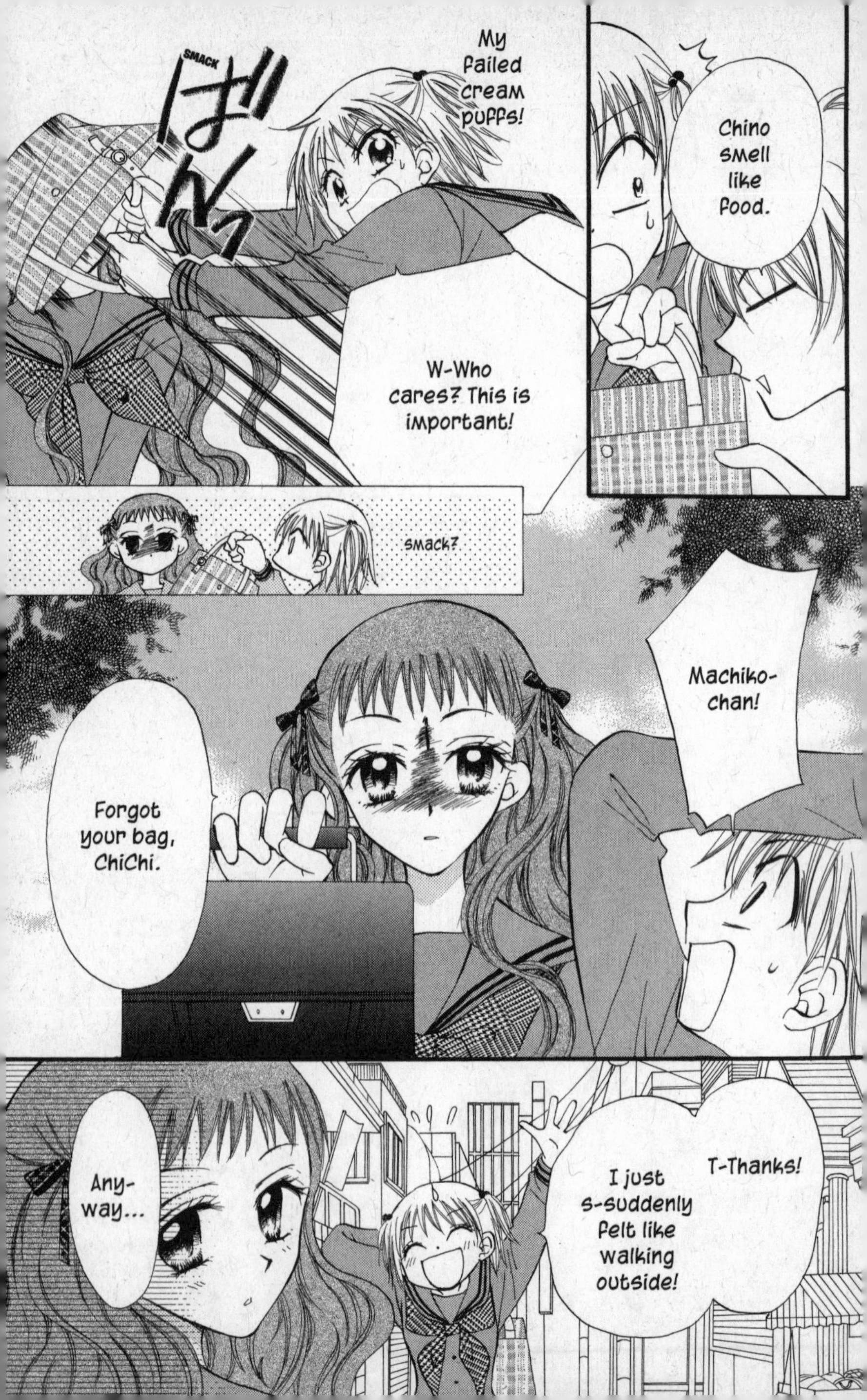
Chino smell like food.
SMACK
My failed cream puffs!
W-Who cares? This is important!
smack?
Machiko-chan!
Forgot your bag, ChiChi.
T-Thanks!
I just s-suddenly felt like walking outside!
Any-way...

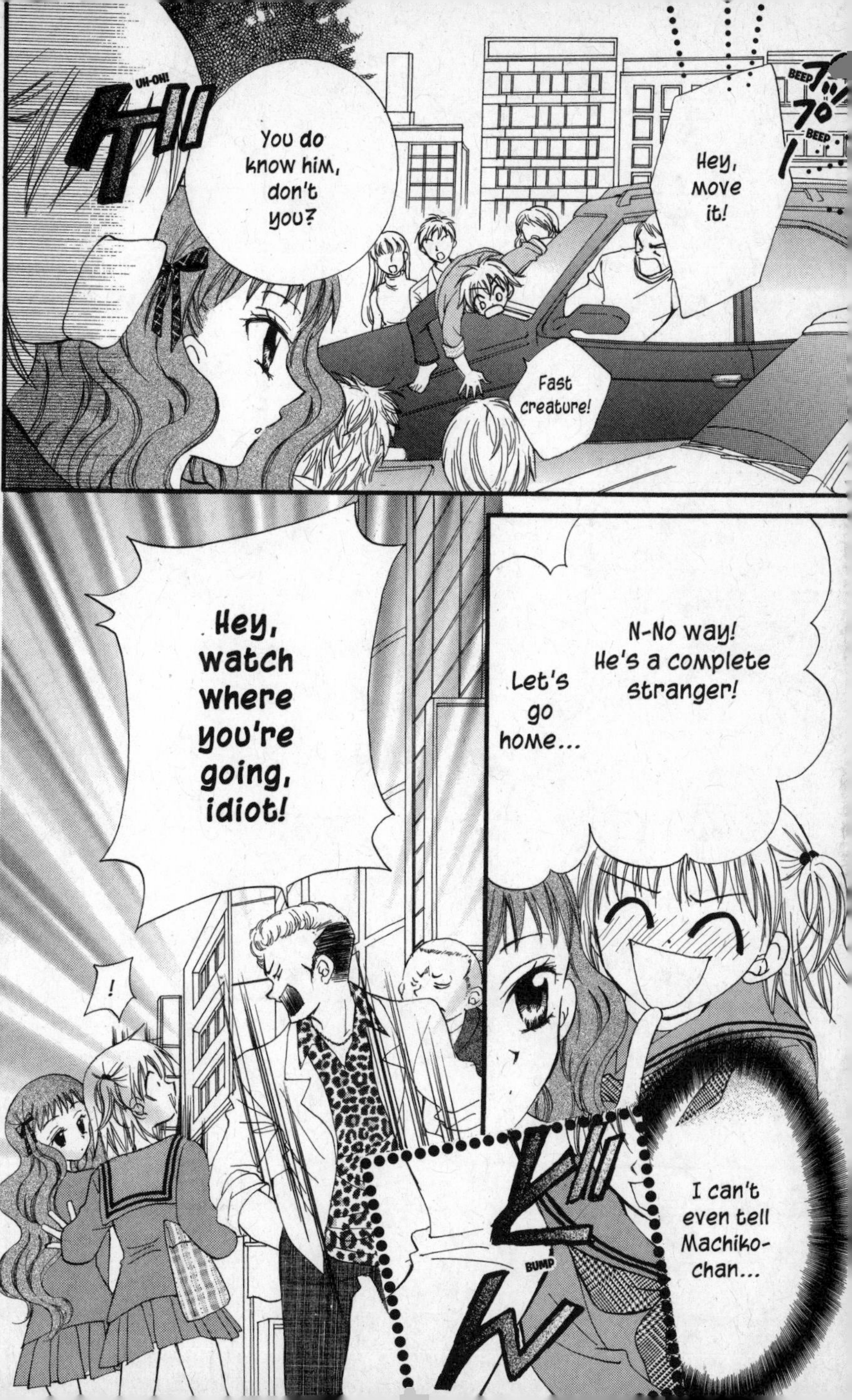
BEEP
BEEP
Hey, move it!
You do know him, don't you?
UH-OH!
Fast creature!
N-No way! He's a complete stranger!
Let's go home...
I can't even tell Machiko-chan...
BUMP
Hey, watch where you're going, idiot!
!

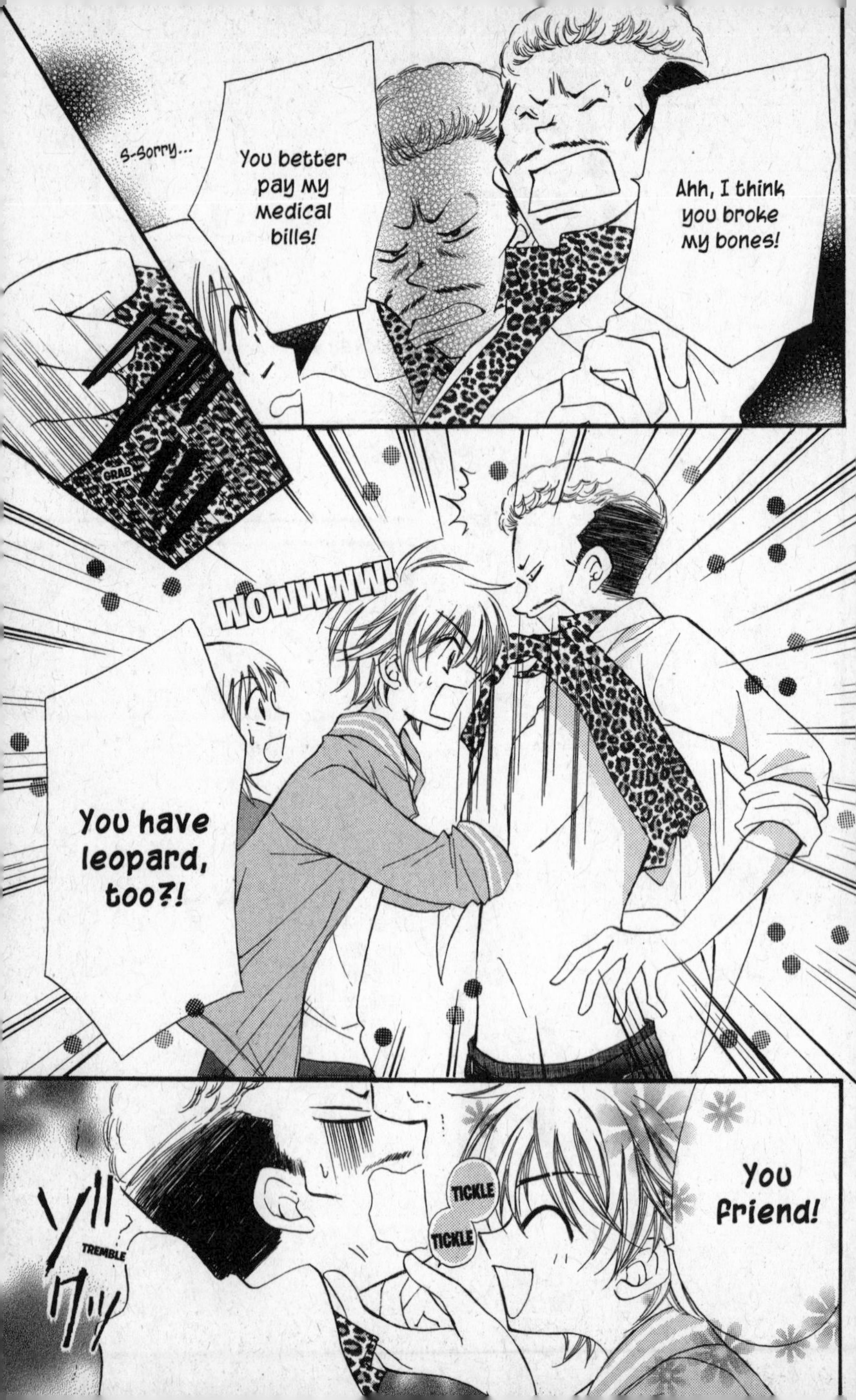
Ahh, I think you broke my bones!
You better pay my medical bills!
S-Sorry...
GRAB
WOWWWW!
You have leopard, too?!
You friend!
TICKLE
TICKLE
TREMBLE

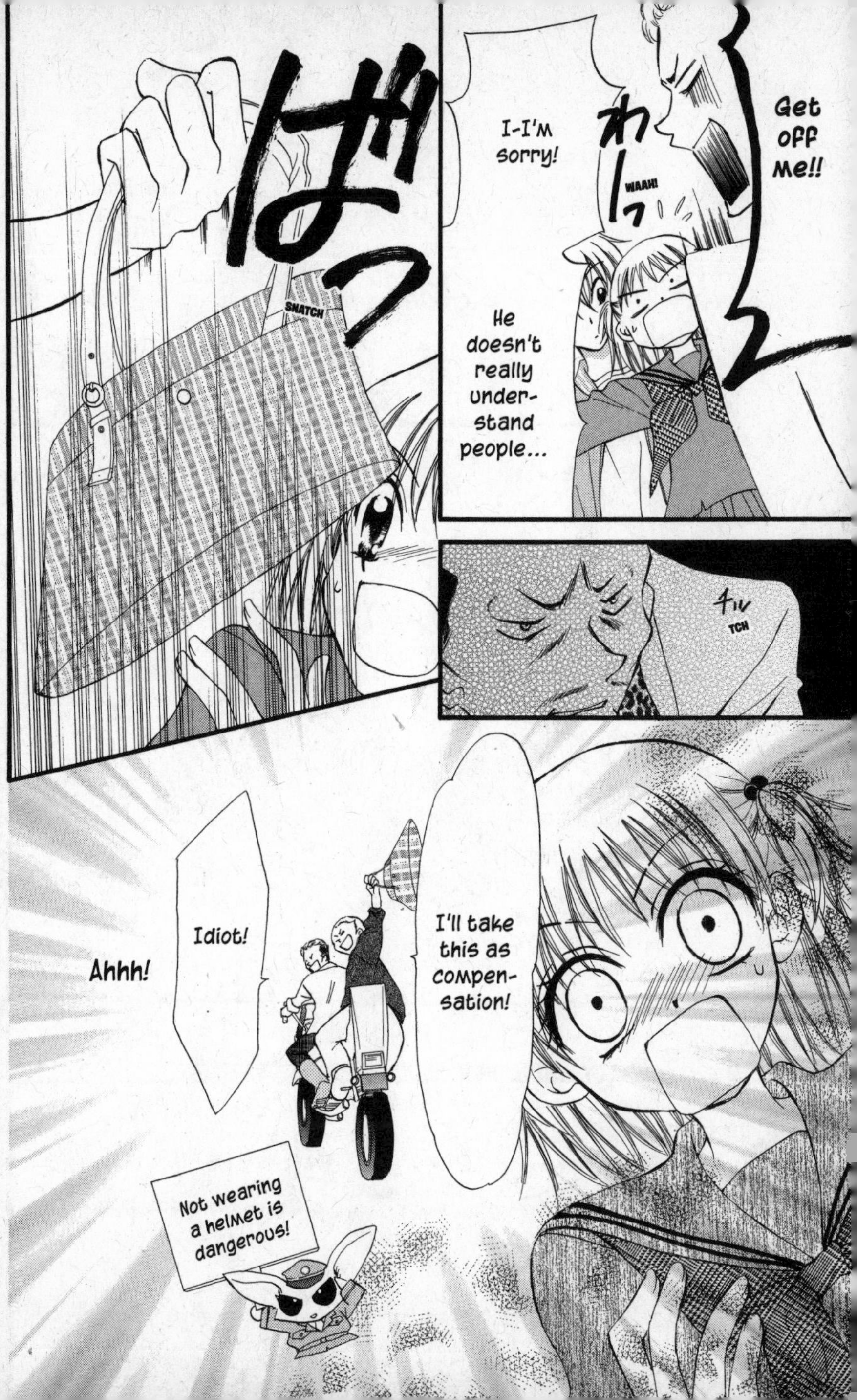
Get off me!!
わーっ
WAAH!
I-I'm sorry!
He doesn't really under-stand people...
チッ
TCH
ばっ
SNATCH
I'll take this as compen-sation!
Idiot!
Ahhh!
Not wearing a helmet is dangerous!

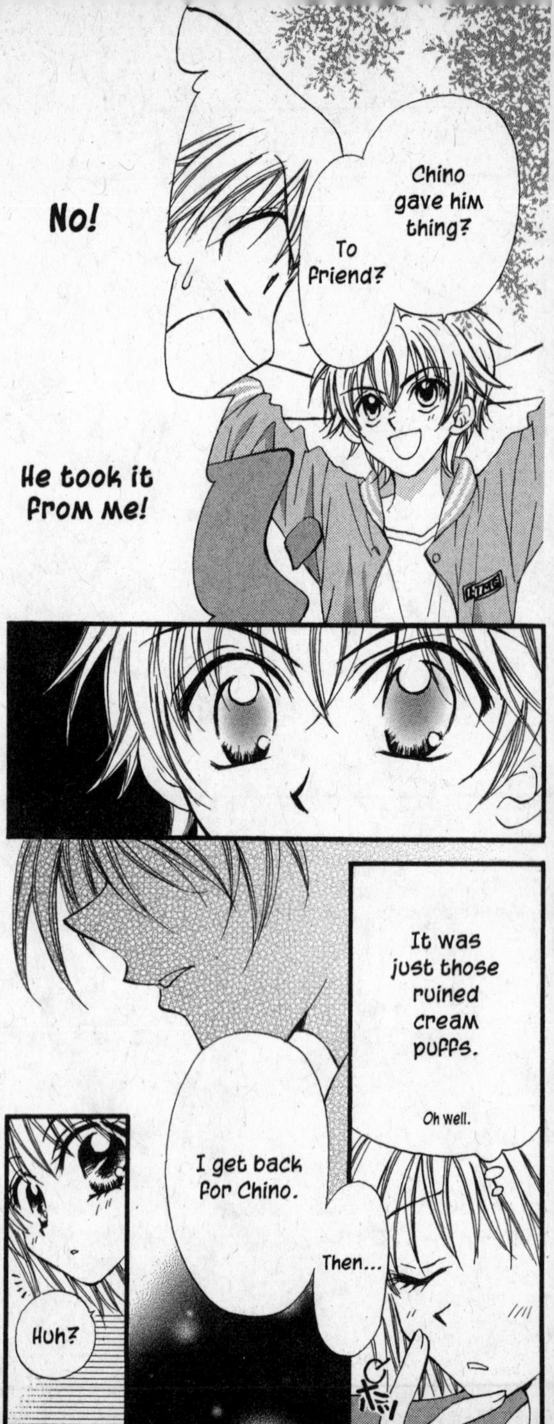
Chino gave him thing?
To friend?
No!
He took it from me!
It was just those ruined cream puffs.
Oh well.
Then...
I get back for Chino.
Huh?

3.

(Still going on about the safari park)
When we got to the lion area, there was only one there and he was covered in cuts, and the guide said...

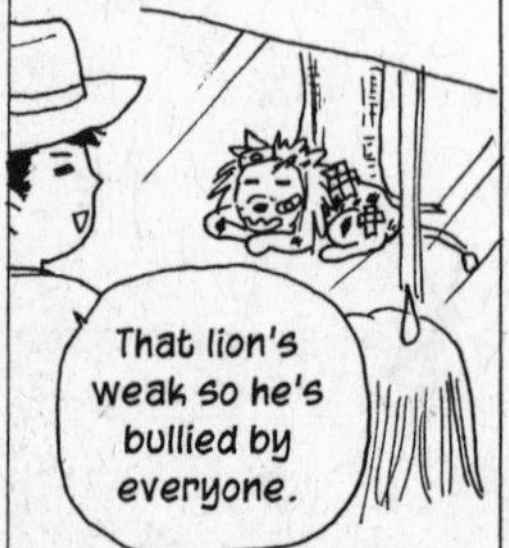
That lion's weak so he's bullied by everyone.

I guess lions have it rough sometimes, too. When I was walking around the park, I saw something from the trees...

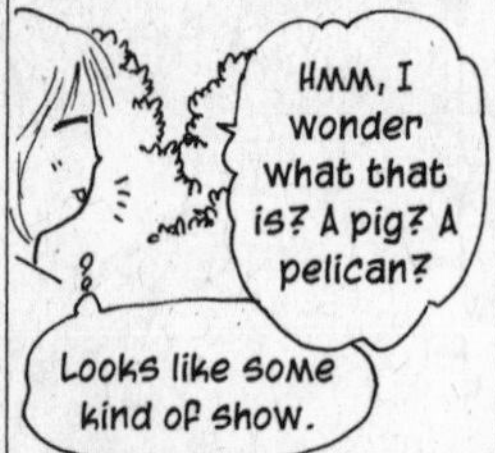
Hmm, I wonder what that is? A pig? A pelican?
Looks like some kind of show.

But when we got closer...

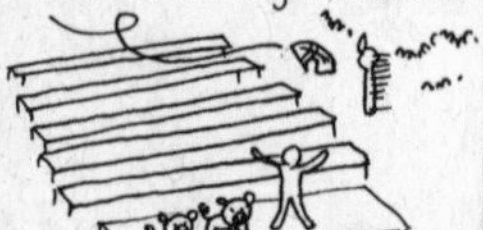

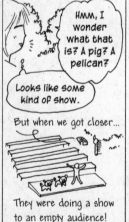

They were doing a show to an empty audience!

Because it was winter.
But it was a great show! ♥

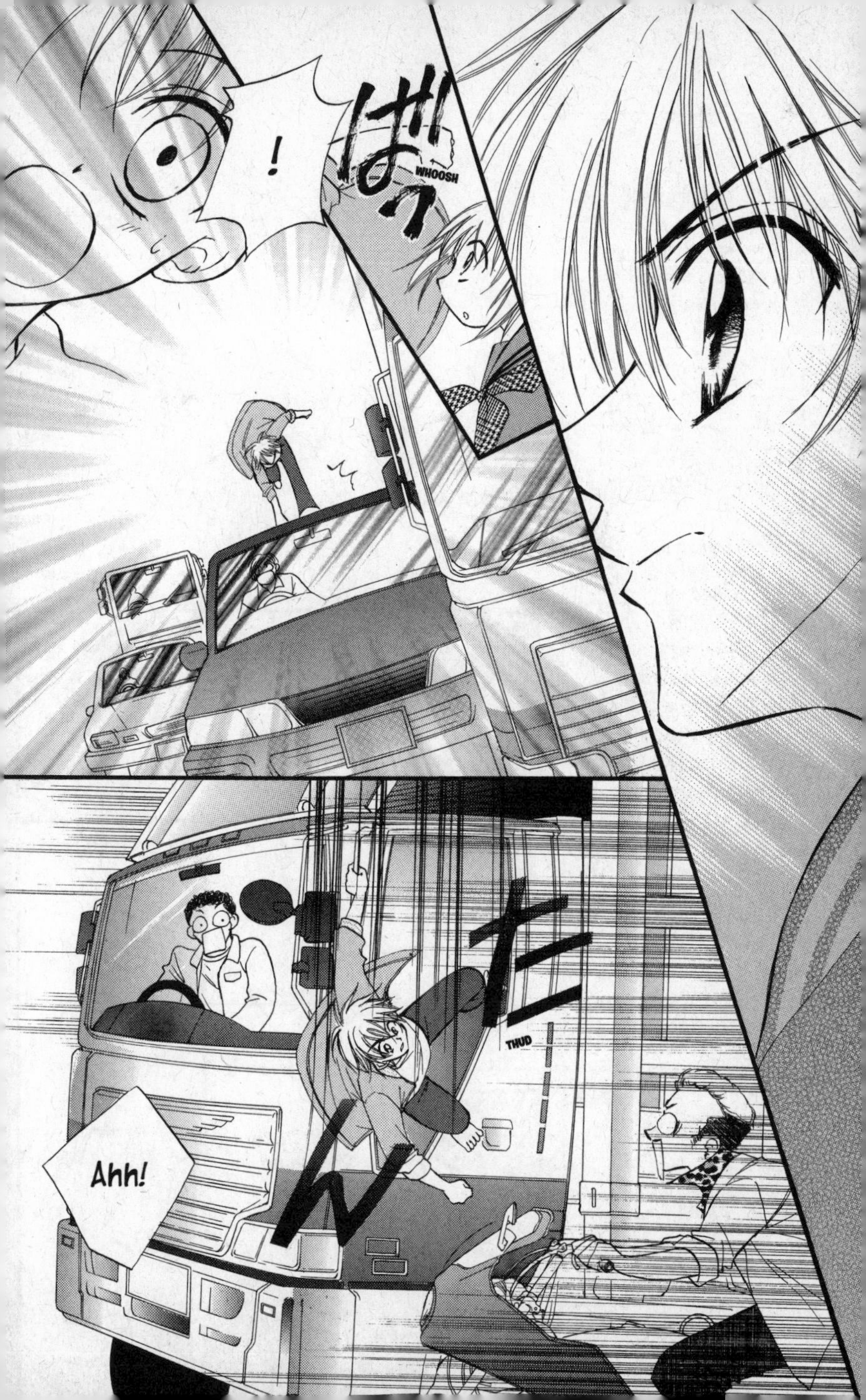
WHOOSH
!
THUD
Ahh!

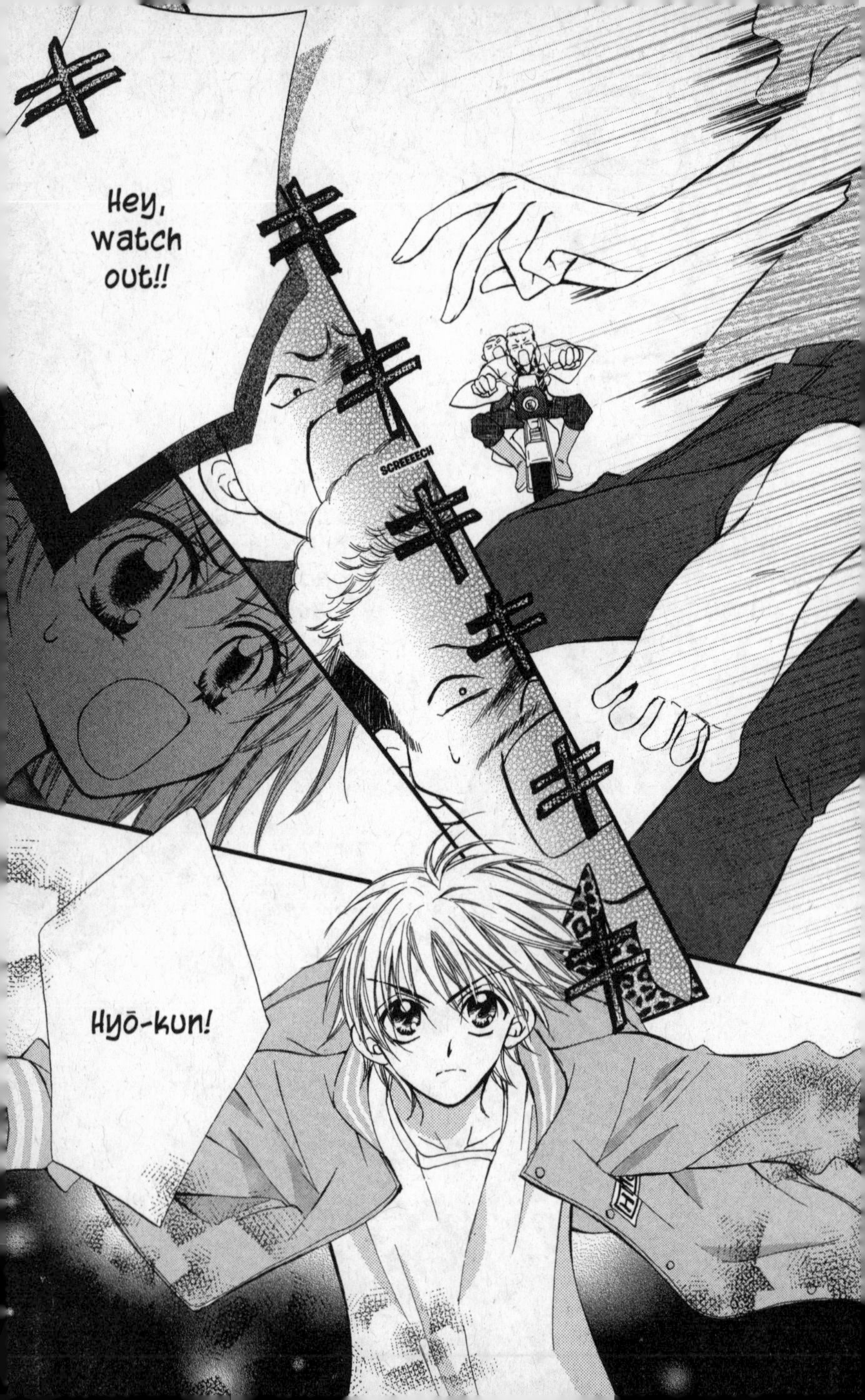
Hey, watch out!!
SCREEECH
Hyō-kun!

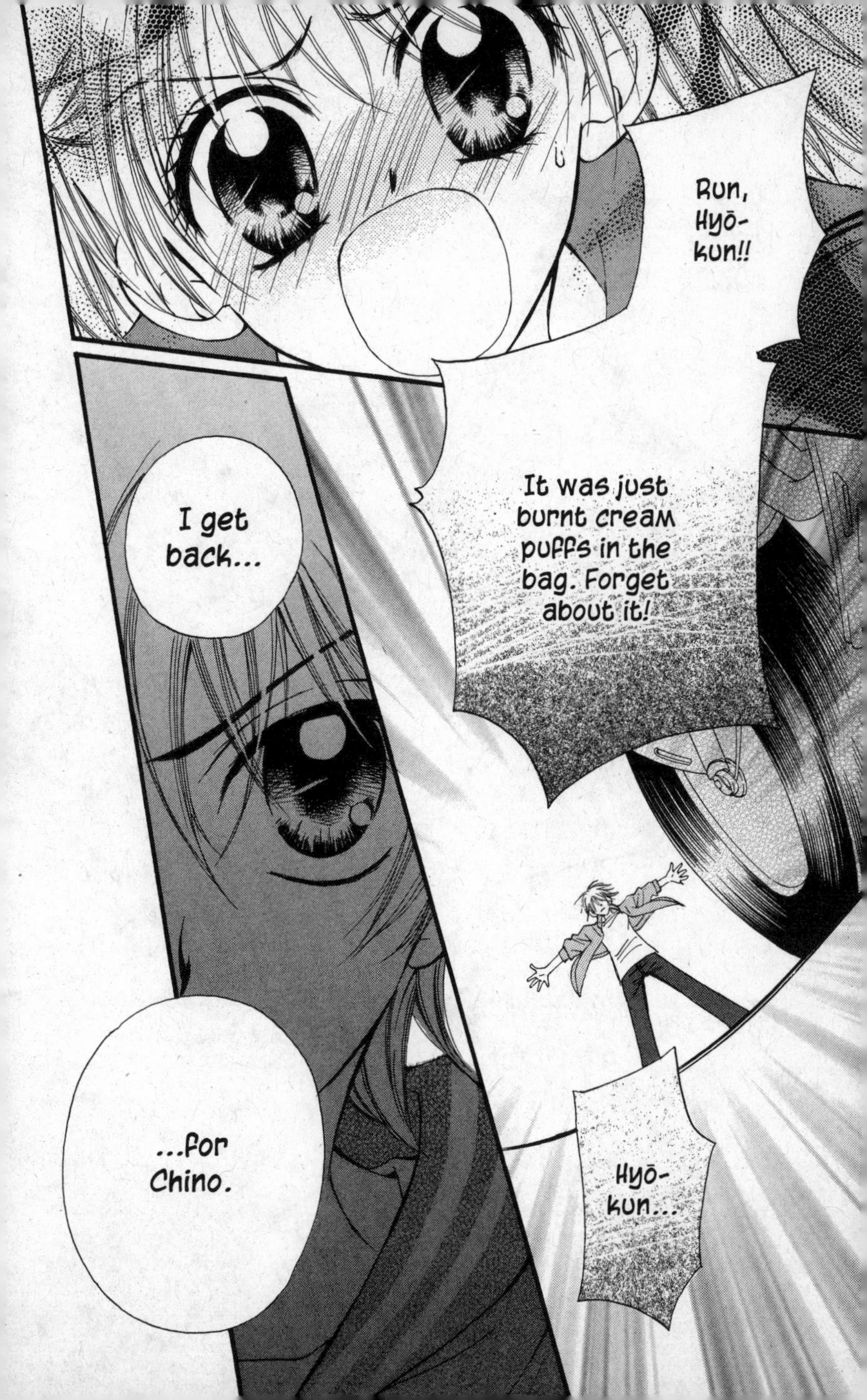
Run, Hyō-kun!!
It was just burnt cream puffs in the bag. Forget about it!
Hyō-kun...
I get back...
...for Chino.

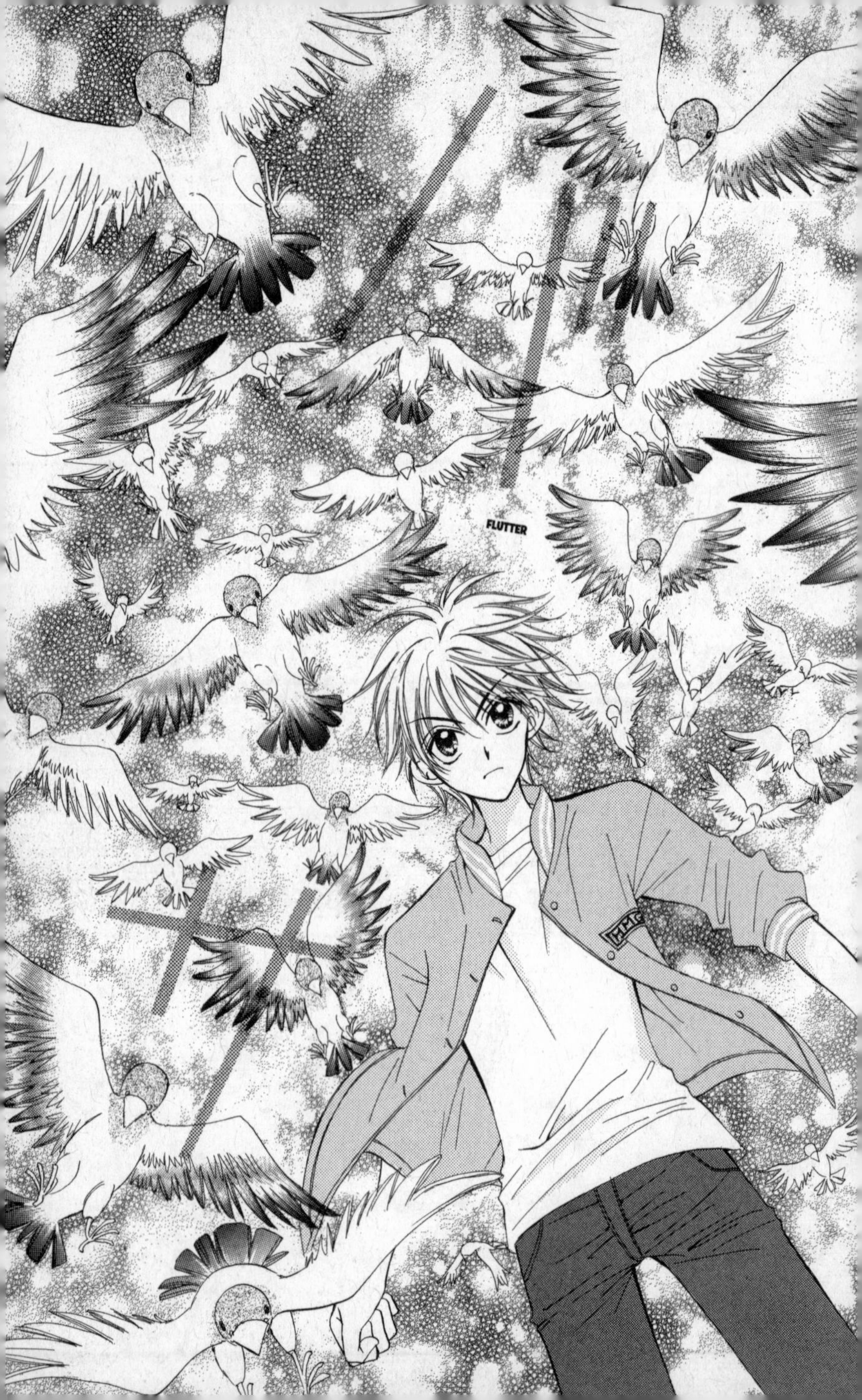
FLUTTER

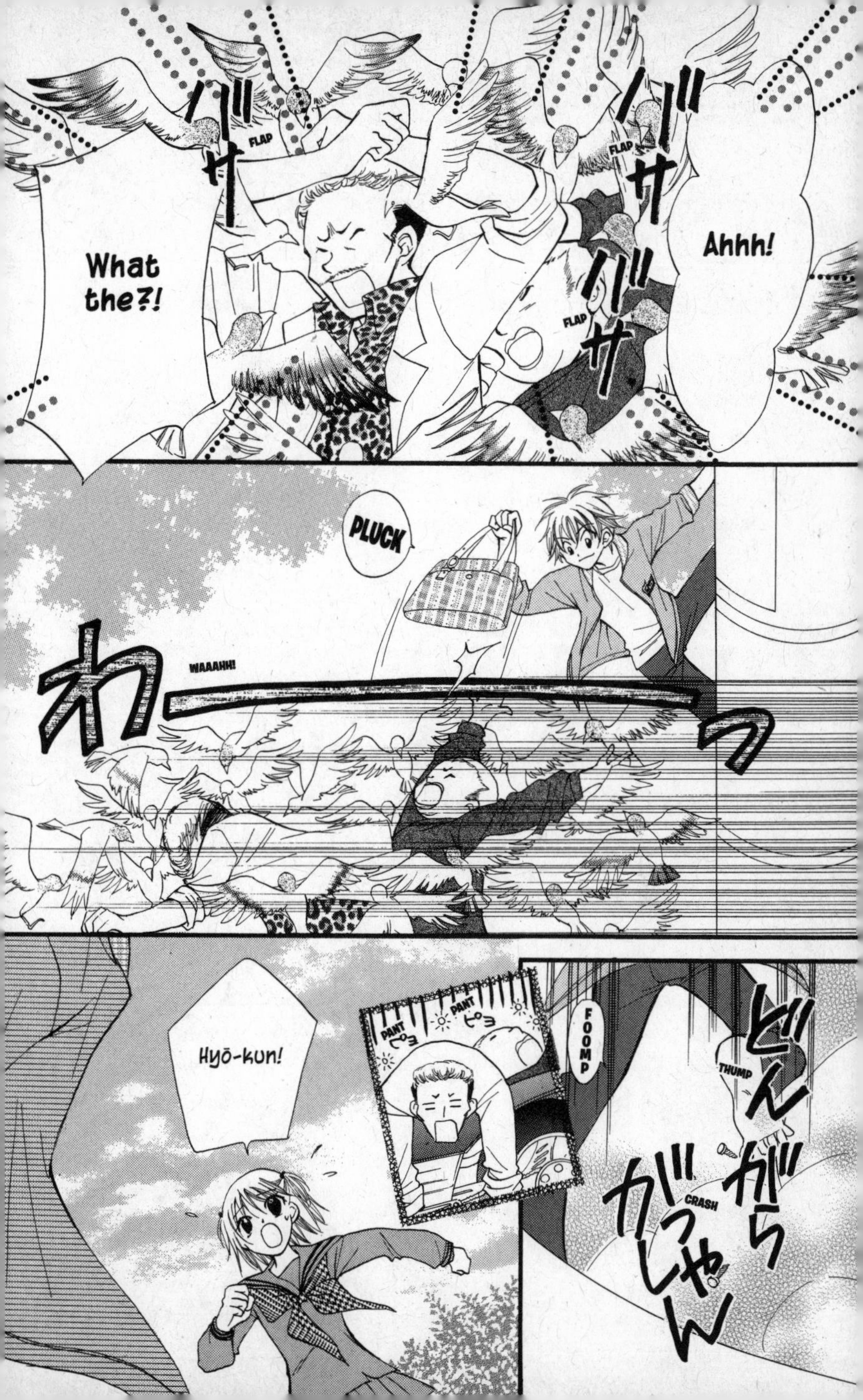
Ahhh!
バサバサ
FLAP
FLAP
FLAP
バサ
What the?!
PLUCK
わーーっ
WAAAHH!
どんがらがっしゃん
THUMP
CRASH
FOOMP
PANT
ピョ
PANT
ピョ
Hyō-kun!

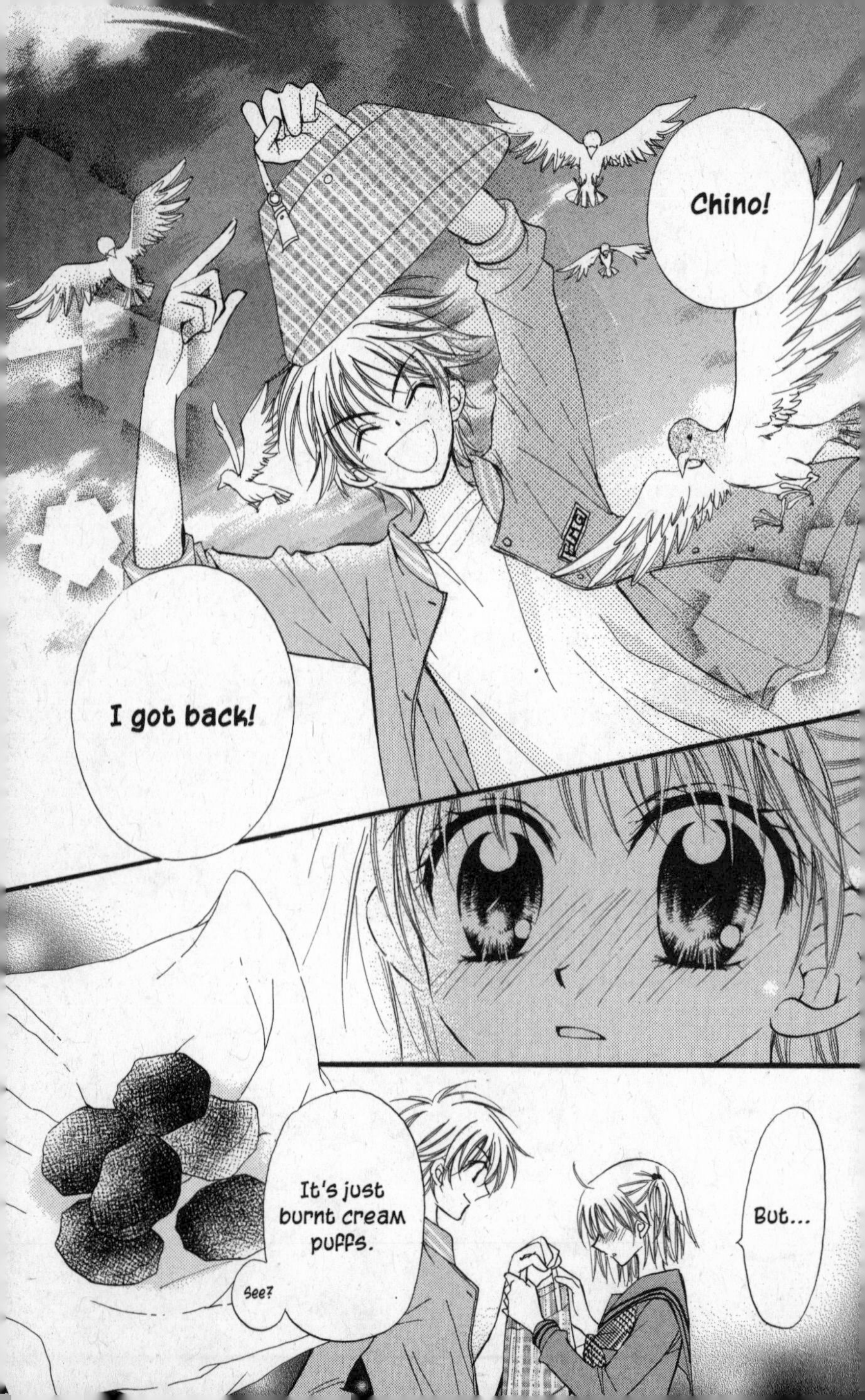
Chino!
I got back!
But...
It's just burnt cream puffs.
See?

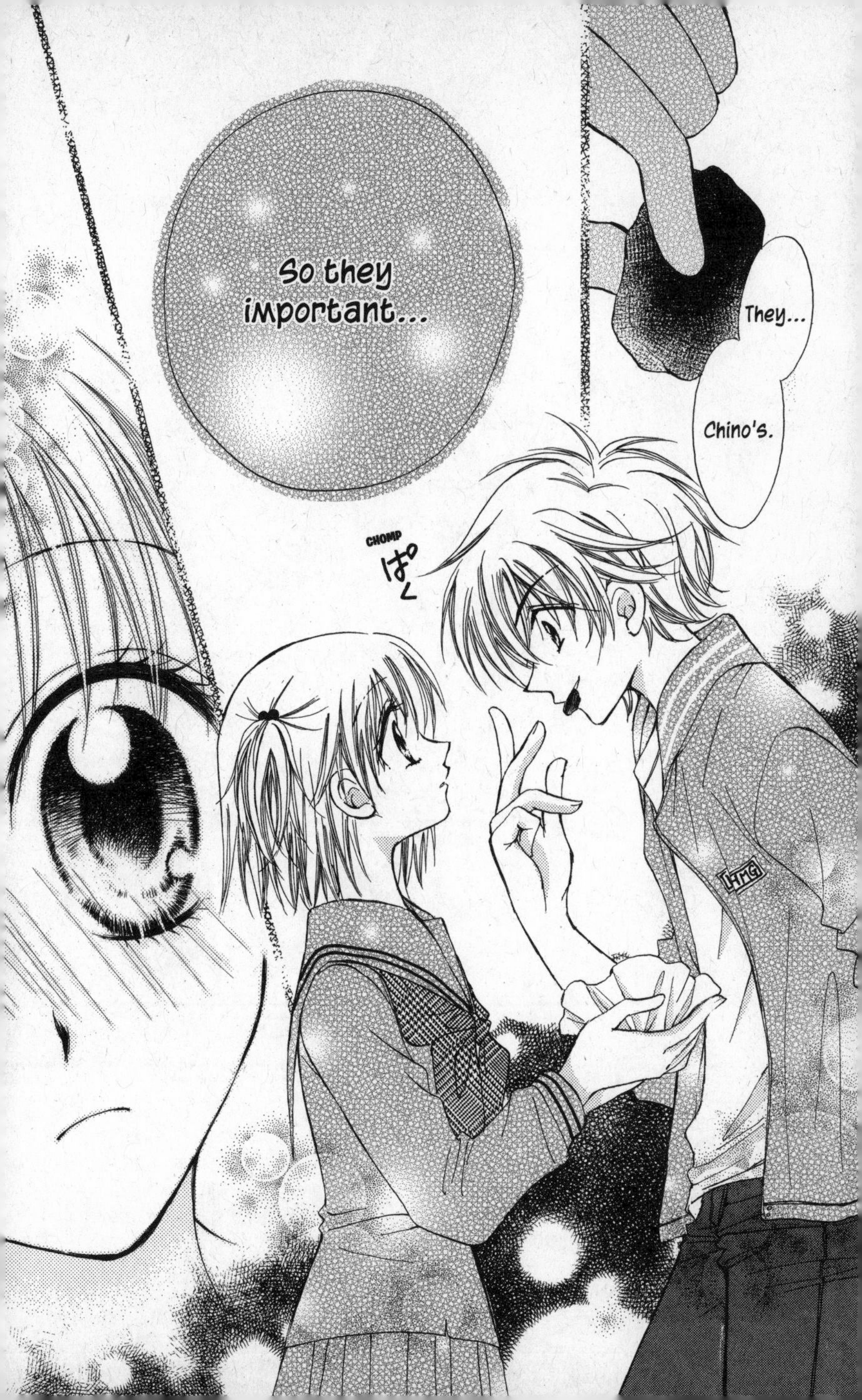
They...
Chino's.
So they important...
CHOMP
ぱく

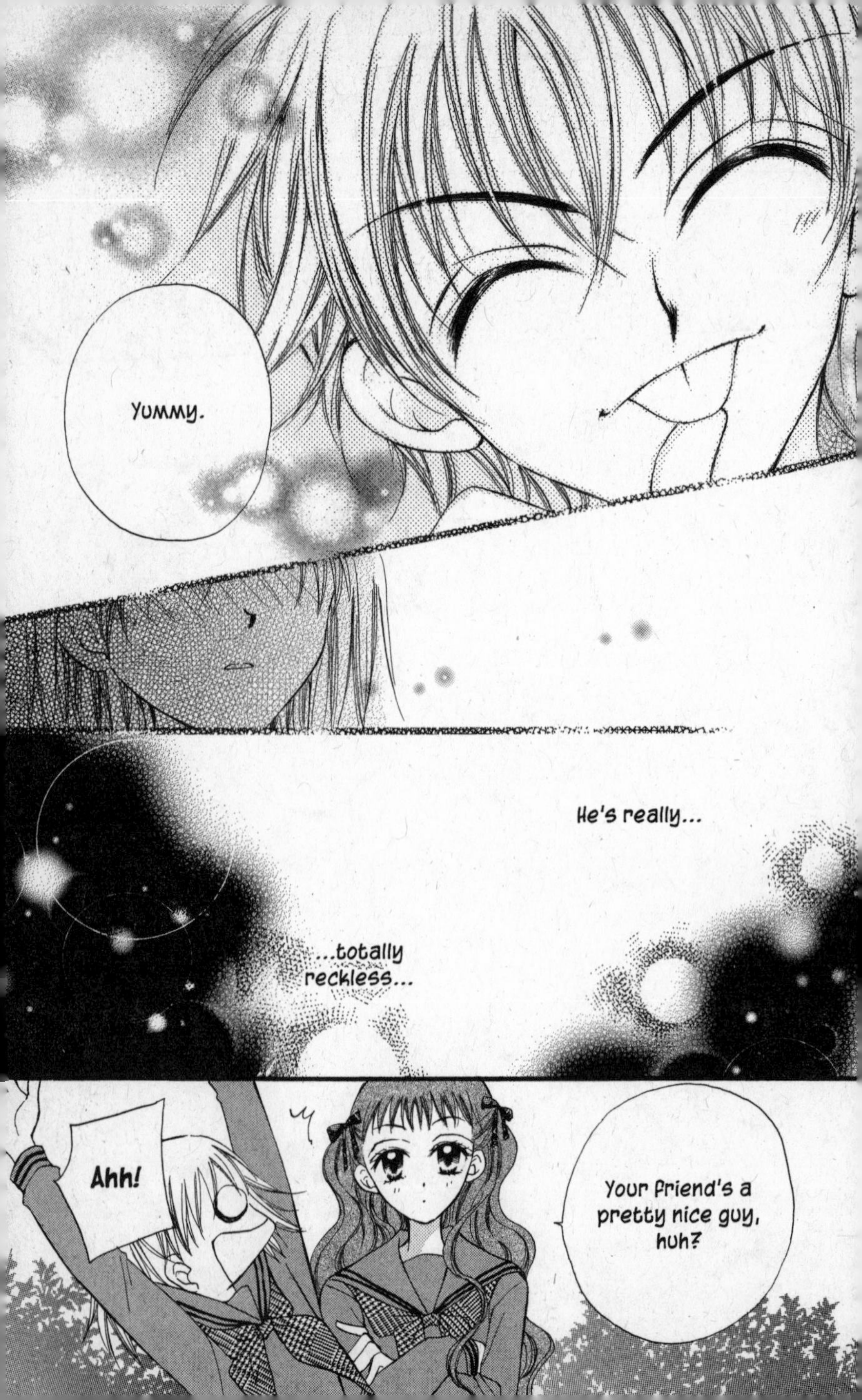
Yummy.
He's really...
...totally reckless...
Your friend's a pretty nice guy, huh?
Ahh!

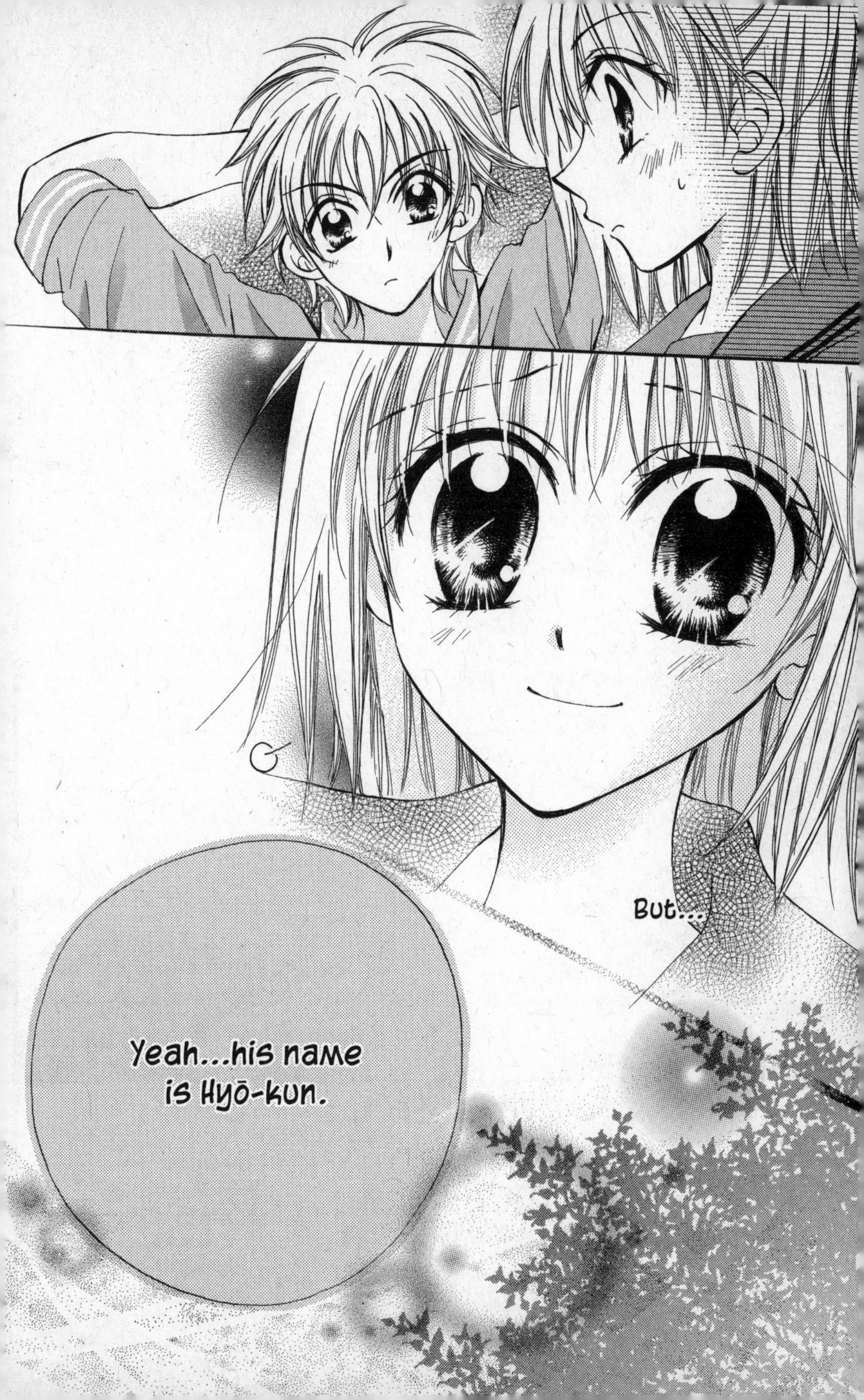
But...
Yeah...his name is Hyō-kun.

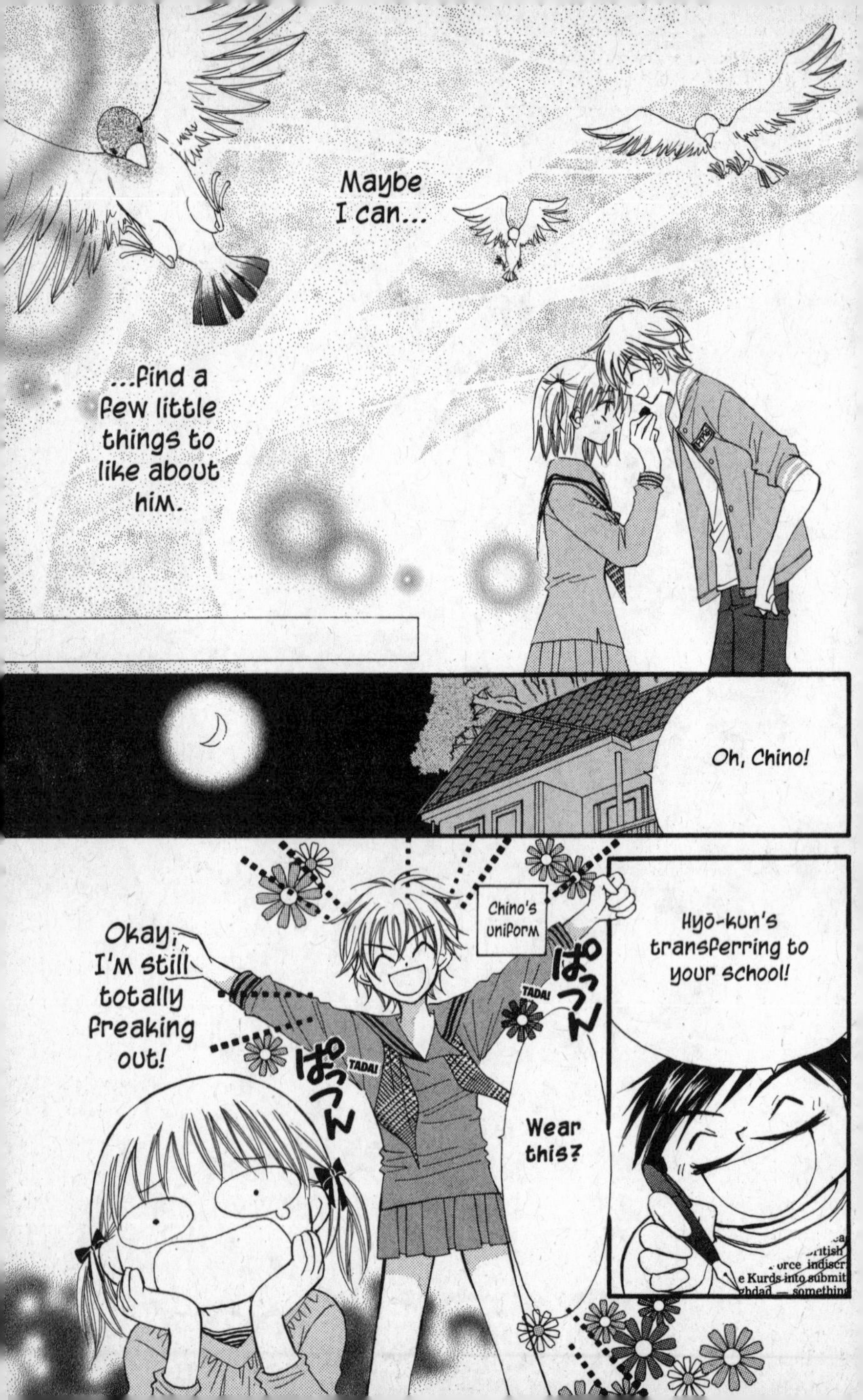
Maybe I can...
...find a few little things to like about him.
Oh, Chino!
Hyō-kun's transferring to your school!
Wear this?
ぱっつん
TADA!
Chino's uniform
ぱっつん
TADA!
Okay, I'm still totally freaking out!

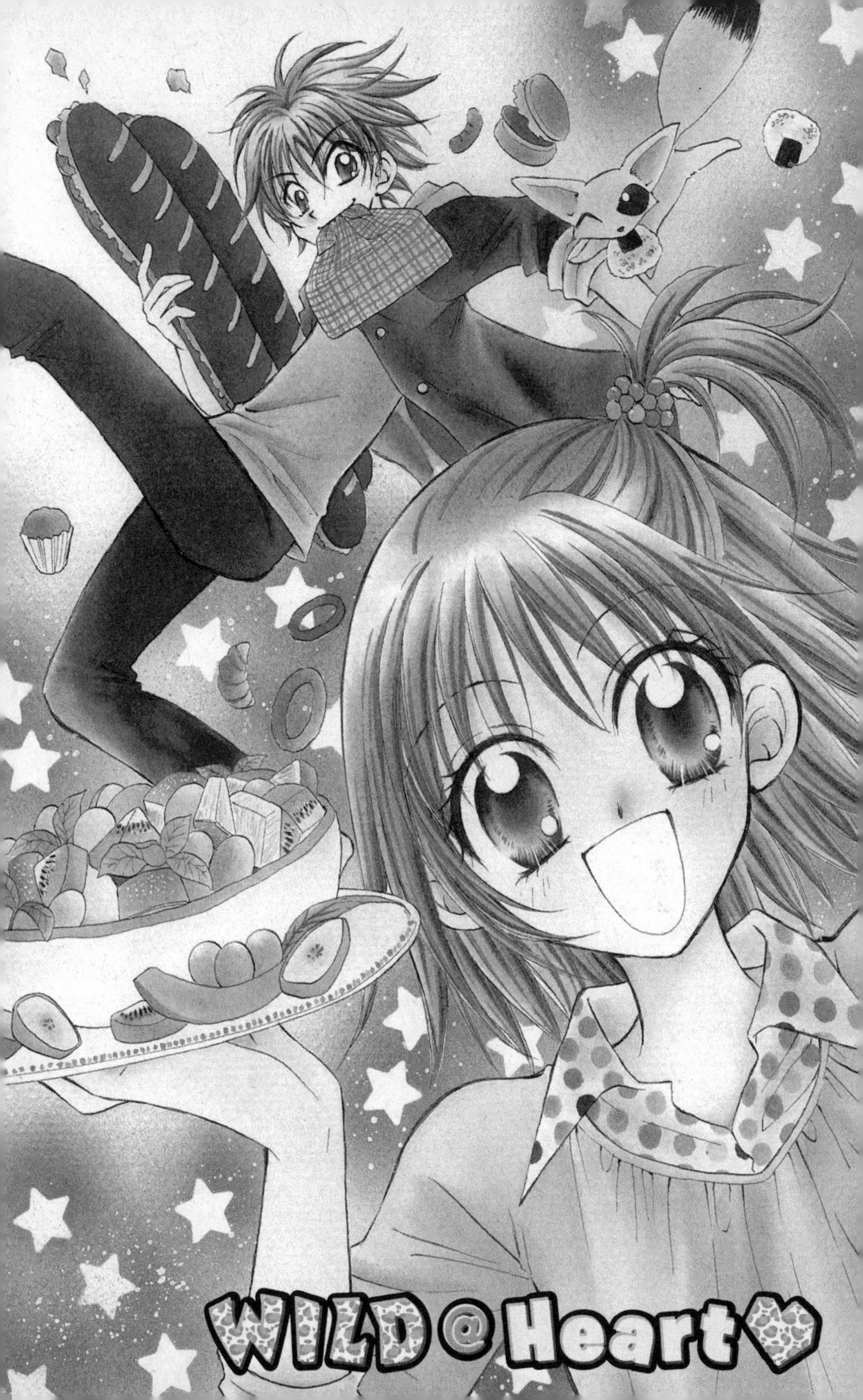
WILD @ Heart♥

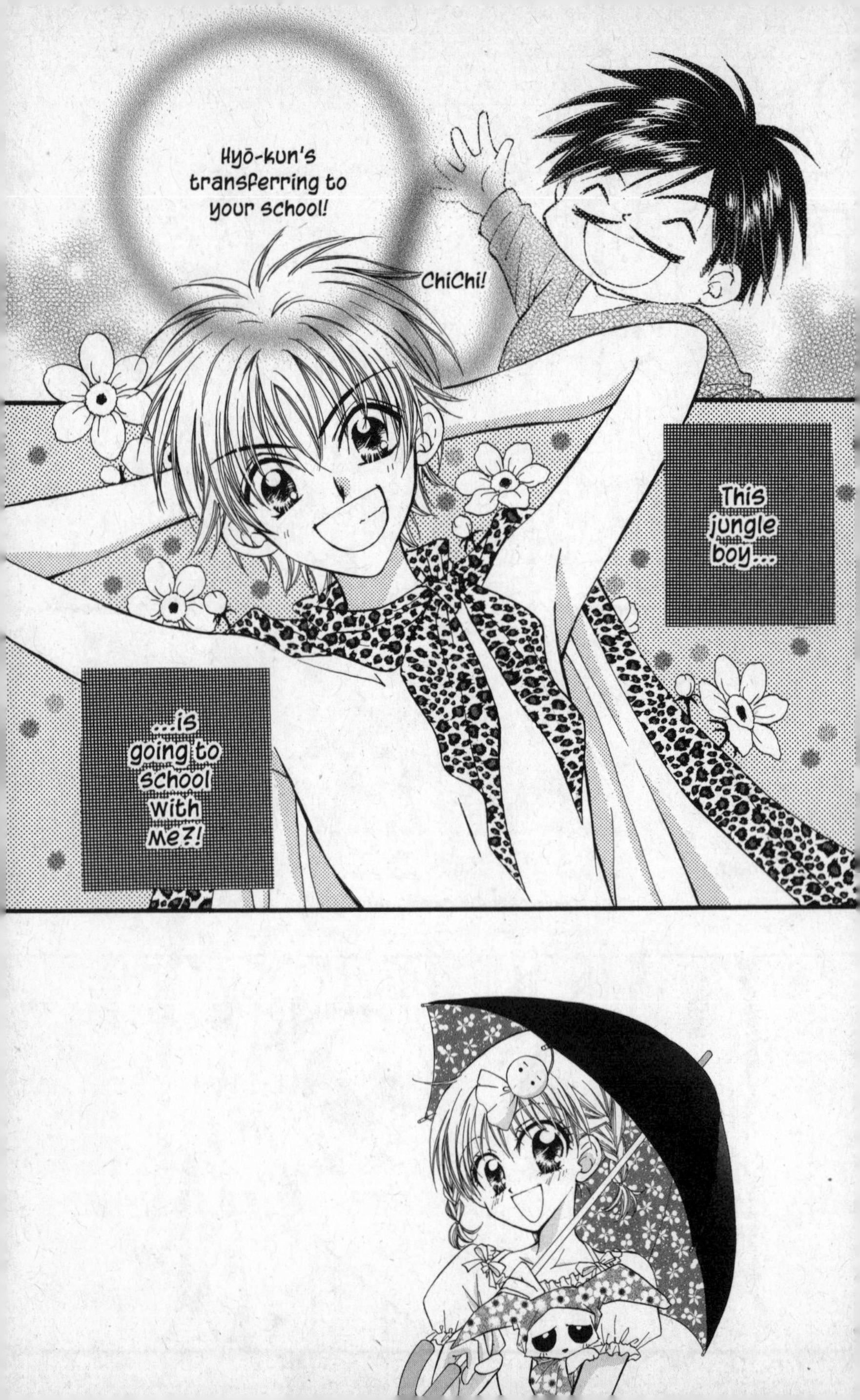
Hyō-kun's transferring to your school!
ChiChi!
This jungle boy...
...is going to school with me?!

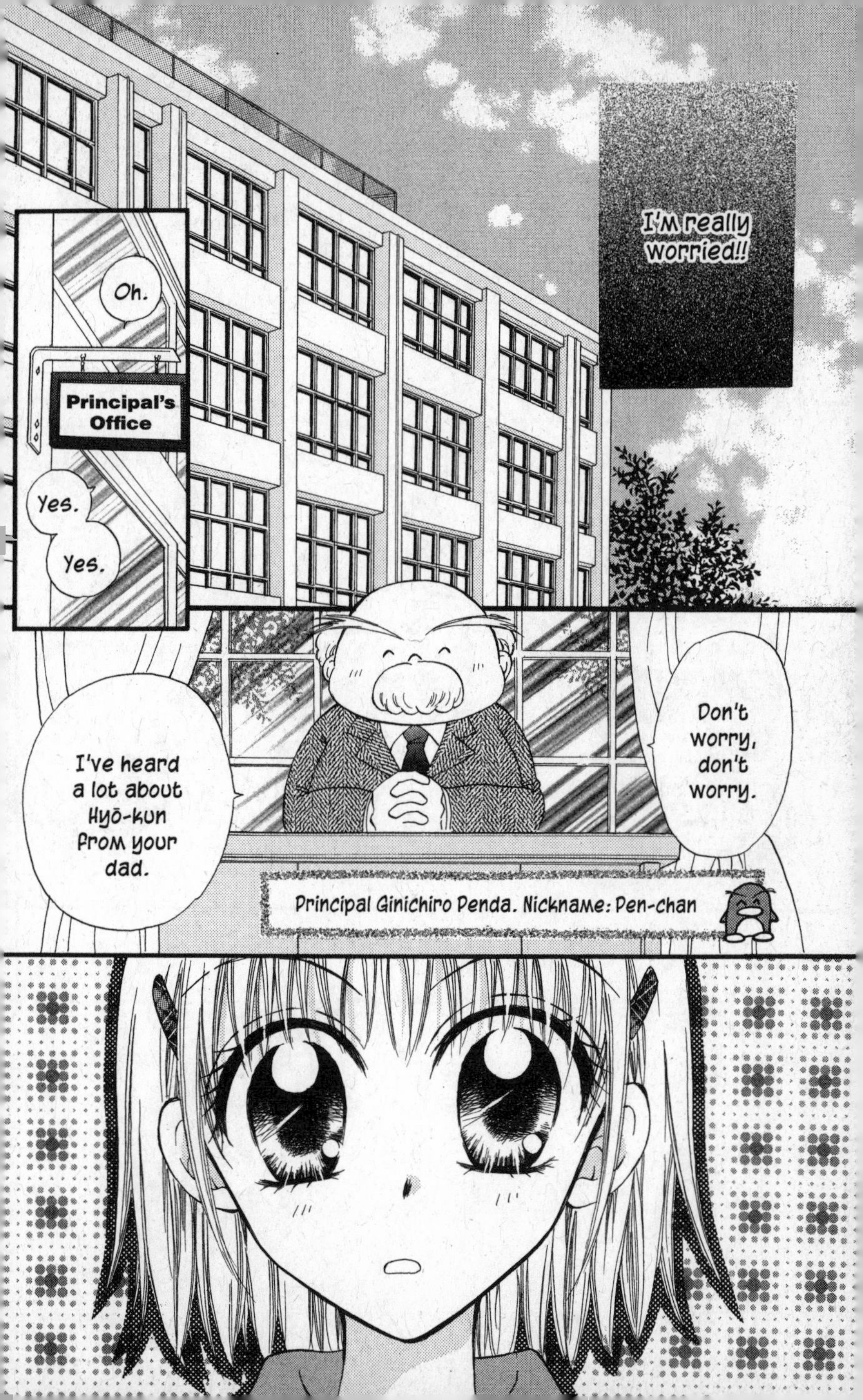
I'm really worried!!
Oh.
Principal's Office
Yes.
Yes.
Don't worry, don't worry.
I've heard a lot about Hyō-kun from your dad.
Principal Ginichiro Penda. Nickname: Pen-chan

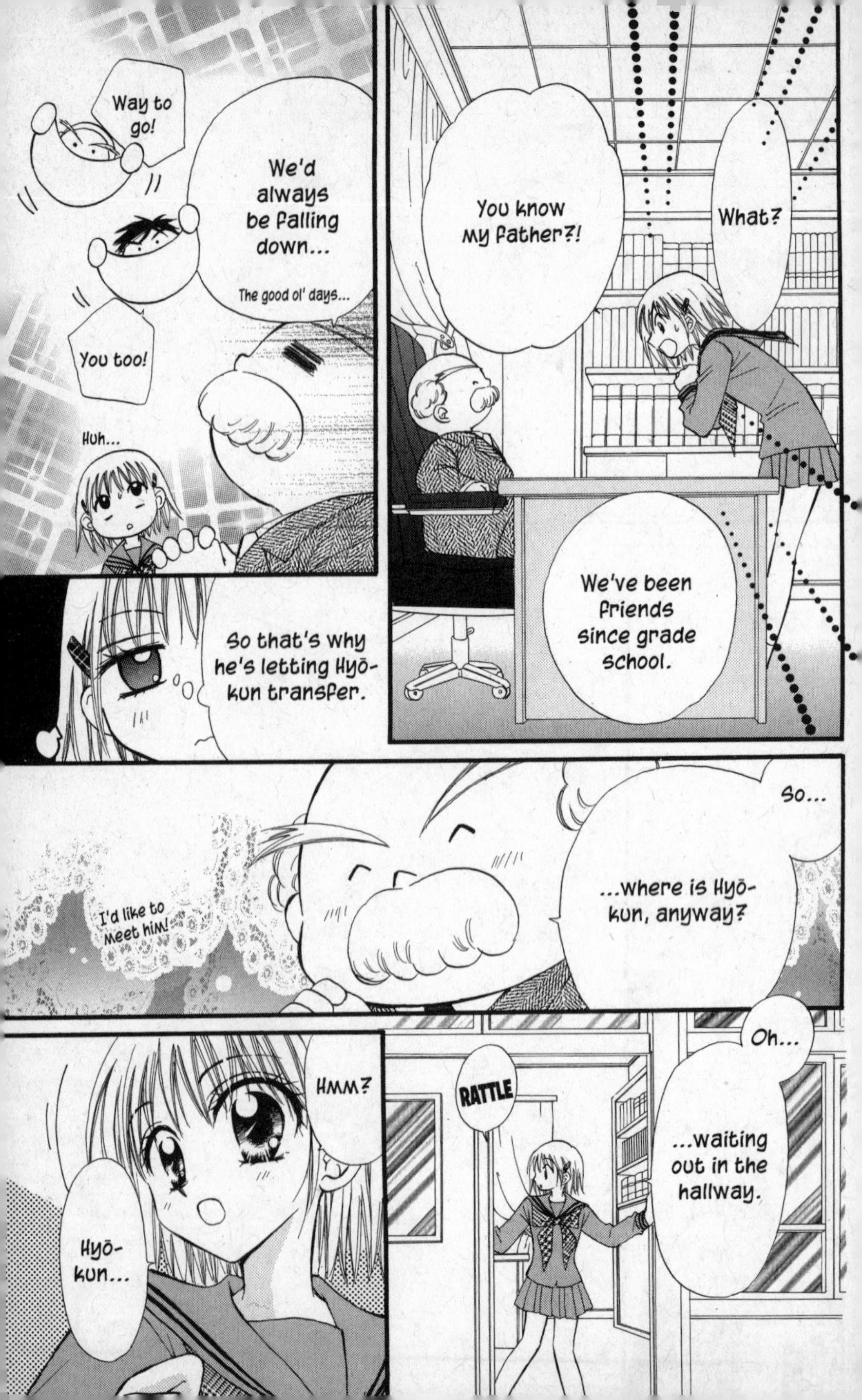
What?
You know my father?!
We've been friends since grade school.
We'd always be falling down...
The good ol' days...
Way to go!
You too!
Huh...
So that's why he's letting Hyō-kun transfer.
So...
...where is Hyō-kun, anyway?
I'd like to meet him!
Oh...
RATTLE
...waiting out in the hallway.
Hmm?
Hyō-kun...

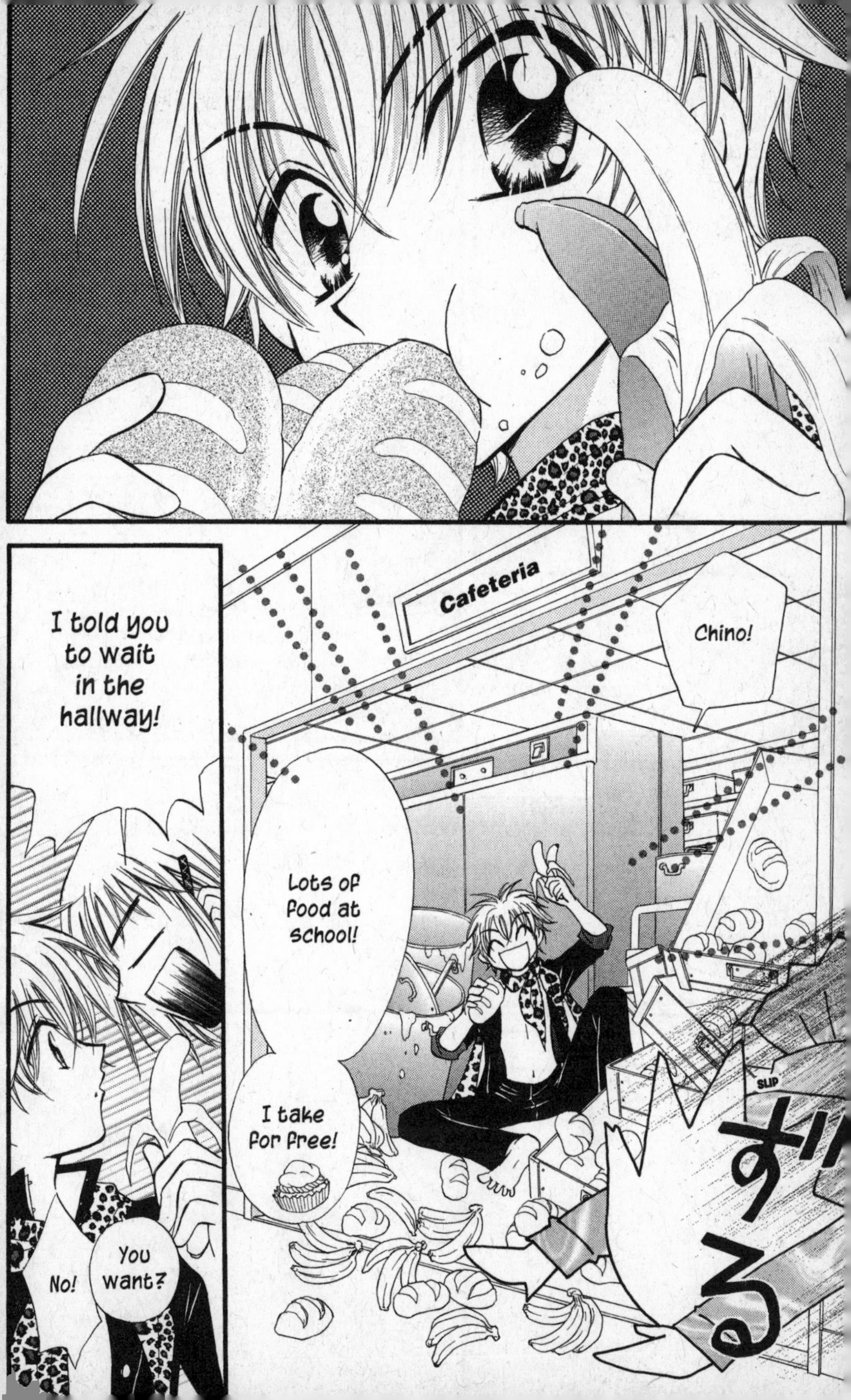
Cafeteria
Chino!
SLIP
Lots of food at school!
I take for free!
I told you to wait in the hallway!
You want?
No!

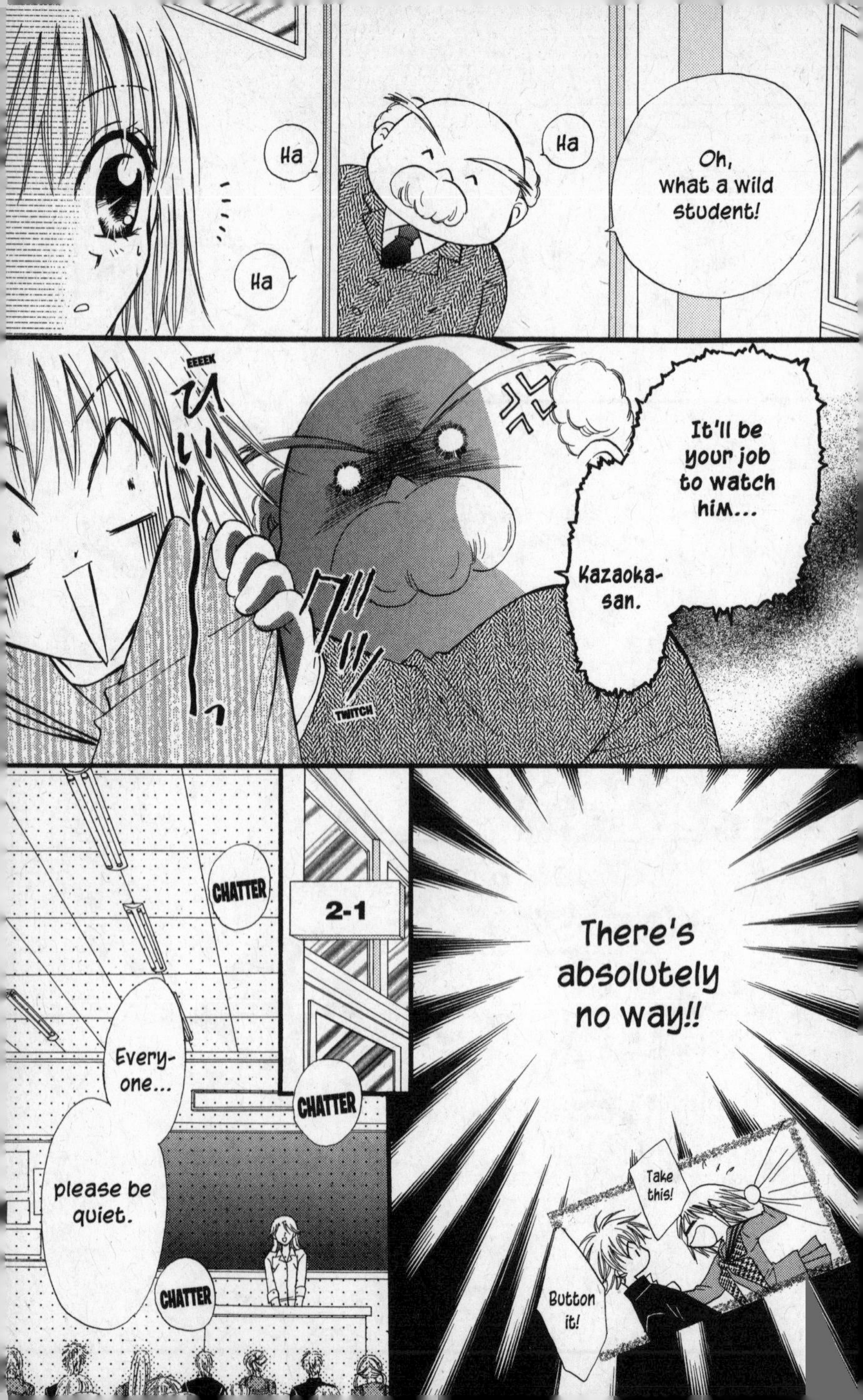

Oh, what a wild student!
Ha
Ha
Ha
It'll be your job to watch him...
Kazaoka-san.
TWITCH
EEEEK
There's absolutely no way!!
Take this!
Button it!
2-1
CHATTER
CHATTER
Every-one...
please be quiet.
CHATTER

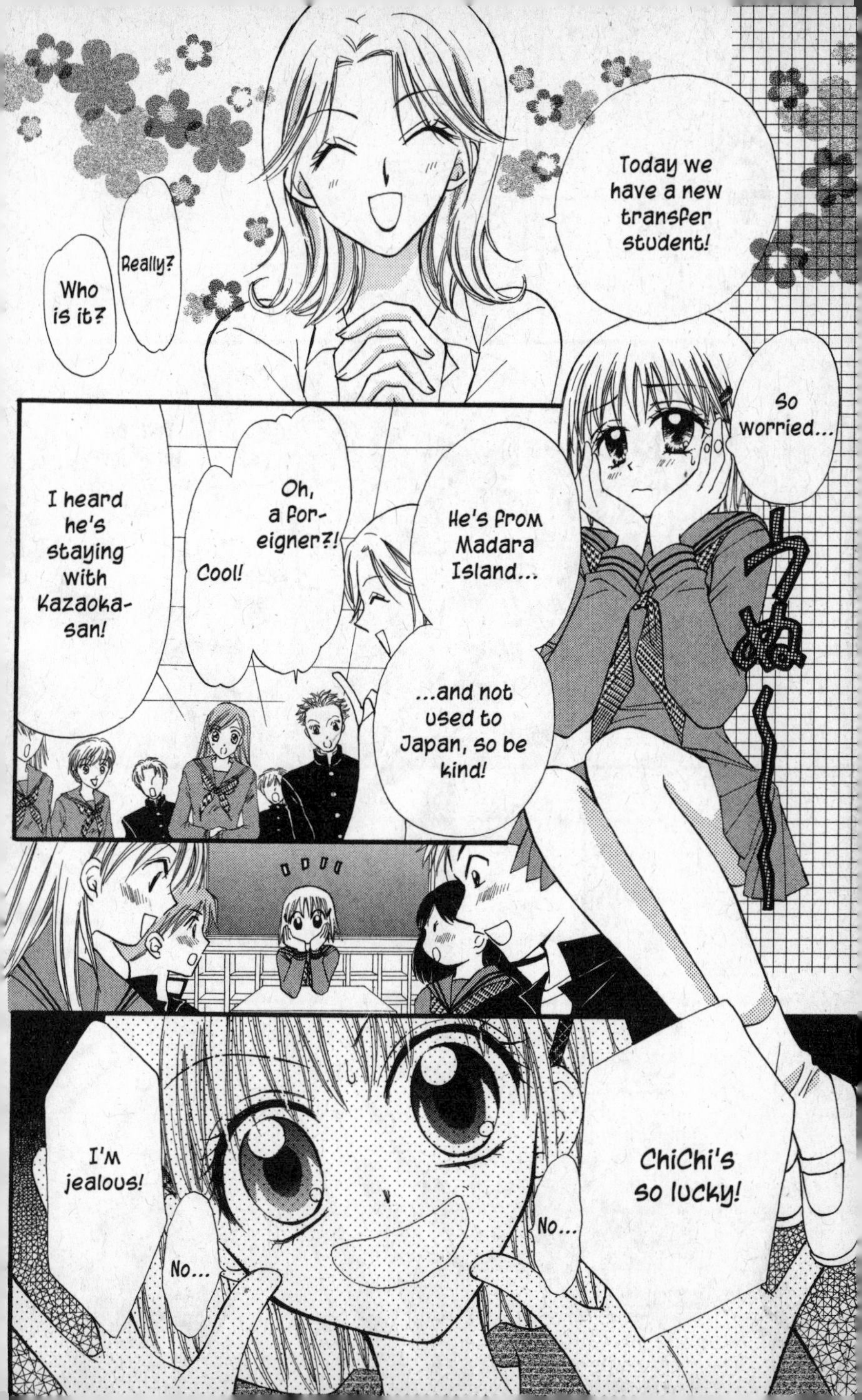
Today we have a new transfer student!
Really?
Who is it?
So worried...
He's from Madara Island...
...and not used to Japan, so be kind!
Oh, a foreigner?!
Cool!
I heard he's staying with Kazaoka-san!
ChiChi's so lucky!
No...
I'm jealous!
No...

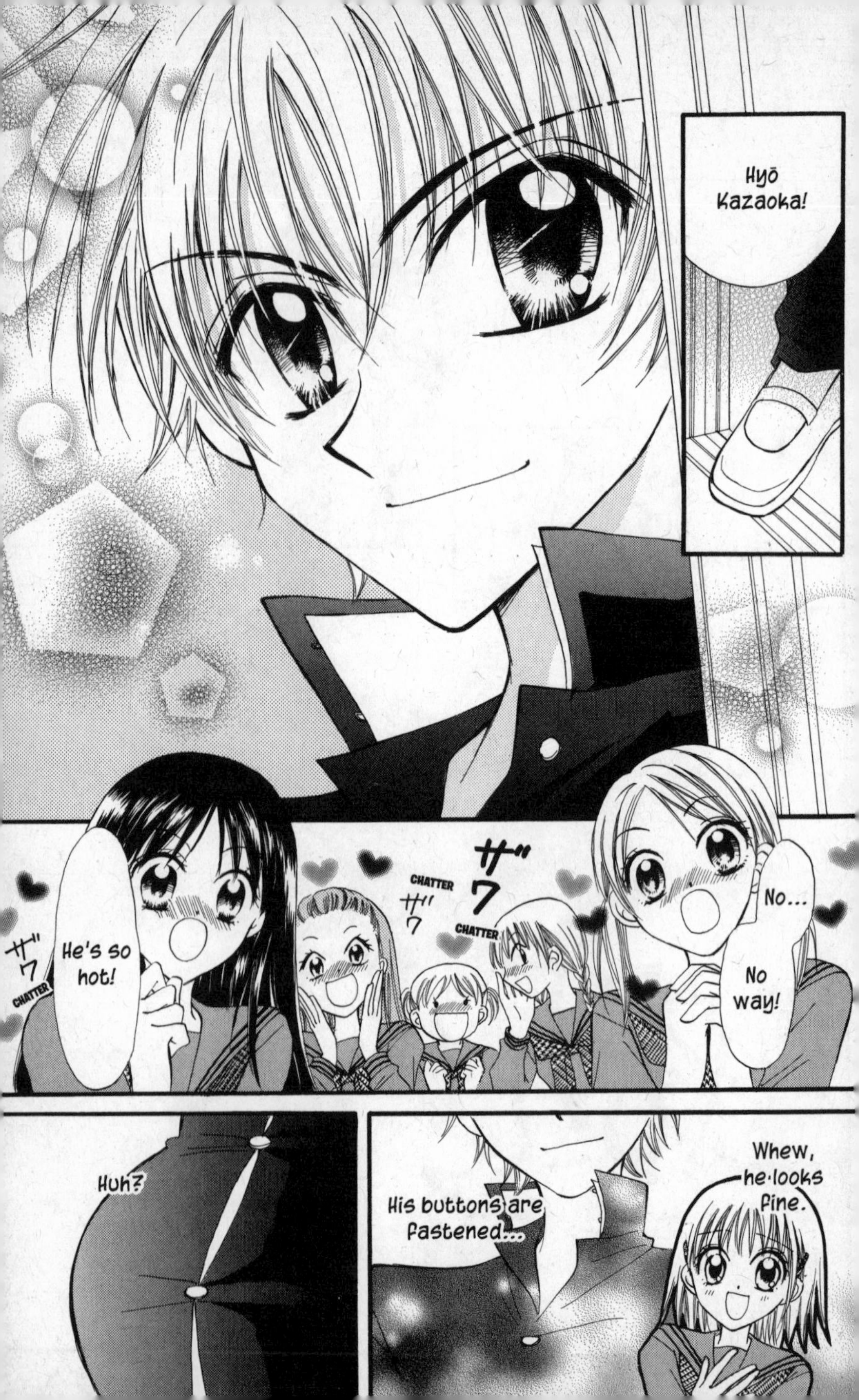
Hyō Kazaoka!
No... No way!
ザワ
CHATTER
ザワ
CHATTER
He's so hot!
ザワ
CHATTER
Whew, he looks fine.
His buttons are fastened...
Huh?

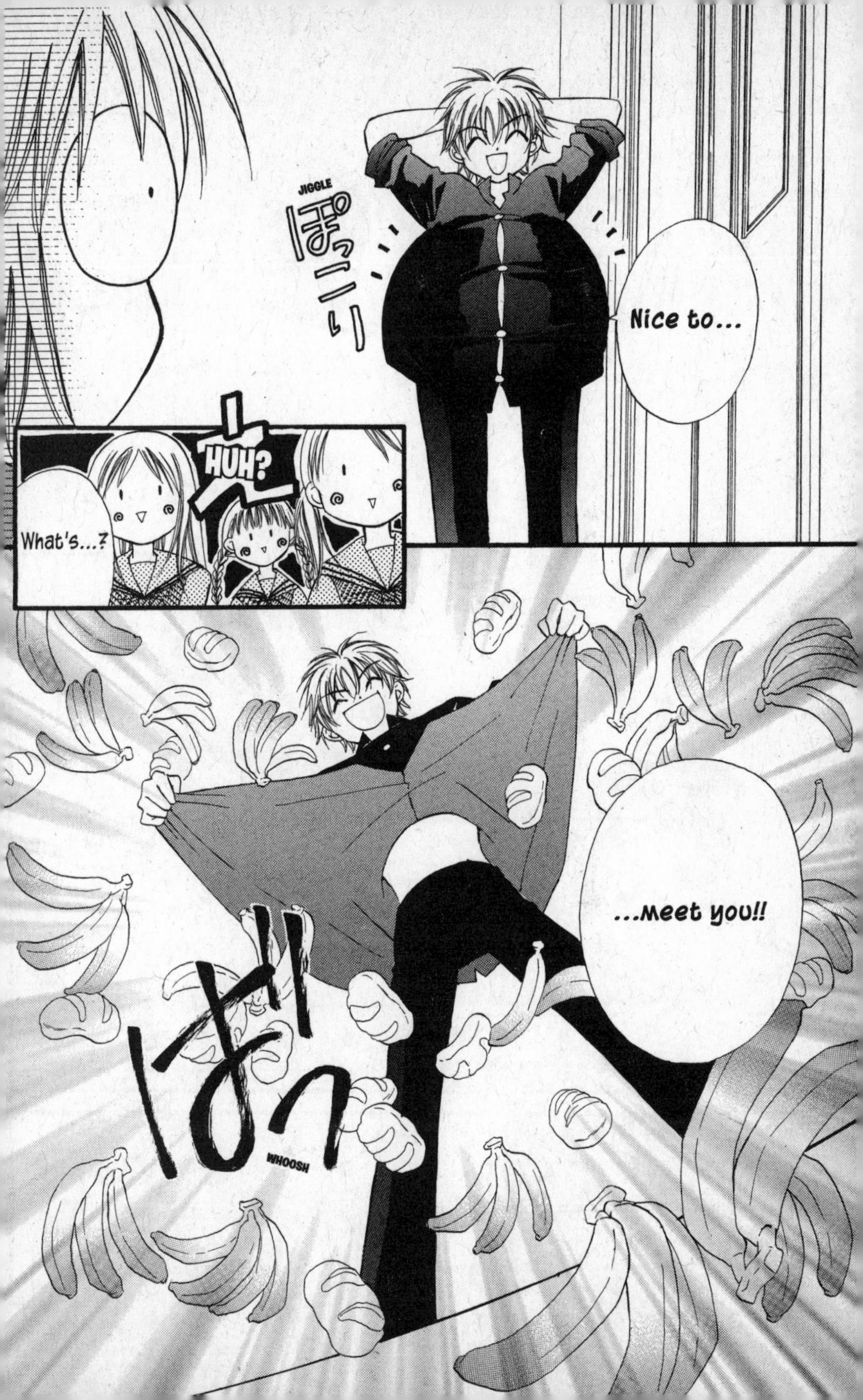
JIGGLE
Nice to...
HUH?
What's...?
...Meet you!!
WHOOSH

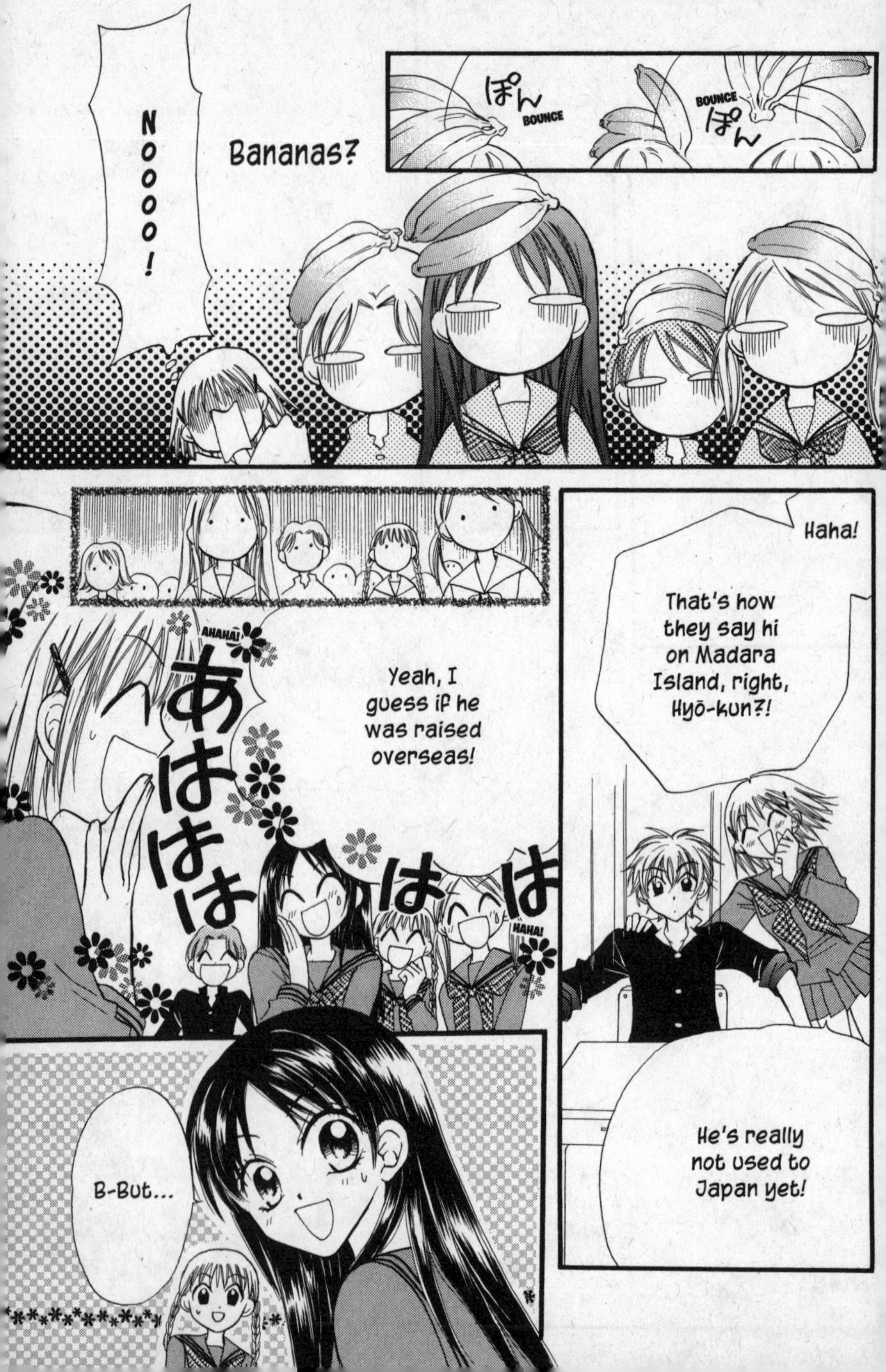
BOUNCE
ぽん
ぽん
BOUNCE
Bananas?
NOOOOO!
Haha!
That's how they say hi on Madara Island, right, Hyō-kun?!
He's really not used to Japan yet!
あははは
AHAHA!
HAHA!
Yeah, I guess if he was raised overseas!
B-But...

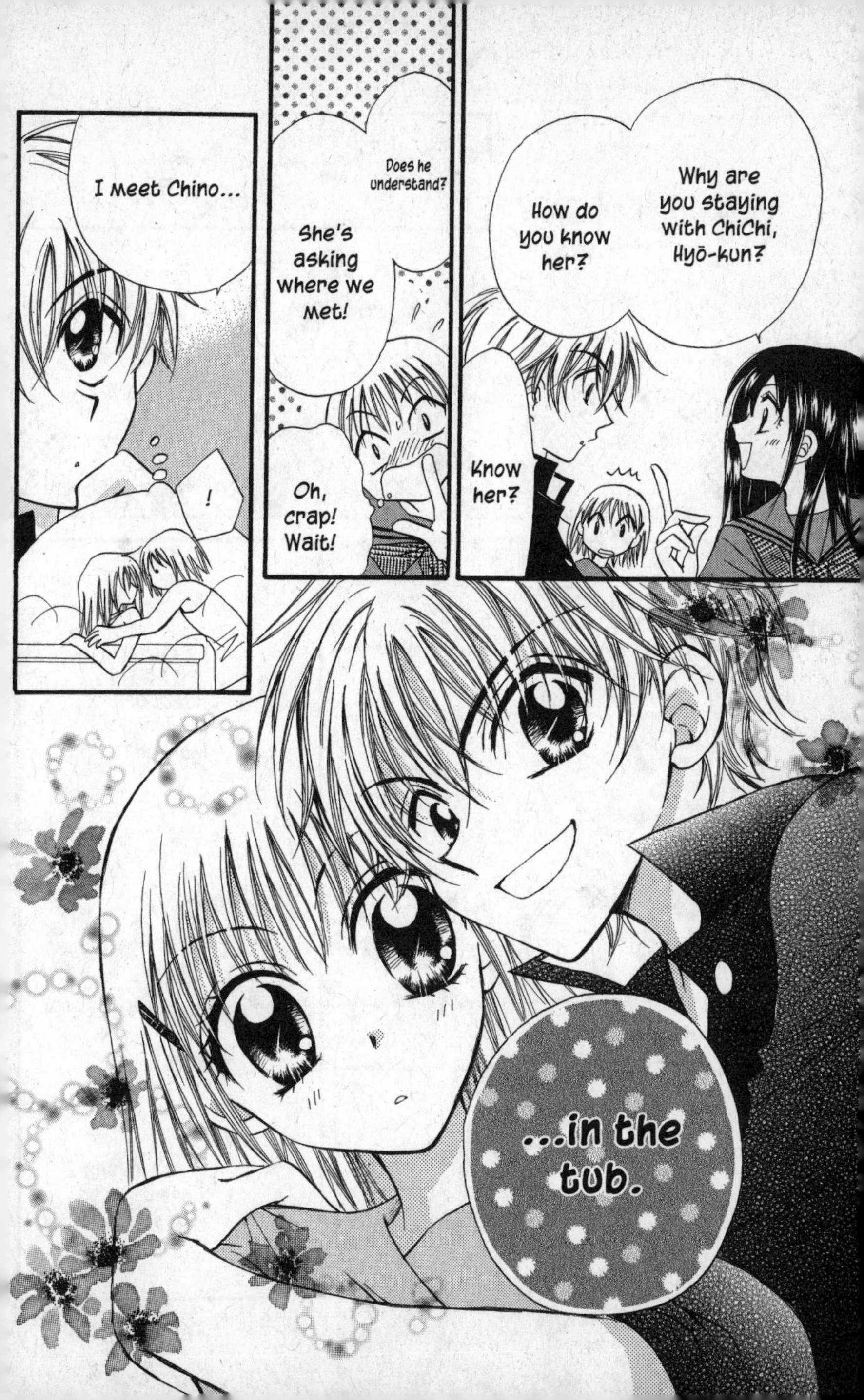
Why are you staying with ChiChi, Hyō-kun?
How do you know her?
Know her?
Does he understand?
She's asking where we met!
Oh, crap! Wait!
I meet Chino...
!
...in the tub.

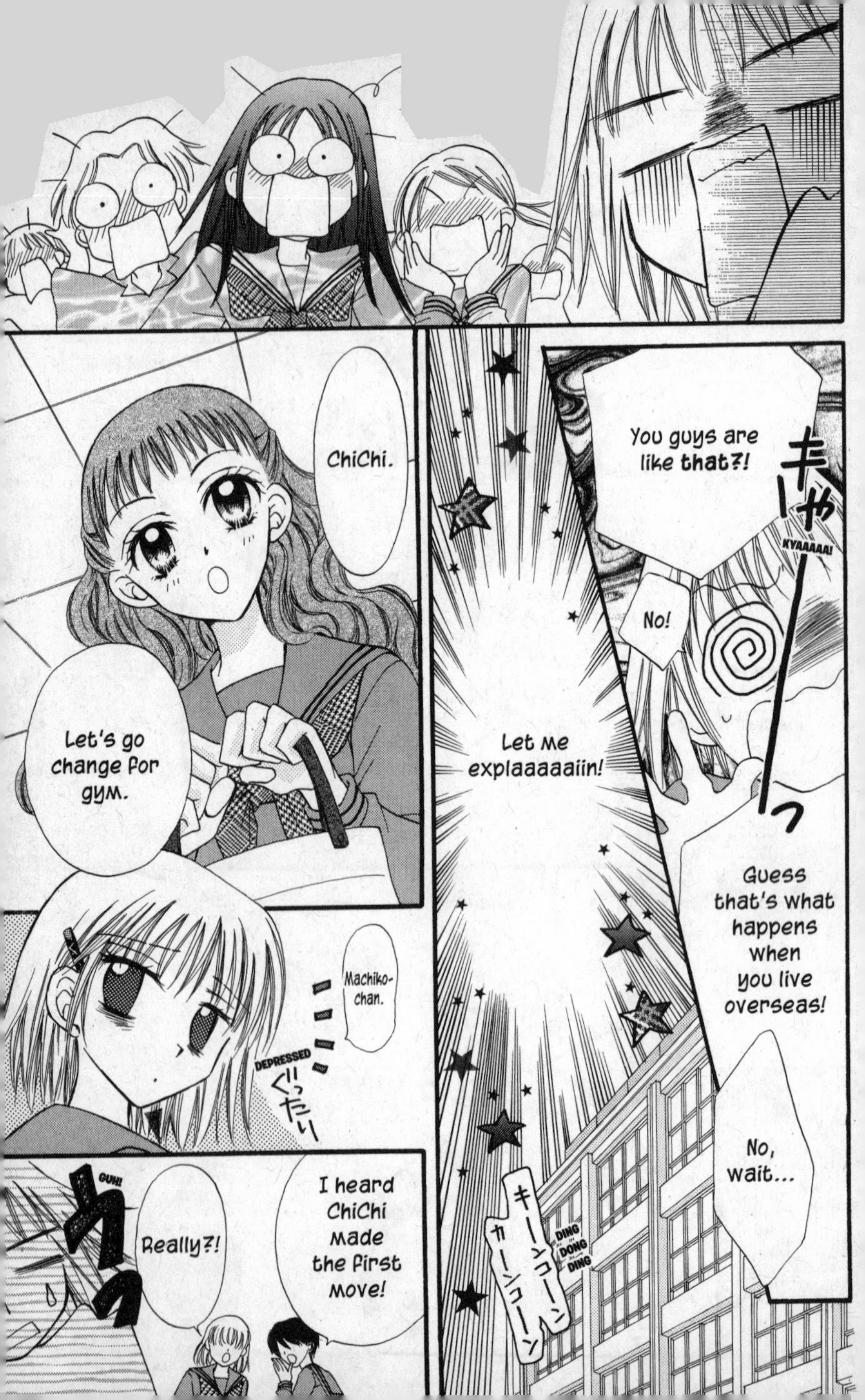

You guys are like that?!
KYAAAAA!
No!
Guess that's what happens when you live overseas!
No, wait...
Let me explaaaaaiin!
キーンコーン
カーンコーン
DING DONG DING
ChiChi.
Let's go change for gym.
Machiko-chan.
DEPRESSED
ぐったり
I heard ChiChi made the first move!
Really?!
GUH!

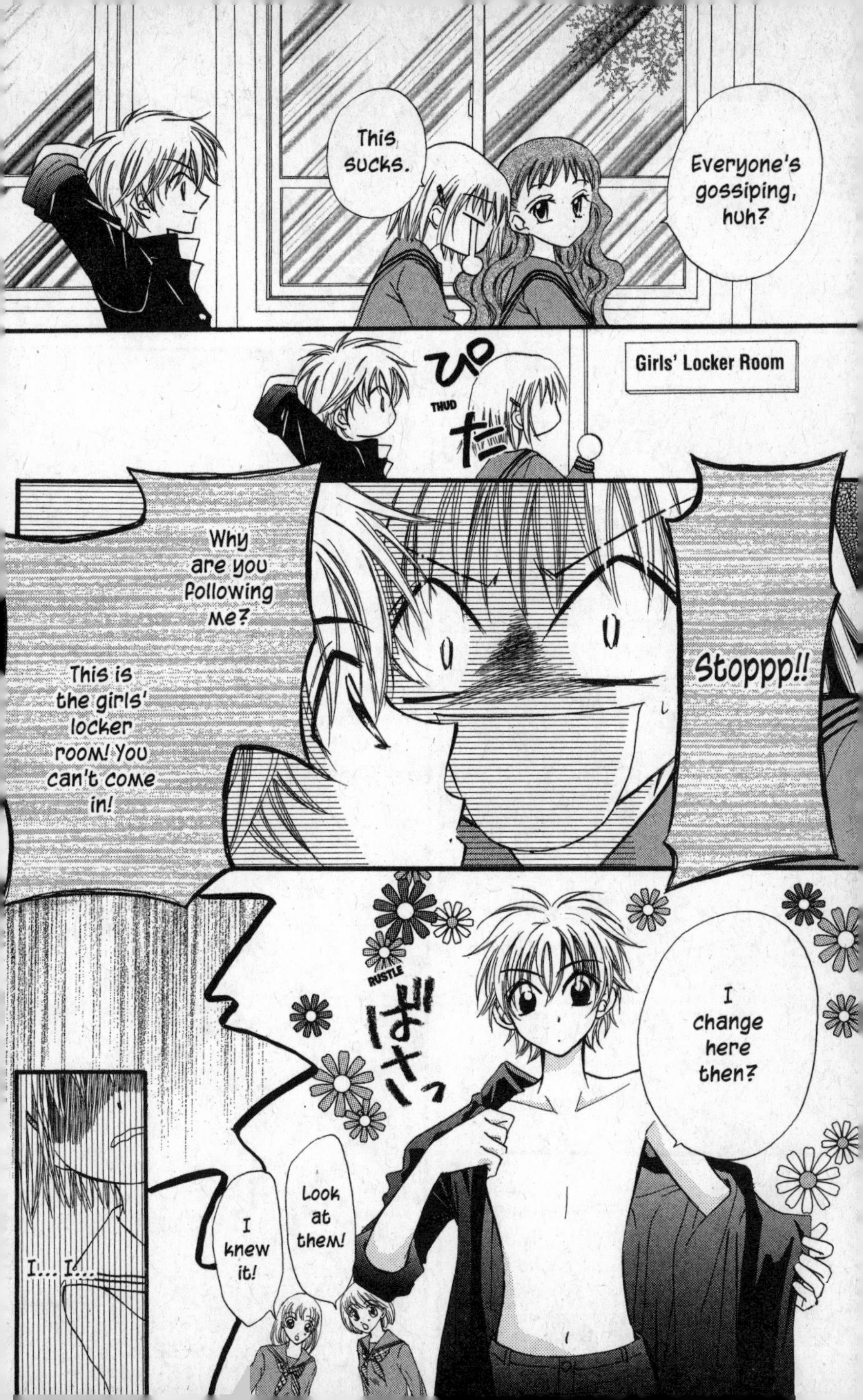
Everyone's gossiping, huh?
This sucks.
Girls' Locker Room
THUD
ぴた
Stoppp!!
Why are you following me?
This is the girls' locker room! You can't come in!
I change here then?
RUSTLE
ばさっ
Look at them!
I knew it!
I... I...

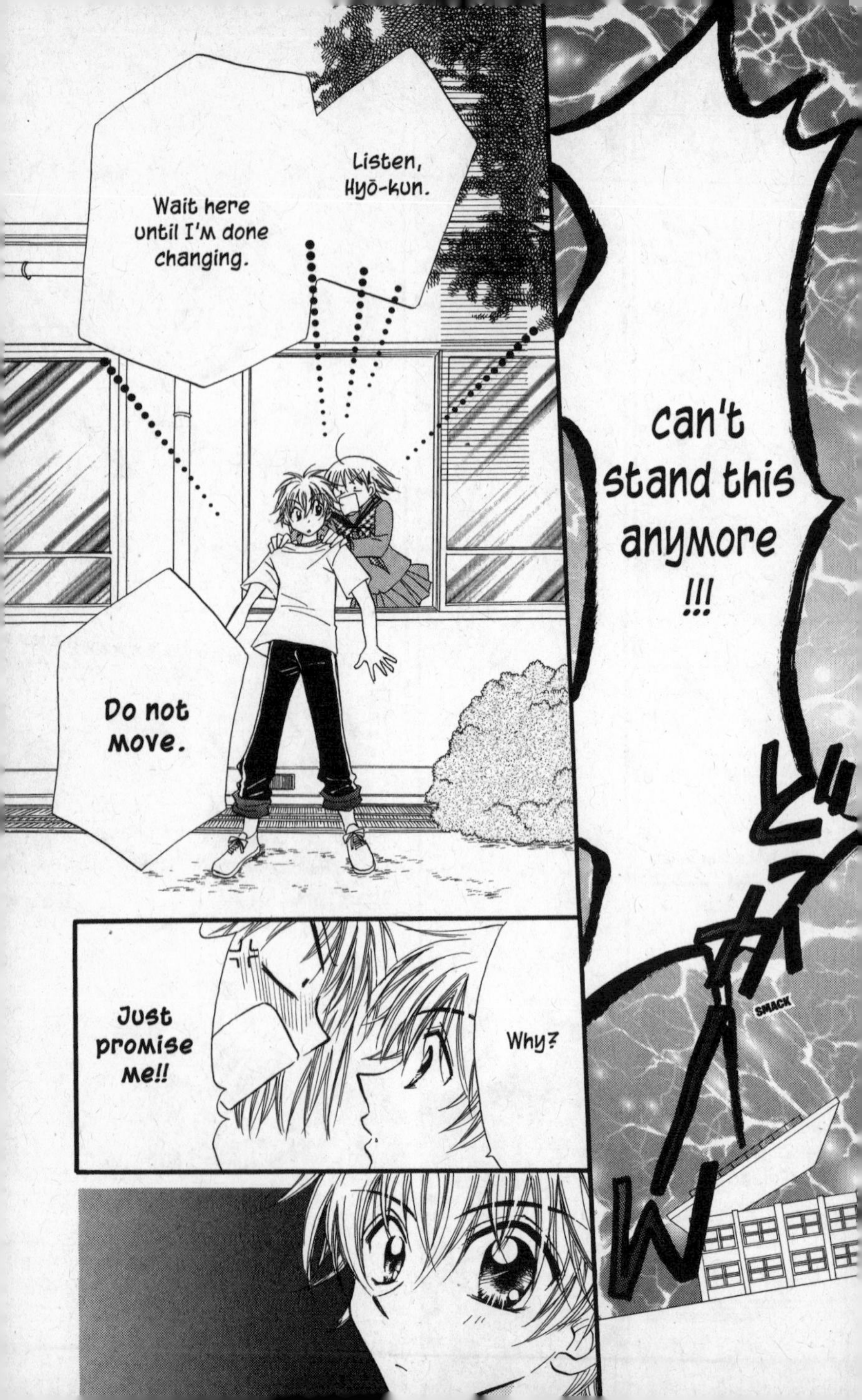
can't stand this anymore !!!
SMACK
Listen, Hyō-kun.
Wait here until I'm done changing.
Do not move.
Why?
Just promise me!!

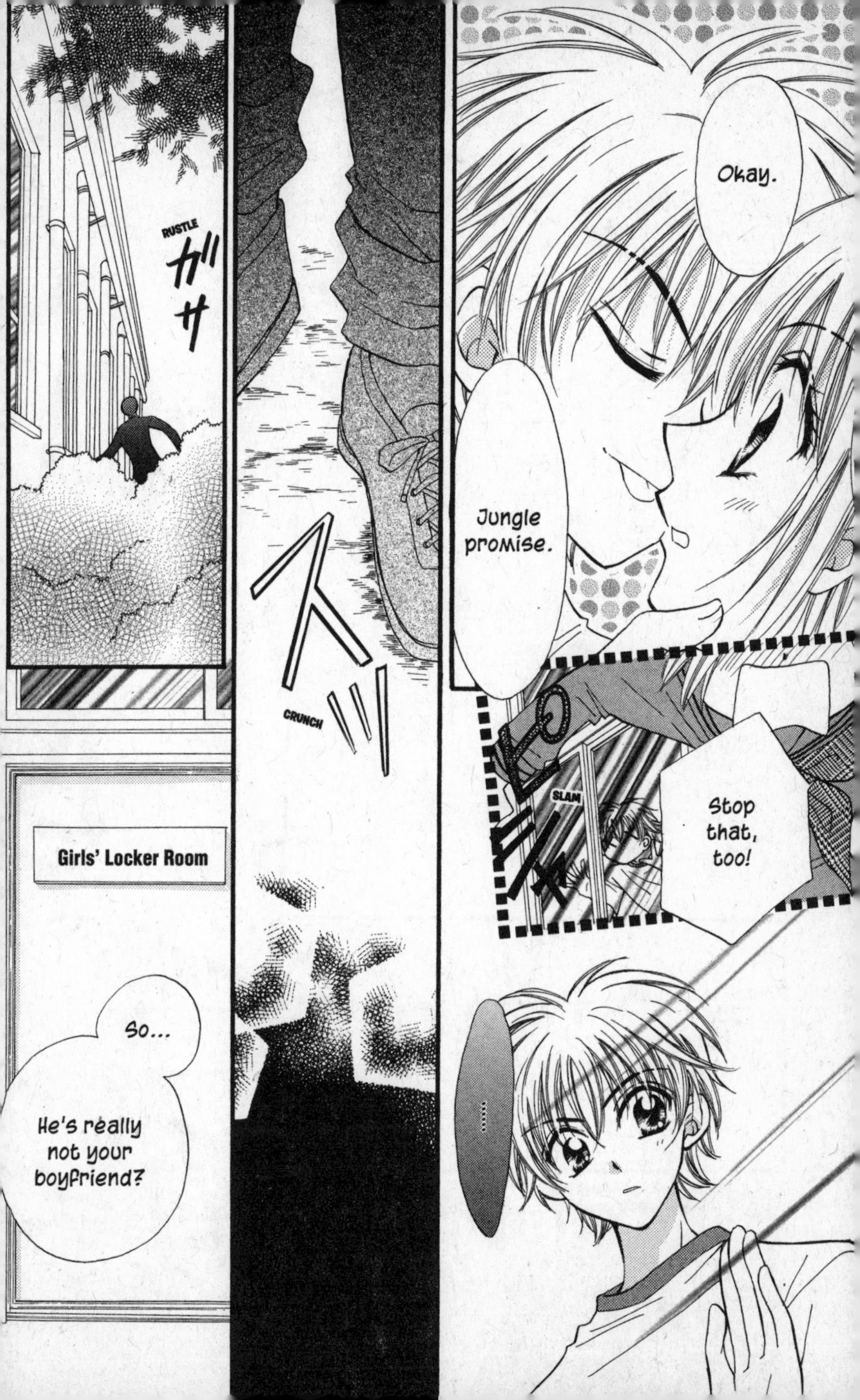

Okay.
Jungle promise.
Stop that, too!
SLAM
......
CRUNCH
RUSTLE
Girls' Locker Room
So...
He's really not your boyfriend?

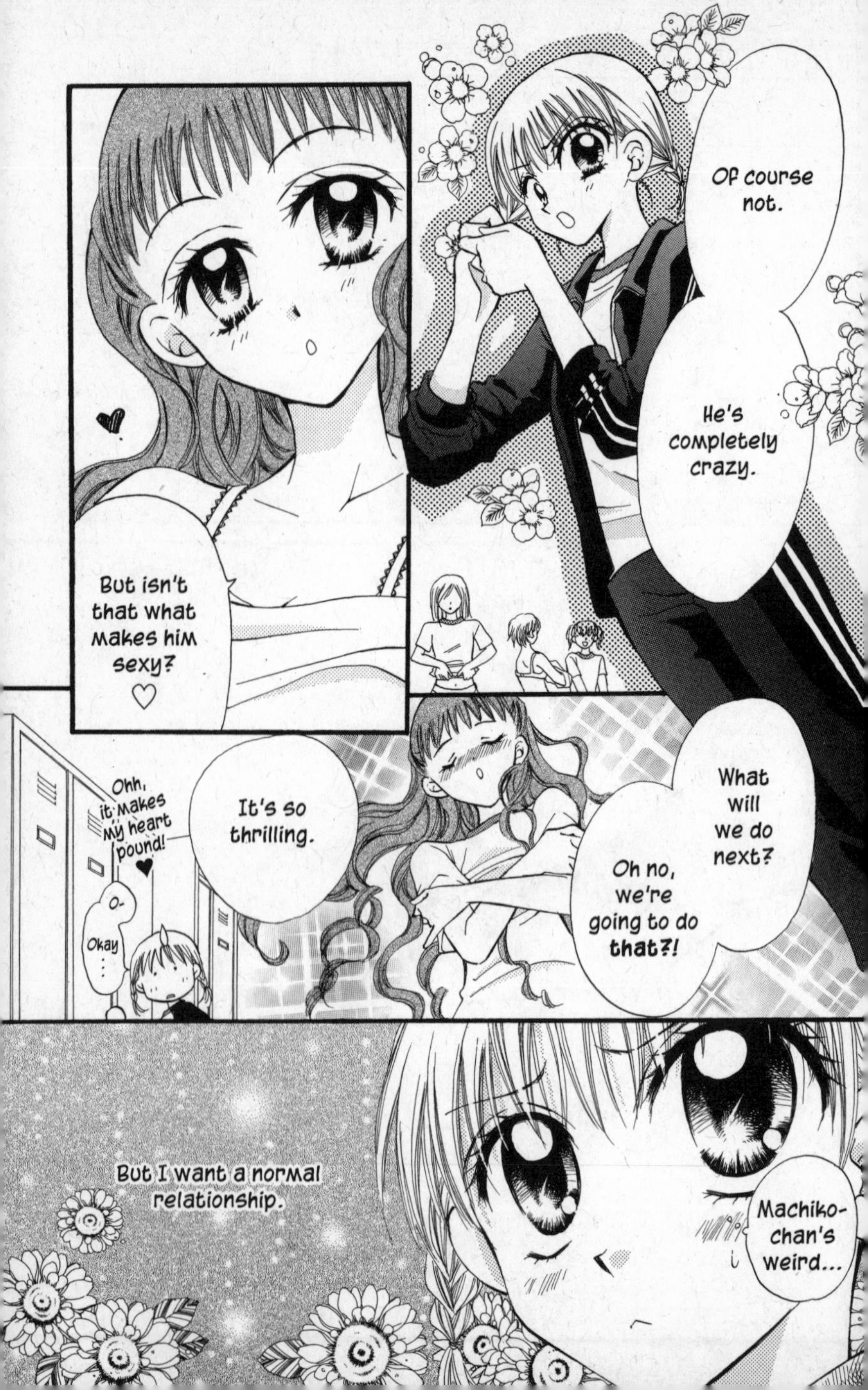
Of course not.
He's completely crazy.
But isn't that what makes him sexy? ♡
What will we do next?
Oh no, we're going to do **that**?!
It's so thrilling.
Ohh, it makes my heart pound! ♥
O- Okay...
Machiko-chan's weird...
But I want a normal relationship.

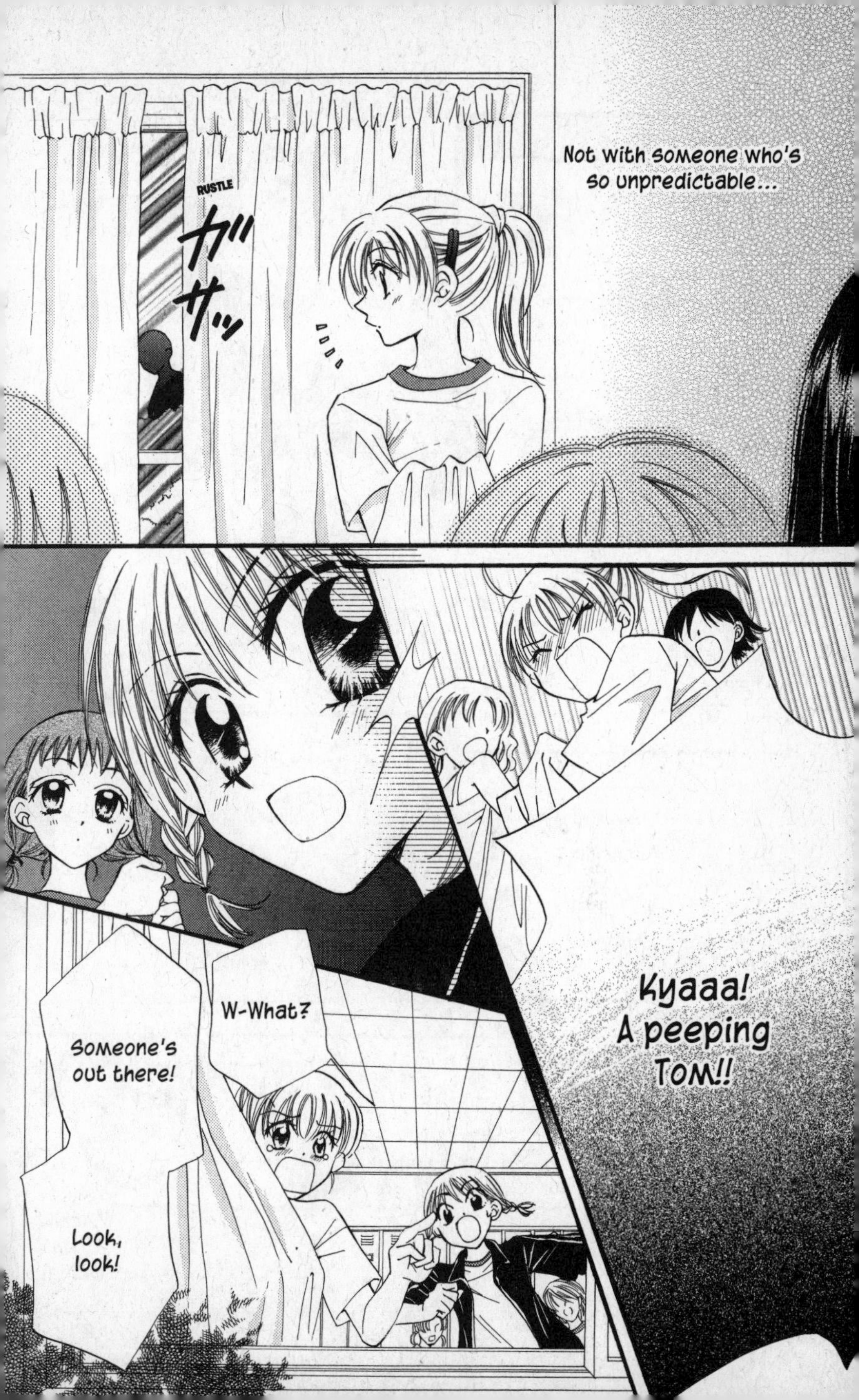
Not with someone who's so unpredictable...
RUSTLE
ガサッ
Kyaaa! A peeping Tom!!
W-What?
Someone's out there!
Look, look!

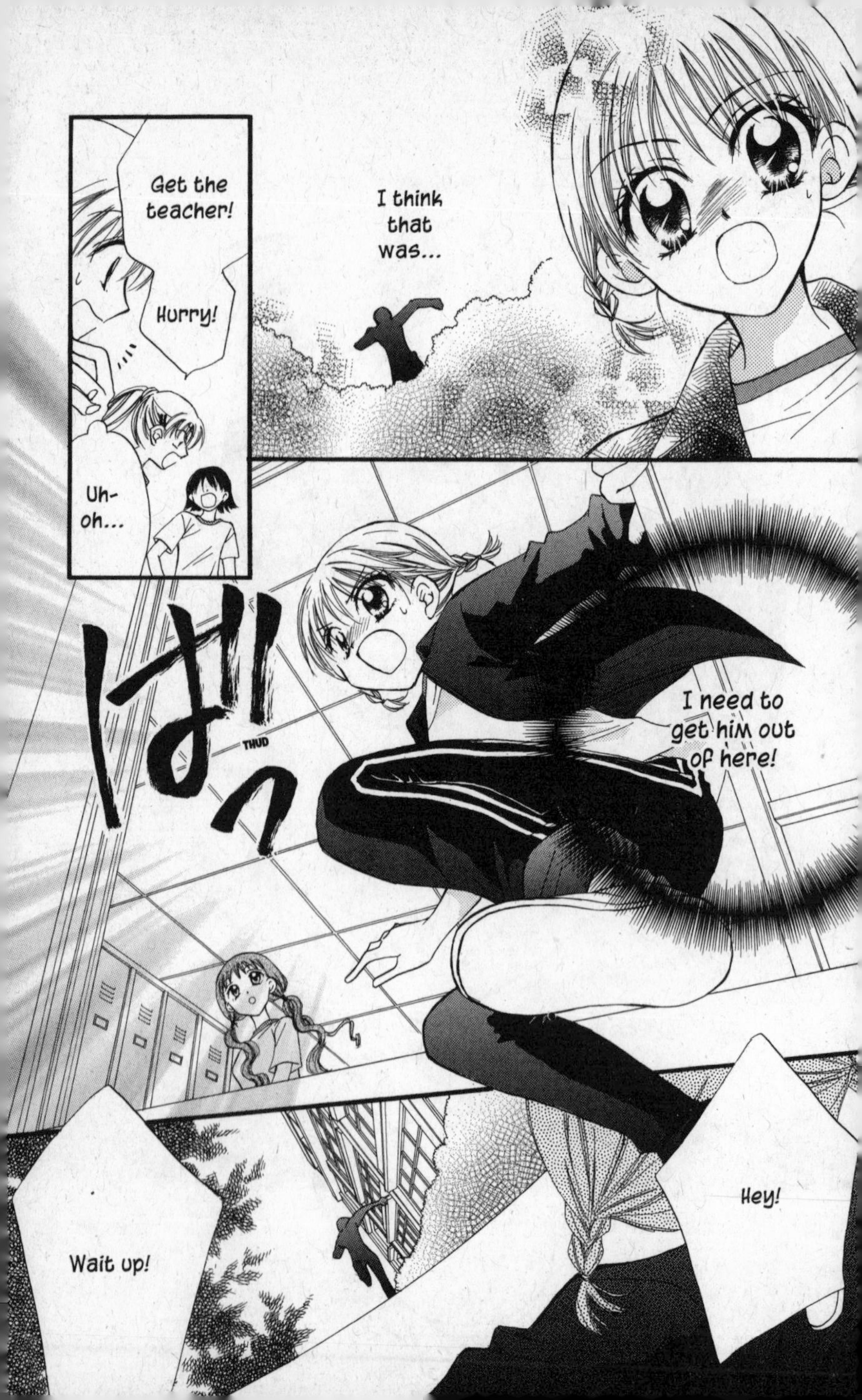
I think that was...
Get the teacher!
Hurry!
Uh-oh...
ぱっ
THUD
I need to get him out of here!
Hey!
Wait up!

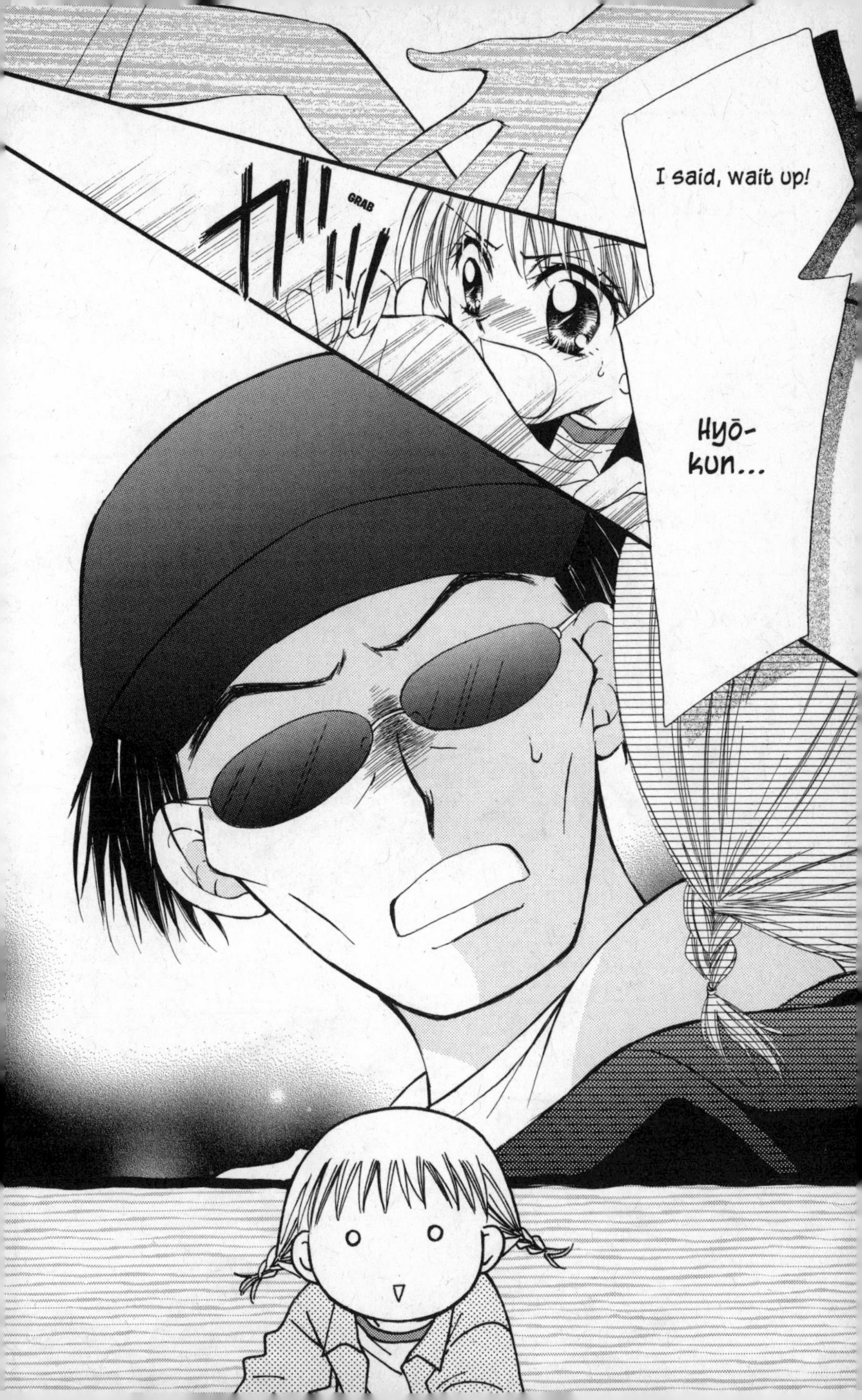
I said, wait up!
ガッ
GRAB
Hyō-
kun...

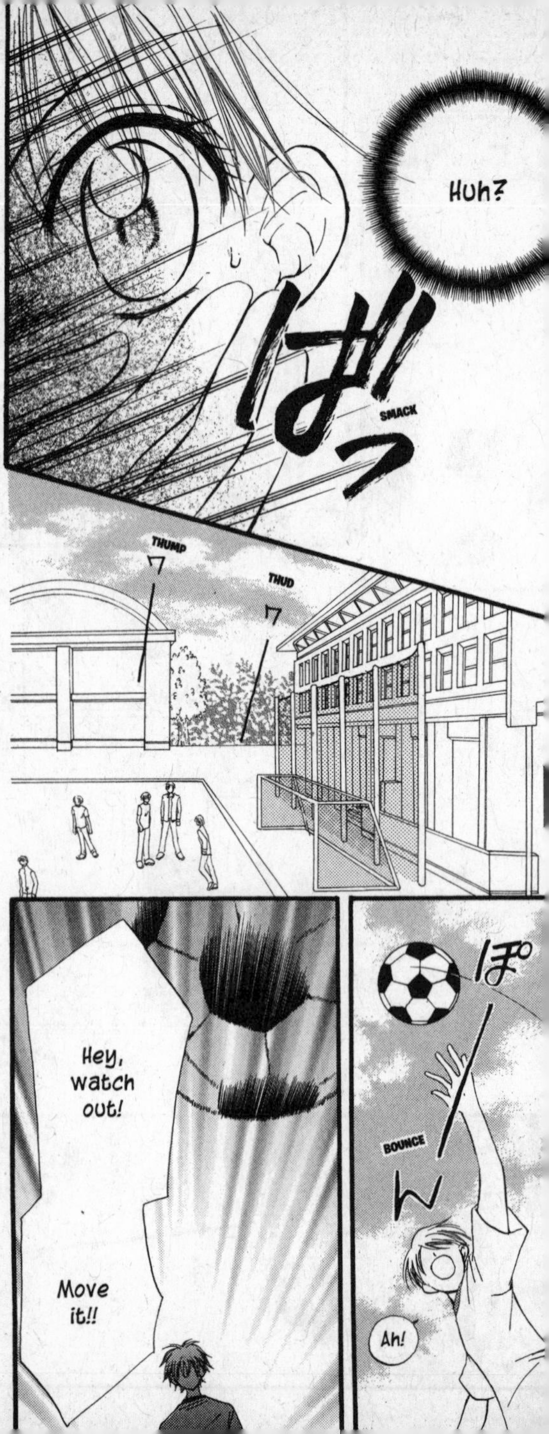
Huh?
SMACK
THUMP
THUD
BOUNCE
Ah!
Hey, watch out!
Move it!!

4.

I received a lot of questions asking what the animal from the first chapter was. I answer it in the second story, but it's an animal called a Fennec Fox. In real life they have larger bodies and are nocturnal animals, so I decided to make my own breed called a "Madaran Fennec Fox." ♥ By the way, I made up Madara Island, too. So that's how both lions and bears are on it. I saw a Fennec Fox on TV once and it was sooo cute! I want one!

At first I drew it without regard to its gender, but I think it's a girl!

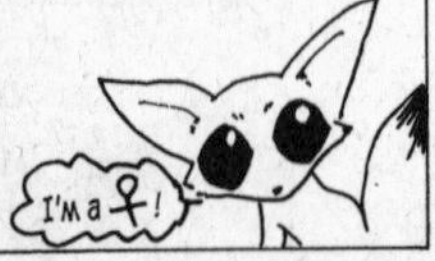
I'm a ♀!

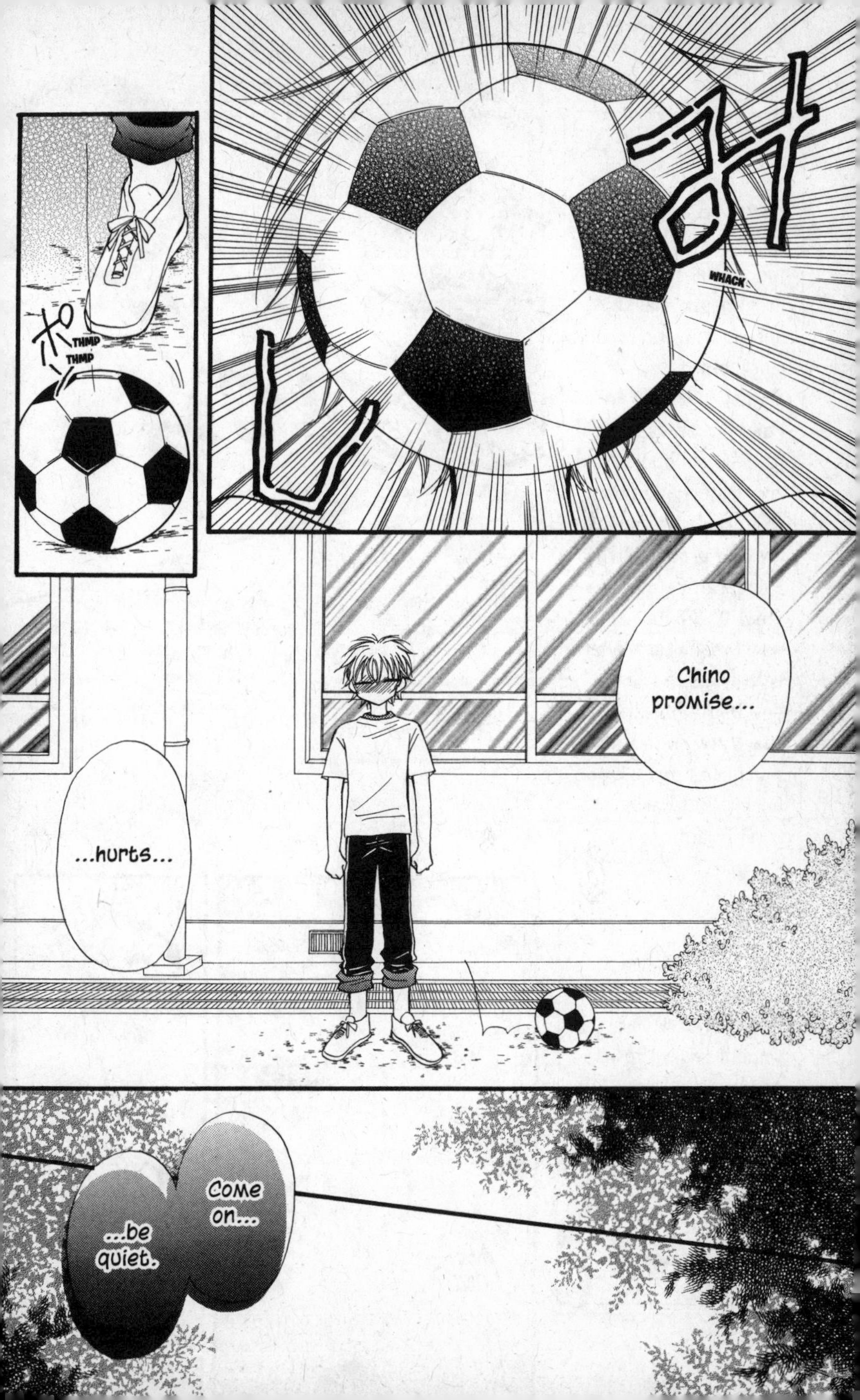
WHACK
THMP
THMP
Chino promise...
...hurts...
Come on...
...be quiet.

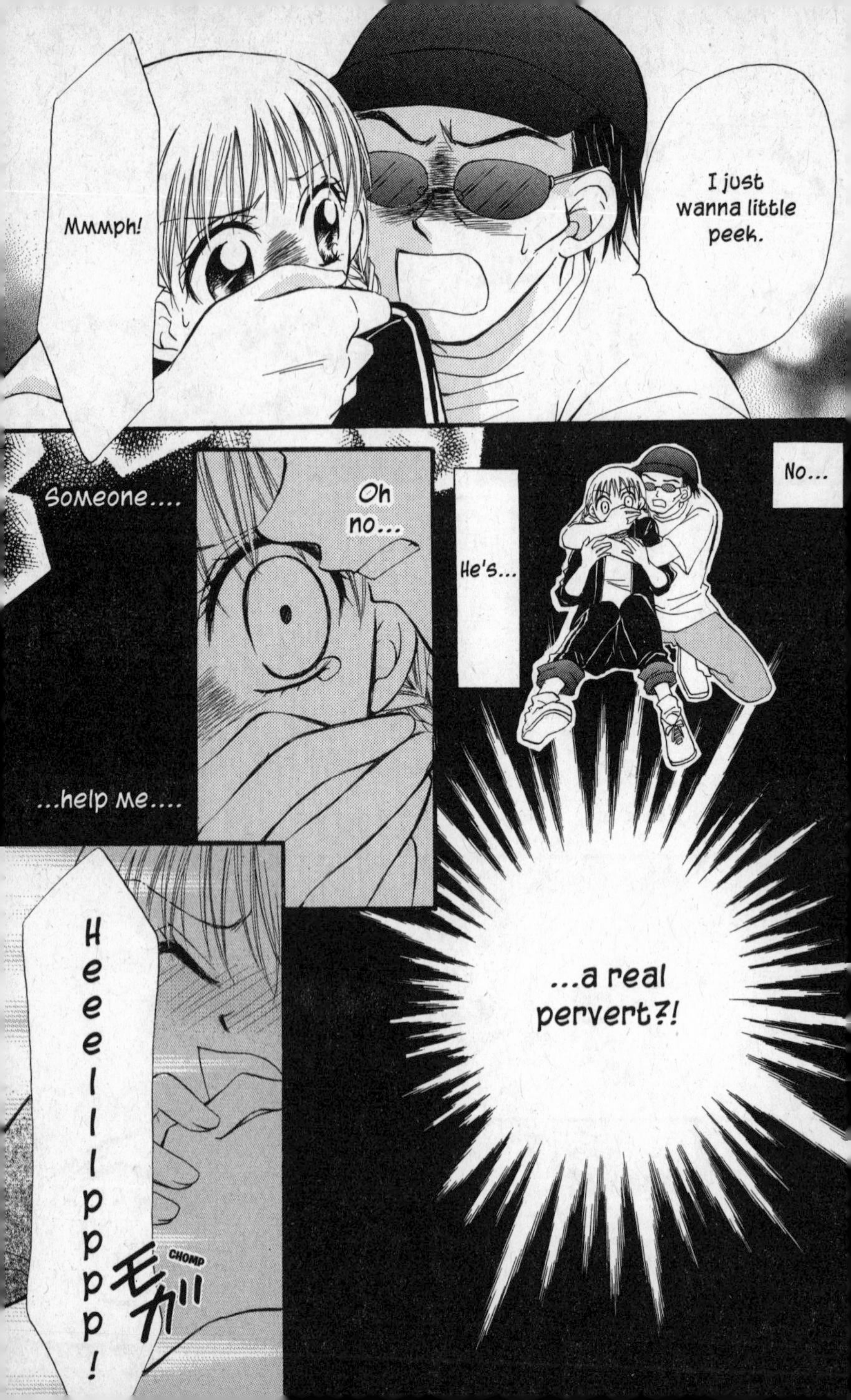

I just wanna little peek.
Mmmph!
No...
He's...
...a real pervert?!
Oh no...
Someone....
...help me....
Heeelllpppp!
CHOMP
モガ

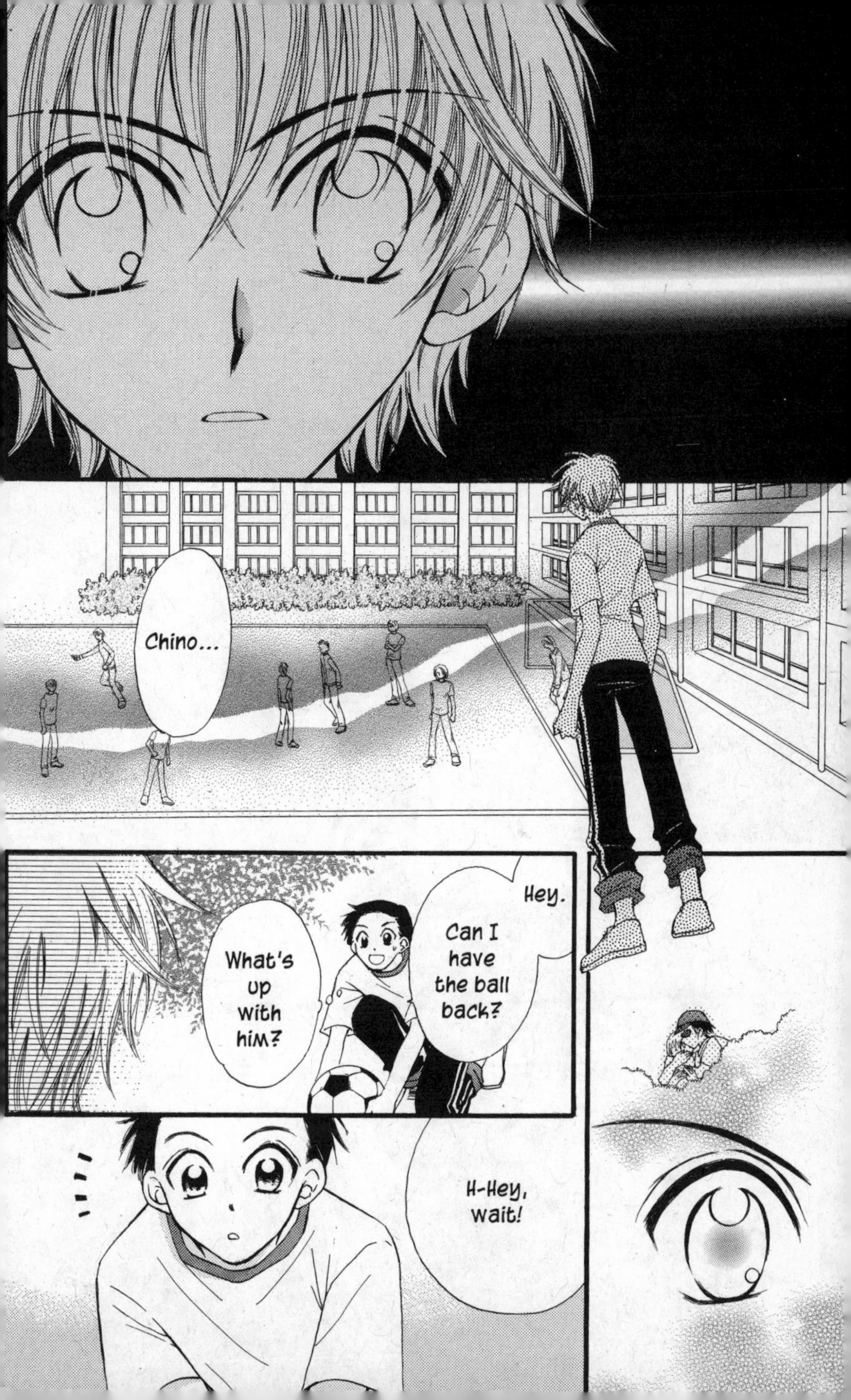
Chino...
Hey.
Can I have the ball back?
What's up with him?
H-Hey, wait!

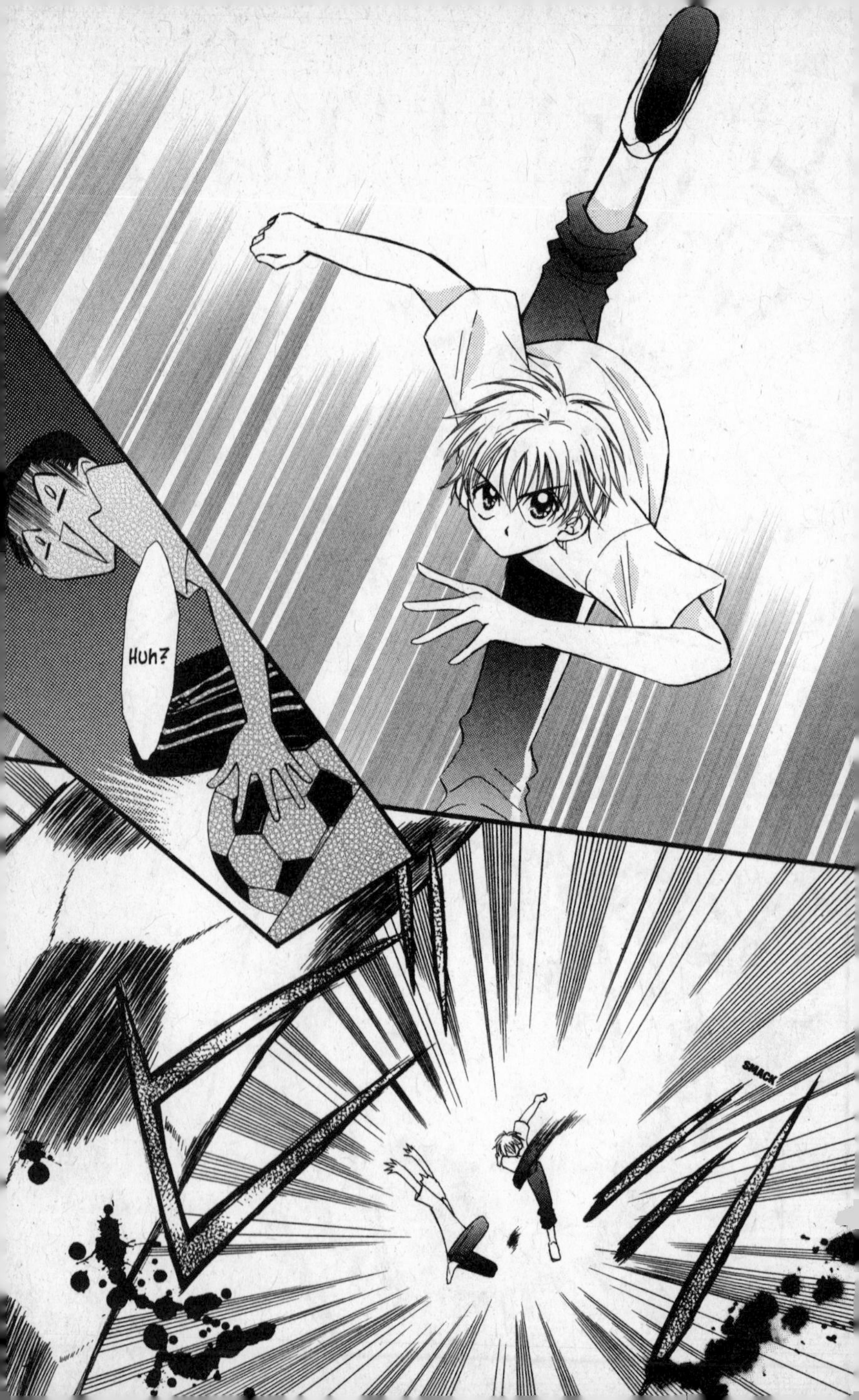
Huh?
SMACK

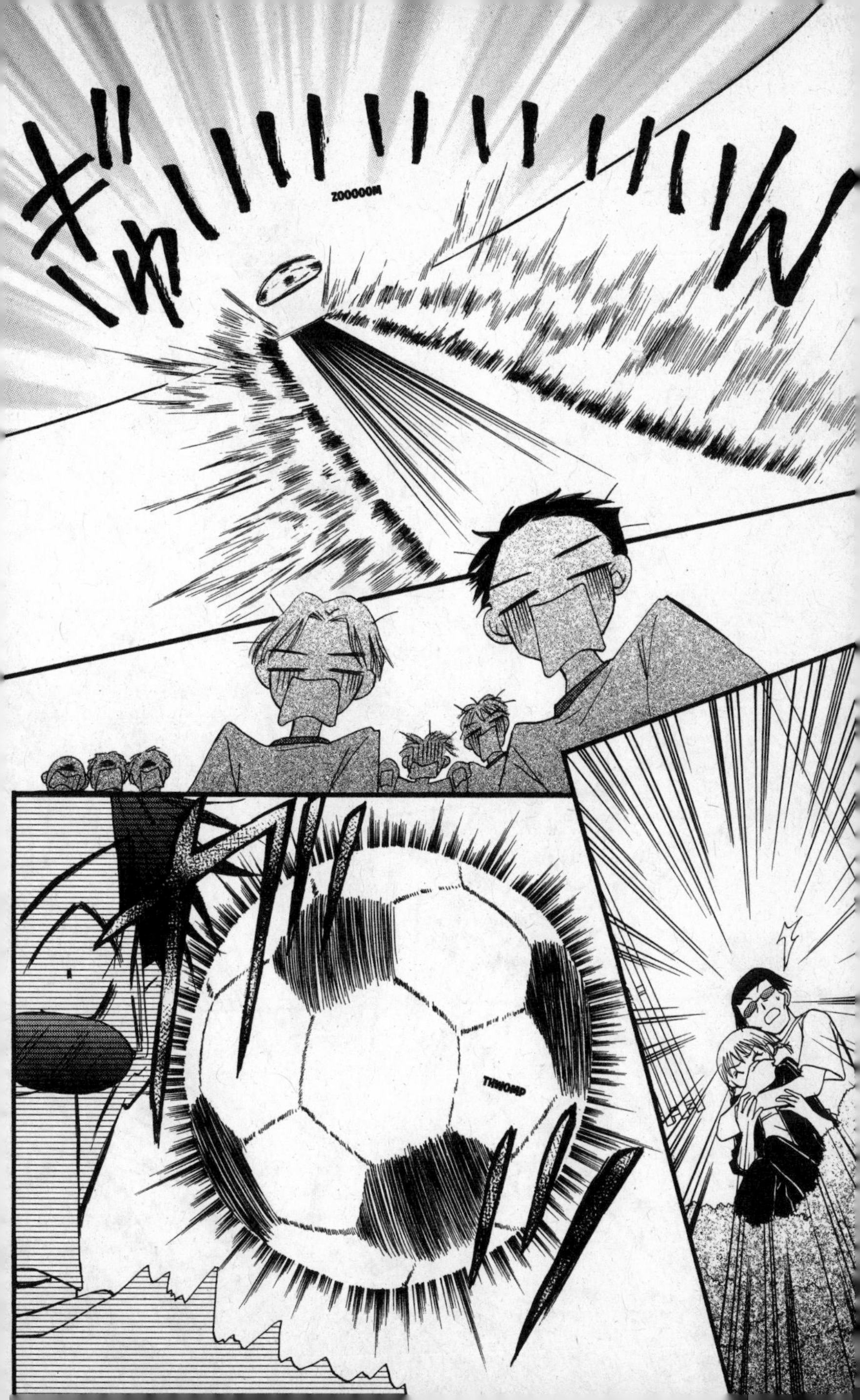
ぎゅいいいいいいん
ZOOOOOM
THWOMP

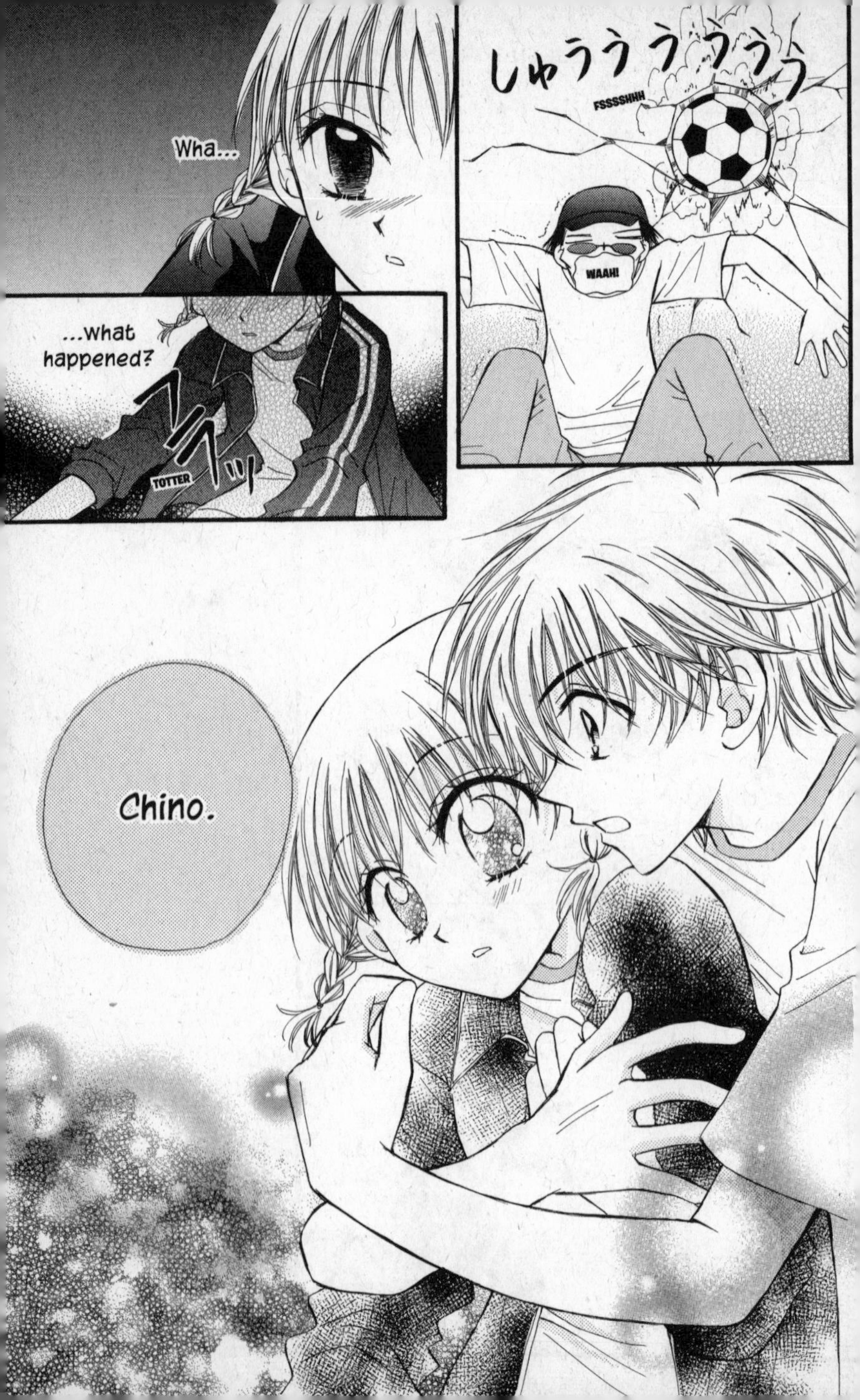
しゅううううう
FSSSSHHH
WAAH!
Wha...
...what happened?
TOTTER
Chino.

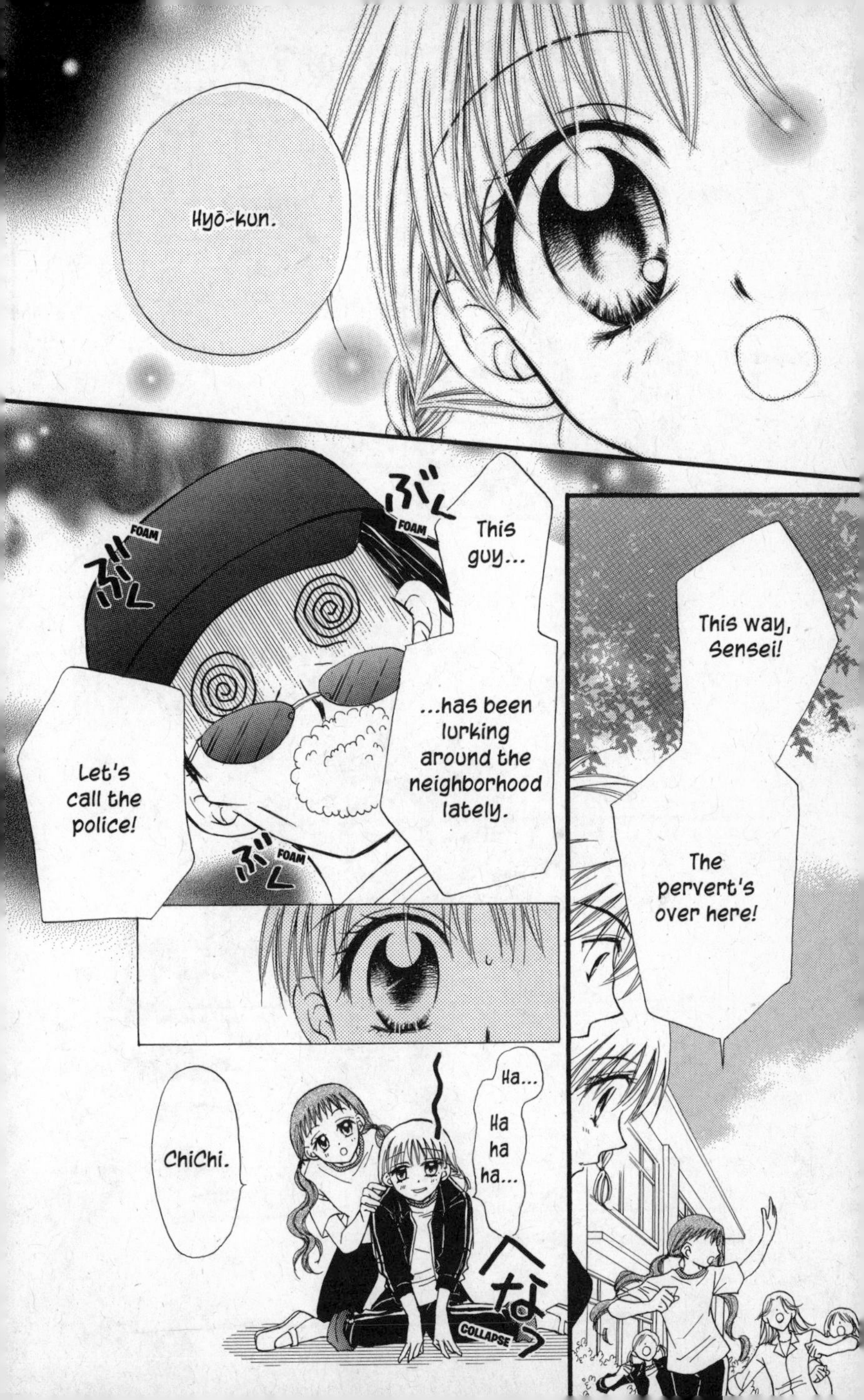
Hyō-kun.
This way, Sensei!
The pervert's over here!
ぶく FOAM
ぶく FOAM
This guy...
...has been lurking around the neighborhood lately.
Let's call the police!
ぶく FOAM
Ha...
Ha ha ha...
ChiChi.
へな COLLAPSE

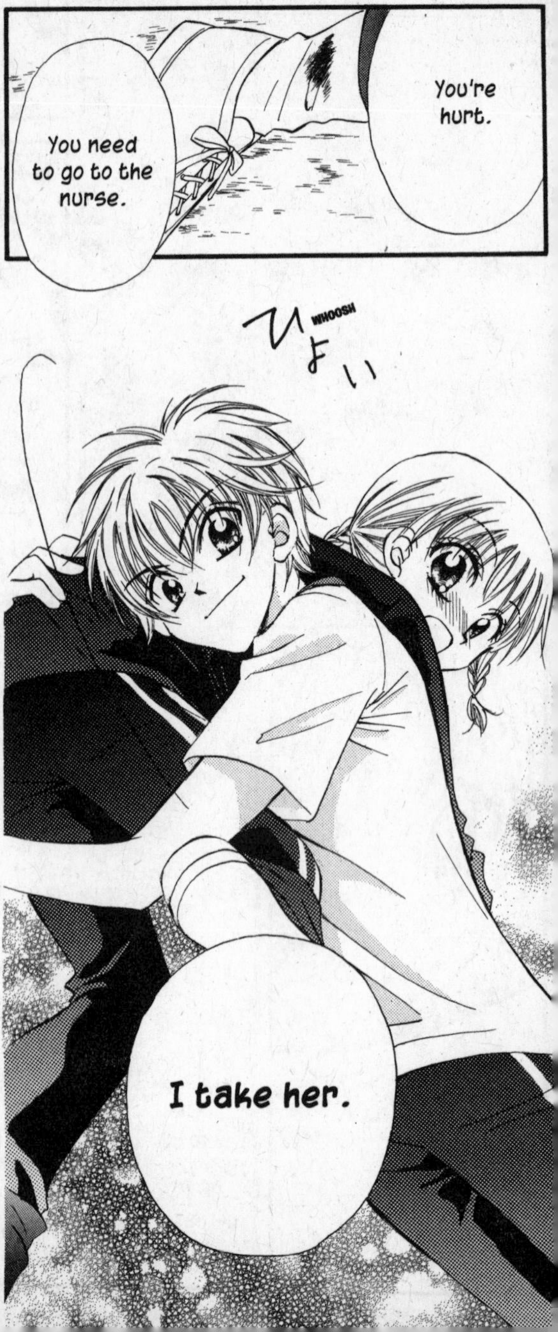
You're hurt.
You need to go to the nurse.
WHOOSH
I take her.

5.

I'm changing the subject, but I love yakiniku (strips of grilled meat). I cook it a lot at home. One day we really wanted yakiniku, but I was working so I couldn't go out so I said to my sister...

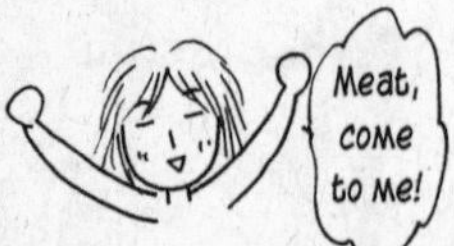
Meat, come to me!

That night, just as I was starving...

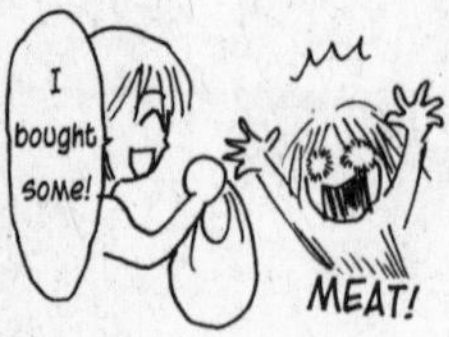
I bought some!
MEAT!

I was sooo happy...

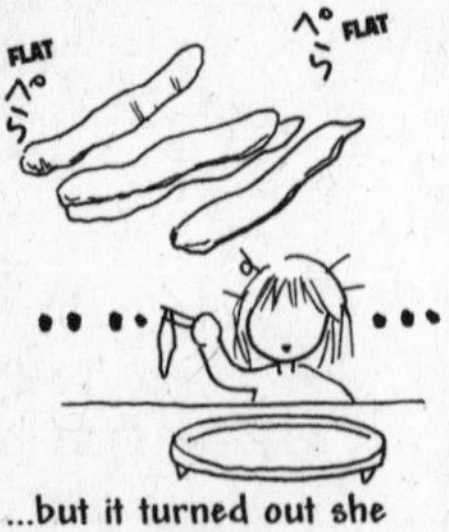
FLAT
FLAT
......

...but it turned out she bought sukiyaki meat instead! (thinly sliced meat for use in hotpot) I made it into yakiniku anyway but it was pretty gross.

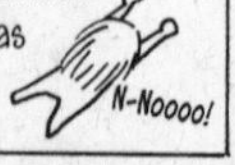
N-Noooo!

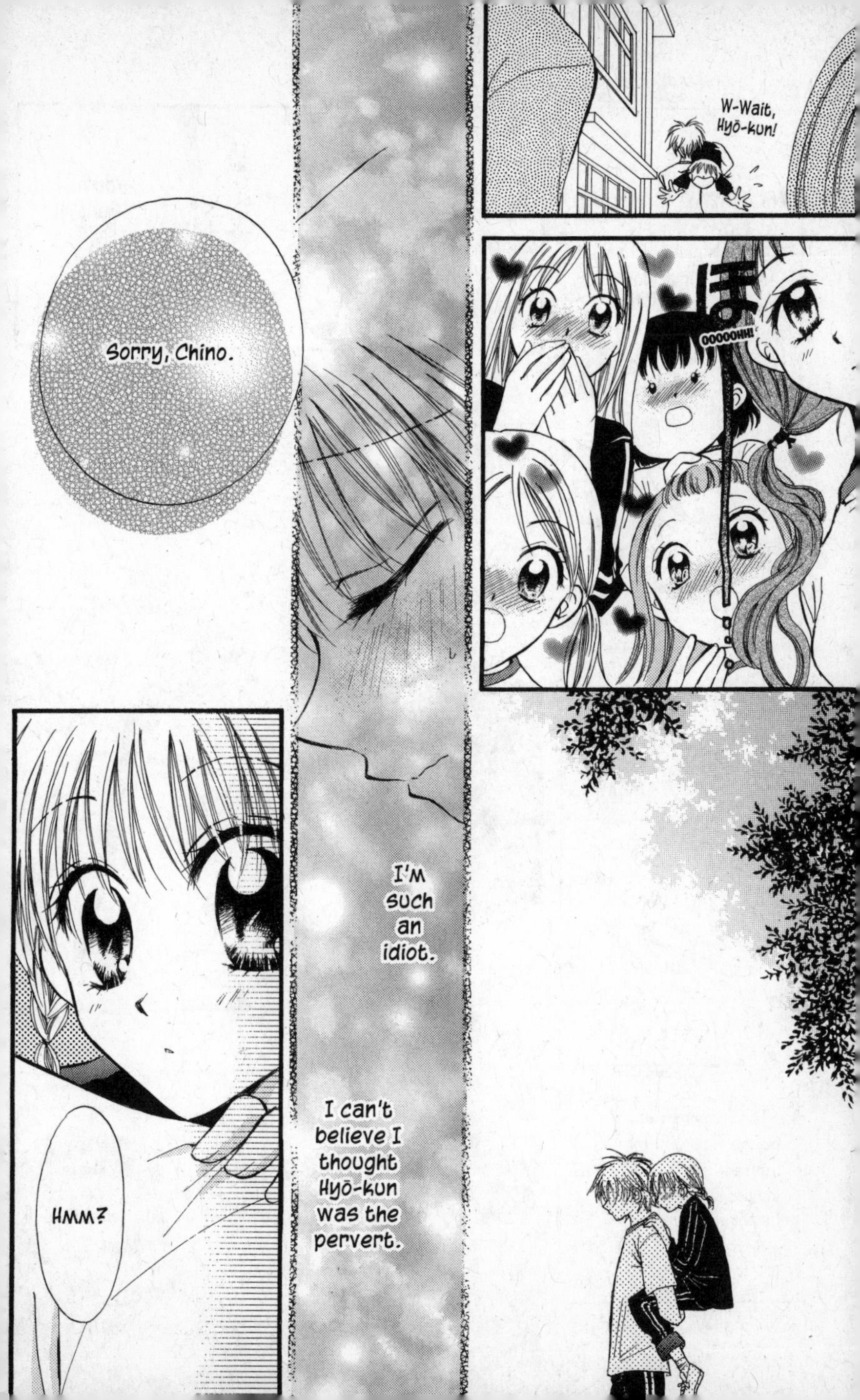
W-Wait, Hyō-kun!
ほ
OOOOOHH!
I'M such an idiot.
I can't believe I thought Hyō-kun was the pervert.
Sorry, Chino.
HMM?

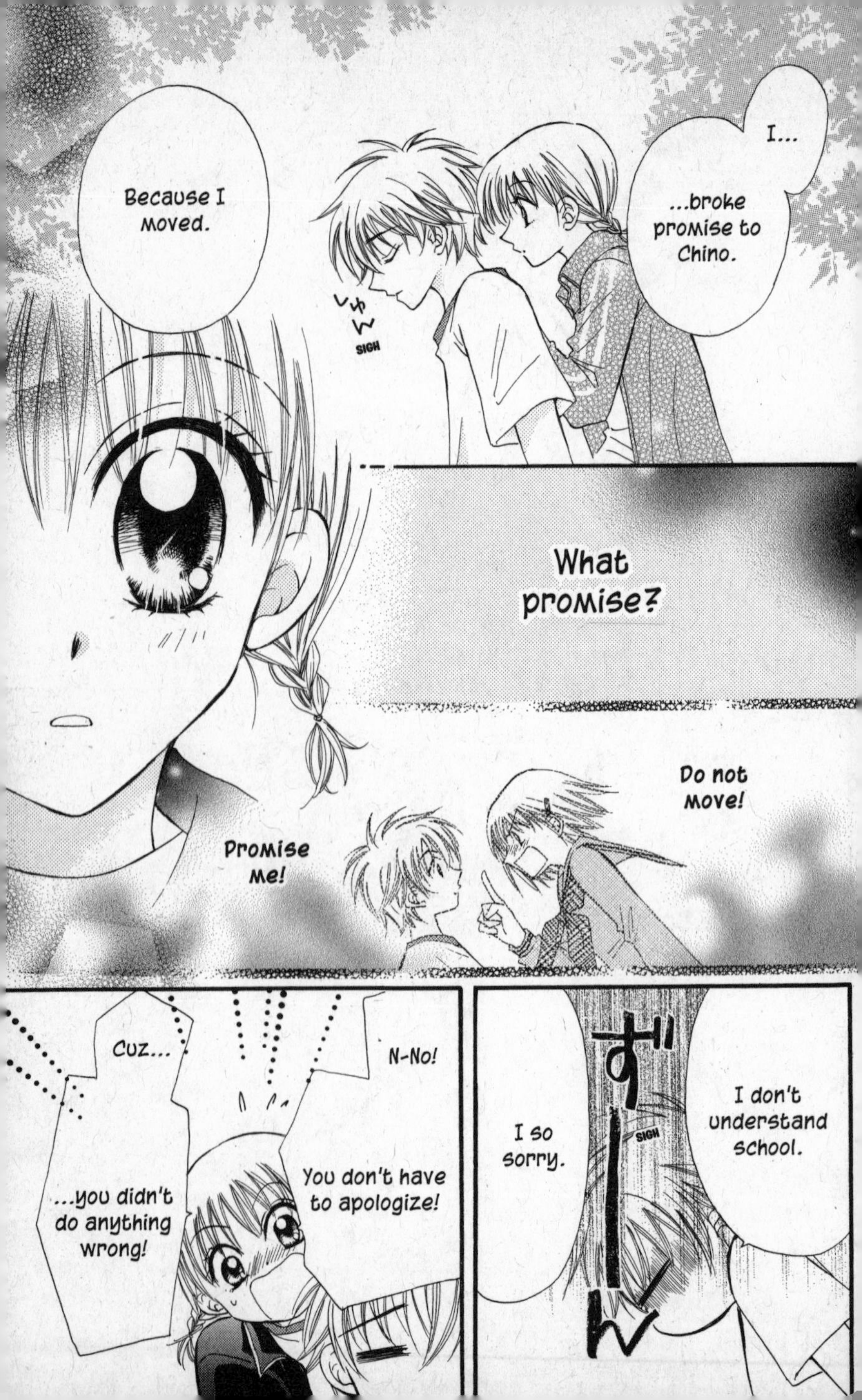
I...
...broke promise to Chino.
Because I moved.
しゅん
SIGH
What promise?
Do not move!
Promise me!
I don't understand school.
ずーん
SIGH
I so sorry.
N-No!
You don't have to apologize!
Cuz...
...you didn't do anything wrong!

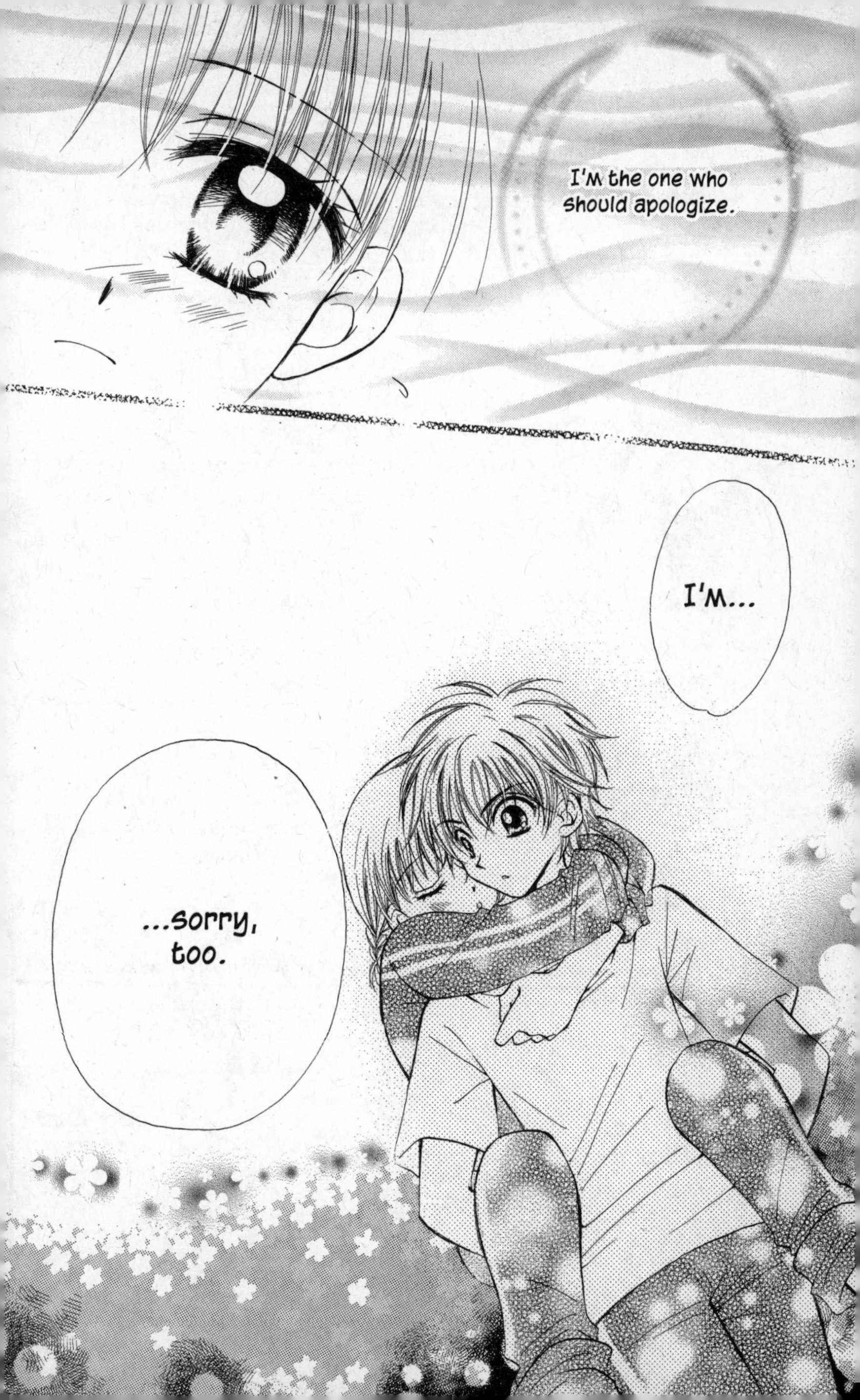
I'M the one who should apologize.
I'M...
...sorry, too.

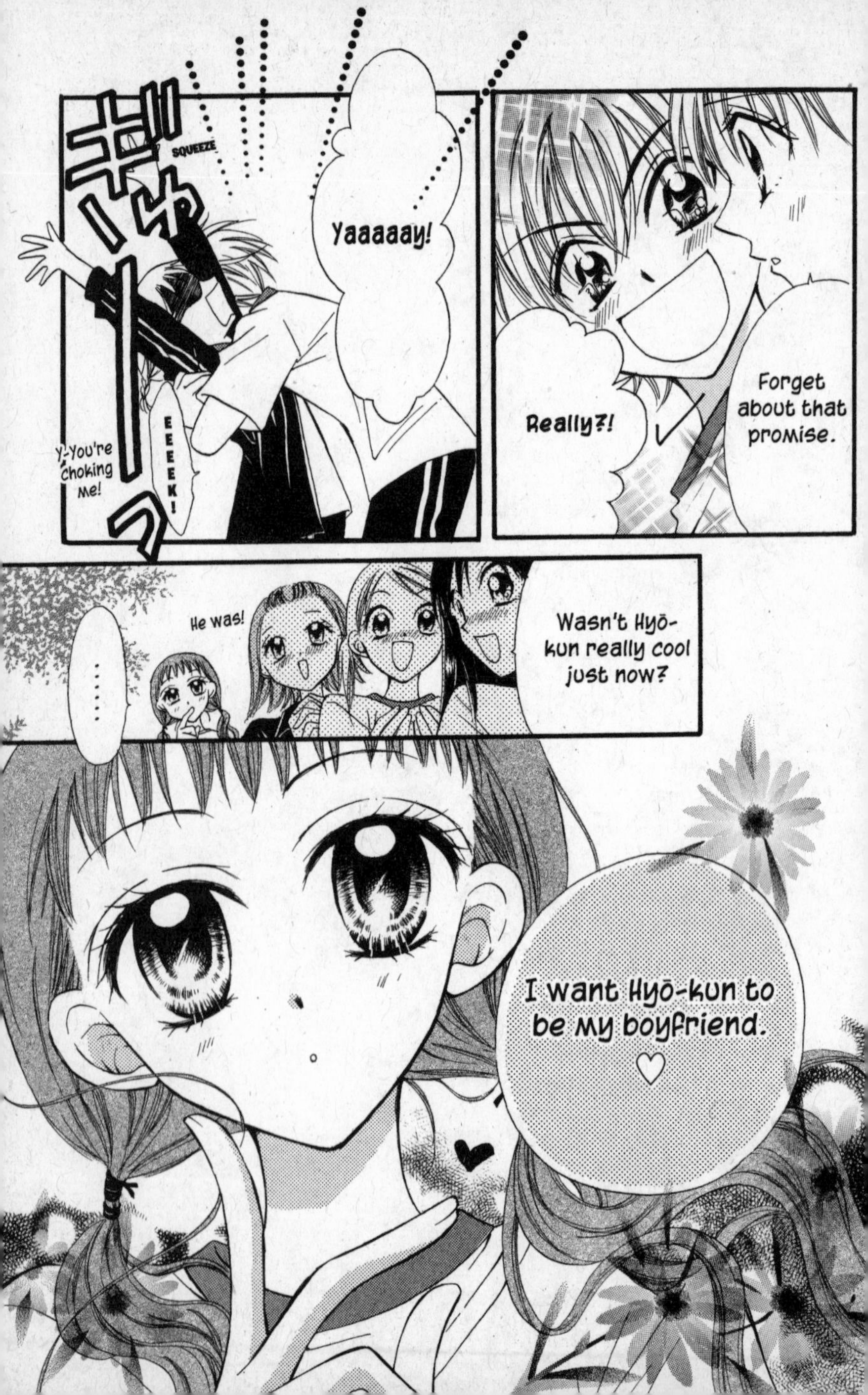
Forget about that promise.
Really?!
Yaaaaay!
ギューッ
SQUEEZE
EEEEEK!
Y-You're choking me!
Wasn't Hyō-kun really cool just now?
He was!
......
I want Hyō-kun to be my boyfriend. ♡

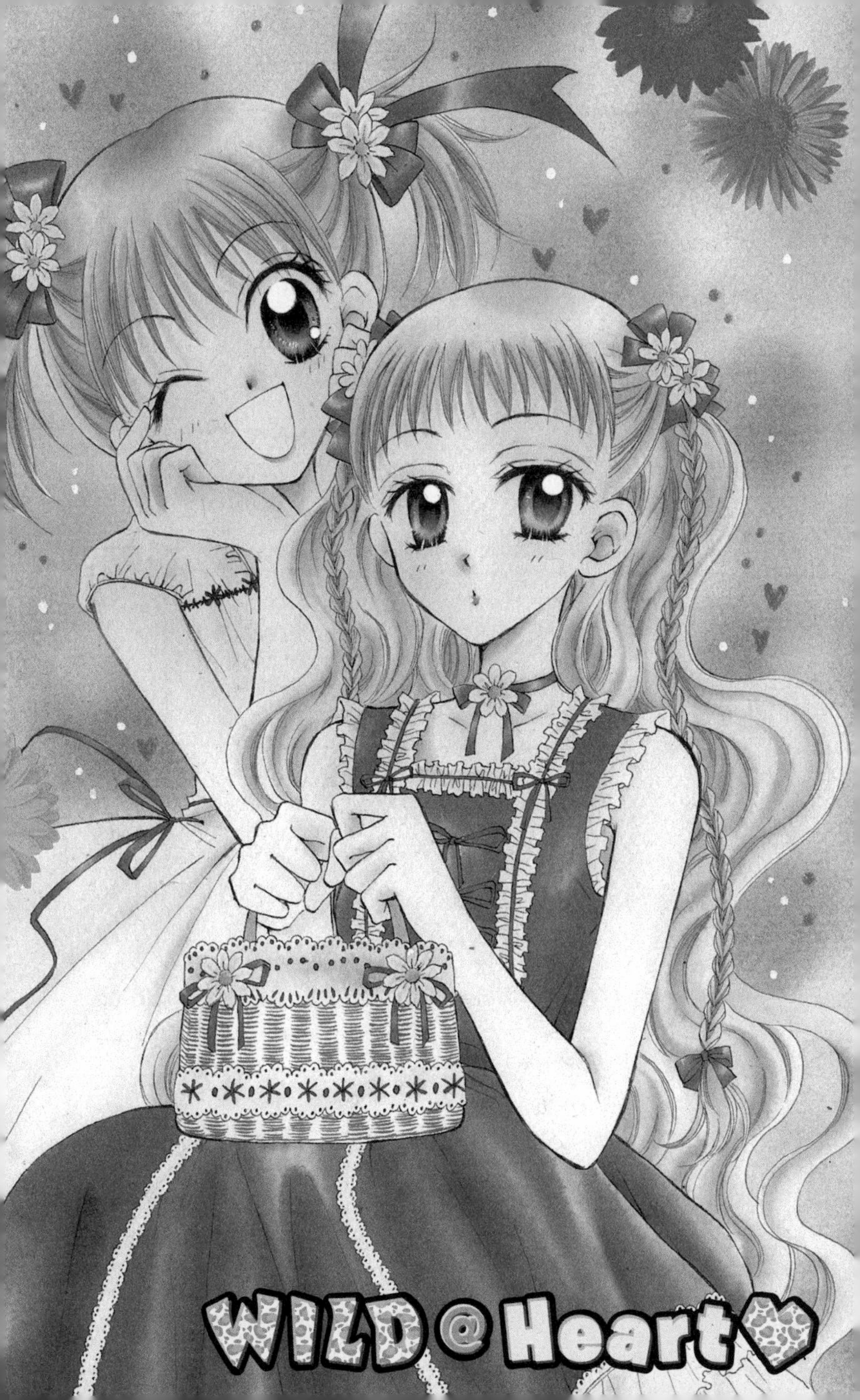
WILD @ Heart♥

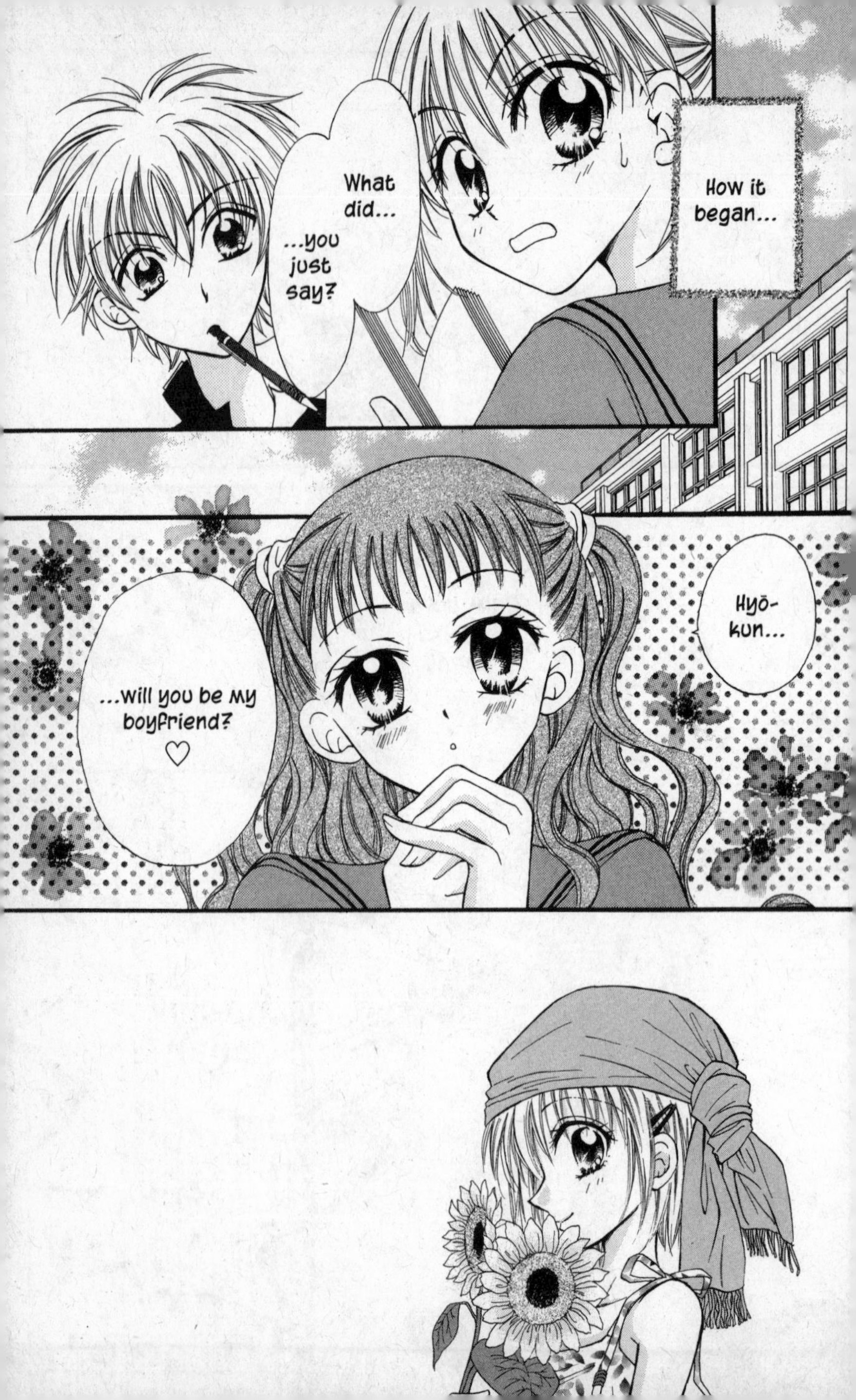
How it began...
What did... ...you just say?
Hyō-kun...
...will you be my boyfriend? ♡

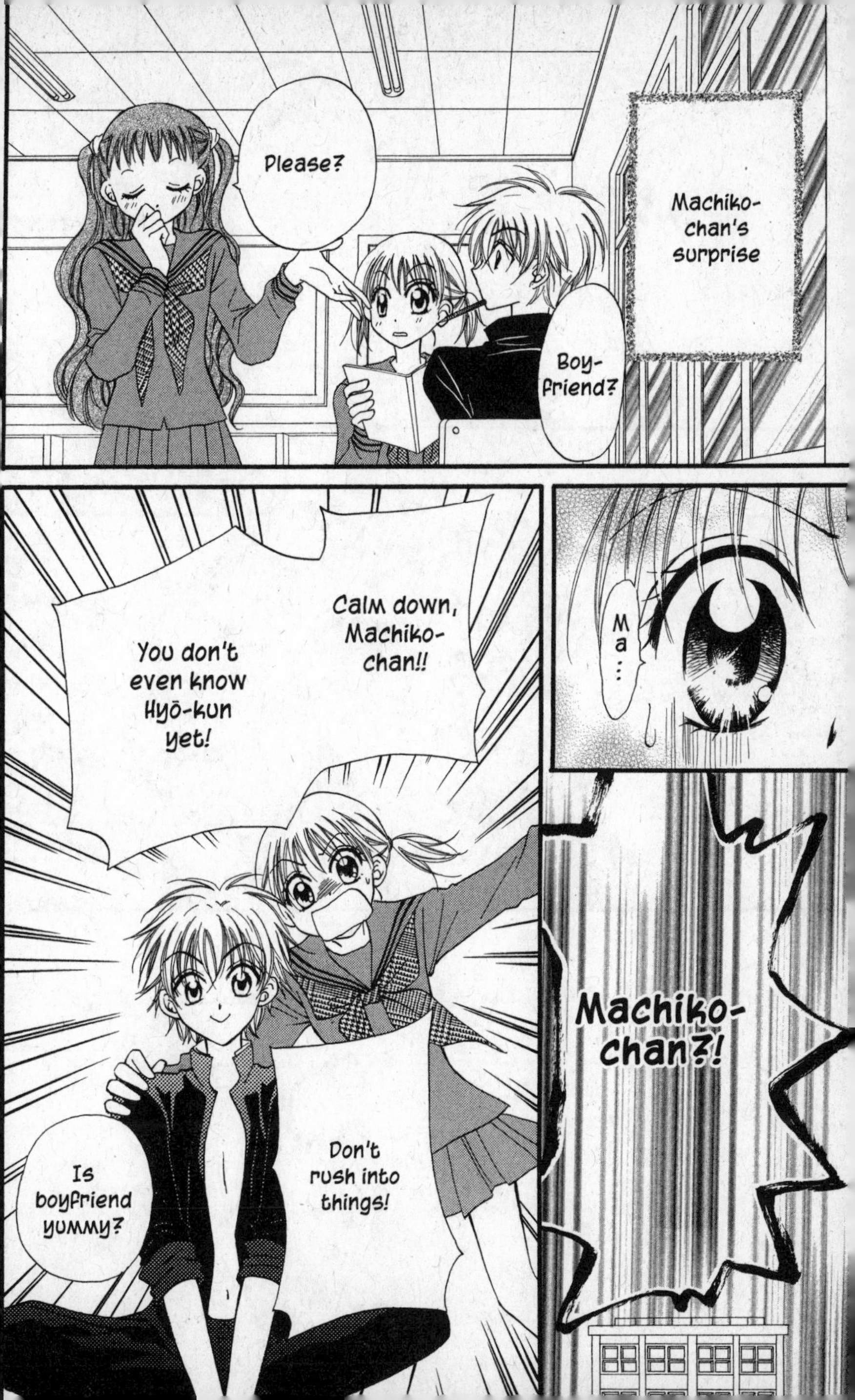

Machiko-chan's surprise
Boy-friend?
Please?
Ma...
Machiko-chan?!
Calm down, Machiko-chan!!
You don't even know Hyō-kun yet!
Don't rush into things!
Is boyfriend yummy?

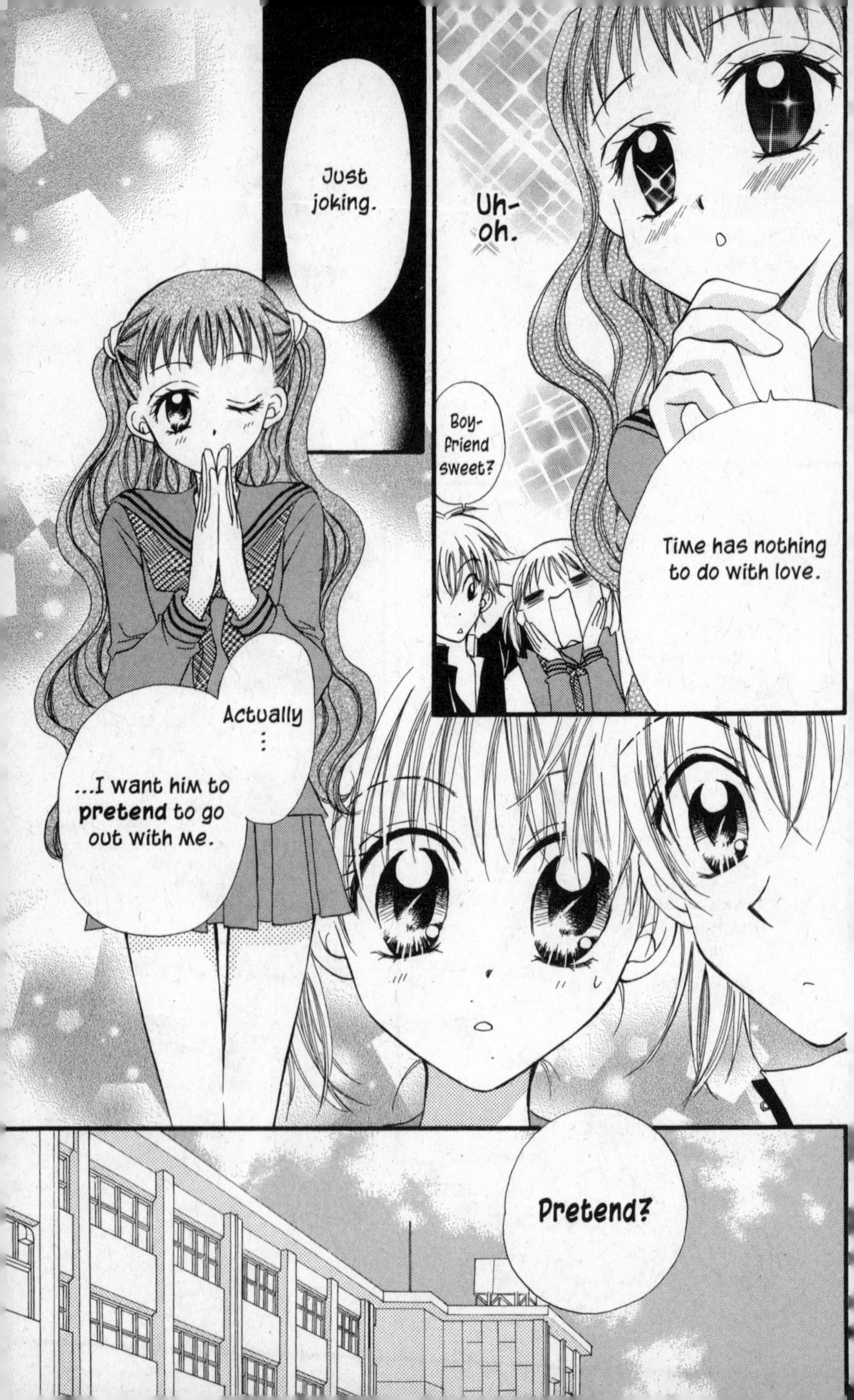
Time has nothing to do with love.
Uh-oh.
Boy-friend sweet?
Just joking.
Actually...
...I want him to pretend to go out with me.
Pretend?

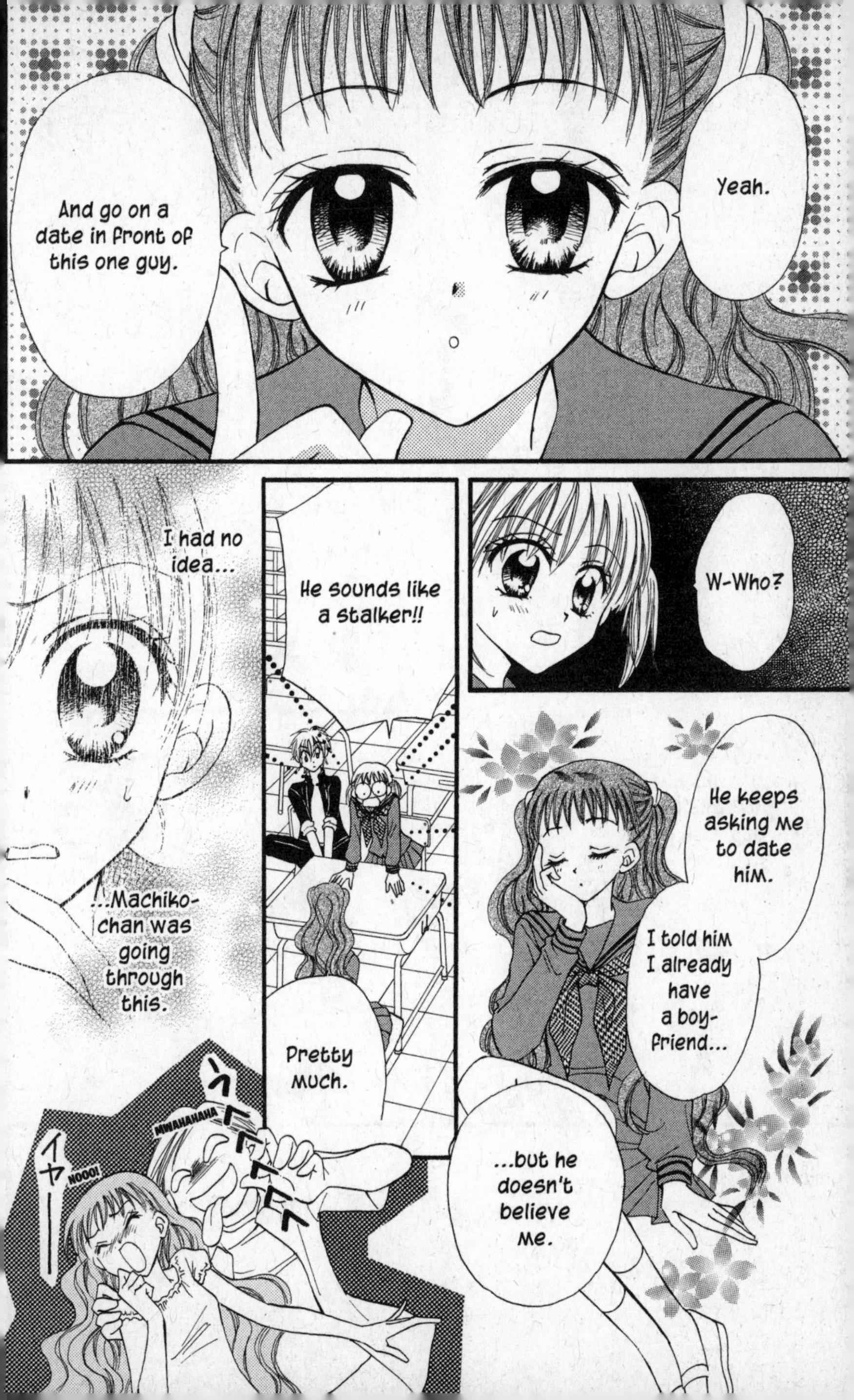

Yeah.
And go on a date in front of this one guy.
W-Who?
He keeps asking me to date him.
I told him I already have a boyfriend...
...but he doesn't believe me.
He sounds like a stalker!!
Pretty much.
I had no idea...
...Machiko-chan was going through this.
イヤー
NOOO!
MWAHAHAHA

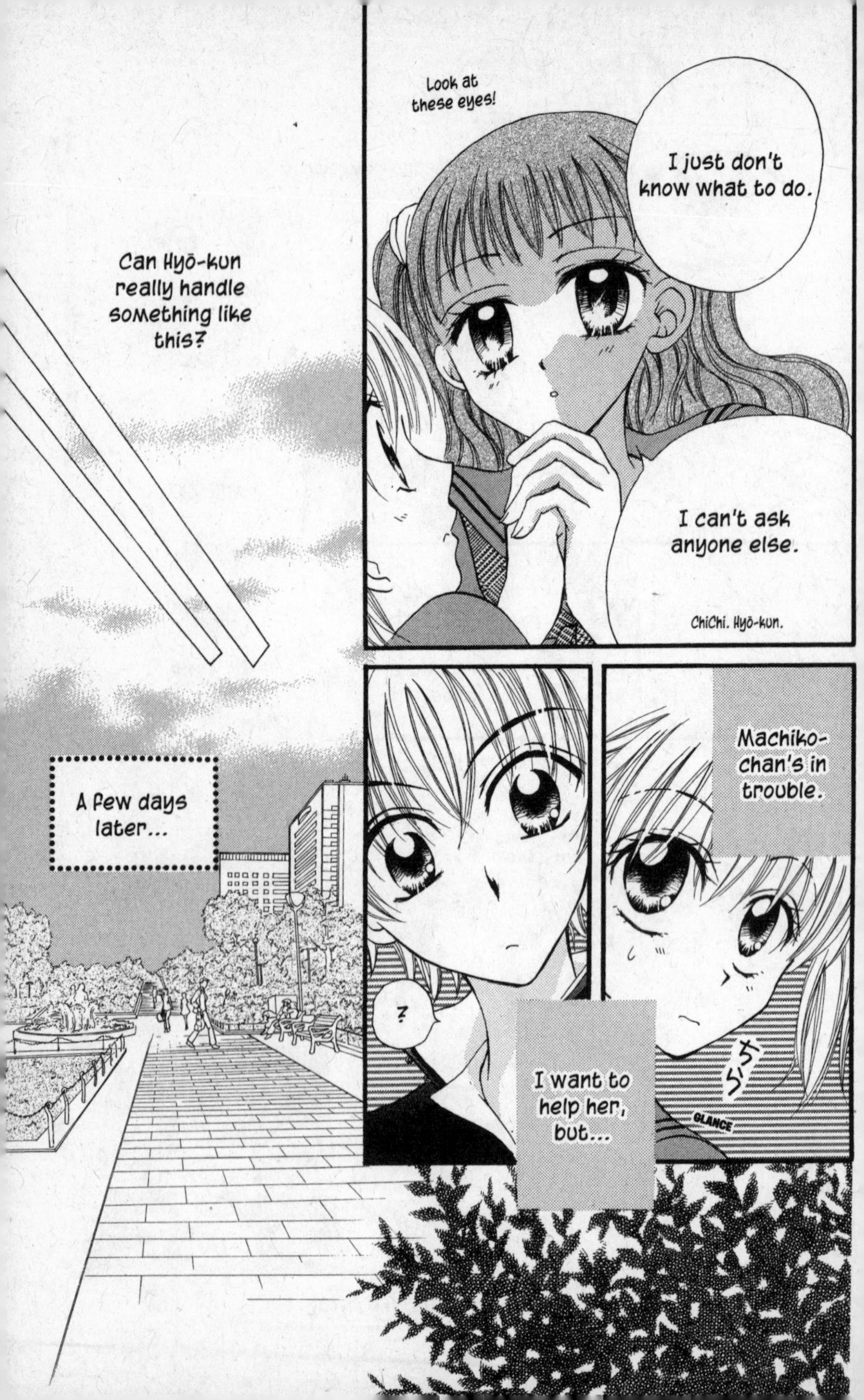
I just don't know what to do.
Look at these eyes!
I can't ask anyone else.
ChiChi. Hyō-kun.
Machiko-chan's in trouble.
ちら
GLANCE
?
I want to help her, but...
Can Hyō-kun really handle something like this?
A few days later...

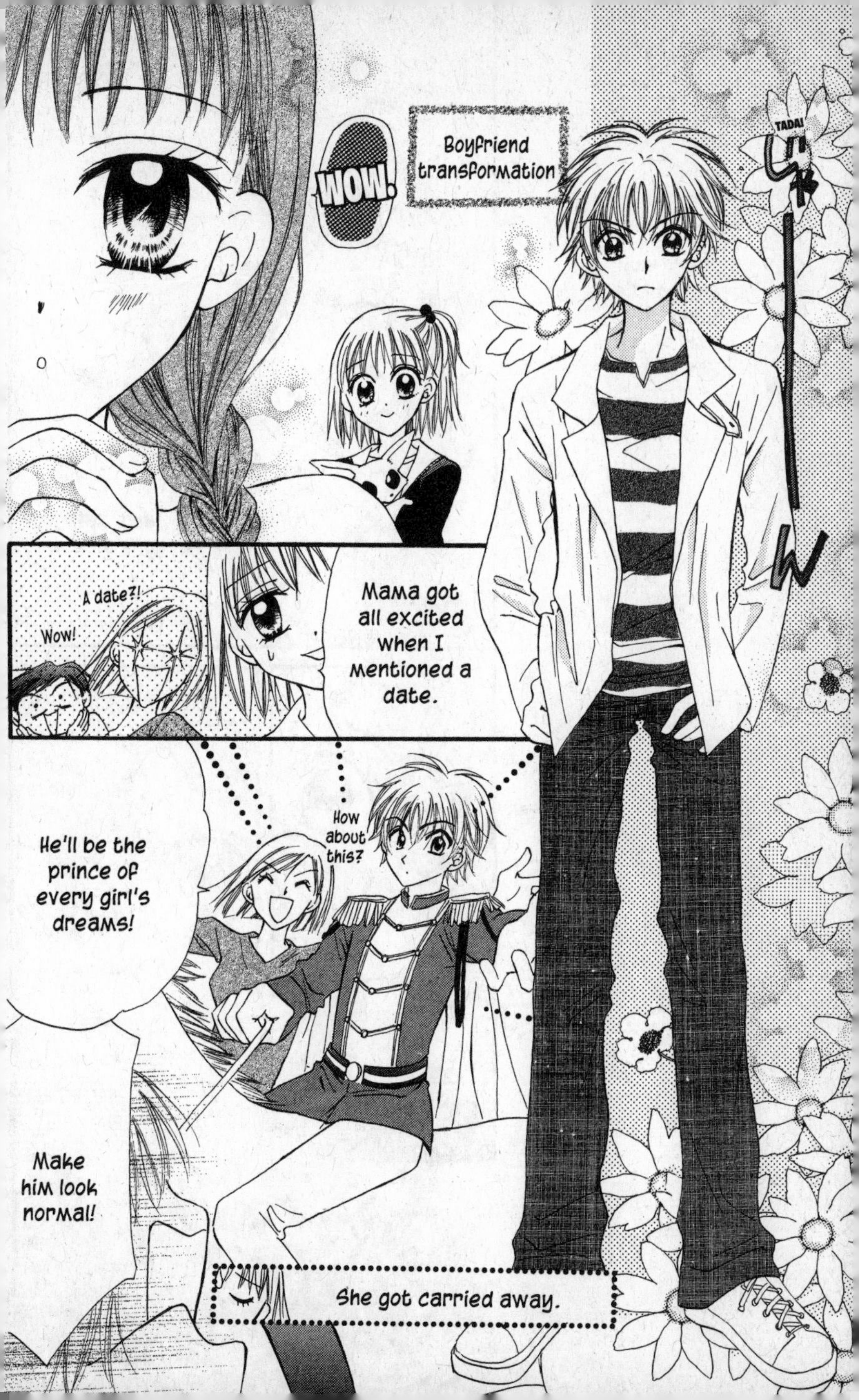

TADA!
Boyfriend transformation
WOW!
Mama got all excited when I mentioned a date.
A date?!
Wow!
How about this?
He'll be the prince of every girl's dreams!
Make him look normal!
She got carried away.

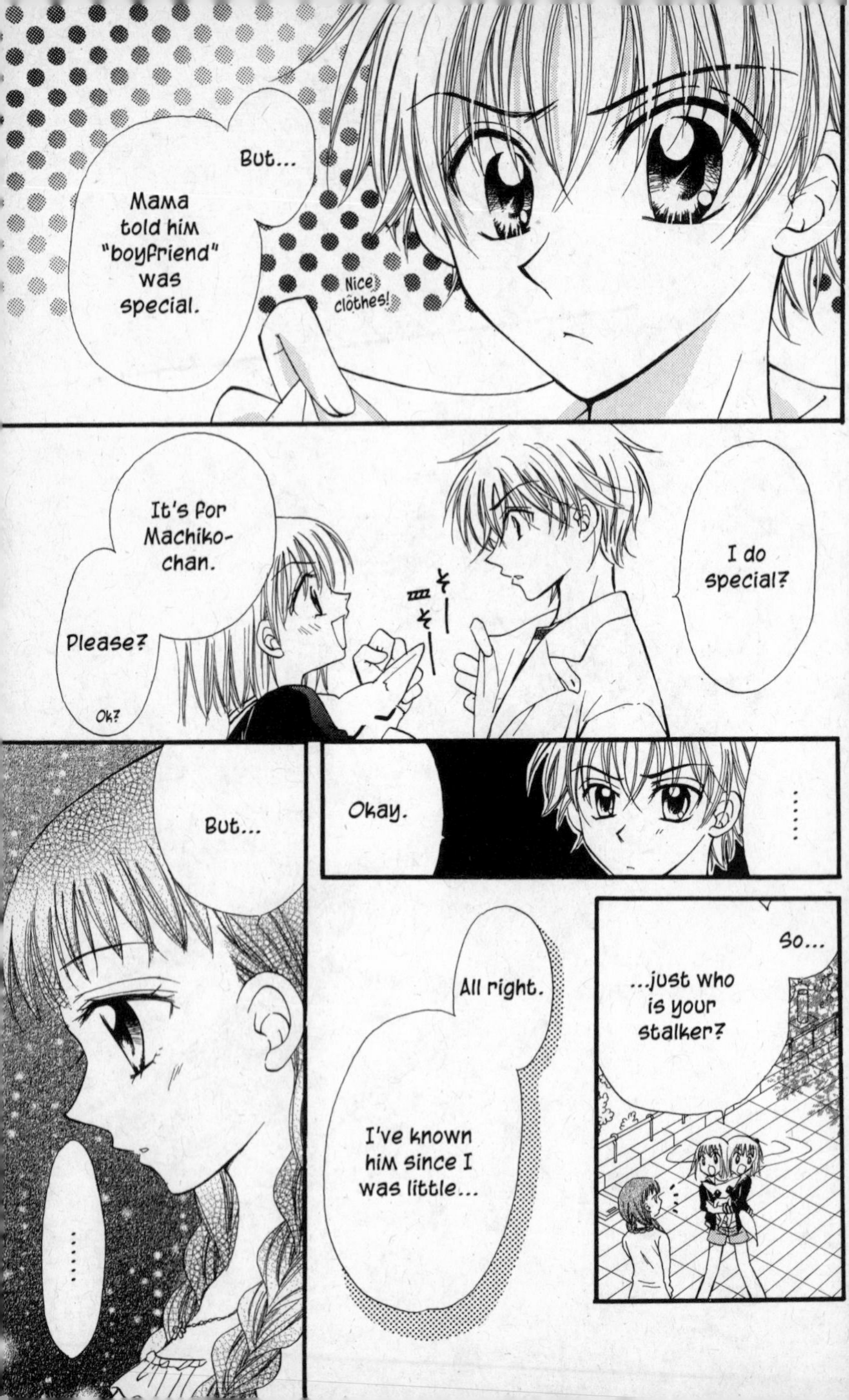
But...
Mama told him "boyfriend" was special.
Nice clothes!
I do special?
It's for Machiko-chan.
Please?
Ok?
......
Okay.
So...
...just who is your stalker?
All right.
I've known him since I was little...
But...
......

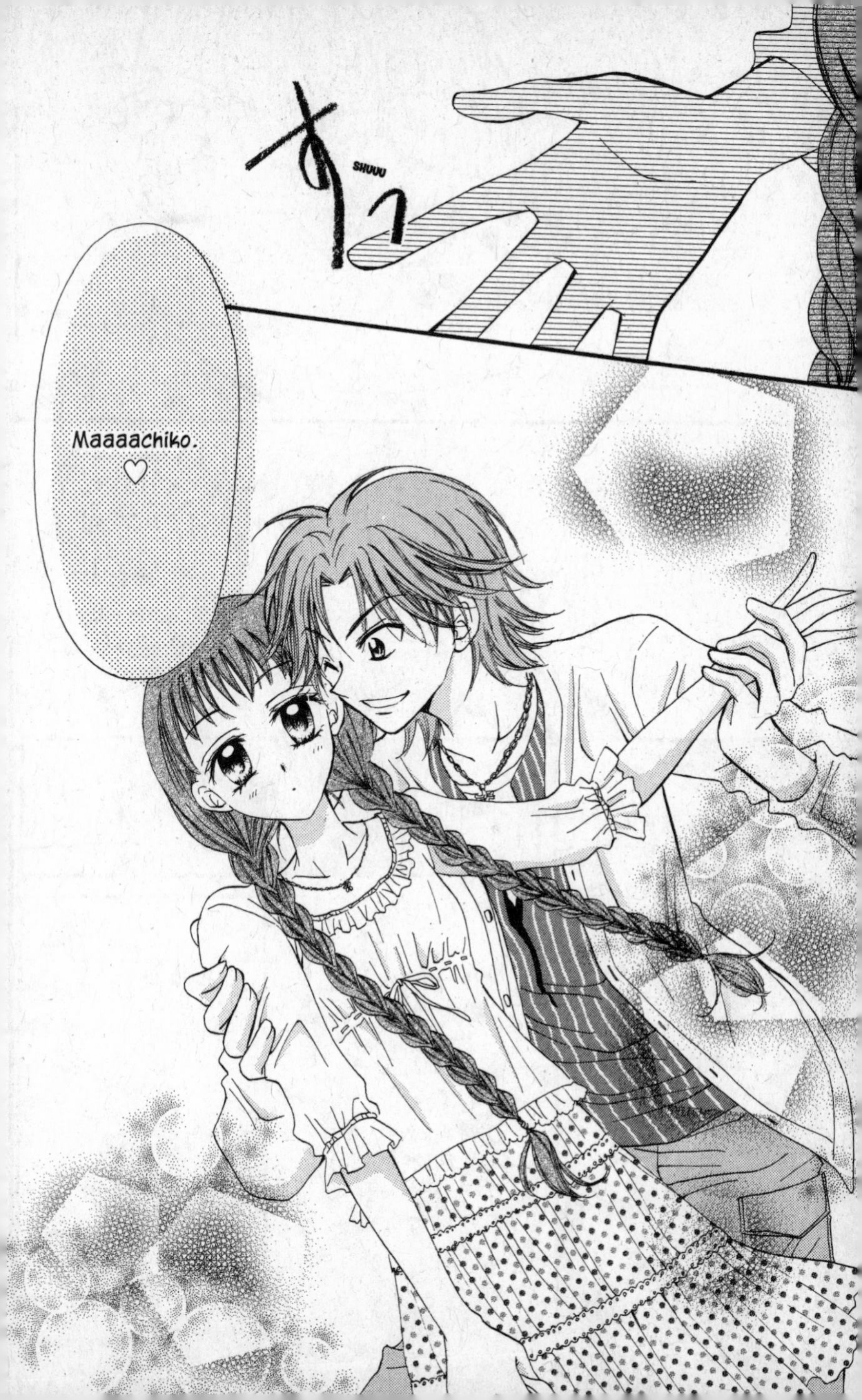
SHUUU
Maaaachiko. ♡

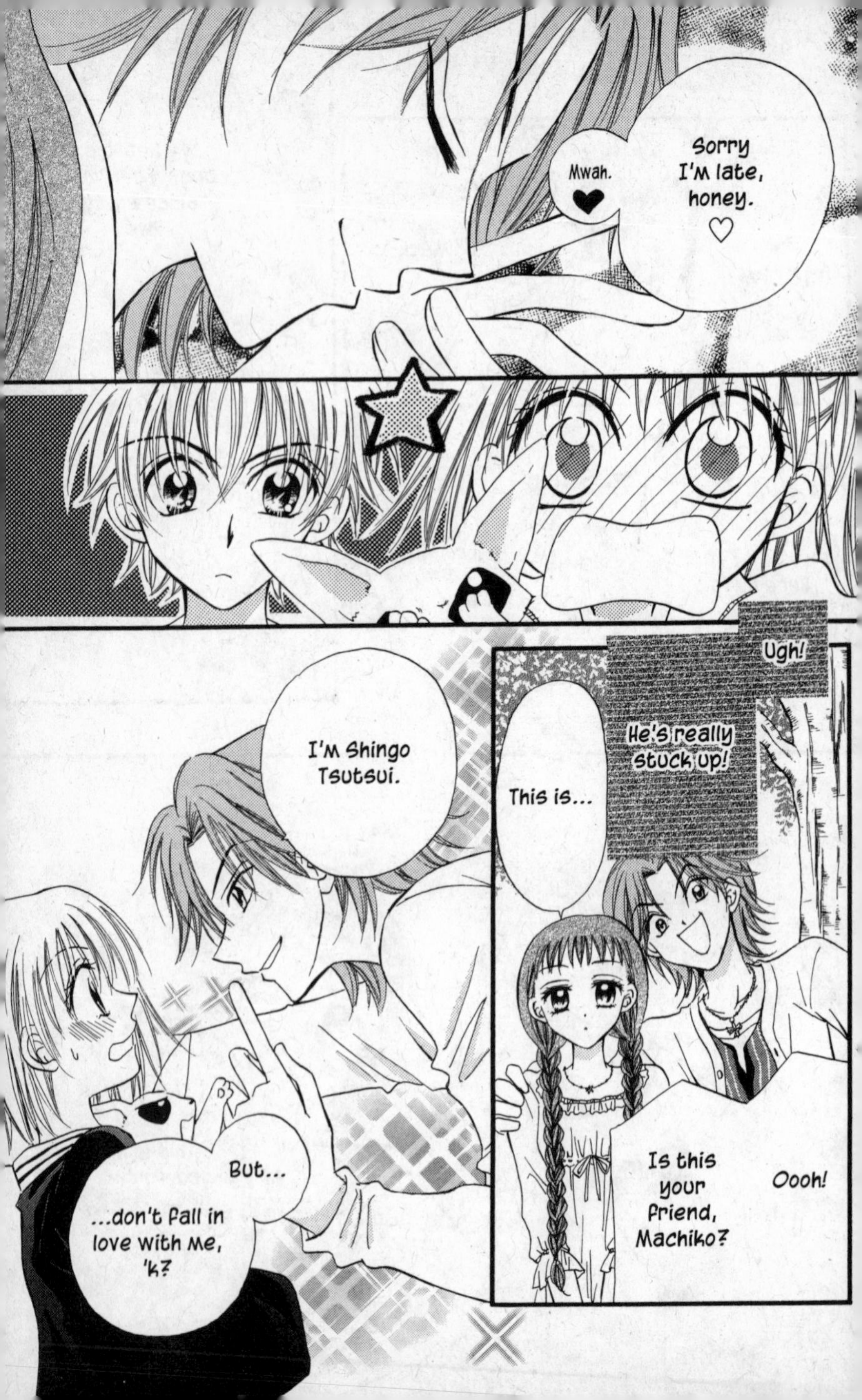
Sorry I'm late, honey. ♡
Mwah. ♥
Ugh!
He's really stuck up!
This is...
Oooh!
Is this your friend, Machiko?
I'm Shingo Tsutsui.
But...
...don't fall in love with me, 'k?

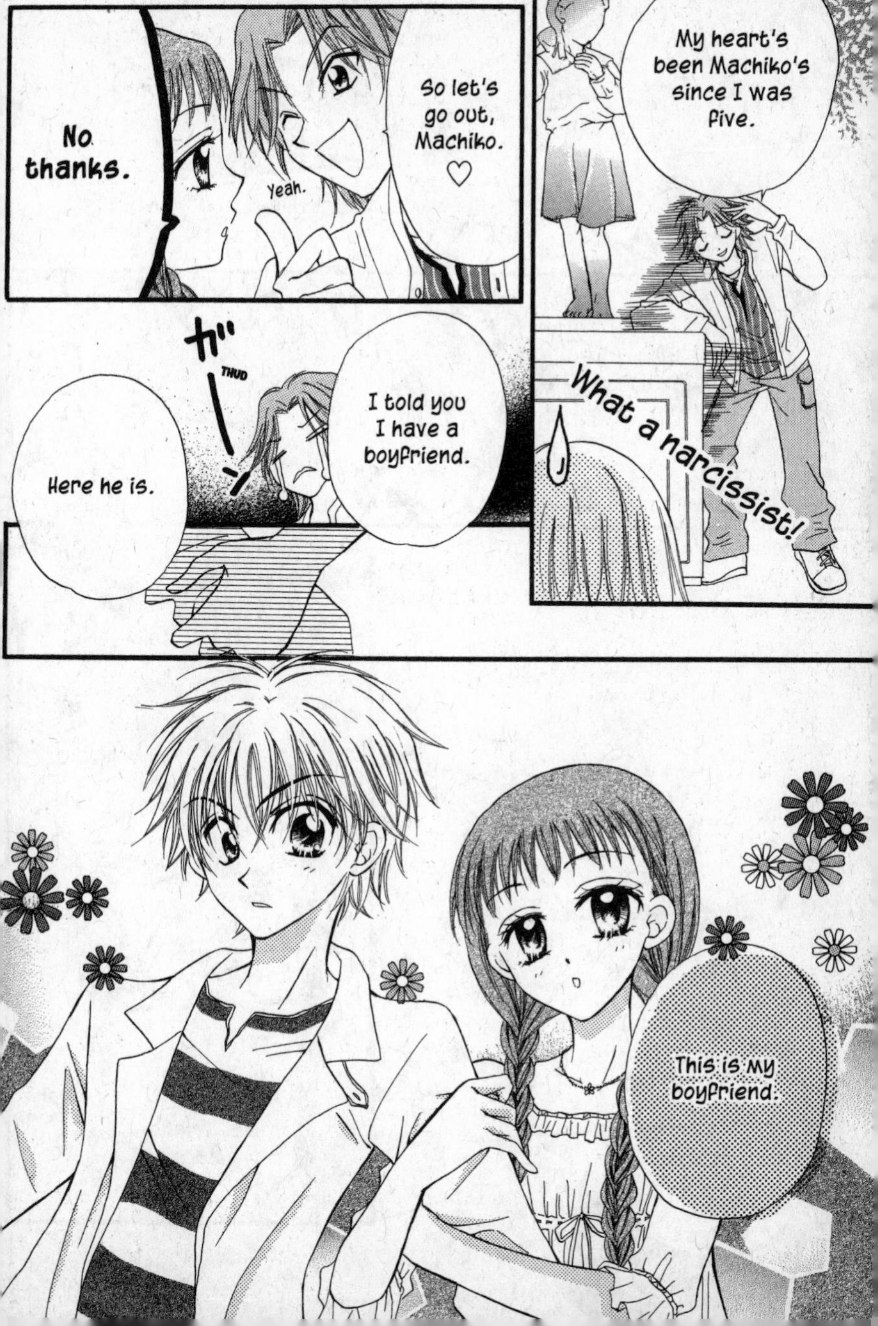
My heart's been Machiko's since I was five.
What a narcissist!
So let's go out, Machiko. ♡
Yeah.
No thanks.
I told you I have a boyfriend.
ガ
THUD
Here he is.
This is my boyfriend.

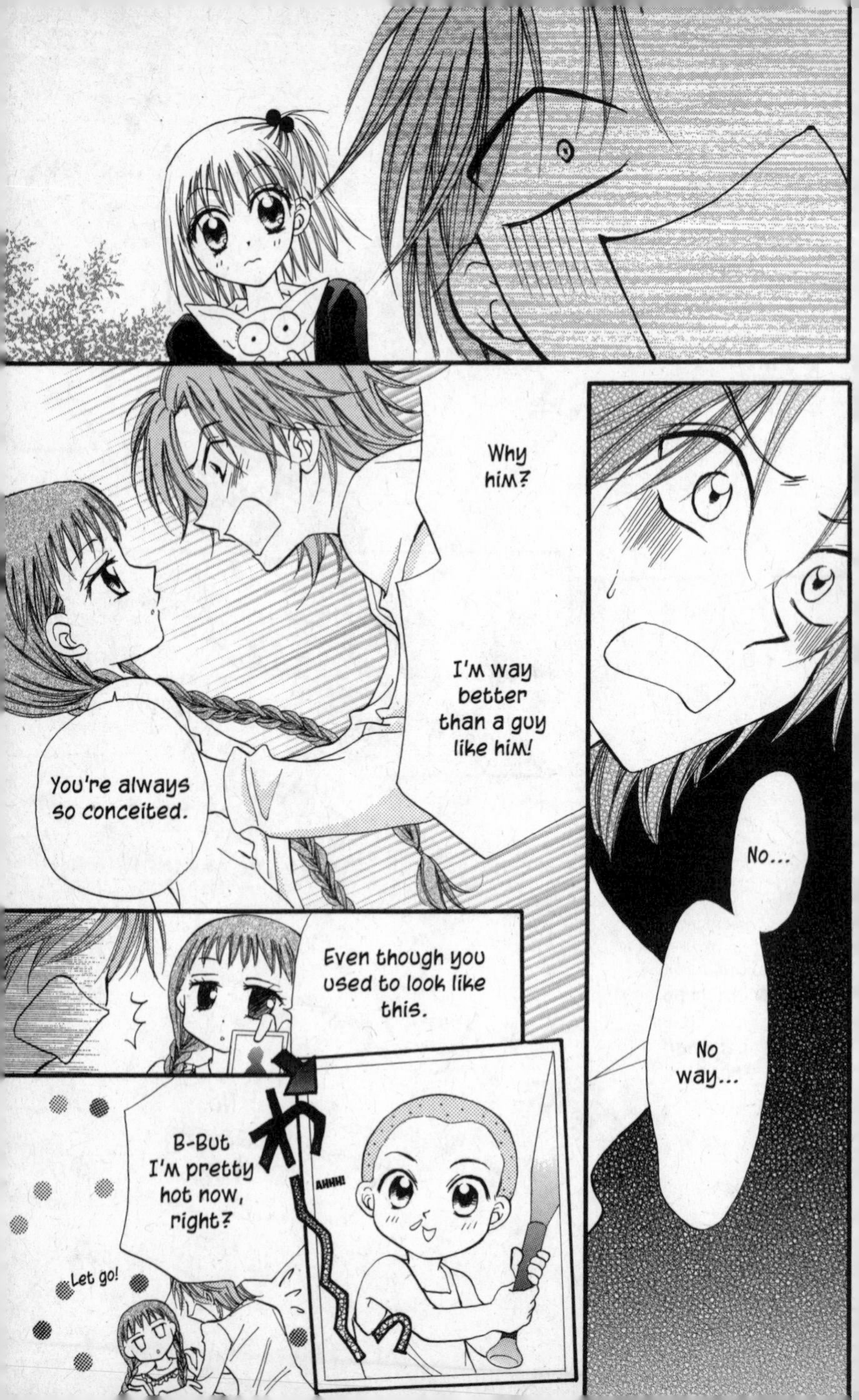
No...
No way...
Why him?
I'm way better than a guy like him!
You're always so conceited.
Even though you used to look like this.
B-But I'm pretty hot now, right?
AHHH!
Let go!

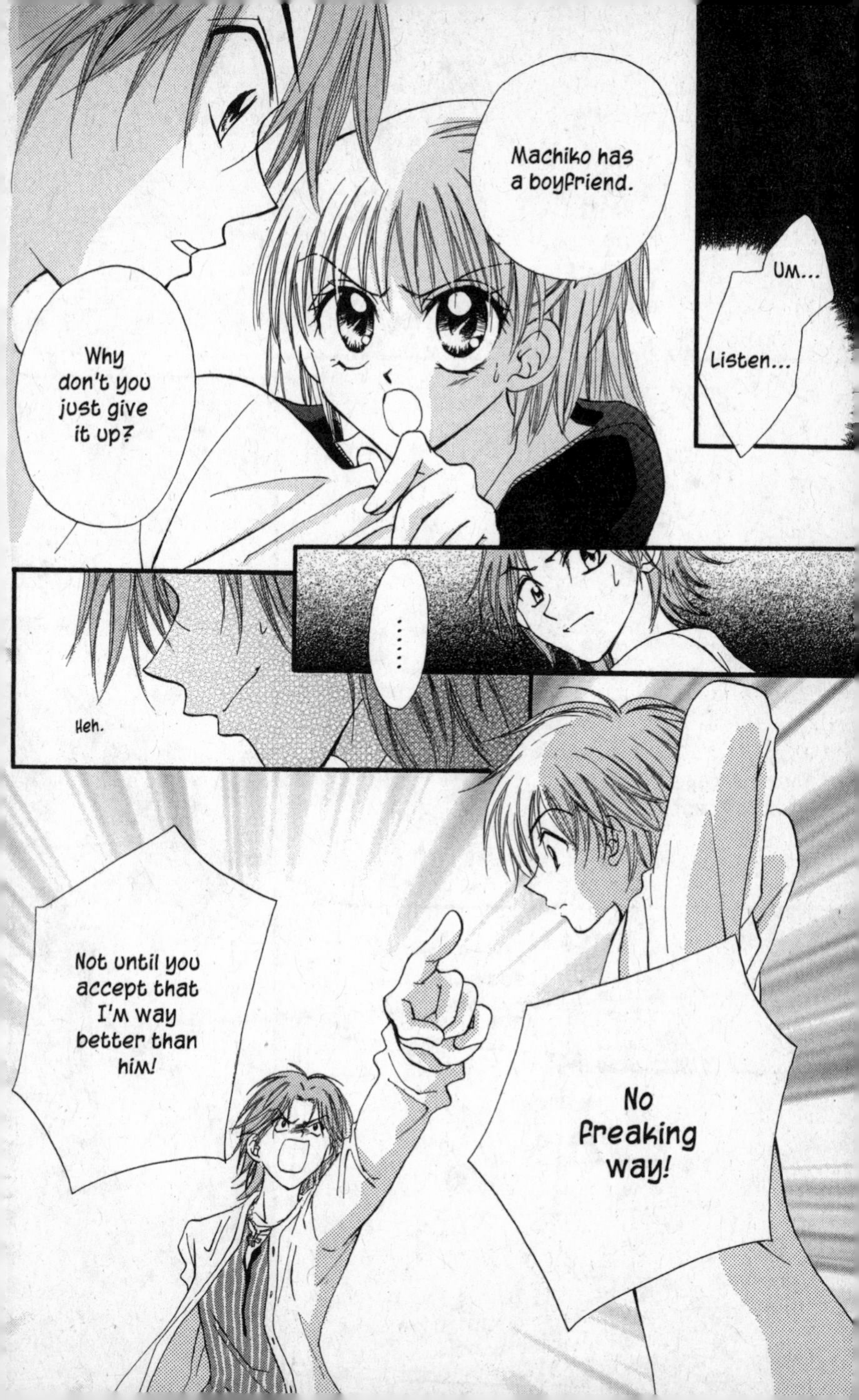
Um...
Listen...
Machiko has a boyfriend.
Why don't you just give it up?
......
Heh.
Not until you accept that I'm way better than him!
No freaking way!

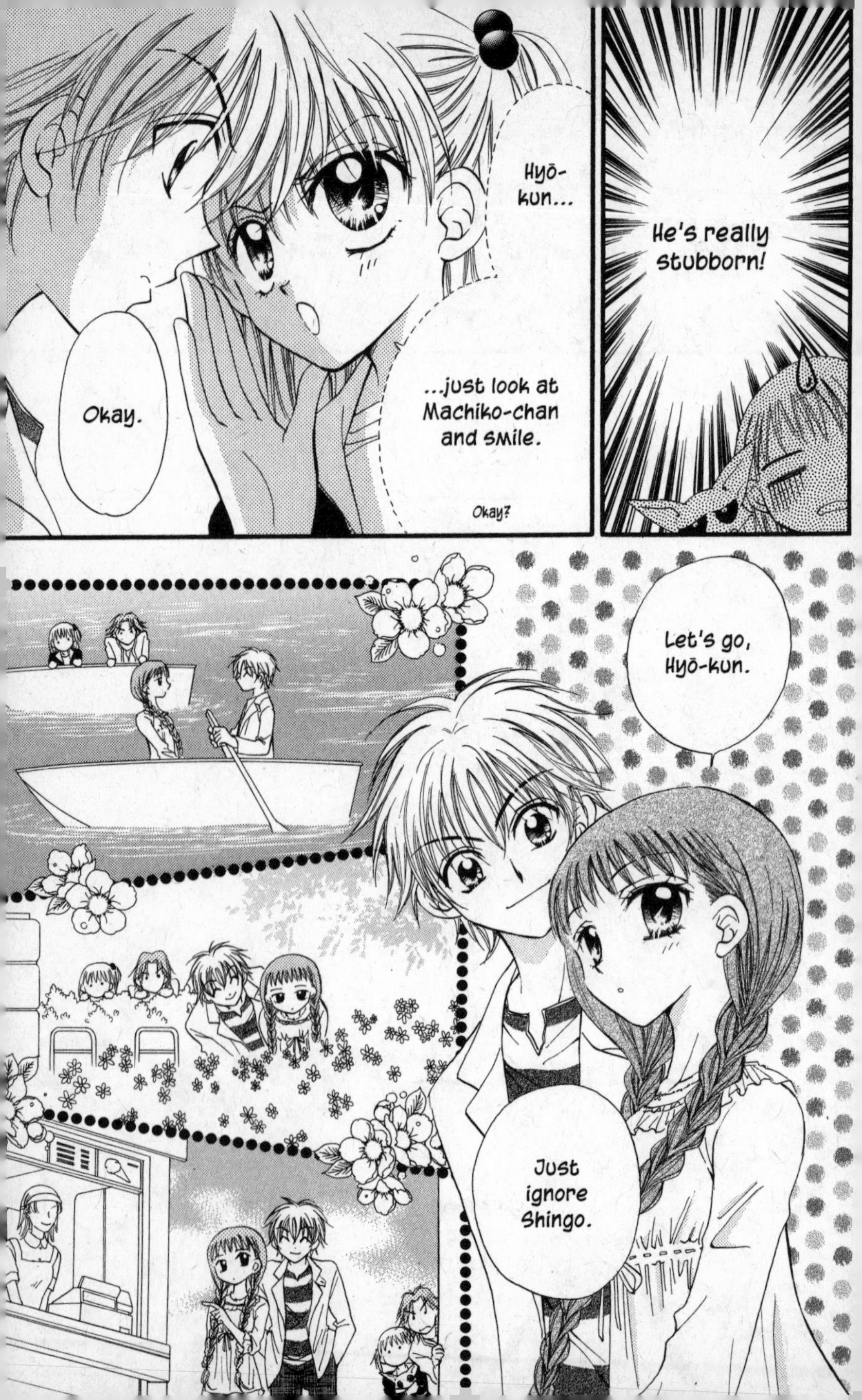
He's really stubborn!
Hyō-kun...
...just look at Machiko-chan and smile.
Okay?
Okay.
Let's go, Hyō-kun.
Just ignore Shingo.

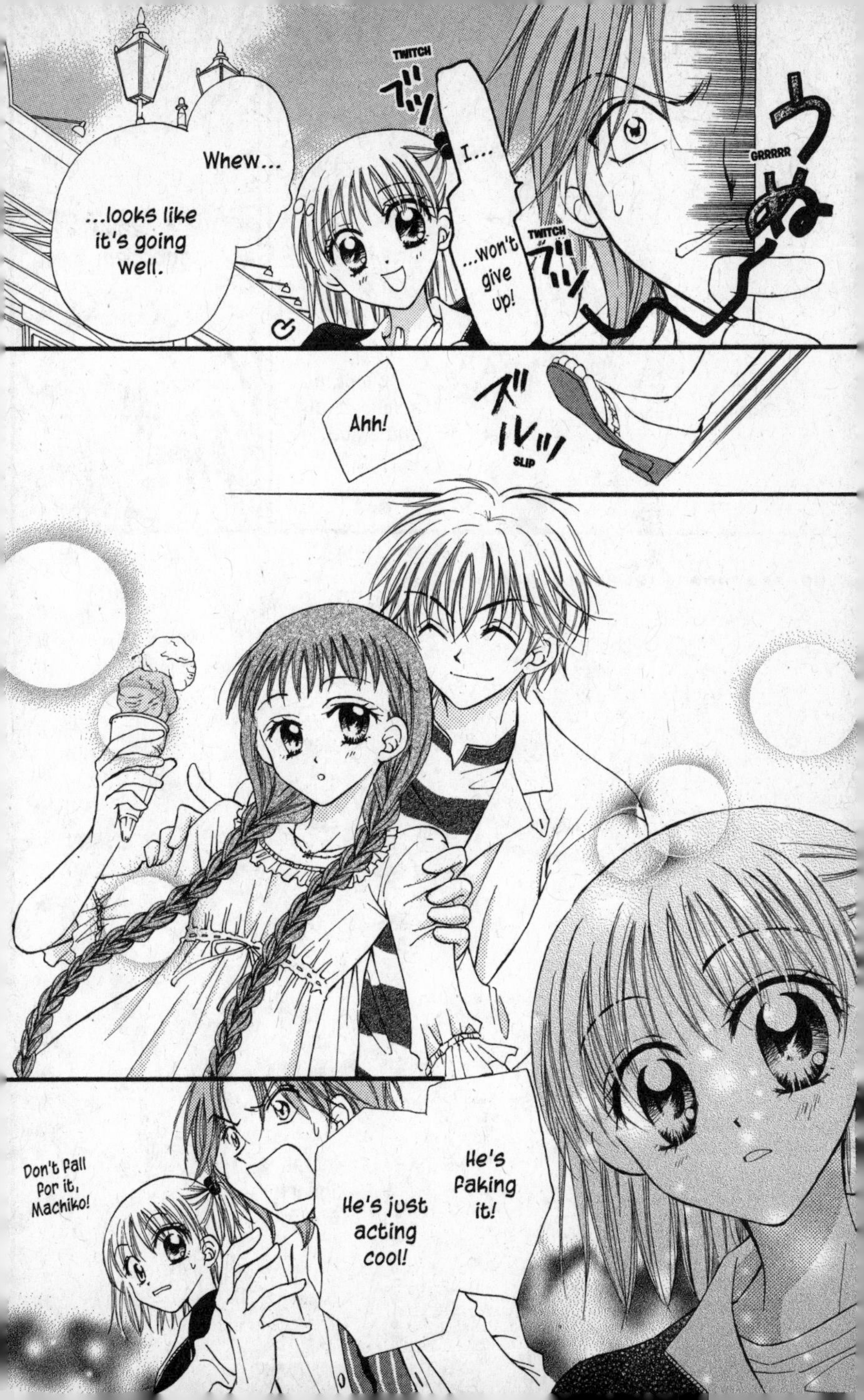
GRRRRR
TWITCH
I...
TWITCH
...won't give up!
Whew...
...looks like it's going well.
SLIP
Ahh!
He's faking it!
He's just acting cool!
Don't fall for it, Machiko!

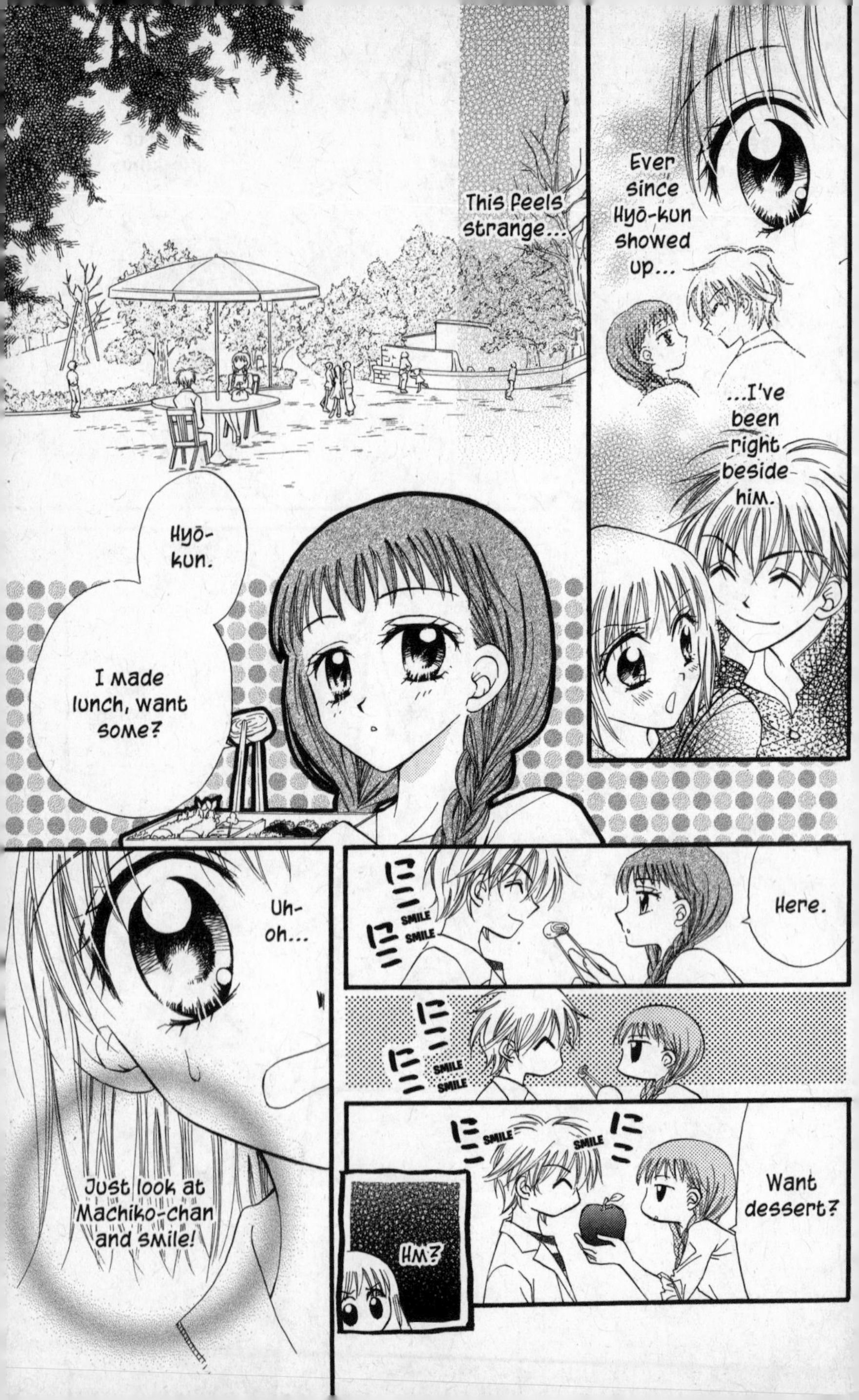
Ever since Hyō-kun showed up...
...I've been right beside him.
This feels strange...
Hyō-kun.
I made lunch, want some?
Here.
にこにこ
SMILE SMILE
にこにこ
SMILE SMILE
Want dessert?
にこ SMILE
SMILE にこ
HM?
Uh-oh...
Just look at Machiko-chan and smile!

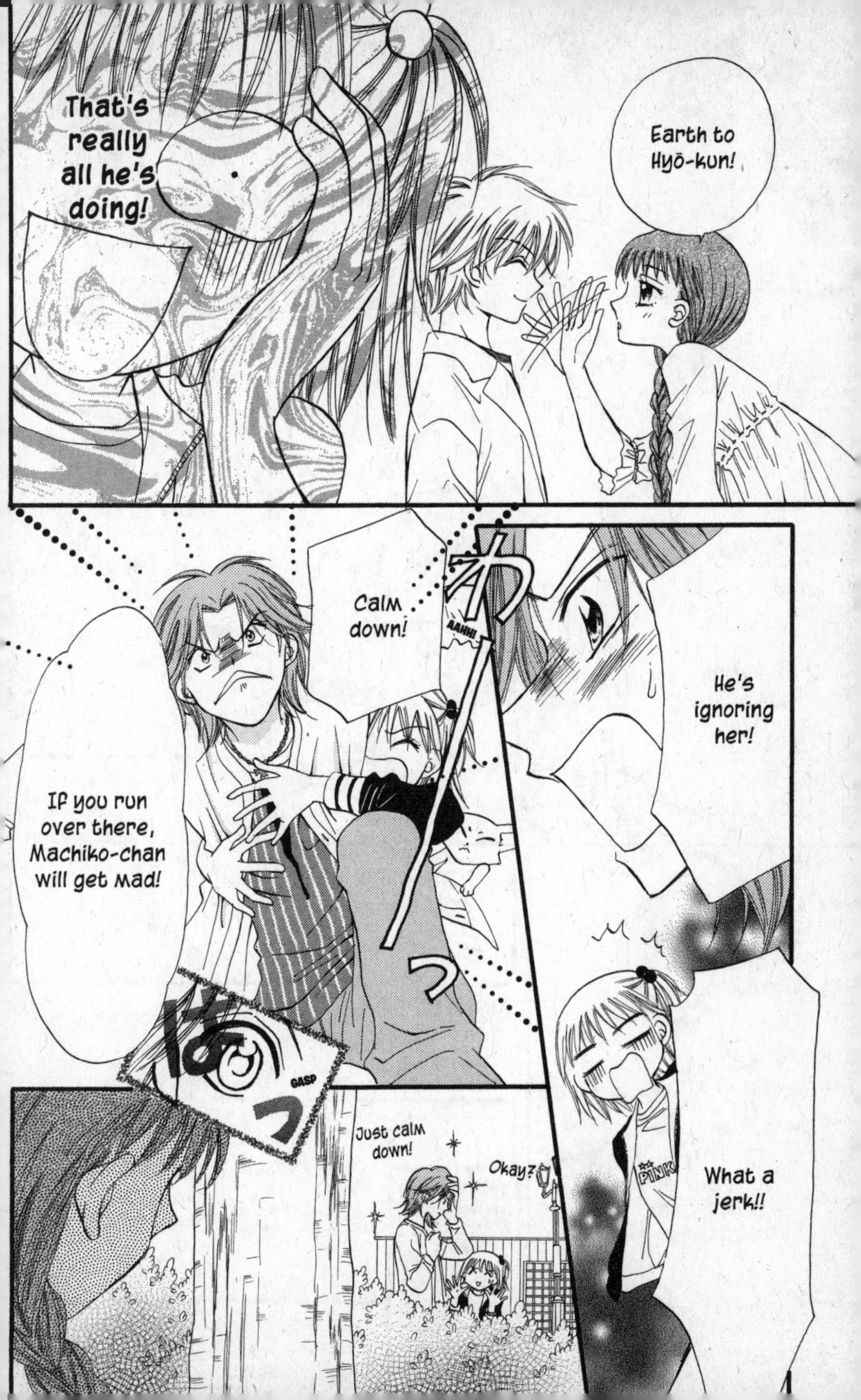
Earth to Hyō-kun!
That's really all he's doing!
He's ignoring her!
What a jerk!!
AAHH!
Calm down!
If you run over there, Machiko-chan will get mad!
GASP
Just calm down!
Okay?

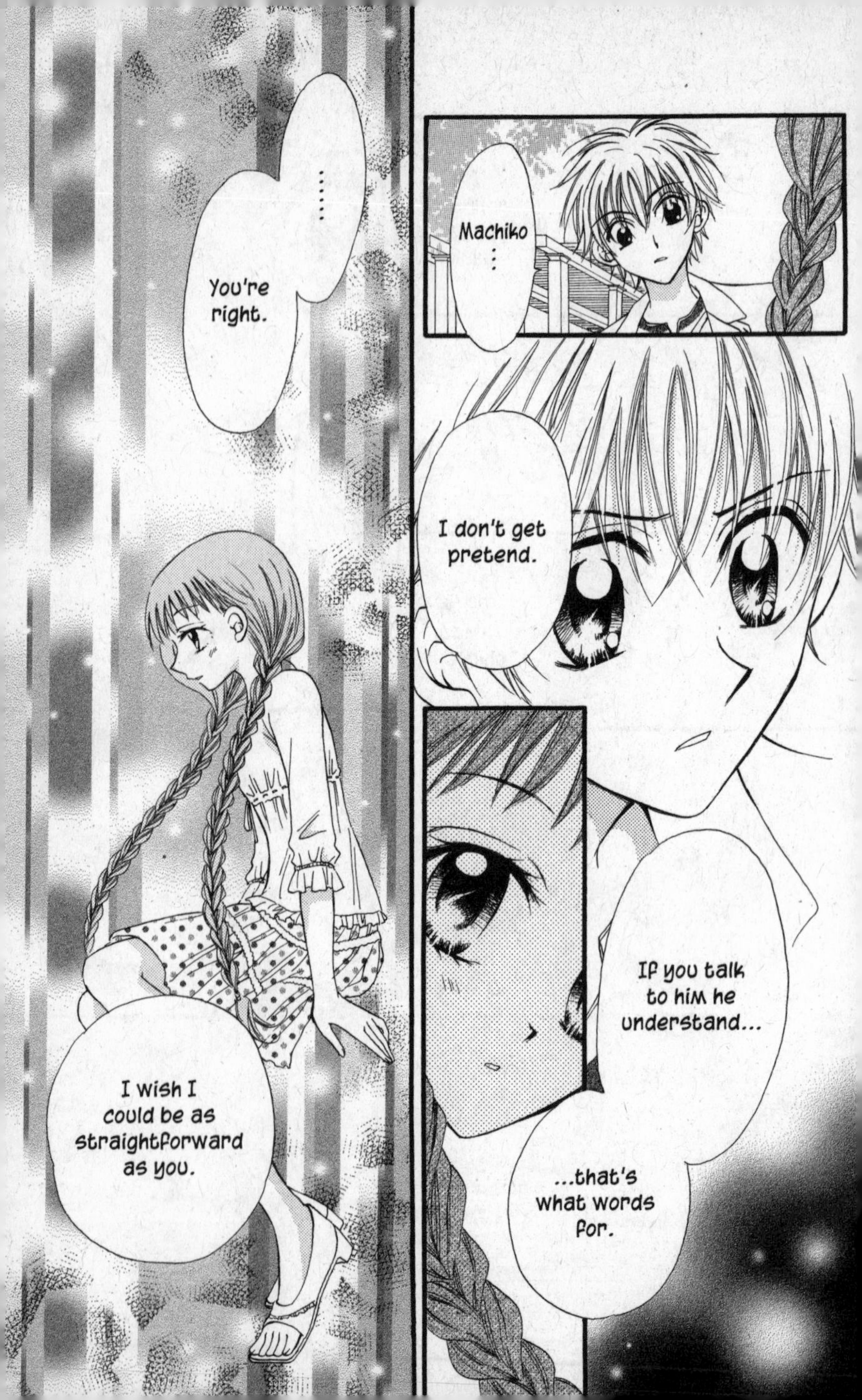
Machiko ...
I don't get pretend.
If you talk to him he understand...
...that's what words for.
......
You're right.
I wish I could be as straightforward as you.

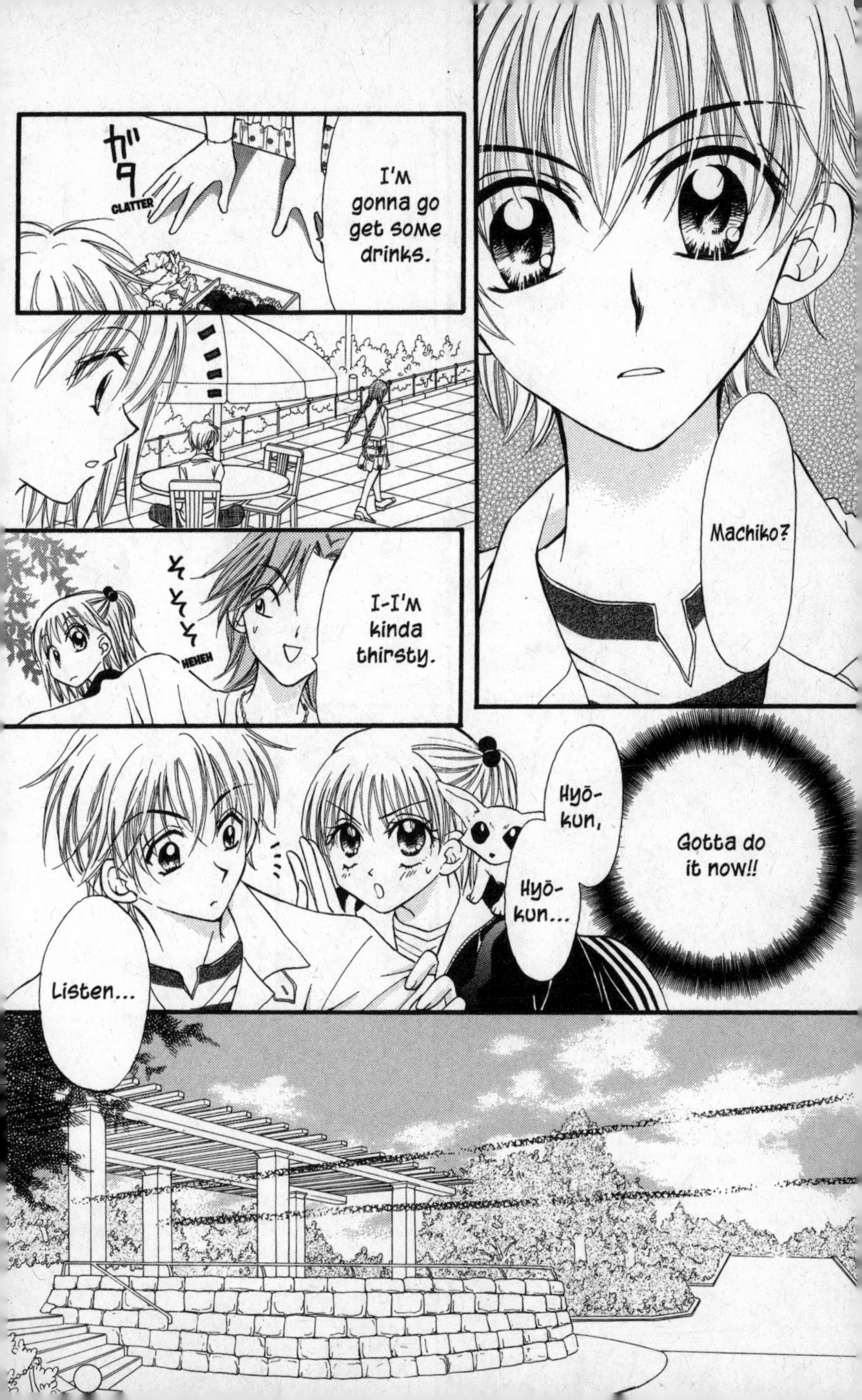

Machiko?
ガタ
CLATTER
I'm gonna go get some drinks.
I-I'm kinda thirsty.
HEHEH
Gotta do it now!!
Hyō-kun,
Hyō-kun...
Listen...

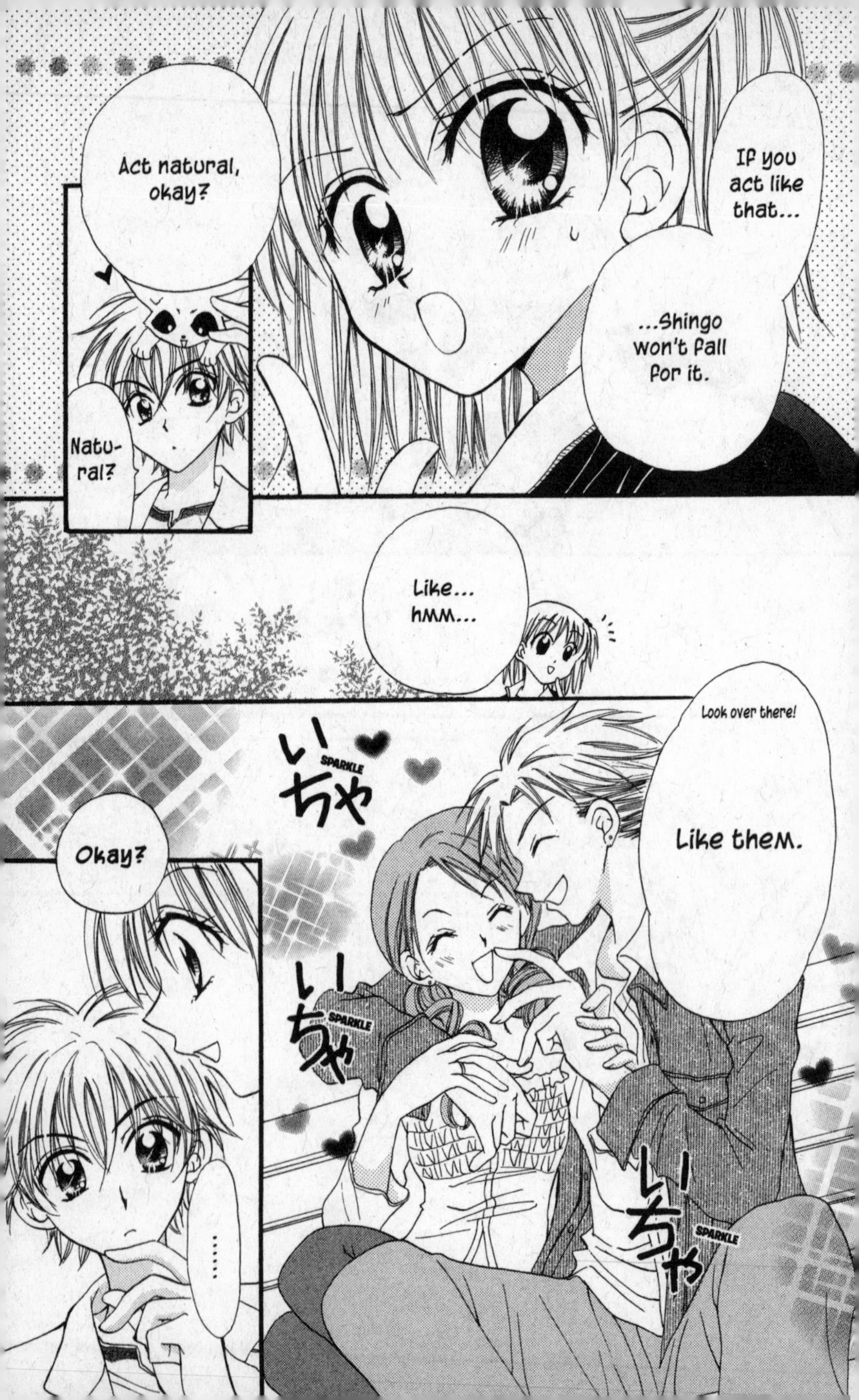
If you act like that...
...Shingo won't fall for it.
Act natural, okay?
Natu-ral?
Like... hmm...
Look over there!
Like them.
いちゃ SPARKLE
いちゃ SPARKLE
いちゃ SPARKLE
Okay?
......

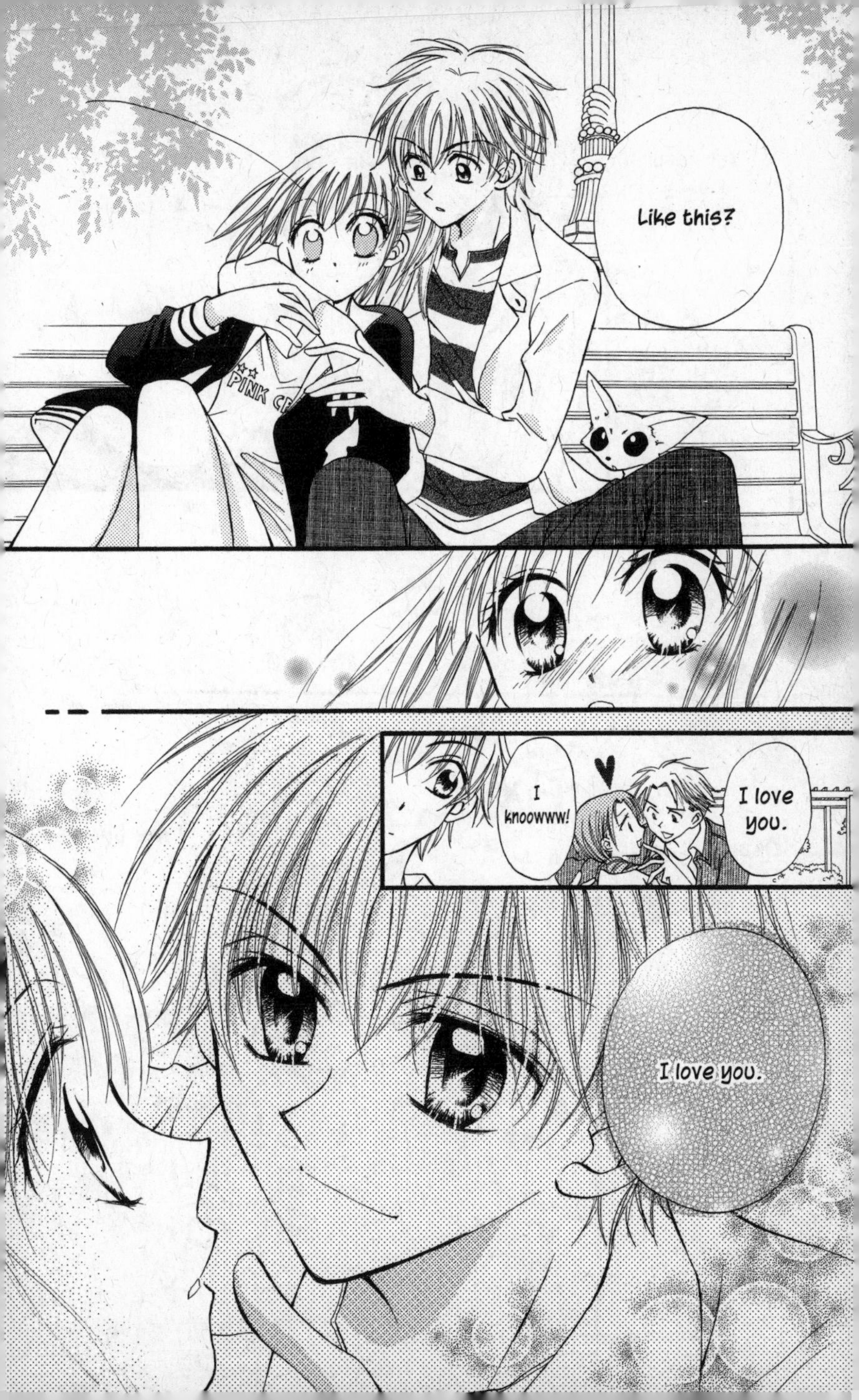
Like this?
PINK CR
I love you.
I knoowww!
I love you.

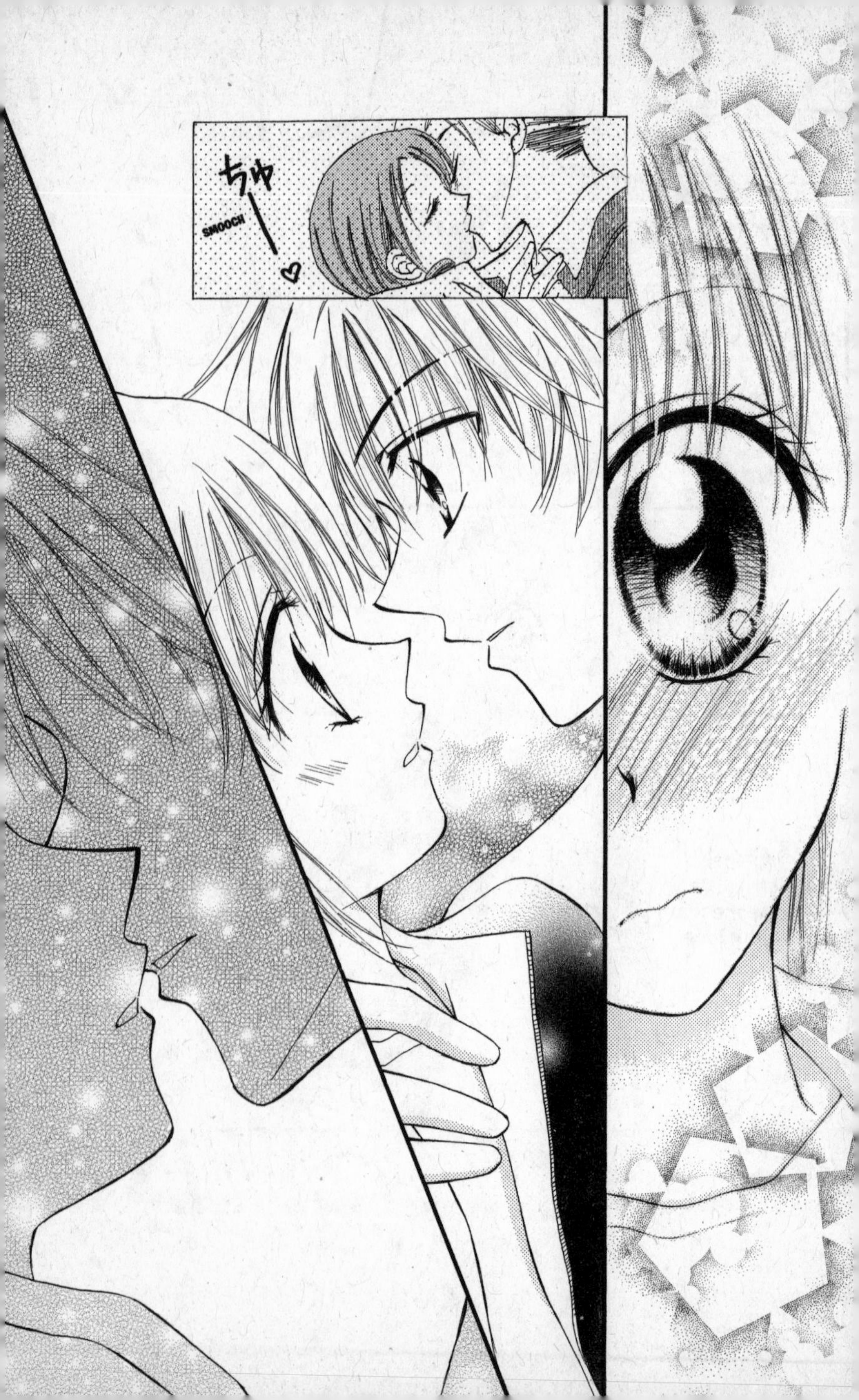
ちゅ—♡
SMOOCH

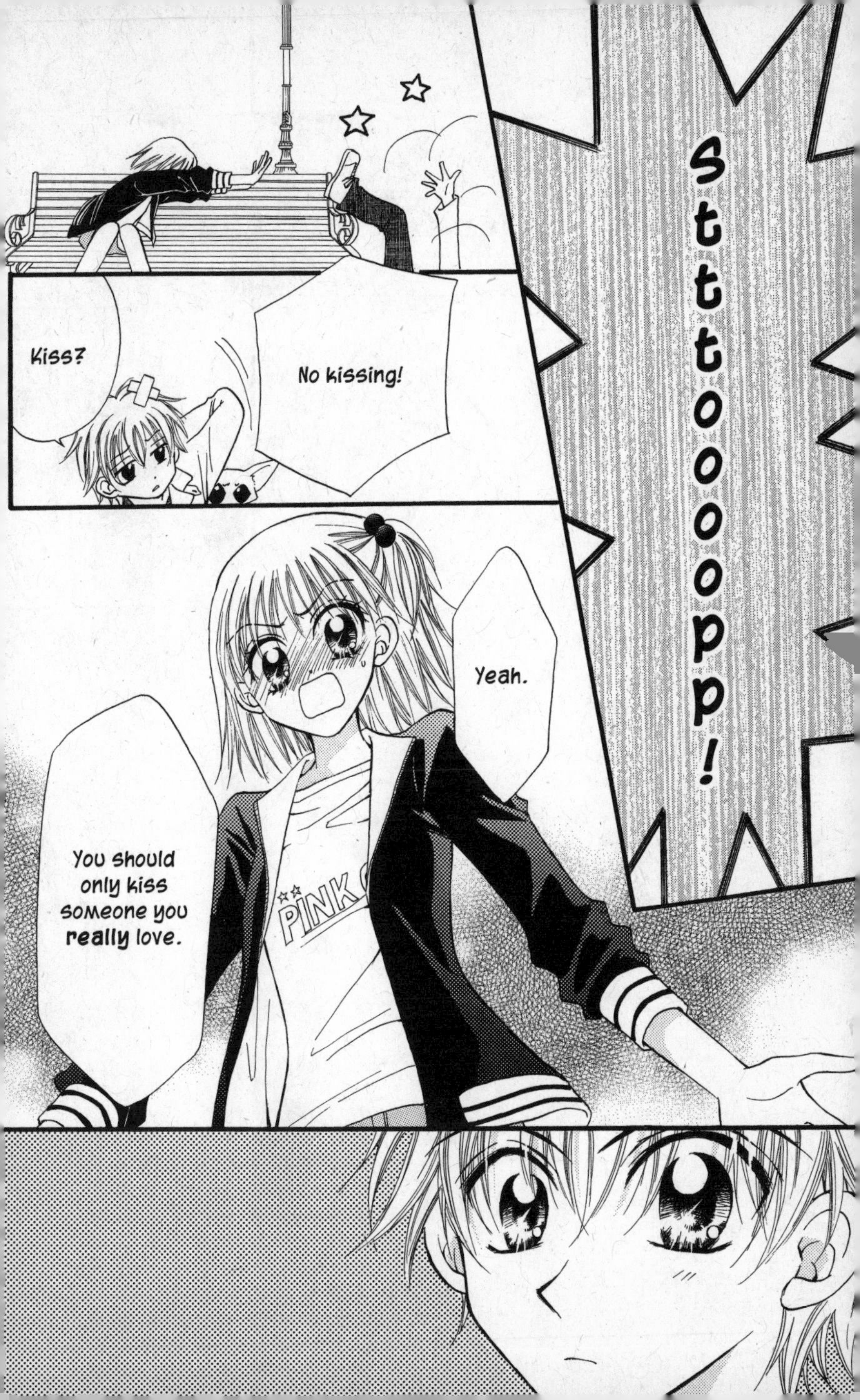
Sttoooopp!
No kissing!
Kiss?
Yeah.
You should only kiss someone you really love.

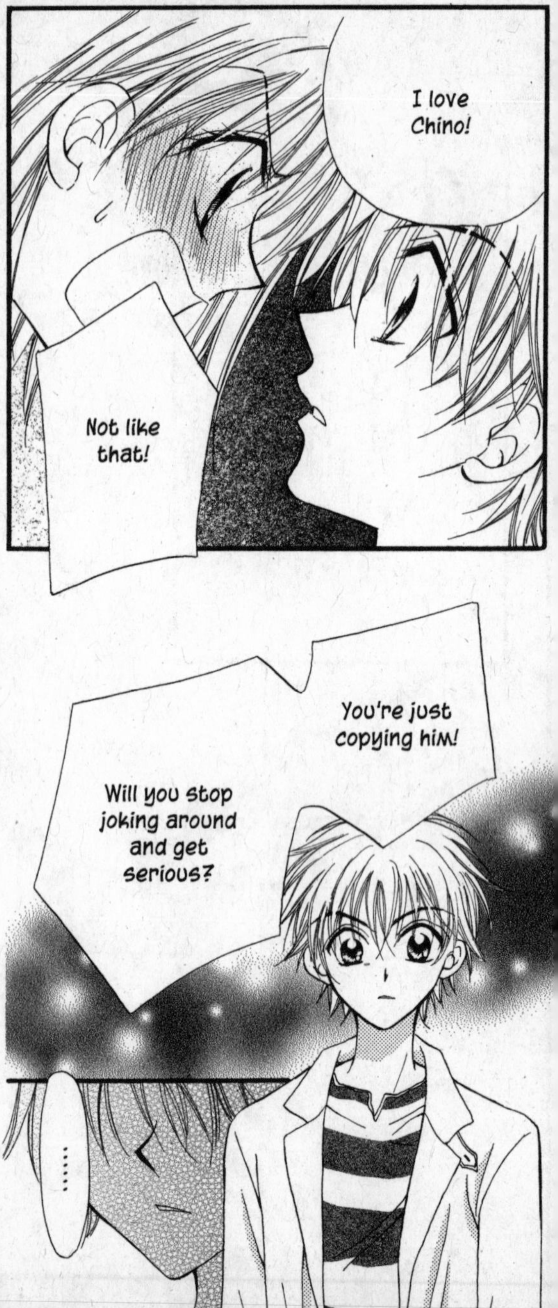
I love Chino!
Not like that!
You're just copying him!
Will you stop joking around and get serious?
......

6.

I love scary stories and watching scary TV shows. Sometimes I watch so many of them I start to get scared by everything. But I guess it's okay because I don't seem to have any psychic abilities. There was that one time late at night...

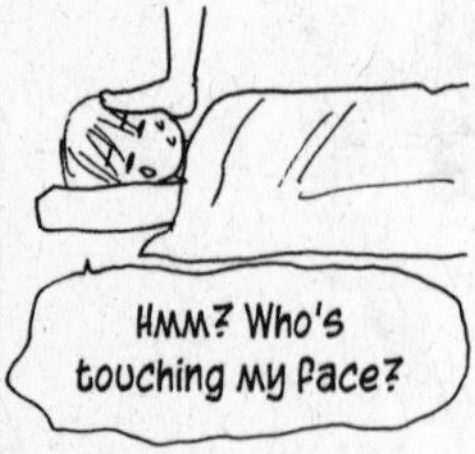
HMM? Who's touching my face?

And when I thought about it...

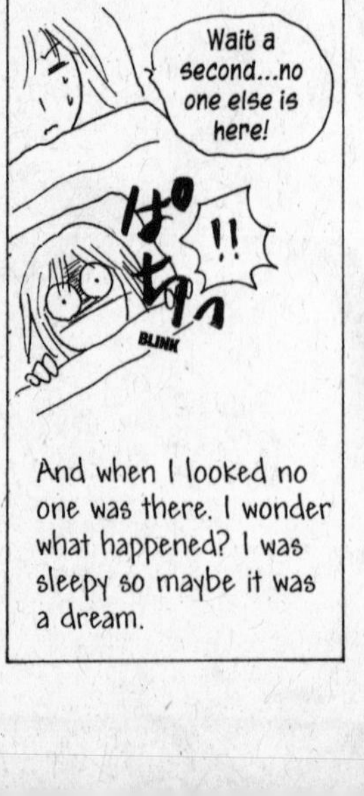
Wait a second...no one else is here!
!!
BLINK

And when I looked no one was there. I wonder what happened? I was sleepy so maybe it was a dream.

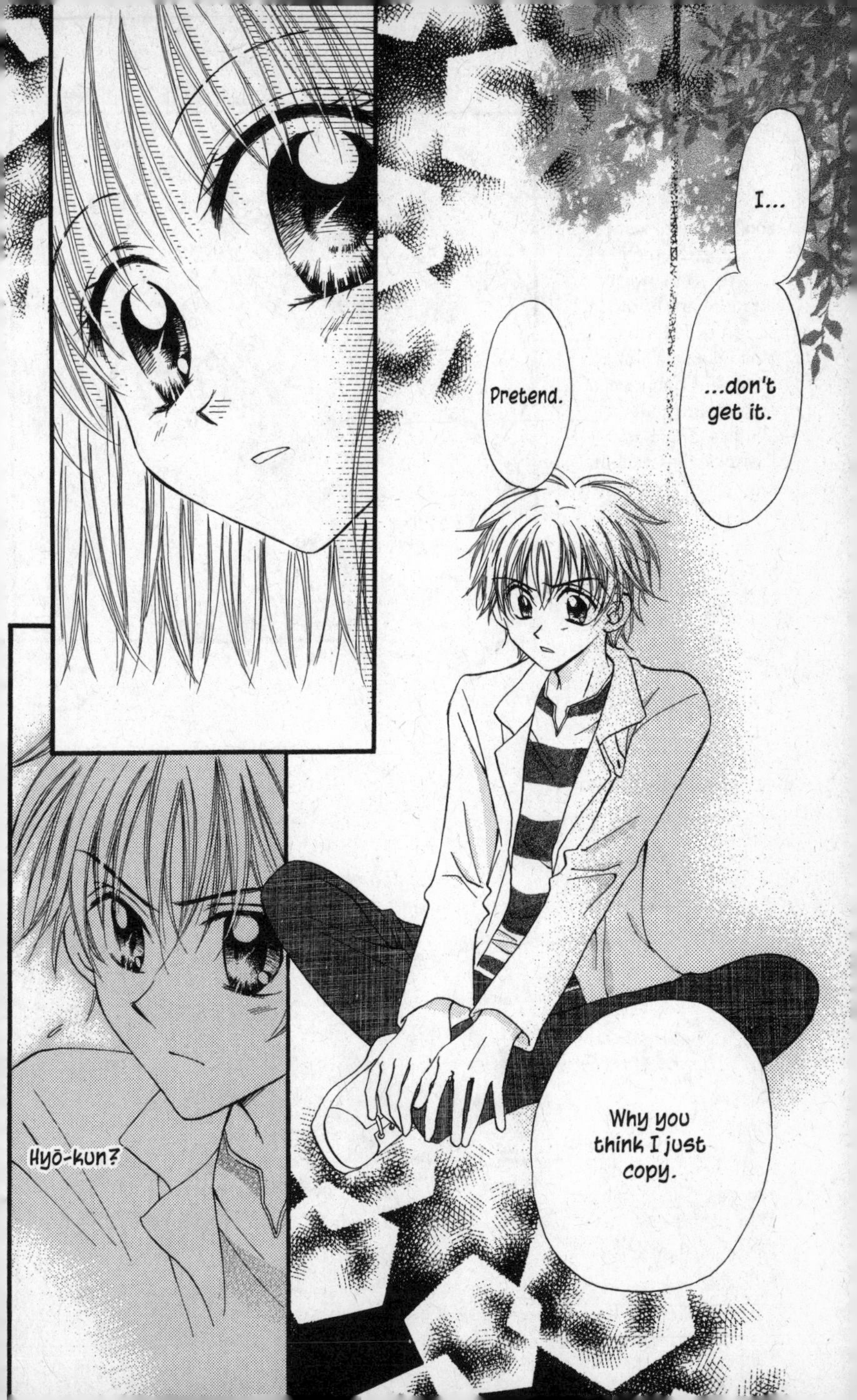
I...
...don't get it.
Pretend.
Why you think I just copy.
Hyō-kun?

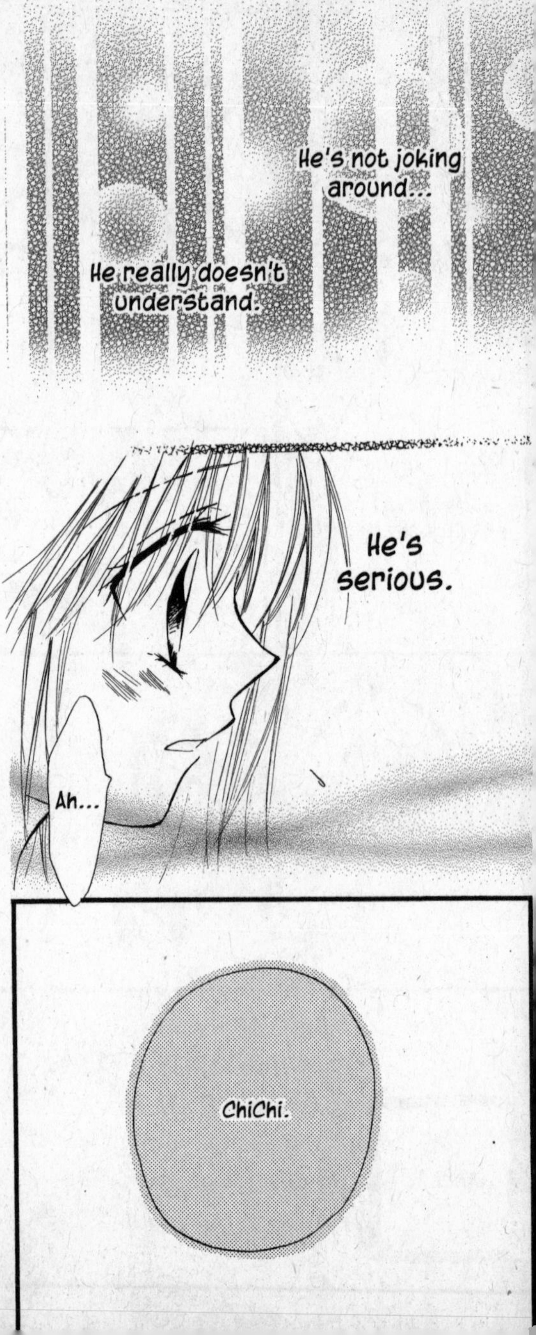
He's not joking around...
He really doesn't understand.
He's serious.
Ah...
ChiChi.

7.

Lately I've been obsessed with going to Disneyland, and there's something I wanna know. Why is Winnie the Pooh's Honey Hunt so popular? There's always a really long line! Last time I got there as soon as it opened and there was still a line! And even when I tried going later in the day...

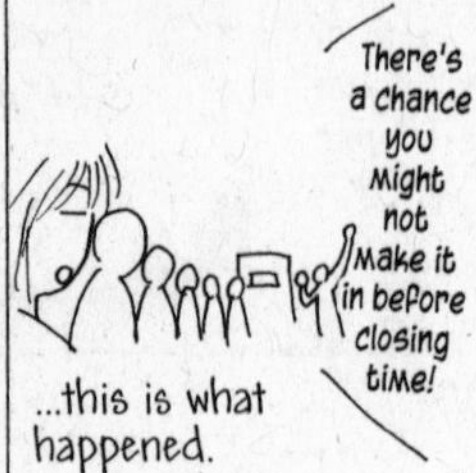
There's a chance you might not make it in before closing time!

...this is what happened.

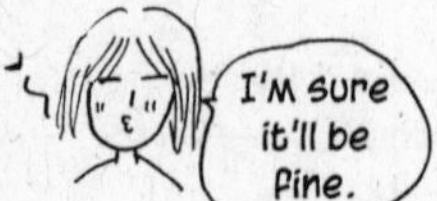
I'm sure it'll be fine.

So I got in line and then right before my turn...

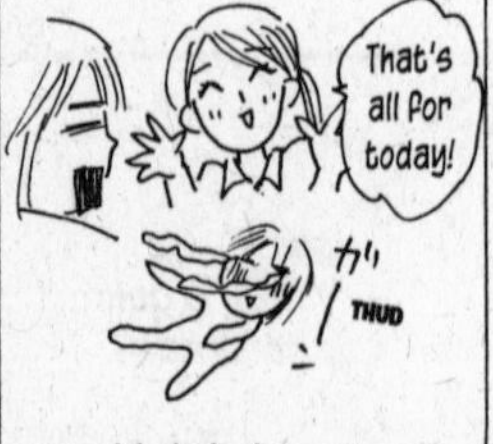
That's all for today!
THUD

I couldn't believe it.

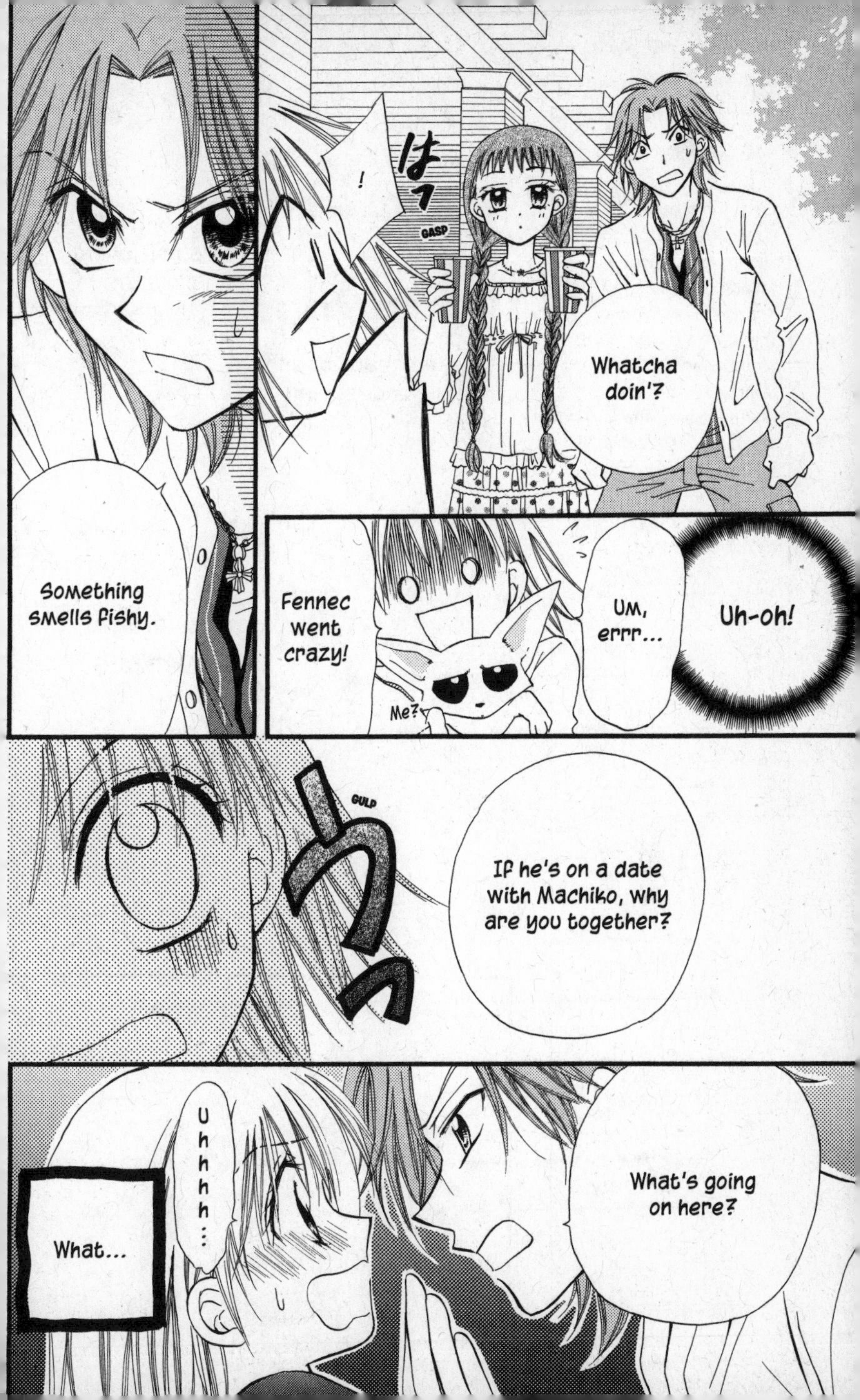
はっ
!
GASP
Whatcha doin'?
Uh-oh!
Um, errr...
Fennec went crazy!
Me?
Something smells fishy.
うっ
GULP
If he's on a date with Machiko, why are you together?
What's going on here?
Uhhhh...
What...

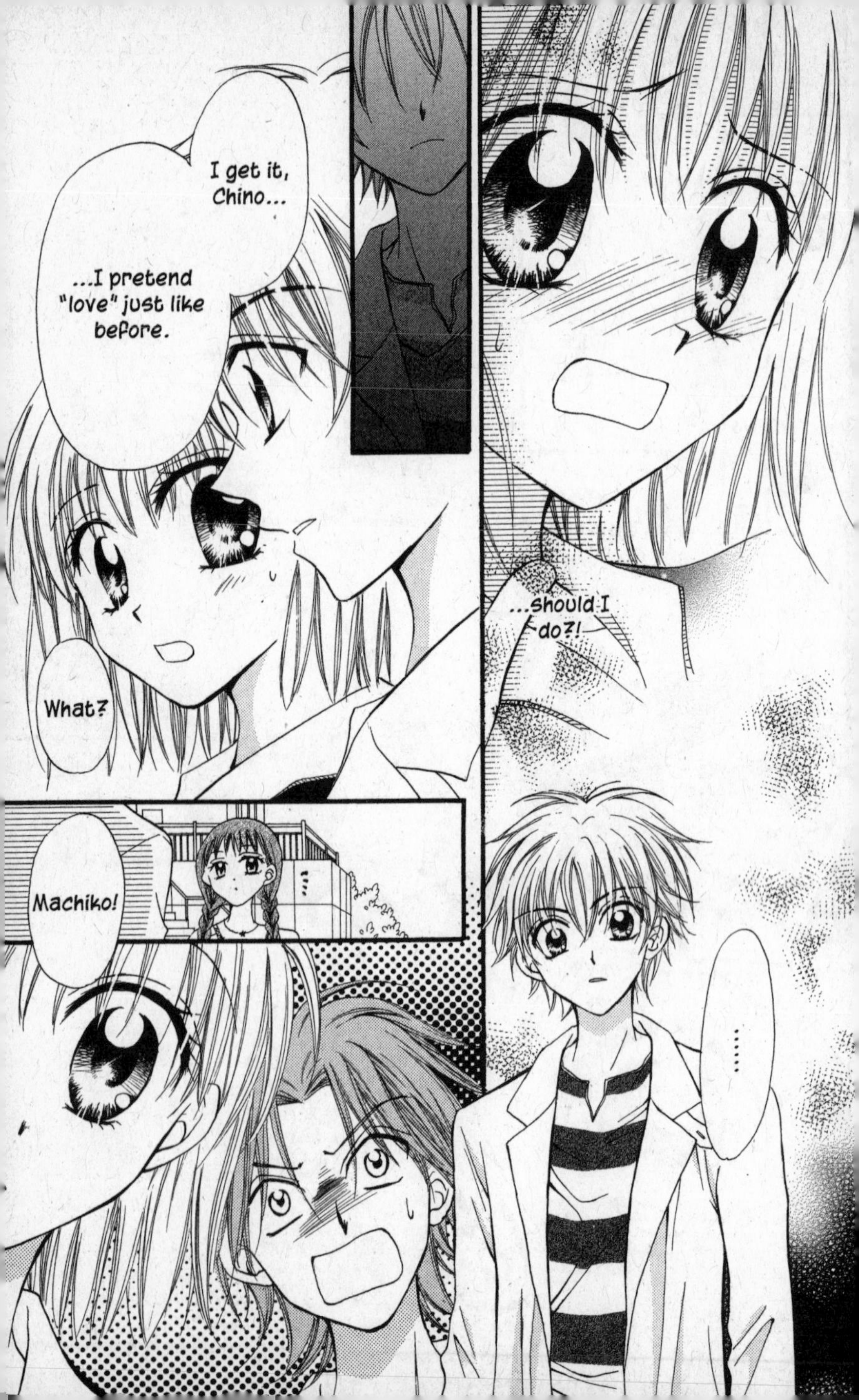

...should I do?!
I get it, Chino...
...I pretend "love" just like before.
What?
......
Machiko!

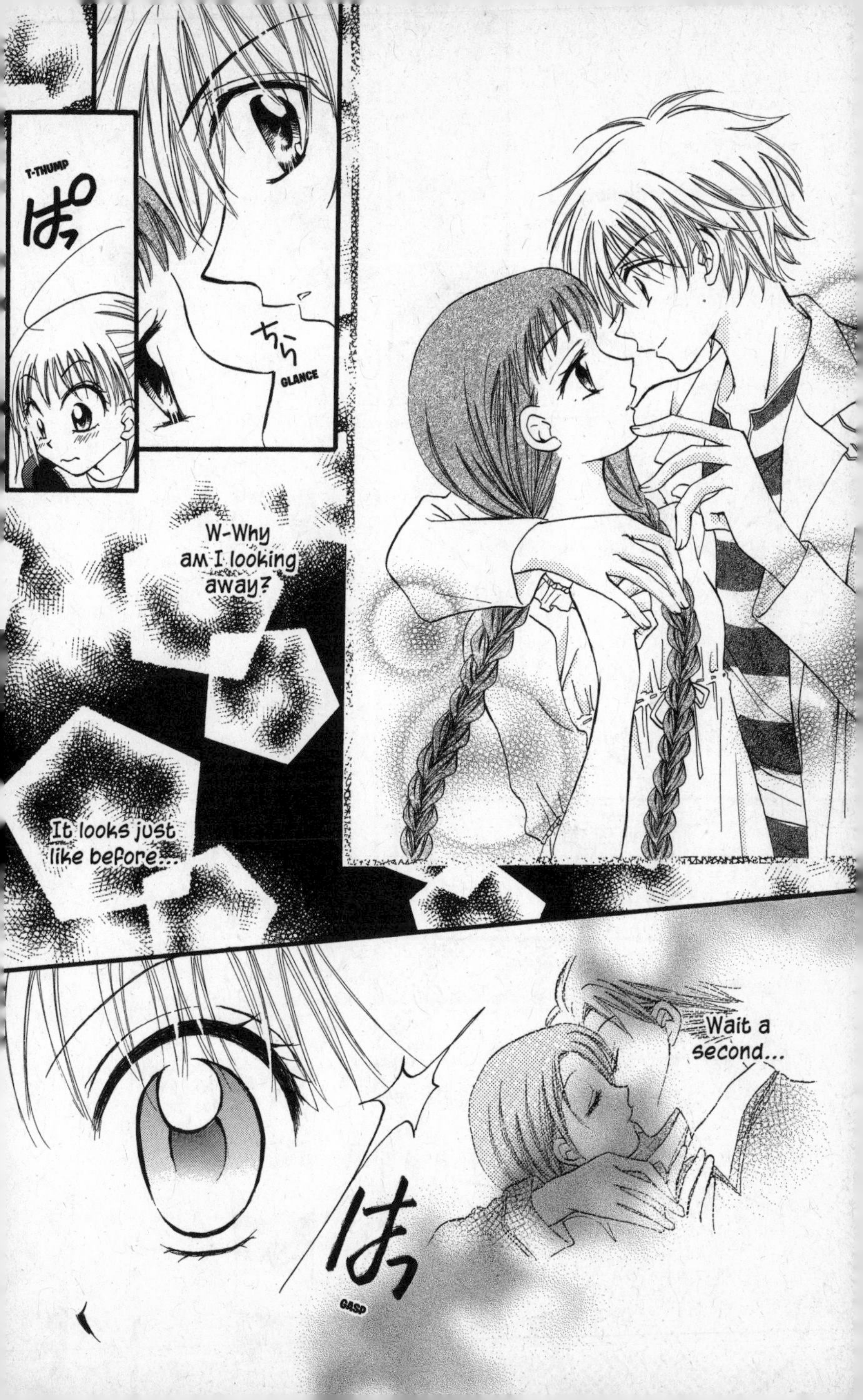
ちら
GLANCE
T-THUMP
ぱっ
W-Why am I looking away?
It looks just like before...
Wait a second...
はっ
GASP

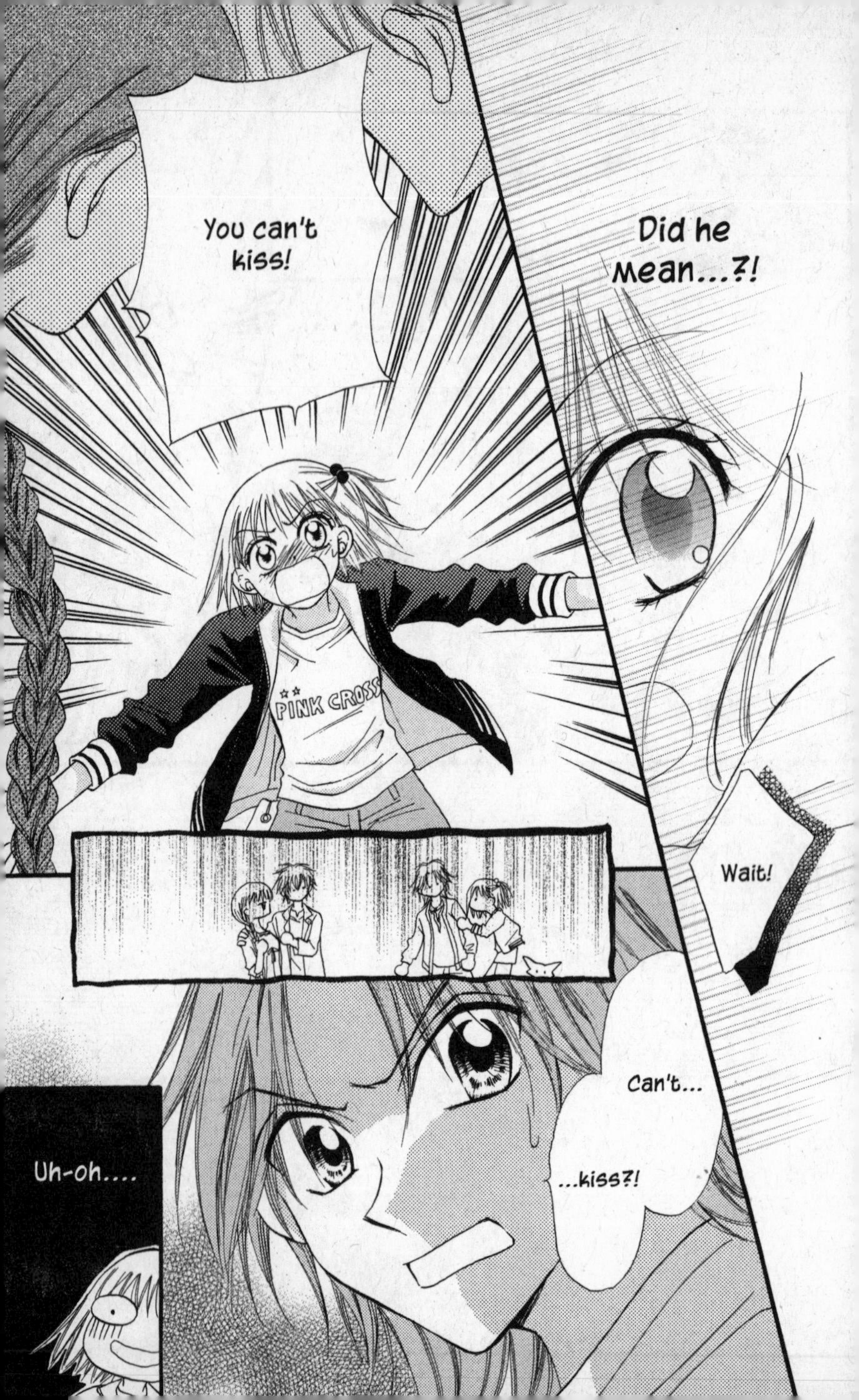
Did he Mean...?!
Wait!
You can't kiss!
PINK CROSS
Can't...
...kiss?!
Uh-oh....

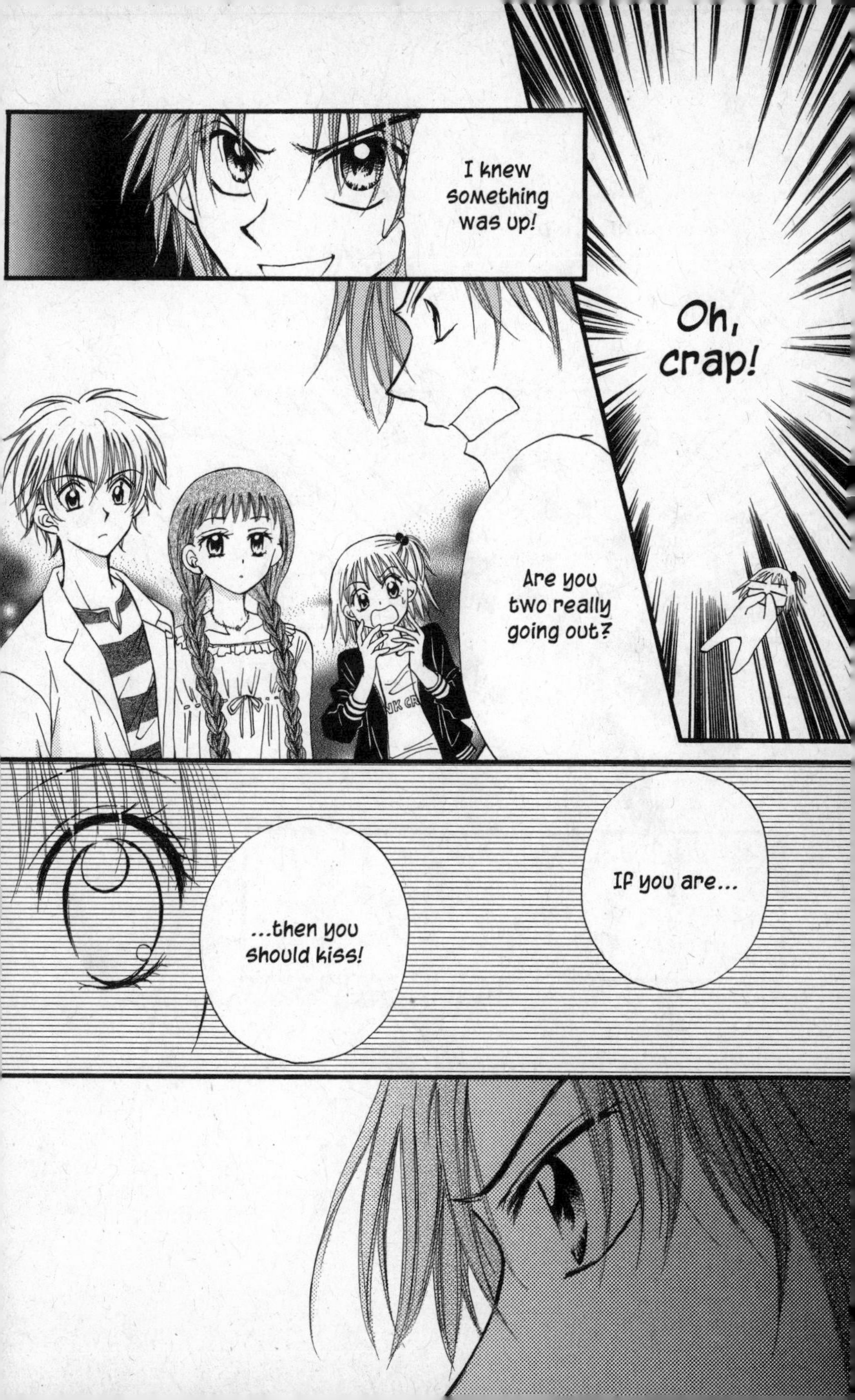
Oh, crap!
I knew something was up!
Are you two really going out?
If you are...
...then you should kiss!

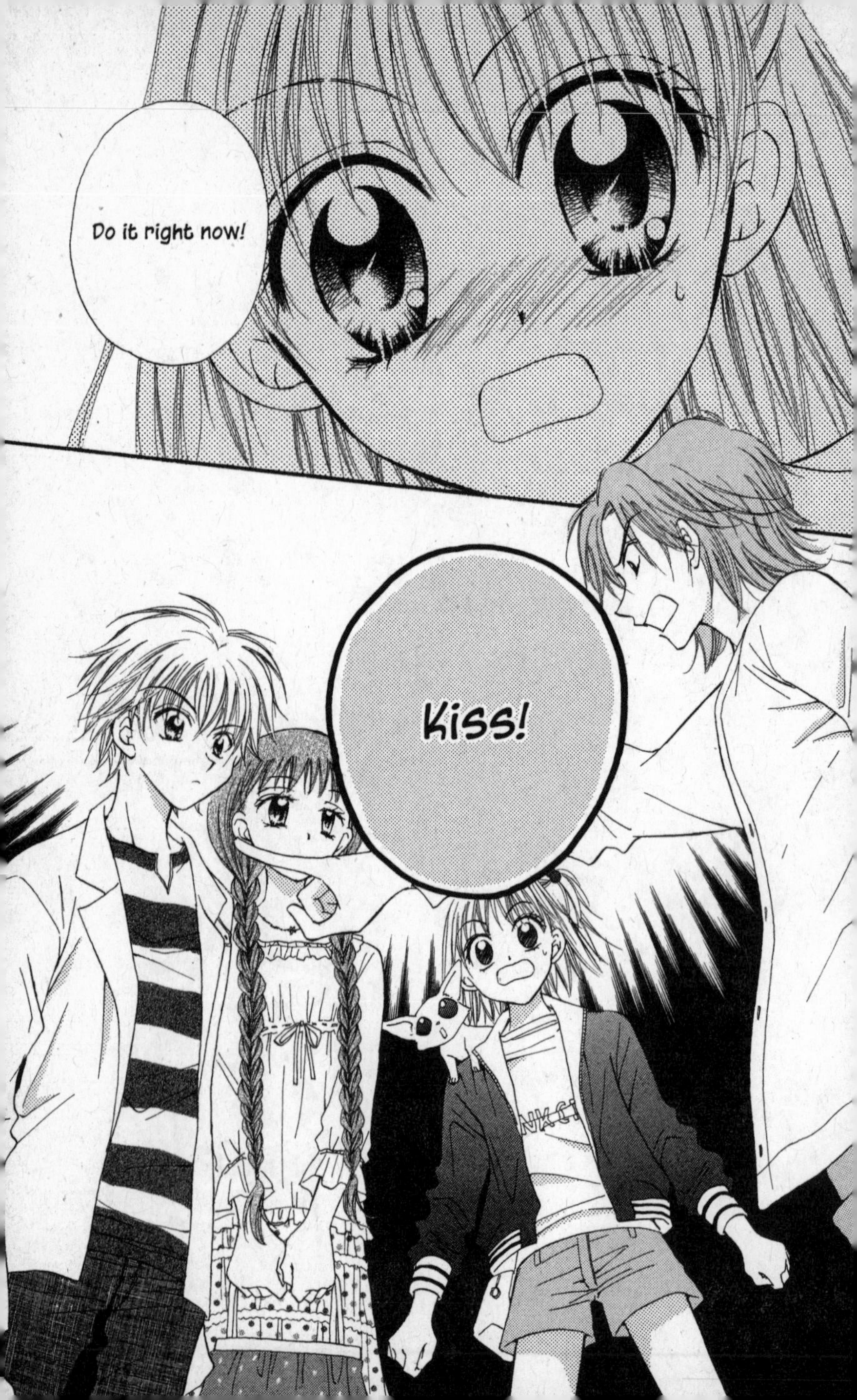
Do it right now!
Kiss!

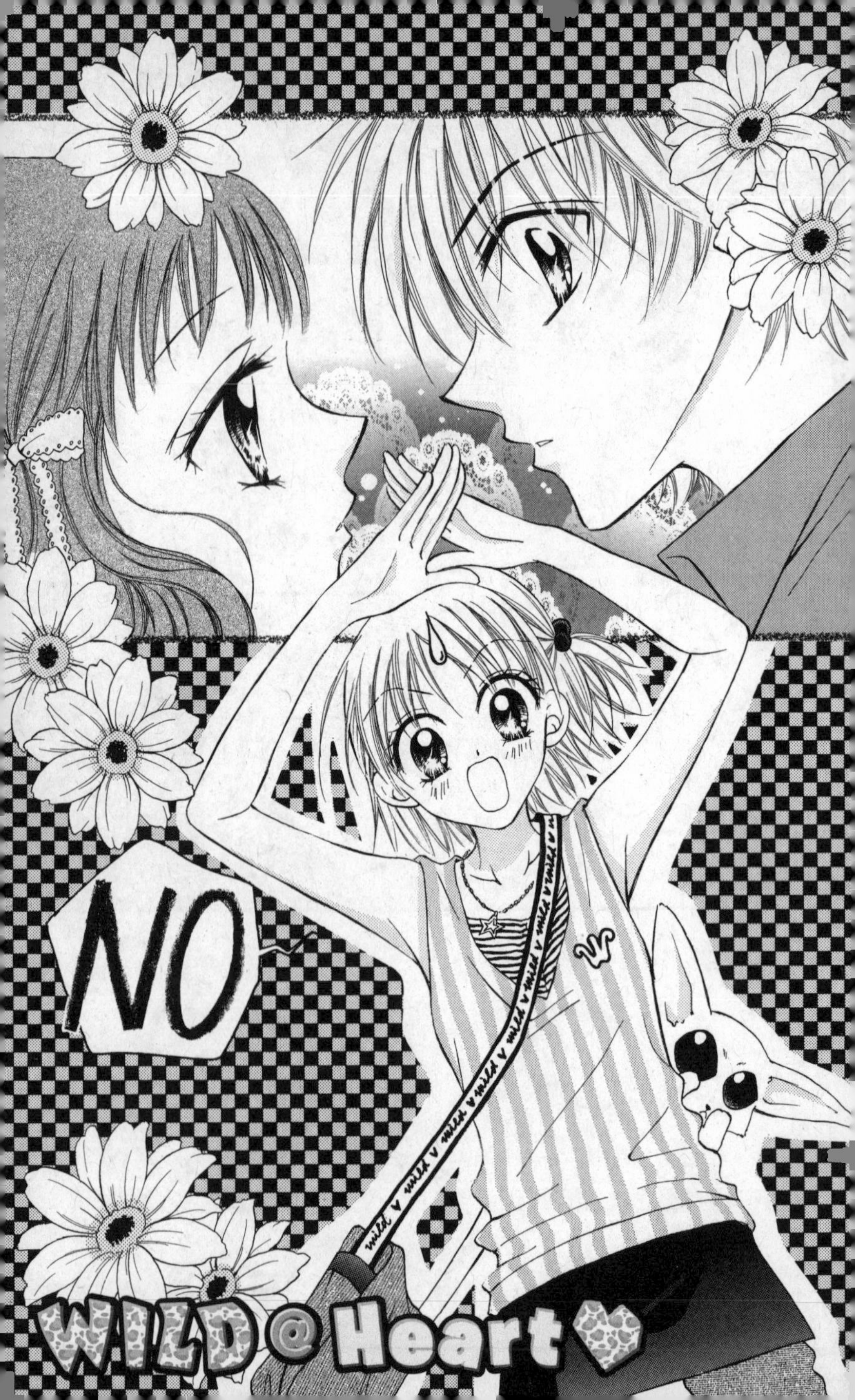
NO
WILD @ Heart

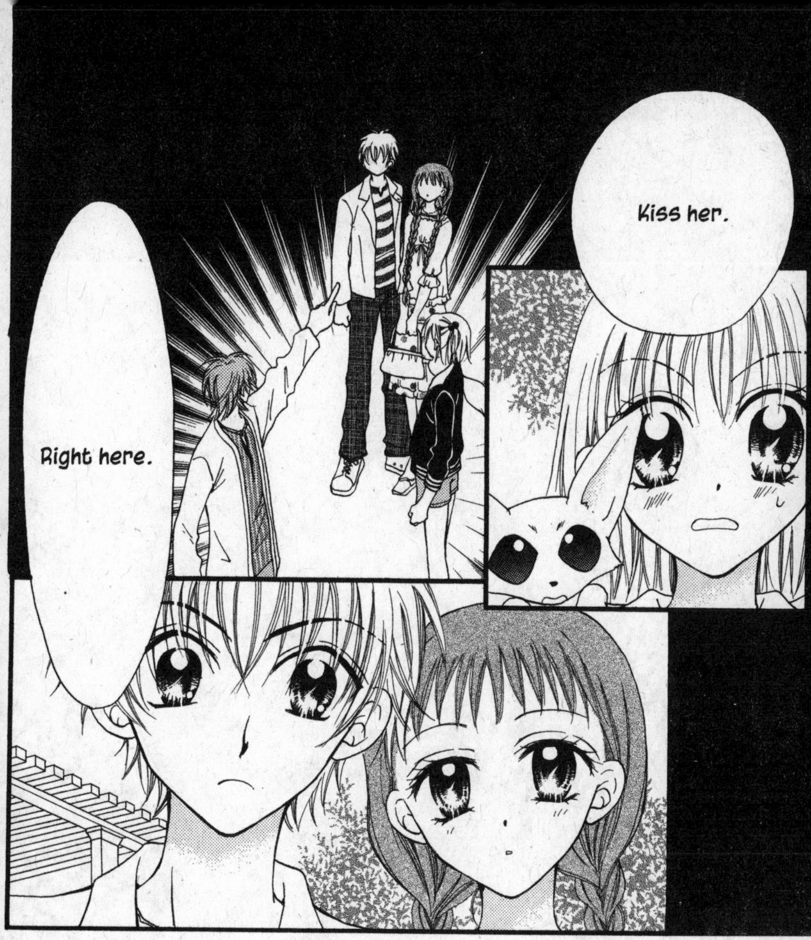
Kiss her.
Right here.

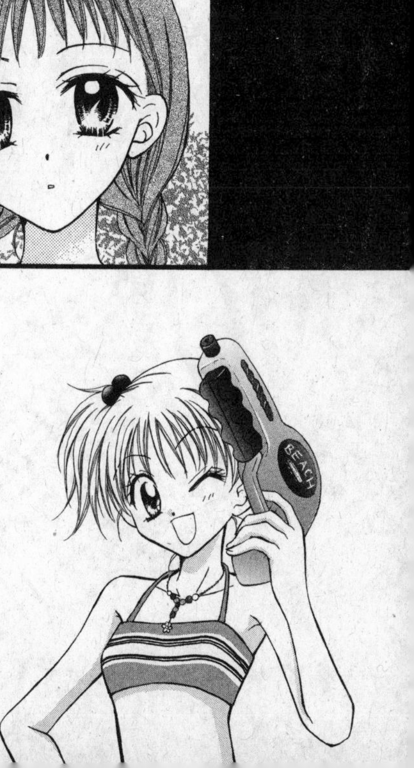

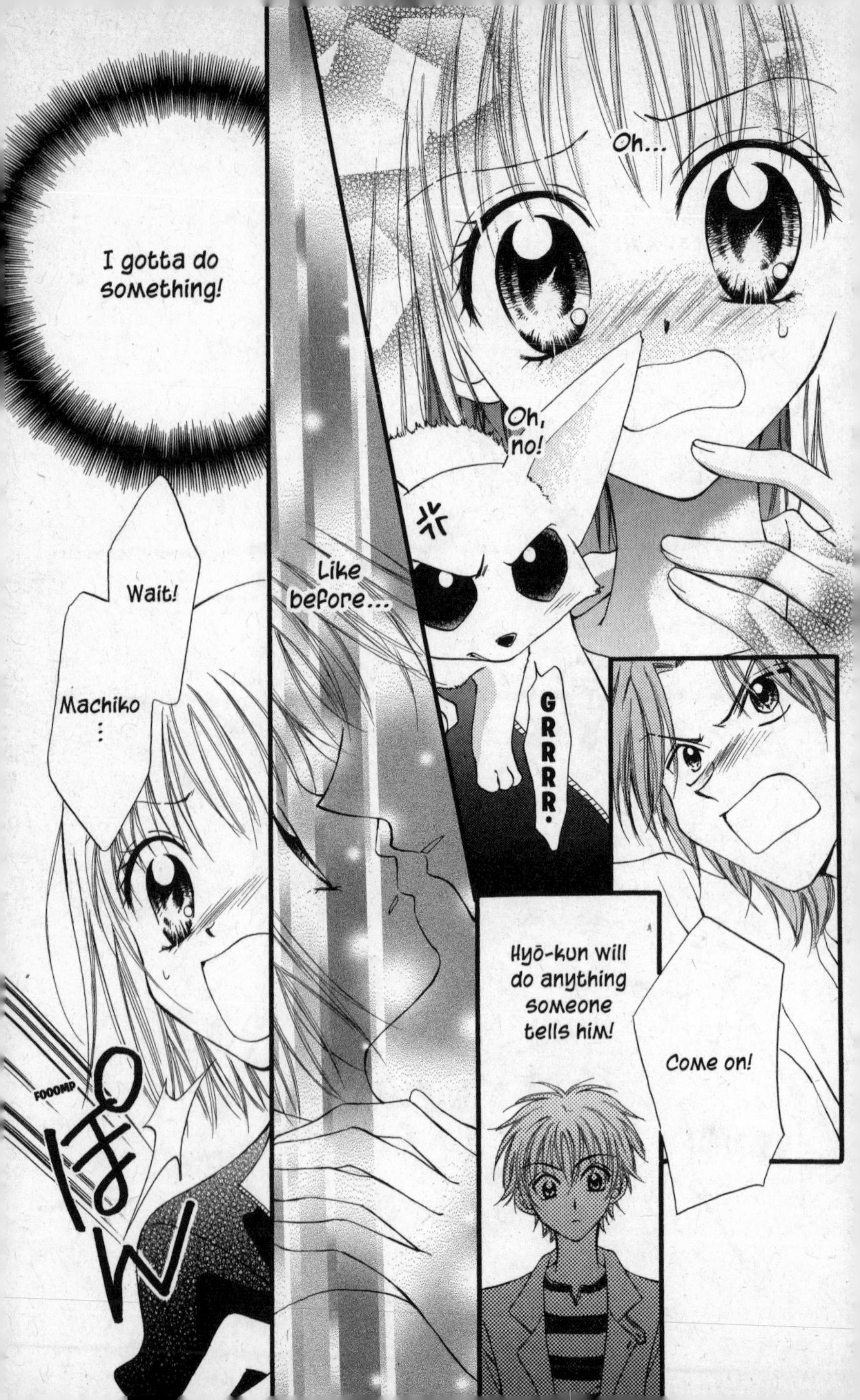

Oh...
Oh, no!
GRRRR.
Come on!
Hyō-kun will do anything someone tells him!
Like before...
I gotta do something!
Wait! Machiko...
FOOOMP

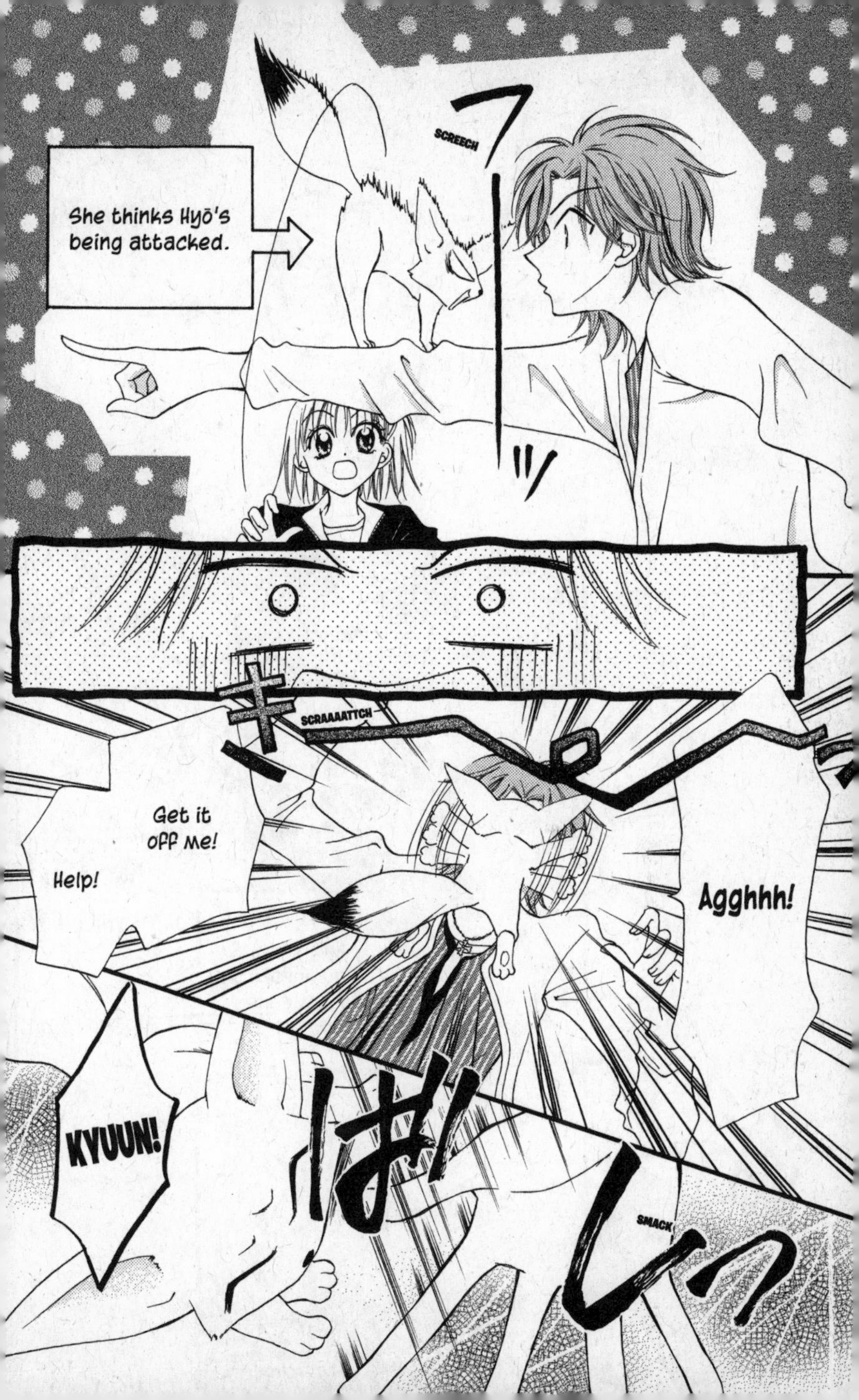
SCREECH
She thinks Hyō's being attacked.
SCRAAAATCH
Agghhh!
Get it off me!
Help!
SMACK
KYUUN!

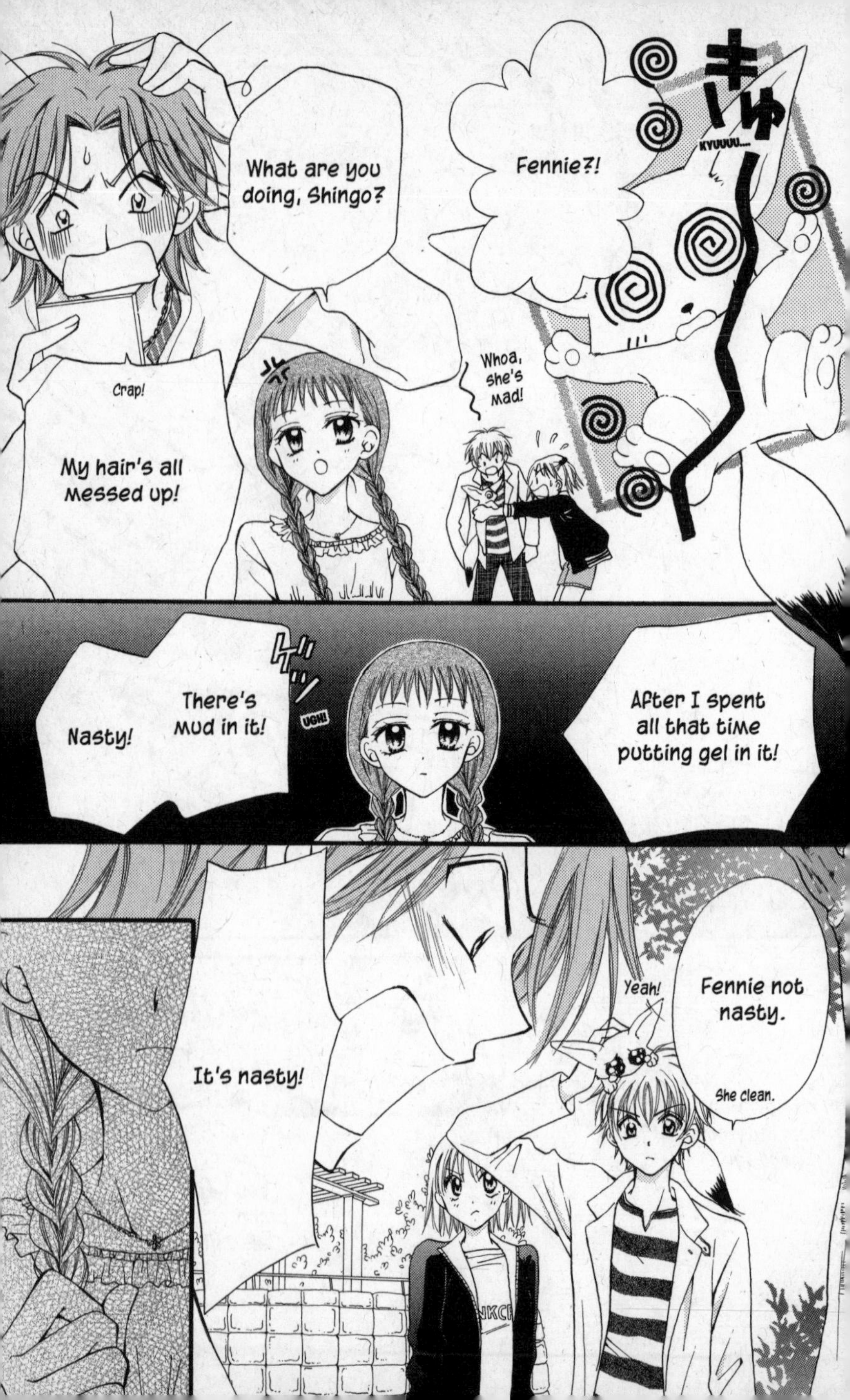
キゅ
KYUUUU...
Fennie?!
What are you doing, Shingo?
Whoa, she's mad!
Crap!
My hair's all messed up!
After I spent all that time putting gel in it!
UGH!
There's mud in it!
Nasty!
Fennie not nasty.
She clean.
Yeah!
It's nasty!

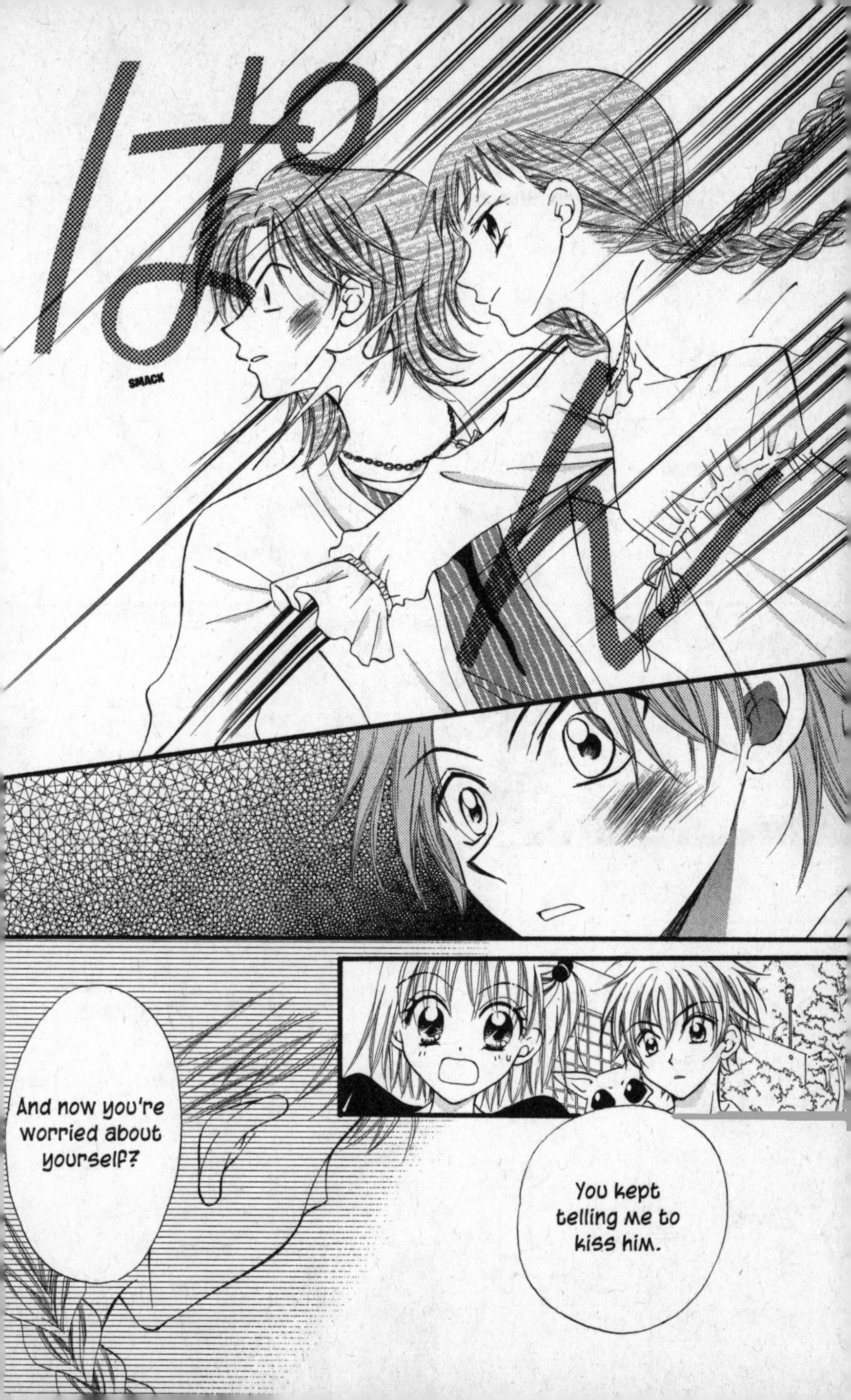
SMACK
You kept telling me to kiss him.
And now you're worried about yourself?

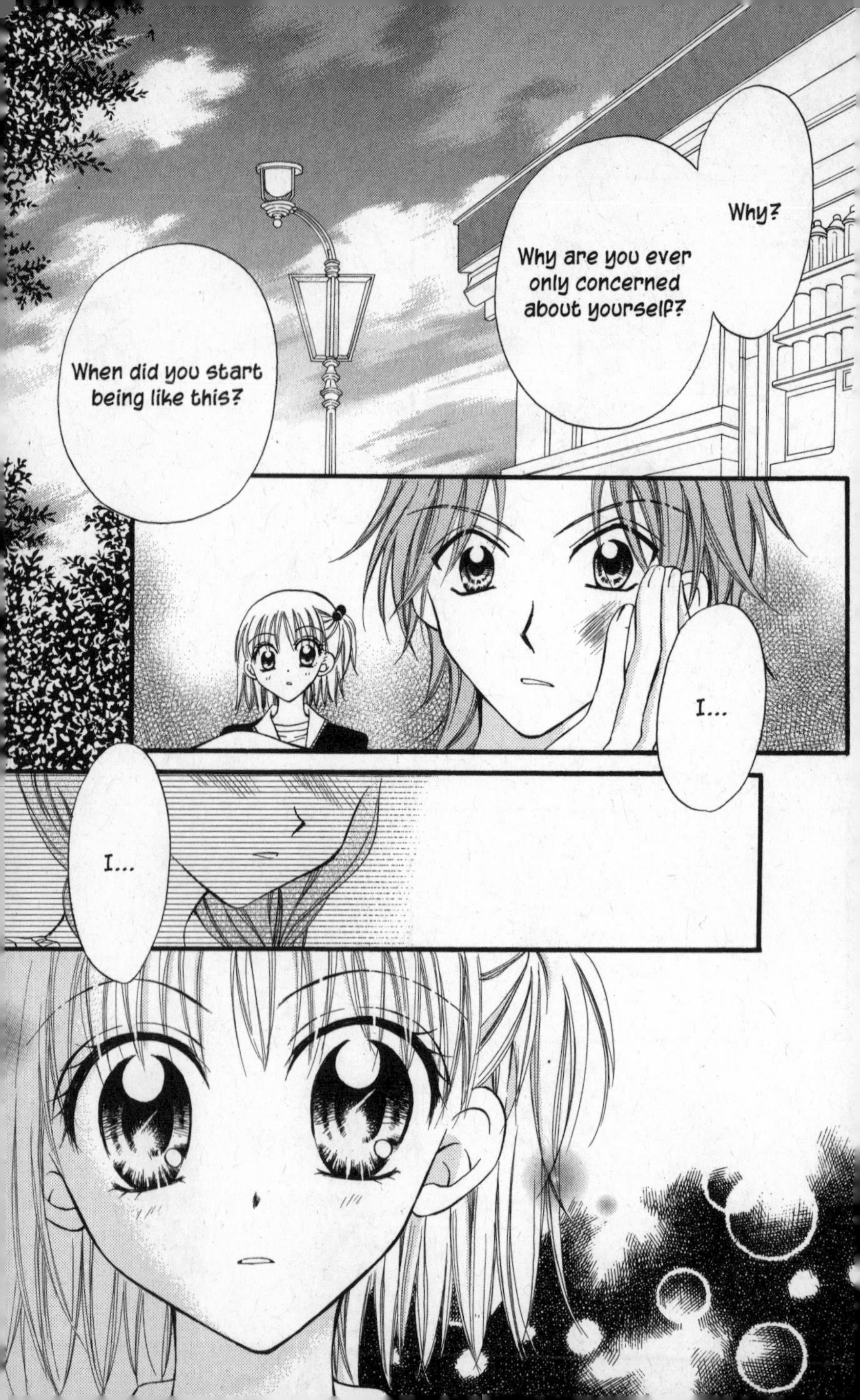
Why?
Why are you ever only concerned about yourself?
When did you start being like this?
I...
I...

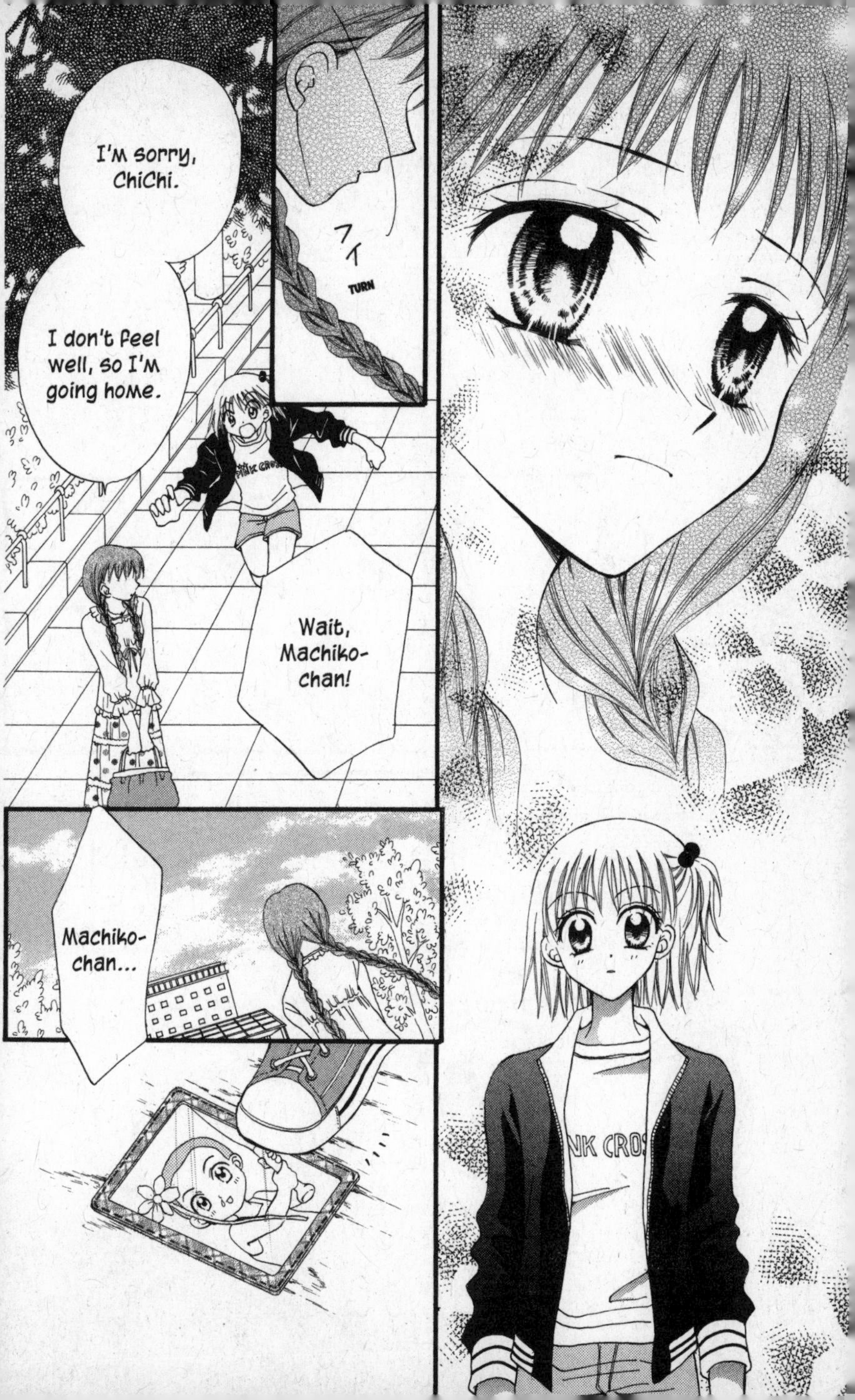
フイ
TURN
I'm sorry, ChiChi.
I don't feel well, so I'm going home.
Wait, Machiko-chan!
Machiko-chan...
...

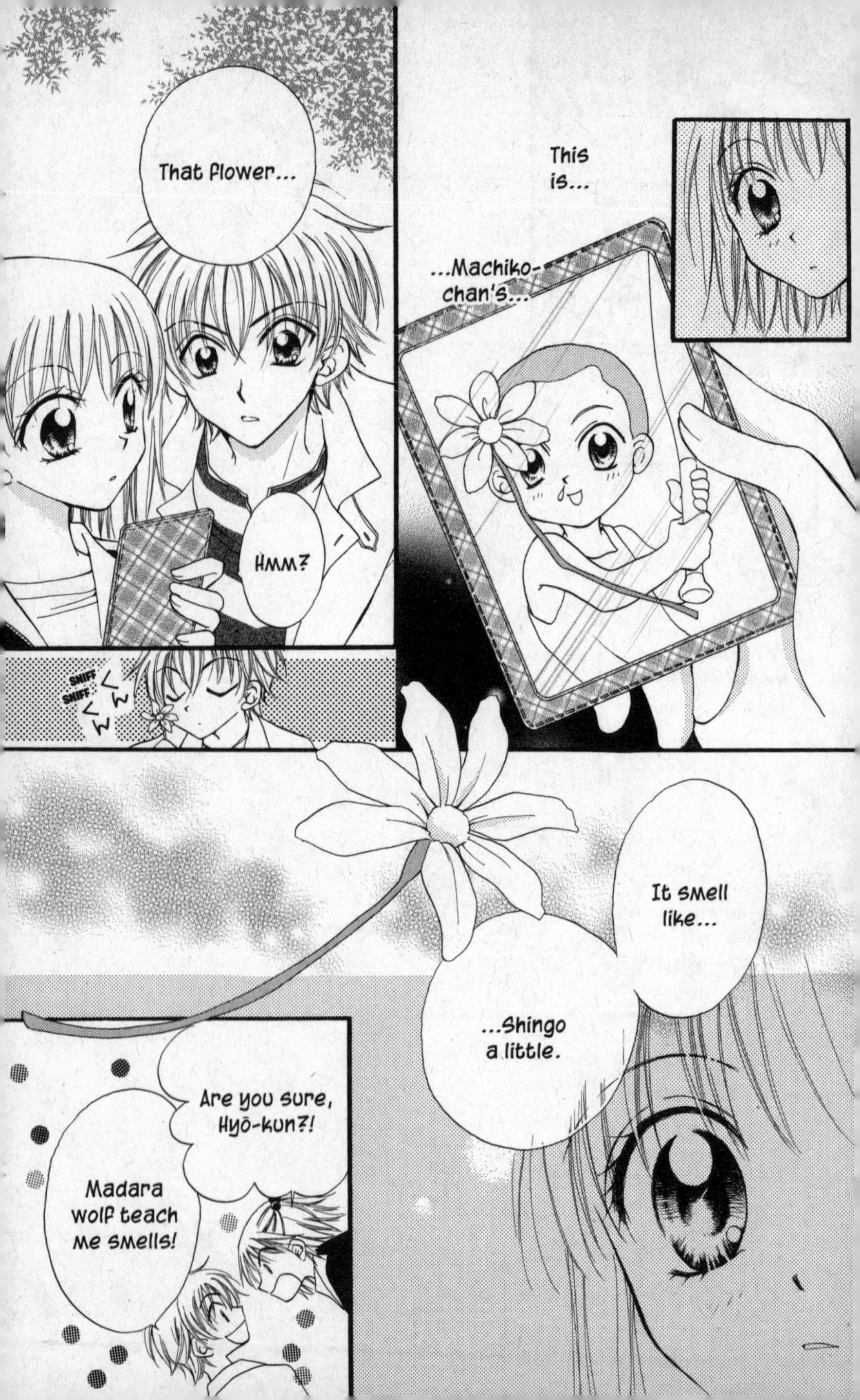

This is...
...Machiko-chan's...
That flower...
HMM?
SNIFF SNIFF
It smell like...
...Shingo a little.
Are you sure, Hyō-kun?!
Madara wolf teach me smells!

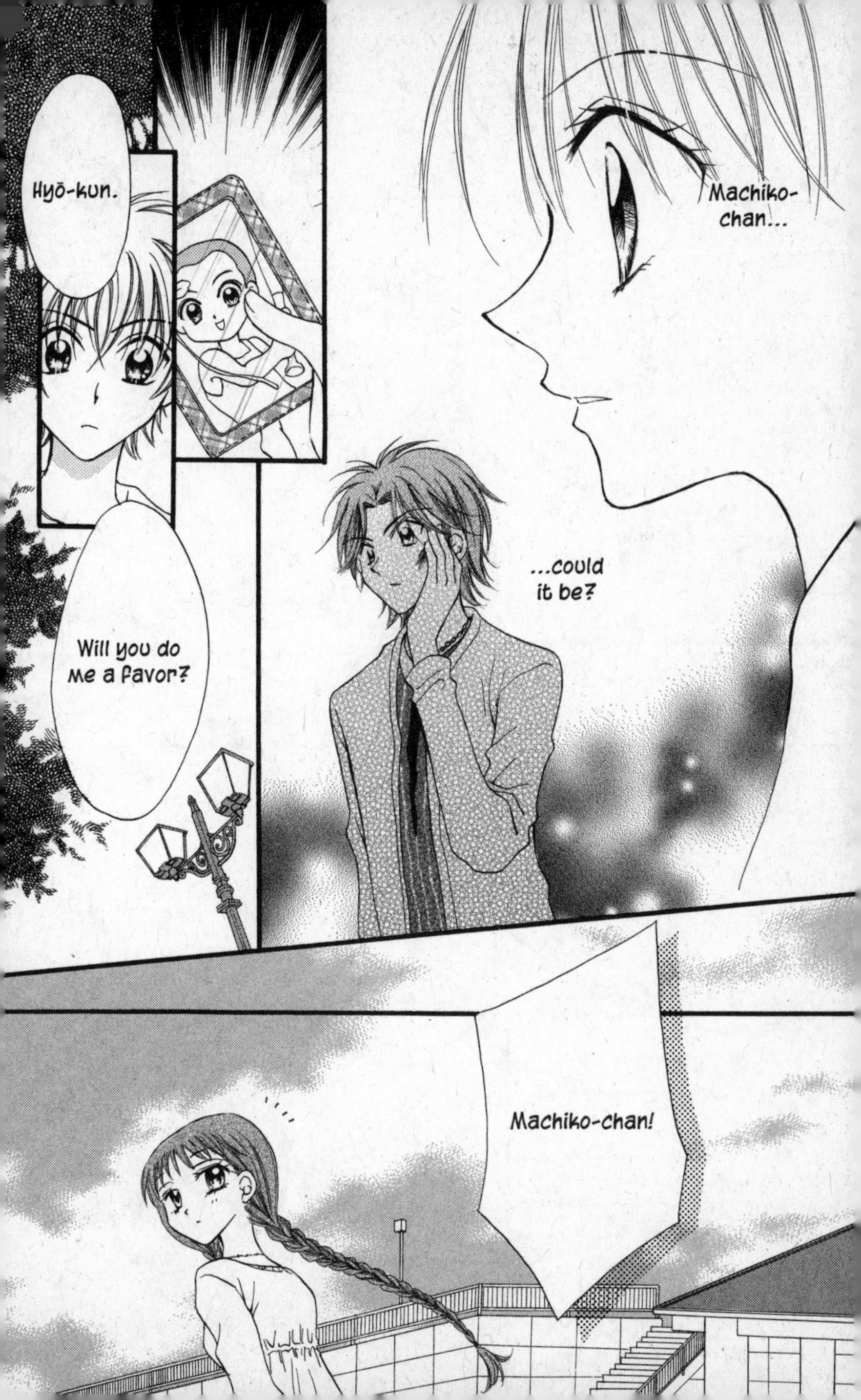
Machiko-chan...
...could it be?
Hyō-kun.
Will you do me a favor?
Machiko-chan!

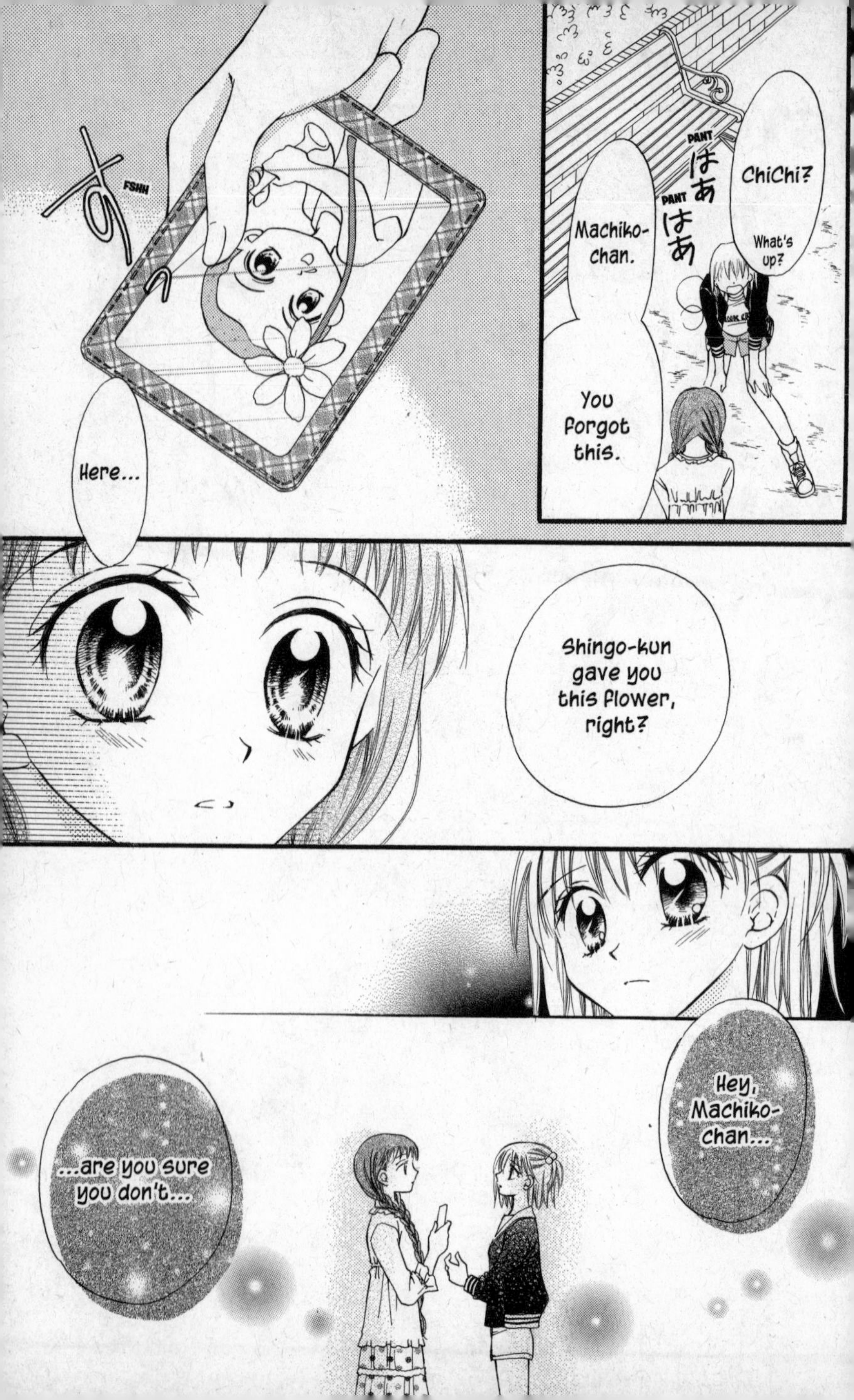
ChiChi?
What's up?
PANT はあ
PANT はあ
Machiko-chan.
You forgot this.
FSHH す
Here...
Shingo-kun gave you this flower, right?
Hey, Machiko-chan...
...are you sure you don't...

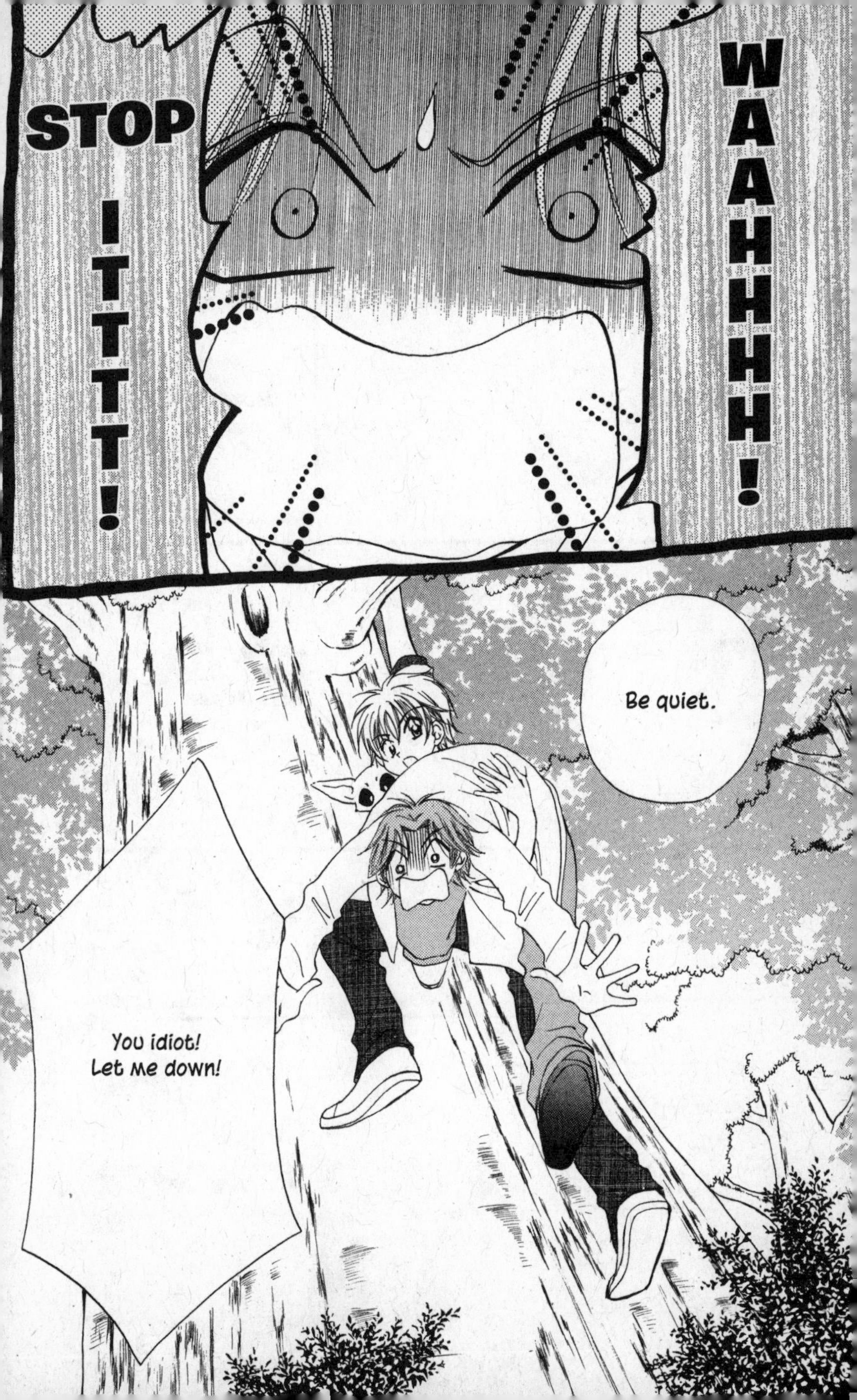
WAAHHHH!
STOP ITTTT!
Be quiet.
You idiot! Let me down!

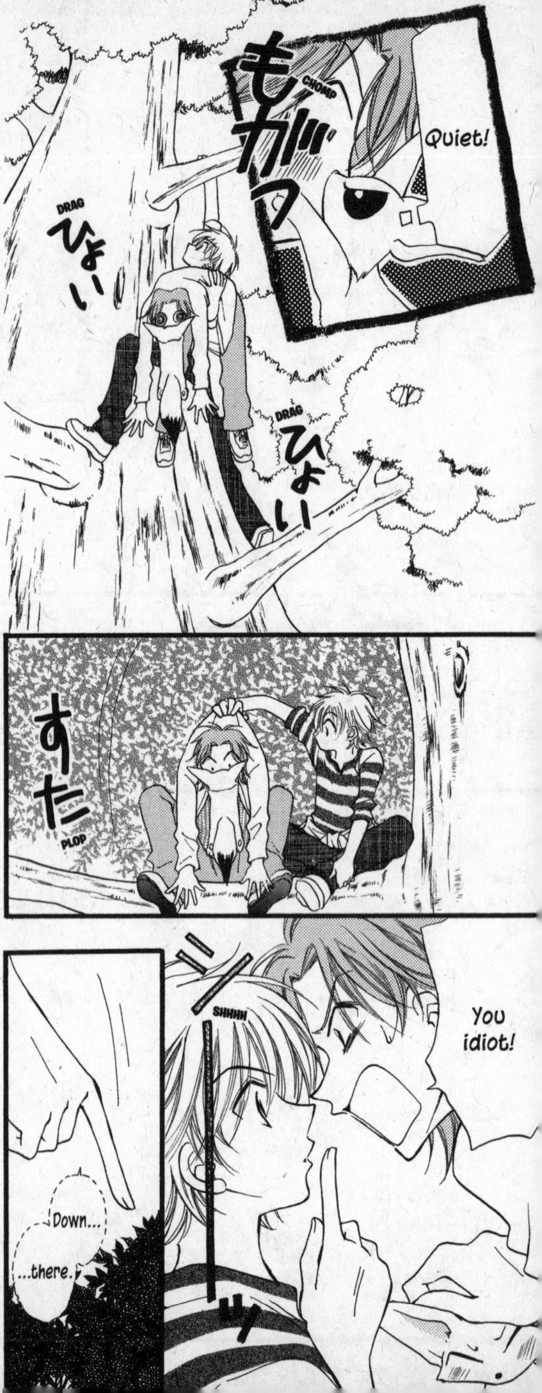
もガッ
CHOMP
Quiet!
DRAG
ひょい
DRAG
ひょい
すた
PLOP
You idiot!
SHHHH
Down...
...there.

8.

There's a big tree in front of my veranda. This spring some ravens made a nest and raised babies there. The ravens were very protective of their nest, but it was really cool to see how they took care of their babies and we checked the nest every day to see if the babies were big enough to leave it.

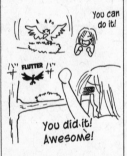

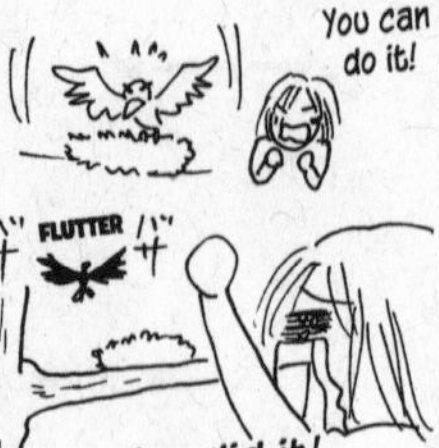
You can do it!
FLUTTER
You did it! Awesome!

I had a dream where it happened like that, but actually they flew a little each day and then just disappeared. Give me back my dreams!

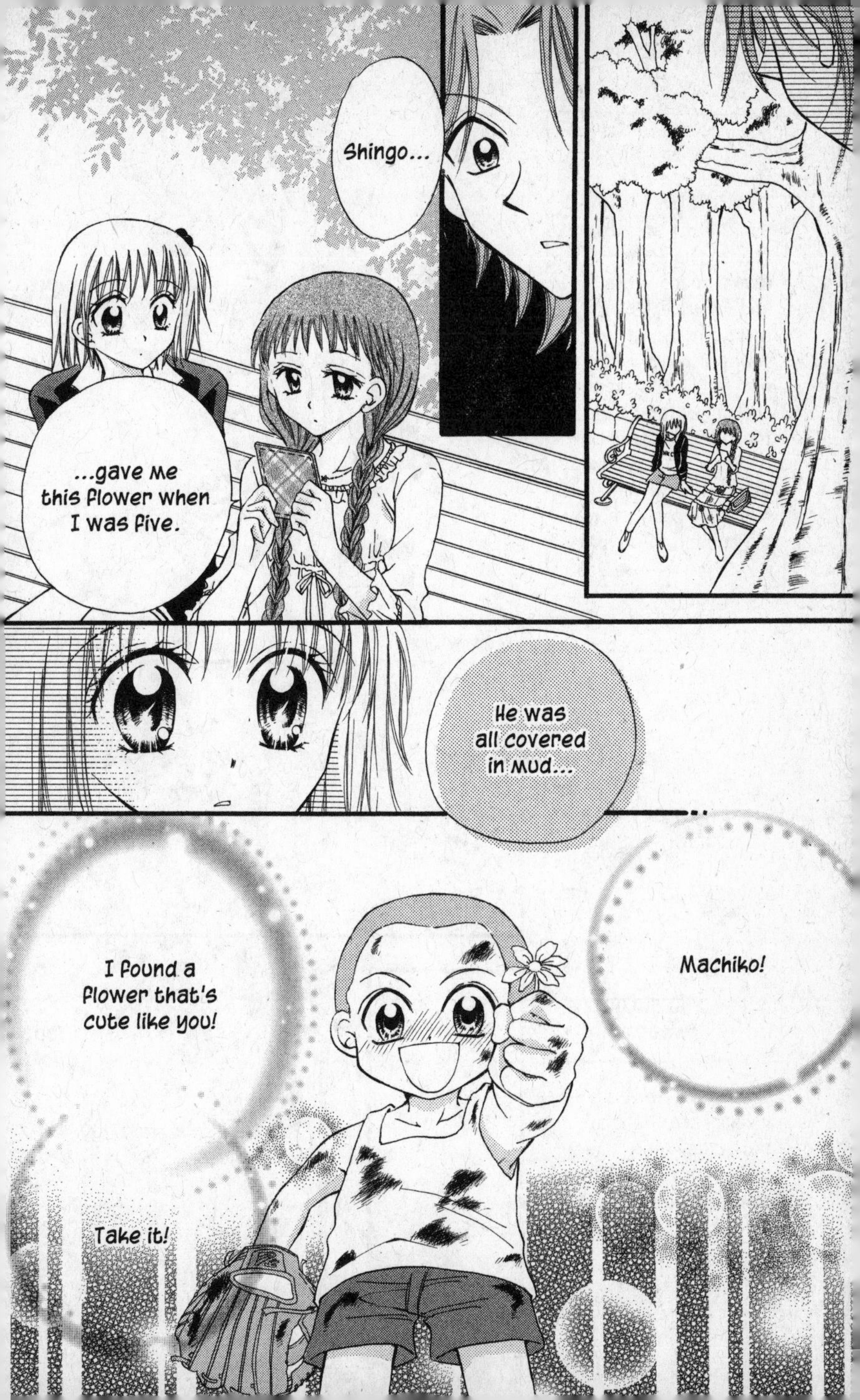
Shingo...
...gave me this flower when I was five.
He was all covered in mud...
Machiko!
I found a flower that's cute like you!
Take it!

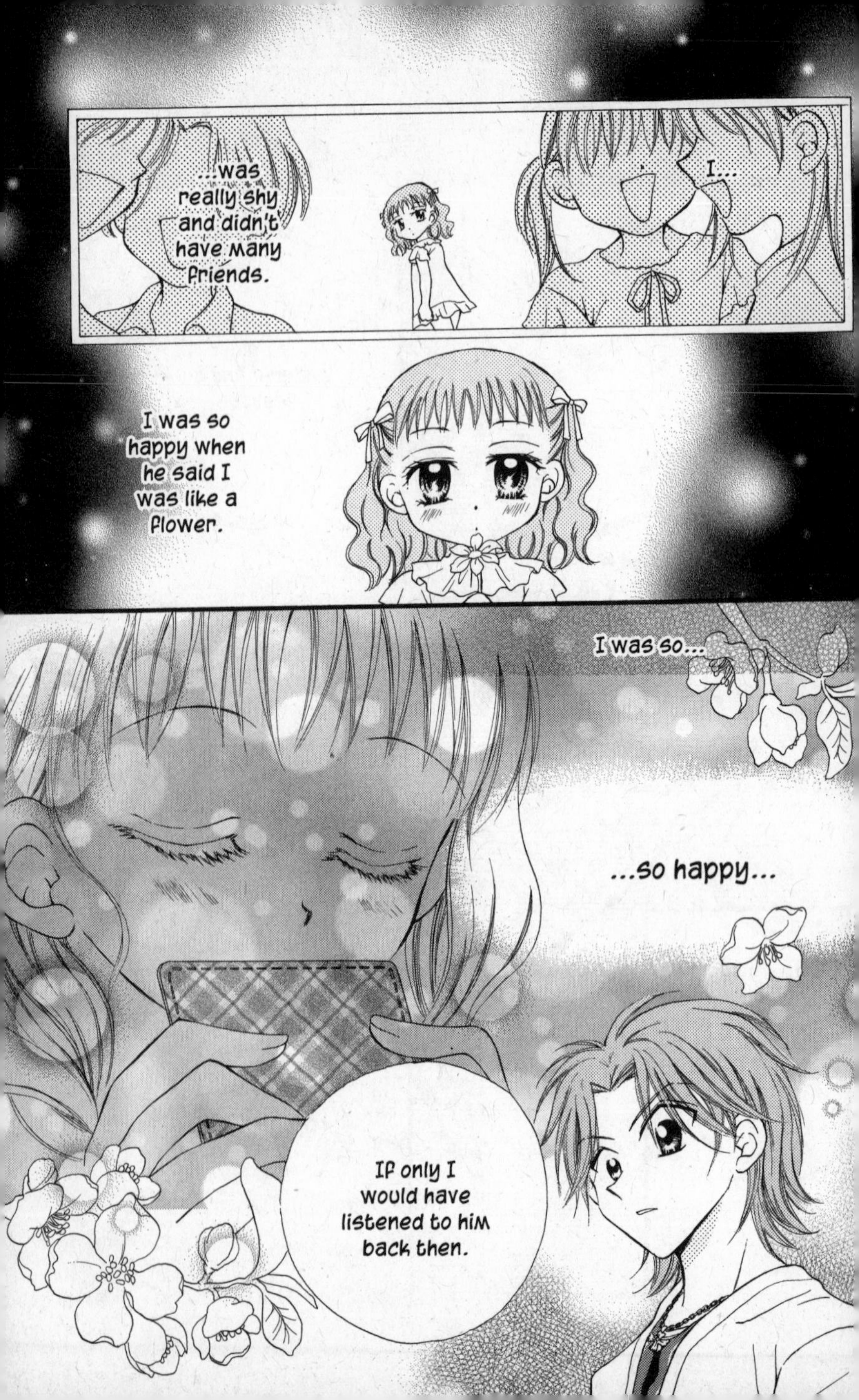
I...
...was really shy and didn't have many friends.
I was so happy when he said I was like a flower.
I was so...
...so happy...
If only I would have listened to him back then.

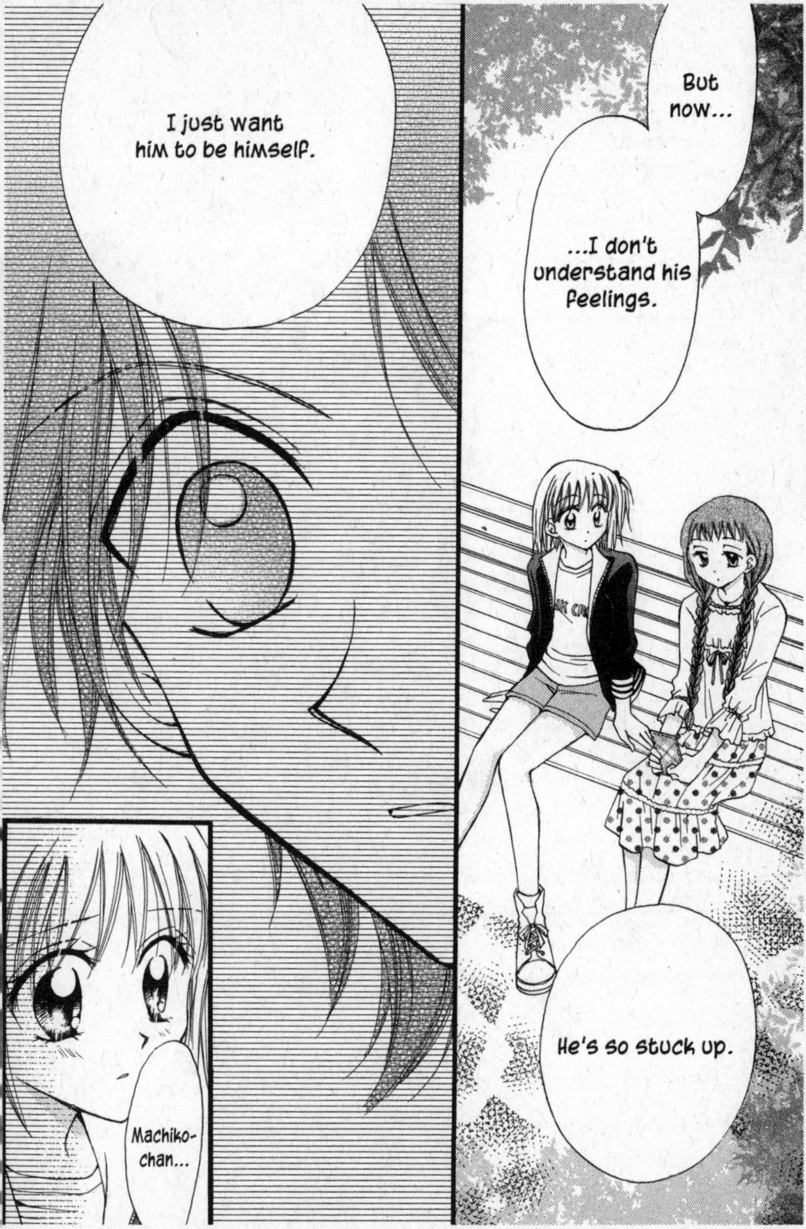
But now...
...I don't understand his feelings.
He's so stuck up.
I just want him to be himself.
Machiko-chan...

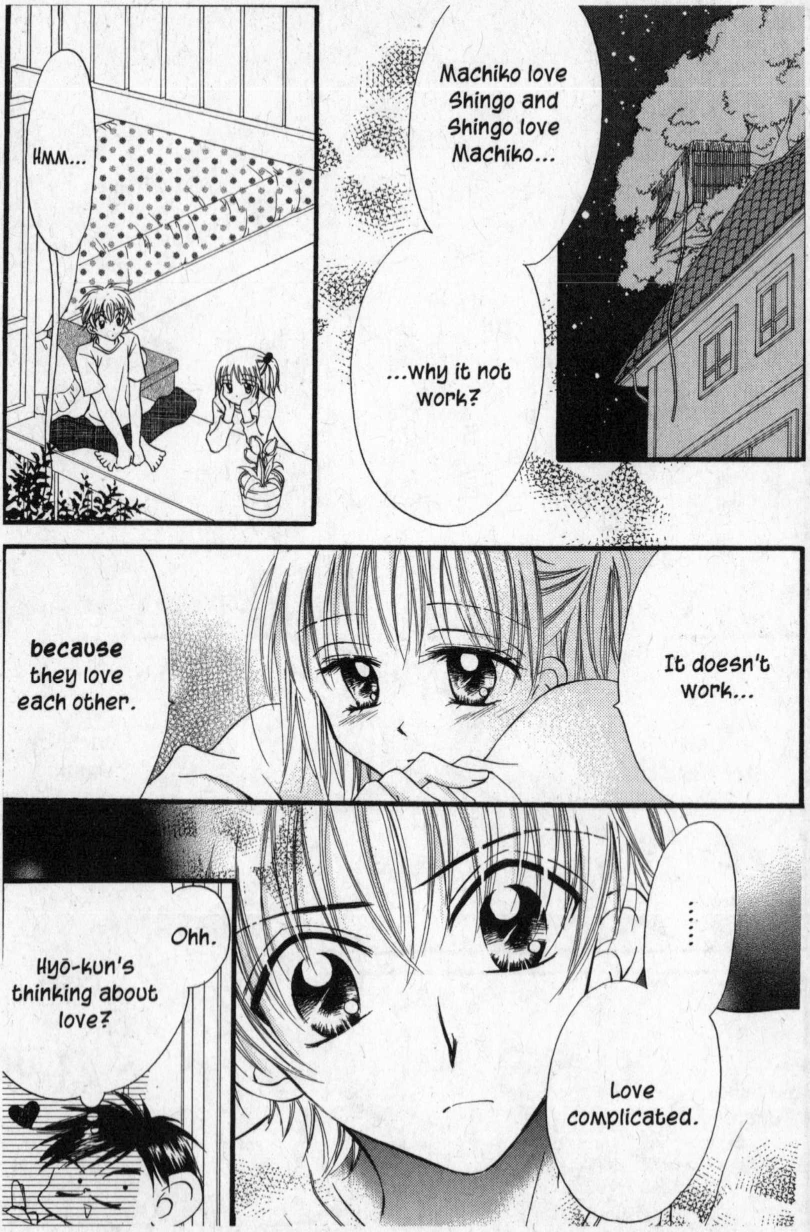
Machiko love Shingo and Shingo love Machiko...
...why it not work?
Hmm...
It doesn't work...
because they love each other.
......
Love complicated.
Ohh.
Hyō-kun's thinking about love?

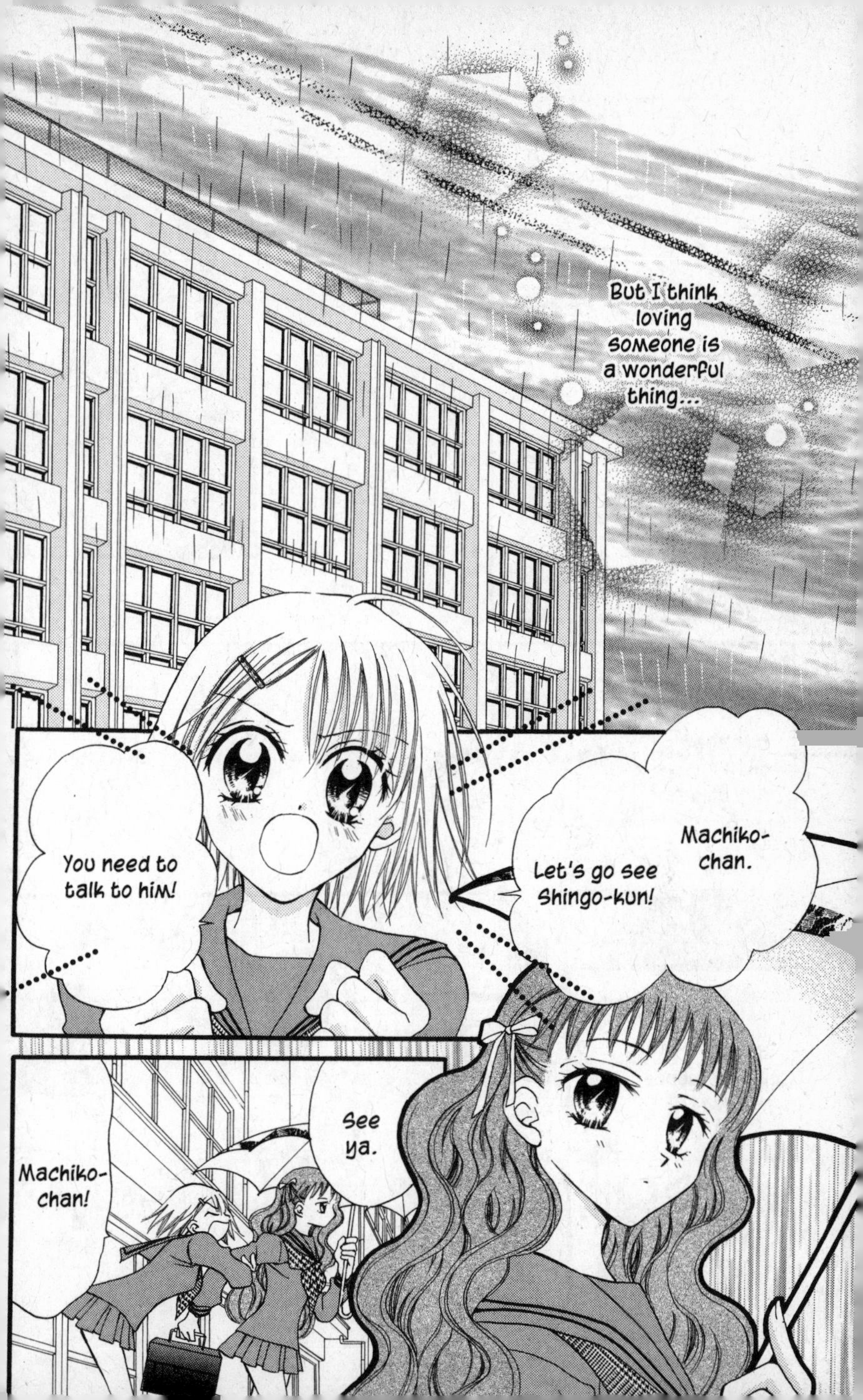
But I think loving someone is a wonderful thing...
Machiko-chan. Let's go see Shingo-kun!
You need to talk to him!
See ya.
Machiko-chan!

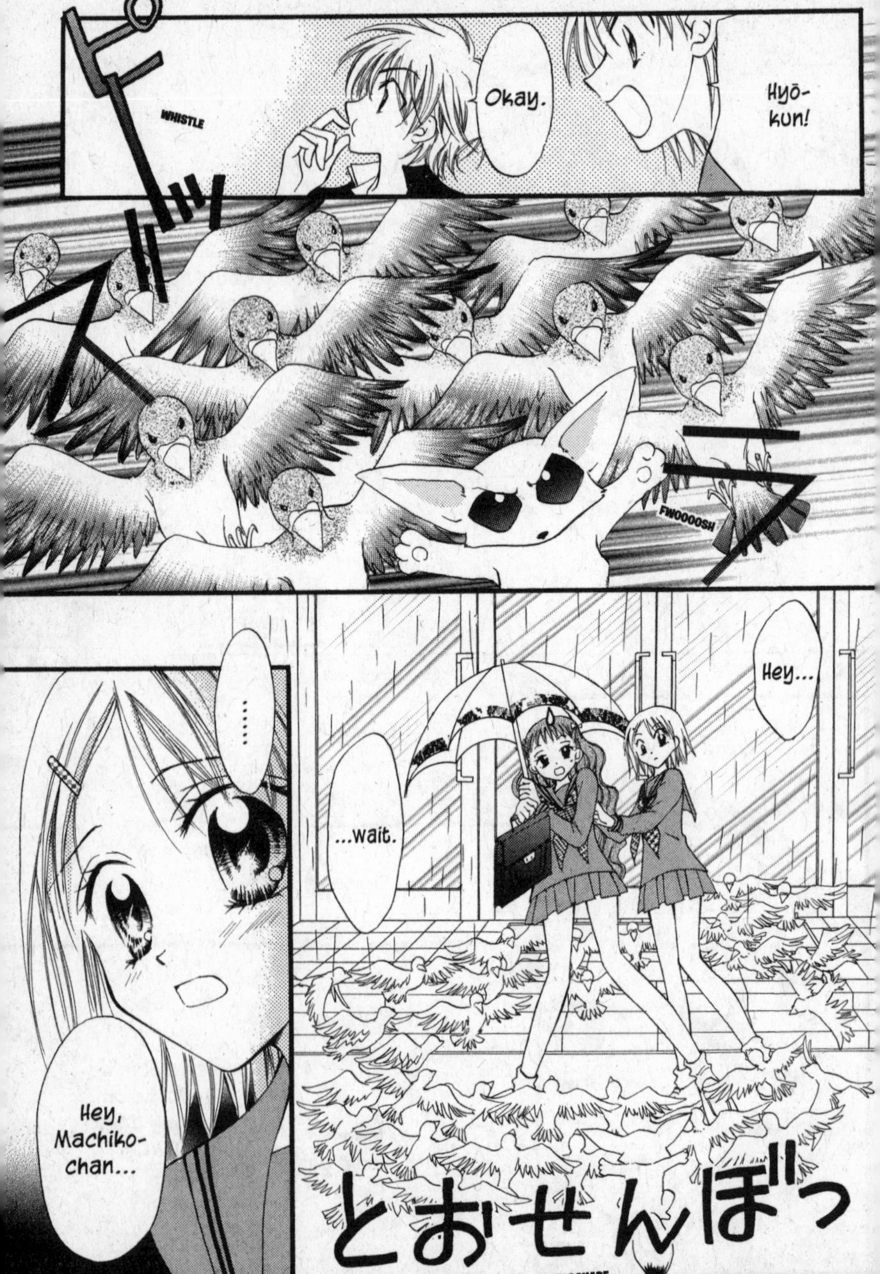
Hyō-kun!
Okay.
WHISTLE
FWOOOOSH
Hey...
...wait.
とおせんぼっ
BLOCKADE
......
Hey, Machiko-chan...

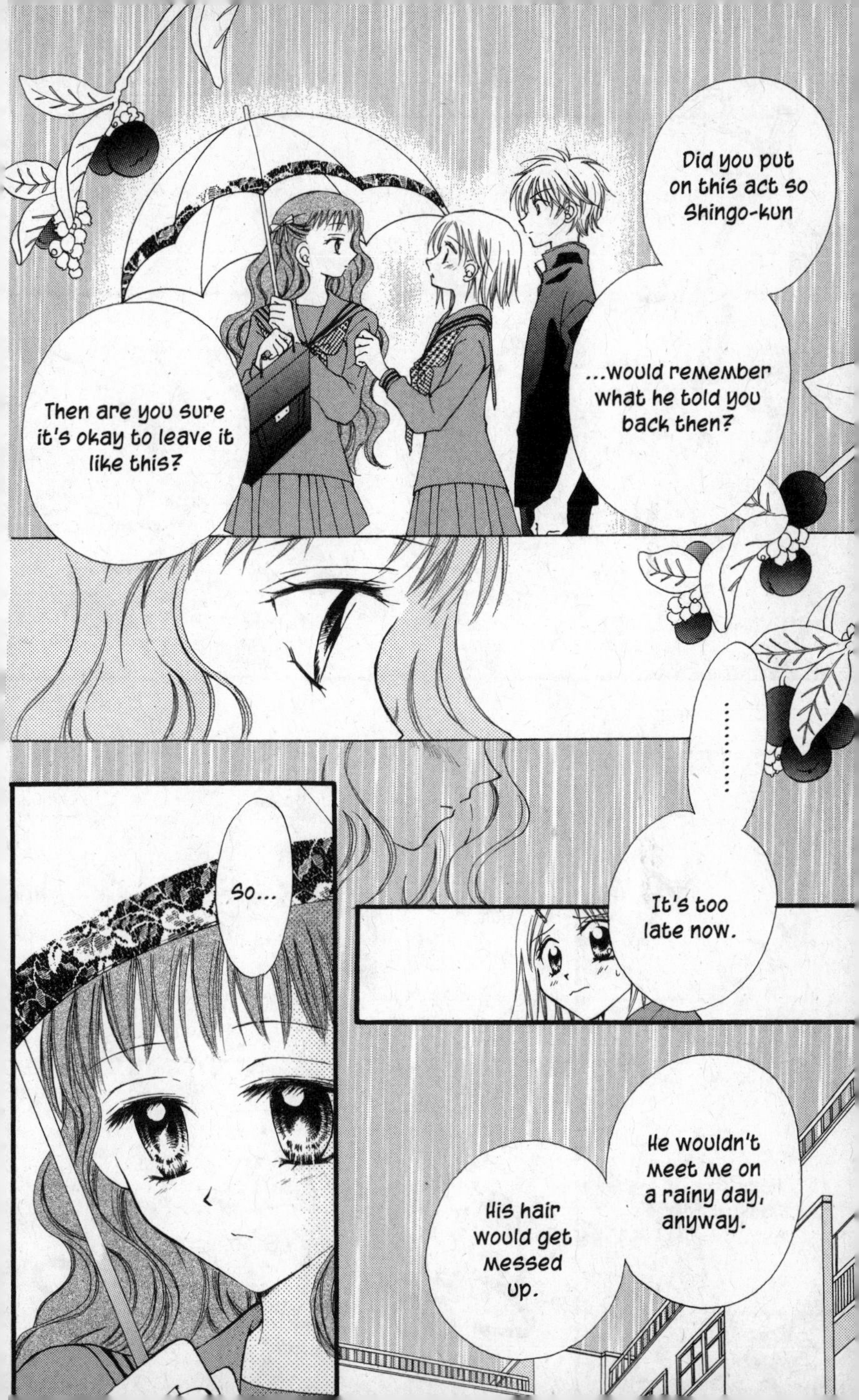
Did you put on this act so Shingo-kun
...would remember what he told you back then?
Then are you sure it's okay to leave it like this?
......
It's too late now.
So...
He wouldn't meet me on a rainy day, anyway.
His hair would get messed up.

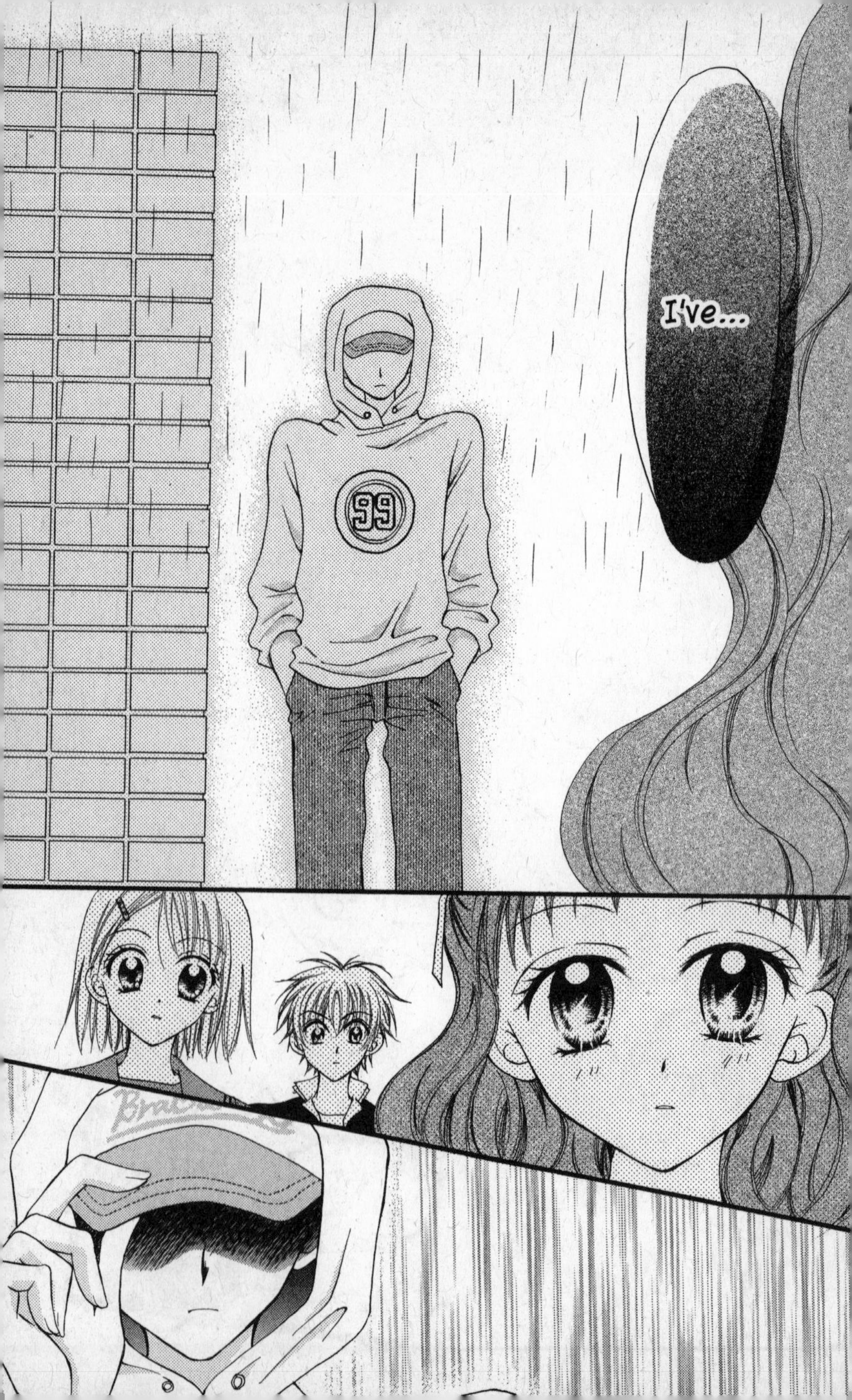
I've...

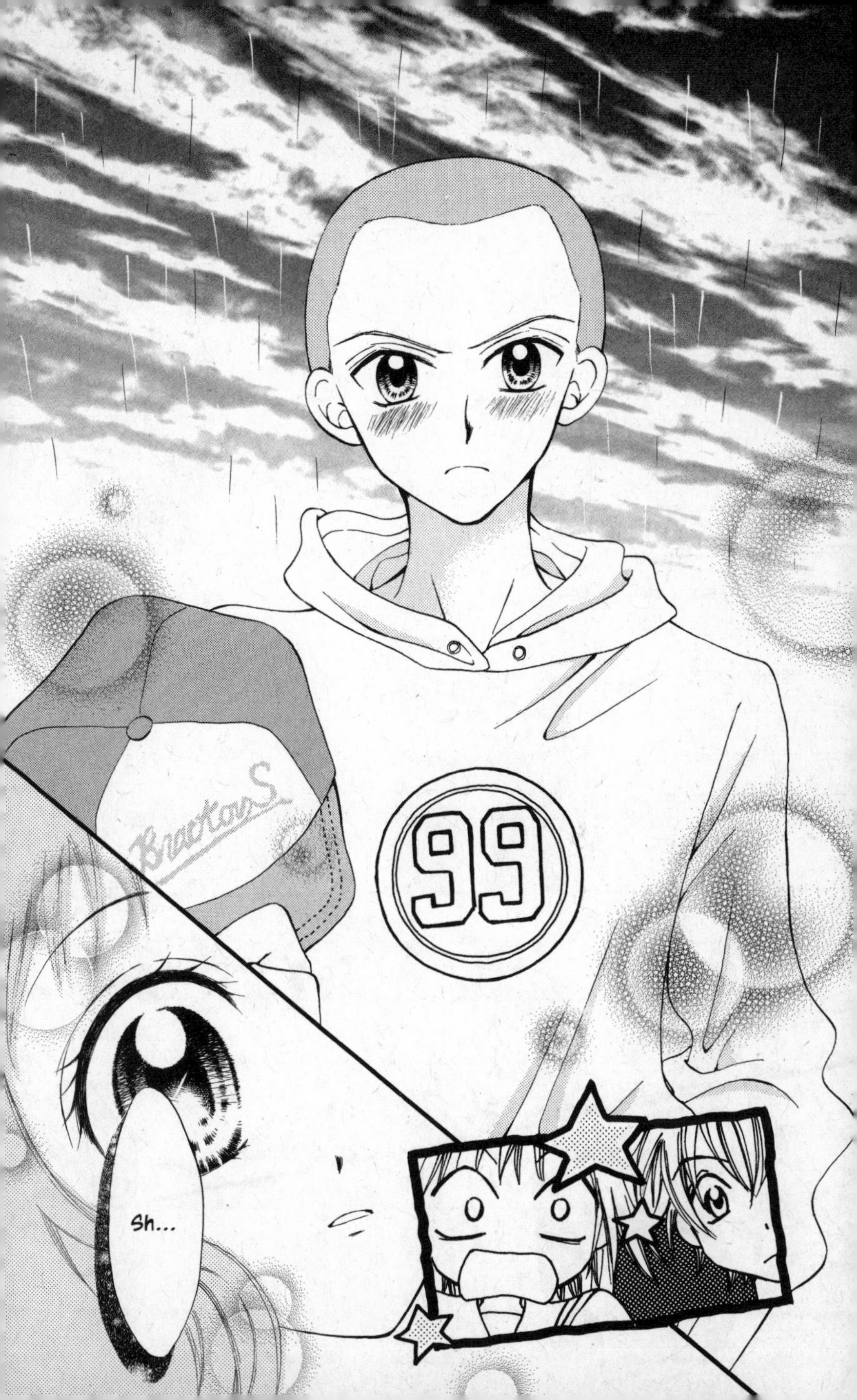
99
Sh...

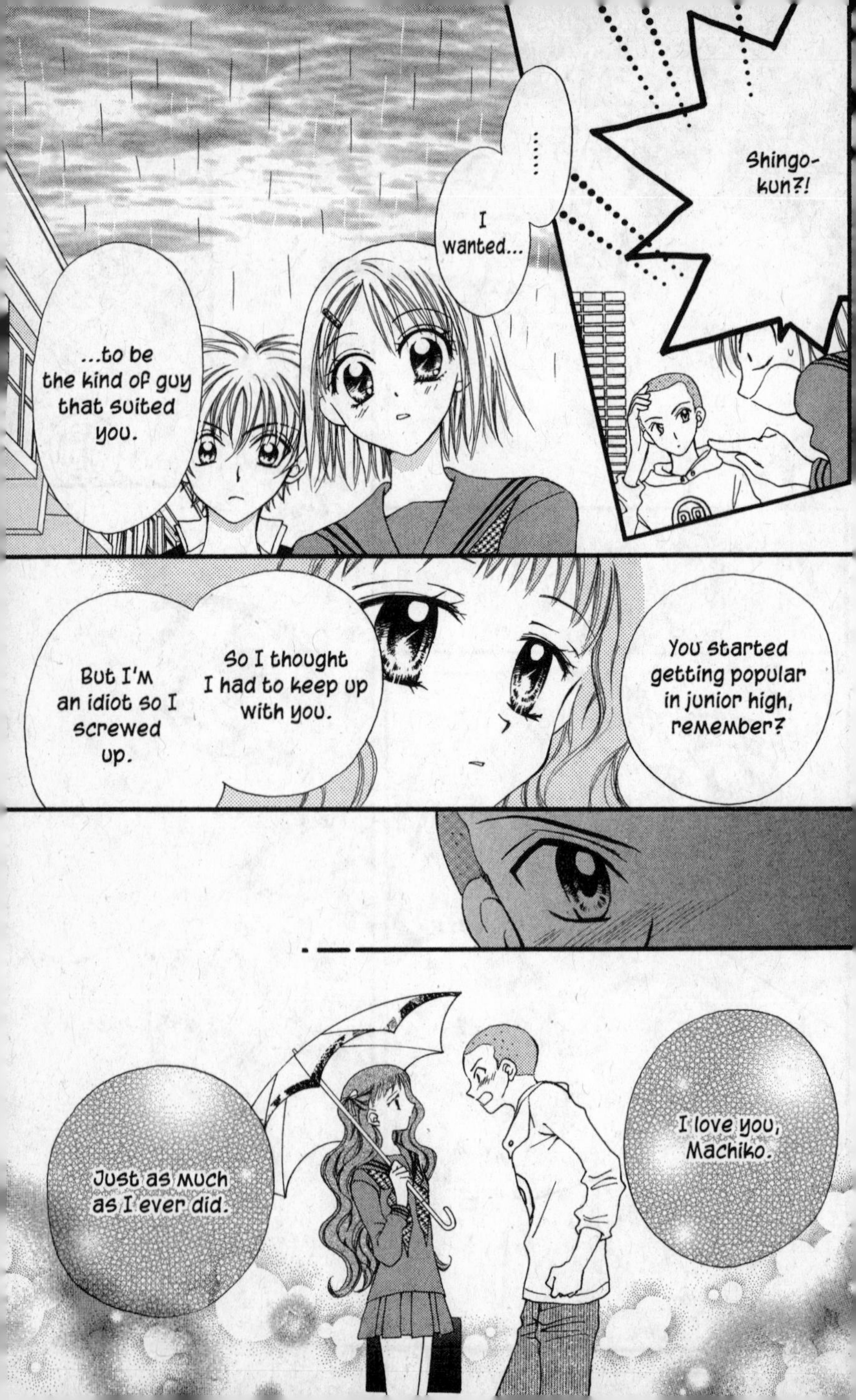
Shingo-kun?!
......
I wanted...
...to be the kind of guy that suited you.
You started getting popular in junior high, remember?
So I thought I had to keep up with you.
But I'm an idiot so I screwed up.
I love you, Machiko.
Just as much as I ever did.

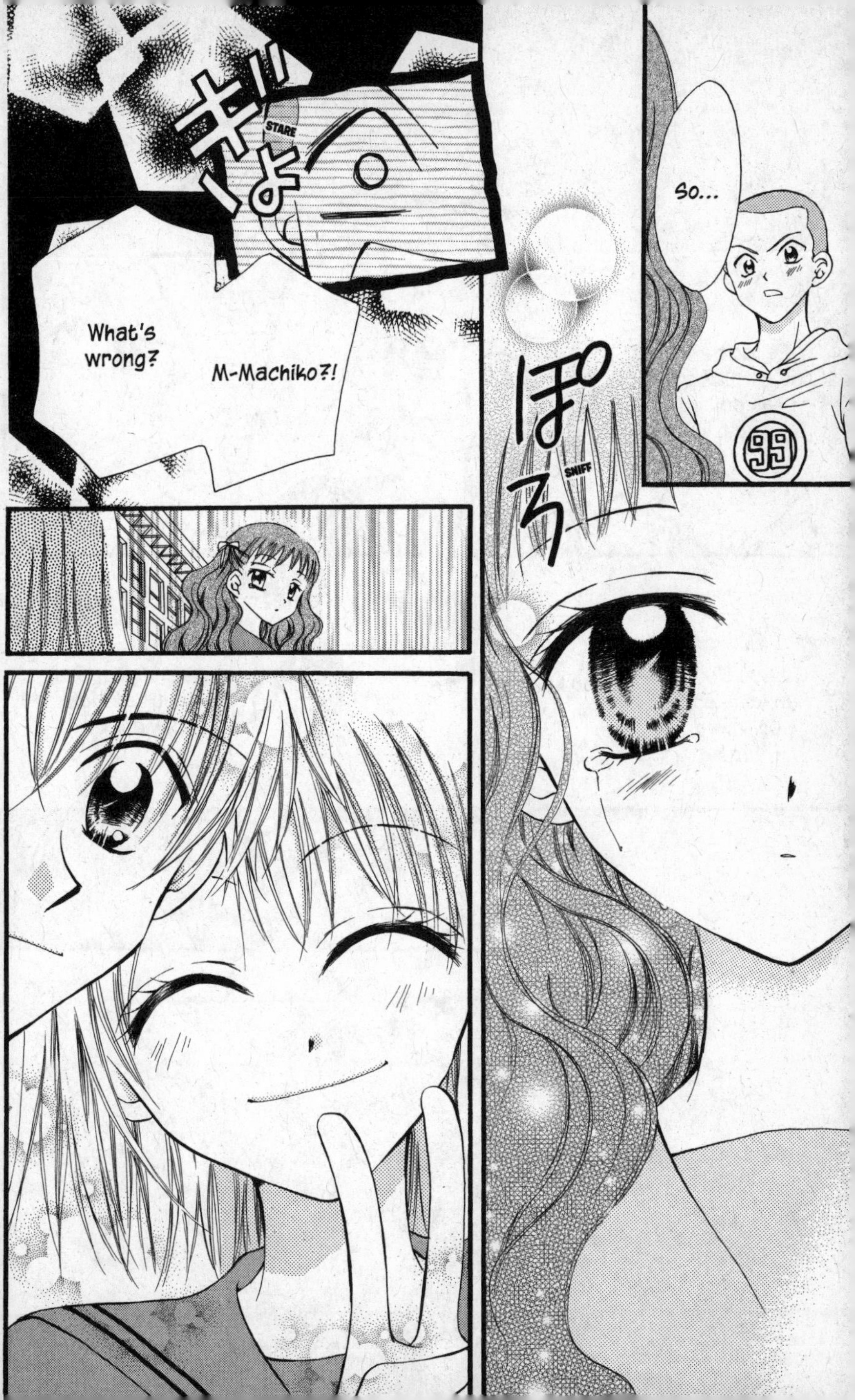
So...
ぽろ
SNIFF
ギョ
STARE
M-Machiko?!
What's wrong?

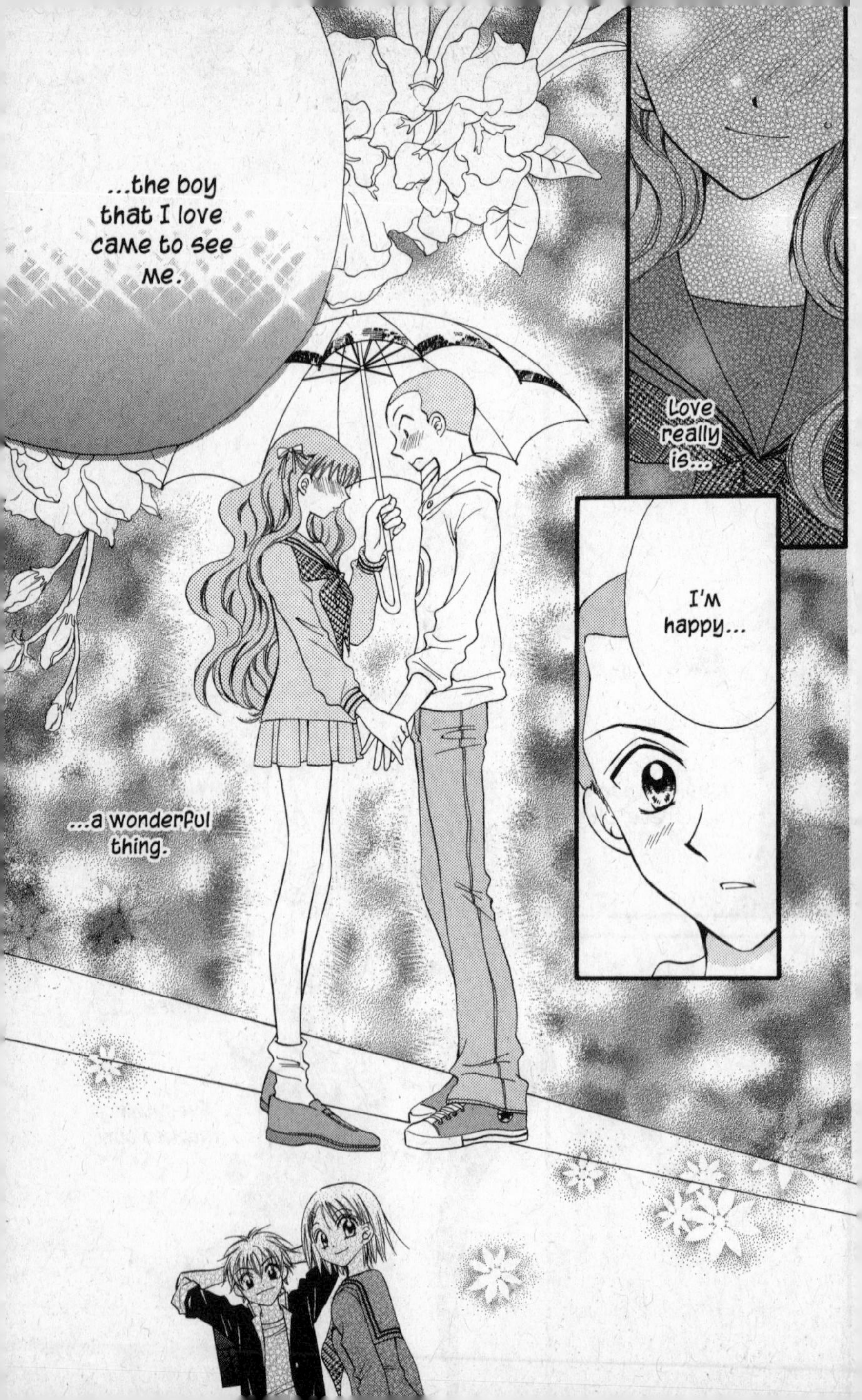
Love really is...
I'm happy...
...the boy that I love came to see me.
...a wonderful thing.

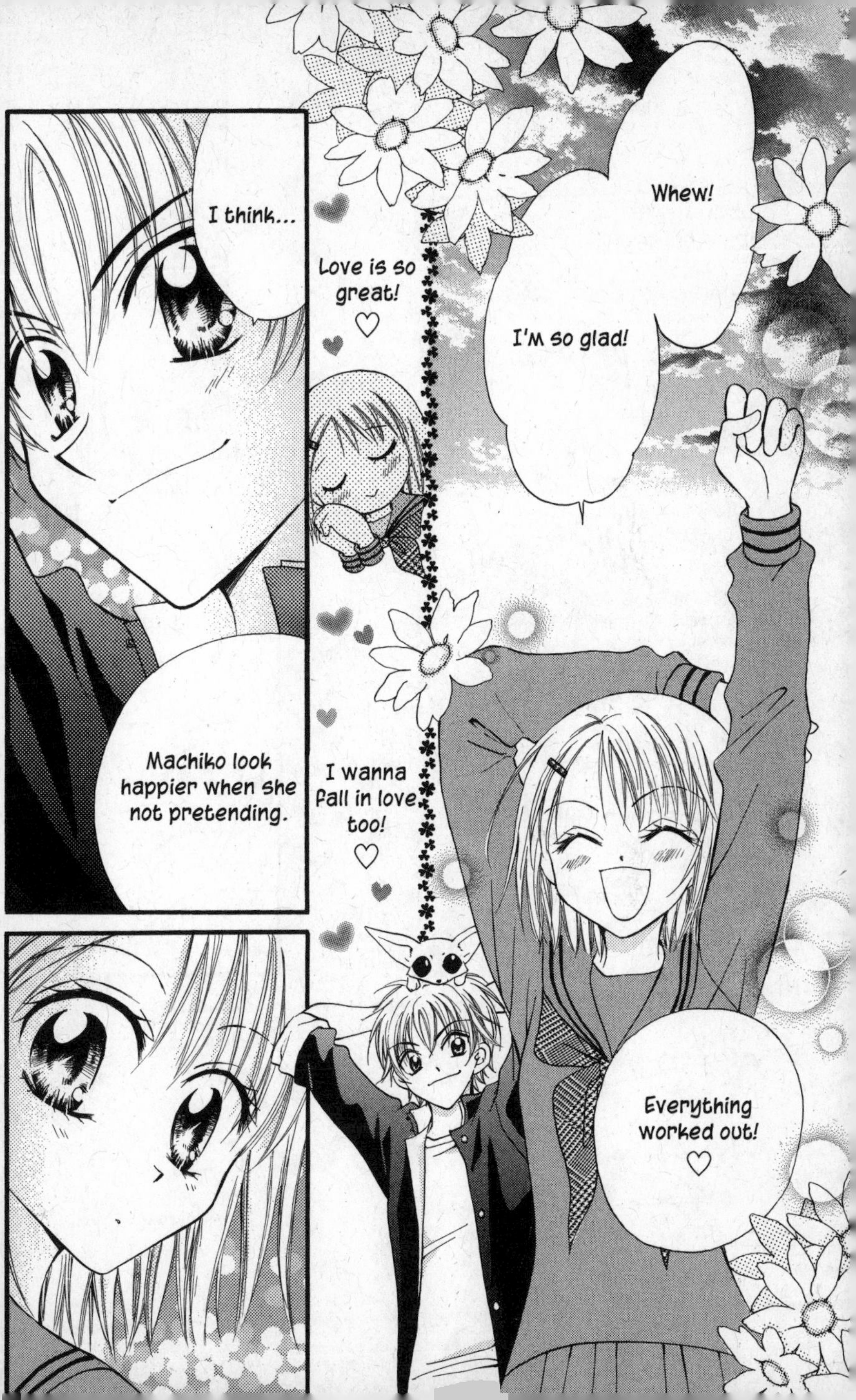
Whew!
I'm so glad!
Everything worked out! ♡
Love is so great! ♡
I wanna fall in love too! ♡
I think...
Machiko look happier when she not pretending.

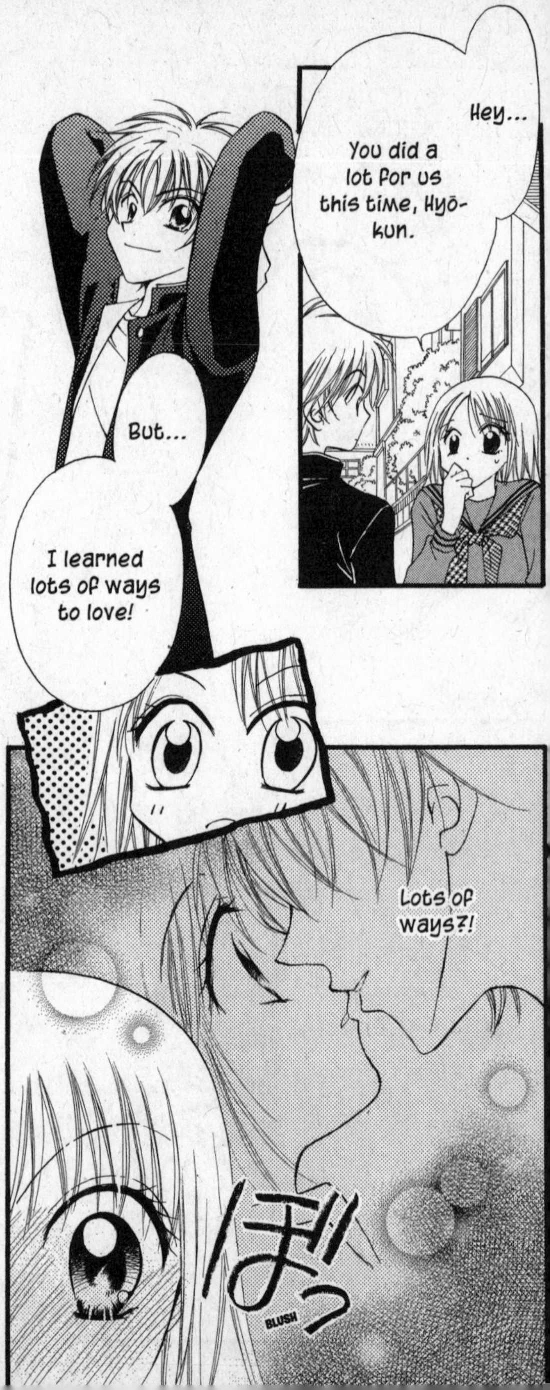
Hey...
You did a lot for us this time, Hyō-kun.
But...
I learned lots of ways to love!
Lots of ways?!
BLUSH

9.

In volume 1, ChiChi had a hard time taking care of Hyō-kun, but the second volume will be a little more romantic. Make sure to check it out!

★ Special thanks ★

★ Maruyama-sama
★ Shoubayashi-sama
★ Kishimoto-sama
★ Suda-sama
★ Kyoko-sama

Please send any comments to:
Natsumi Ando
Del Rey Manga
1745 Broadway
New York, NY 10019

There're bonus pages at the end of the volume; make sure to read them!

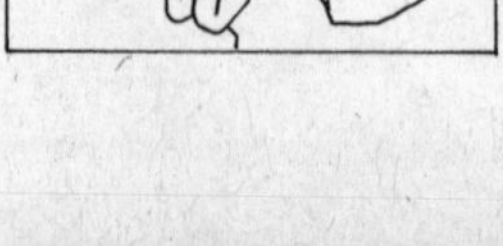
See ya next volume!
Hehe!

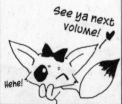

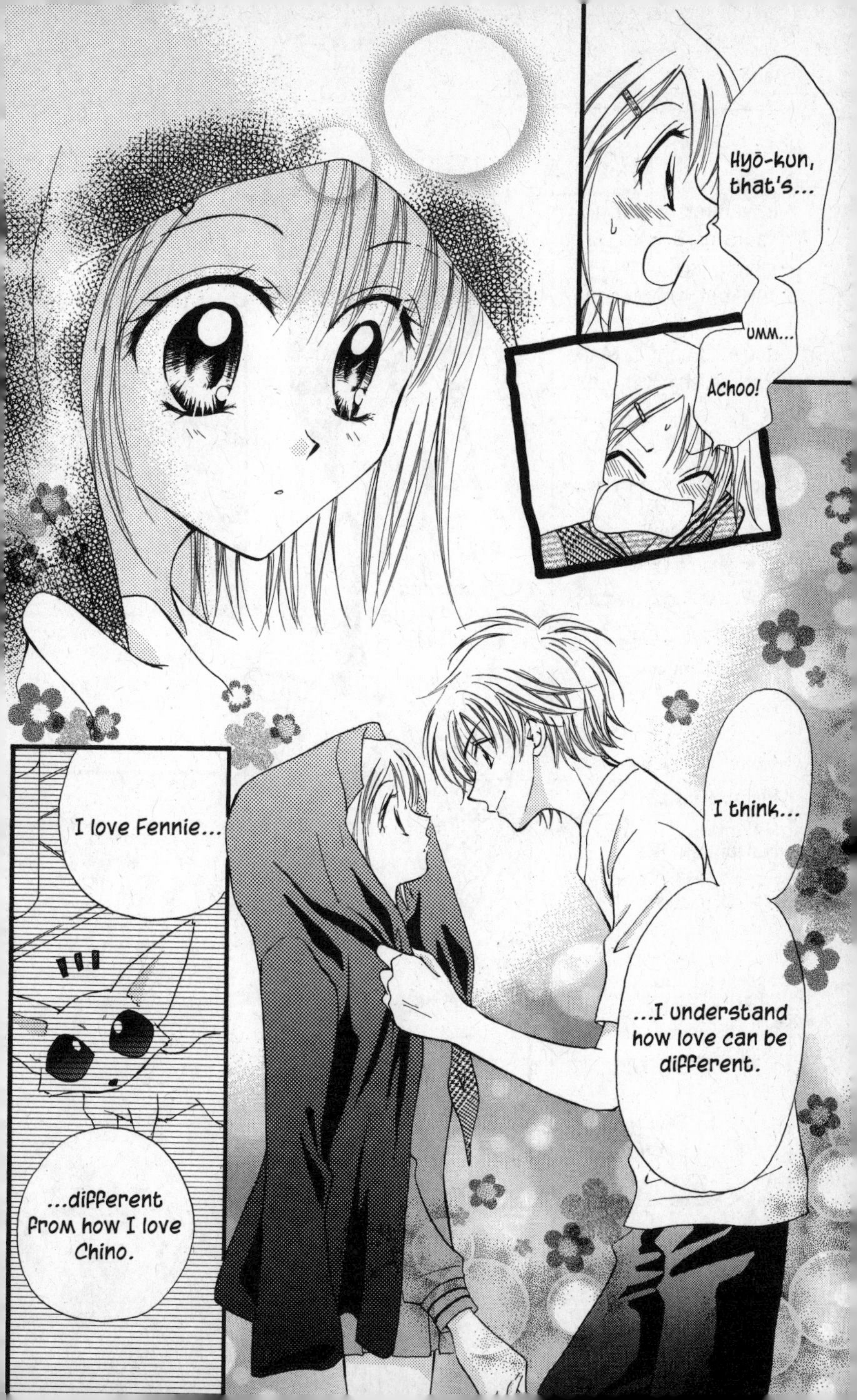
Hyō-kun, that's...
Umm...
Achoo!
I think...
...I understand how love can be different.
I love Fennie...
...different from how I love Chino.

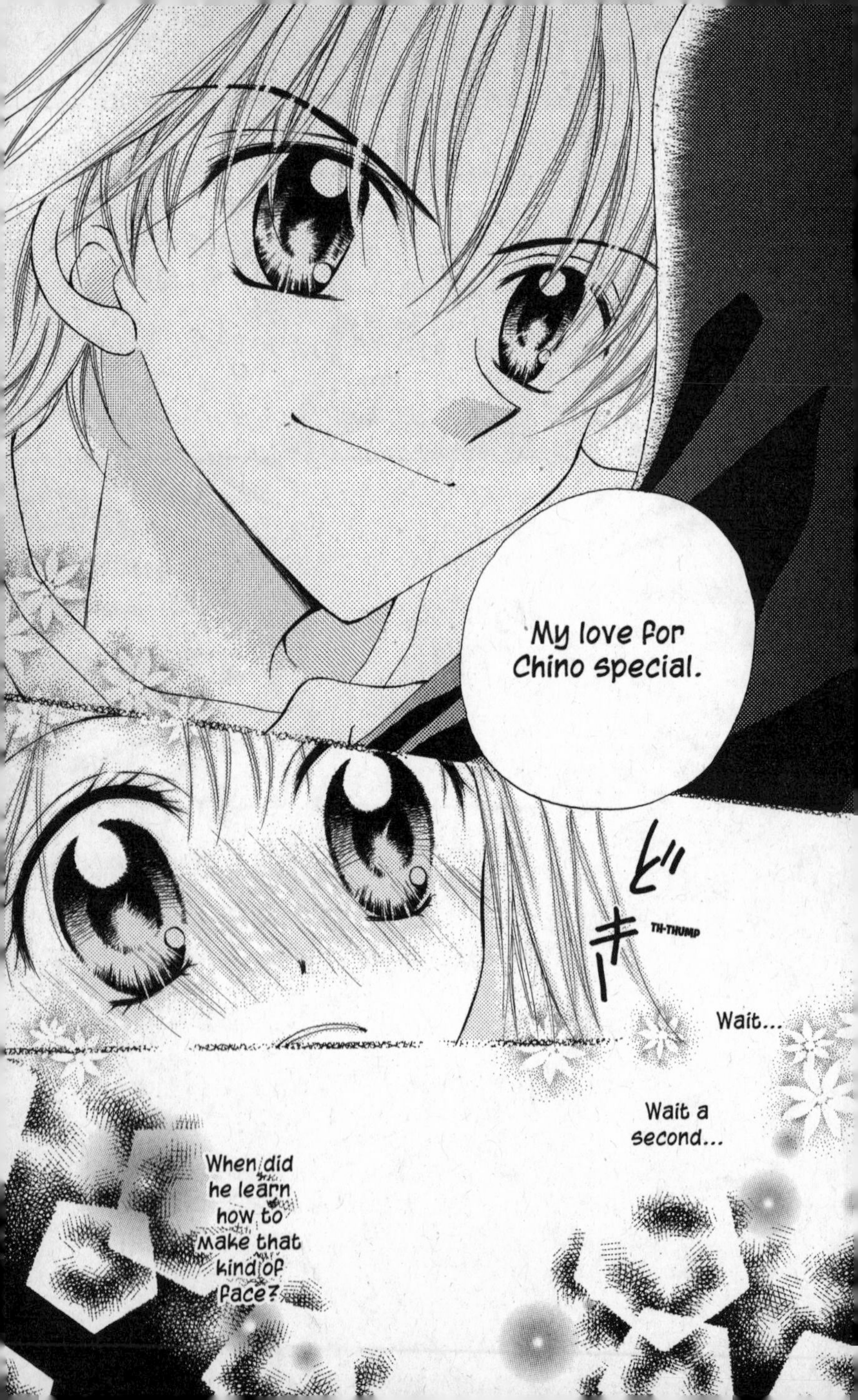
My love for Chino special.
ドキ
TH-THUMP
Wait...
Wait a second...
When did he learn how to make that kind of face?

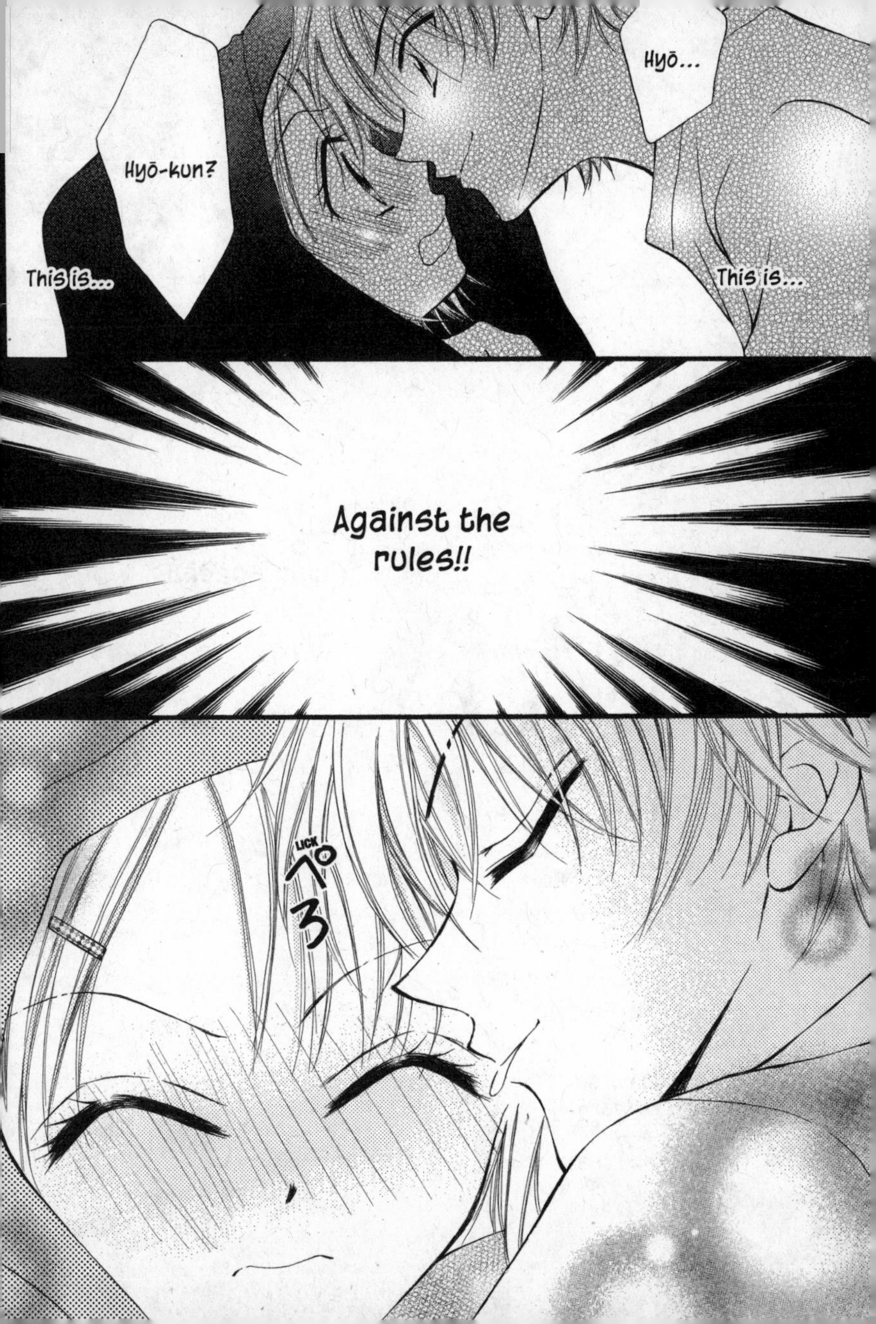
Hyō...
This is...
Hyō-kun?
This is...
Against the rules!!
LICK

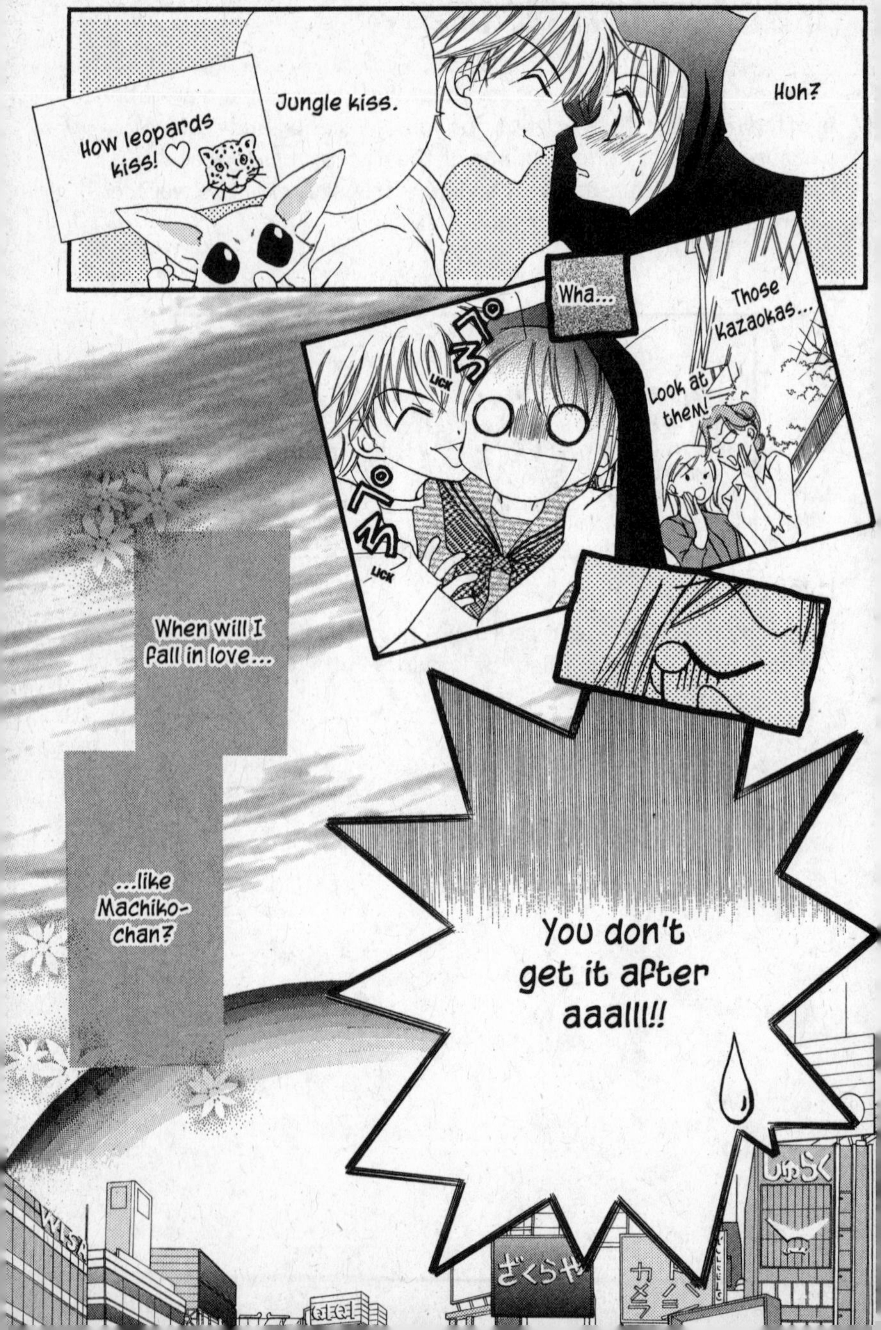
Huh?
Jungle kiss.
How leopards kiss! ♡
Those Kazaokas...
Wha...
Look at them!
LICK
LICK
You don't get it after aaalll!!
When will I fall in love...
...like Machiko-chan?
ざくらや

Translation Notes

Japanese is a tricky language for most Westerners, and translation is often more art than science. For your edification and reading pleasure, here are notes on some of the places where we could have gone in a different direction in our translation of the work, or where a Japanese cultural reference is used.

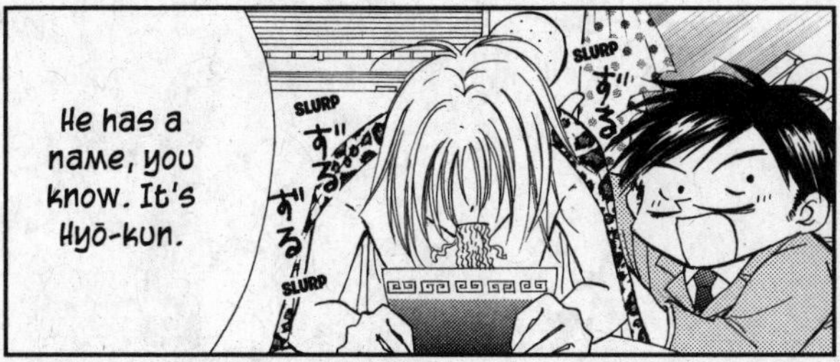
SLURP
ずる
He has a name, you know. It's Hyō-kun.
SLURP
ずる
ずる
SLURP

Hyō, page 16

Papa named the boy who rescued him from the lions "Hyō," or "leopard," since he was raised by leopards in the wild.

WiLD @ Heart

Volume 2

WiLD

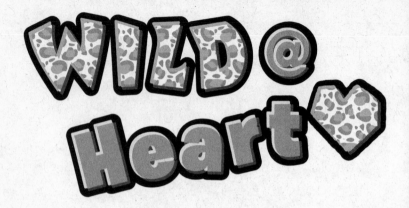

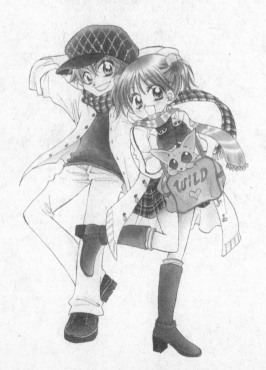

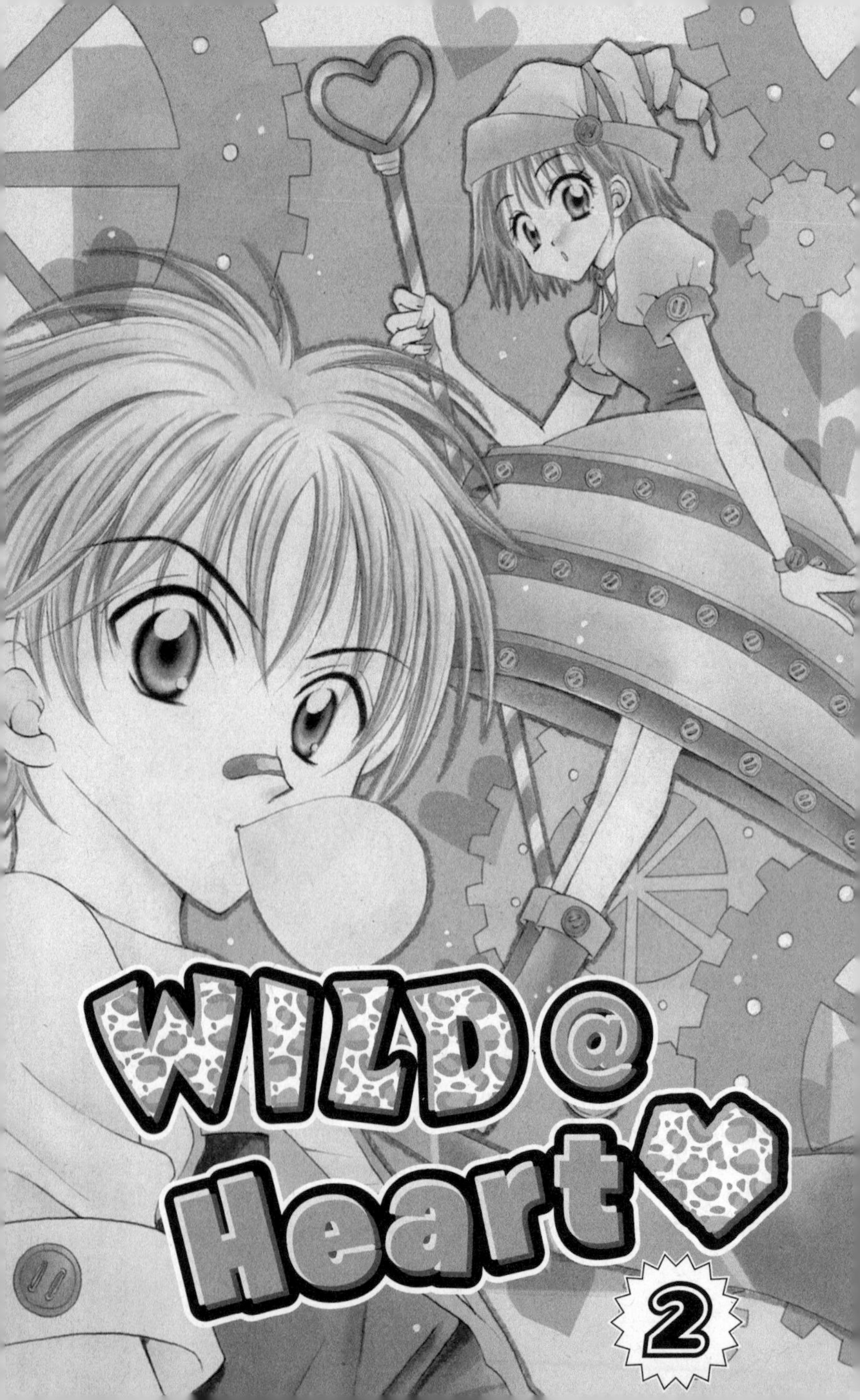
WILD @ Heart
2

WILD @ Heart ♥

The Story So Far ♡

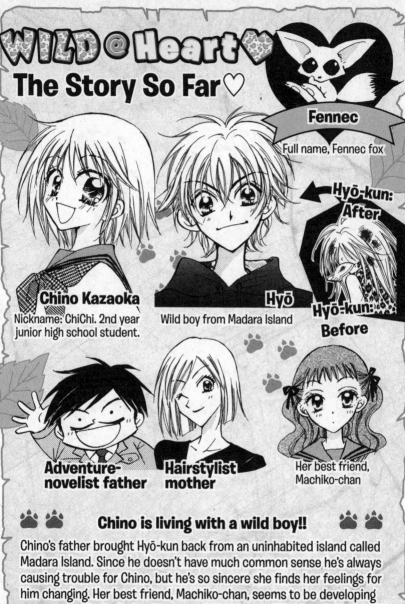

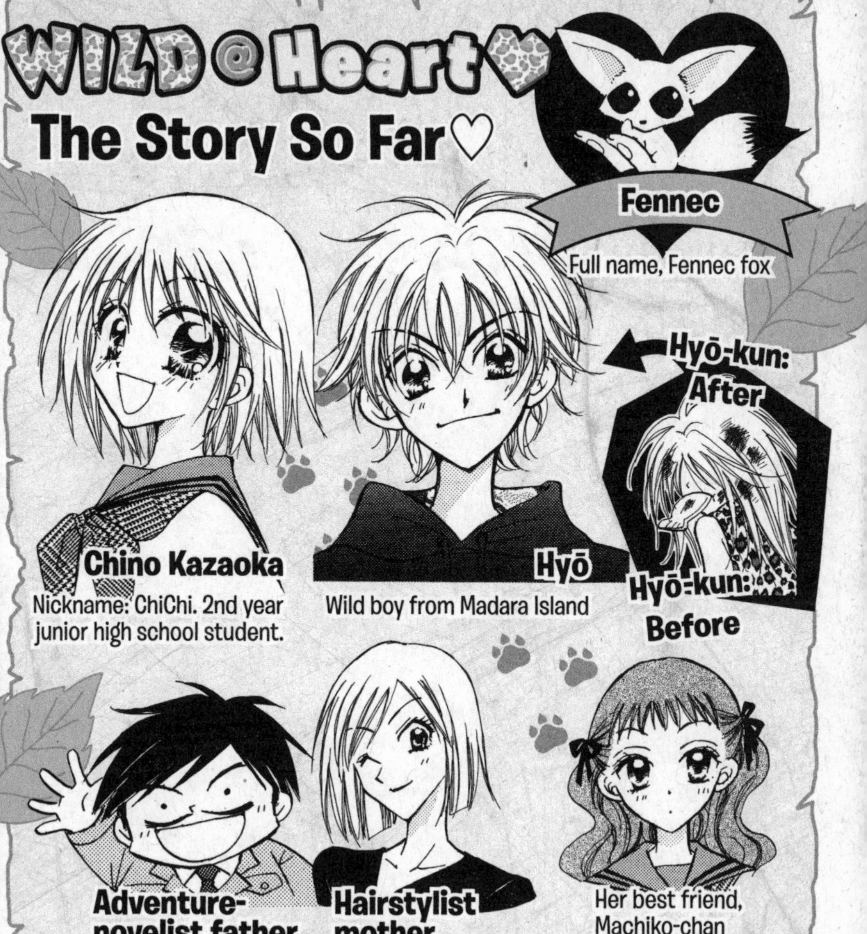
Fennec
Full name, Fennec fox
Hyō-kun: After
Hyō-kun: Before
Hyō
Wild boy from Madara Island
Chino Kazaoka
Nickname: ChiChi. 2nd year junior high school student.
Her best friend, Machiko-chan
Hairstylist mother
Adventure-novelist father

Chino is living with a wild boy!!

Chino's father brought Hyō-kun back from an uninhabited island called Madara Island. Since he doesn't have much common sense he's always causing trouble for Chino, but he's so sincere she finds her feelings for him changing. Her best friend, Machiko-chan, seems to be developing some romantic feelings of her own. Will Chino and Hyō-kun fall in love?!

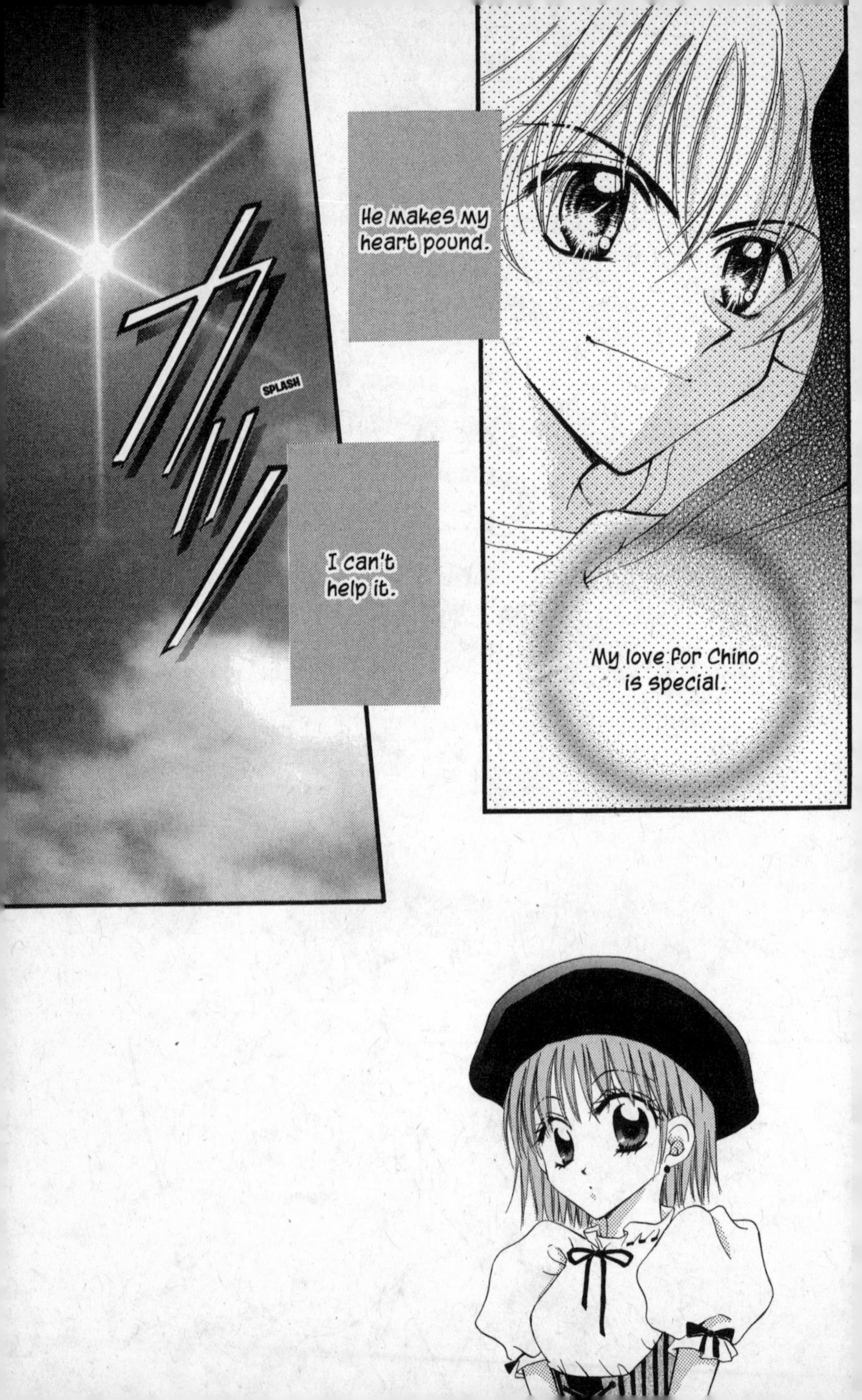
My love for Chino is special.
He makes my heart pound.
I can't help it.
カッ
SPLASH

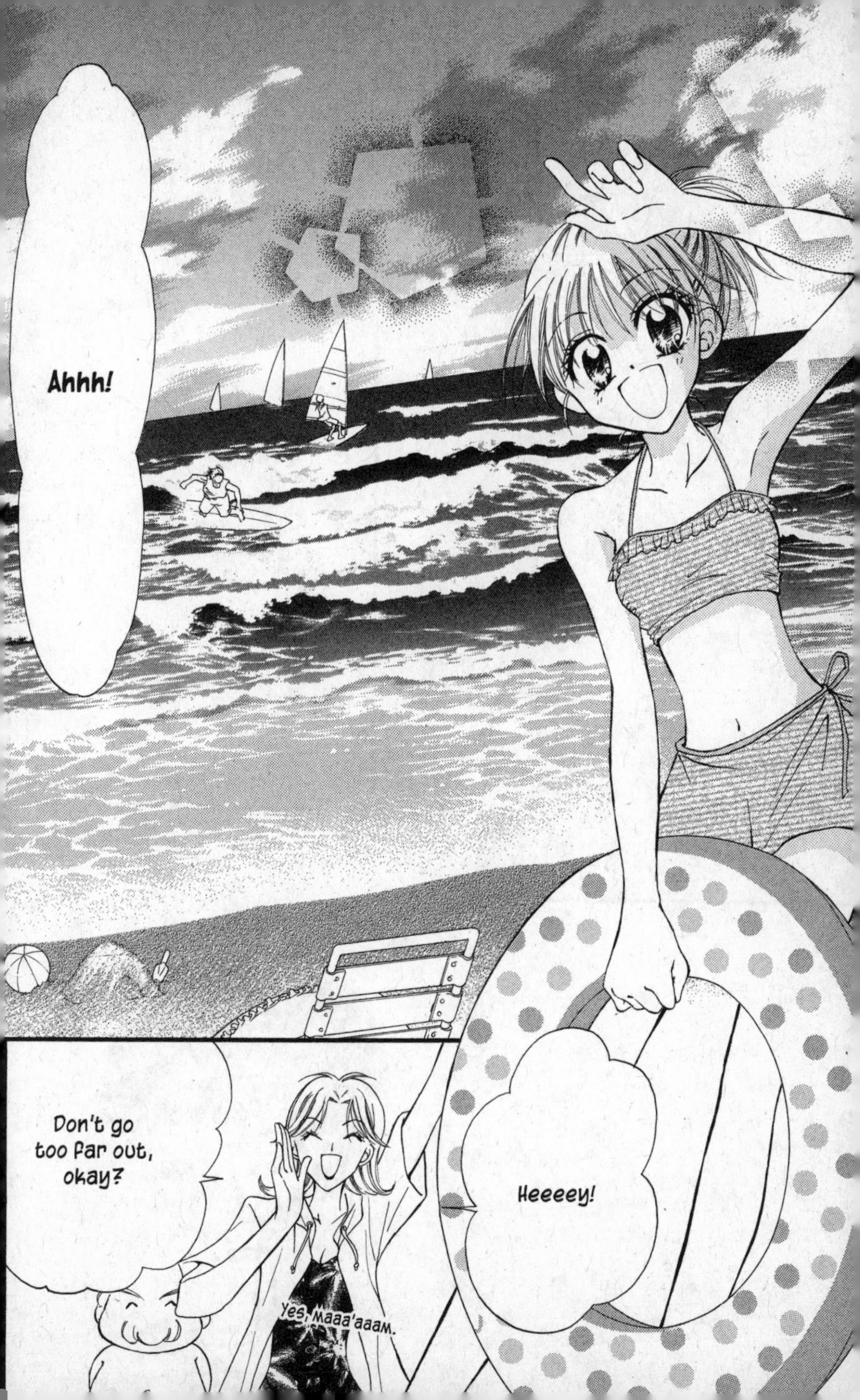
Ahhh!
Heeeey!
Don't go too far out, okay?
Yes, Maaa'aaam.

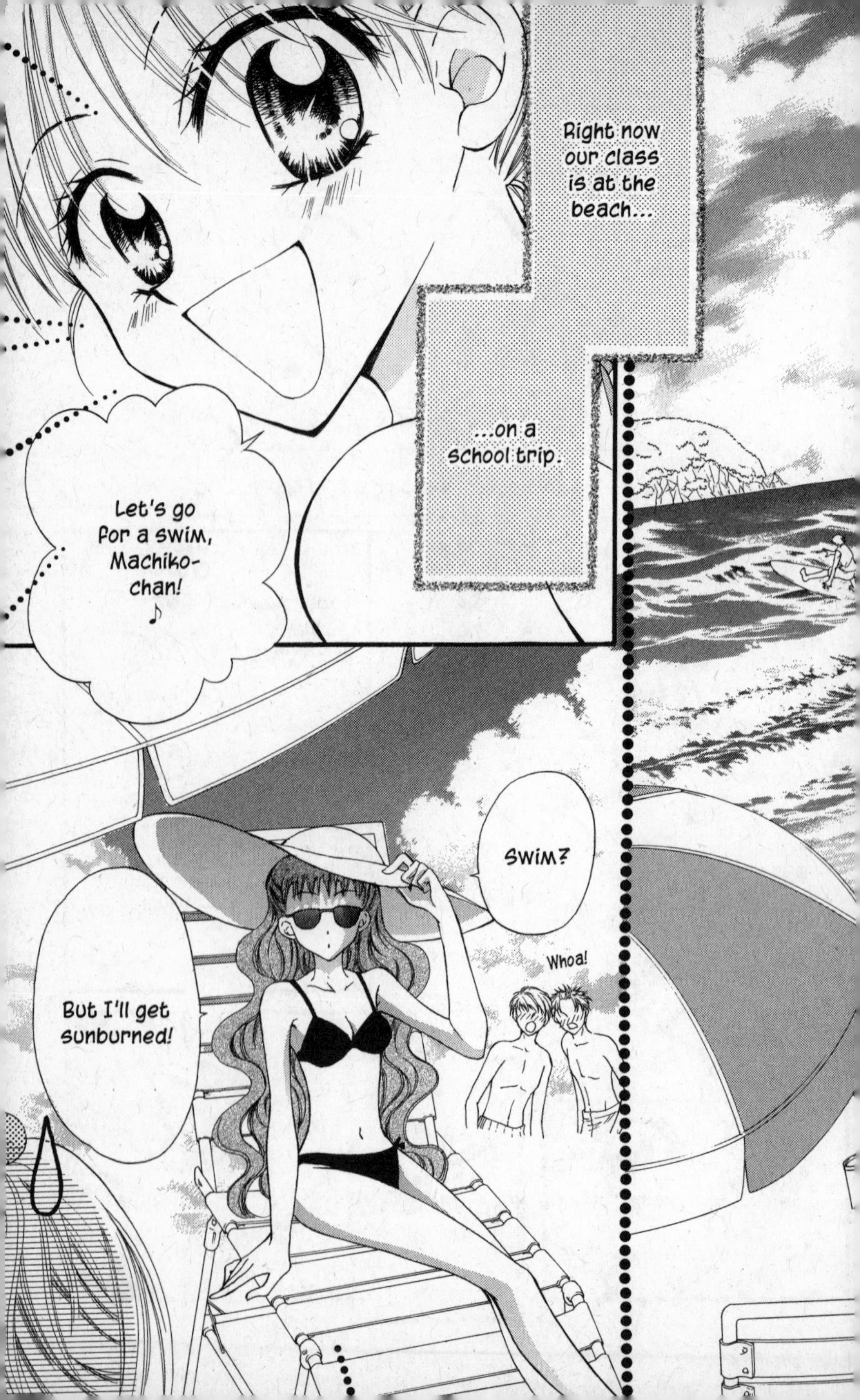
Right now our class is at the beach...
...on a school trip.
Let's go for a swim, Machiko-chan! ♪
Swim?
Whoa!
But I'll get sunburned!

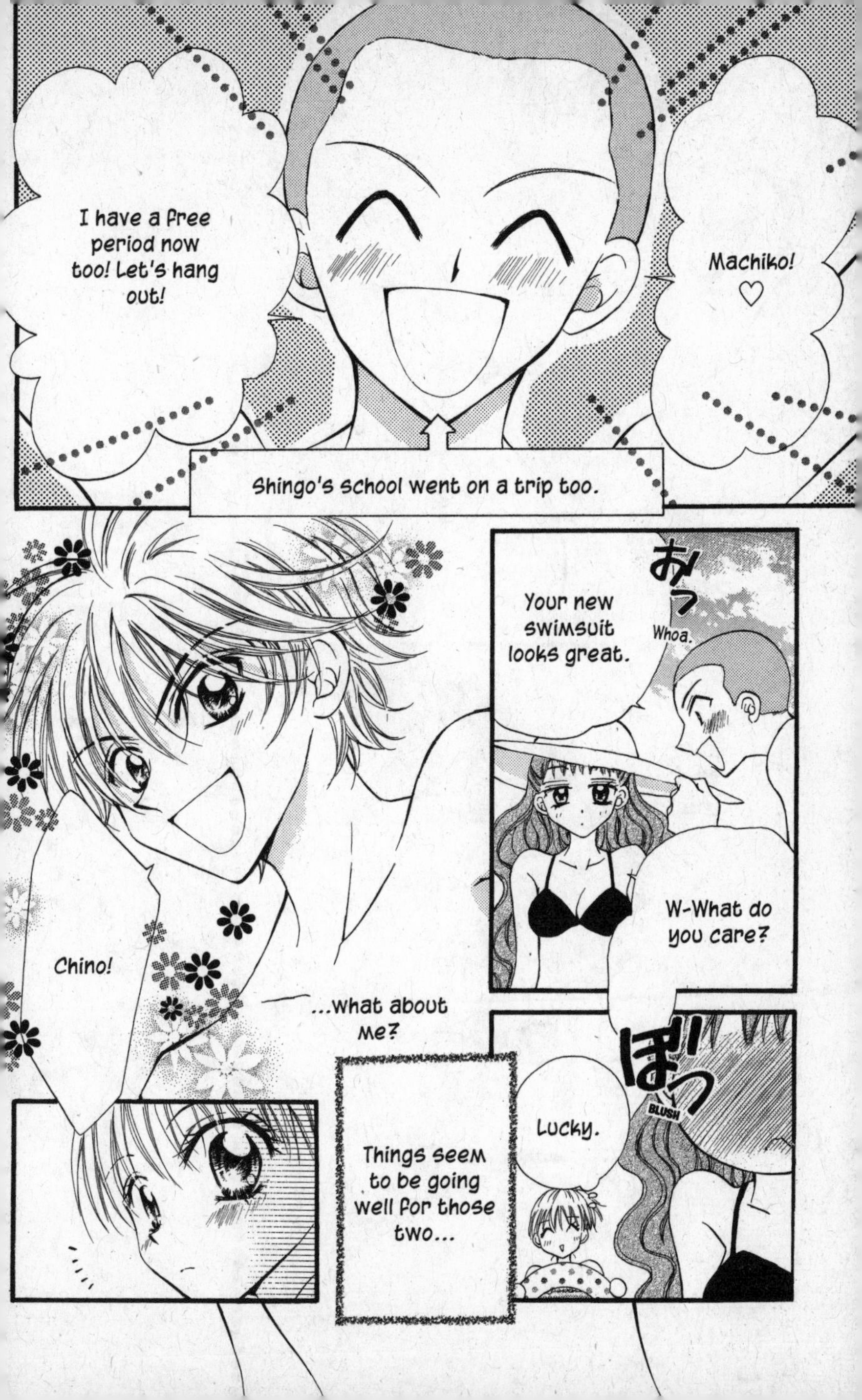
Machiko! ♡
I have a free period now too! Let's hang out!
Shingo's school went on a trip too.
おっ
Whoa.
Your new swimsuit looks great.
W-What do you care?
ぼっ
BLUSH
Lucky.
Things seem to be going well for those two...
Chino!
...what about me?

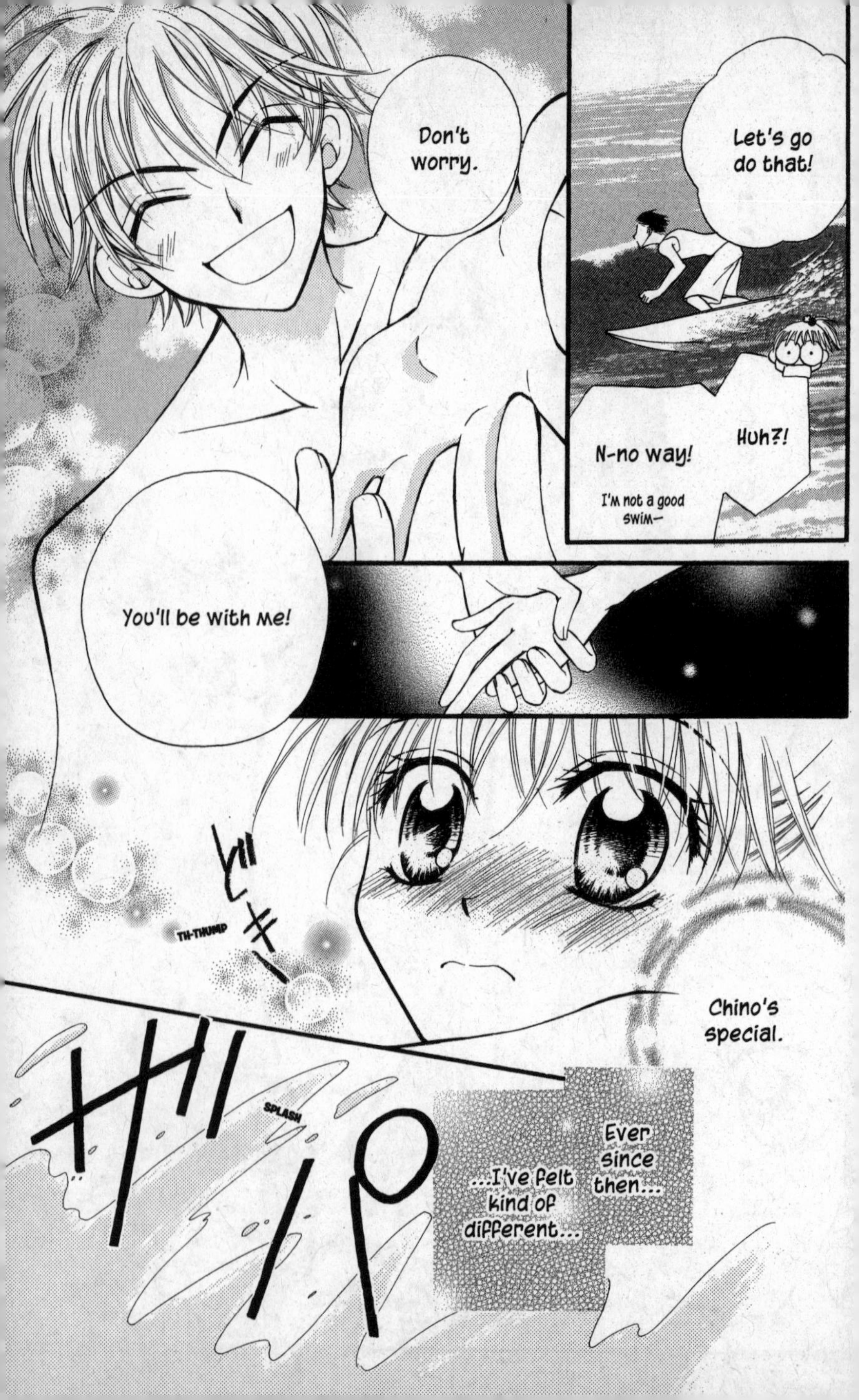
Let's go do that!
Huh?!
N-no way!
I'm not a good swim—
Don't worry.
You'll be with me!
TH-THUMP
Chino's special.
Ever since then...
...I've felt kind of different...
SPLASH

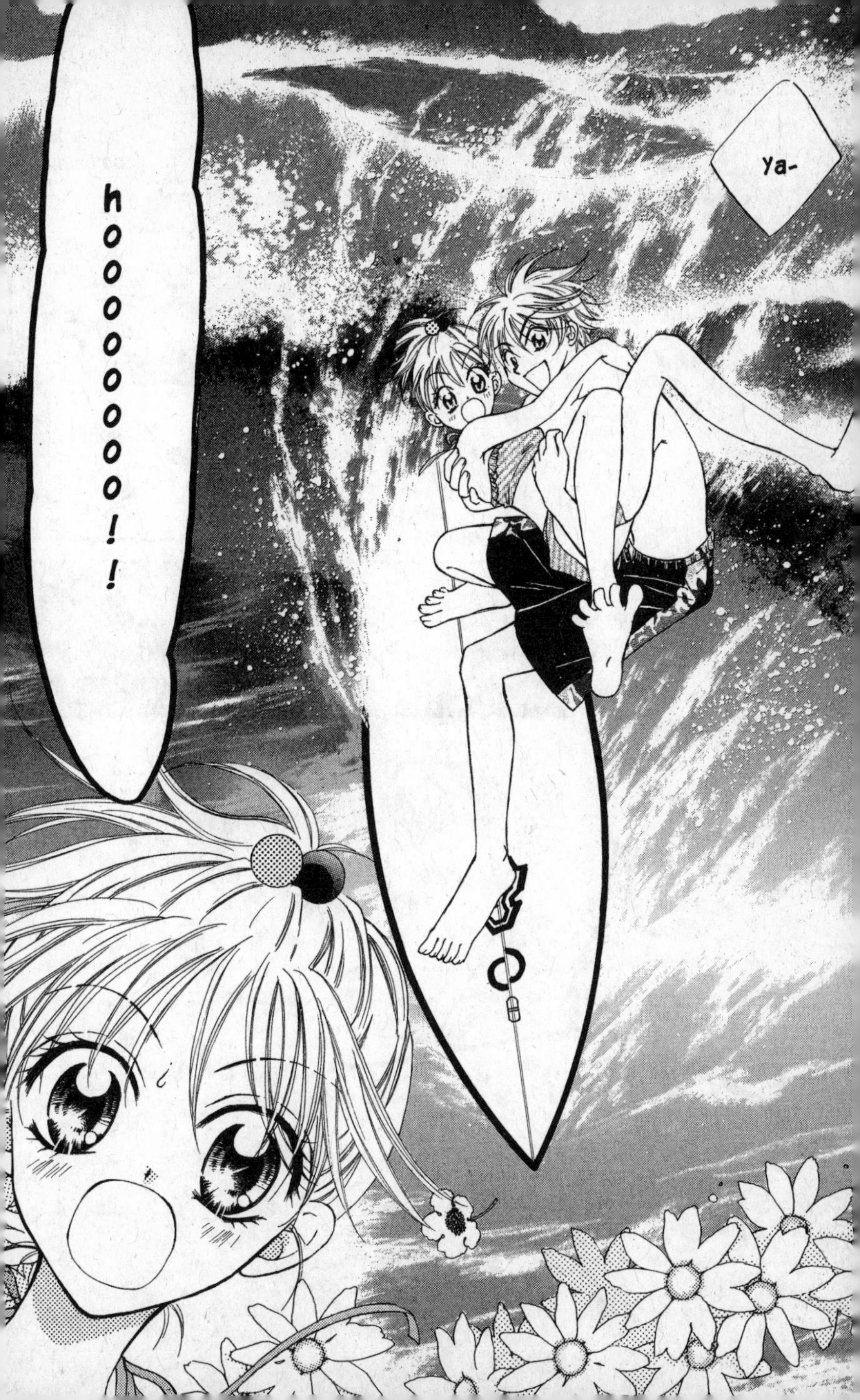
Ya-
hooooooooo!!

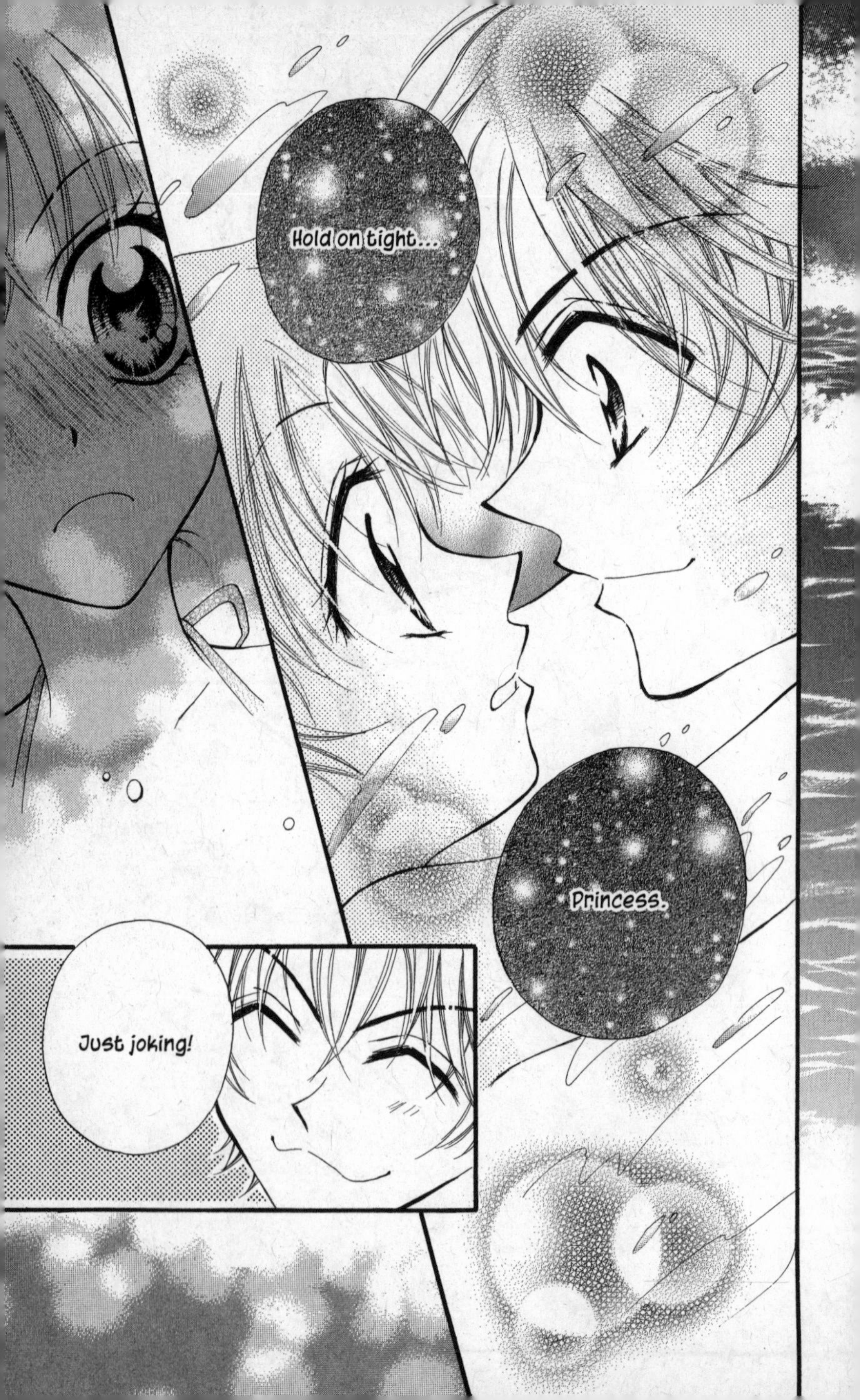
Hold on tight...
Princess.
Just joking!

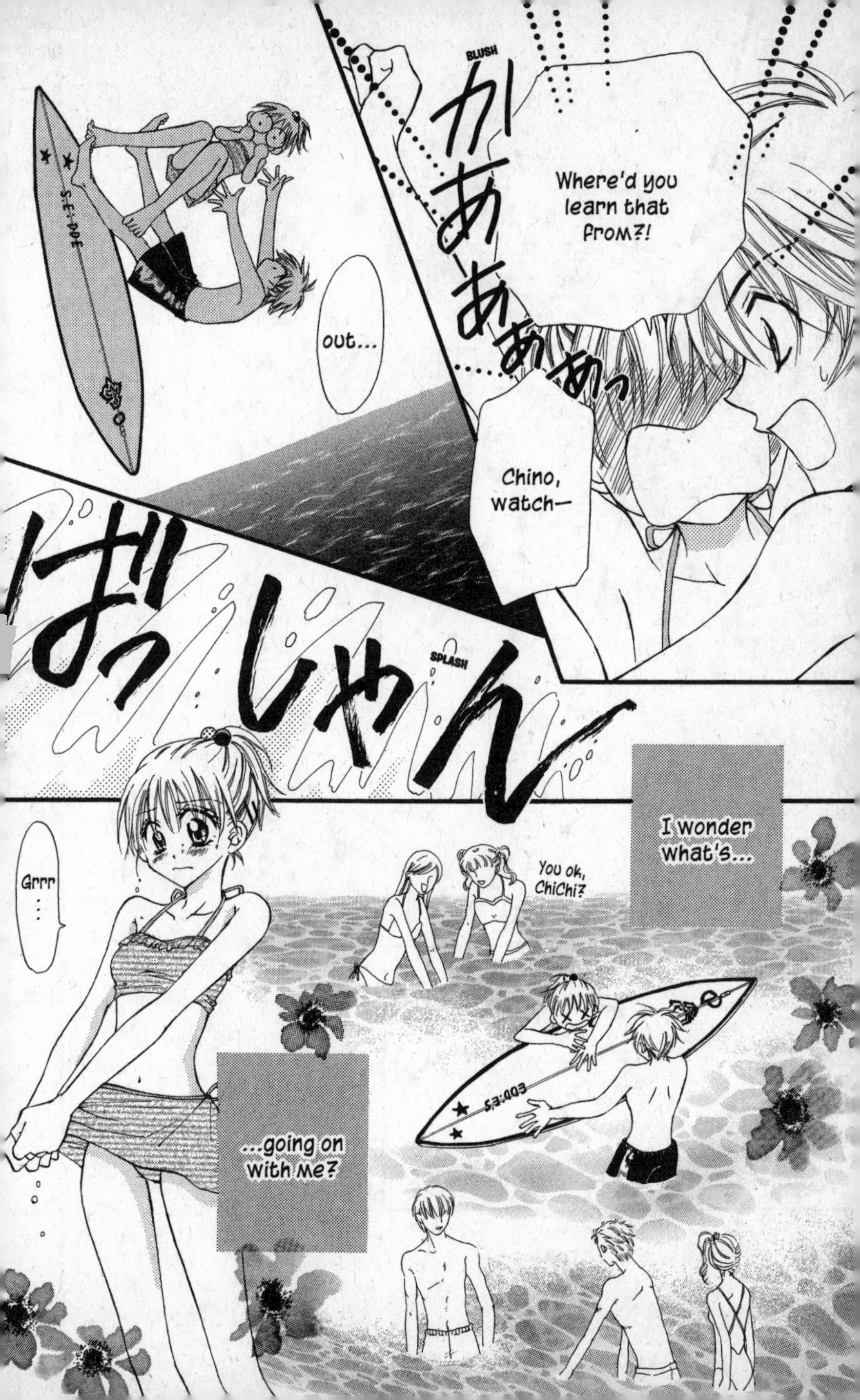
BLUSH
Where'd you learn that from?!
Chino, watch—
out...
SPLASH
ばっしゃん
I wonder what's...
You ok, ChiChi?
...going on with me?
Grrr...

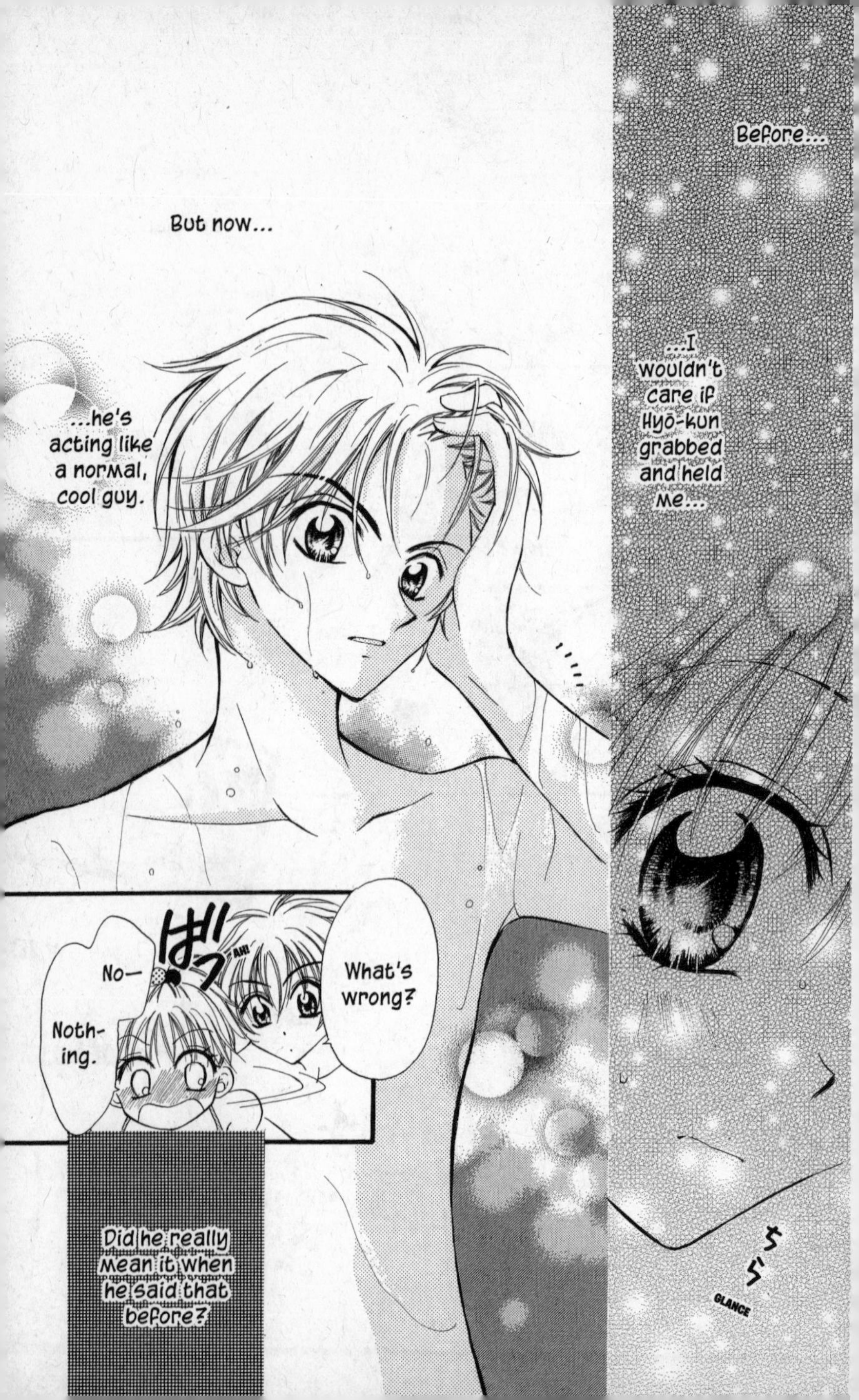
Before...
...I wouldn't care if Hyō-kun grabbed and held me...
ちら
GLANCE
But now...
...he's acting like a normal, cool guy.
.....
What's wrong?
ぱっ
AH!
No— Noth-ing.
Did he really mean it when he said that before?

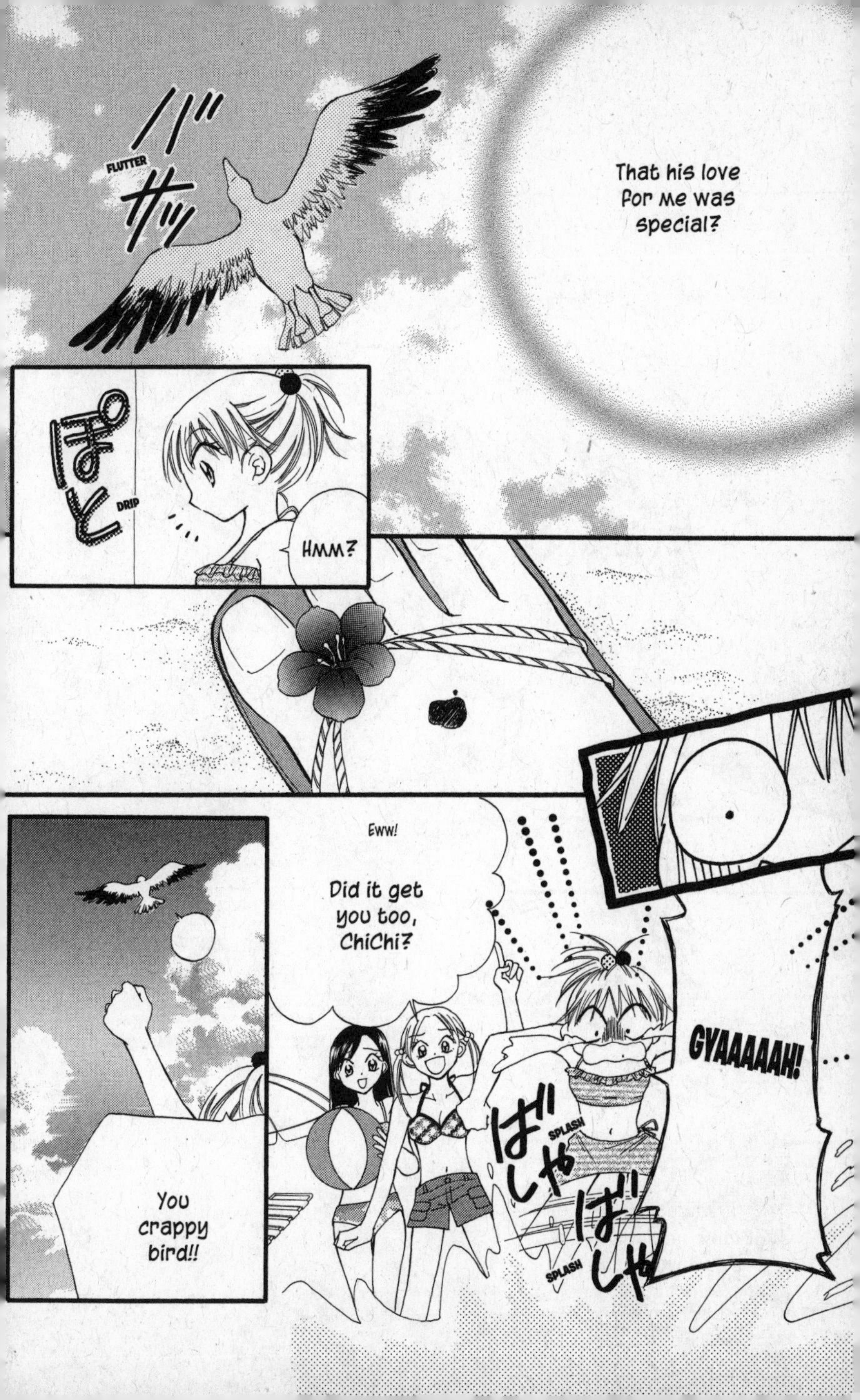
That his love for me was special?
バザッ
FLUTTER
HMM?
ぽと
DRIP
GYAAAAH!
Eww!
Did it get you too, ChiChi?
ばしゃ
SPLASH
ばしゃ
SPLASH
You crappy bird!!

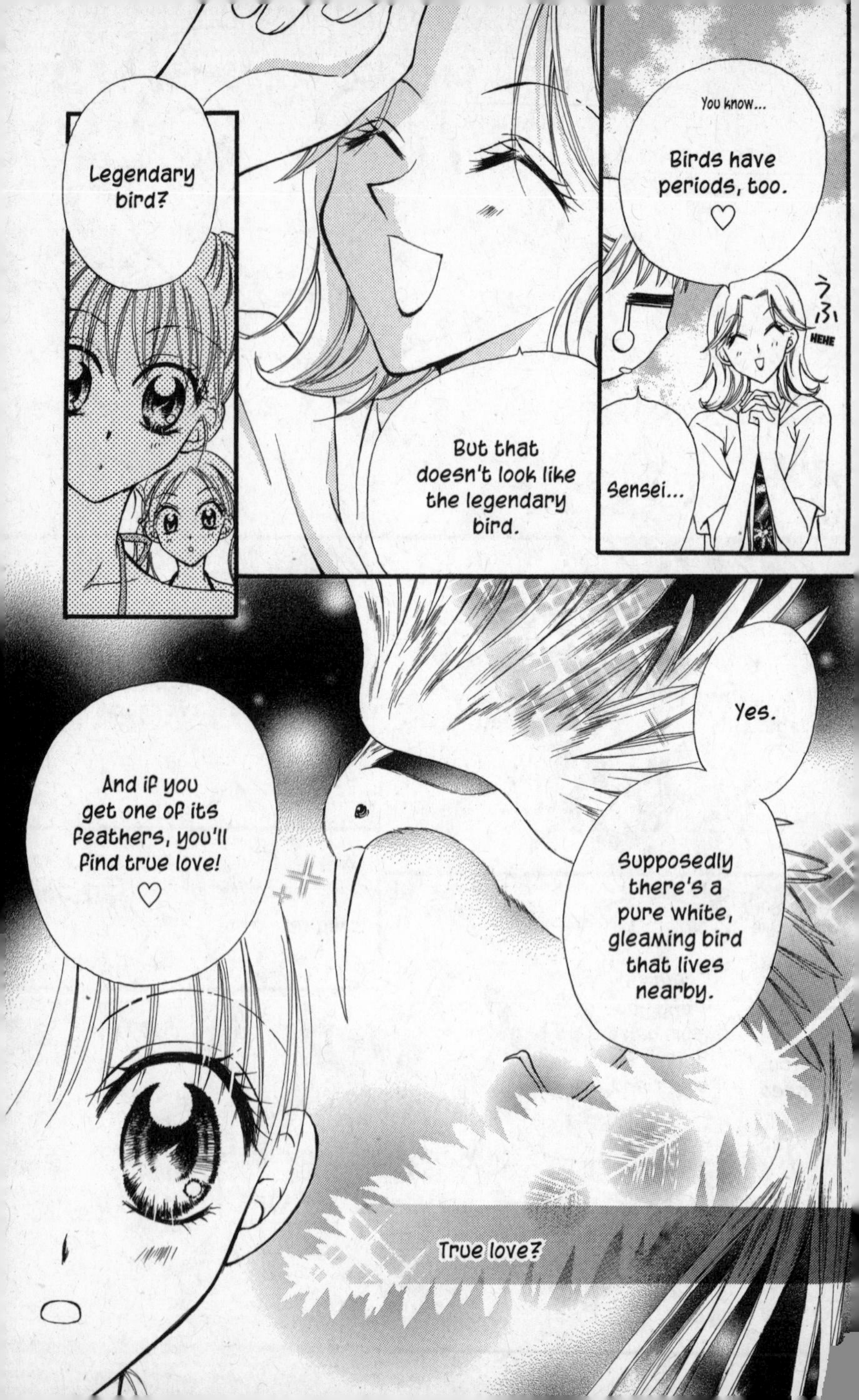
You know...
Birds have periods, too. ♡
うふ
HEHE
Sensei...
But that doesn't look like the legendary bird.
Legendary bird?
Yes.
Supposedly there's a pure white, gleaming bird that lives nearby.
And if you get one of its feathers, you'll find true love! ♡
True love?

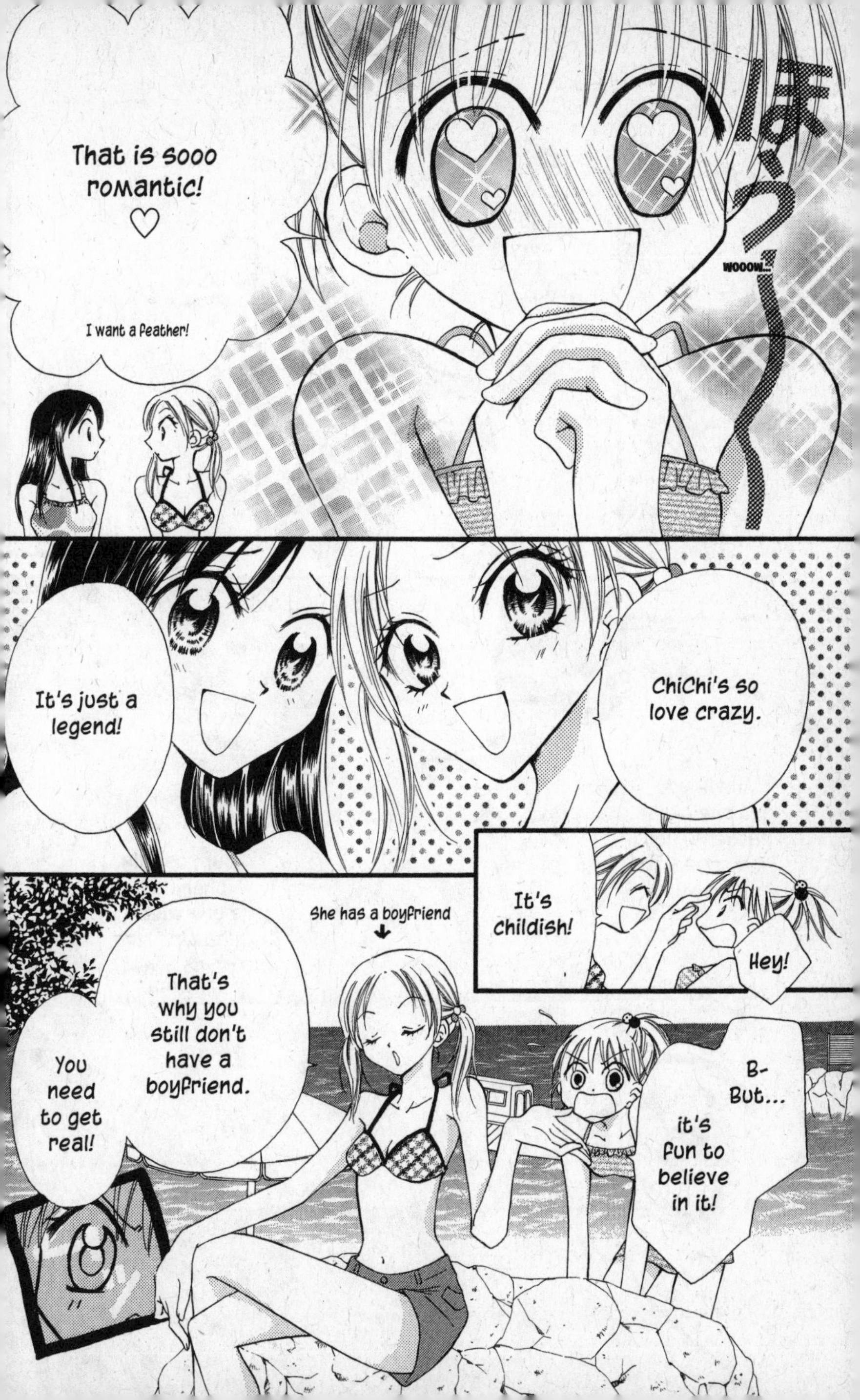
ほう
wooow...
That is sooo romantic! ♡
I want a feather!
ChiChi's so love crazy.
It's just a legend!
It's Childish!
Hey!
B- But... it's fun to believe in it!
She has a boyfriend
That's why you still don't have a boyfriend.
You need to get real!

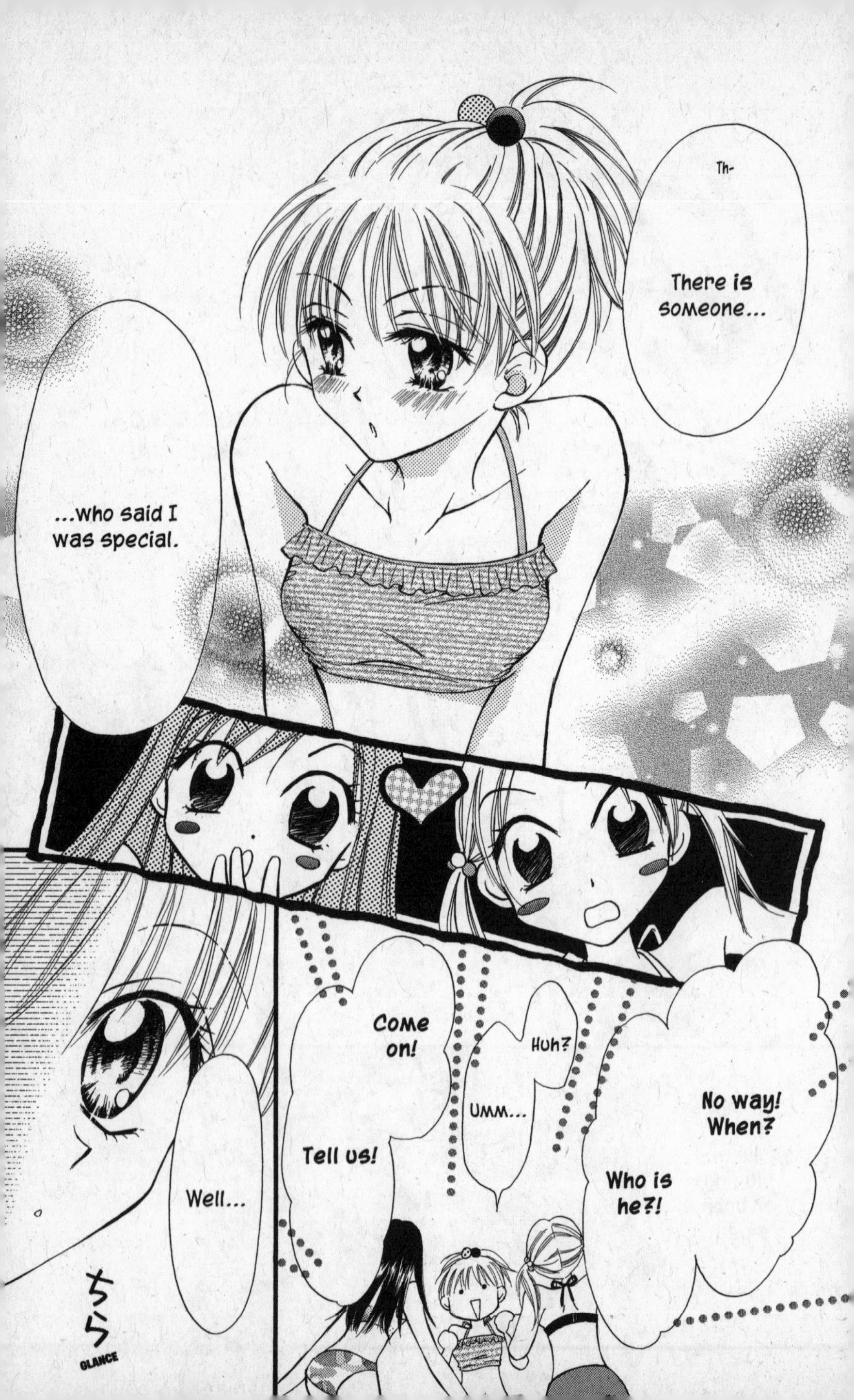
Th-
There is someone...
...who said I was special.
No way! When?
Who is he?!
Huh?
Umm...
Come on!
Tell us!
Well...
ちら
GLANCE

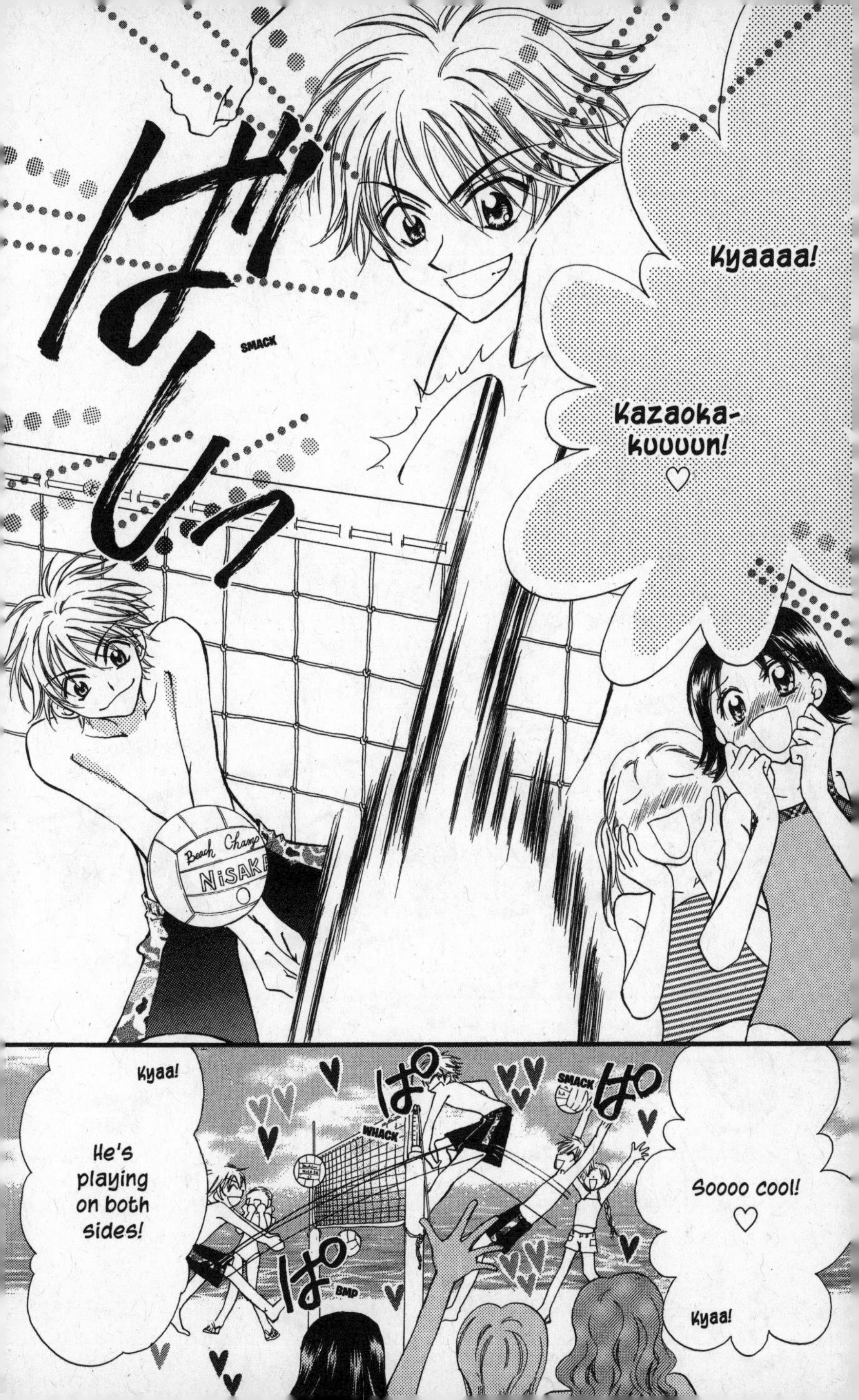
Kyaaaa!
Kazaoka-kuuuun! ♡
ばしっ
SMACK
Soooo cool! ♡
Kyaa!
ぱ
SMACK
ぱ
WHACK
ぱ
BMP
Kyaa!
He's playing on both sides!

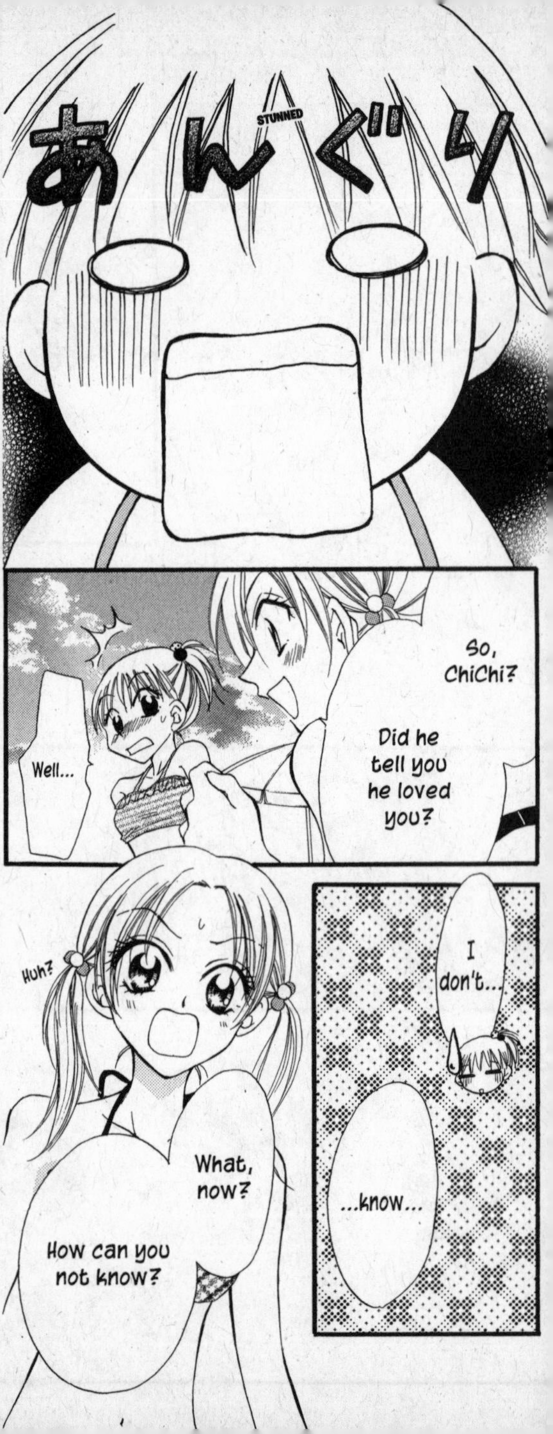
あんぐり
STUNNED
So, ChiChi?
Did he tell you he loved you?
Well...
I don't...
...know...
Huh?
What, now?
How can you not know?

1.

Hi everyone! ♪
Welcome to Wild @ Heart volume 2!

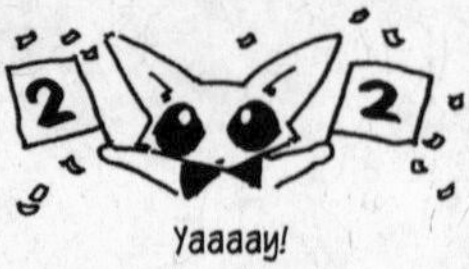
2
2
Yaaaay!

I illustrated the cover with a Chinese theme this time. Not that it has anything to do with China. But I did have a craving for Chinese food when I drew it. ♡ Haha. I never got to have any, though. I did have ujikintoki, though. It had an interesting taste... Machiko ♡ and Shingo are on the back. But now, looking back on it, they didn't really show up much in this volume.
Their profiles are in this volume, though, so make sure to check it! ♡
I had lots of free space for sidebars this volume so please read if you have time~

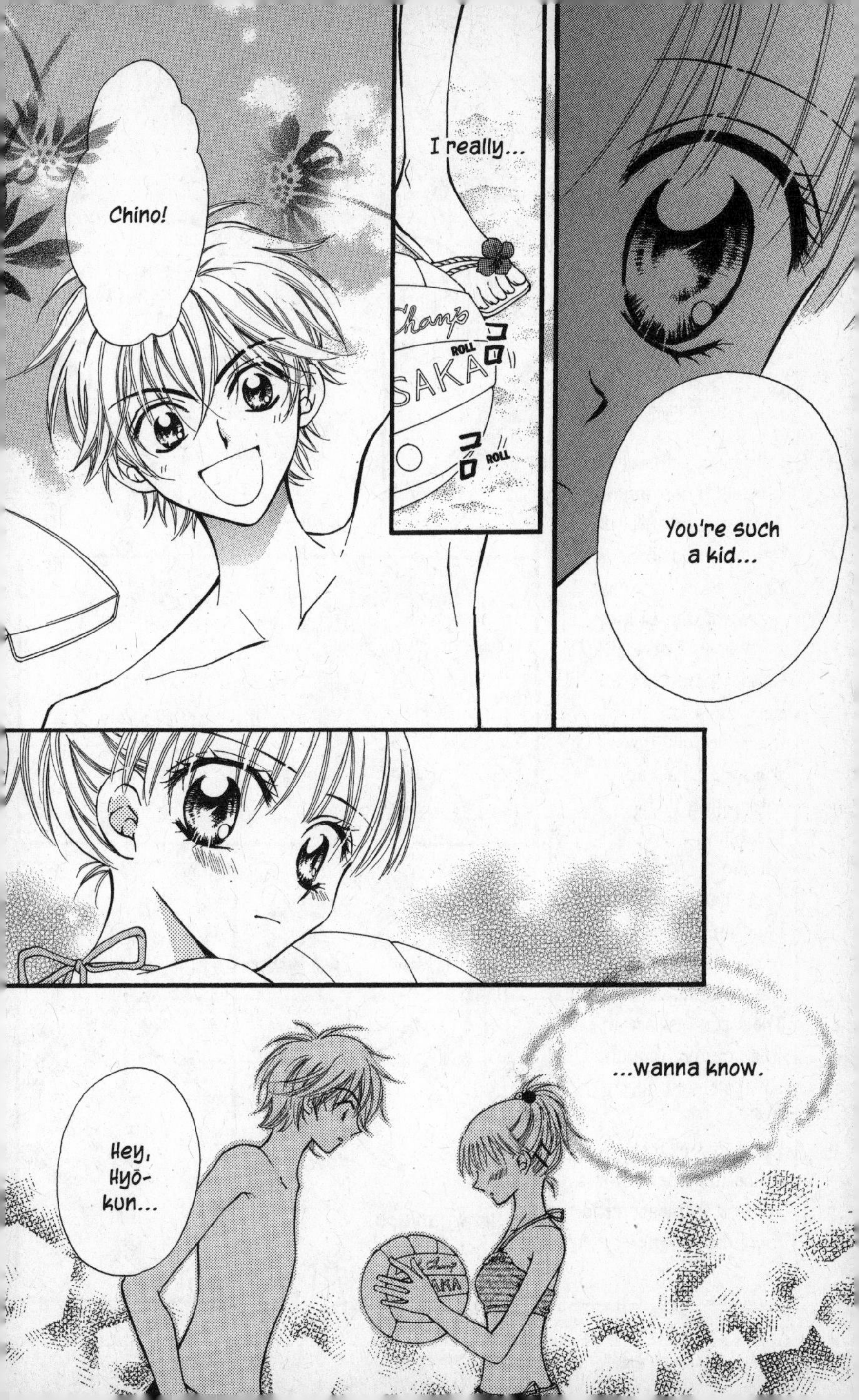
You're such a kid...
I really...
Champ
SAKA
コロ ROLL
コロ ROLL
Chino!
...wanna know.
Hey, Hyō-kun...

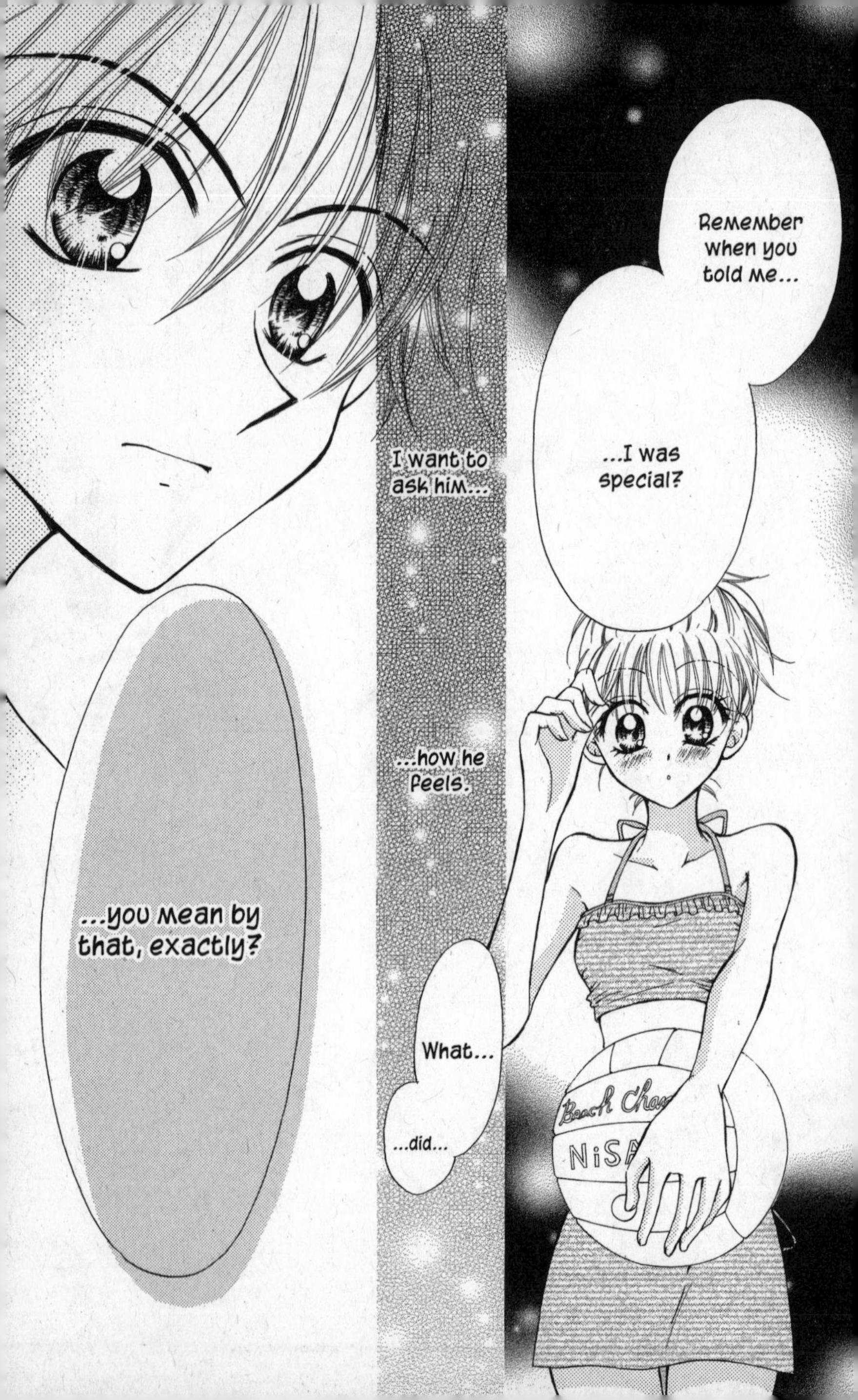
Remember when you told me...
...I was special?
I want to ask him...
...how he feels.
What...
...did...
...you mean by that, exactly?

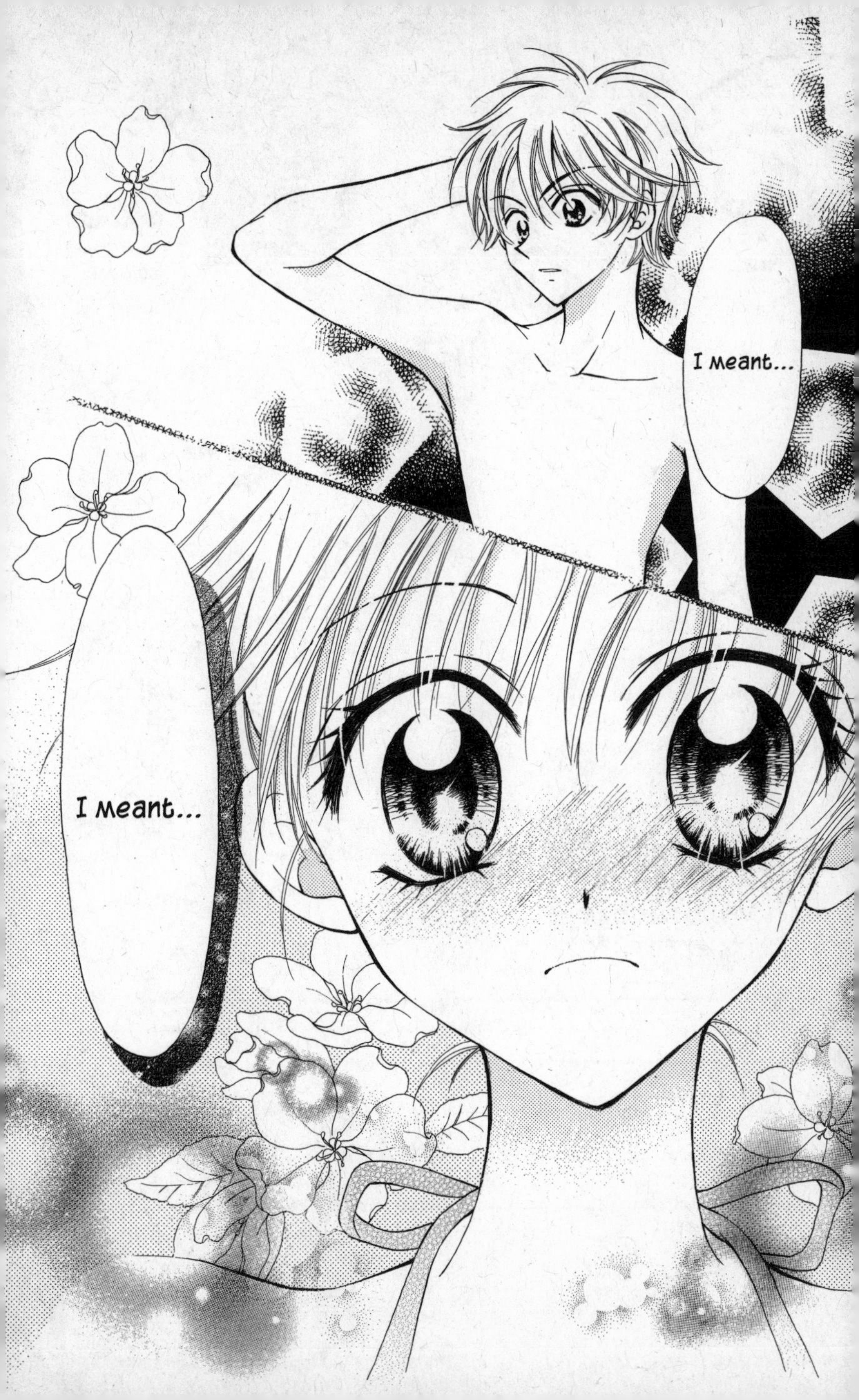
I meant...
I meant...

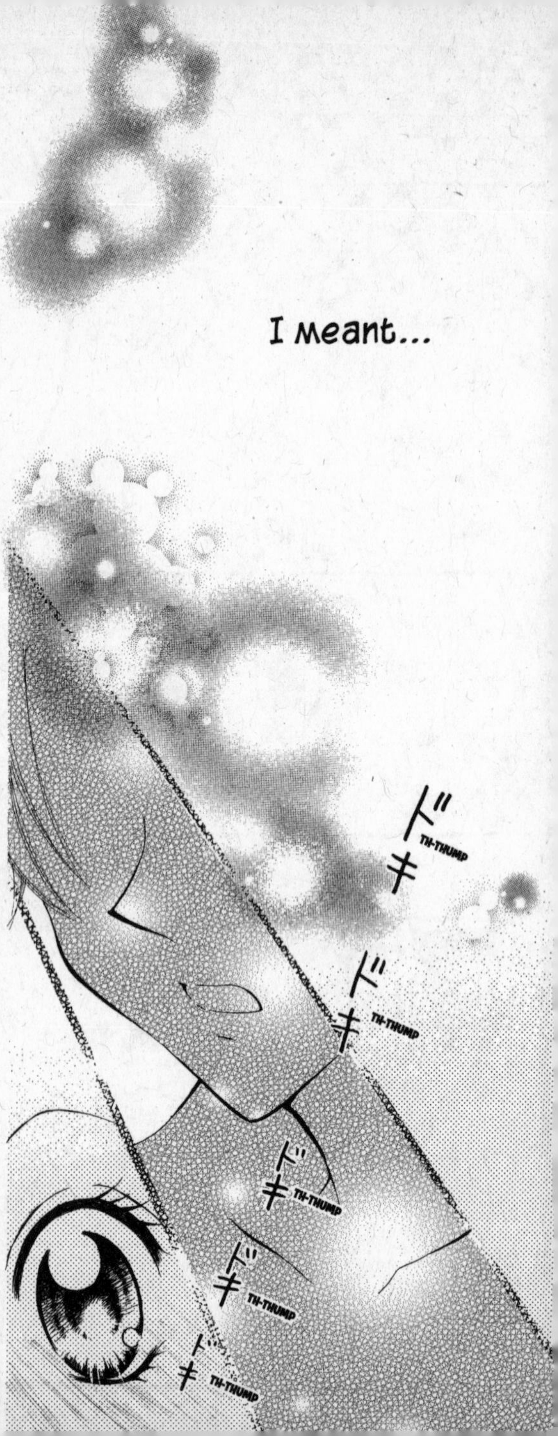
I meant...
ドキ TH-THUMP
ドキ TH-THUMP
ドキ TH-THUMP
ドキ TH-THUMP
ドキ TH-THUMP

2.

School trips...I never got to go to the beach. In middle school we went camping in the mountains!! We had a campfire at night, and I'm pretty sure we did little skits. We did Snow White and Cinderella and Kaguya-hime. I played Kaguya-hime! ♡ HOWEVER, for some reason in that skit Kaguya-hime was the villain. 💧 I don't remember the details but I think Cinderella, Snow White and Kaguya-hime were like the three wicked stepsisters...

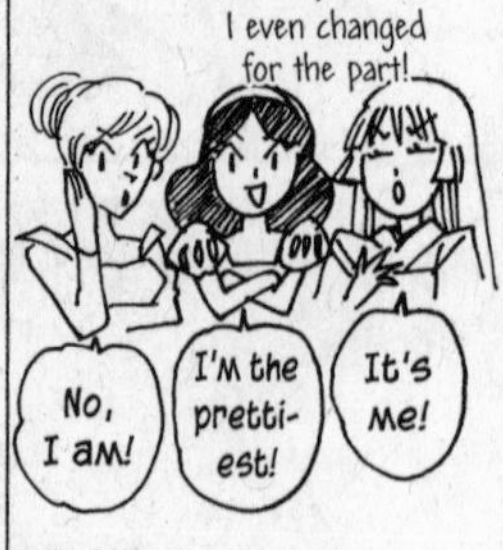
I even changed for the part!
No, I am!
I'm the pretti-est!
It's me!

That's how it was...
But it was so fun. ♪ I loved that part.
We always told scary stories, too. When we saw a light on the mountain across the way someone said, "There are marionettes over there!" and I actually believed them and didn't go to the bathroom that night!

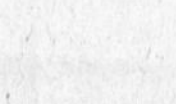
Tears

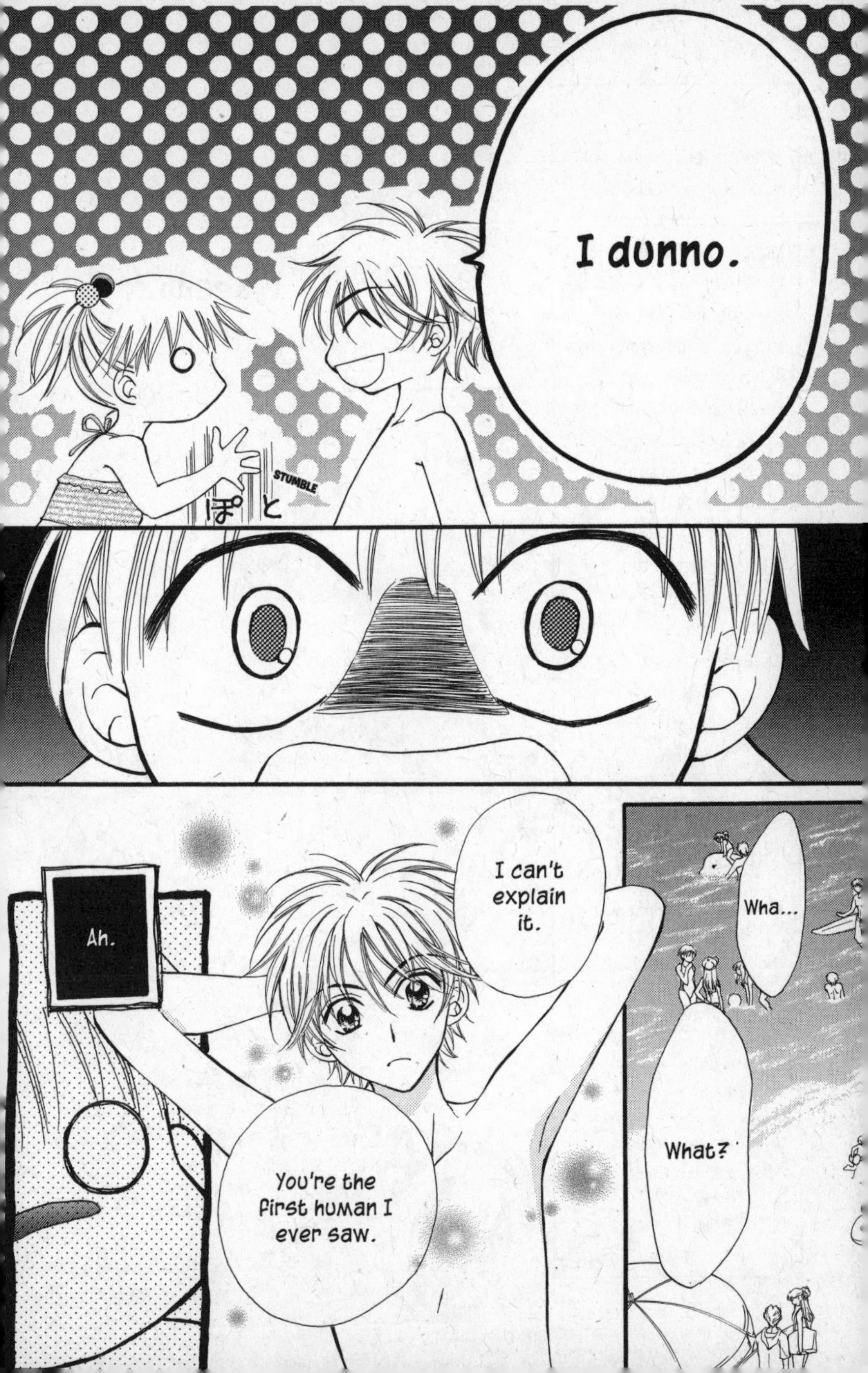
I dunno.
STUMBLE
ぽと
Wha...
What?
I can't explain it.
You're the first human I ever saw.
Ah.

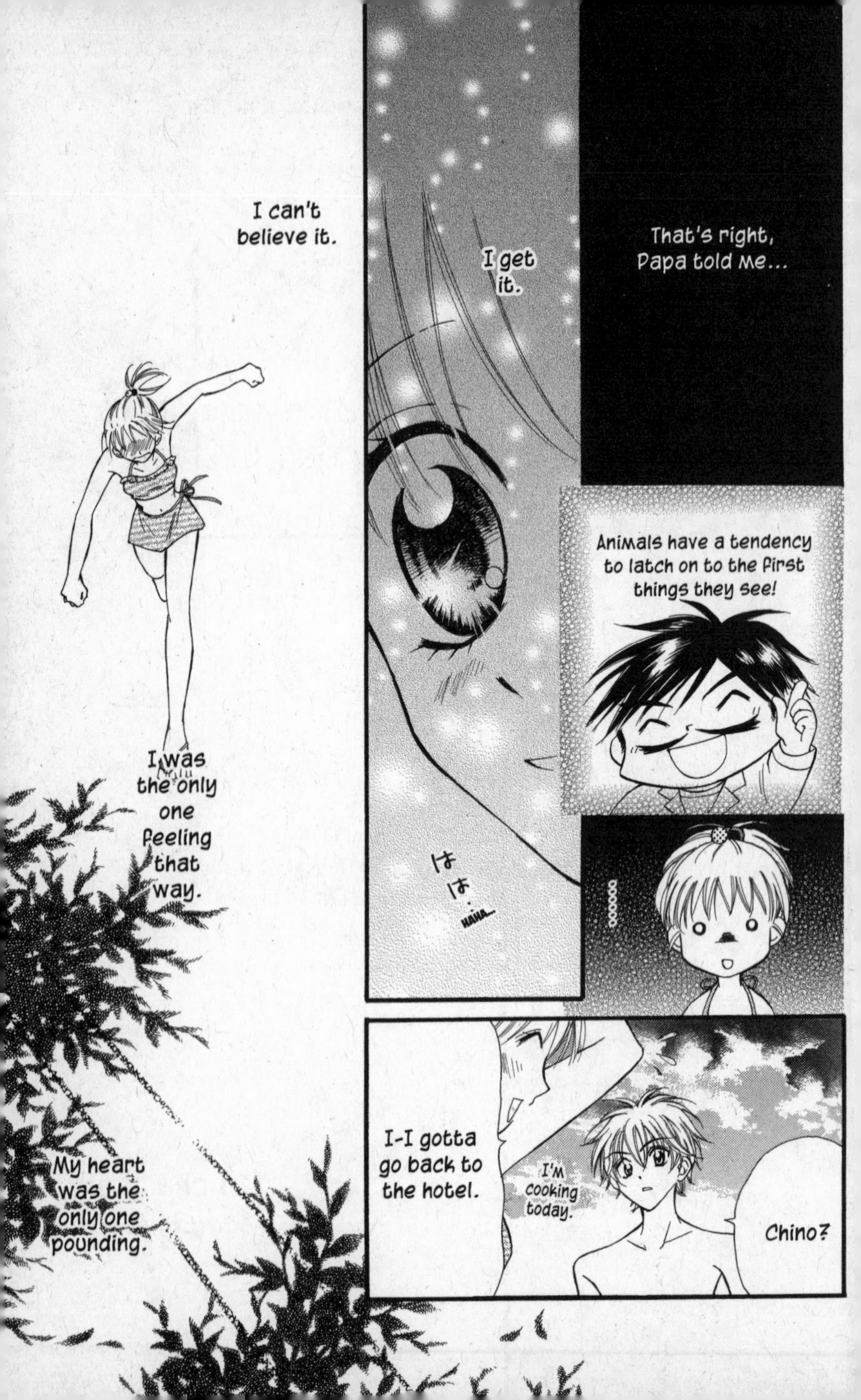
That's right, Papa told me...
Animals have a tendency to latch on to the first things they see!
ooooo
I get it.
はは
HAHA
Chino?
I'm cooking today.
I-I gotta go back to the hotel.
I can't believe it.
I was the only one feeling that way.
My heart was the only one pounding.

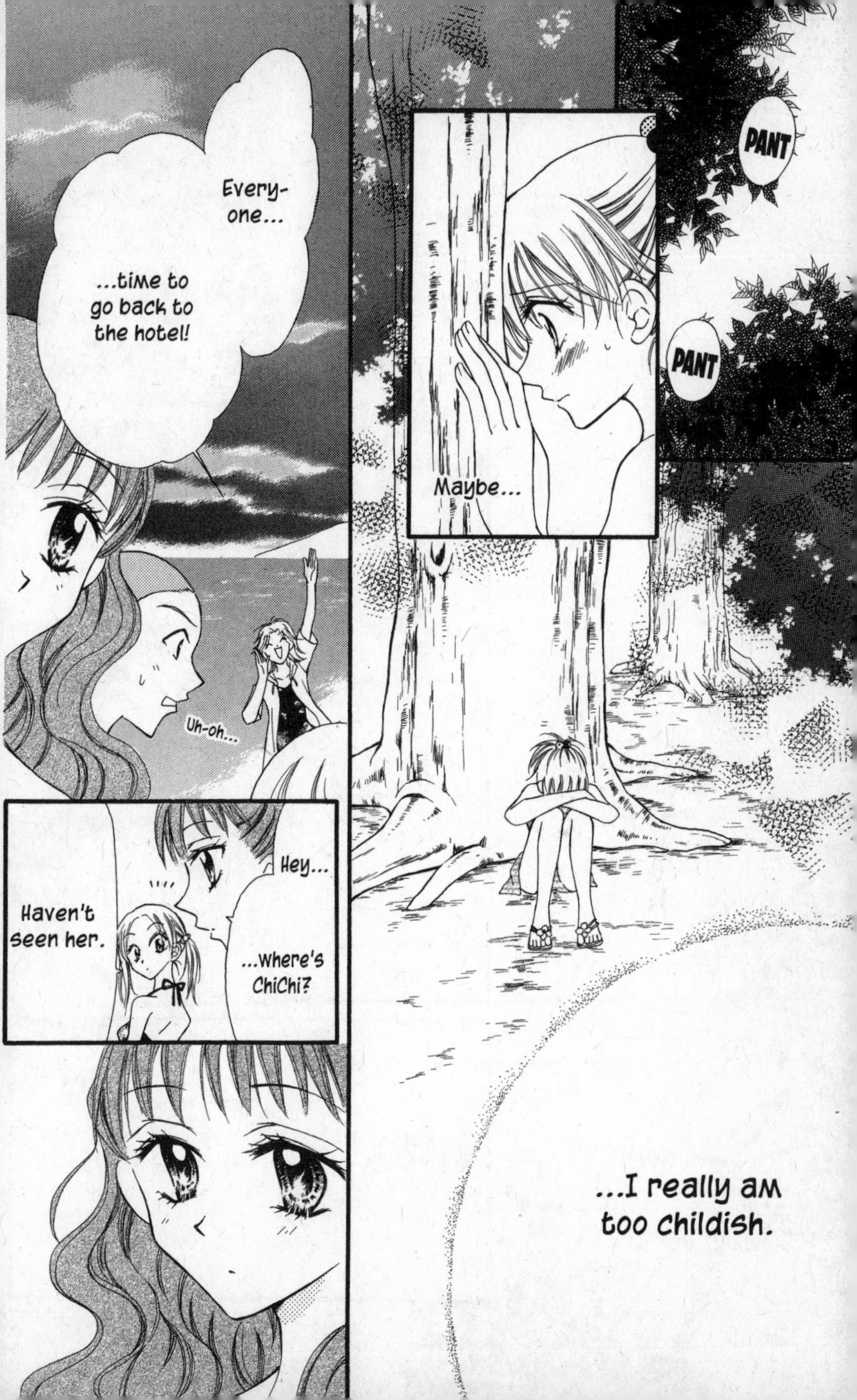
PANT
PANT
Maybe...
...I really am too childish.
Every-one...
...time to go back to the hotel!
Uh-oh...
Hey...
...where's ChiChi?
Haven't seen her.

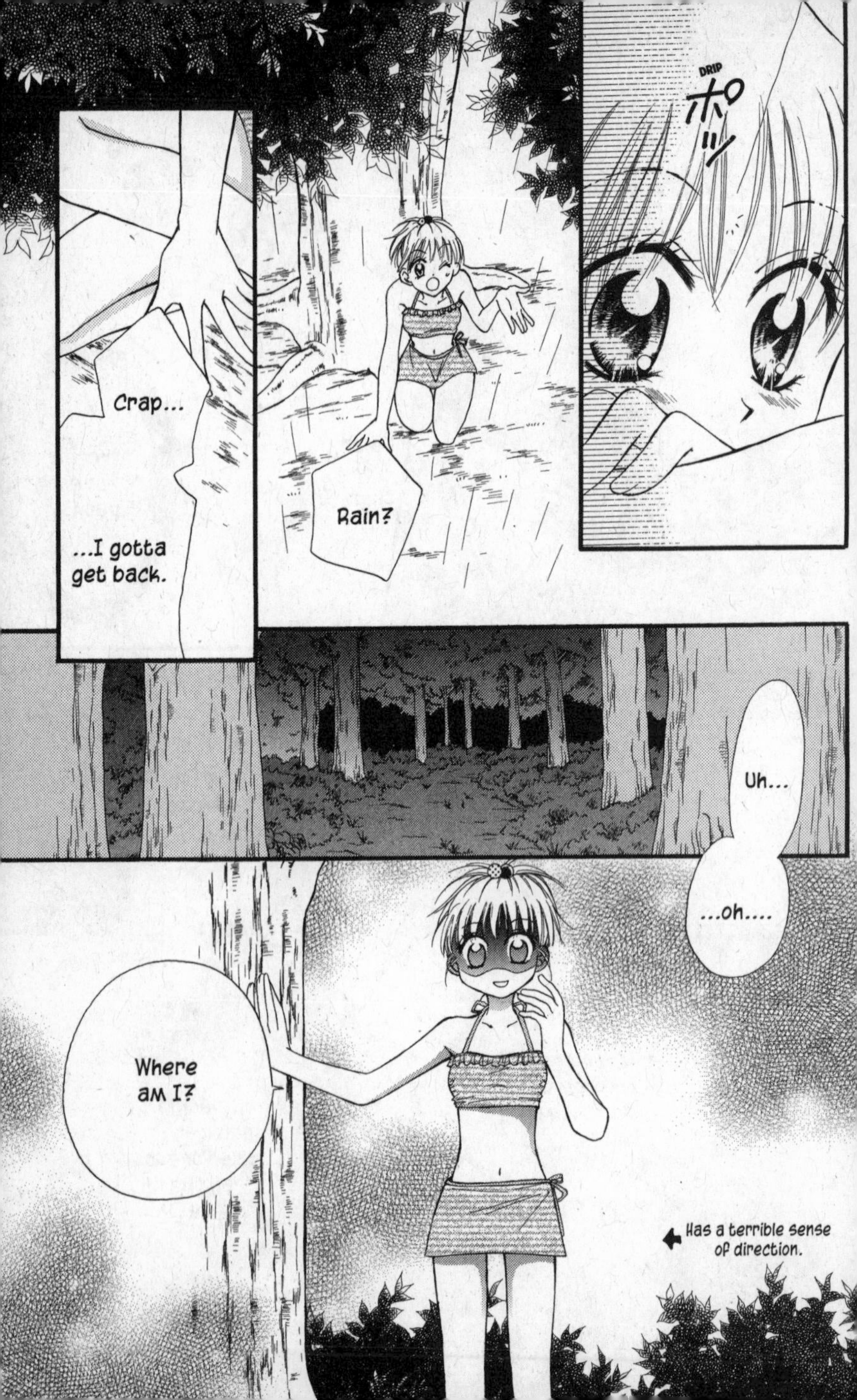
DRIP
ポッ
Rain?
Crap...
...I gotta get back.
Uh...
...oh....
Where am I?
Has a terrible sense of direction.

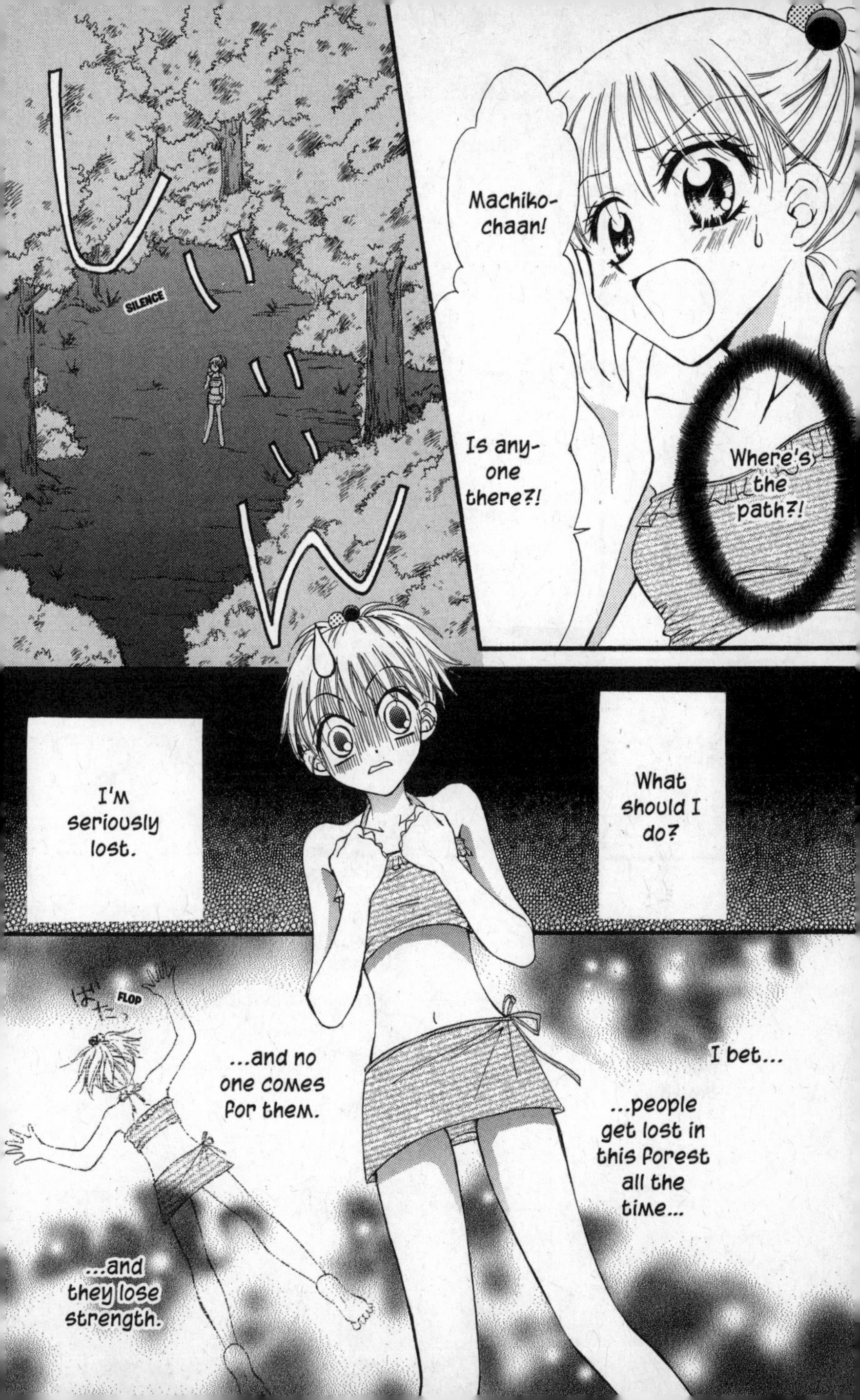

Machiko-chaan!
Is any-one there?!
Where's the path?!
SILENCE
What should I do?
I'M seriously lost.
I bet...
...people get lost in this forest all the time...
...and no one comes for them.
FLOP
...and they lose strength.

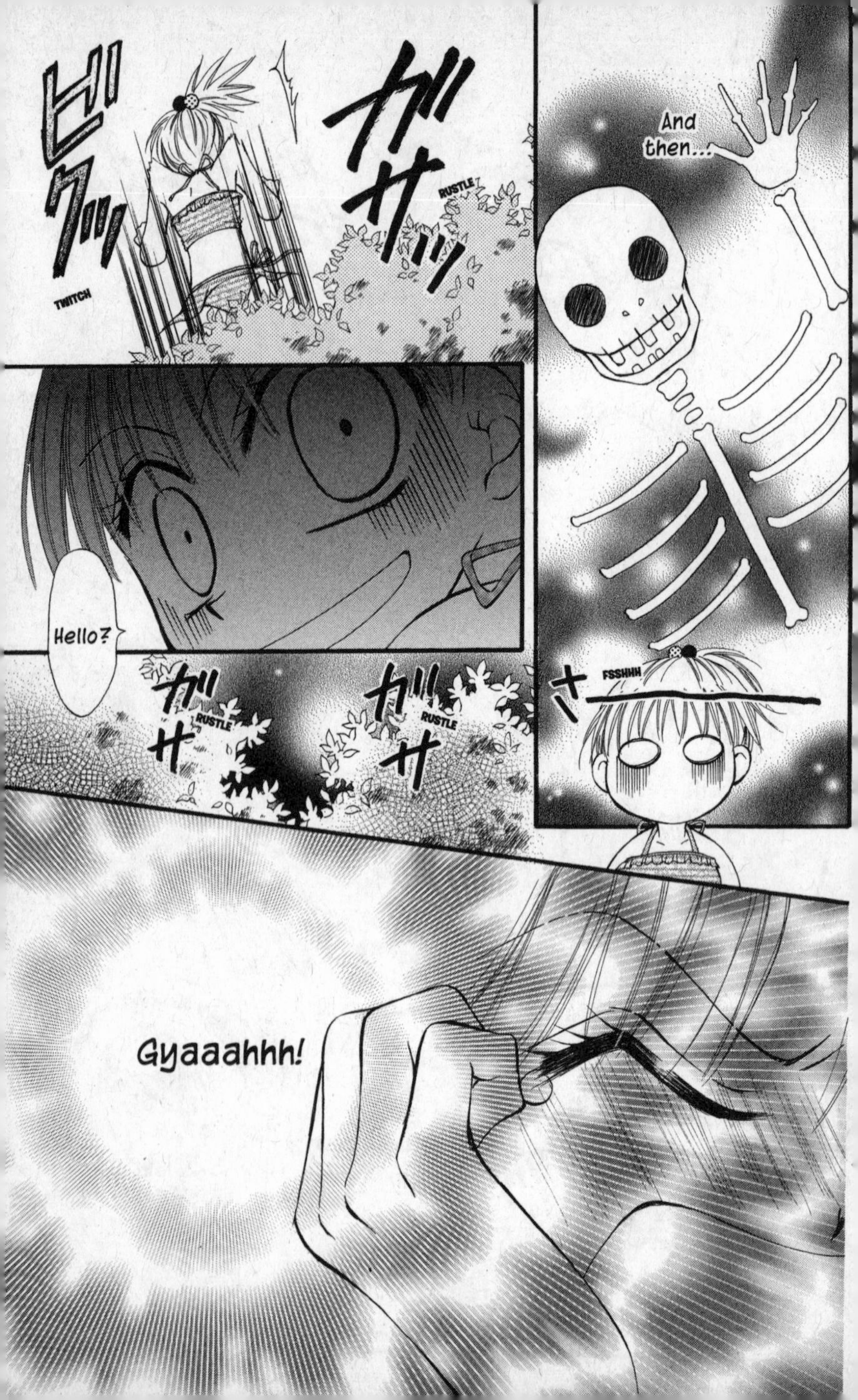
And then...
FSSHHH
RUSTLE
TWITCH
Hello?
RUSTLE
RUSTLE
Gyaaahhh!

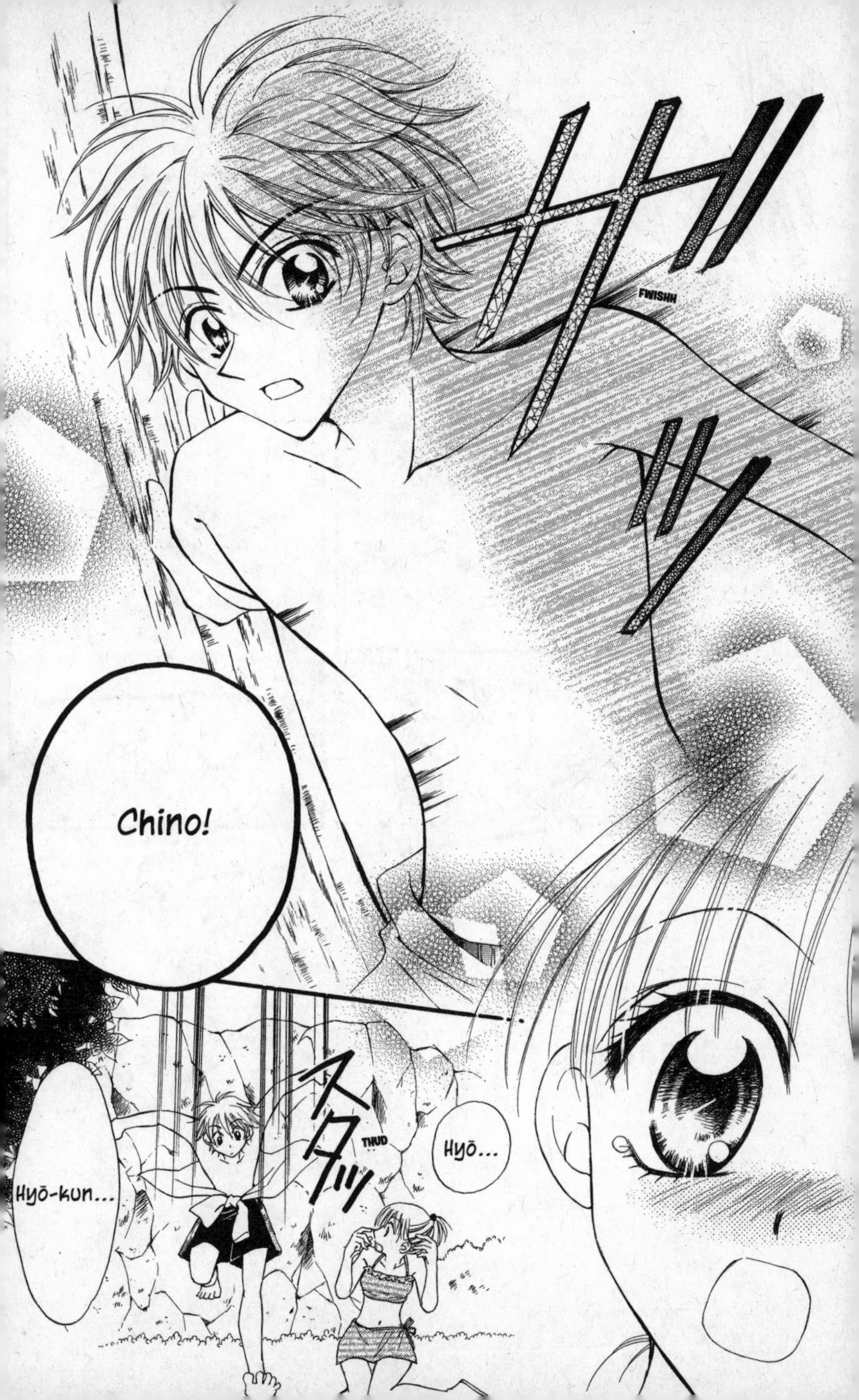
FWISHH
Chino!
Hyō...
THUD
Hyō-kun...

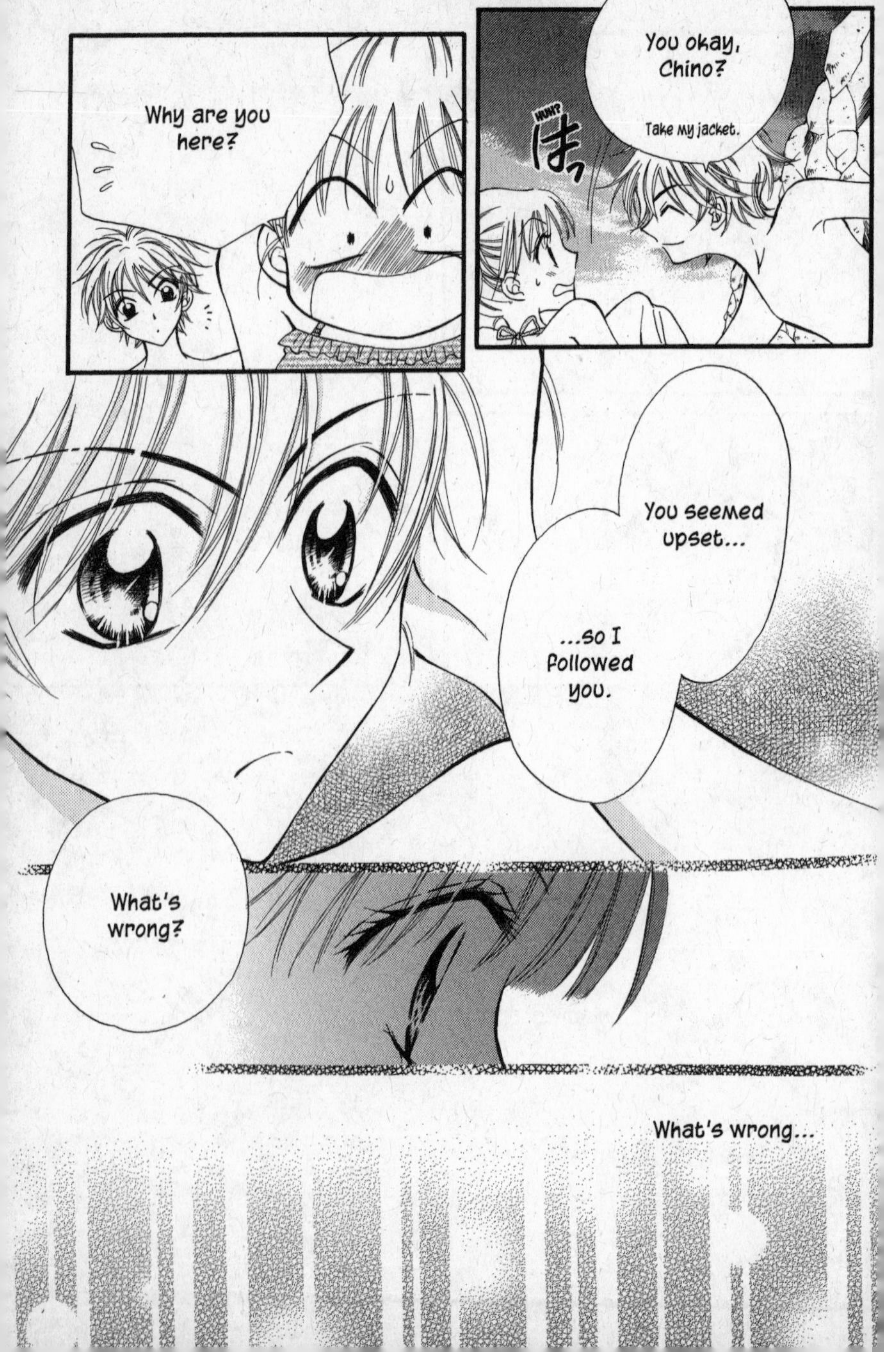

You okay, Chino?
Take my jacket.
HUH?
は
Why are you here?
You seemed upset...
...so I followed you.
What's wrong?
What's wrong...

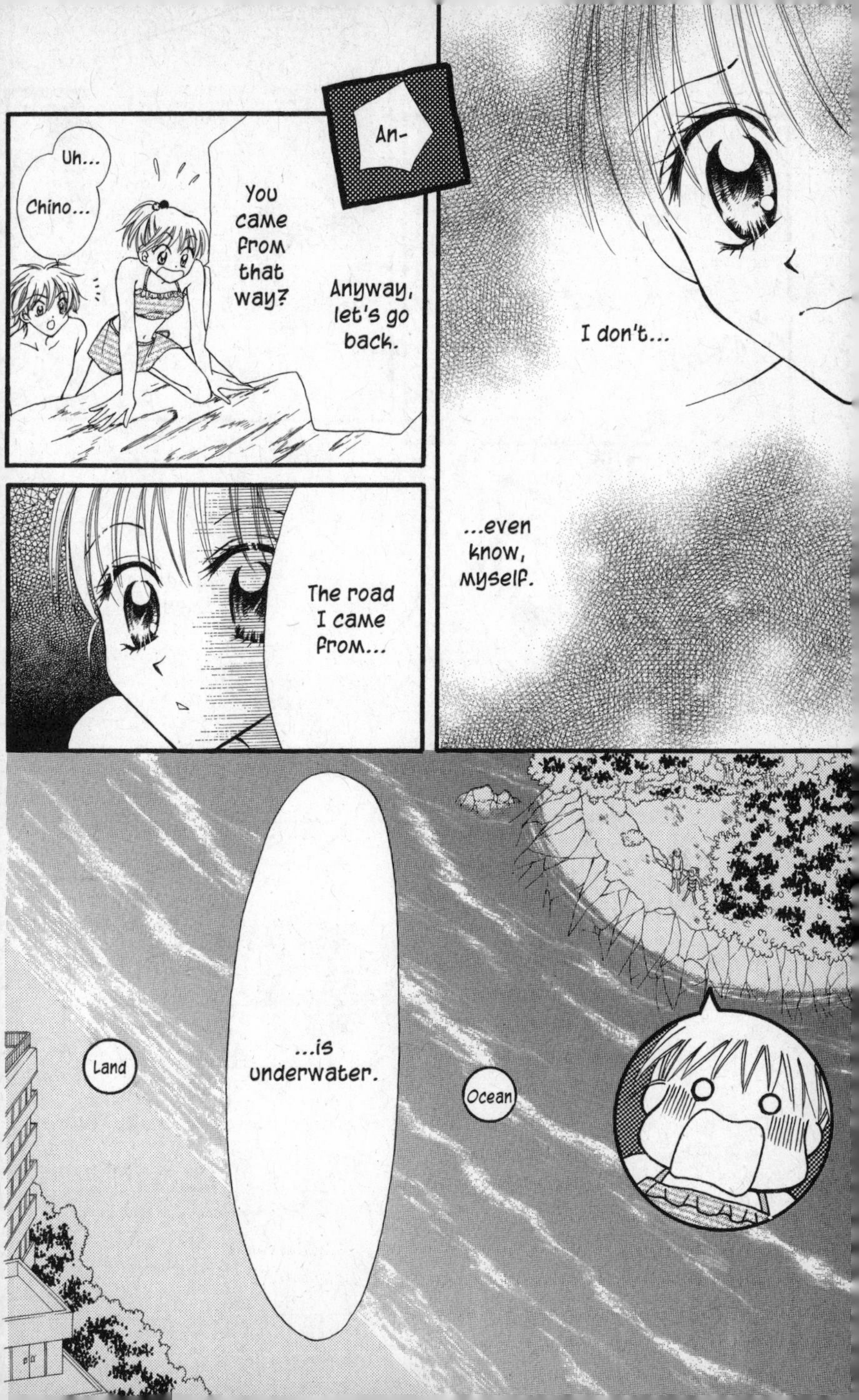
I don't...
...even know, myself.
An-
Uh...
Chino...
You came from that way?
Anyway, let's go back.
The road I came from...
...is underwater.
Ocean
Land

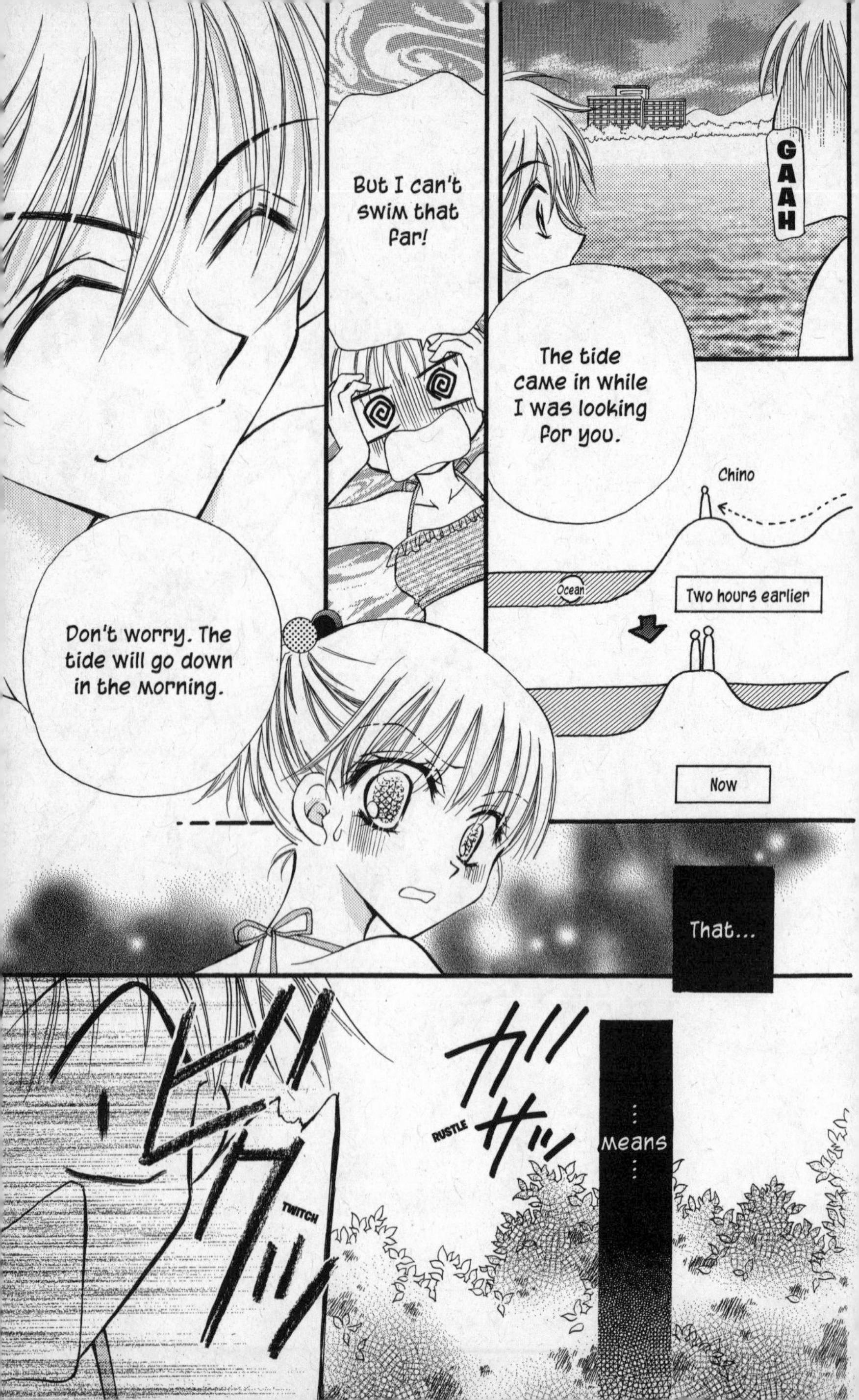
GAAH
The tide came in while I was looking for you.
Chino
Ocean
Two hours earlier
Now
But I can't swim that far!
Don't worry. The tide will go down in the morning.
That...
...Means...
RUSTLE
TWITCH

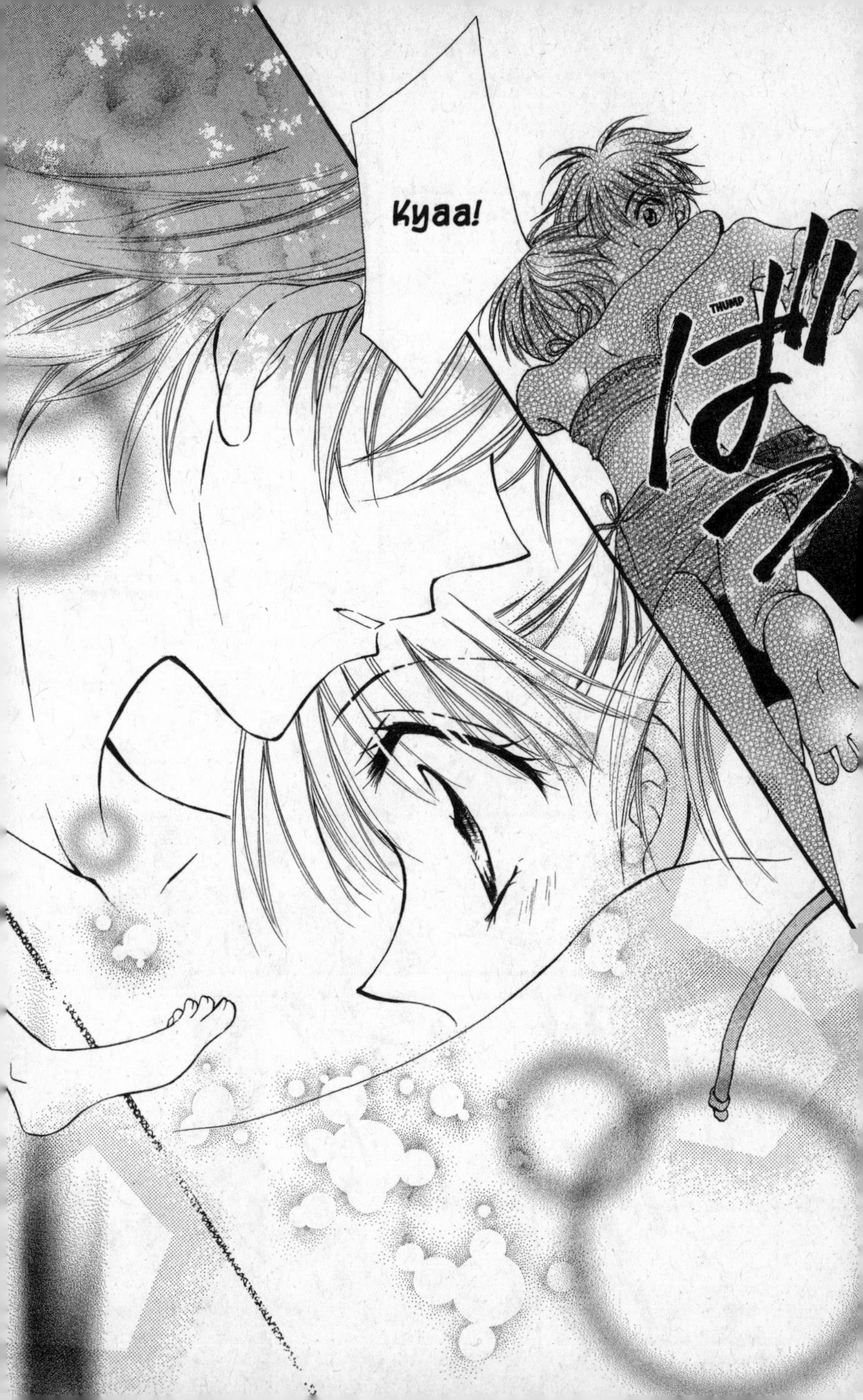
Kyaa!
THUMP
ばっ

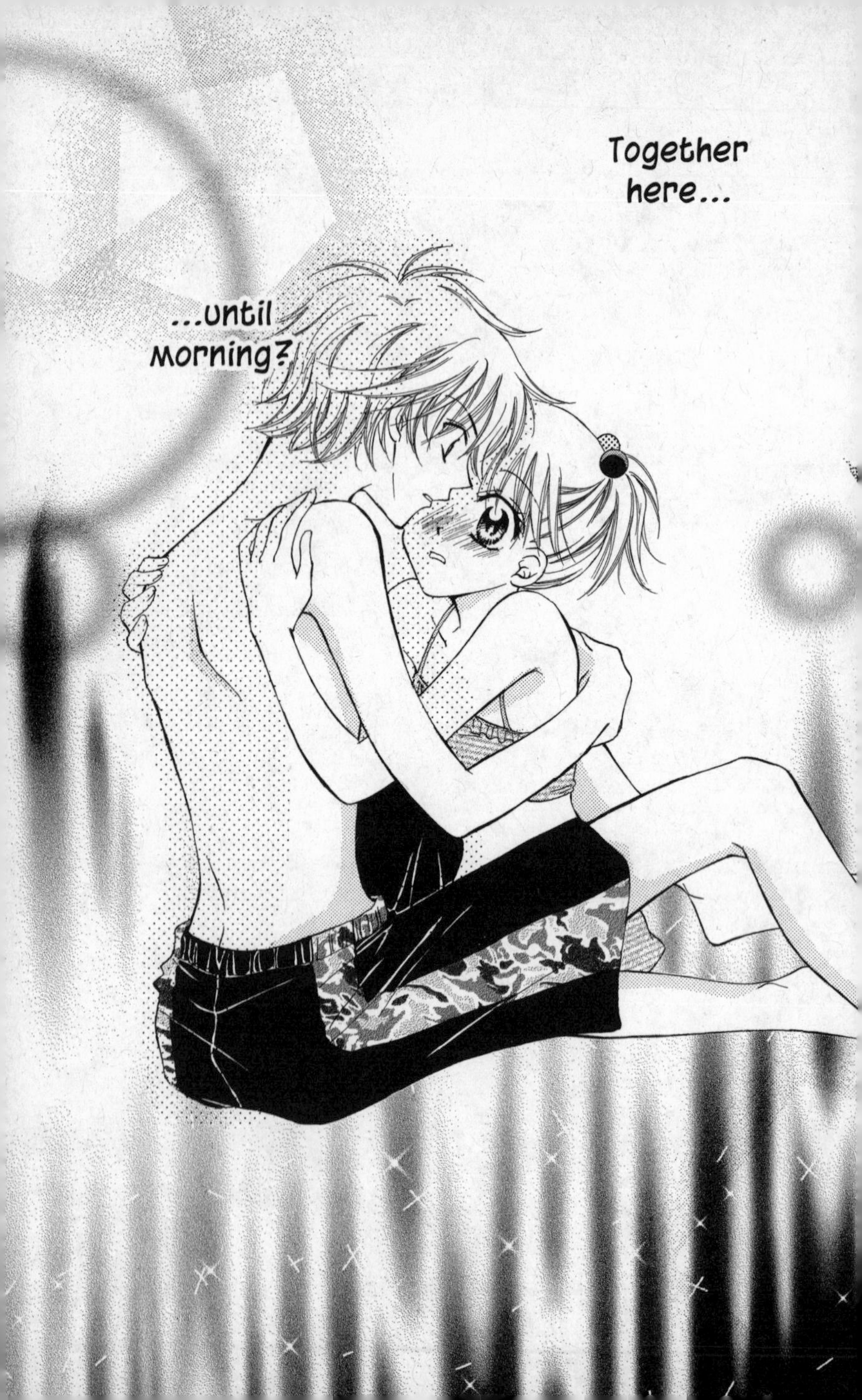
Together here...
...until morning?

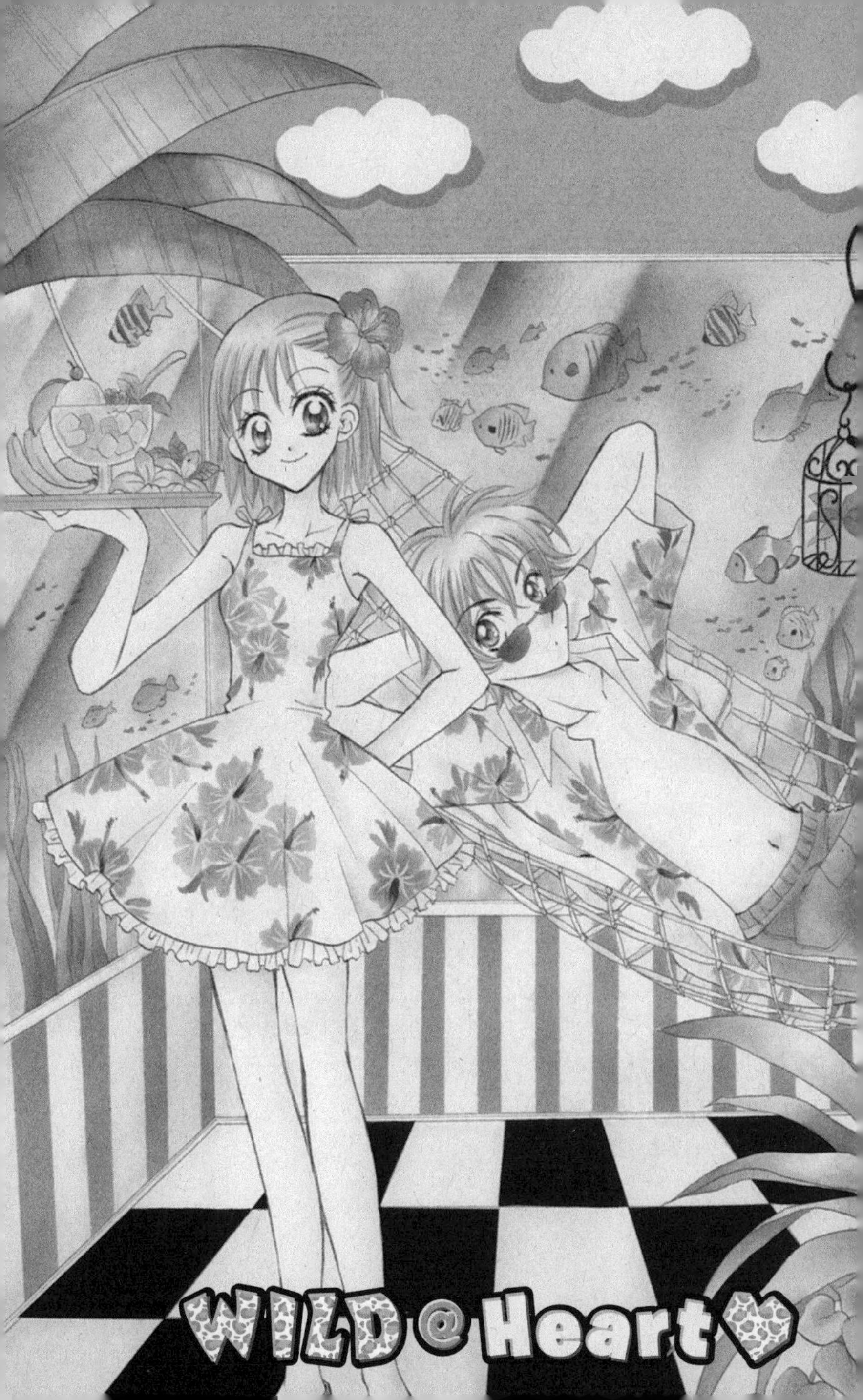
WILD @ Heart

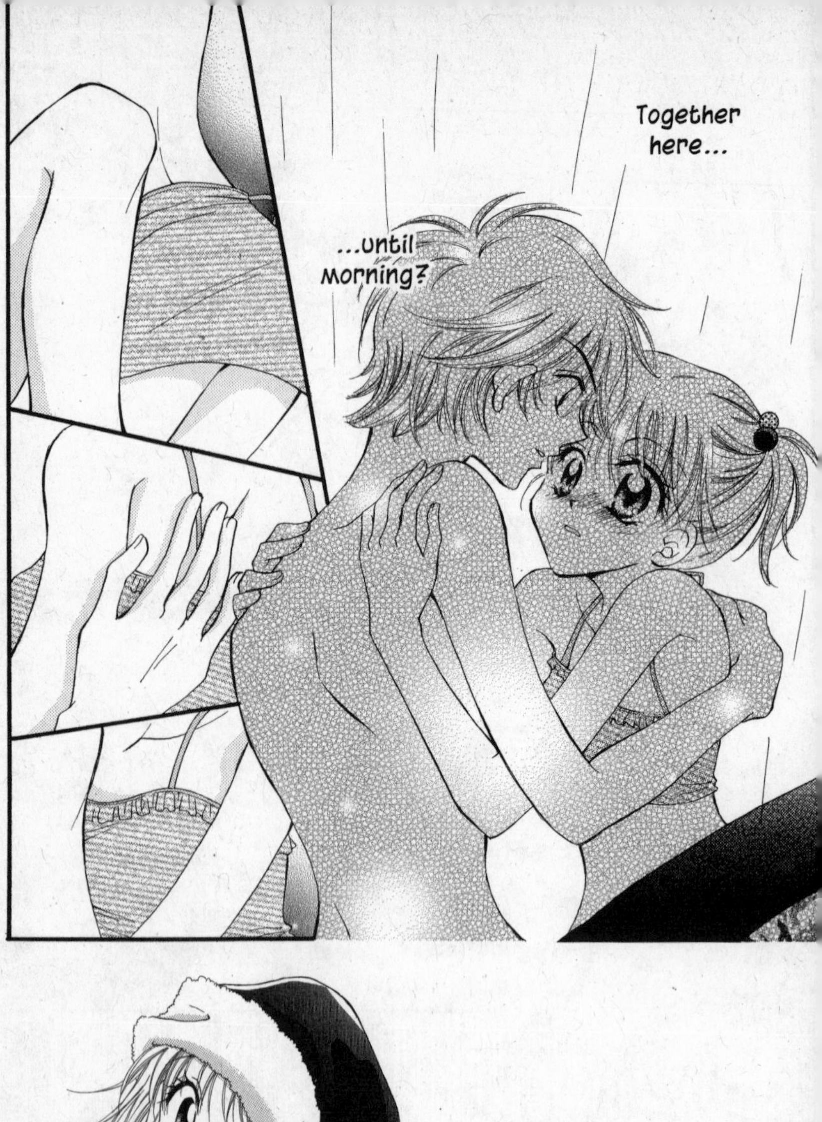
Together here...
...until morning?

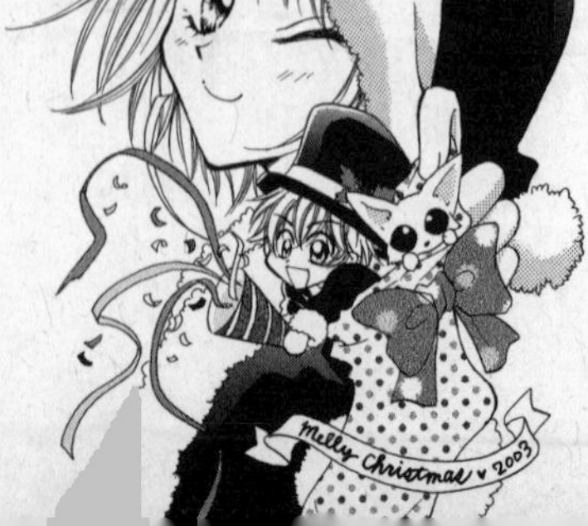
Melly Christmas ♥ 2003

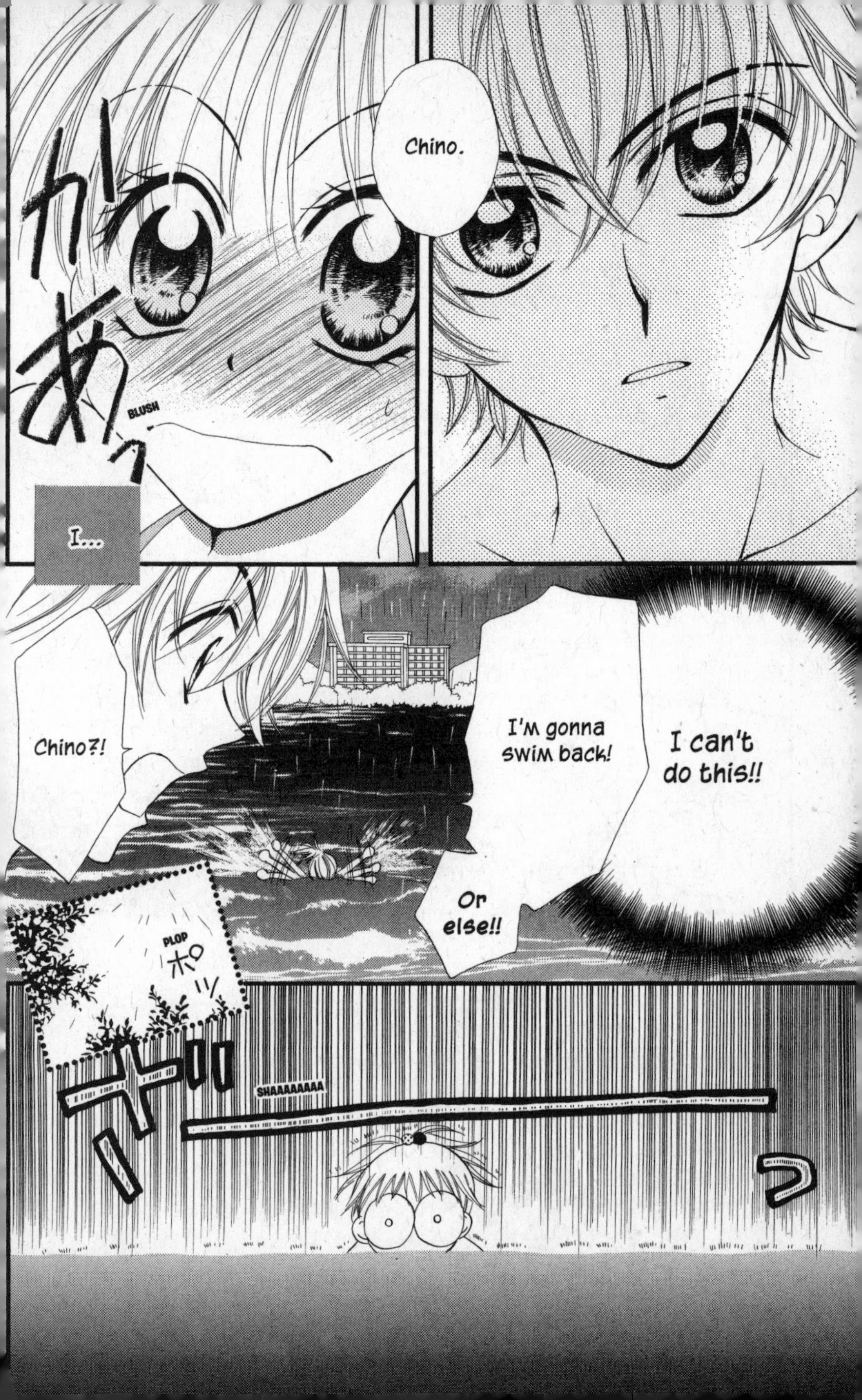
Chino.
BLUSH
I...
I can't do this!!
I'm gonna swim back!
Or else!!
Chino?!
PLOP
SHAAAAAAAA

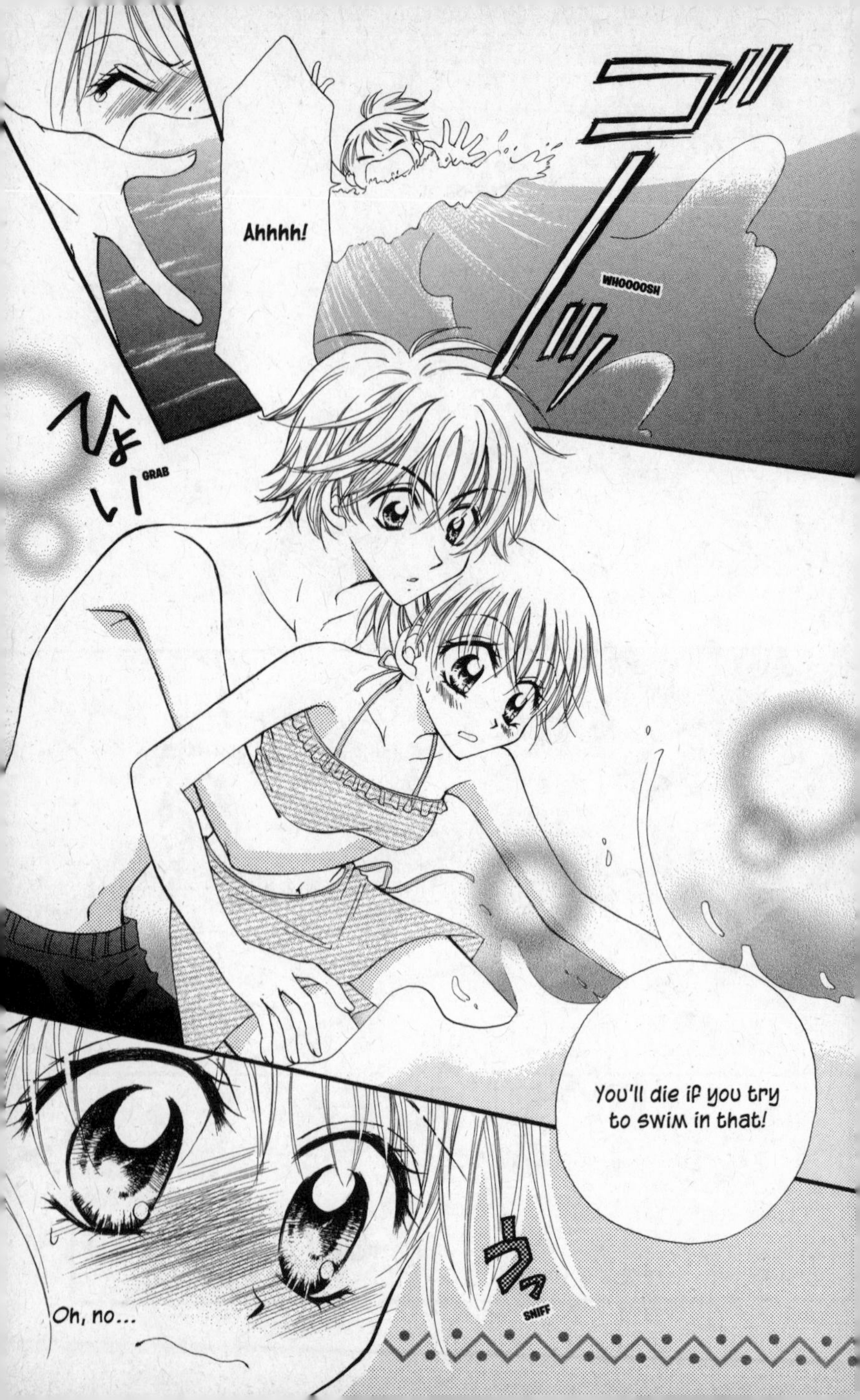

ゴーッ
WHOOOOSH
Ahhhh!
ひょい
GRAB
You'll die if you try to swim in that!
うっ
SNIFF
Oh, no...

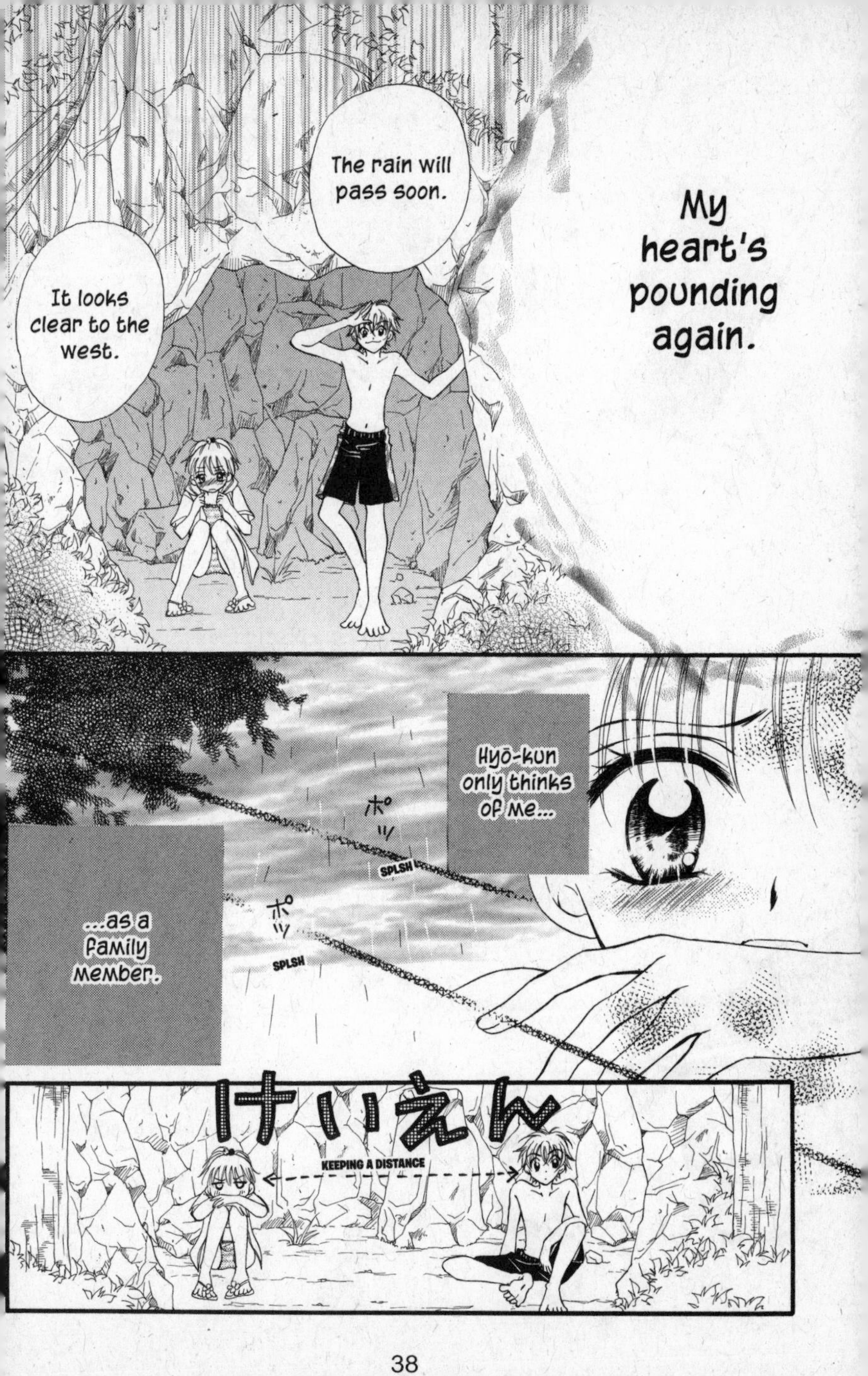
My heart's pounding again.
The rain will pass soon.
It looks clear to the west.
Hyō-kun only thinks of me...
ポツ
SPLSH
ポツ
SPLSH
...as a family member.
けいえん
KEEPING A DISTANCE

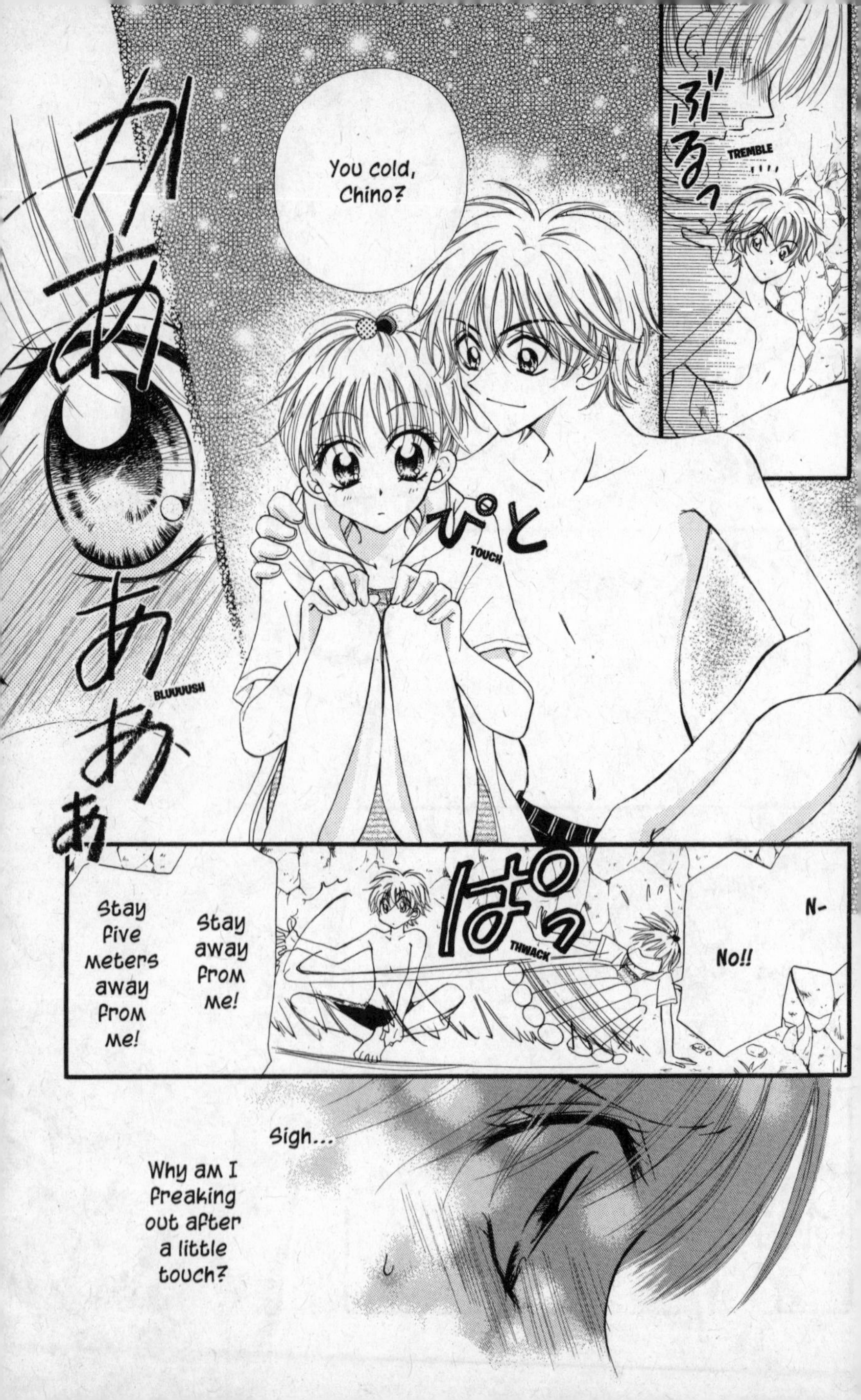
ぶるっ
TREMBLE
....
You cold, Chino?
ぴと
TOUCH
かあああああ
BLUUUSH
N-
No!!
ぱっ
THWACK
Stay away from me!
Stay five meters away from me!
Sigh...
Why am I freaking out after a little touch?

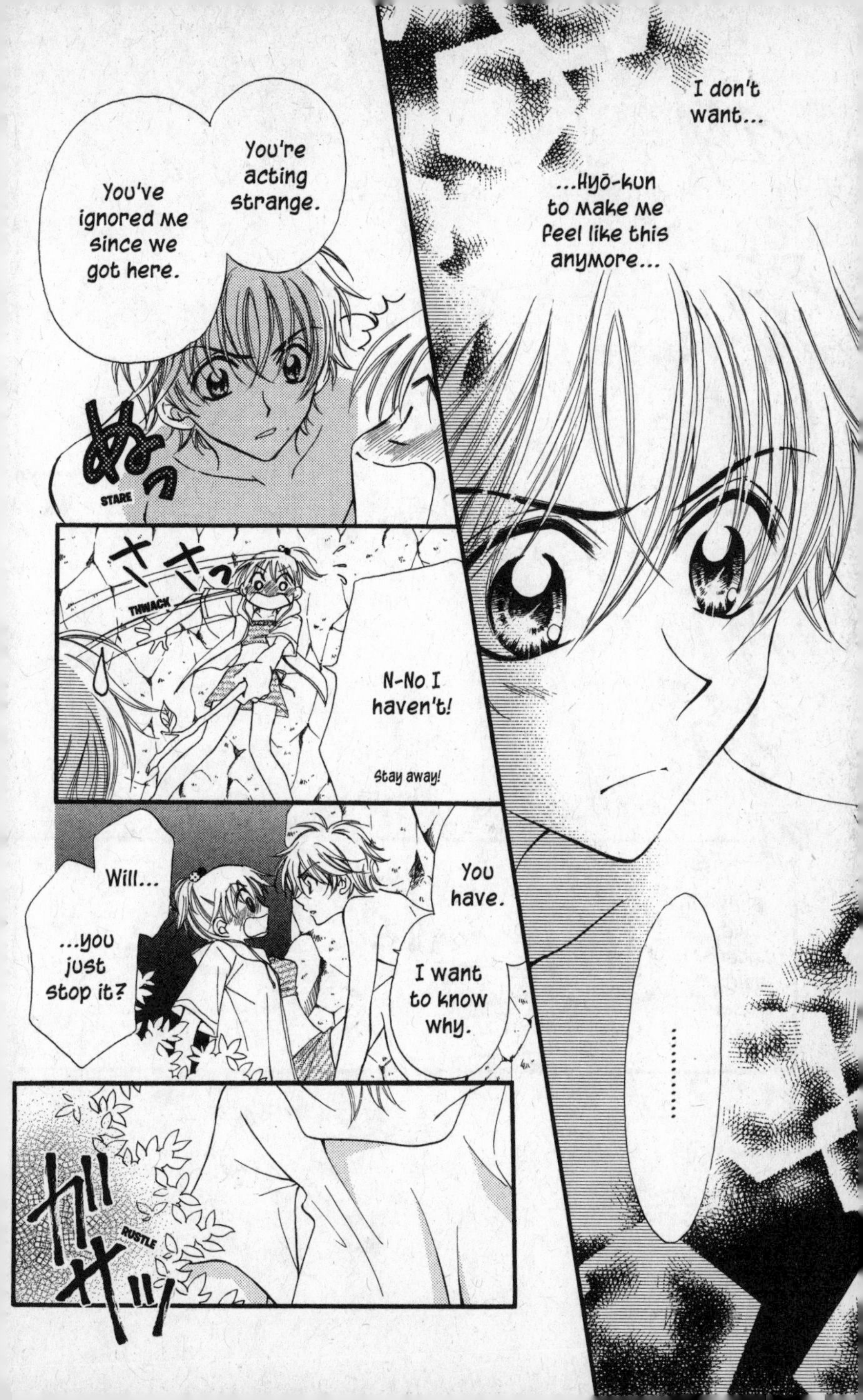
I don't want...
...Hyō-kun to make me feel like this anymore...
......
You're acting strange.
You've ignored me since we got here.
ぬっ
STARE
N-No I haven't!
ささっ
THWACK
Stay away!
You have.
I want to know why.
Will...
...you just stop it?
ガサッ
RUSTLE

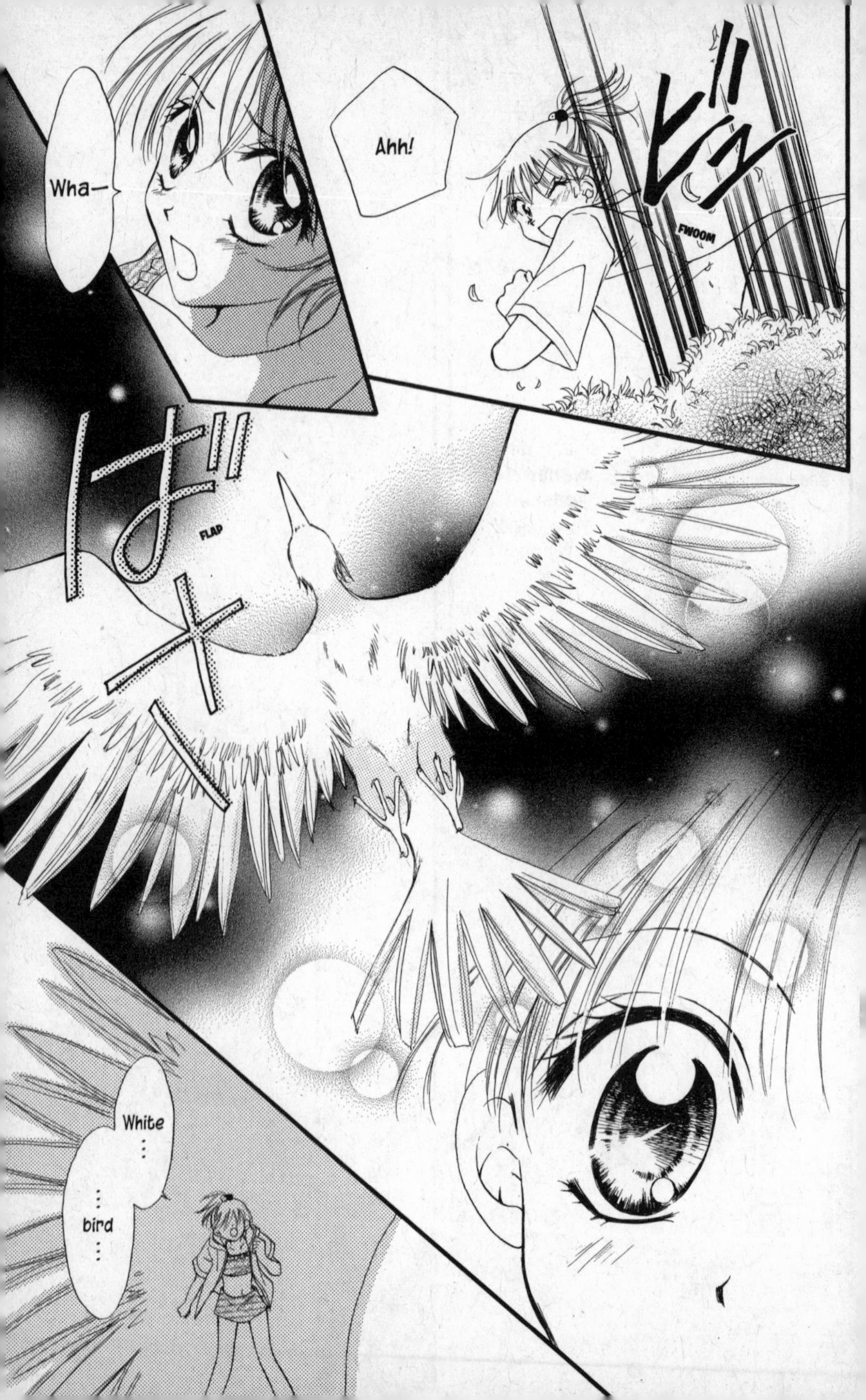

Ahh!
FWOOM
Wha—
FLAP
White…
…bird…

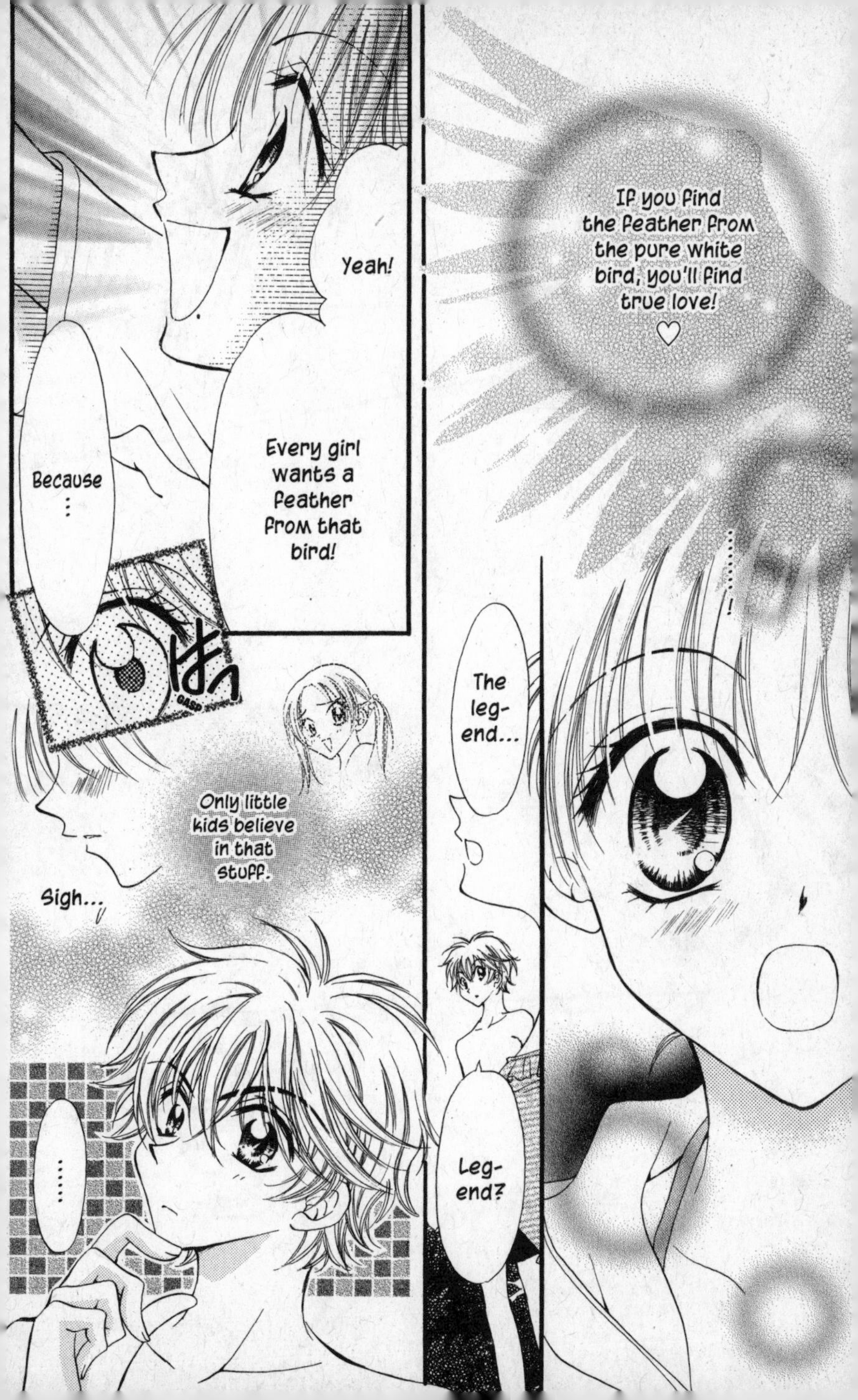
If you find the feather from the pure white bird, you'll find true love! ♡
......!
The leg-end...
Leg-end?
Yeah!
Every girl wants a feather from that bird!
Because ...
はっ
GASP
Only little kids believe in that stuff.
Sigh...
......

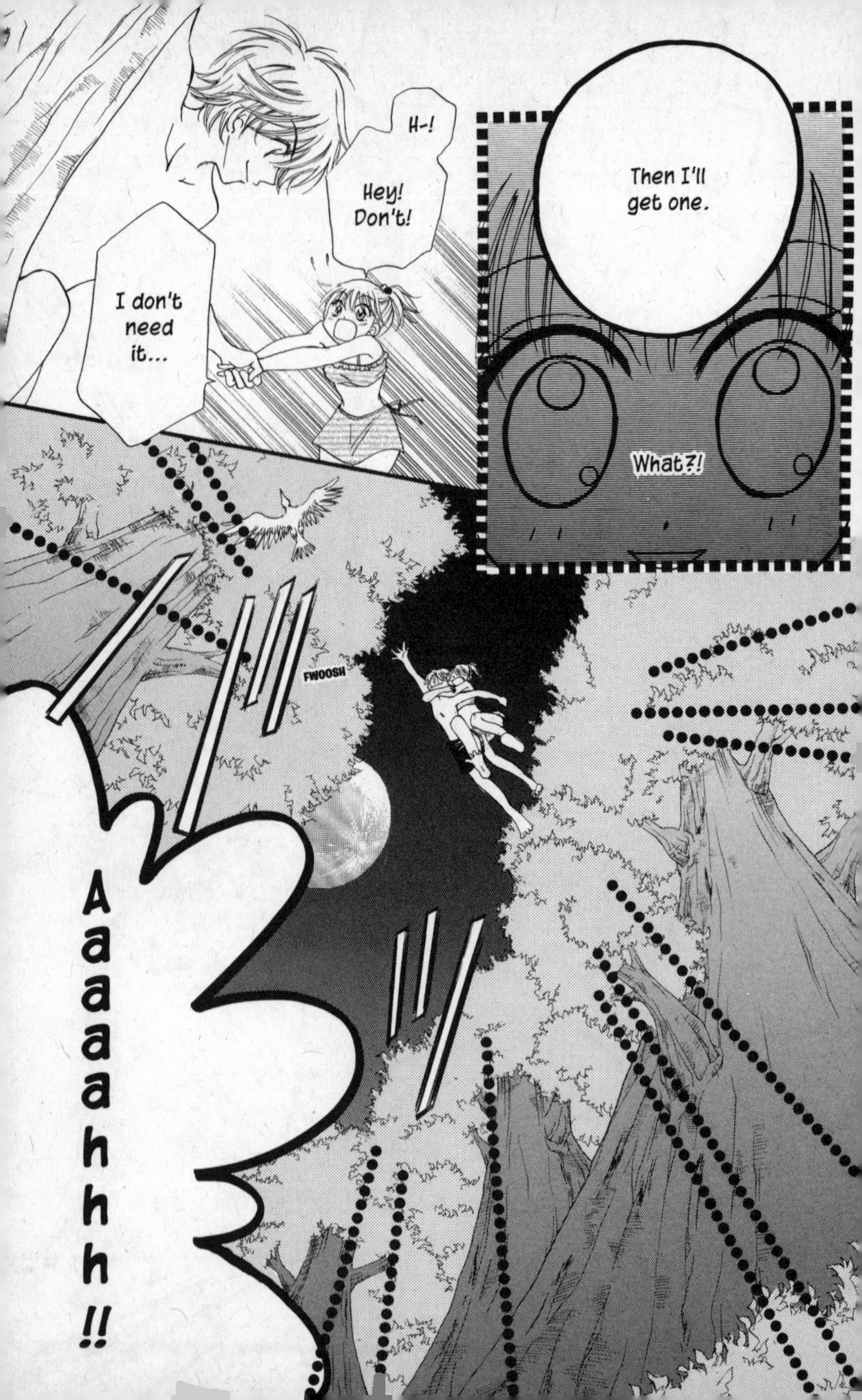
Then I'll get one.
What?!
H-!
Hey! Don't!
I don't need it...
FWOOSH
Aaaaahhh!!

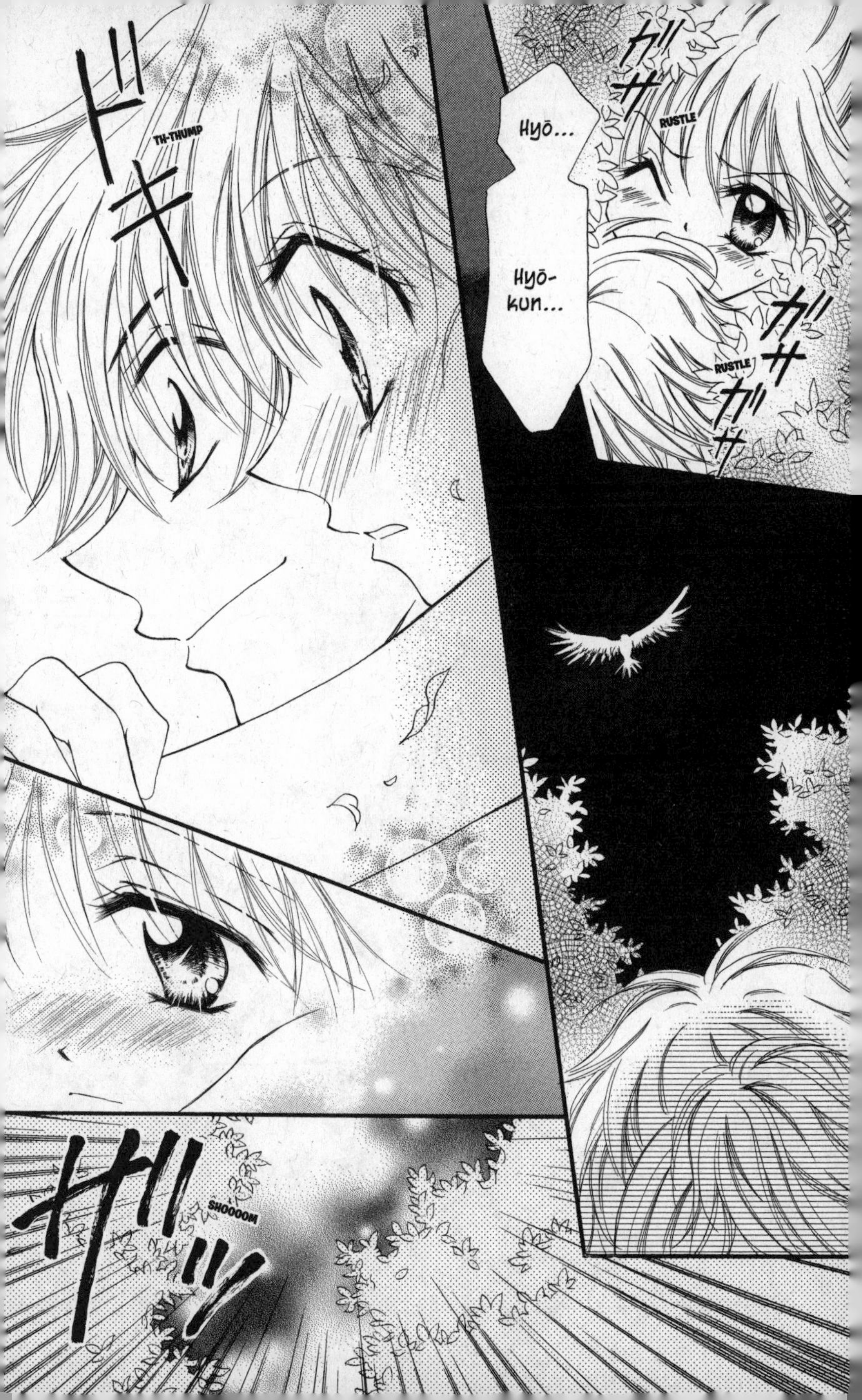

RUSTLE
Hyō...
Hyō-kun...
RUSTLE
TH-THUMP
SHOOOOM

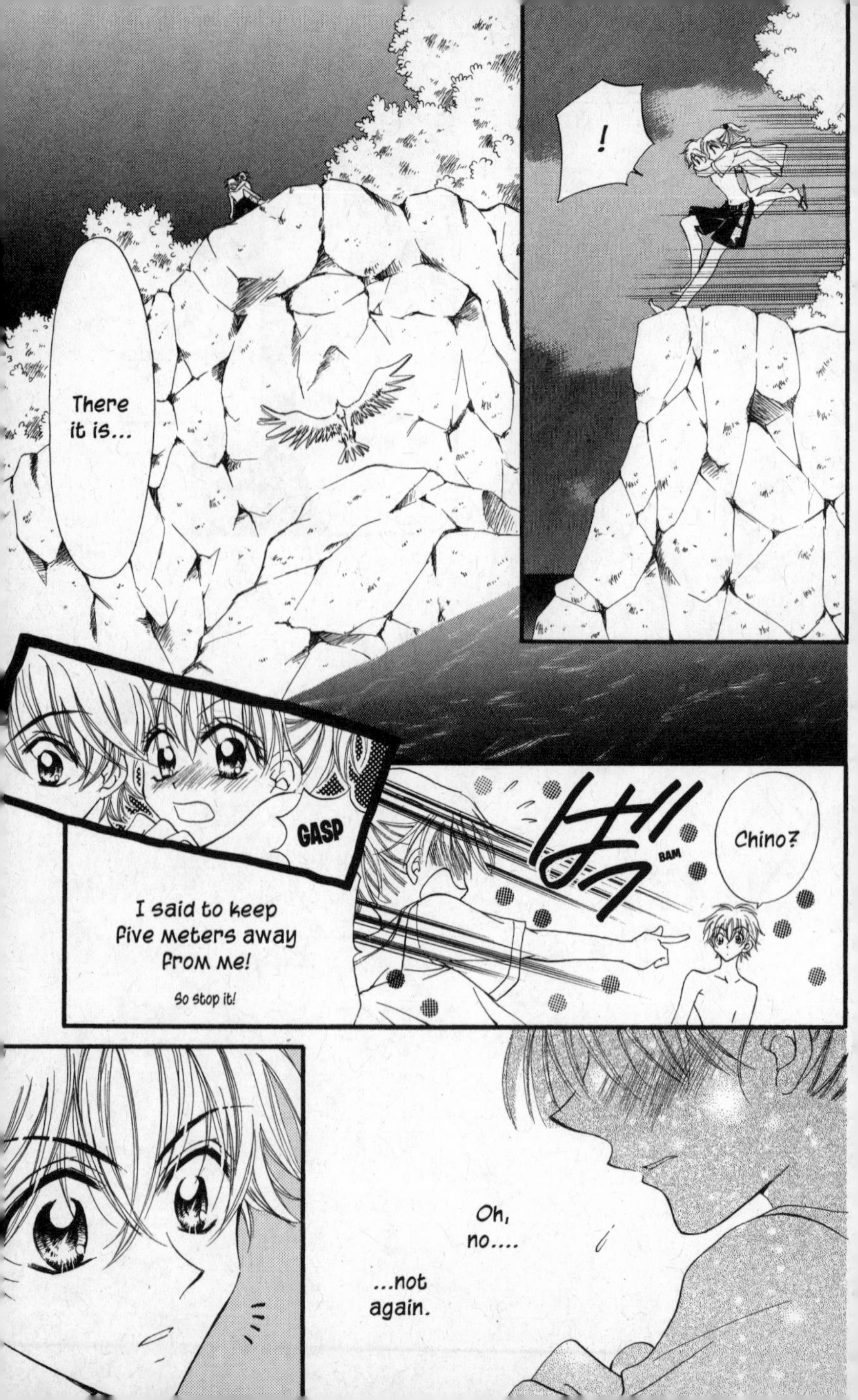
!
There it is...
GASP
Chino?
BAM
I said to keep five meters away from me!
So stop it!
Oh, no....
...not again.

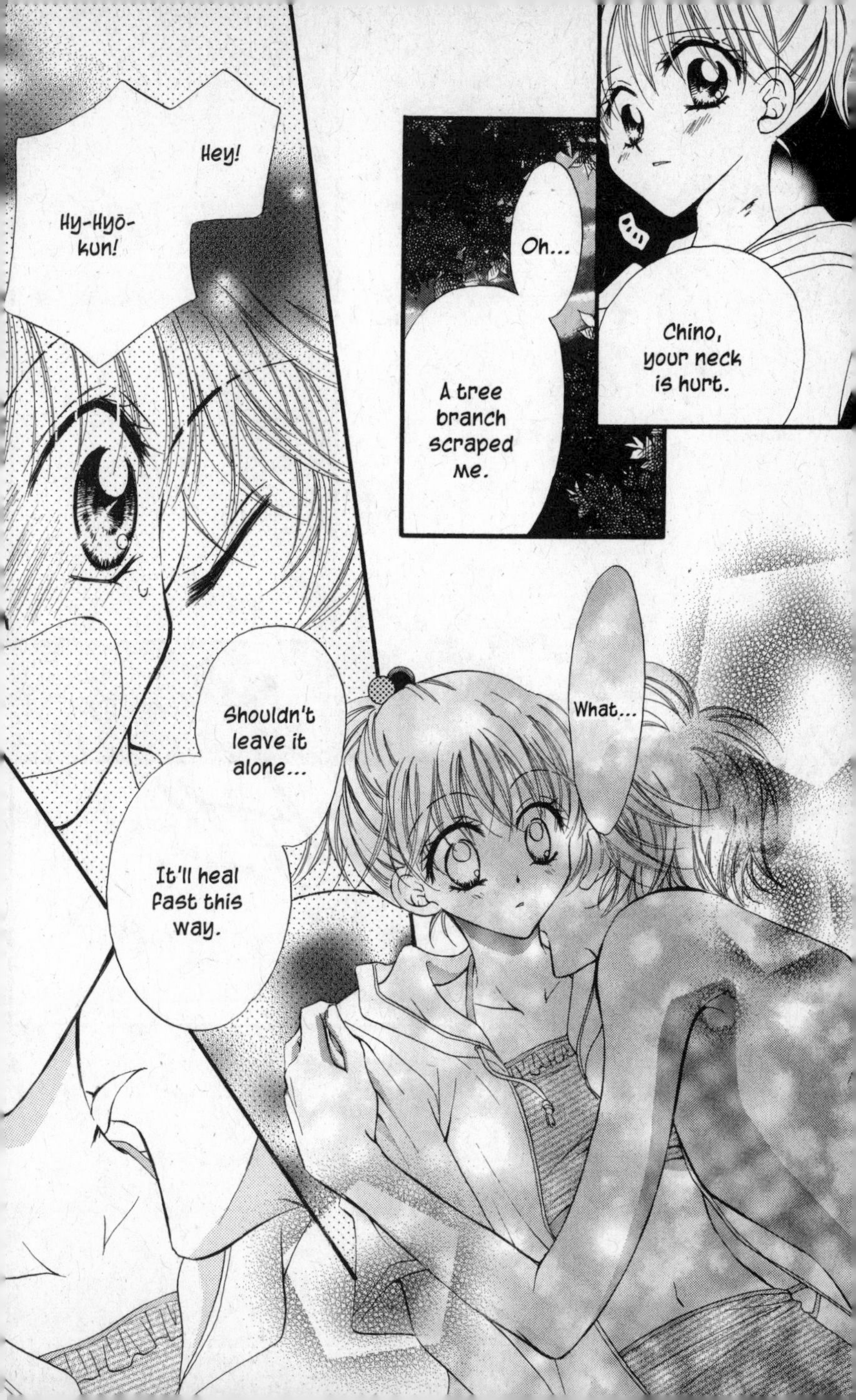
Chino, your neck is hurt.
Oh...
A tree branch scraped me.
What...
Shouldn't leave it alone...
It'll heal fast this way.
Hey!
Hy-Hyō-kun!

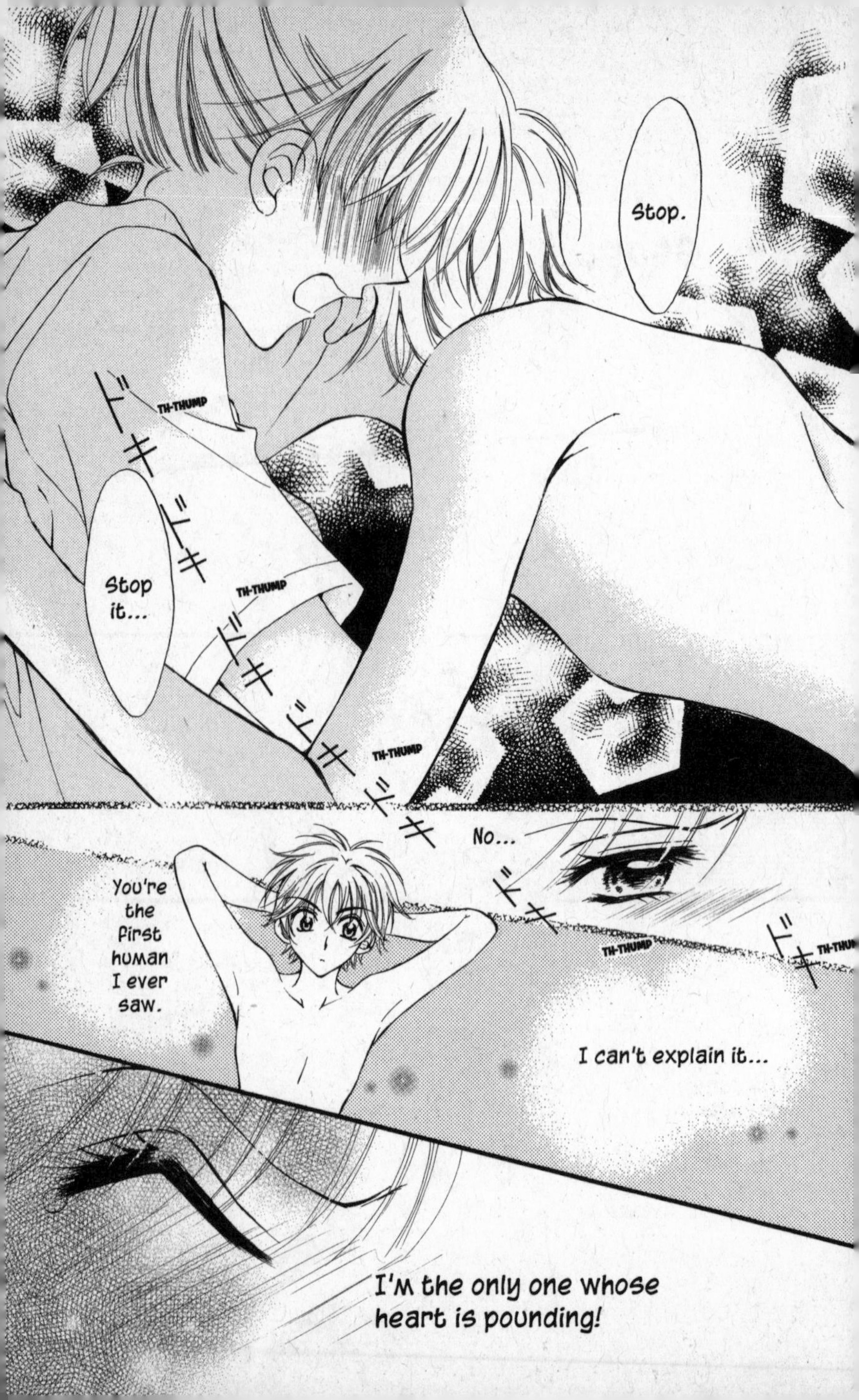
Stop.
ドキ
TH-THUMP
Stop it...
ドキ
TH-THUMP
ドキ
ドキ
TH-THUMP
ドキ
No...
ドキ
TH-THUMP
ドキ
TH-THUMP
You're the first human I ever saw.
I can't explain it...
I'm the only one whose heart is pounding!

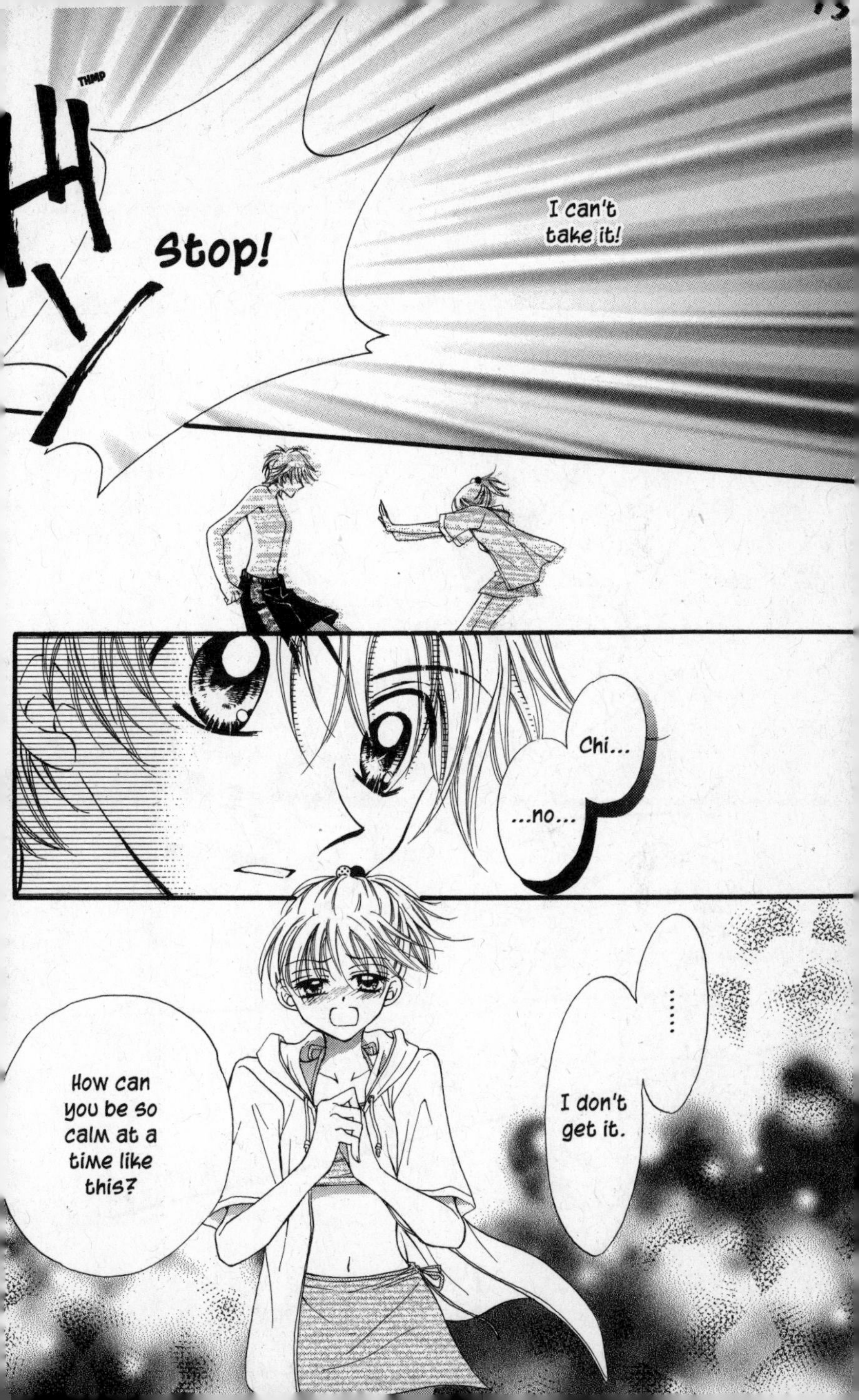
I can't take it!
THUMP
Stop!
Chi...
...no...
......
I don't get it.
How can you be so calm at a time like this?

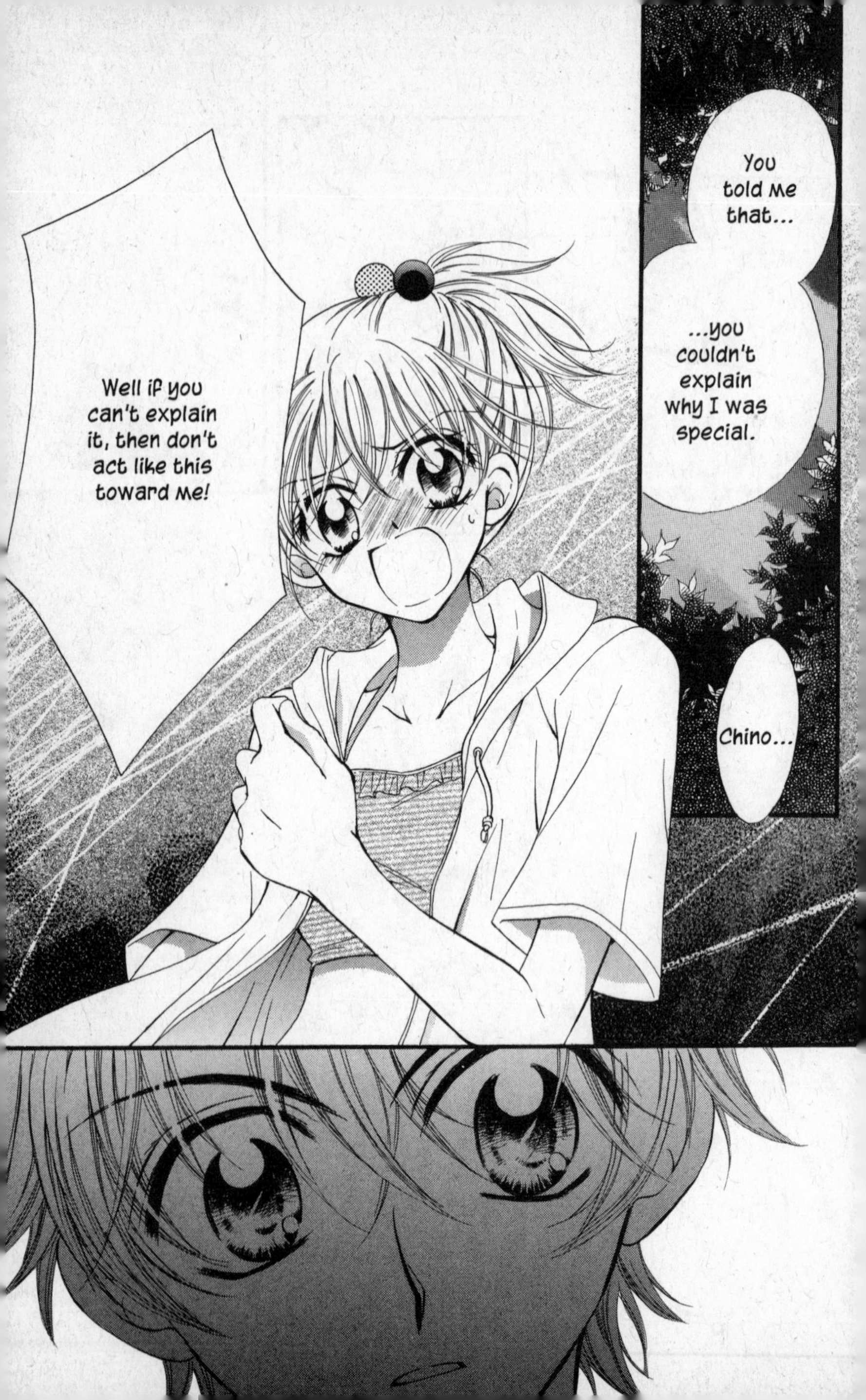
You told me that...
...you couldn't explain why I was special.
Chino...
Well if you can't explain it, then don't act like this toward me!

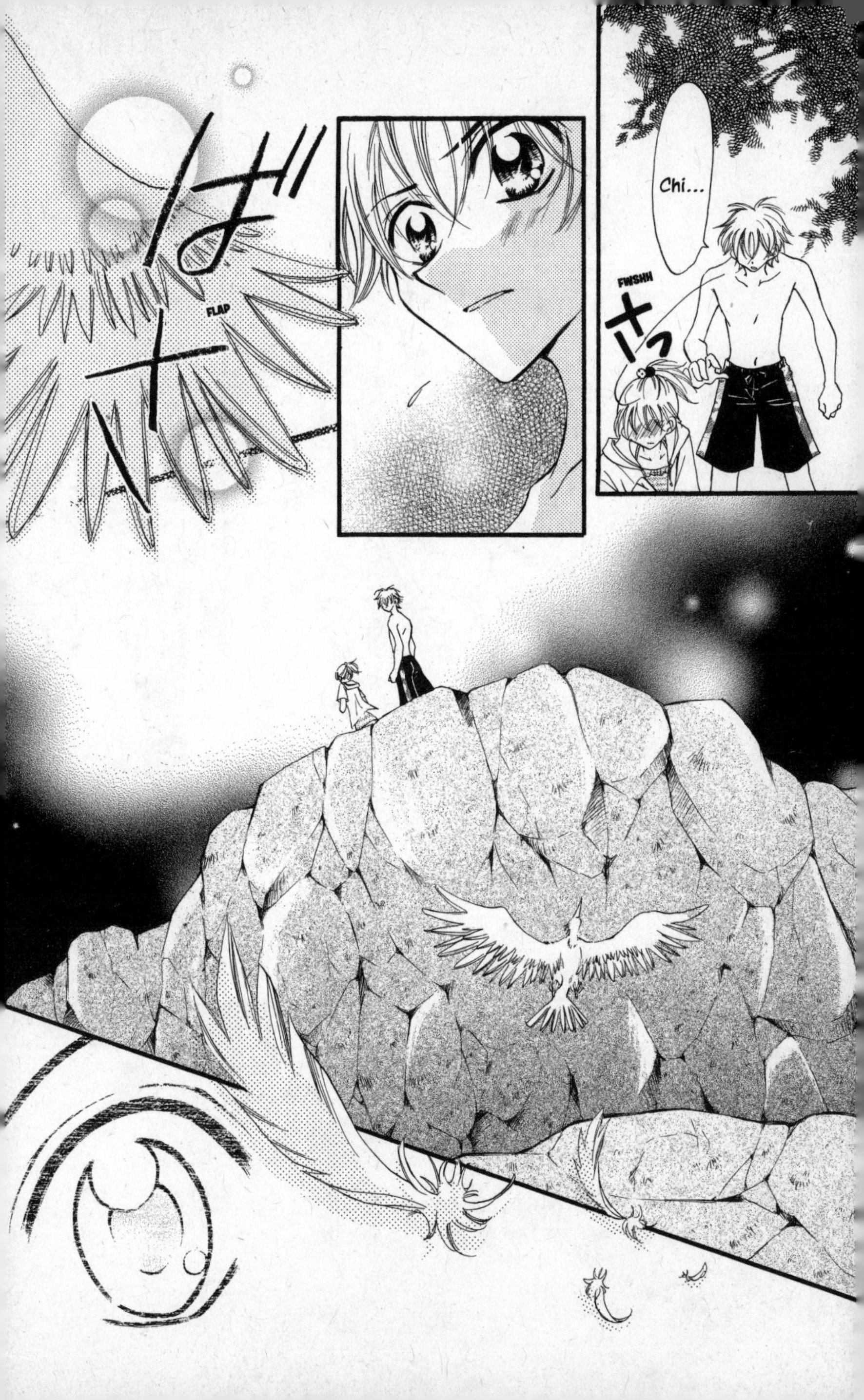
Chi...
FWSHH
さっ
FLAP
ばさ

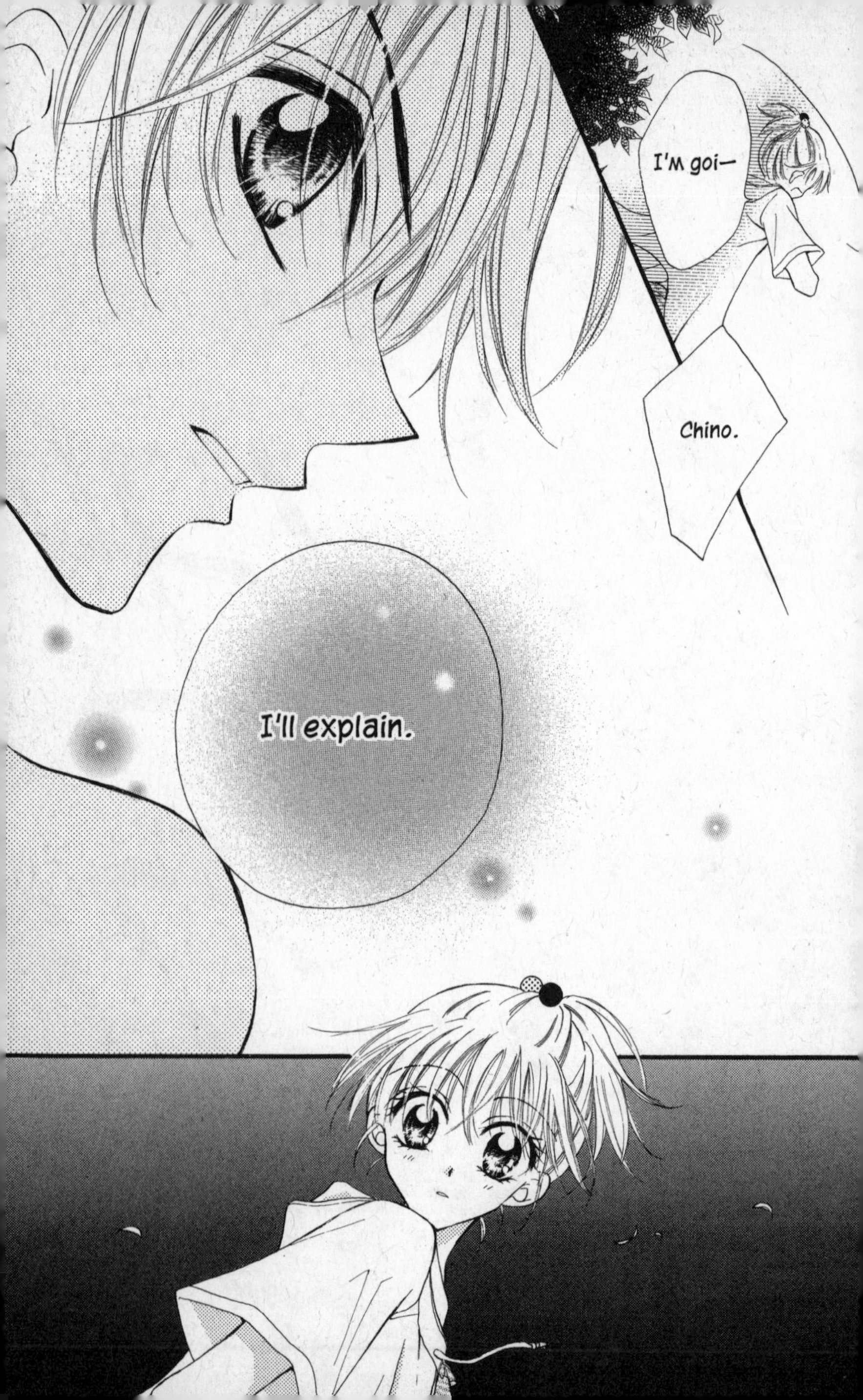
I'M goi—
Chino.
I'll explain.

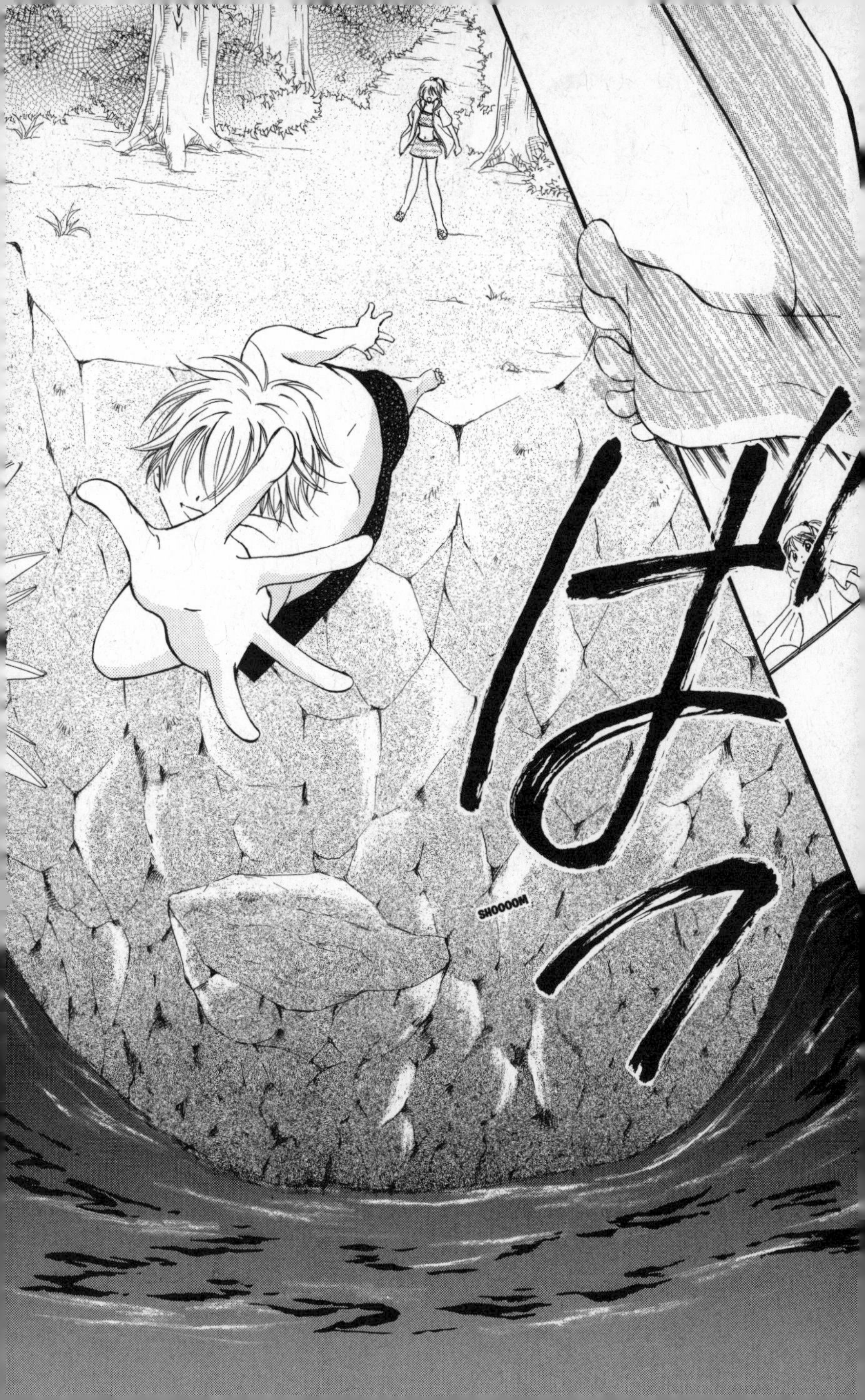
はっ
SHOOOOM

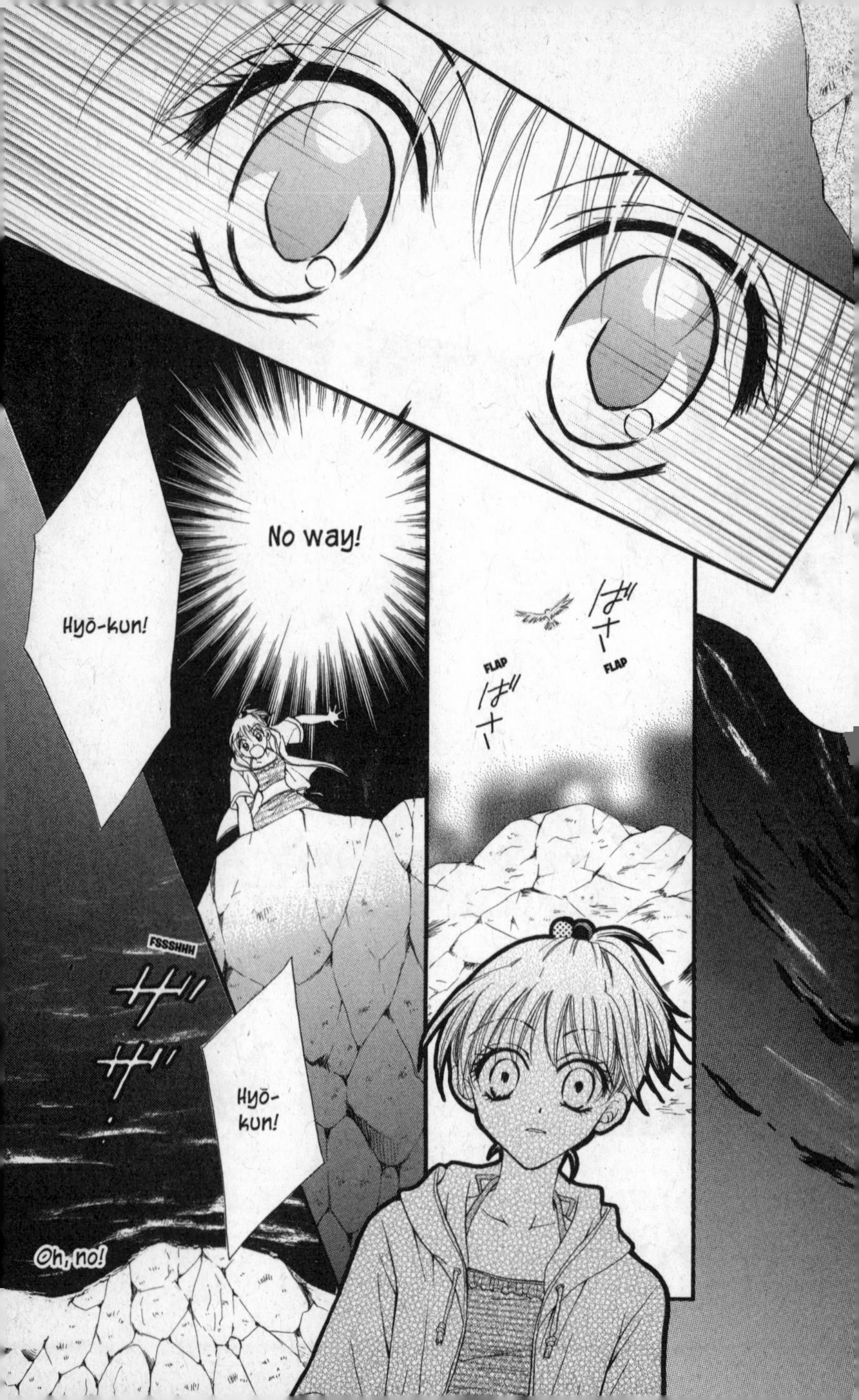
ばさ
FLAP
ばさ
FLAP
No way!
Hyō-kun!
Hyō-kun!
FSSSHHH
ザザ
Oh, no!

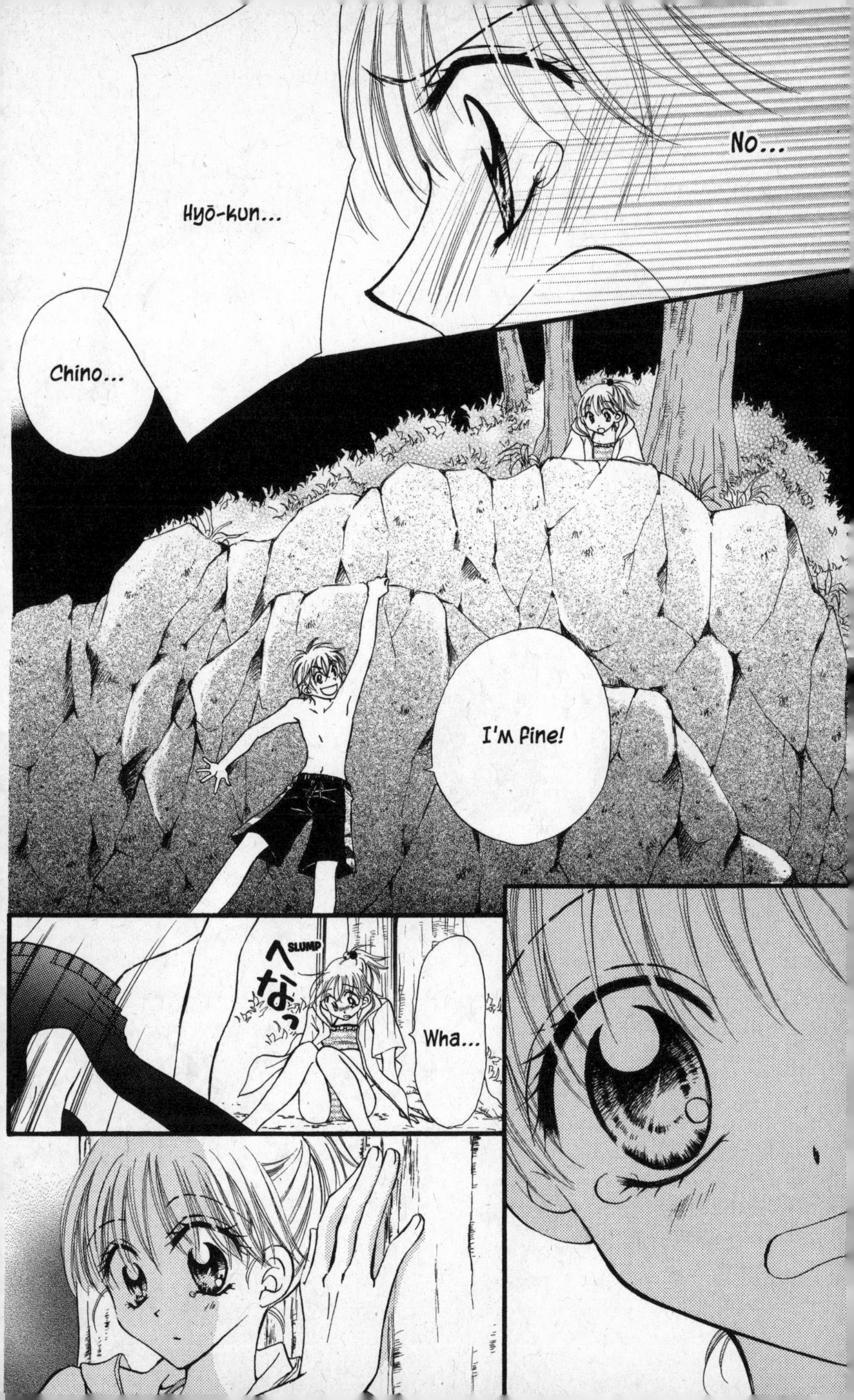
No...
Hyō-kun...
Chino...
I'm fine!
Wha...
へなっ
SLUMP

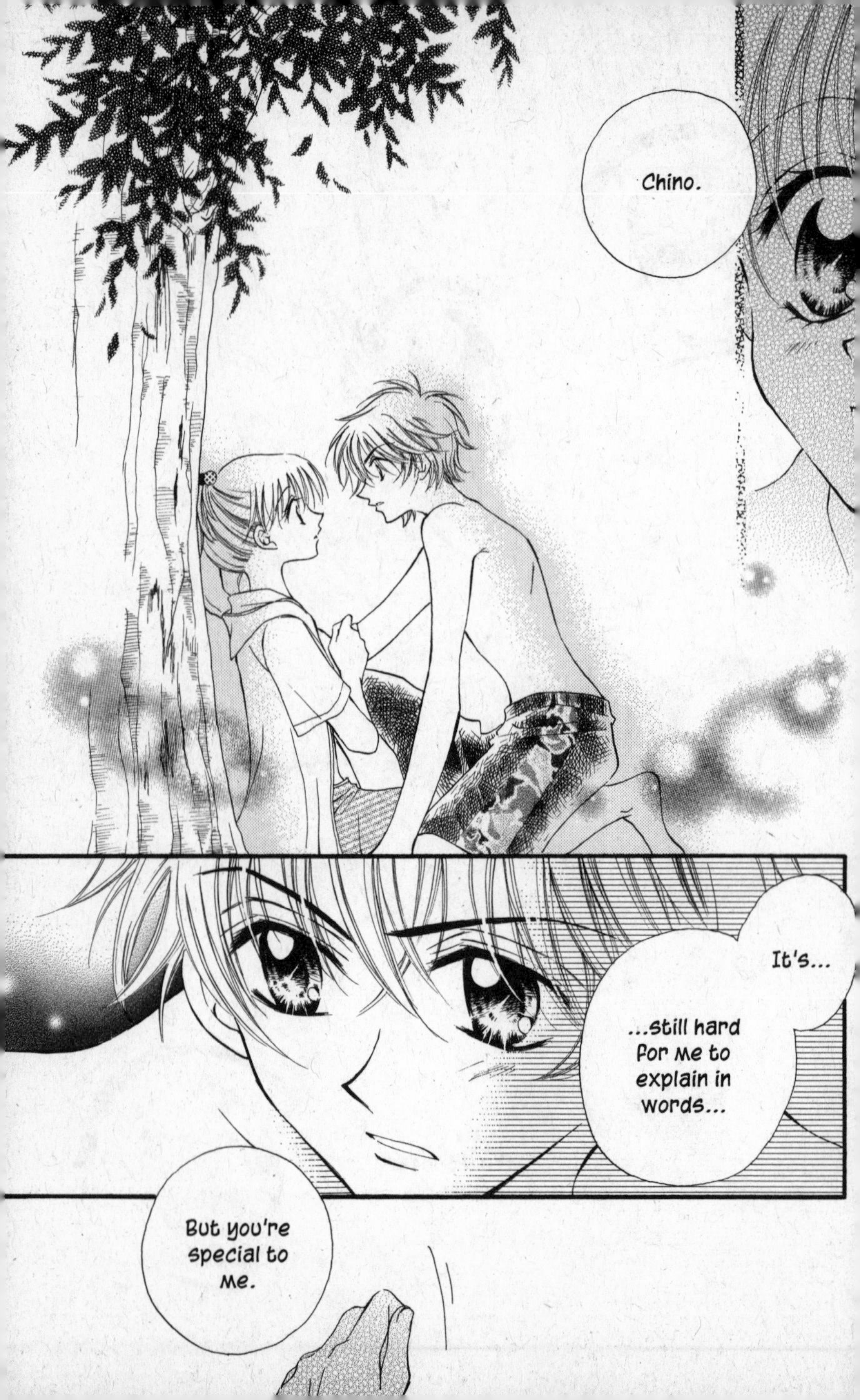
Chino.
It's...
...still hard for me to explain in words...
But you're special to me.

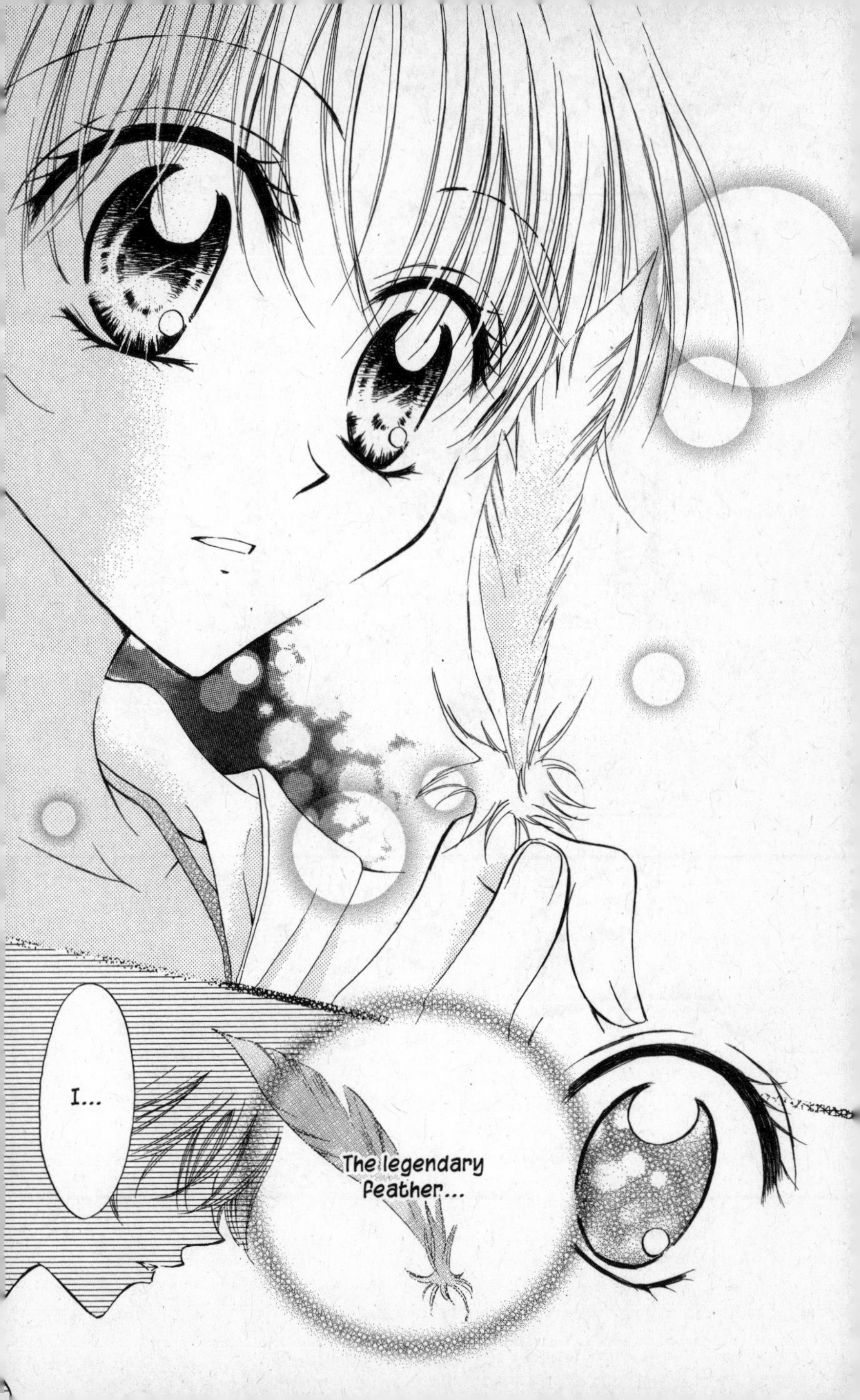
The legendary feather...
I...

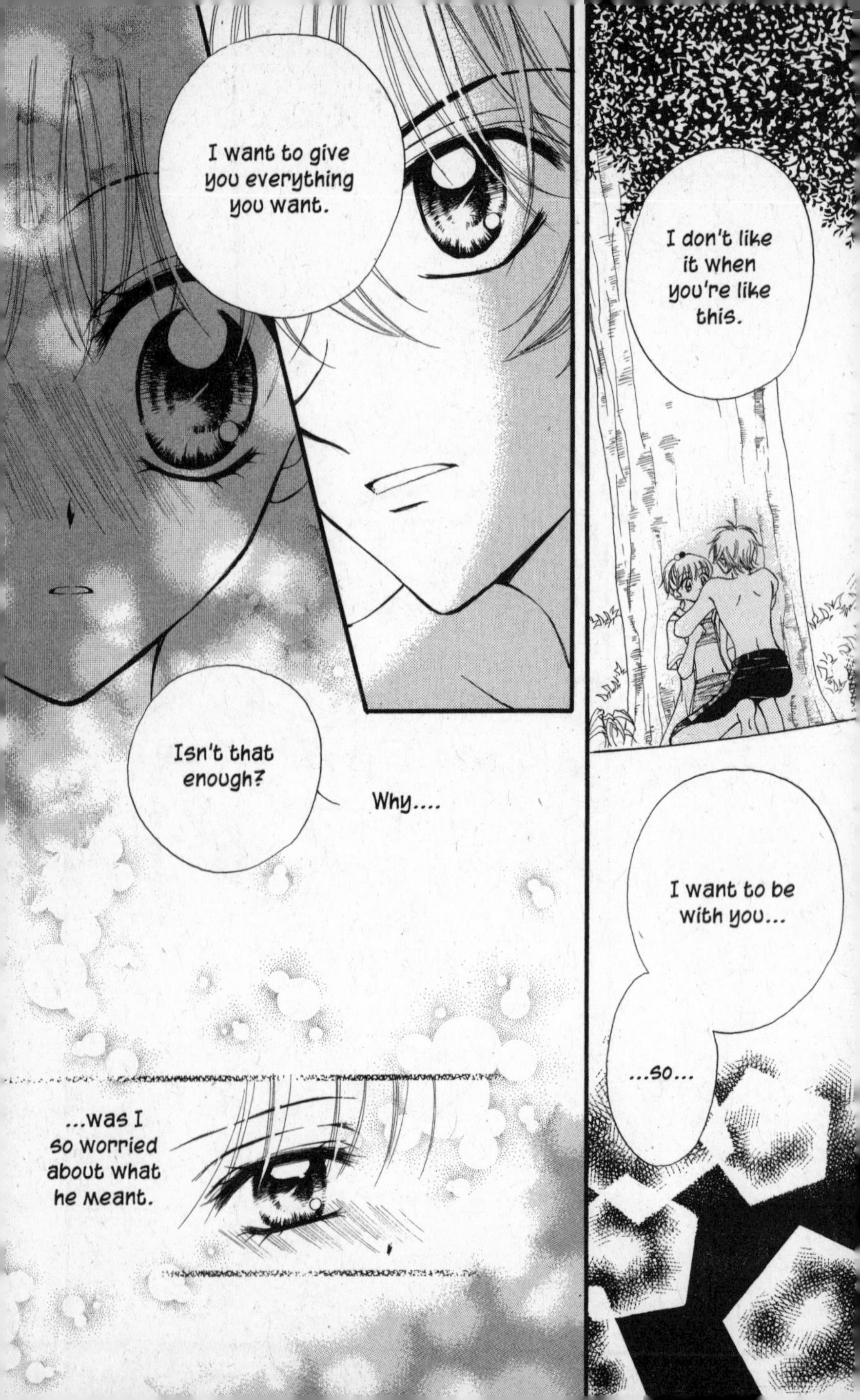
I don't like it when you're like this.
I want to be with you...
...so...
I want to give you everything you want.
Isn't that enough?
Why....
...was I so worried about what he meant.

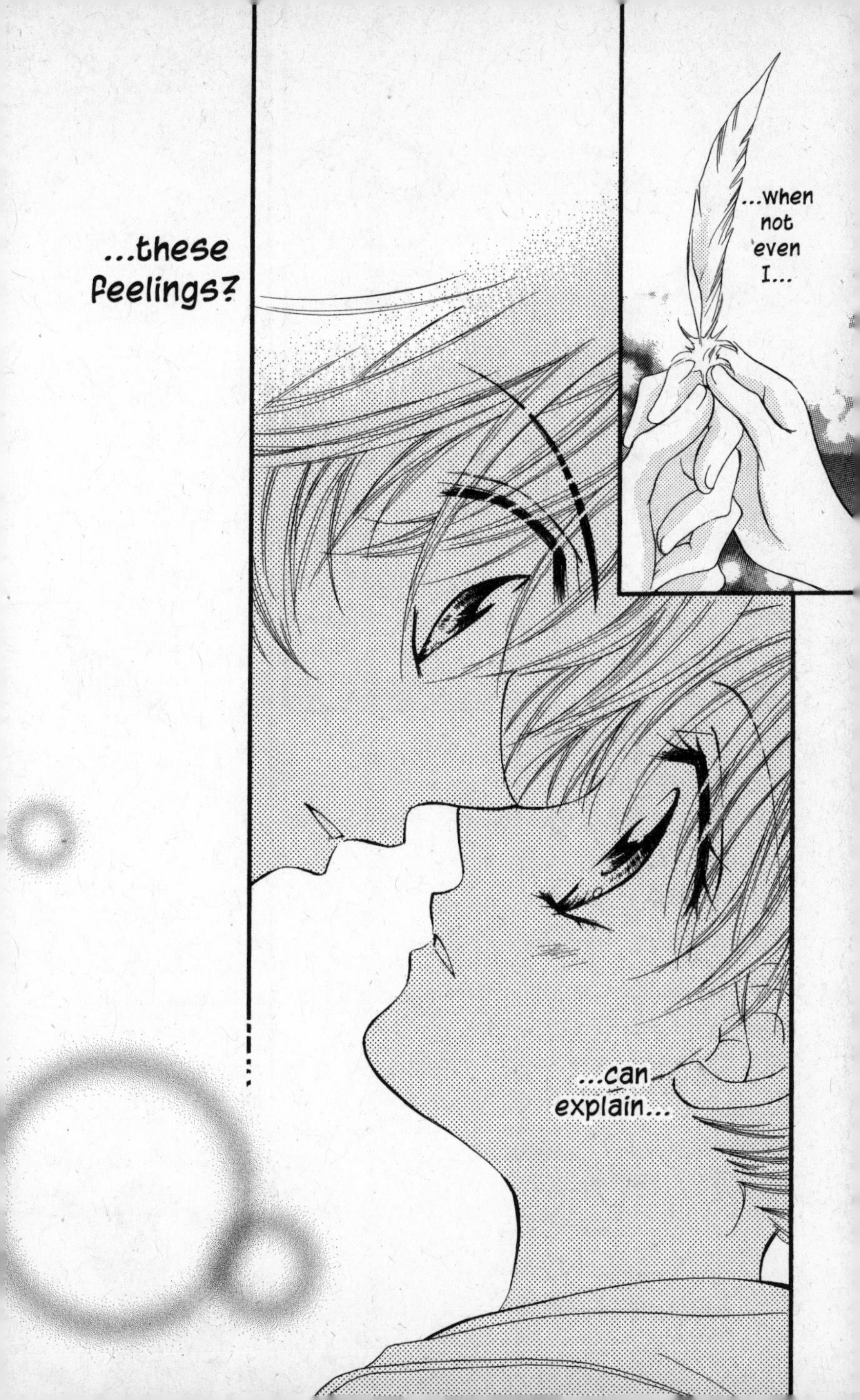
...when not even I...
...can explain...
...these feelings?

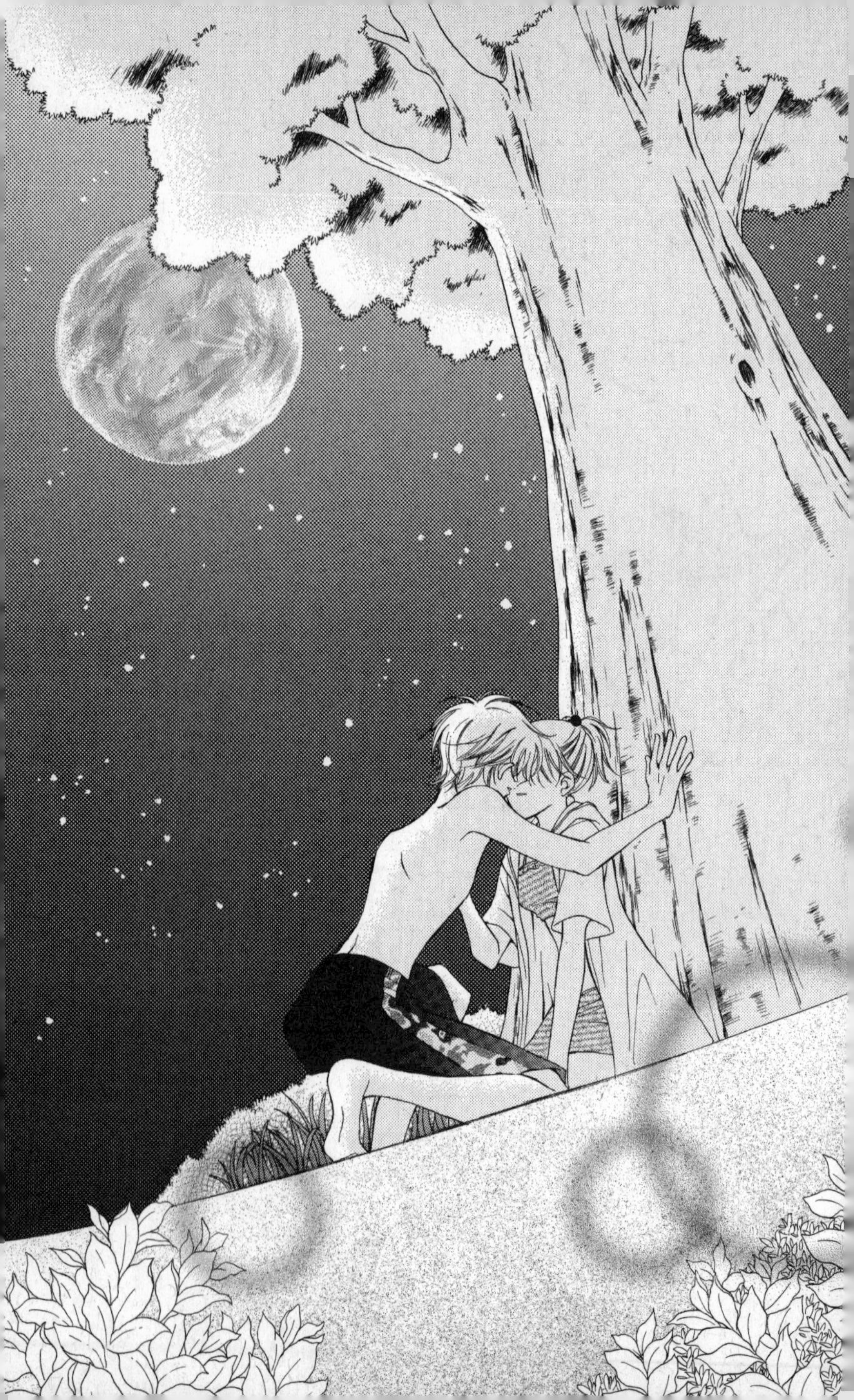

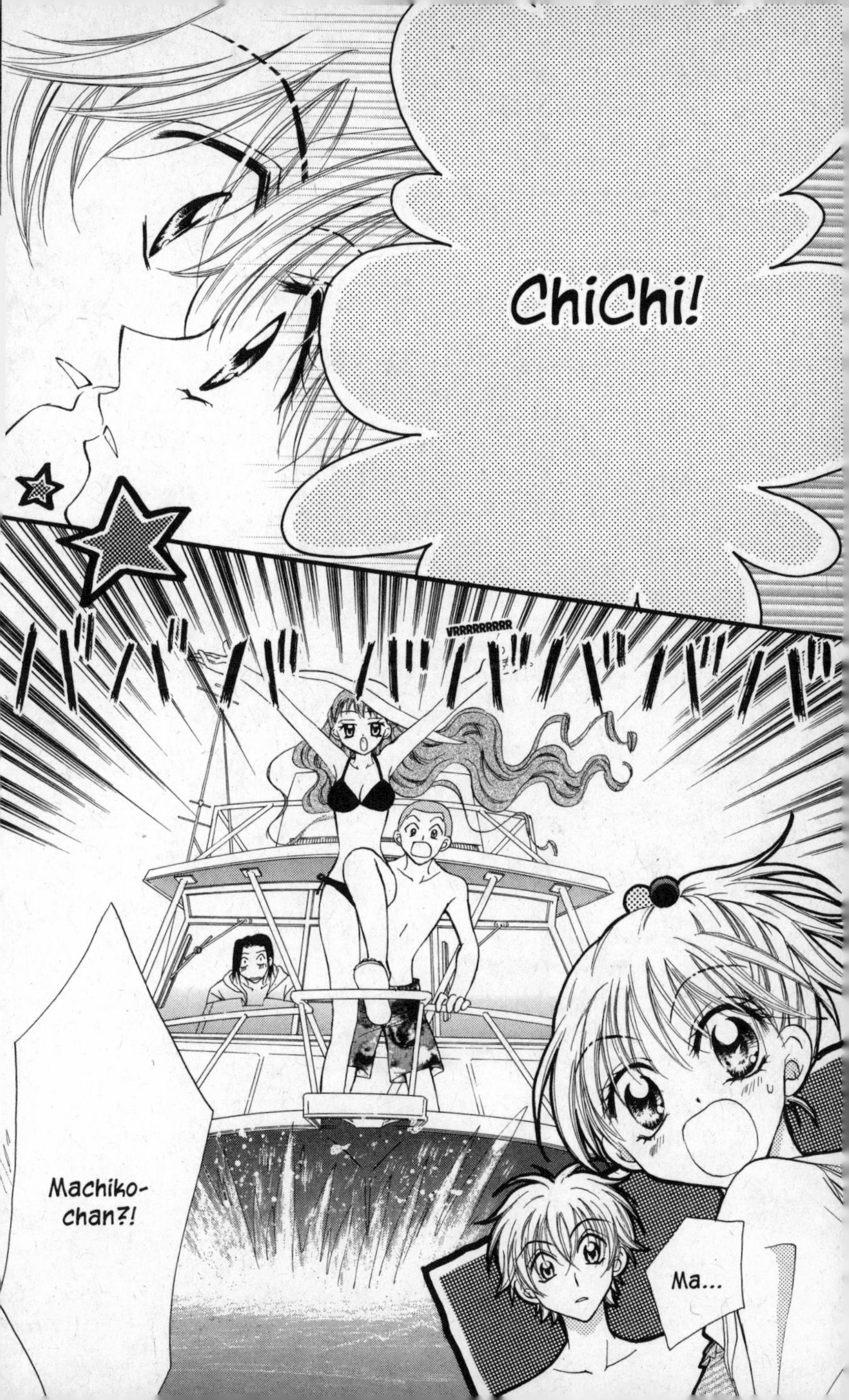
ChiChi!
VRRRRRRRRR
Ma...
Machiko-chan?!

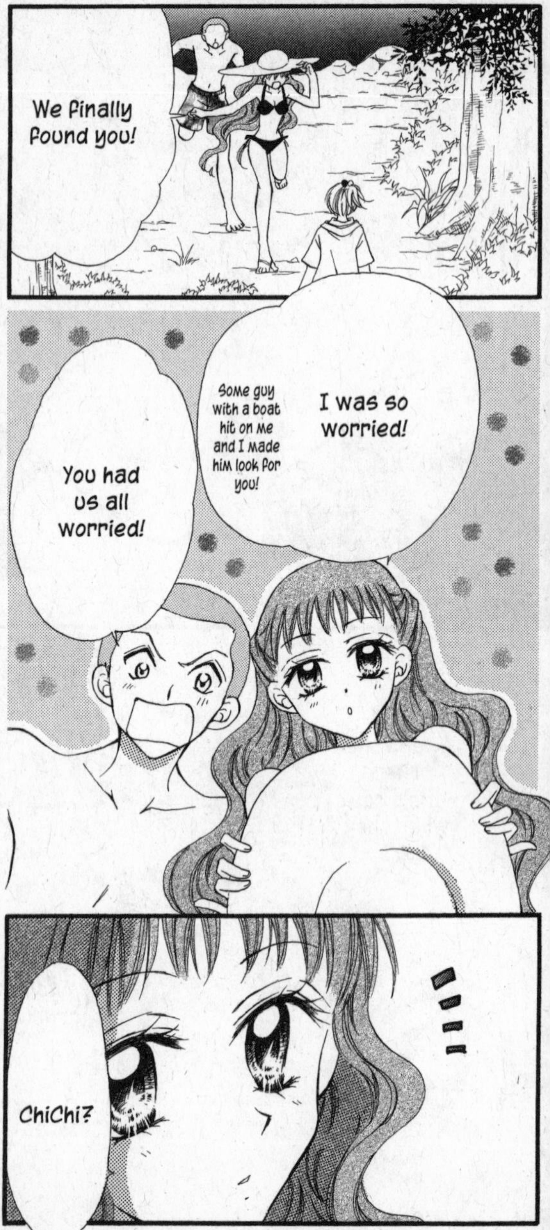
We finally found you!
I was so worried!
Some guy with a boat hit on me and I made him look for you!
You had us all worried!
ChiChi?

3.

Since it's onsen season, I decided to travel to Izu! I stayed in a small hotel (it only had about 5 rooms) but it was so relaxing! And there were...

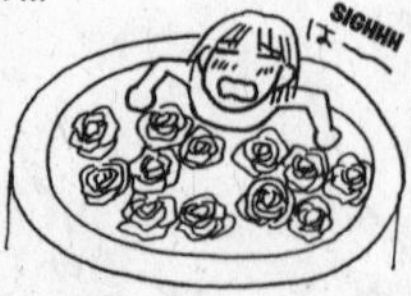
SIGHHH

ROSE PETALS in the water! ★★ It wasn't that expensive, either. It felt so good I went in over and over again, even while it was raining! It was good to relax after working so hard. And the people in Izu are all so kind! I had trouble finding a restaurant I saw in a guide book and got lost when...

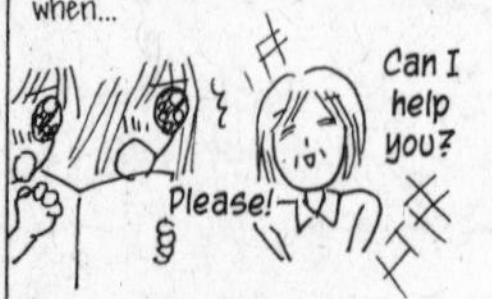
Can I help you?
Please!

...someone offered to help! That would never happen in Tokyo! She was so nice. Even the dogs were nice!

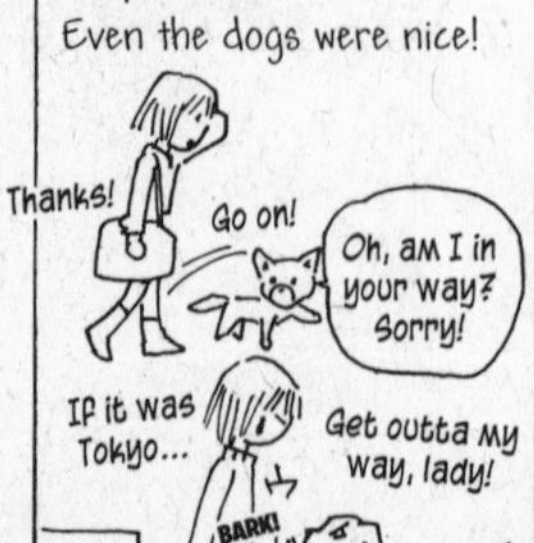
Thanks!
Go on!
Oh, am I in your way? Sorry!
If it was Tokyo...
Get outta my way, lady!
BARK!
Continued...

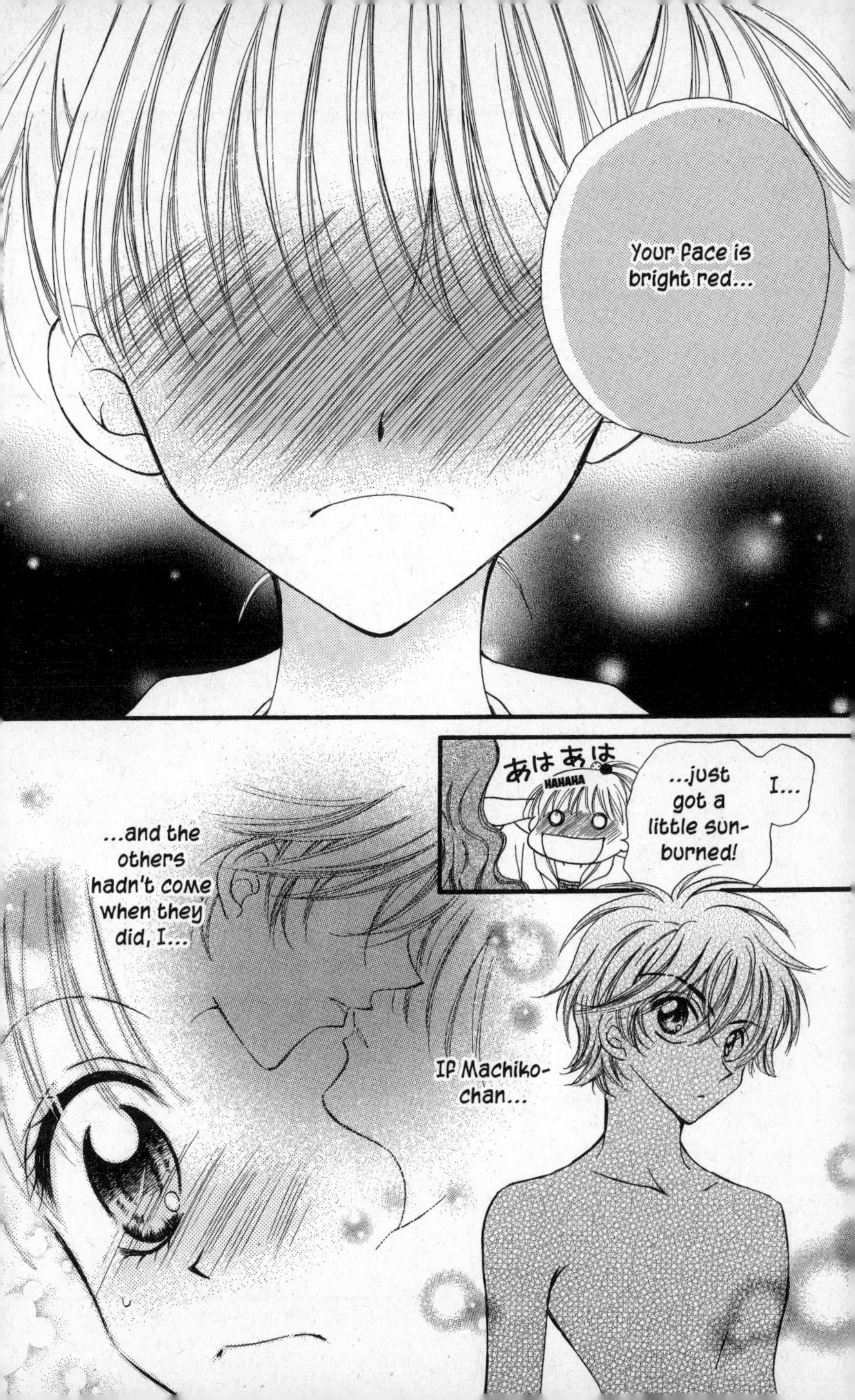
Your face is bright red...
あはあは
HAHAHA
I...
...just got a little sun-burned!
If Machiko-chan...
...and the others hadn't come when they did, I...

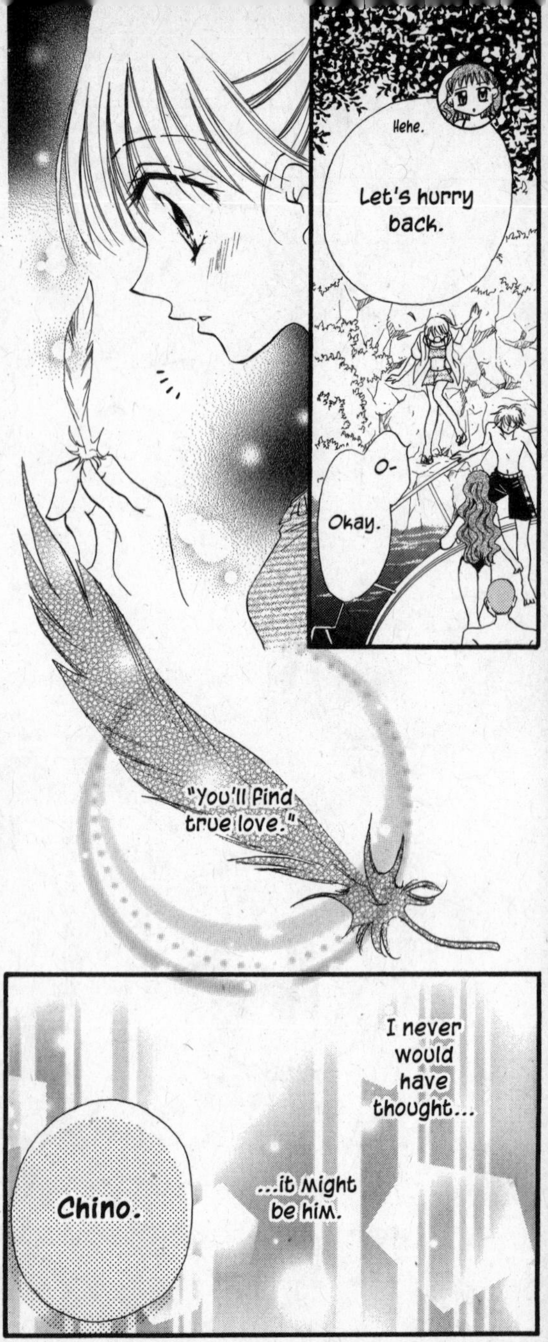
Hehe.
Let's hurry back.
O-
Okay.
"You'll find true love."
I never would have thought...
...it might be him.
Chino.

4.

Thanks to the kind woman I was able to figure out the way to the restaurant, but I didn't end up going because...

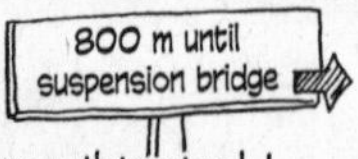
800 m until suspension bridge

...I saw this sign! I was really hungry and wanted to eat at that restaurant, and seeing a suspension bridge is pretty rare, so I headed for it.

It was so scary! I'm afraid of heights!

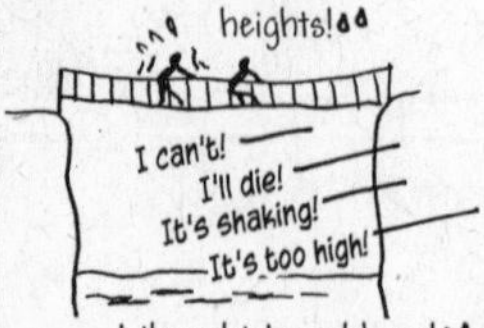
I can't!
I'll die!
It's shaking!
It's too high!

I thought I would cry!

I went across it but didn't see anything on the other side so I had to turn back the way I came! ♡

The next day I got on the train to go to a rose garden, but I must have been really tired (it was the day after a deadline) and I fell asleep and missed my station.

I ended way up in the mountains!

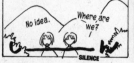

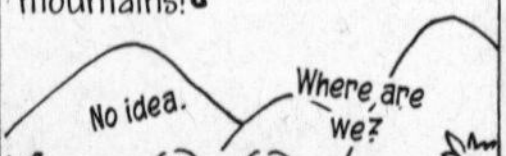
No idea.
Where are we?
SILENCE

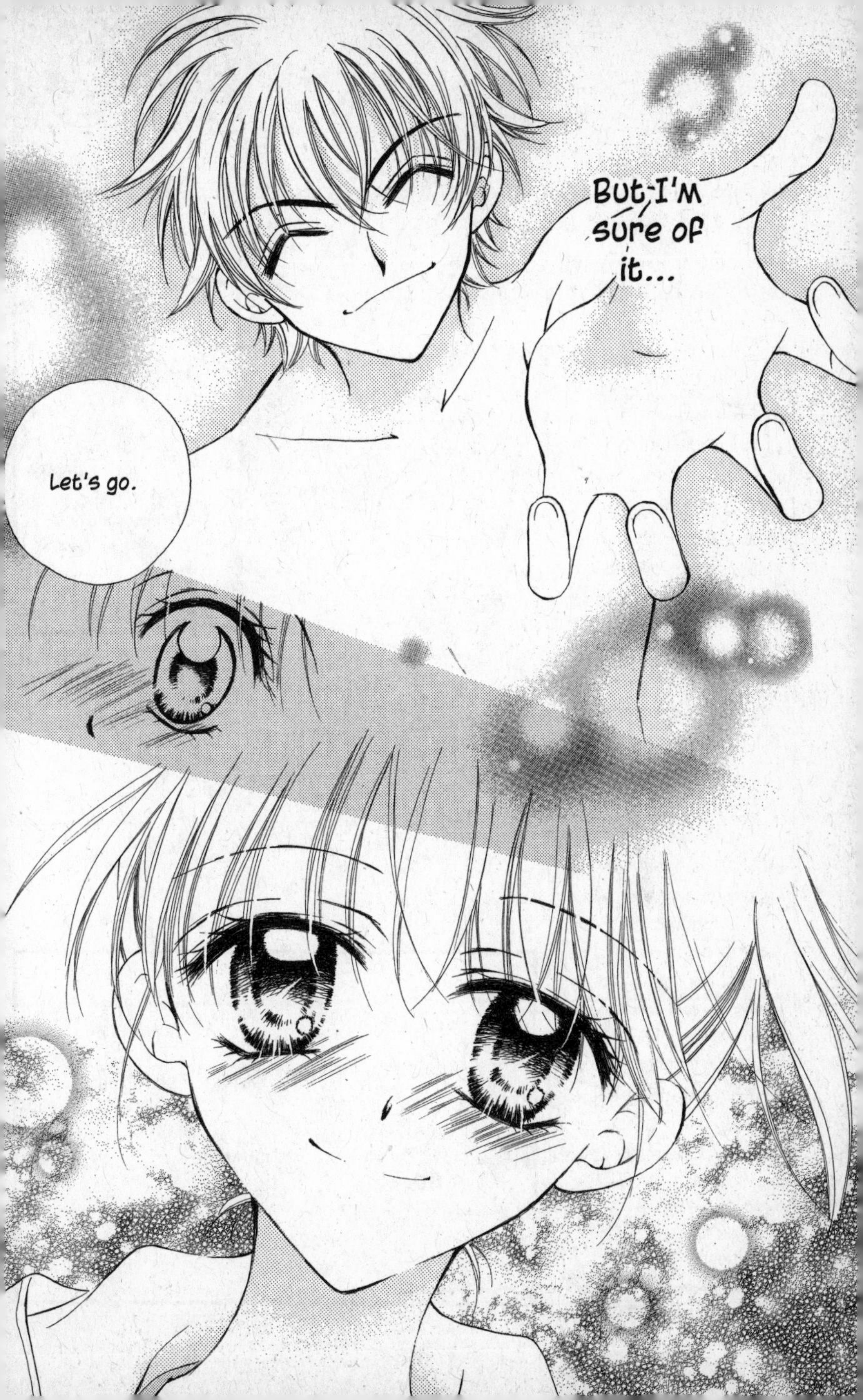
But I'm sure of it...
Let's go.

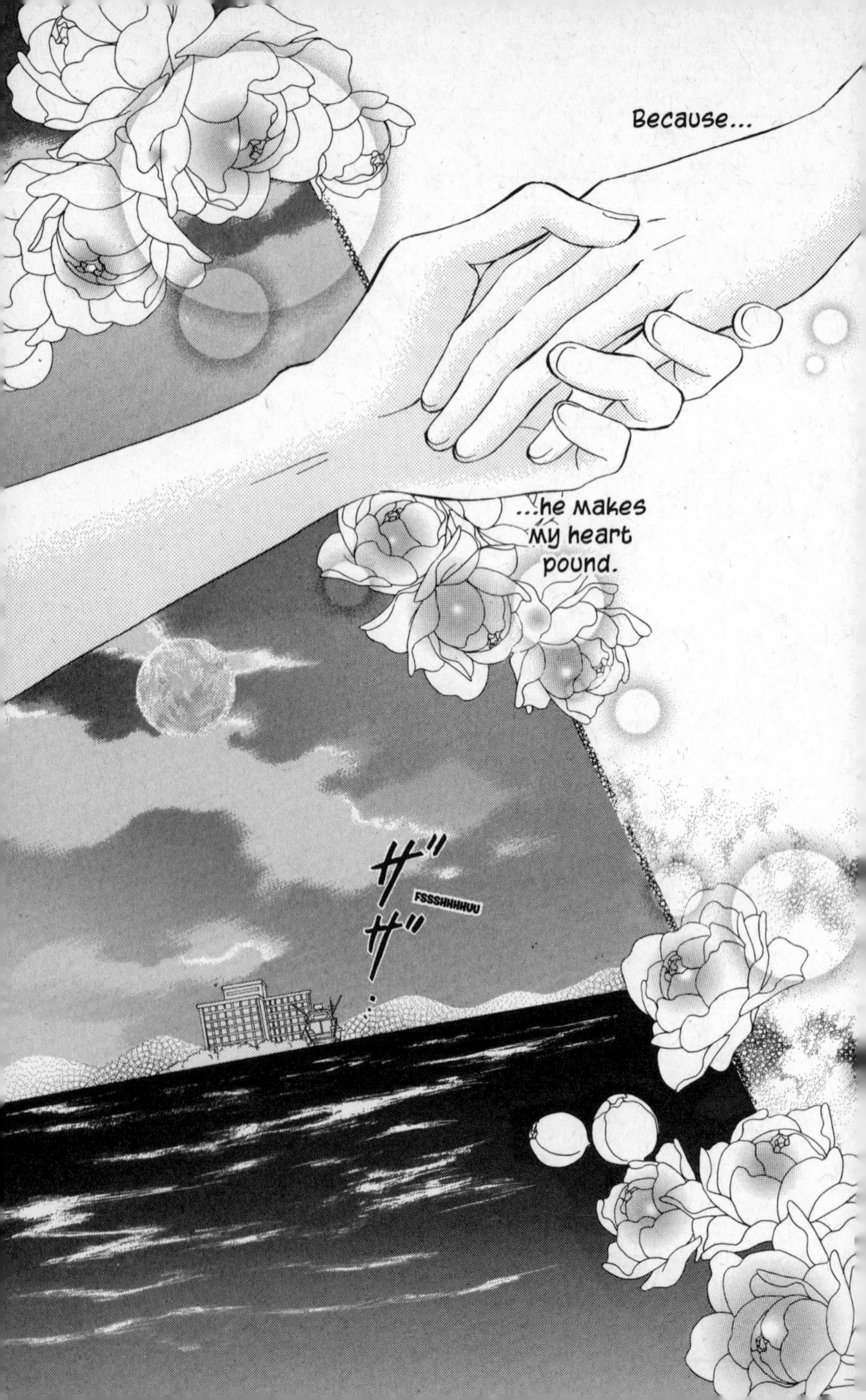
Because...
...he makes my heart pound.
ザザ...
FSSSHHHHUU

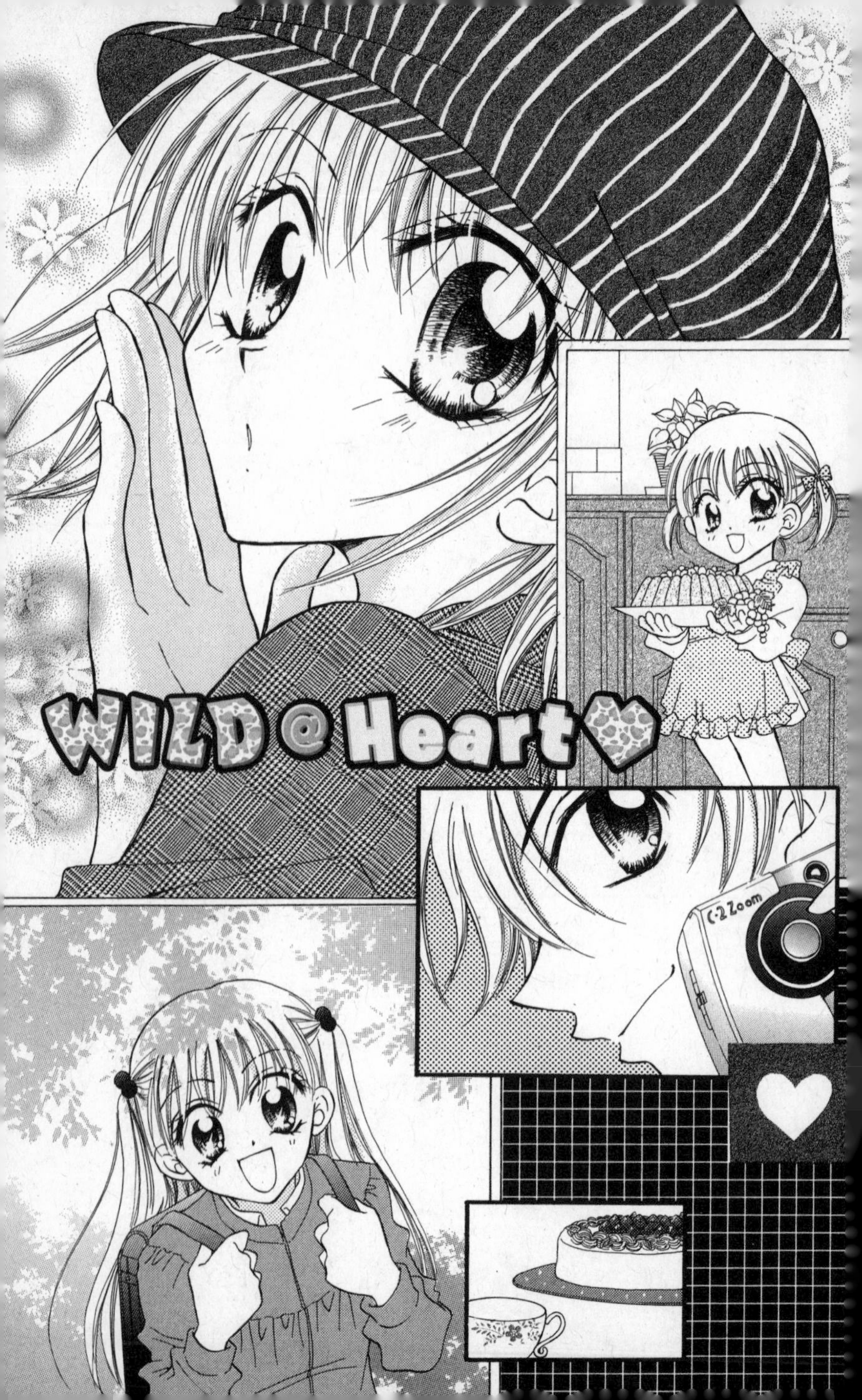
WILD @ Heart♥
C-2 Zoom

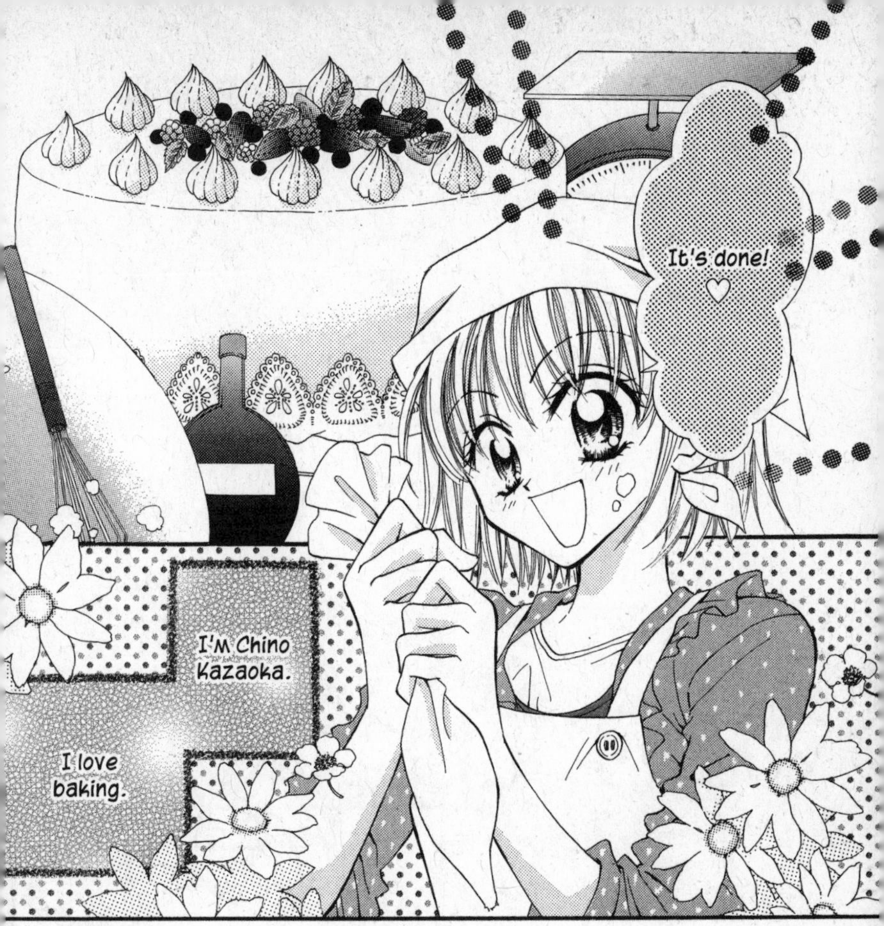
It's done! ♡
I'm Chino Kazaoka.
I love baking.

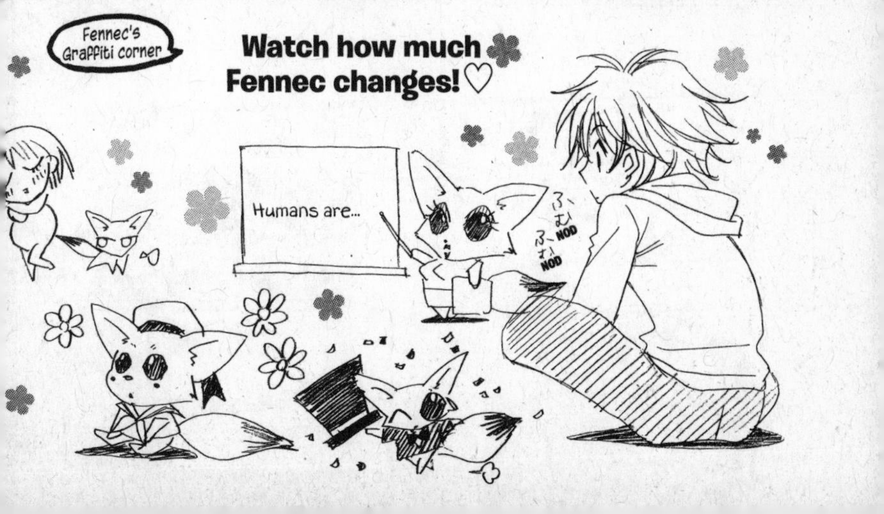
Fennec's Graffiti corner
Watch how much Fennec changes! ♡
Humans are...
NOD
NOD

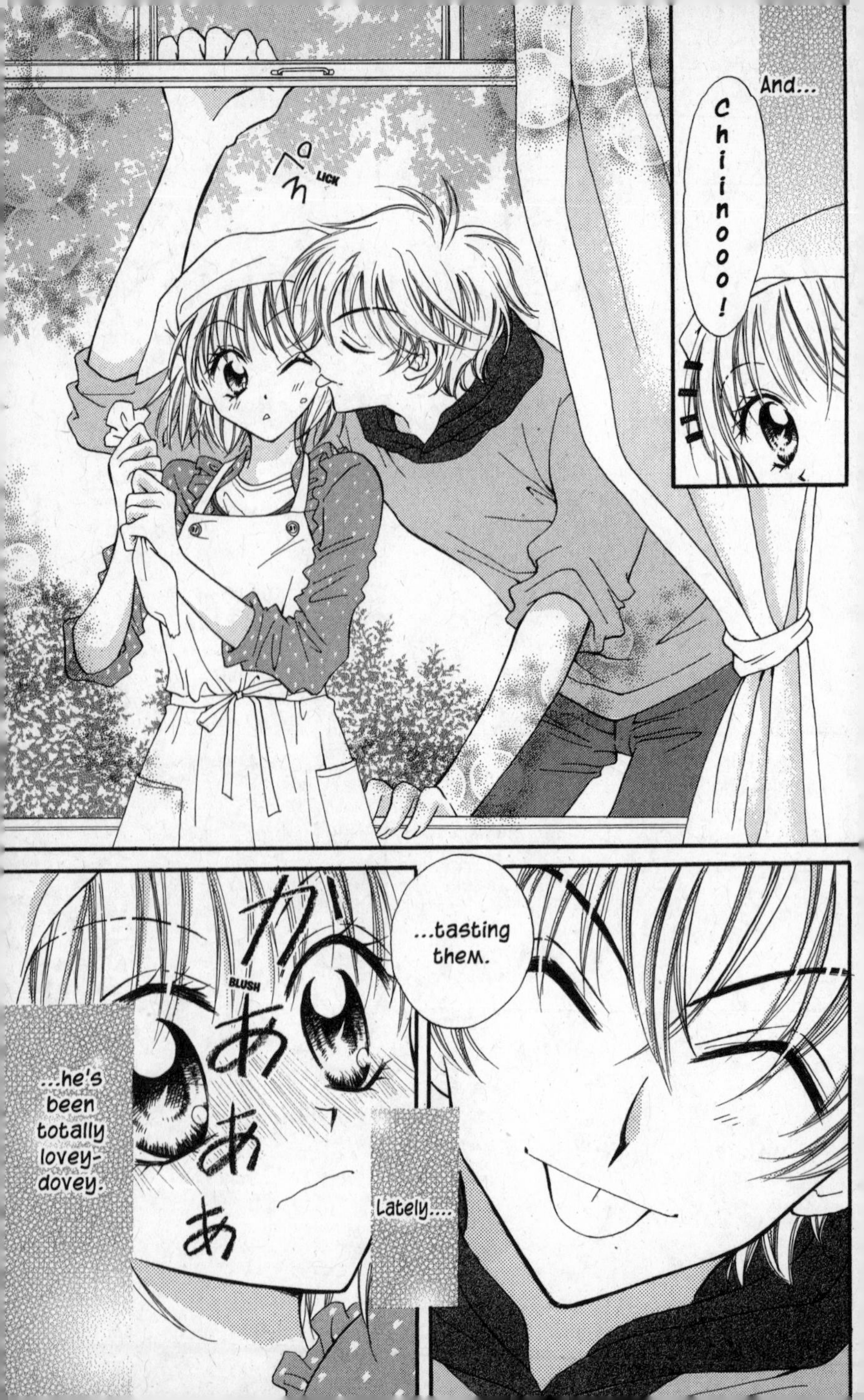
And...
Chiinooo!
LICK
...tasting them.
Lately....
かあああ
BLUSH
...he's been totally lovey-dovey.

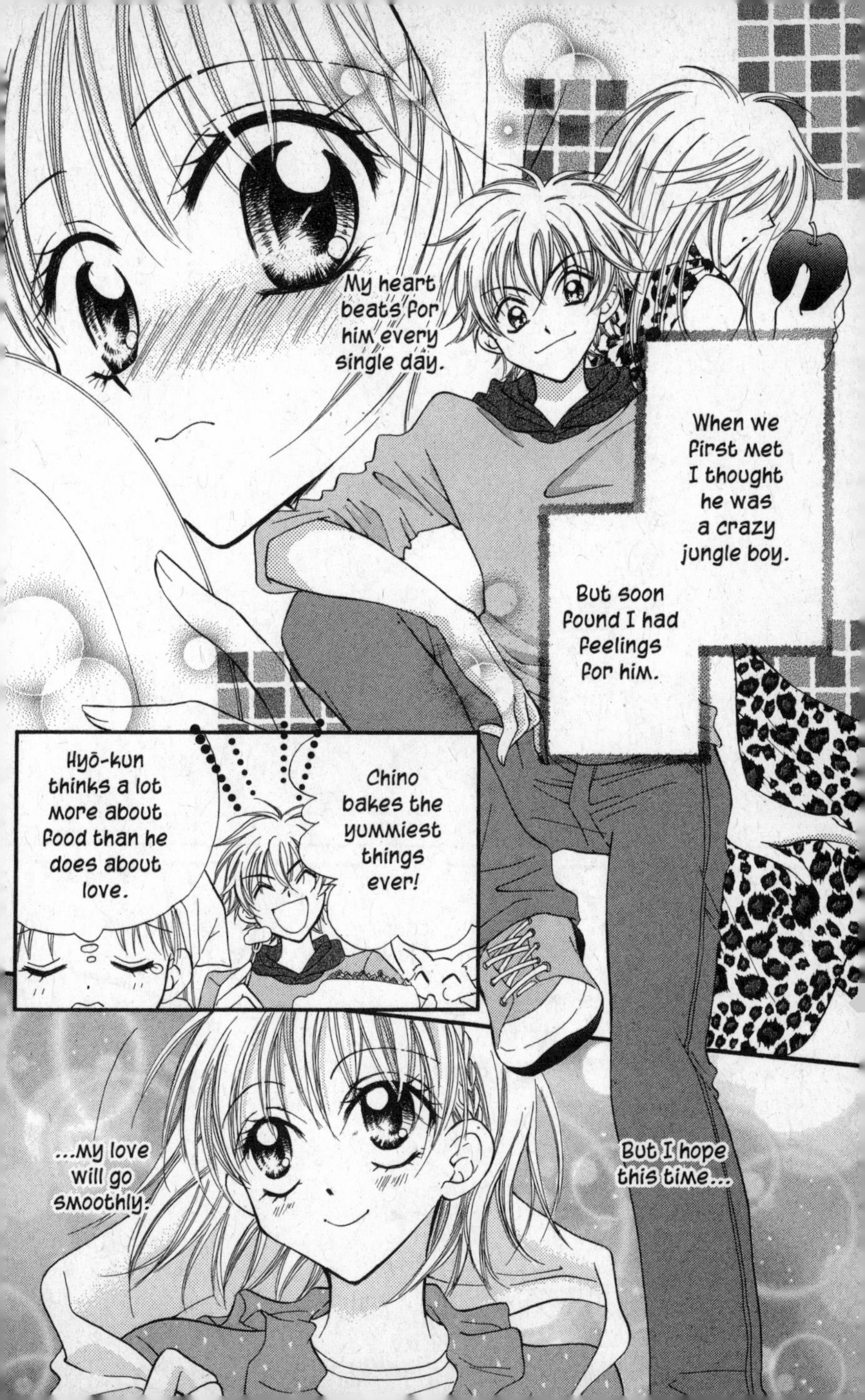
When we first met I thought he was a crazy jungle boy.
But soon found I had feelings for him.
My heart beats for him every single day.
Chino bakes the yummiest things ever!
Hyō-kun thinks a lot more about food than he does about love.
But I hope this time...
...my love will go smoothly.

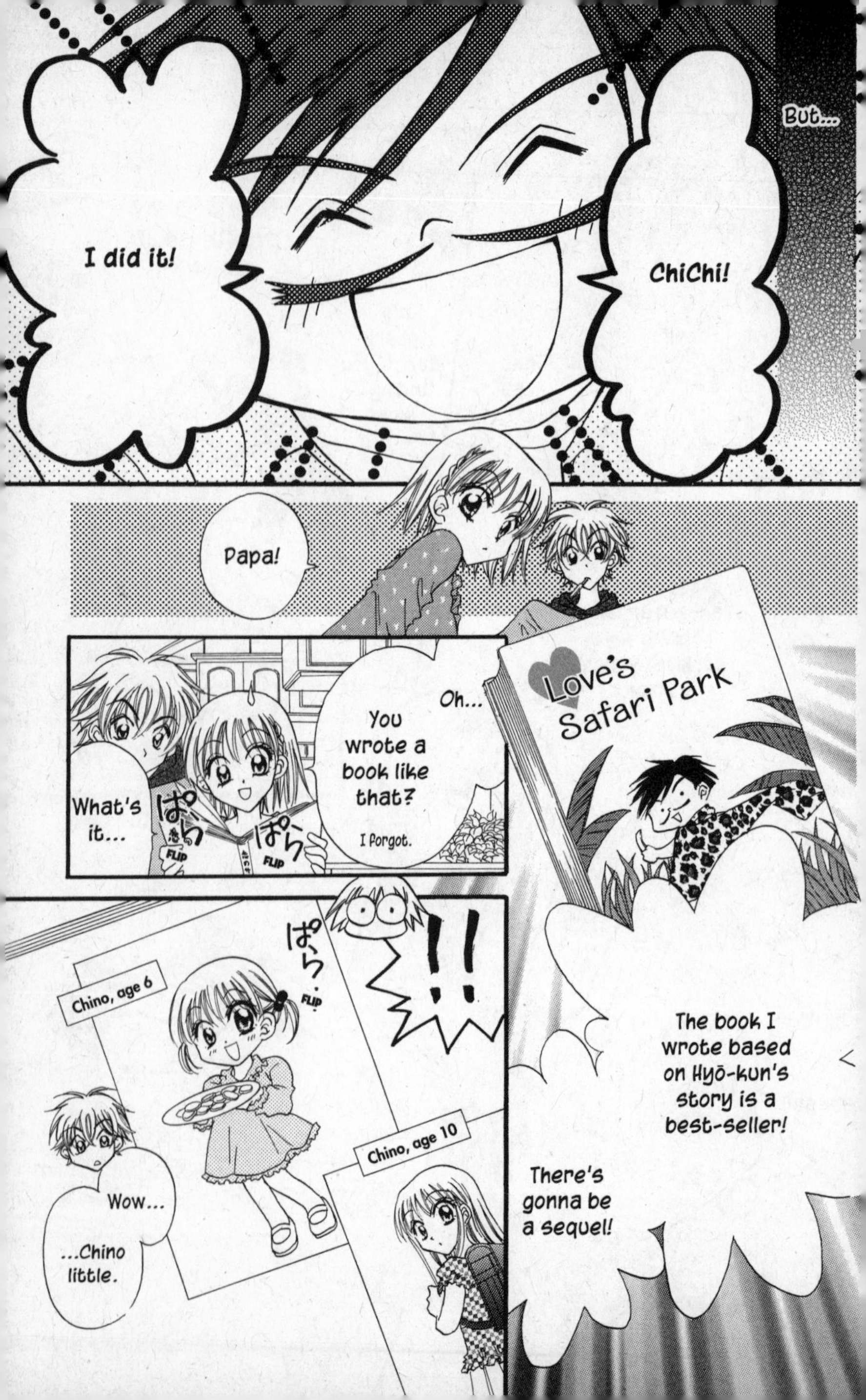
But...
ChiChi!
I did it!
Love's Safari Park
The book I wrote based on Hyō-kun's story is a best-seller!
There's gonna be a sequel!
Papa!
Oh...
You wrote a book like that?
I forgot.
ぱら FLIP
ぱら FLIP
What's it...
!!
ぱら FLIP
Chino, age 6
Chino, age 10
Wow...
...Chino little.

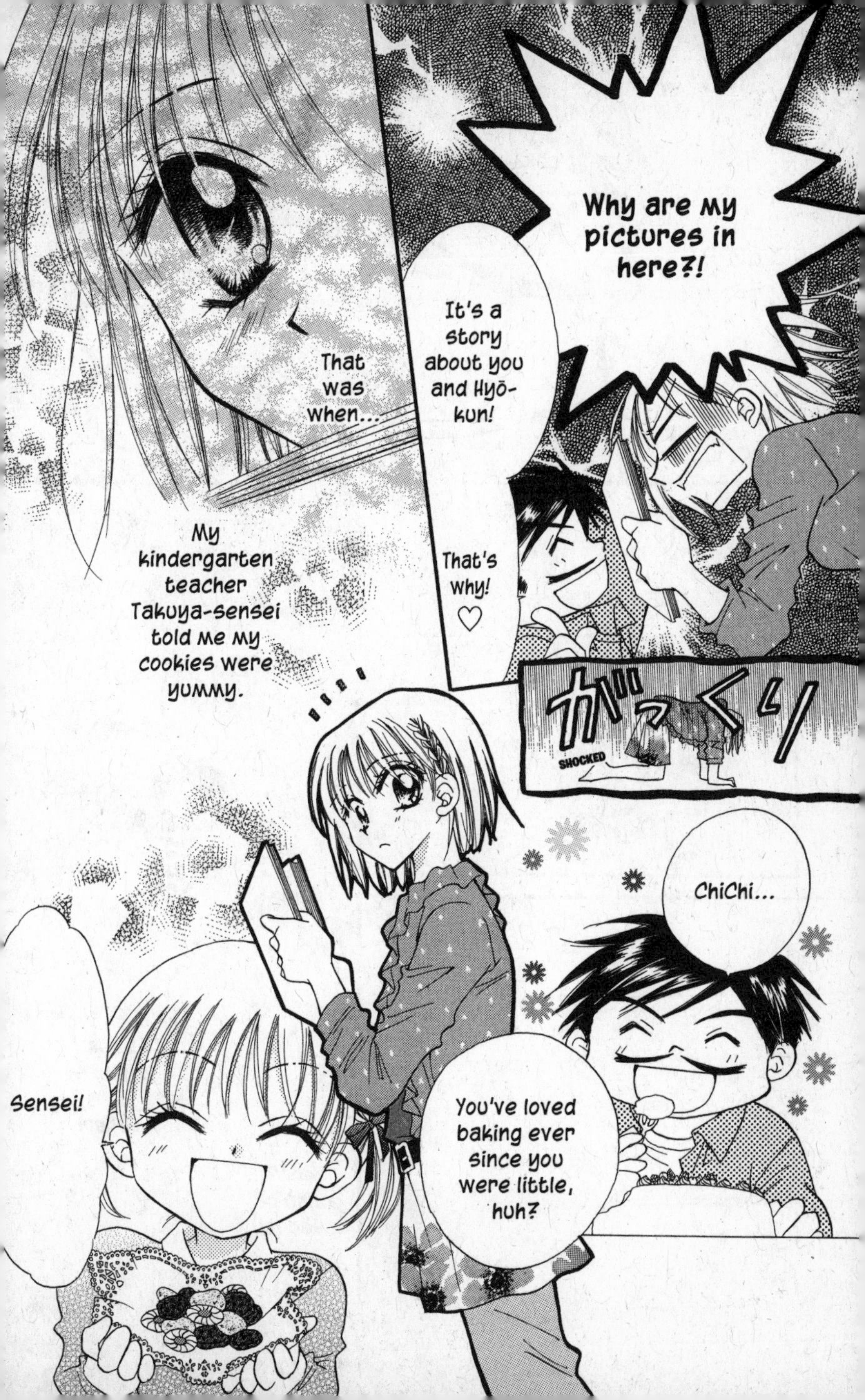
Why are my pictures in here?!
It's a story about you and Hyō-kun!
That's why! ♡
がっくり
SHOCKED
That was when...
My kindergarten teacher Takuya-sensei told me my cookies were yummy.
ChiChi...
You've loved baking ever since you were little, huh?
Sensei!

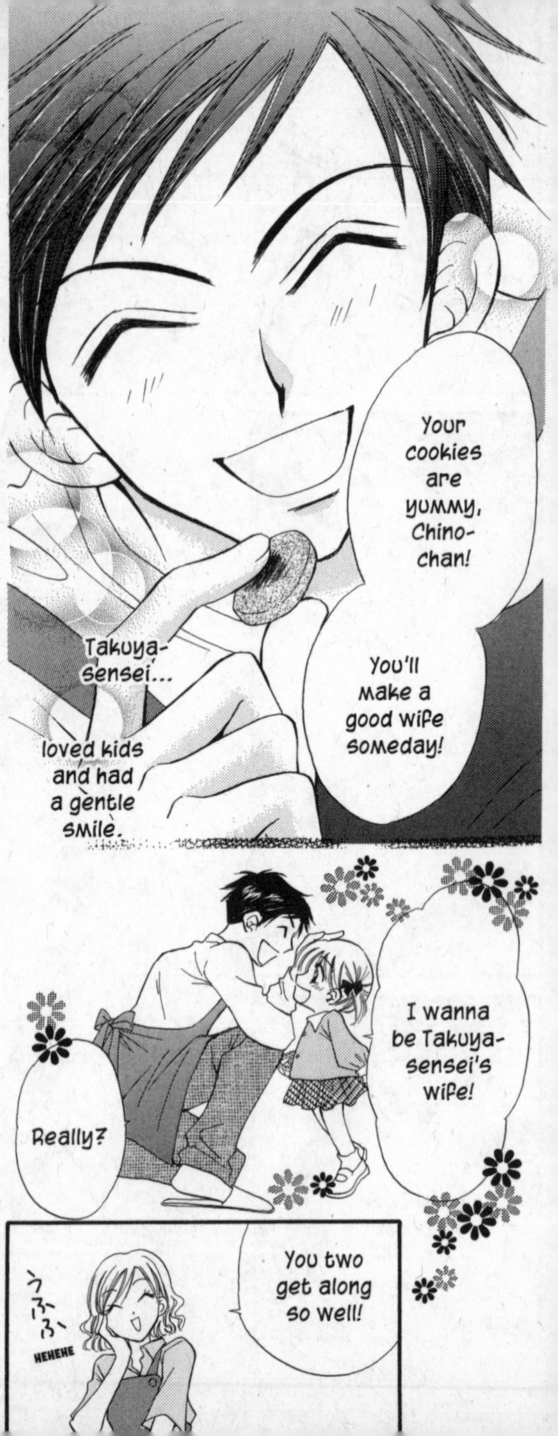
Your cookies are yummy, Chino-chan!
You'll make a good wife someday!
Takuya-sensei...
loved kids and had a gentle smile.
I wanna be Takuya-sensei's wife!
Really?
You two get along so well!
うふふ
HEHEHE

5.

In this volume Chino's story about Hasebe-kun appears. That's about 1/10 made up from my own personal experiences.
The boy wasn't as mean to me as he was to Chino, though. But the part about me having a crush on the boy who sat next to me and then growing apart after having our seats changed is true. In elementary and middle school it was a big deal when your assigned seats changed, right? No one wanted to be put in the front row by the teacher! My favorite place was in the back row next to the window. That way no one ever caught you if you weren't paying attention!!
I was always writing a story or something during class.
One time the teacher caught me and hit me! It knocked the book right out of my hands! She told me to go stand out in the hall, just like on TV. That teacher used to hit students all the time but these days that would cause a huge problem!!

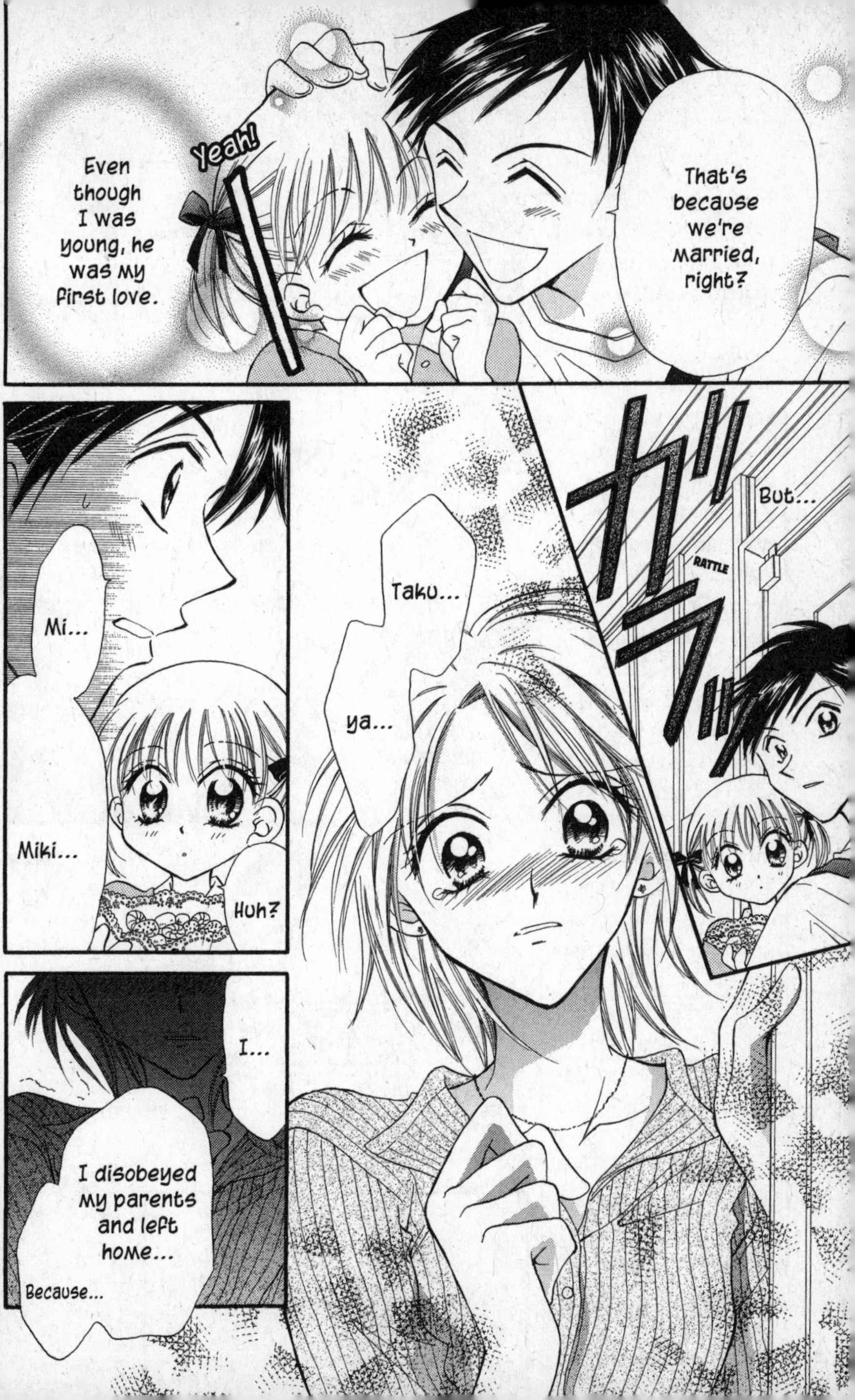
That's because we're married, right?
Yeah!
Even though I was young, he was my first love.
But...
ガラッ
RATTLE
Taku...
ya...
Mi...
Miki...
Huh?
I...
I disobeyed my parents and left home...
Because...

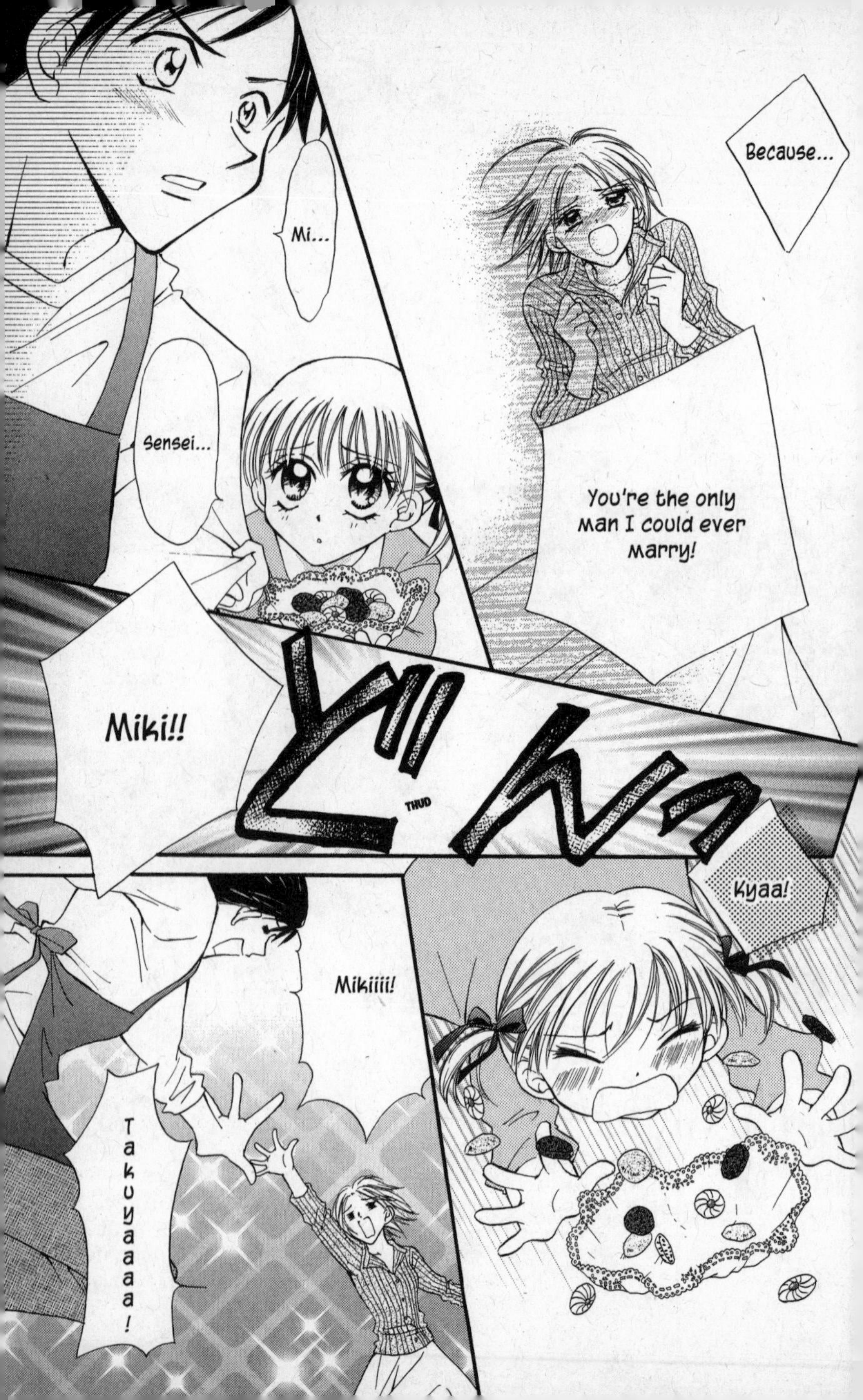

Because...
You're the only man I could ever marry!
Mi...
Sensei...
THUD
Miki!!
Kyaa!
Mikiiii!
Takuyaaaaa!

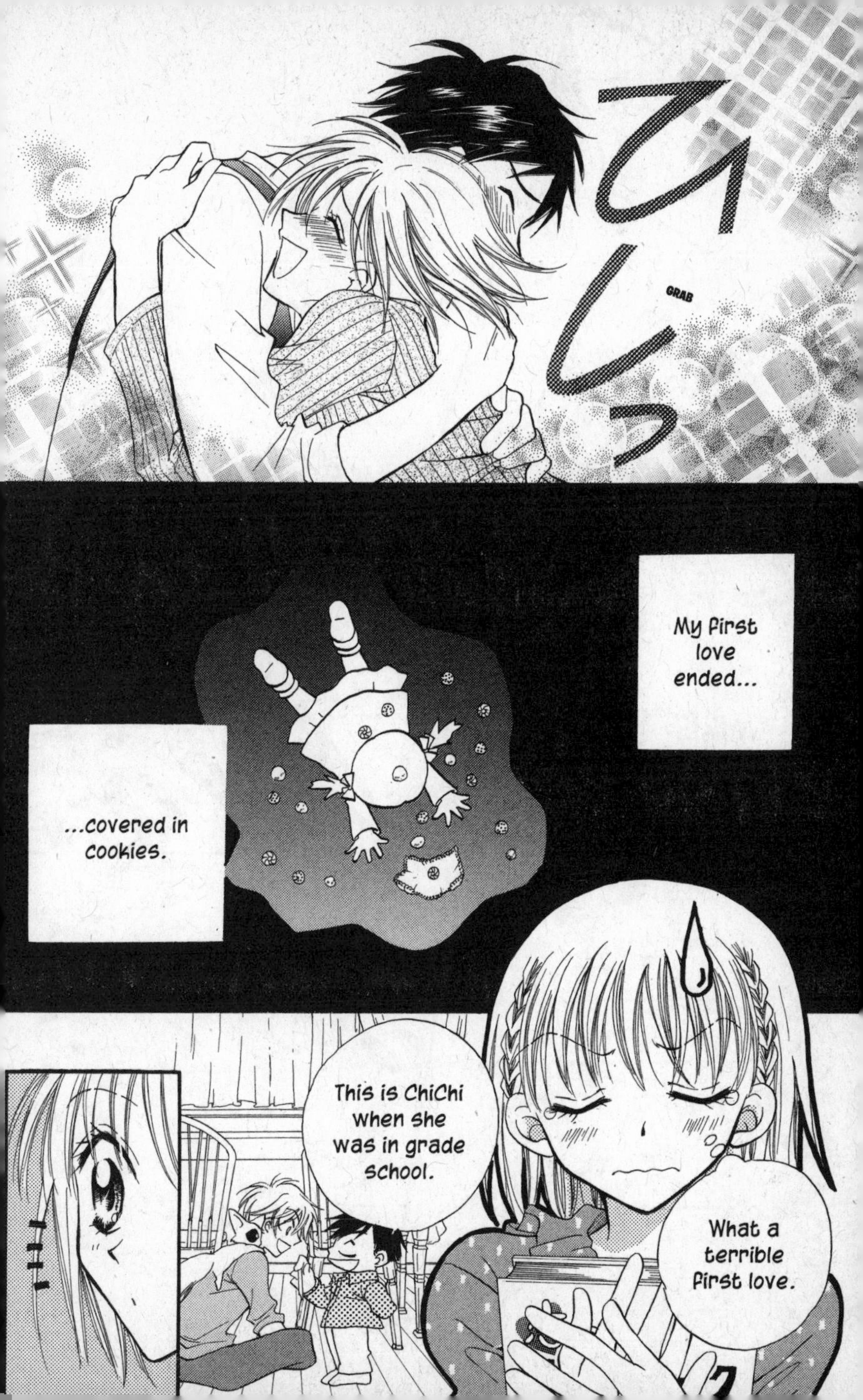
GRAB
My first love ended...
...covered in cookies.
This is ChiChi when she was in grade school.
What a terrible first love.

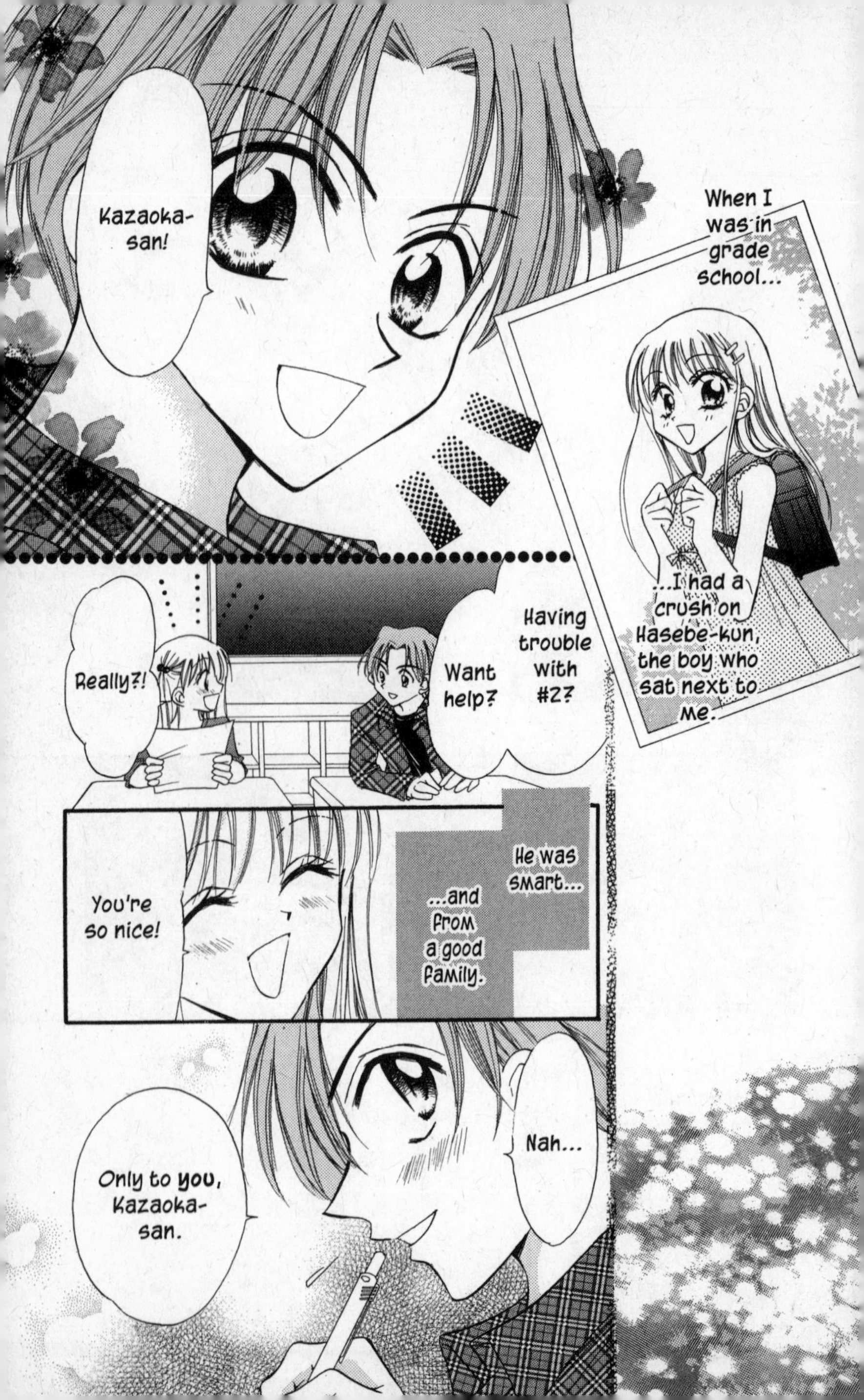
When I was in grade school...
...I had a crush on Hasebe-kun, the boy who sat next to me.
Kazaoka-san!
Having trouble with #2?
Want help?
...
Really?!
He was smart...
...and from a good family.
You're so nice!
Nah...
Only to you, Kazaoka-san.

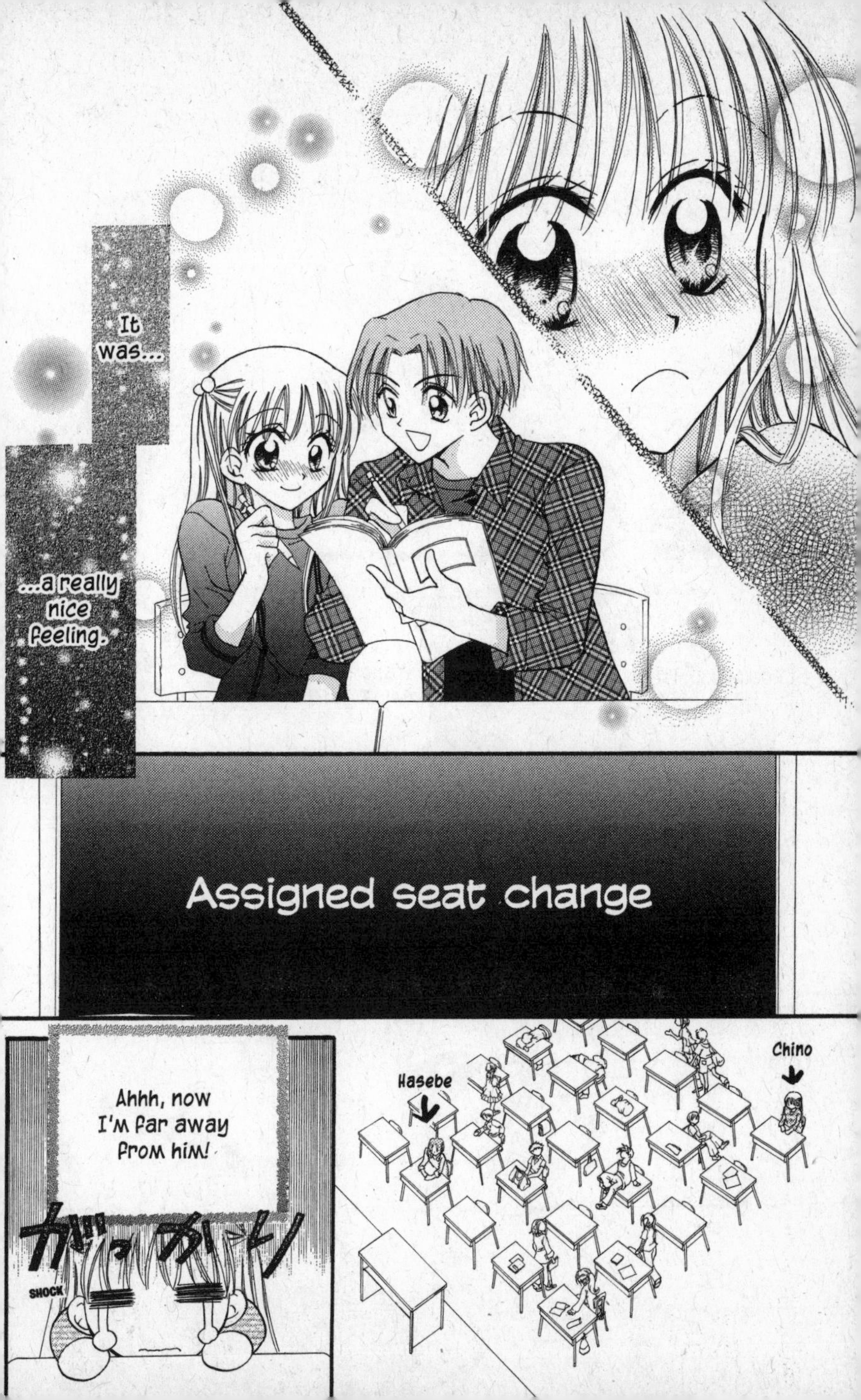
It was...
...a really nice feeling.
Assigned seat change
Chino
Hasebe
Ahhh, now I'm far away from him!
SHOCK

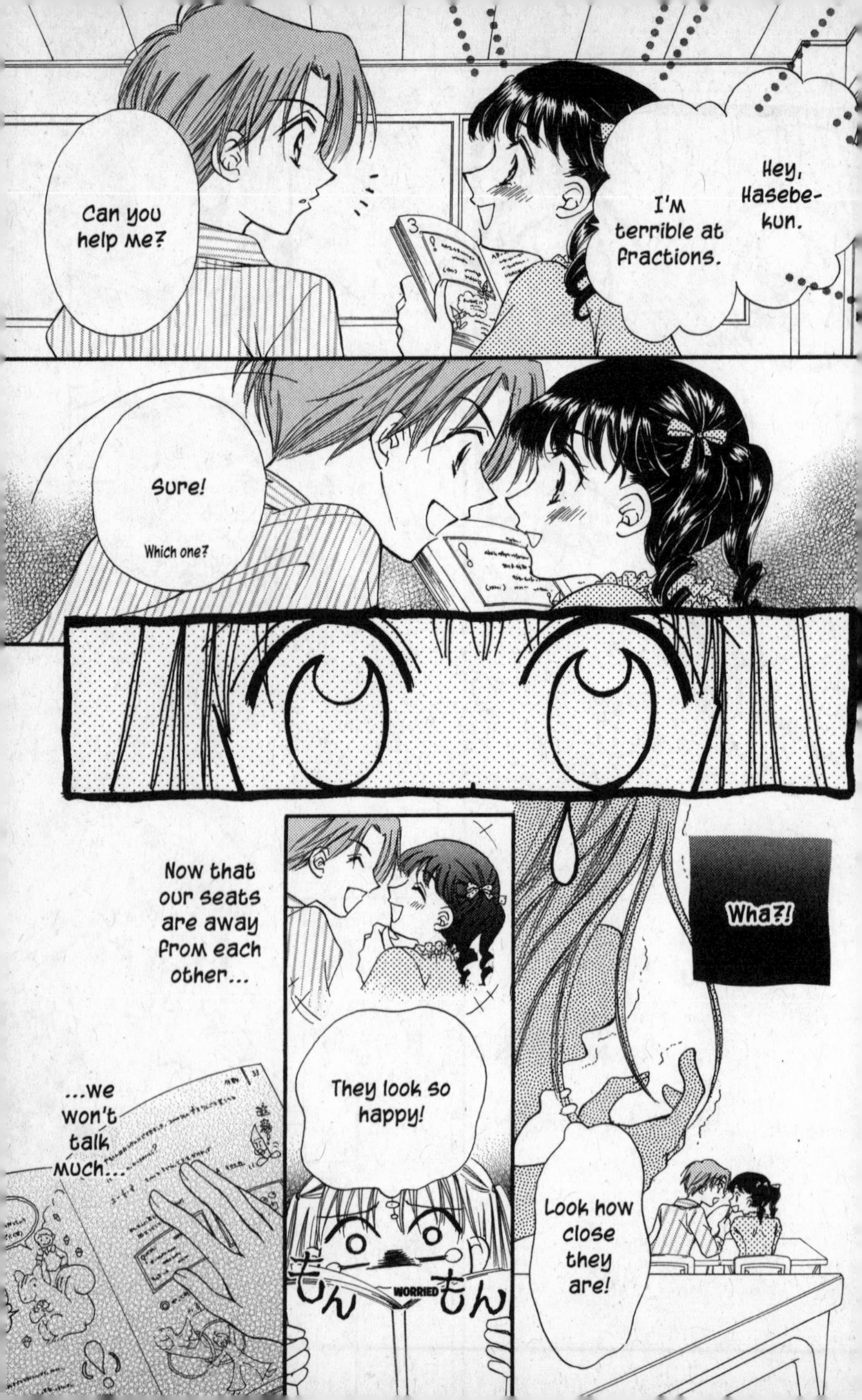
Hey, Hasebe-kun.
I'm terrible at fractions.
Can you help me?
Sure!
Which one?
Wha?!
Look how close they are!
They look so happy!
もん WORRIED もん
Now that our seats are away from each other...
...we won't talk much...

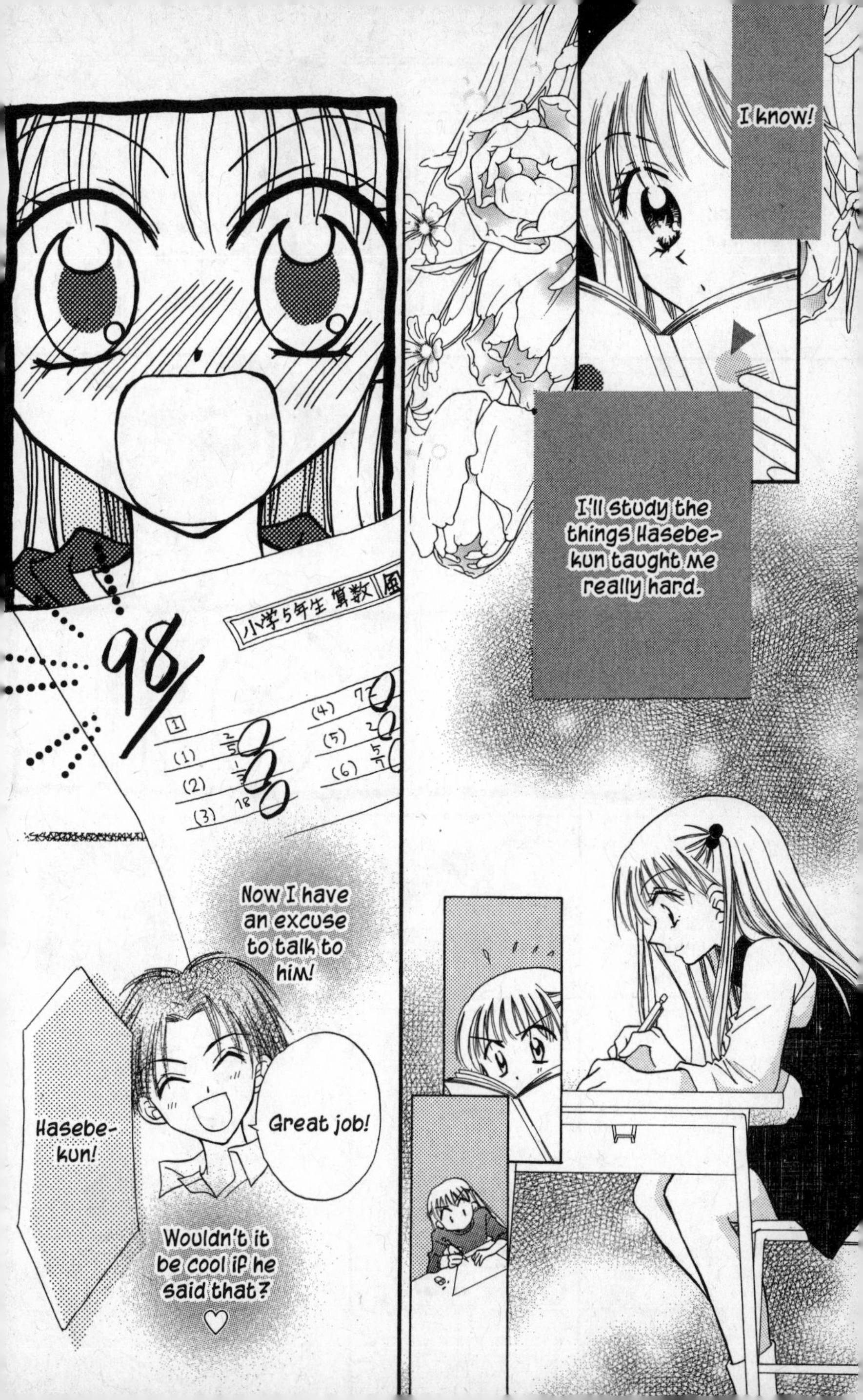
I know!
I'll study the things Hasebe-kun taught me really hard.
小学5年生 算数
98
Now I have an excuse to talk to him!
Great job!
Hasebe-kun!
Wouldn't it be cool if he said that? ♡

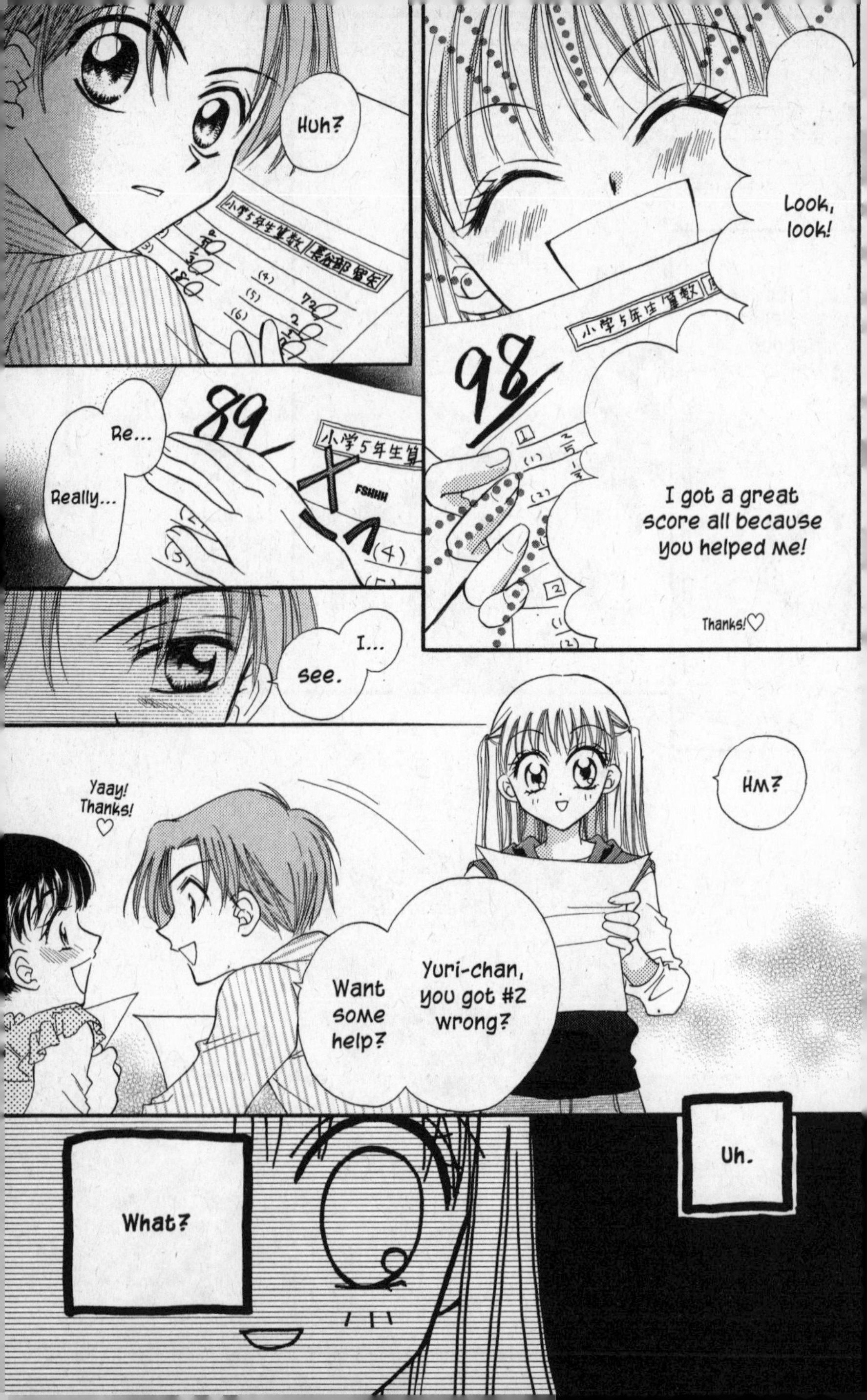
Look, look!
I got a great score all because you helped me!
Thanks!♡
Huh?
98
89
Re...
Really...
FSHHH
I... see.
Hm?
Yuri-chan, you got #2 wrong?
Want some help?
Yaay! Thanks! ♡
Uh.
What?

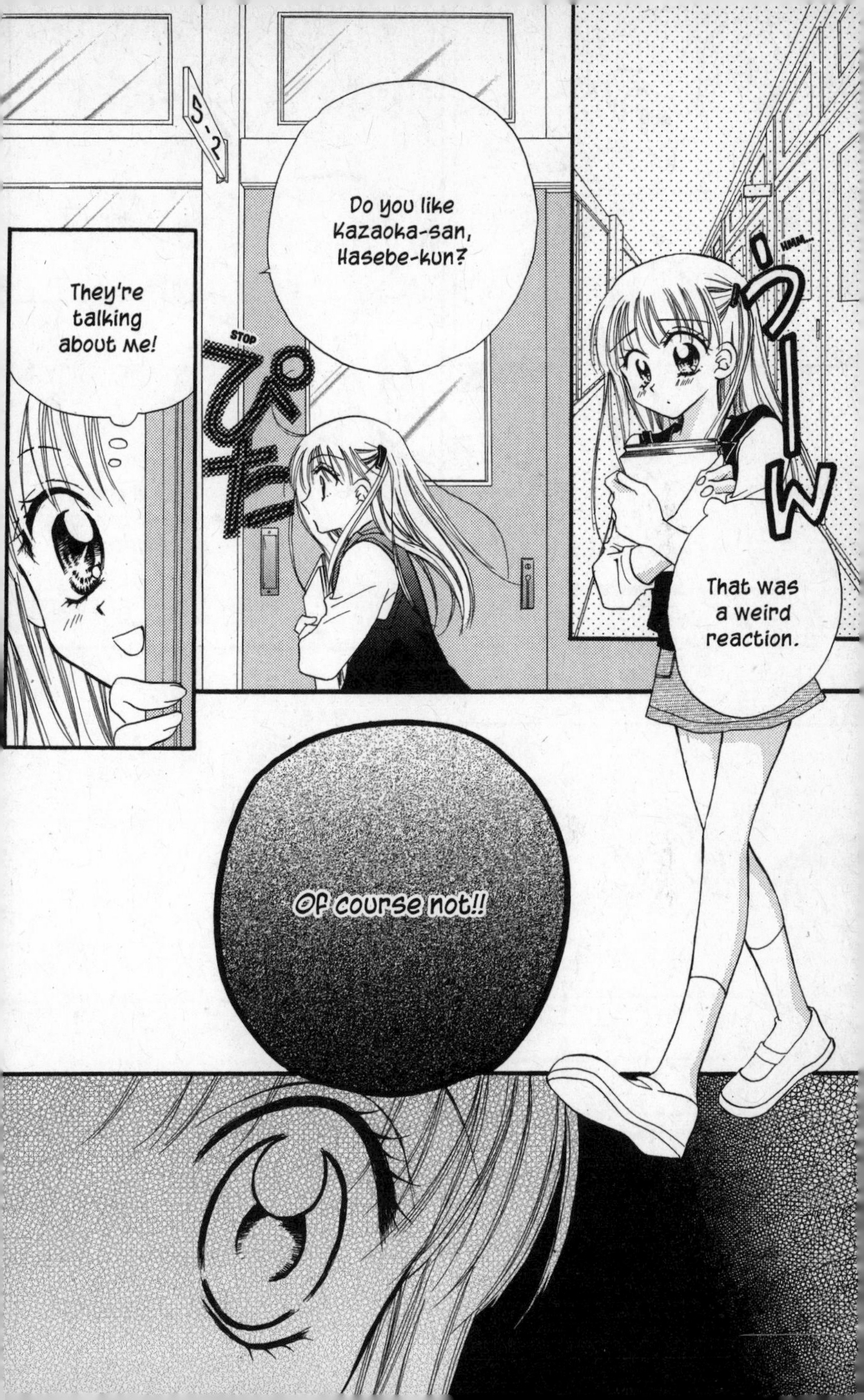
HMM...
うーん
That was a weird reaction.
Do you like Kazaoka-san, Hasebe-kun?
STOP
ぴた
They're talking about me!
Of course not!!

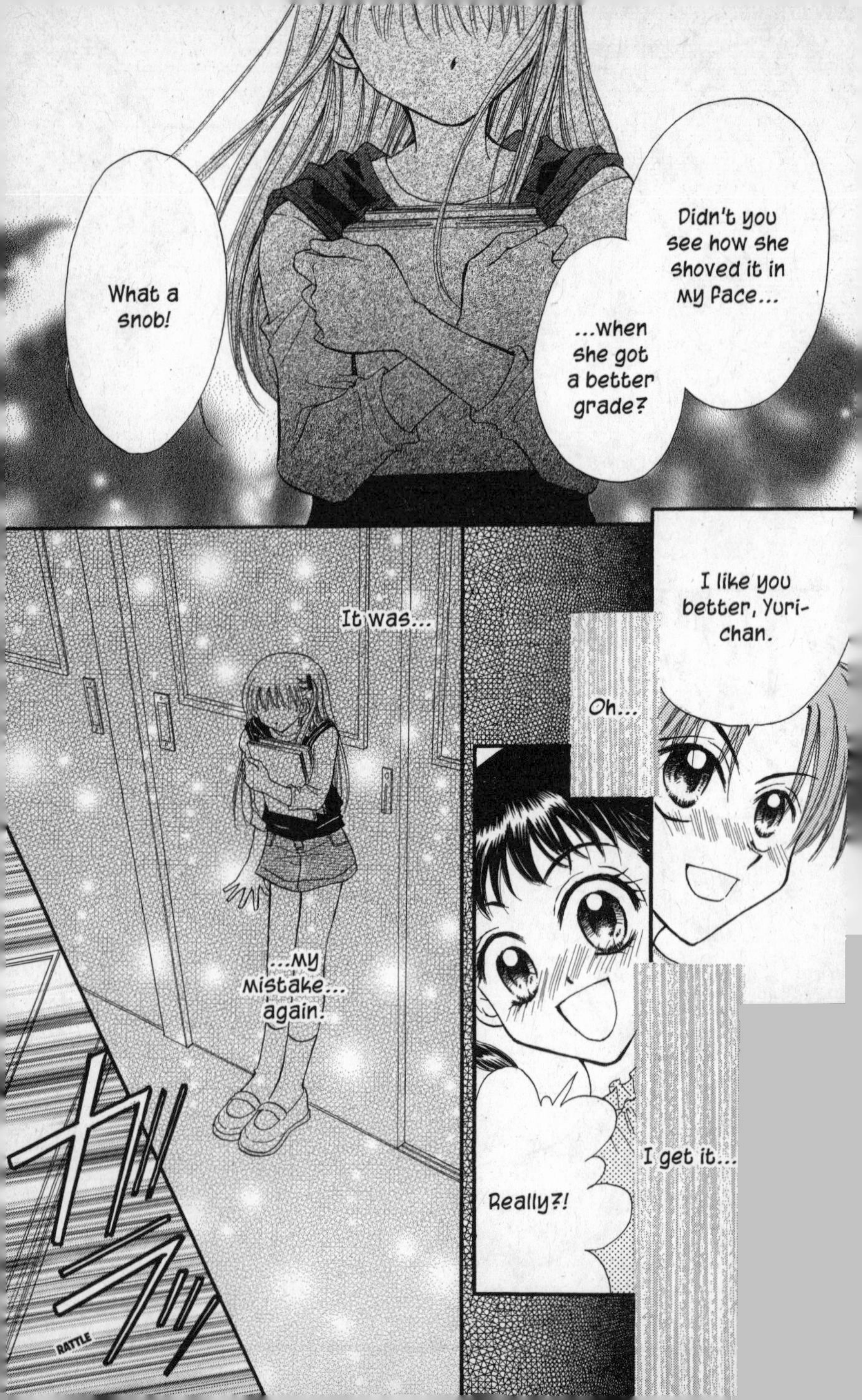
Didn't you see how she shoved it in my face...
...when she got a better grade?
What a snob!
I like you better, Yuri-chan.
Oh...
I get it...
Really?!
It was...
...my mistake... again.
RATTLE

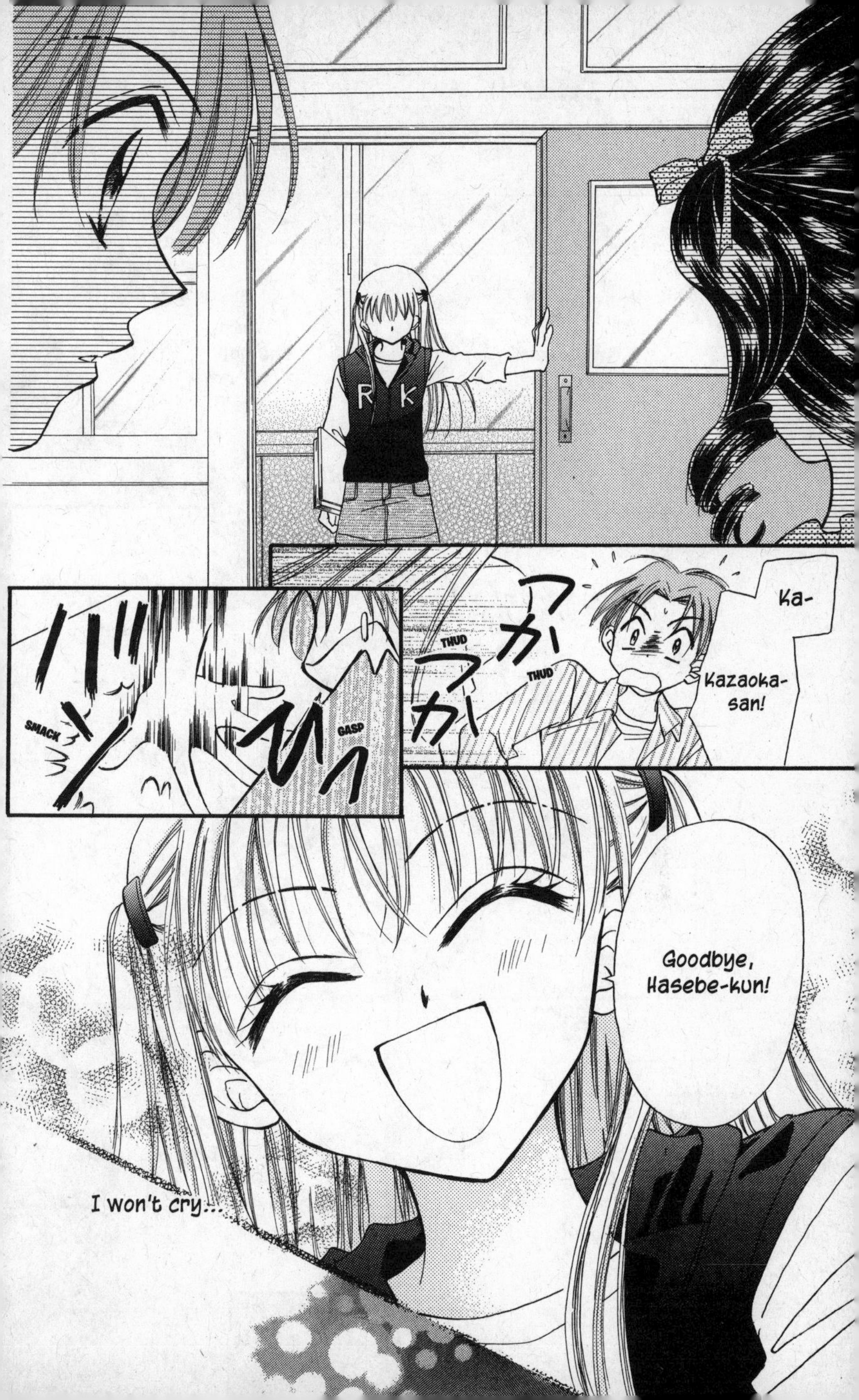
Ka-
Kazaoka-san!
THUD
THUD
GASP
SMACK
Goodbye, Hasebe-kun!
I won't cry...

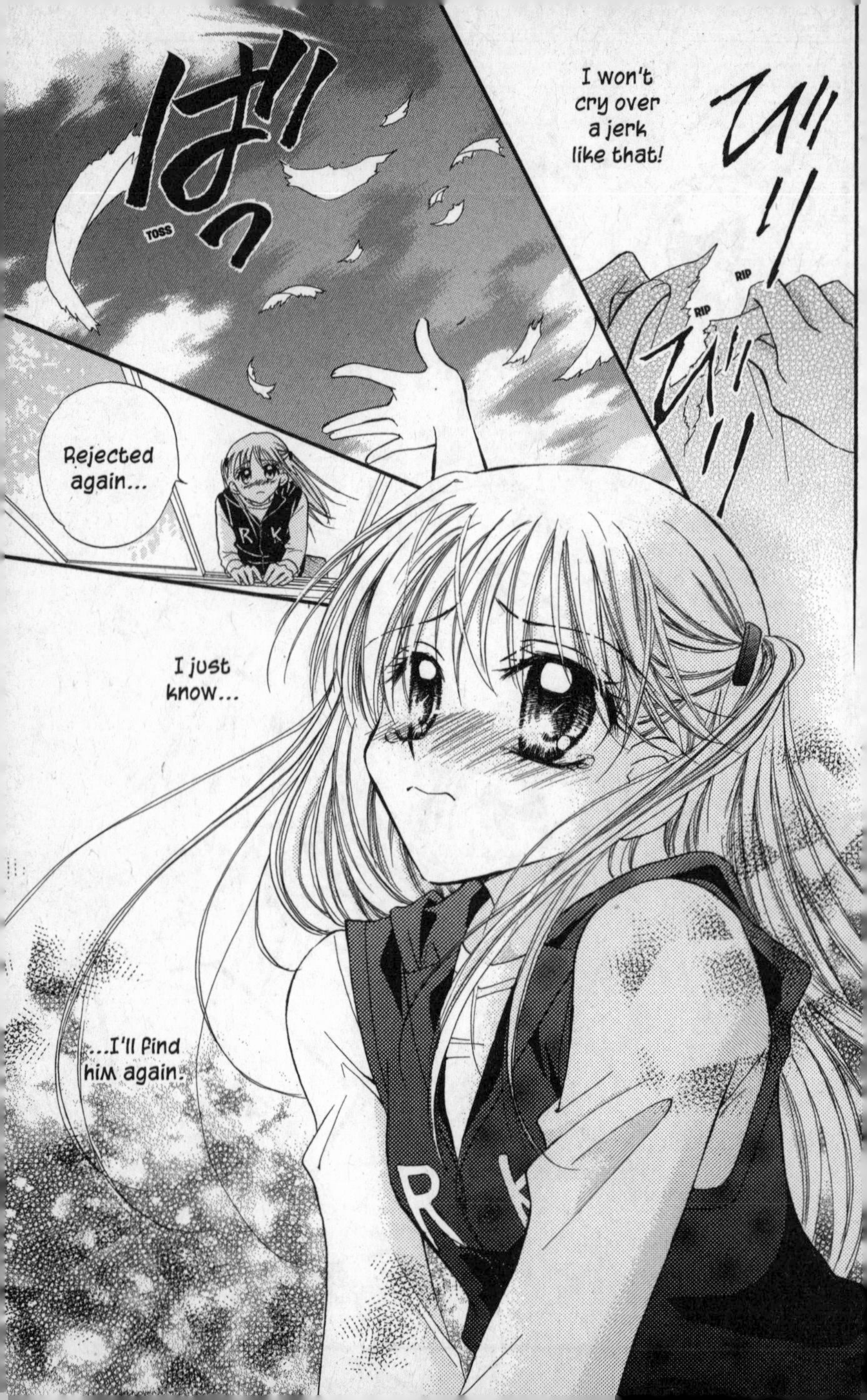
I won't cry over a jerk like that!
RIP
RIP
TOSS
Rejected again...
I just know...
...I'll find him again.

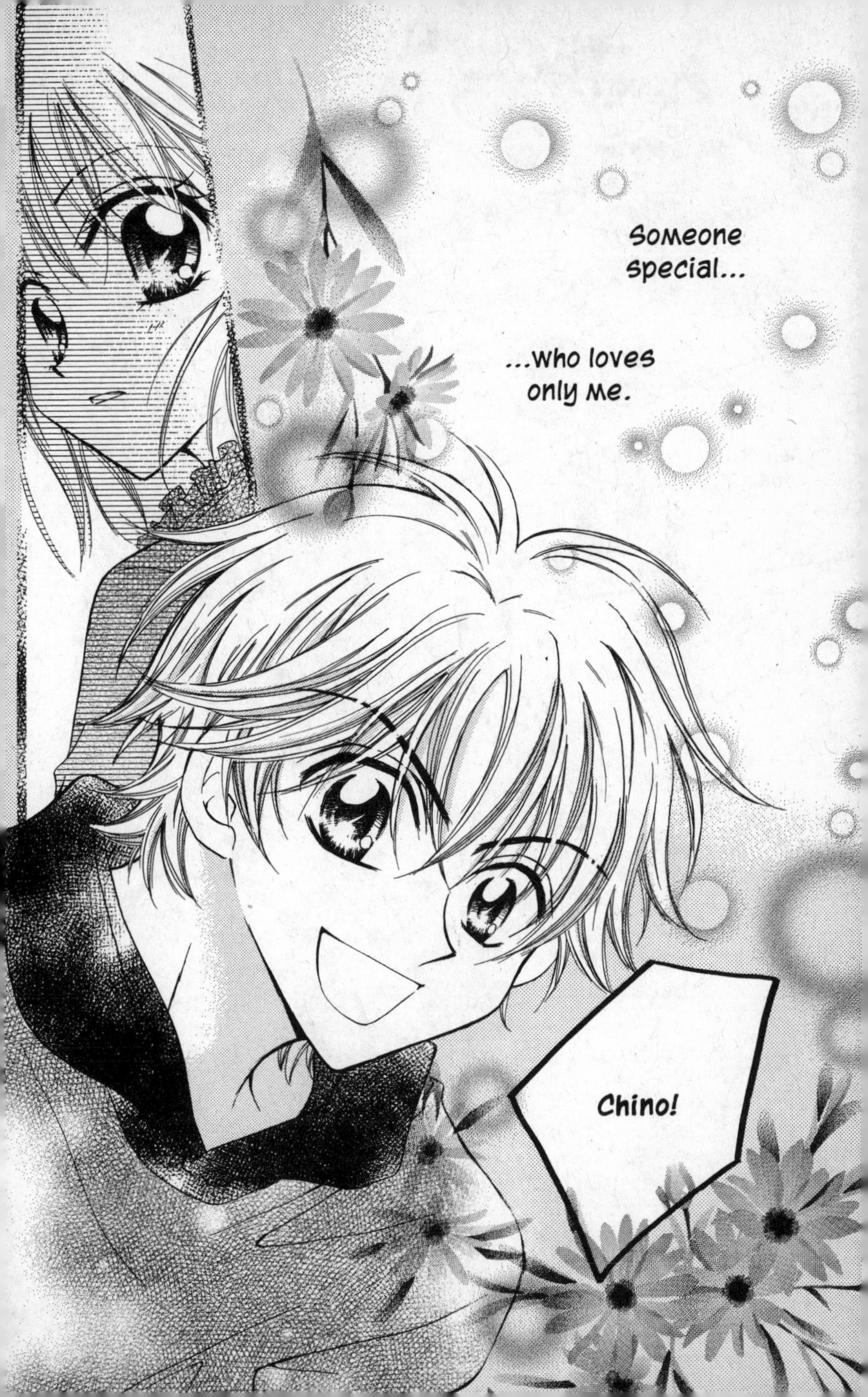
Someone special...
...who loves only me.
Chino!

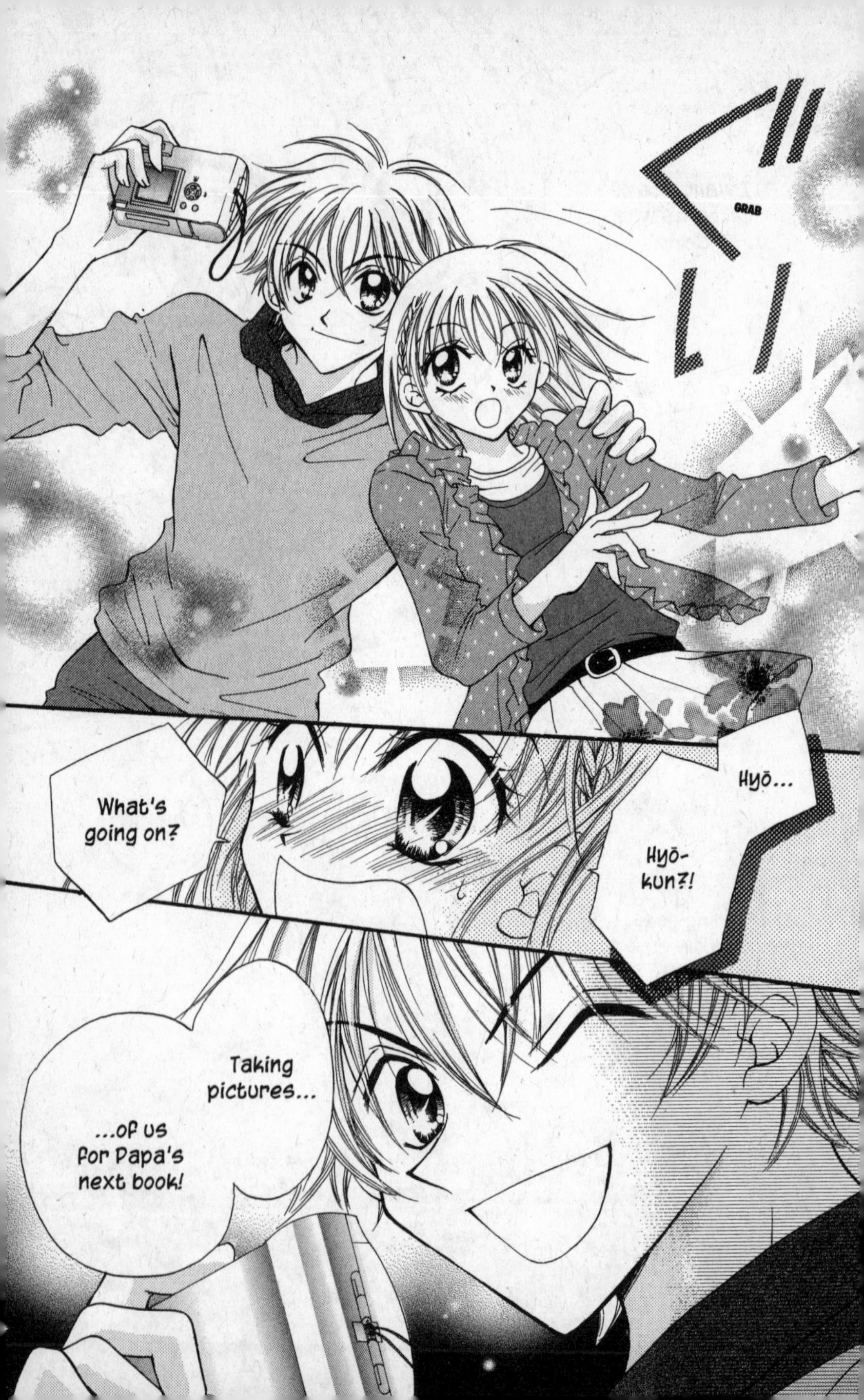
GRAB
Hyō...
Hyō-kun?!
What's going on?
Taking pictures...
...of us for Papa's next book!

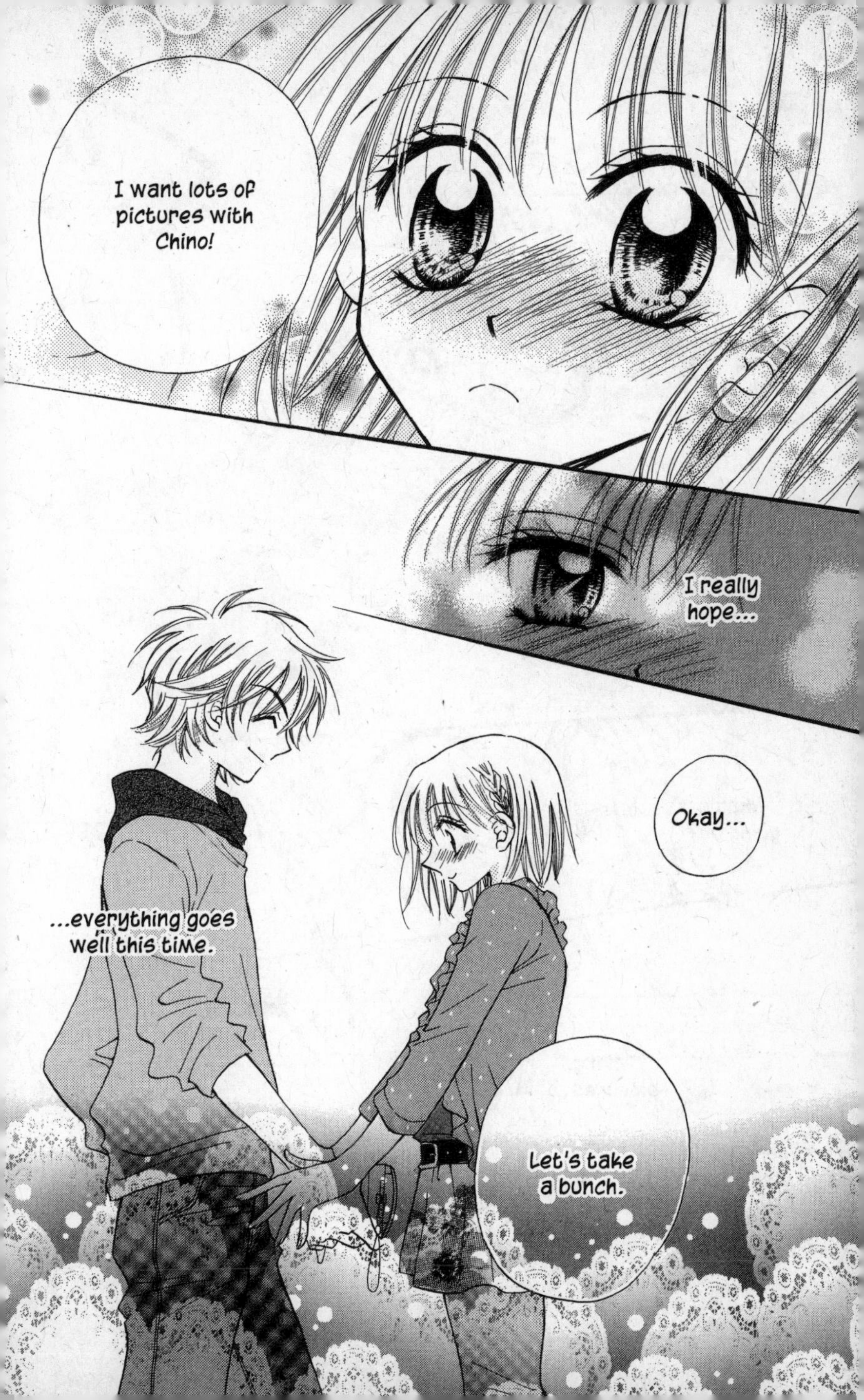
I want lots of pictures with Chino!
I really hope...
Okay...
...everything goes well this time.
Let's take a bunch.

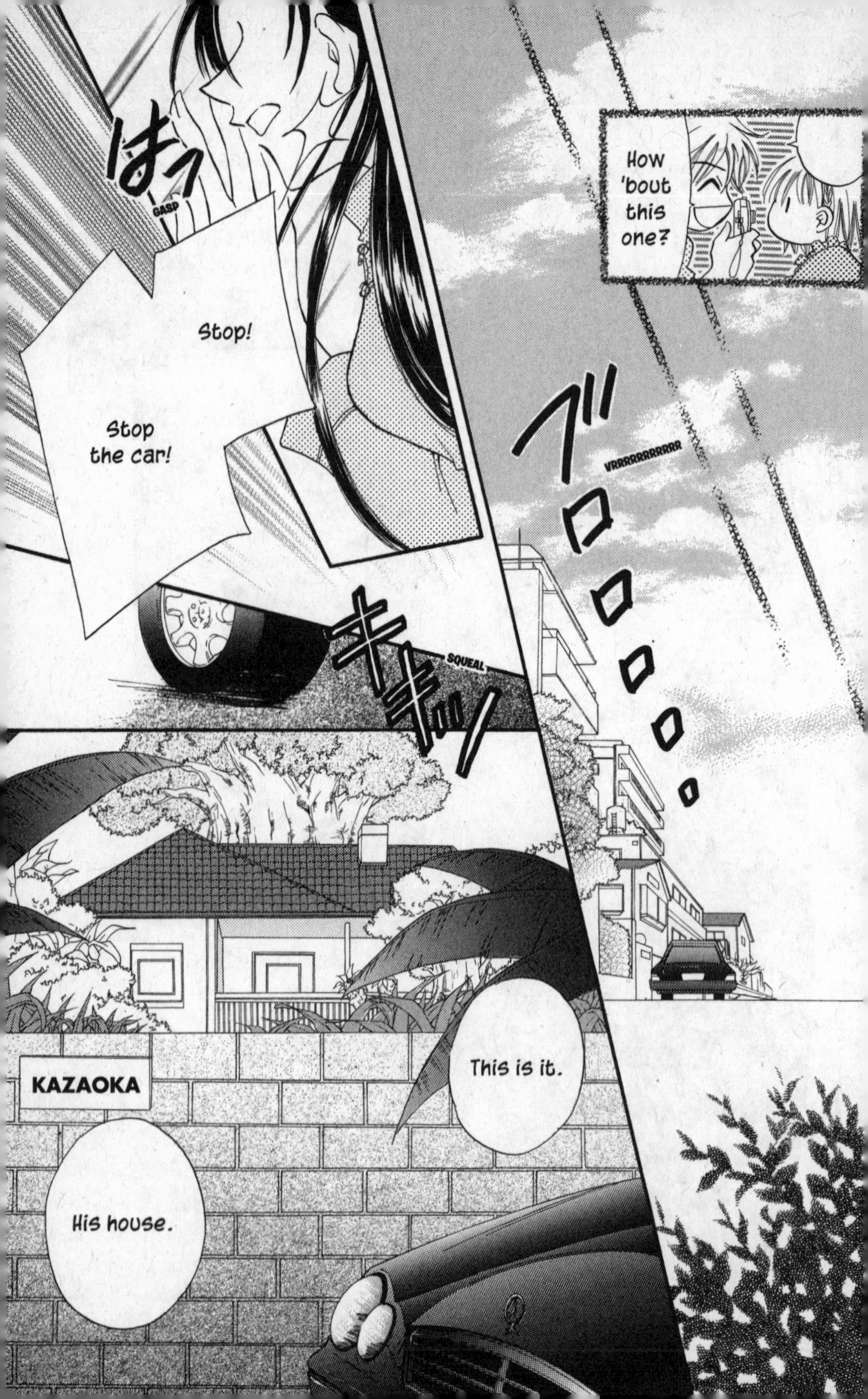
How 'bout this one?
ブロロロロロ
VRRRRRRRRRRR
はっ
GASP
Stop!
Stop the car!
キキッ
SQUEAL
This is it.
KAZAOKA
His house.

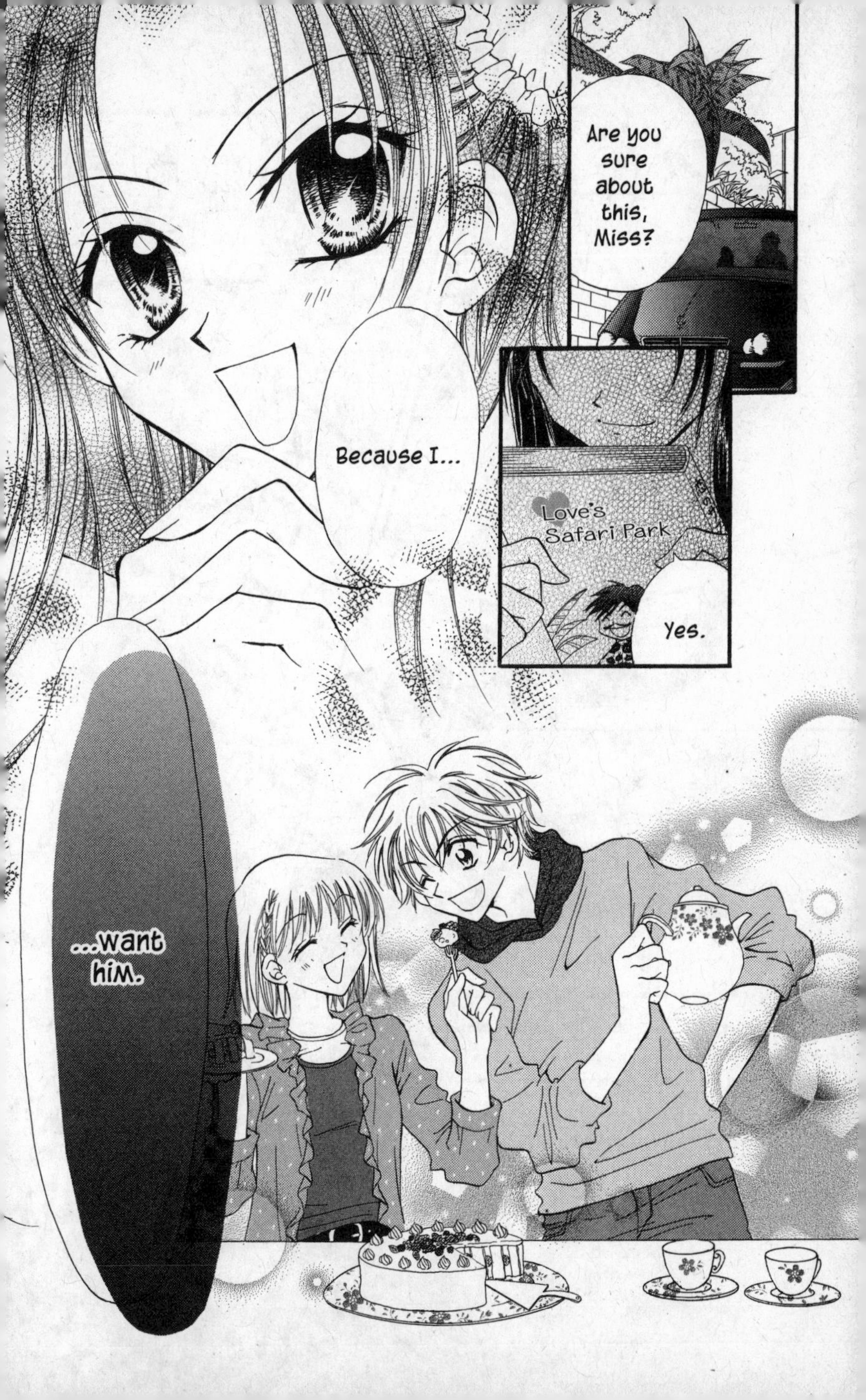
Are you sure about this, Miss?
Love's Safari Park
Yes.
Because I...
...want him.

Character Profile 2

✳ Shingo Tsutsui

Birthday: December 6
14 years old.
Sagittarius. Blood Type: O
Height : 5'5"
Hobbies: Dancing and texting.
Texts Machiko every day but she never replies...♦
Crybaby, often cries over movies and manga.
Loves hamburgers and curry, but his favorite is curry!!

✳ Machiko Nonohara

Birthday: October 28
14 years old.
Scorpio. Blood Type: A
Height: 5'1"
Hobbies: Cleaning.
In cooking club with Chino.
Cooks like a pro but likes strange food so her creations are always weird, such as putting soy sauce on pudding.
Likes wearing girly clothes.

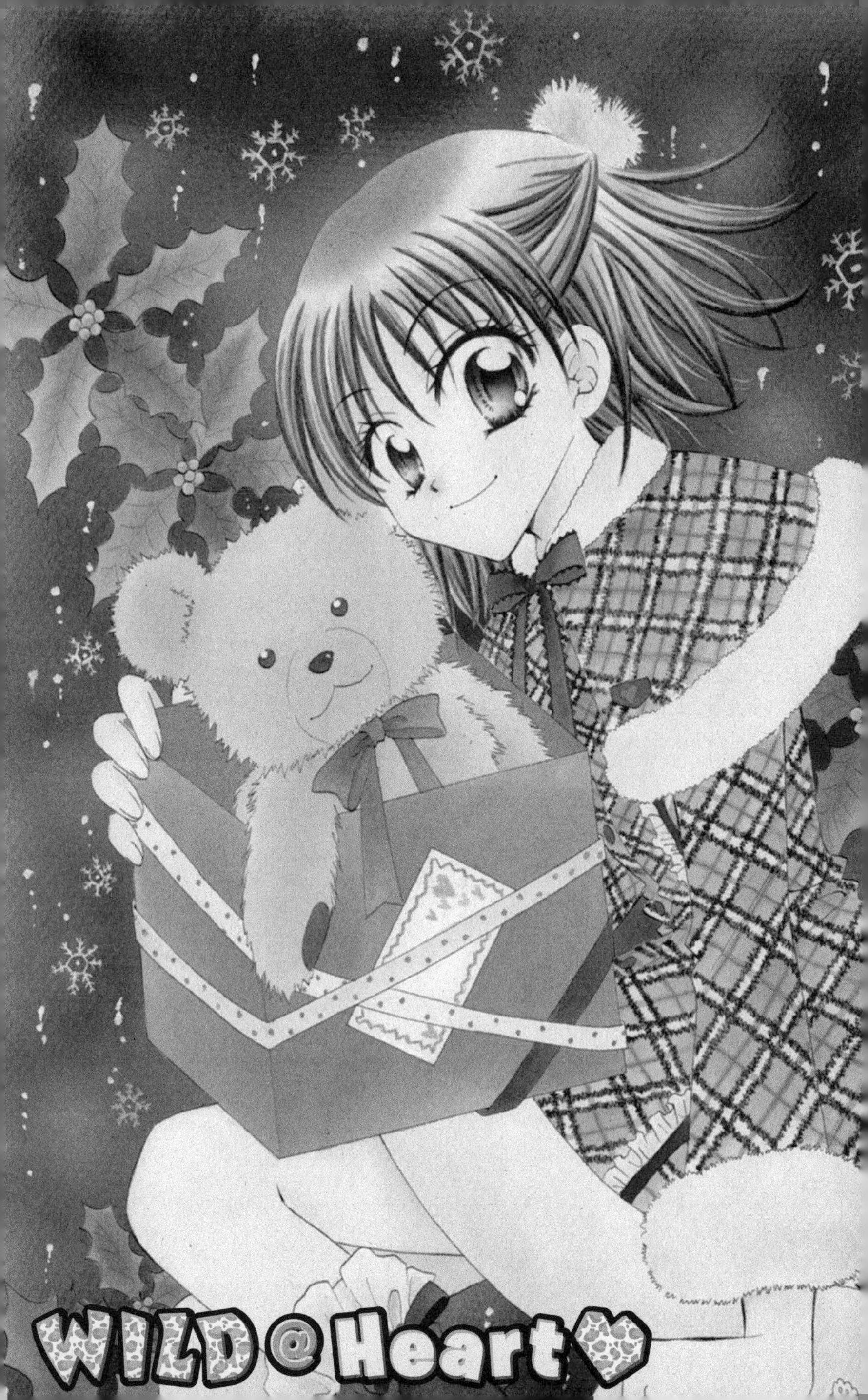
WILD @ Heart♥

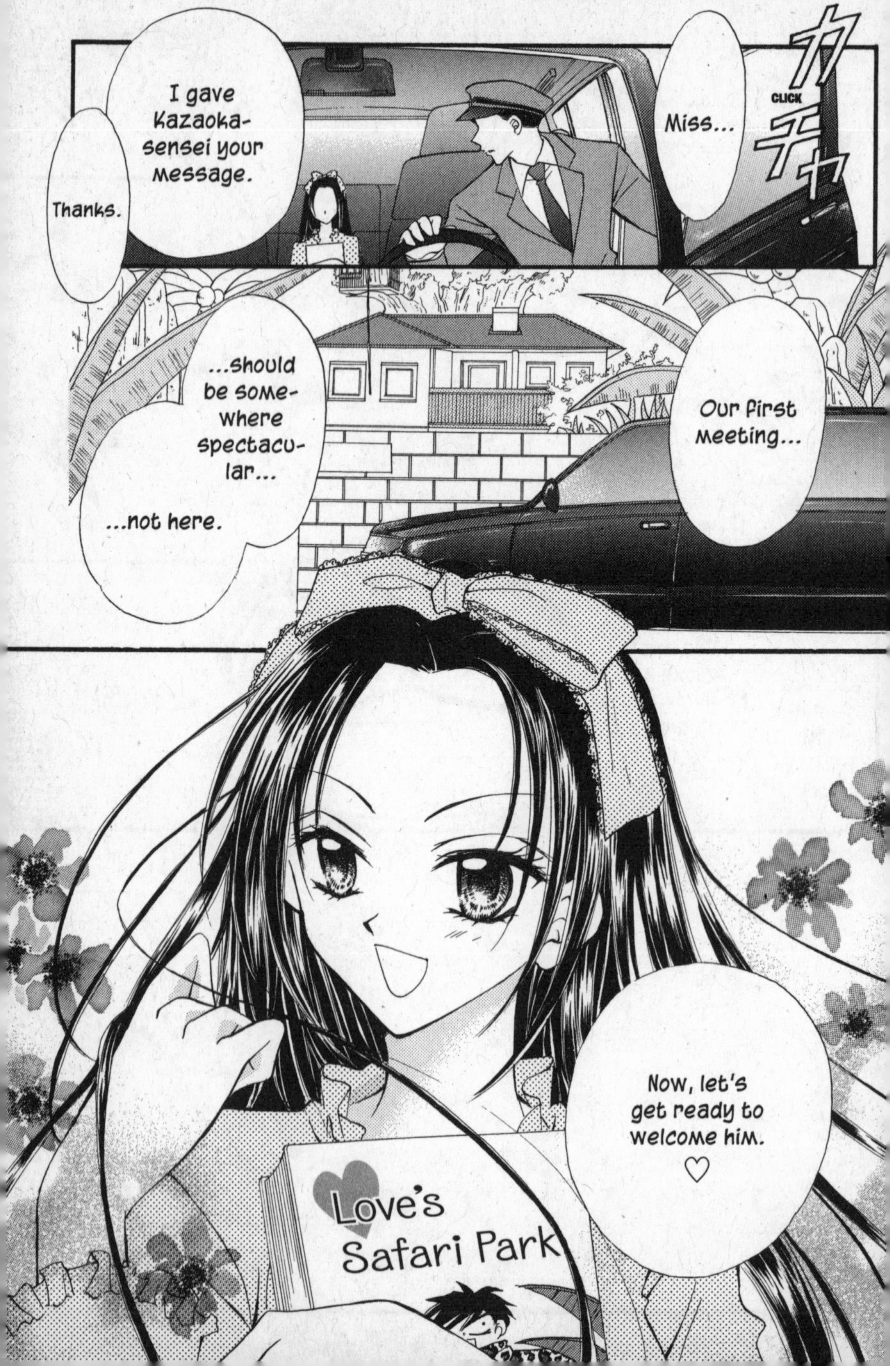
カチャ
CLICK
Miss...
I gave Kazaoka-sensei your message.
Thanks.
Our first meeting...
...should be some-where spectacu-lar...
...not here.
Now, let's get ready to welcome him. ♡
Love's Safari Park

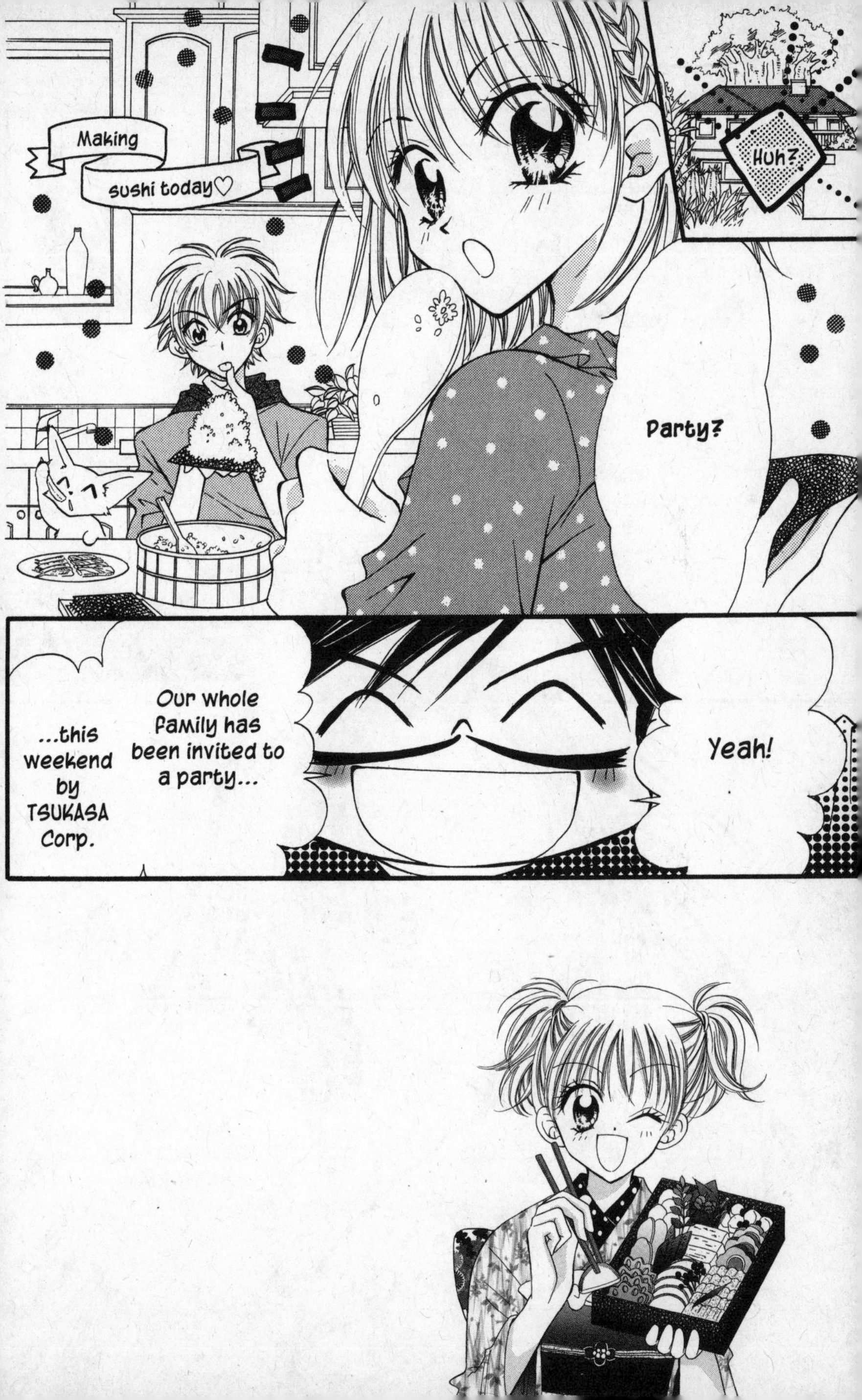
Huh?
Party?
Making sushi today♡
Yeah!
Our whole family has been invited to a party...
...this weekend by TSUKASA Corp.

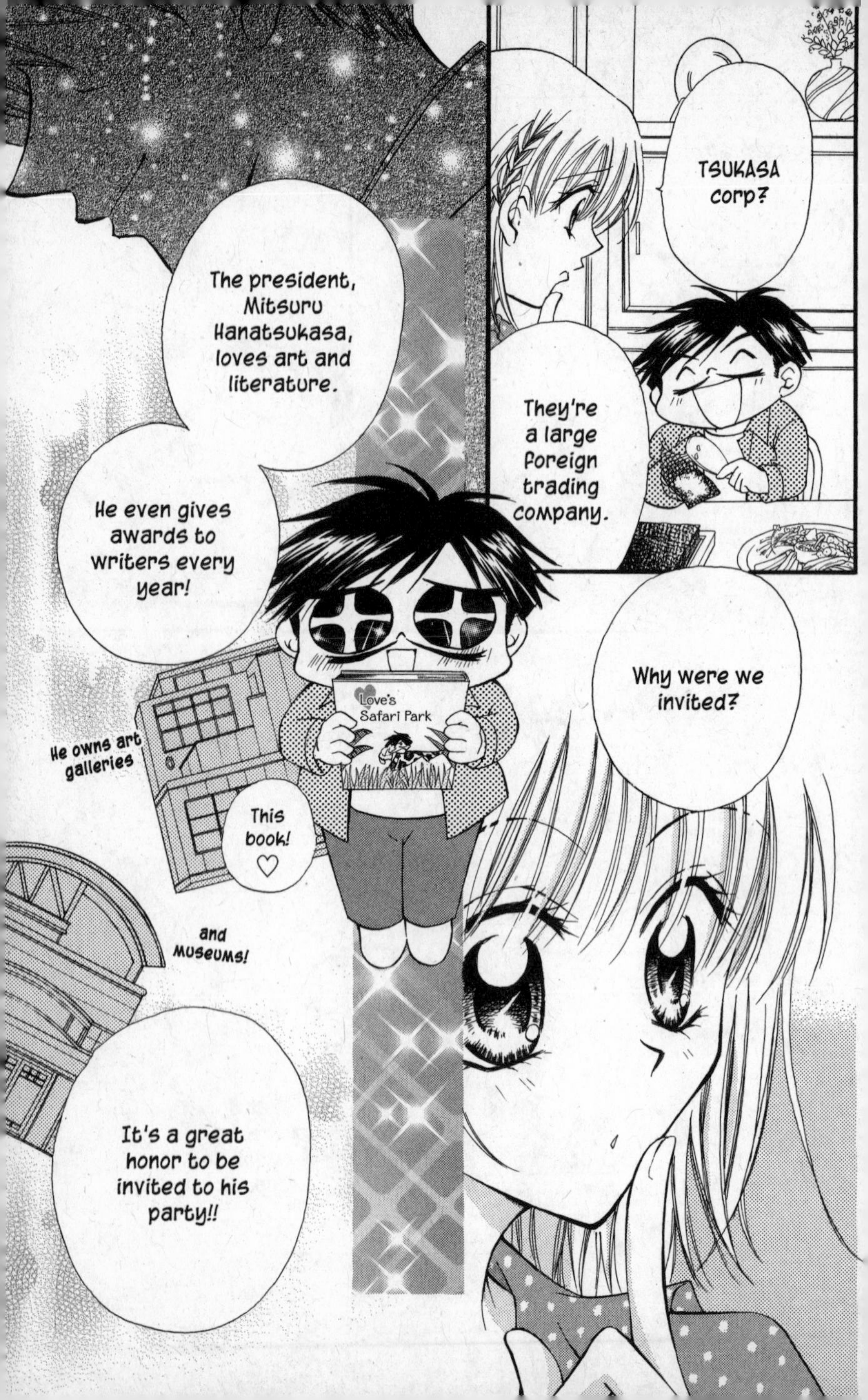
TSUKASA corp?
They're a large foreign trading company.
Why were we invited?
The president, Mitsuru Hanatsukasa, loves art and literature.
He even gives awards to writers every year!
Love's Safari Park
He owns art galleries
This book! ♡
and museums!
It's a great honor to be invited to his party!!

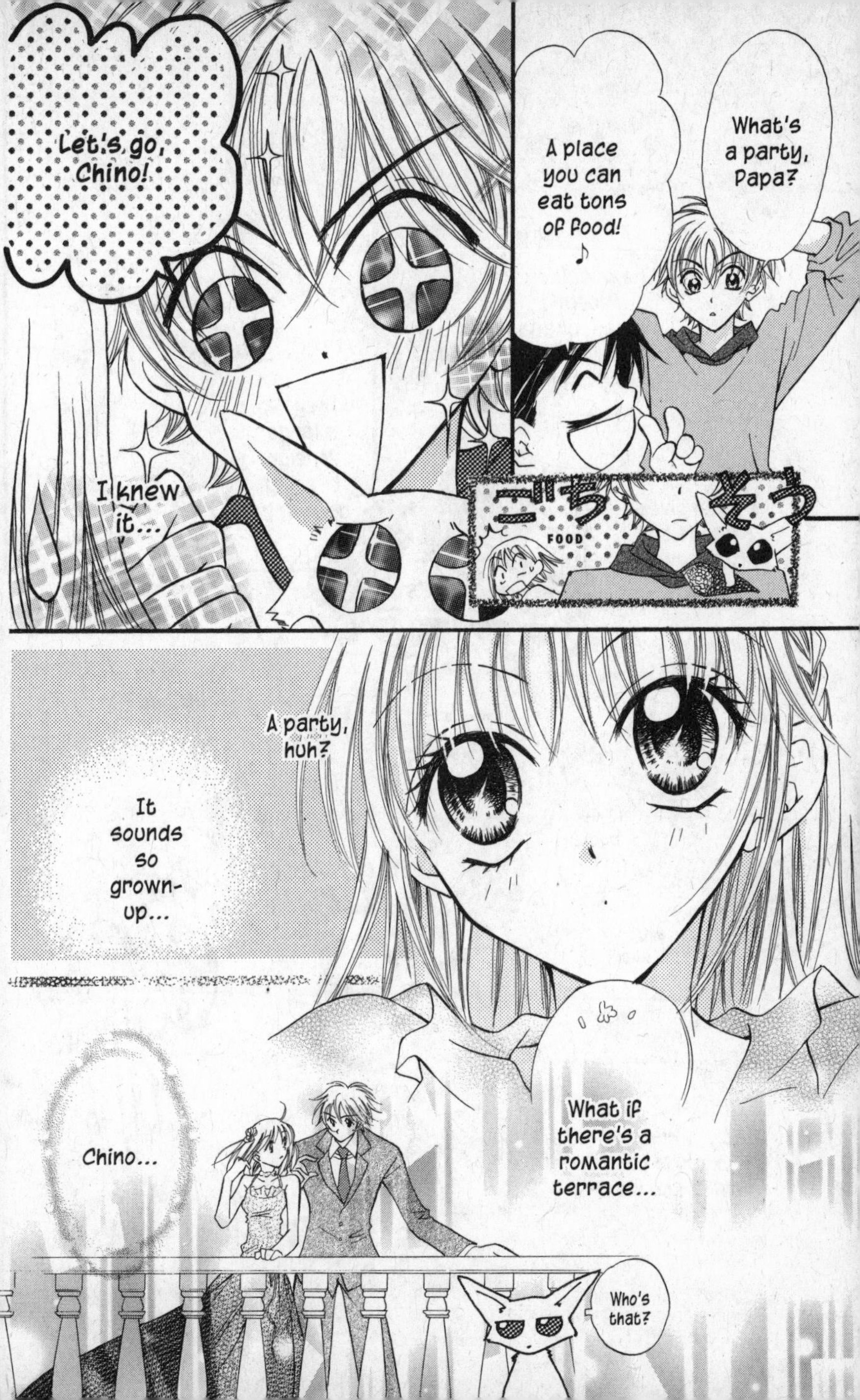
What's a party, Papa?
A place you can eat tons of food! ♪
ごち そう
FOOD
Let's go, Chino!
I knew it...
A party, huh?
It sounds so grown-up...
What if there's a romantic terrace...
Chino...
Who's that?

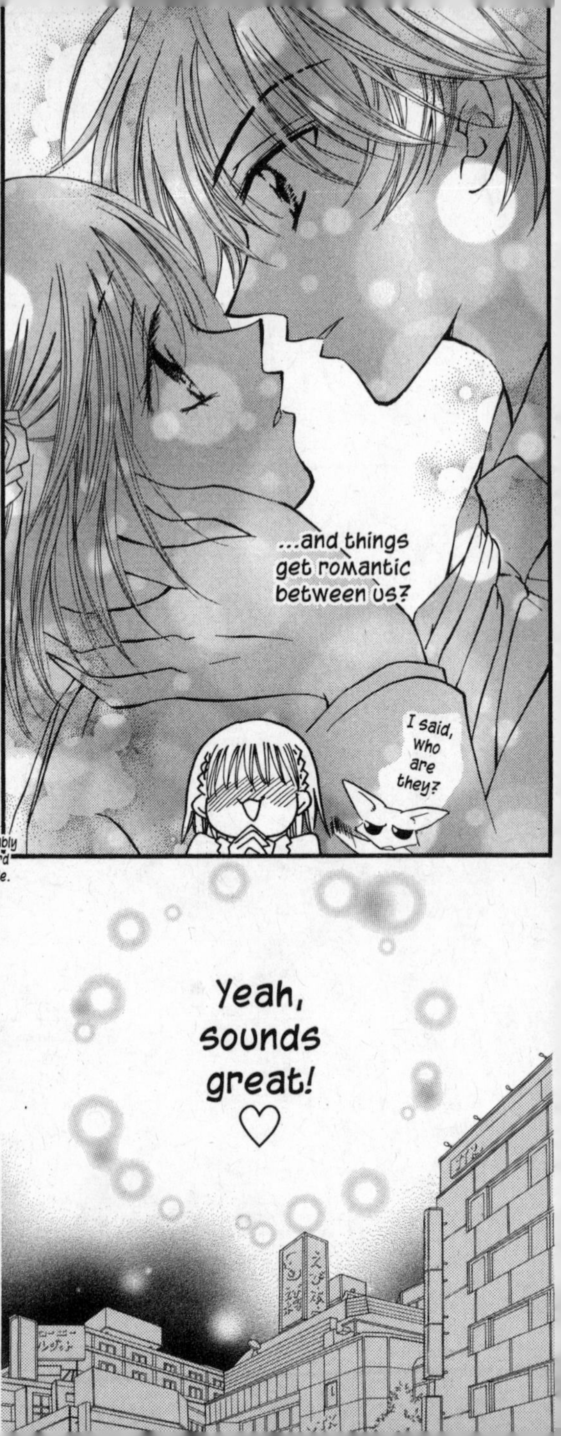
...and things get romantic between us?
I said, who are they?
Yeah, sounds great! ♡

6.

There are a bunch of TVs playing old cartoons and commercials in the Disneyland gallery. One time when I was there I saw a brother and sister.

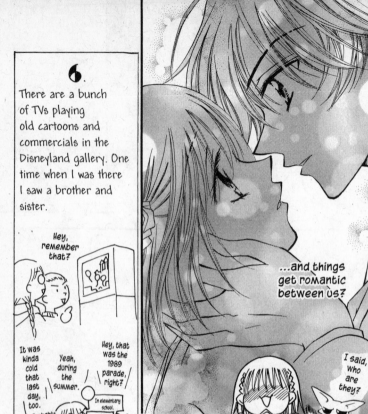

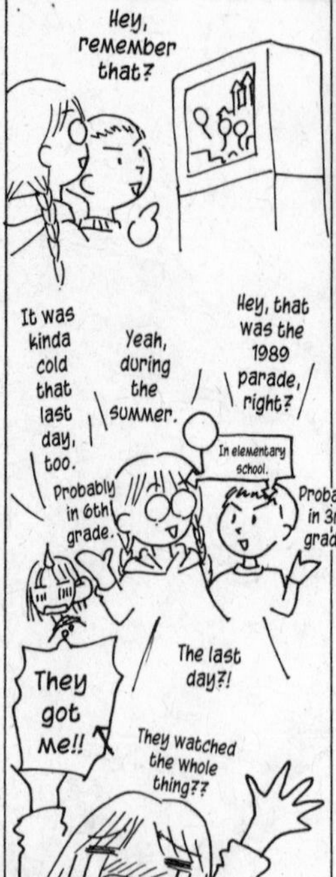
Hey, remember that?
Hey, that was the 1989 parade, right?
Yeah, during the summer.
It was kinda cold that last day, too.
Probably in 3rd grade.
In elementary school.
Probably in 6th grade.
The last day?!
They got me!!
They watched the whole thing??

They knew way more than me....

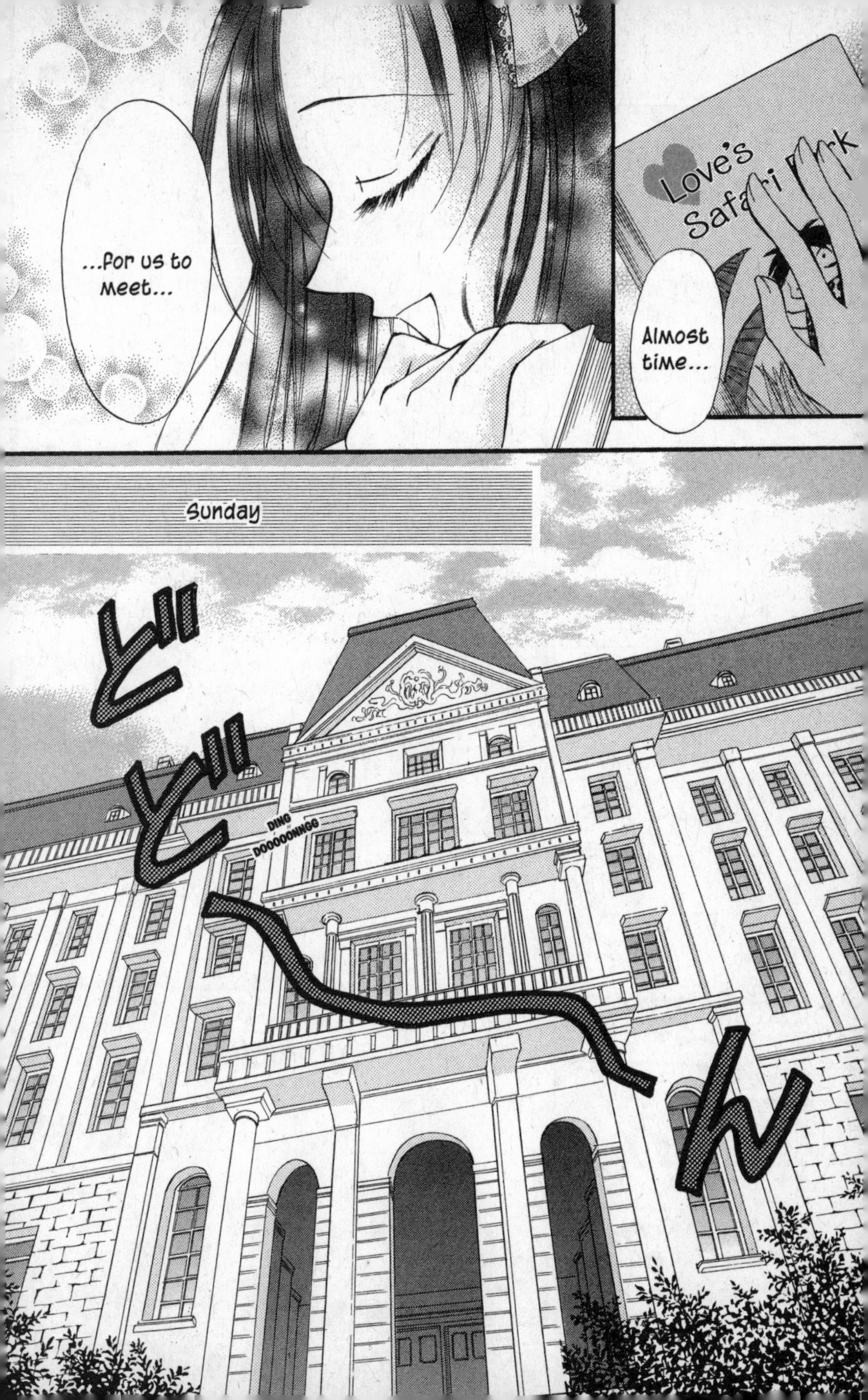
Love's
Almost time...
...for us to meet...
Sunday
DING DOOOOONNGG

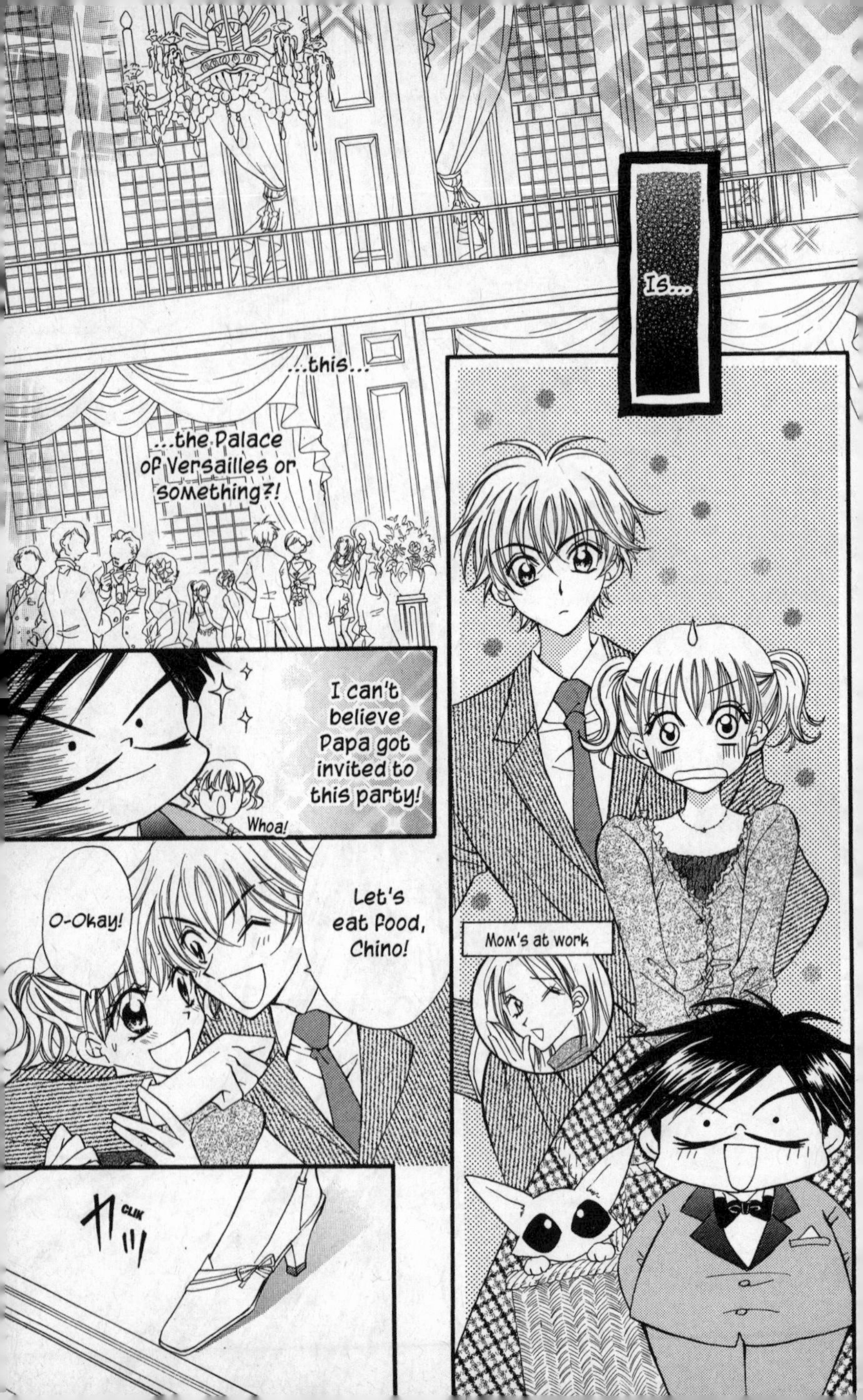
Is...
...this...
...the Palace of Versailles or something?!
Mom's at work
I can't believe Papa got invited to this party!
Whoa!
Let's eat food, Chino!
O-Okay!
CLIK

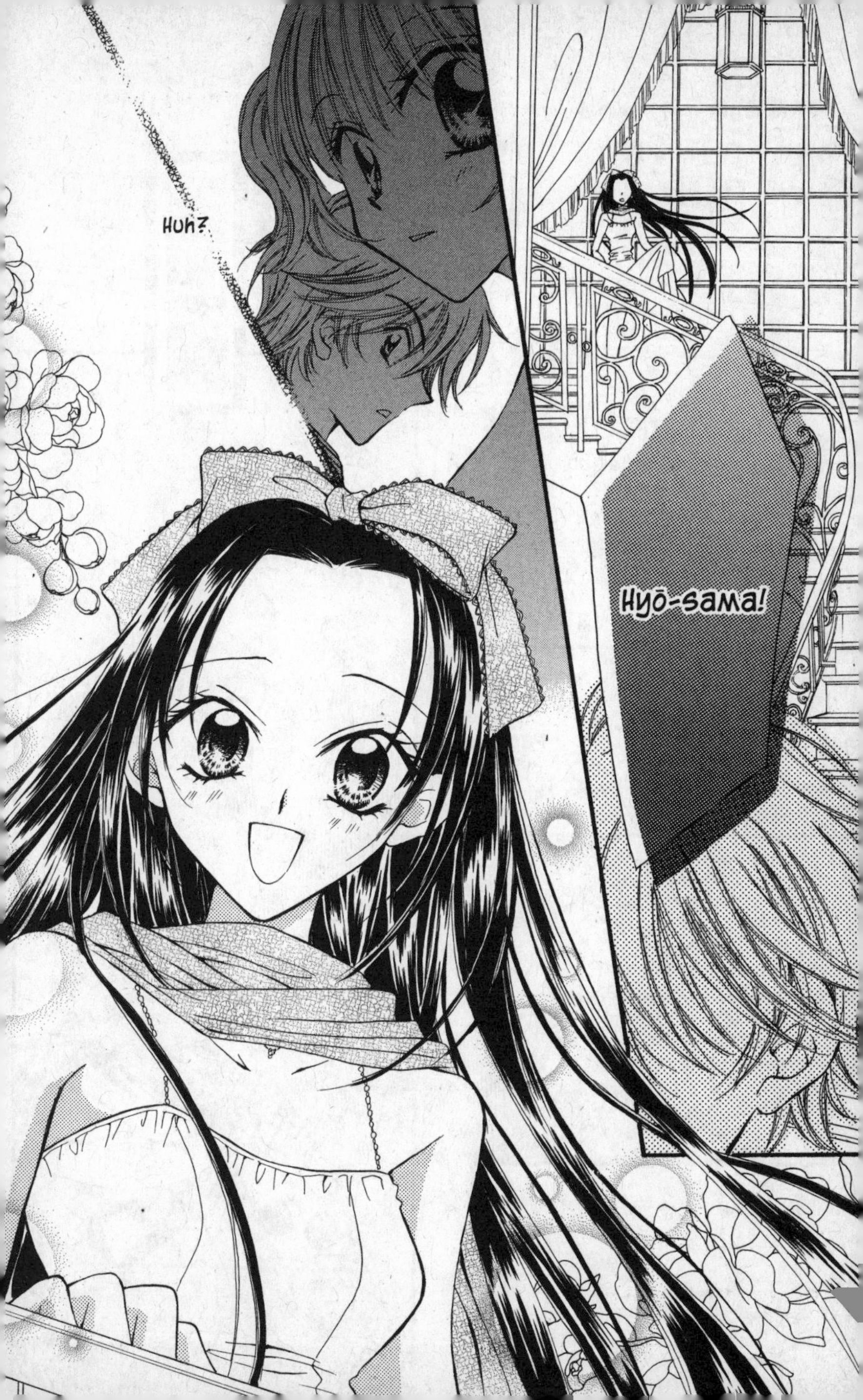
Hyō-sama!
Huh?

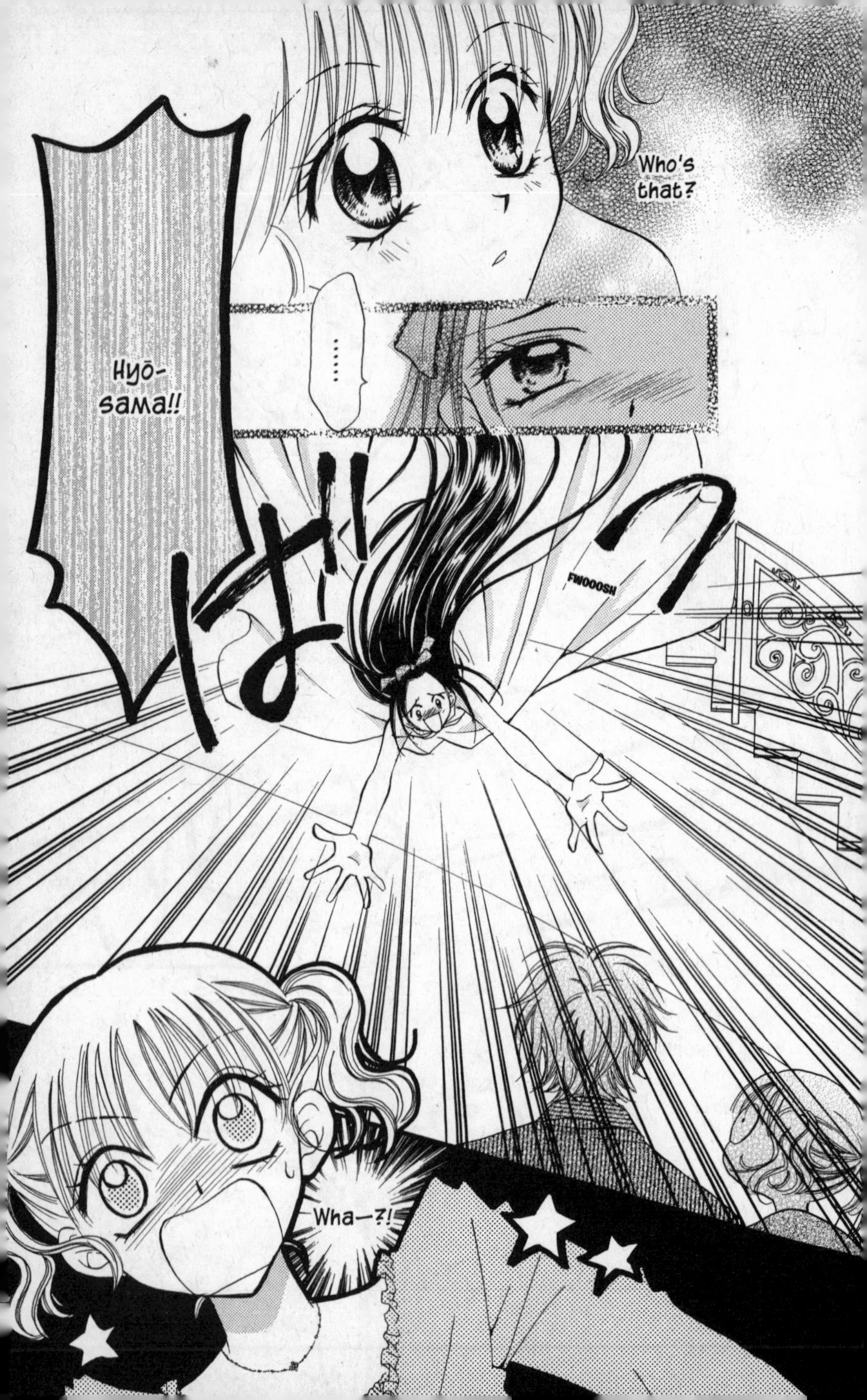
Who's that?
......
Hyō-sama!!
FWOOOSH
Wha—?!

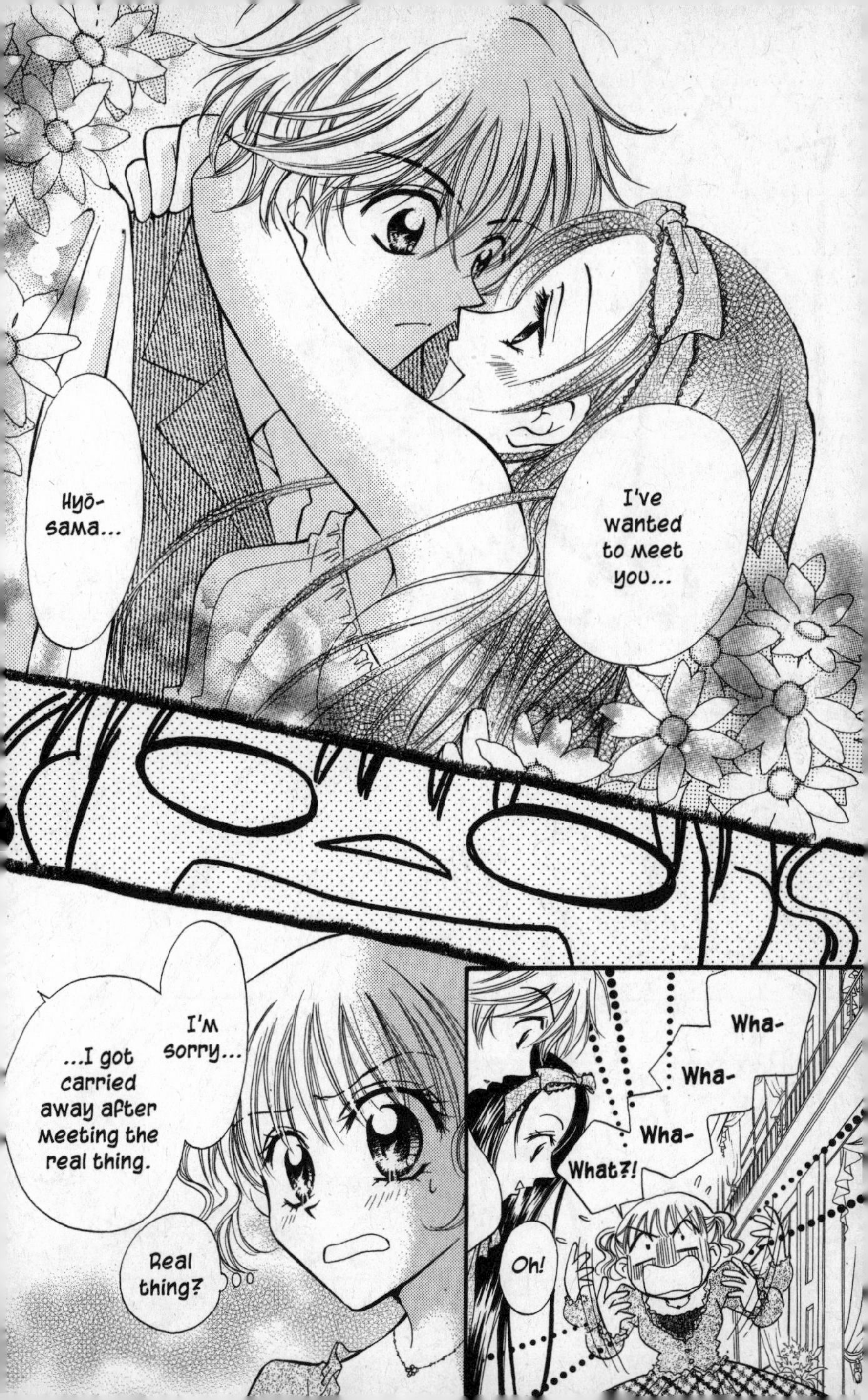
I've wanted to meet you...
Hyō-sama...
Wha-
Wha-
Wha-
What?!
Oh!
I'm sorry...
...I got carried away after meeting the real thing.
Real thing?

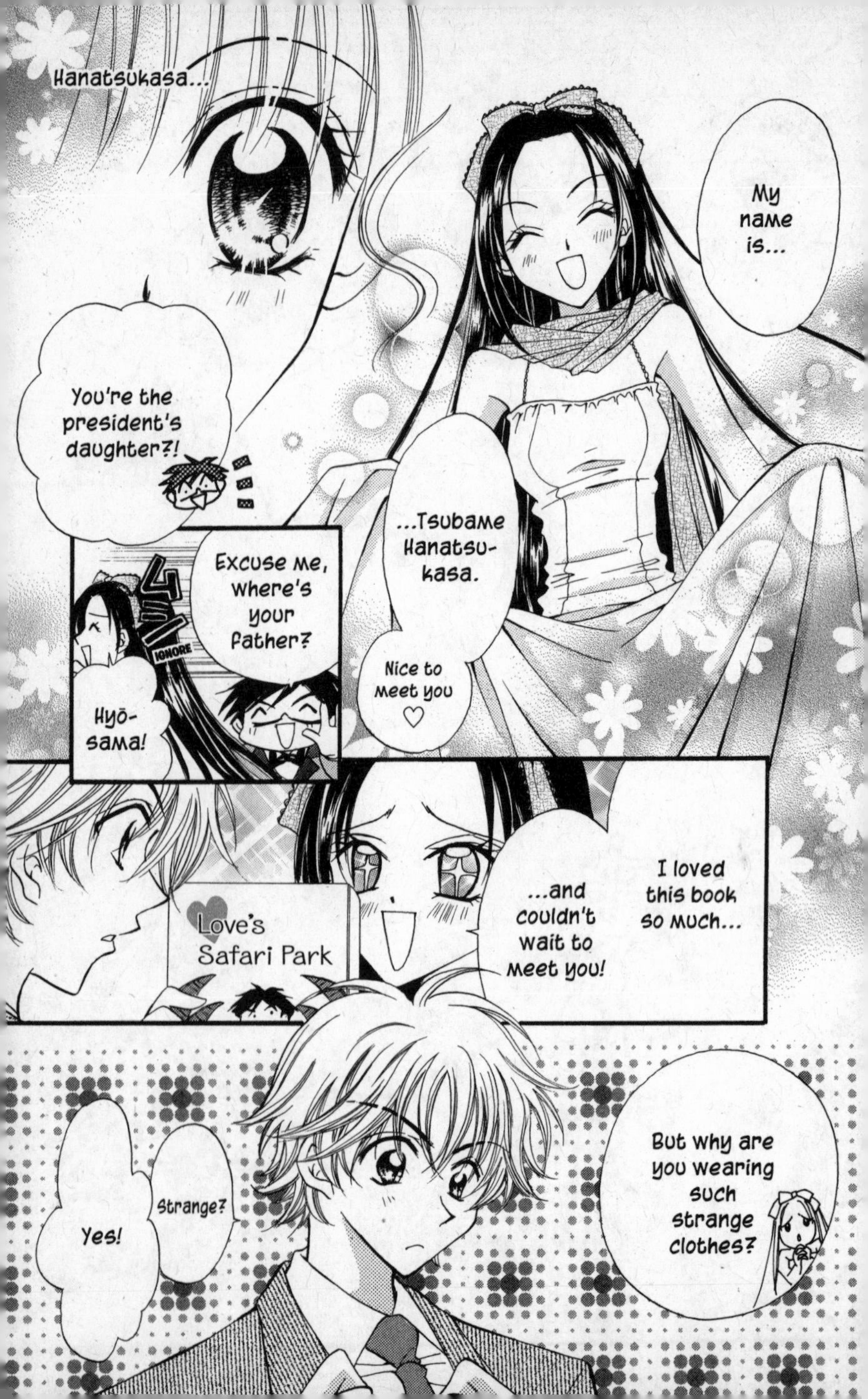

My name is...
...Tsubame Hanatsukasa.
Nice to meet you ♡
Hanatsukasa...
You're the president's daughter?!
Excuse me, where's your father?
IGNORE
Hyō-sama!
I loved this book so much...
...and couldn't wait to meet you!
Love's Safari Park
But why are you wearing such strange clothes?
Strange?
Yes!

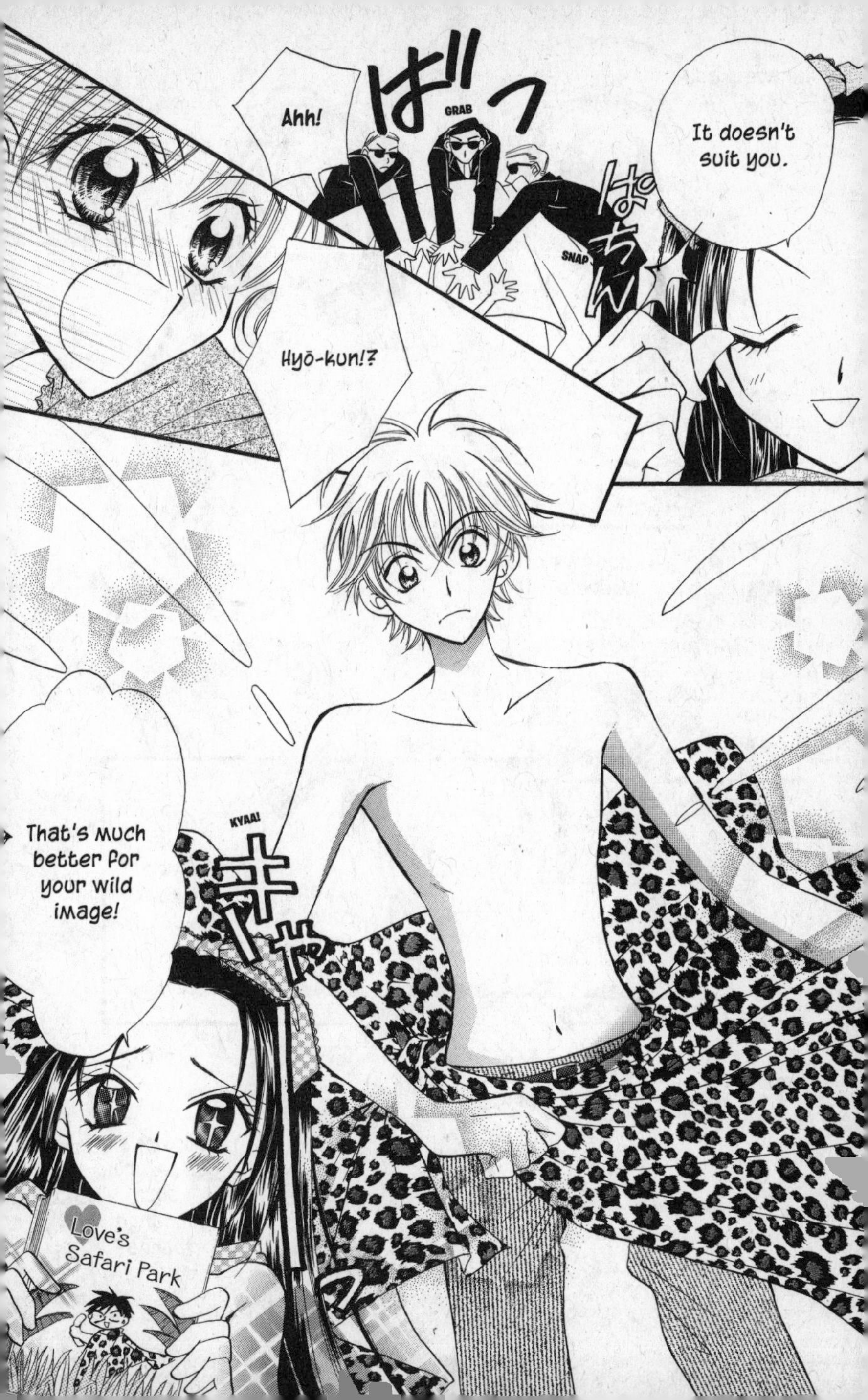
It doesn't suit you.
ぱちん
SNAP
ばっ
GRAB
Ahh!
Hyō-kun!?
キャー
KYAA!
That's much better for your wild image!
Love's Safari Park

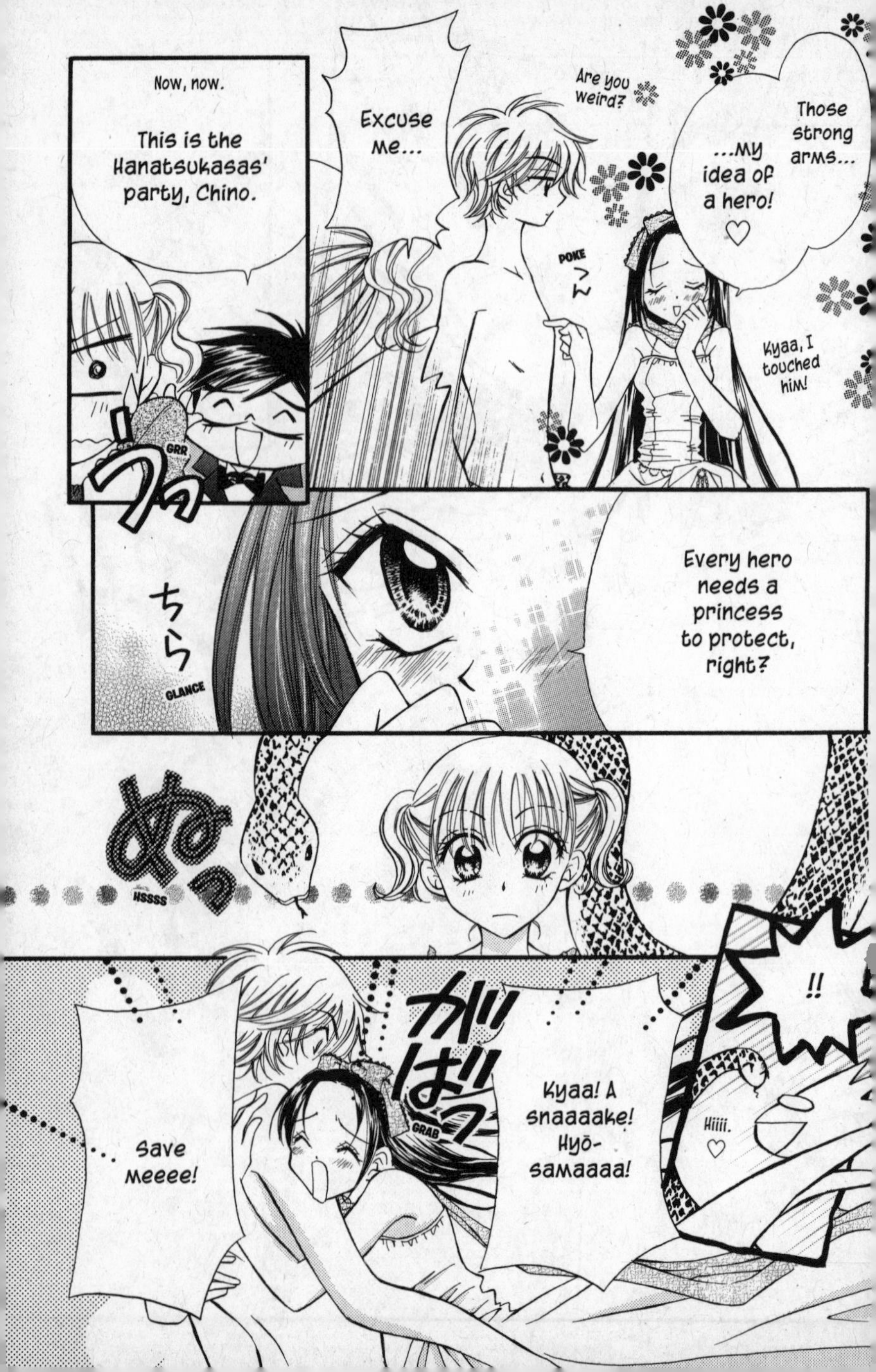

Those strong arms... ...my idea of a hero! ♡
Are you weird?
Kyaa, I touched him!
POKE
Excuse me...
Now, now.
This is the Hanatsukasas' party, Chino.
GRR
Every hero needs a princess to protect, right?
ちら
GLANCE
HSSSS
!!
Hiiii. ♡
Kyaa! A snaaaake! Hyō-samaaaa!
GRAB
Save meeee!

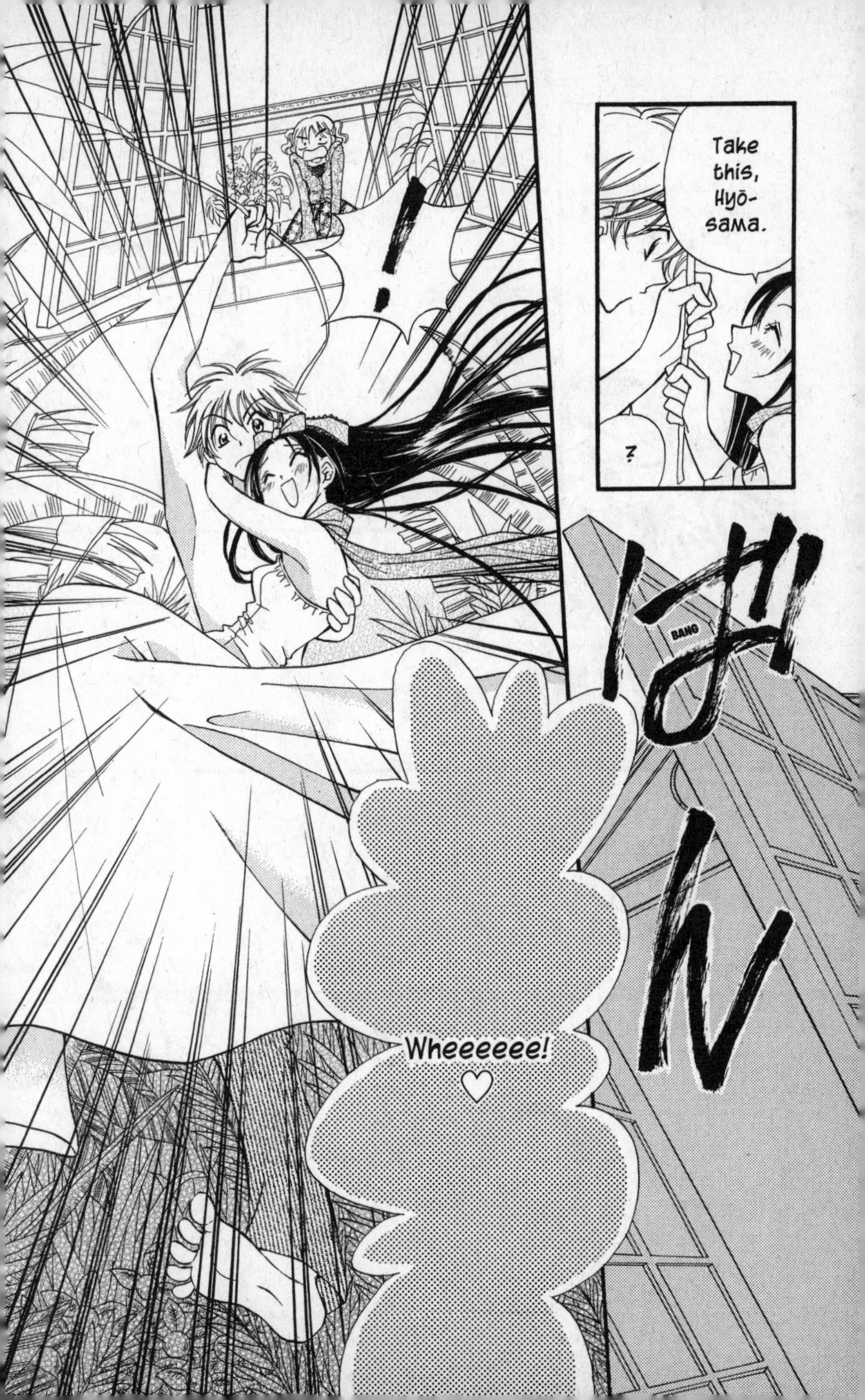
Take this, Hyō-sama.
?
!
BANG
Wheeeeee! ♥

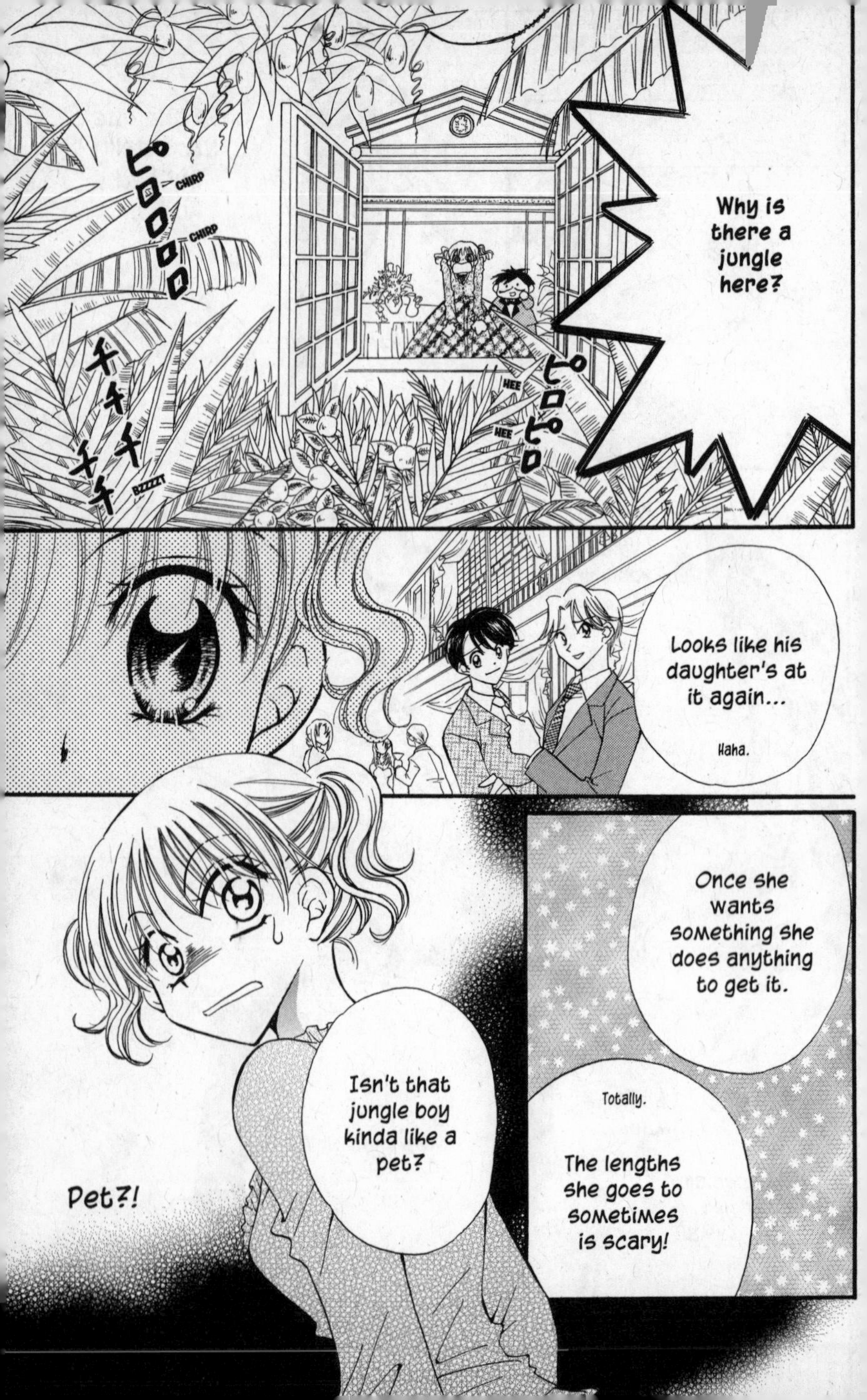
Why is there a jungle here?
HEE
HEE
CHIRP
CHIRP
BZZZZT
Looks like his daughter's at it again...
Haha.
Once she wants something she does anything to get it.
Totally.
The lengths she goes to sometimes is scary!
Isn't that jungle boy kinda like a pet?
Pet?!

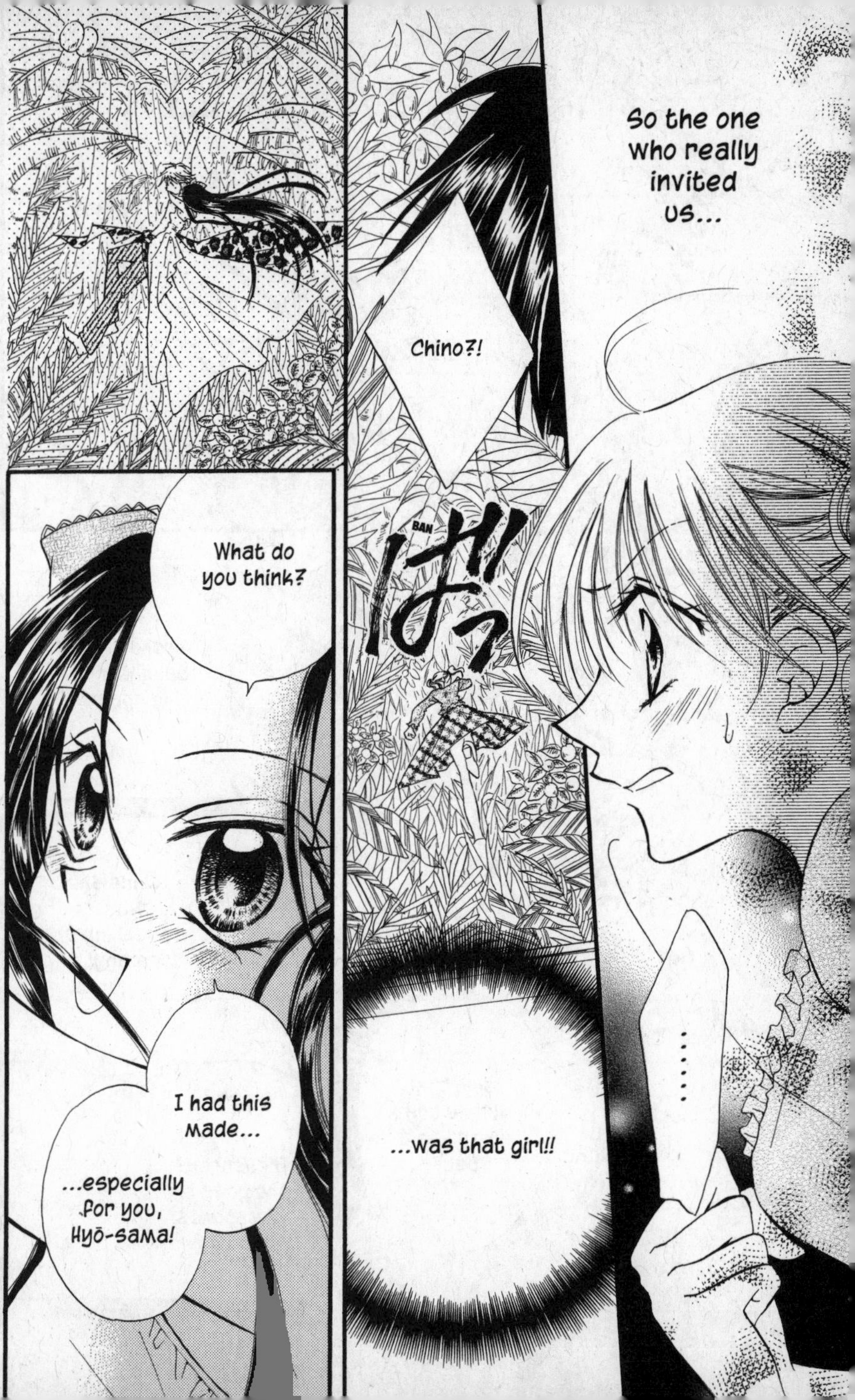
So the one who really invited us...
......
Chino?!
BAN
...was that girl!!
What do you think?
I had this made...
...especially for you, Hyō-sama!

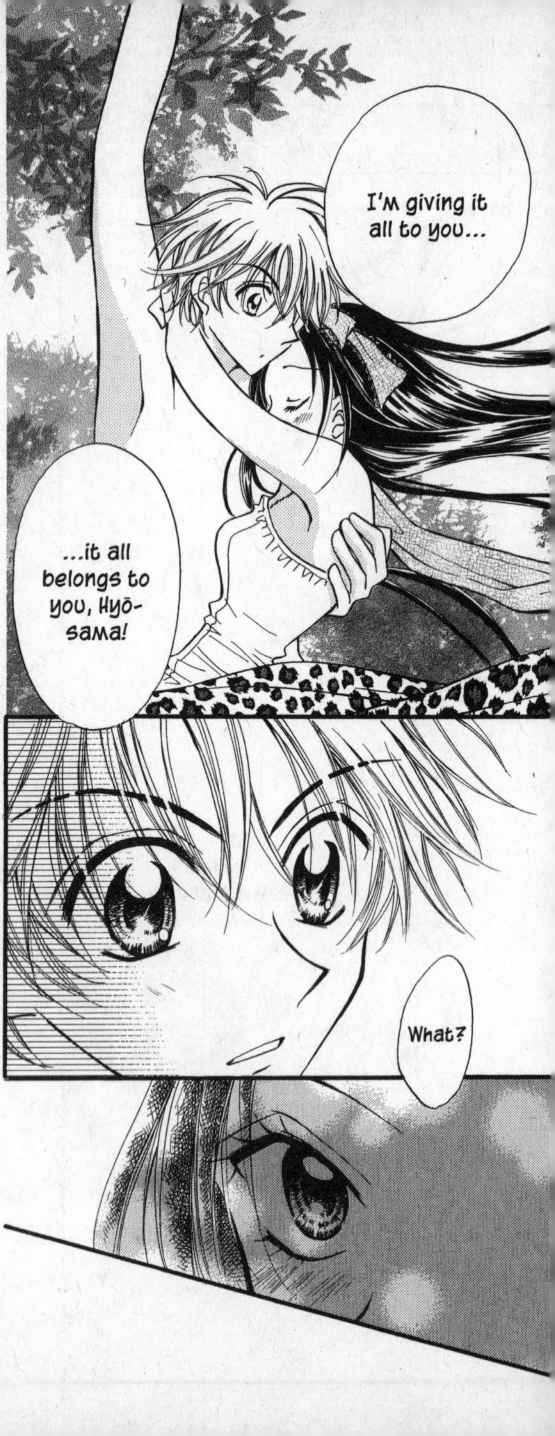
I'm giving it all to you...
...it all belongs to you, Hyō-sama!
What?

7.

One time on the way to my place for work, my assistant, M-san, got into a fight with an old man. They accidentally bumped into each other and he yelled "Apologize!" to her.

That reminded me of a time when I was waiting at the train station, leaning up against a pole reading.

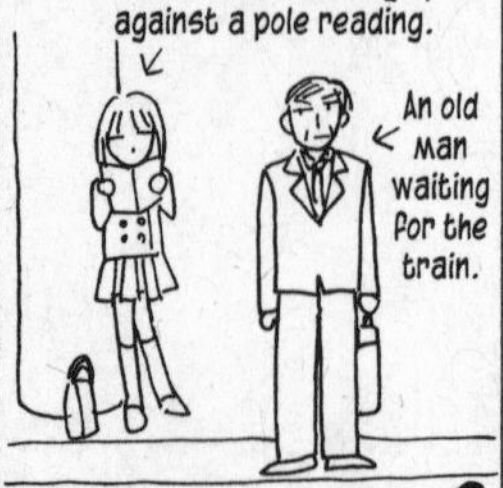
An old man waiting for the train.

And then...

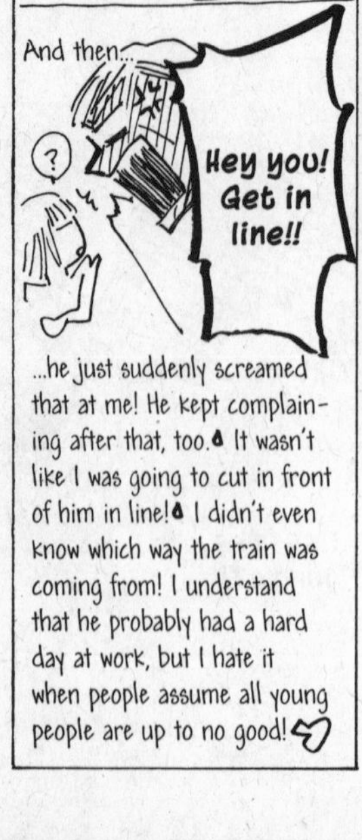
?
Hey you! Get in line!!

...he just suddenly screamed that at me! He kept complaining after that, too. It wasn't like I was going to cut in front of him in line! I didn't even know which way the train was coming from! I understand that he probably had a hard day at work, but I hate it when people assume all young people are up to no good!

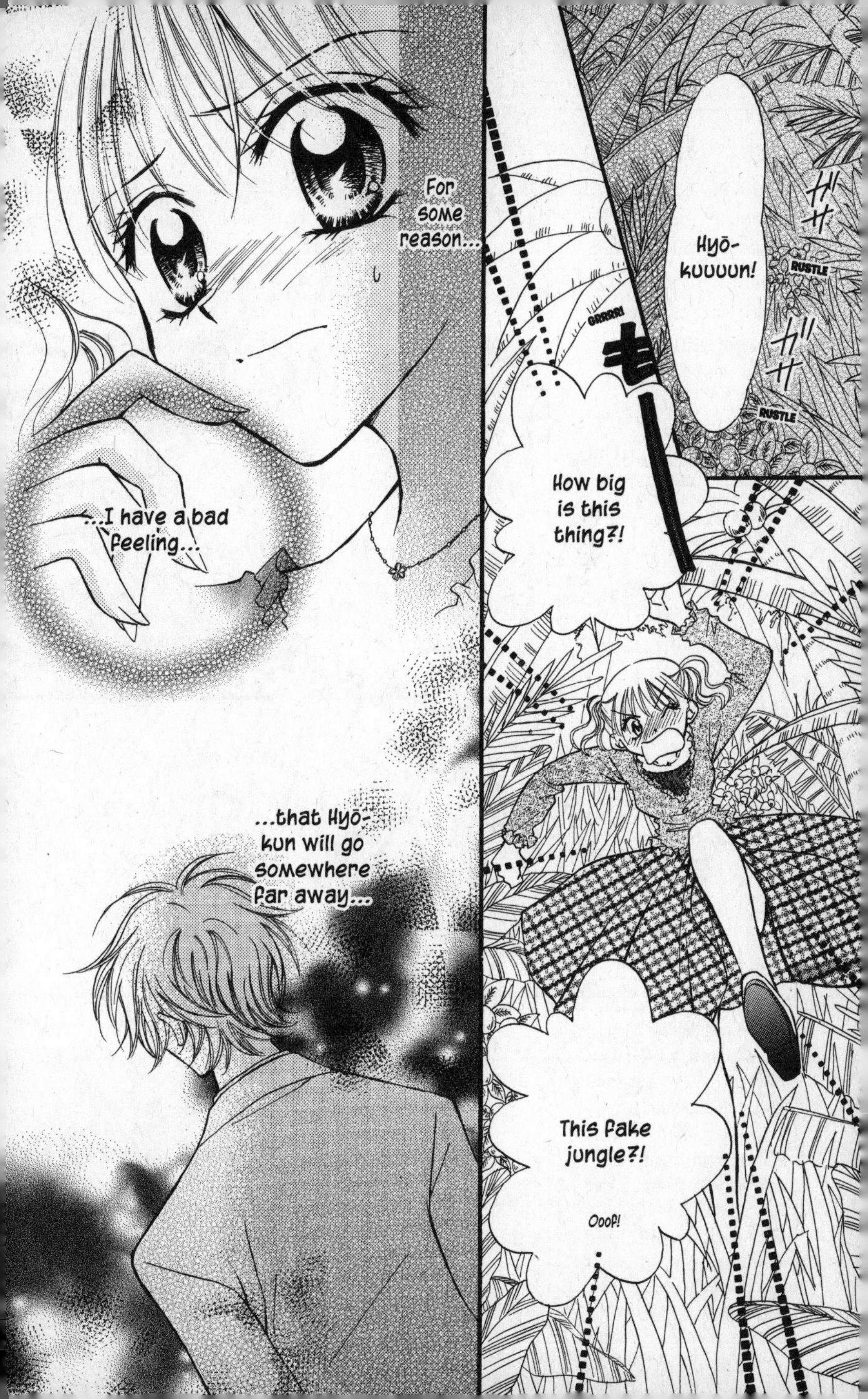

Hyō-kuuuun!
RUSTLE
RUSTLE
GRRRR!
How big is this thing?!
This fake jungle?!
Ooof!
For some reason...
...I have a bad feeling...
...that Hyō-kun will go somewhere far away...

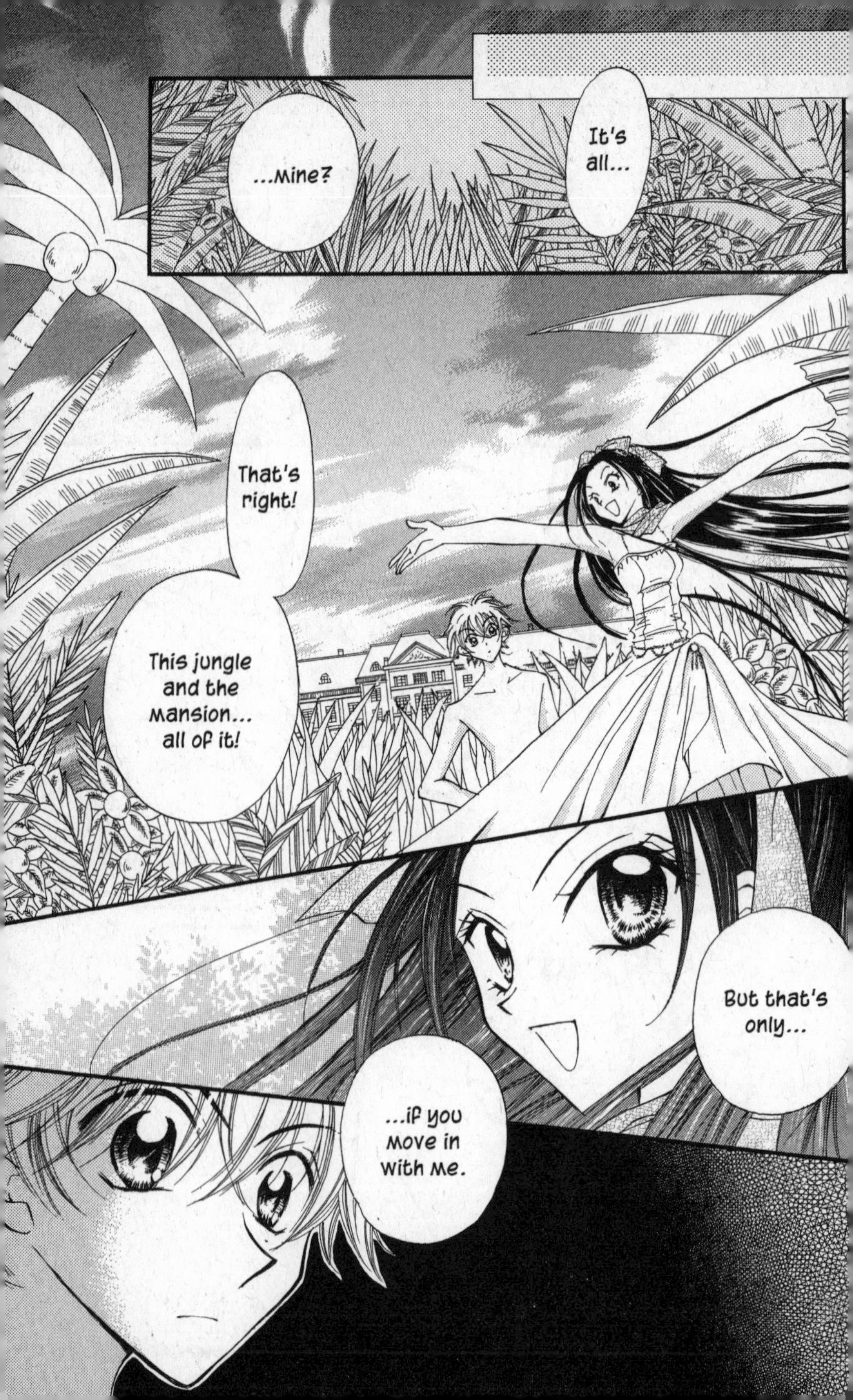
It's all...
...Mine?
That's right!
This jungle and the Mansion... all of it!
But that's only...
...if you Move in with Me.

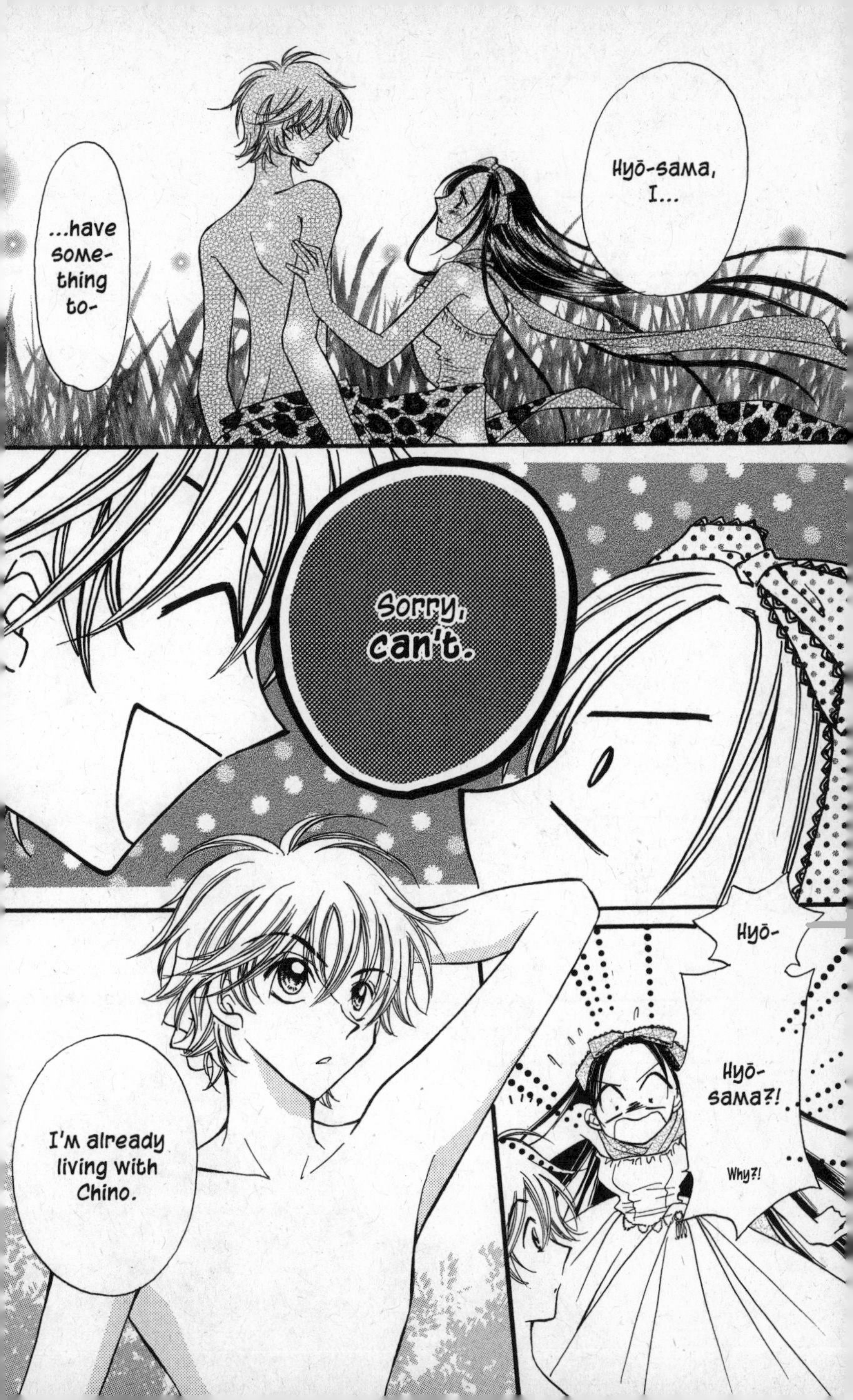
Hyō-sama, I...
...have some-thing to-
Sorry, can't.
Hyō-
Hyō-sama?!
Why?!
I'm already living with Chino.

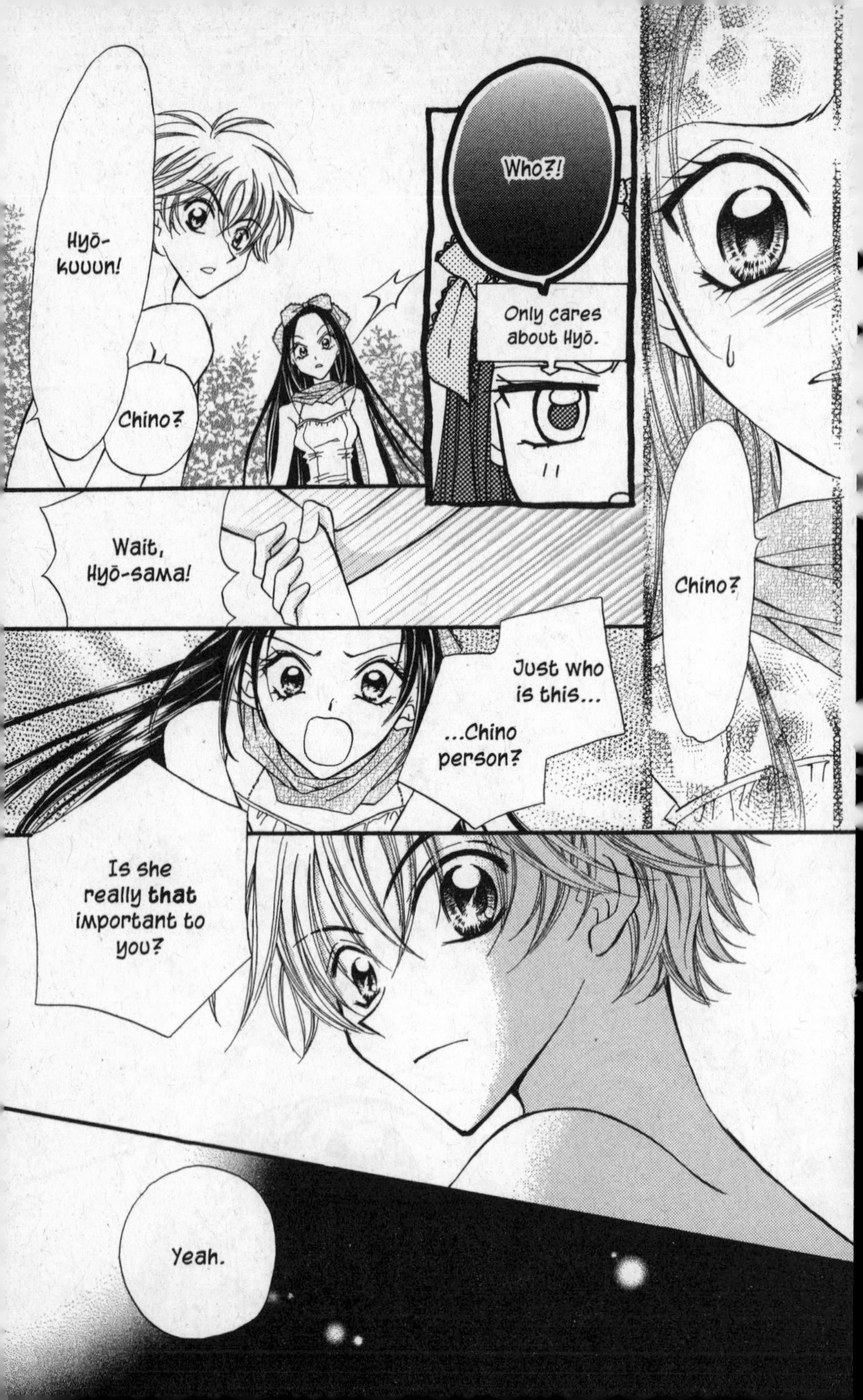
Chino?
Who?!
Only cares about Hyō.
Hyō-kuuun!
Chino?
Wait, Hyō-sama!
Just who is this...
...Chino person?
Is she really that important to you?
Yeah.

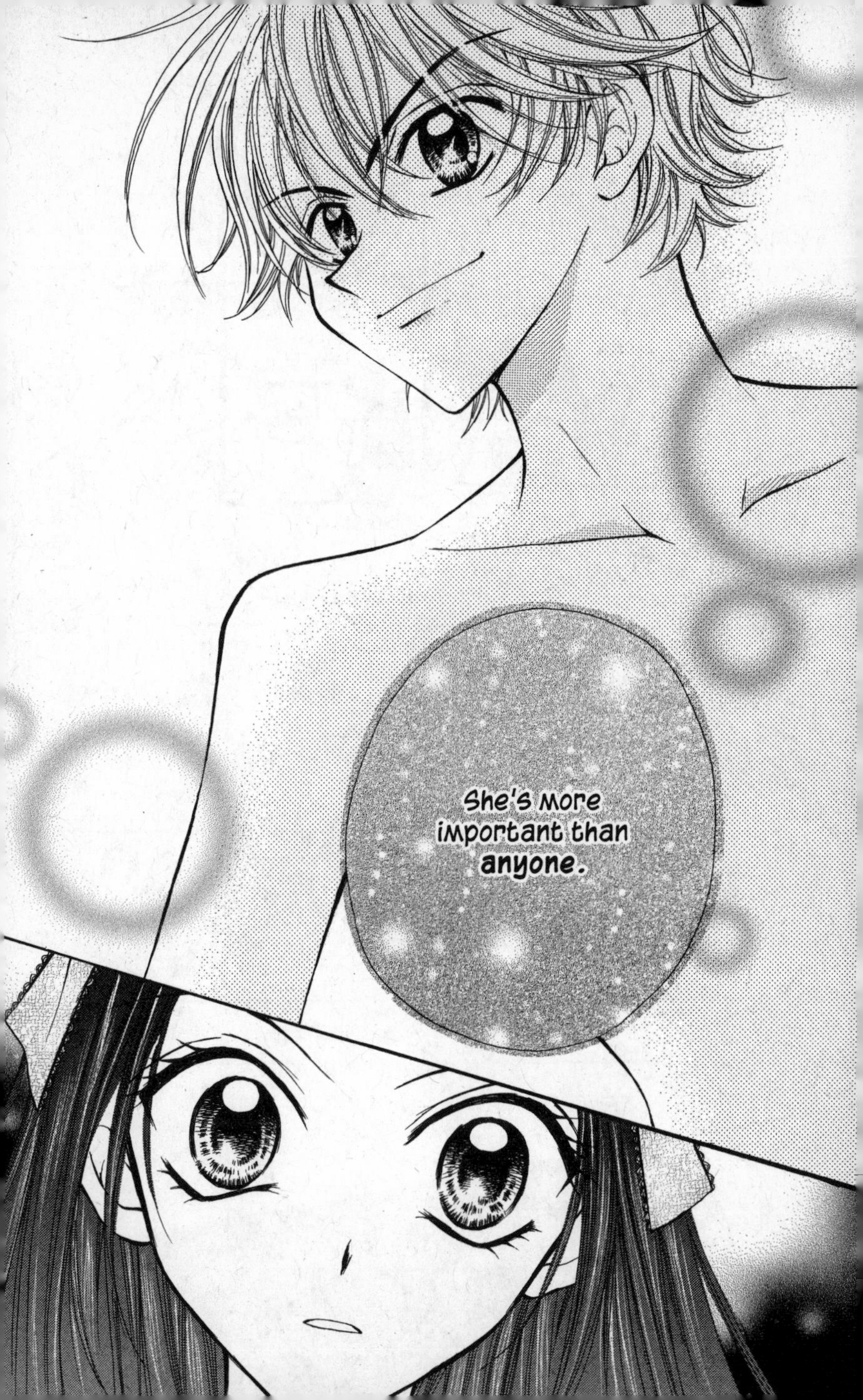
She's more important than anyone.

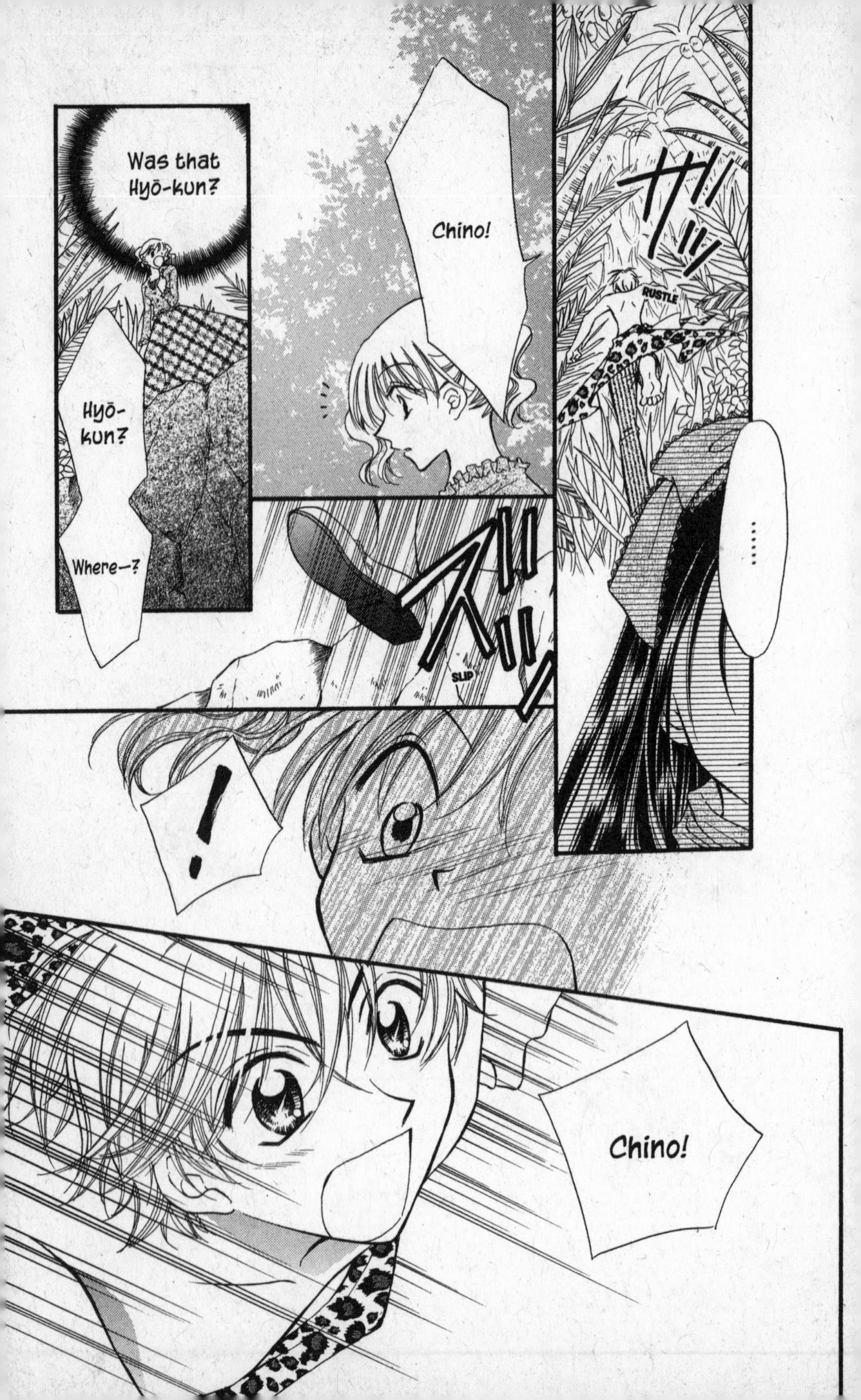
RUSTLE
.....
Chino!
SLIP
Was that Hyō-kun?
Hyō-kun?
Where—?
!
Chino!

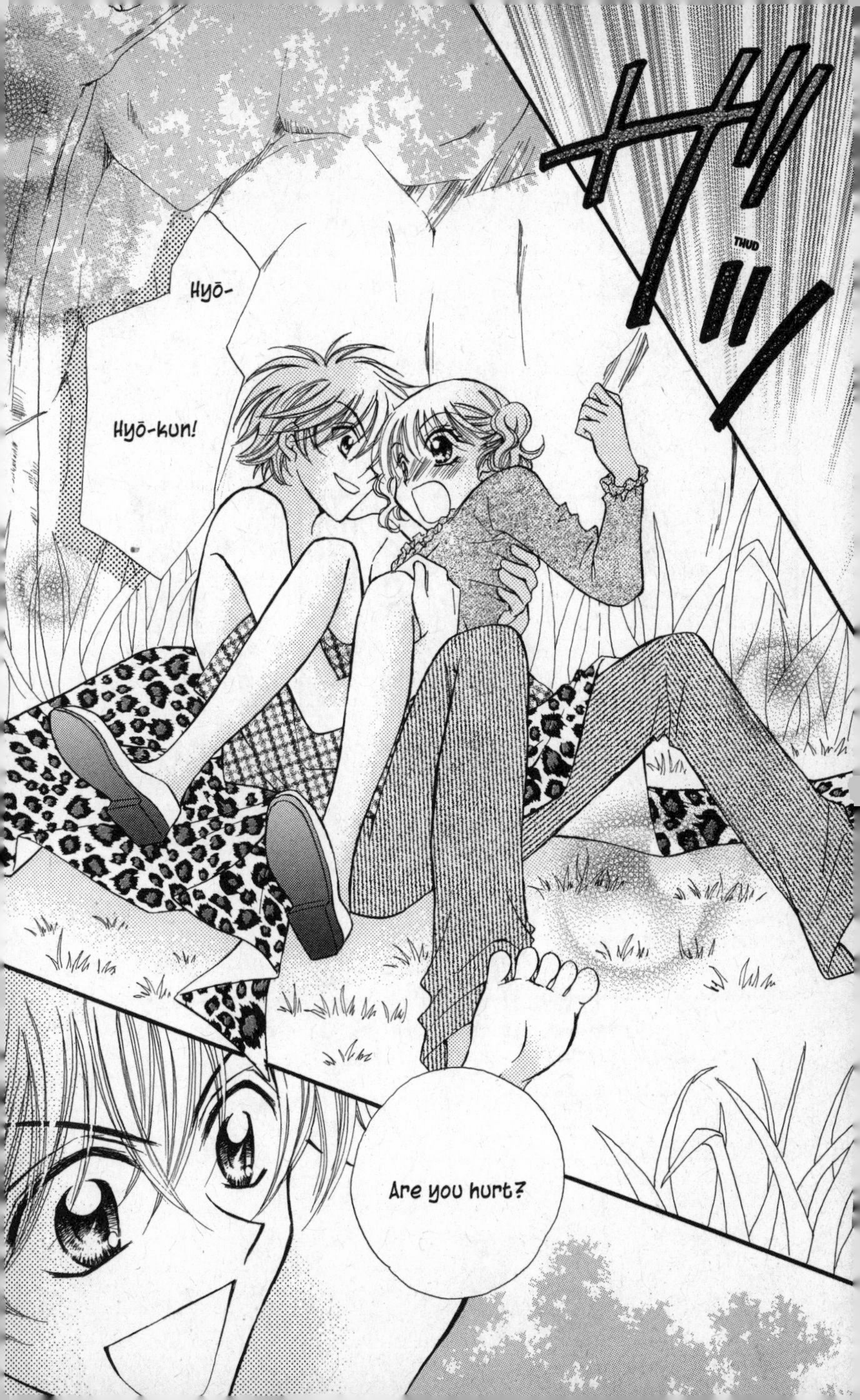
THUD
Hyō-
Hyō-kun!
Are you hurt?

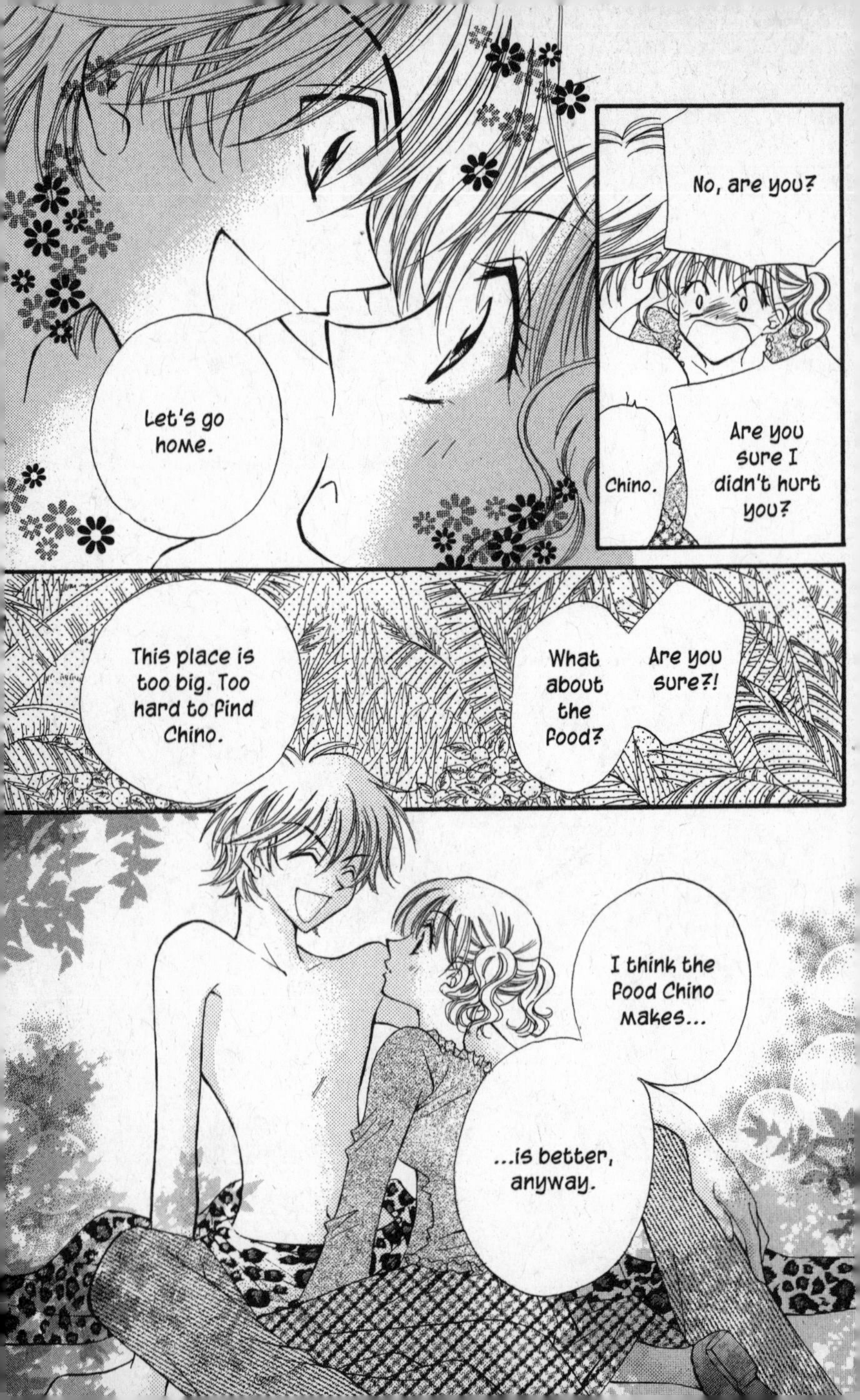
No, are you?
Are you sure I didn't hurt you?
Chino.
Let's go home.
Are you sure?!
What about the food?
This place is too big. Too hard to find Chino.
I think the food Chino makes...
...is better, anyway.

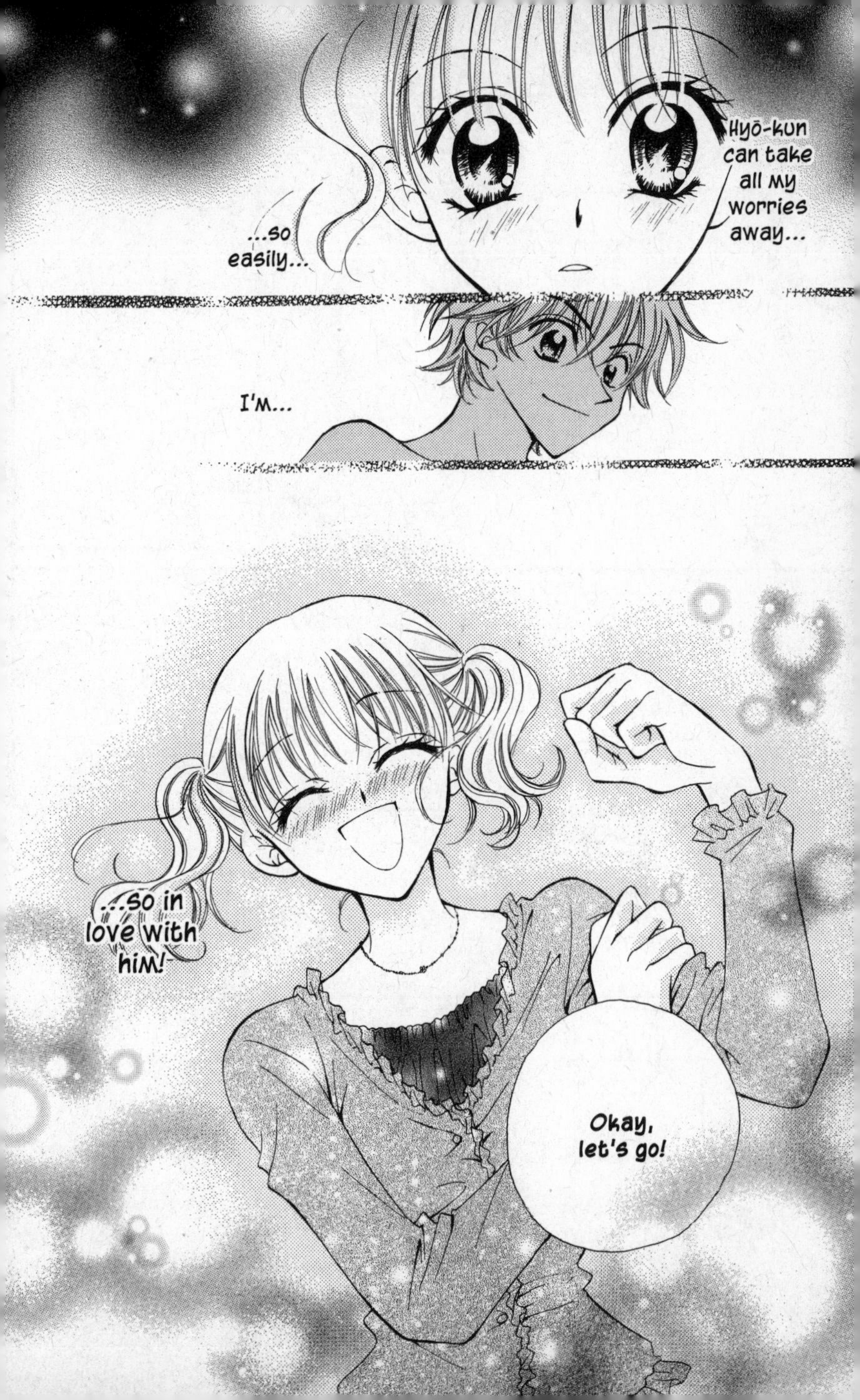
Hyō-kun can take all my worries away...
...so easily...
I'm...
...so in love with him!
Okay, let's go!

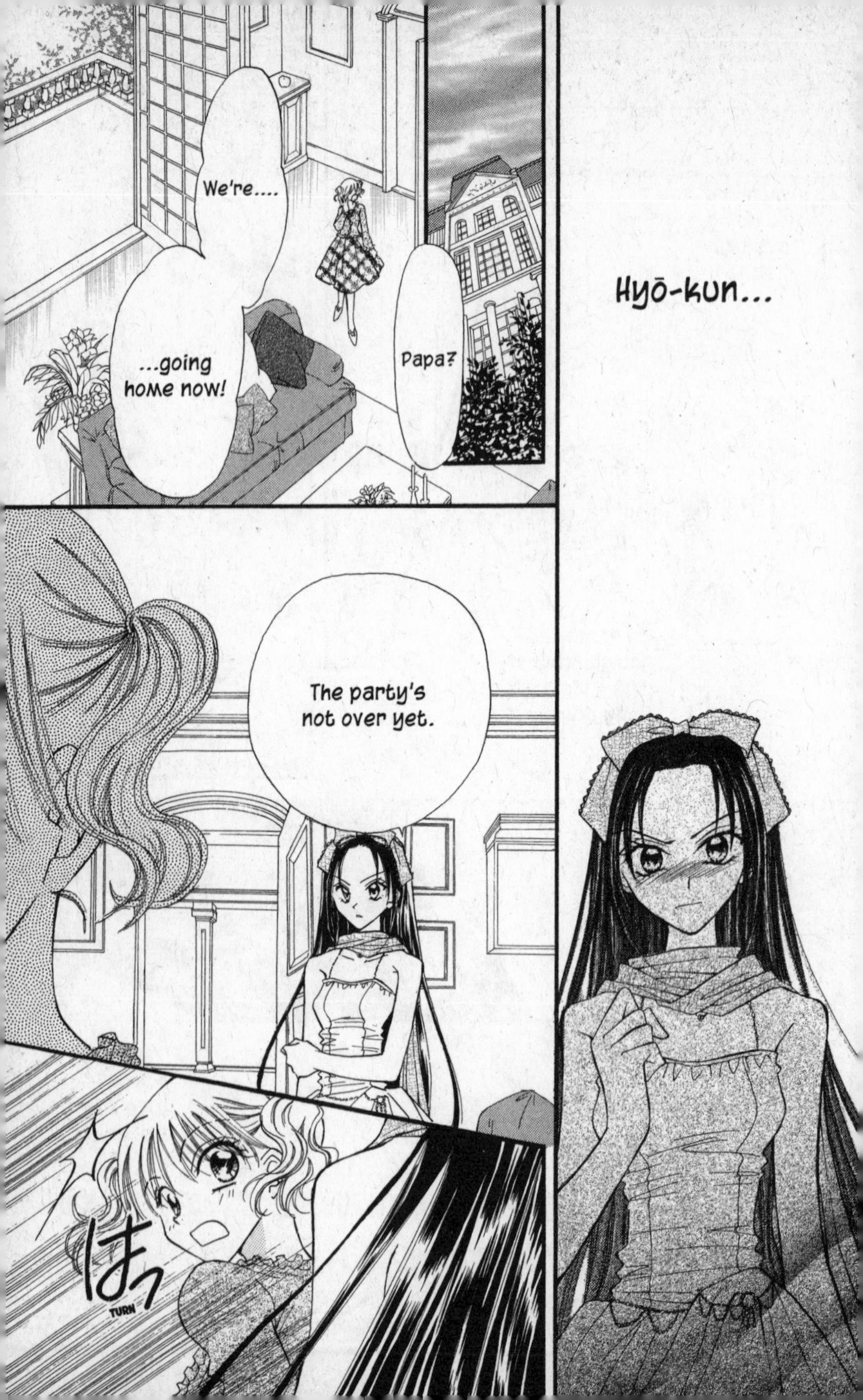
Hyō-kun...
Papa?
We're....
...going home now!
The party's not over yet.
はっ
TURN

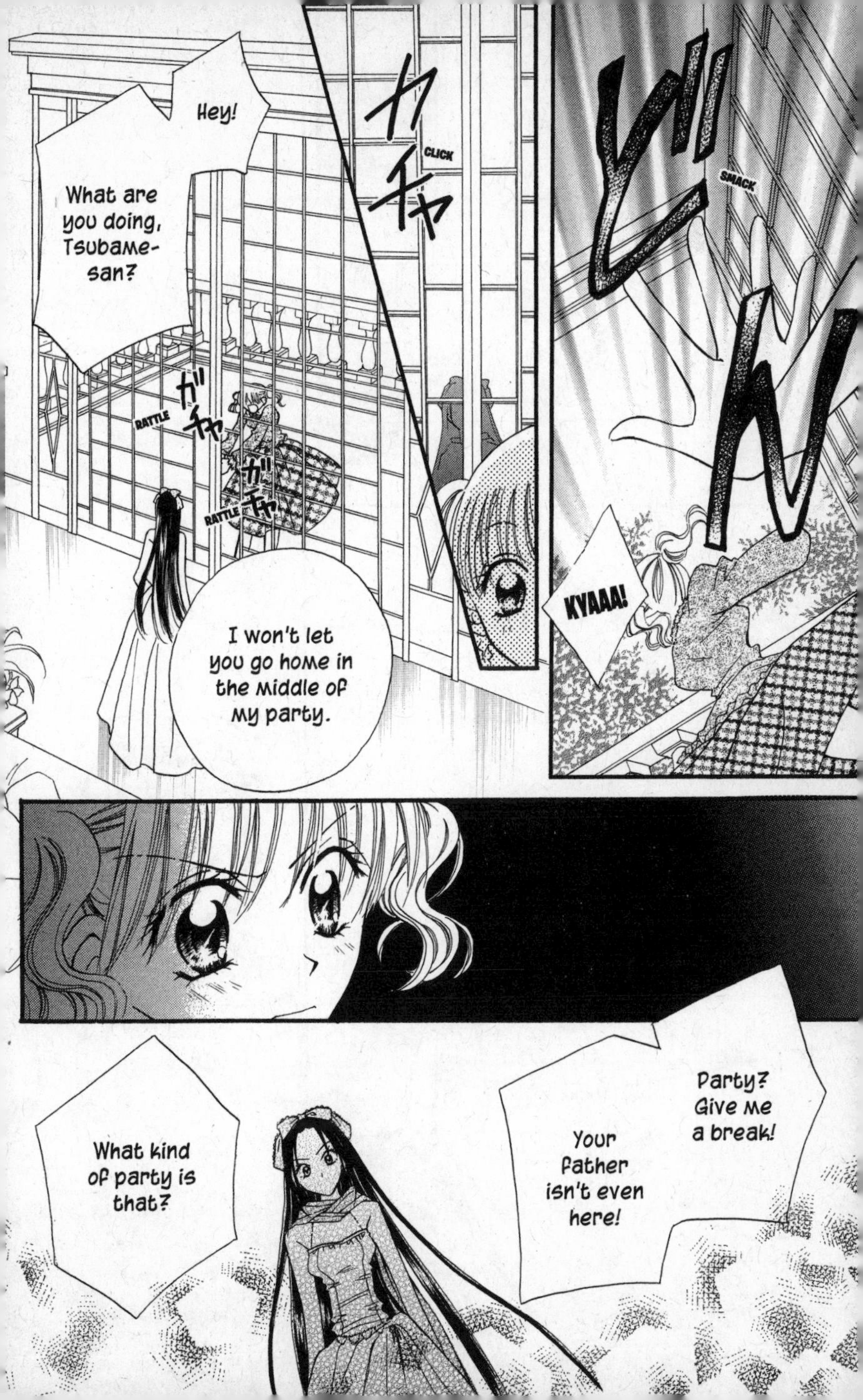
SMACK
KYAAA!
カチャ
CLICK
Hey!
What are you doing, Tsubame-san?
ガチャ
RATTLE
ガチャ
RATTLE
I won't let you go home in the middle of my party.
Party? Give me a break!
Your father isn't even here!
What kind of party is that?

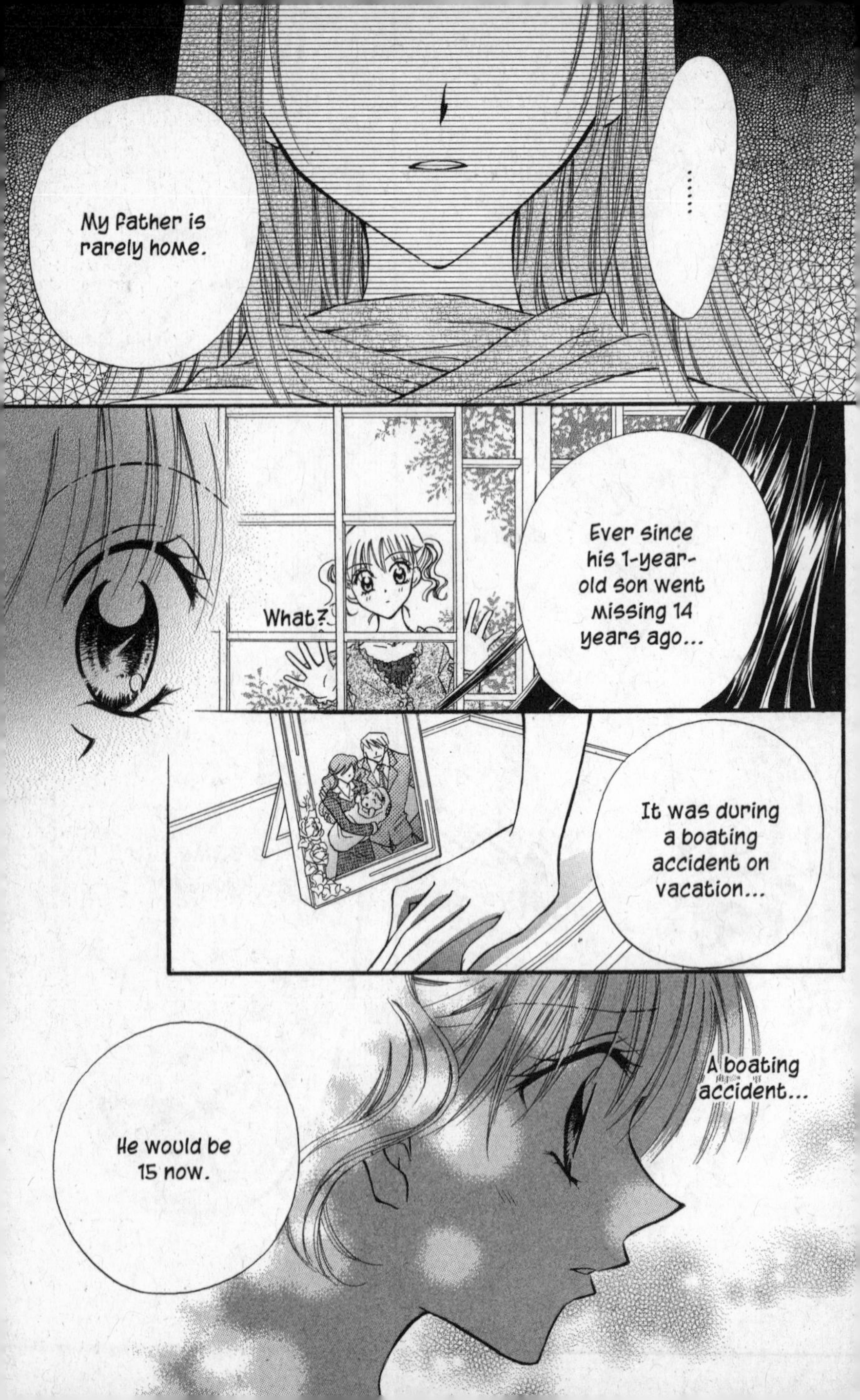
......
My father is rarely home.
Ever since his 1-year-old son went missing 14 years ago...
What?
It was during a boating accident on vacation...
A boating accident...
He would be 15 now.

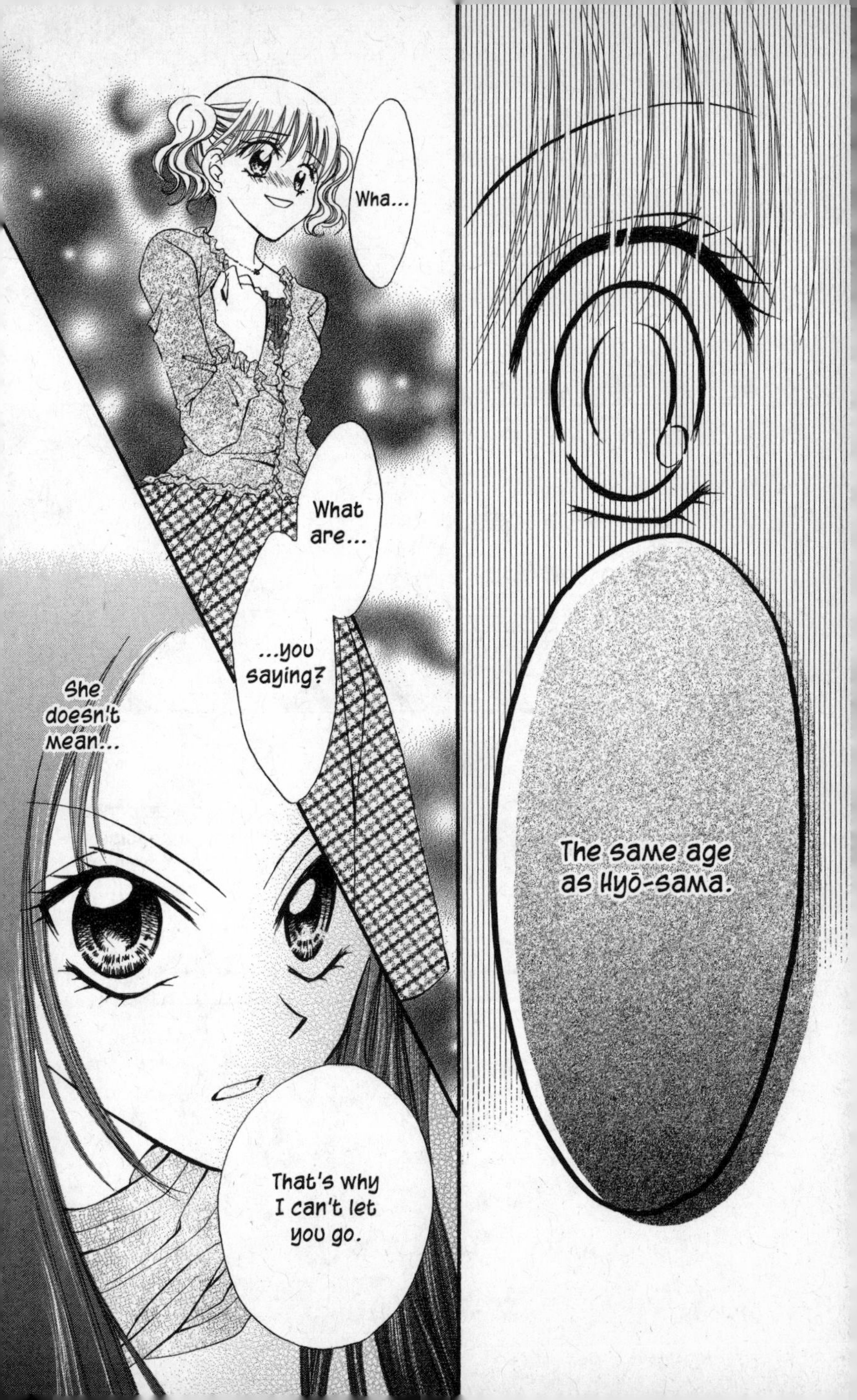
The same age as Hyō-sama.
Wha...
What are...
...you saying?
She doesn't mean...
That's why I can't let you go.

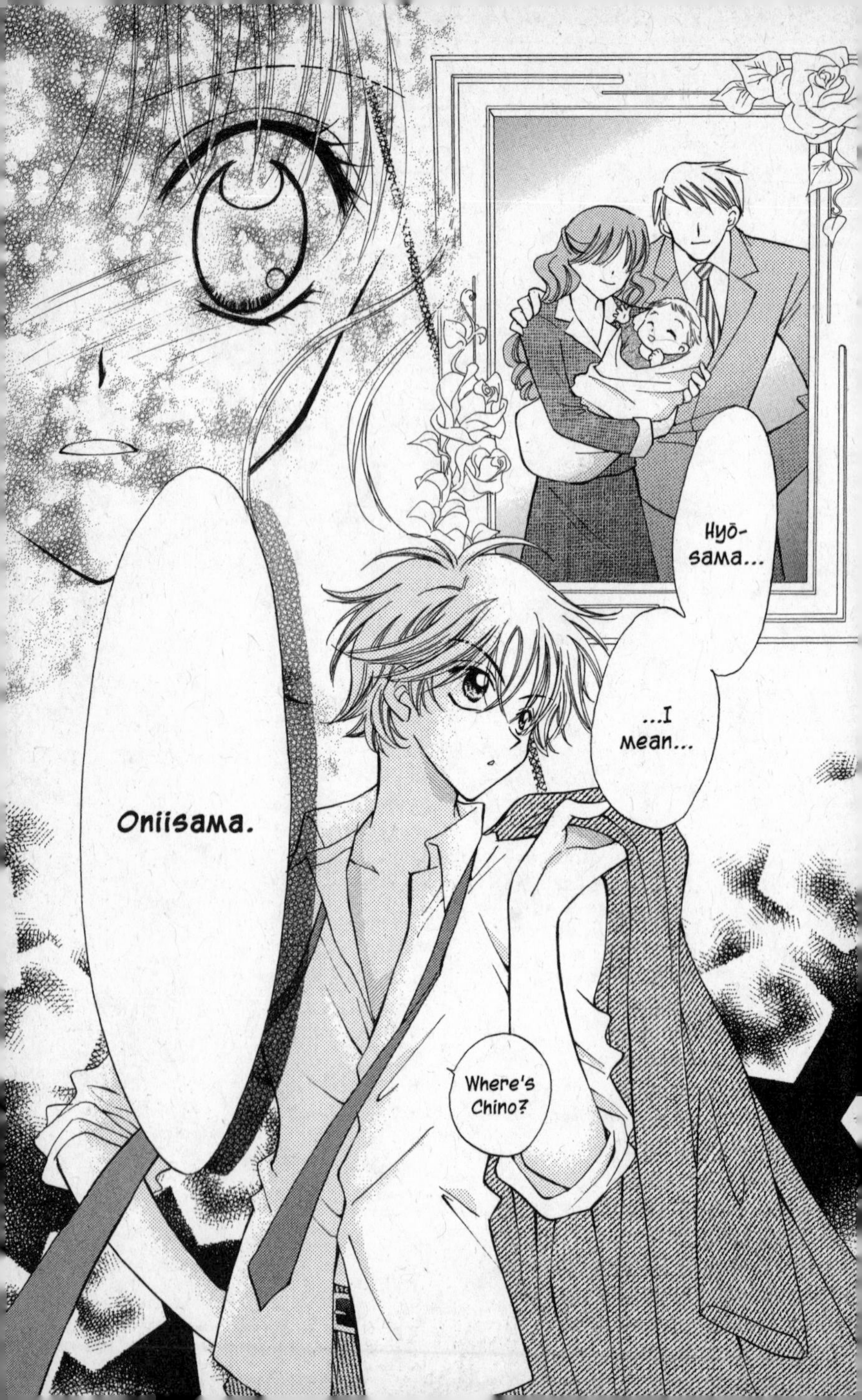
Hyō-sama...
...I mean...
Oniisama.
Where's Chino?

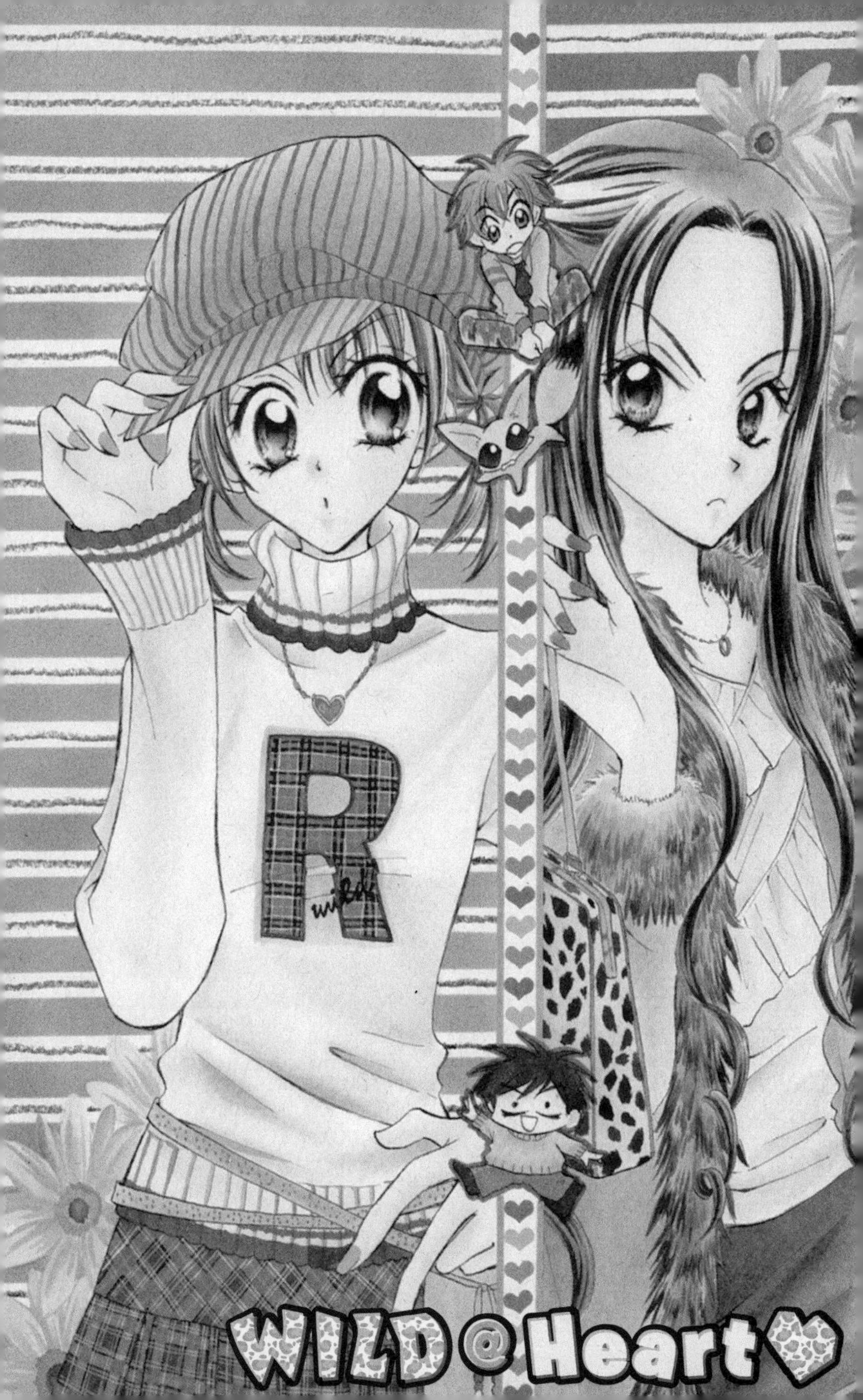
R
WILD @ Heart

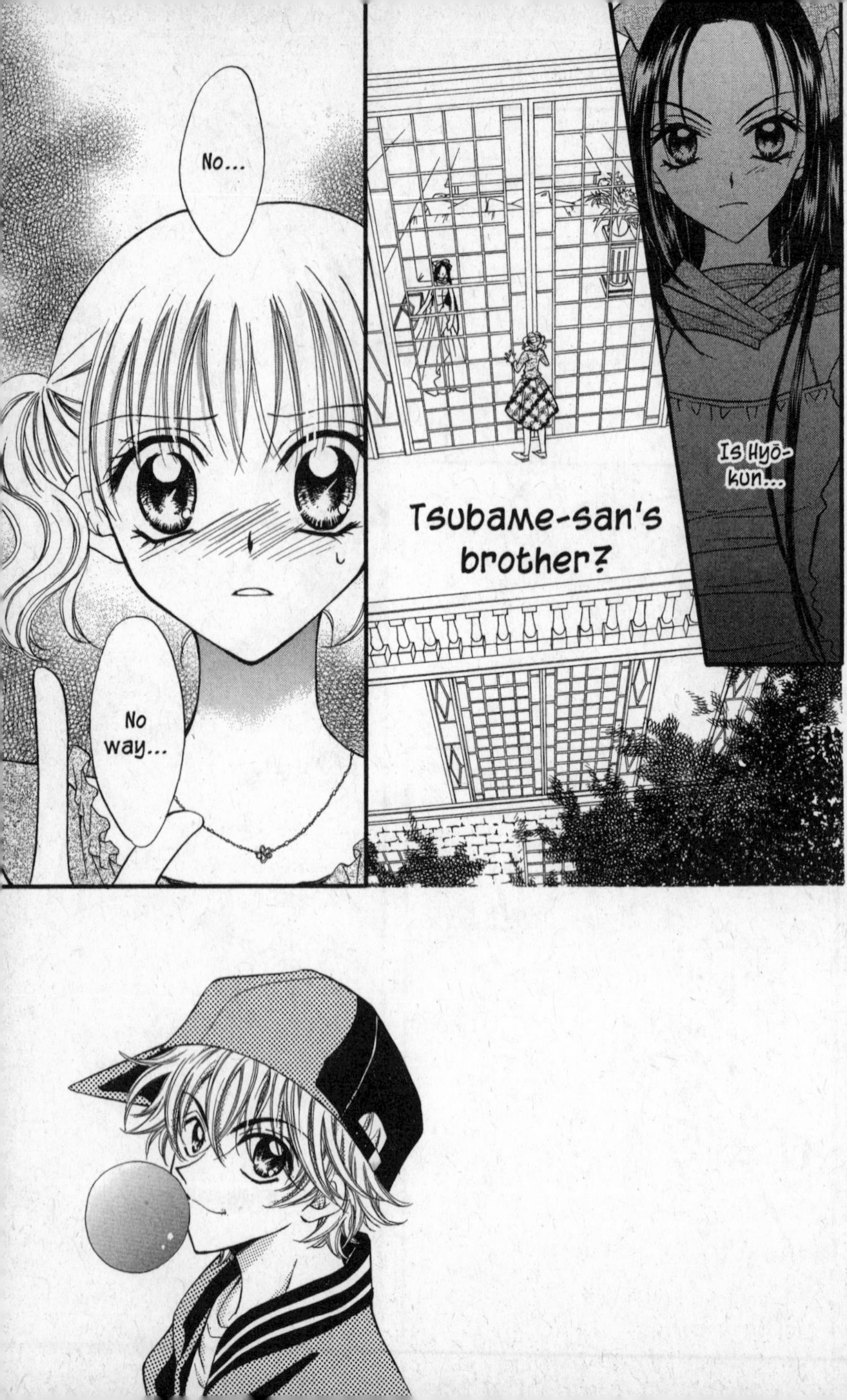
Is Hyō-kun...
Tsubame-san's brother?
No...
No way...

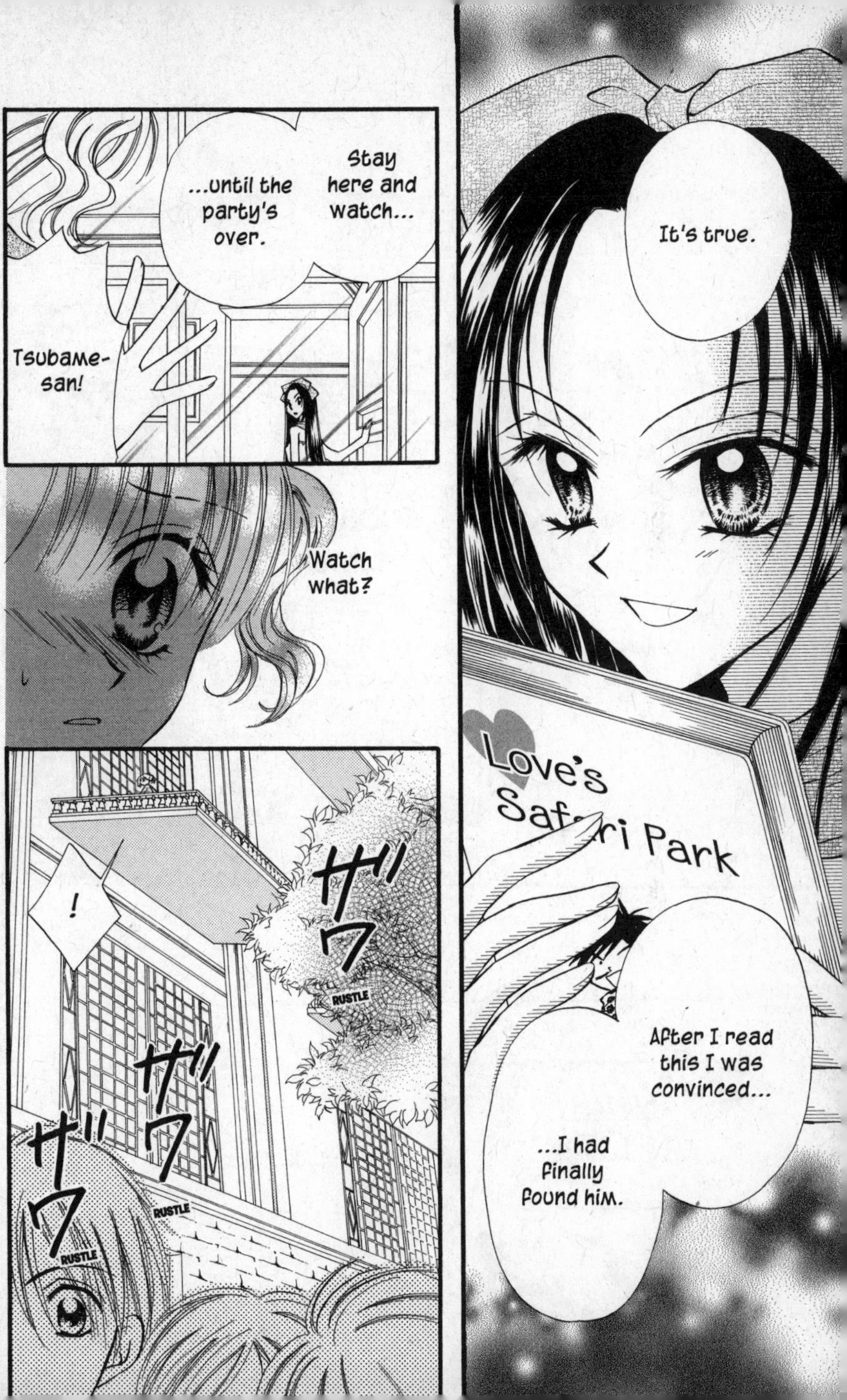
It's true.
Love's
After I read this I was convinced...
...I had finally found him.
Stay here and watch...
...until the party's over.
Tsubame-san!
Watch what?
!
RUSTLE
RUSTLE
RUSTLE

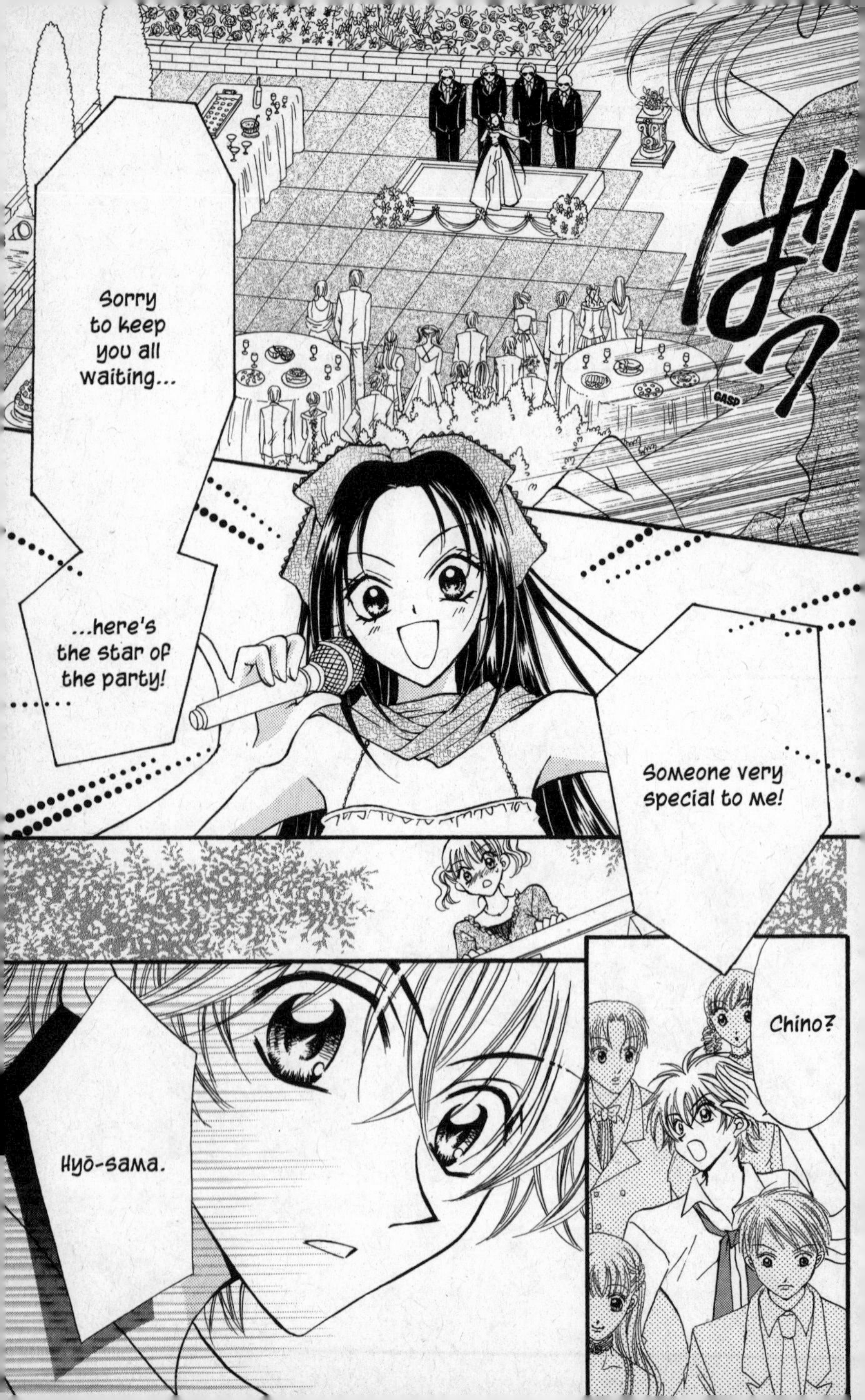

はっ
GASP
Sorry to keep you all waiting...
...here's the star of the party!
Someone very special to me!
Chino?
Hyō-sama.

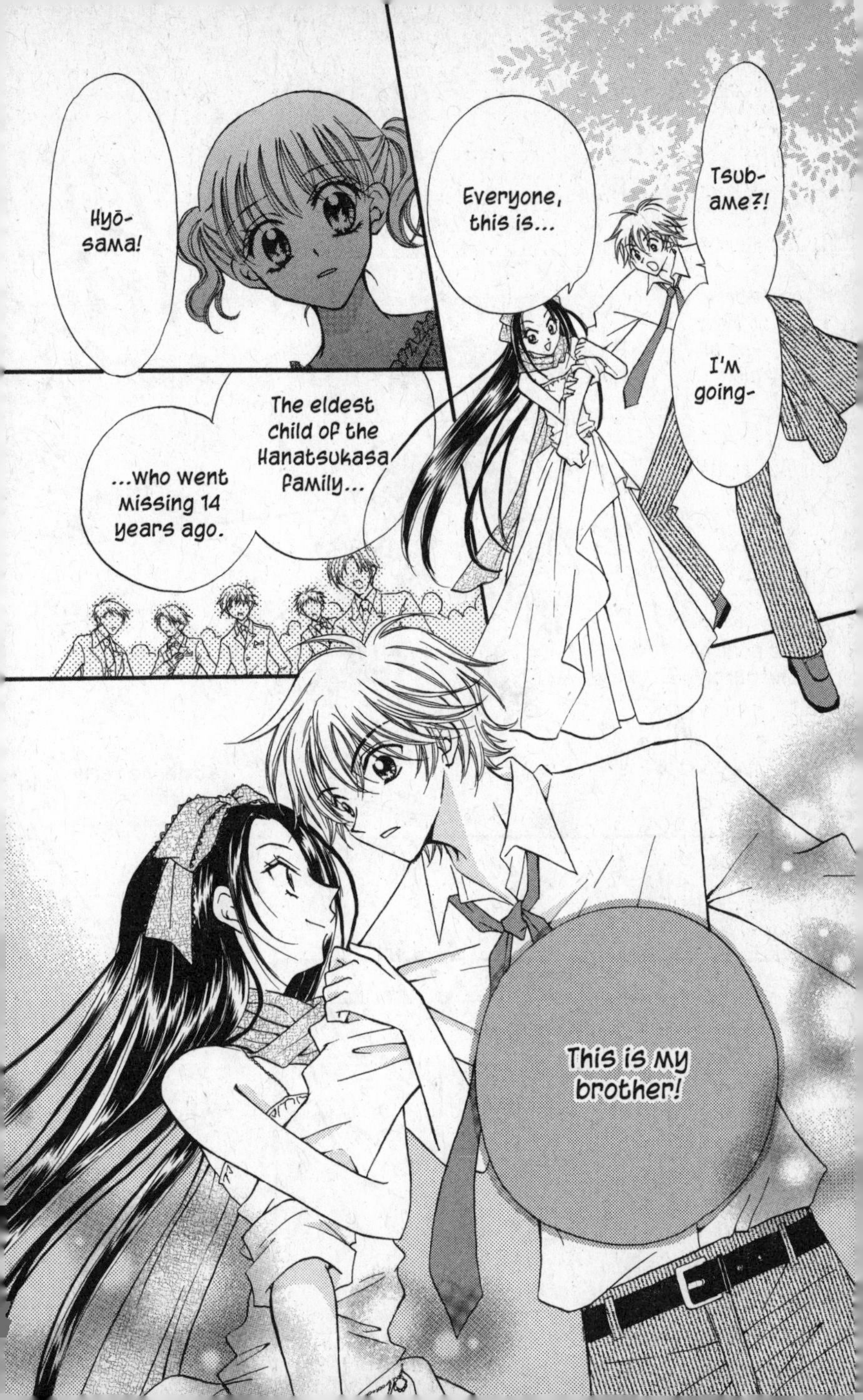
Tsub-ame?!
Everyone, this is...
I'm going-
Hyō-sama!
The eldest child of the Hanatsukasa family...
...who went missing 14 years ago.
This is my brother!

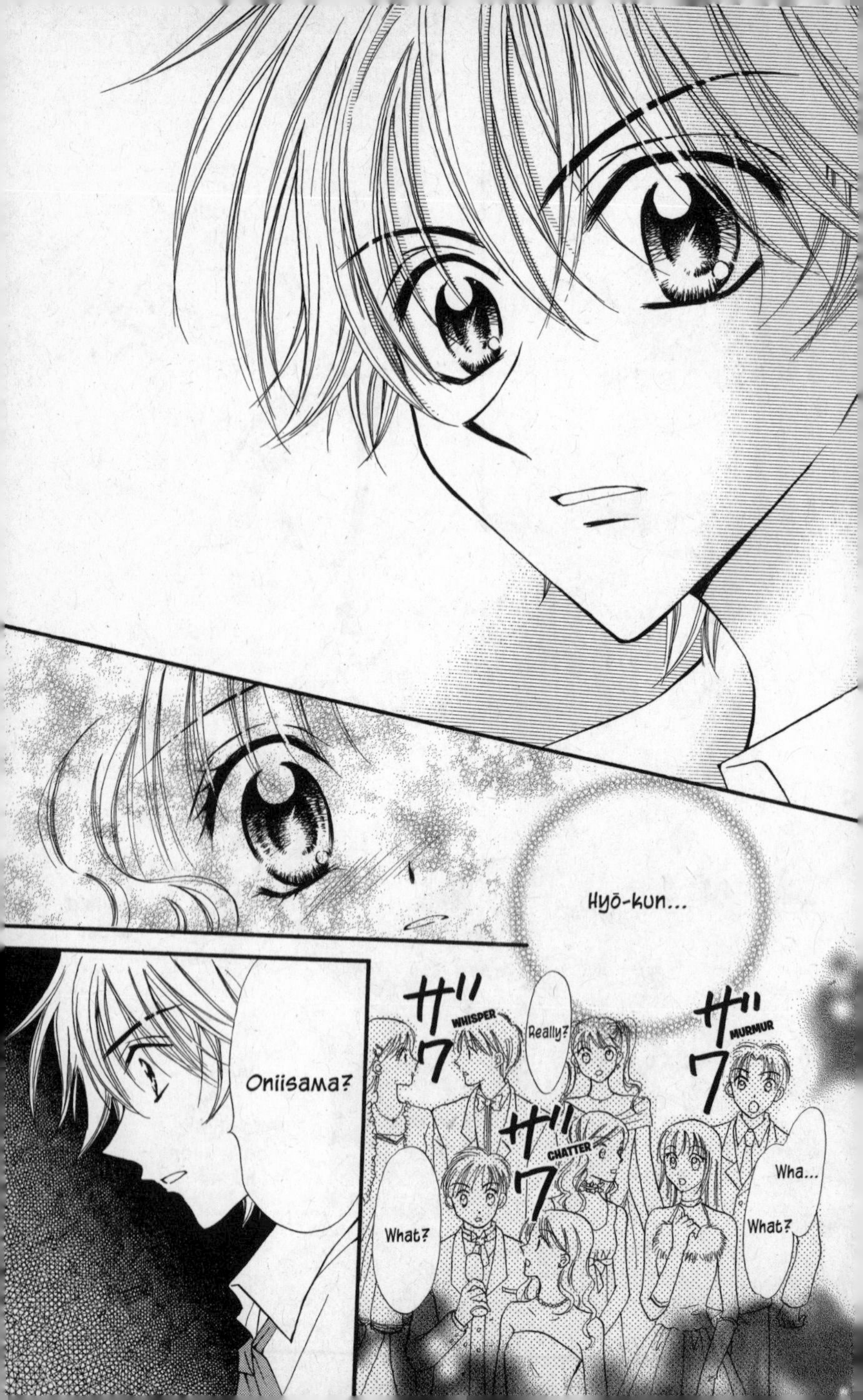
Hyō-kun...
ザワ MURMUR
Wha...
What?
ザワ CHATTER
What?
Really?
ザワ WHISPER
Oniisama?

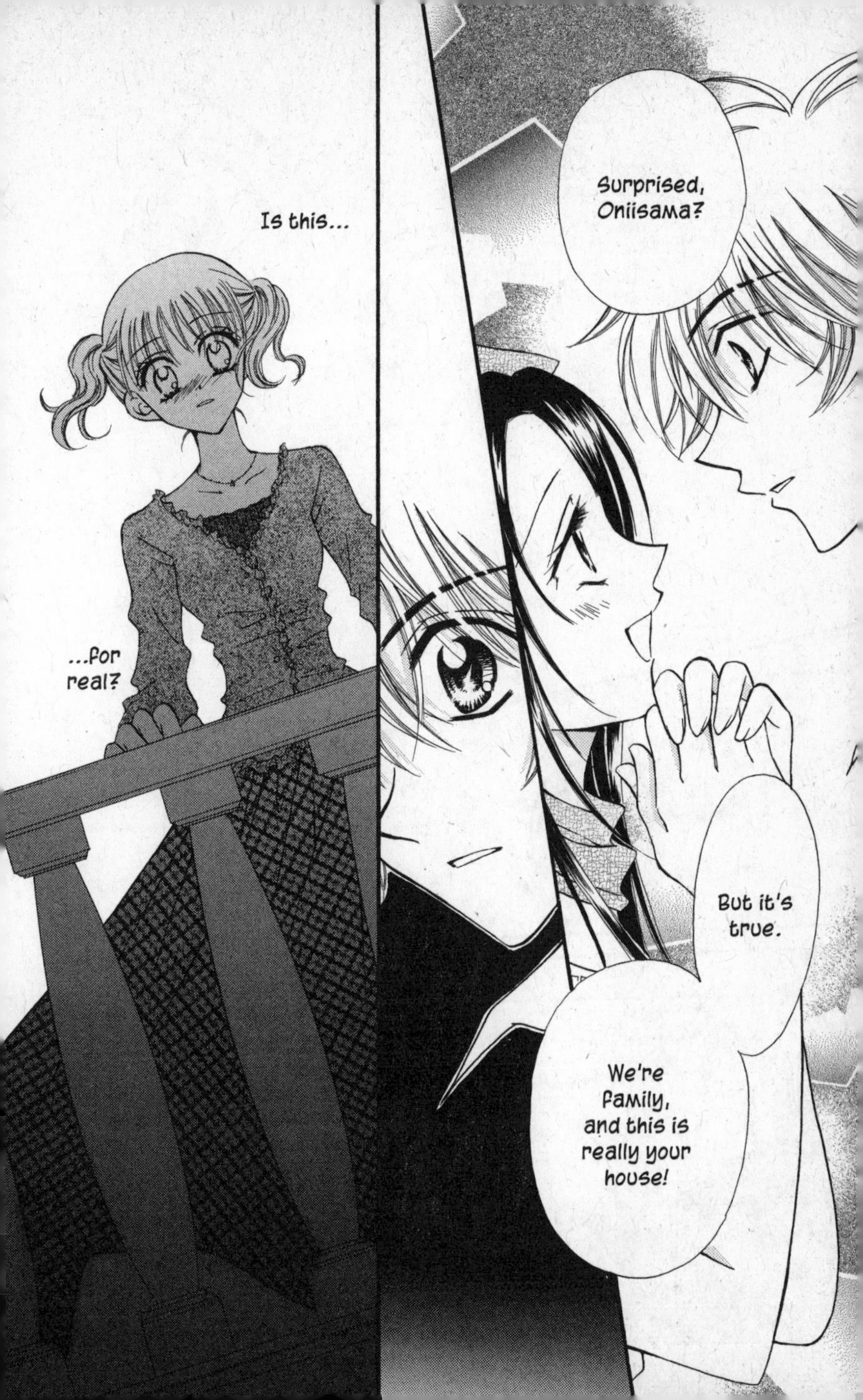
Surprised, Oniisama?
But it's true.
We're family, and this is really your house!
Is this...
...for real?

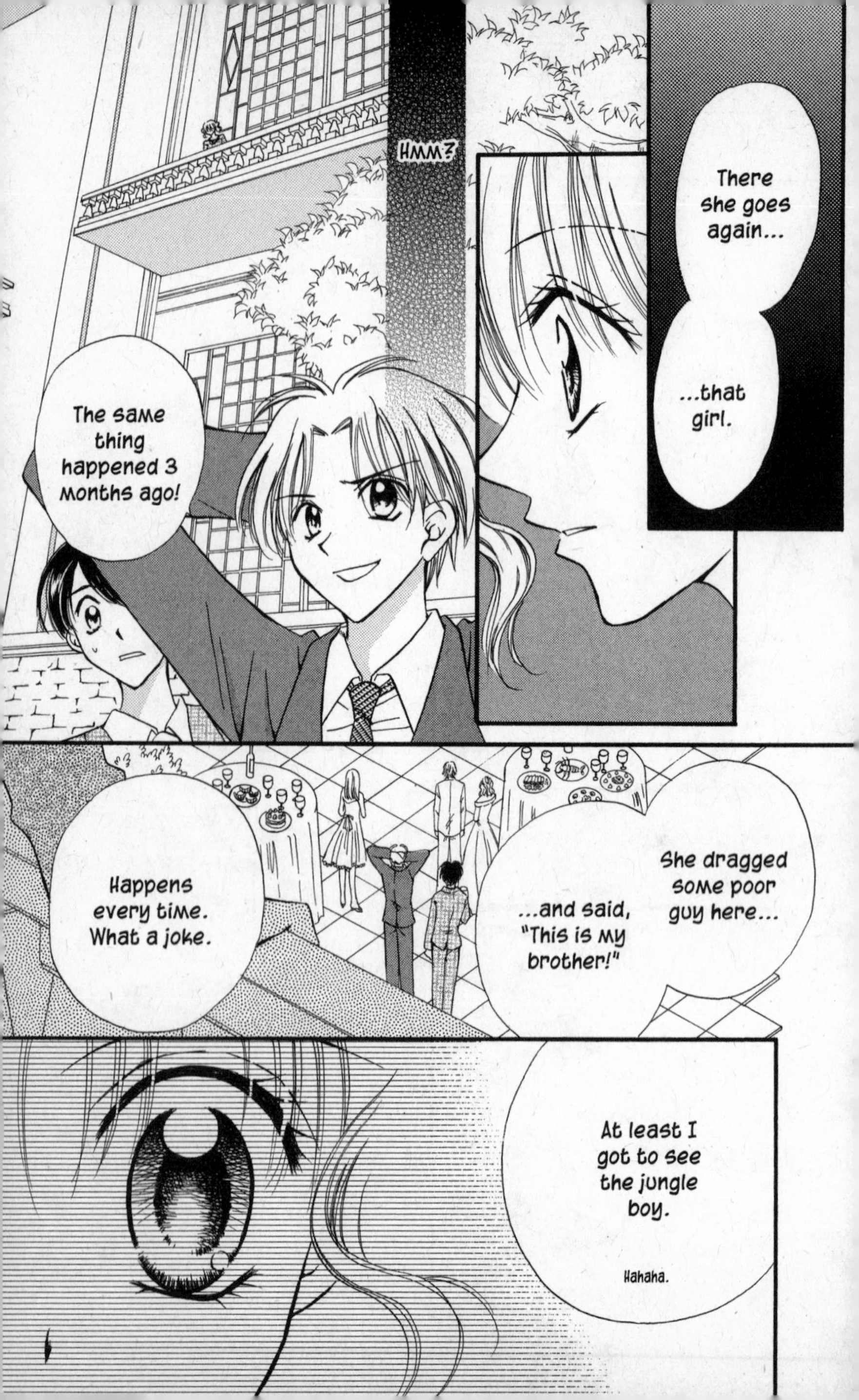
There she goes again...
...that girl.
HMM?
The same thing happened 3 months ago!
She dragged some poor guy here...
...and said, "This is my brother!"
Happens every time. What a joke.
At least I got to see the jungle boy.
Hahaha.

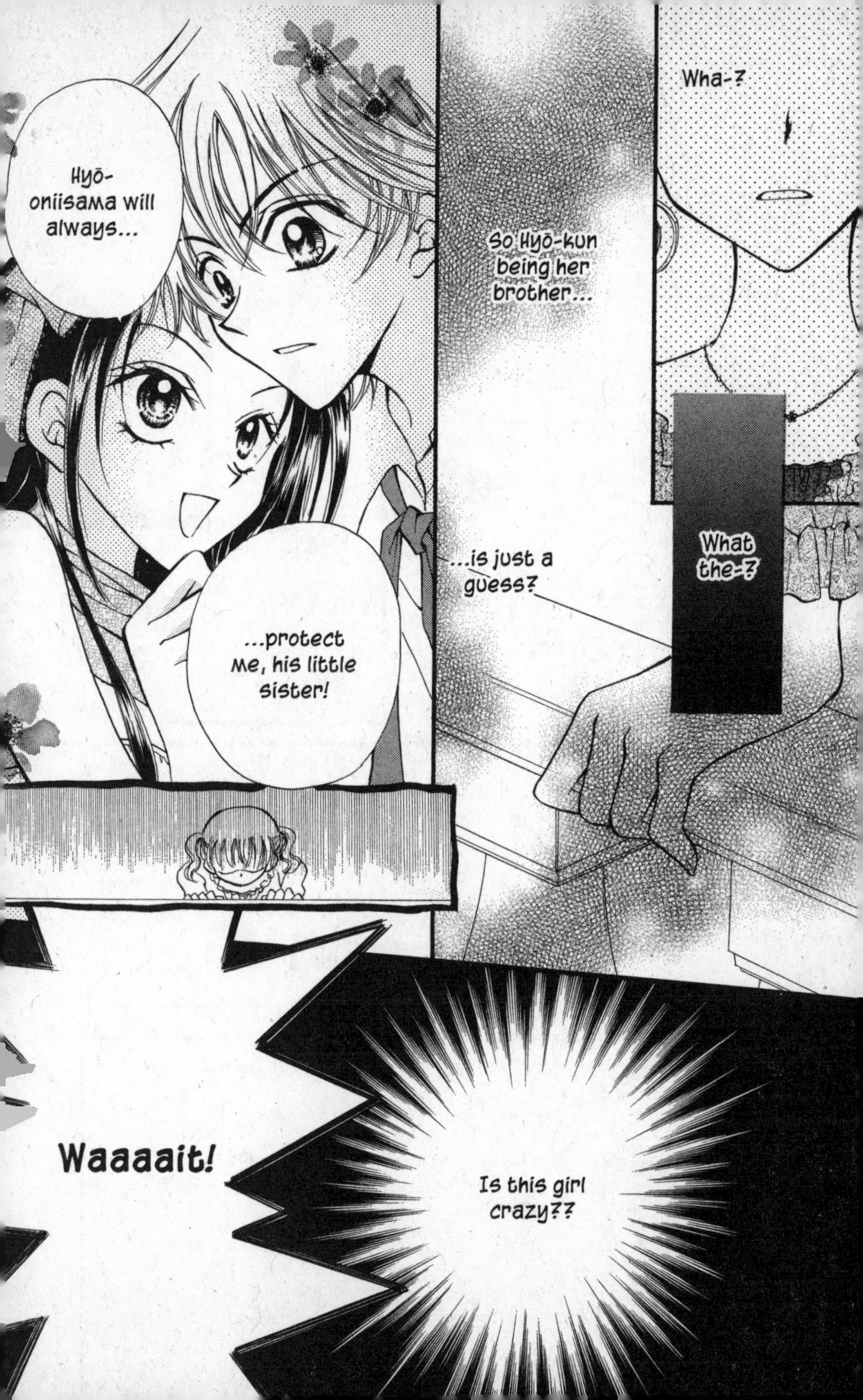
Wha-?
What the-?
So Hyō-kun being her brother...
...is just a guess?
Hyō-oniisama will always...
...protect me, his little sister!
Waaaait!
Is this girl crazy??

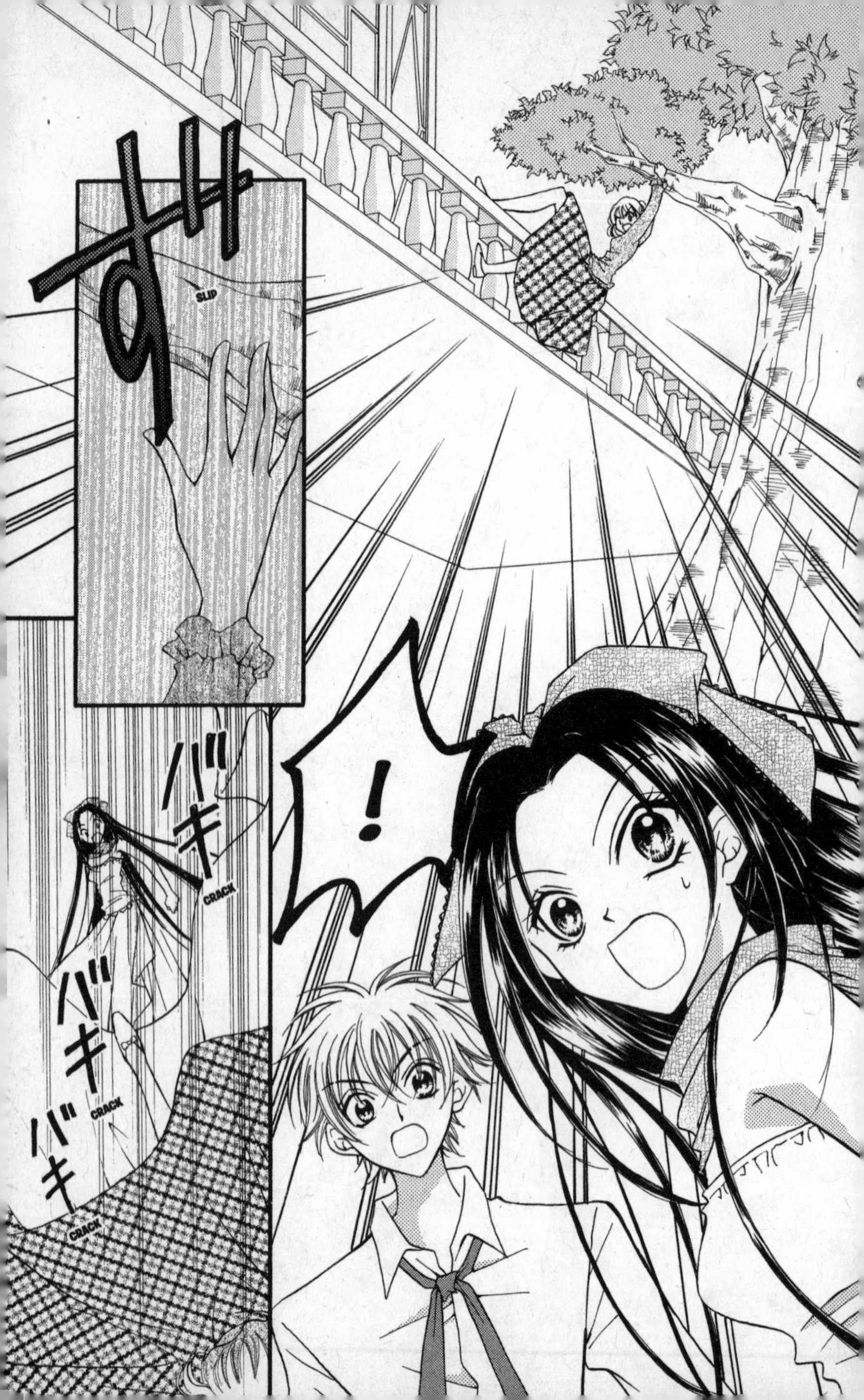
すっ
SLIP
!
バキ
CRACK
バキ
CRACK
バキ
CRACK

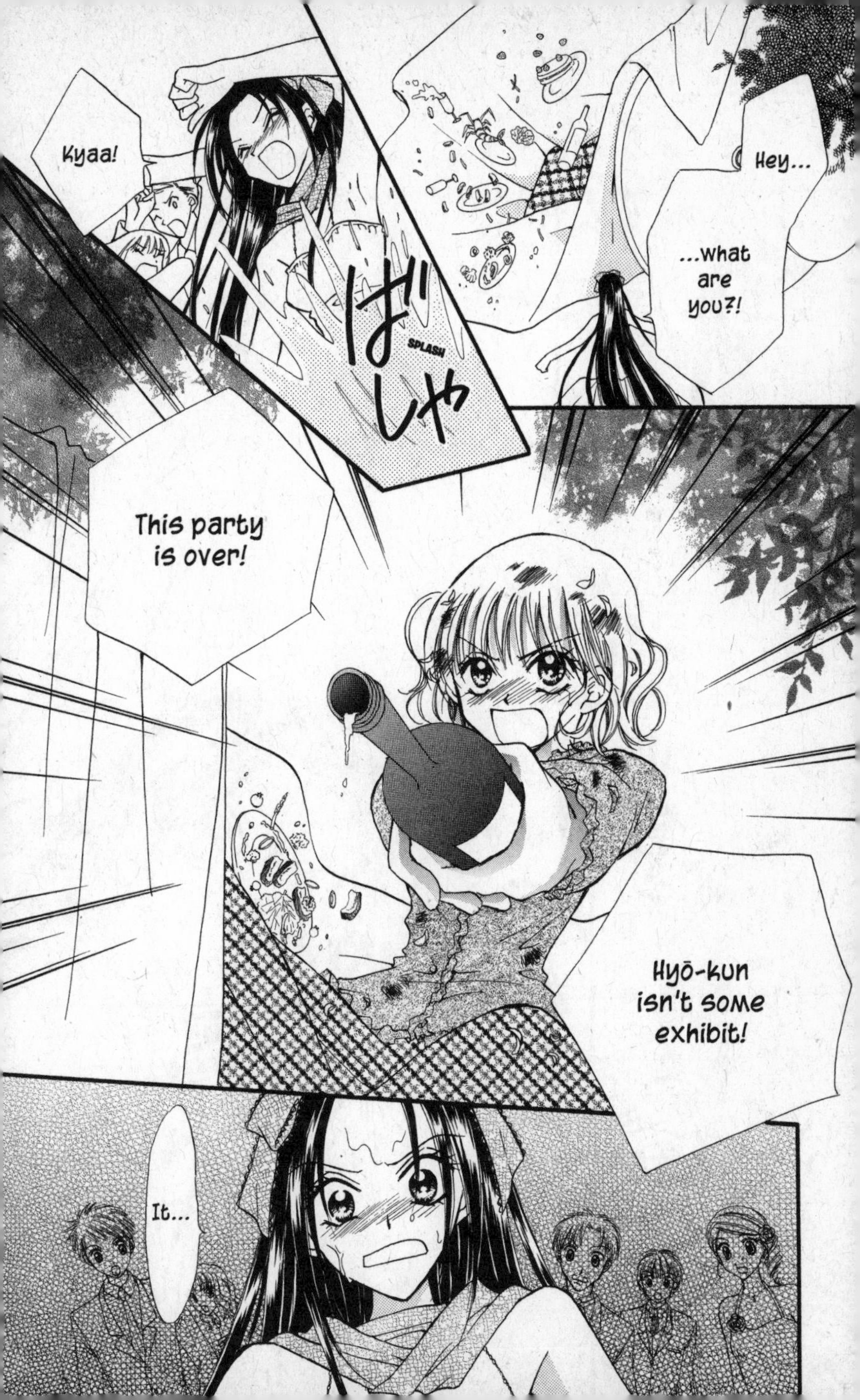
Hey...
...what are you?!
Kyaa!
ばしゃ
SPLASH
This party is over!
Hyō-kun isn't some exhibit!
It...

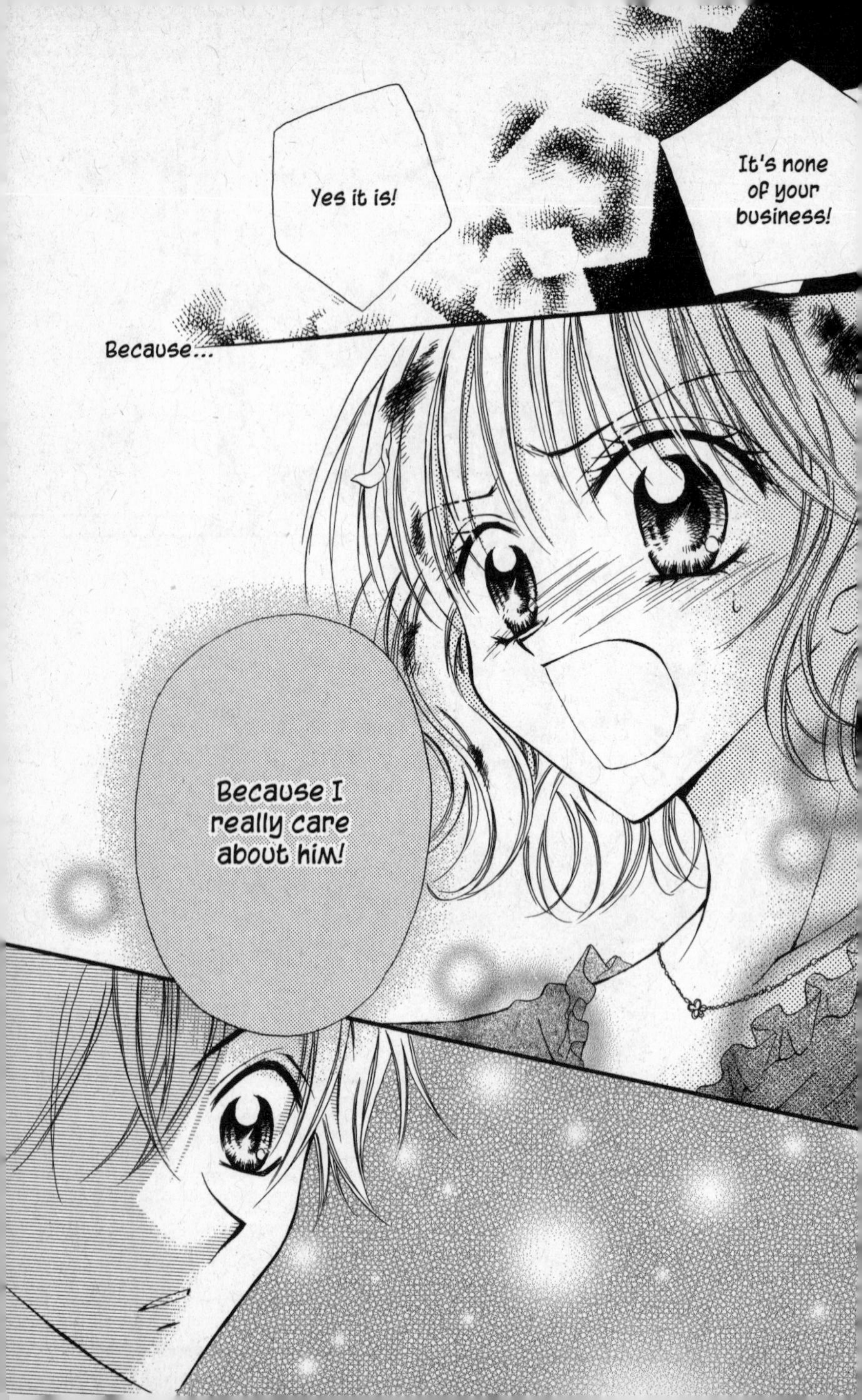
It's none of your business!
Yes it is!
Because...
Because I really care about him!

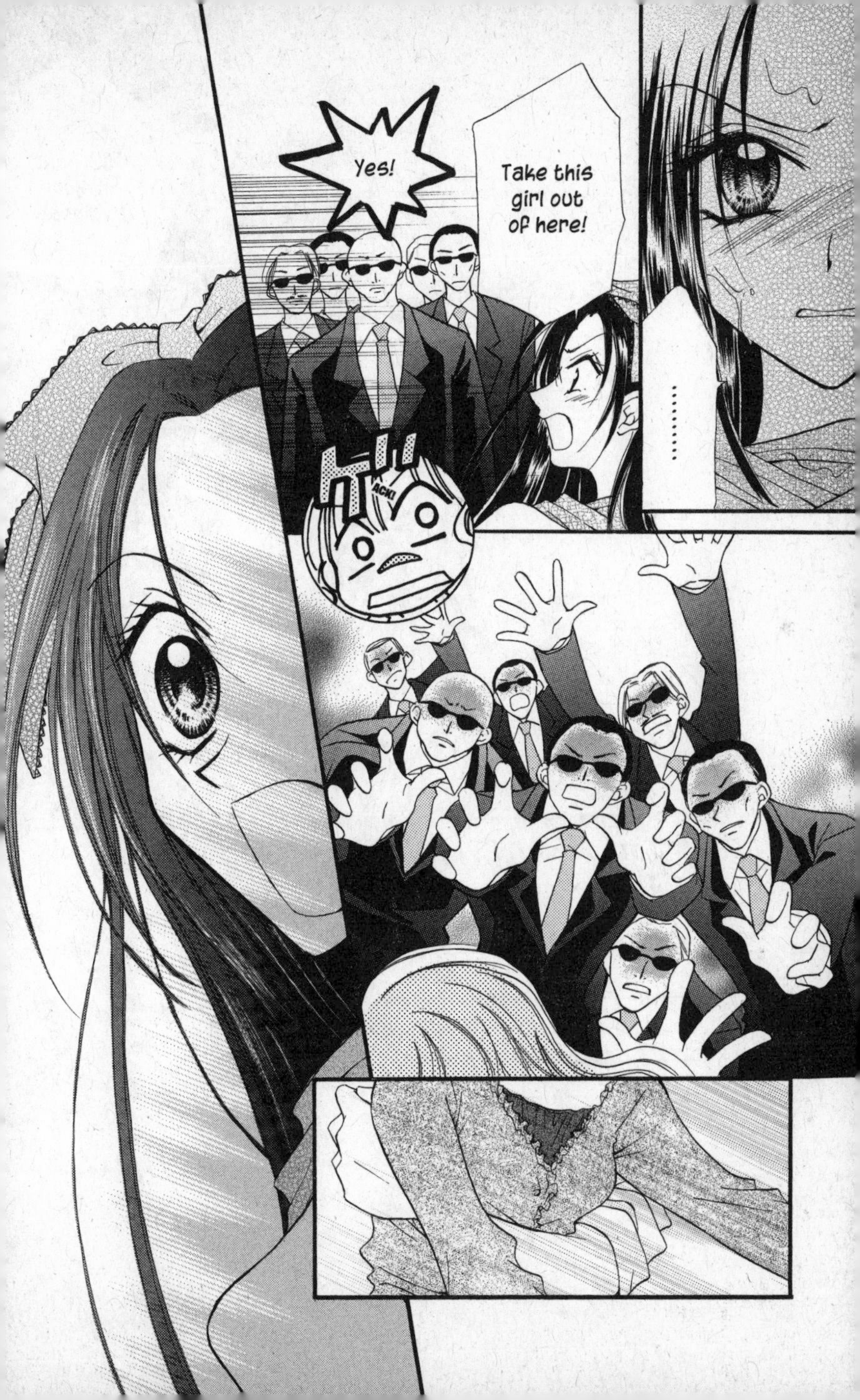
......
Take this girl out of here!
Yes!
ACK!

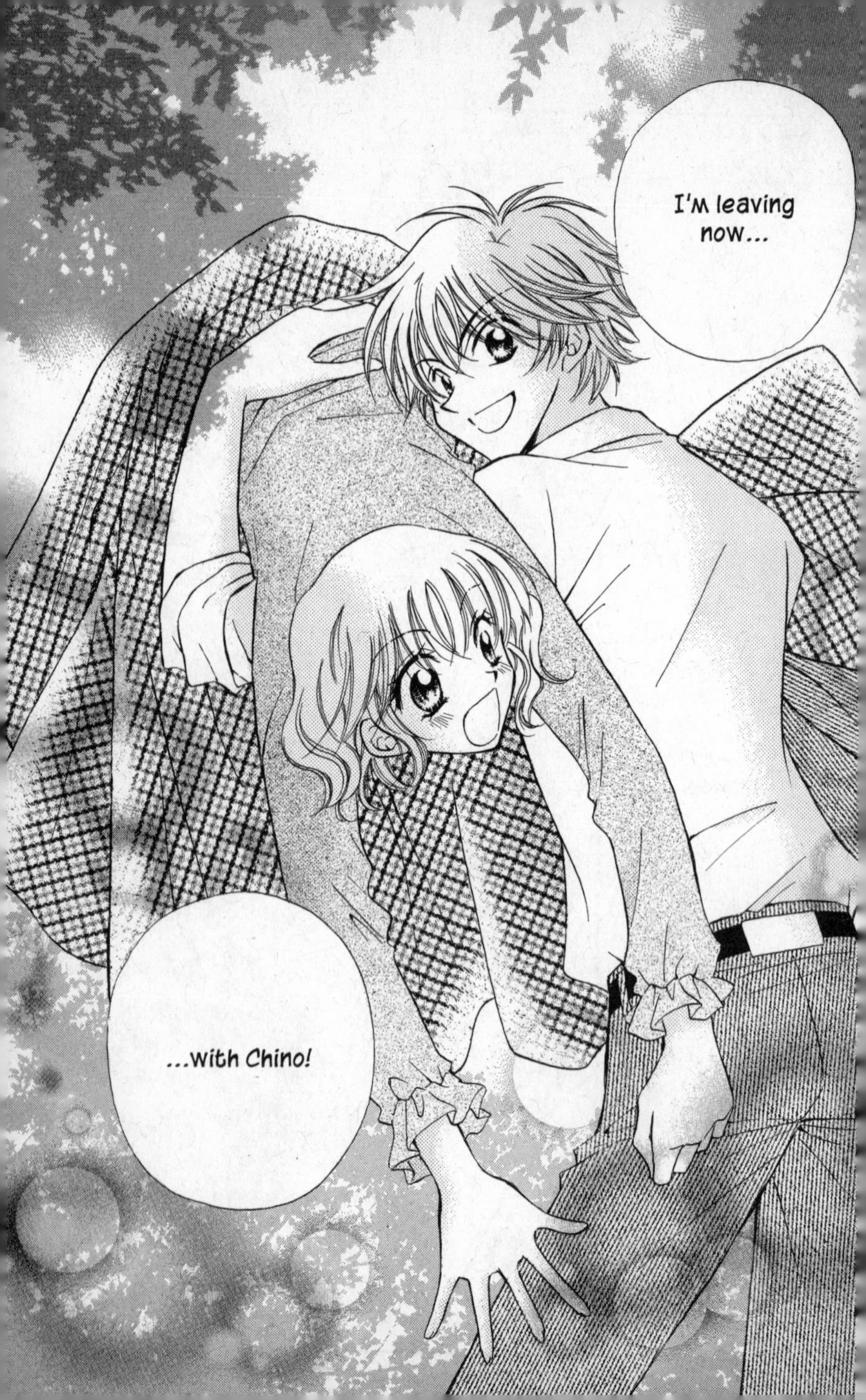
I'M leaving now...
...with Chino!

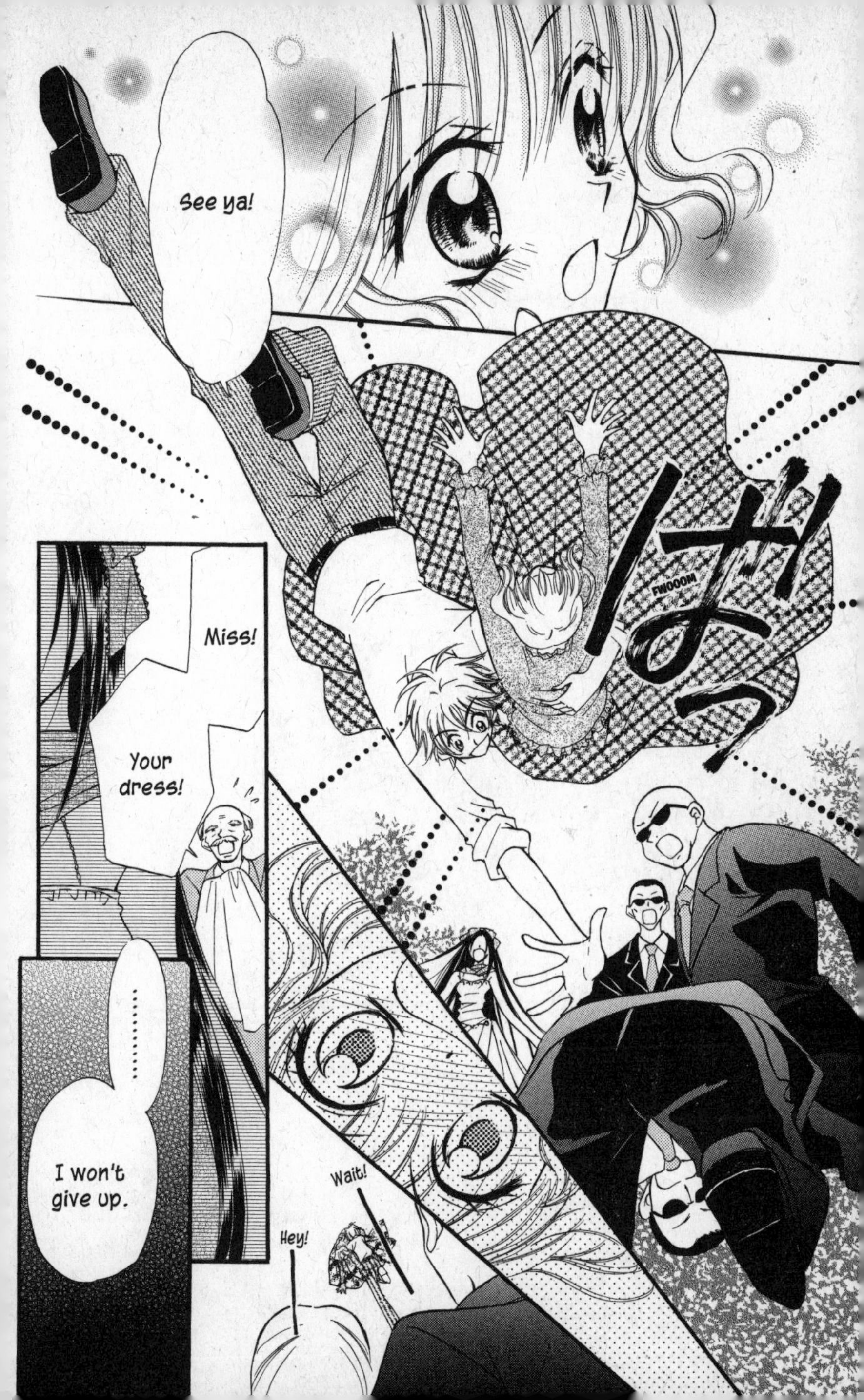
See ya!
FWOOOM
Miss!
Your dress!
Wait!
Hey!
......
I won't give up.

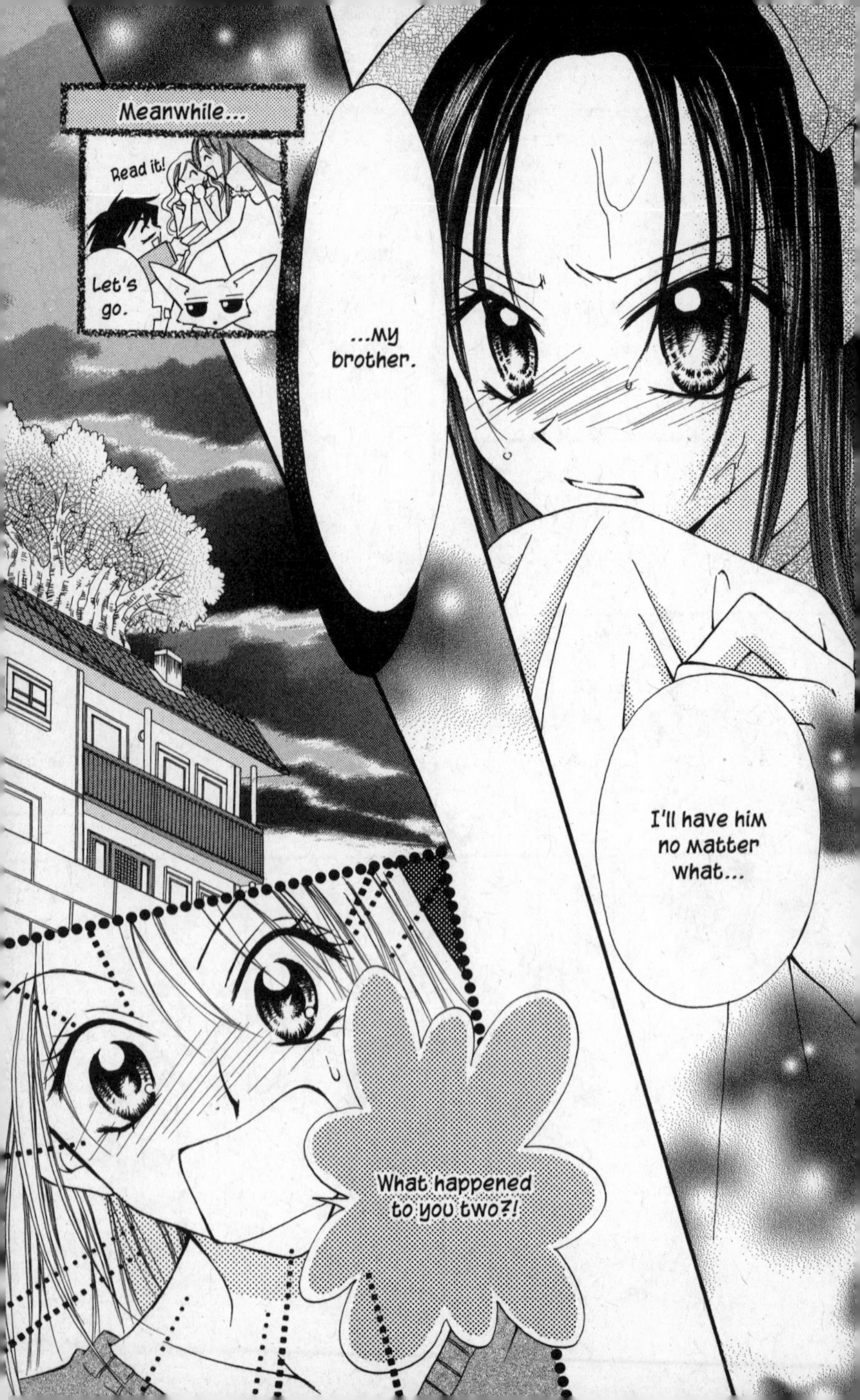
...My brother.
I'll have him no matter what...
Meanwhile...
Read it!
Let's go.
What happened to you two?!

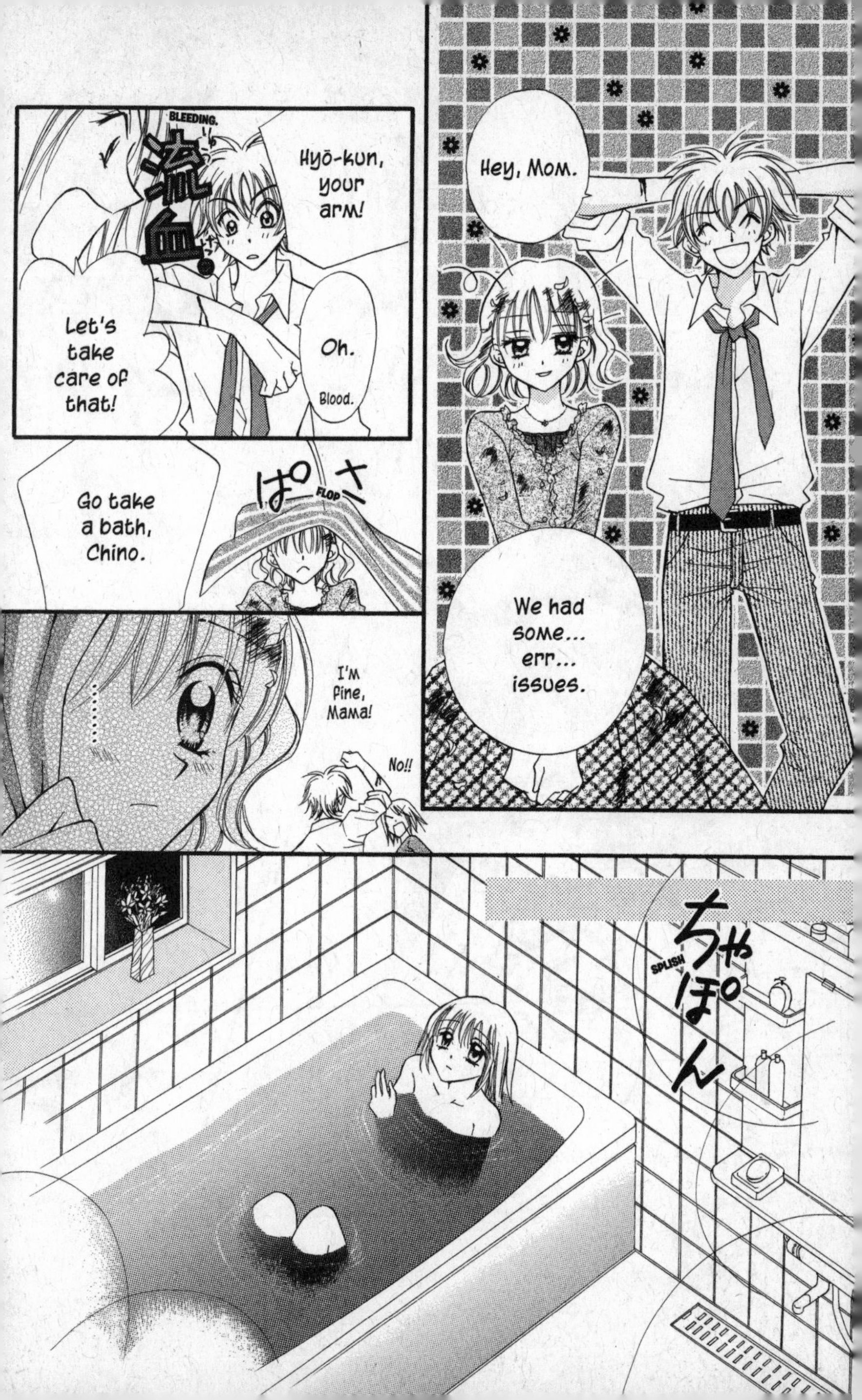

Hey, Mom.
We had some... err... issues.
Hyō-kun, your arm!
BLEEDING.
流血
Oh.
Blood.
Let's take care of that!
ぱさ
FLOP
Go take a bath, Chino.
I'm fine, Mama!
No!!
......
ちゃぽん
SPLISH

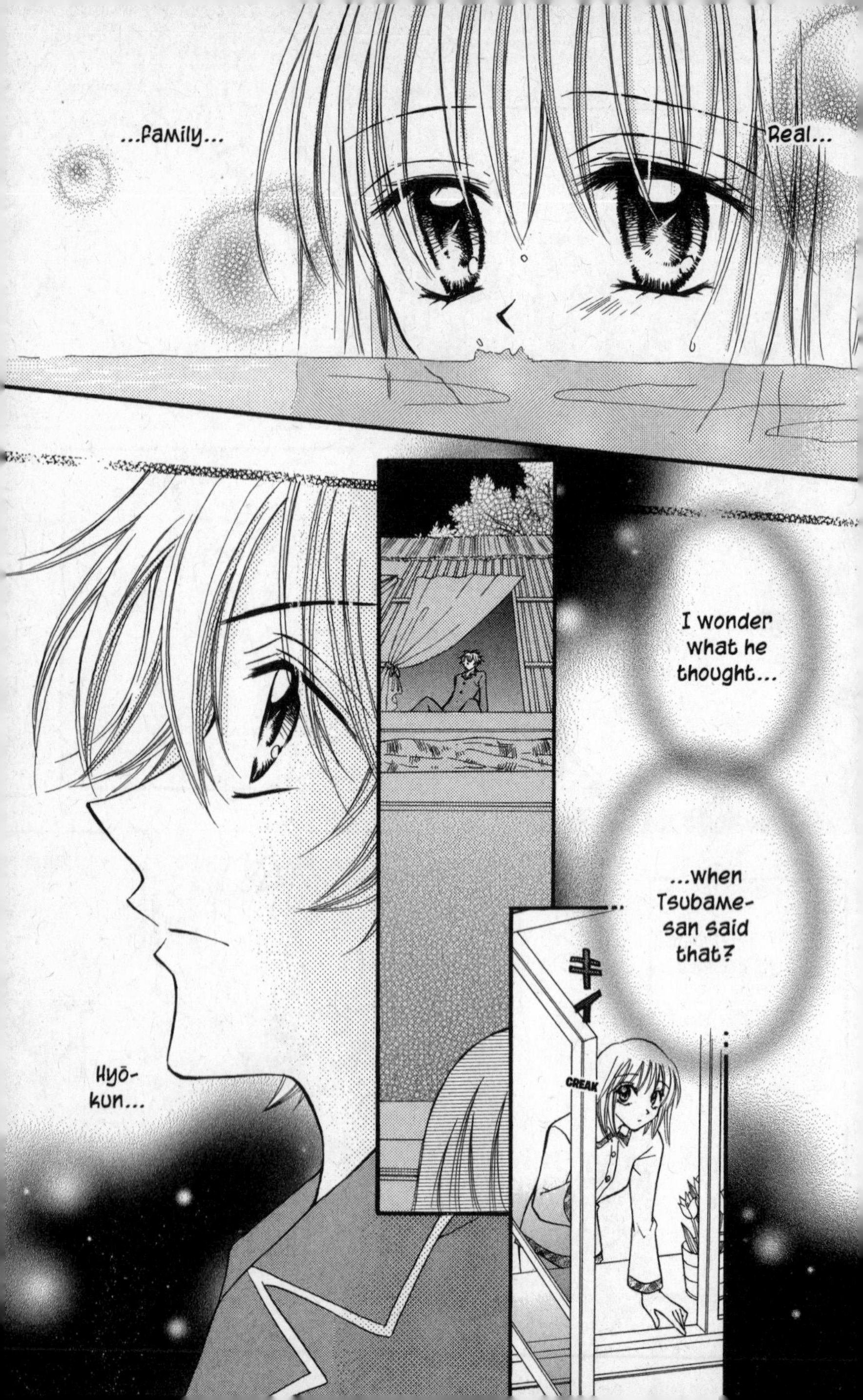
Real...
...family...
I wonder what he thought...
...when Tsubame-san said that?
CREAK
Hyō-kun...

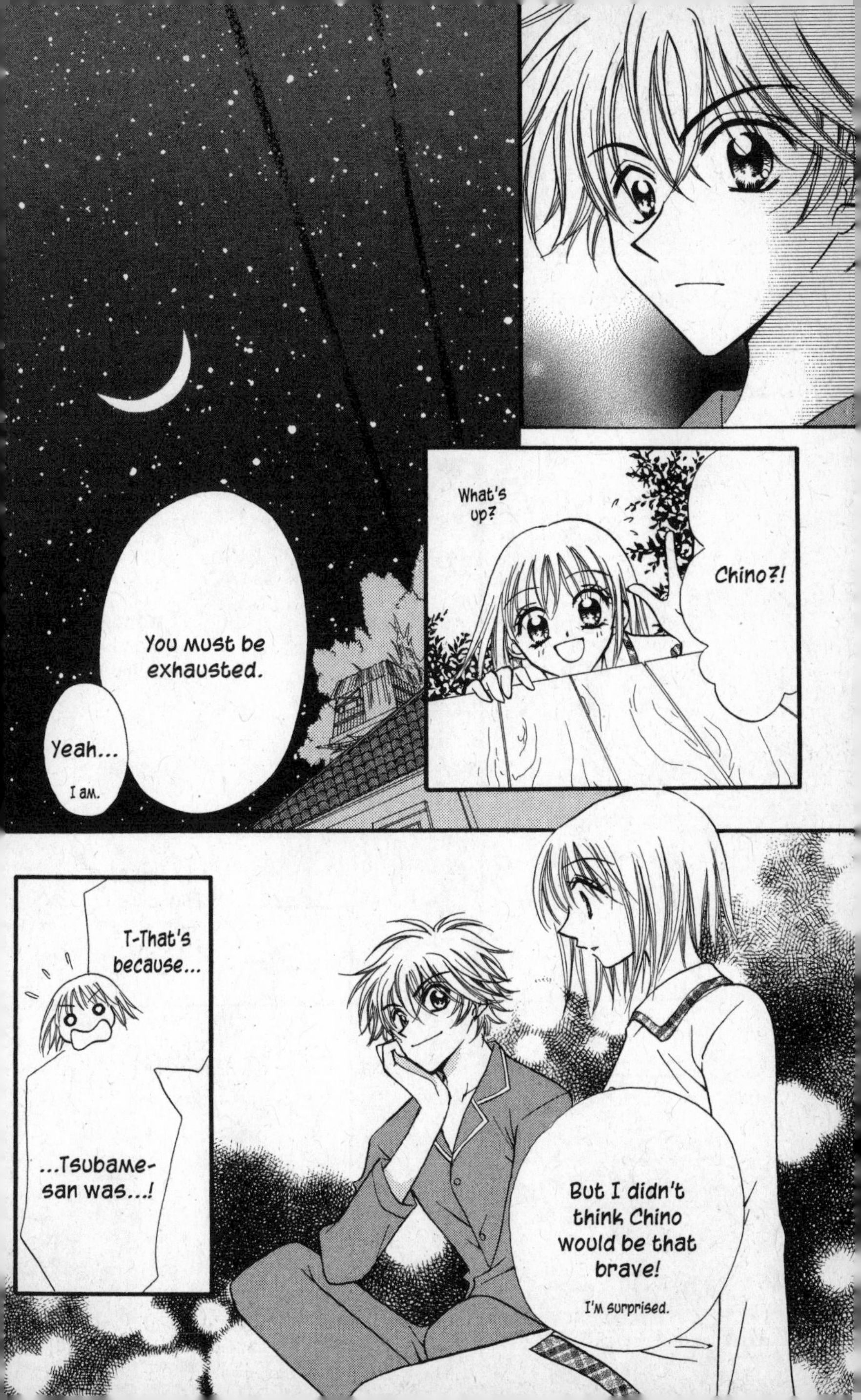

Chino?!
What's up?
You must be exhausted.
Yeah...
I am.
But I didn't think Chino would be that brave!
I'm surprised.
T-That's because...
...Tsubame-san was...!

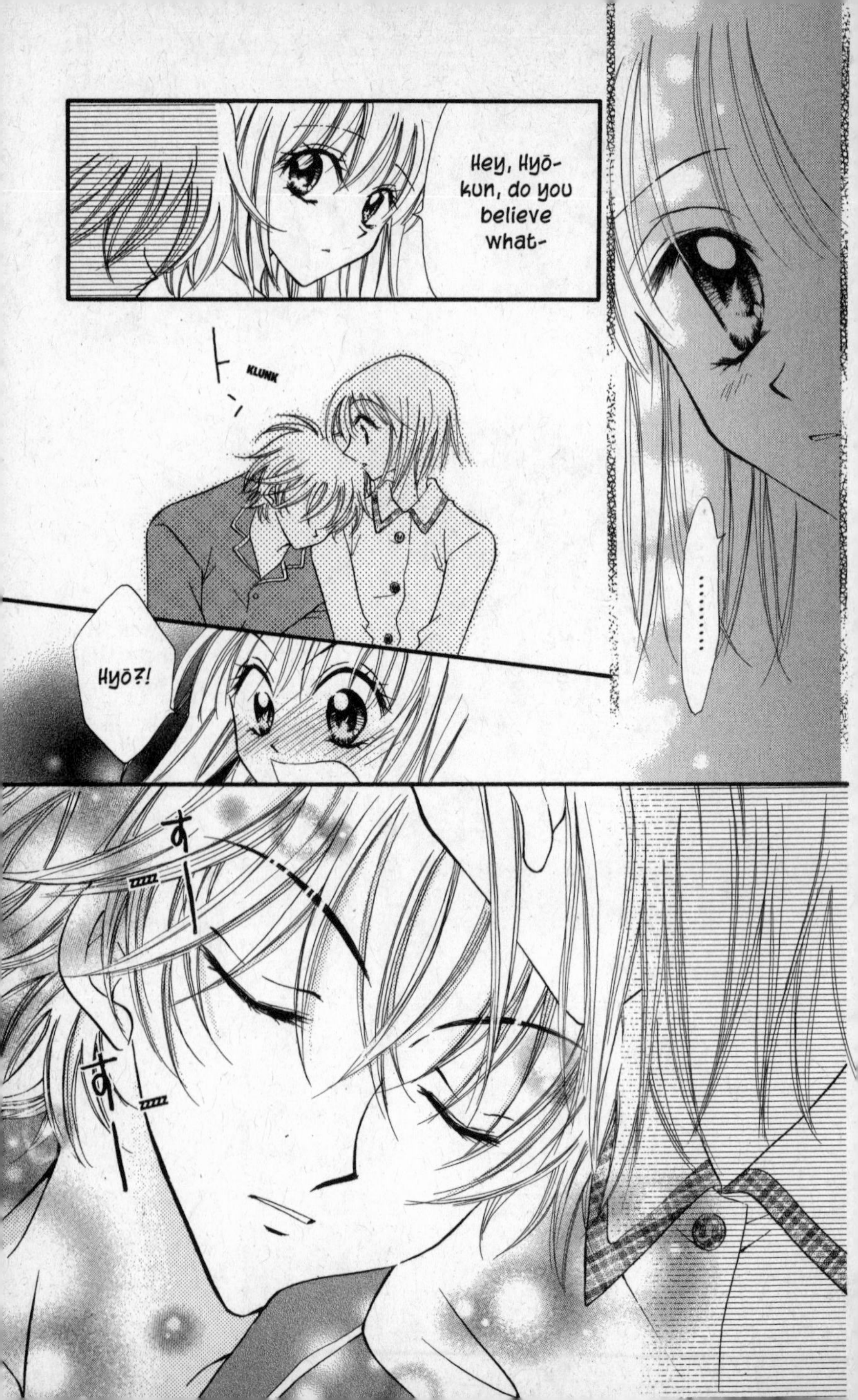
......
Hey, Hyō-kun, do you believe what-
KLUNK
Hyō?!
すー
zzzz
すー
zzzz

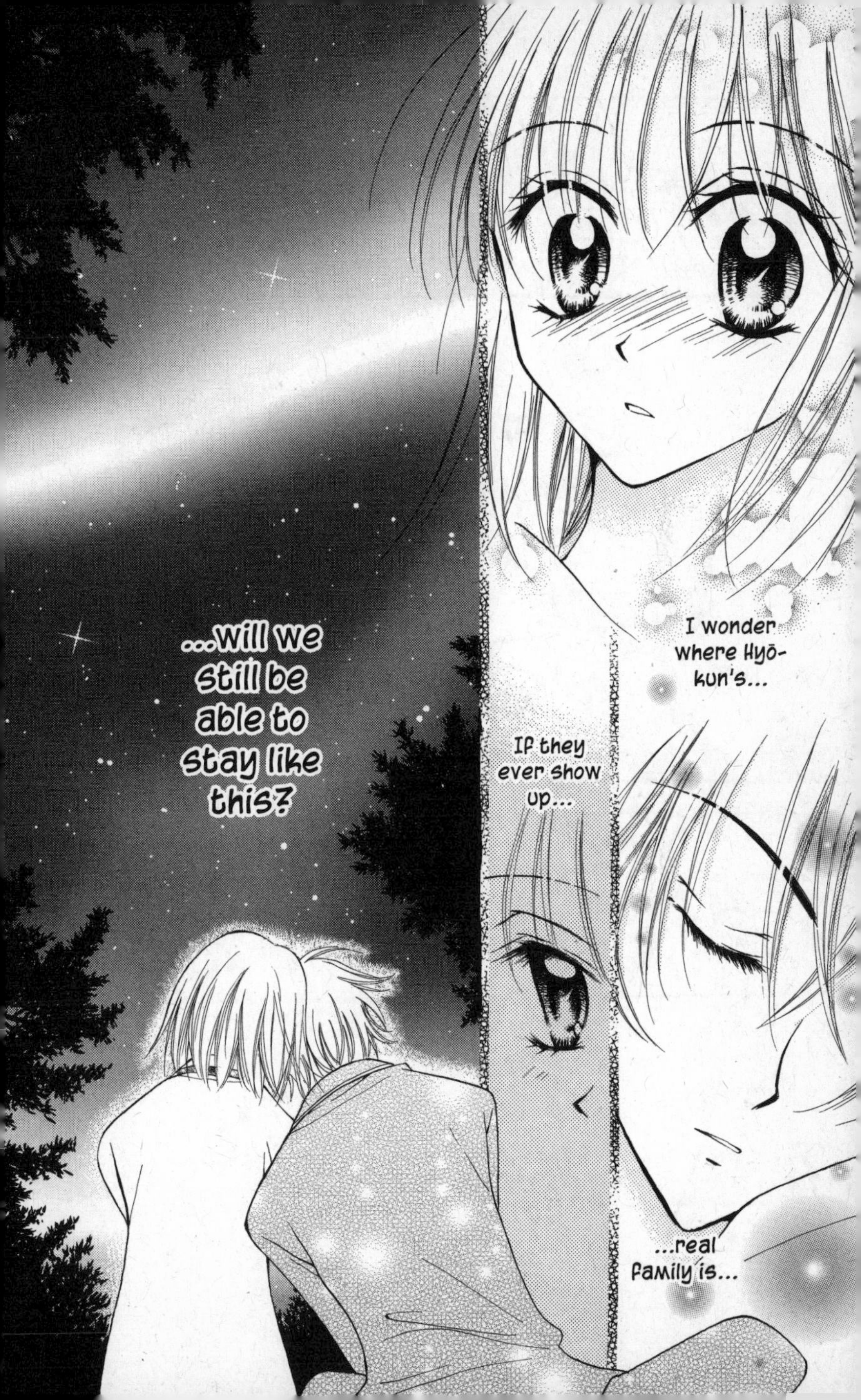
I wonder where Hyō-kun's...
...real family is...
If they ever show up...
...will we still be able to stay like this?

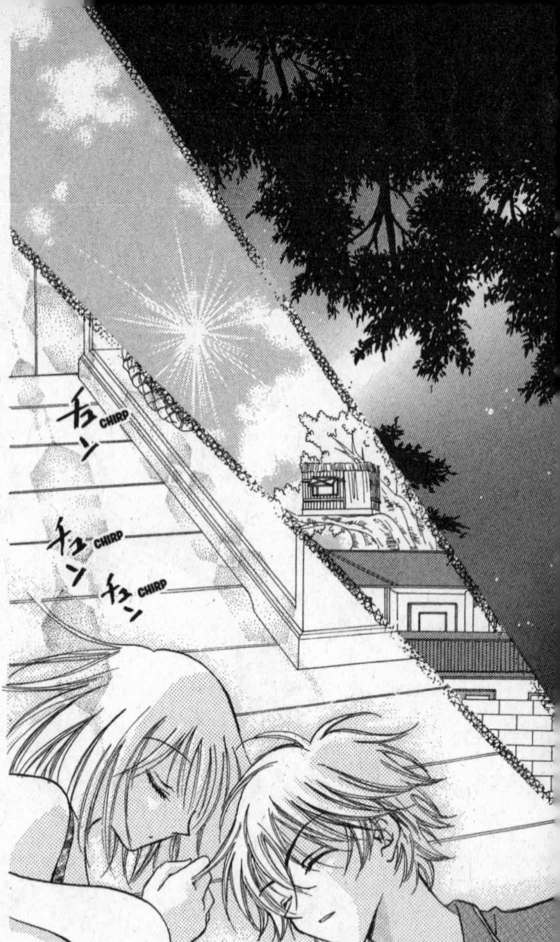
チュン CHIRP
チュン CHIRP
チュン CHIRP

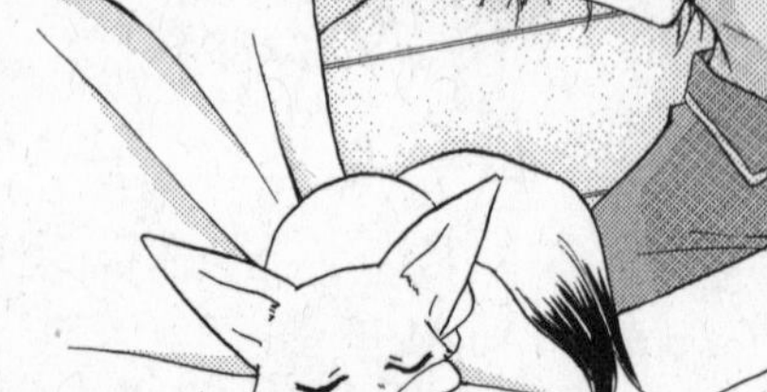
NMM...

8.

The other day I finished a draft and went to go make copies of it. I brought it home and started to fill in the dialogue in the bubbles. Finally I was done!! But then I remembered I forgot something. The copy of the original! I had left them at the copy place! It had taken me a while to realize it since I was working with the original! Anyone could have found the copies and read them! I was so worried and finally one of my assistants offered to go get it for me. Apparently someone had found it and brought it up to the register for safekeeping. So an employee saw it! So embarrassing! But luckily I wasn't the one picking it up so they didn't know who had written it. S-san, thanks for picking it up for me! ♡

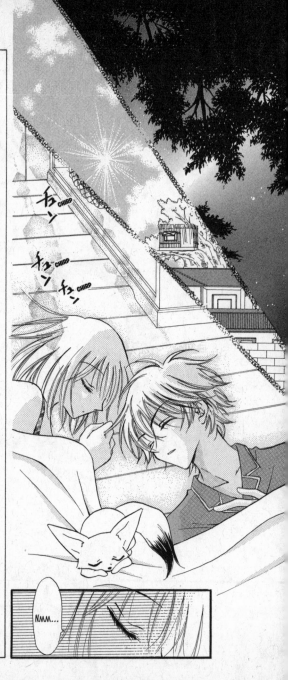

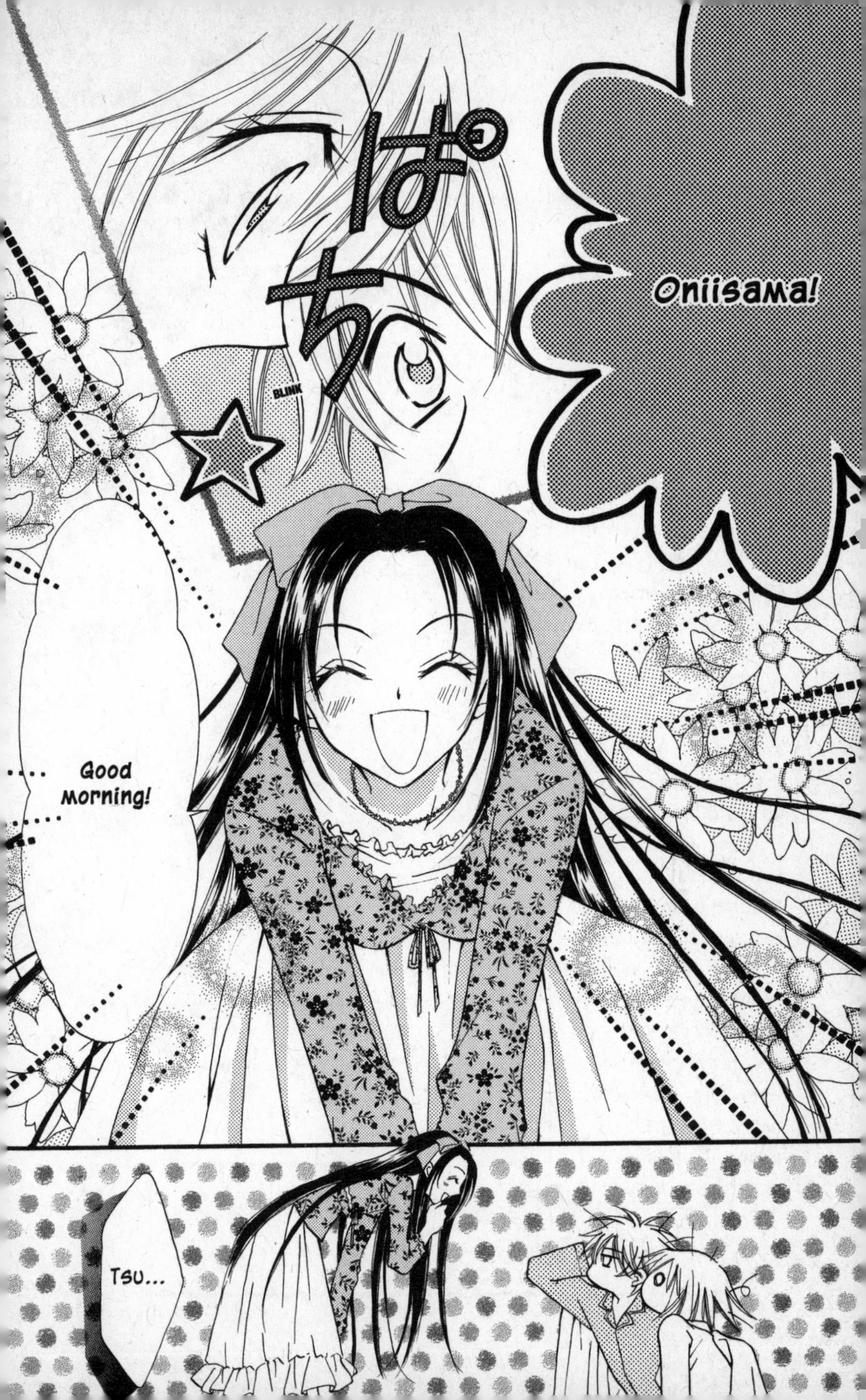
Oniisama!
ぱち
BLINK
... Good morning!
Tsu...

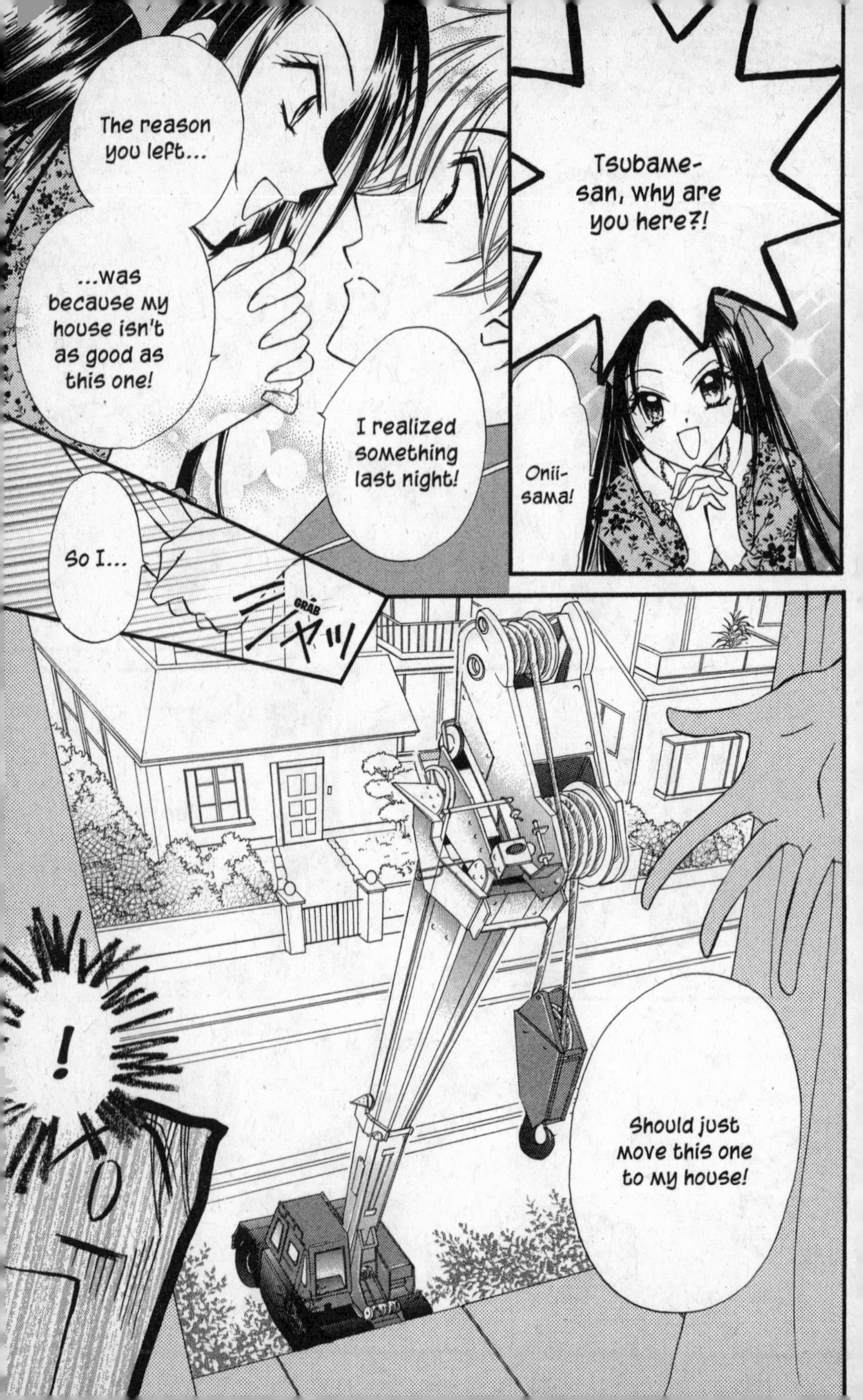
Tsubame-san, why are you here?!
Onii-sama!
The reason you left...
...was because my house isn't as good as this one!
I realized something last night!
So I...
GRAB
!
Should just move this one to my house!

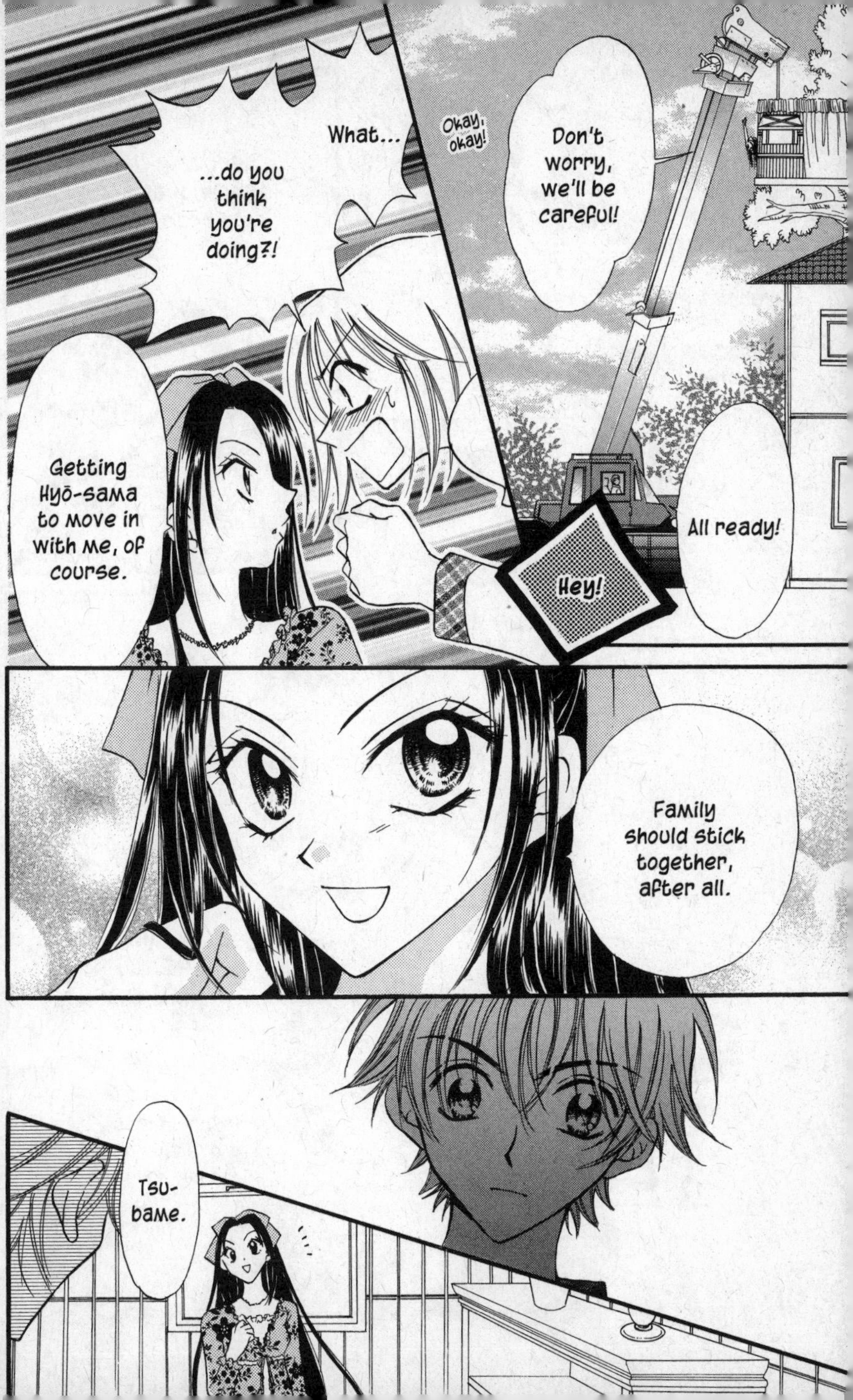
Don't worry, we'll be careful!
Okay, okay!
All ready!
Hey!
What...
...do you think you're doing?!
Getting Hyō-sama to move in with me, of course.
Family should stick together, after all.
Tsu-bame.

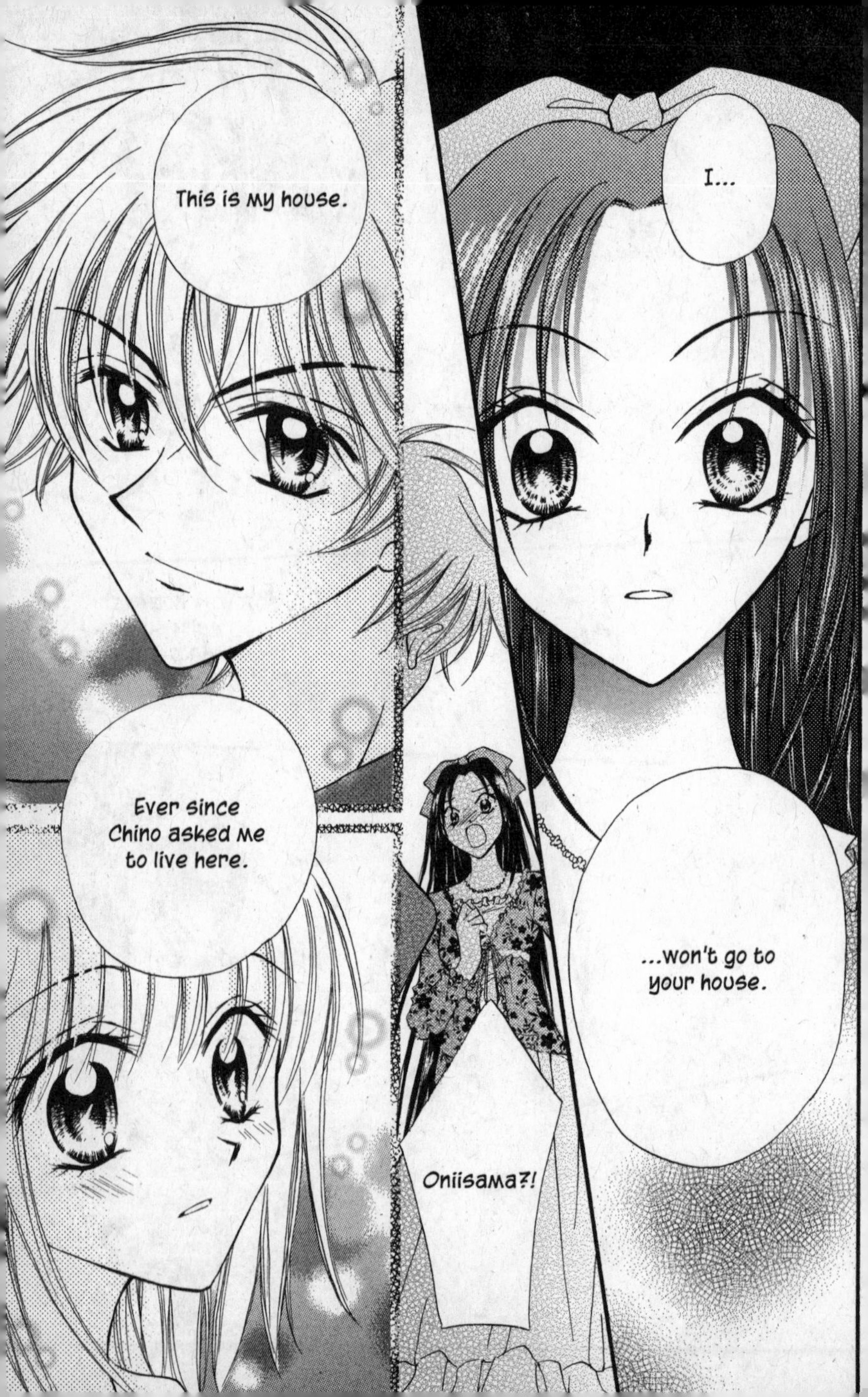
I...
...won't go to your house.
Oniisama?!
This is my house.
Ever since Chino asked me to live here.

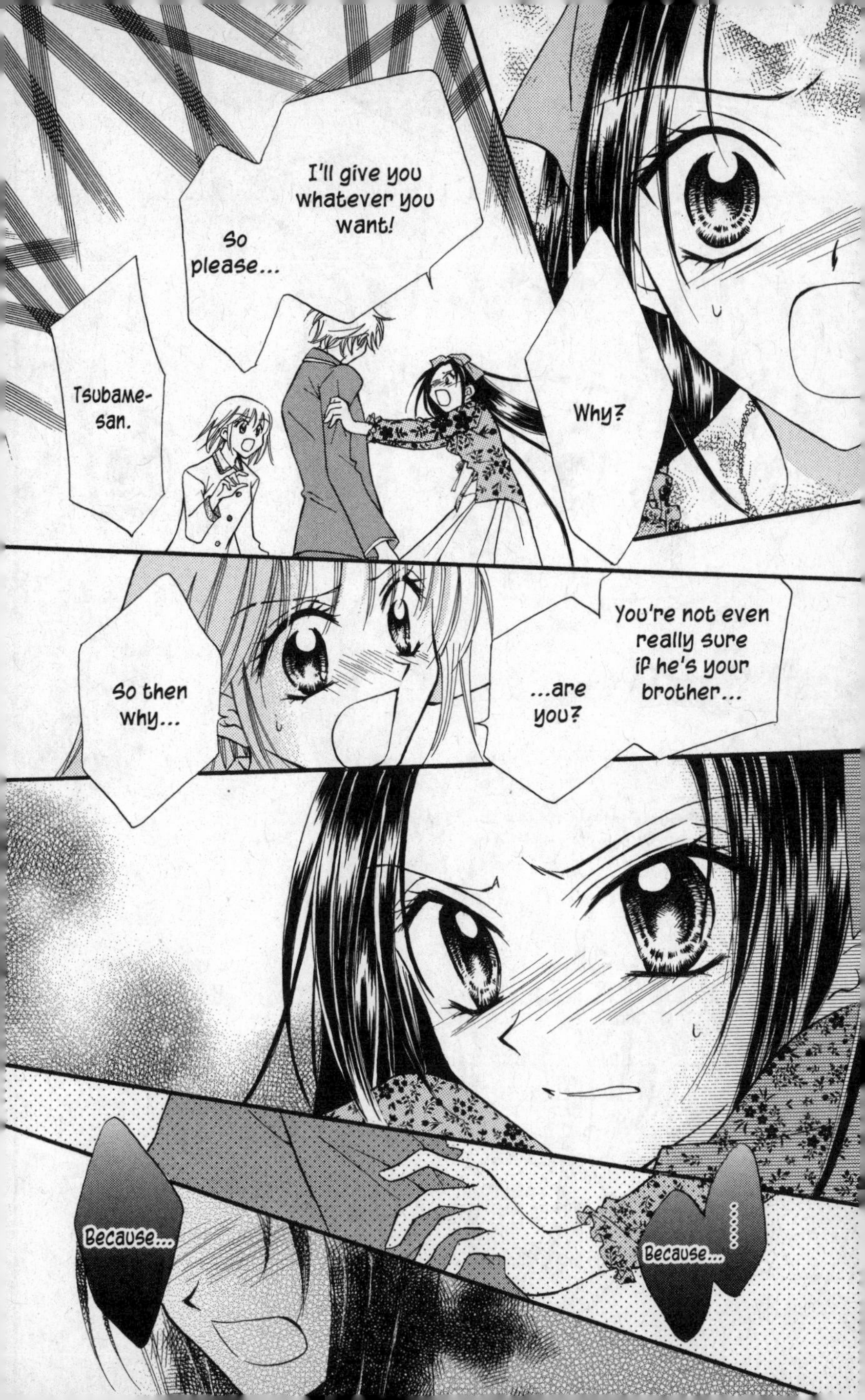
Why?
I'll give you whatever you want!
So please...
Tsubame-san.
You're not even really sure if he's your brother...
...are you?
So then why...
......
Because...
Because...

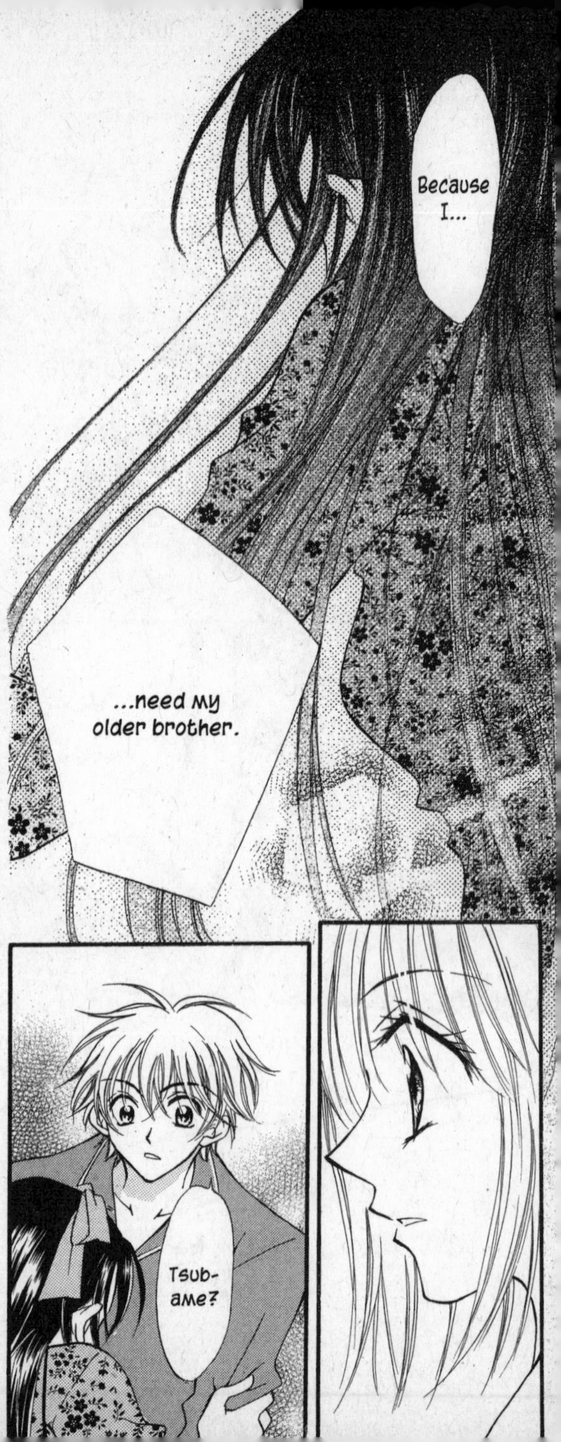
Because I...
...need my older brother.
Tsub-ame?

9.

This summer I could see fireworks from my window. They were so pretty I put down my work and went to watch them! I turned off all the lights. But then some people from my building came to watch them–right in front of my room!

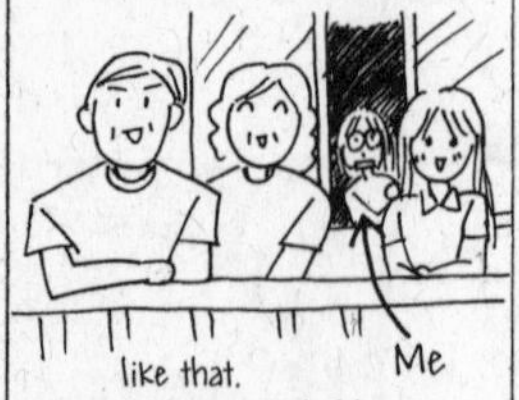
like that.
Me

My room was pitch black so they didn't even see that I was trying to watch from behind them. I was embarrassed about watching it like that...

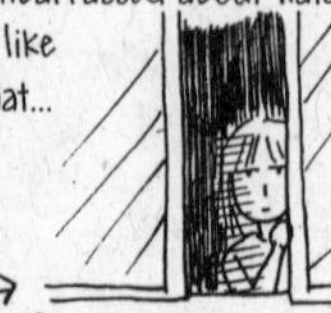

...But I wanted to see the fireworks so bad! At some point their daughter noticed me and I think I might have scared her. Then they went away. Sorry I'm such a weird neighbor! But the fireworks were so pretty! ♡

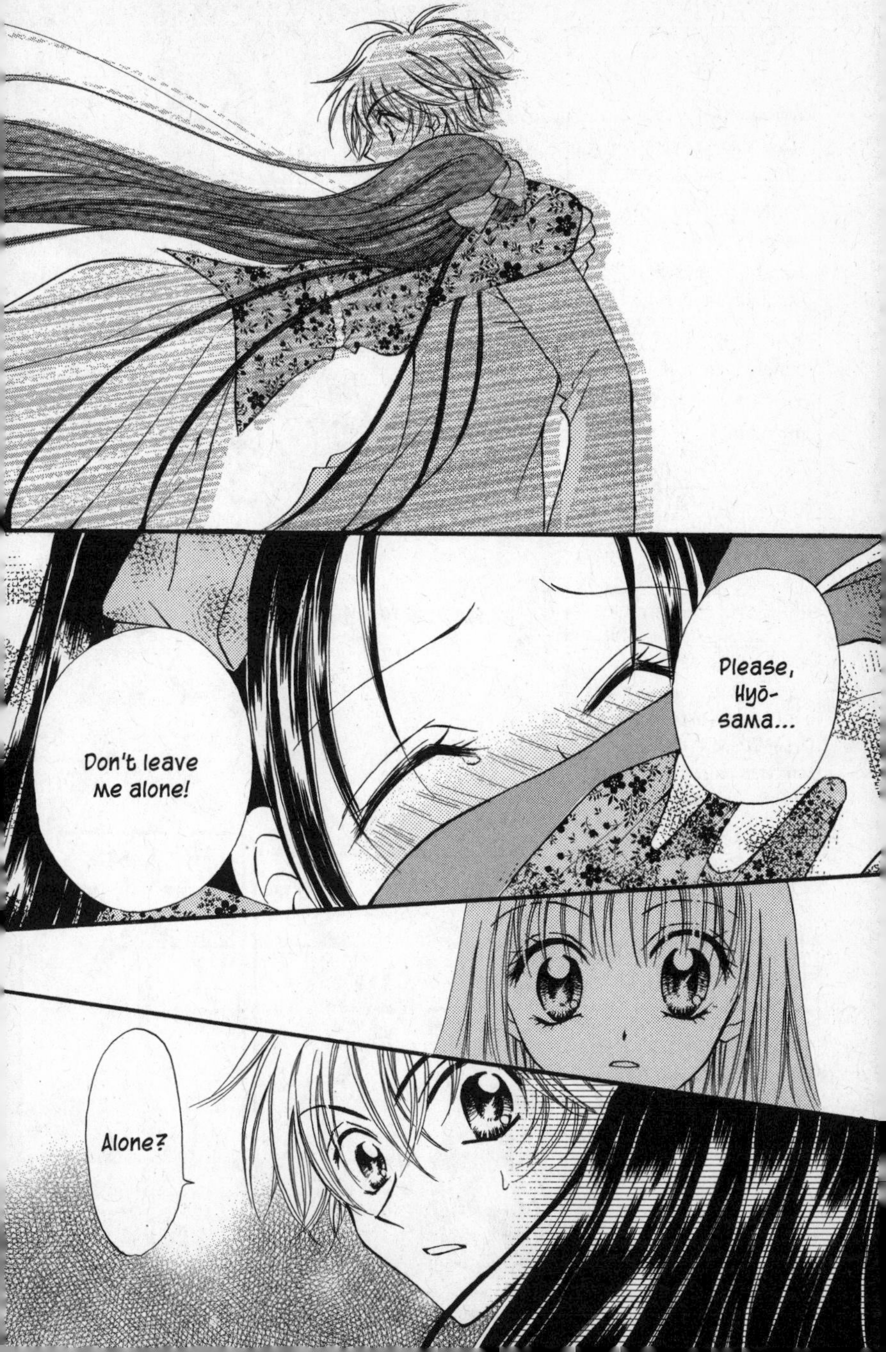
Please, Hyō-sama...
Don't leave me alone!
Alone?

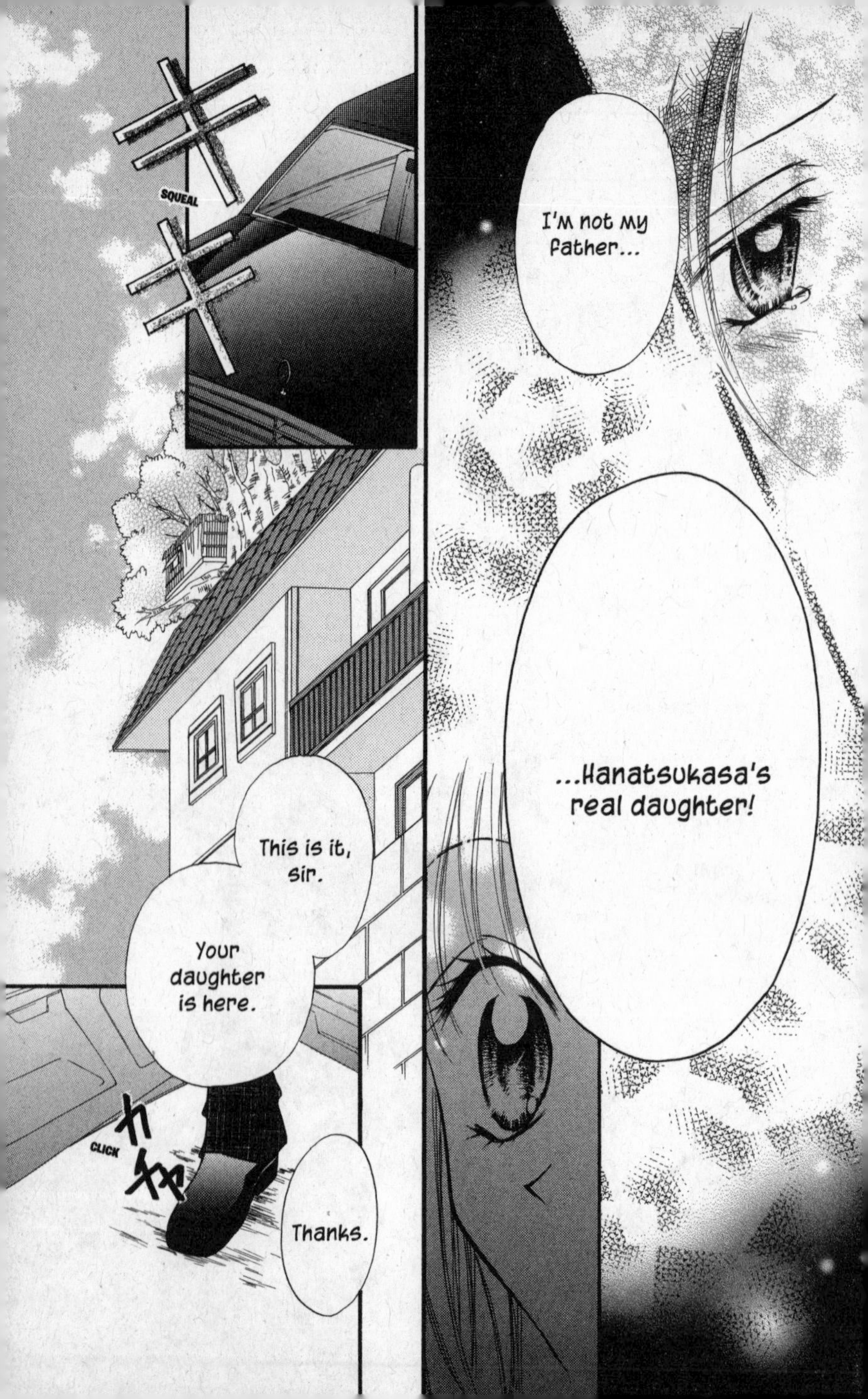
I'm not my father...
...Hanatsukasa's real daughter!
SQUEAL
This is it, sir.
Your daughter is here.
CLICK
Thanks.

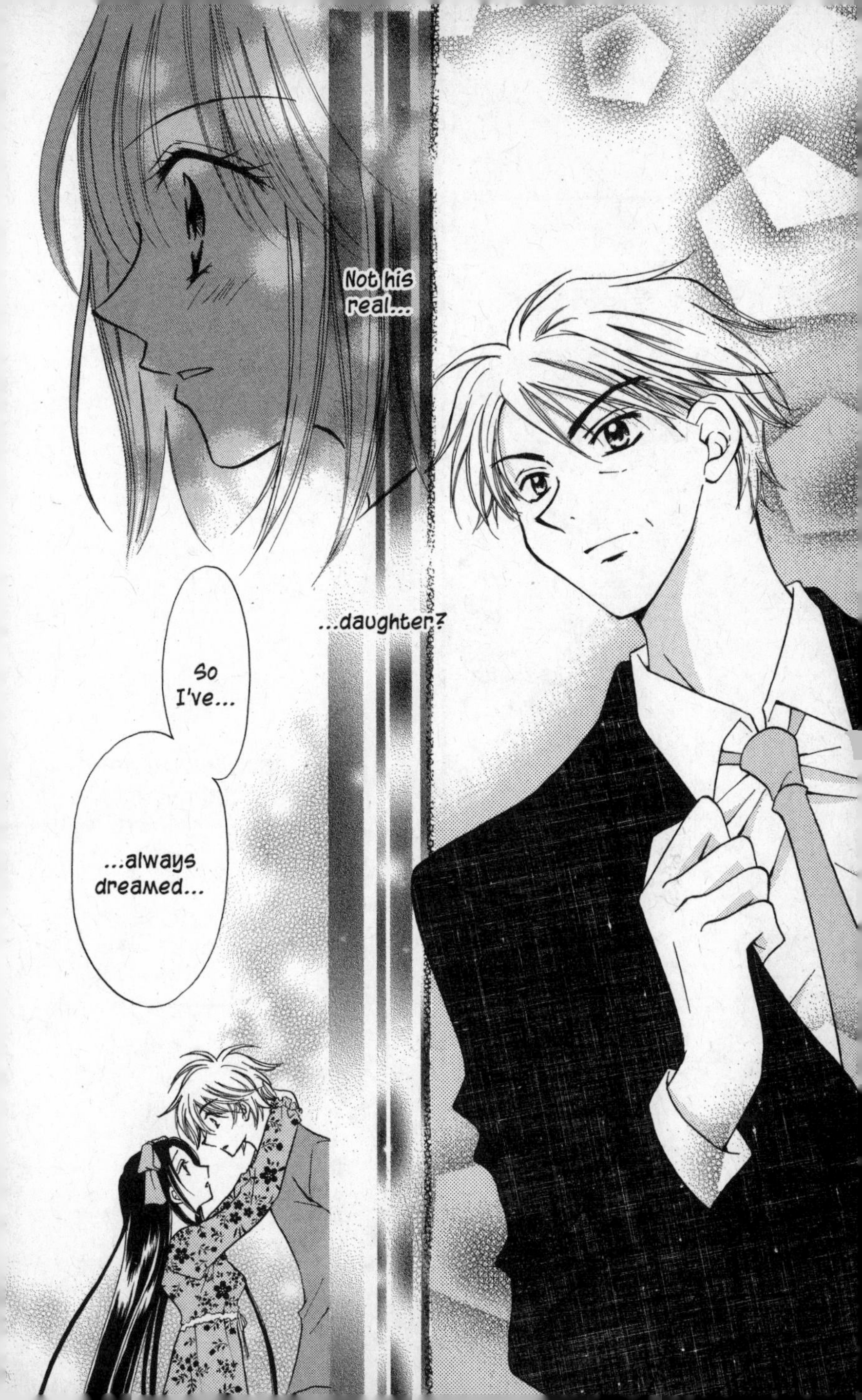
Not his real...
...daughter?
So I've...
...always dreamed...

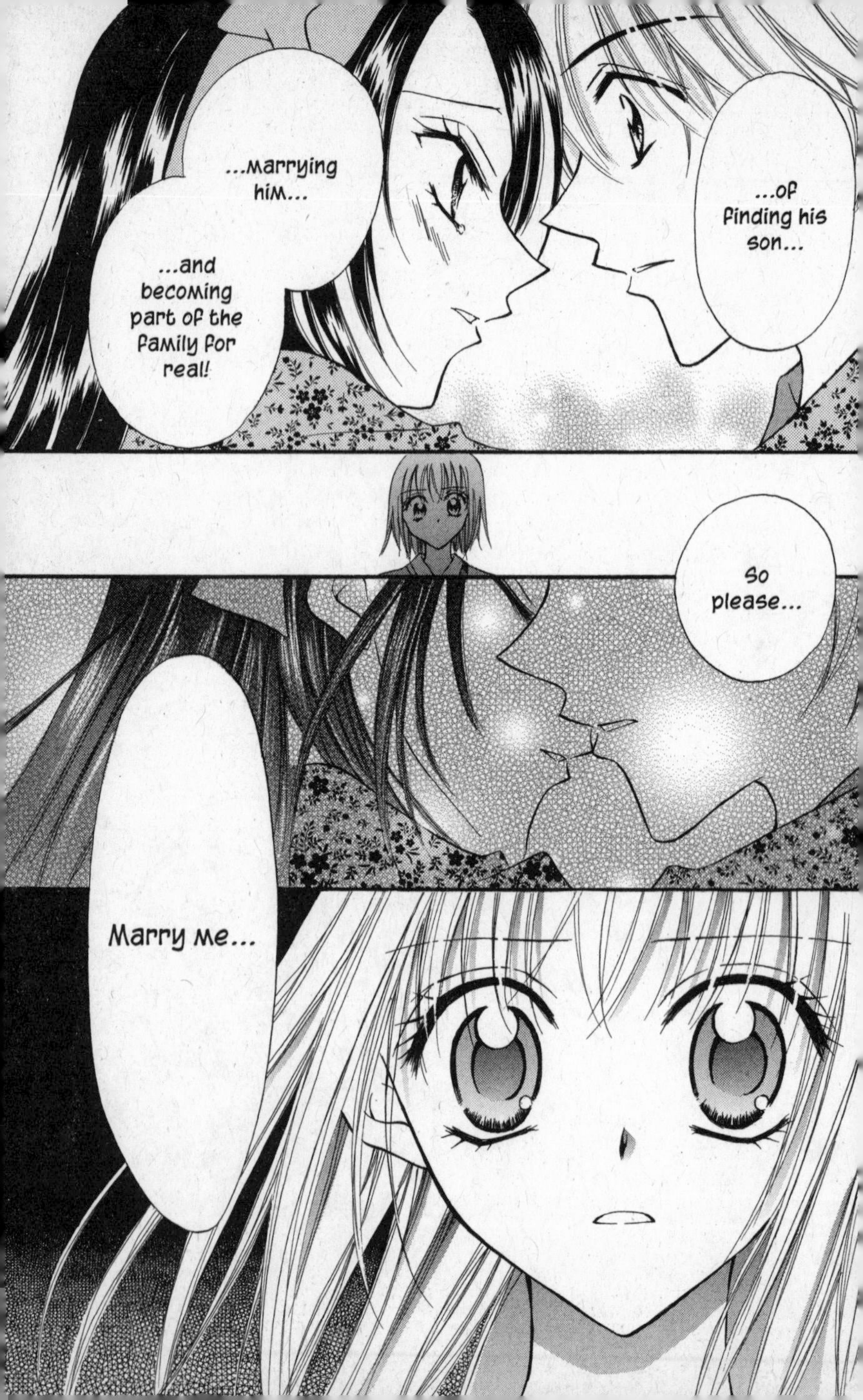
...of finding his son...
...marrying him...
...and becoming part of the family for real!
So please...
Marry me...

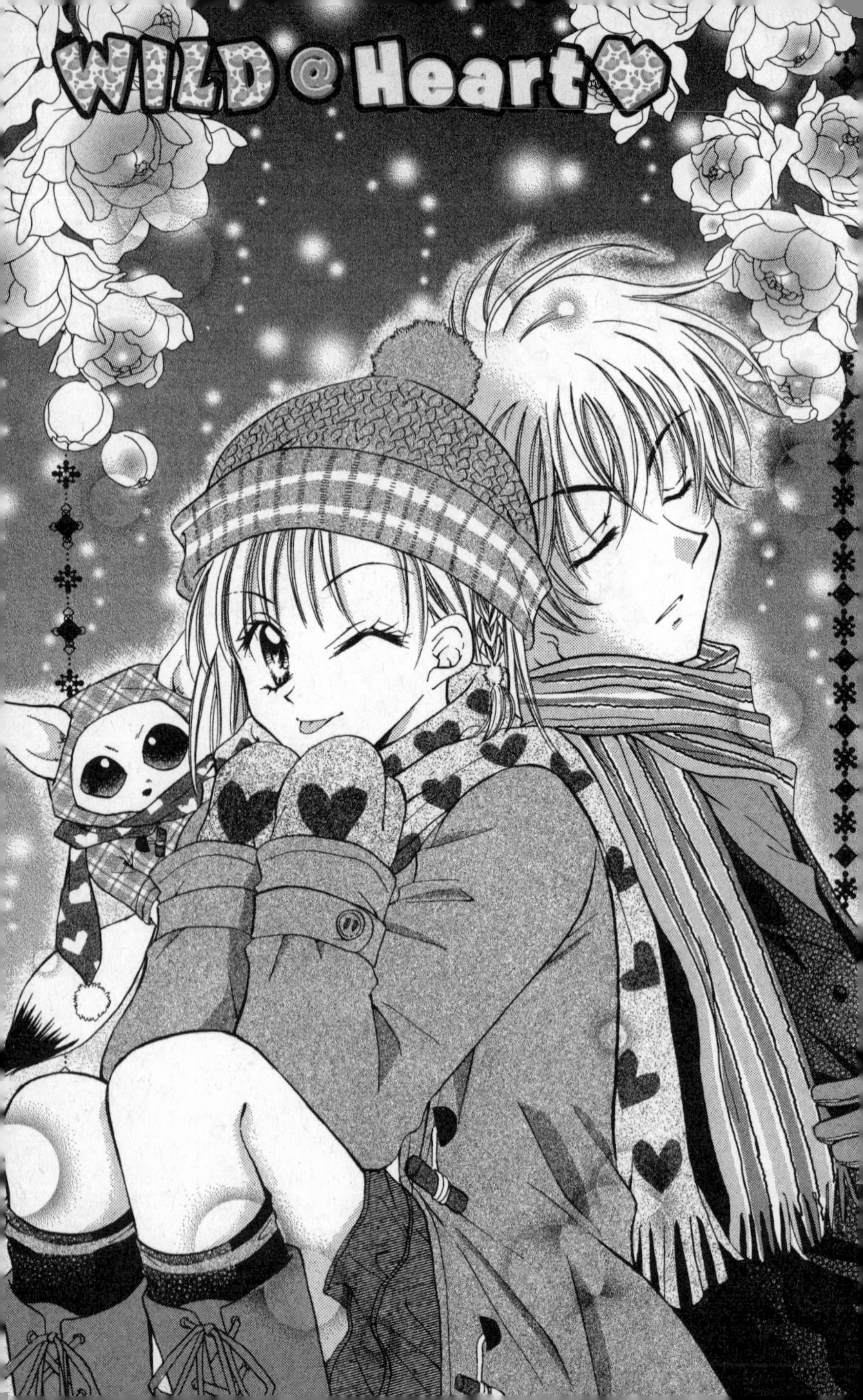
WILD @ Heart

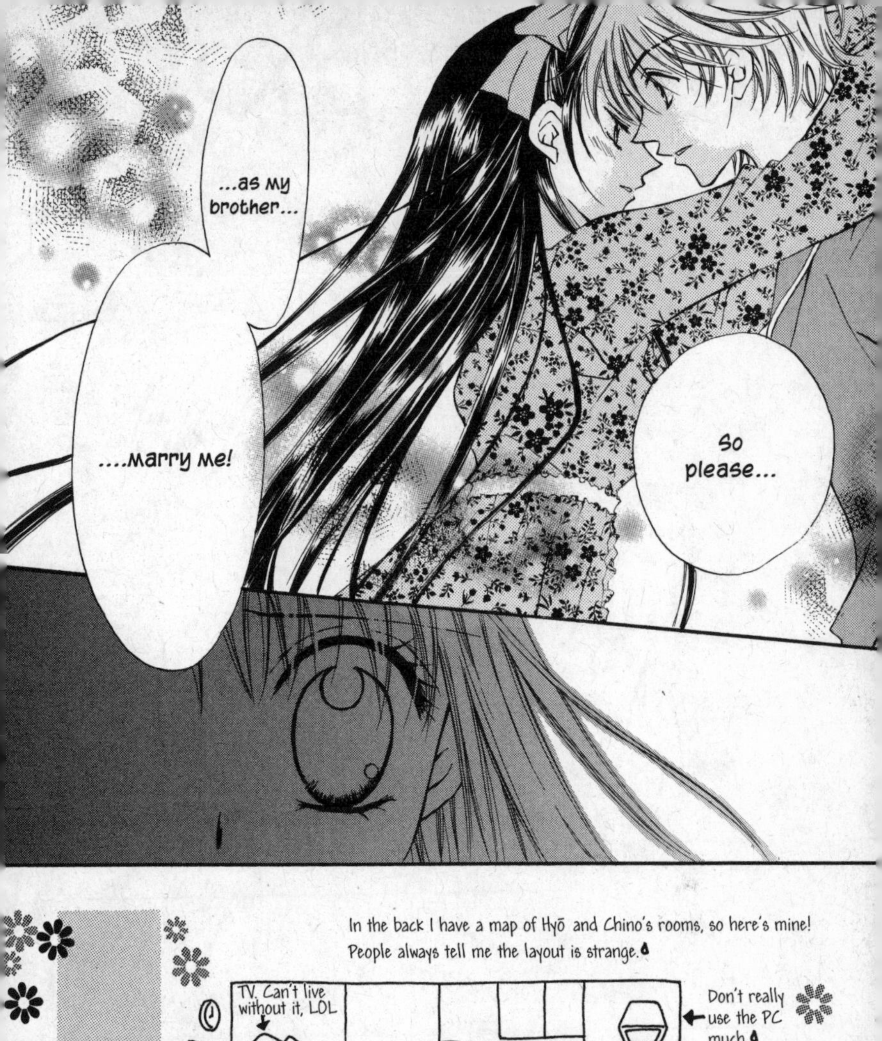
So please...
...as my brother...
....marry me!

Here's my office!!

In the back I have a map of Hyō and Chino's rooms, so here's mine! People always tell me the layout is strange.

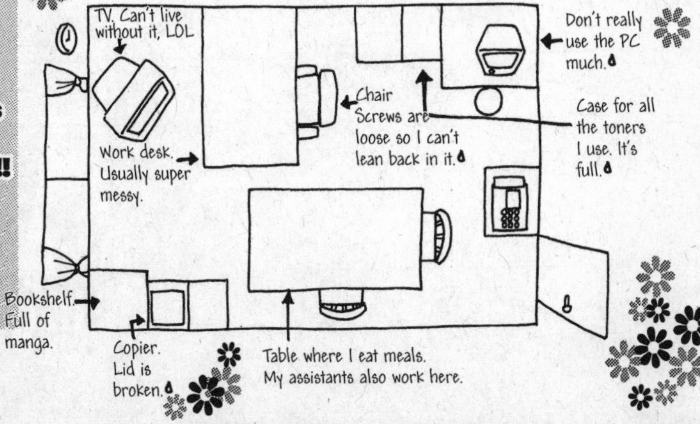
TV. Can't live without it, LOL
Work desk. Usually super messy.
Chair
Screws are loose so I can't lean back in it.
Don't really use the PC much.
Case for all the toners I use. It's full.
Bookshelf. Full of manga.
Copier. Lid is broken.
Table where I eat meals. My assistants also work here.

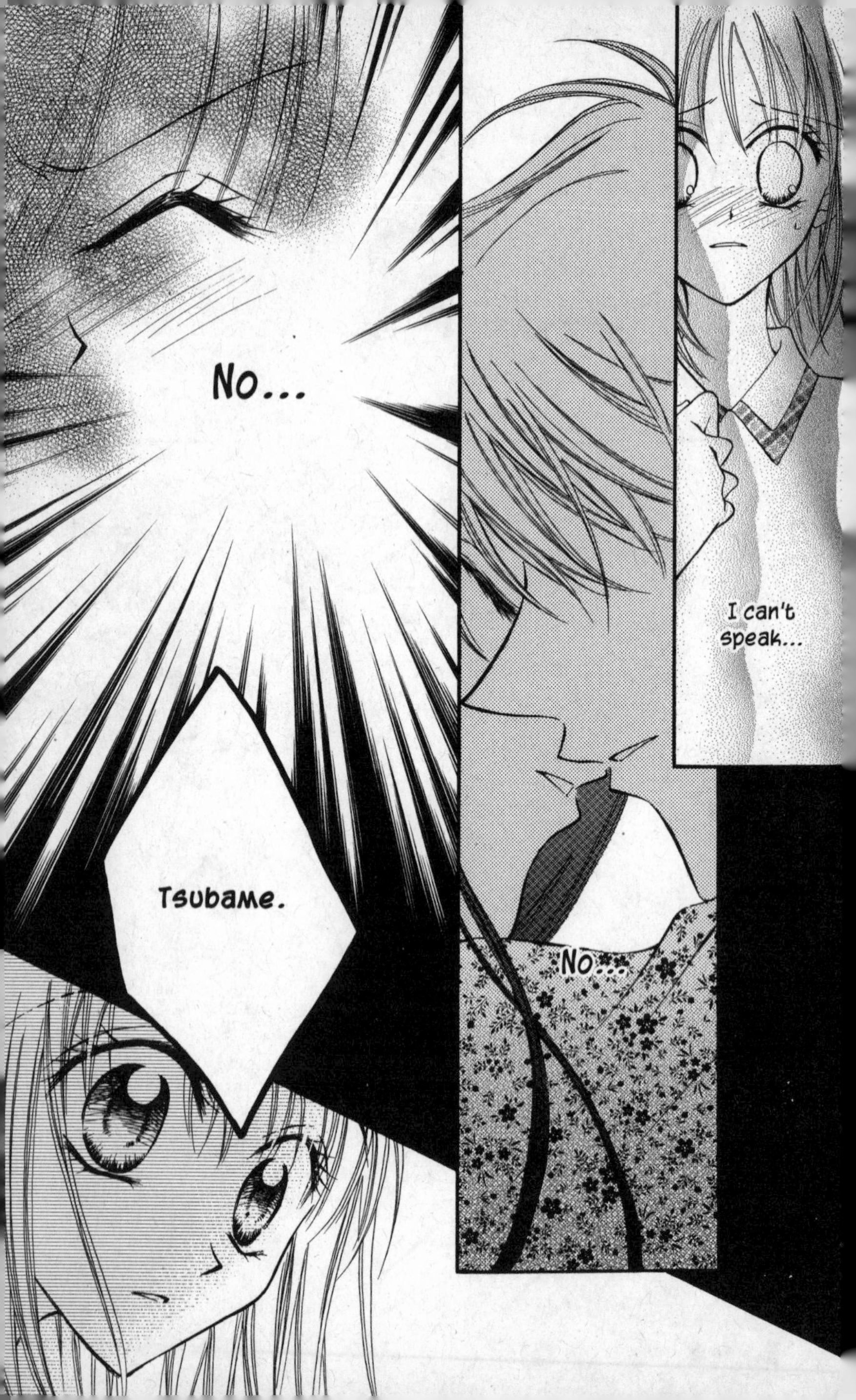
I can't speak...
No...
No...
Tsubame.

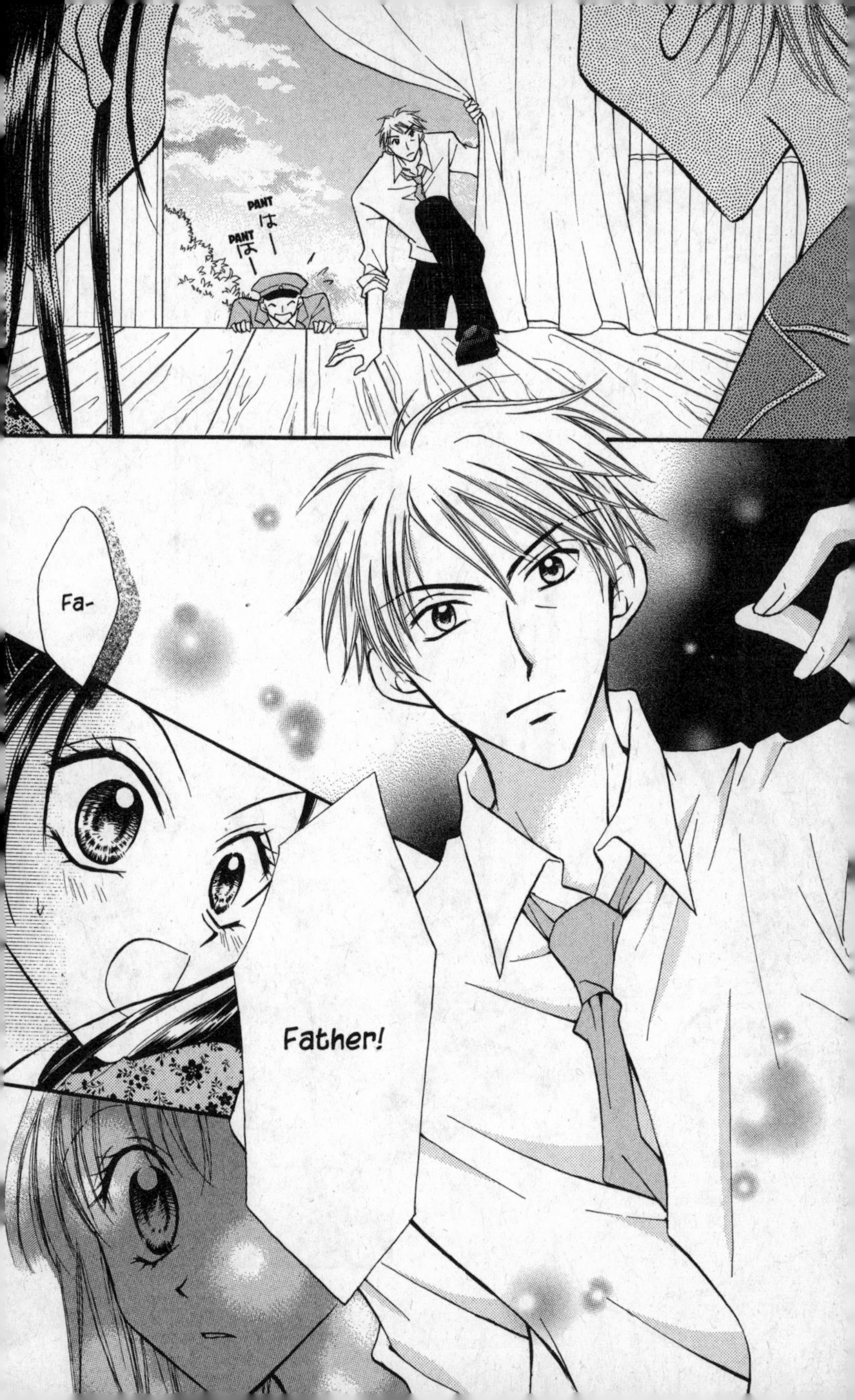
PANT はー
PANT はー
Fa-
Father!

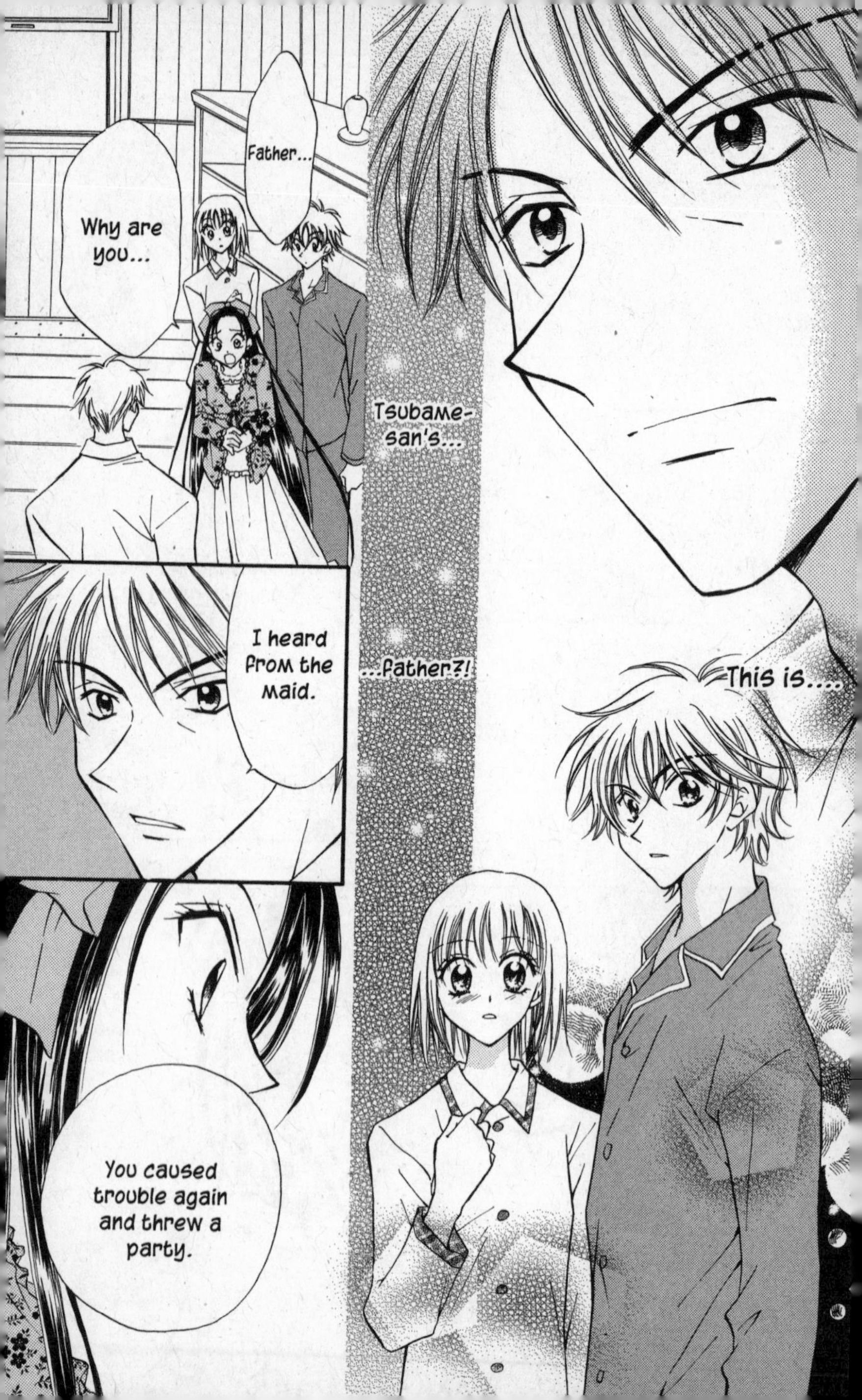
This is....
Tsubame-san's...
...father?!
Father...
Why are you...
I heard from the maid.
You caused trouble again and threw a party.

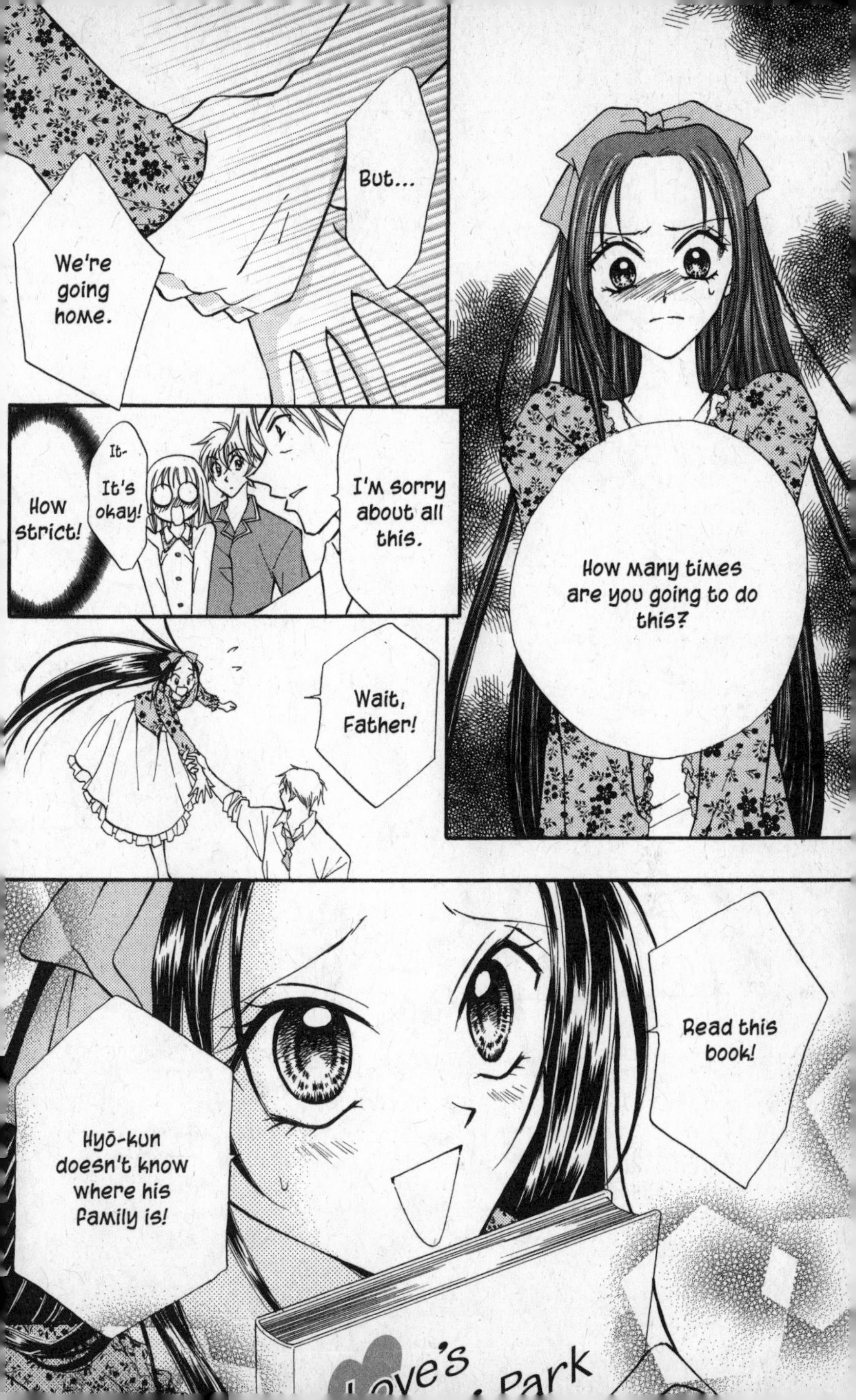
How many times are you going to do this?
But...
We're going home.
I'm sorry about all this.
It-
It's okay!
How strict!
Wait, Father!
Read this book!
Hyō-kun doesn't know where his family is!
Love's
Park

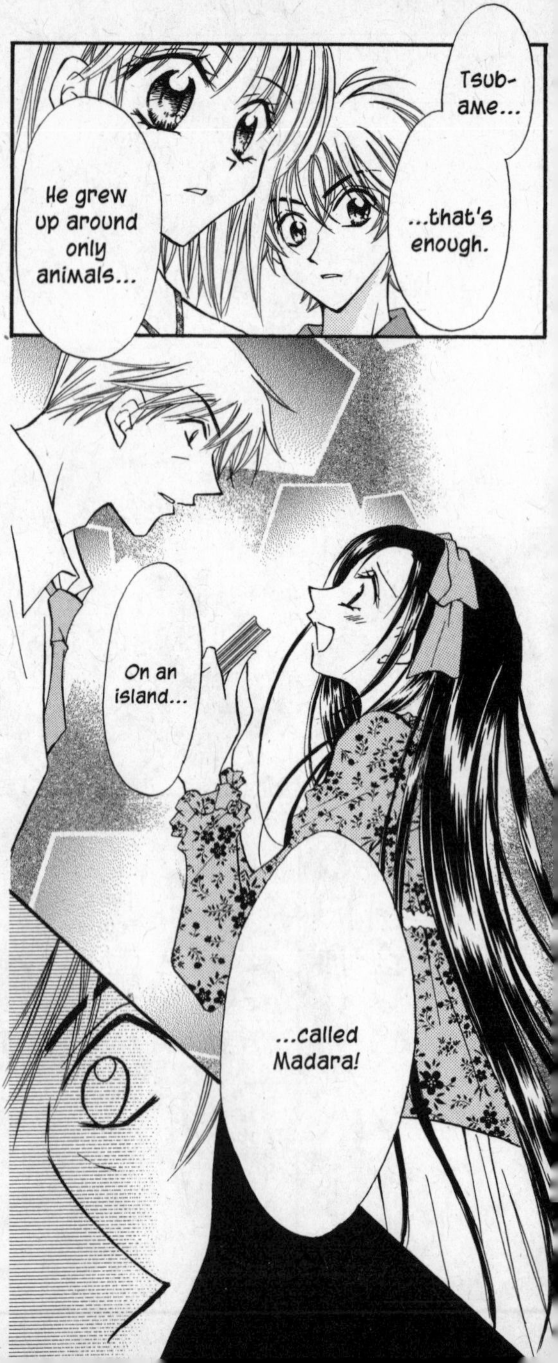
Tsub-ame...
...that's enough.
He grew up around only animals...
On an island...
...called Madara!

10.

A few new characters were introduced in this volume and the story got a little more serious, huh? Did you notice that Hyō-kun's speech has gotten a lot more natural? He basically talks like a normal boy now. Please keep reading to find out what happens next with Hyō-kun and Chino!

Please send all questions/comments to:

Natsumi Ando
c/o Del Rey Manga
1745 Broadway
New York, NY 10019

It might take me a while to respond, sorry!

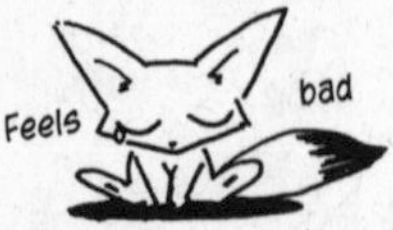
Feels
bad

See you next volume! ♪

Special thanks:

Maruyama-sama
Sh_bashi-sama
Kishimoto-sama

and you!

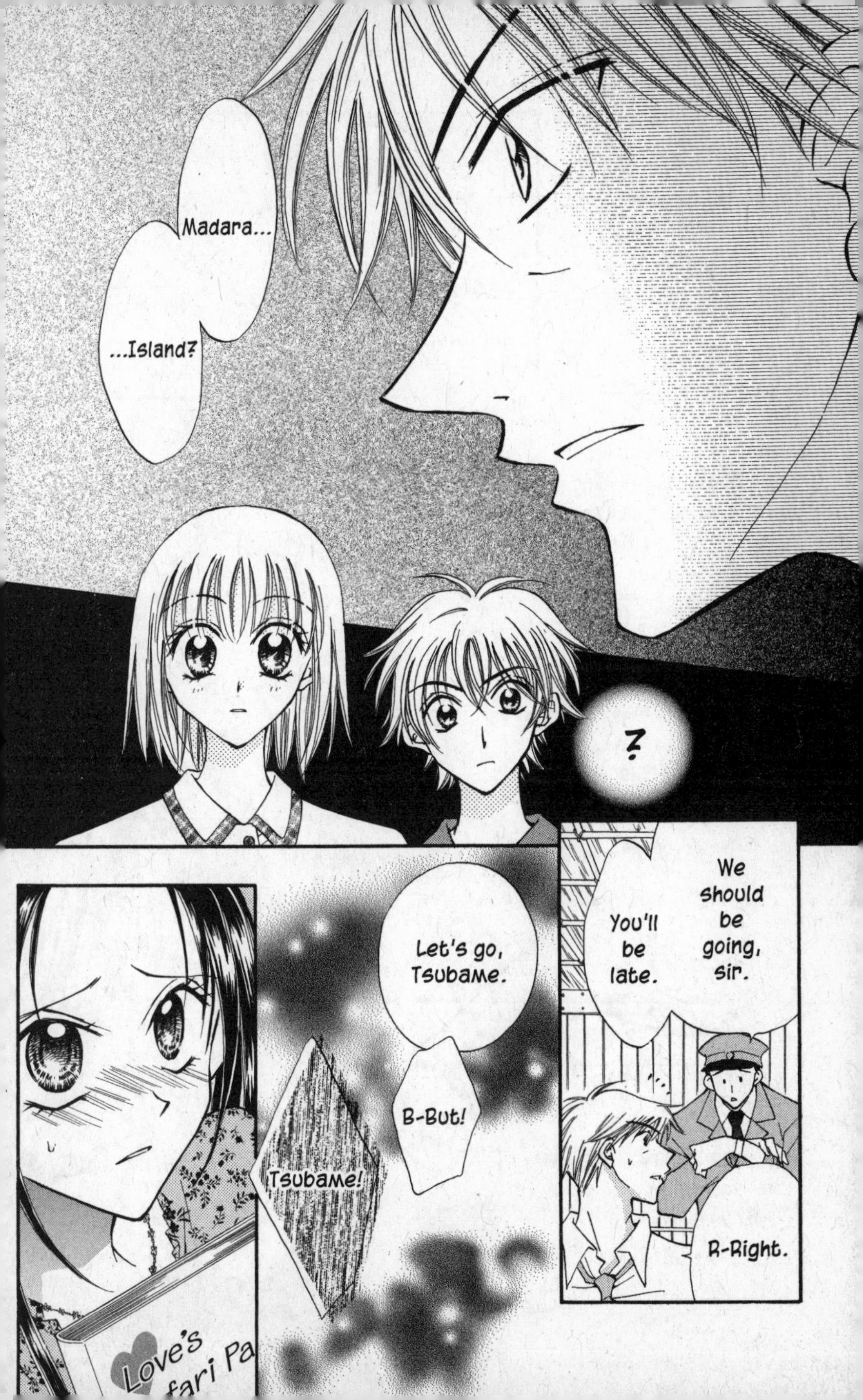
Madara...
...Island?
?
We should be going, sir.
You'll be late.
R-Right.
Let's go, Tsubame.
B-But!
Tsubame!
Love's
fari Pa

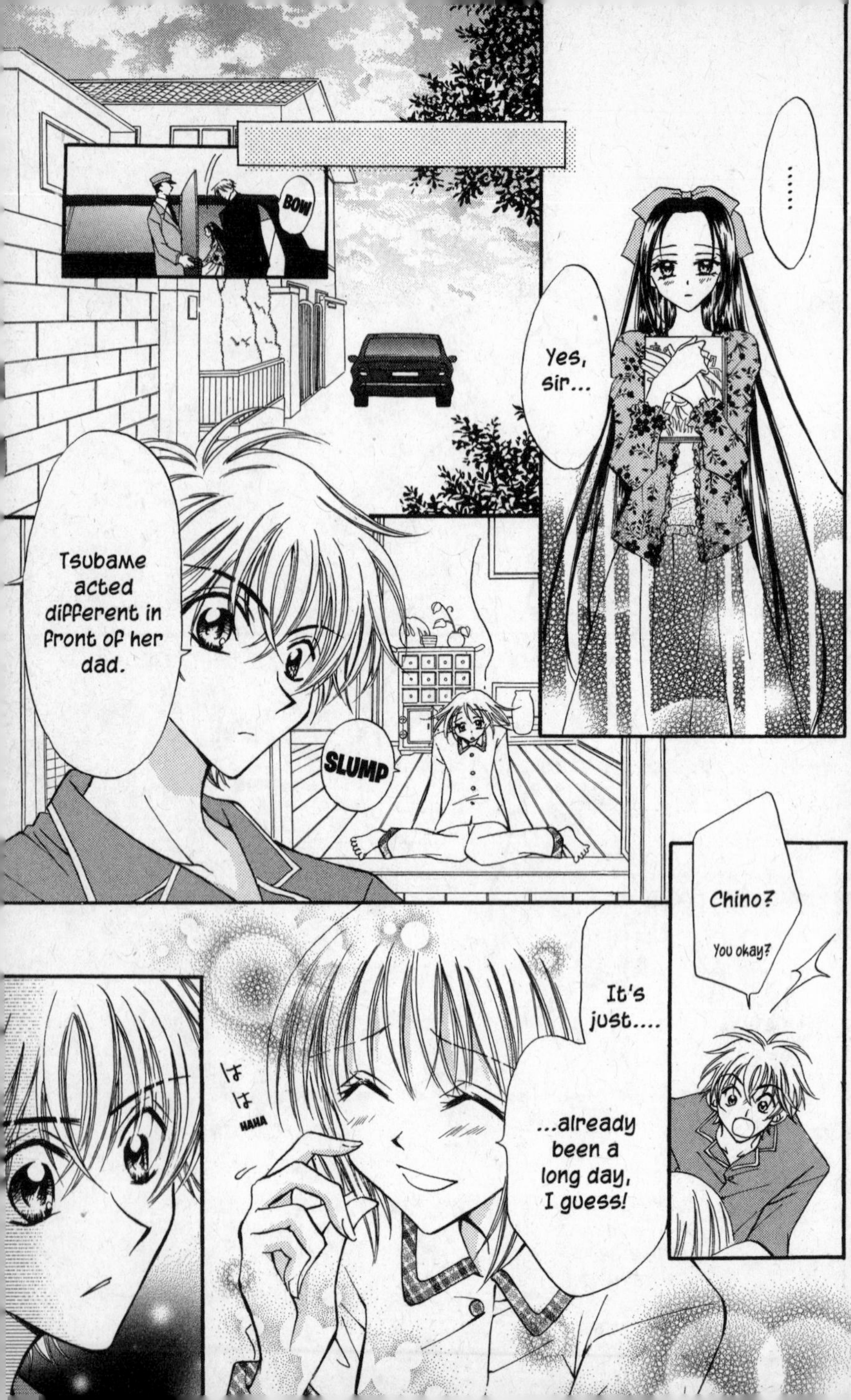
......
Yes, sir...
BOW
Tsubame acted different in front of her dad.
SLUMP
Chino?
You okay?
It's just....
...already been a long day, I guess!
はは
HAHA

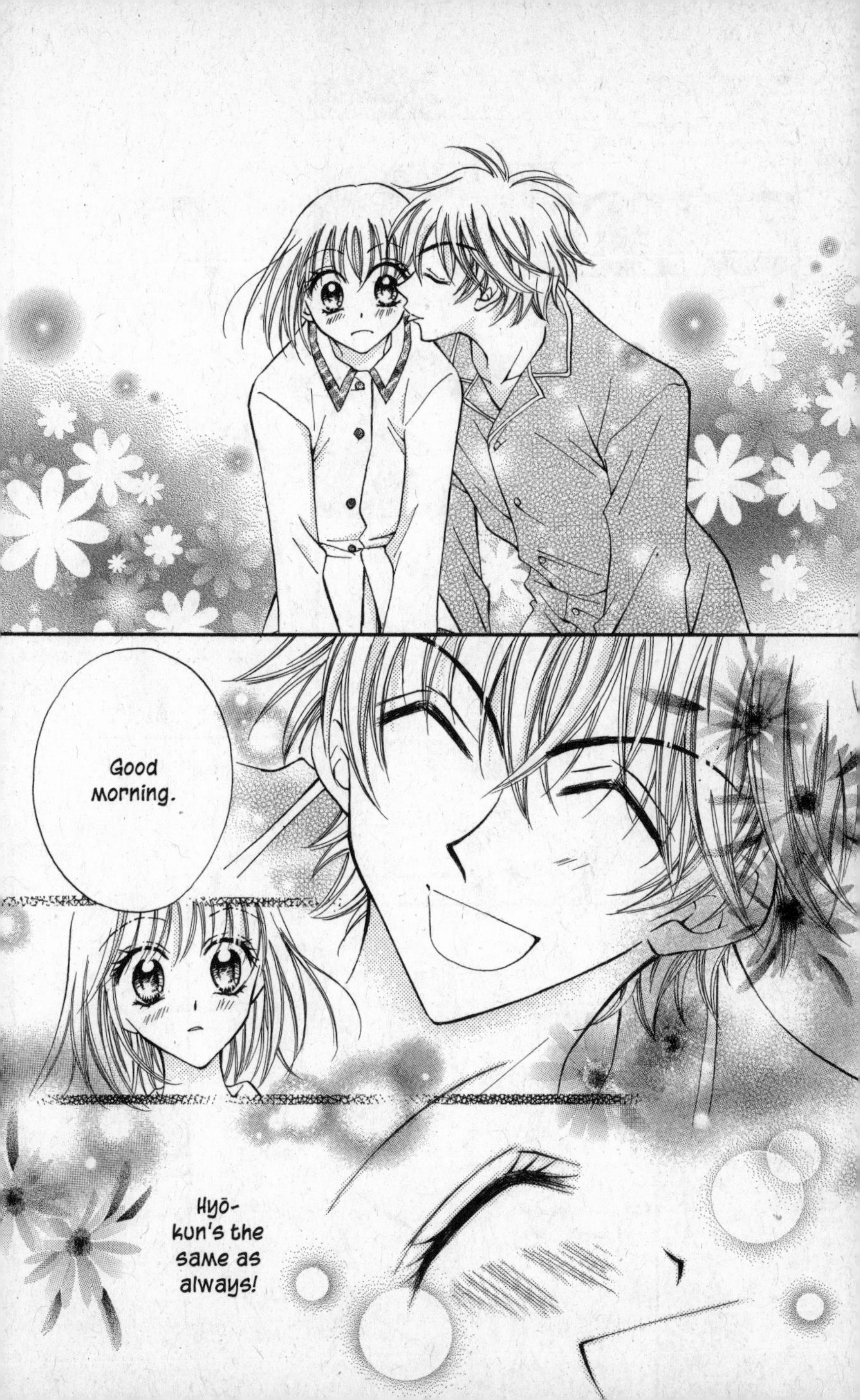
Good morning.
Hyō-kun's the same as always!

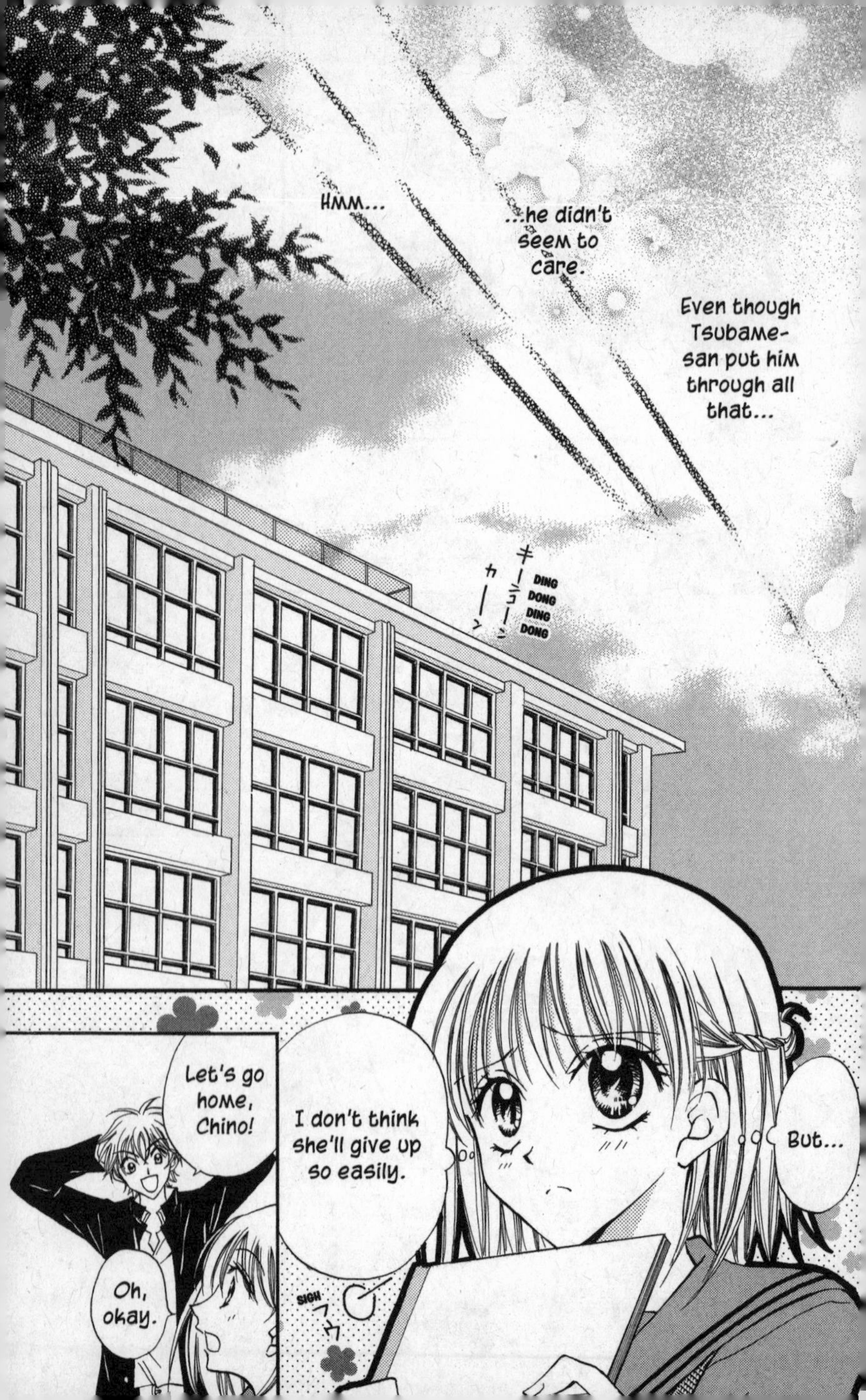

Even though Tsubame-san put him through all that...
...he didn't seem to care.
HMM...
キーンコーン カーン
DING DONG DING DONG
But...
I don't think she'll give up so easily.
SIGH
Let's go home, Chino!
Oh, okay.

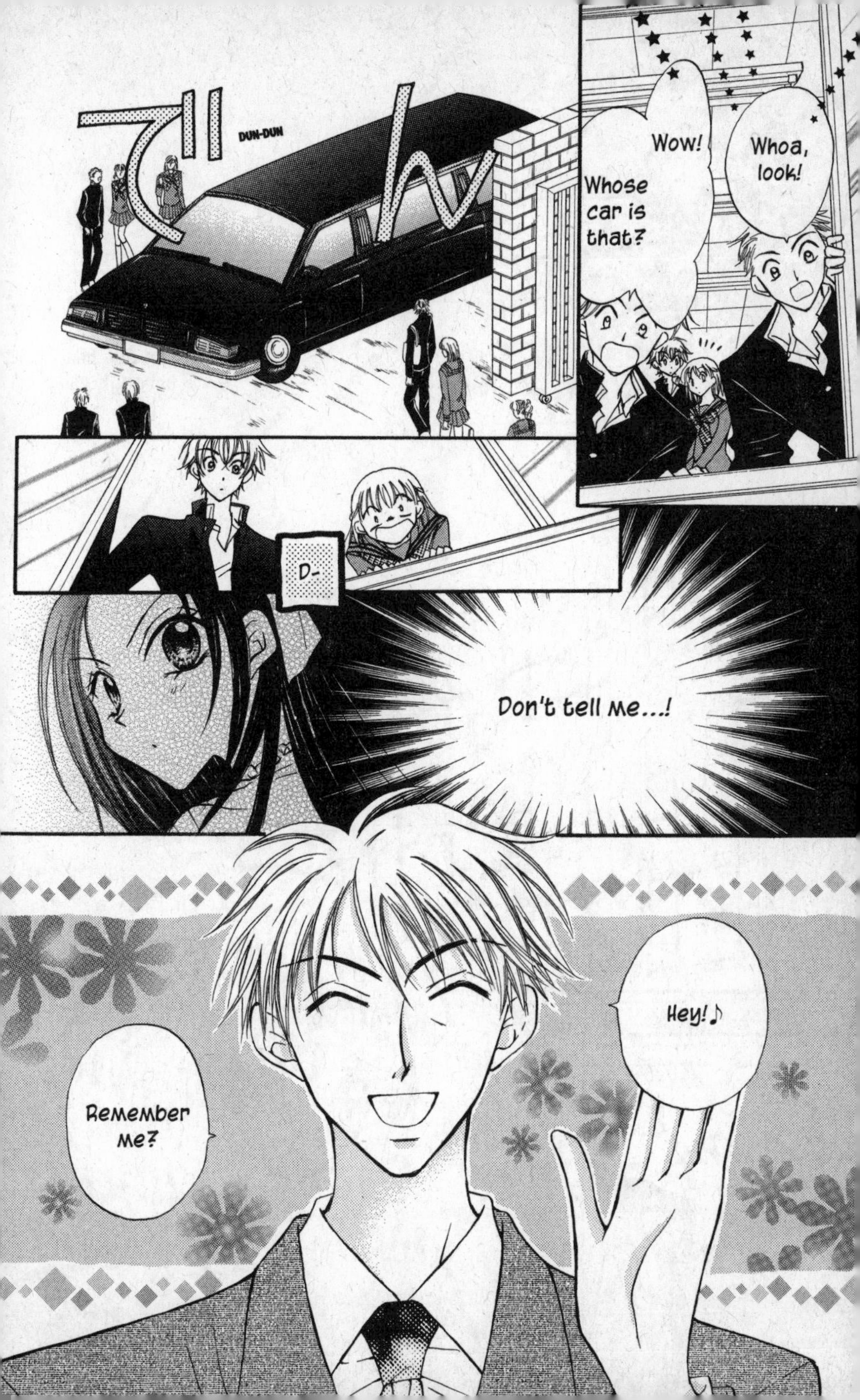
Whoa, look!
Wow!
Whose car is that?
DUN-DUN
D-
Don't tell me...!
Hey!♪
Remember me?

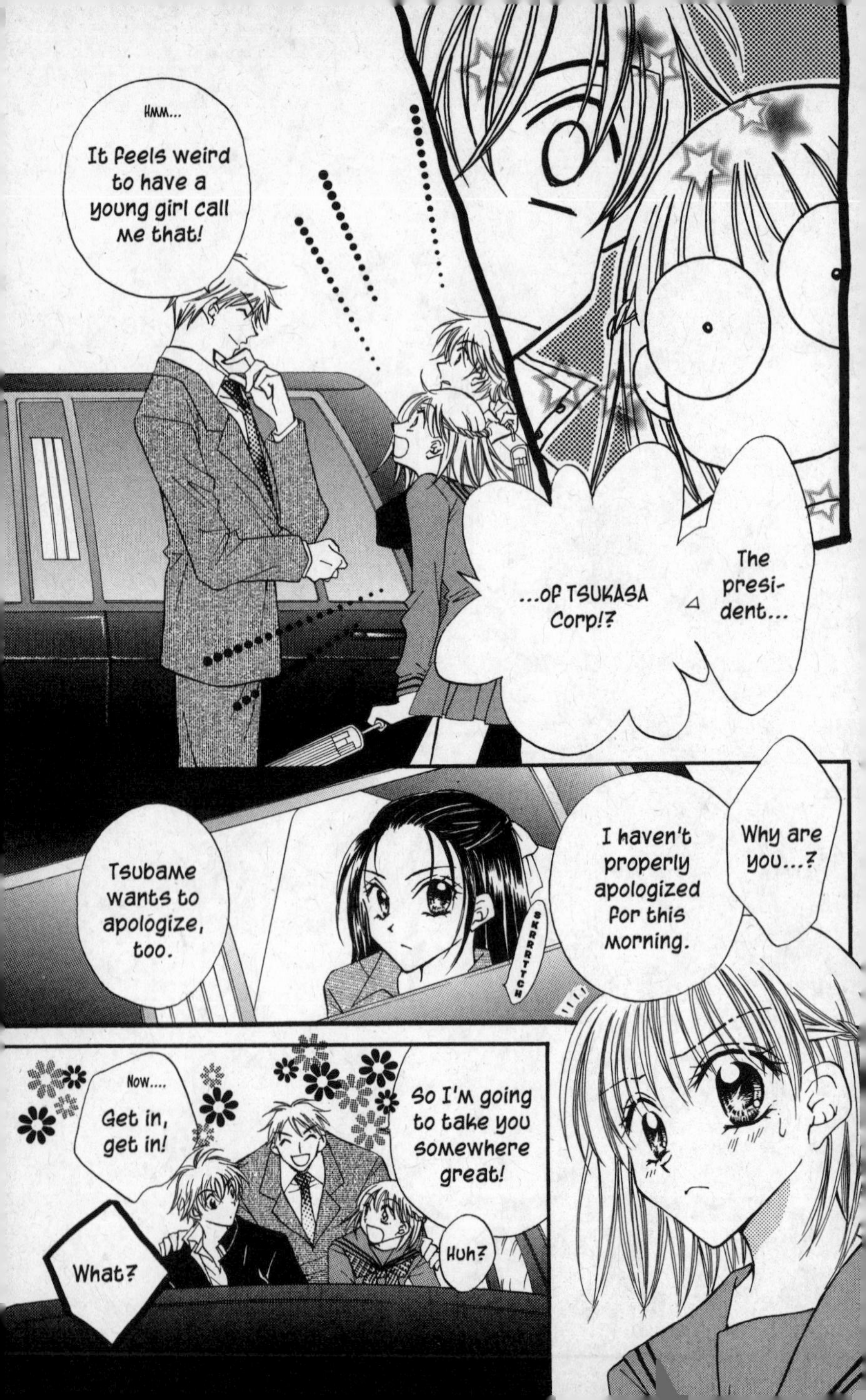
The president...
...of TSUKASA Corp!?
Hmm...
It feels weird to have a young girl call me that!
Why are you...?
I haven't properly apologized for this morning.
SKRRRTTCH
Tsubame wants to apologize, too.
So I'm going to take you somewhere great!
Now....
Get in, get in!
Huh?
What?

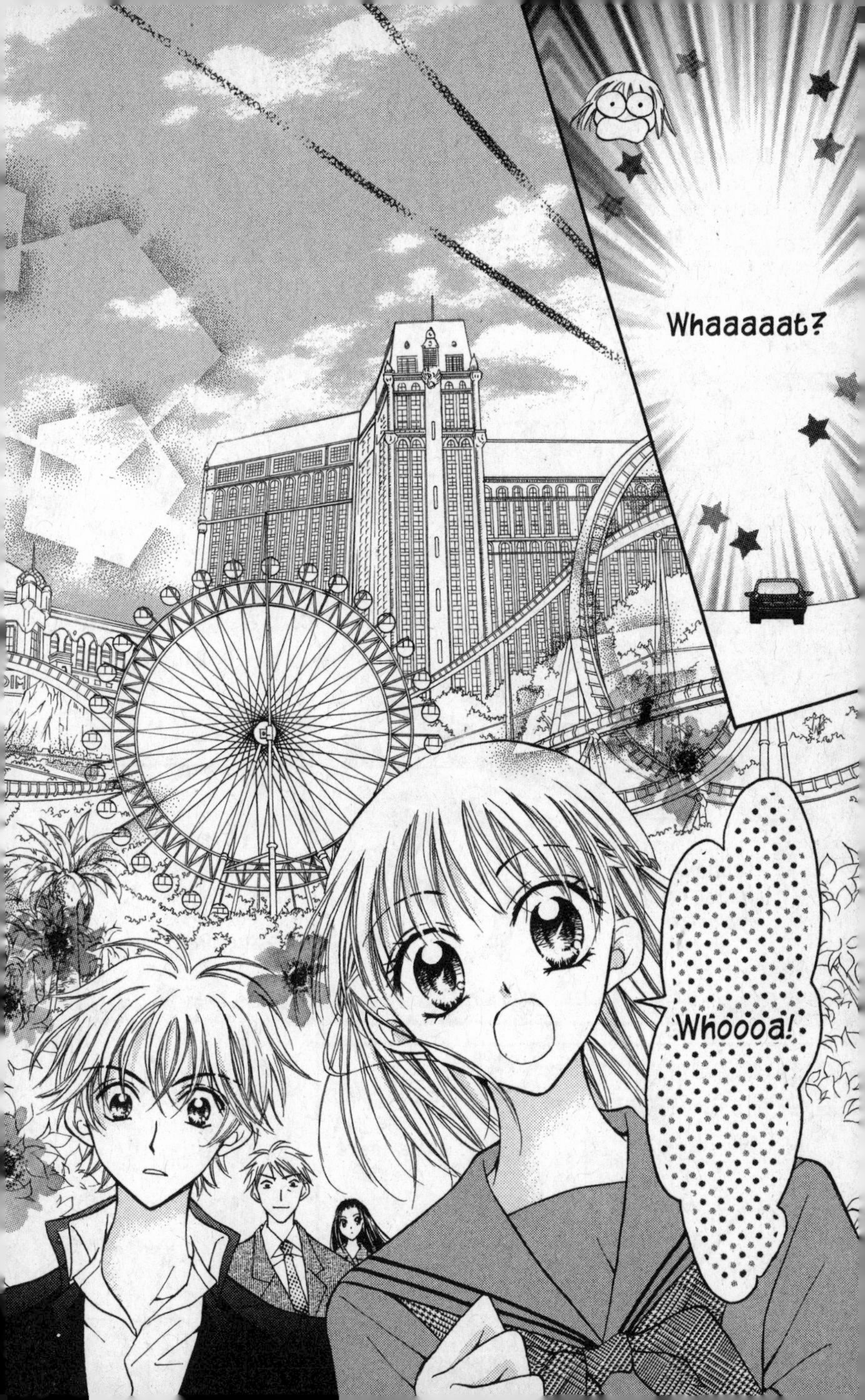
Whaaaaat?
Whoooa!

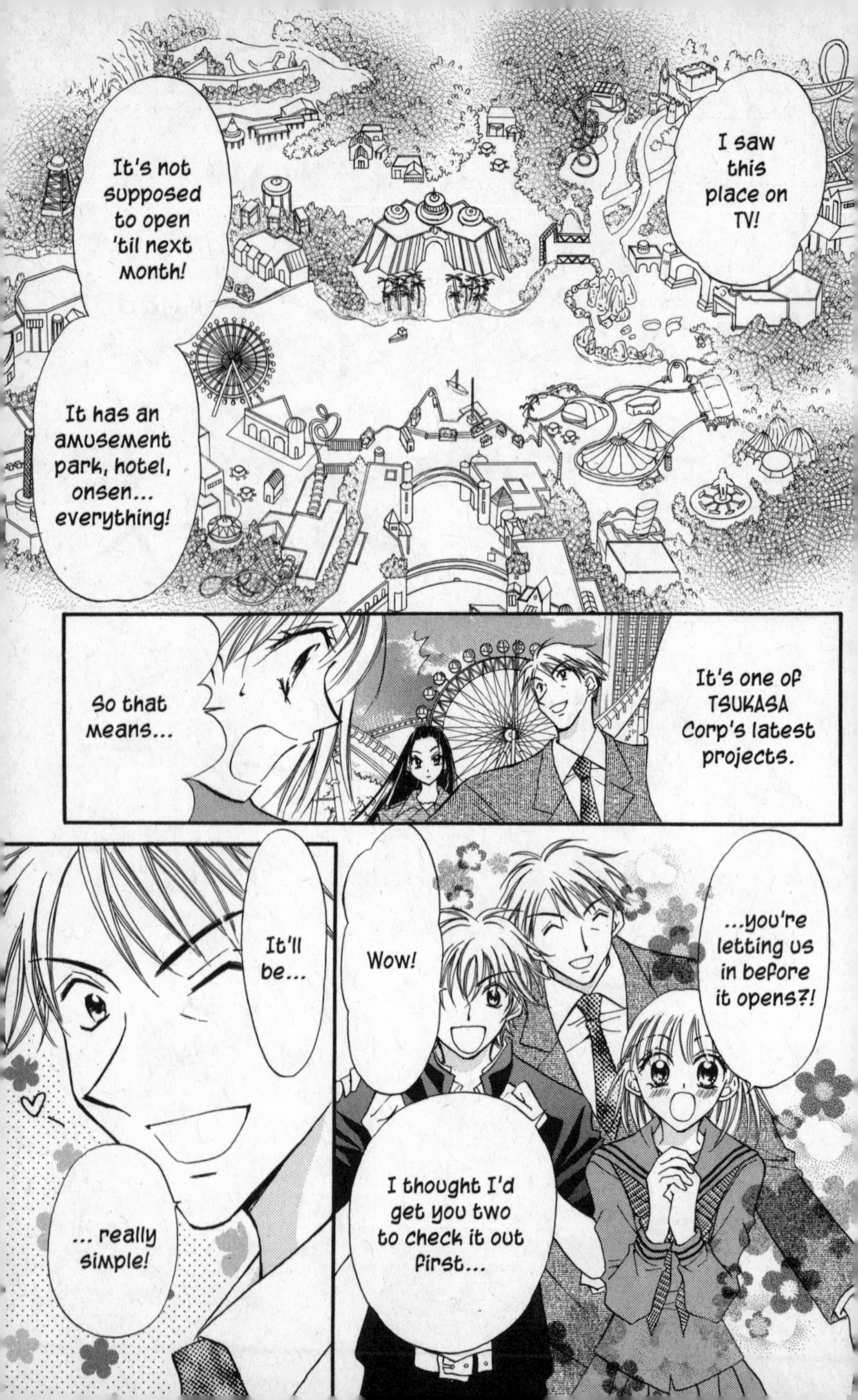
I saw this place on TV!
It's not supposed to open 'til next month!
It has an amusement park, hotel, onsen... everything!
It's one of TSUKASA Corp's latest projects.
So that means...
...you're letting us in before it opens?!
Wow!
I thought I'd get you two to check it out first...
It'll be...
... really simple!

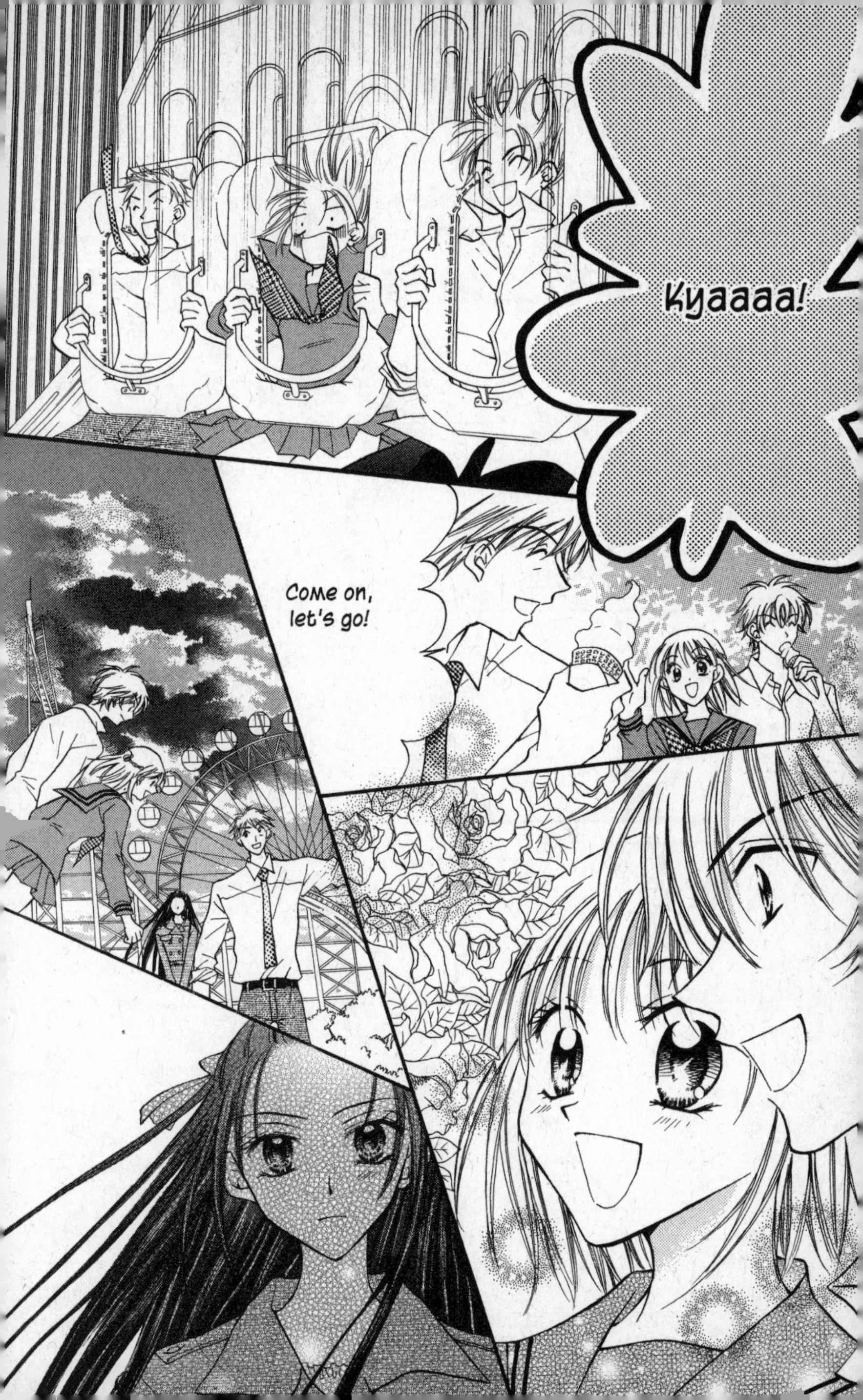
Kyaaaa!
Come on, let's go!

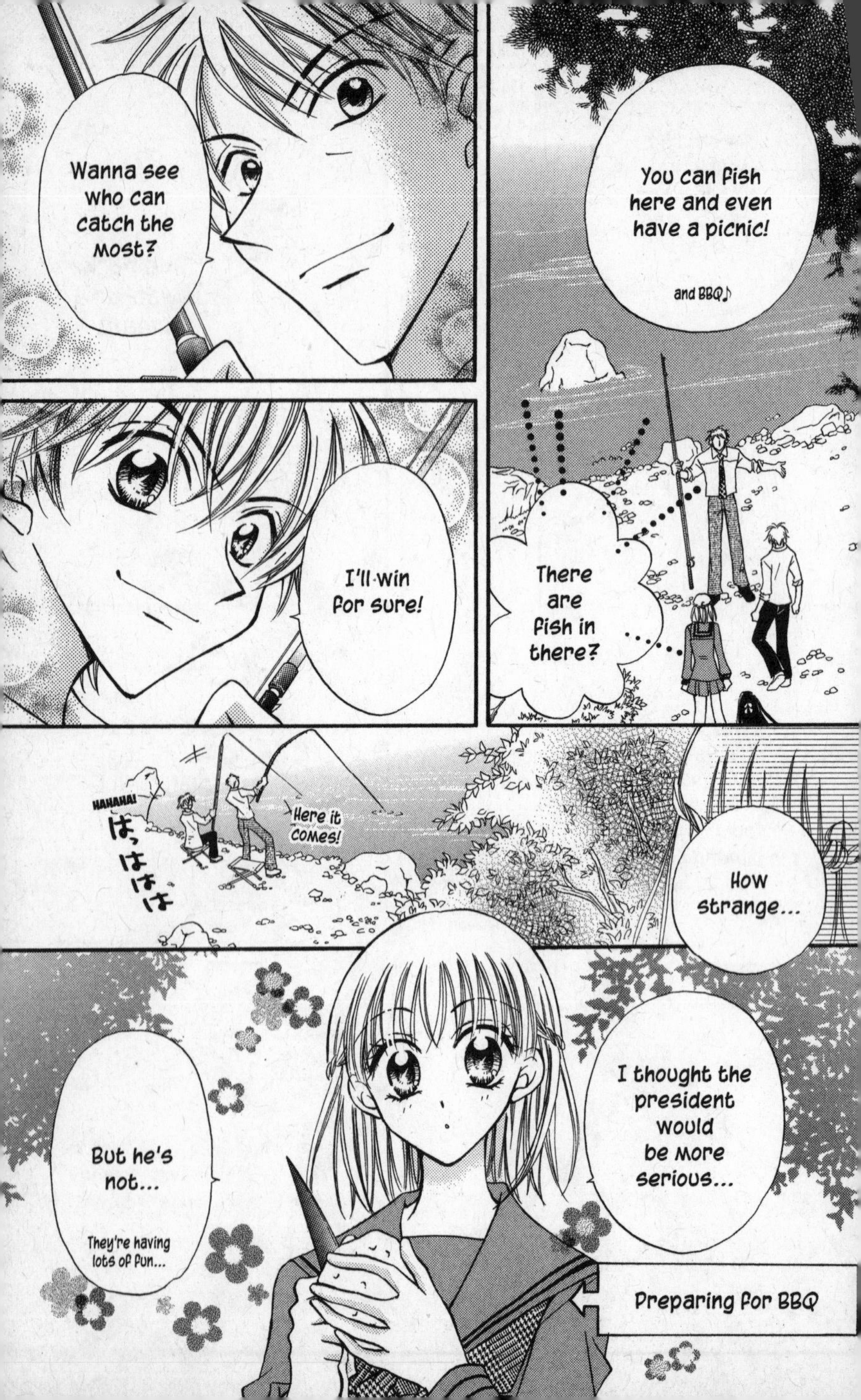
You can fish here and even have a picnic!
and BBQ♪
There are fish in there?
Wanna see who can catch the most?
I'll win for sure!
How strange...
Here it comes!
HAHAHA!
はっははは
I thought the president would be more serious...
But he's not...
They're having lots of fun...
Preparing for BBQ

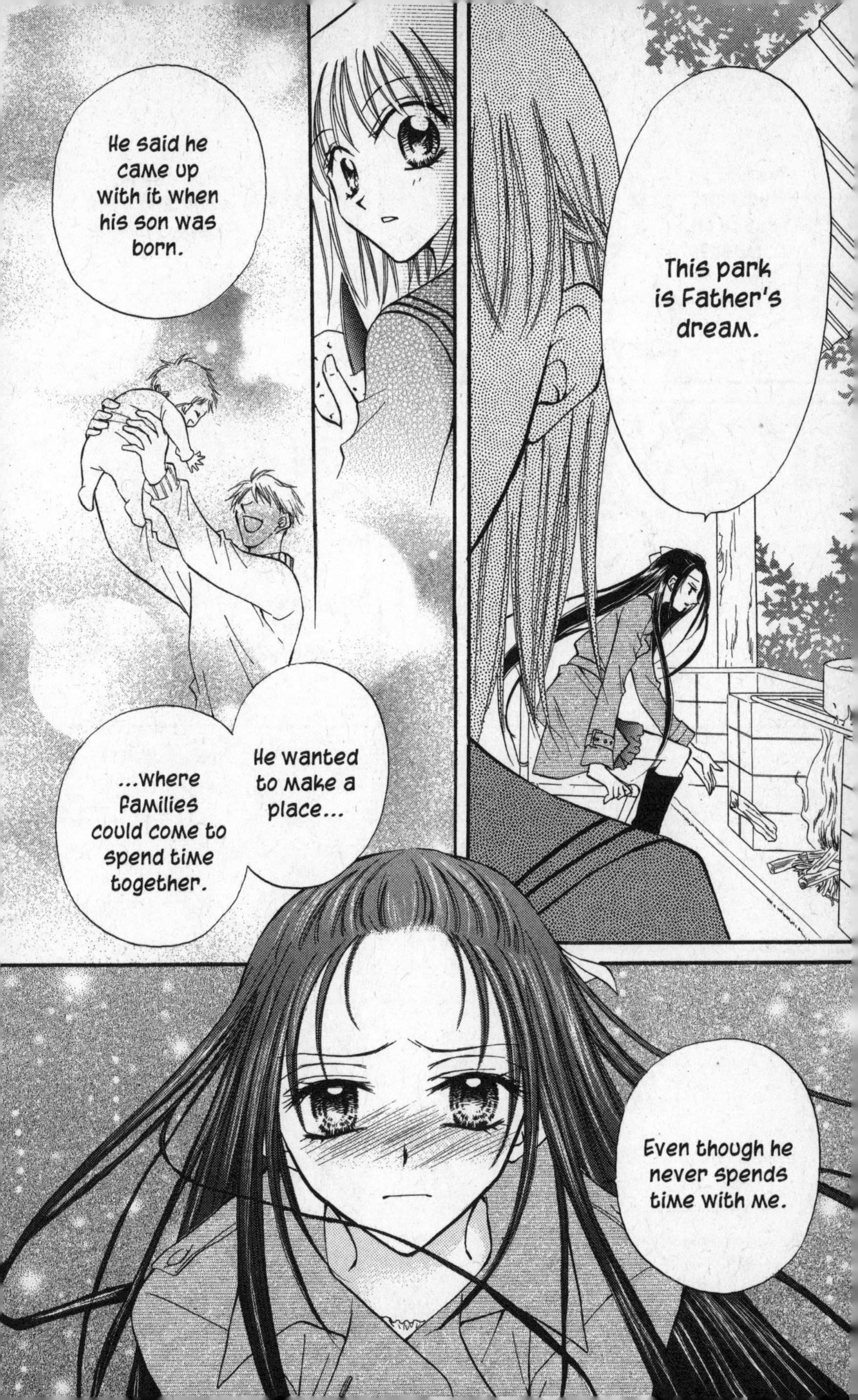
This park is Father's dream.
He said he came up with it when his son was born.
He wanted to make a place...
...where families could come to spend time together.
Even though he never spends time with me.

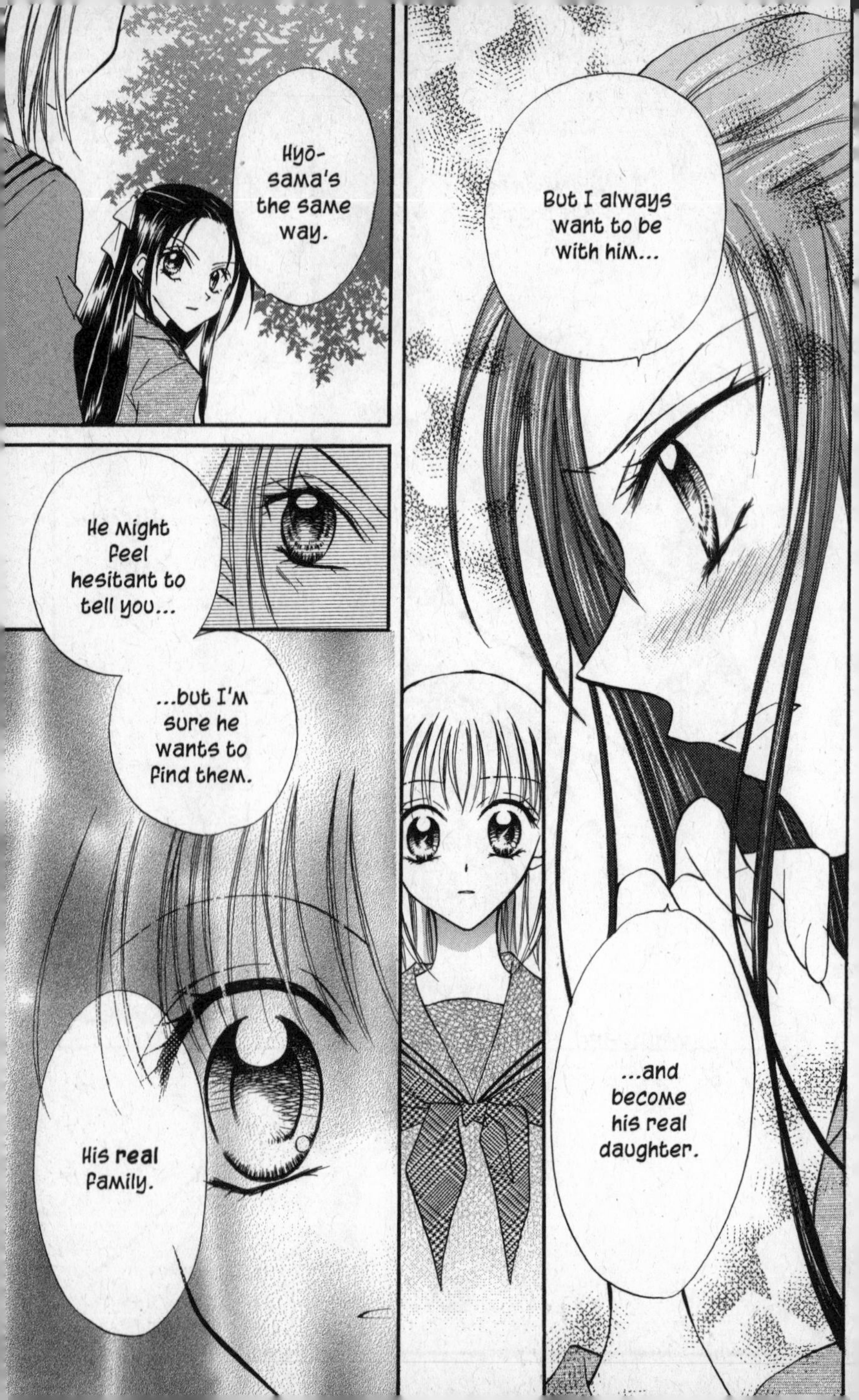
But I always want to be with him...
...and become his real daughter.
Hyō-sama's the same way.
He might feel hesitant to tell you...
...but I'm sure he wants to find them.
His real family.

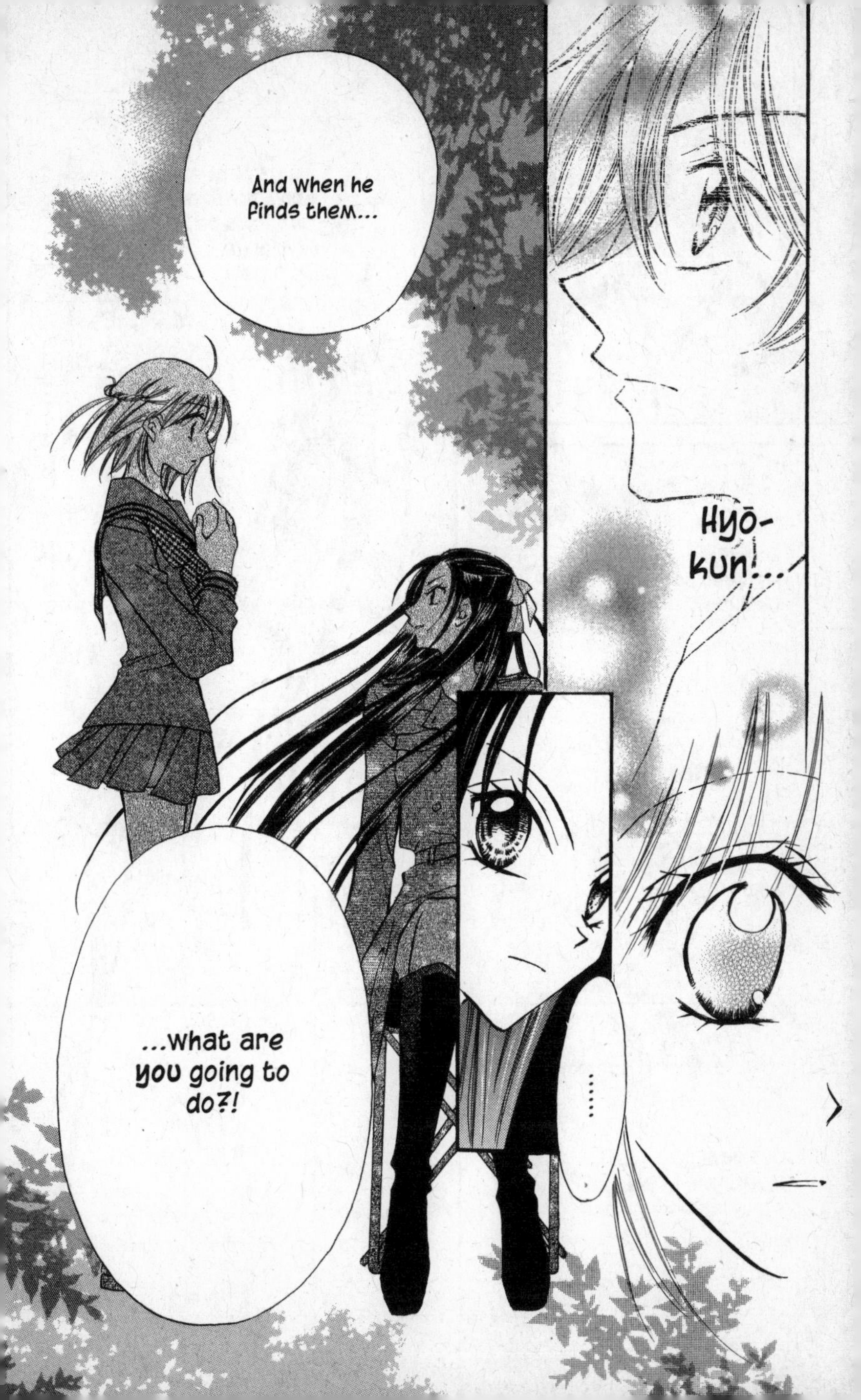
Hyō-kun...
......
And when he finds them...
...what are you going to do?!

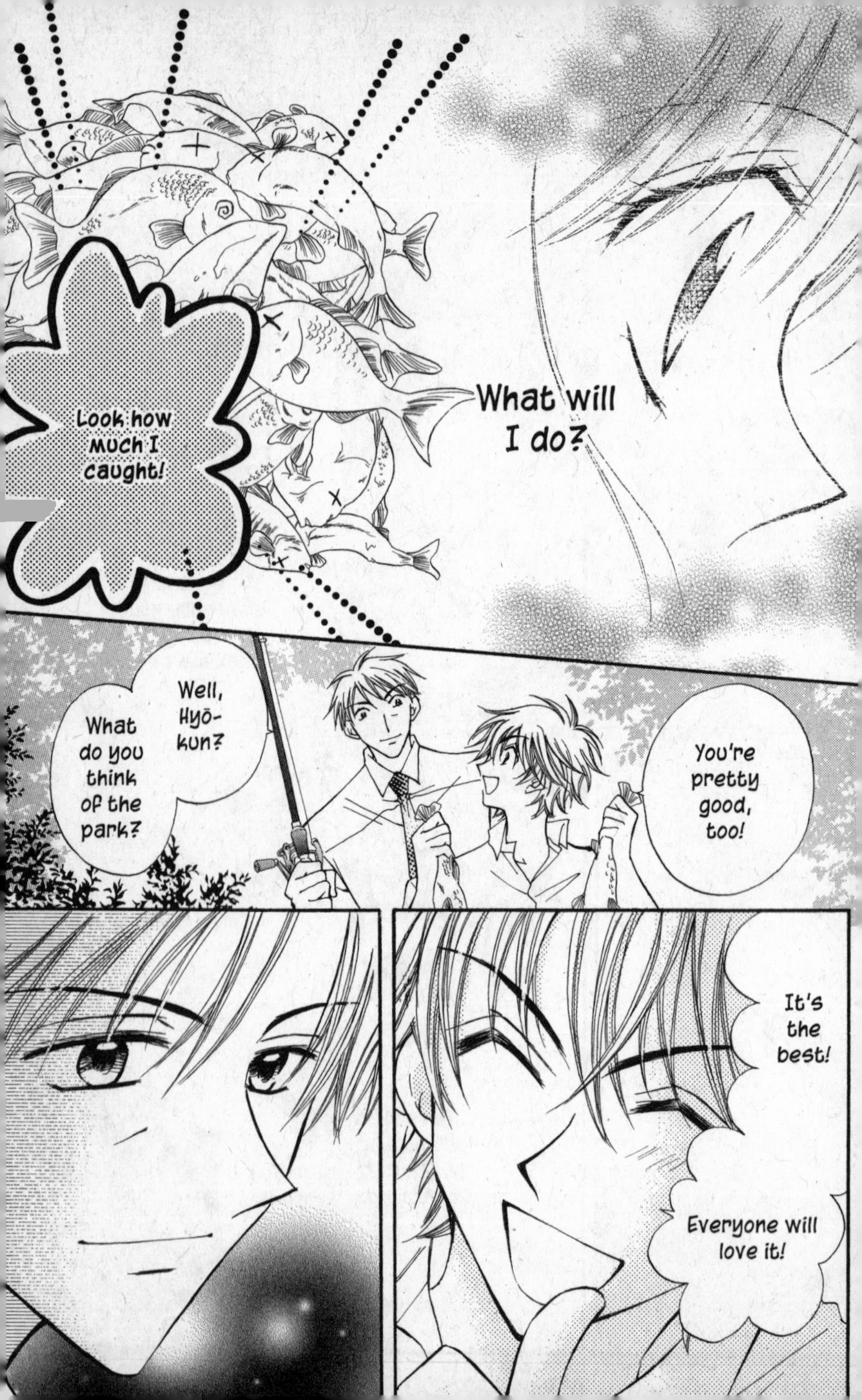
What will I do?
Look how much I caught!
You're pretty good, too!
Well, Hyō-kun? What do you think of the park?
It's the best!
Everyone will love it!

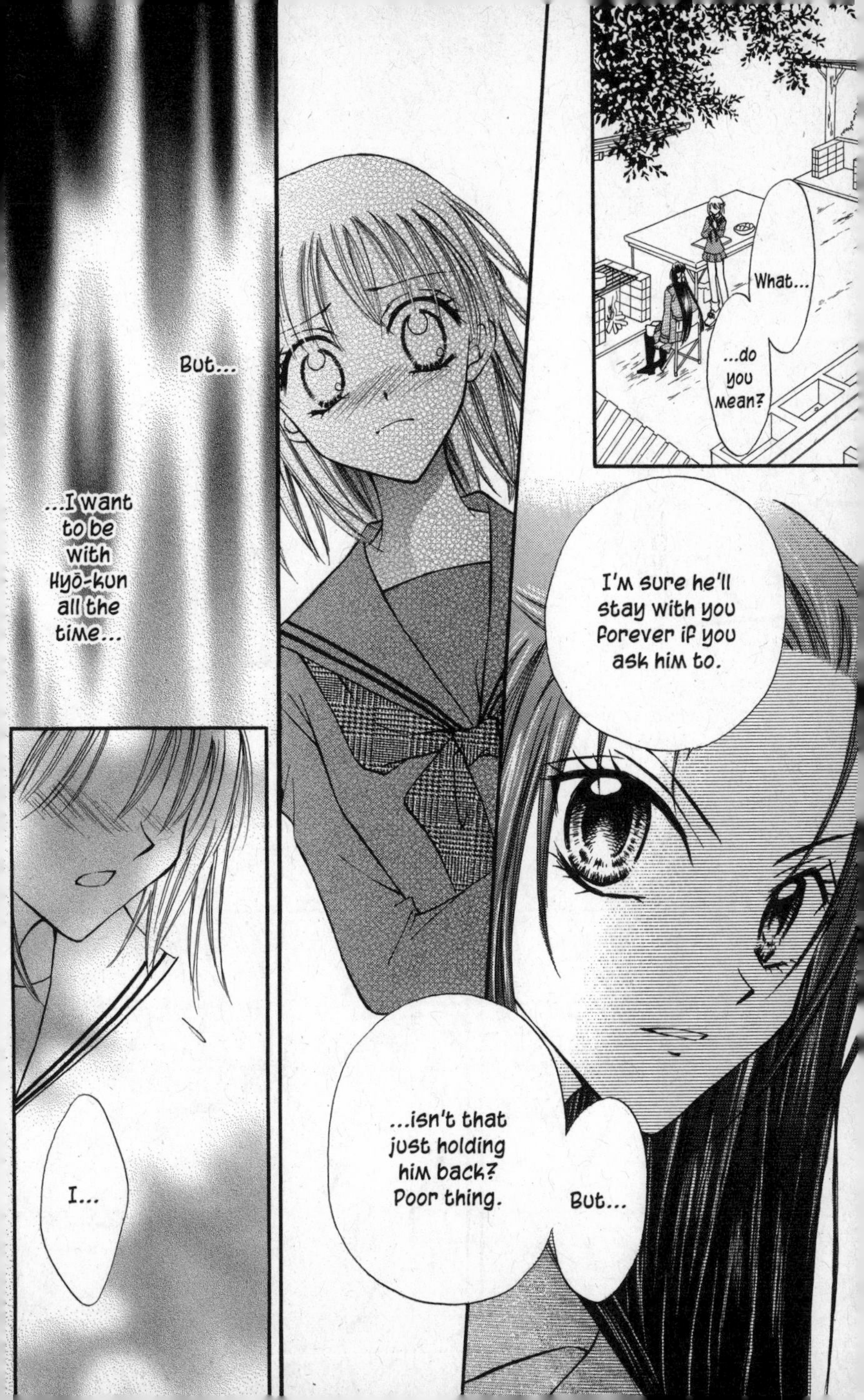
What...
...do you mean?
I'm sure he'll stay with you forever if you ask him to.
But...
...isn't that just holding him back? Poor thing.
But...
...I want to be with Hyō-kun all the time...
I...

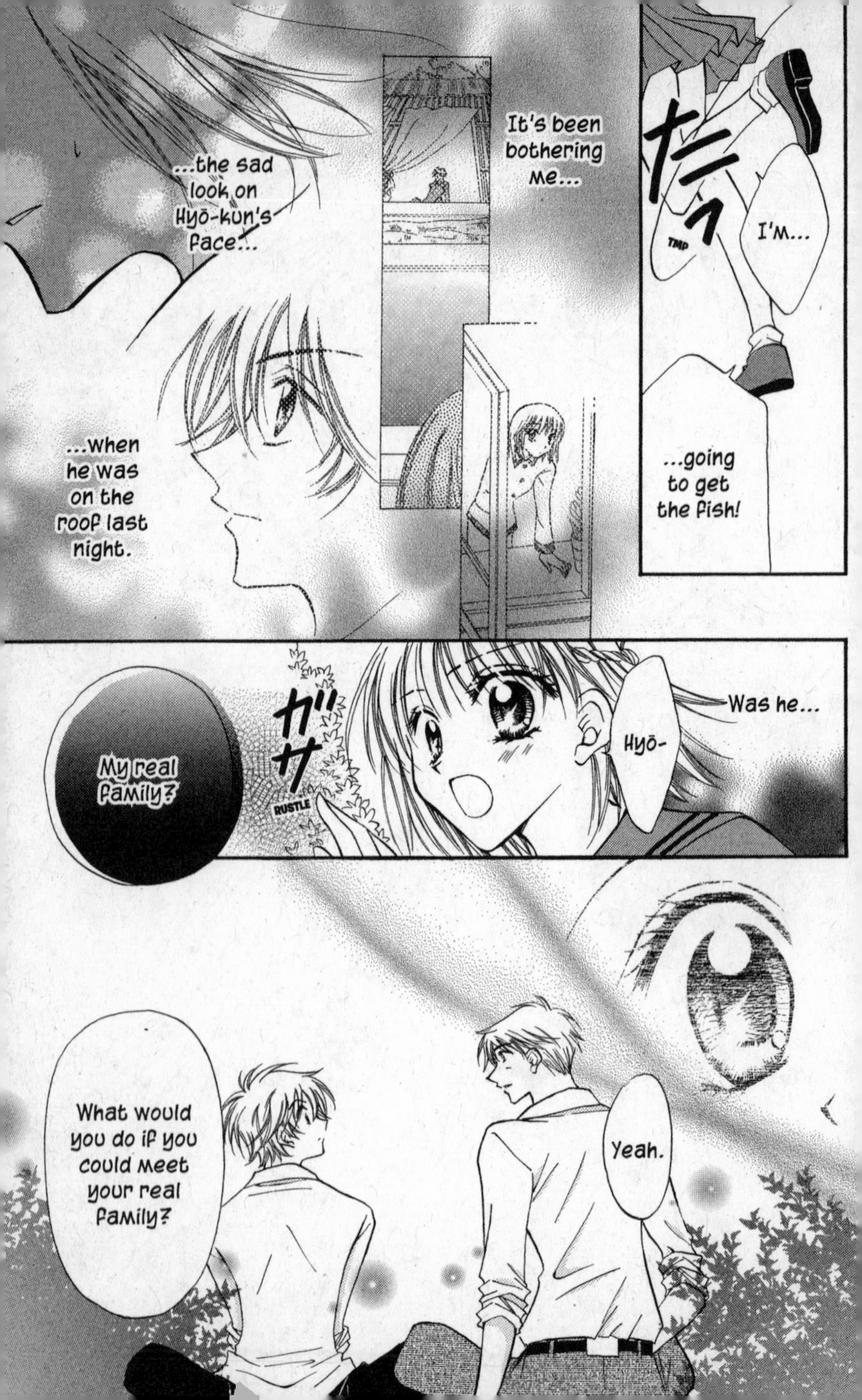

TMP
I'M...
...going to get the fish!
It's been bothering me...
...the sad look on Hyō-kun's face...
...when he was on the roof last night.
Was he...
Hyō-
ガサ
RUSTLE
My real family?
Yeah.
What would you do if you could meet your real family?

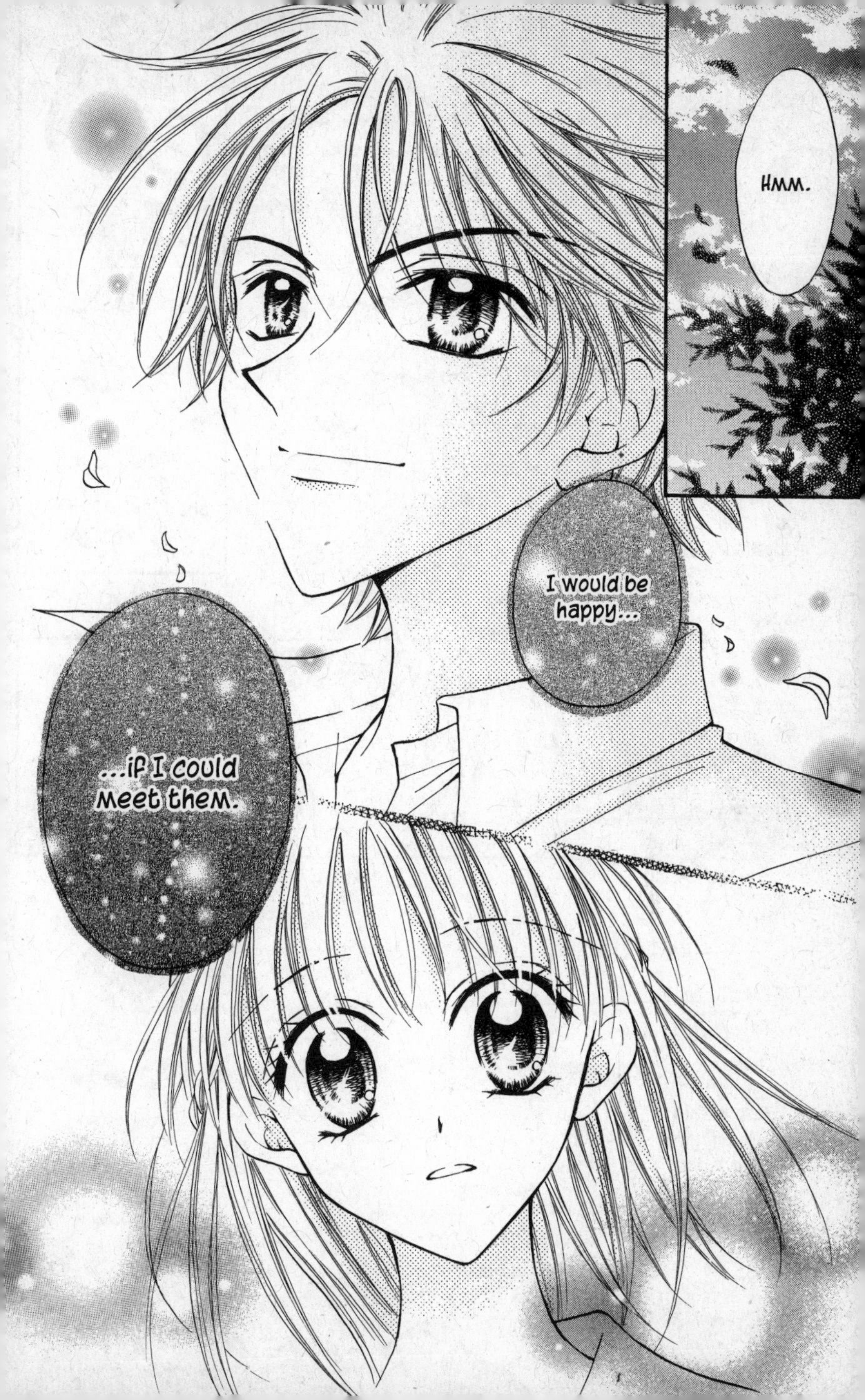
Hmm.
I would be happy...
...if I could meet them.

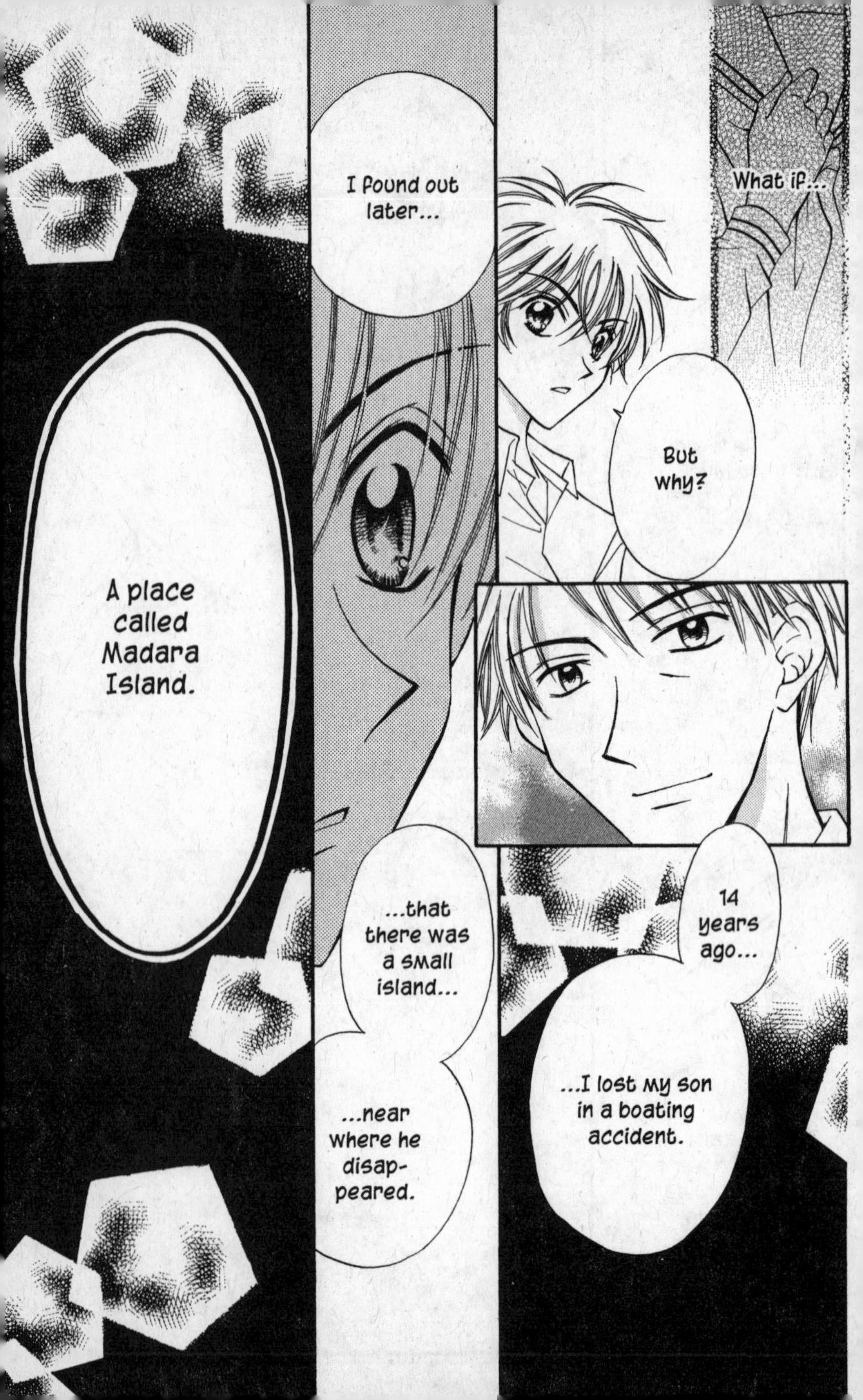
What if...
But why?
14 years ago...
...I lost my son in a boating accident.
I found out later...
...that there was a small island...
...near where he disappeared.
A place called Madara Island.

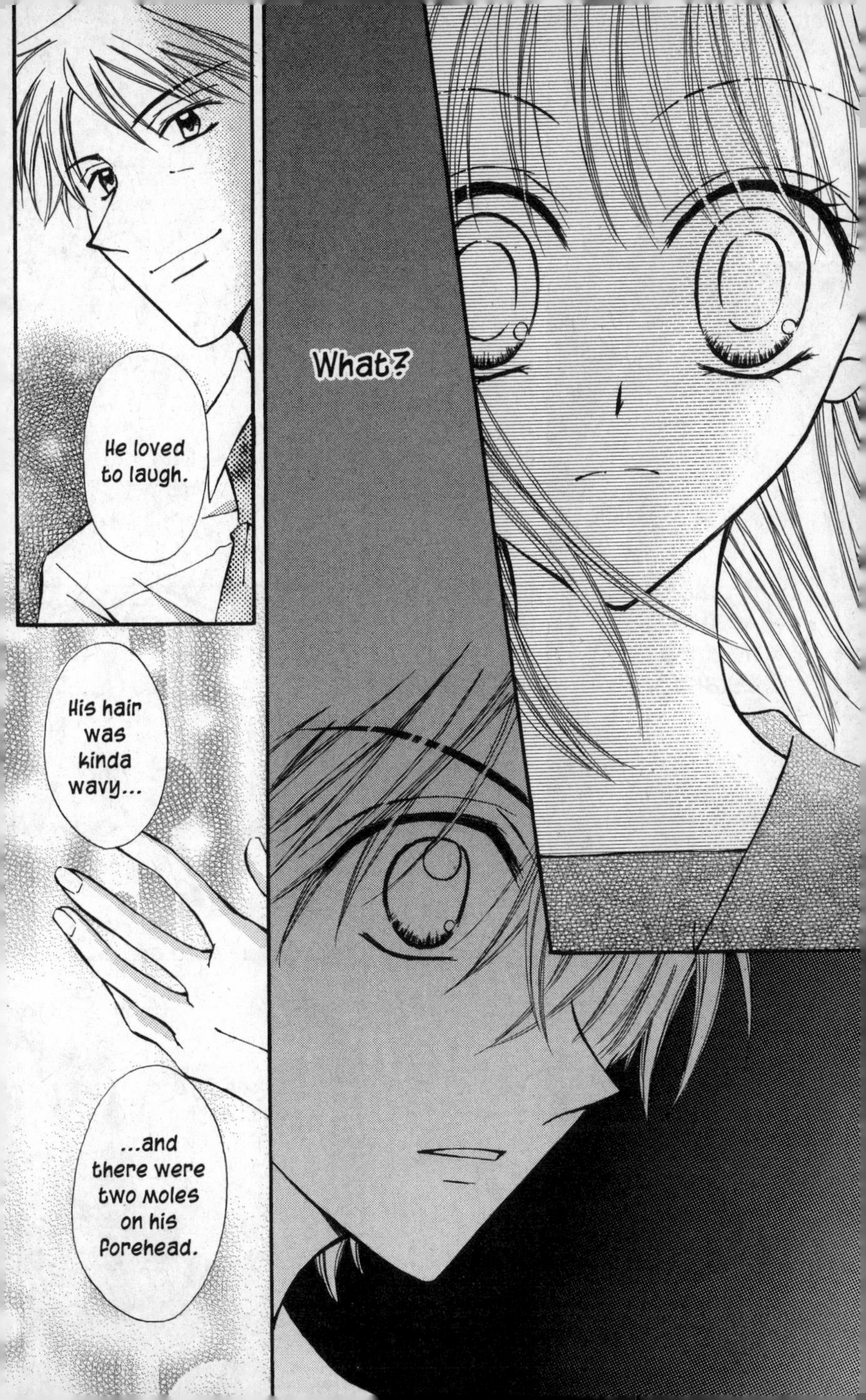
What?
He loved to laugh.
His hair was kinda wavy...
...and there were two moles on his forehead.

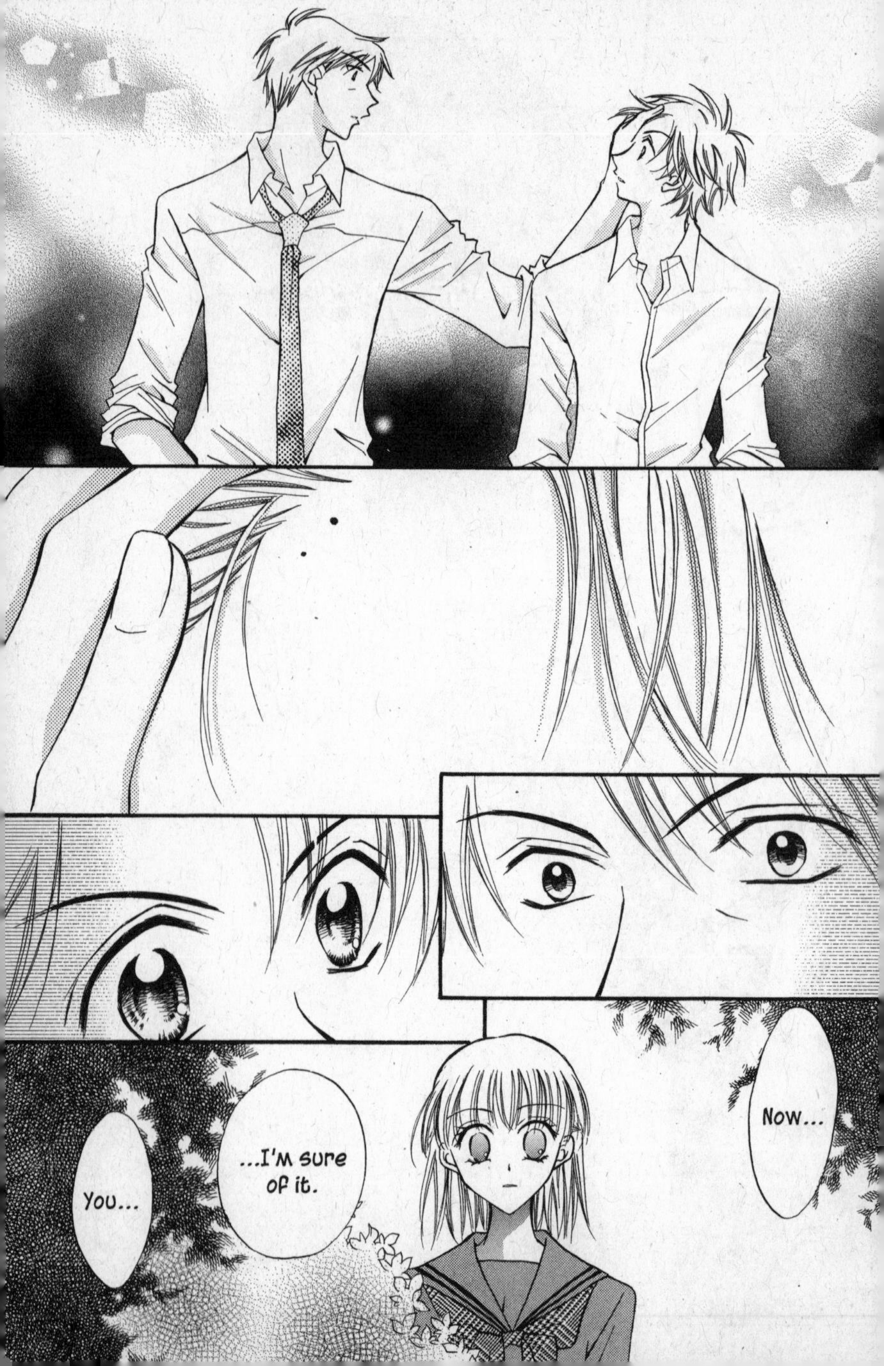
Now...
...I'm sure of it.
You...

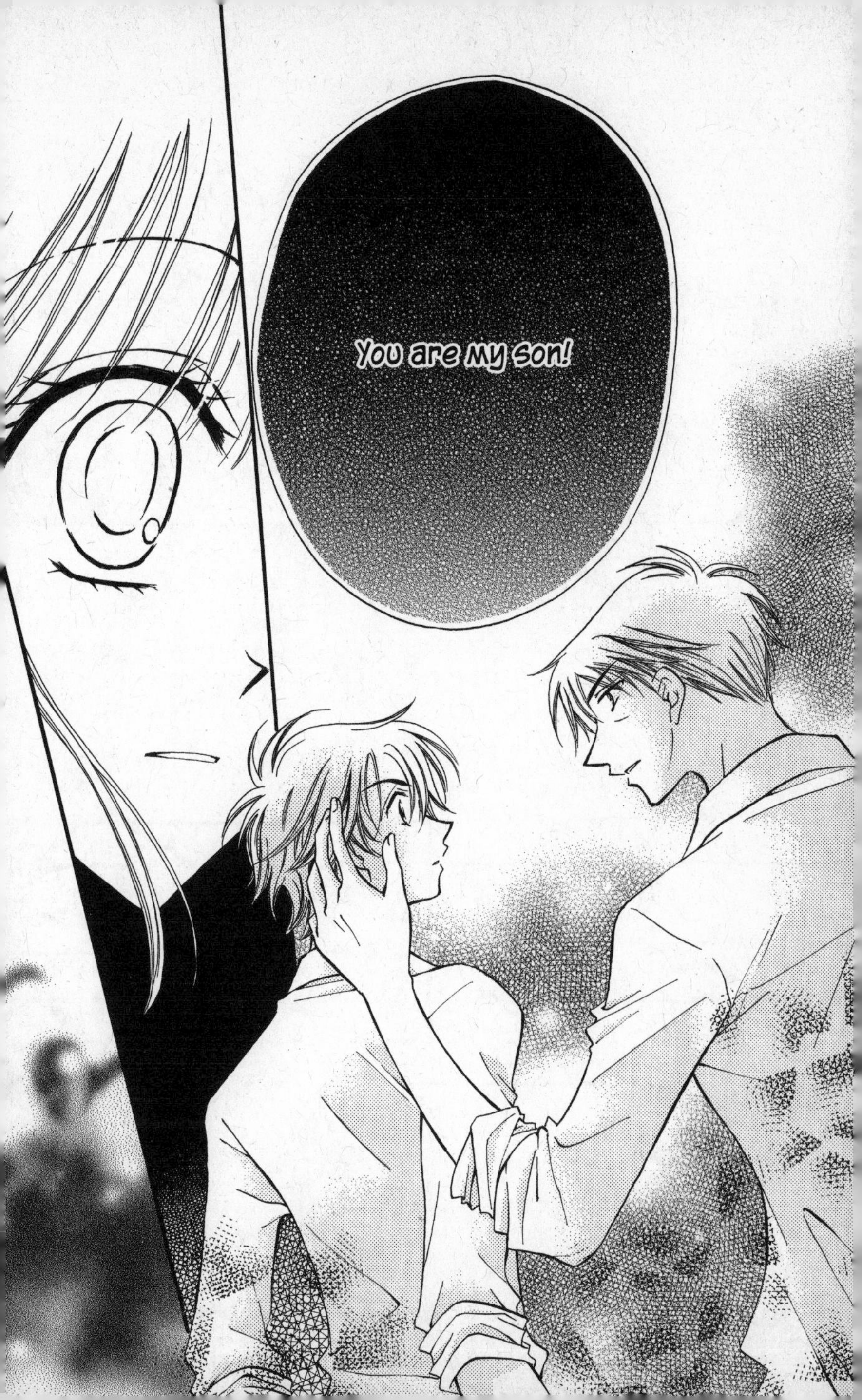
You are my son!

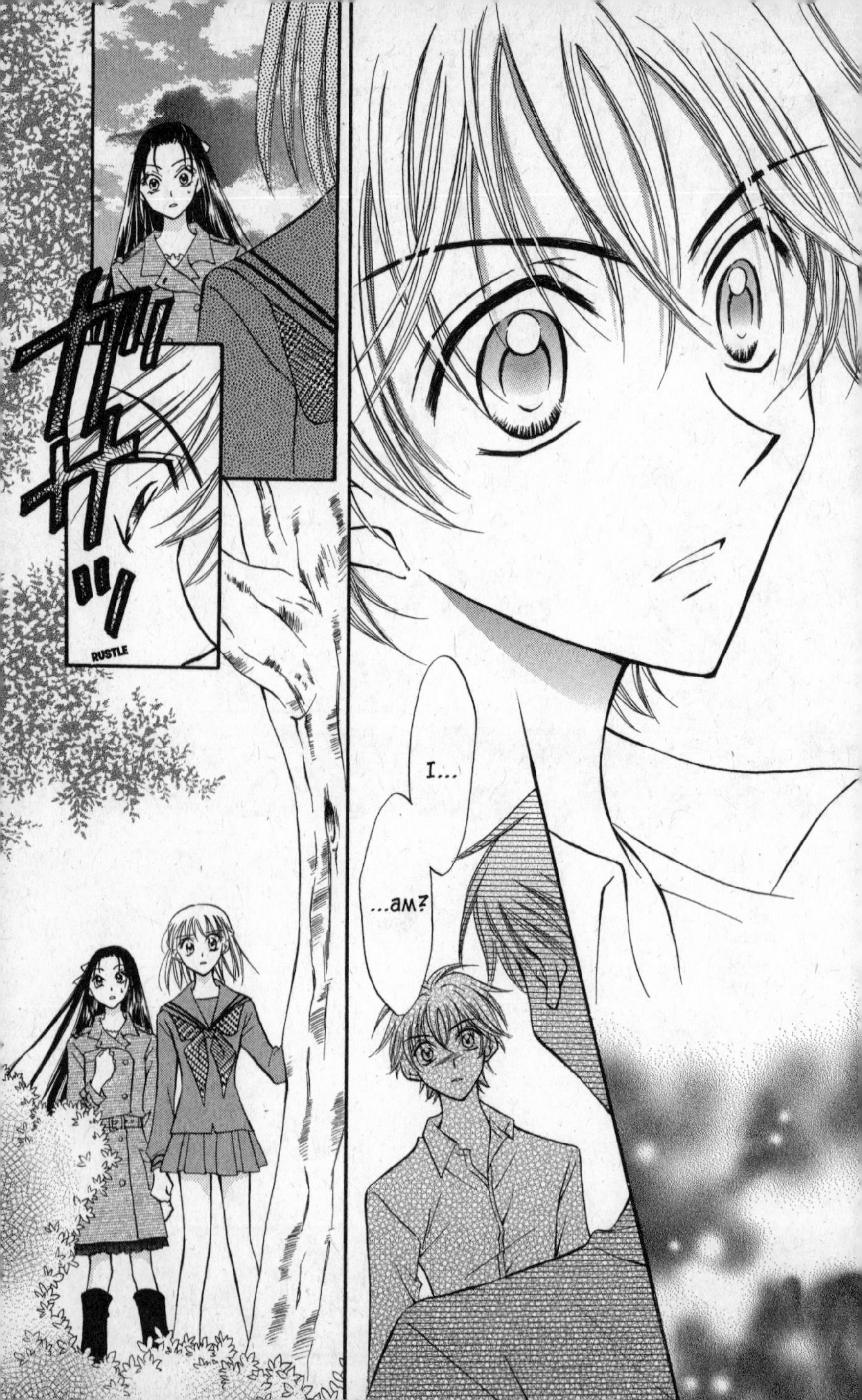
I...
...am?
RUSTLE

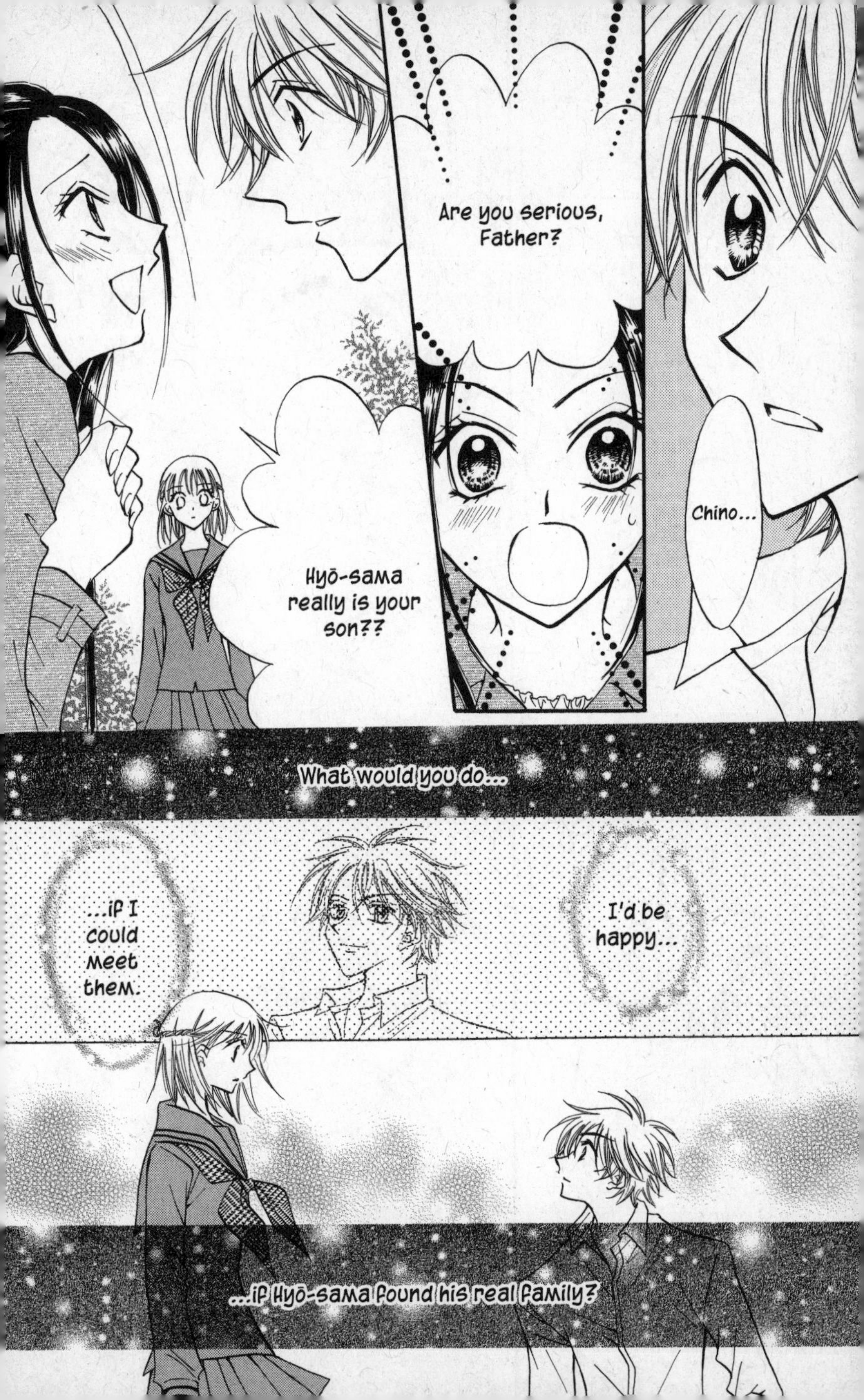
Chino...
Are you serious, Father?
Hyō-sama really is your son??
What would you do...
I'd be happy...
...if I could meet them.
...if Hyō-sama found his real family?

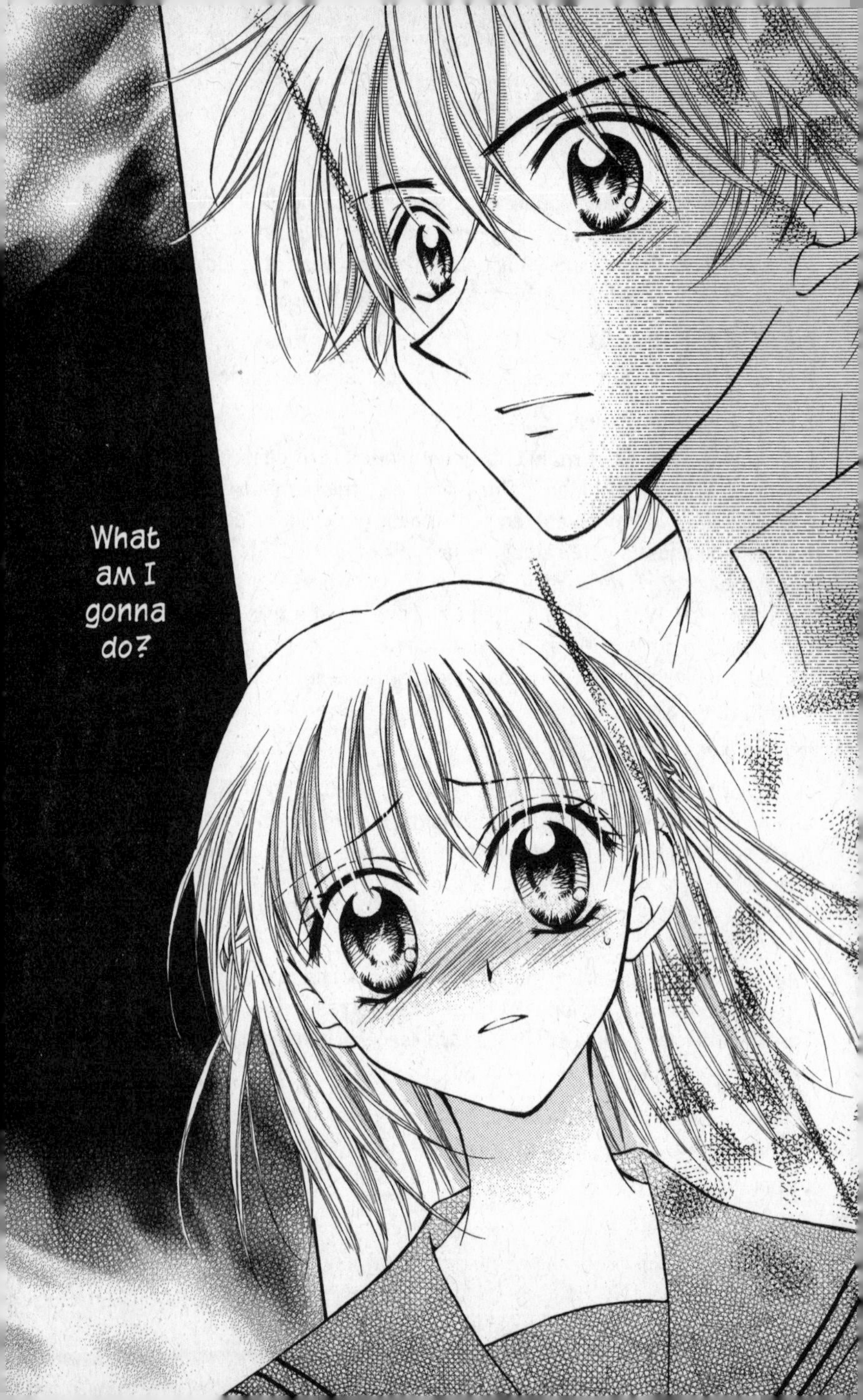
What am I gonna do?

Translation Notes

School trips

Many Japanese schools sponsor school trips during which an entire grade will travel somewhere together, sometimes staying as long as 2-3 days. These trips usually happen in the final year of middle school and high school during the summer or late spring.

ujikintoki, page 17

Shaved ice topped with green tea syrup and Japanese kintoki beans.

Kaguya-hime, page 21

Princess Kaguya is the main character from a 10th-century Japanese folktale called Taketori Monogatari, or Tale of the Bamboo Cutter. In the story an elderly bamboo cutter finds a baby growing inside a stalk of bamboo. He and his wife raise her as their own child. After he found Kaguya, each time he went to cut bamboo he would find gold in it, making them rich. When Princess Kaguya grows up she tells her parents that she is from the Moon and must go back to her kingdom. Her parents hoped it wasn't true, but one night she returned to the moon, leaving them alone.

Blood types, page 91

Many Japanese believe that blood type is an indication of the positive and negative aspects of one's personality, so this is why characters' blood types are often included in manga. Here's a quick guide to what each blood type means.

Type A: Perfectionists. Conservative, introverted. Stubborn and obsessive.

Type B: Outgoing, creative, individualistic. Forgetful and whimsical.

Type AB: Logical and rational. Critical, easily stressed.

Type O: Ambitious and athletic. Natural leaders, confident. Reckless and insensitive.

Palace of Versailles, page 99

A huge palace in Versailles, France, that served as the official residence of the kings of France.

Onsen, page 171

Hot springs – popular vacation resorts for many Japanese.

188

WILD @ Heart♥

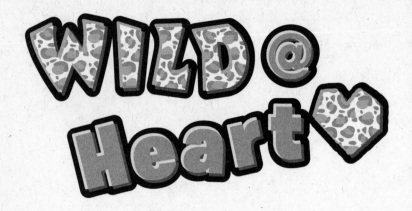

Volume 3

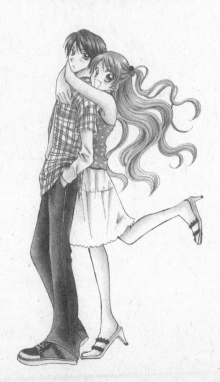

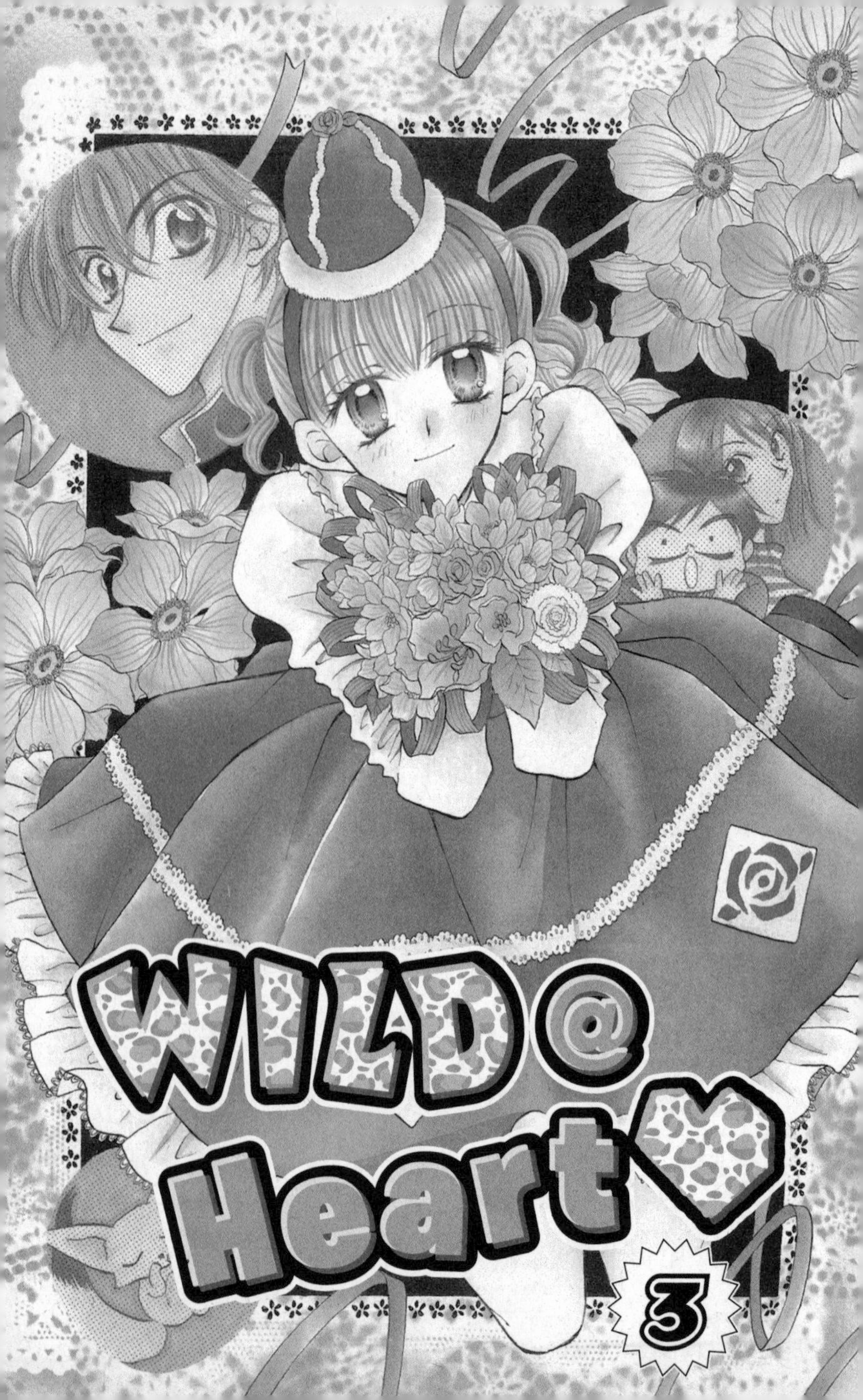

WILD @ Heart
3

Contents

WILD @ Heart
The Story So Far♡

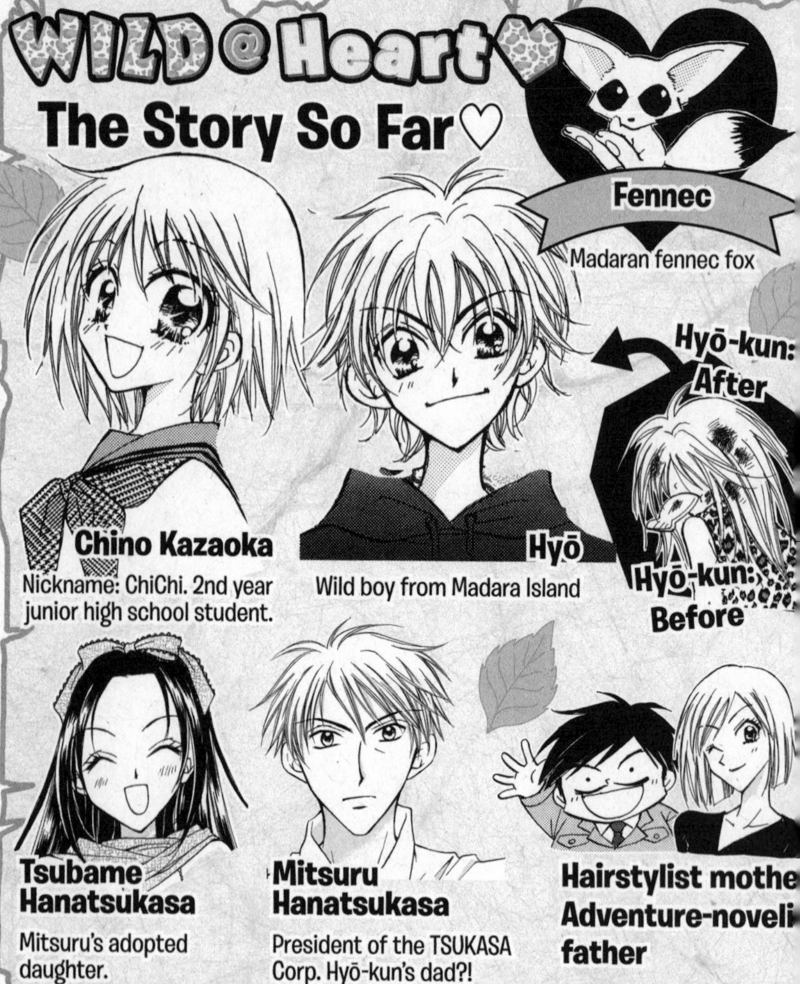
Fennec
Madaran fennec fox
Hyō-kun: After
Chino Kazaoka
Nickname: ChiChi. 2nd year junior high school student.
Hyō
Wild boy from Madara Island
Hyō-kun: Before
Tsubame Hanatsukasa
Mitsuru's adopted daughter.
Mitsuru Hanatsukasa
President of the TSUKASA Corp. Hyō-kun's dad?!
Hairstylist mothe
Adventure-noveli
father

Where is Hyō-kun's real family??

Chino's dad brought Hyō-kun back from an uninhabited island filled with animals, called Madara Island. Since he doesn't have much common sense he's always causing trouble for Chino, but he's so sincere she finds her feelings for him changing...They've finally grown closer when a girl named Tsubame Hanatsukasa appears and says Hyō is her long-lost brother!!

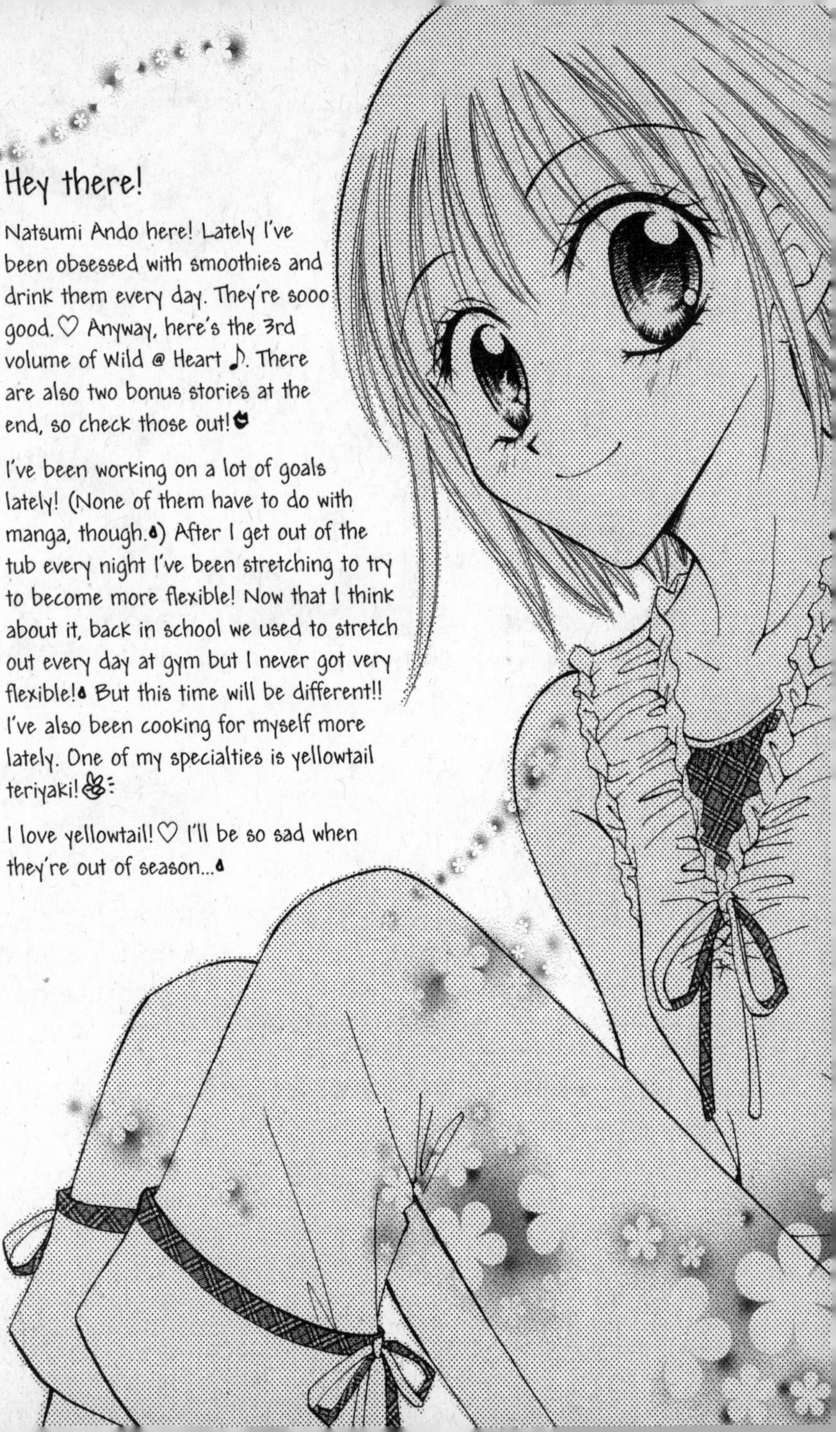

Hey there!

Natsumi Ando here! Lately I've been obsessed with smoothies and drink them every day. They're sooo good.♡ Anyway, here's the 3rd volume of Wild @ Heart ♪. There are also two bonus stories at the end, so check those out!

I've been working on a lot of goals lately! (None of them have to do with manga, though.) After I get out of the tub every night I've been stretching to try to become more flexible! Now that I think about it, back in school we used to stretch out every day at gym but I never got very flexible! But this time will be different!! I've also been cooking for myself more lately. One of my specialties is yellowtail teriyaki!

I love yellowtail!♡ I'll be so sad when they're out of season...

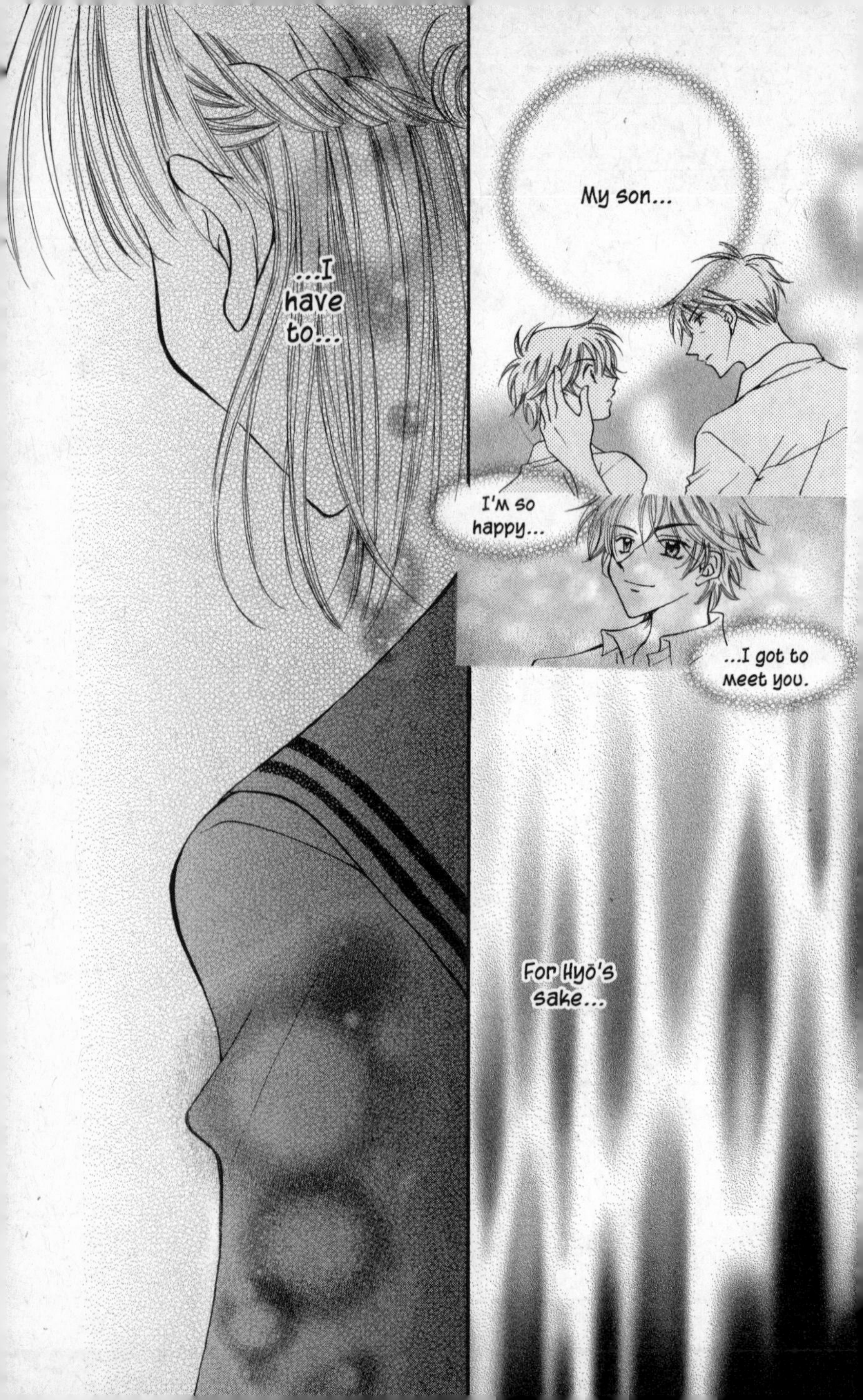
My son...
I'm so happy...
...I got to meet you.
For Hyō's sake...
...I have to...

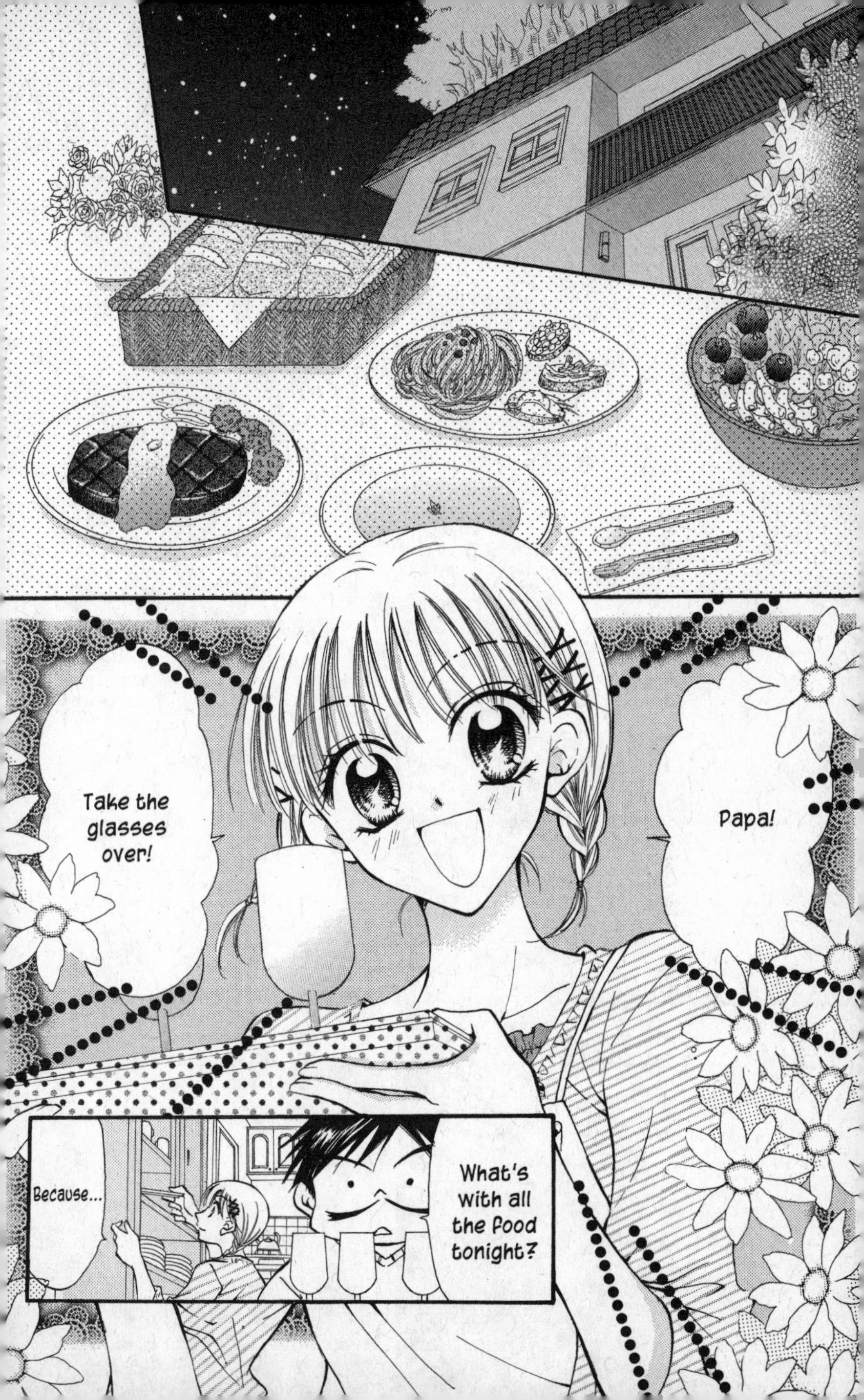
Papa!
Take the glasses over!
What's with all the food tonight?
Because...

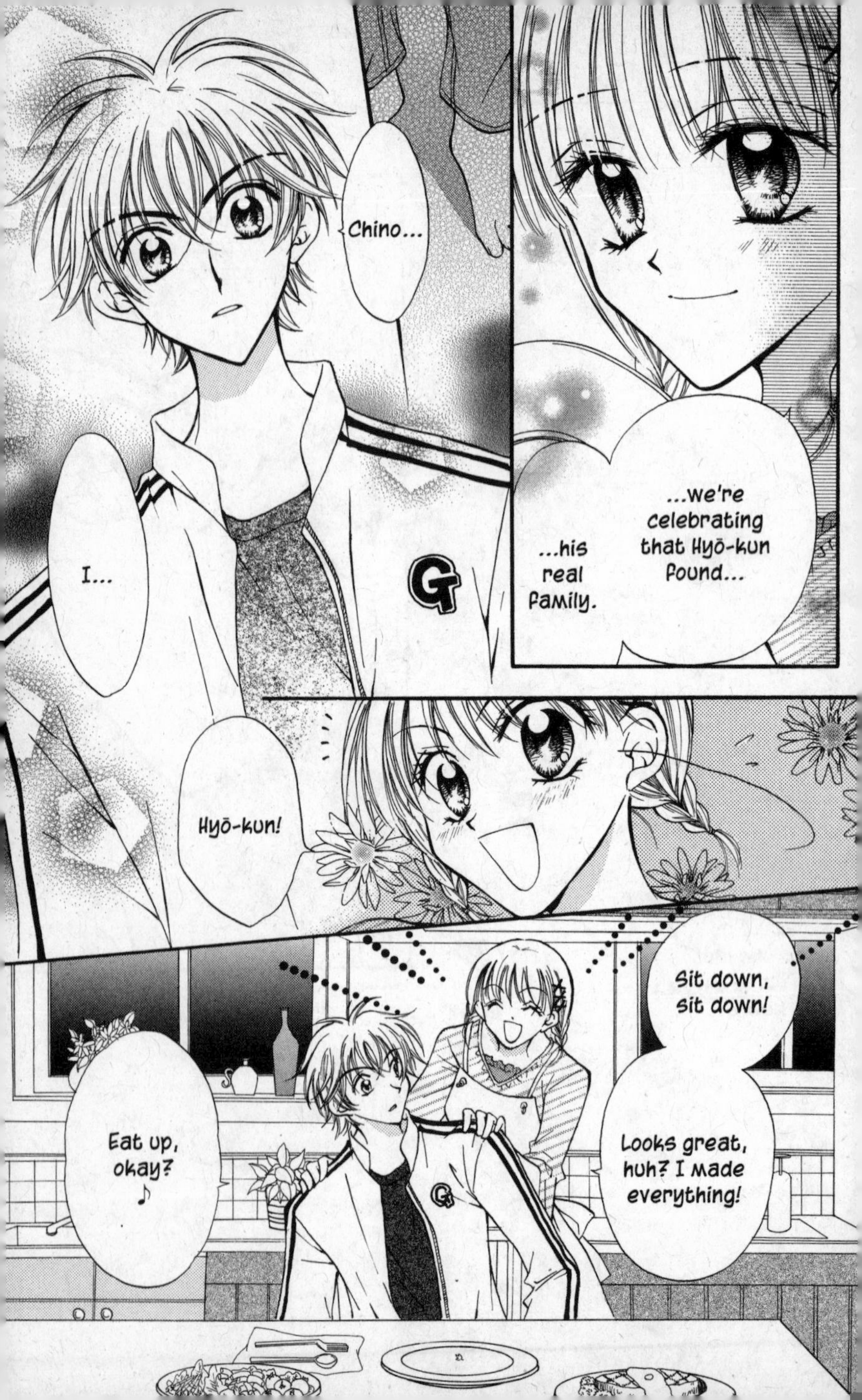
Chino...
...we're celebrating that Hyō-kun found...
...his real family.
I...
Hyō-kun!
Sit down, sit down!
Looks great, huh? I made everything!
Eat up, okay? ♪

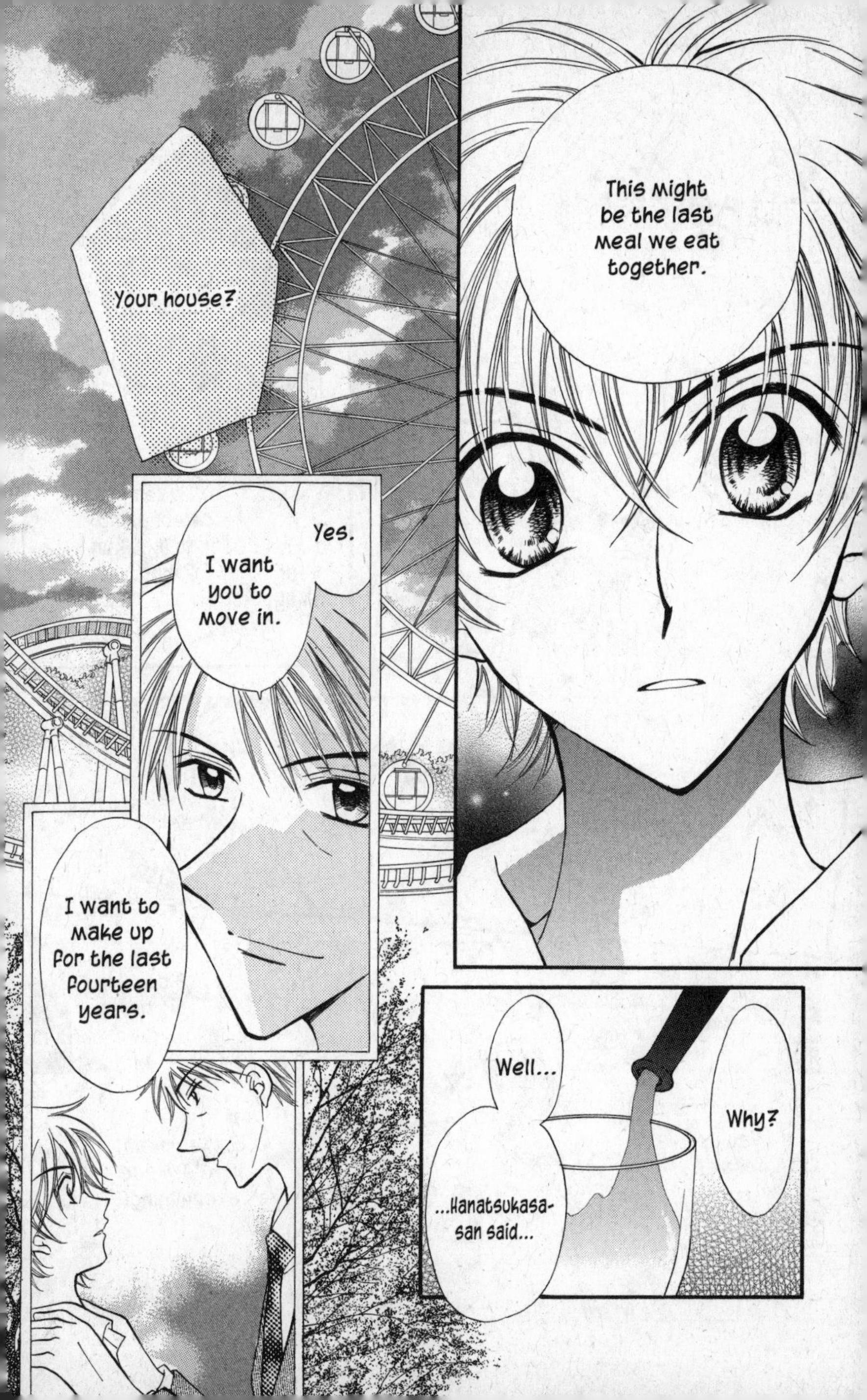
This might be the last meal we eat together.
Why?
Well...
...Hanatsukasa-san said...
Your house?
Yes.
I want you to move in.
I want to make up for the last fourteen years.

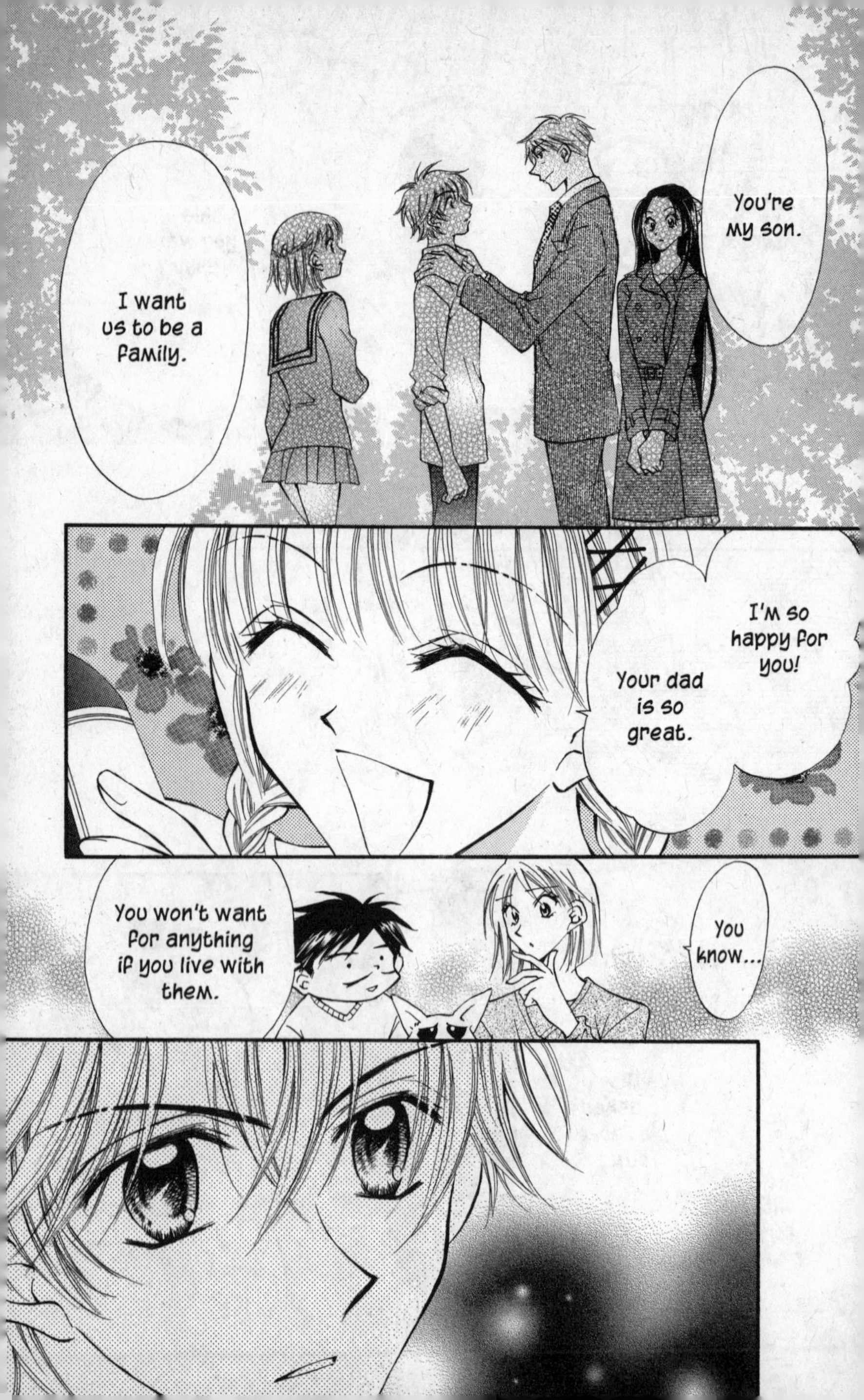
You're my son.
I want us to be a family.
I'm so happy for you!
Your dad is so great.
You know...
You won't want for anything if you live with them.

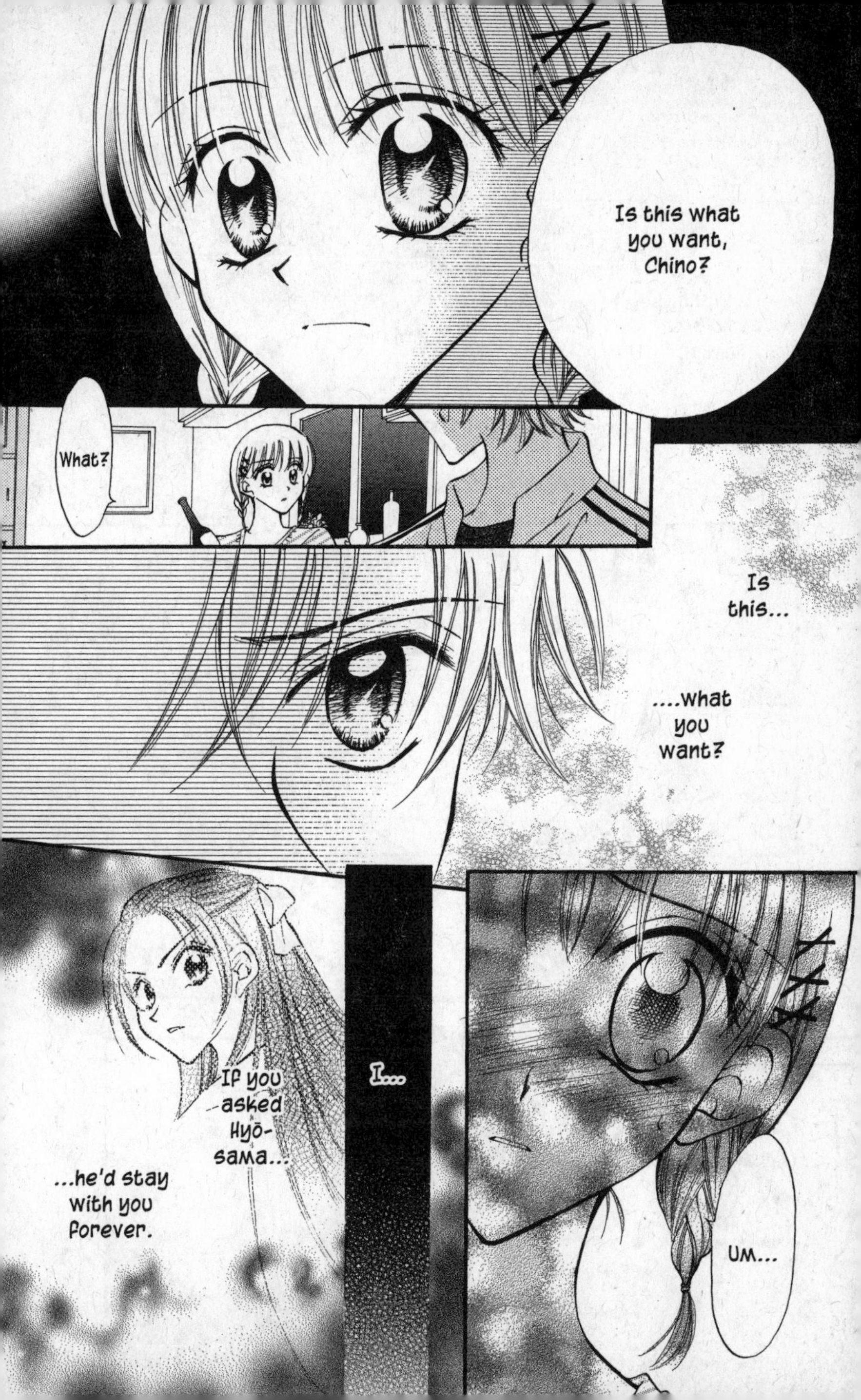
Is this what you want, Chino?
What?
Is this...
....what you want?
Um...
I...
If you asked Hyō-sama...
...he'd stay with you forever.

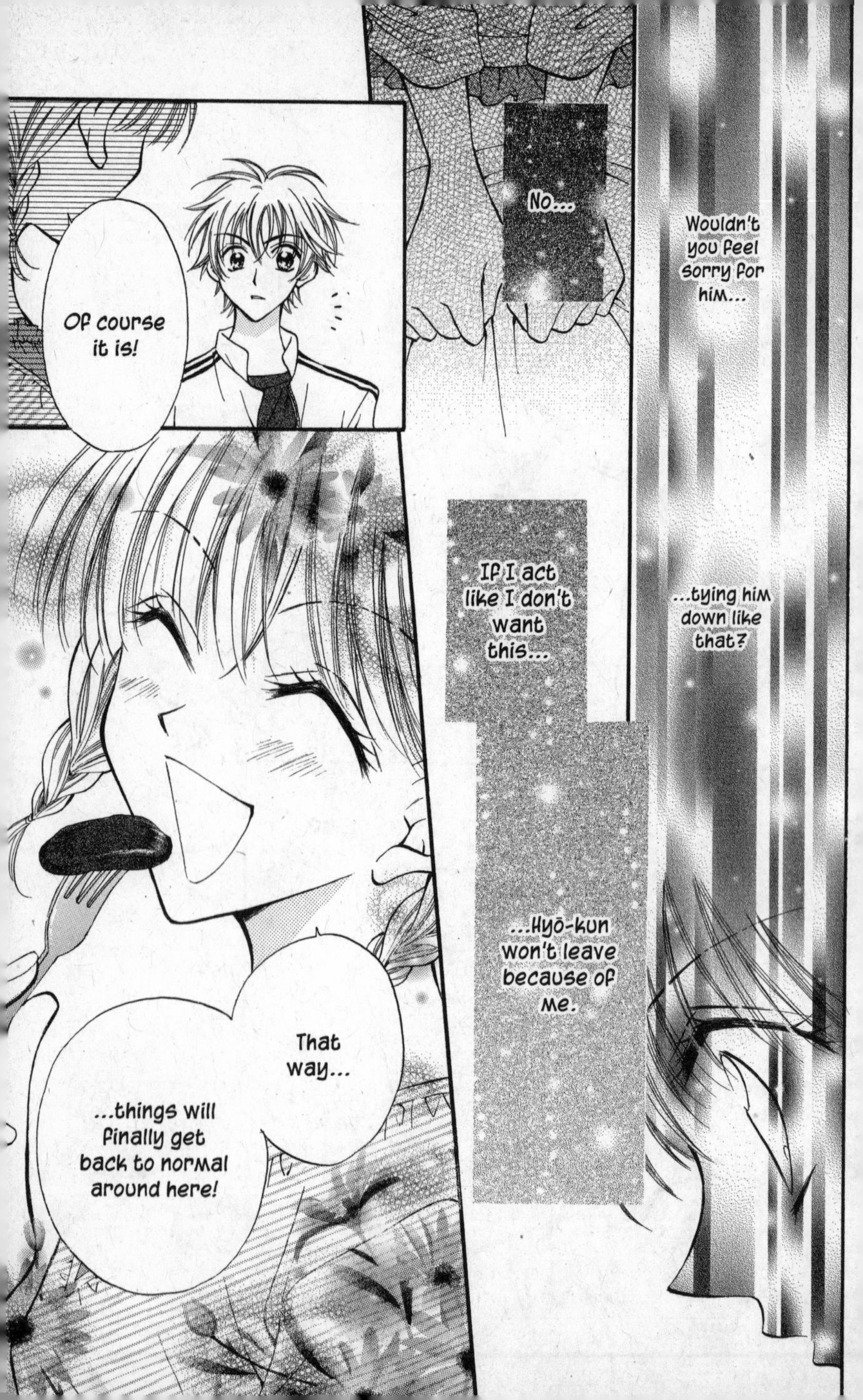
Wouldn't you feel sorry for him...
...tying him down like that?
No...
Of course it is!
If I act like I don't want this...
...Hyō-kun won't leave because of me.
That way...
...things will finally get back to normal around here!

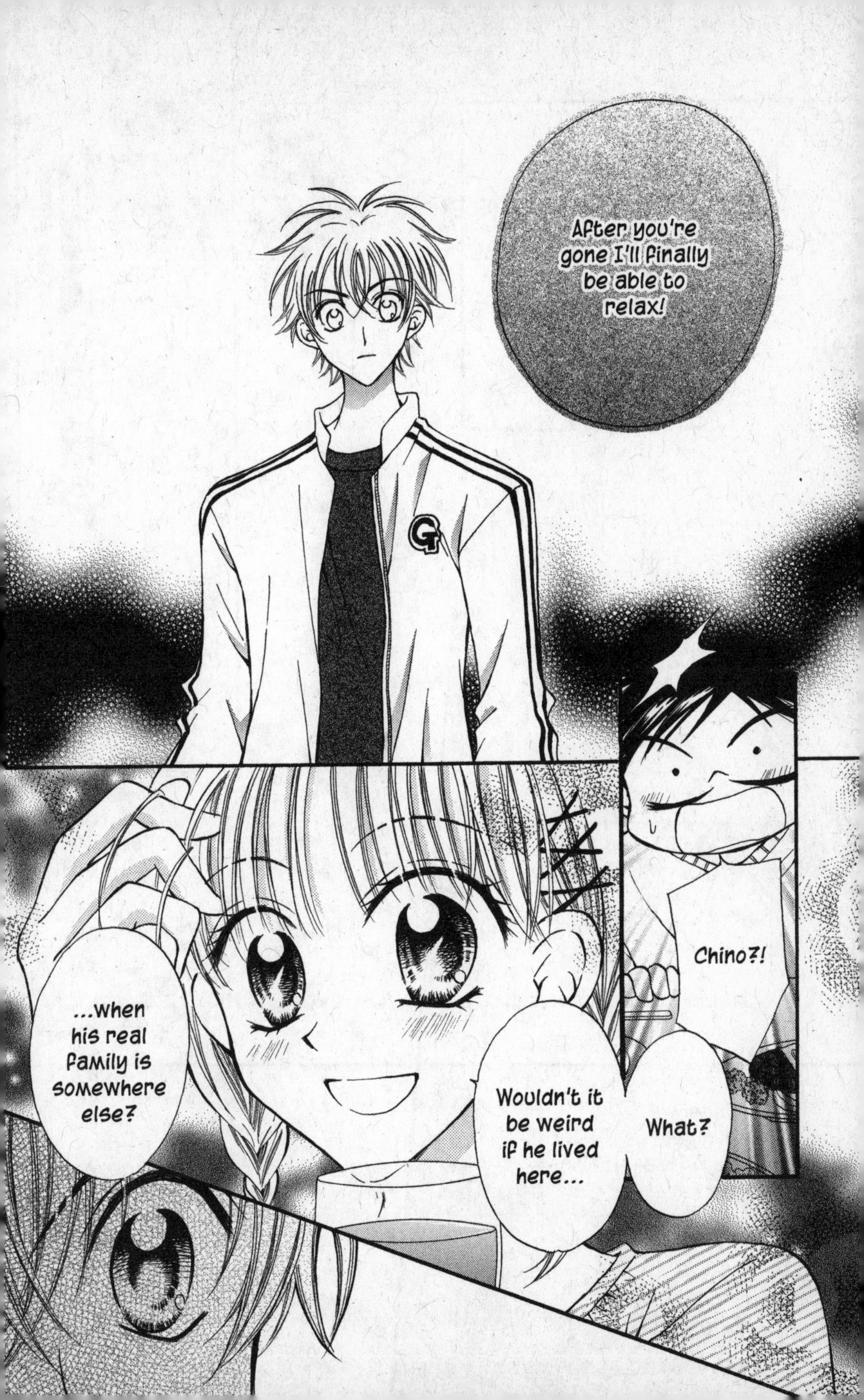
After you're gone I'll finally be able to relax!
Chino?!
What?
Wouldn't it be weird if he lived here...
...when his real family is somewhere else?

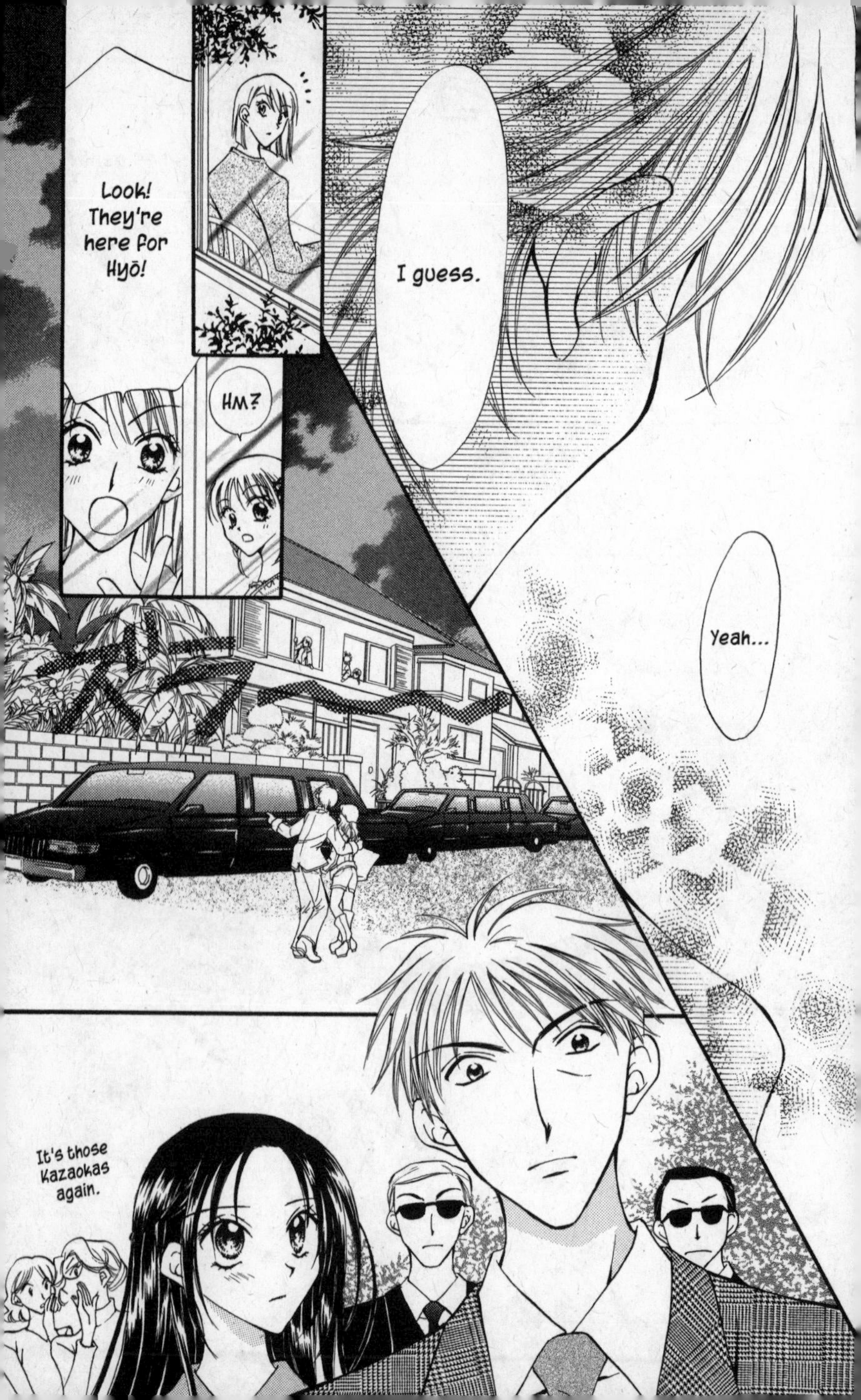
I guess.
Yeah...
Look! They're here for Hyō!
HM?
It's those Kazaokas again.

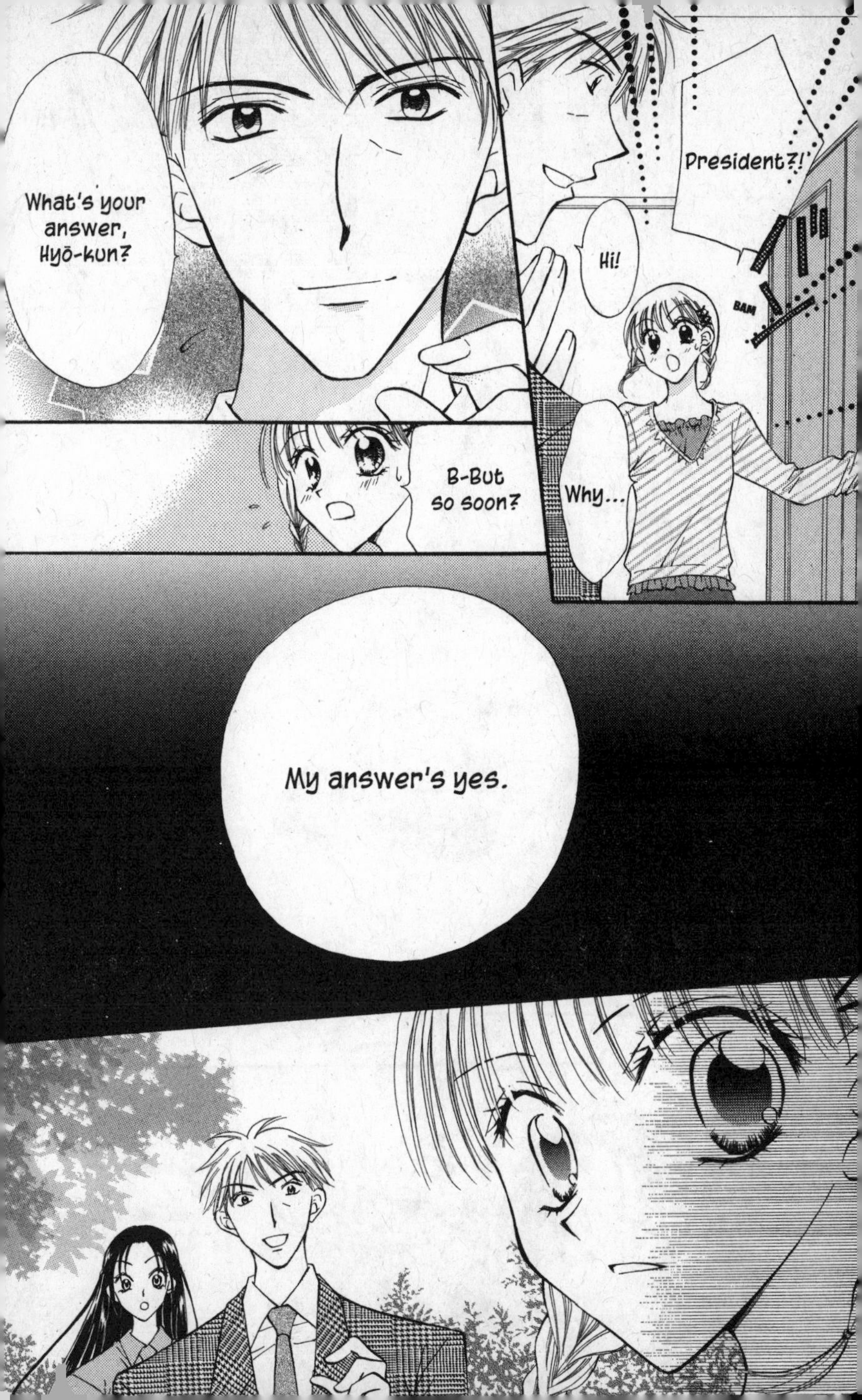
President?!
BAM
Hi!
Why...
What's your answer, Hyō-kun?
B-But so soon?
My answer's yes.

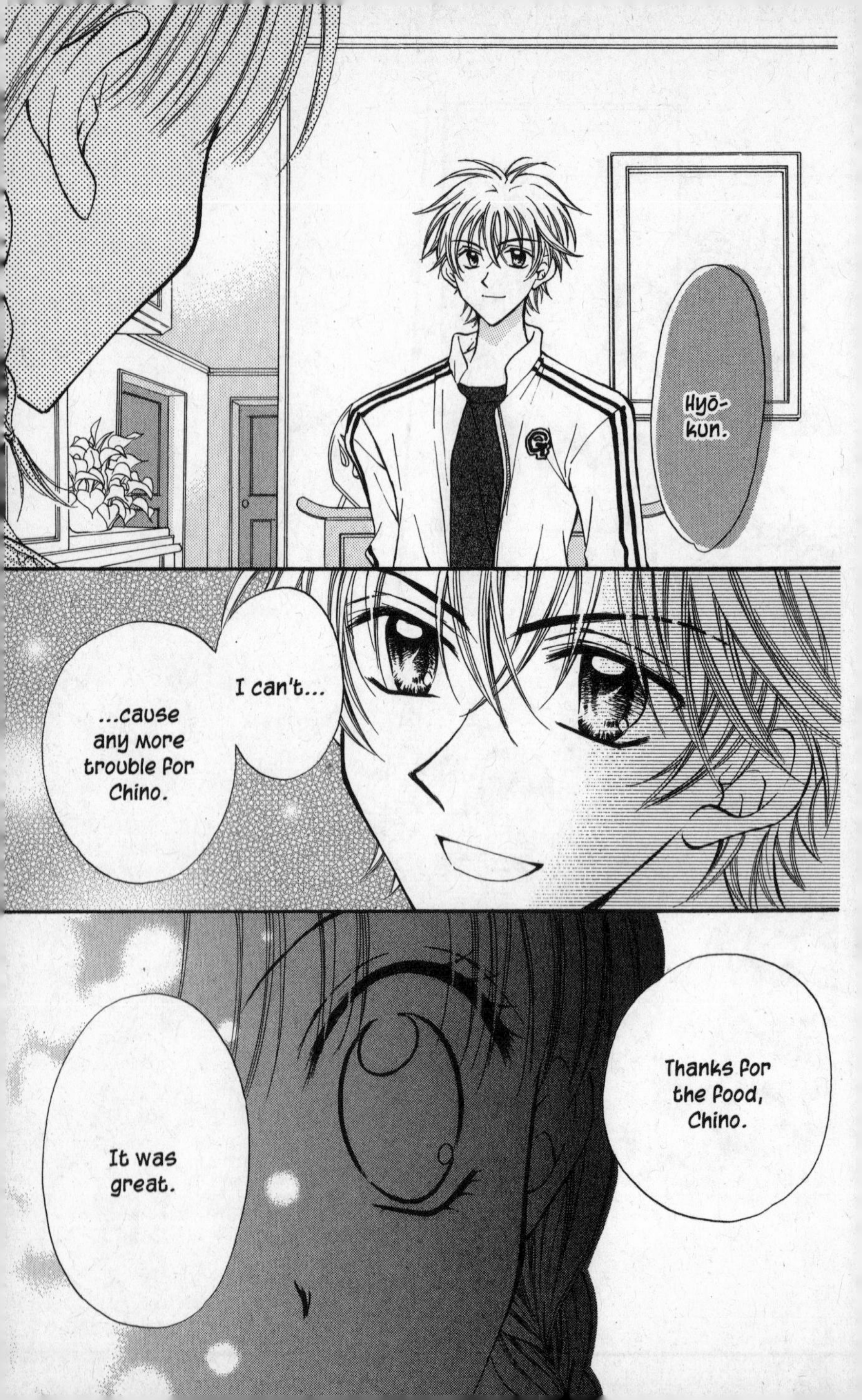
Hyō-kun.
I can't...
...cause any more trouble for Chino.
Thanks for the food, Chino.
It was great.

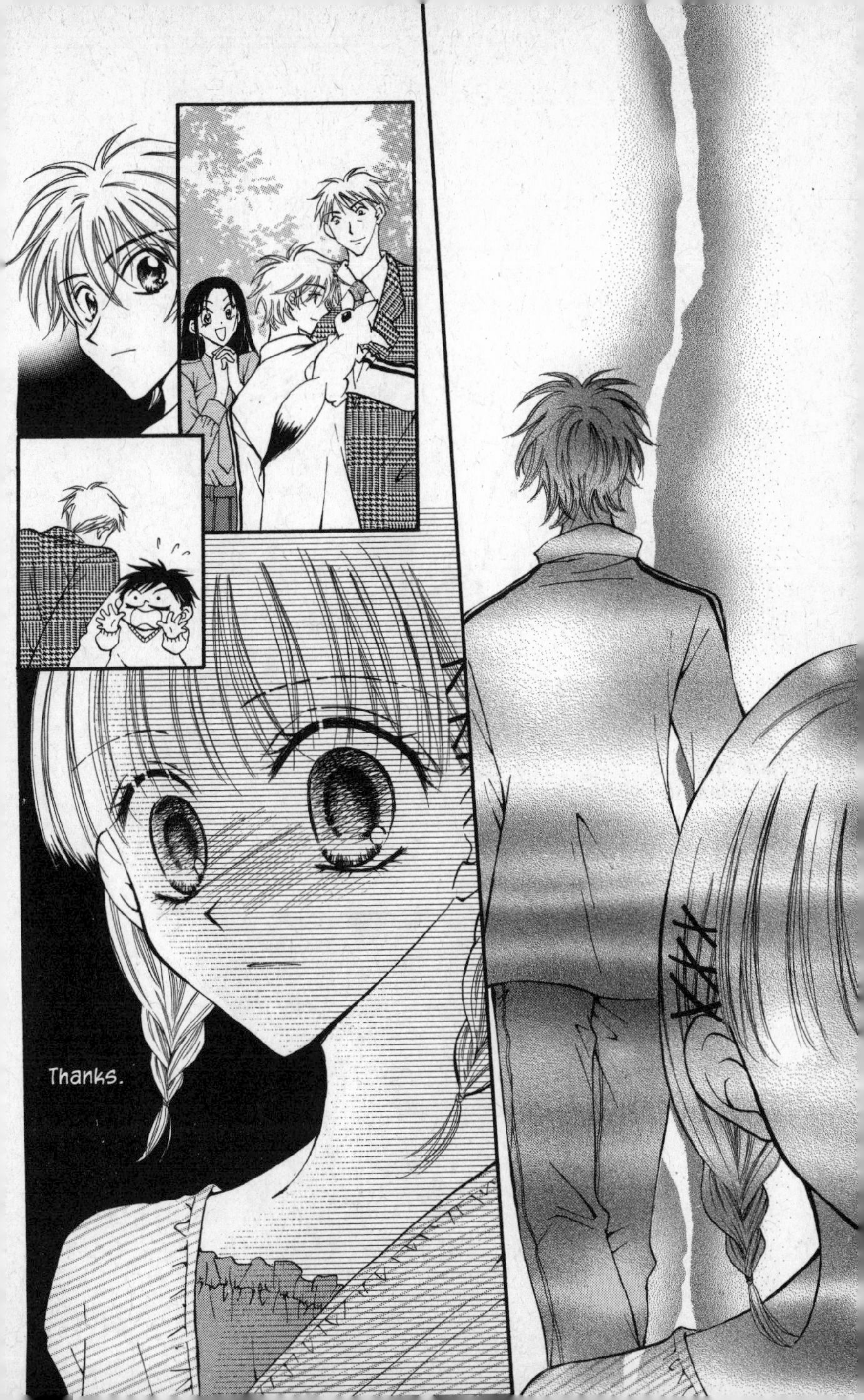
Thanks.

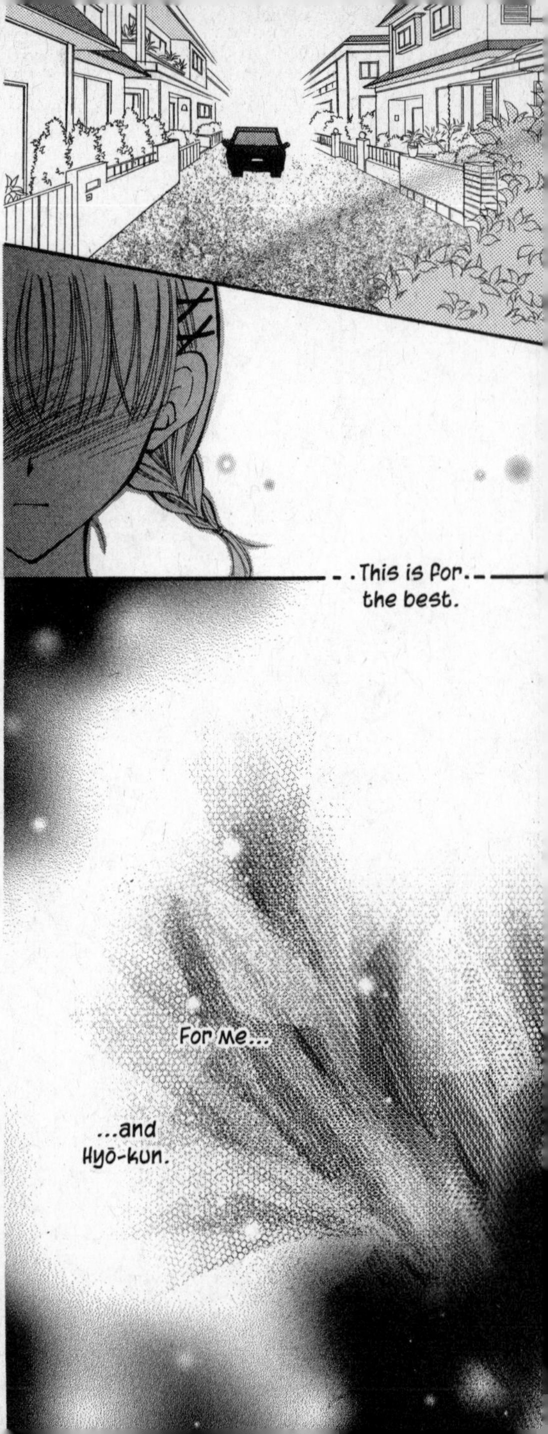

...This is for the best.
For me...
...and Hyō-kun.

1.

I went to the U.S. at the beginning of 2004! It was for work so I had to go on a certain train to Narita Airport. I knew I couldn't be late so I thought I left early enough, but it took longer than I expected. Also, I got the time the train left wrong! There was only a few minutes before it came before I even got to the station. Then I had to go a different way because there was construction being done! I thought all I had to do was just get on the escalator to the platform, so I dragged my suitcases along and saw...

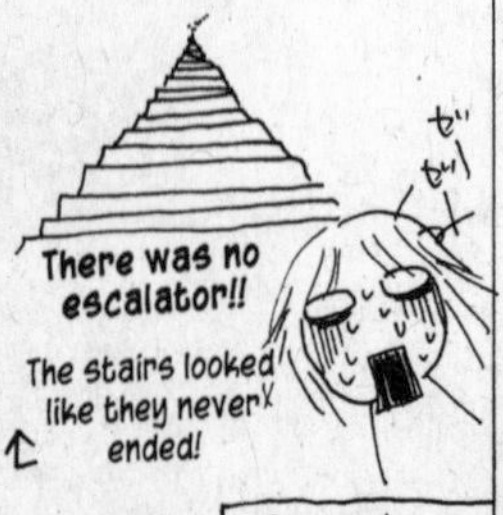

There was no escalator!!
The stairs looked like they never ended!

Continued in 2

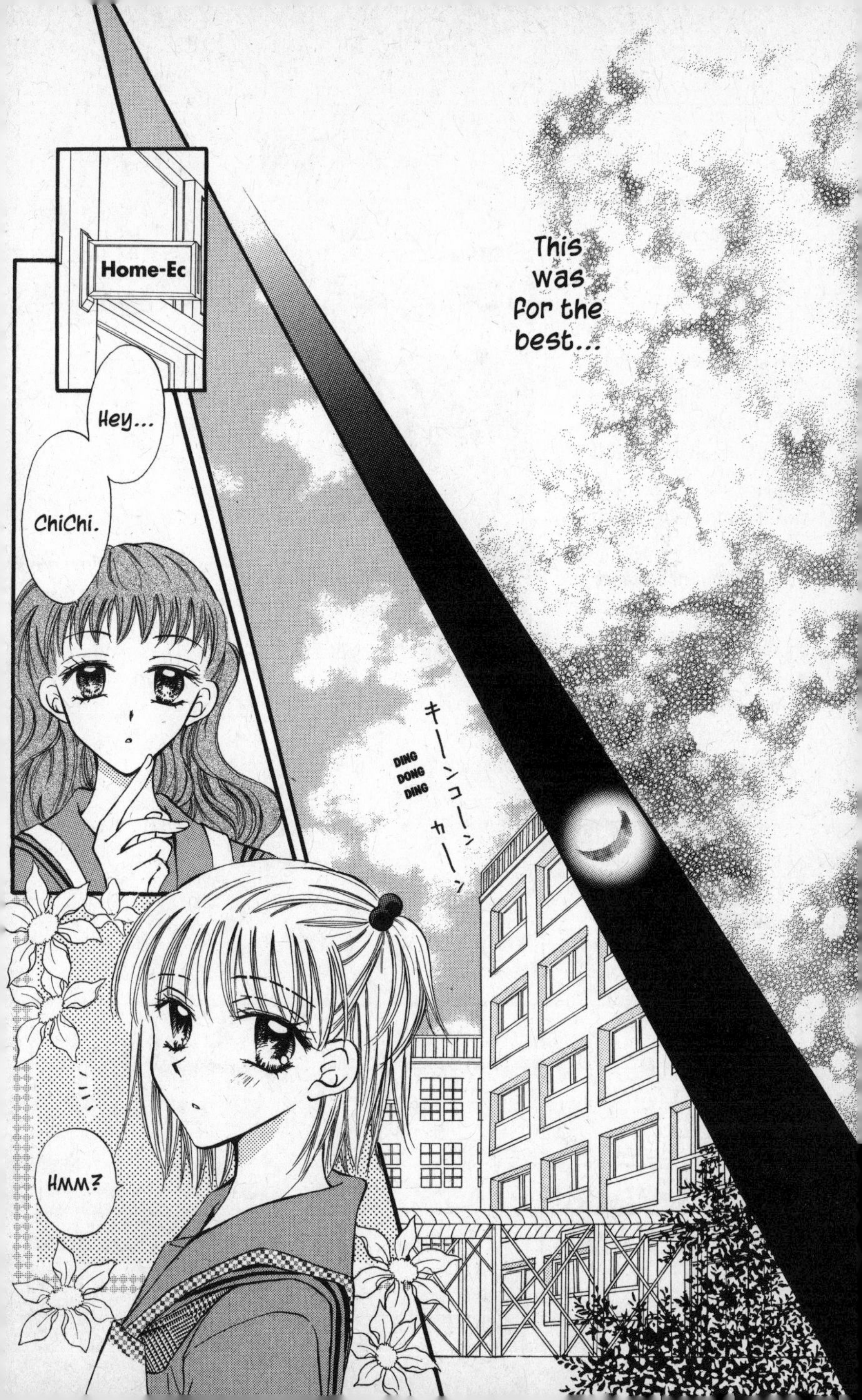
This was for the best...
Home-Ec
Hey...
ChiChi.
キーンコーン
カーン
DING DONG DING
...
Hmm?

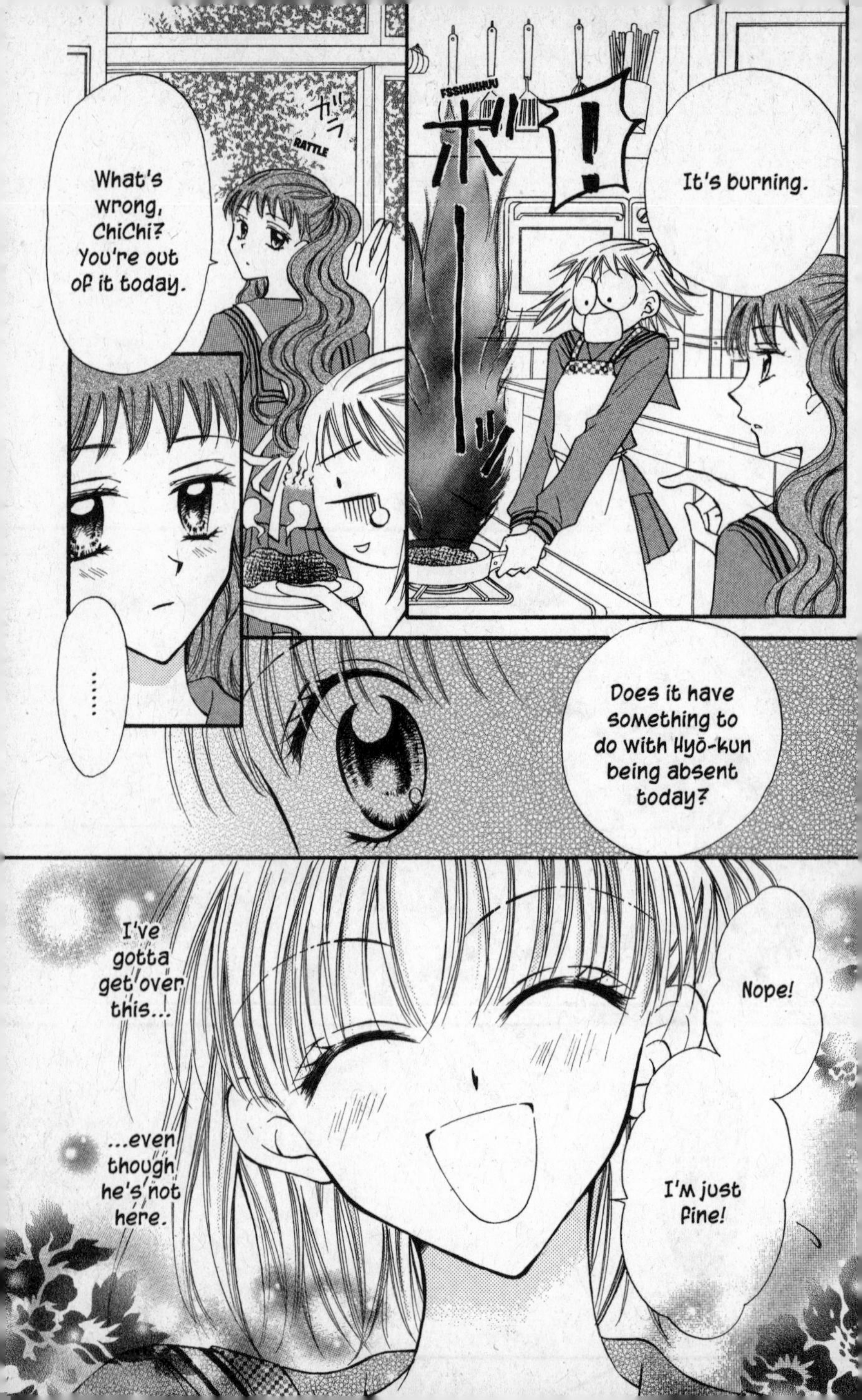
FSSHHHHUU
It's burning.
ガラ
RATTLE
What's wrong, ChiChi? You're out of it today.
……
Does it have something to do with Hyō-kun being absent today?
Nope!
I'm just fine!
I've gotta get over this...
...even though he's not here.

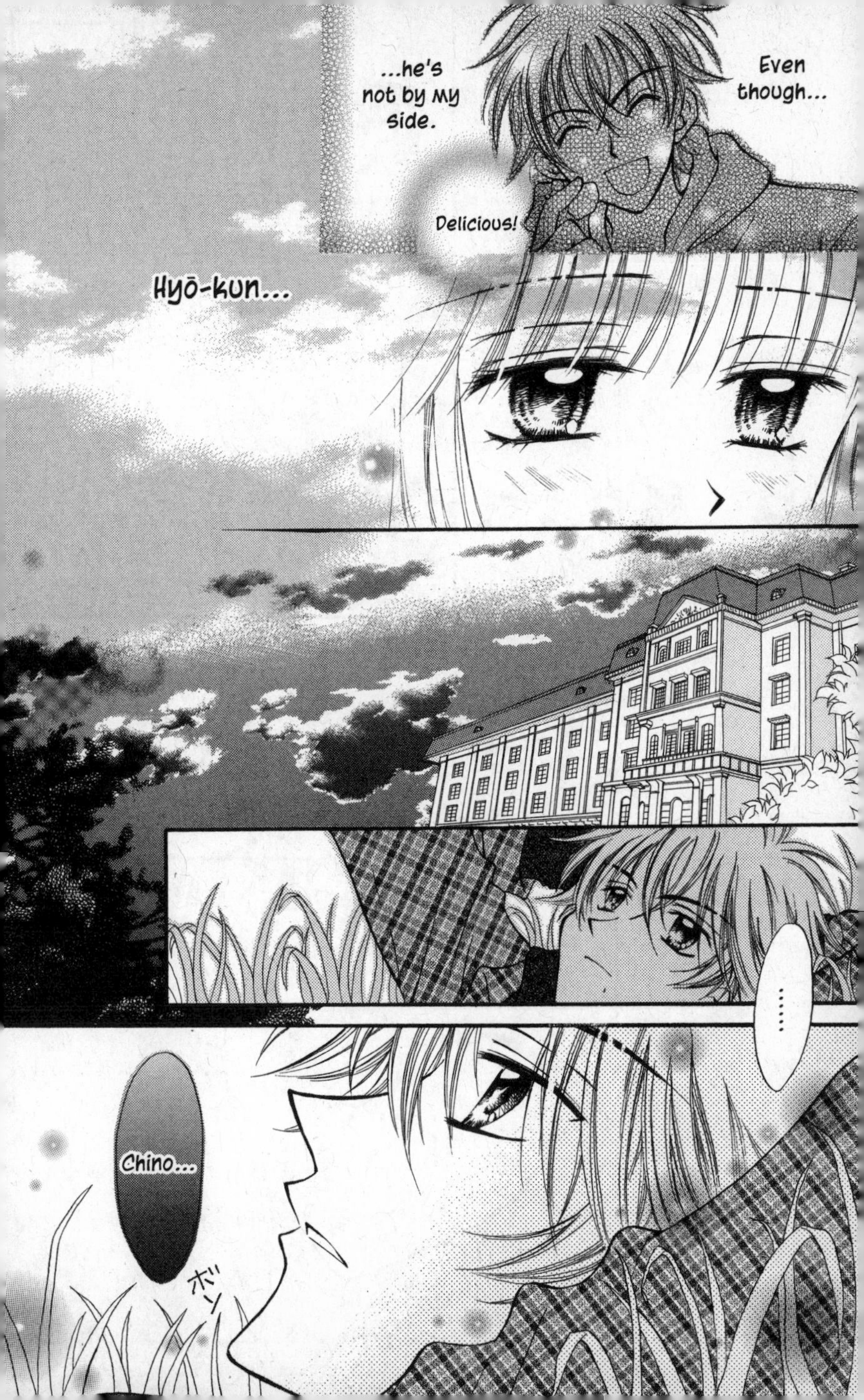
Even though...
...he's not by my side.
Delicious!
Hyō-kun...
......
Chino...
ボソ

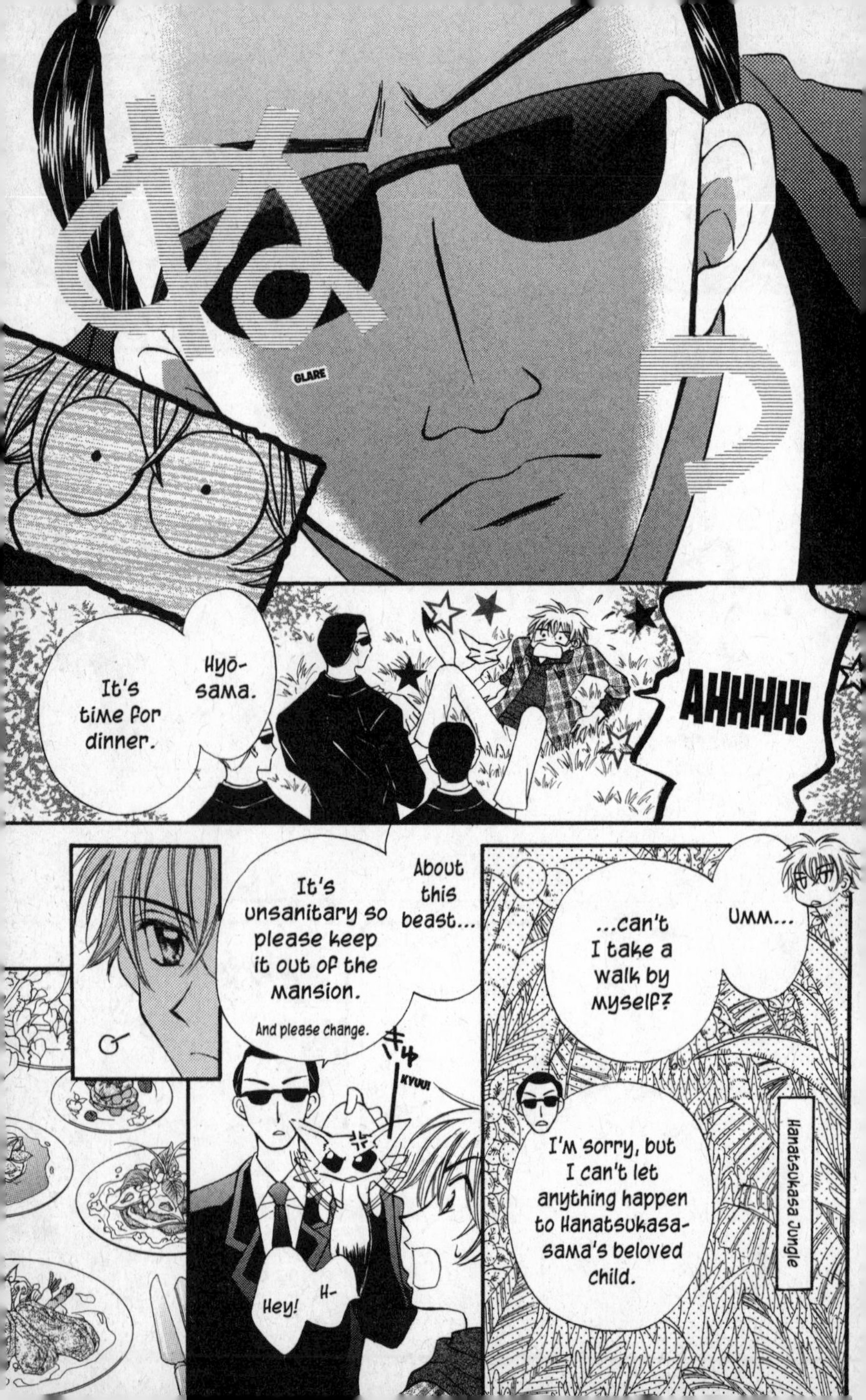
GLARE
AHHHH!
Hyō-sama.
It's time for dinner.
Umm...
...can't I take a walk by myself?
Hanatsukasa Jungle
I'm sorry, but I can't let anything happen to Hanatsukasa-sama's beloved child.
About this beast...
It's unsanitary so please keep it out of the mansion.
And please change.
キュ
KYUU!
H-
Hey!

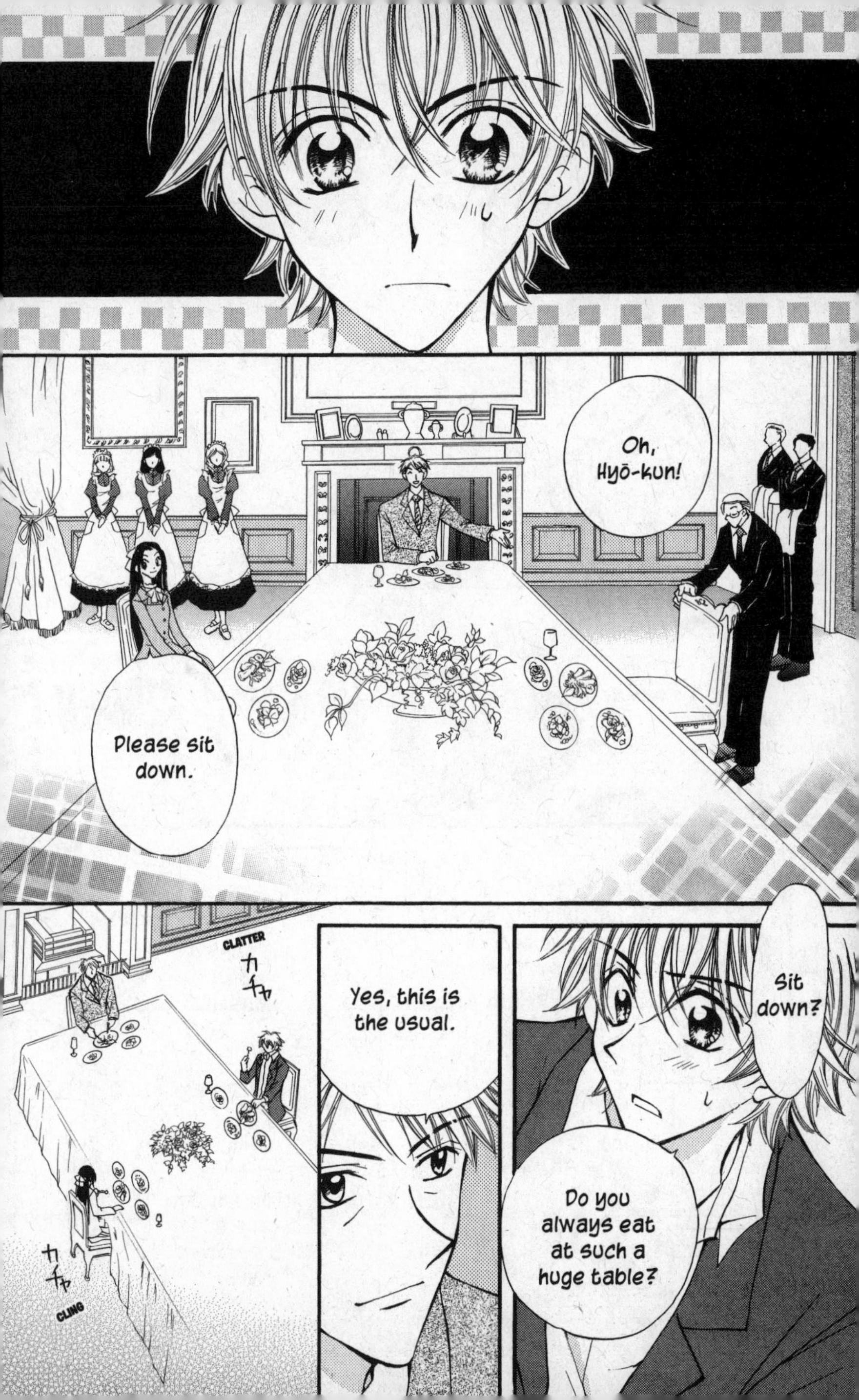
Oh, Hyō-kun!
Please sit down.
Sit down?
Do you always eat at such a huge table?
Yes, this is the usual.
CLATTER
カチャ
カチャ
CLING

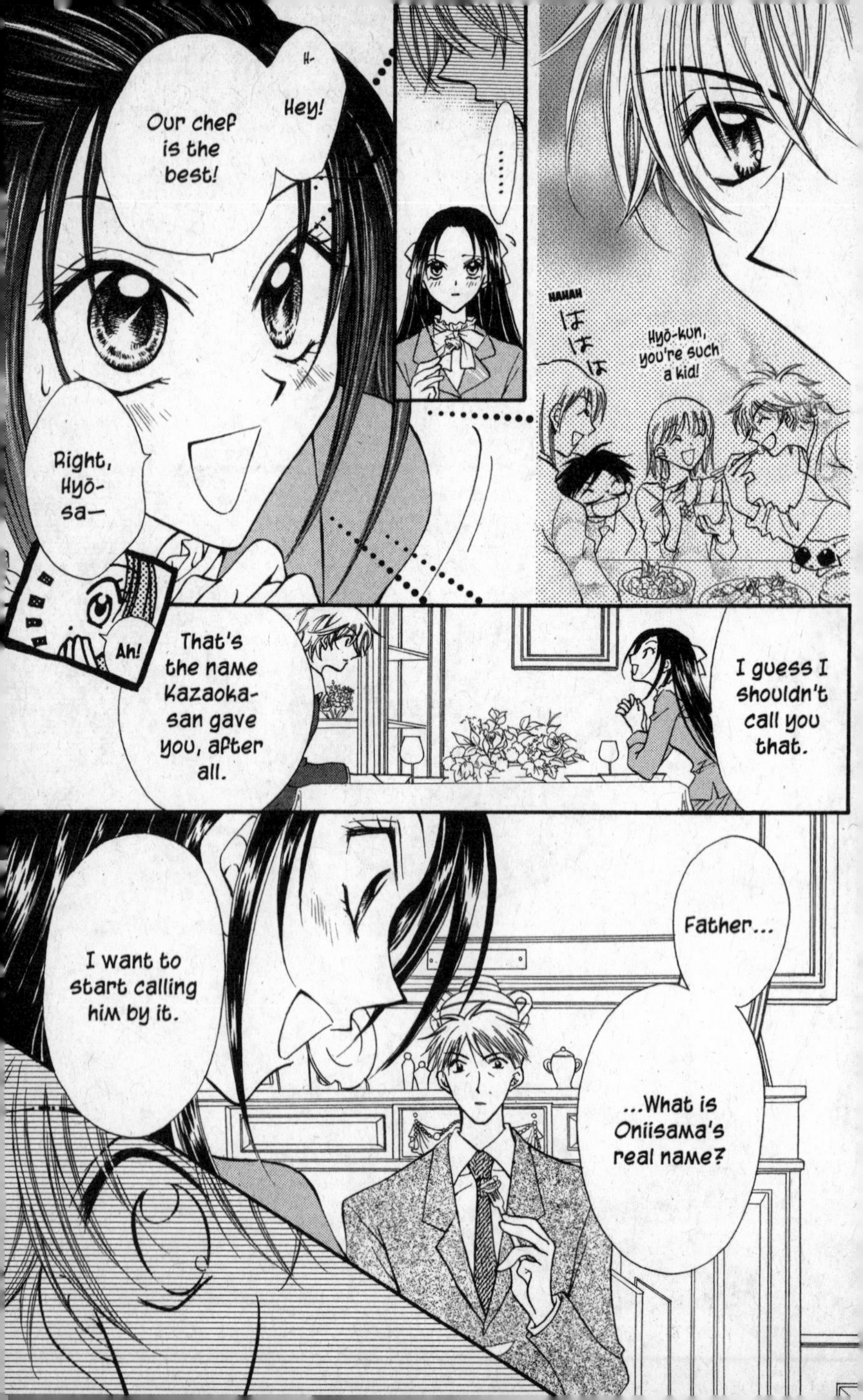
HAHAH
ははは
Hyō-kun, you're such a kid!
......
H-
Hey!
Our chef is the best!
Right, Hyō-sa—
...
Ah!
I guess I shouldn't call you that.
That's the name Kazaoka-san gave you, after all.
Father...
...What is Oniisama's real name?
I want to start calling him by it.

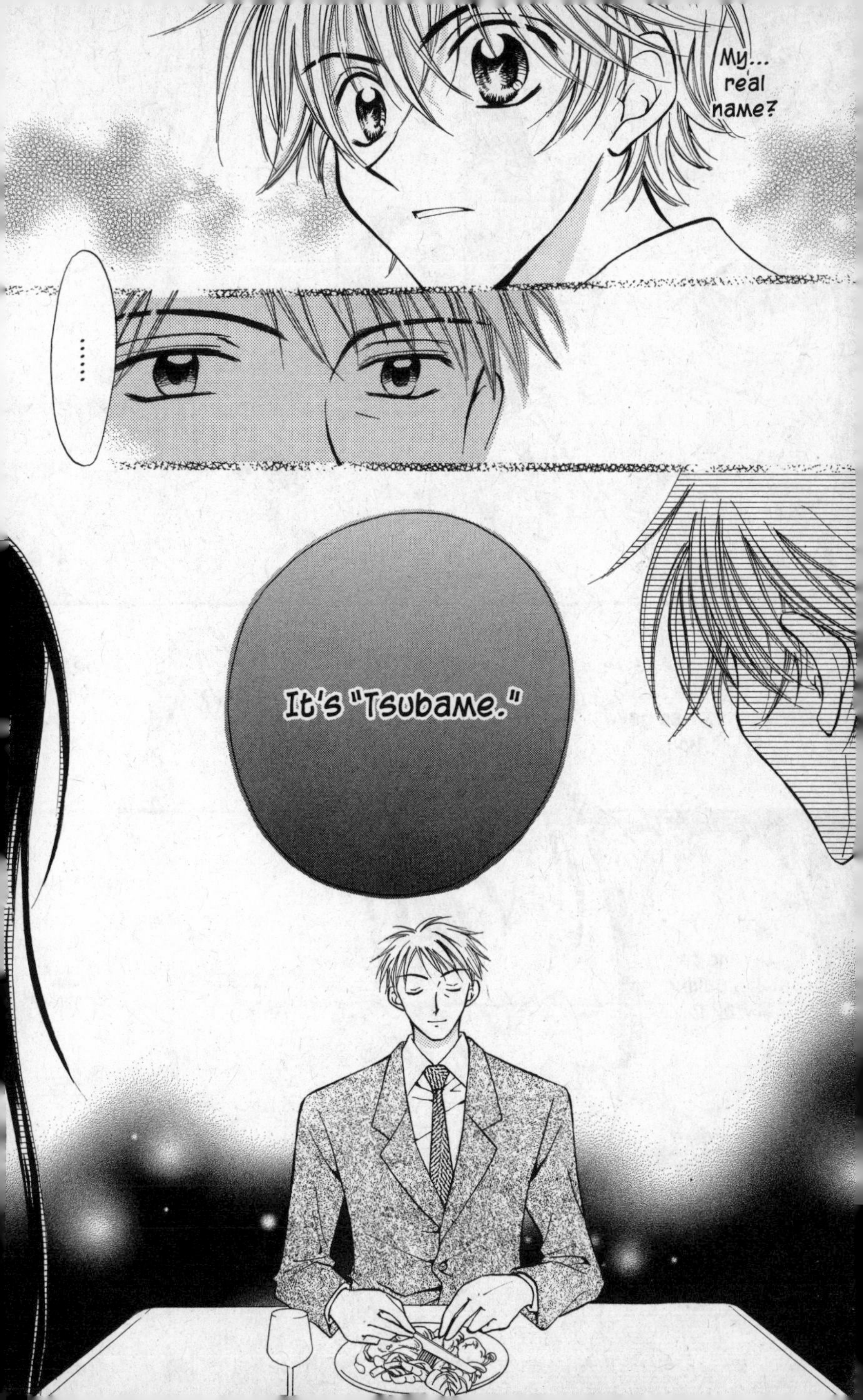
My... real name?
......
It's "Tsubame."

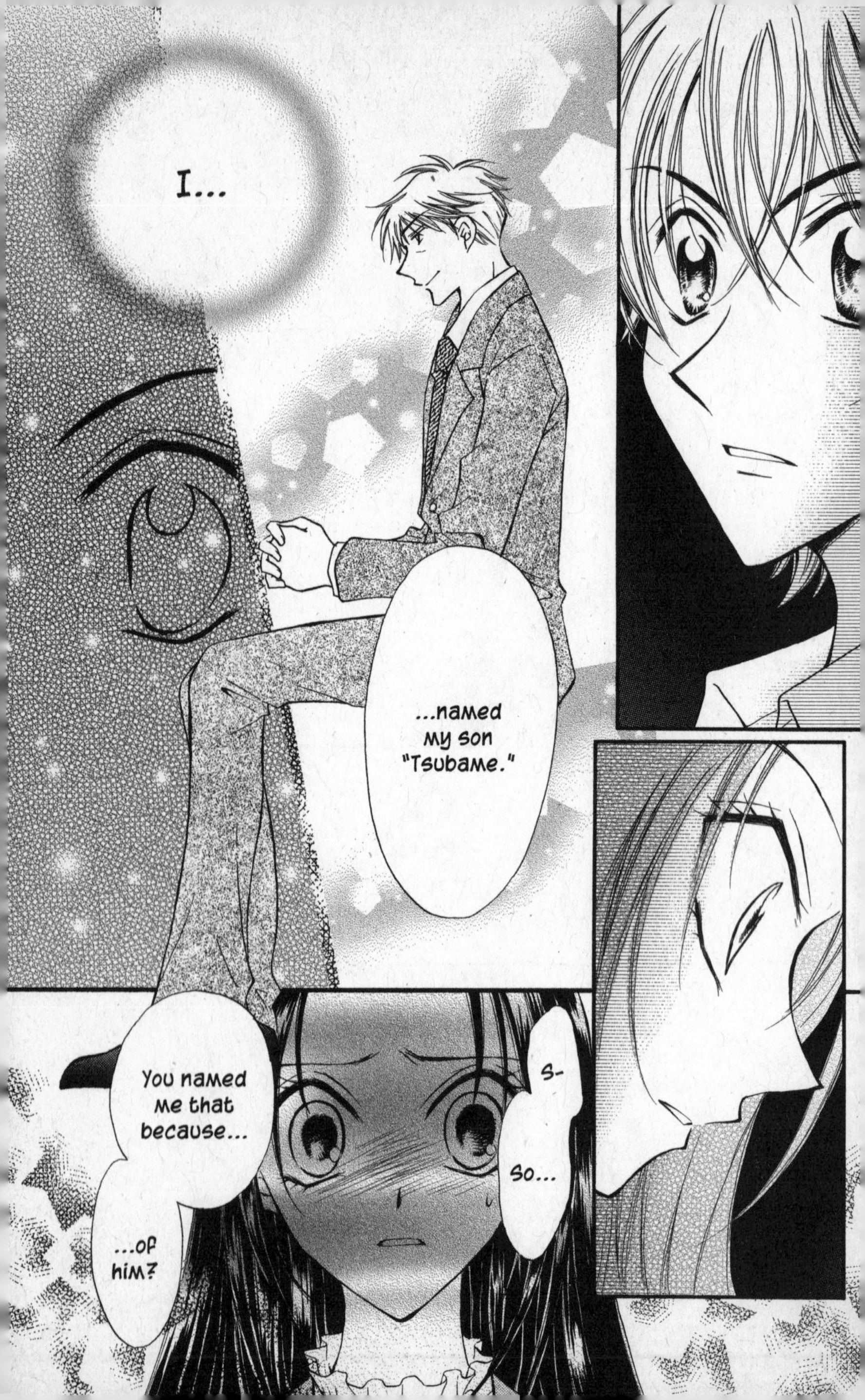
I...
...named my son "Tsubame."
S-
So...
You named me that because...
...of him?

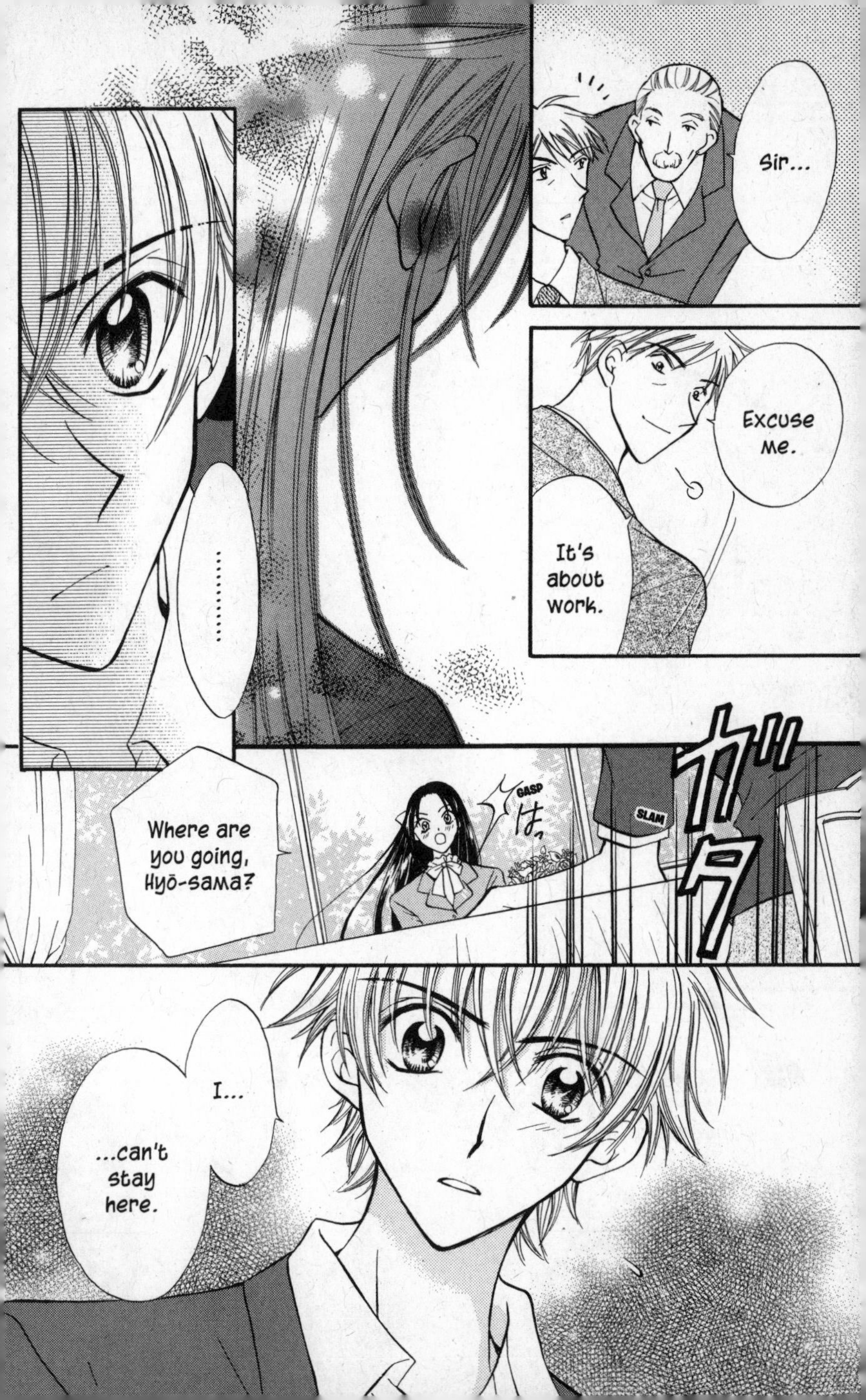
Sir...
Excuse me.
It's about work.
......
ガタ
SLAM
GASP
はっ
Where are you going, Hyō-sama?
I...
...can't stay here.

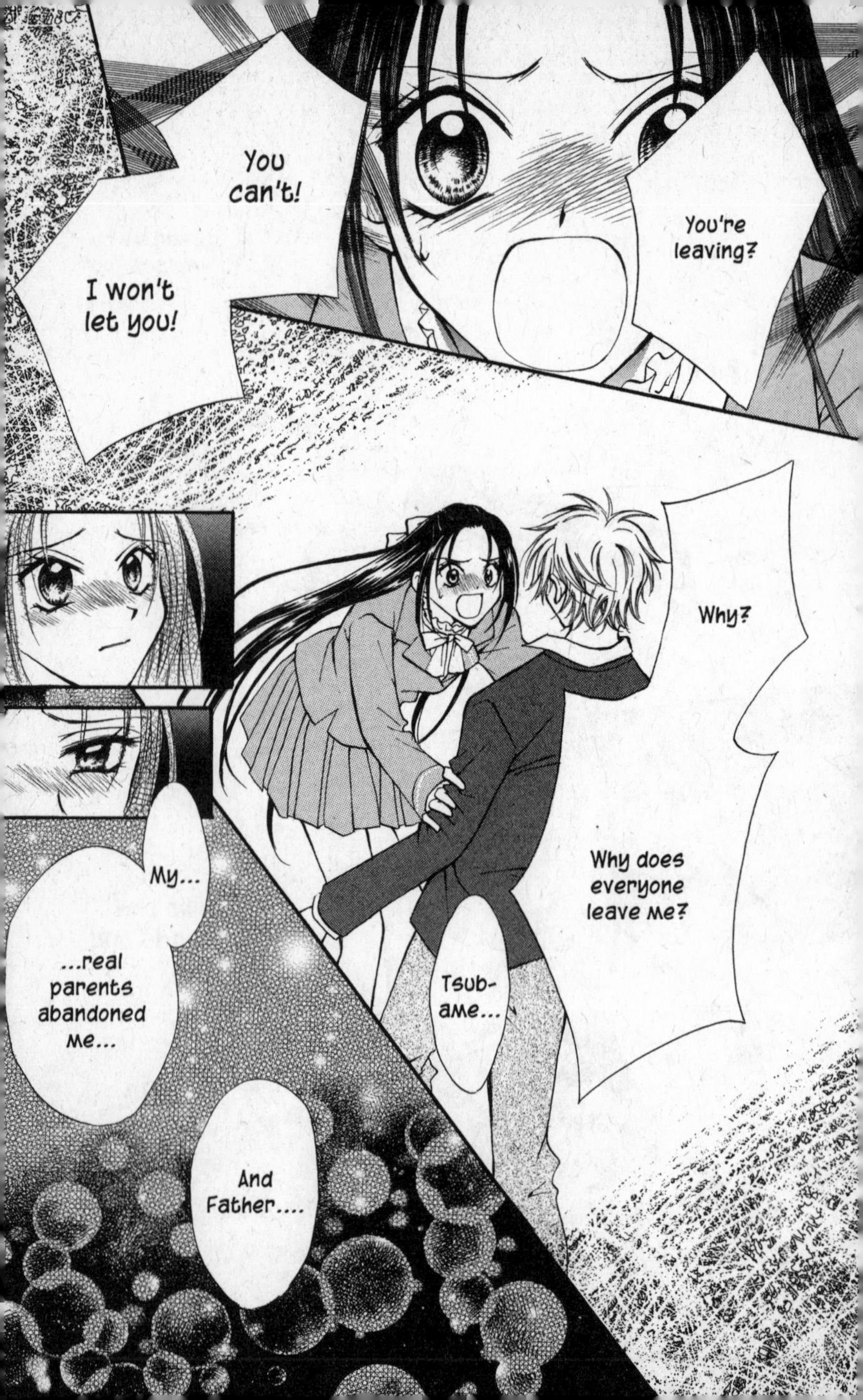
You're leaving?
You can't!
I won't let you!
Why?
Why does everyone leave me?
Tsub-ame...
My...
...real parents abandoned me...
And Father....

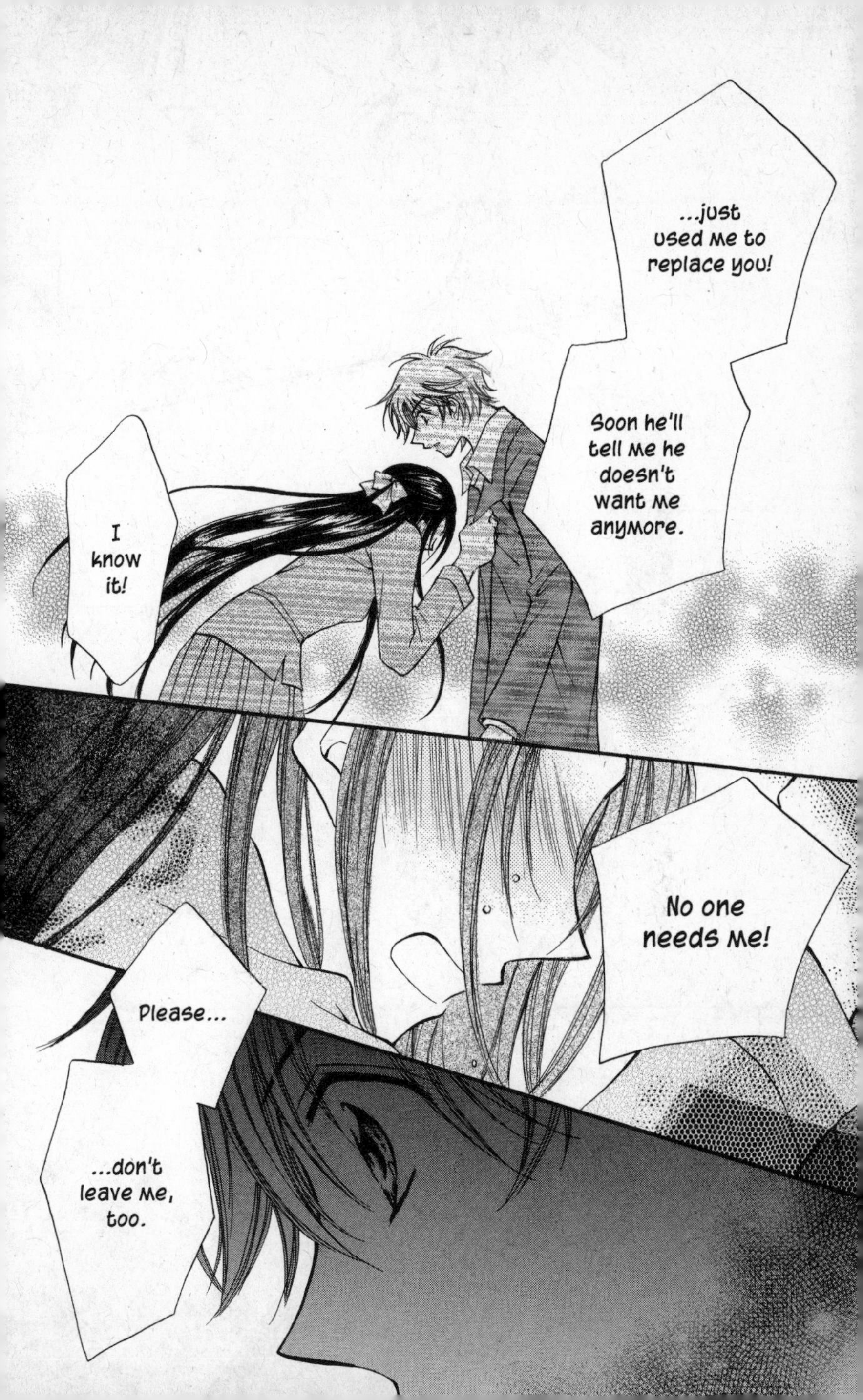
...just used me to replace you!
Soon he'll tell me he doesn't want me anymore.
I know it!
No one needs me!
Please...
...don't leave me, too.

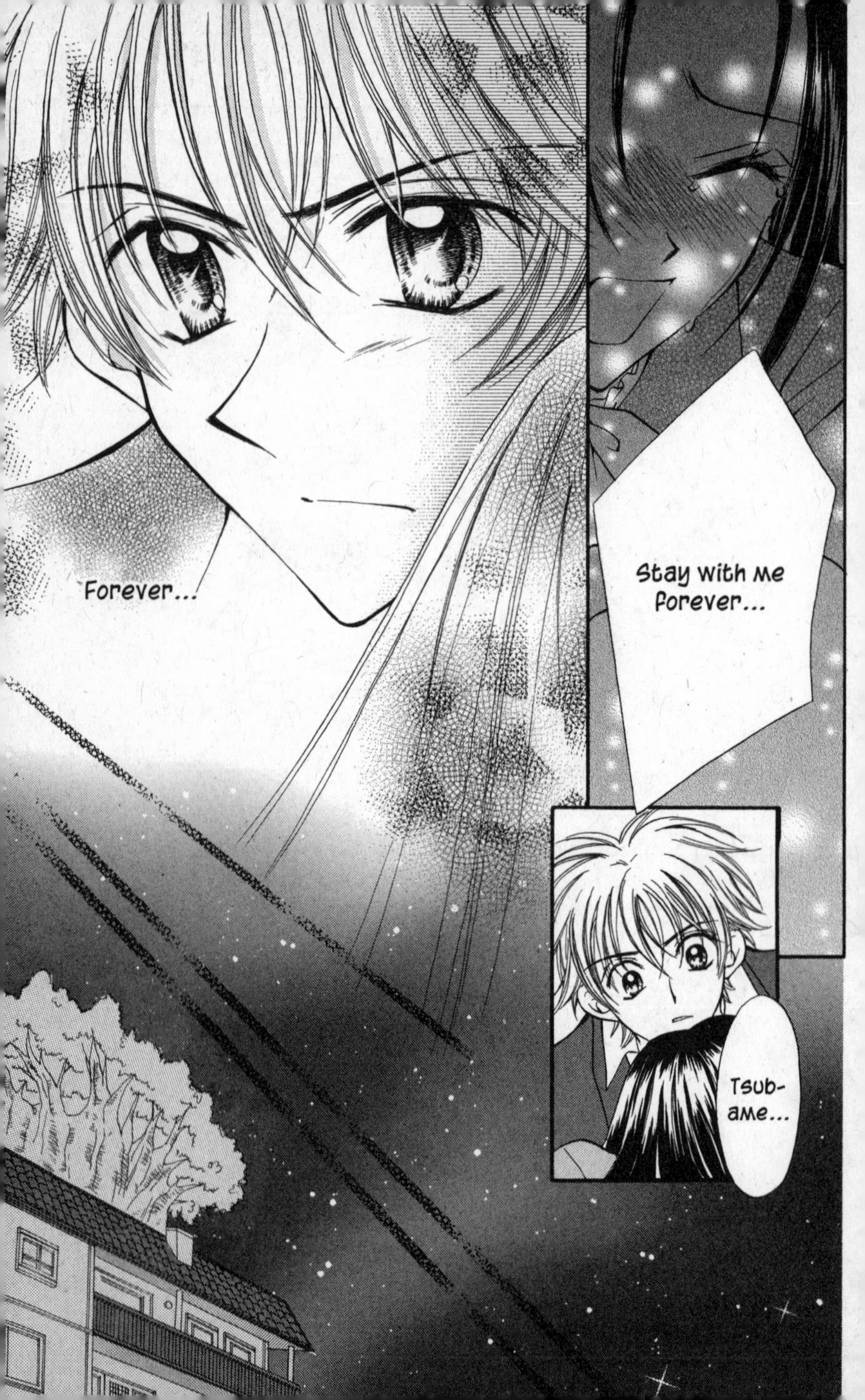
Stay with me forever...
Tsub-ame...
Forever...

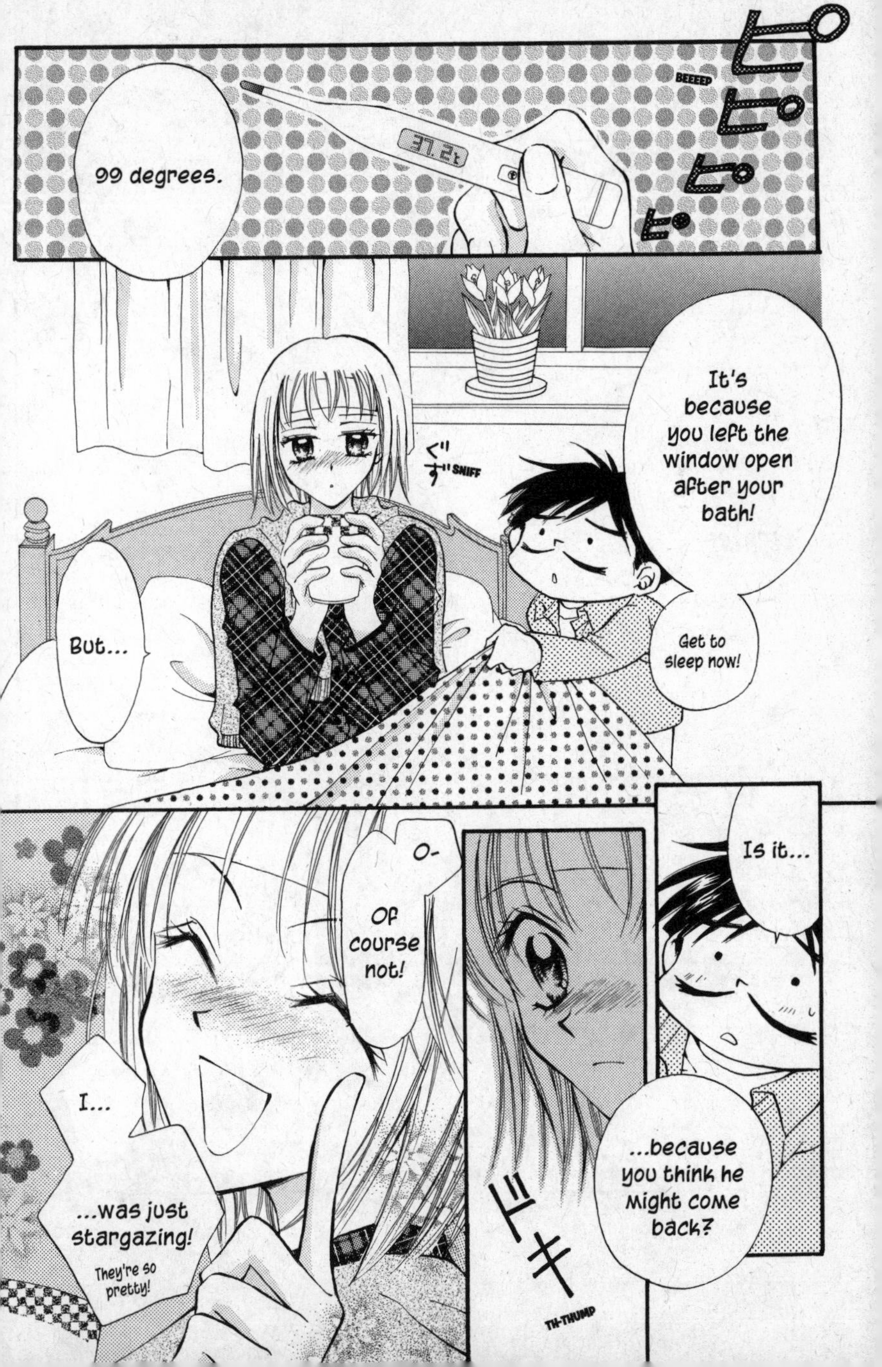
ピピピピ
BEEEP
99 degrees.
It's because you left the window open after your bath!
ぐず
SNIFF
Get to sleep now!
But...
Is it...
...because you think he might come back?
ドキ
TH-THUMP
O-
Of course not!
I...
...was just stargazing!
They're so pretty!

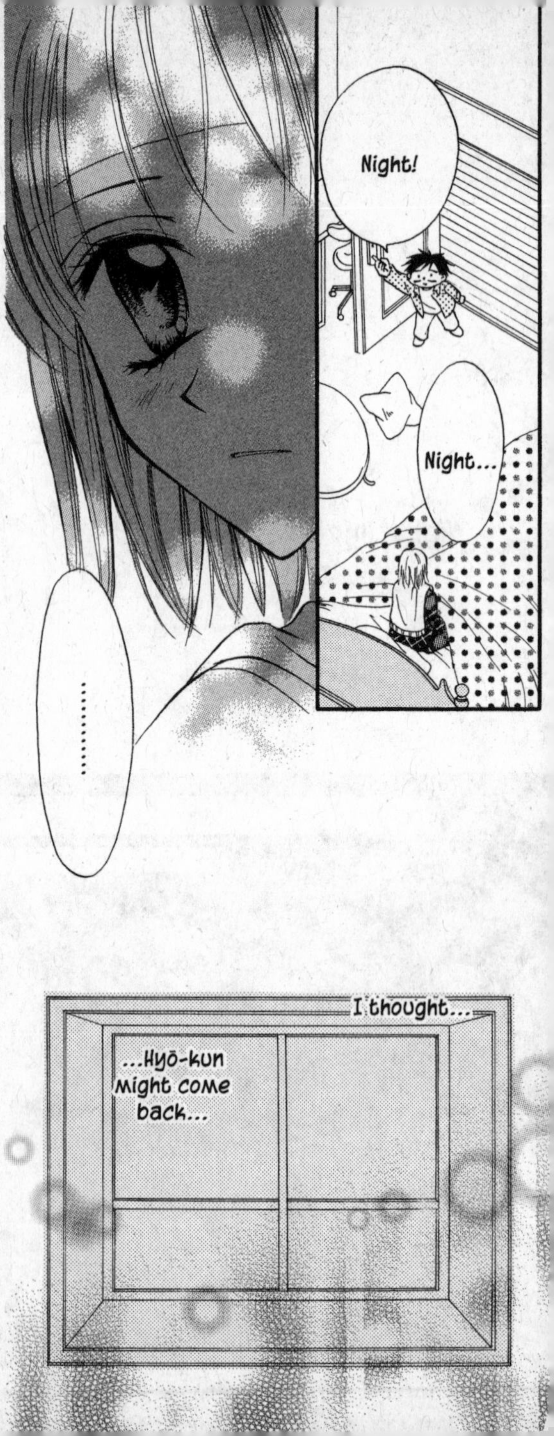
Night!
Night...
......
I thought...
...Hyō-kun might come back...

2.

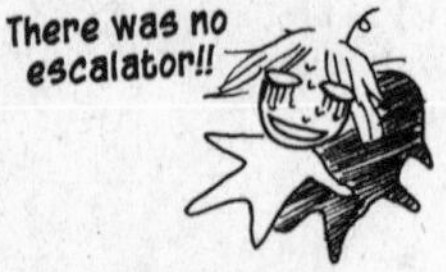
There was no escalator!!

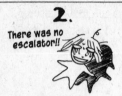

I prepared myself to be late. (Even if I might miss the train [sweatmark].) But I didn't give up! I got to the top of the stairs just as the bell rang!!!

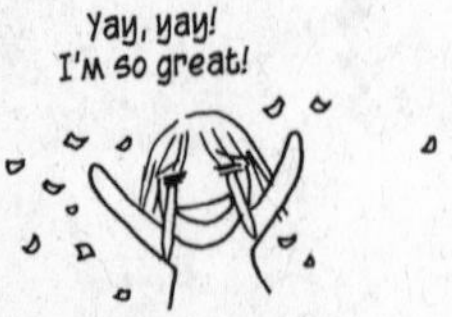
Yay, yay! I'm so great!

I was sore for a while. While I was climbing up I noticed another man struggling with a suitcase up the stairs. I wonder if he made it on time, too? He gave me the strength to keep going!

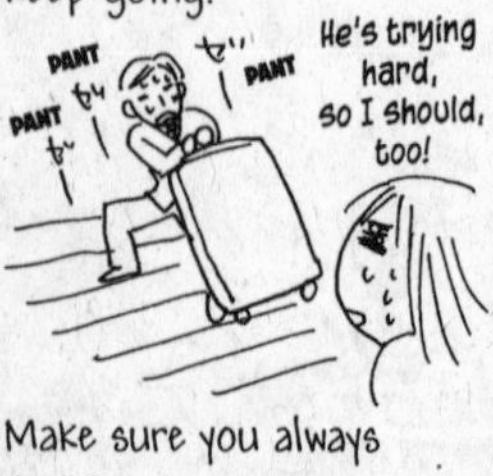
PANT
PANT
PANT
He's trying hard, so I should, too!

Make sure you always double-check the time the trains come!

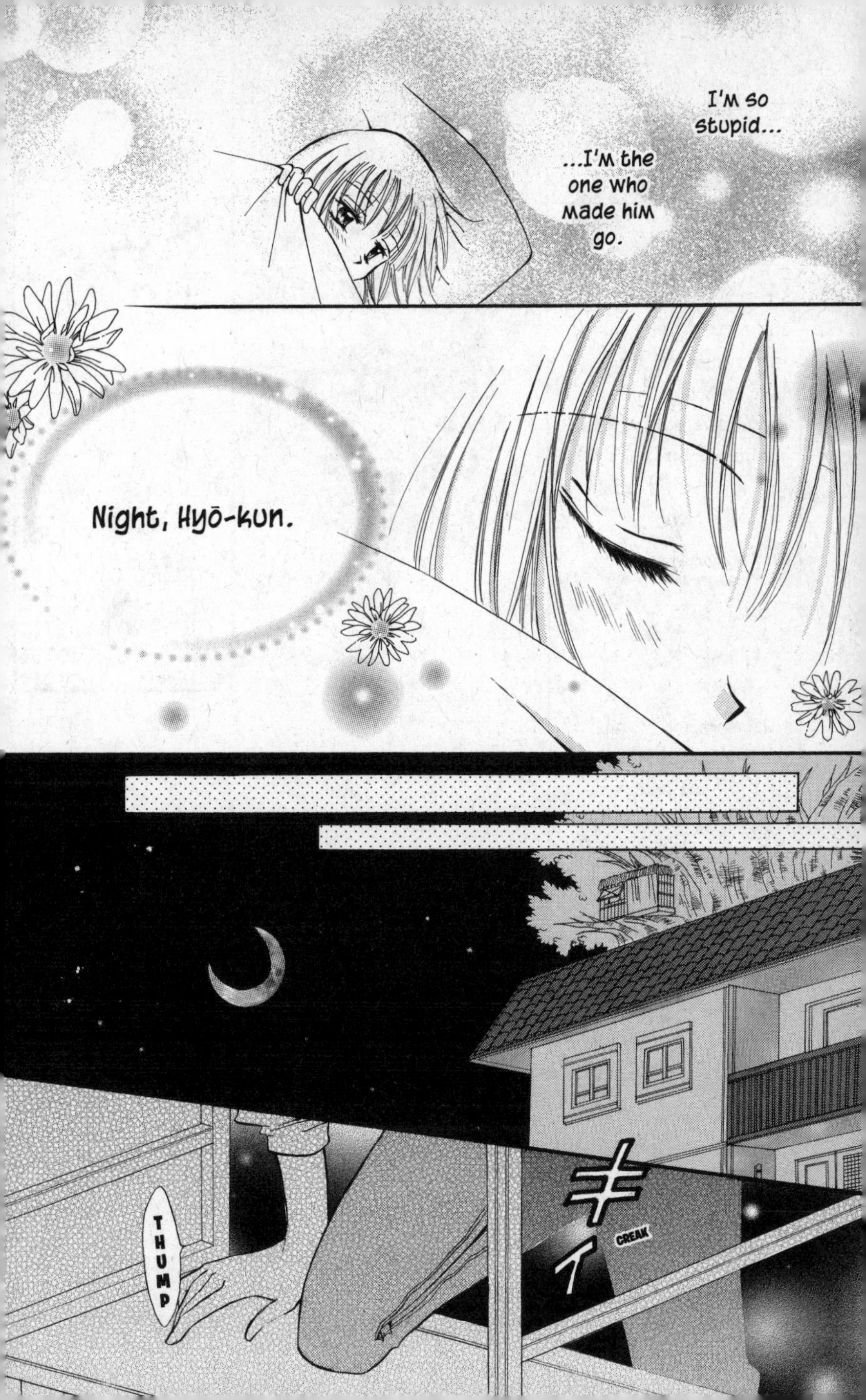
I'm so stupid...
...I'm the one who made him go.
Night, Hyō-kun.
CREAK
THUMP

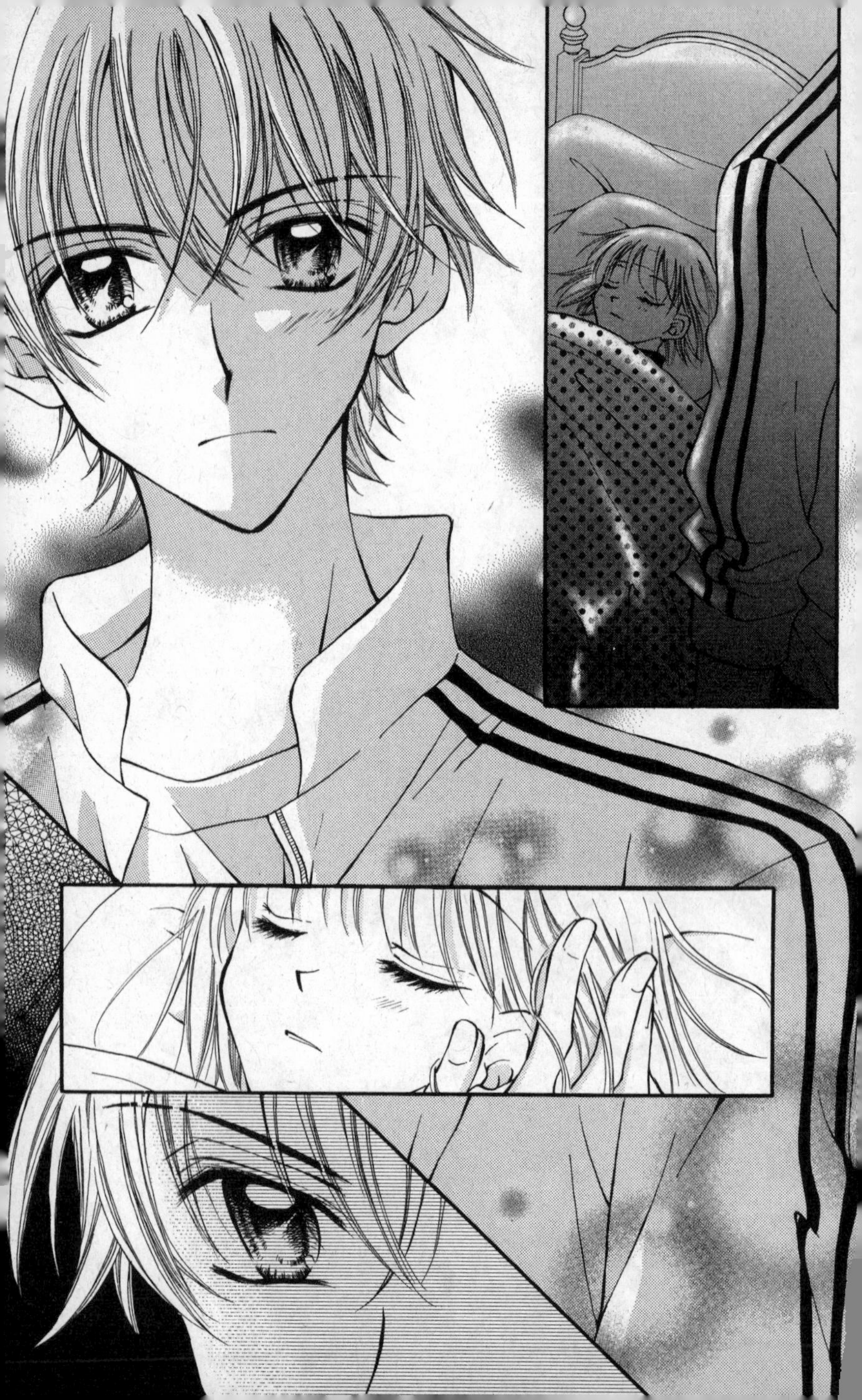

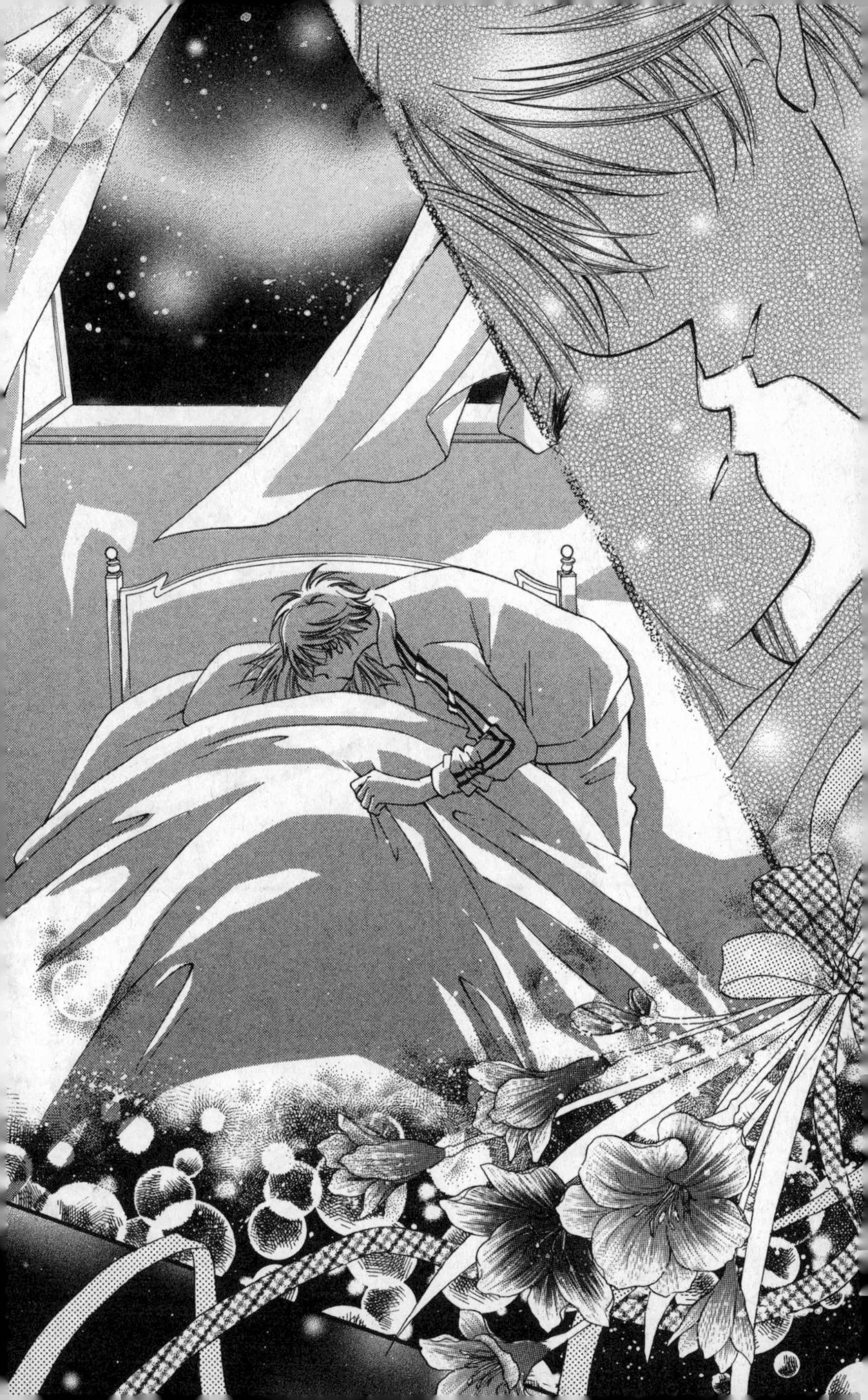

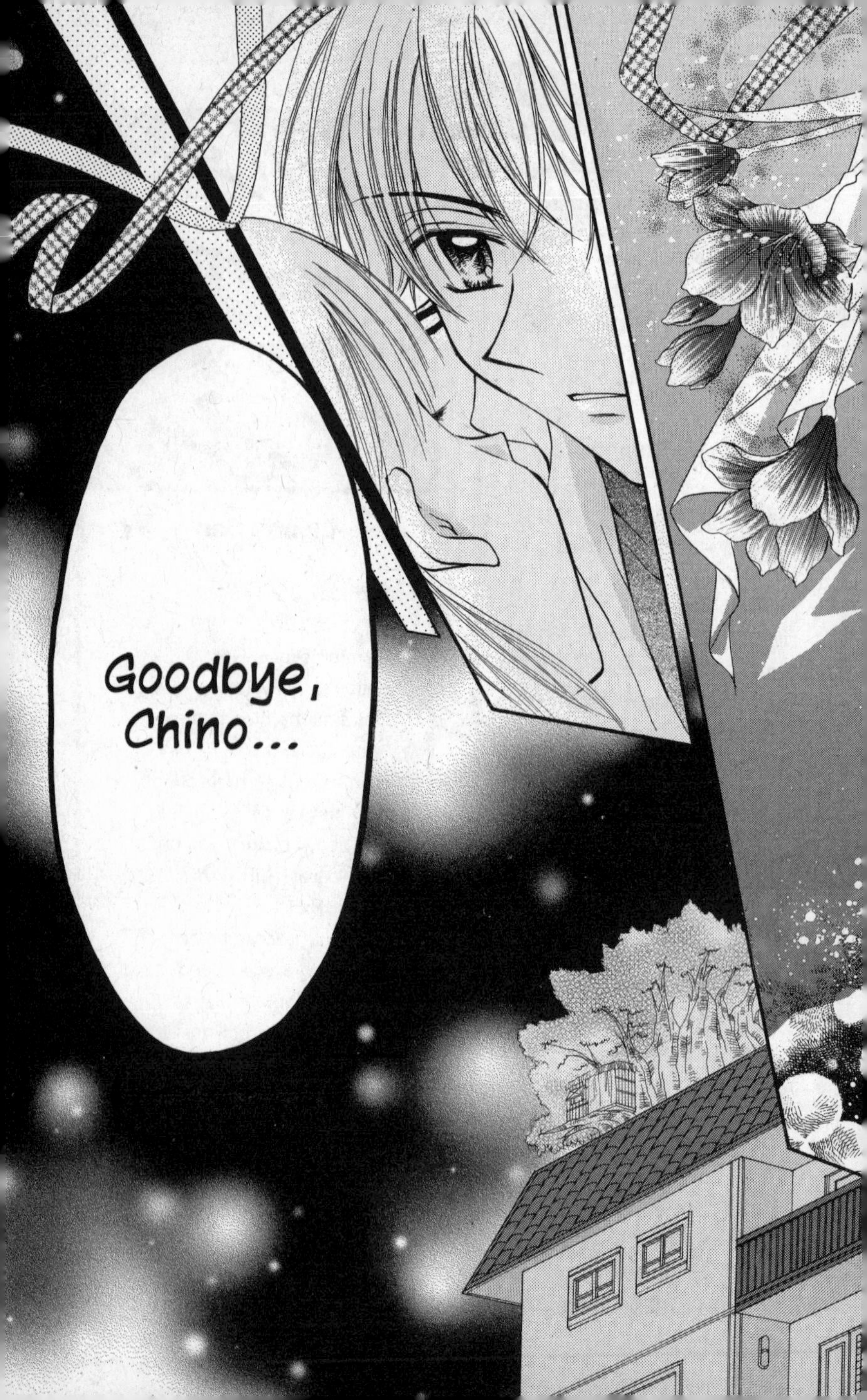
Goodbye, Chino...

✿ Chino's Mom ✿

Birthday: September 29th
35 years old.
Libra. Blood Type: AB
Hobbies: Tennis, watching TV.
Wears jeans 98% of the time. Goes to the gym often to keep up her figure. Her dream is to go to a beauty school in France to study! The reason she doesn't have a big part in the manga might be because she's so busy at work? ◖◗

✿ Chino's Dad ✿

Birthday: June 8th
50 years old.
Gemini. Blood Type: O
Hobbies: Traveling.
One time he didn't come home for 2 years, 7 months. (When he brought Hyō-kun back.)
The above picture was on his biography in *Love's Safari Park.*
He was a teacher before becoming a writer, and Mom was one of his students! They got married and had Chino.♡

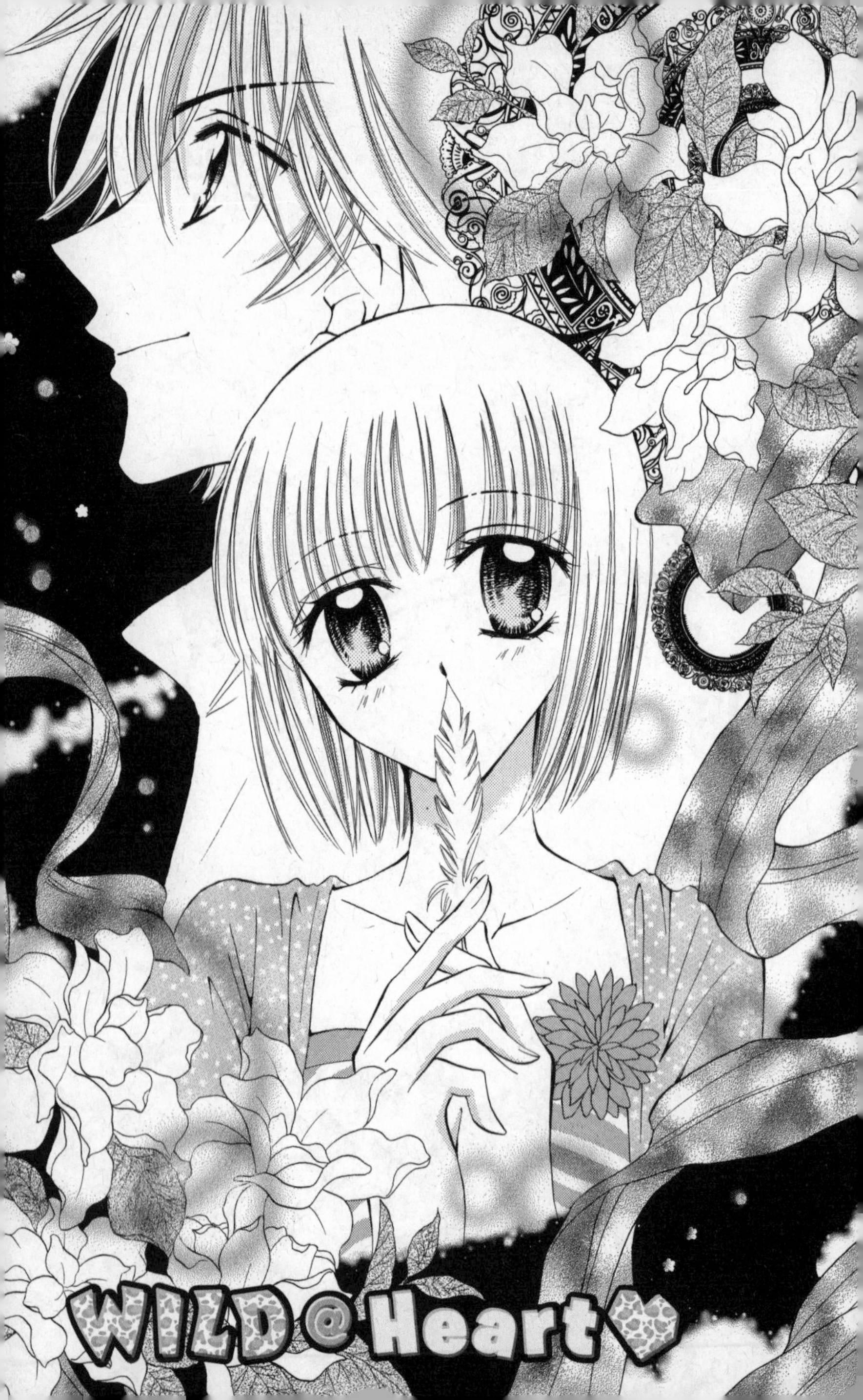
WILD@Heart♥

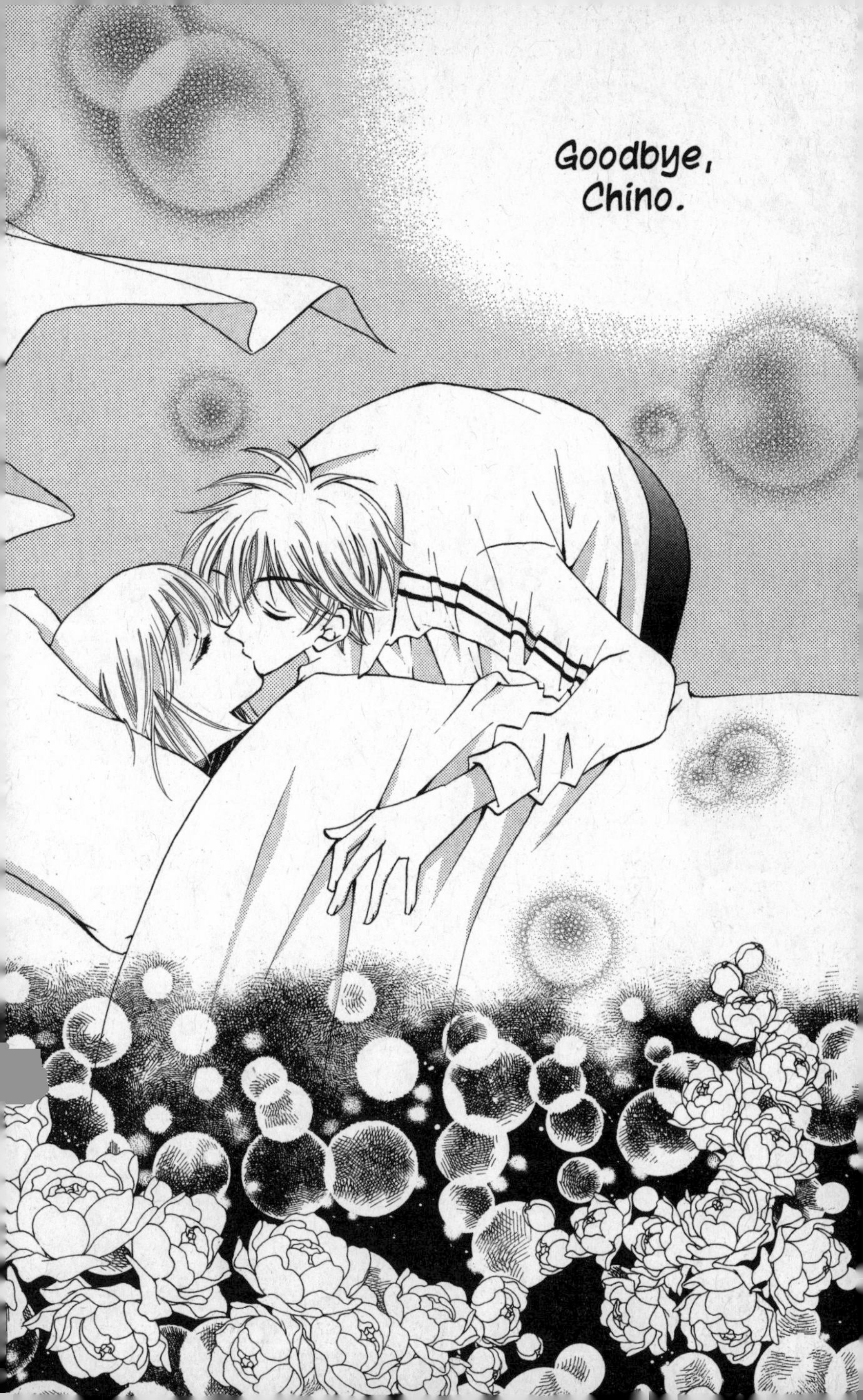
Goodbye, Chino.

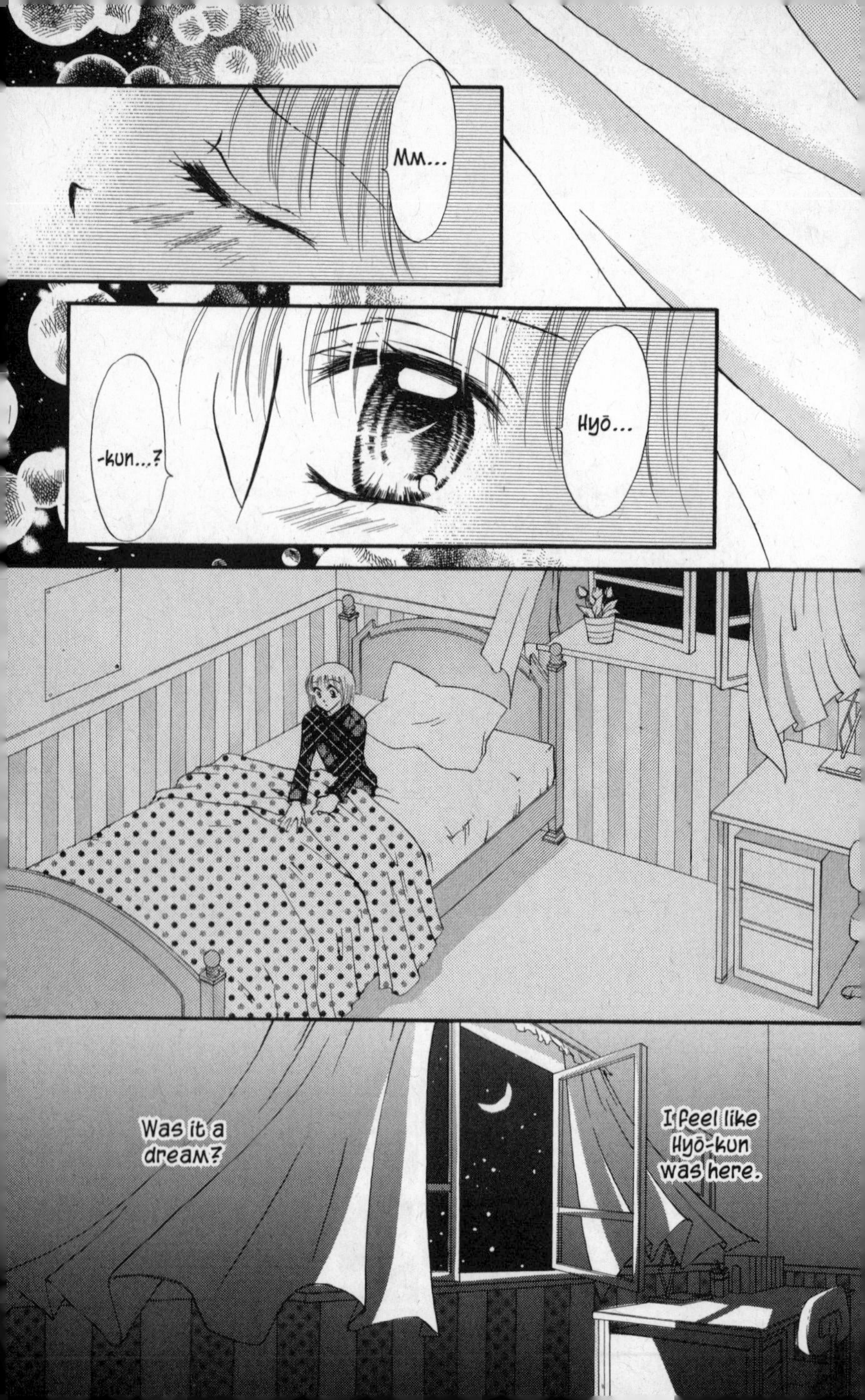

Mm...
Hyō...
-kun...?
I feel like Hyō-kun was here.
Was it a dream?

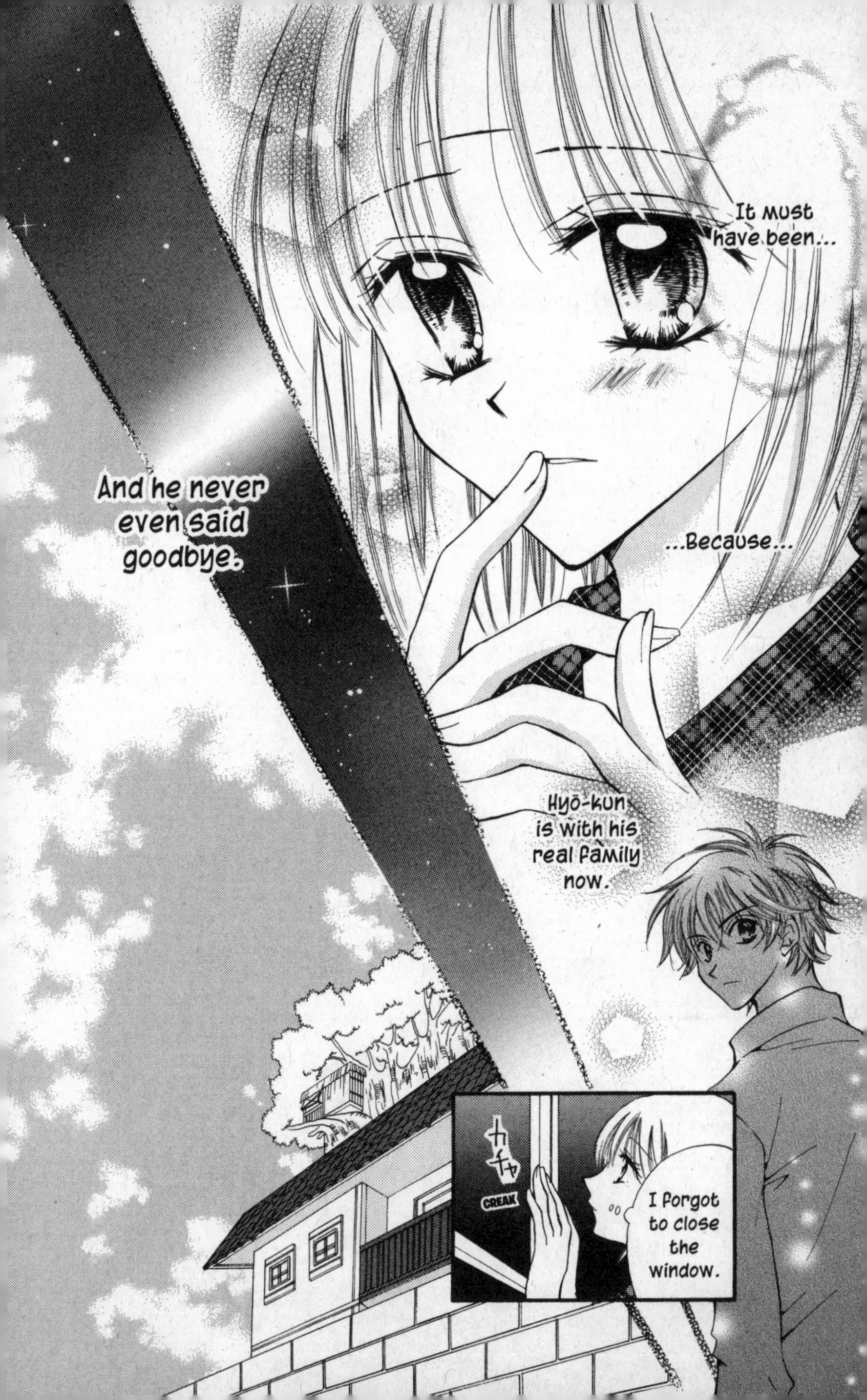
It must have been...
...Because...
Hyō-kun is with his real family now.
And he never even said goodbye.
カチャ
CREAK
I forgot to close the window.

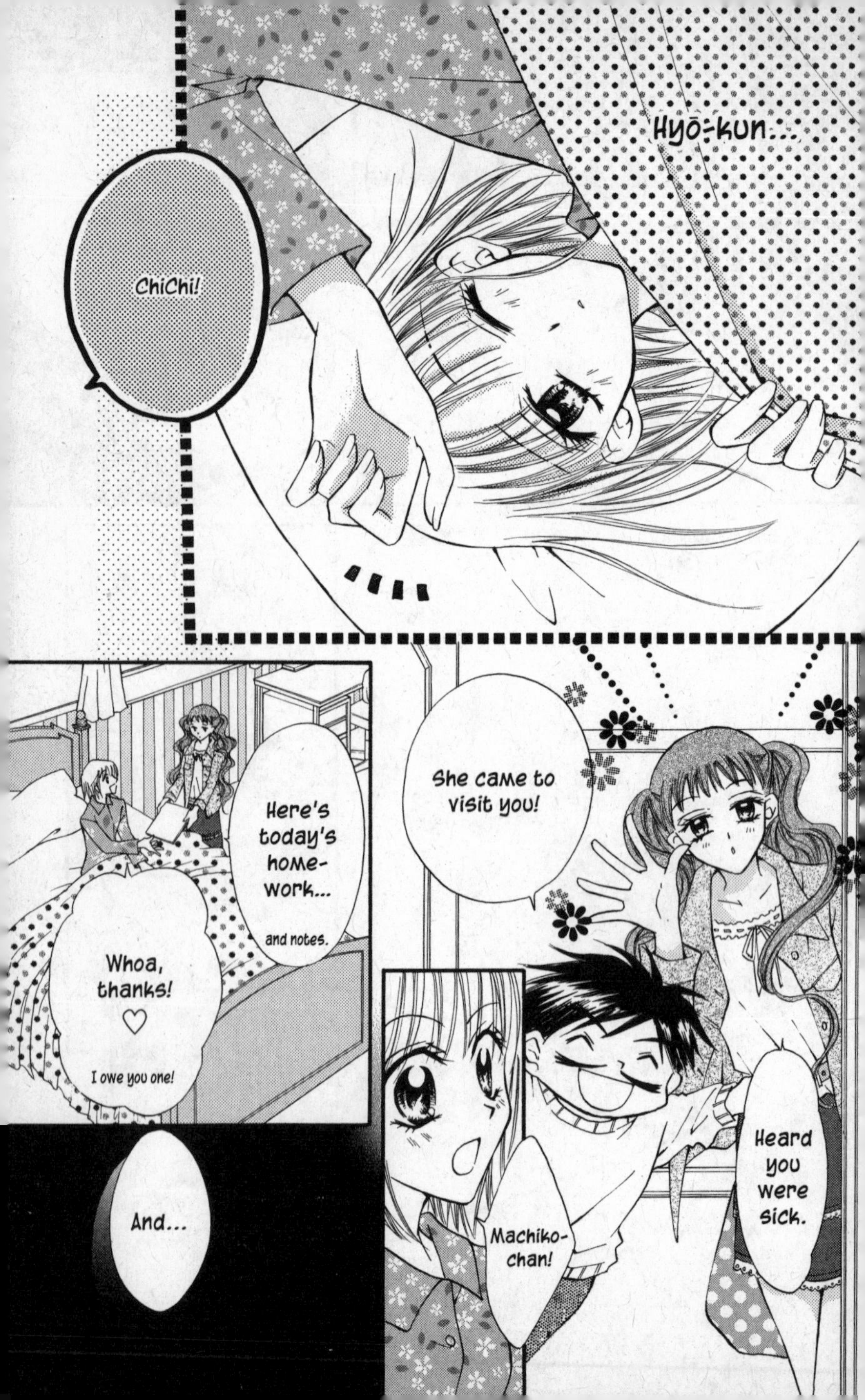
Hyō-kun...
ChiChi!
She came to visit you!
Heard you were sick.
Machiko-chan!
Here's today's home-work...
and notes.
Whoa, thanks! ♡
I owe you one!
And...

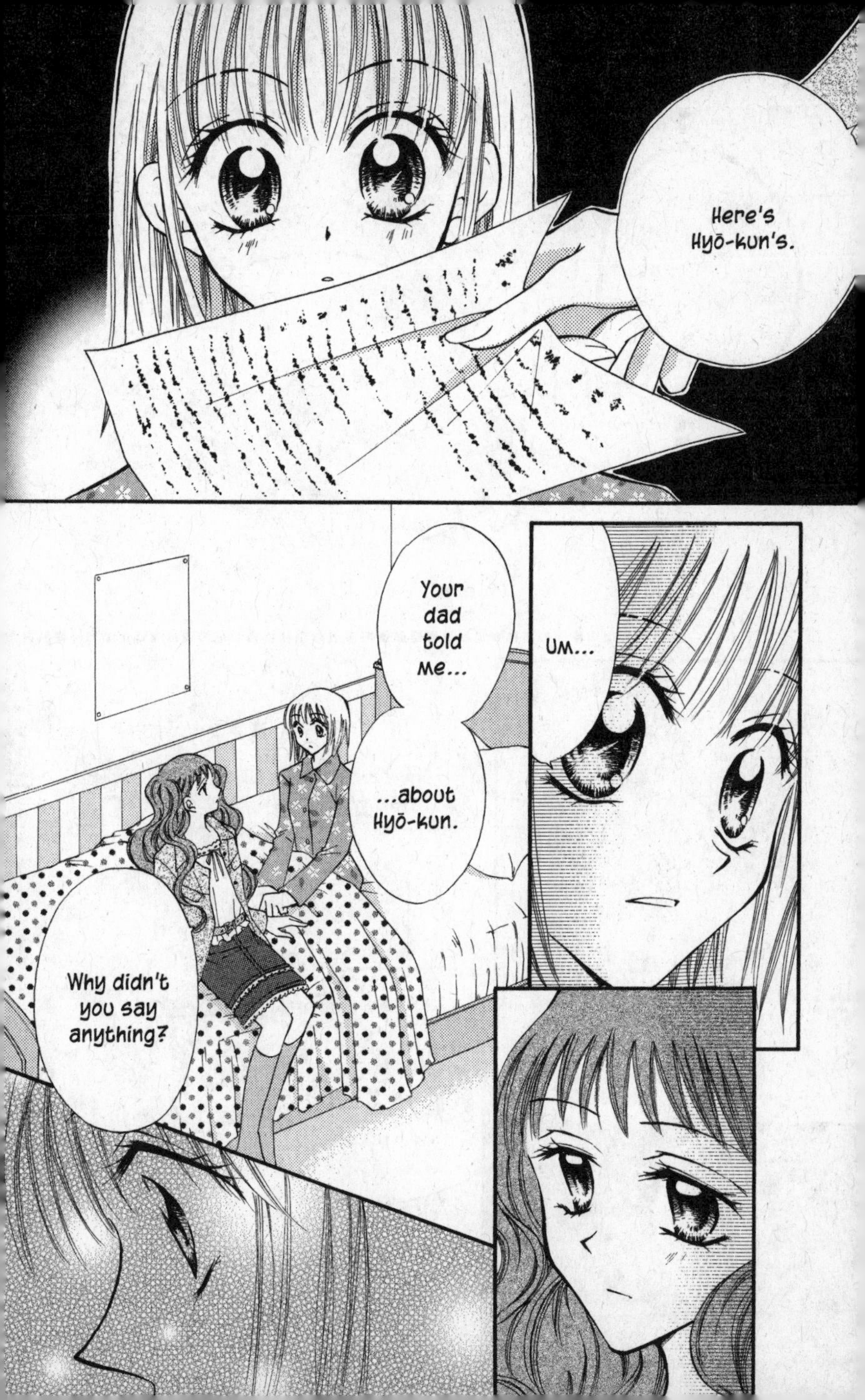
Here's Hyō-kun's.
Um...
Your dad told me...
...about Hyō-kun.
Why didn't you say anything?

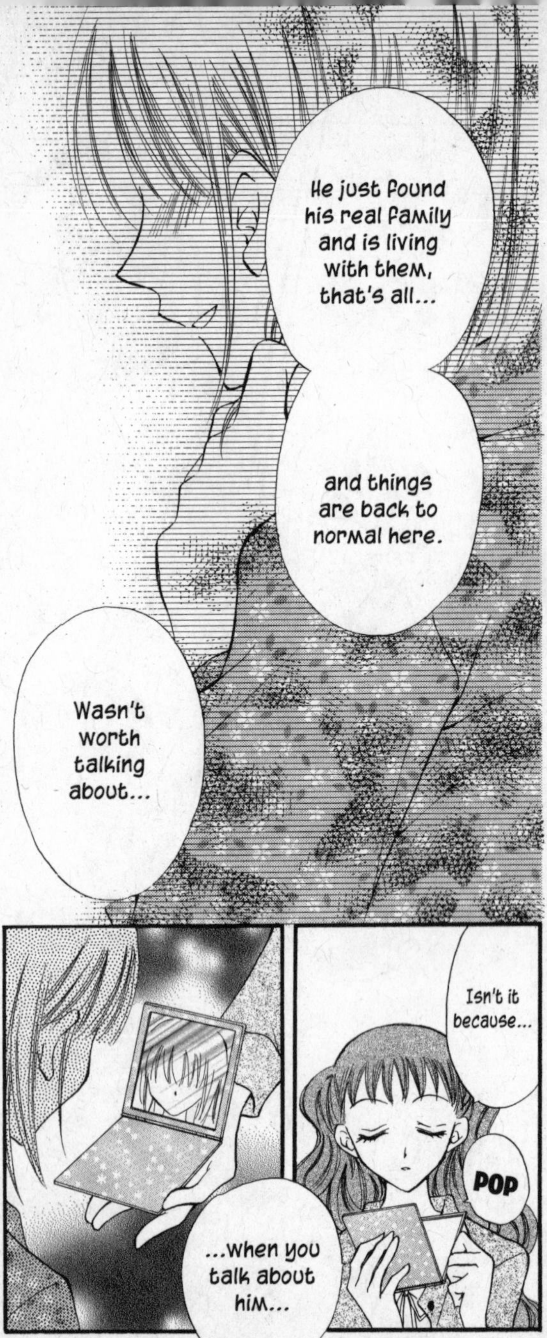
He just found his real family and is living with them, that's all...
and things are back to normal here.
Wasn't worth talking about...
Isn't it because...
POP
...when you talk about him...

3.

A lot happened on the way there, but the U.S. is a great place! ♪ I stayed in Long Beach near Los Angeles. Apparently they only get rain 14 days out of the year! My hairstylist said they went to Long Beach too but that it rained the whole time! The chances of that happening are so slim! I got some coffee and I ordered a small but it seemed like a large to me! I heard that everything was bigger in the U.S., and I guess it was true! I really wanted to see how big the large was but I didn't have enough guts to order it! I'm thinking of visiting there again! ♪

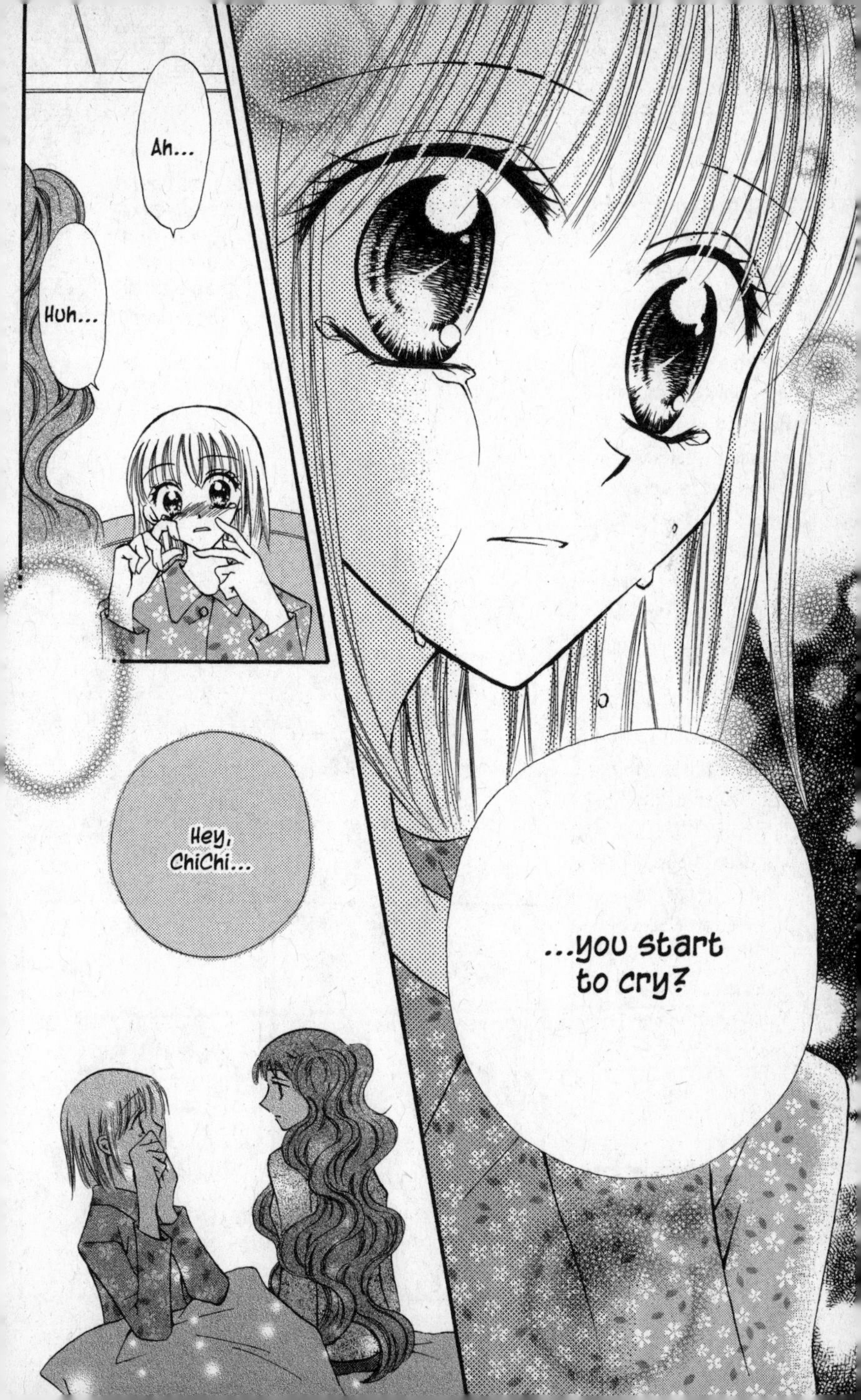
Ah...
Huh...
Hey, ChiChi...
...you start to cry?

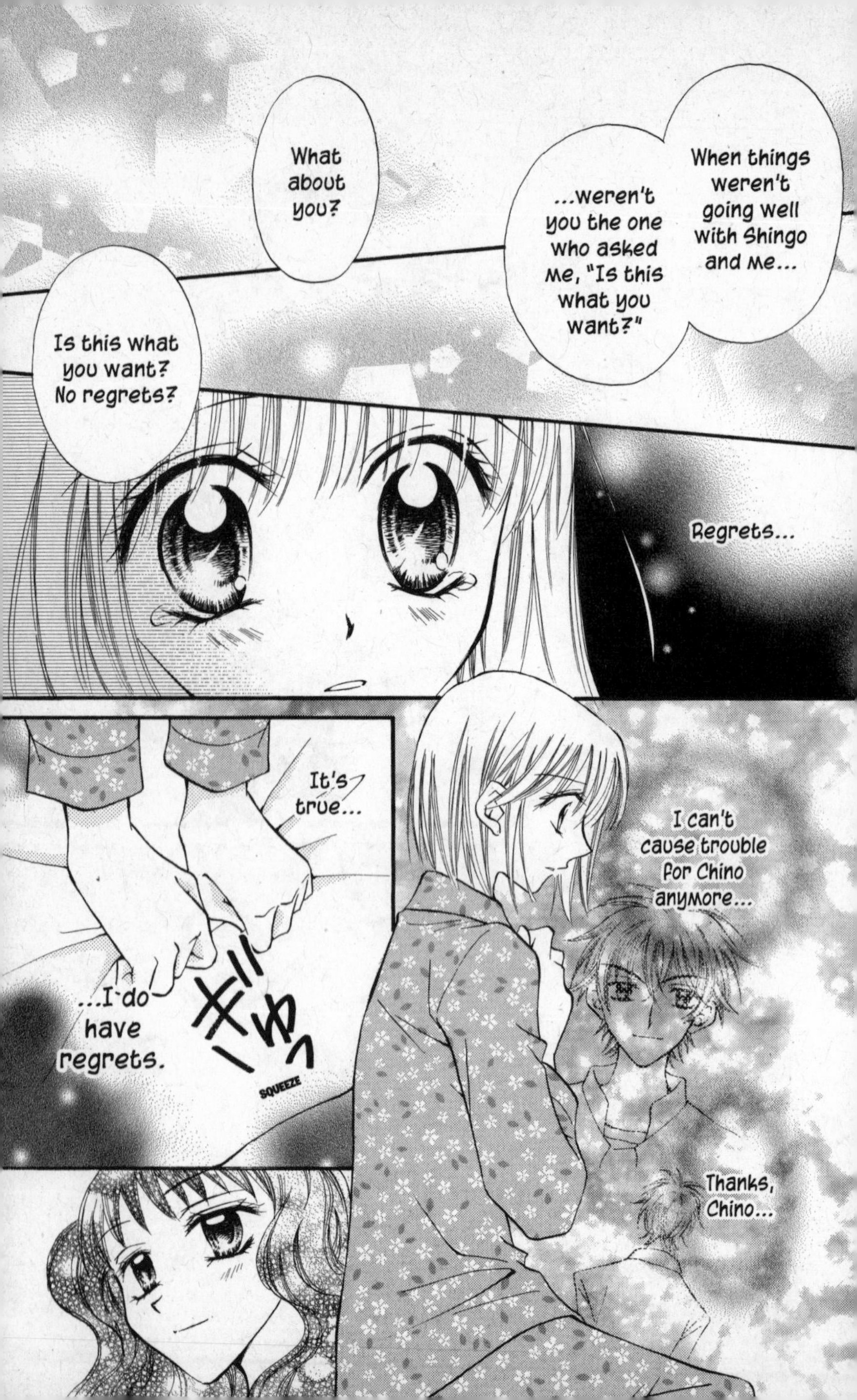
When things weren't going well with Shingo and me...
...weren't you the one who asked me, "Is this what you want?"
What about you?
Is this what you want? No regrets?
Regrets...
I can't cause trouble for Chino anymore...
Thanks, Chino...
It's true...
ぎゅっ
SQUEEZE
...I do have regrets.

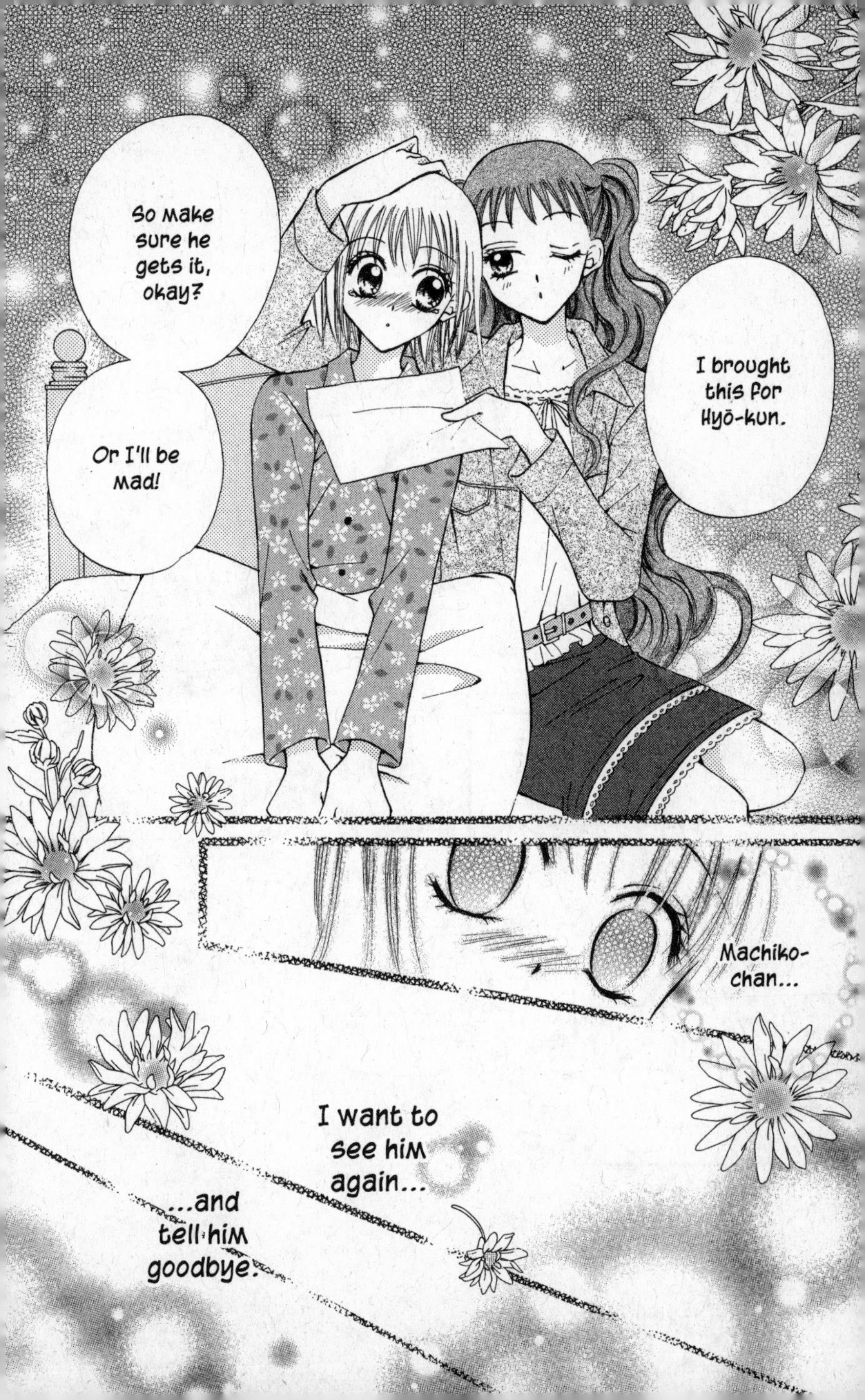
I brought this for Hyō-kun.
So make sure he gets it, okay?
Or I'll be mad!
Machiko-chan...
I want to see him again...
...and tell him goodbye.

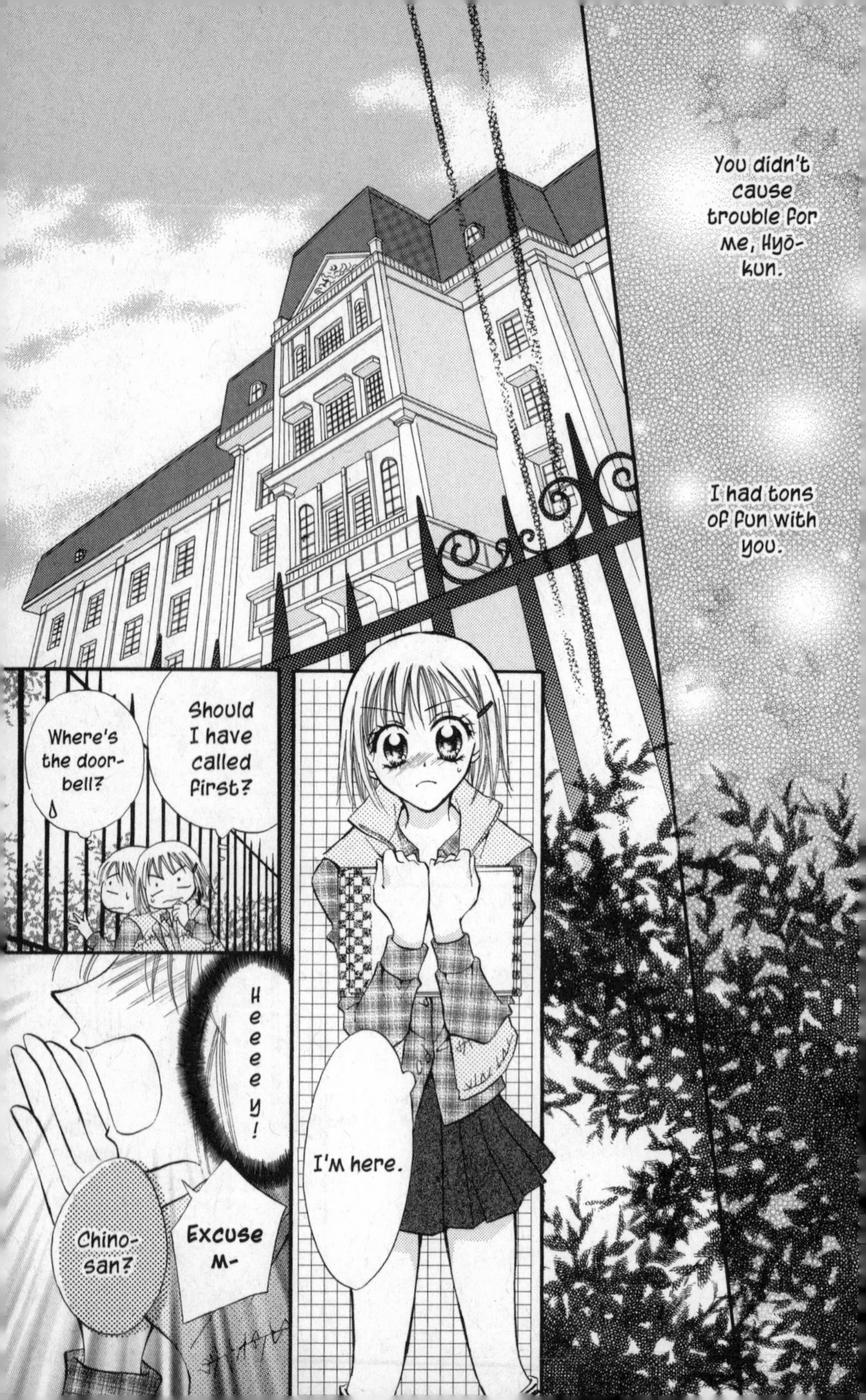
You didn't cause trouble for me, Hyō-kun.
I had tons of fun with you.
I'm here.
Should I have called first?
Where's the doorbell?
Heeeey!
Excuse m-
Chino-san?

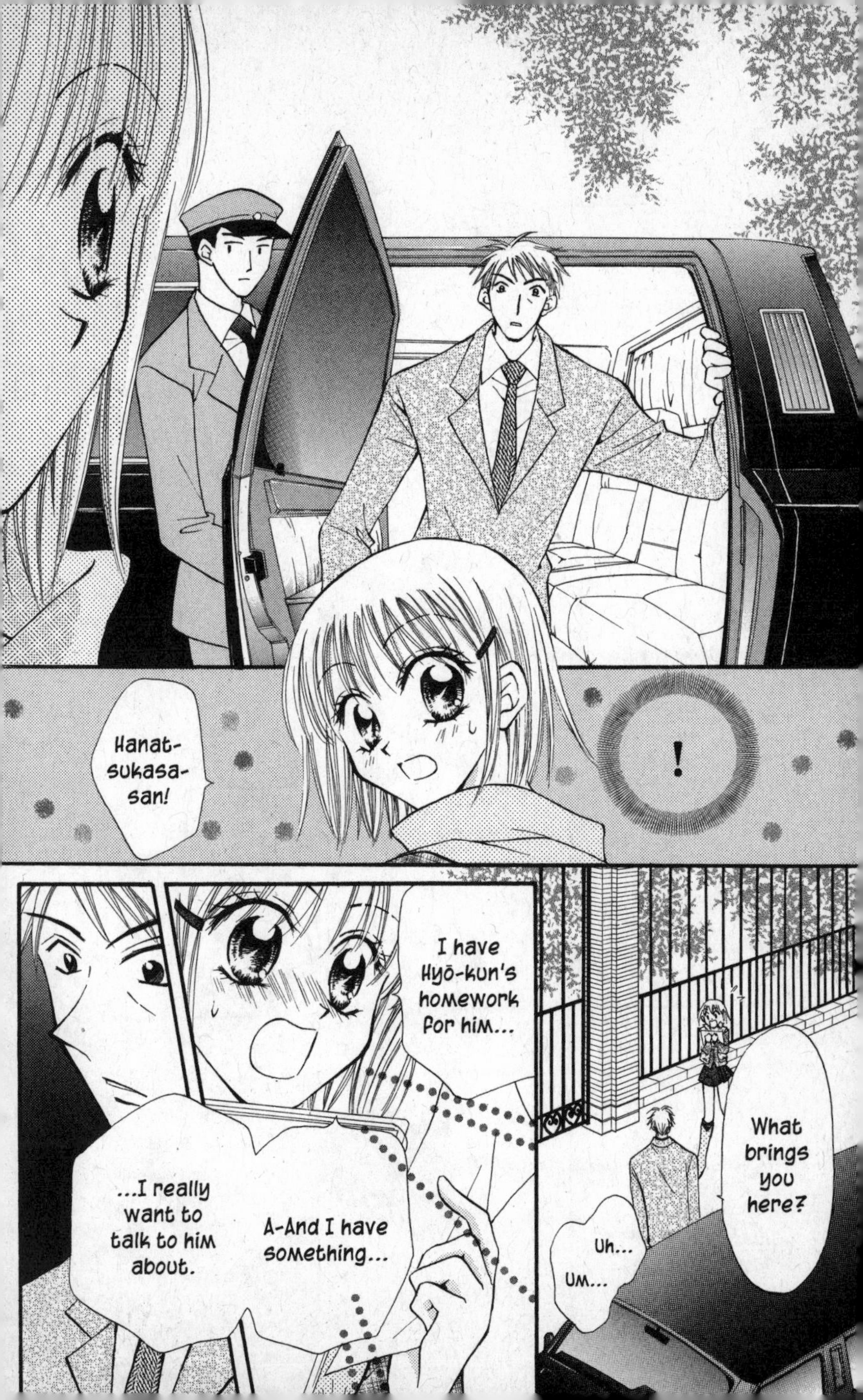
!
Hanat-sukasa-san!
What brings you here?
Uh...
Um...
I have Hyō-kun's homework for him...
A-And I have something...
...I really want to talk to him about.

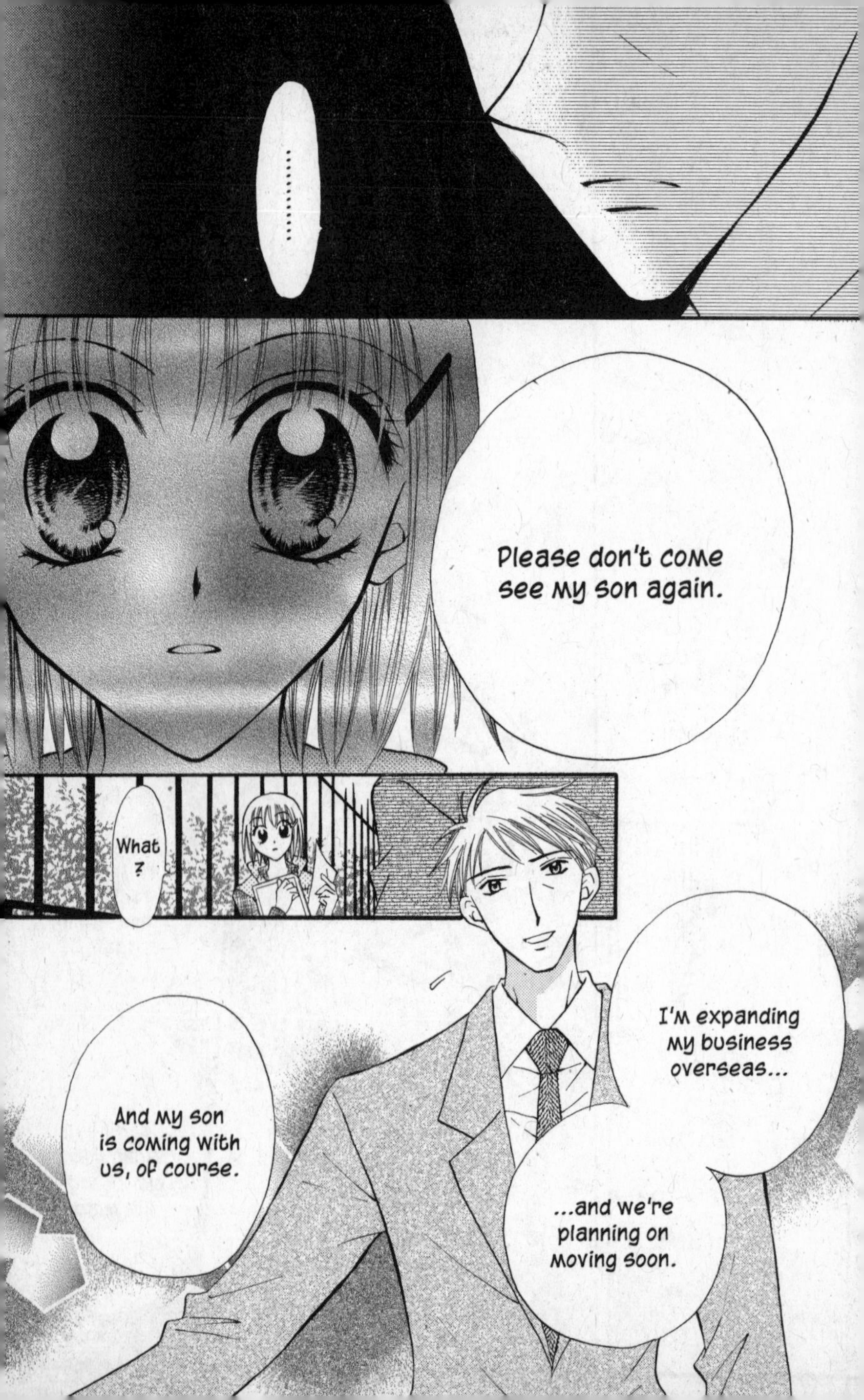

......
Please don't come see my son again.
What?
I'm expanding my business overseas...
...and we're planning on moving soon.
And my son is coming with us, of course.

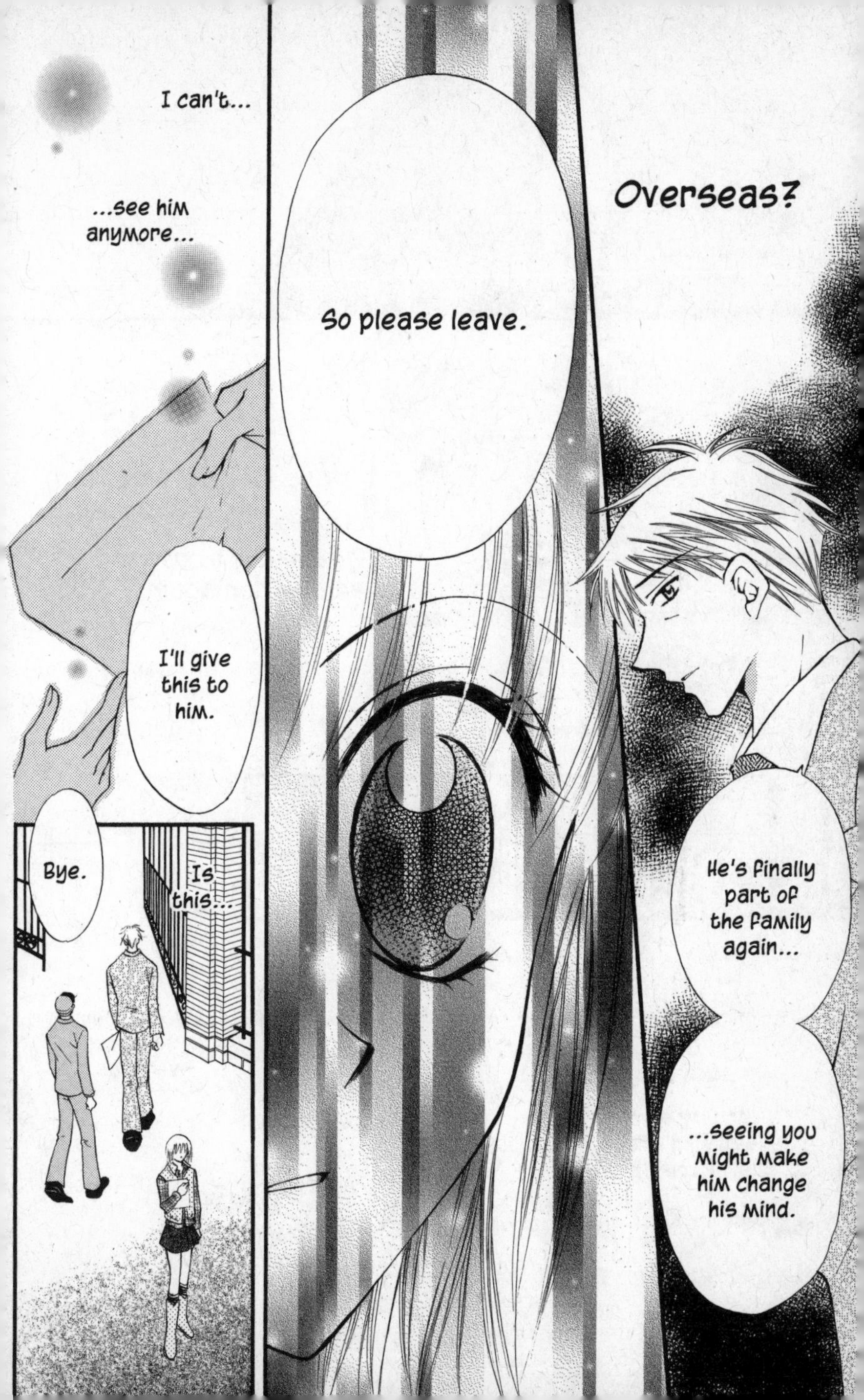

Overseas?
He's finally part of the family again...
...seeing you might make him change his mind.
So please leave.
I can't...
...see him anymore...
I'll give this to him.
Bye.
Is this...

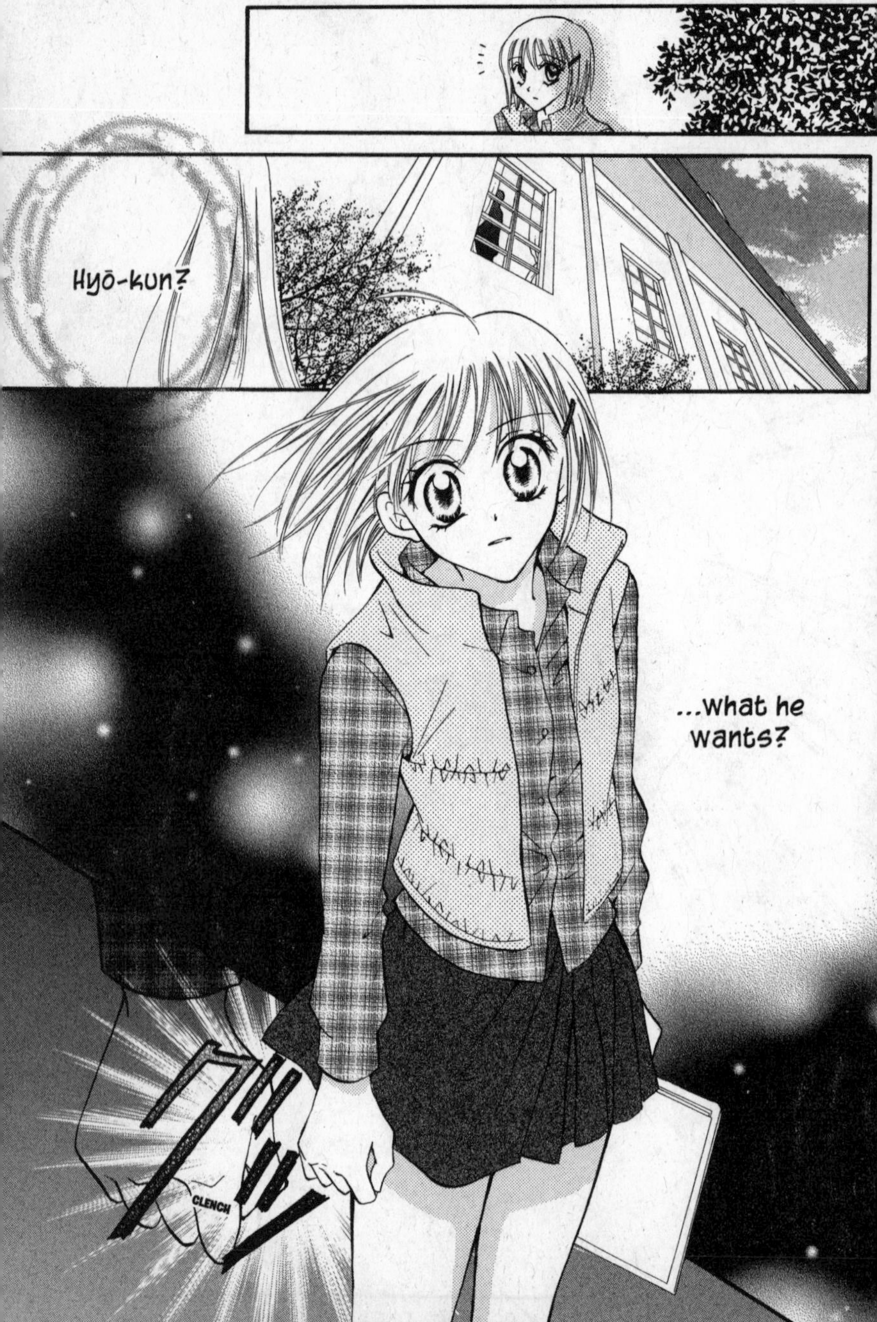
Hyō-kun?
...what he wants?
CLENCH

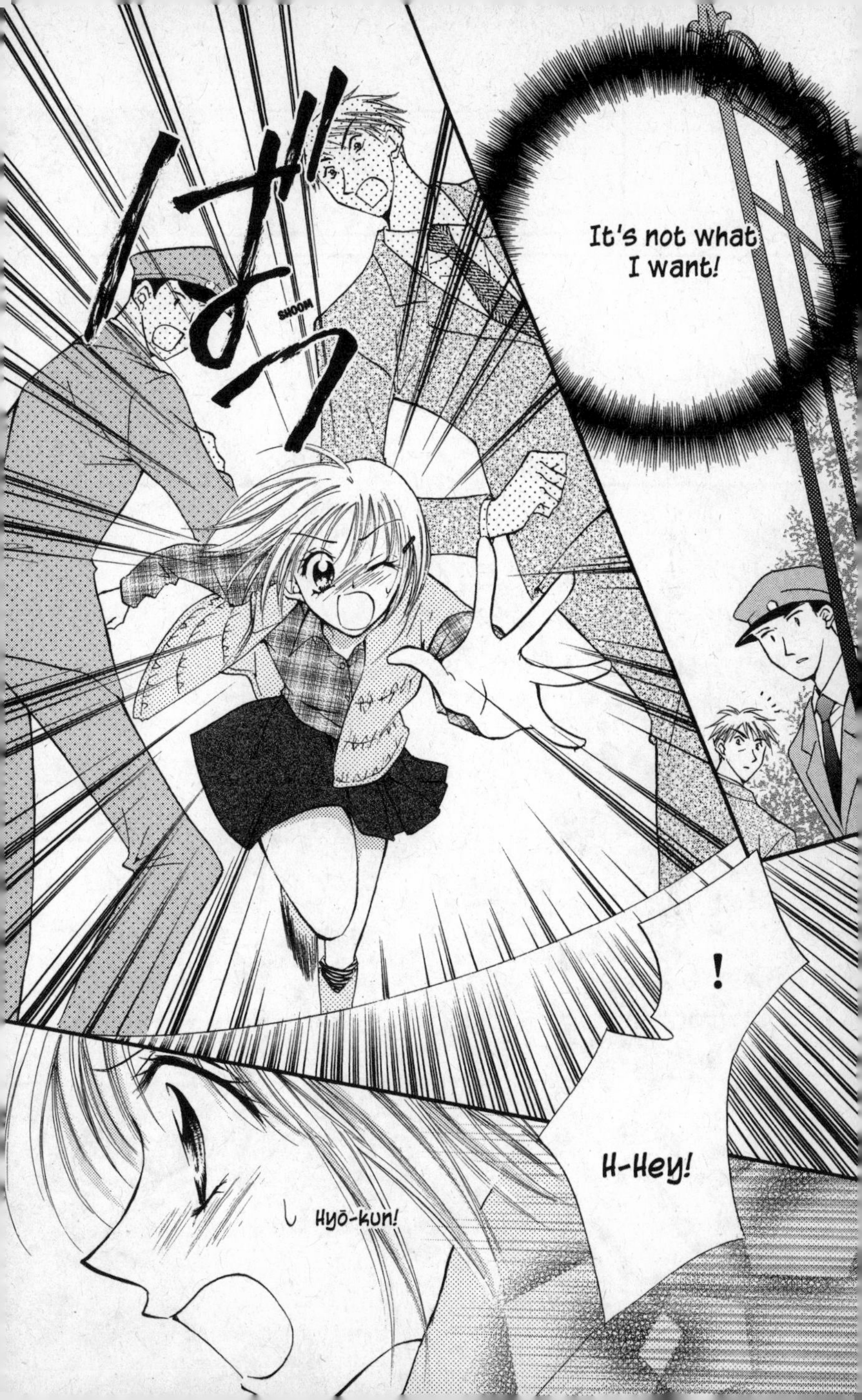
It's not what I want!
SHOOM
!
H-Hey!
Hyō-kun!

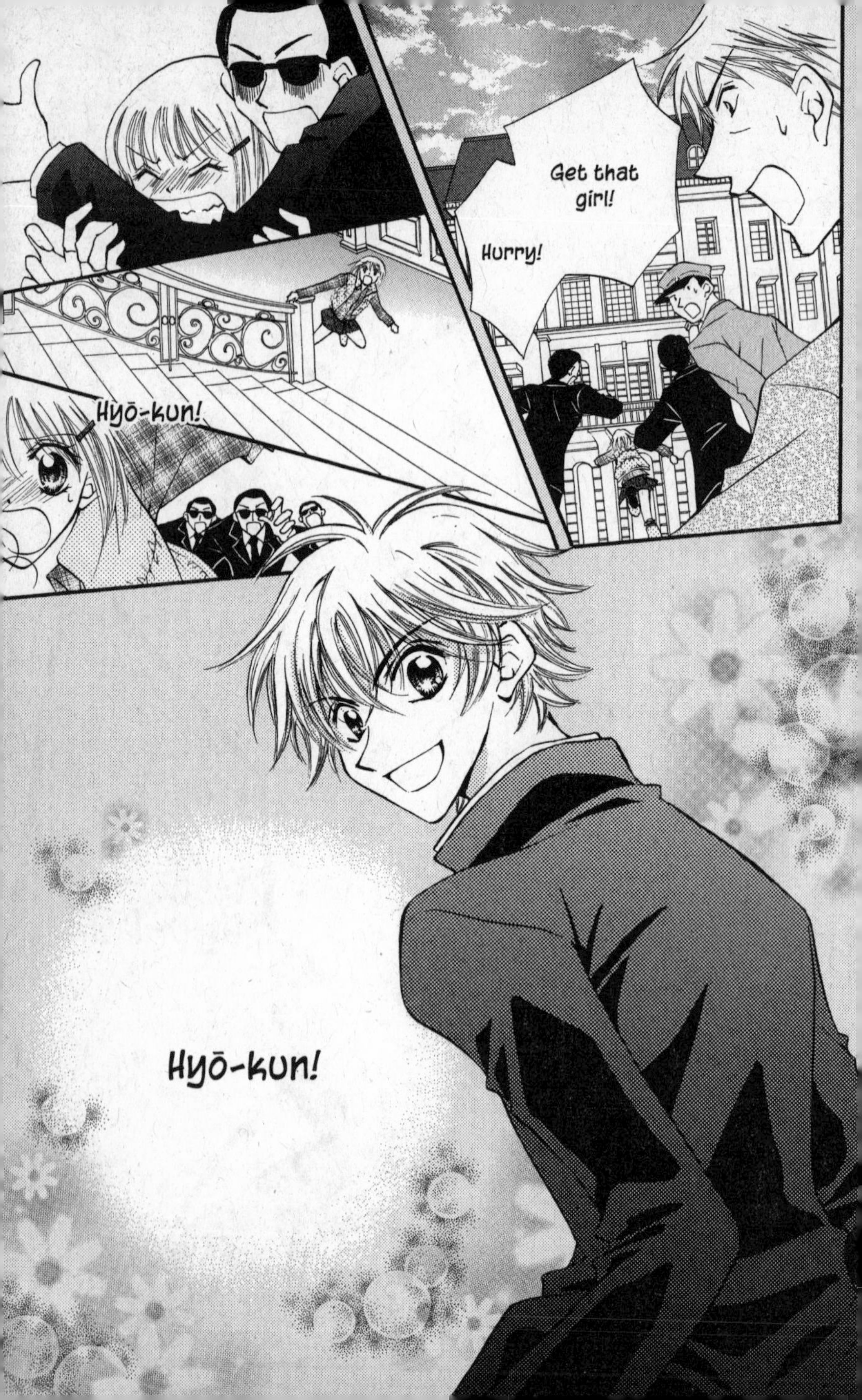
Get that girl!
Hurry!
Hyō-kun!
Hyō-kun!

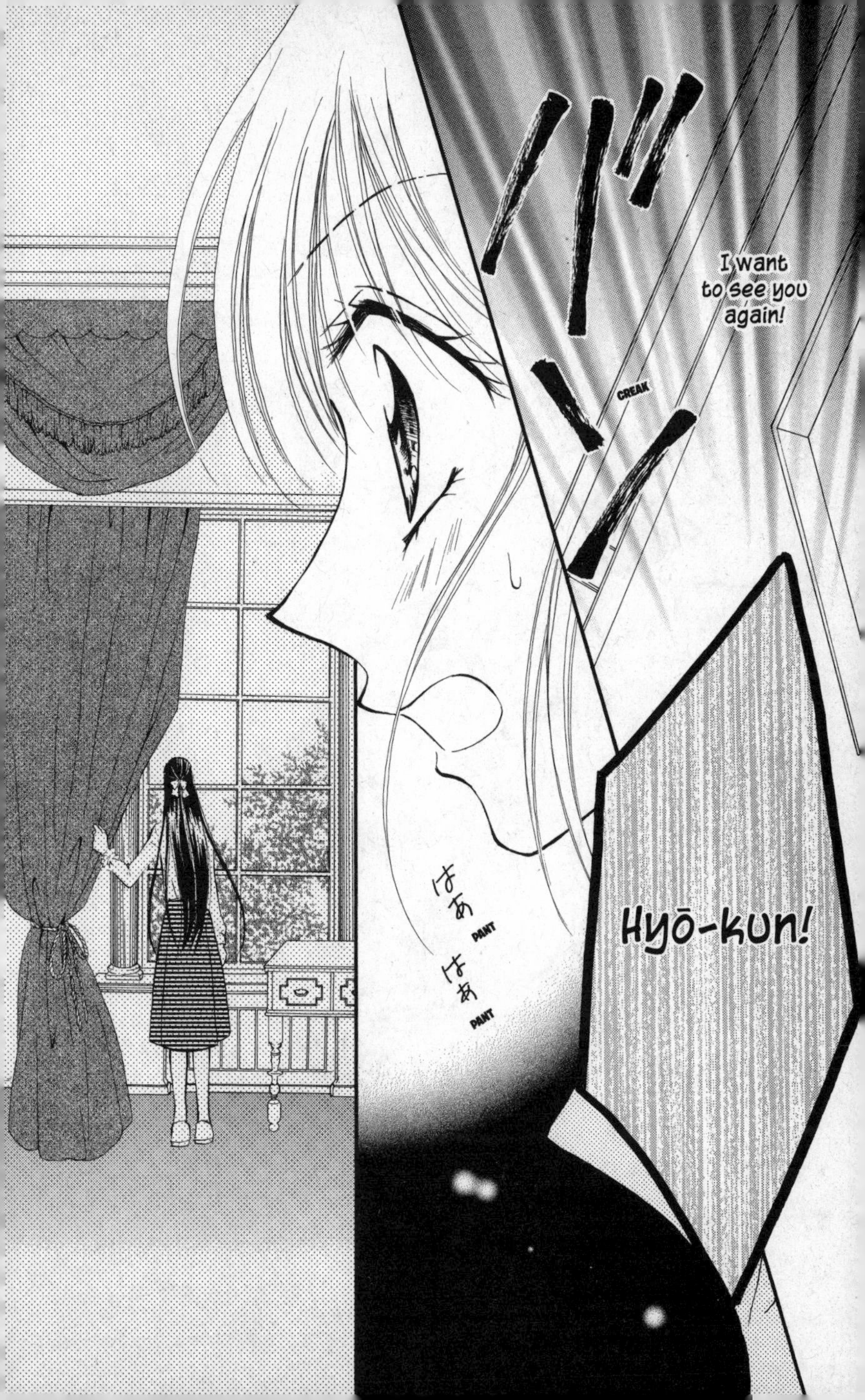
I want to see you again!
CREAK
Hyō-kun!
はあ
PANT
はあ
PANT

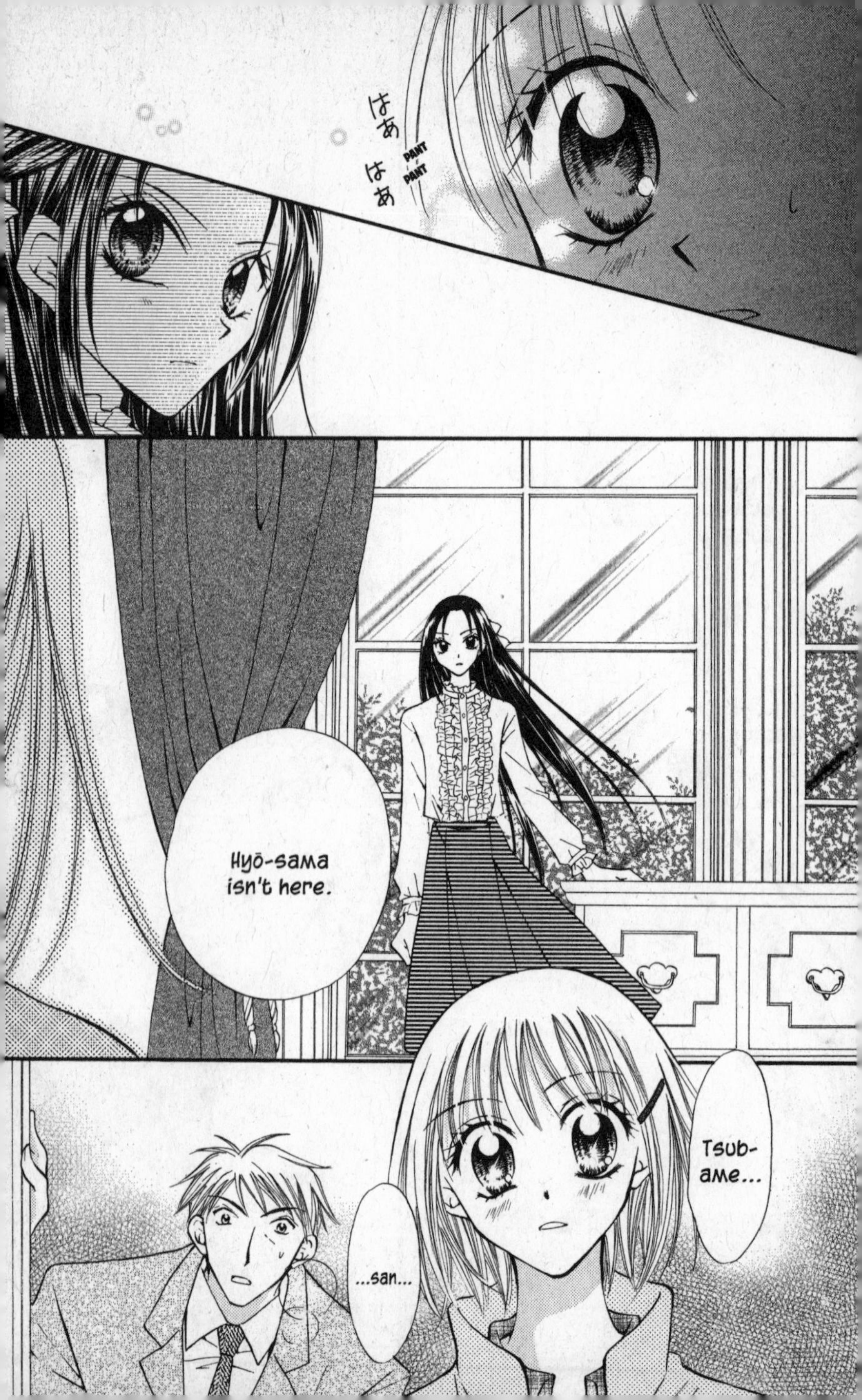
はあ はあ
PANT PANT
Hyō-sama isn't here.
Tsub-ame...
...san...

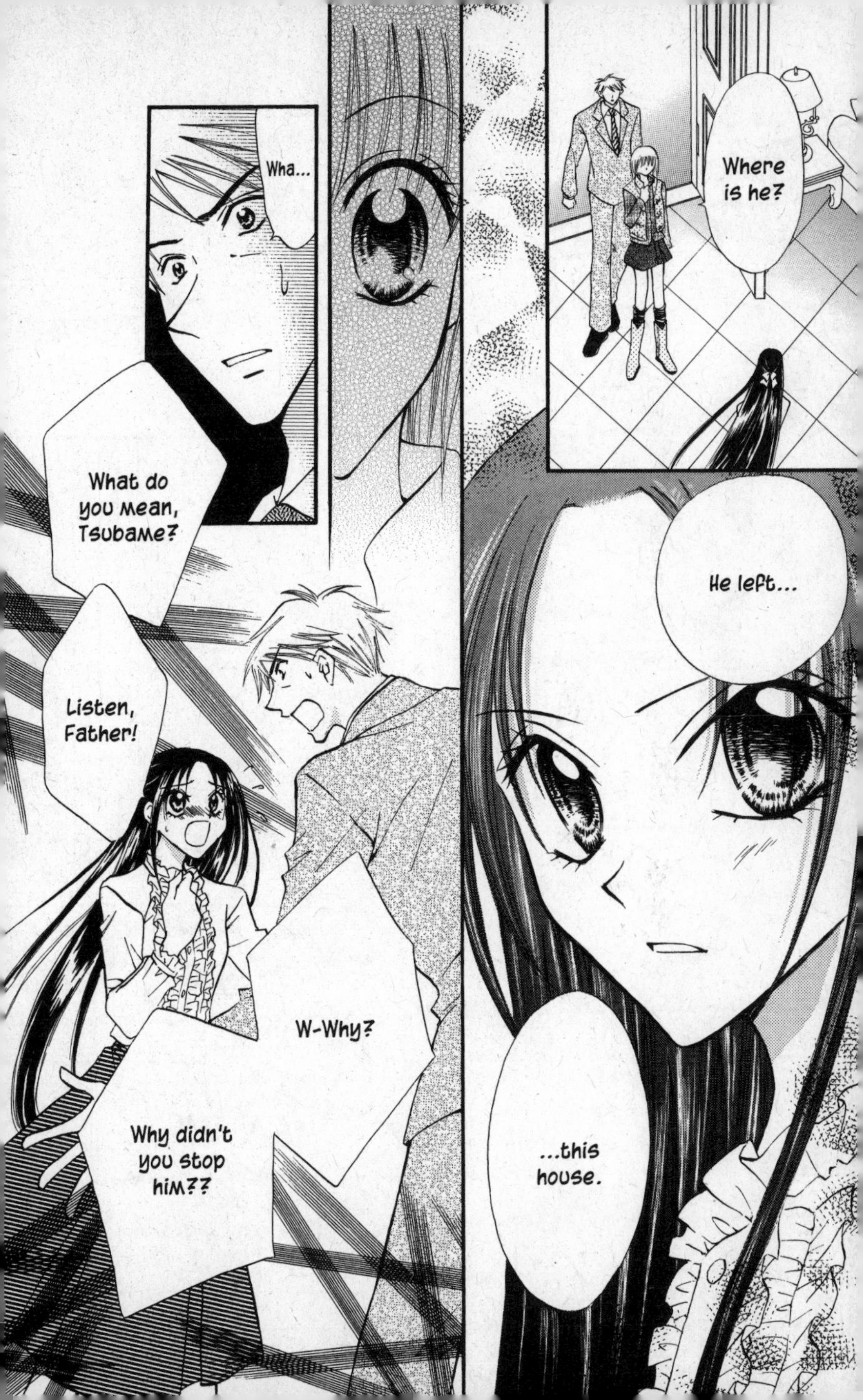
Where is he?
He left...
...this house.
Wha...
What do you mean, Tsubame?
Listen, Father!
W-Why?
Why didn't you stop him??

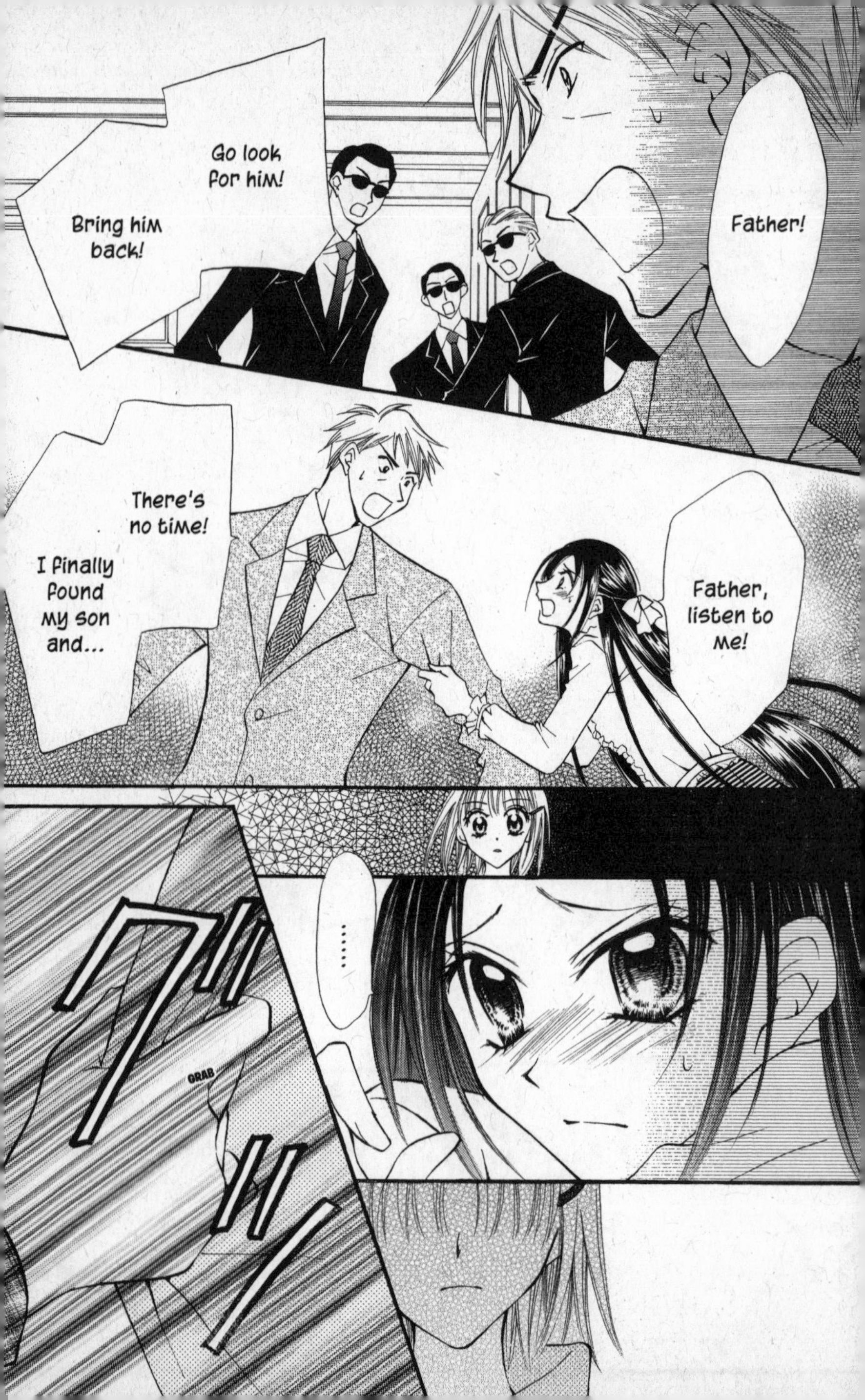
Father!
Go look for him!
Bring him back!
Father, listen to me!
There's no time!
I finally found my son and...
......
GRAB

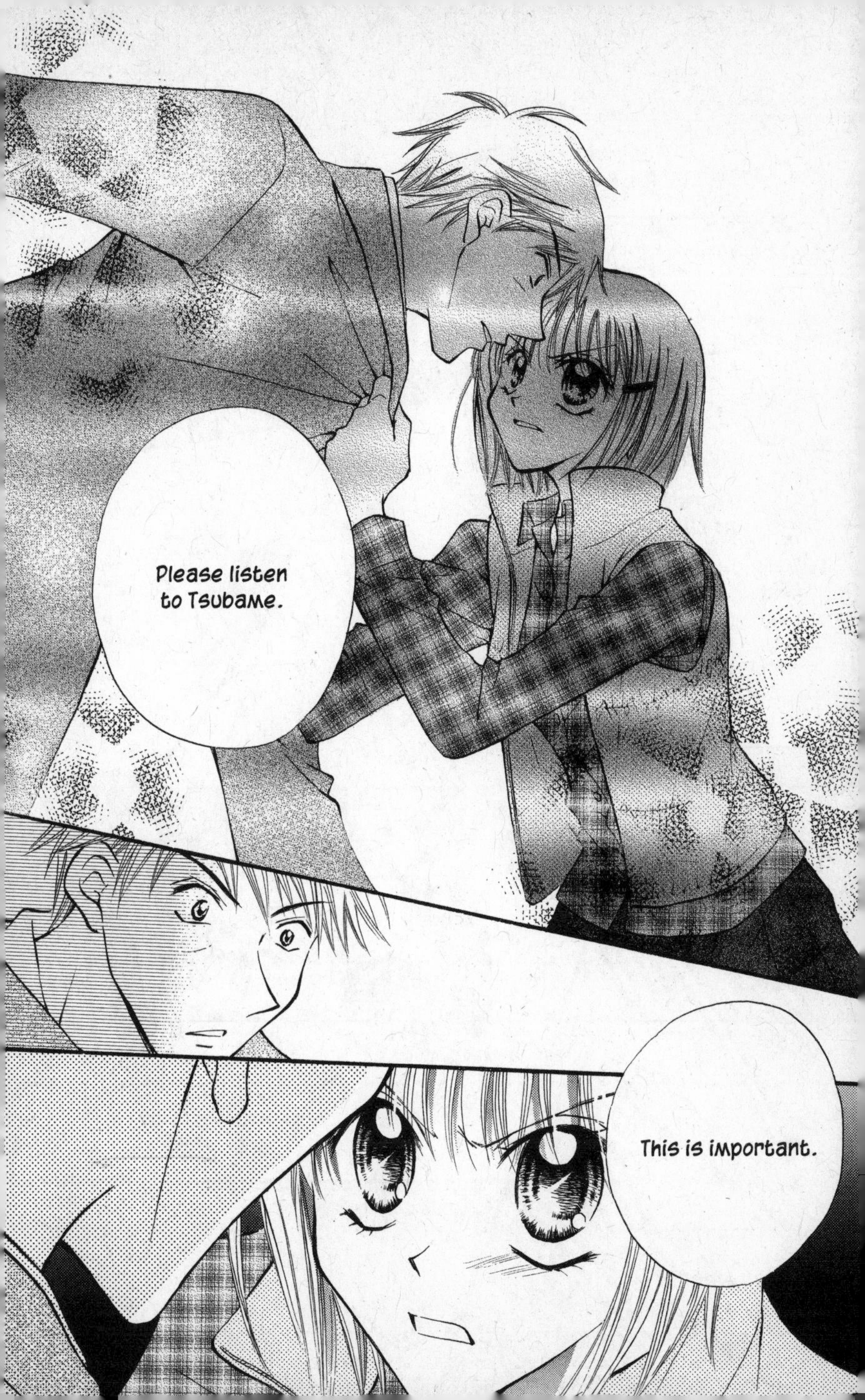
Please listen to Tsubame.
This is important.

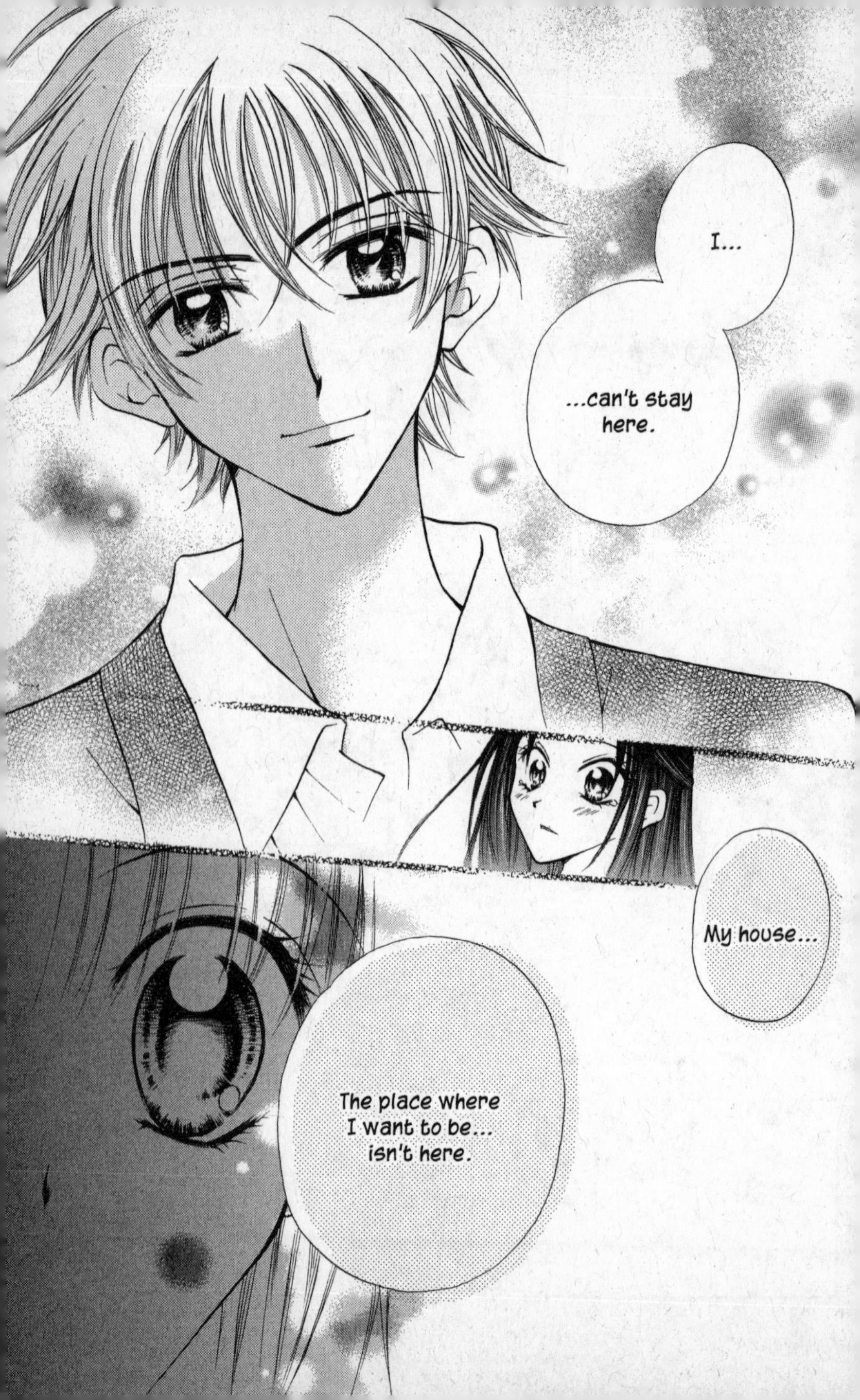
I...
...can't stay here.
My house...
The place where I want to be... isn't here.

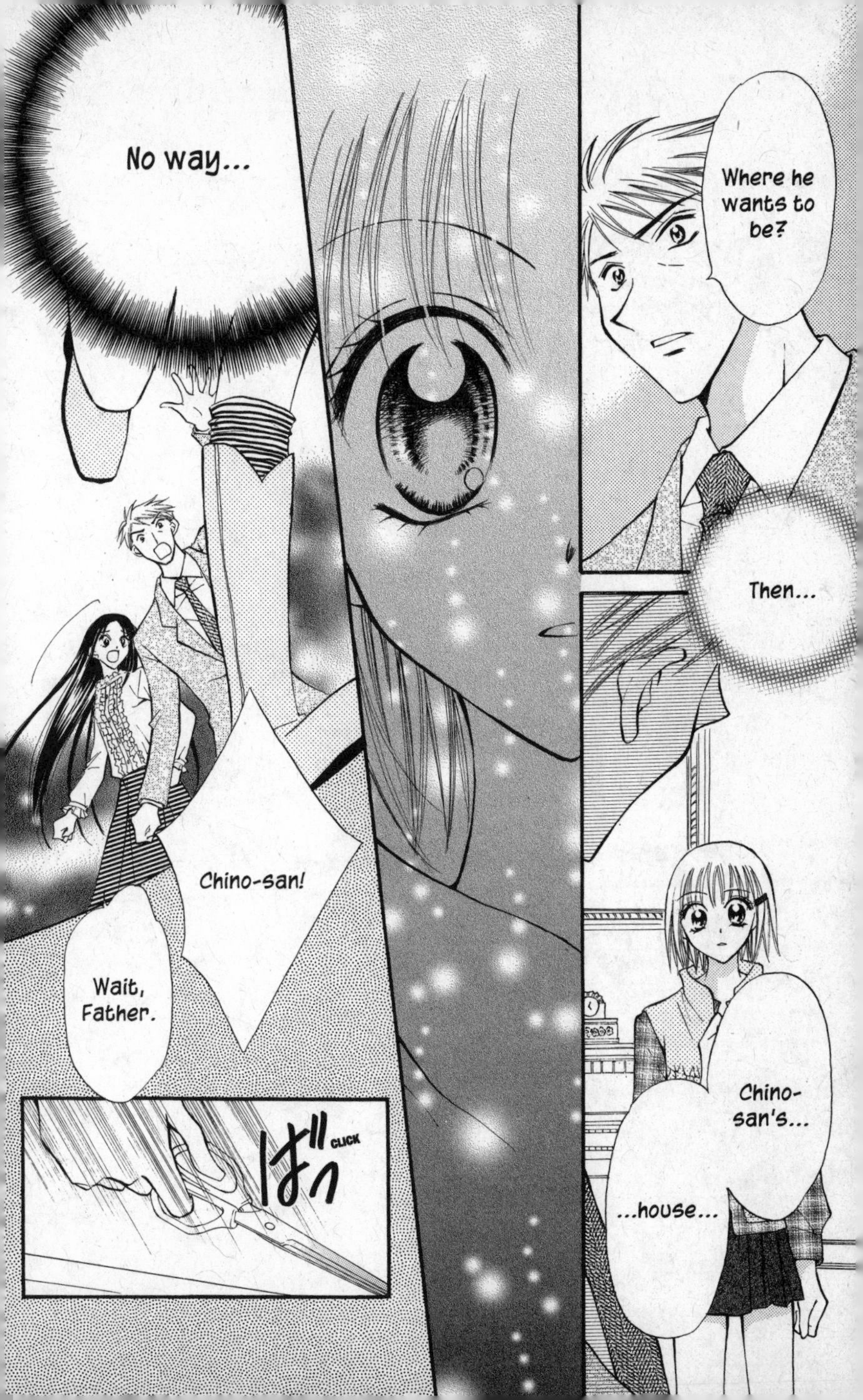
Where he wants to be?
Then...
Chino-san's...
...house...
No way...
Chino-san!
Wait, Father.
ぱっ
CLICK

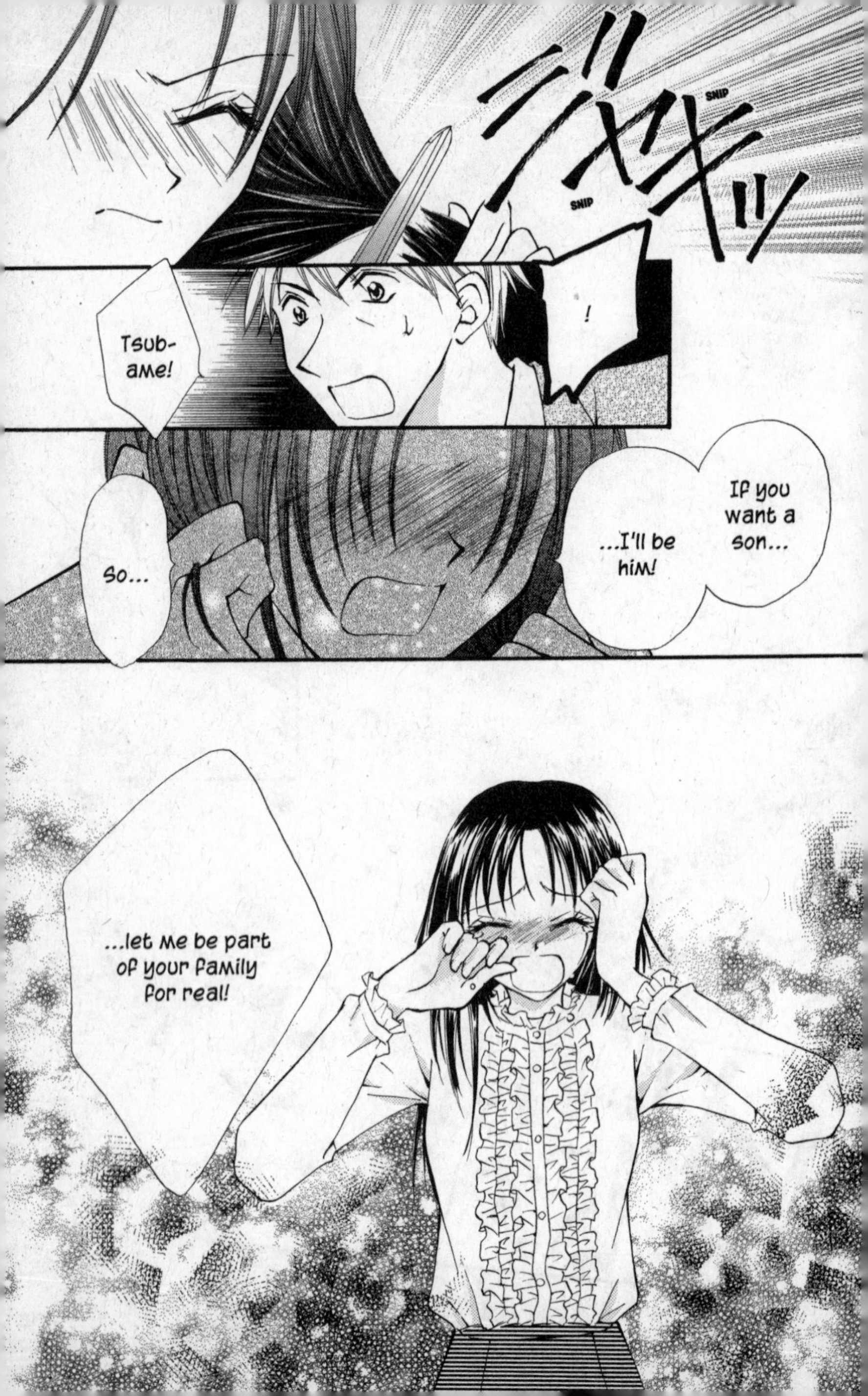
ジャキッ
SNIP
SNIP
!
Tsub-ame!
If you want a son...
...I'll be him!
So...
...let me be part of your family for real!

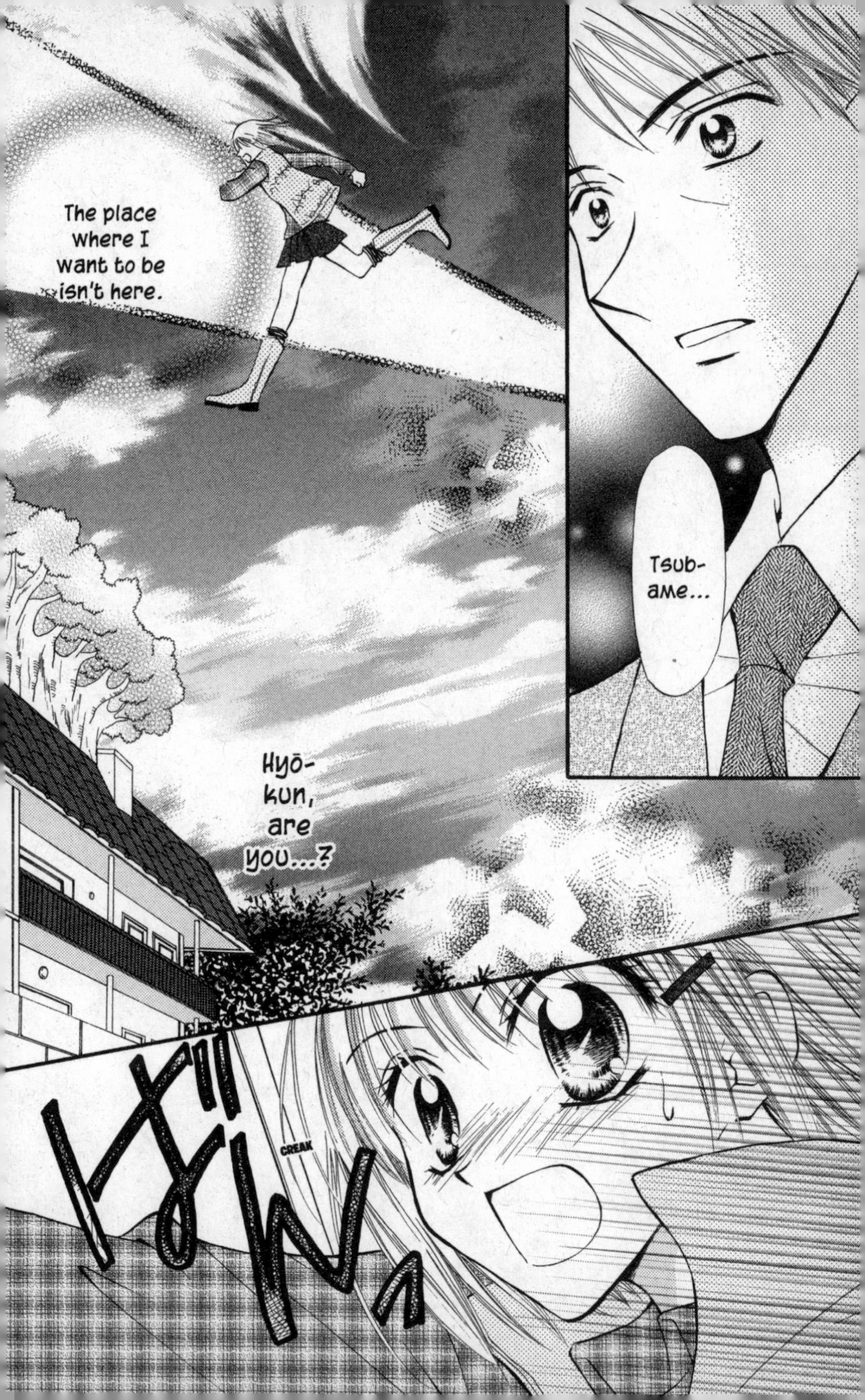

Tsub-ame...
The place where I want to be isn't here.
Hyō-kun, are you...?
CREAK

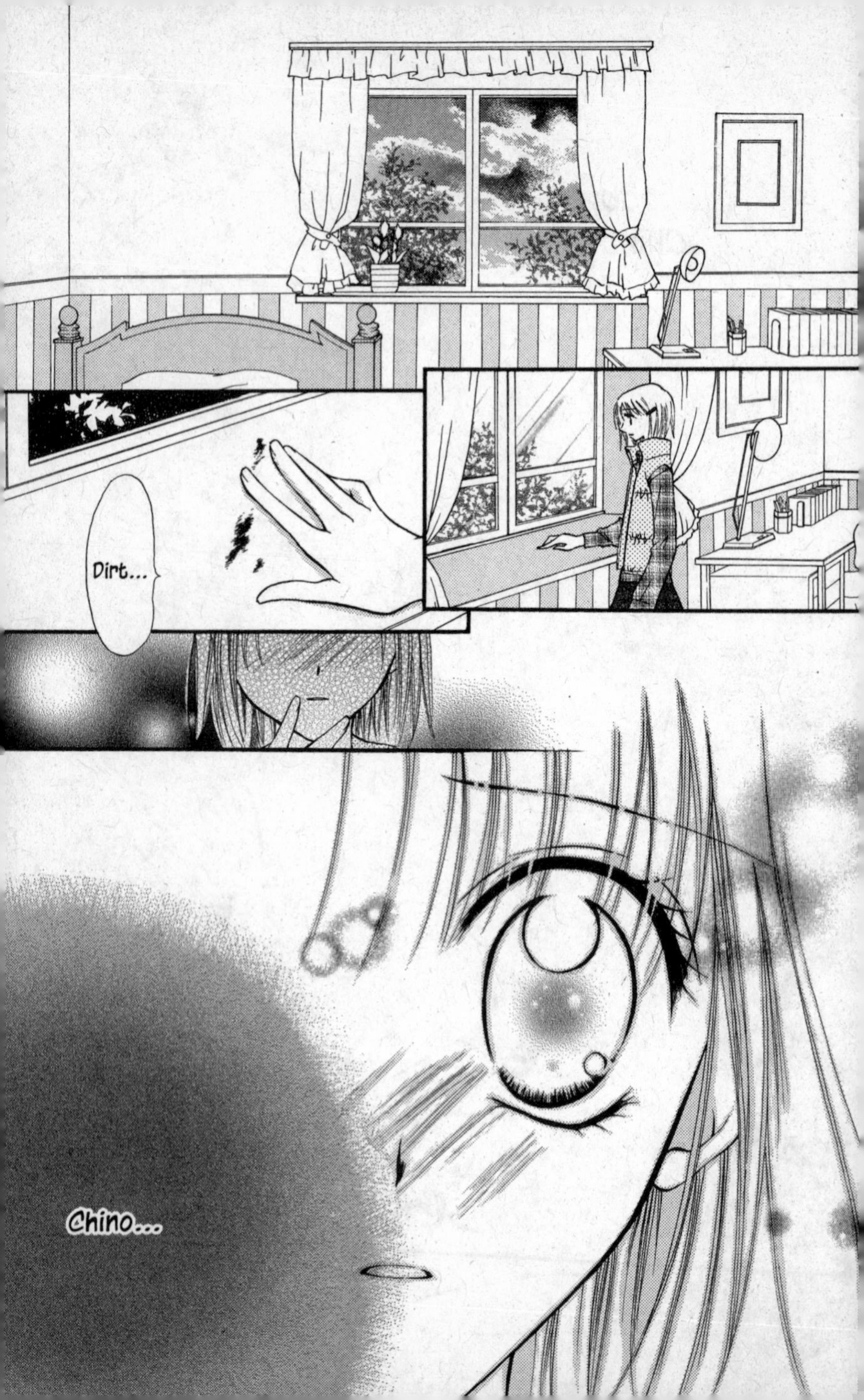
Dirt...
Chino...

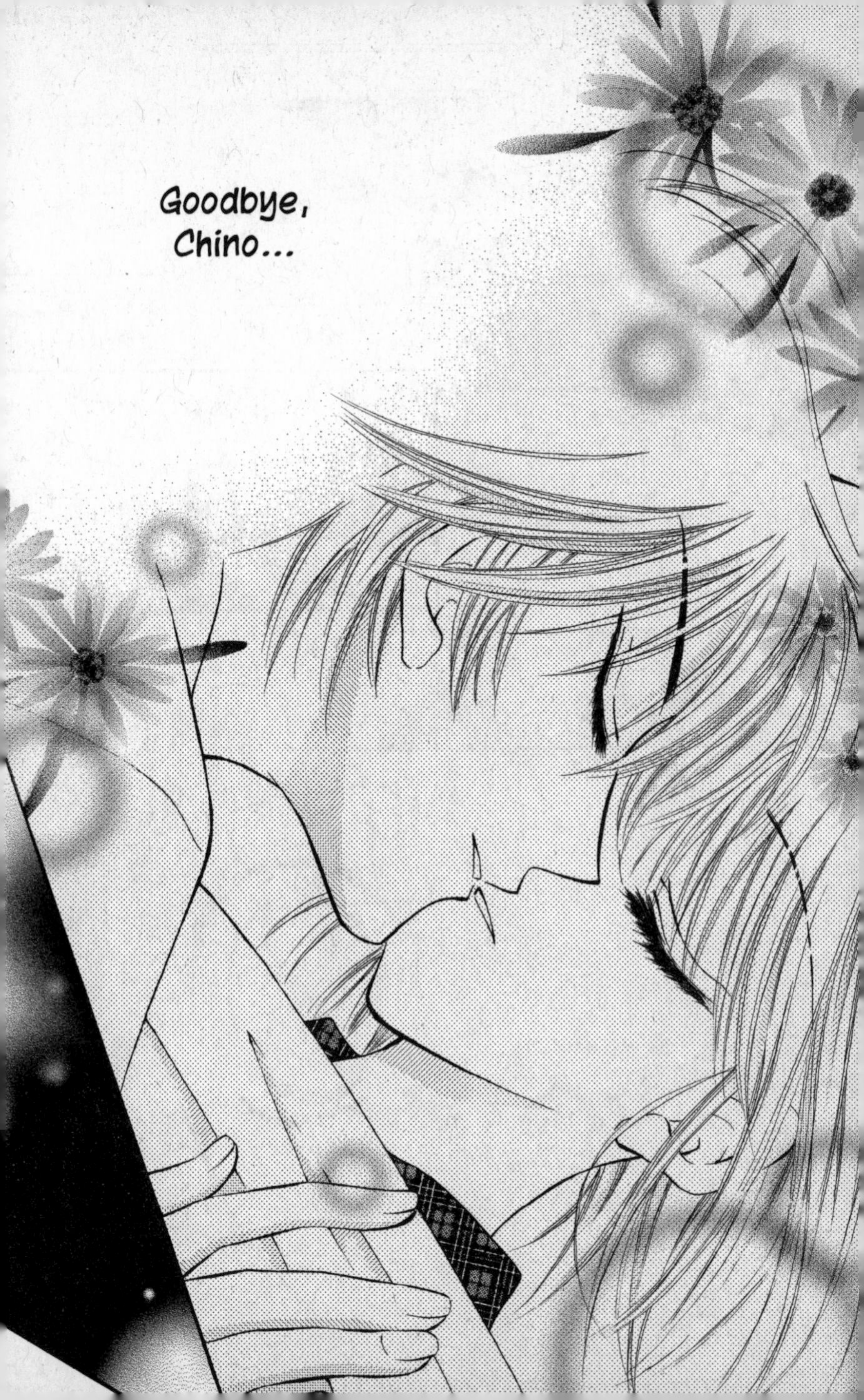
Goodbye,
Chino...

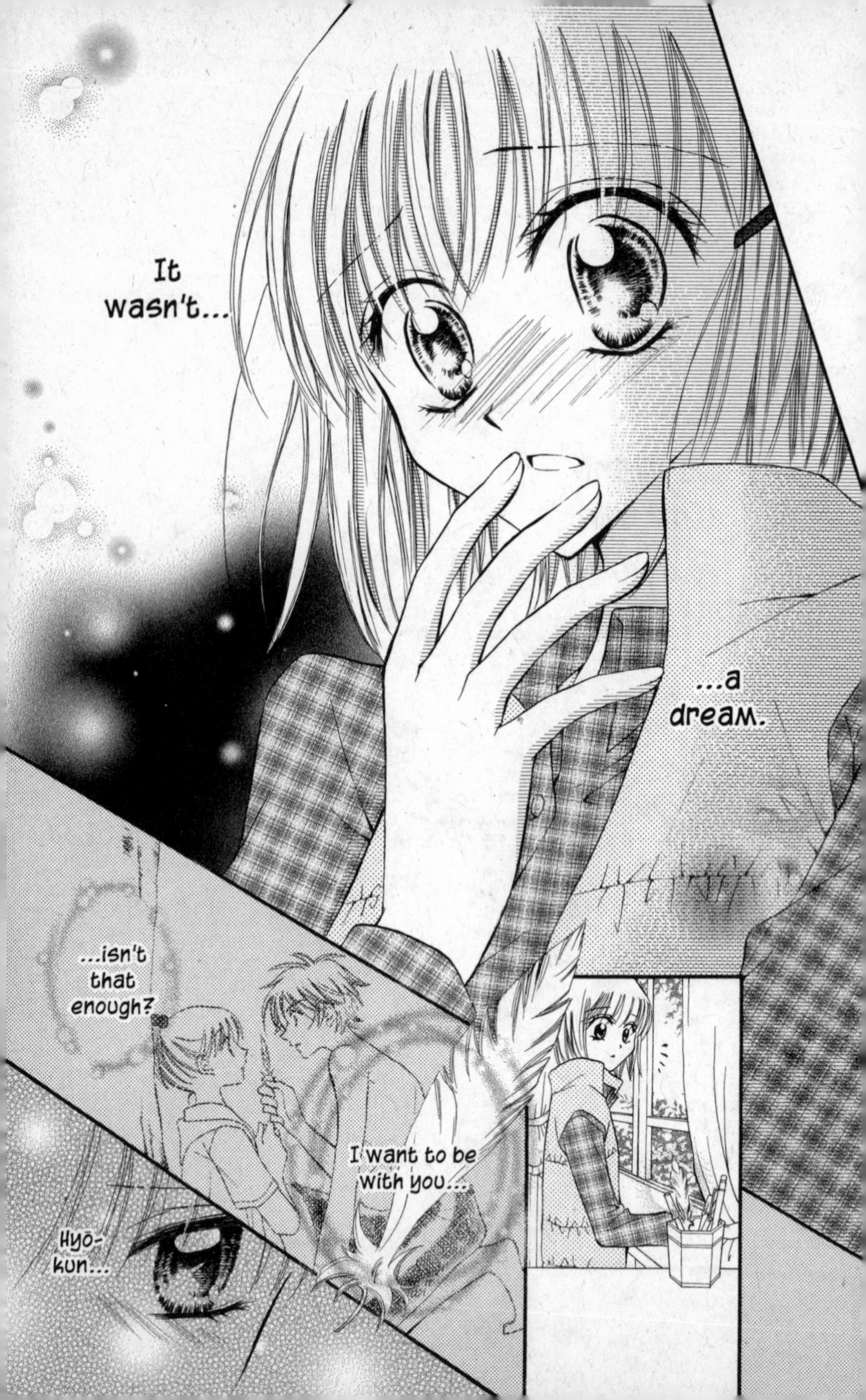
It wasn't...
...a dream.
...isn't that enough?
I want to be with you...
Hyō-kun...

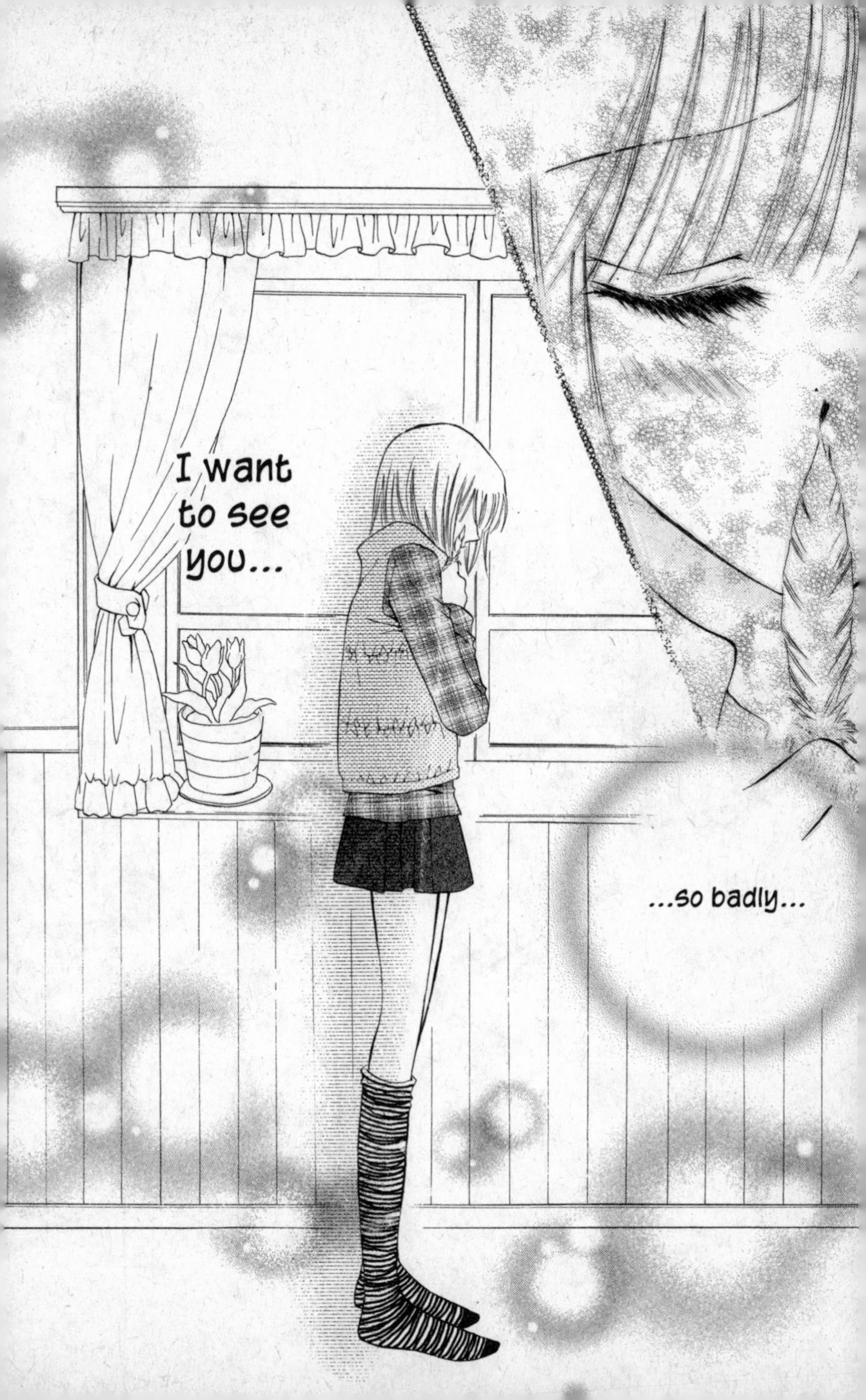
I want to see you...
...so badly...

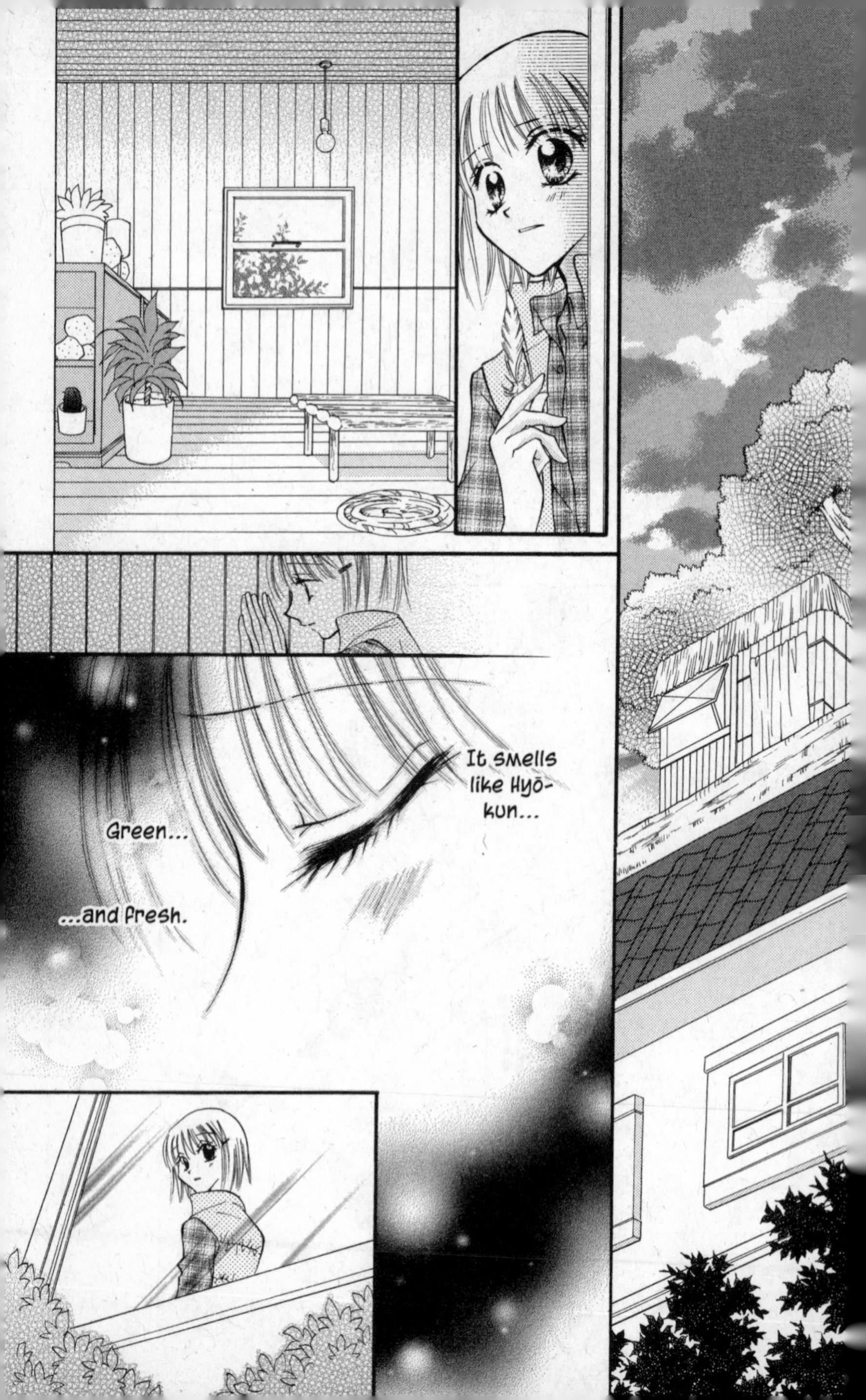
It smells like Hyō-kun...
Green...
...and fresh.

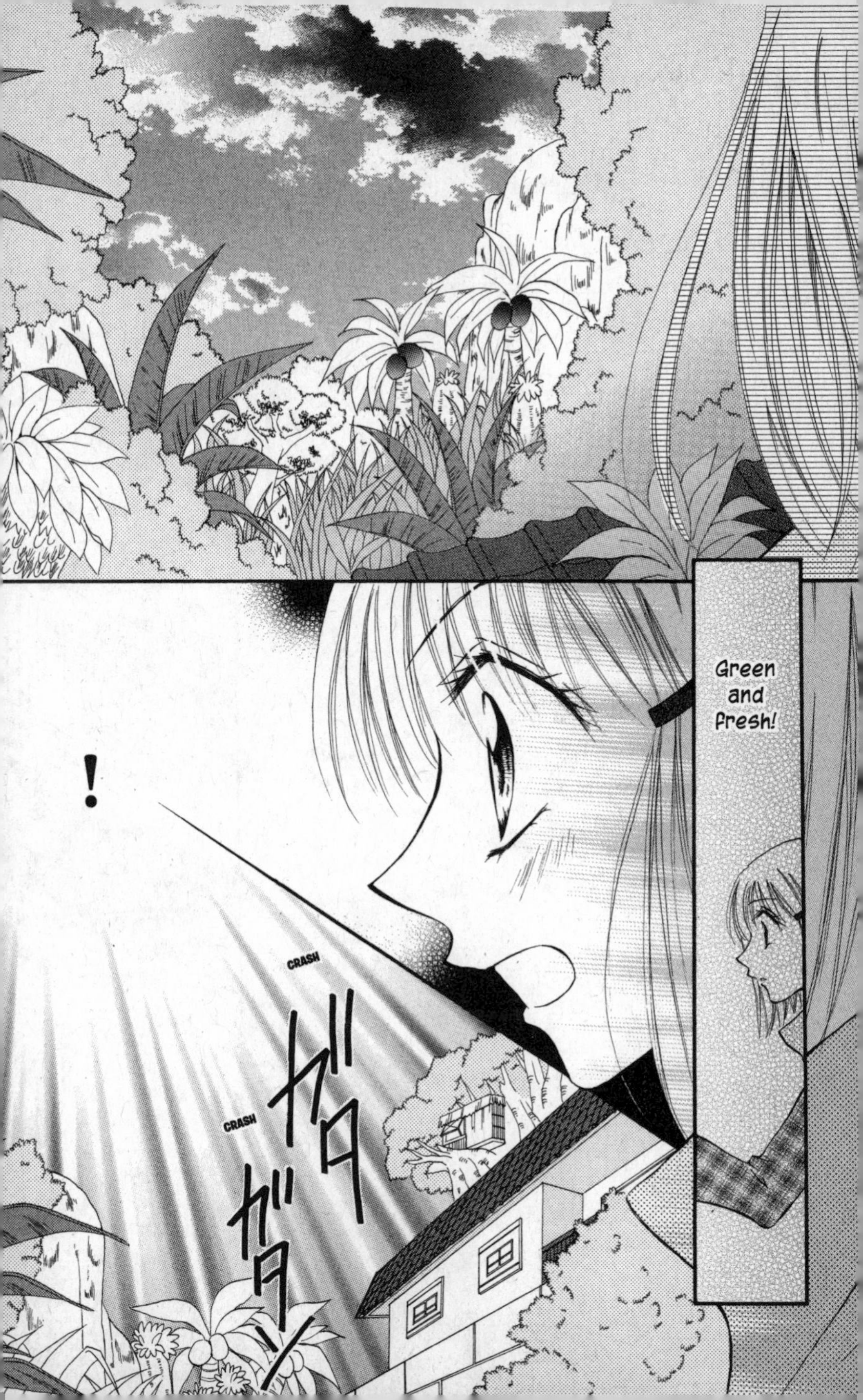
Green and fresh!
!
CRASH
CRASH
ガタガタン

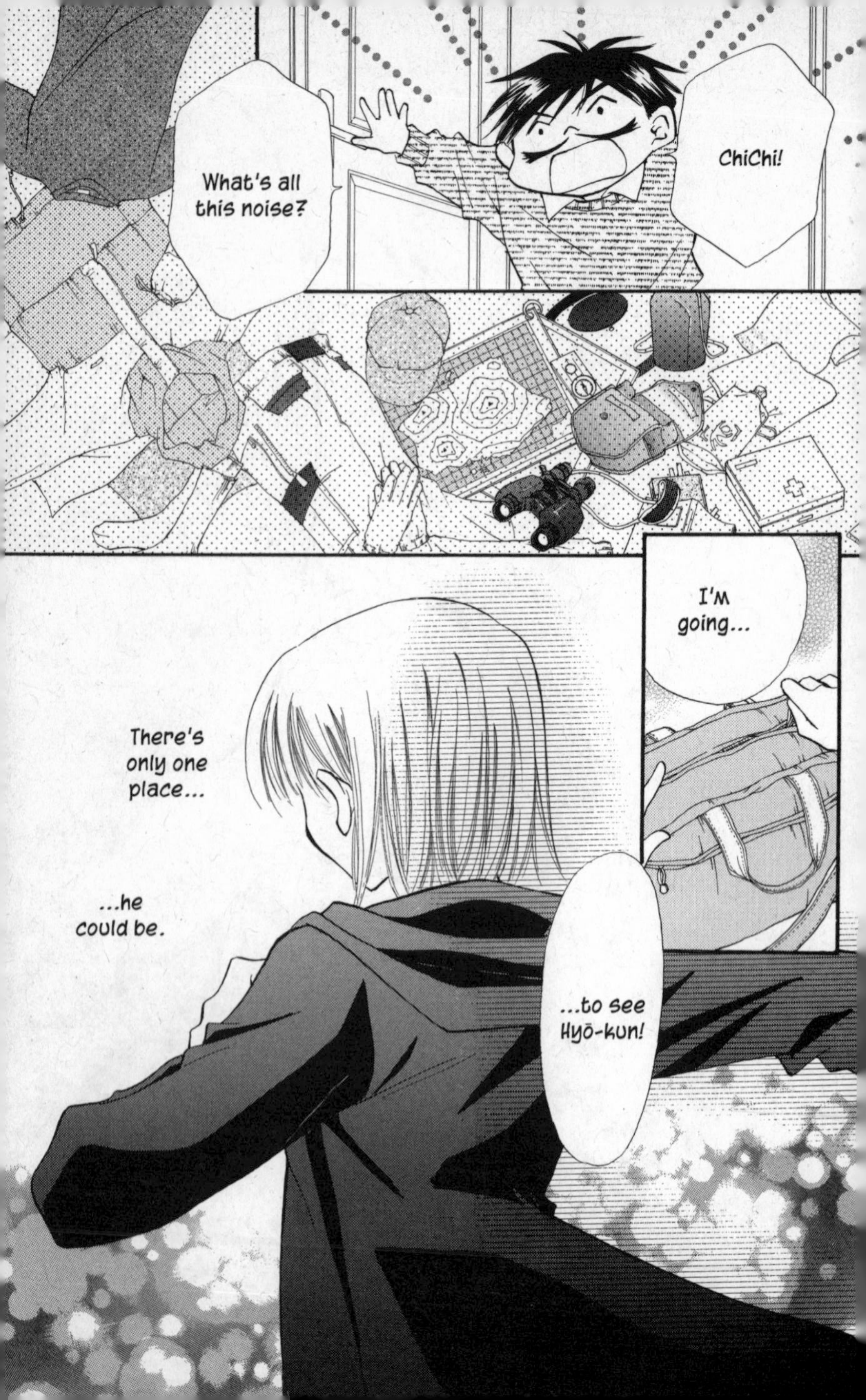
ChiChi!
What's all this noise?
I'M going...
...to see Hyō-kun!
There's only one place...
...he could be.

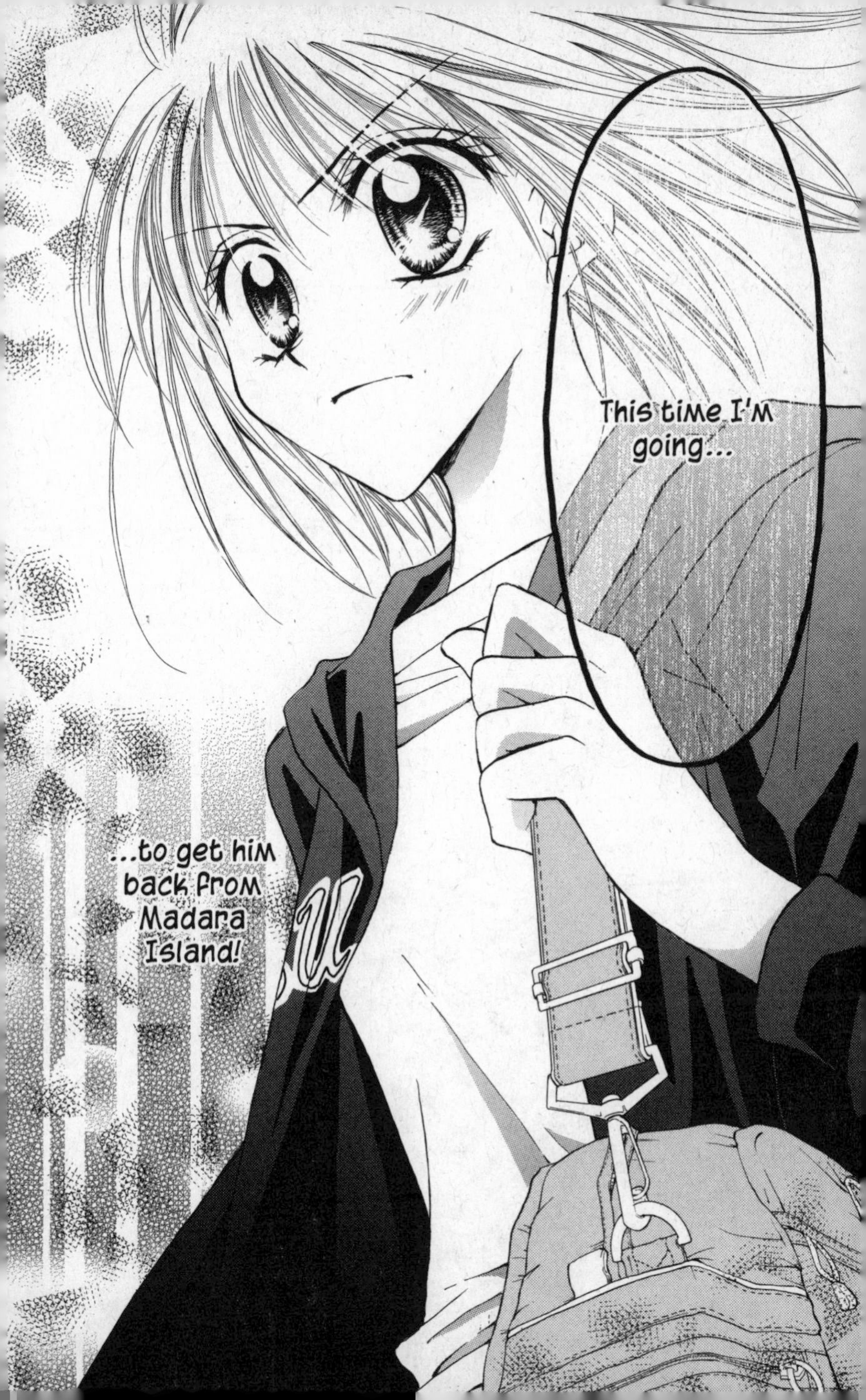
This time I'm going...
...to get him back from Madara Island!

Character Profile 4

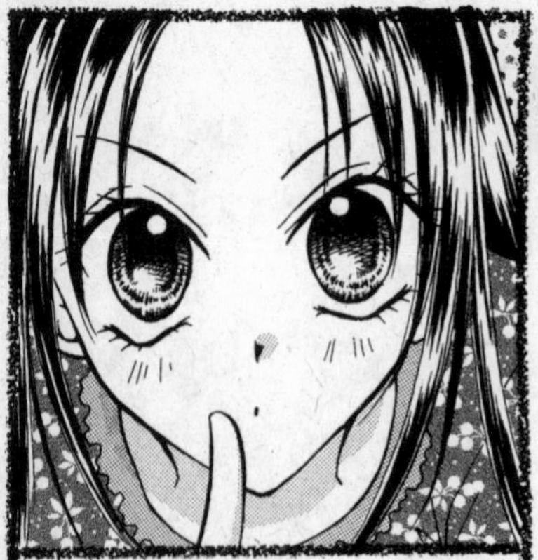

Tsubame Hanatsukasa

Birthday: February 28th
13 years old.
Pisces. Blood Type: B
Hobbies: Throwing parties.
Most of the time she has parties just to get attention.
She's even had birthday parties a month before and after her birthday.
Hanatsukasa's wife took her in after her parents abandoned her.
The type of guy she likes is just like her father.♡

Mitsuru Hanatsukasa

Birthday: August 3rd
45 years old.
Leo. Blood Type: A
Hobbies: Fishing.
Likes to go fishing around the world when he has time off.
His wife died the year their son went missing.
The shock of his disappearance was too much for her weak health.
Since then he's dedicated himself to his work.

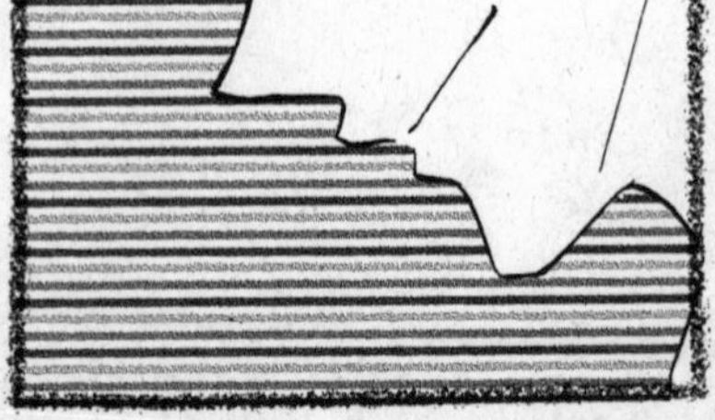

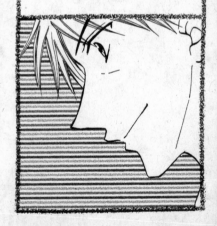

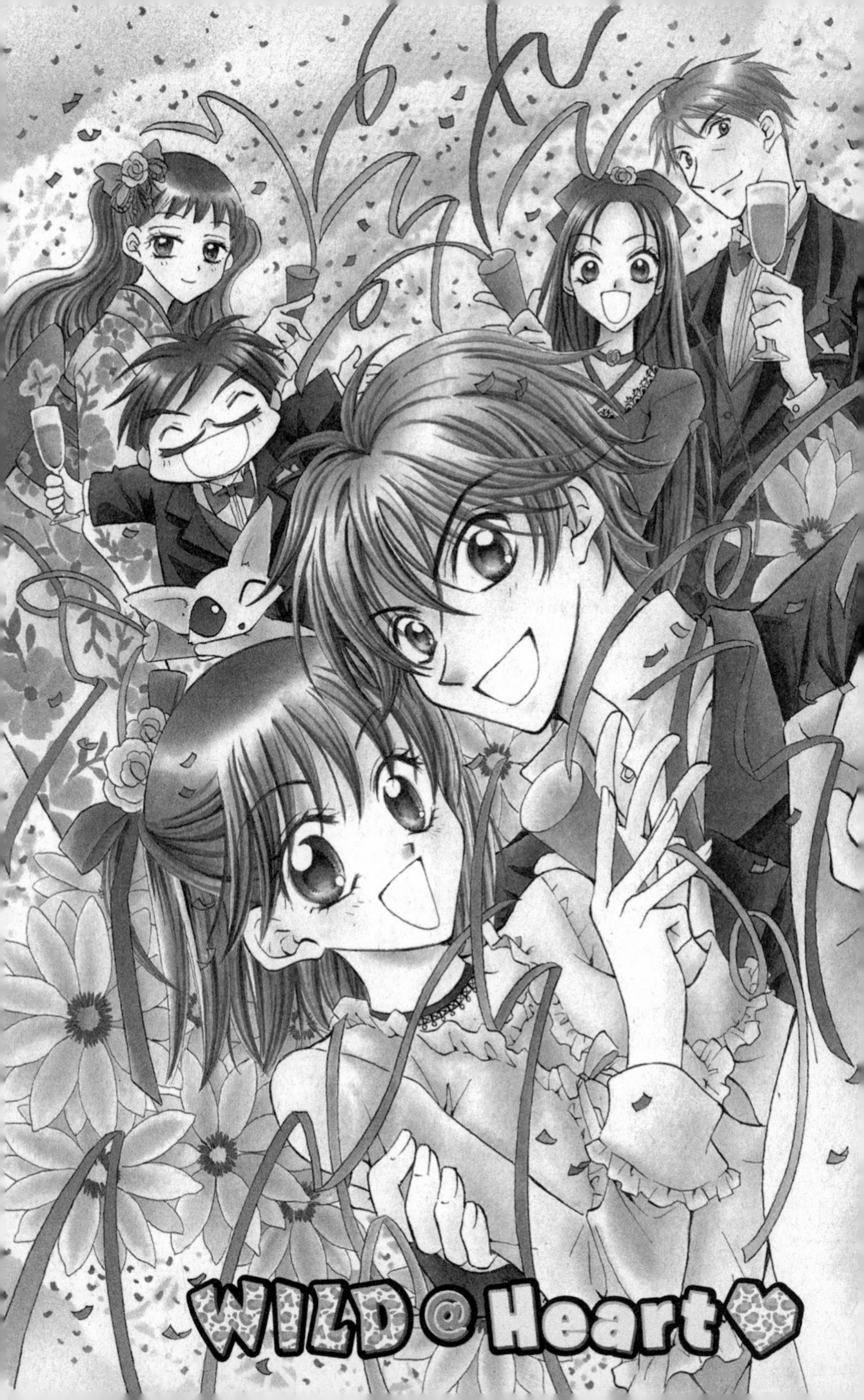
WILD @ Heart

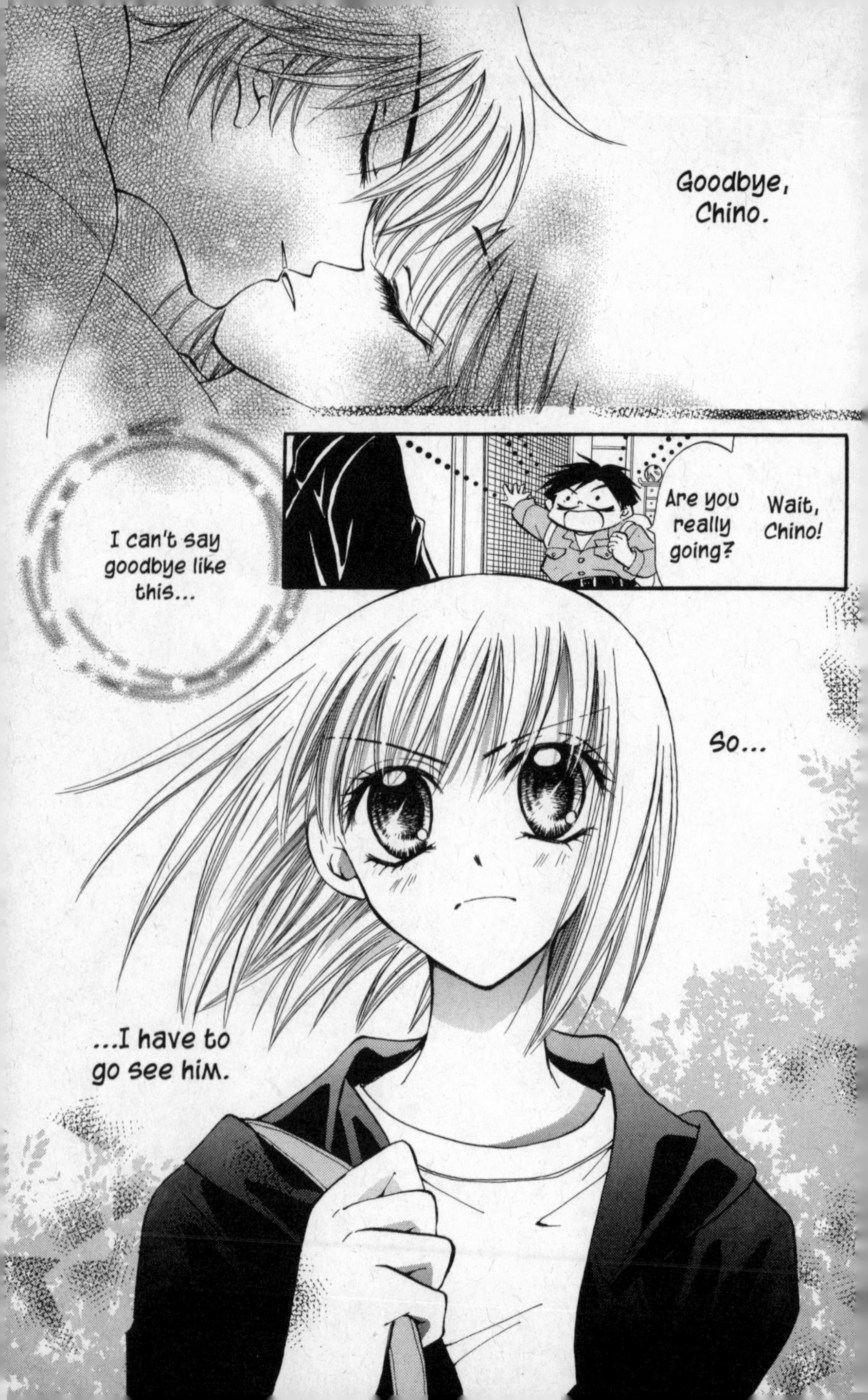
Goodbye, Chino.
Wait, Chino!
Are you really going?
I can't say goodbye like this...
So...
...I have to go see him.

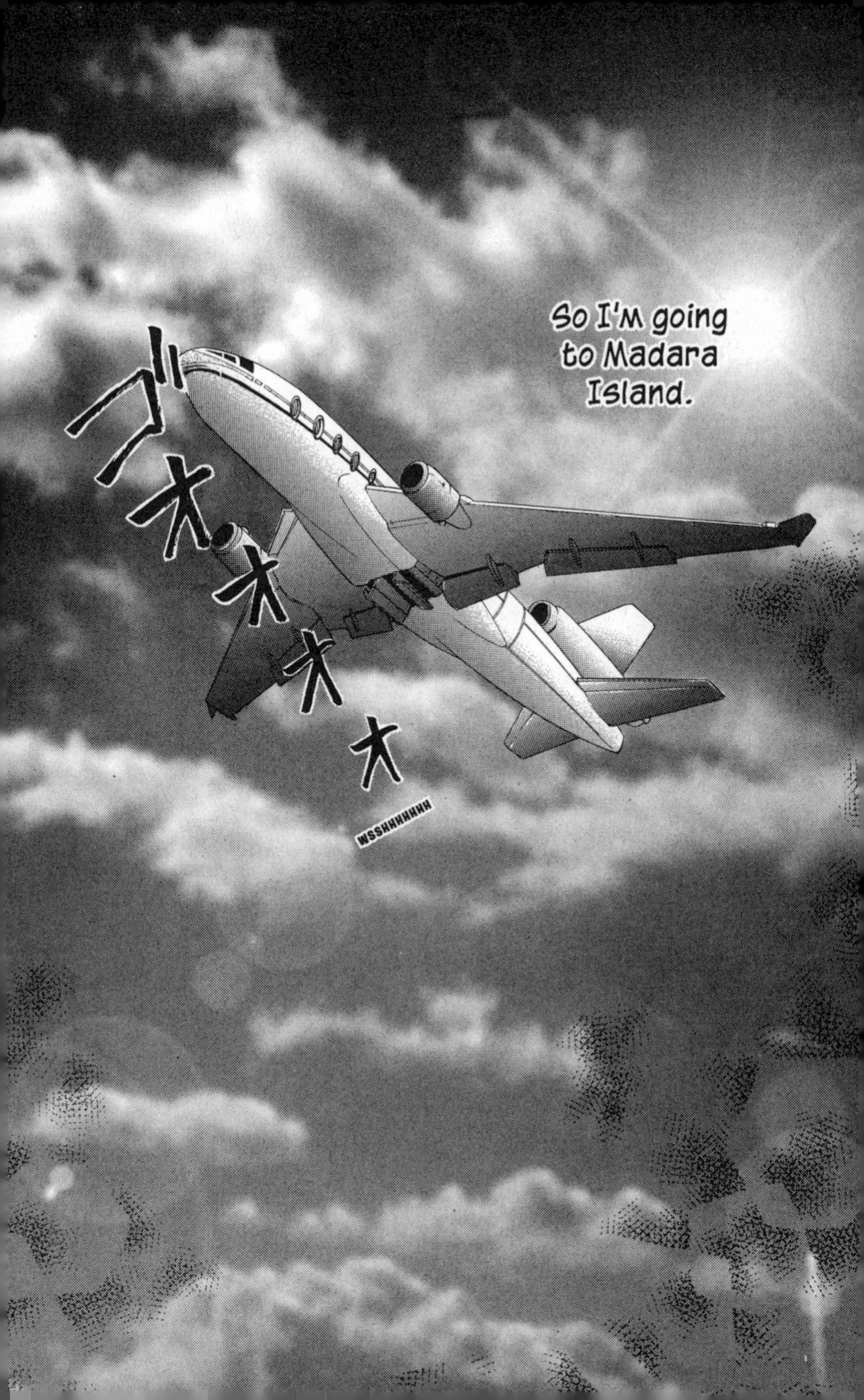
So I'm going to Madara Island.
ゴオオオオ
WSSHHHHHHH

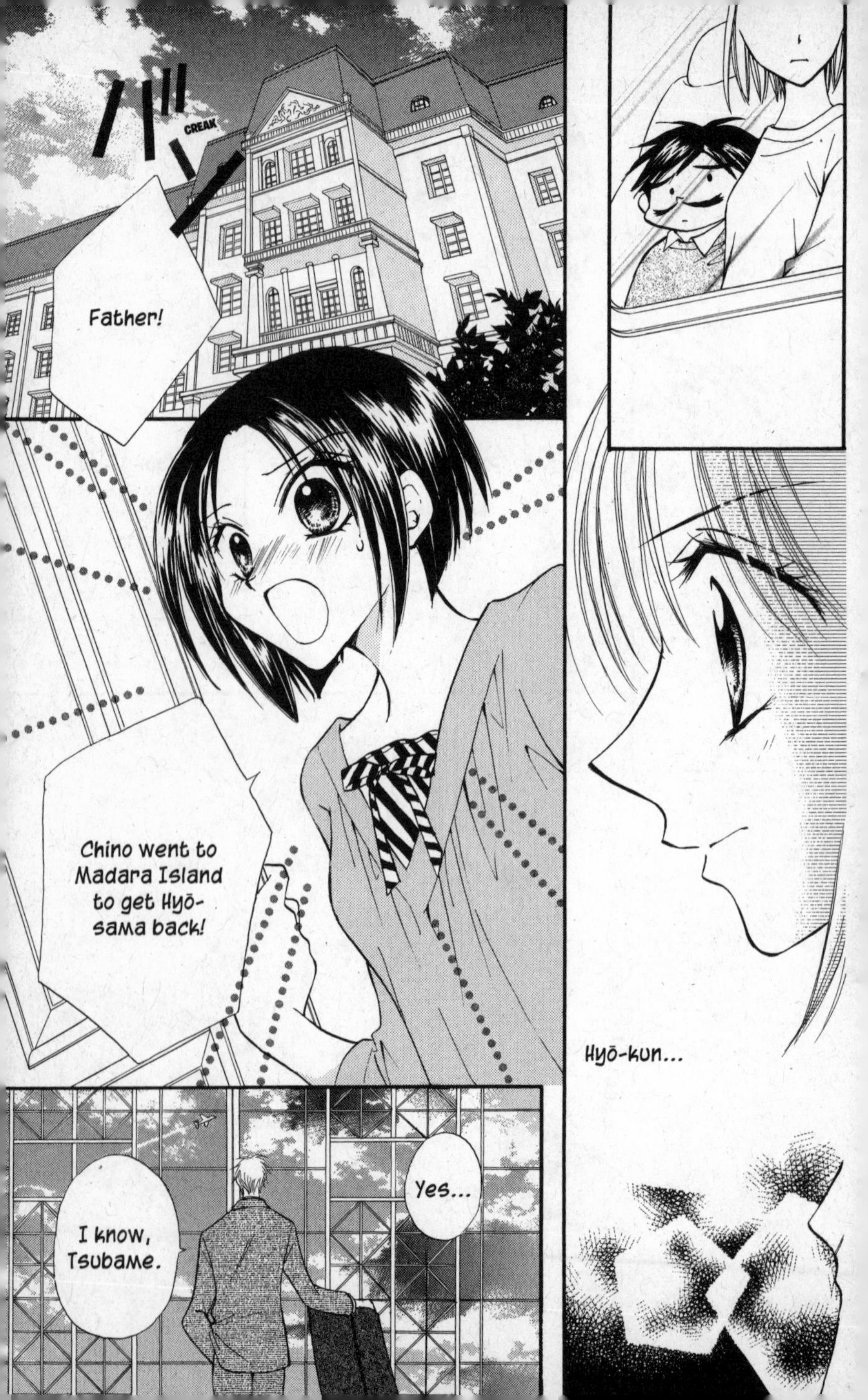
CREAK
Father!
Chino went to Madara Island to get Hyō-sama back!
Hyō-kun...
Yes...
I know, Tsubame.

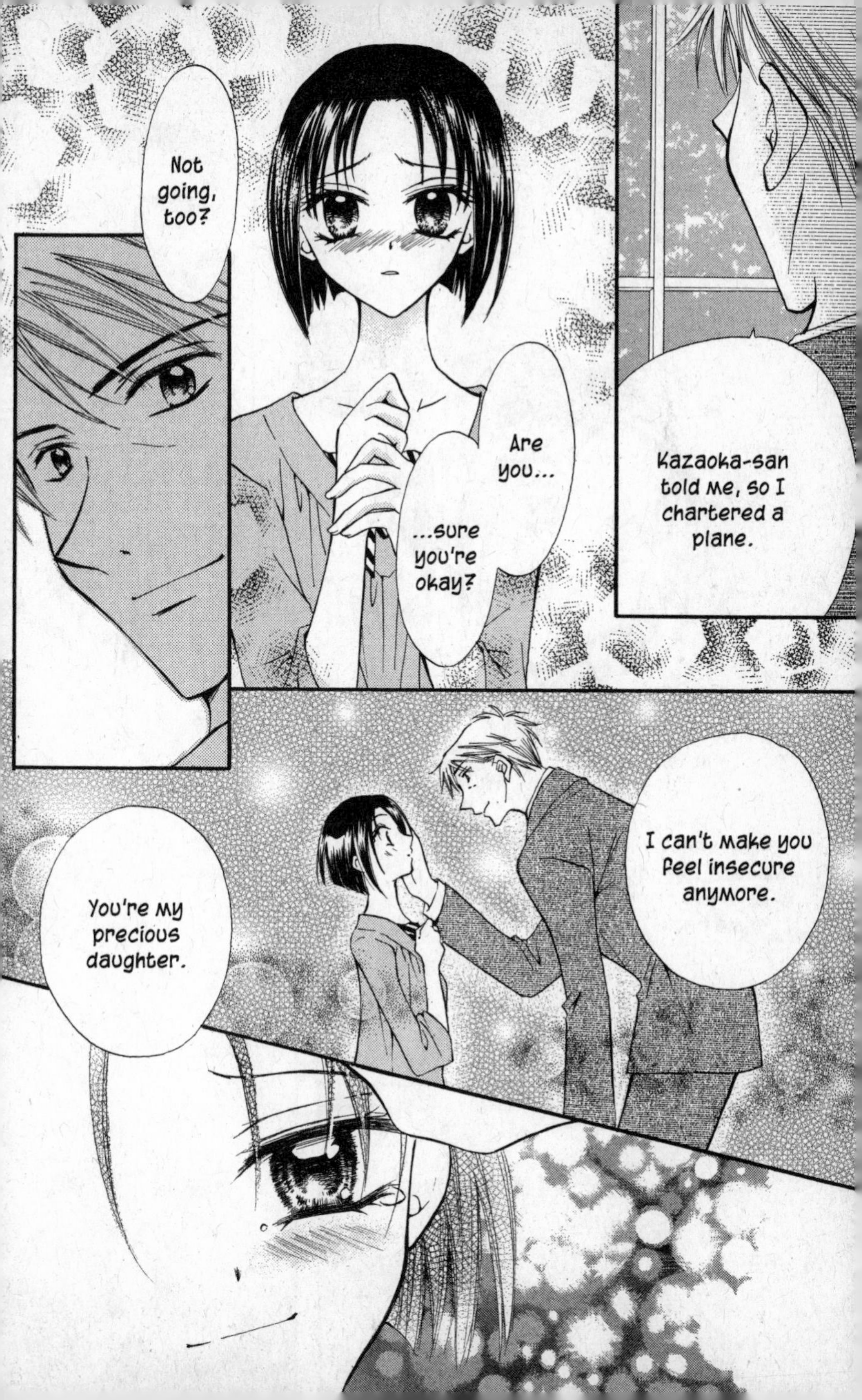
Kazaoka-san told me, so I chartered a plane.
Are you...
...sure you're okay?
Not going, too?
I can't make you feel insecure anymore.
You're my precious daughter.

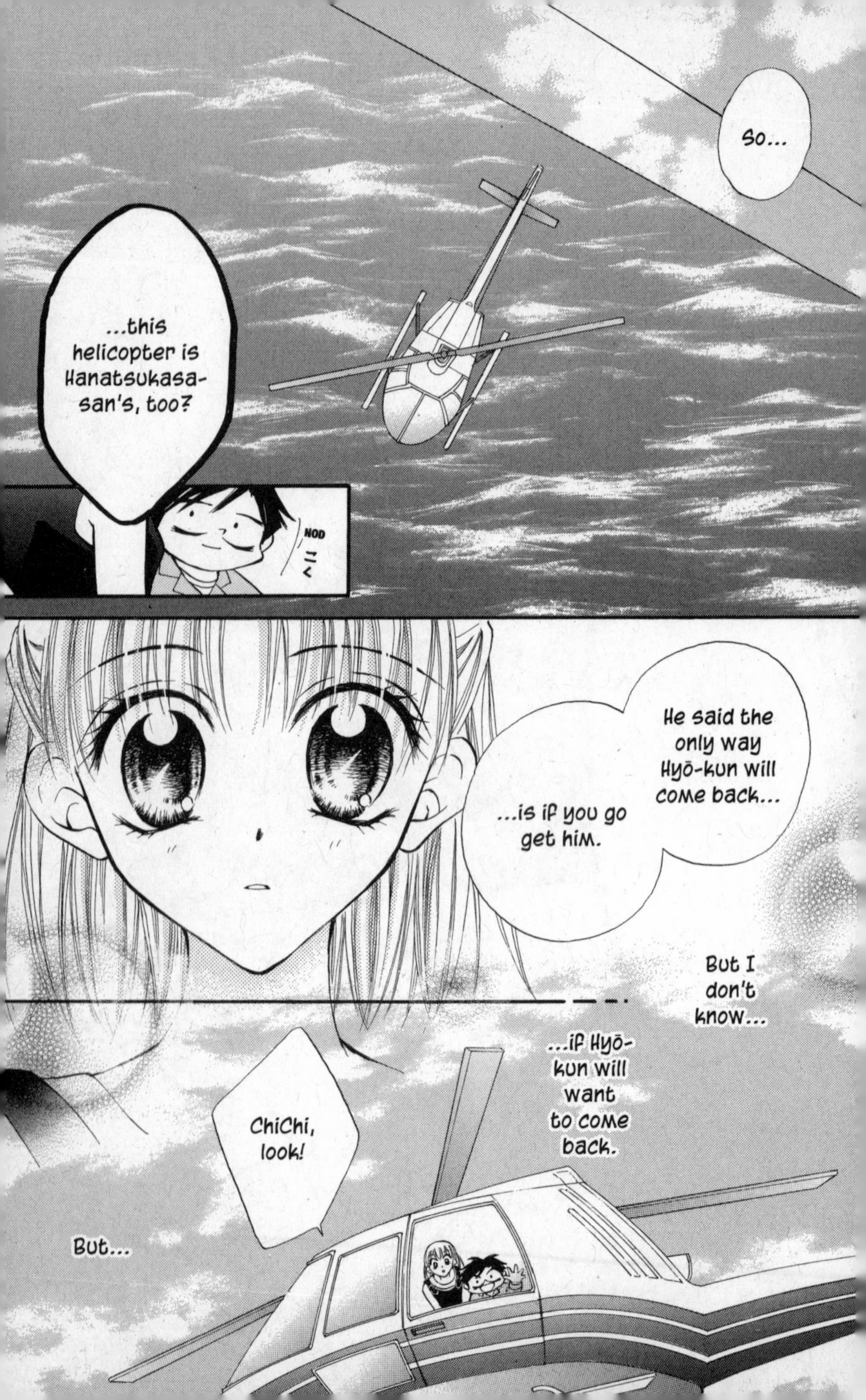
So...
...this helicopter is Hanatsukasa-san's, too?
NOD
He said the only way Hyō-kun will come back...
...is if you go get him.
But I don't know...
...if Hyō-kun will want to come back.
ChiChi, look!
But...

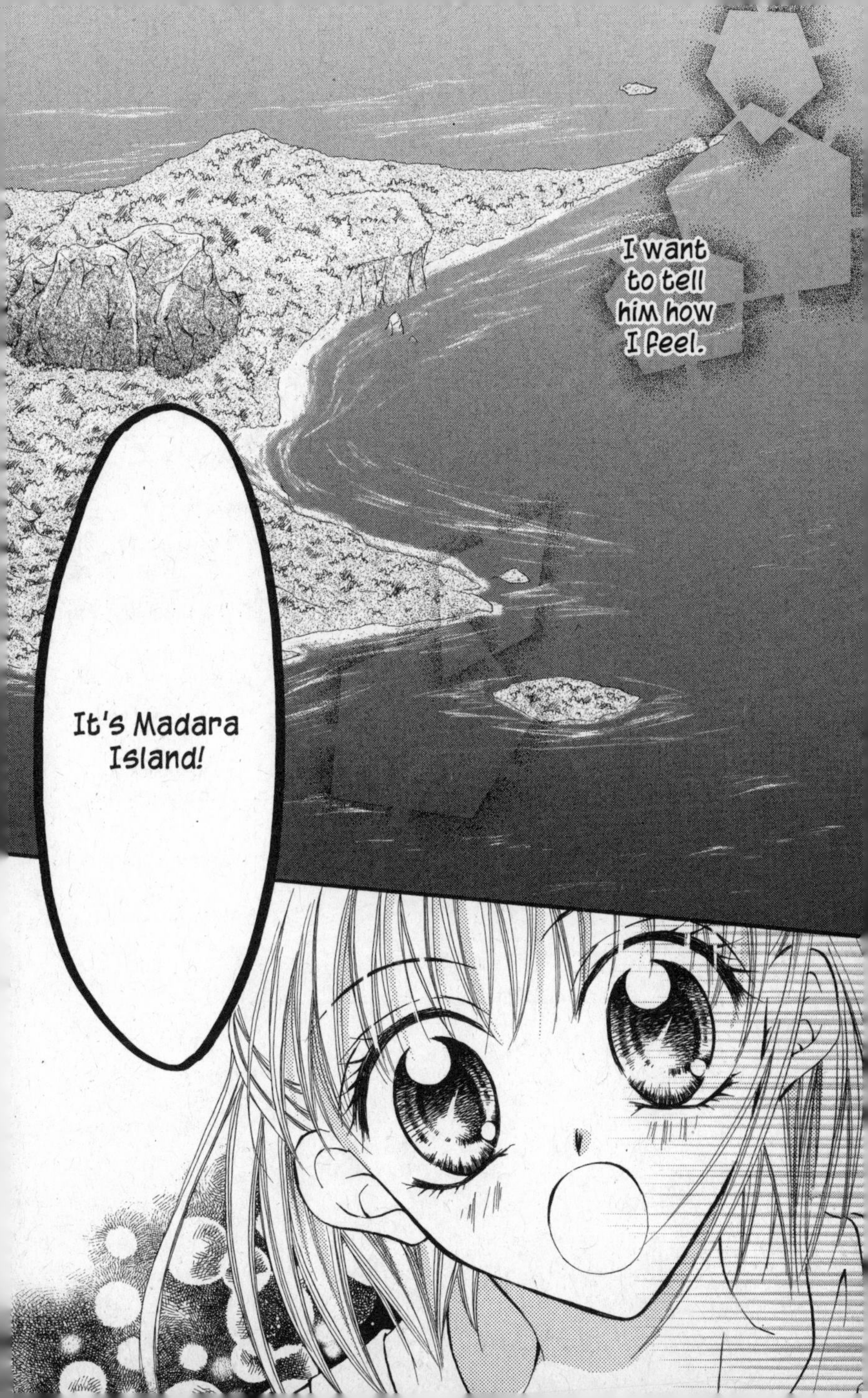
I want to tell him how I feel.
It's Madara Island!

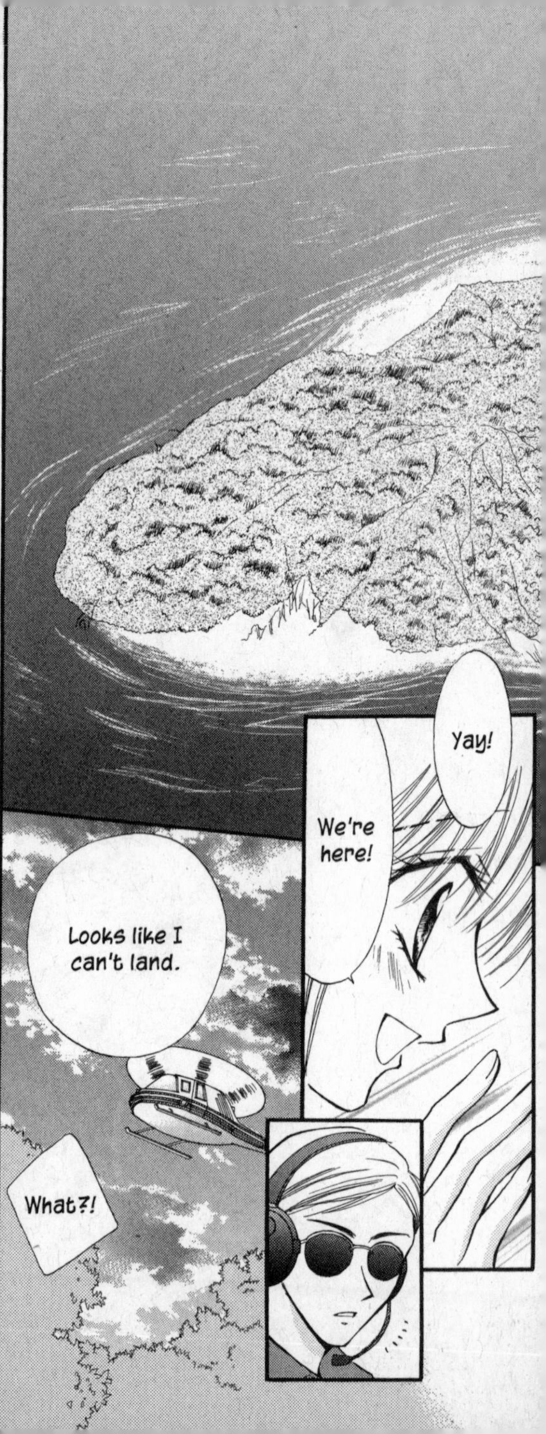
Yay!
We're here!
Looks like I can't land.
What?!

5.

My friend had a baby so I went to visit her. I had a cold that day and when I coughed...

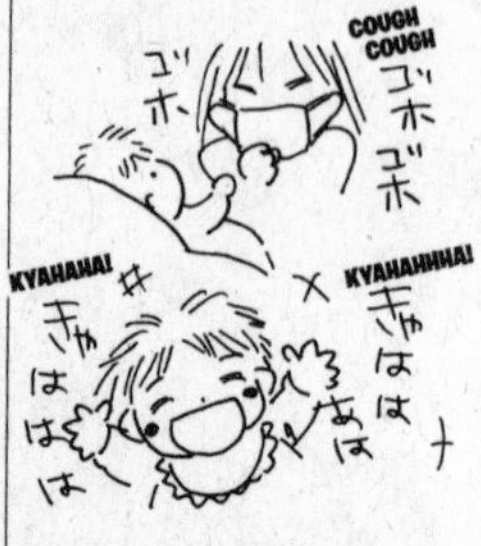
COUGH COUGH
KYAHAHA!
KYAHAHHHA!

the baby cracked up!

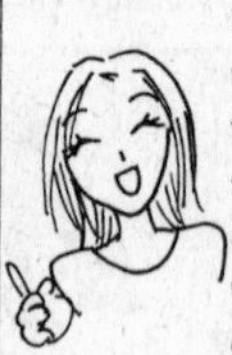

My friend told me the baby used to laugh when someone imitated a gorilla but now she thought coughing was funny!

The baby really did laugh every time I coughed.

I'd never seen that before!

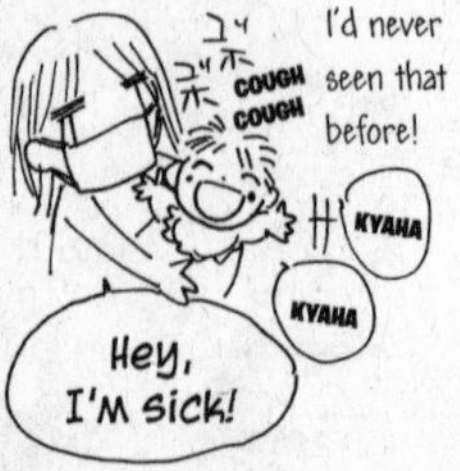
COUGH COUGH
KYAHA
KYAHA
Hey, I'm sick!

But it was so cute! ♡ I wonder what she'll laugh at next! ♪

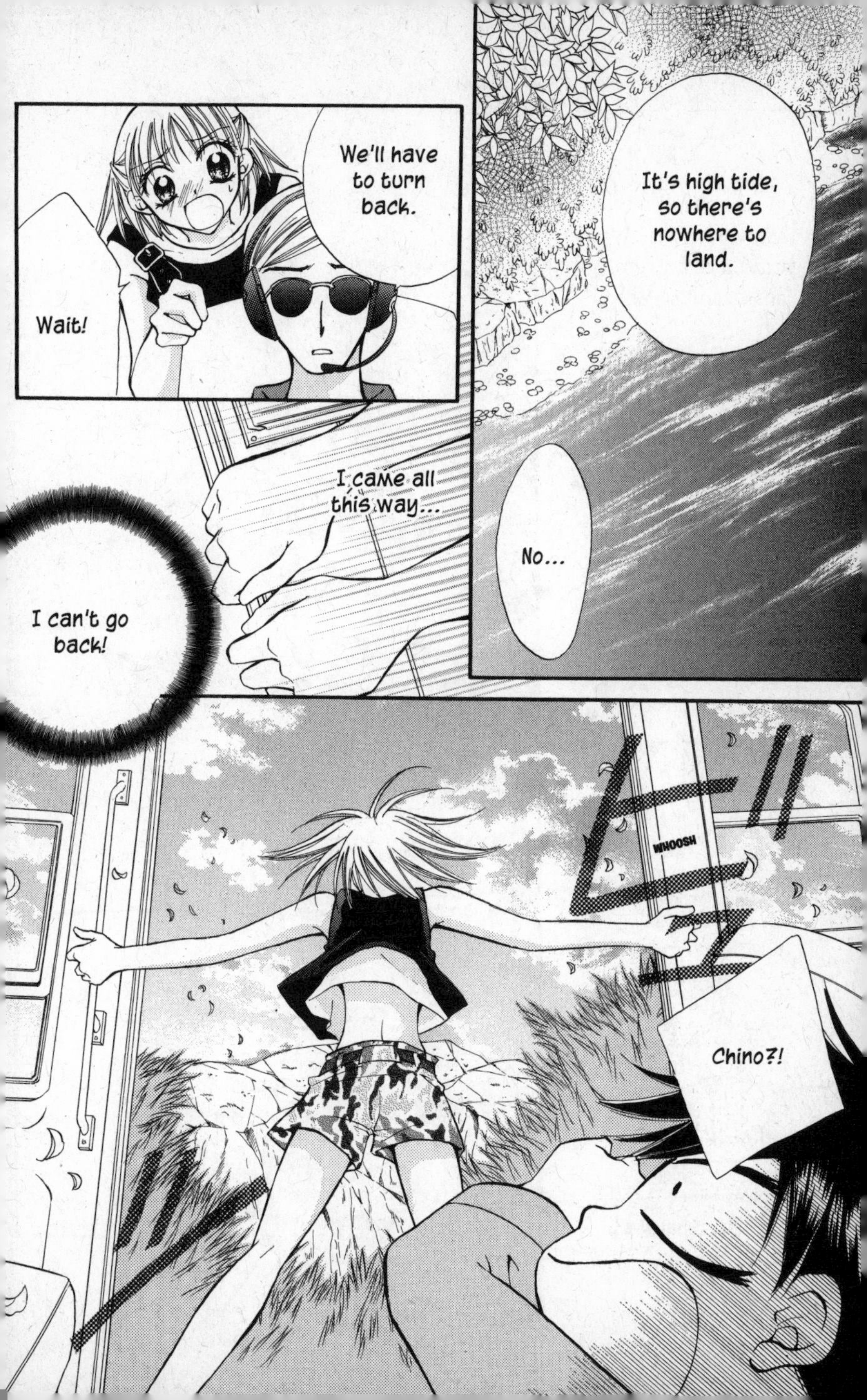
It's high tide, so there's nowhere to land.
No...
We'll have to turn back.
Wait!
I came all this way...
I can't go back!
WHOOSH
Chino?!

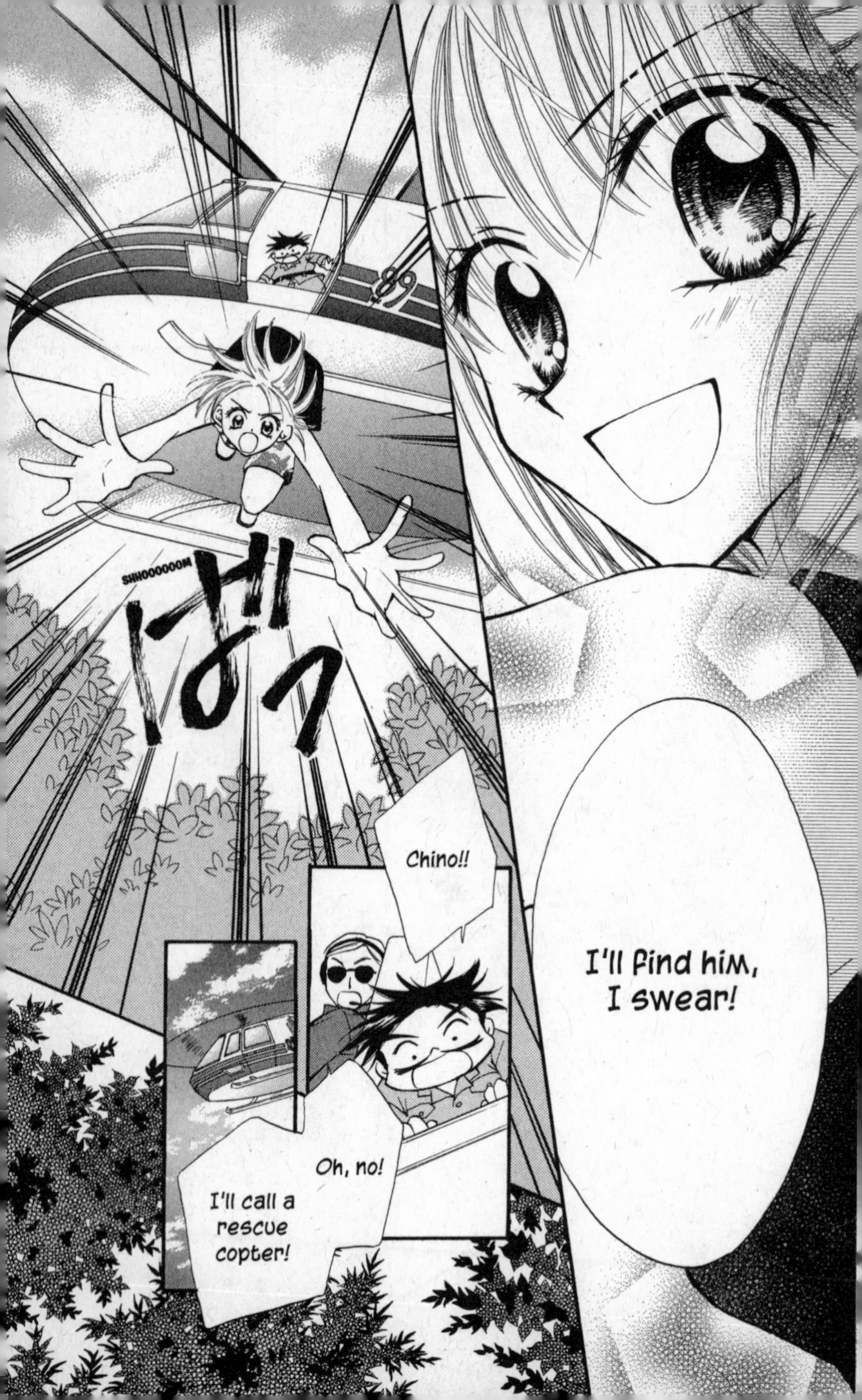
I'll find him, I swear!
SHHOOOOOOOM
Chino!!
Oh, no!
I'll call a rescue copter!

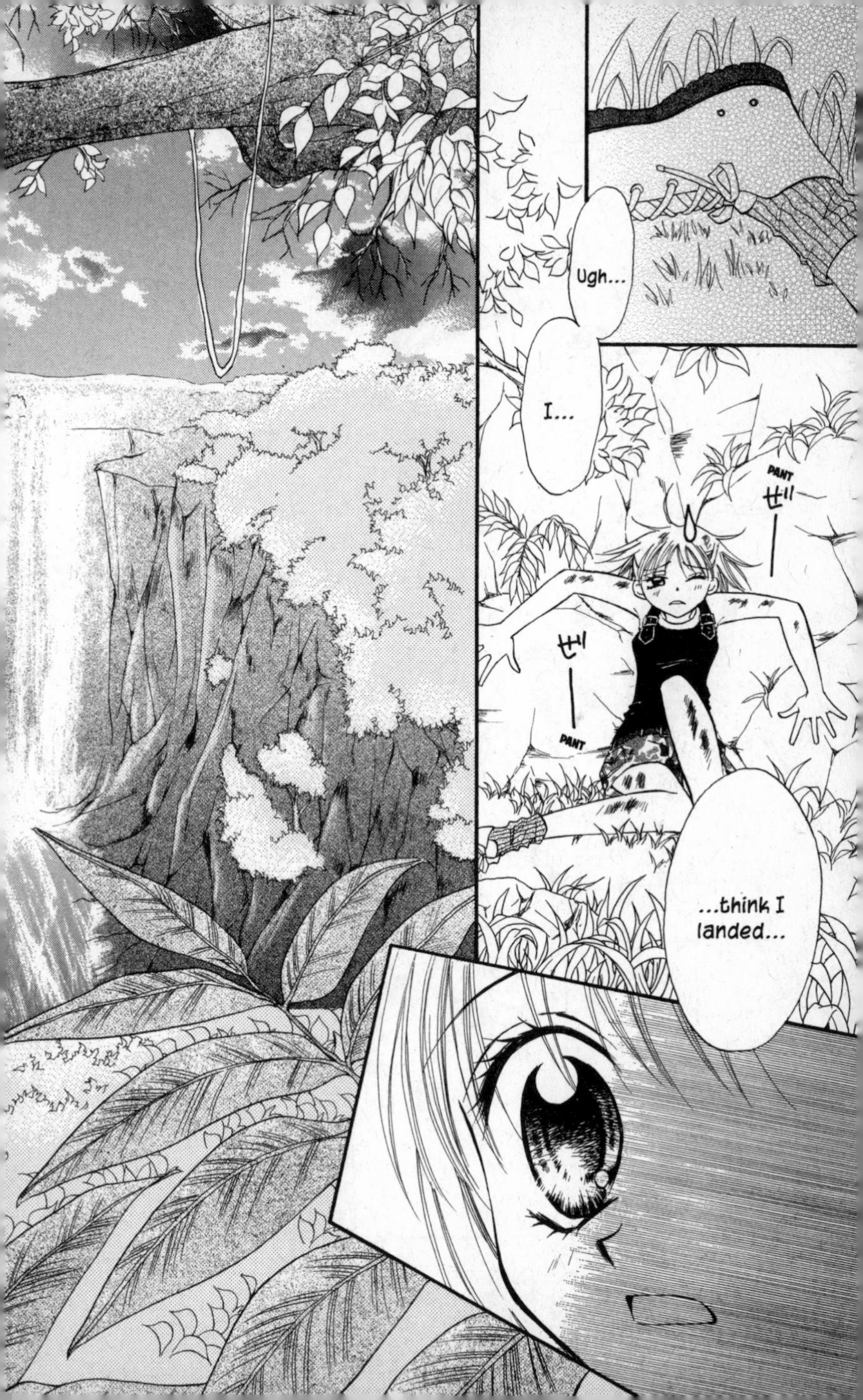

Ugh...
I...
PANT
ゼー
ゼー
PANT
...think I landed...

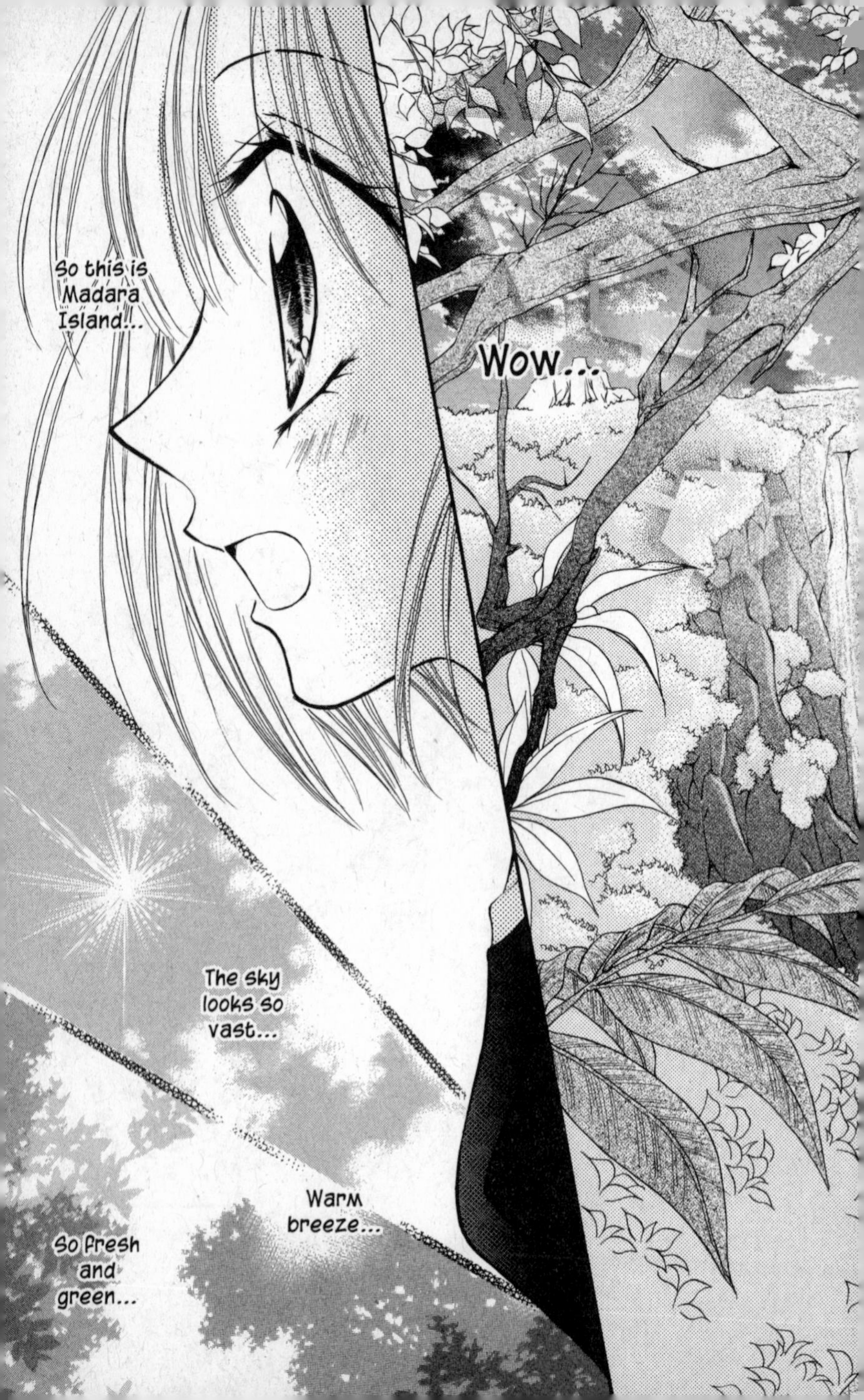
Wow...
So this is Madara Island...
The sky looks so vast...
Warm breeze...
So fresh and green...

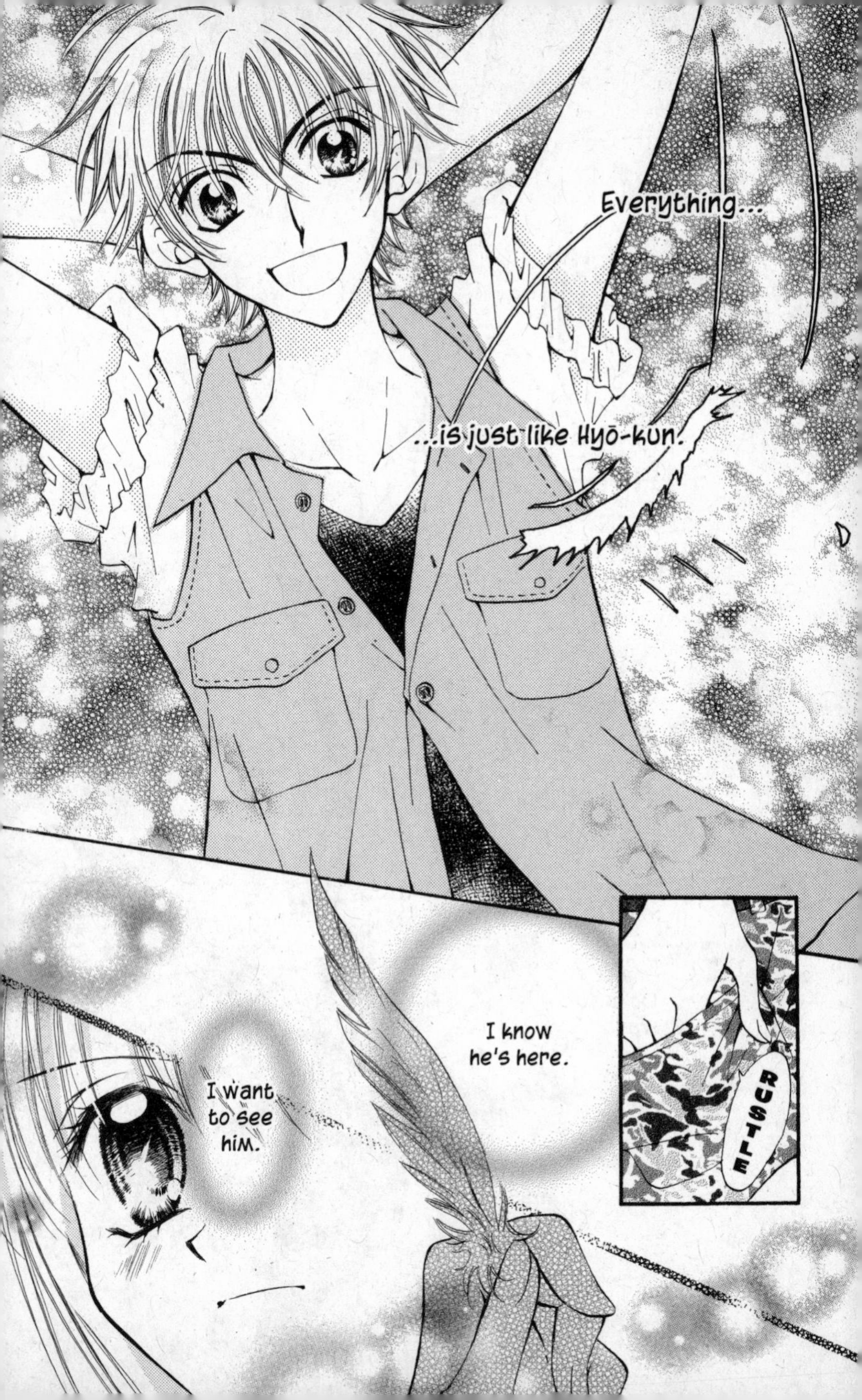
Everything...
...is just like Hyō-kun.
RUSTLE
I know he's here.
I want to see him.

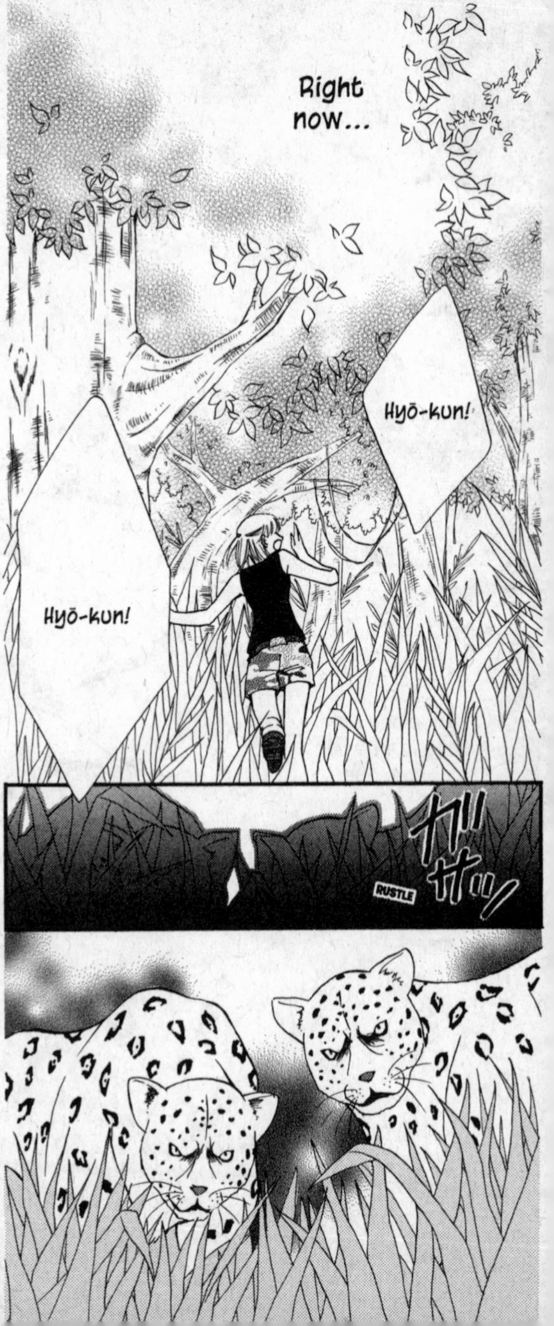
Right now...
Hyō-kun!
Hyō-kun!
ガサッ
RUSTLE

6.

The other day I was walking through town...

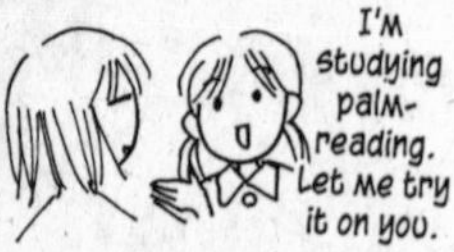
I'm studying palm-reading. Let me try it on you.

...when a girl came up to me and said that. She said it to me twice before I realized she was talking to me! Do I really look that unhappy? I turned her down, of course. My little sister got her palm read once. The lady said, "Hmm, there is something troubling you," and when my sister said, "Not really," the lady insisted there was! Then someone else showed up and said, "Want to come to a meeting where we can help you with your problems?" I wonder what kind of meeting it was? Anyway, my sister ran away!

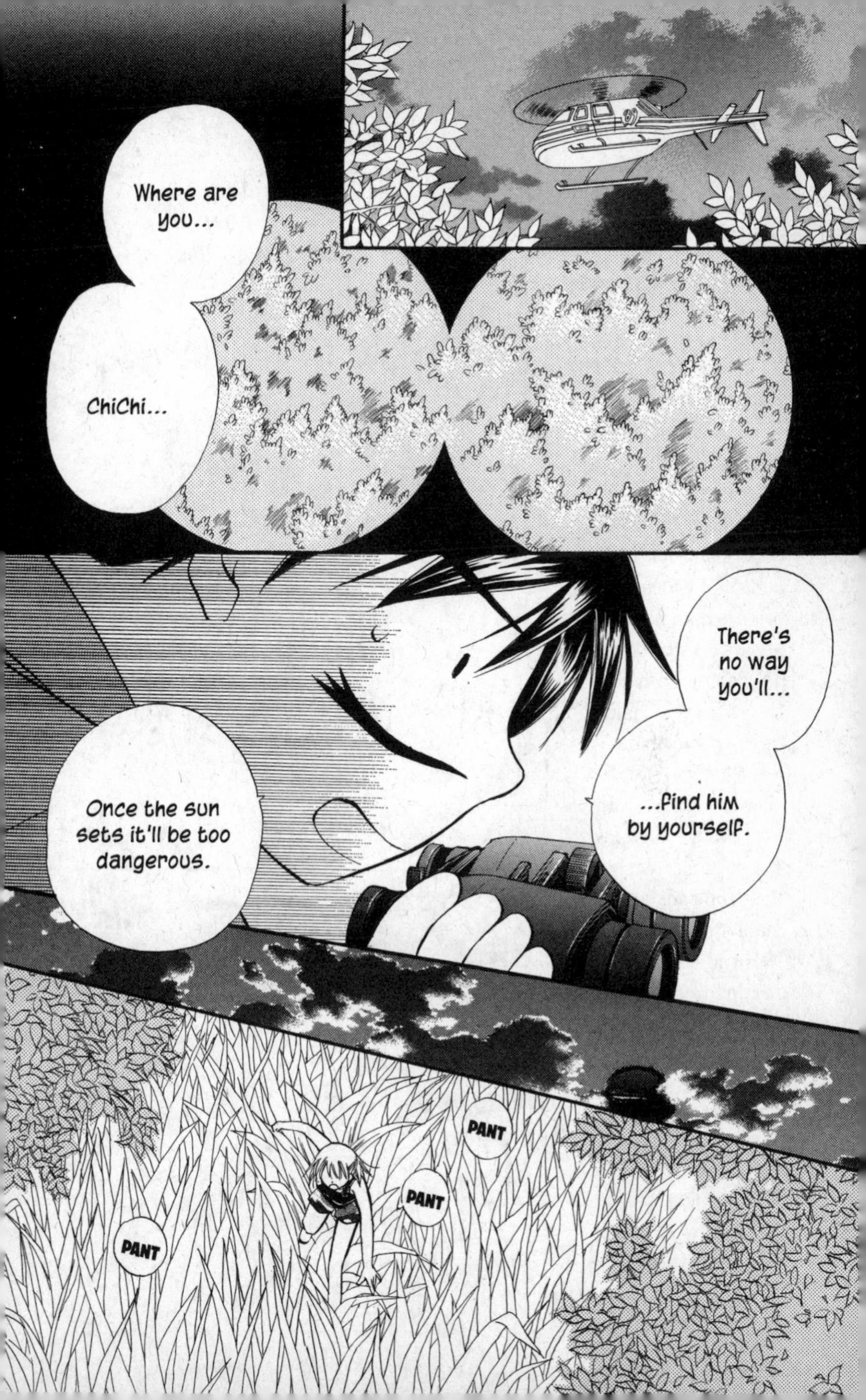
Where are you...
ChiChi...
There's no way you'll...
...find him by yourself.
Once the sun sets it'll be too dangerous.
PANT
PANT
PANT

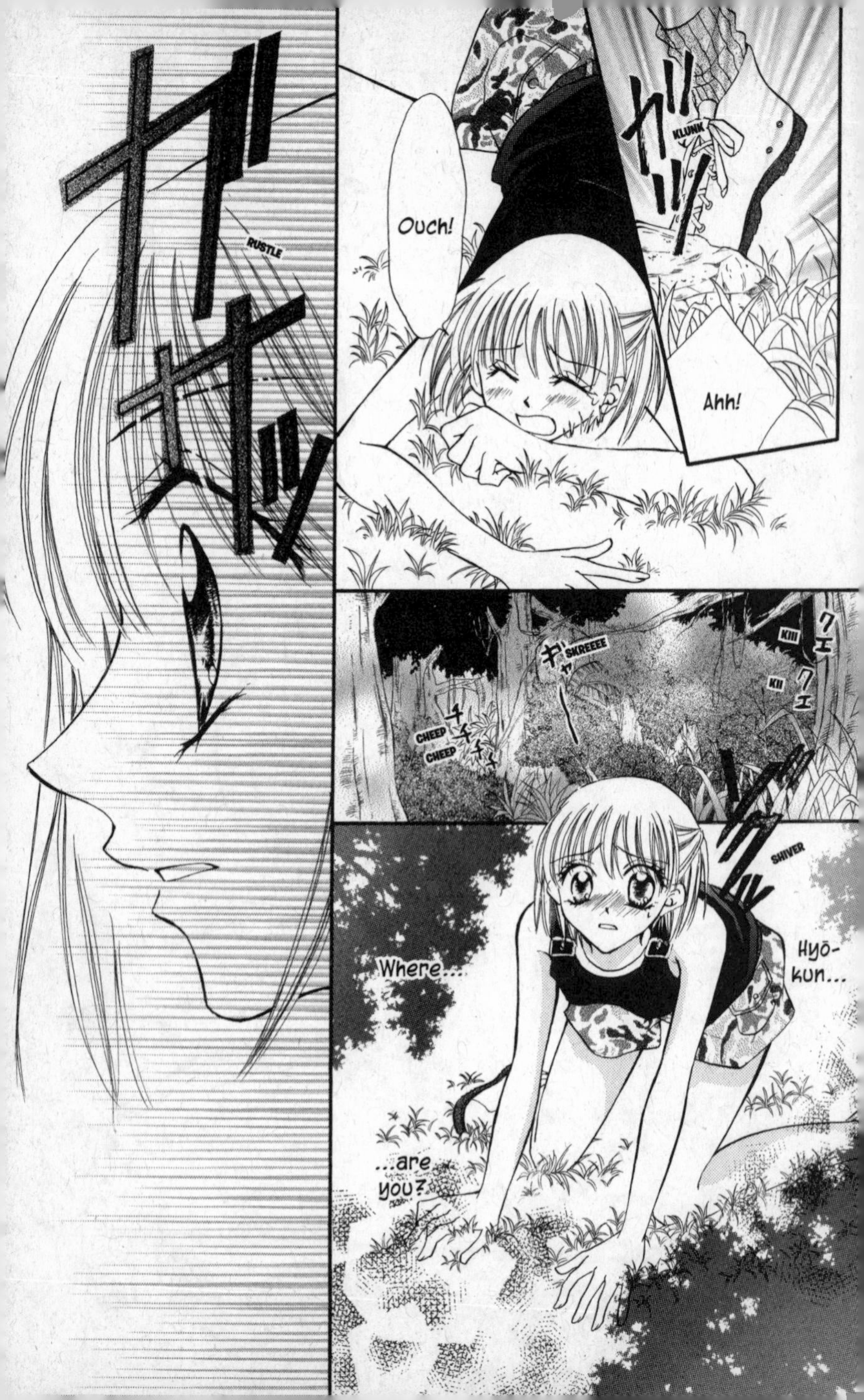
KLUNK
Ahh!
Ouch!
KIII
KIII
SKREEEE
CHEEP
CHEEP
SHIVER
Hyō-kun...
Where...
...are you?
RUSTLE

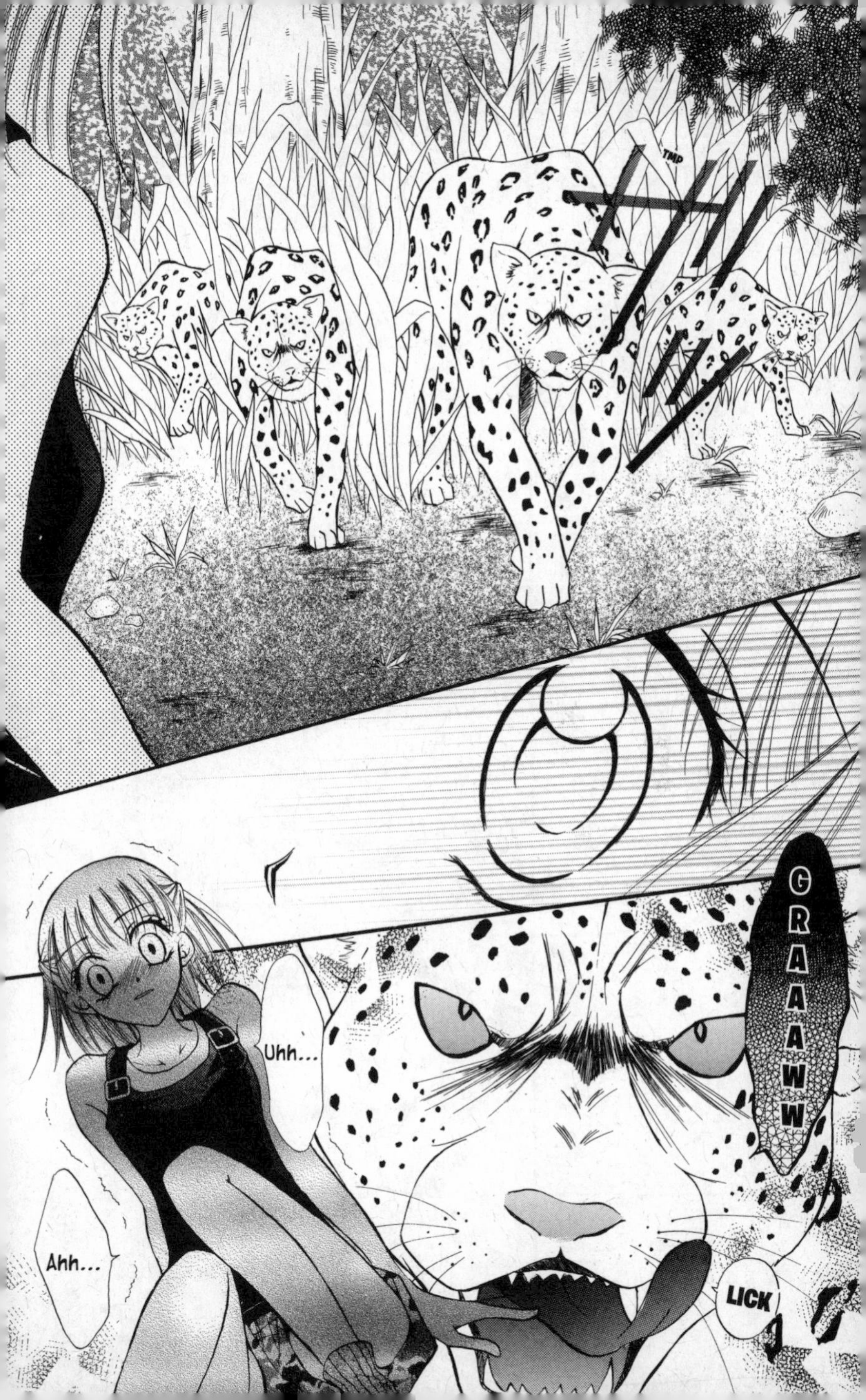
TMP
GRAAAAWW
Uhh...
LICK
Ahh...

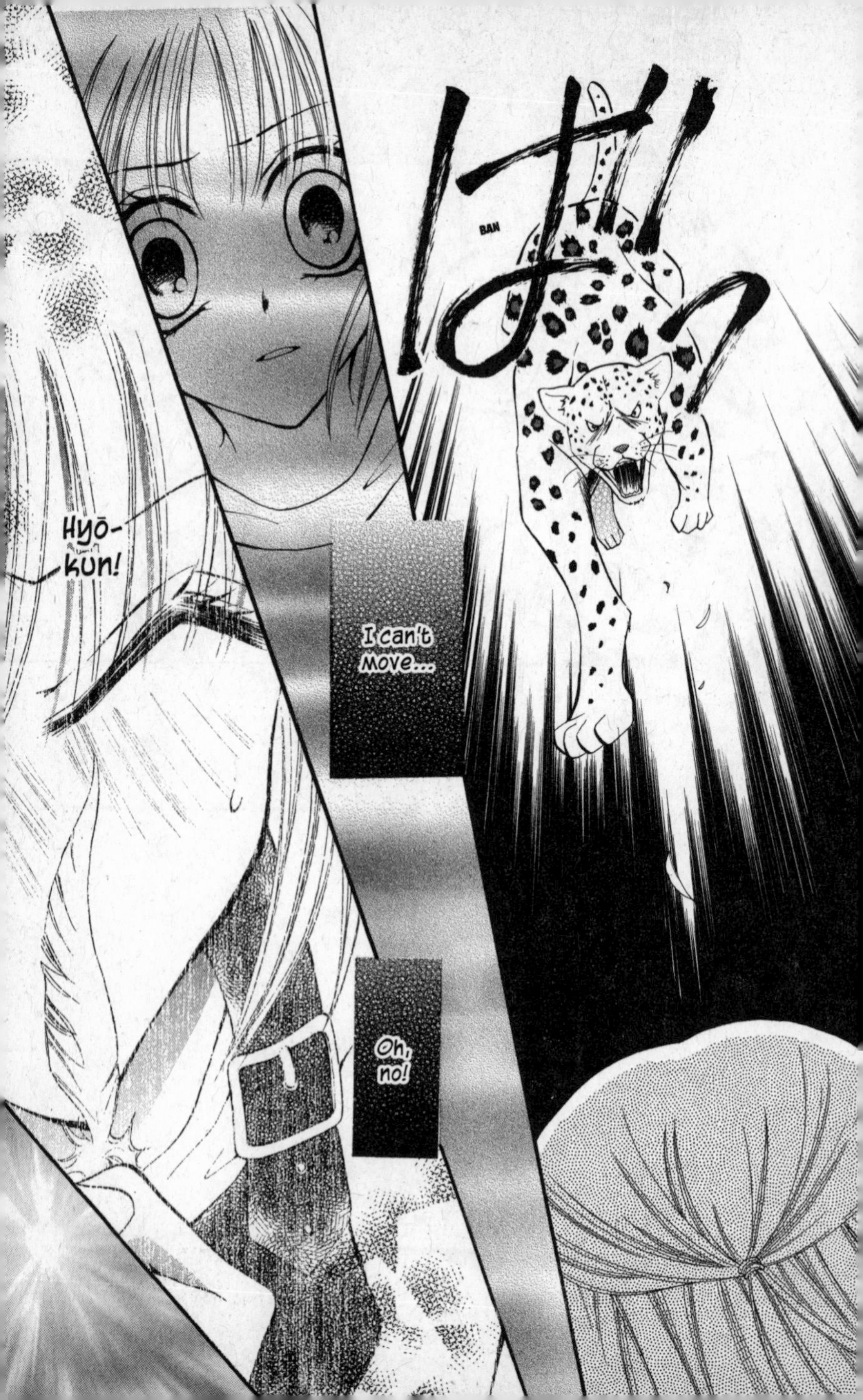
BAN
I can't move...
Oh, no!
Hyō-kun!

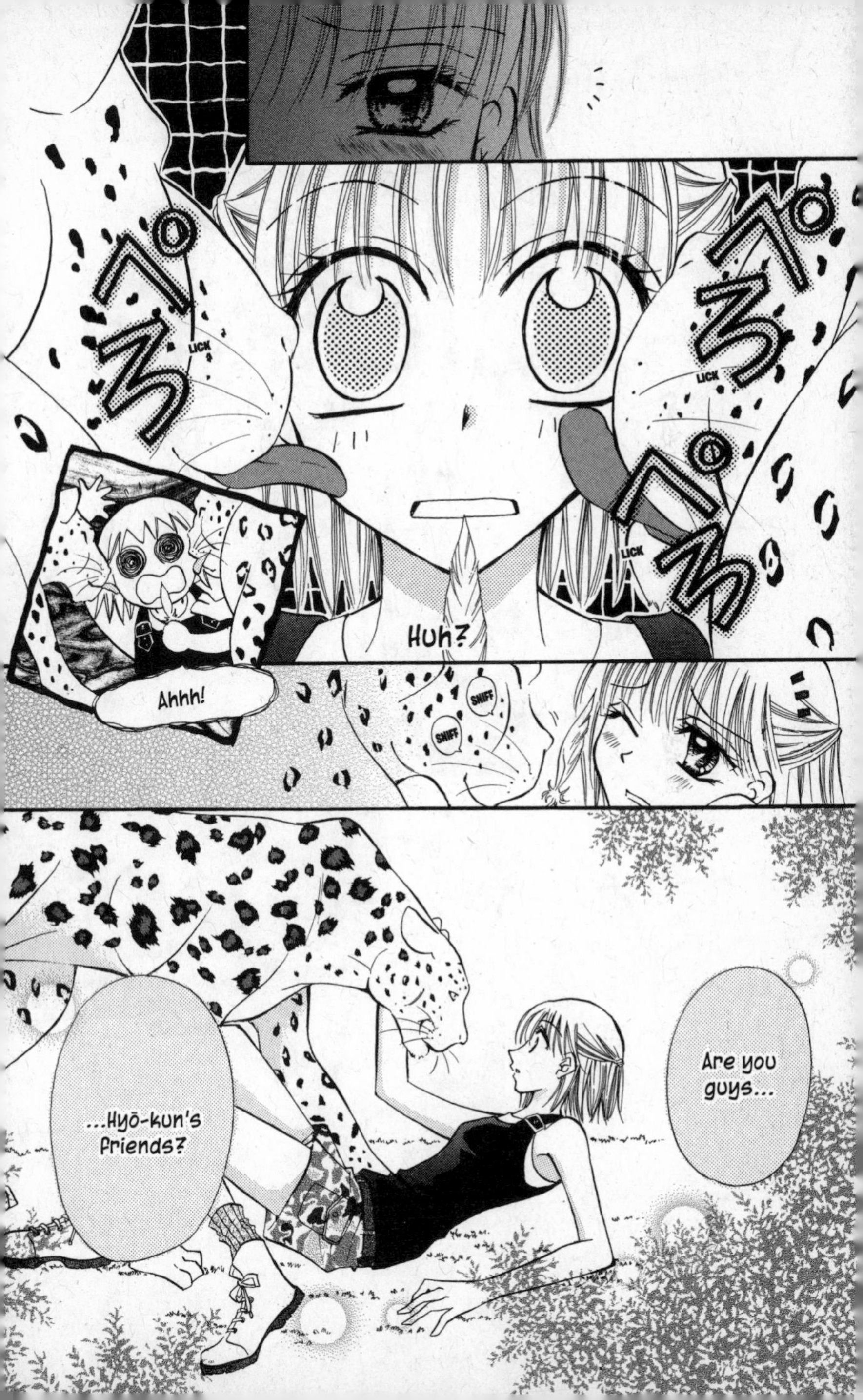
LICK
LICK
LICK
Huh?
Ahhh!
SNIFF
SNIFF
Are you guys...
...Hyō-kun's friends?

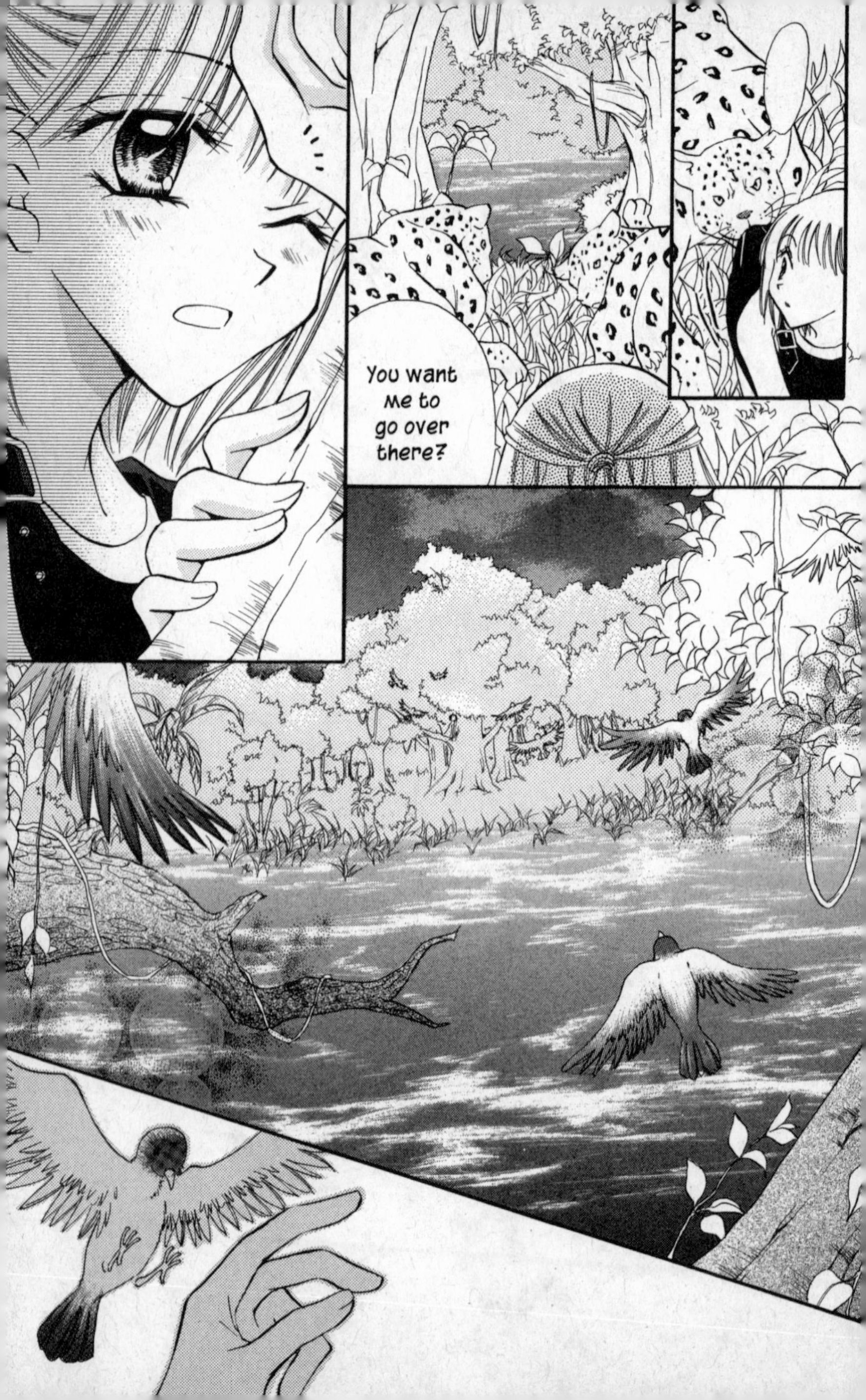
You want me to go over there?

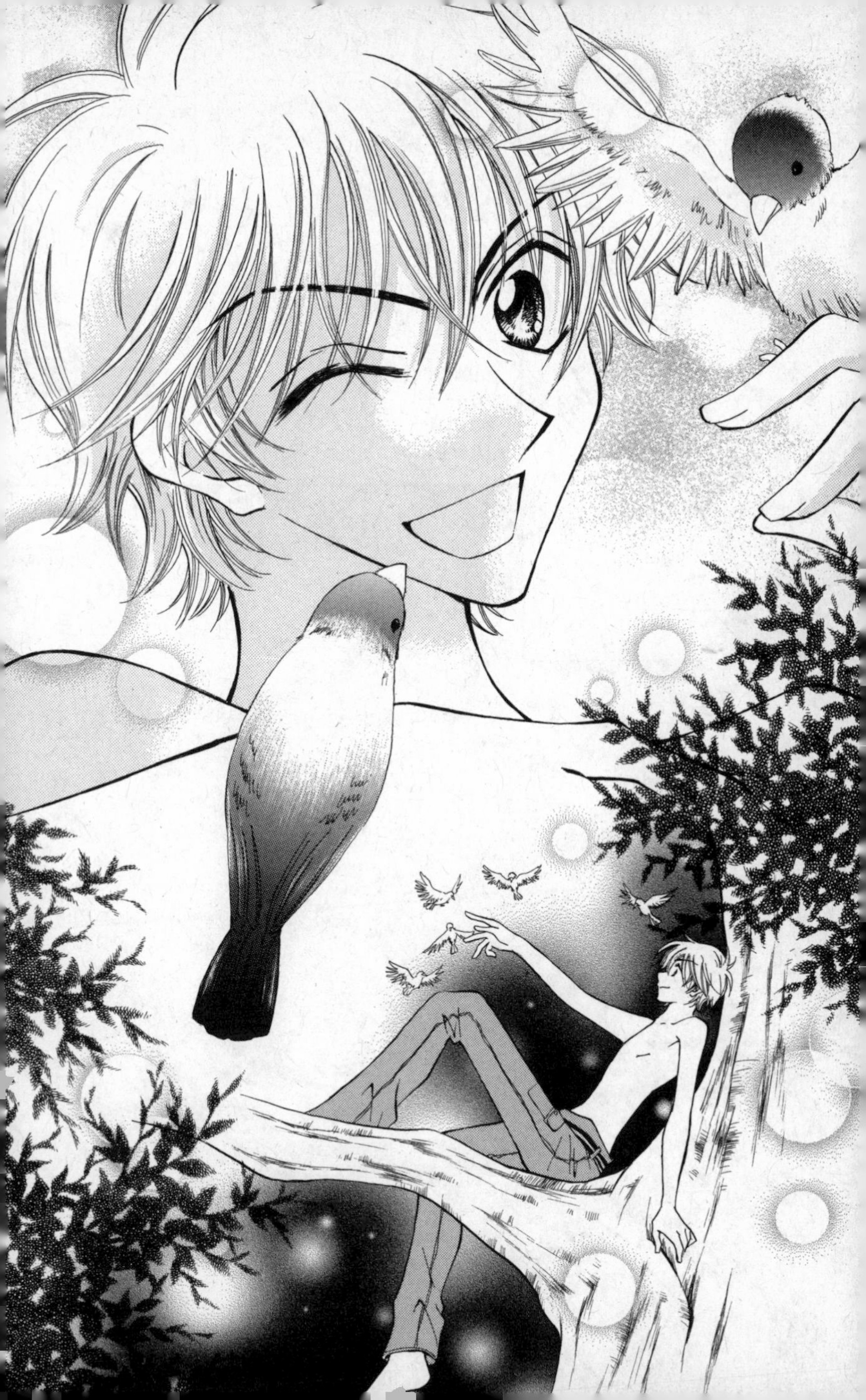

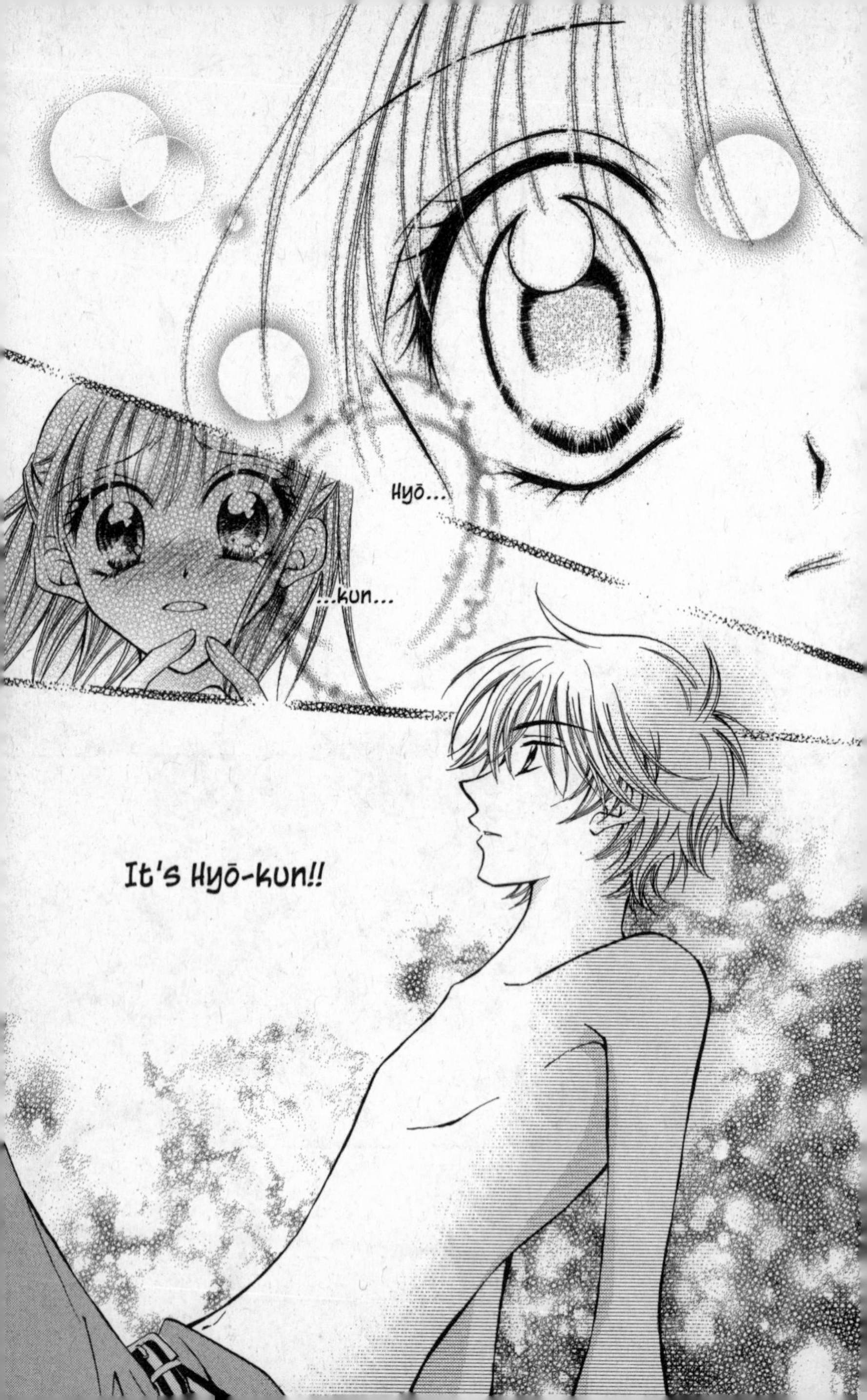
Hyō...
...kun...
It's Hyō-kun!!

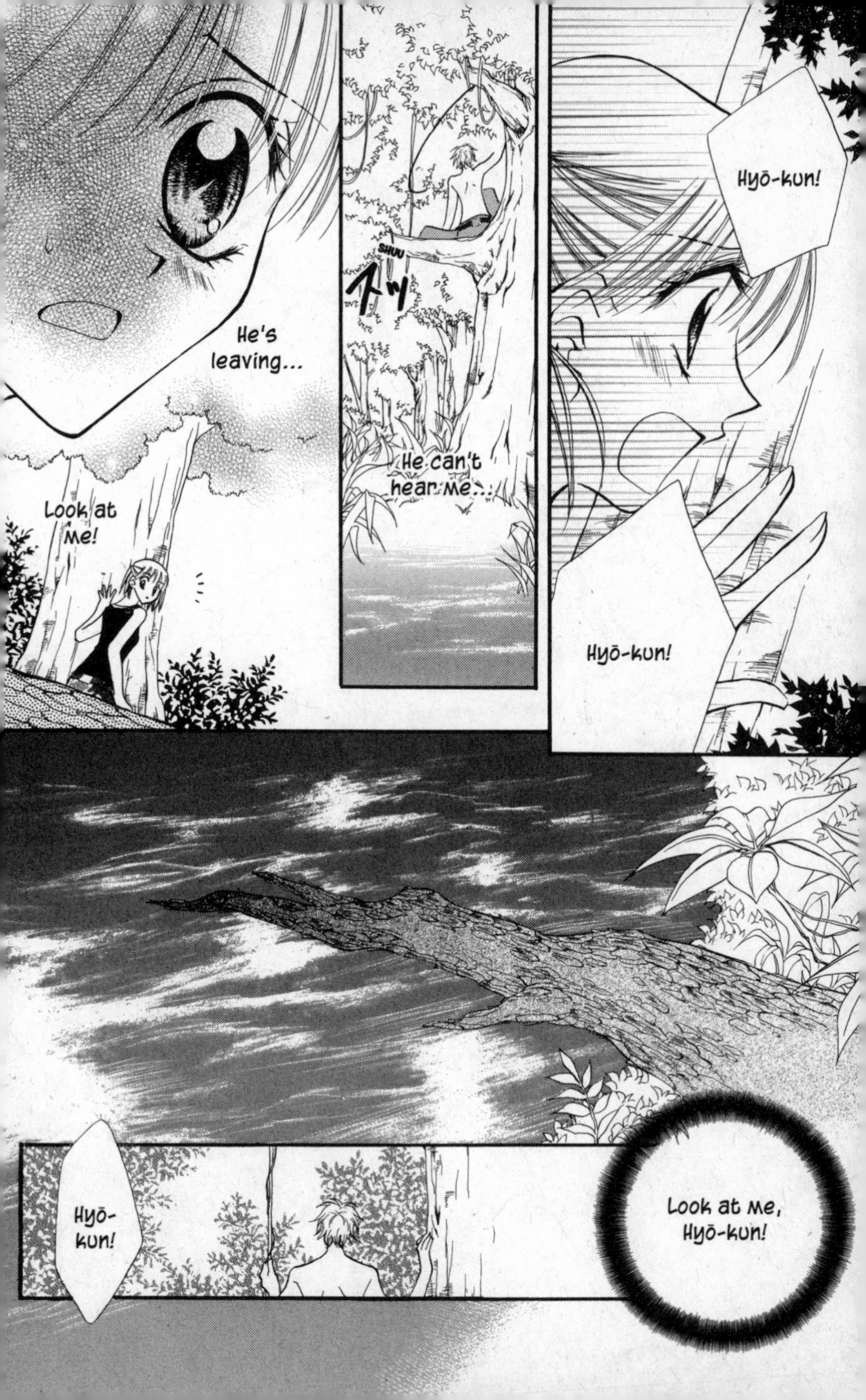
Hyō-kun!
Hyō-kun!
SHUU
He can't hear me...
He's leaving...
Look at me!
Look at me, Hyō-kun!
Hyō-kun!

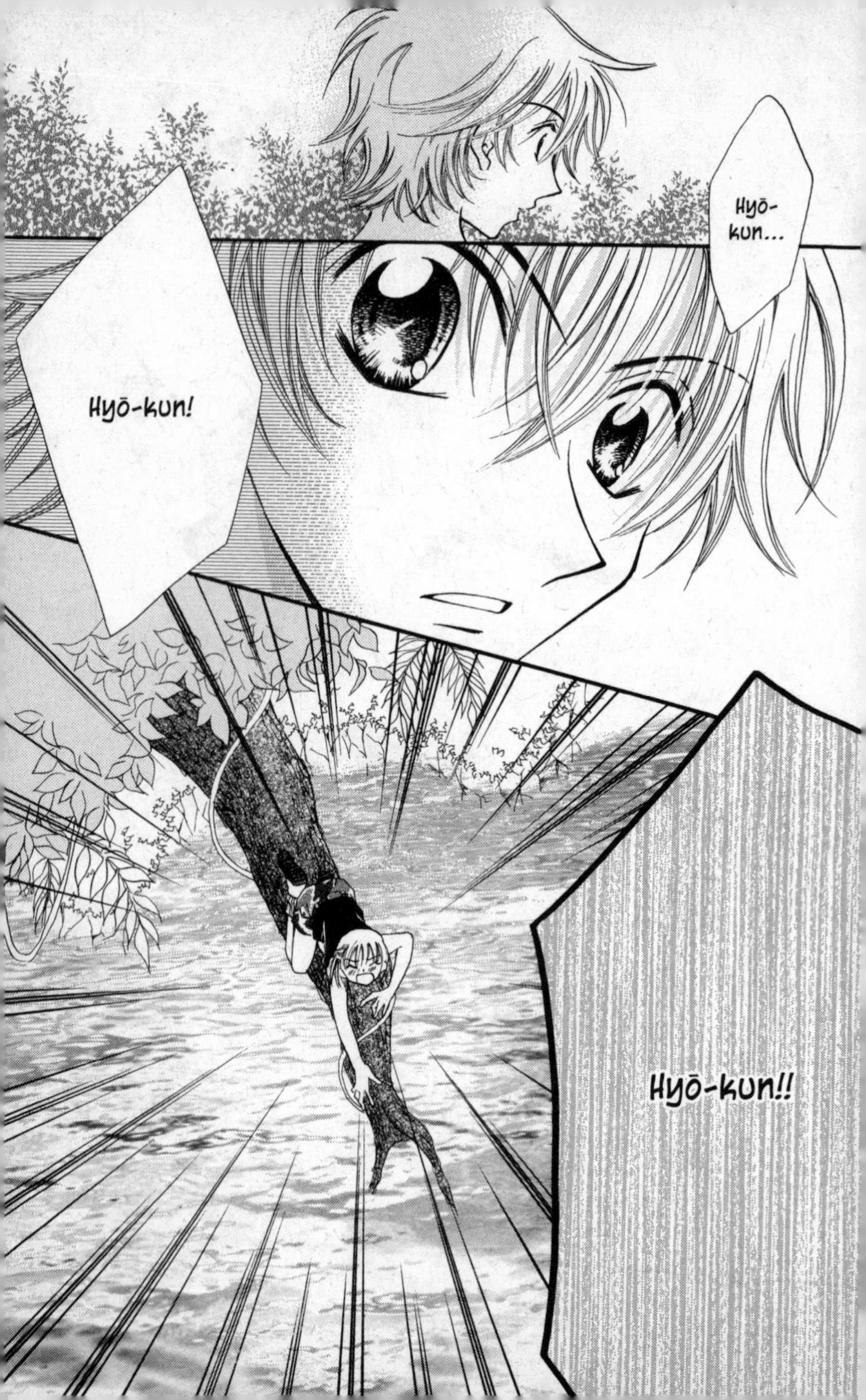
Hyō-kun...
Hyō-kun!
Hyō-kun!!

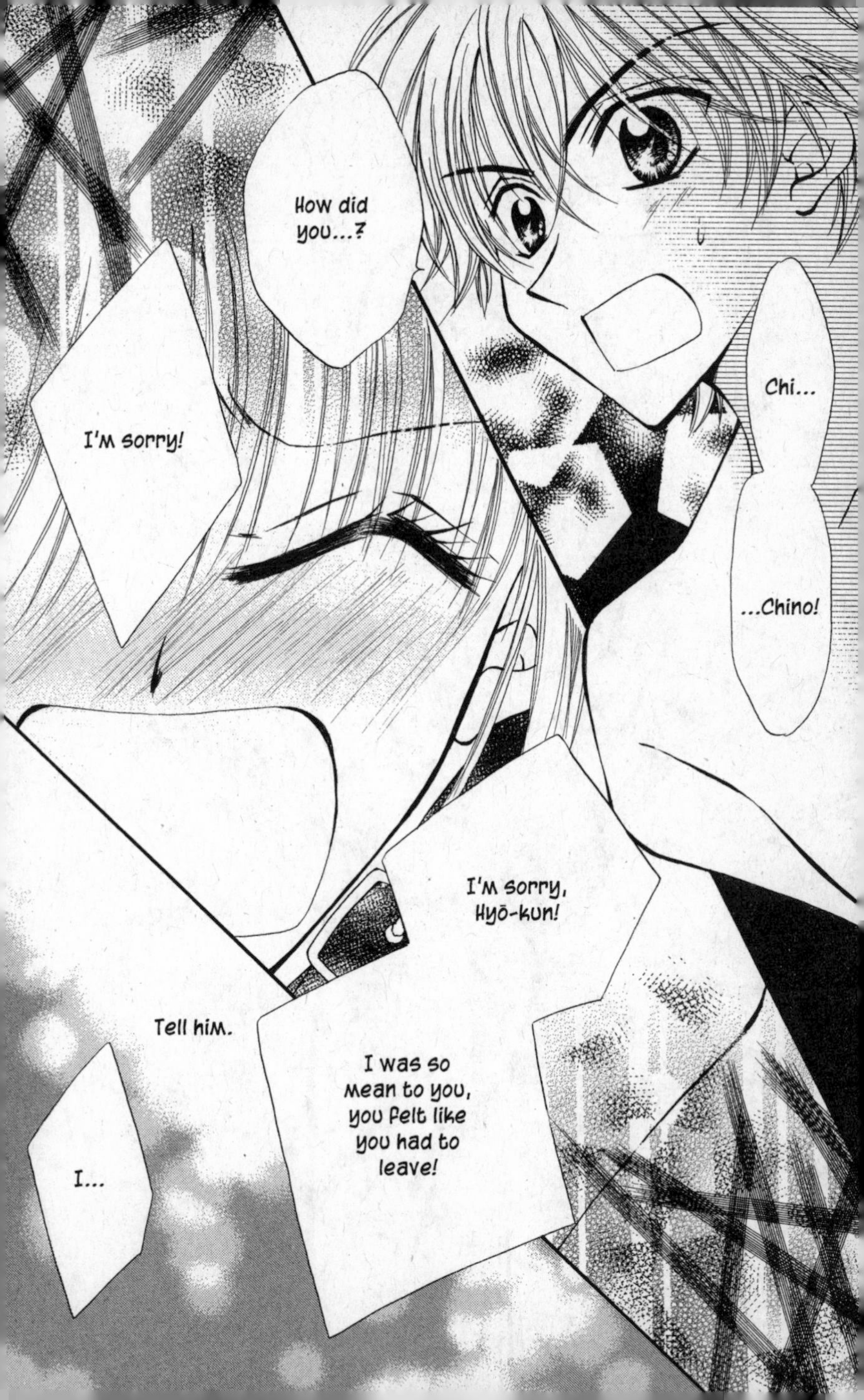
How did you...?
Chi...
...Chino!
I'm sorry!
I'm sorry, Hyō-kun!
I was so mean to you, you felt like you had to leave!
Tell him.
I...

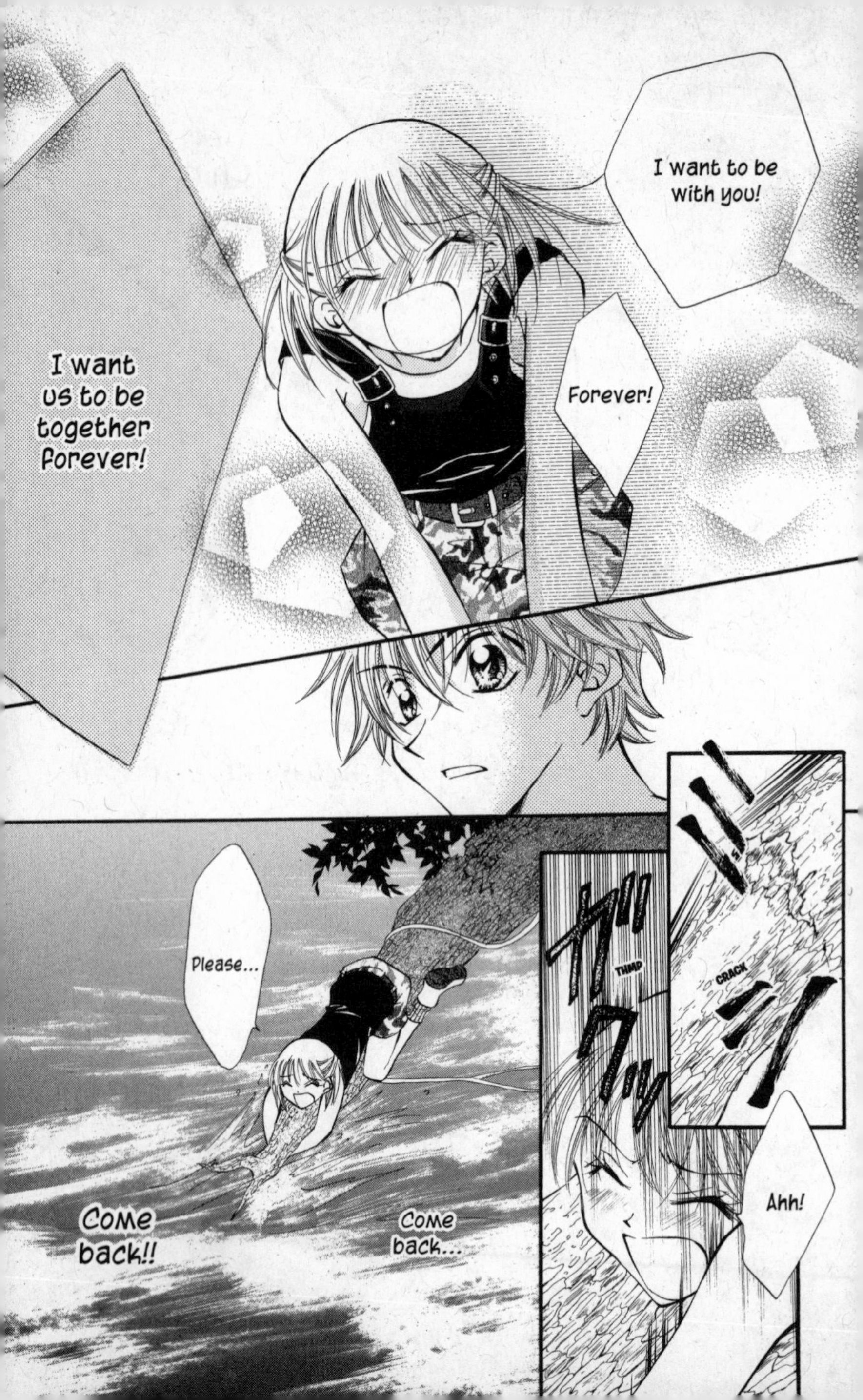
I want to be with you!
Forever!
I want us to be together forever!
CRACK
THMP
Ahh!
Please...
Come back...
Come back!!

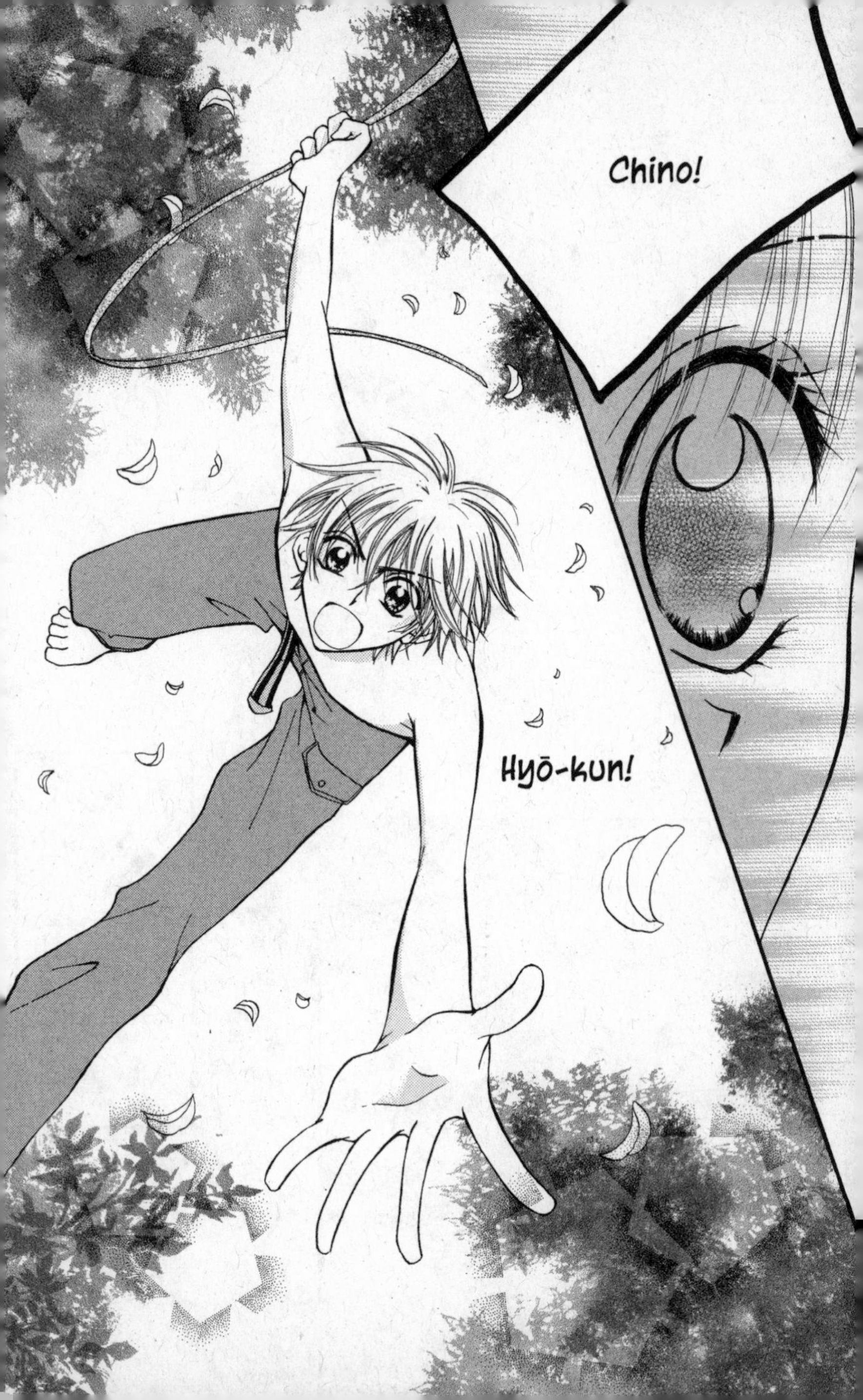
Chino!
Hyō-kun!

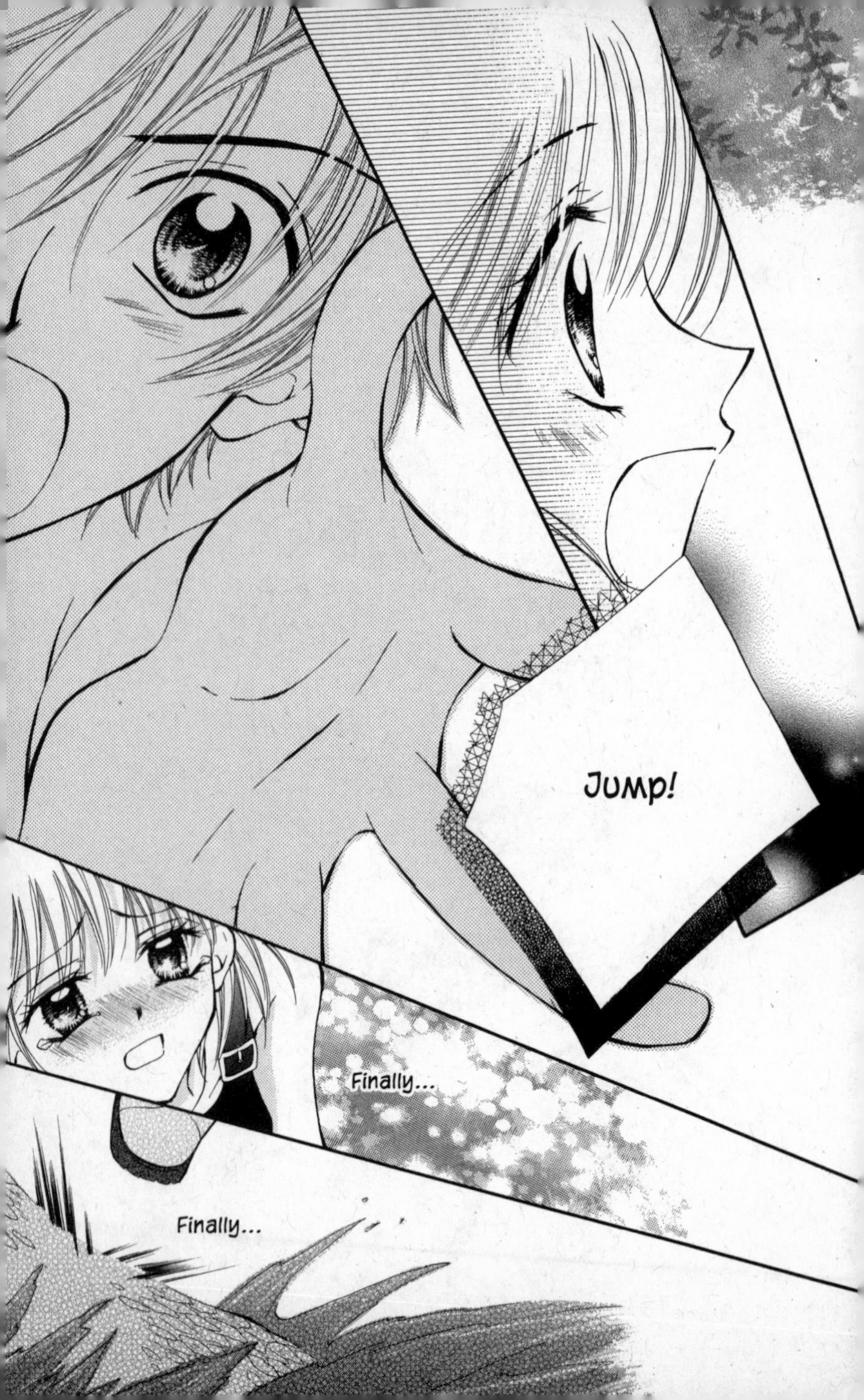
JUMP!
Finally...
Finally...

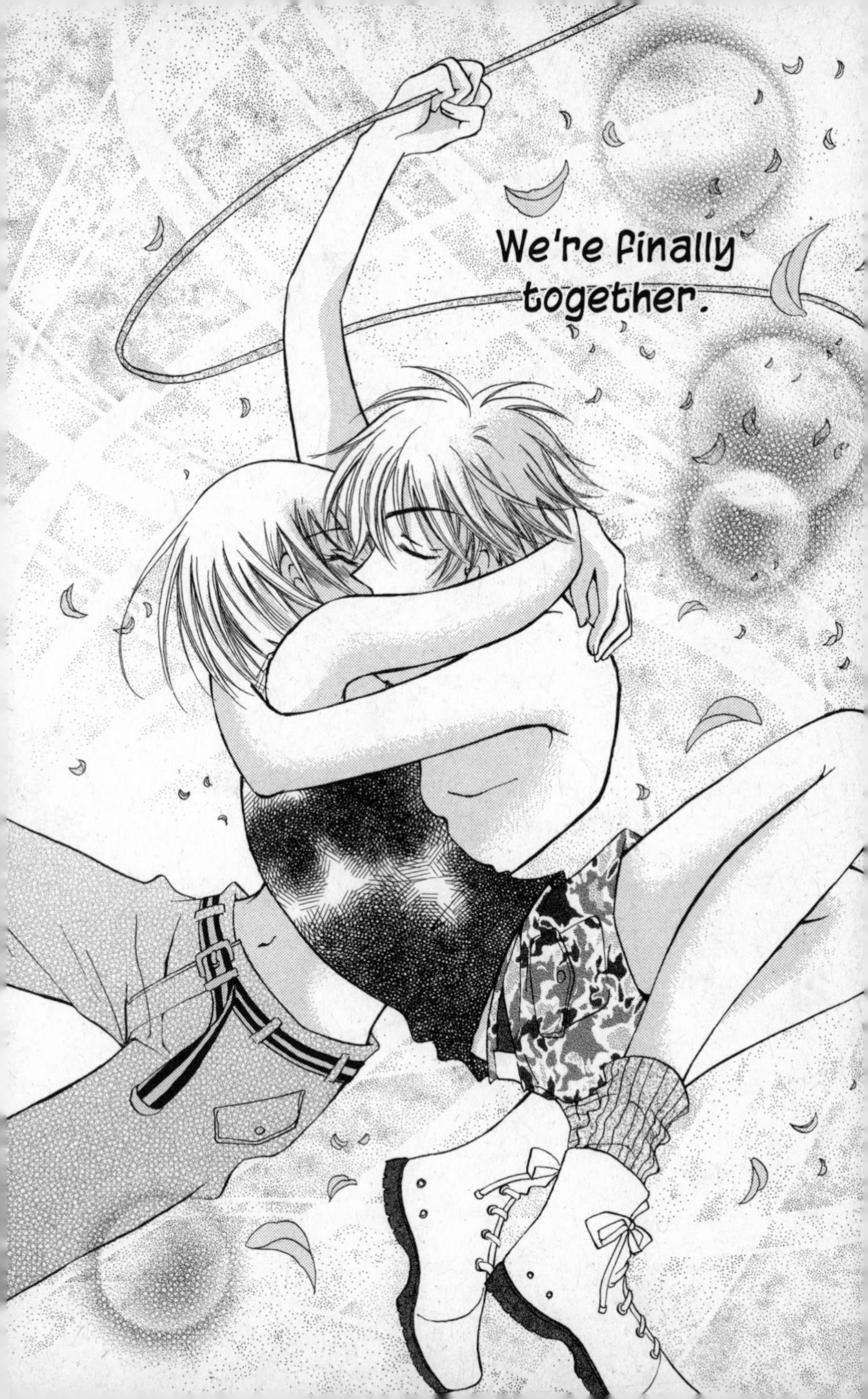
We're finally together.

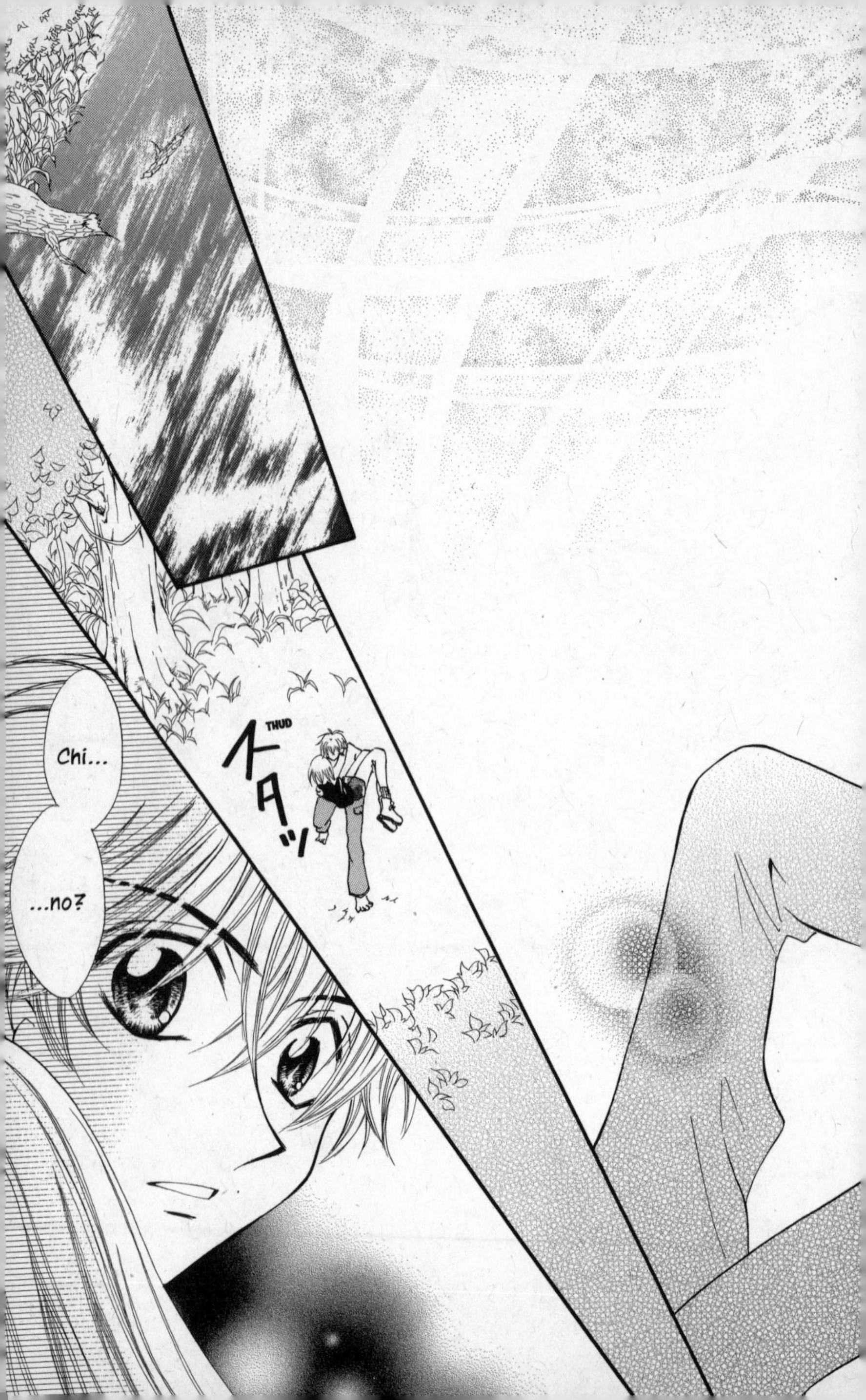
THUD
Chi...
...no?

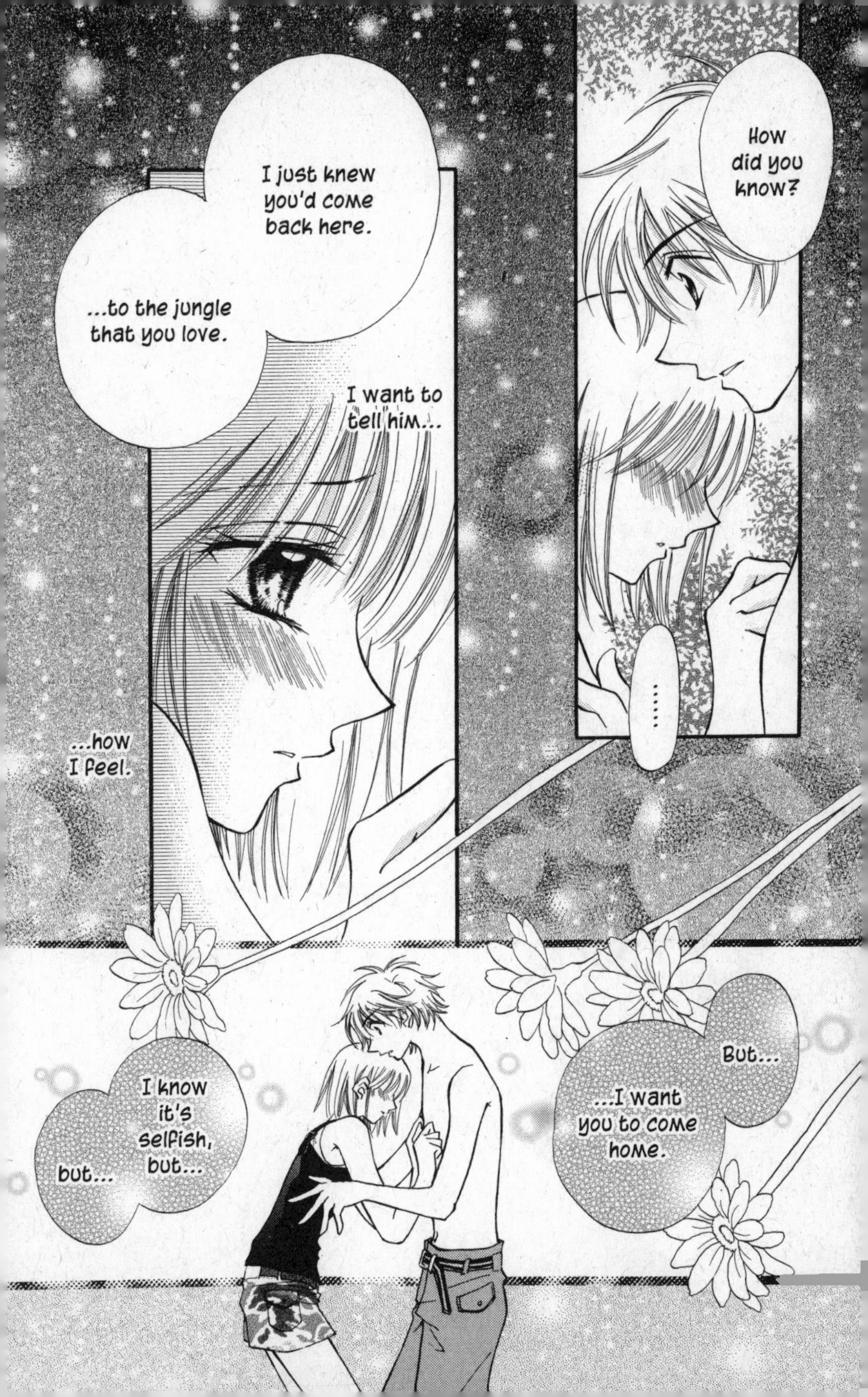

How did you know?
......
I just knew you'd come back here.
...to the jungle that you love.
I want to tell him...
...how I feel.
But...
...I want you to come home.
I know it's selfish, but...
but...

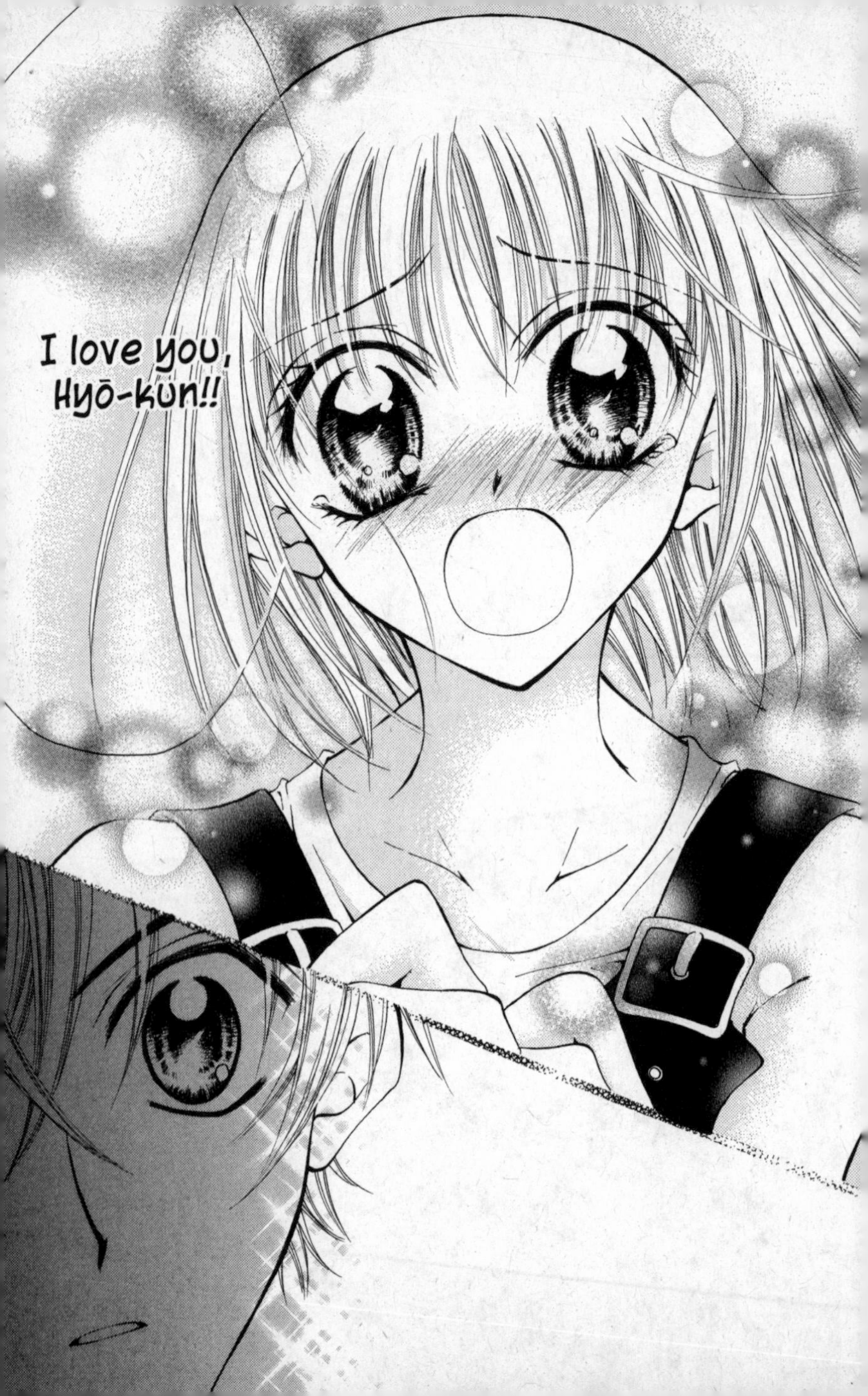
I love you, Hyō-kun!!

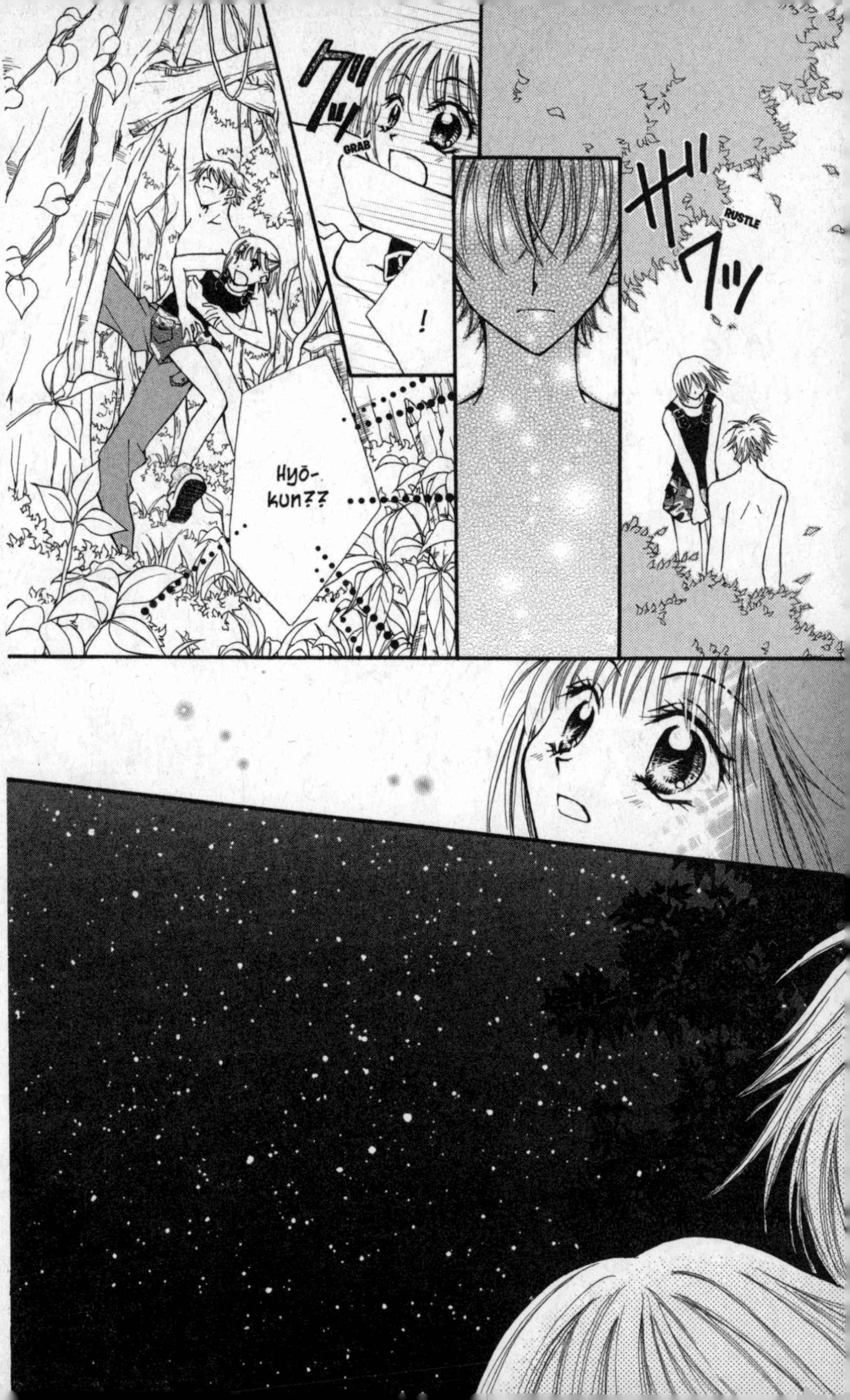
ザワッ
RUSTLE
グッ
GRAB
!
Hyō-
kun??

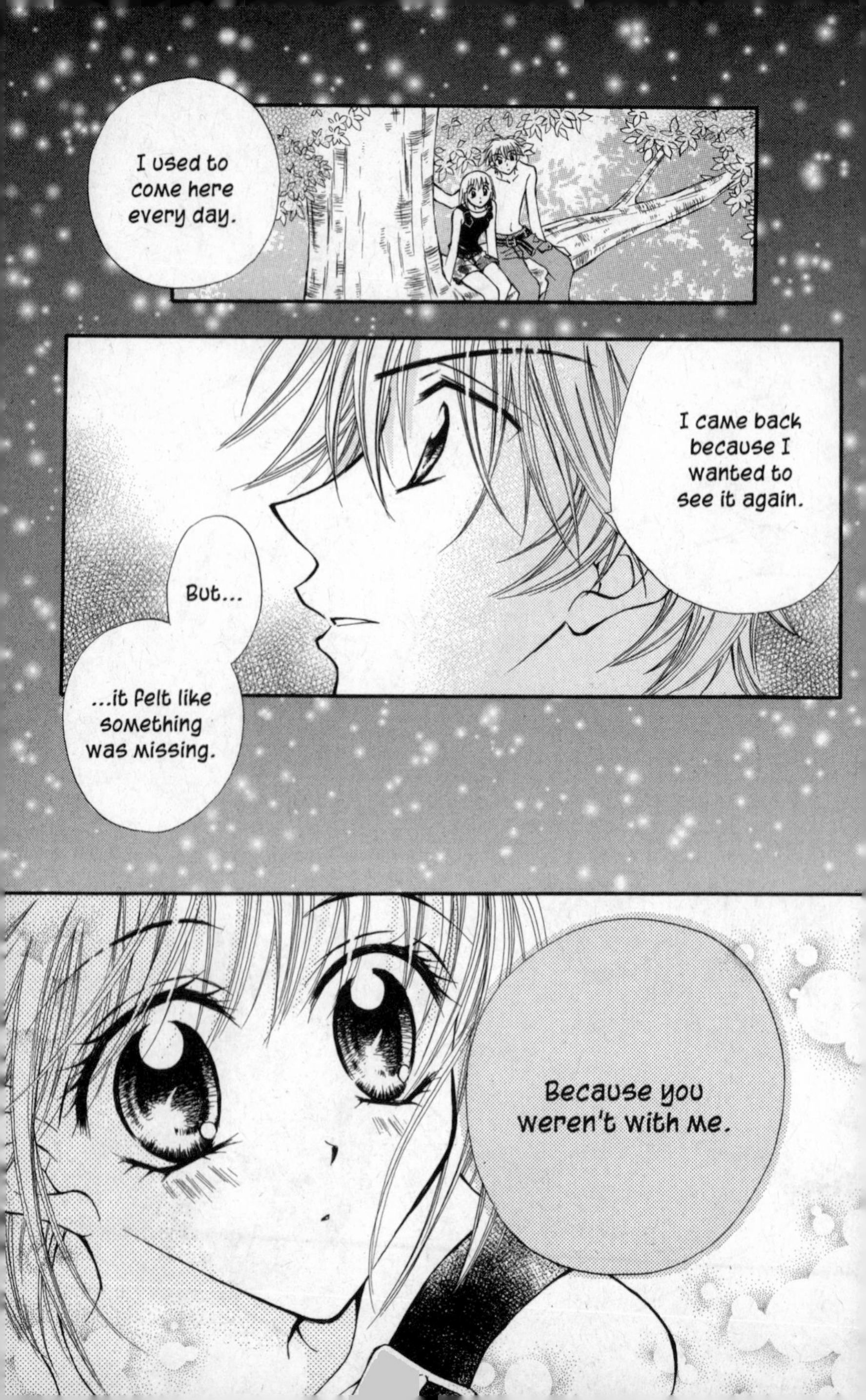
I used to come here every day.
I came back because I wanted to see it again.
But...
...it felt like something was missing.
Because you weren't with me.

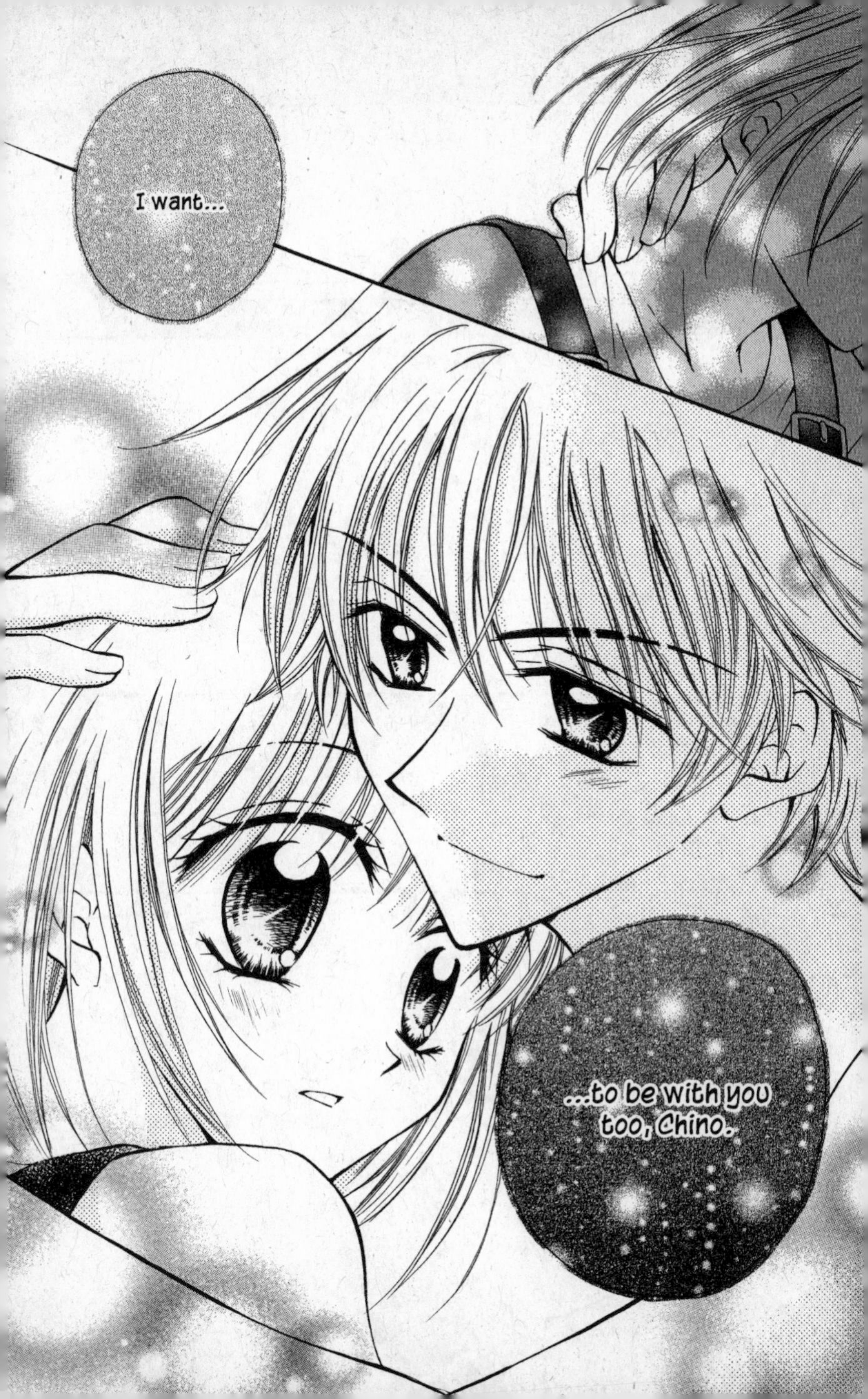
I want...
...to be with you too, Chino.

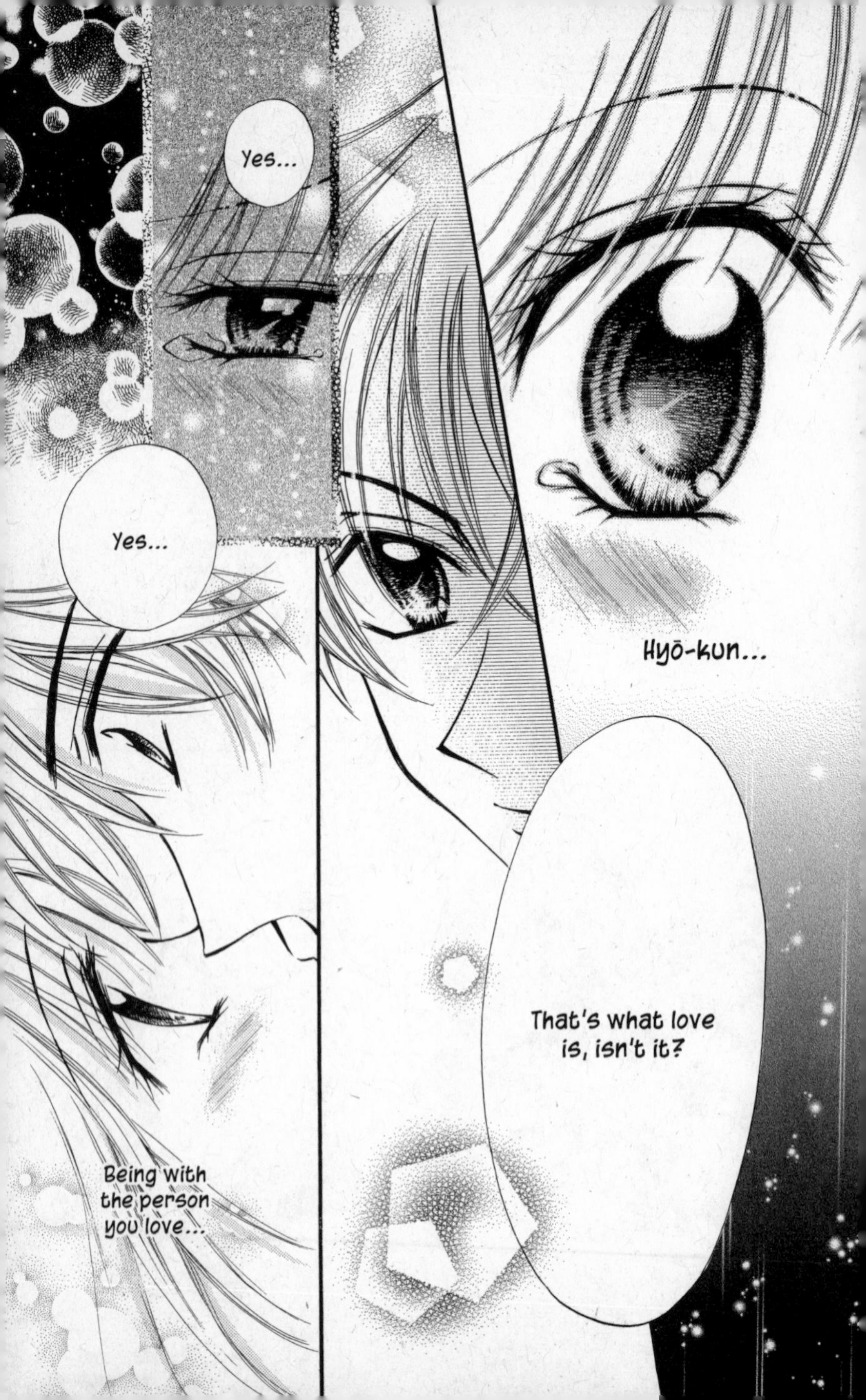
Hyō-kun...
That's what love is, isn't it?
Yes...
Yes...
Being with the person you love...

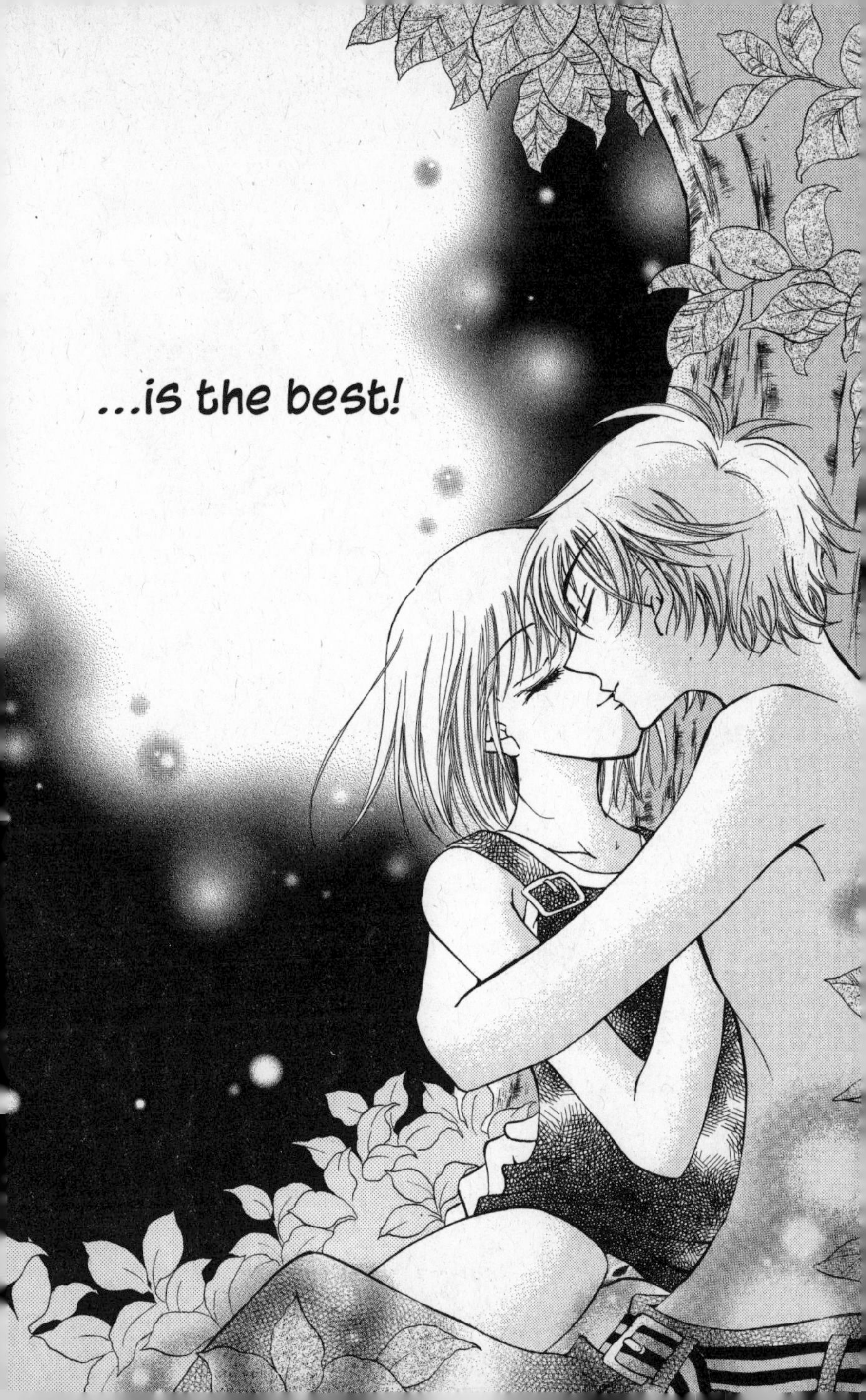
...is the best!

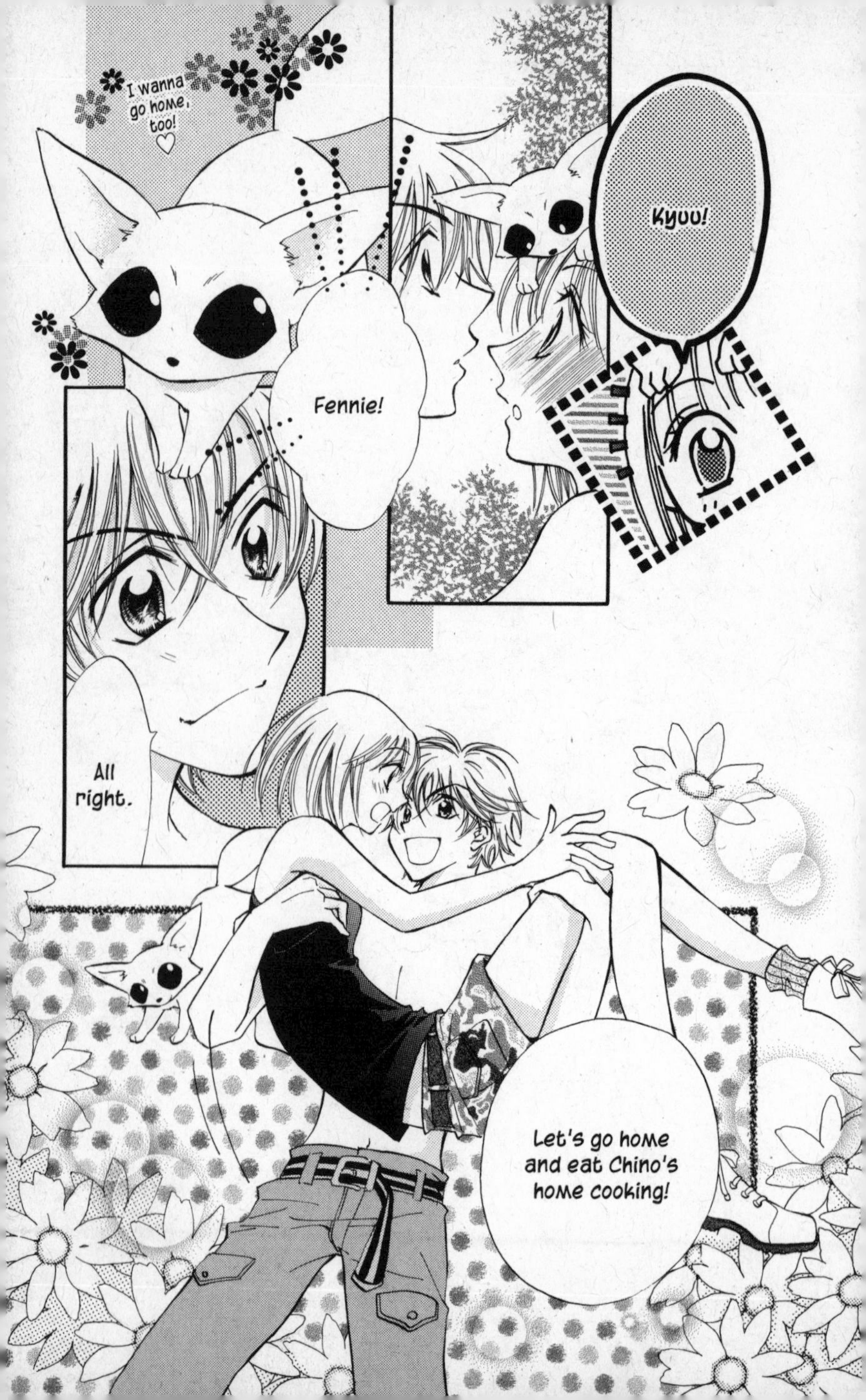
Kyuu!
I wanna go home, too! ♡
Fennie!
All right.
Let's go home and eat Chino's home cooking!

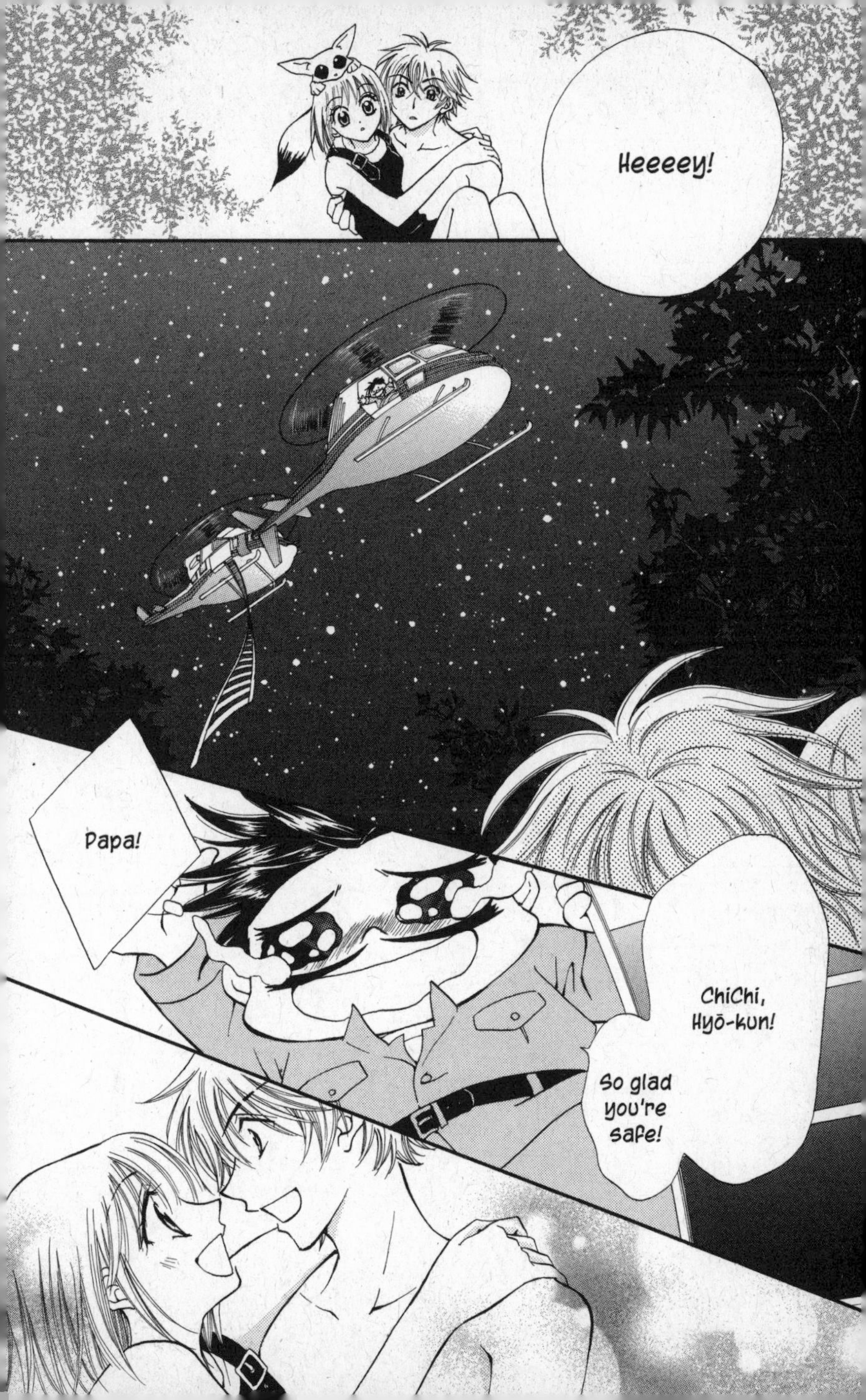
Heeeey!
Papa!
ChiChi, Hyō-kun!
So glad you're safe!

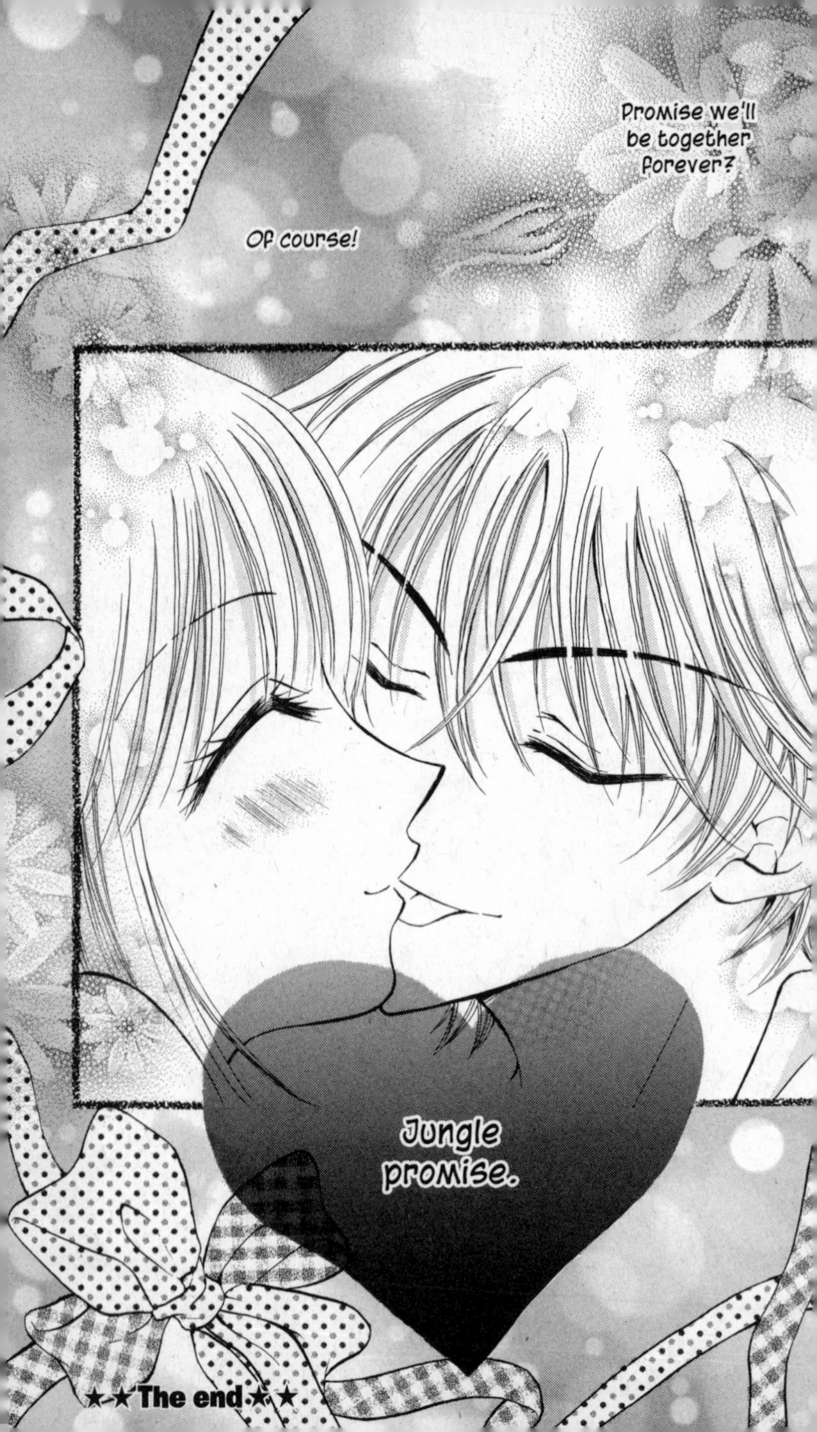
Promise we'll be together forever?
Of course!
Jungle promise.
★★The end★★

That's the end of Wild @ Heart!! I know it's cliché, but I wanted to draw their wedding scene! I bet it's possible they'll live together on Madara Island together! ♡ Chino is a pretty tough girl, after all! I want Chino to swing through the jungle, too! Thanks so much for cheering them both on! ♡

Natsumi Ando

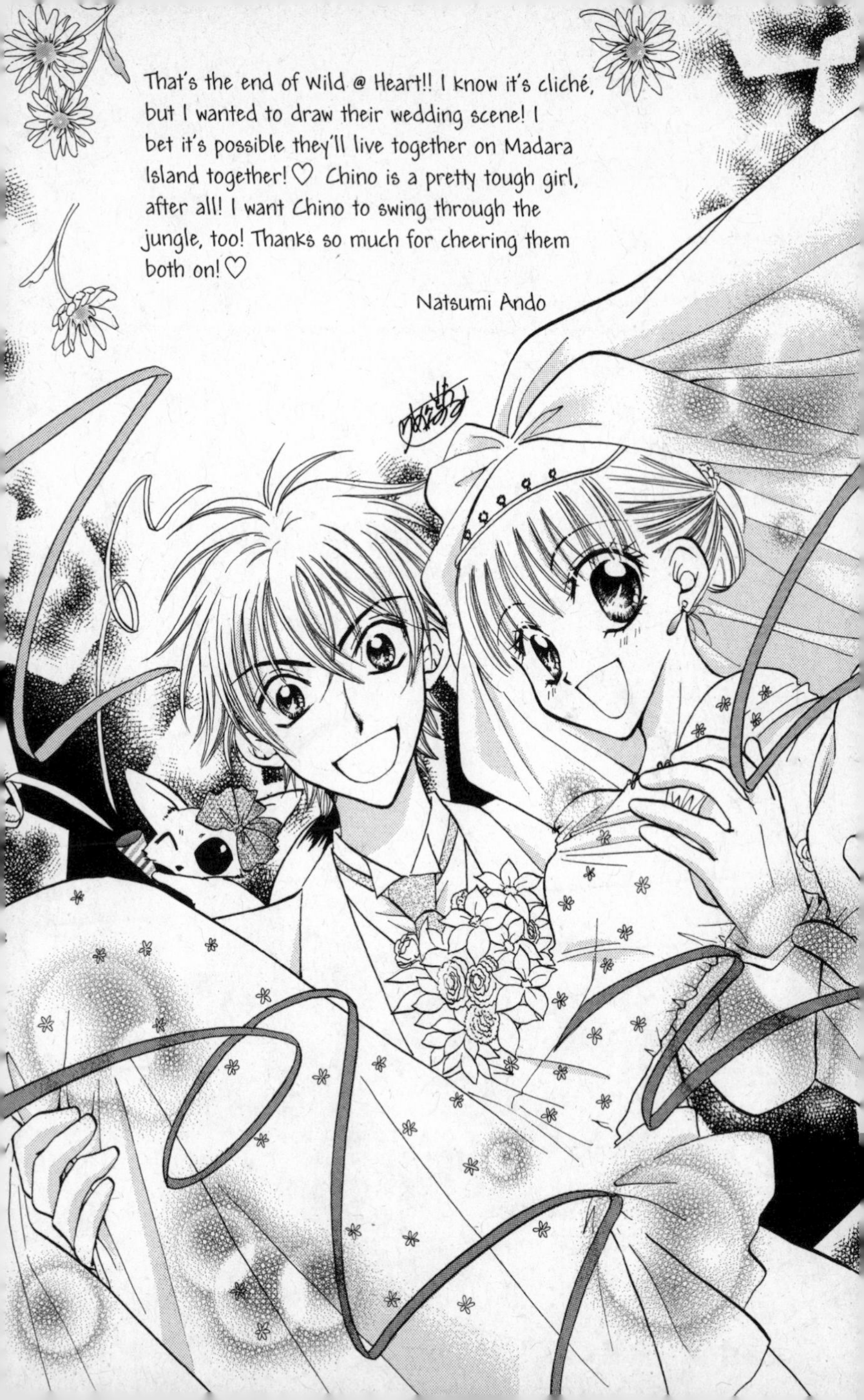

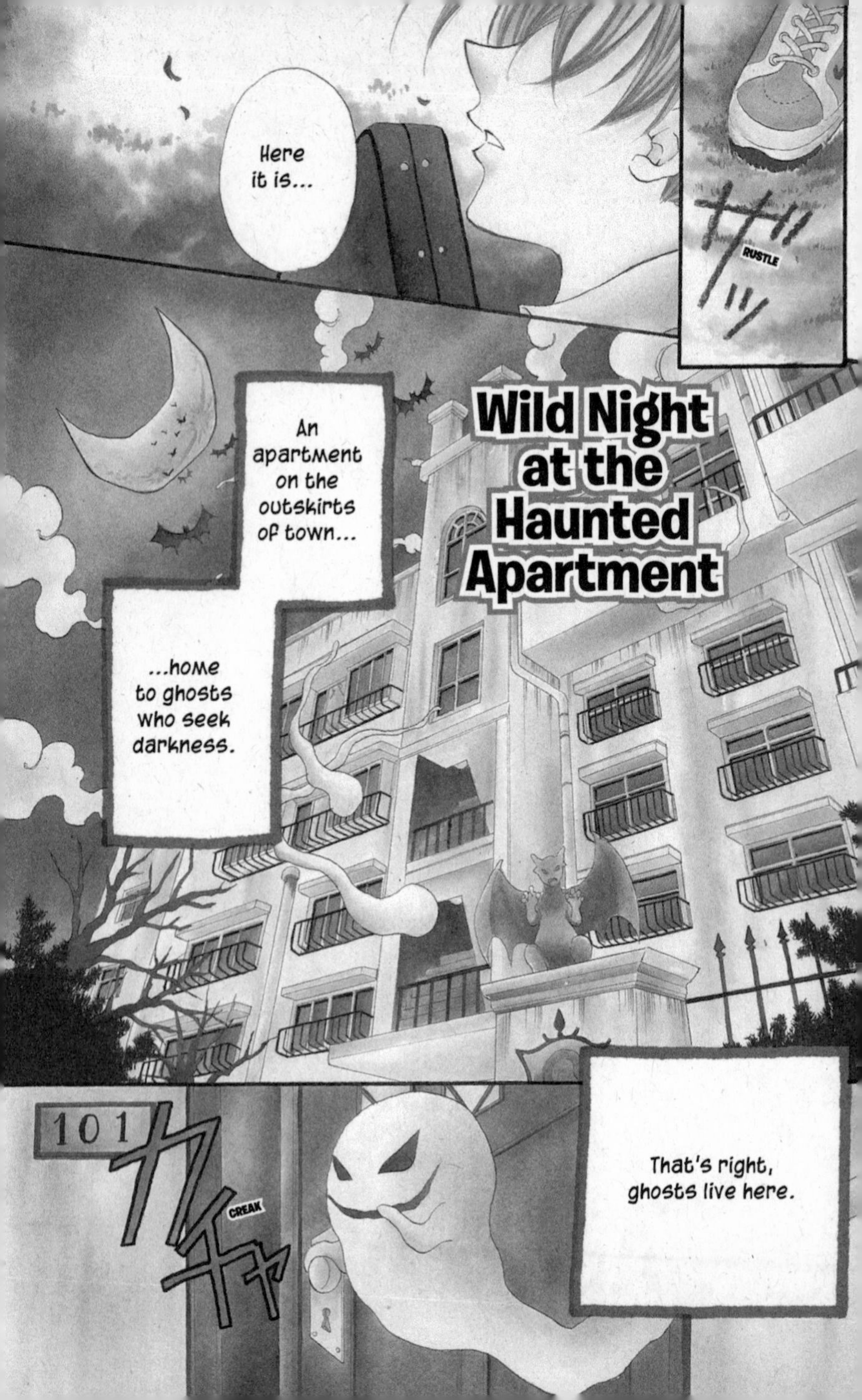
RUSTLE
Here it is...
Wild Night at the Haunted Apartment
An apartment on the outskirts of town...
...home to ghosts who seek darkness.
That's right, ghosts live here.
101
CREAK

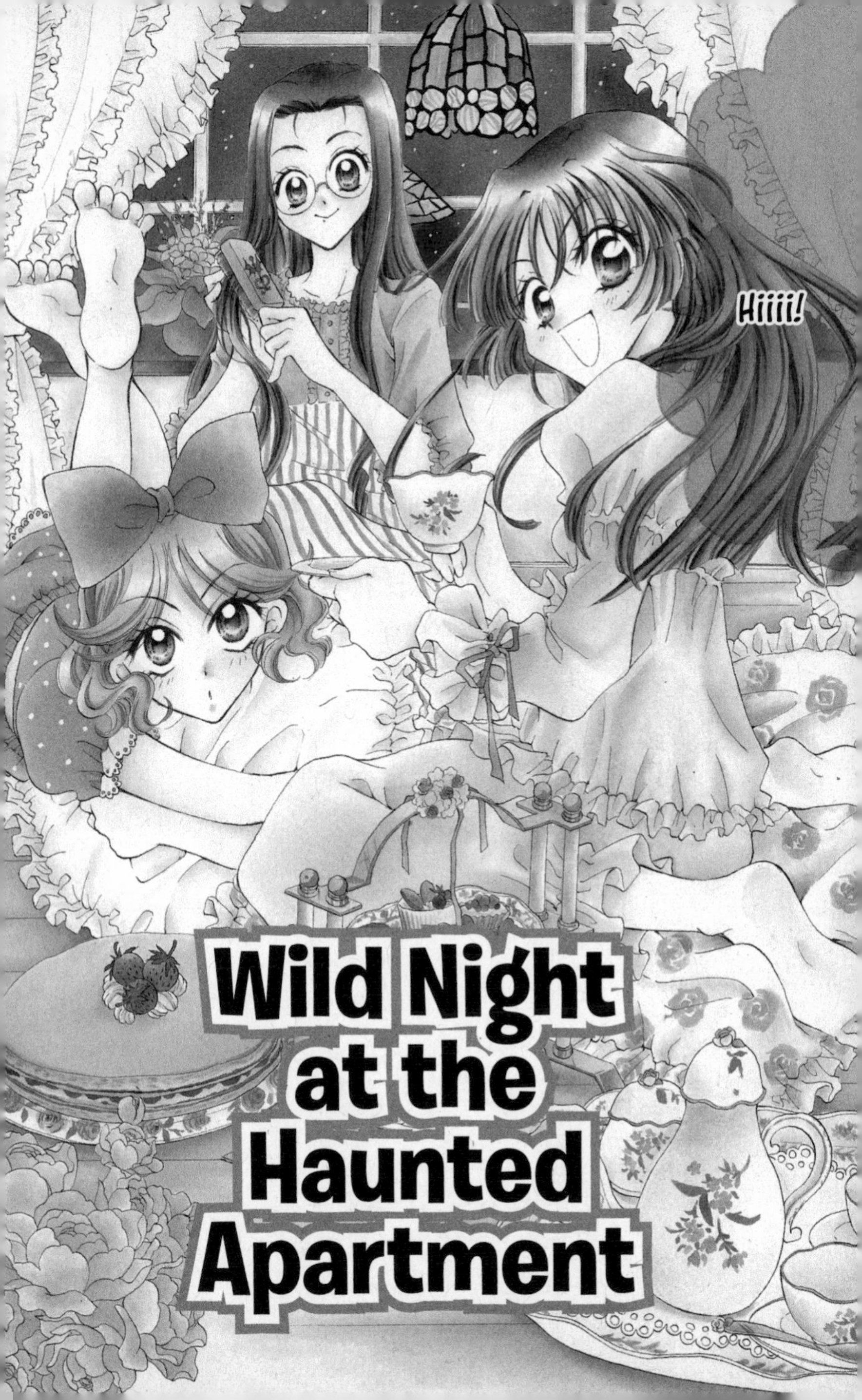
Hiiii!
Wild Night at the Haunted Apartment

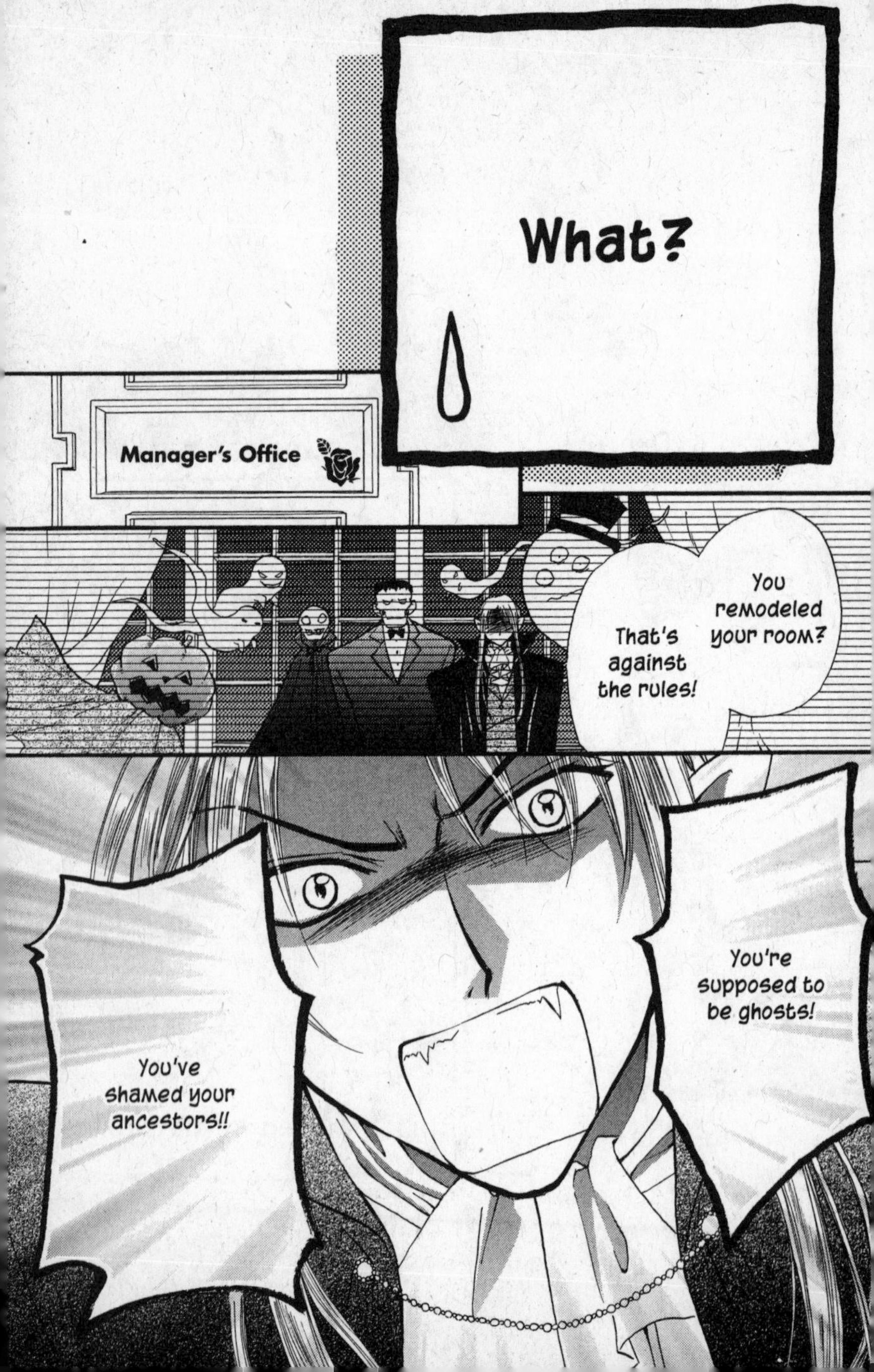
What?
Manager's Office
You remodeled your room?
That's against the rules!
You're supposed to be ghosts!
You've shamed your ancestors!!

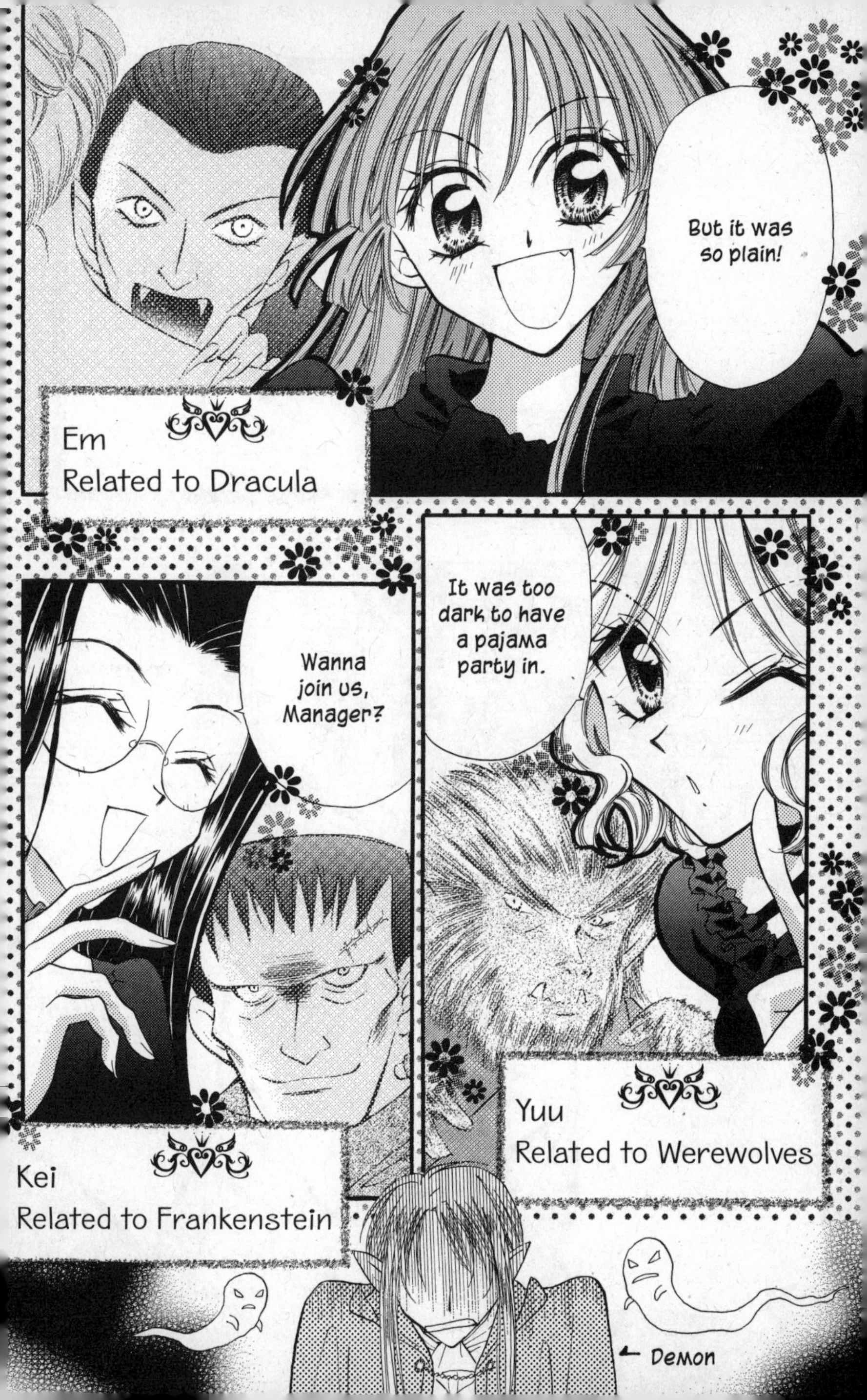
But it was so plain!
Em
Related to Dracula
It was too dark to have a pajama party in.
Yuu
Related to Werewolves
Wanna join us, Manager?
Kei
Related to Frankenstein
← Demon

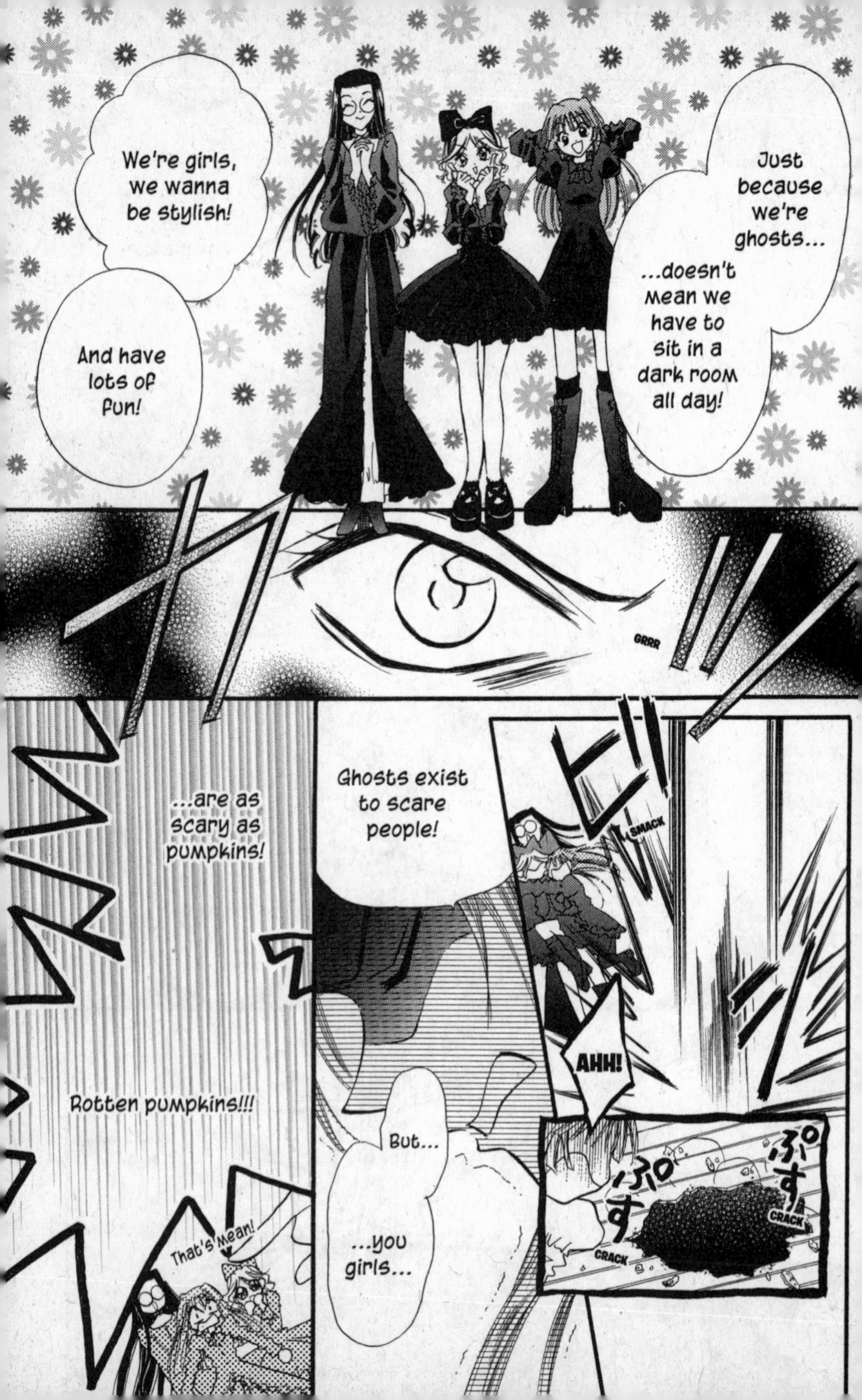
Just because we're ghosts...
...doesn't mean we have to sit in a dark room all day!
We're girls, we wanna be stylish!
And have lots of fun!
GRRR
SMACK
AHH!
ぷす
CRACK
ぷす
CRACK
Ghosts exist to scare people!
But...
...you girls...
...are as scary as pumpkins!
Rotten pumpkins!!!
That's mean!

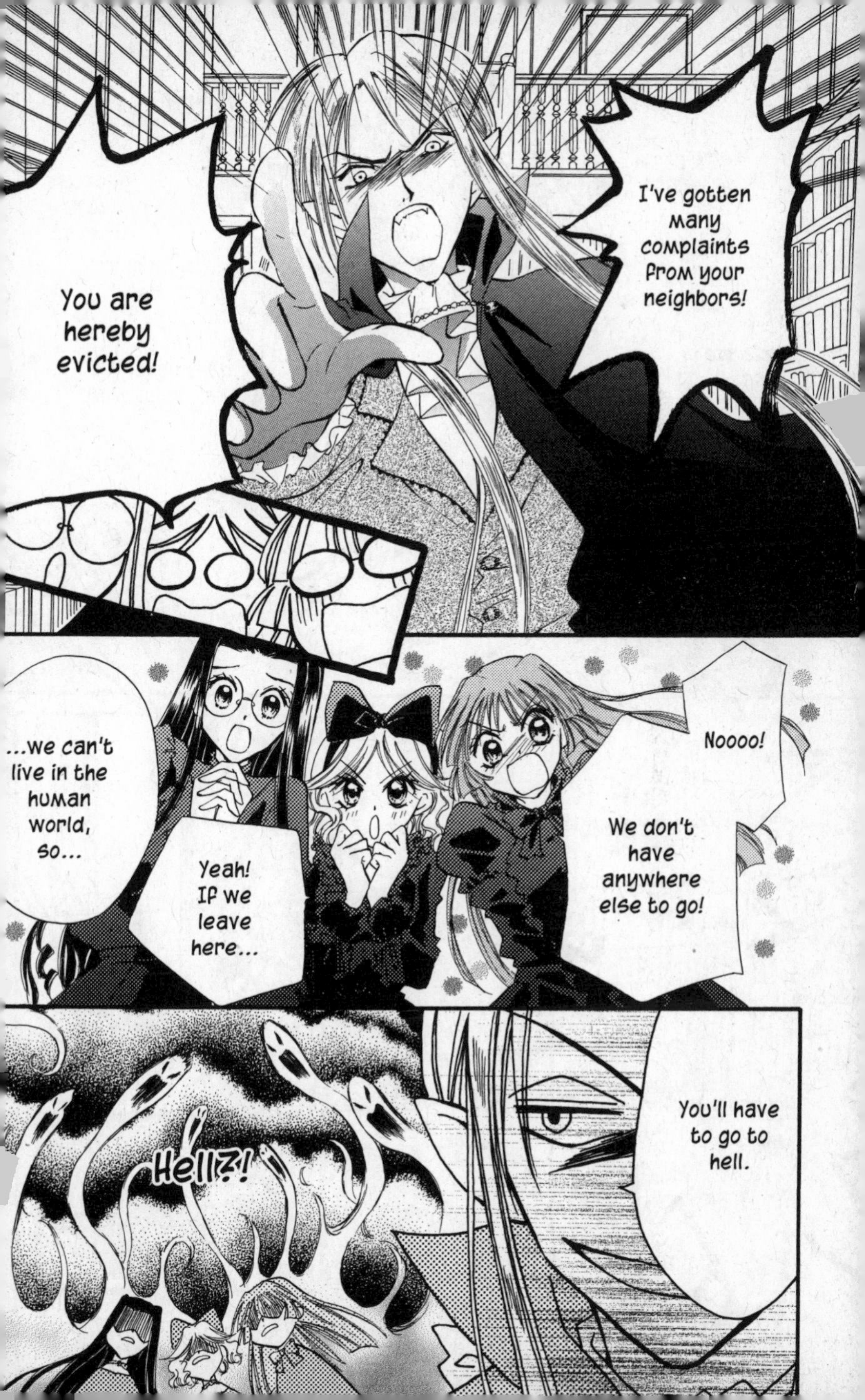
I've gotten many complaints from your neighbors!
You are hereby evicted!
Noooo!
We don't have anywhere else to go!
Yeah! If we leave here...
...we can't live in the human world, so...
You'll have to go to hell.
Hell?!

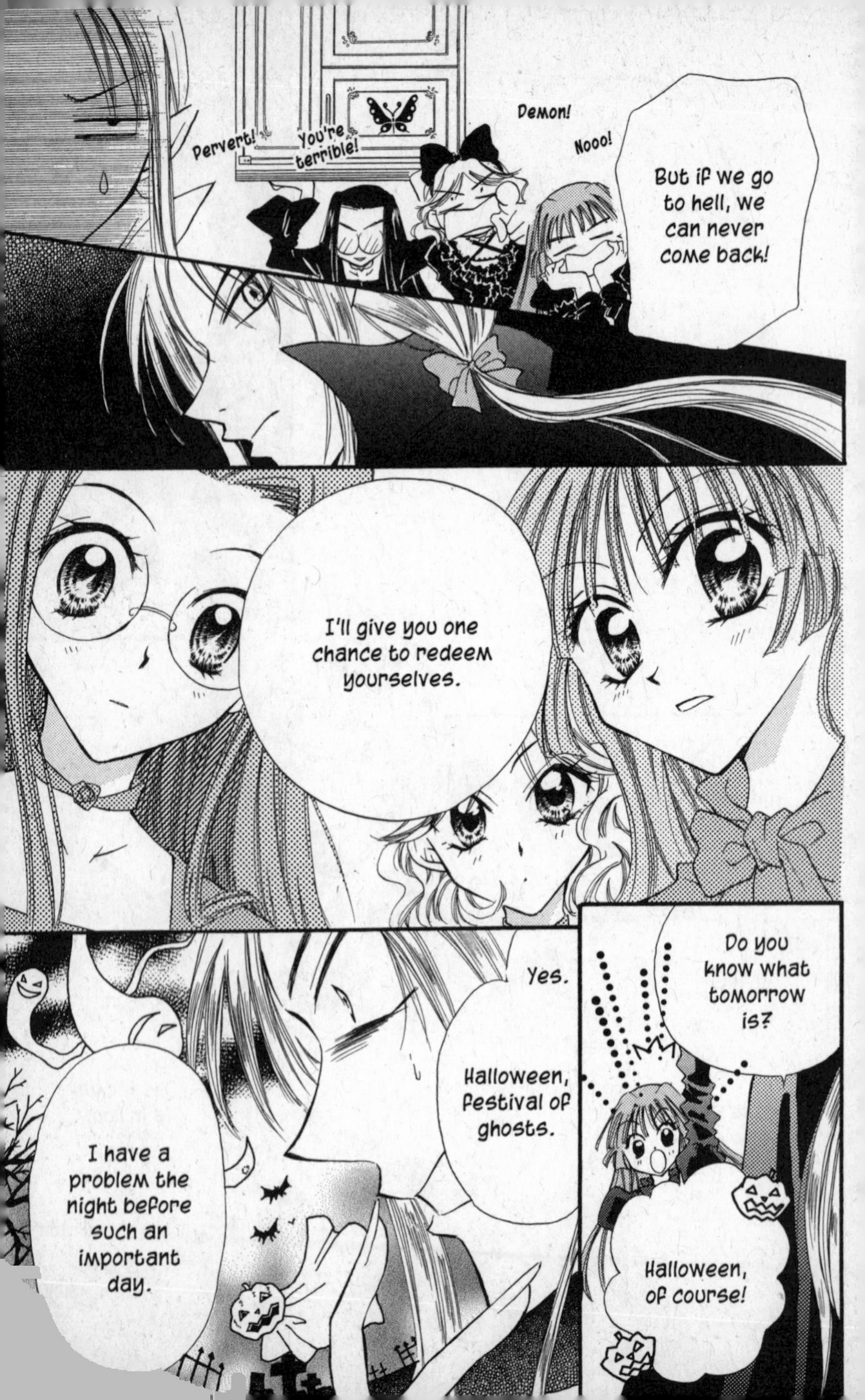

But if we go to hell, we can never come back!
Demon!
Nooo!
You're terrible!
Pervert!
I'll give you one chance to redeem yourselves.
Do you know what tomorrow is?
Halloween, of course!
Yes.
Halloween, festival of ghosts.
I have a problem the night before such an important day.

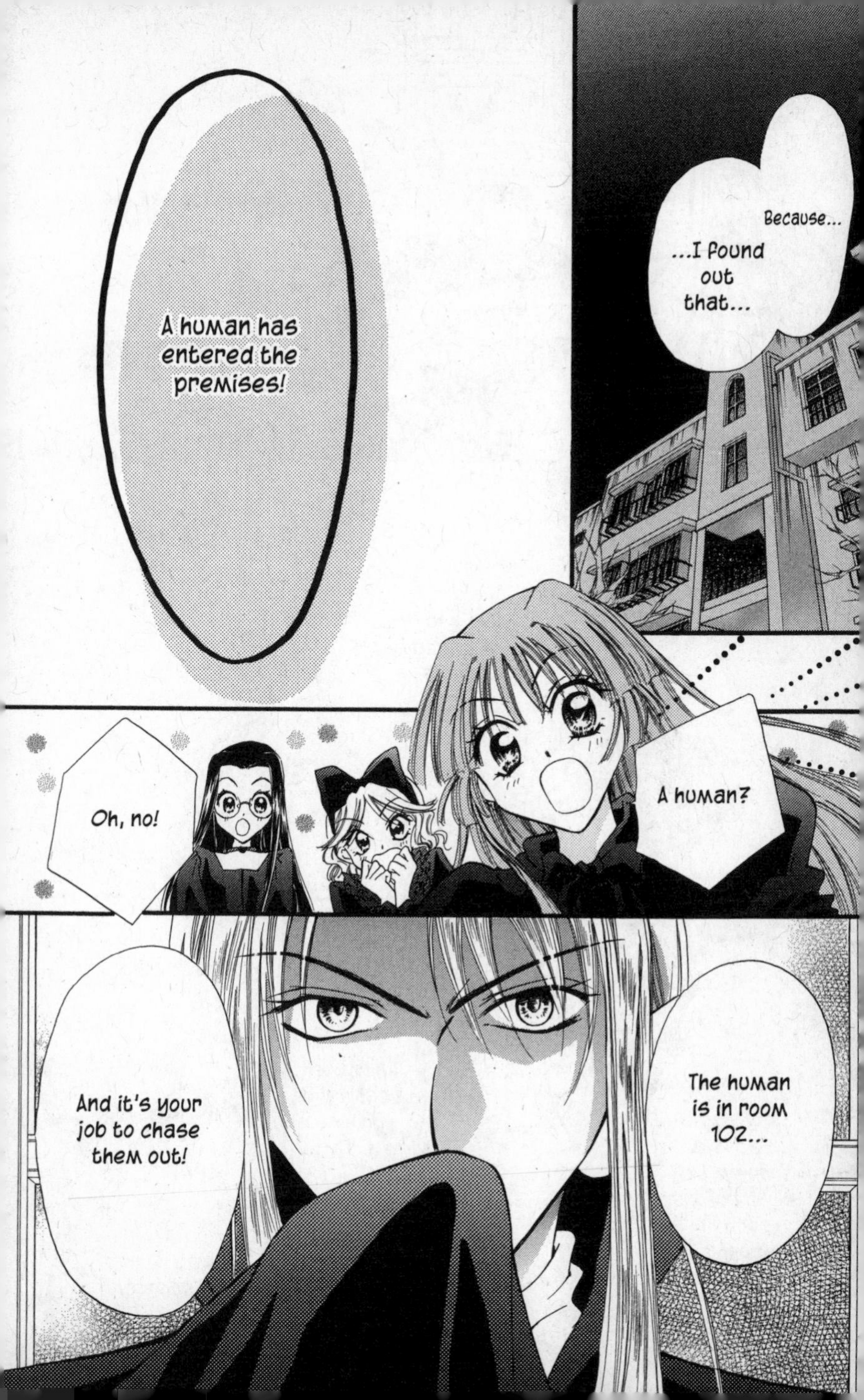
Because...
...I found out that...
A human has entered the premises!
A human?
Oh, no!
The human is in room 102...
And it's your job to chase them out!

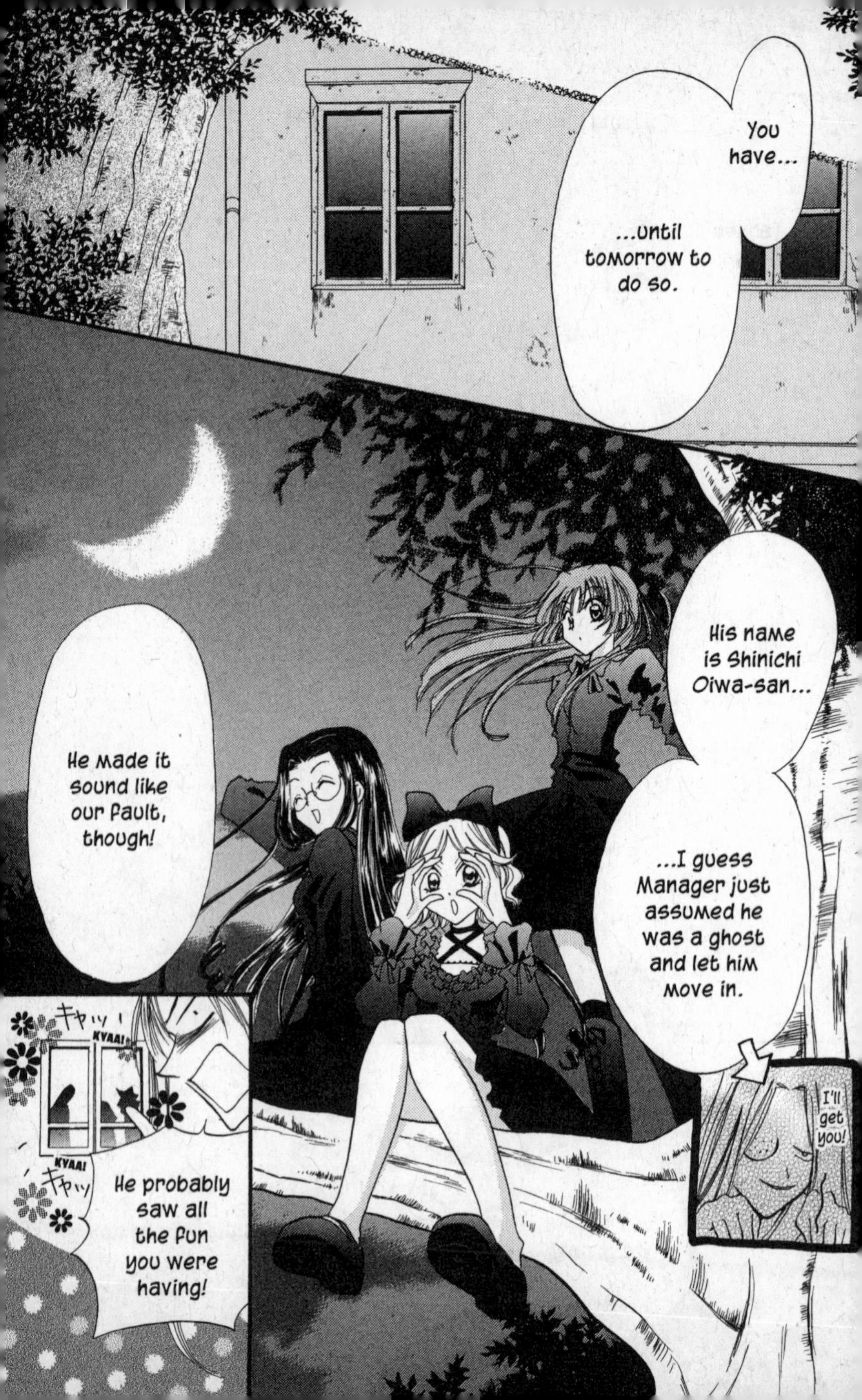
You have...
...until tomorrow to do so.
His name is Shinichi Oiwa-san...
...I guess Manager just assumed he was a ghost and let him move in.
I'll get you!
He made it sound like our fault, though!
キャッ
KYAA!
KYAA!
キャッ
He probably saw all the fun you were having!

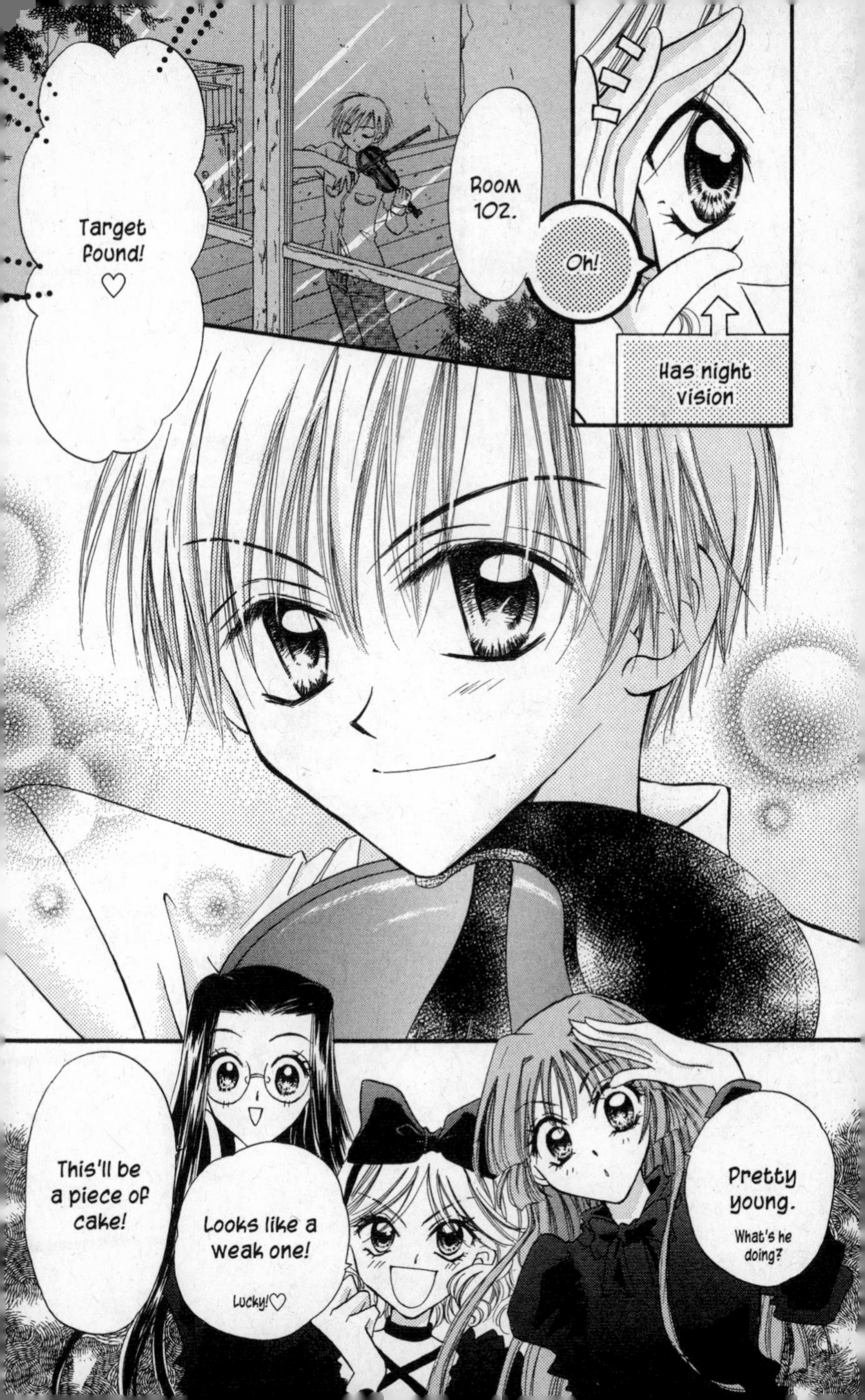
Oh!
Has night vision
Room 102.
Target found! ♡
Pretty young.
What's he doing?
Looks like a weak one!
Lucky!♡
This'll be a piece of cake!

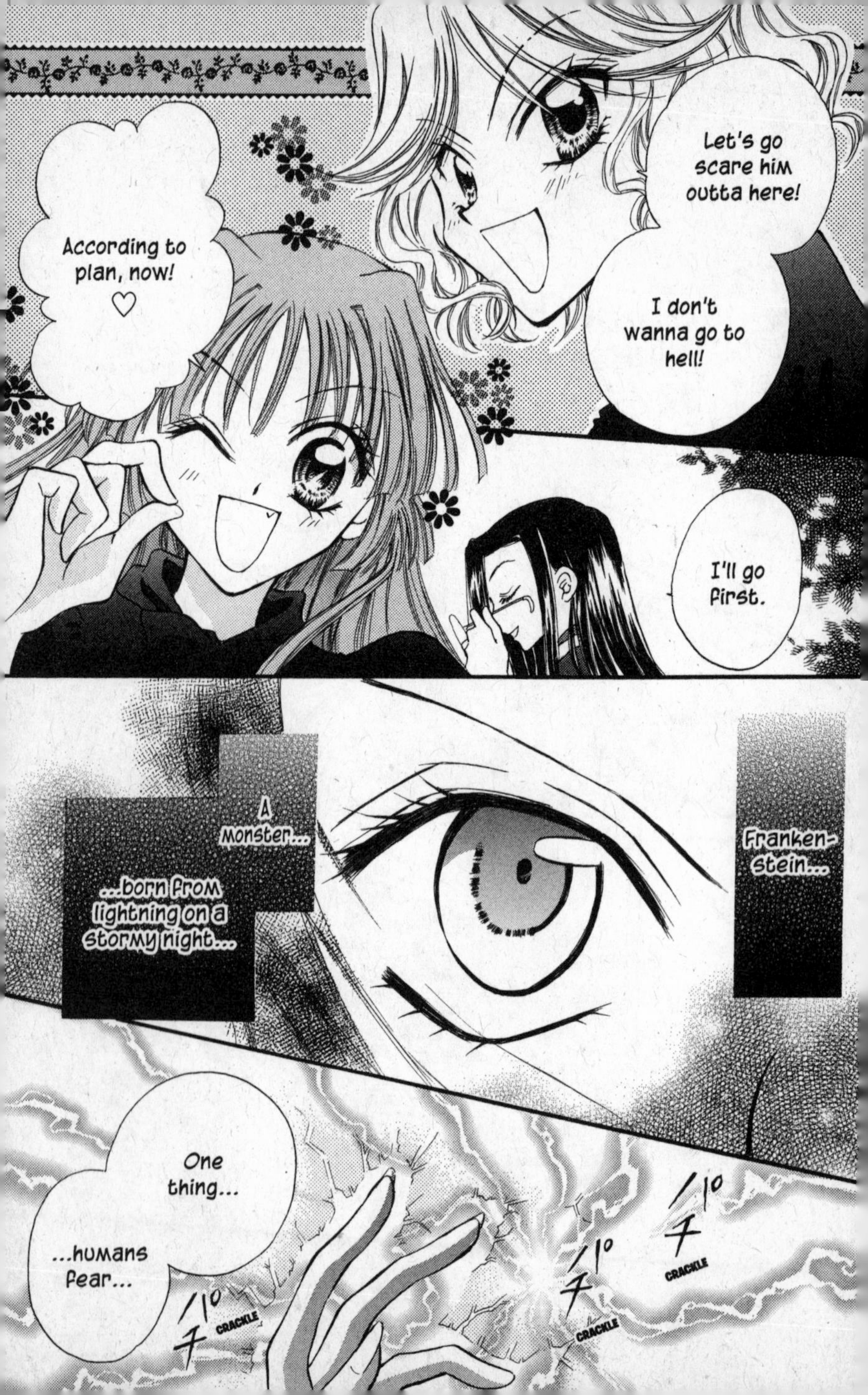
Let's go scare him outta here!
I don't wanna go to hell!
According to plan, now! ♡
I'll go first.
Franken-stein...
A monster...
...born from lightning on a stormy night...
CRACKLE
CRACKLE
One thing...
...humans fear...
CRACKLE

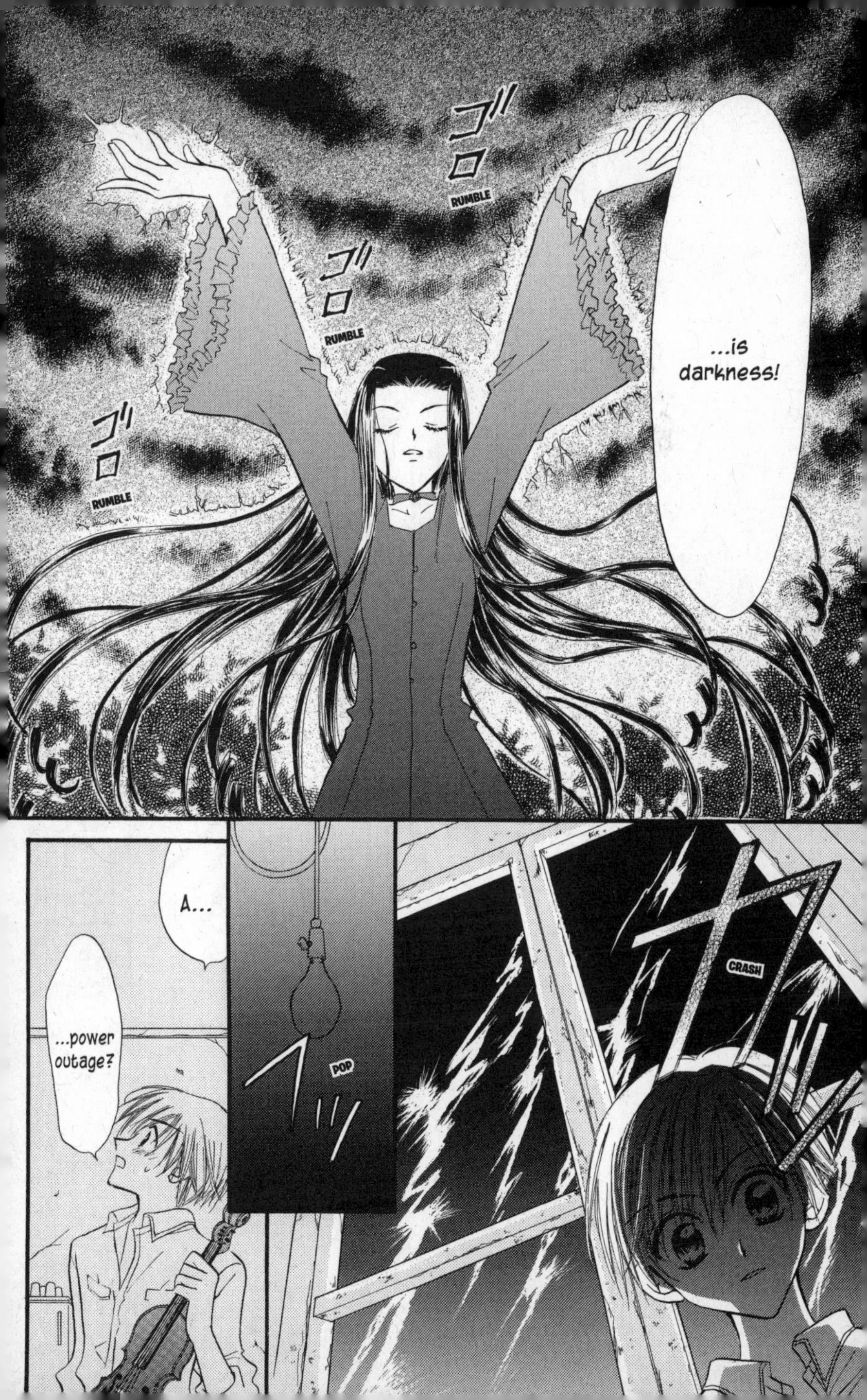
...is darkness!
ゴロ
RUMBLE
ゴロ
RUMBLE
ゴロ
RUMBLE
CRASH
POP
A...
...power outage?

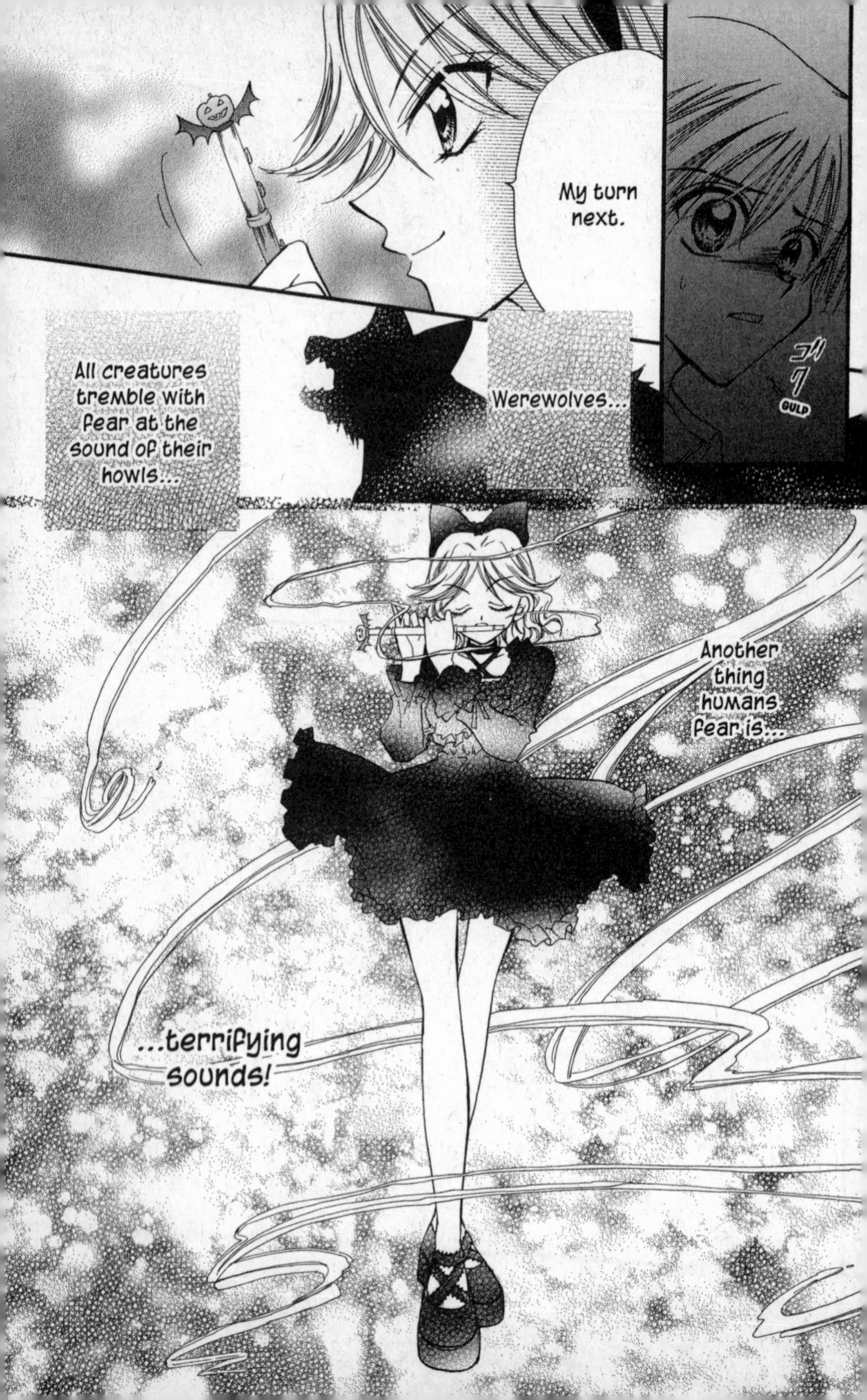
ゴク
GULP
My turn next.
Werewolves...
All creatures tremble with fear at the sound of their howls...
Another thing humans fear is...
...terrifying sounds!

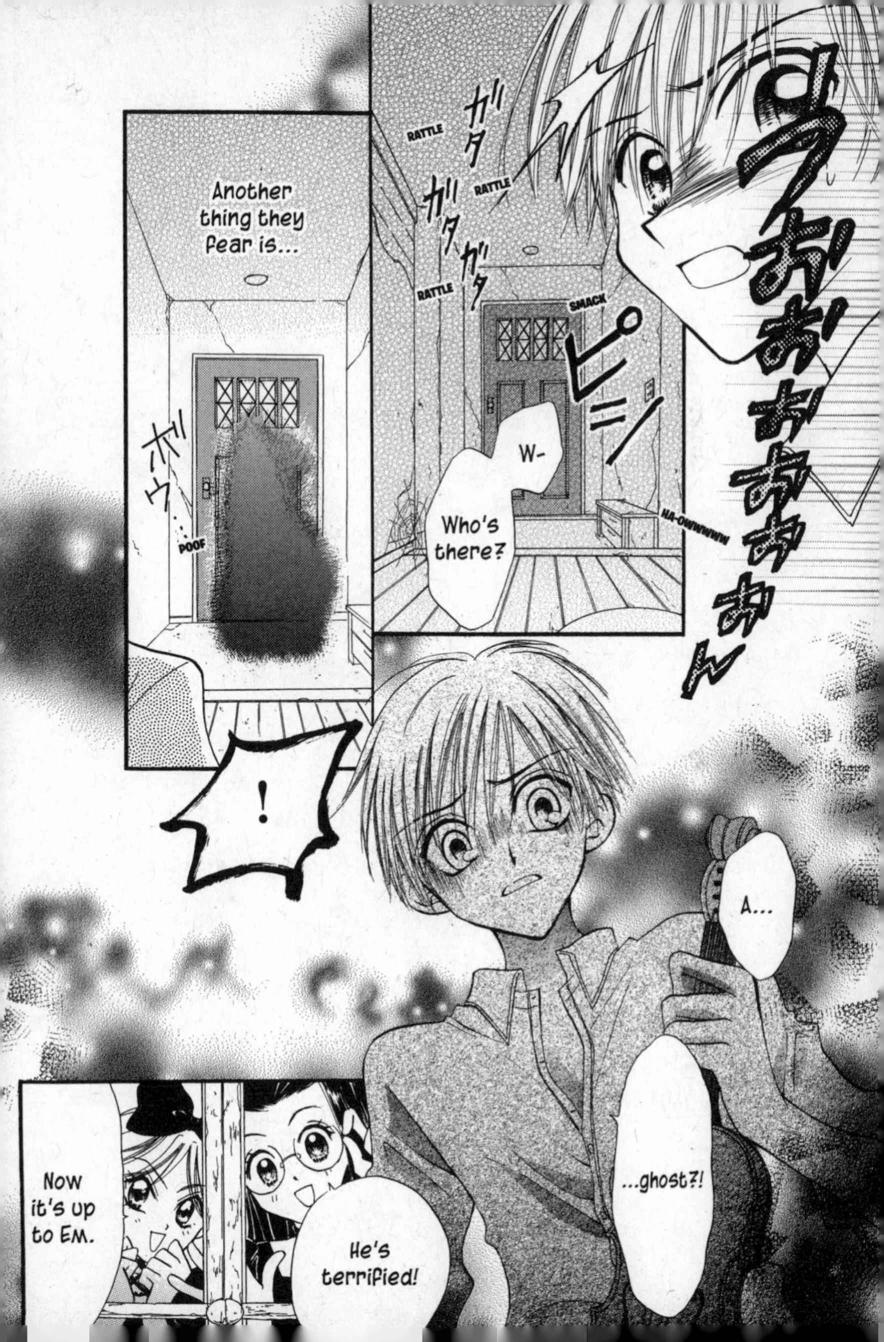

うおおおおおおん
HA-OWWWWWW
ガタ
RATTLE
ガタ
RATTLE
ガタ
RATTLE
SMACK
W-
Who's there?
Another thing they fear is...
POOF
!
A...
...ghost?!
He's terrified!
Now it's up to Em.

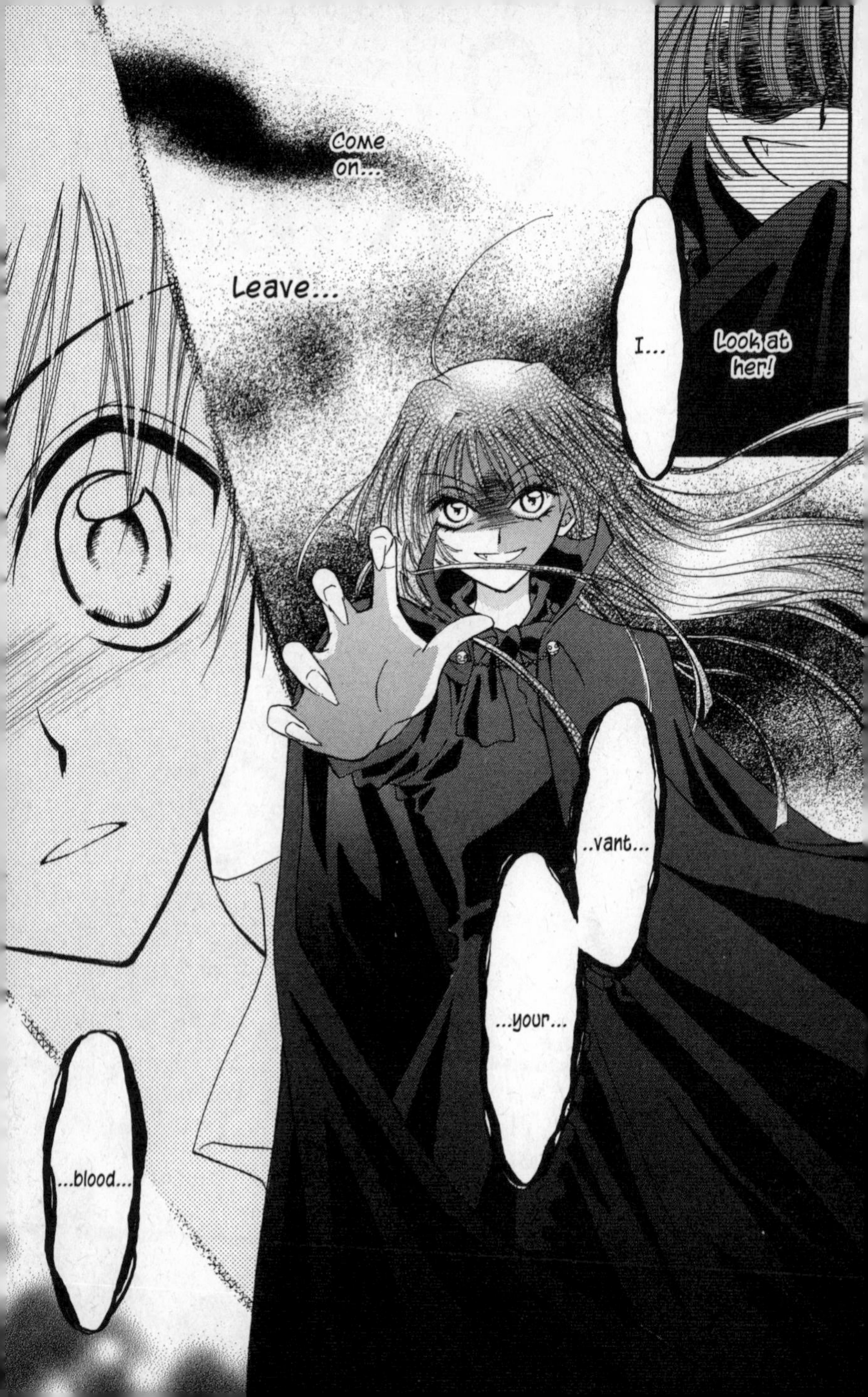
Look at her!
Come on...
Leave...
I...
..vant...
...your...
...blood...

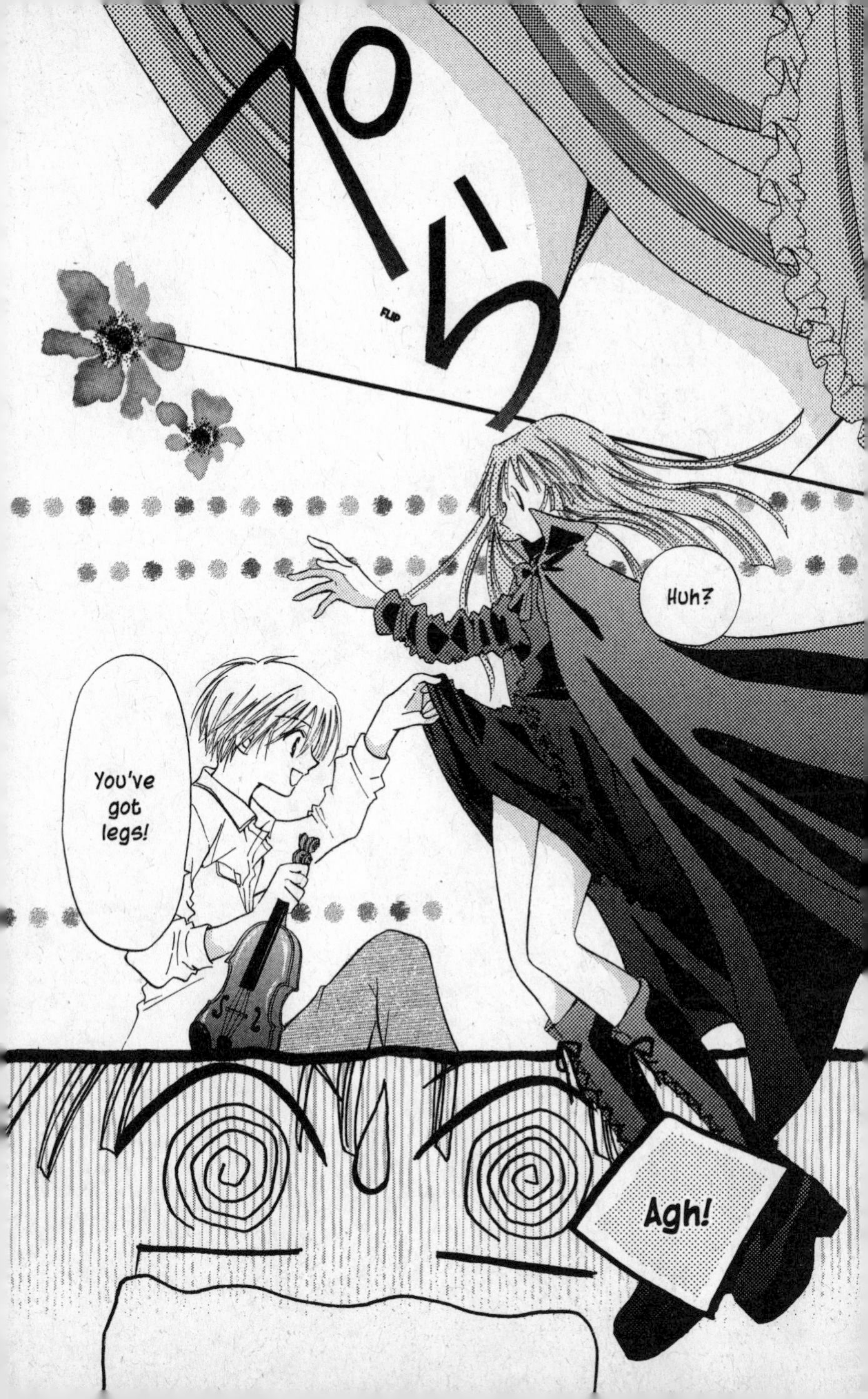
FLIP
Huh?
You've got legs!
Agh!

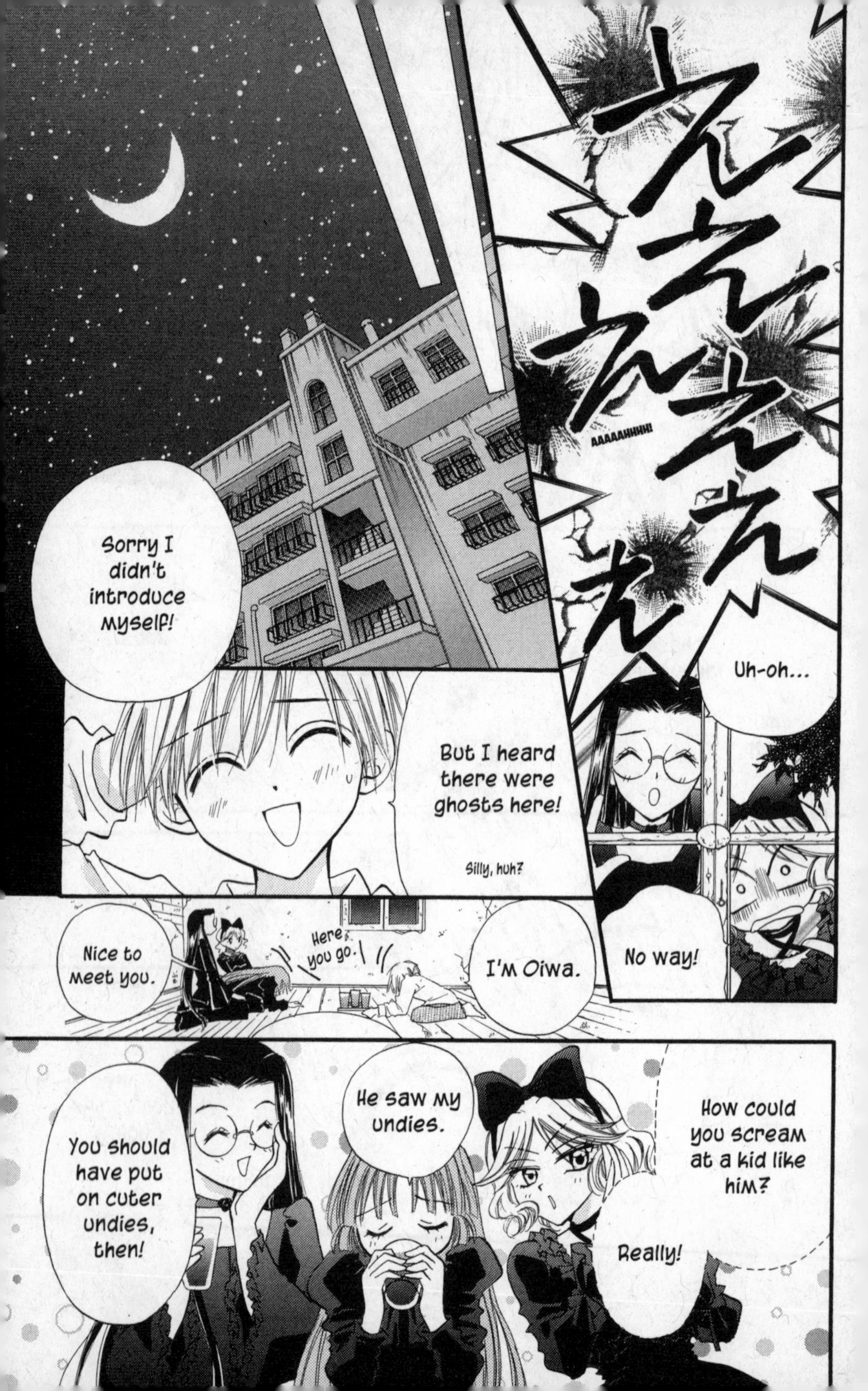
AAAAAHHHH!
Sorry I didn't introduce myself!
Uh-oh...
No way!
But I heard there were ghosts here!
Silly, huh?
I'm Oiwa.
Here you go.
Nice to meet you.
How could you scream at a kid like him?
Really!
He saw my undies.
You should have put on cuter undies, then!

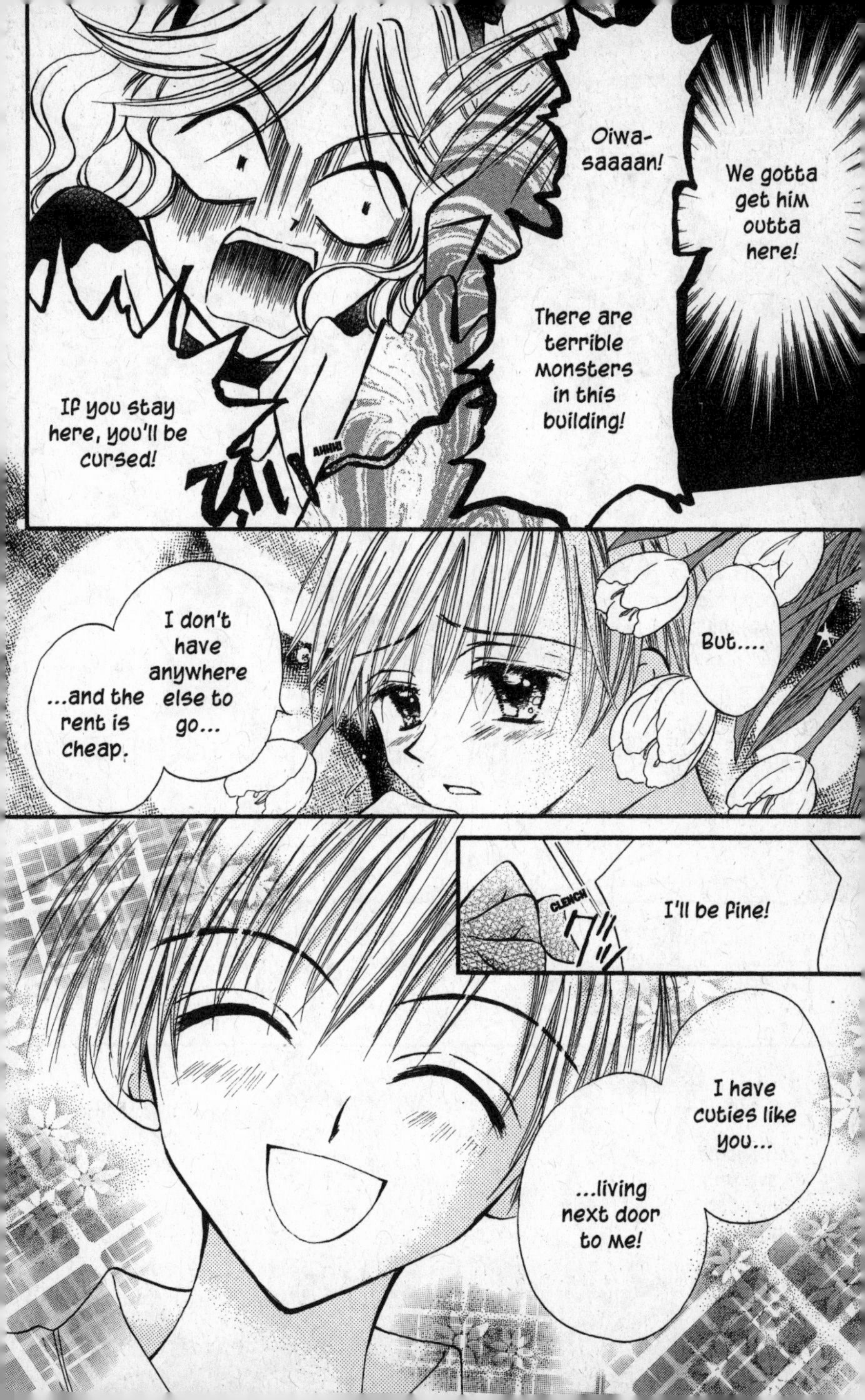
We gotta get him outta here!
Oiwa-saaaaan!
There are terrible monsters in this building!
If you stay here, you'll be cursed!
But....
I don't have anywhere else to go...
...and the rent is cheap.
CLENCH
I'll be fine!
I have cuties like you...
...living next door to me!

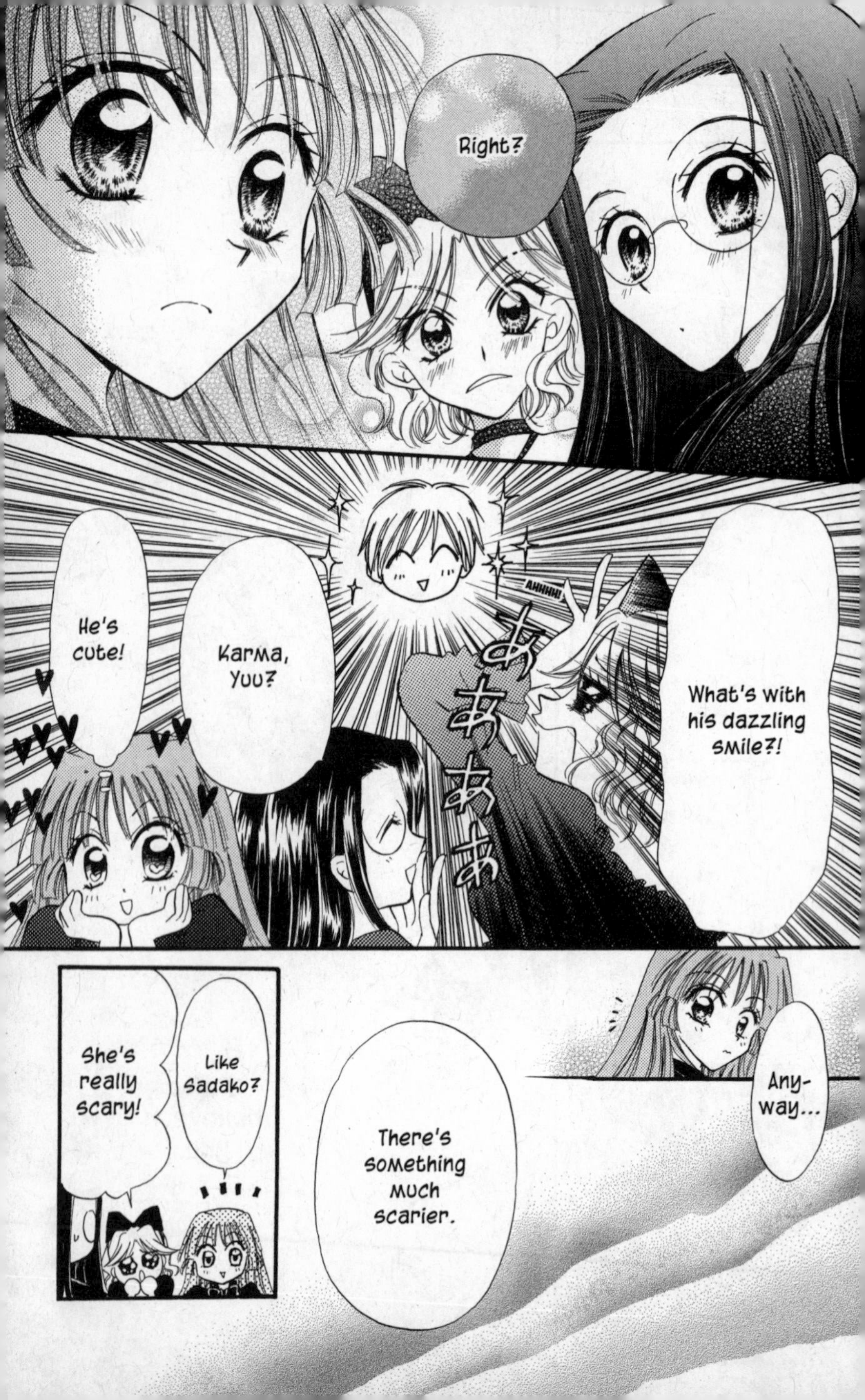
Right?
What's with his dazzling smile?!
AHHHH!
ああああ
Karma, Yuu?
He's cute!
Any-way...
There's something much scarier.
Like Sadako?
She's really scary!

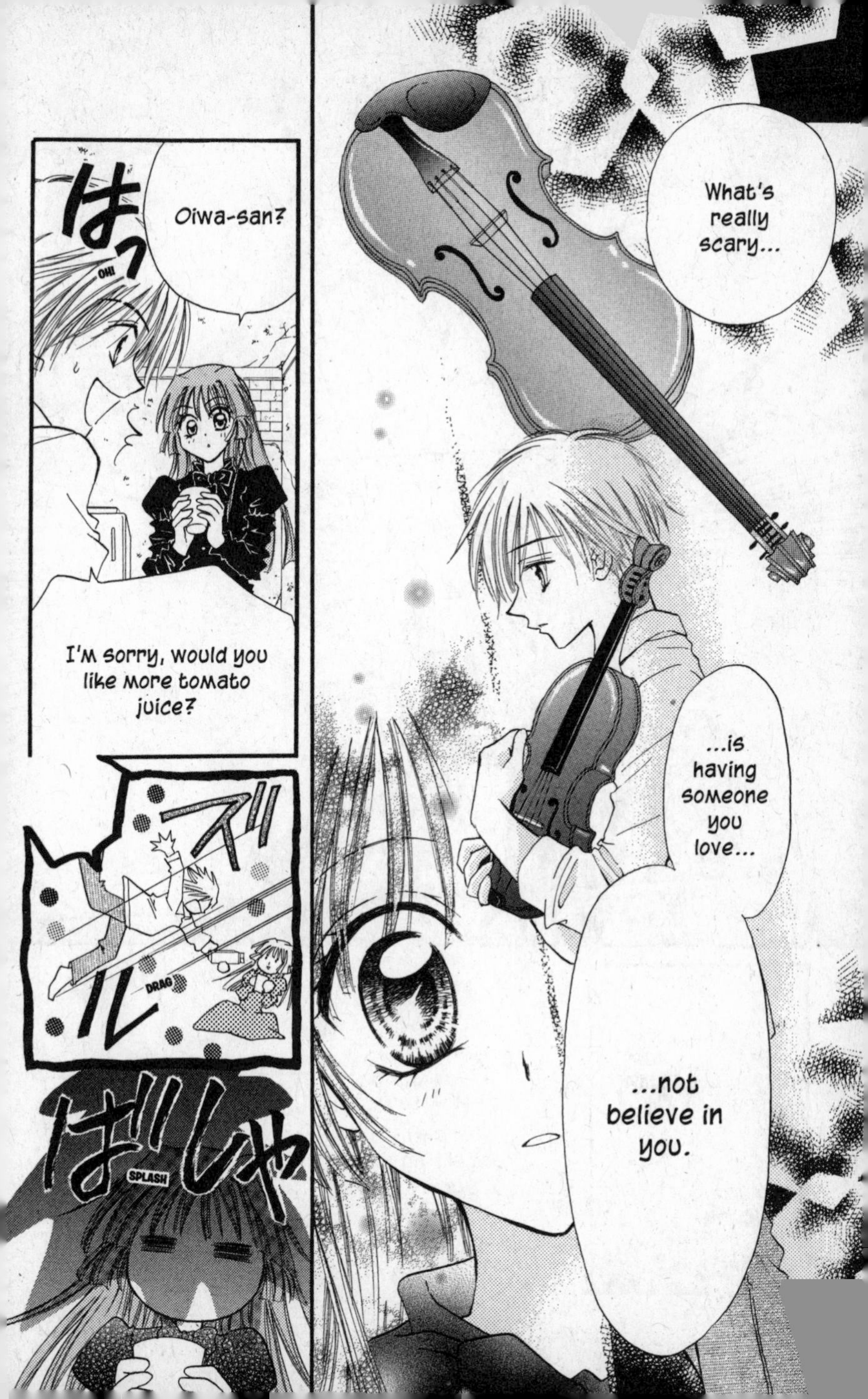
What's really scary...
...is having someone you love...
...not believe in you.
はっ
OH!
Oiwa-san?
I'm sorry, would you like more tomato juice?
ズル
DRAG
ばしゃ
SPLASH

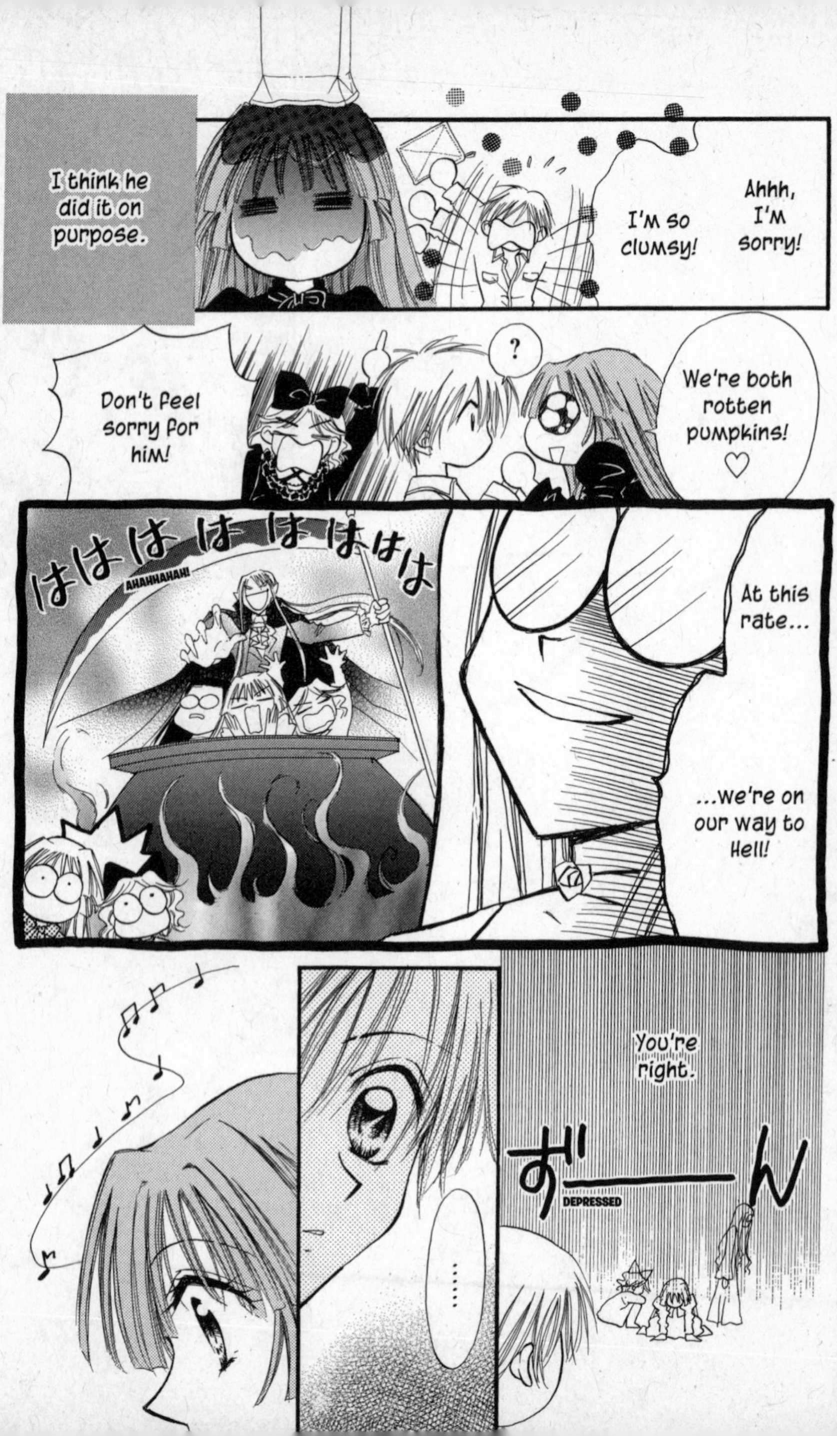
Ahhh, I'm sorry!
I'm so clumsy!
I think he did it on purpose.
We're both rotten pumpkins! ♡
?
Don't feel sorry for him!
At this rate...
...we're on our way to Hell!
はははははははは
AHAHHAHAH!
You're right.
ず――ん
DEPRESSED
......

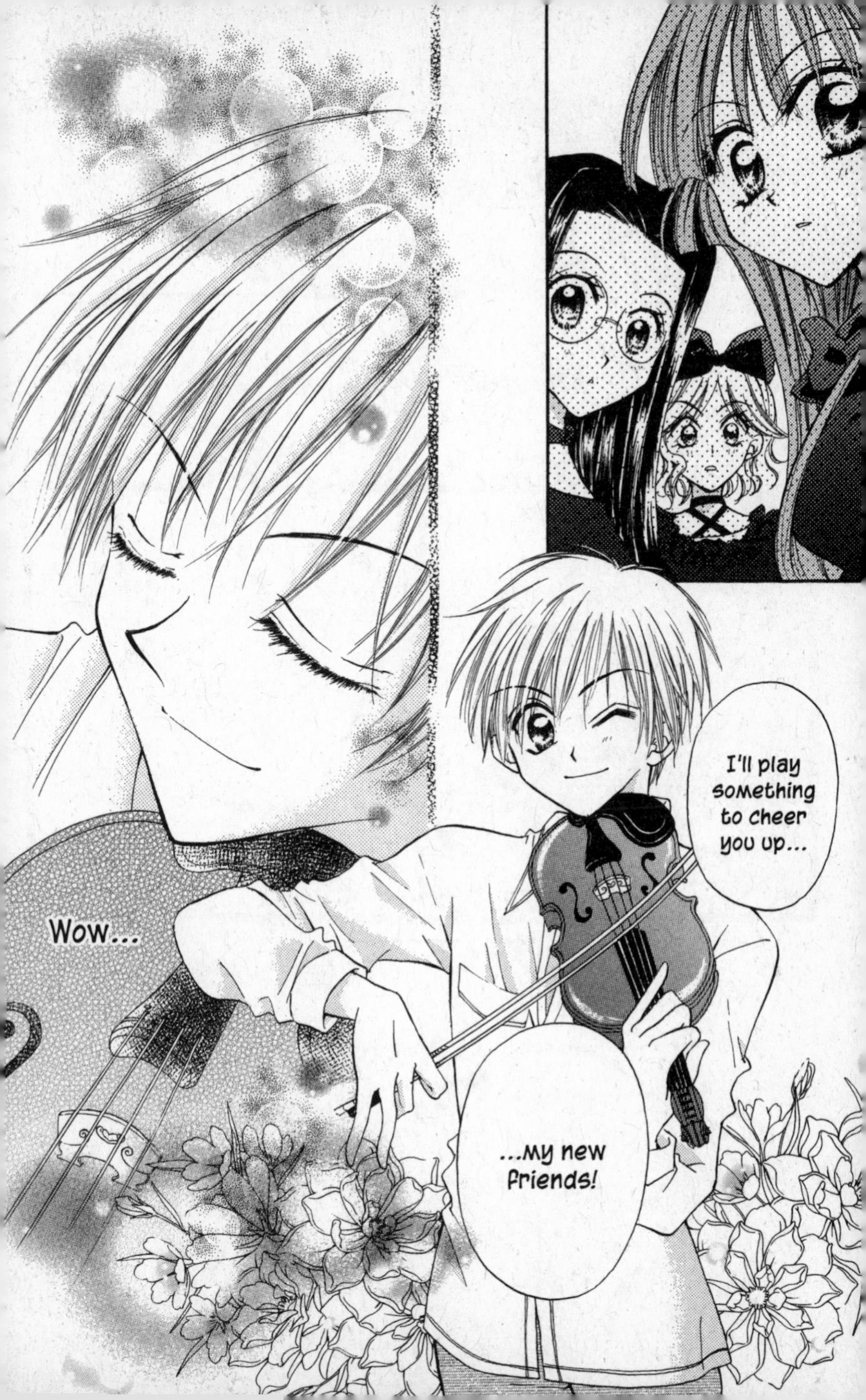
I'll play something to cheer you up...
...my new friends!
Wow...

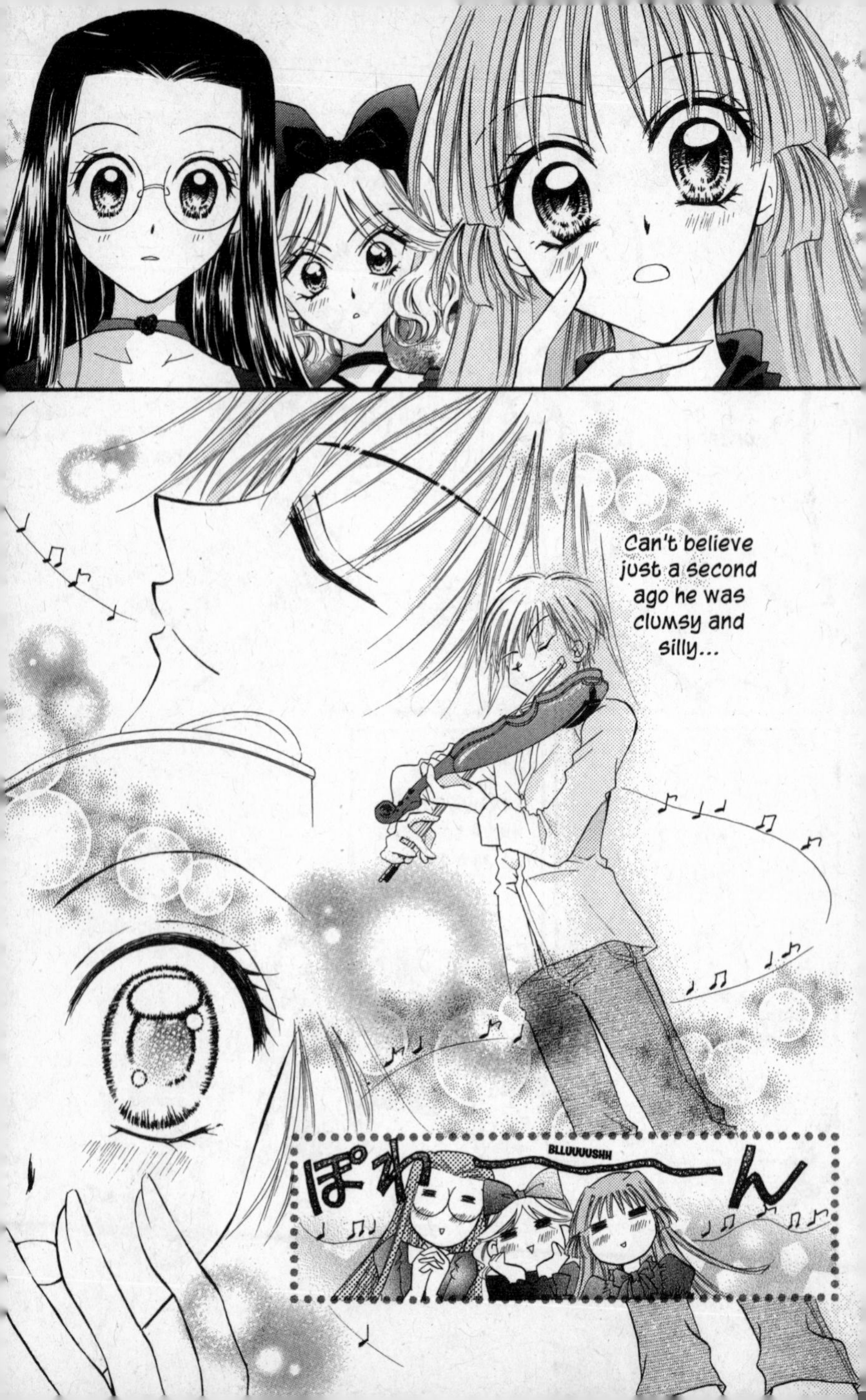
Can't believe just a second ago he was clumsy and silly...
ぽわーーん
BLLUUUUSHH

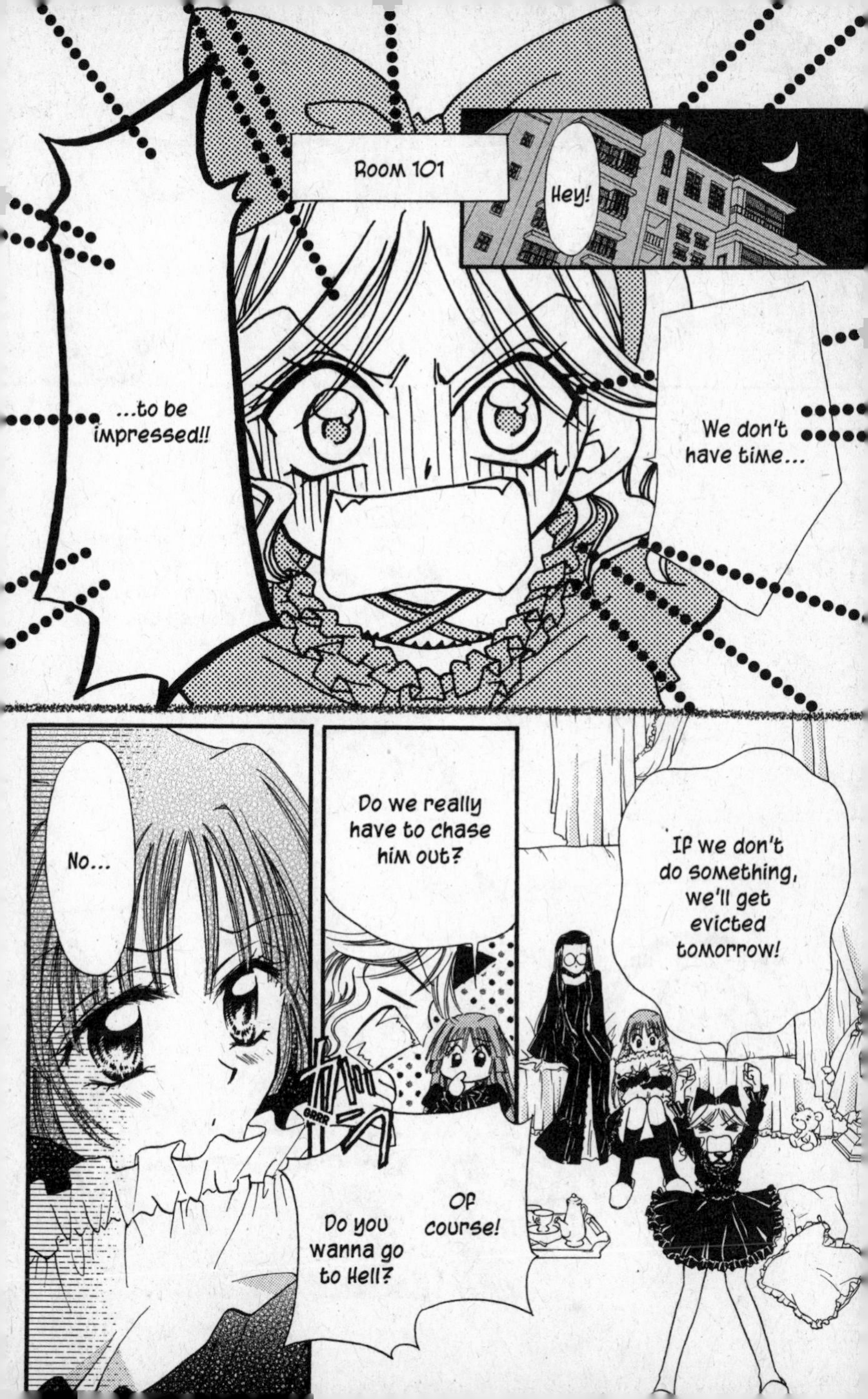
Room 101
Hey!
We don't have time...
...to be impressed!!
If we don't do something, we'll get evicted tomorrow!
Do we really have to chase him out?
GRRR
Of course!
Do you wanna go to Hell?
No...

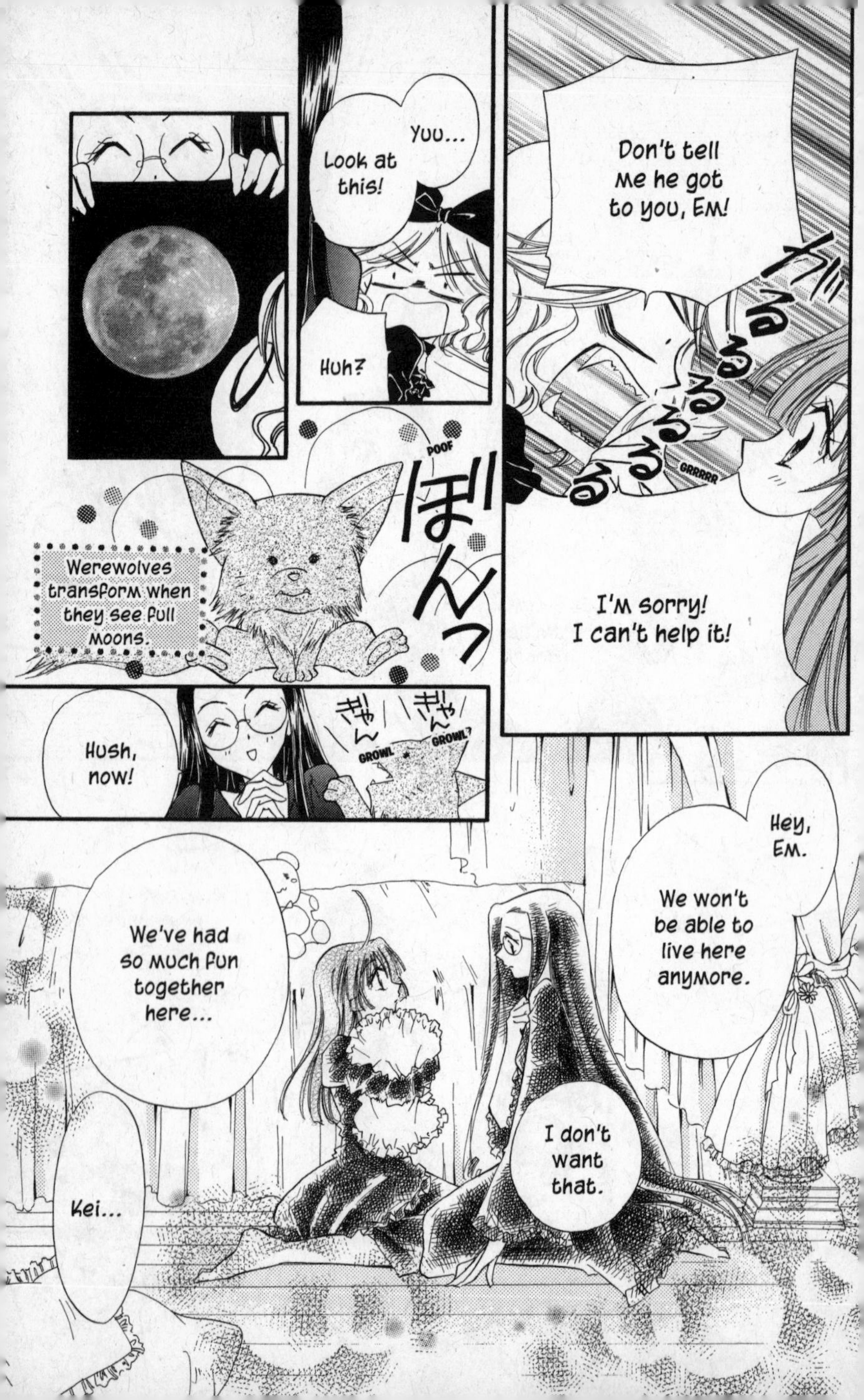
Don't tell me he got to you, Em!
ガるるるるる
GRRRRR
I'm sorry! I can't help it!
You...
Look at this!
Huh?
ぽんっ
POOF
Werewolves transform when they see full moons.
ぎゃん
GROWL
ぎゃん
GROWL
Hush, now!
Hey, Em.
We won't be able to live here anymore.
We've had so much fun together here...
I don't want that.
Kei...

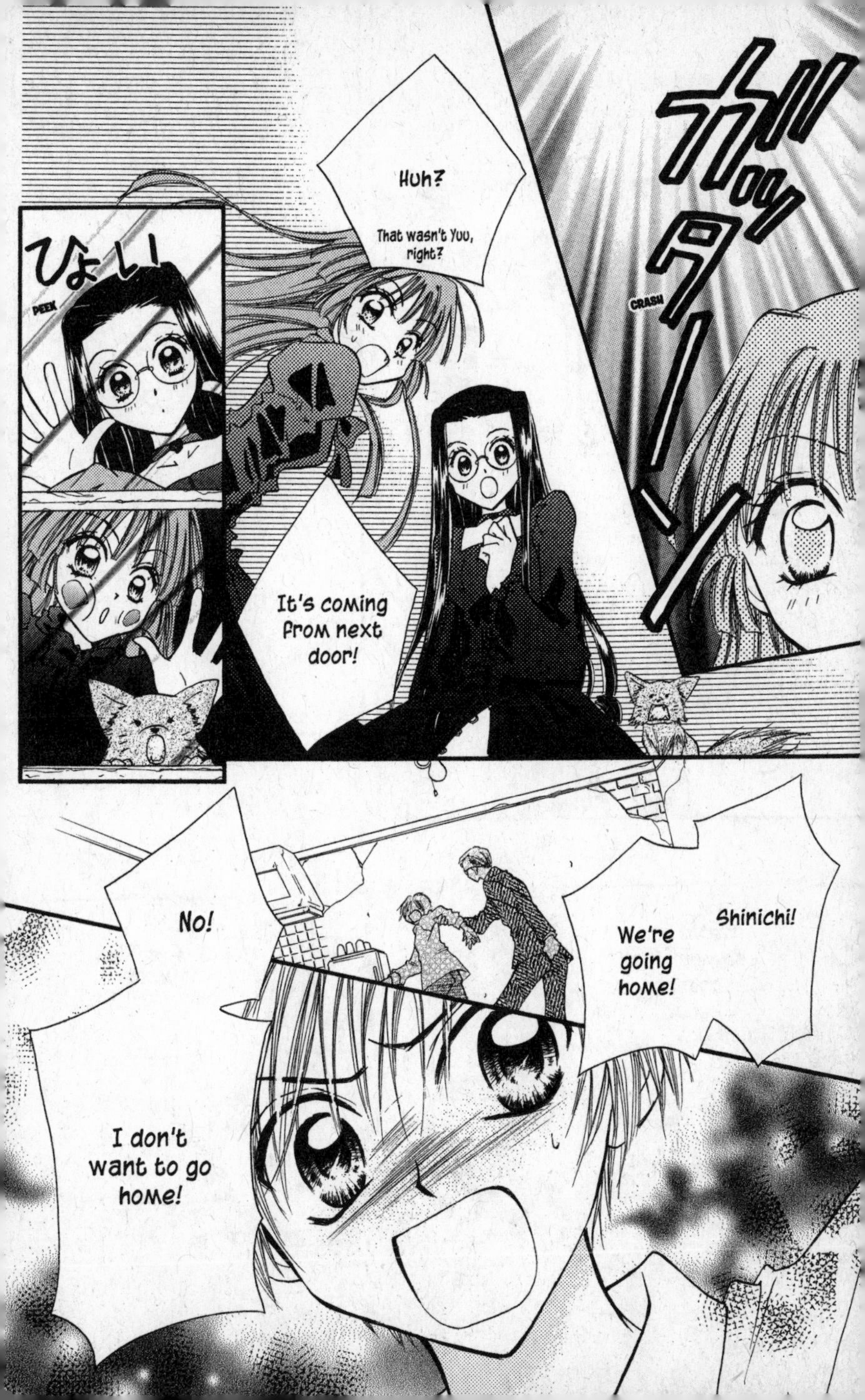

ガッターン
CRASH
Huh?
That wasn't you, right?
It's coming from next door!
ひょい
PEEK
Shinichi! We're going home!
No!
I don't want to go home!

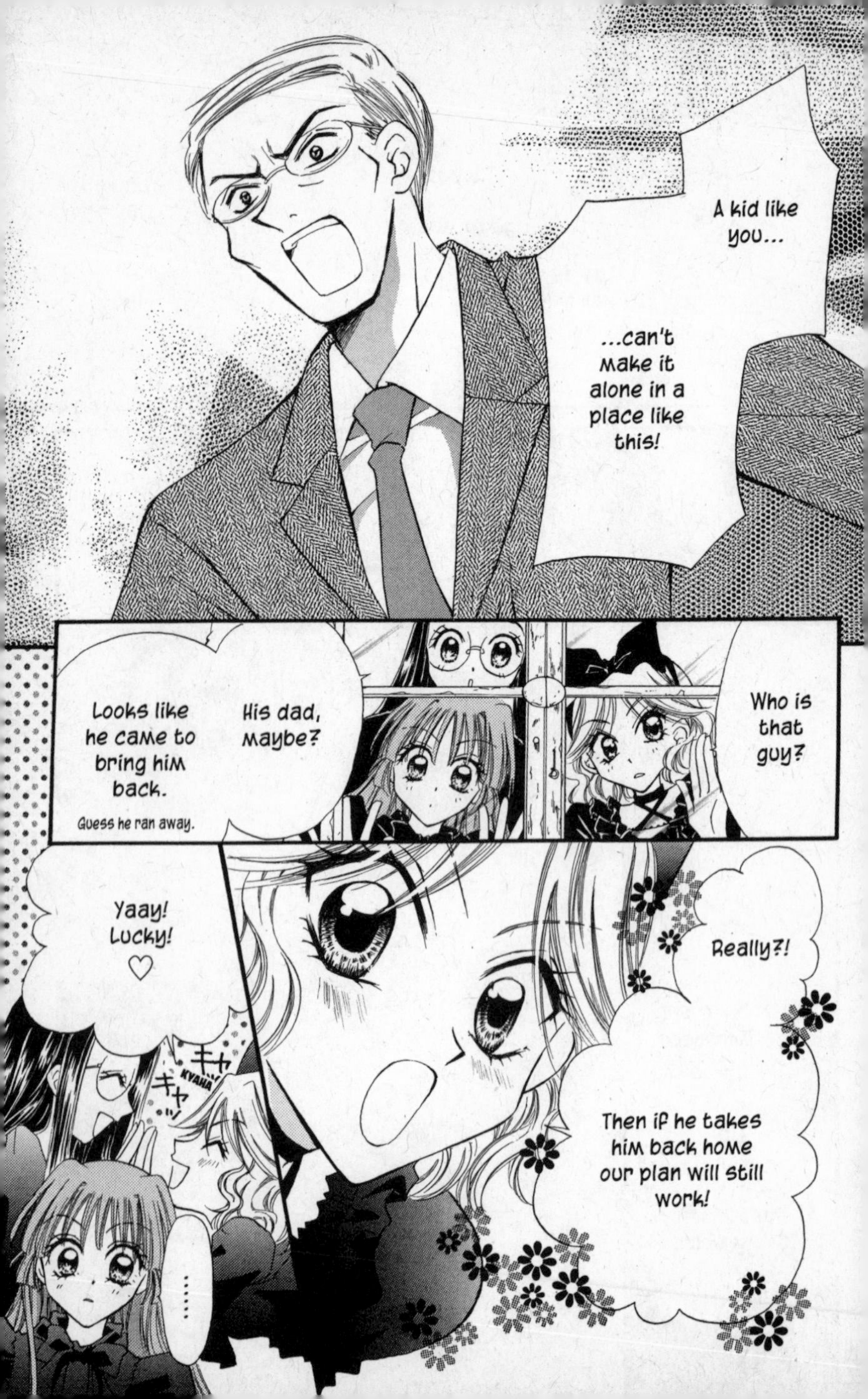
A kid like you...
...can't make it alone in a place like this!
Who is that guy?
His dad, maybe?
Looks like he came to bring him back.
Guess he ran away.
Really?!
Then if he takes him back home our plan will still work!
Yaay! Lucky! ♡
KYAHA
......

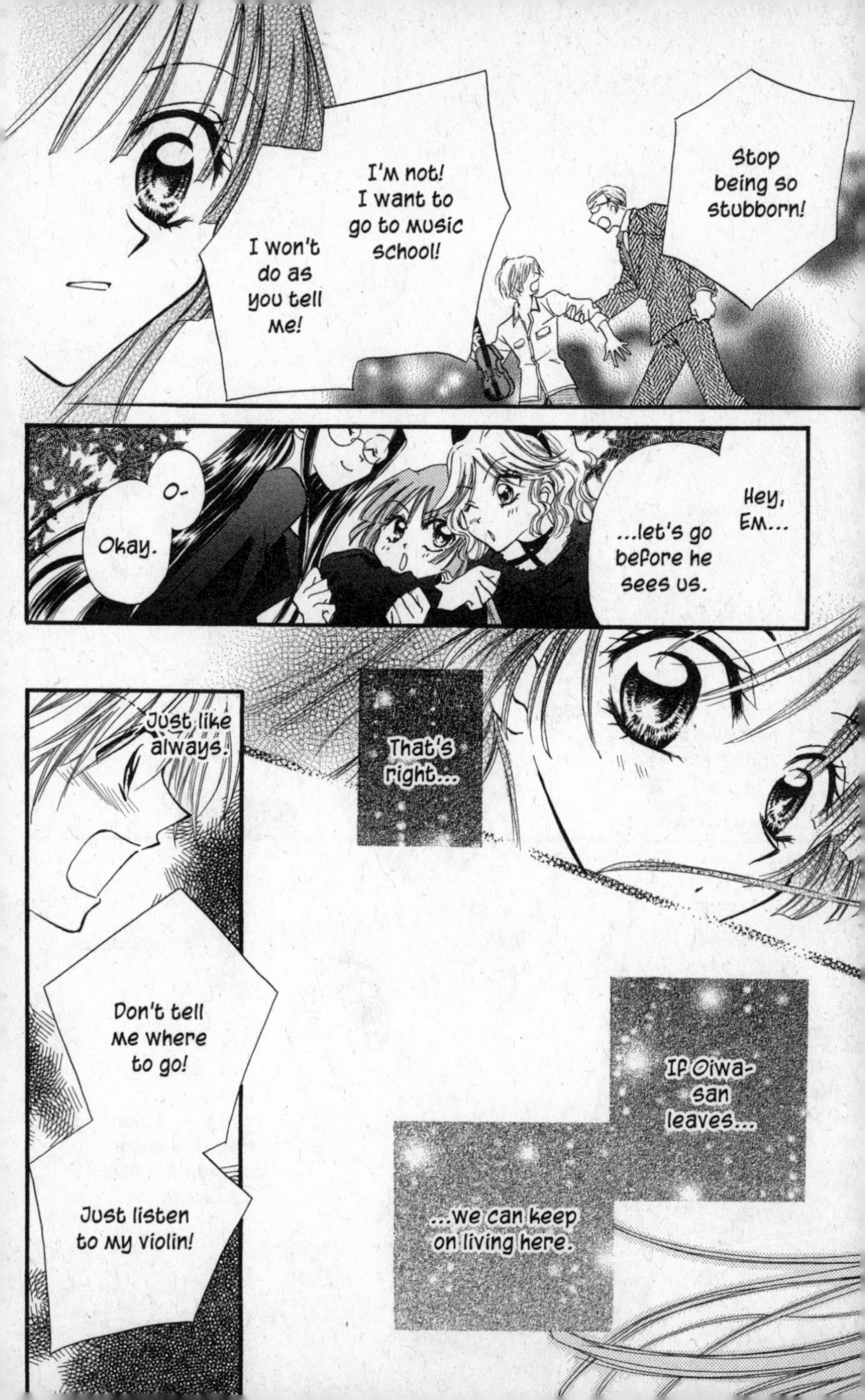
Stop being so stubborn!
I'm not! I want to go to music school!
I won't do as you tell me!
Hey, Em...
...let's go before he sees us.
O-
Okay.
That's right...
If Oiwa-san leaves...
...we can keep on living here.
Just like always.
Don't tell me where to go!
Just listen to my violin!

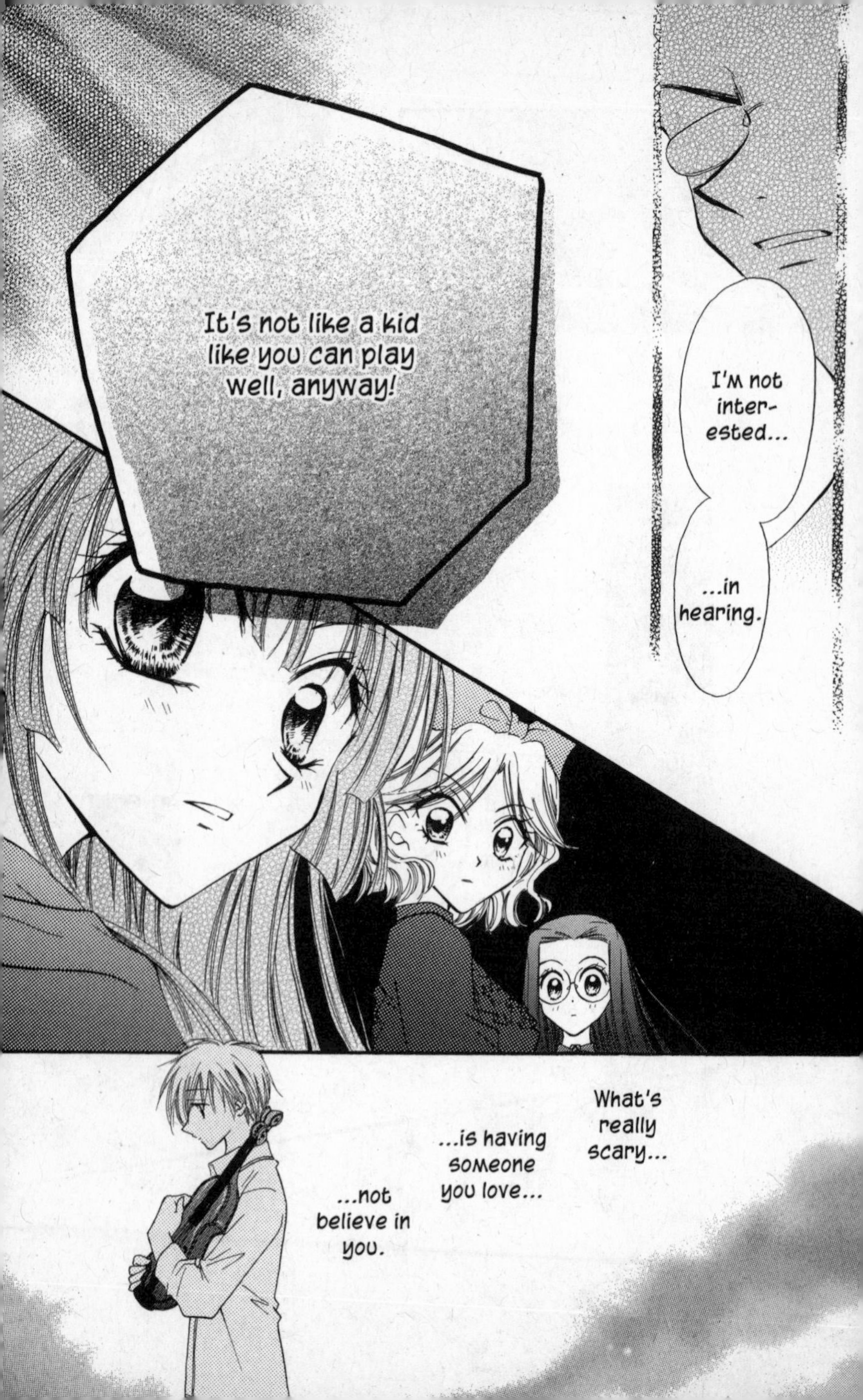
I'm not interested...
...in hearing.
It's not like a kid like you can play well, anyway!
What's really scary...
...is having someone you love...
...not believe in you.

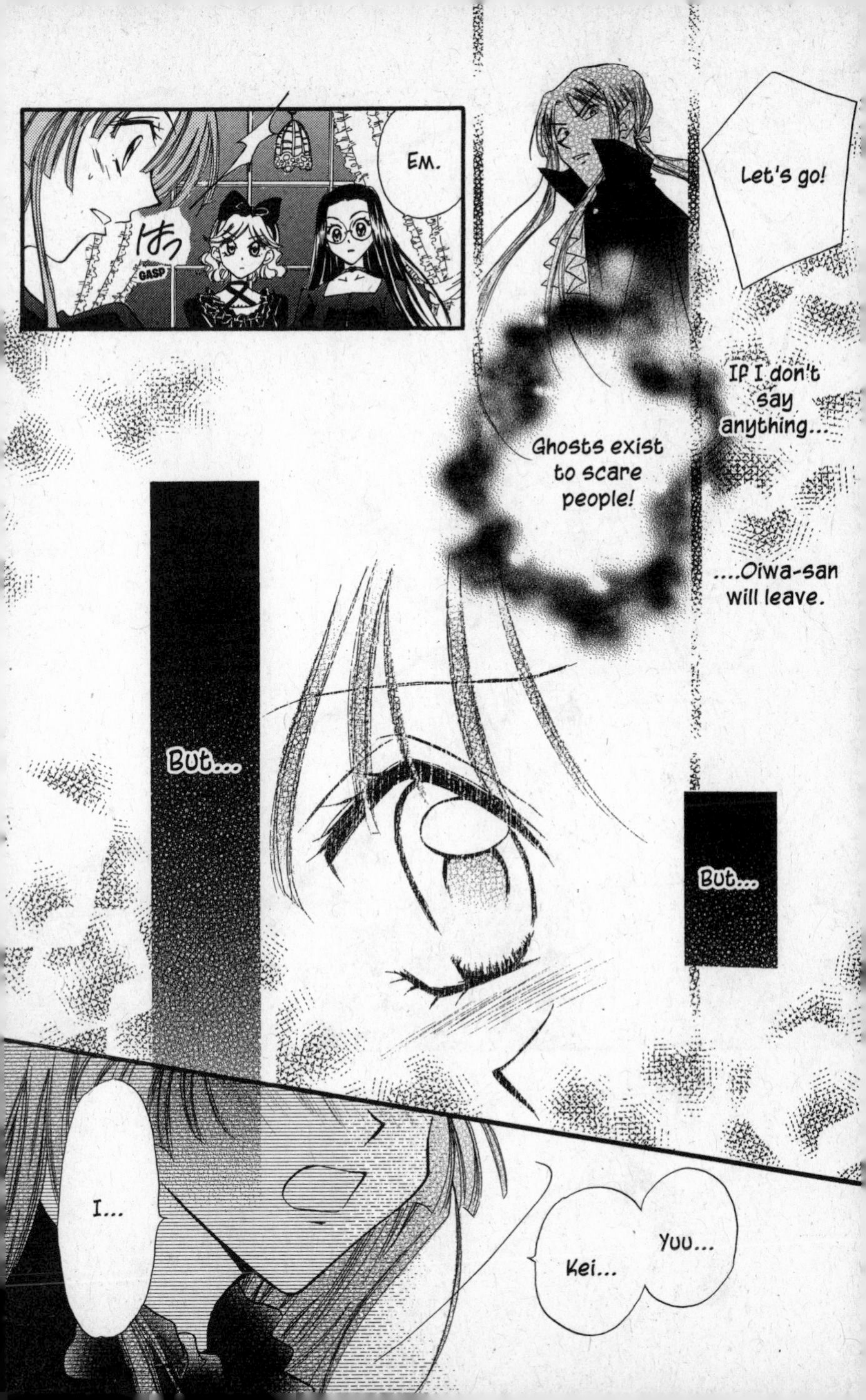
Let's go!
Ghosts exist to scare people!
Em.
はっ
GASP
If I don't say anything...
....Oiwa-san will leave.
But...
But...
You...
Kei...
I...

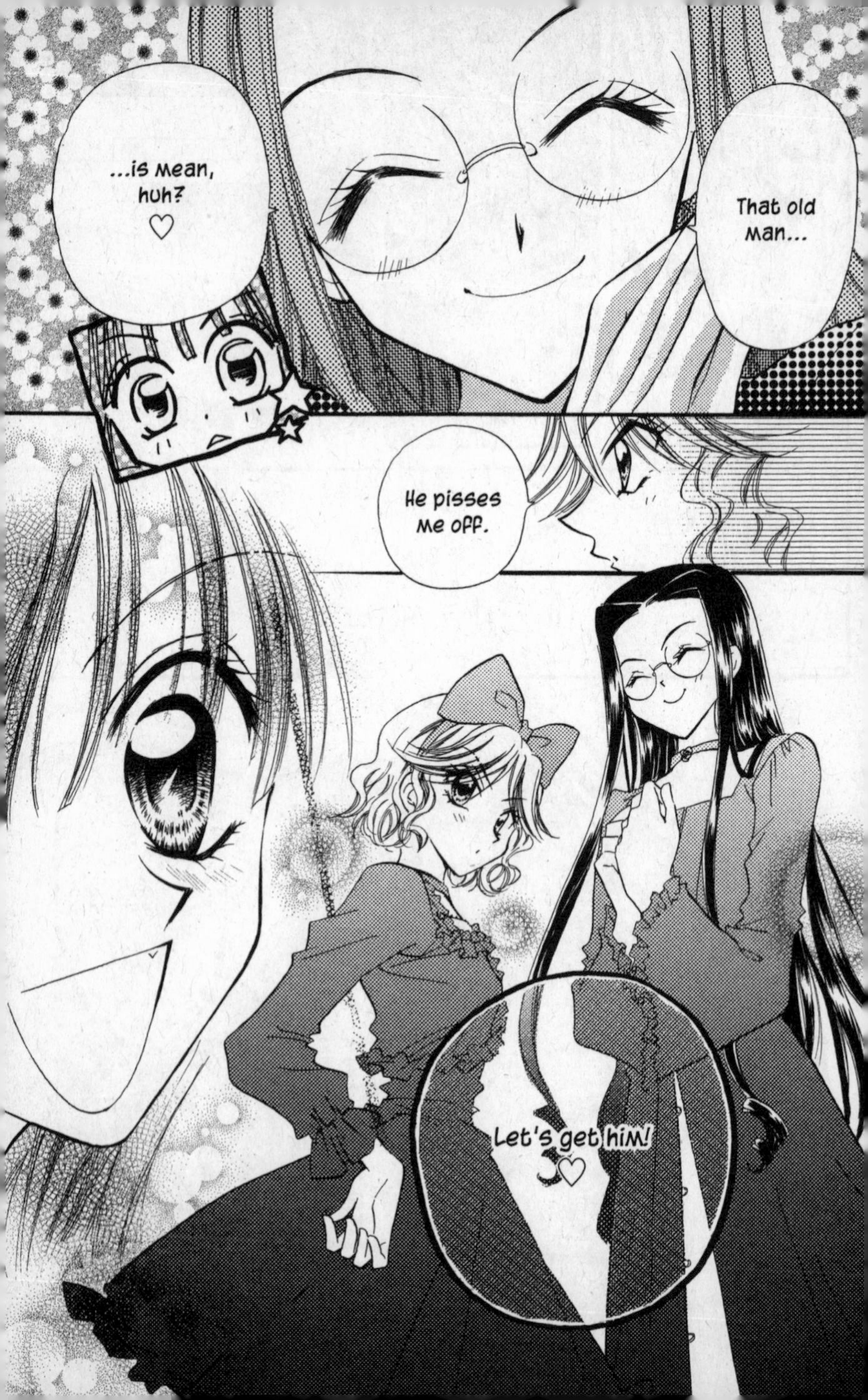
That old man...
...is mean, huh? ♡
He pisses me off.
Let's get him! ♡

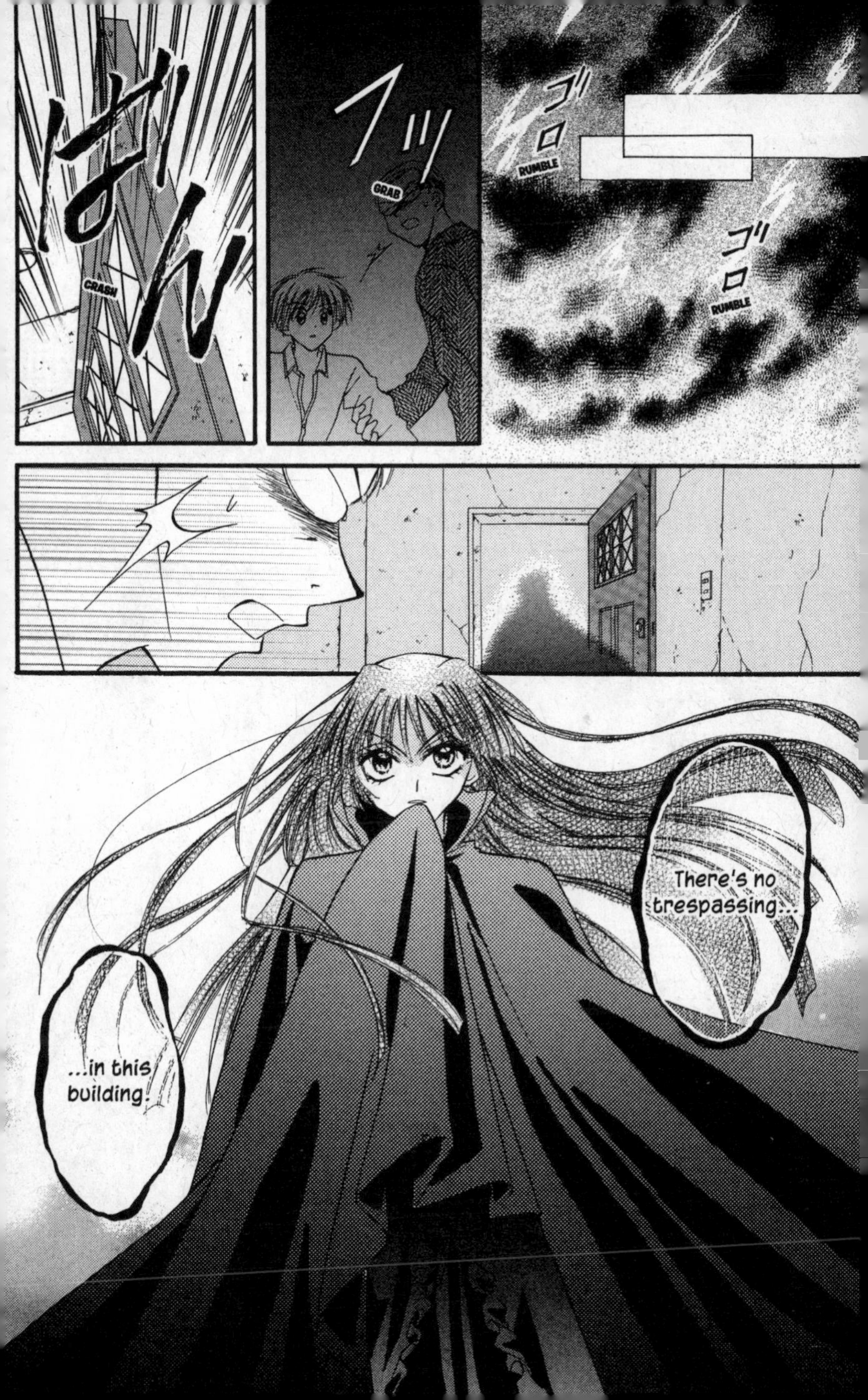
ゴロ
RUMBLE
ゴロ
RUMBLE
GRAB
ばん
CRASH
There's no trespassing...
...in this building.

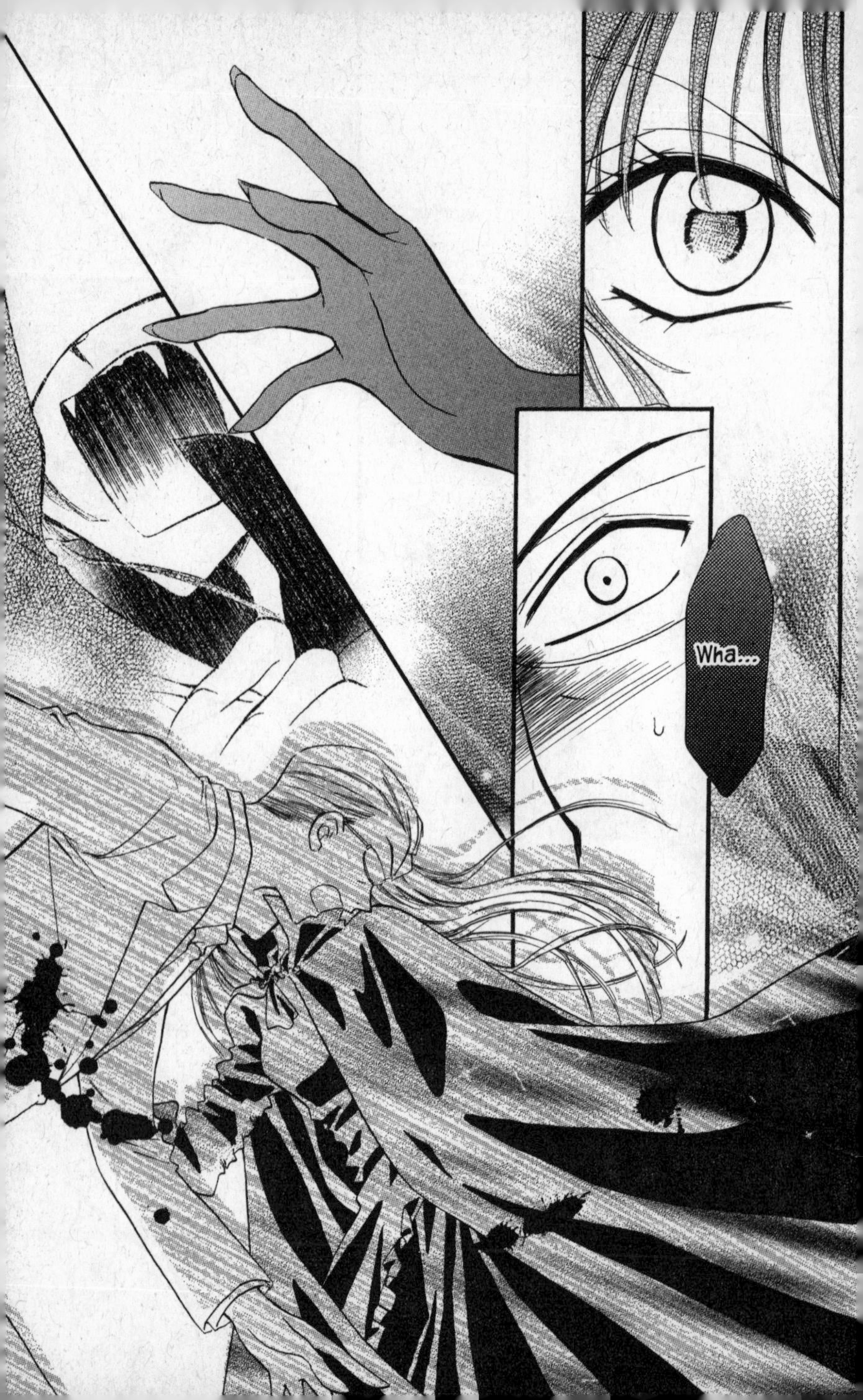
Wha...

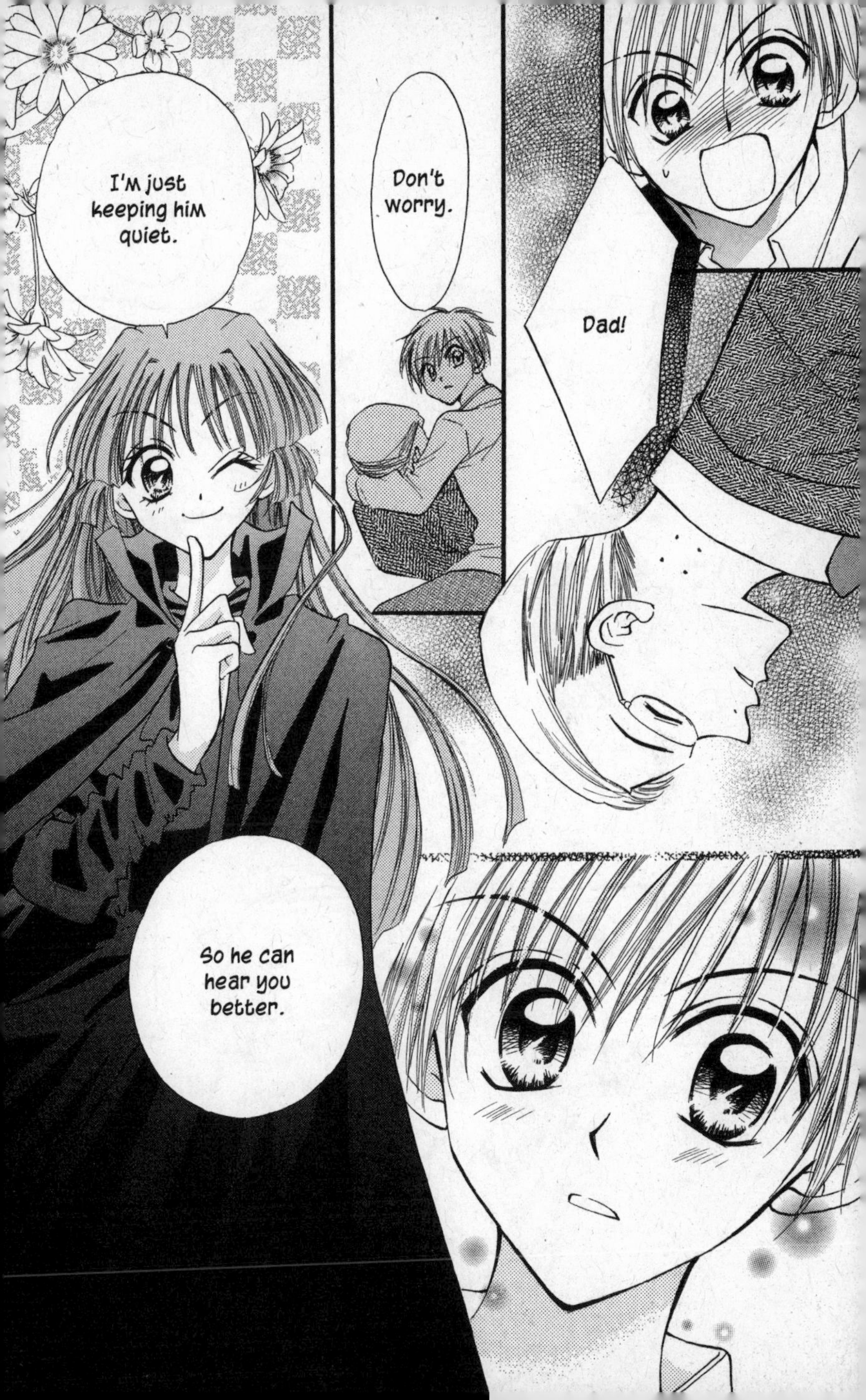
Dad!
Don't worry.
I'm just keeping him quiet.
So he can hear you better.

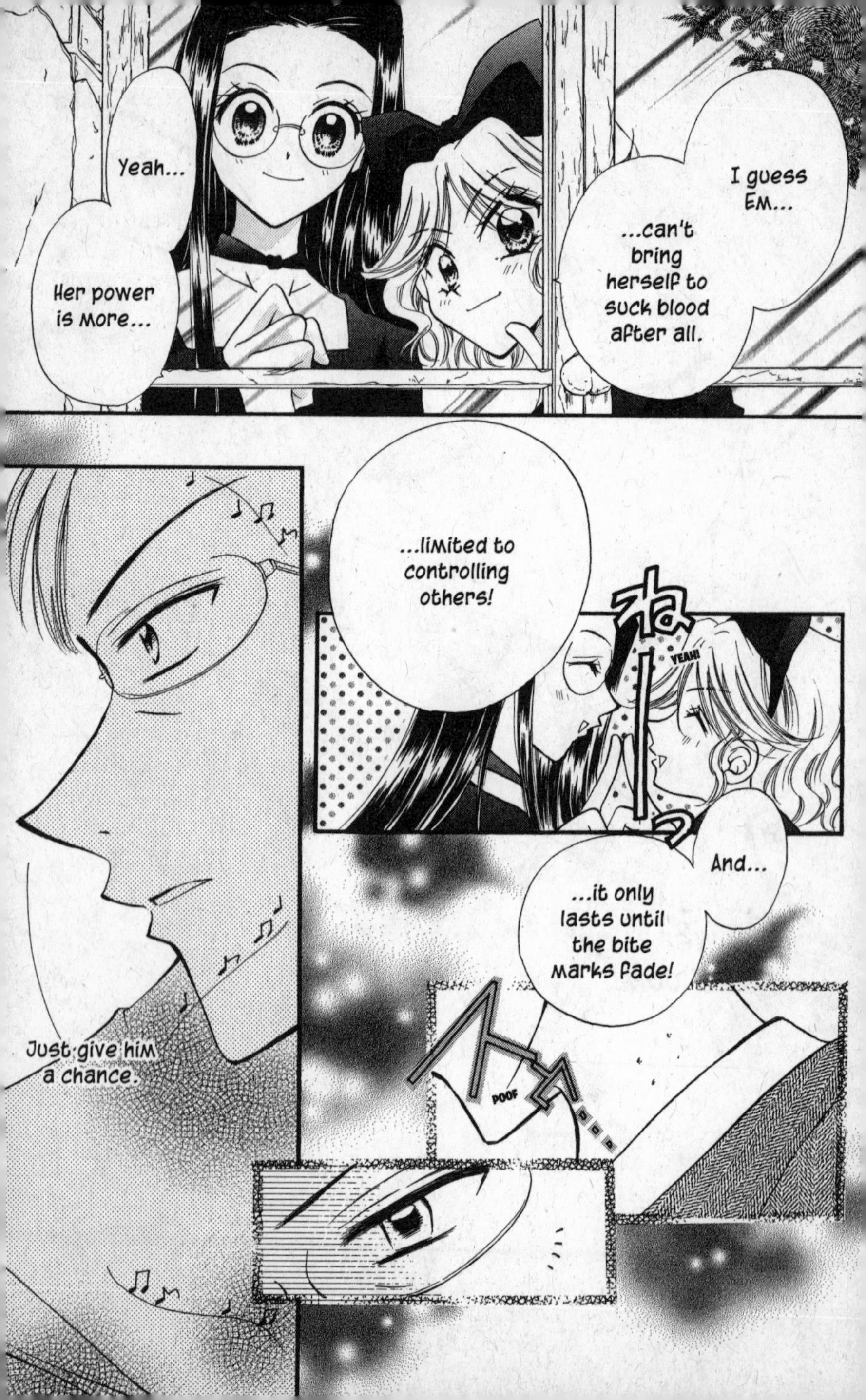
I guess Em...
...can't bring herself to suck blood after all.
Yeah...
Her power is more...
...limited to controlling others!
YEAH!
And...
...it only lasts until the bite marks fade!
POOF
Just give him a chance.

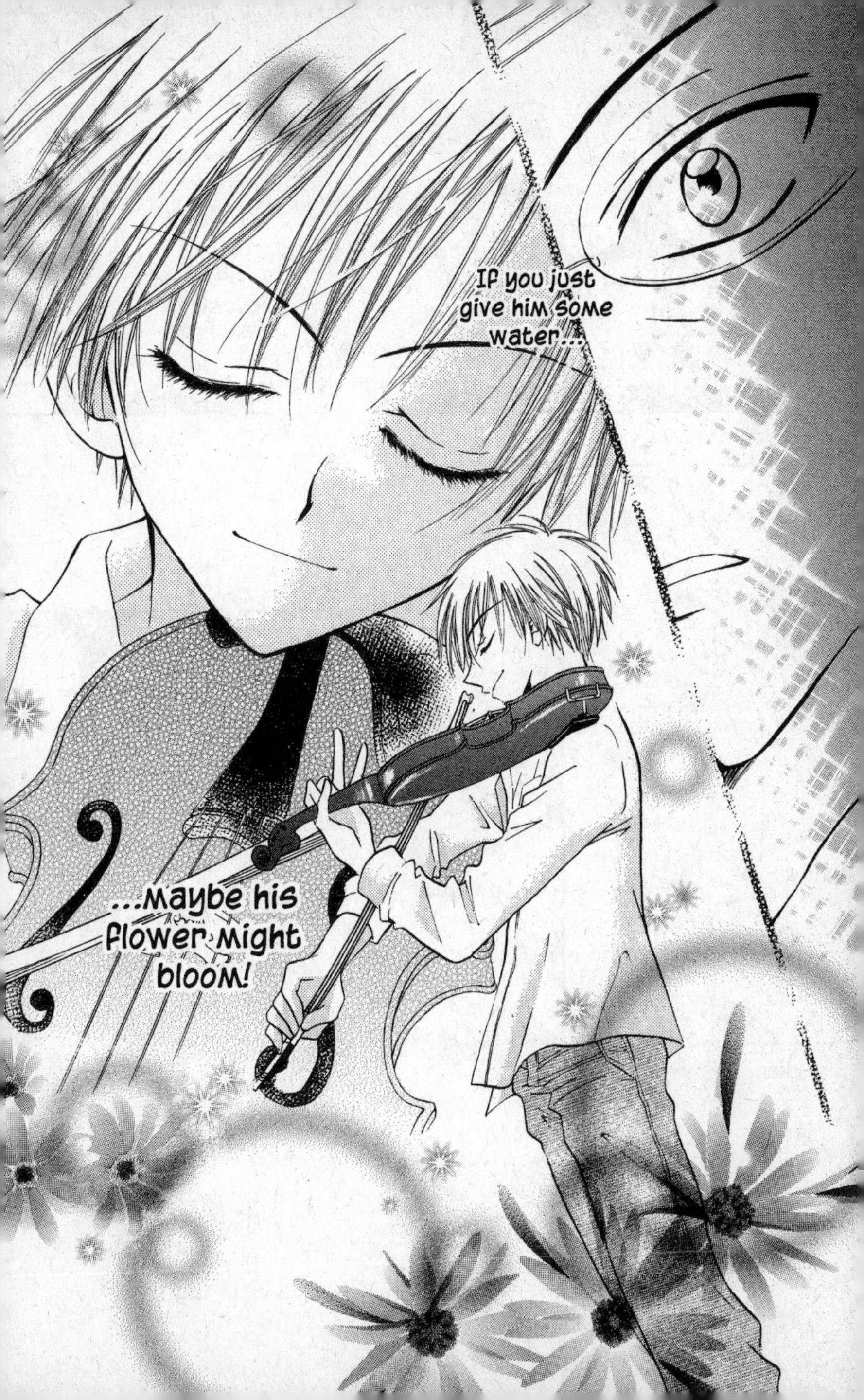
If you just give him some water...
...Maybe his flower might bloom!

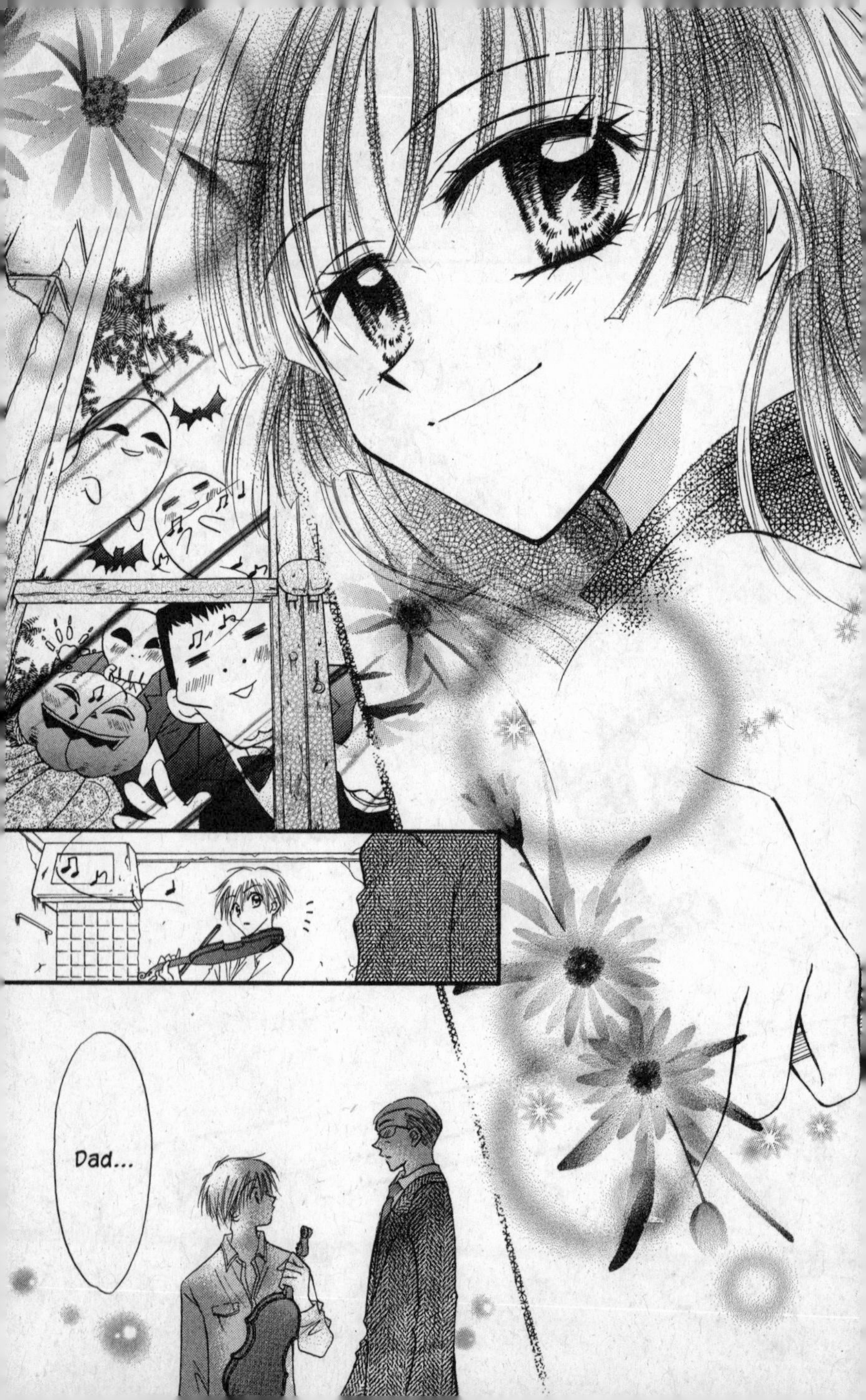
Dad...

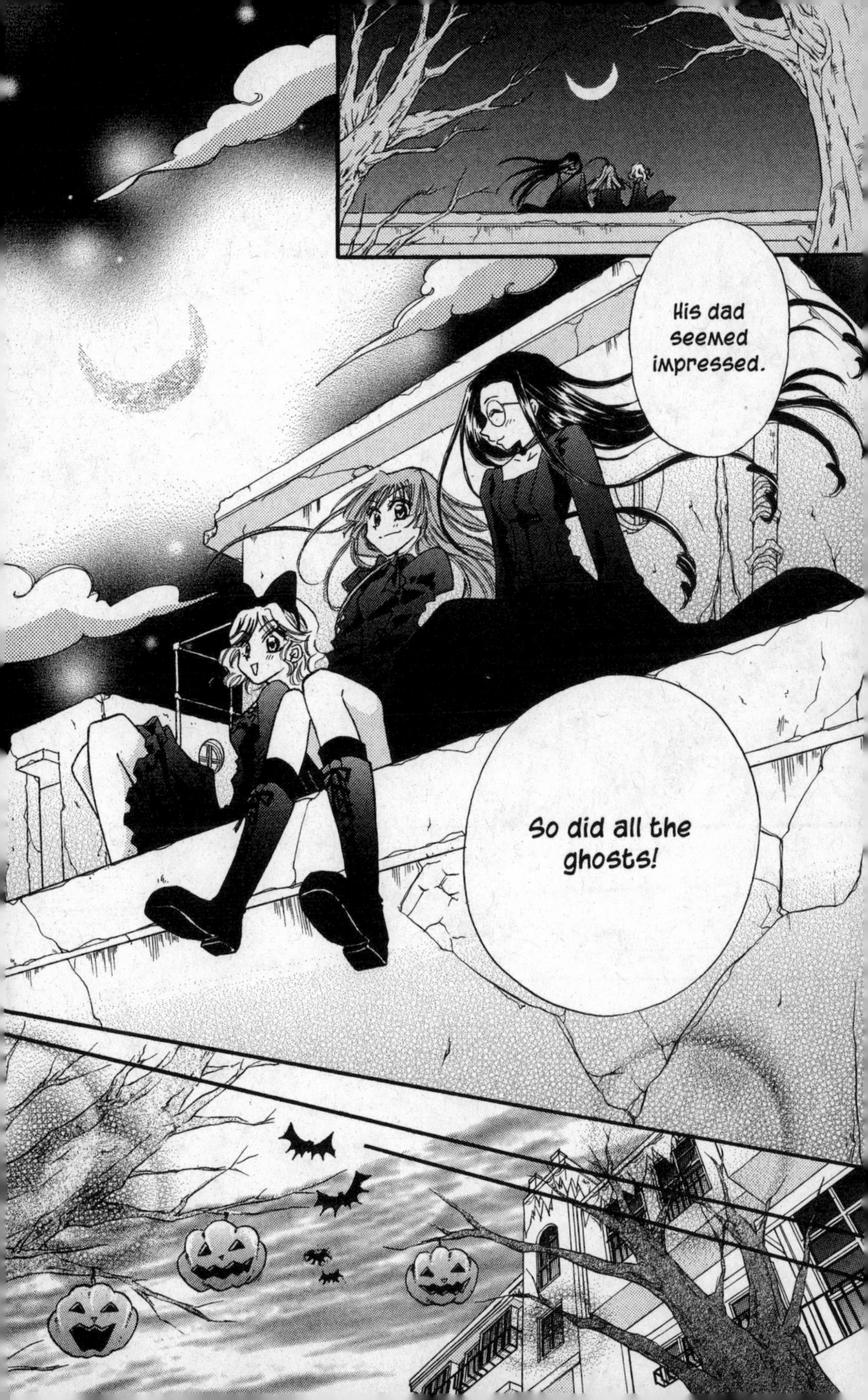
His dad seemed impressed.
So did all the ghosts!

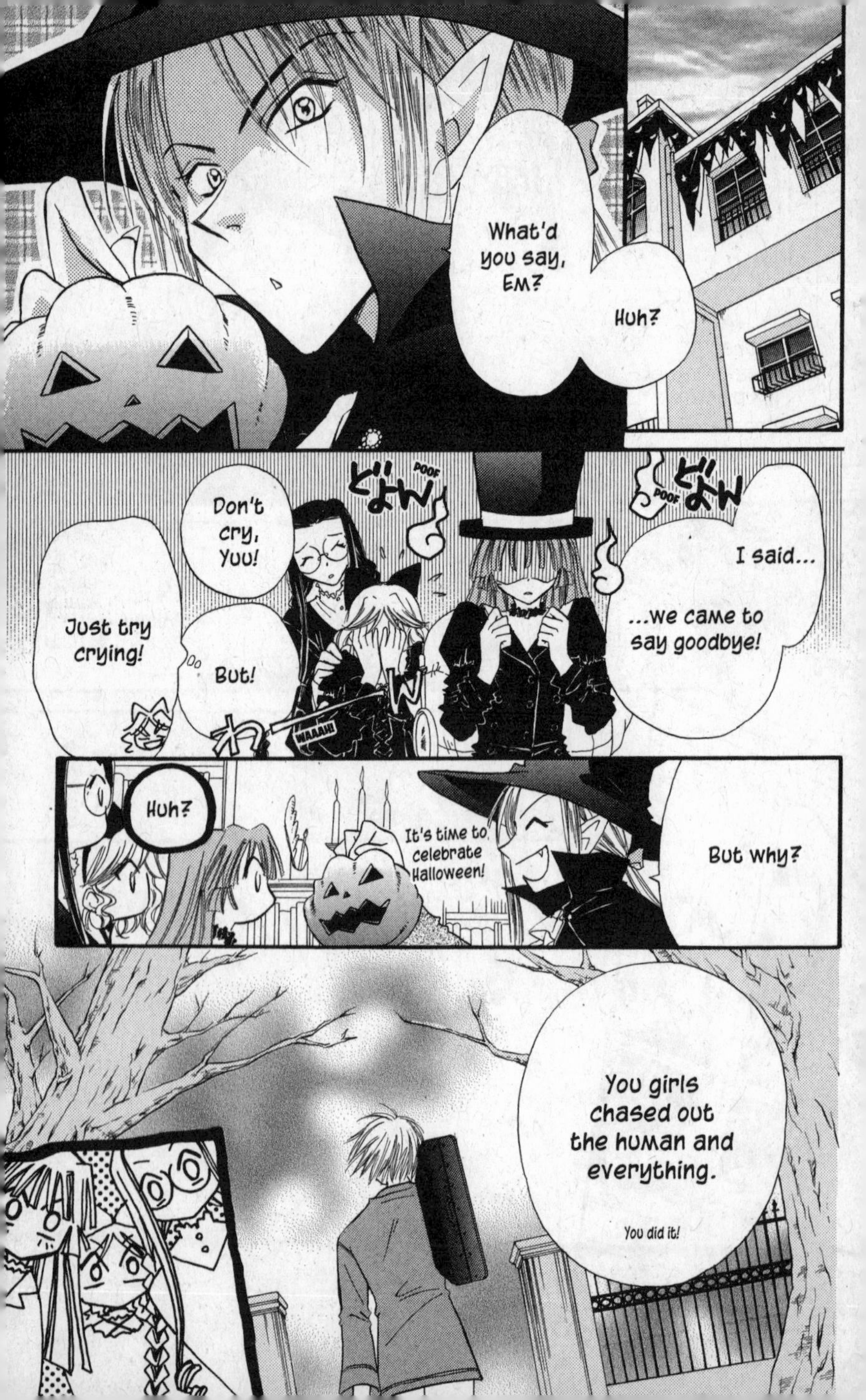

What'd you say, Em?
Huh?
POOF
I said...
...we came to say goodbye!
POOF
Don't cry, Yuu!
WAAAH!
But!
Just try crying!
But why?
It's time to celebrate Halloween!
Huh?
You girls chased out the human and everything.
You did it!

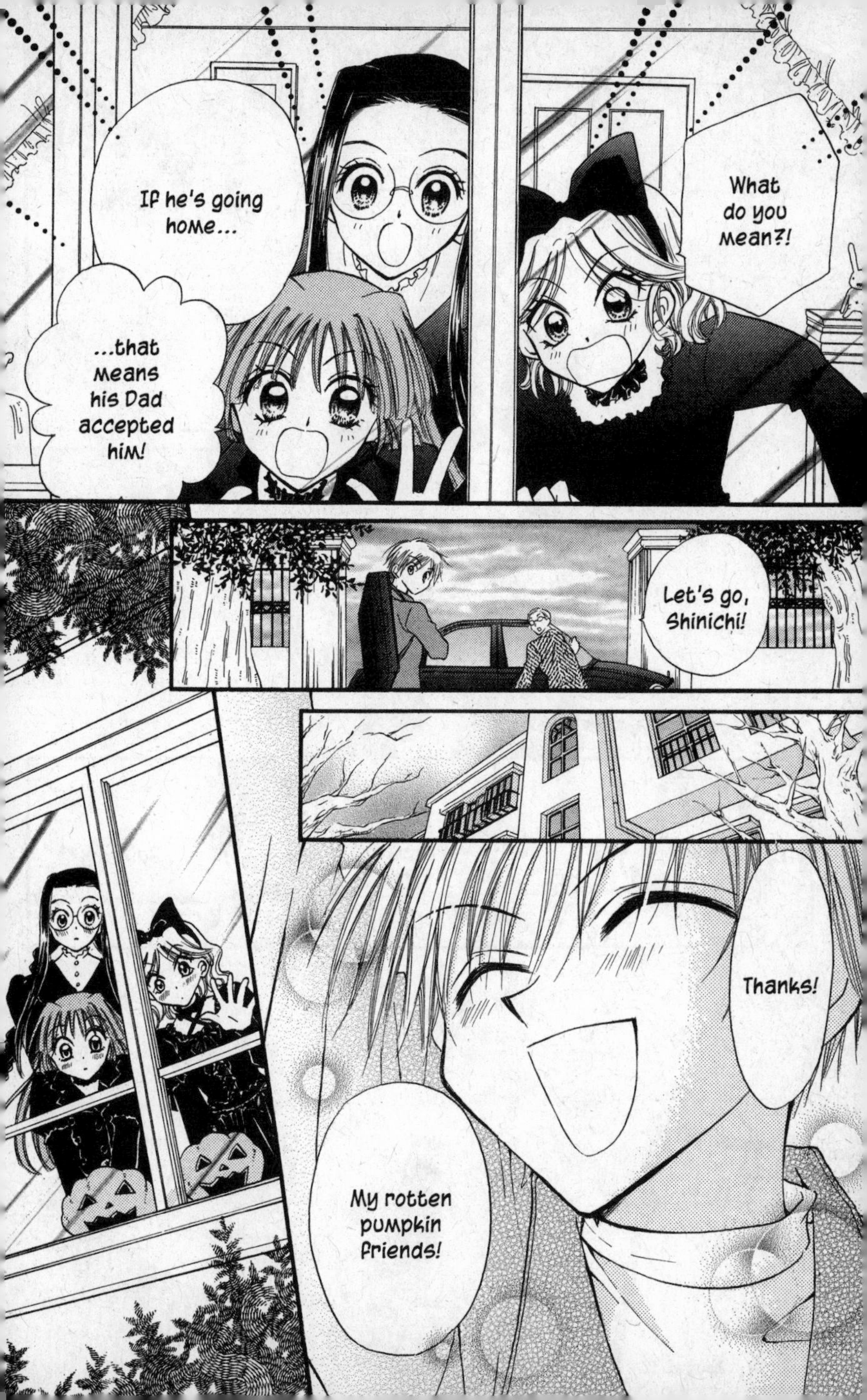
What do you mean?!
If he's going home...
...that means his Dad accepted him!
Let's go, Shinichi!
Thanks!
My rotten pumpkin friends!

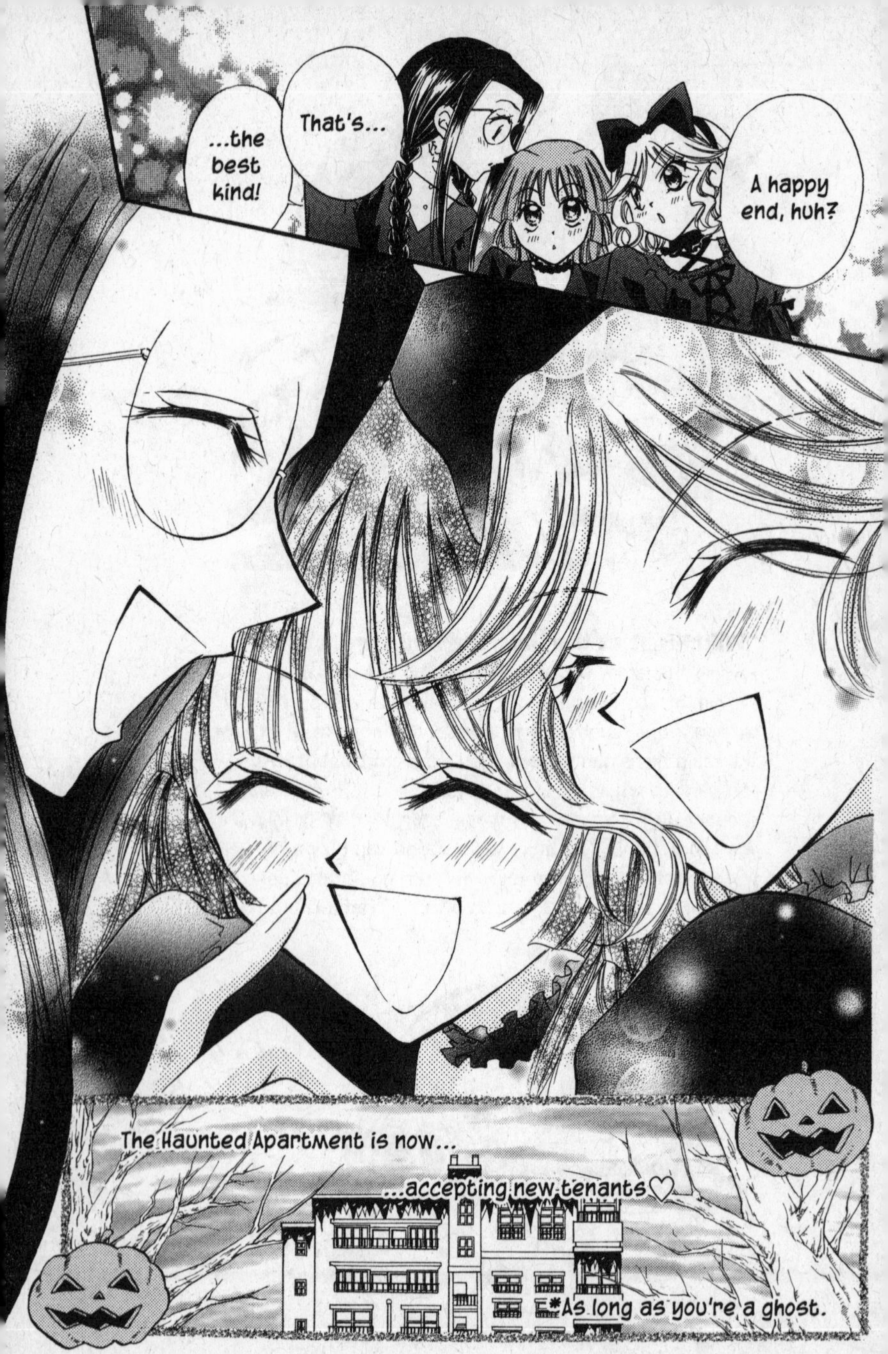
A happy end, huh?
That's...
...the best kind!
The Haunted Apartment is now...
...accepting new tenants♡
*As long as you're a ghost.

★★The end★★

"Wild Night at the Haunted Apartment"

I wrote this story because this volume comes out in November, so I wanted to try a Halloween story. I haven't written a one-shot story in a while, so I enjoyed it. At first the main girl's names were Elle, Em, and En, but it was too hard to tell them apart, so I changed it. My assistant thought up the name for the manager, Kyu! ✱ Thanks for the suggestion! ♡ I admire anyone who can play a musical instrument. I decided to make the setting an abandoned apartment building. ♪ I figured a lot of drama could happen there!

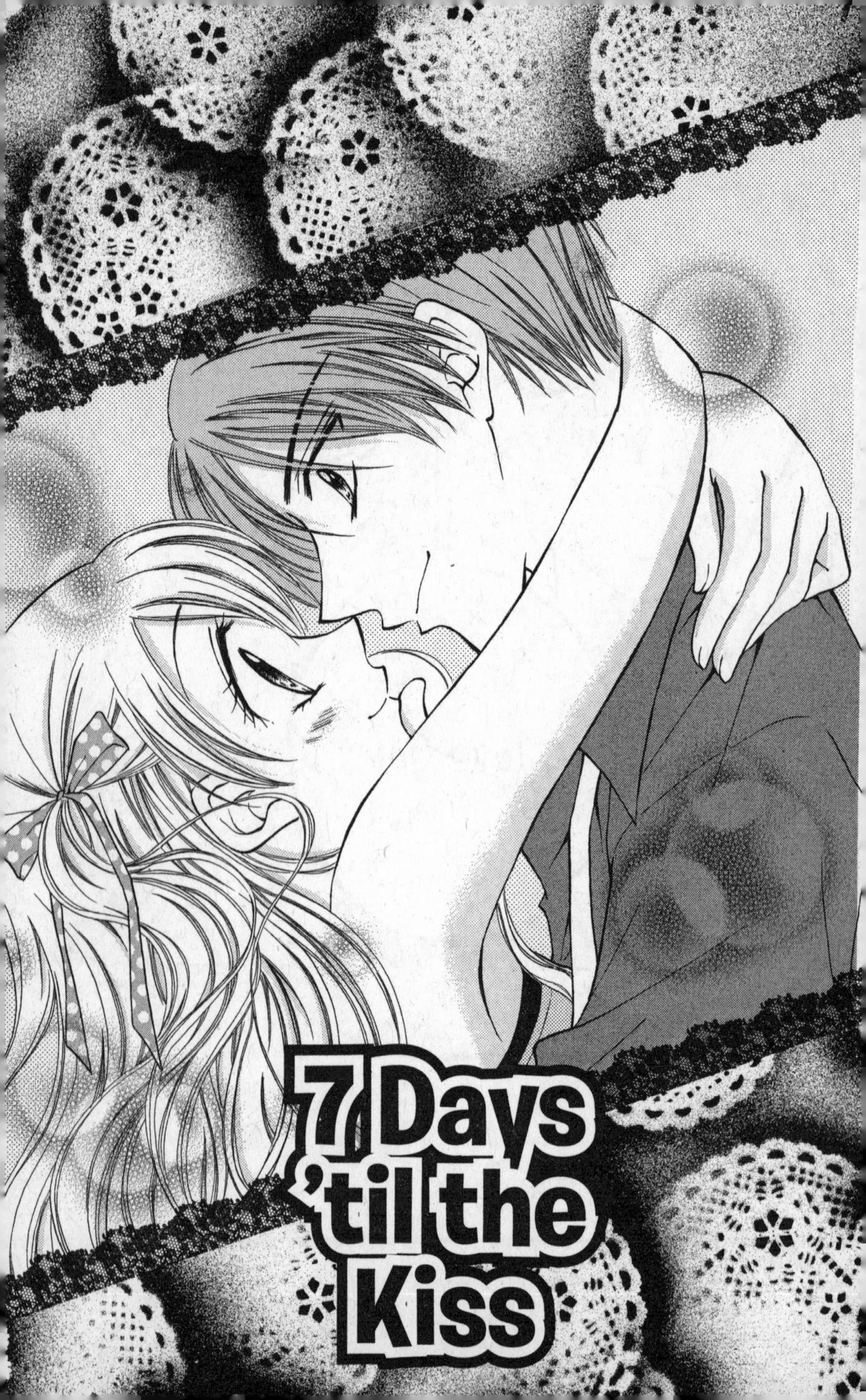
7 Days
'til the
Kiss

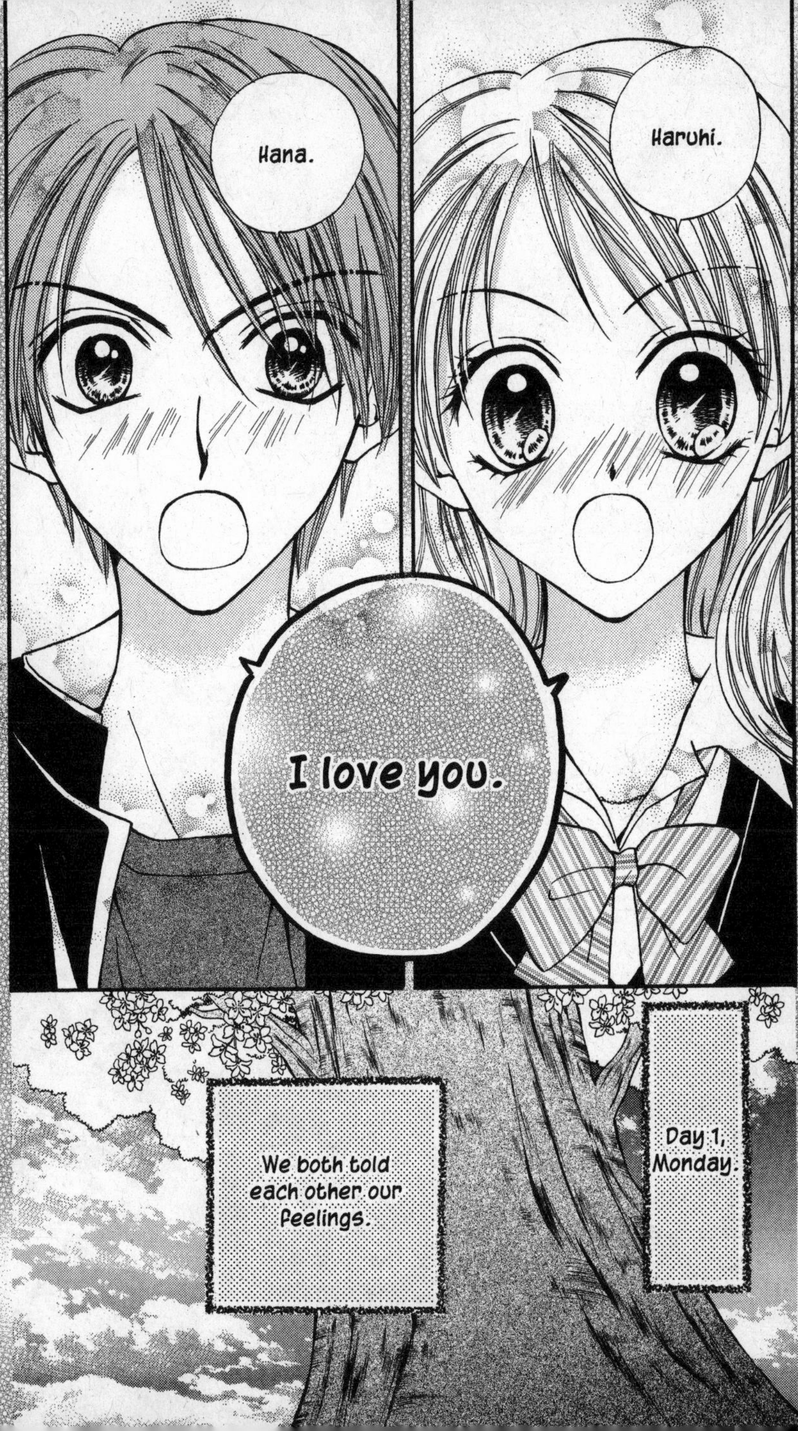
Haruhi.
Hana.
I love you.
Day 1, Monday.
We both told each other our feelings.

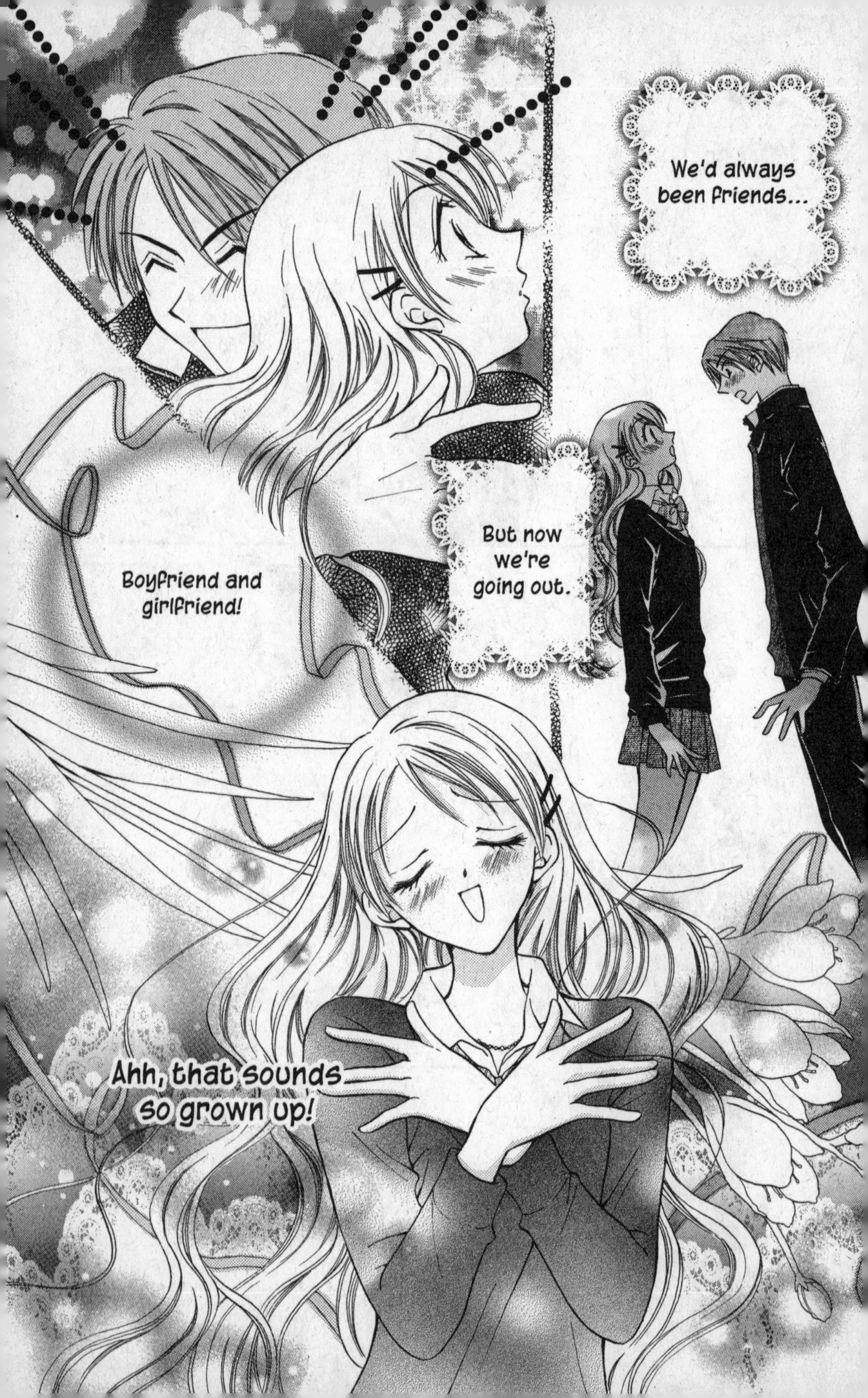
We'd always been friends...
But now we're going out.
Boyfriend and girlfriend!
Ahh, that sounds so grown up!

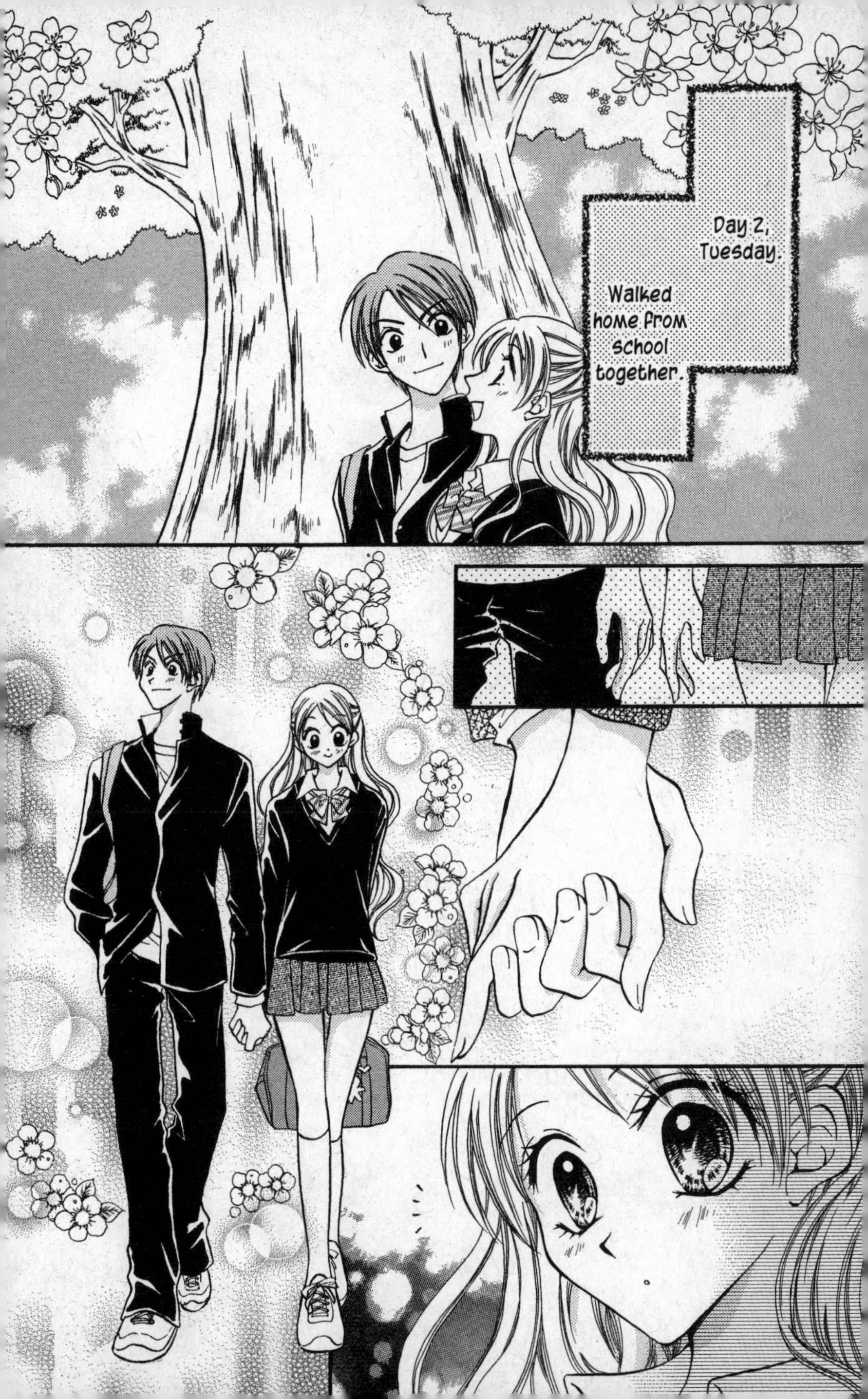
Day 2, Tuesday:
Walked home from school together.

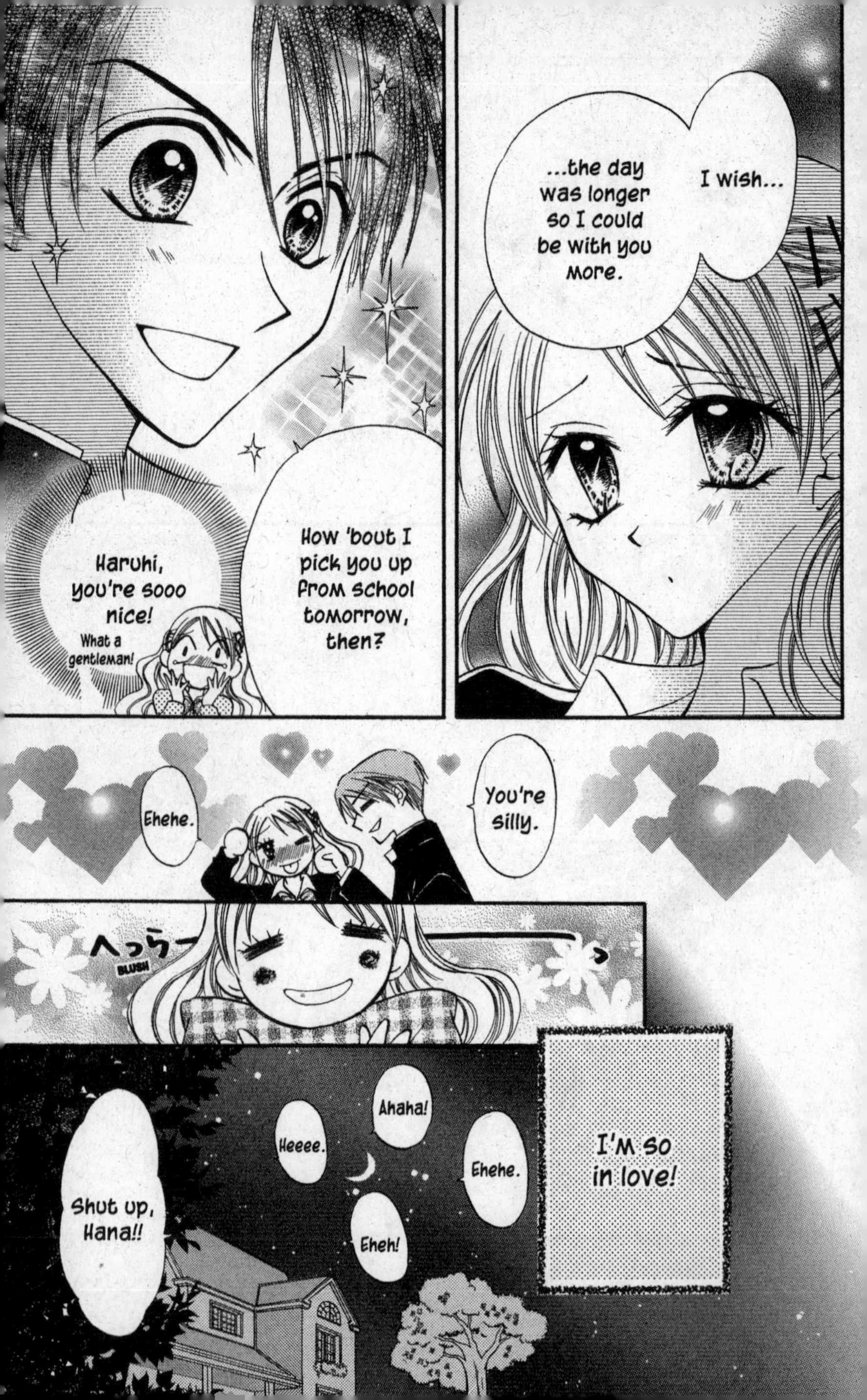
I wish...
...the day was longer so I could be with you more.
How 'bout I pick you up from school tomorrow, then?
Haruhi, you're sooo nice!
What a gentleman!
You're silly.
Ehehe.
へっらー
BLUSH
I'm so in love!
Ahaha!
Ehehe.
Heeee.
Eheh!
Shut up, Hana!!

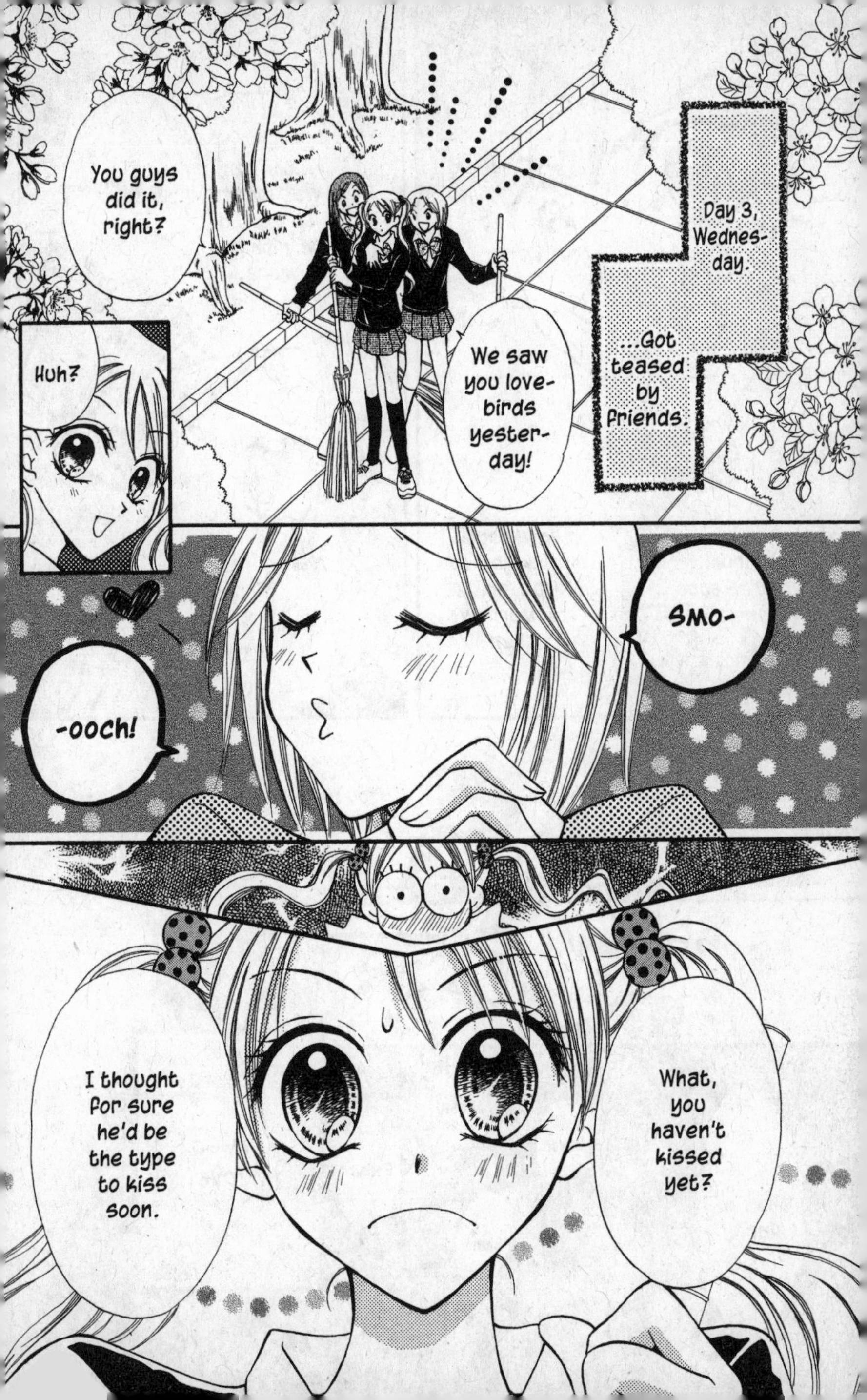

Day 3, Wednesday.
...Got teased by friends.
We saw you lovebirds yesterday!
You guys did it, right?
Huh?
Smo-
-ooch!
What, you haven't kissed yet?
I thought for sure he'd be the type to kiss soon.

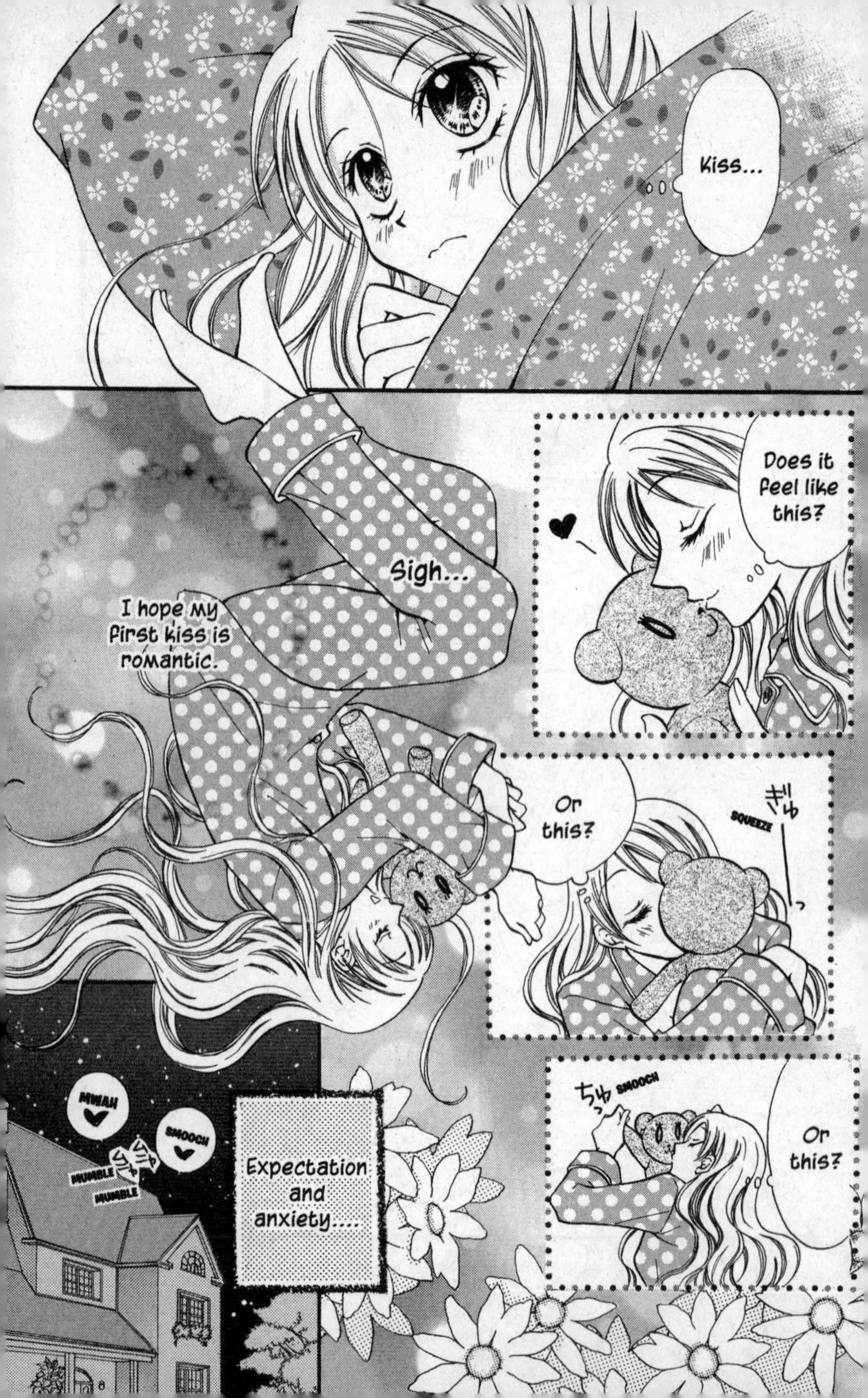
Kiss...
Does it feel like this?
Or this?
ぎゅ
SQUEEZE
Or this?
ちゅ
SMOOCH
Sigh...
I hope my first kiss is romantic.
Expectation and anxiety....
MWAH
SMOOCH
MUMBLE
MUMBLE

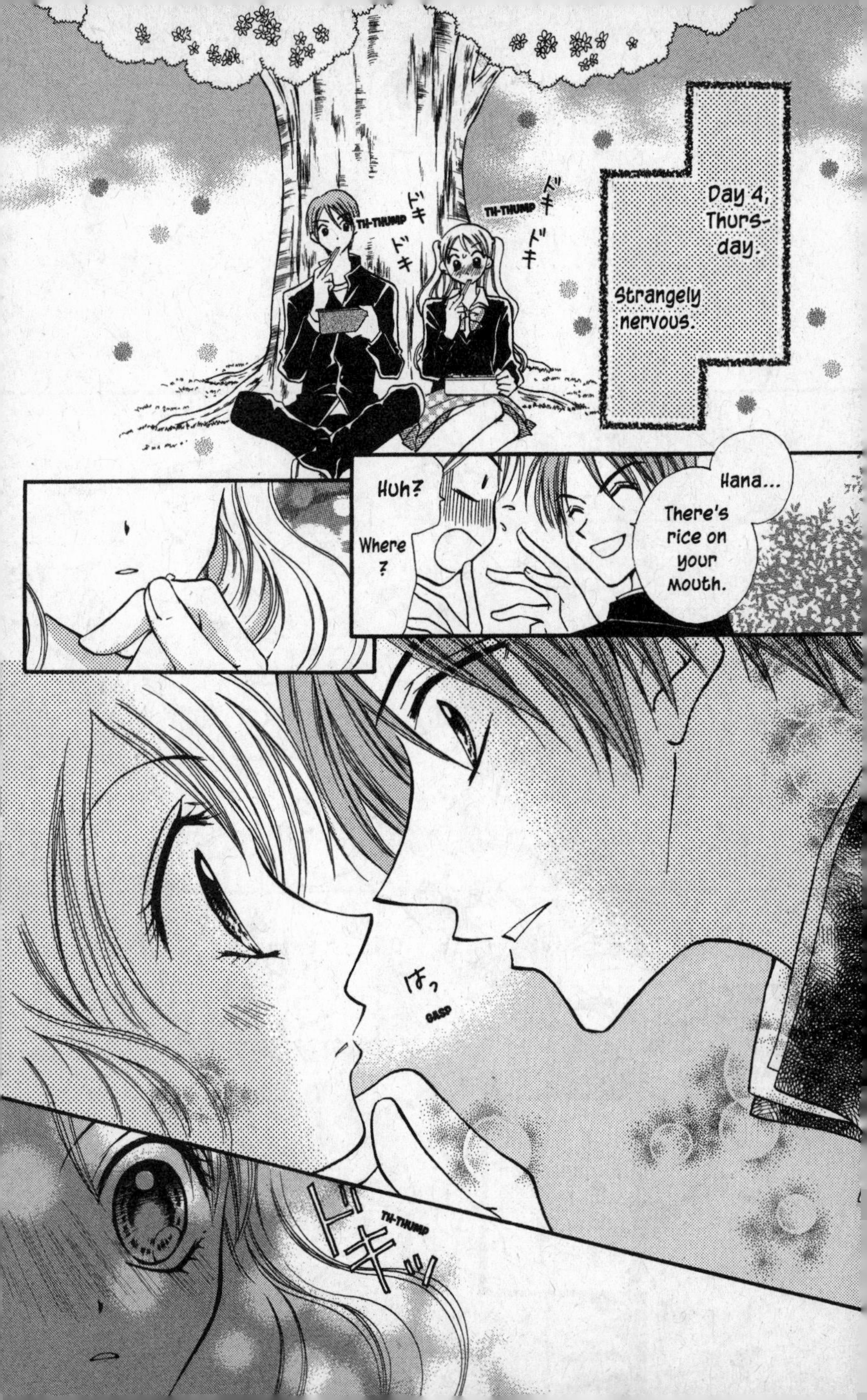
Day 4, Thurs-day.
Strangely nervous.
ドキドキ
TH-THUMP
ドキドキ
TH-THUMP
Hana...
There's rice on your mouth.
Huh?
Where?
はっ
GASP
ドキッ
TH-THUMP

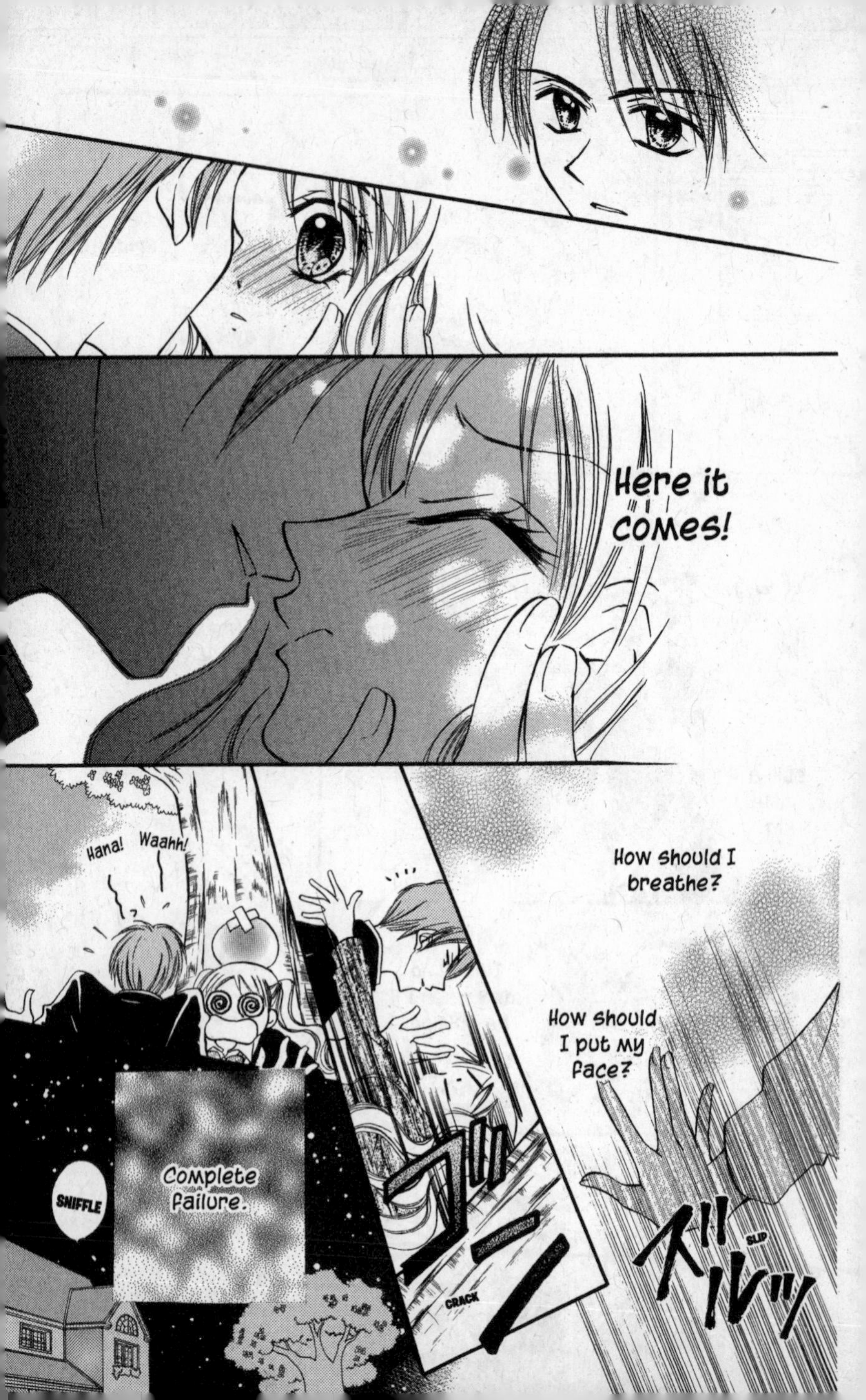
Here it comes!
How should I breathe?
How should I put my face?
SLIP
CRACK
Waahh!
Hana!
Complete failure.
SNIFFLE

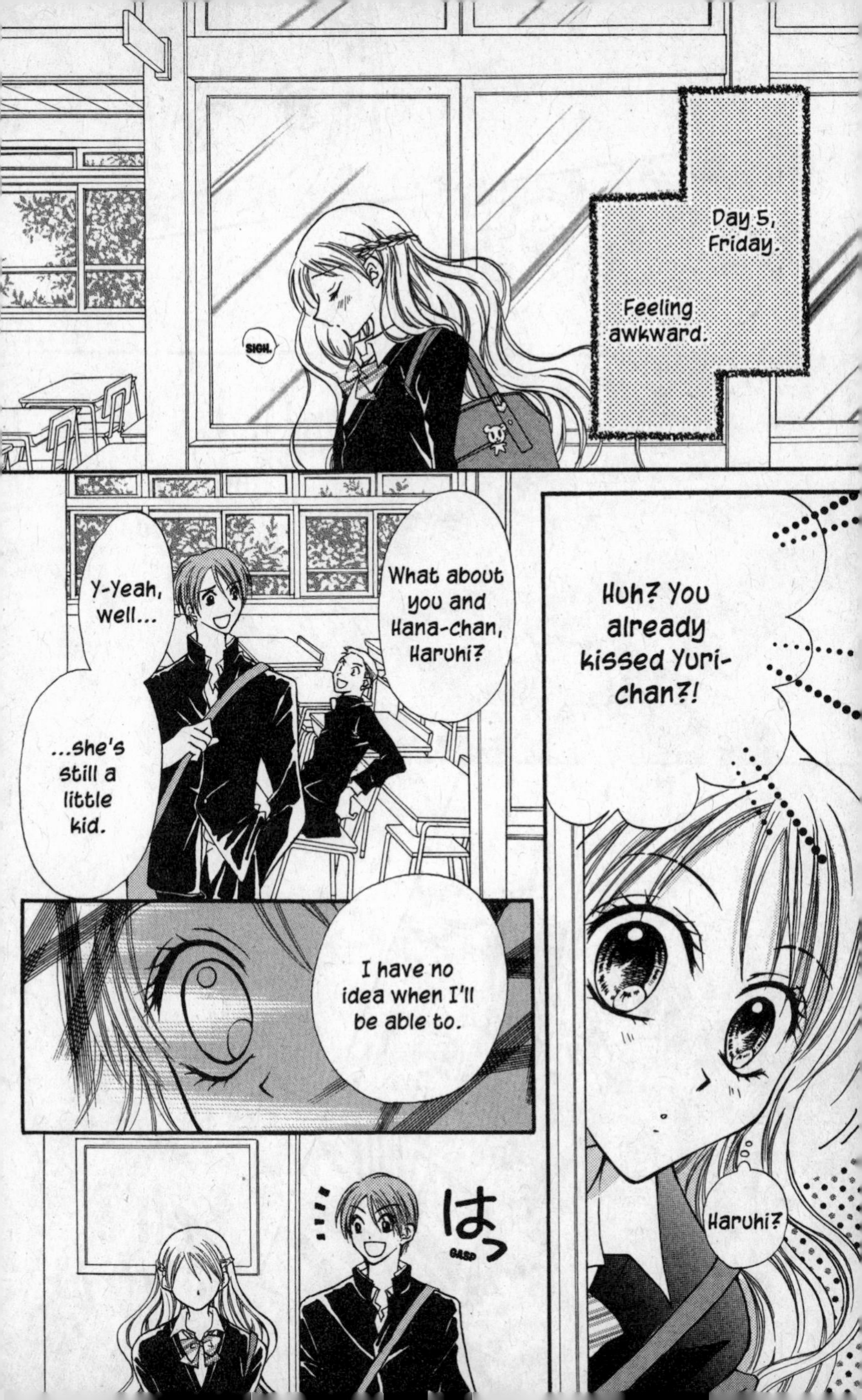
Day 5, Friday.
Feeling awkward.
SIGH.
Huh? You already kissed Yuri-chan?!
Haruhi?
What about you and Hana-chan, Haruhi?
Y-Yeah, well...
...she's still a little kid.
I have no idea when I'll be able to.
はっ
GASP

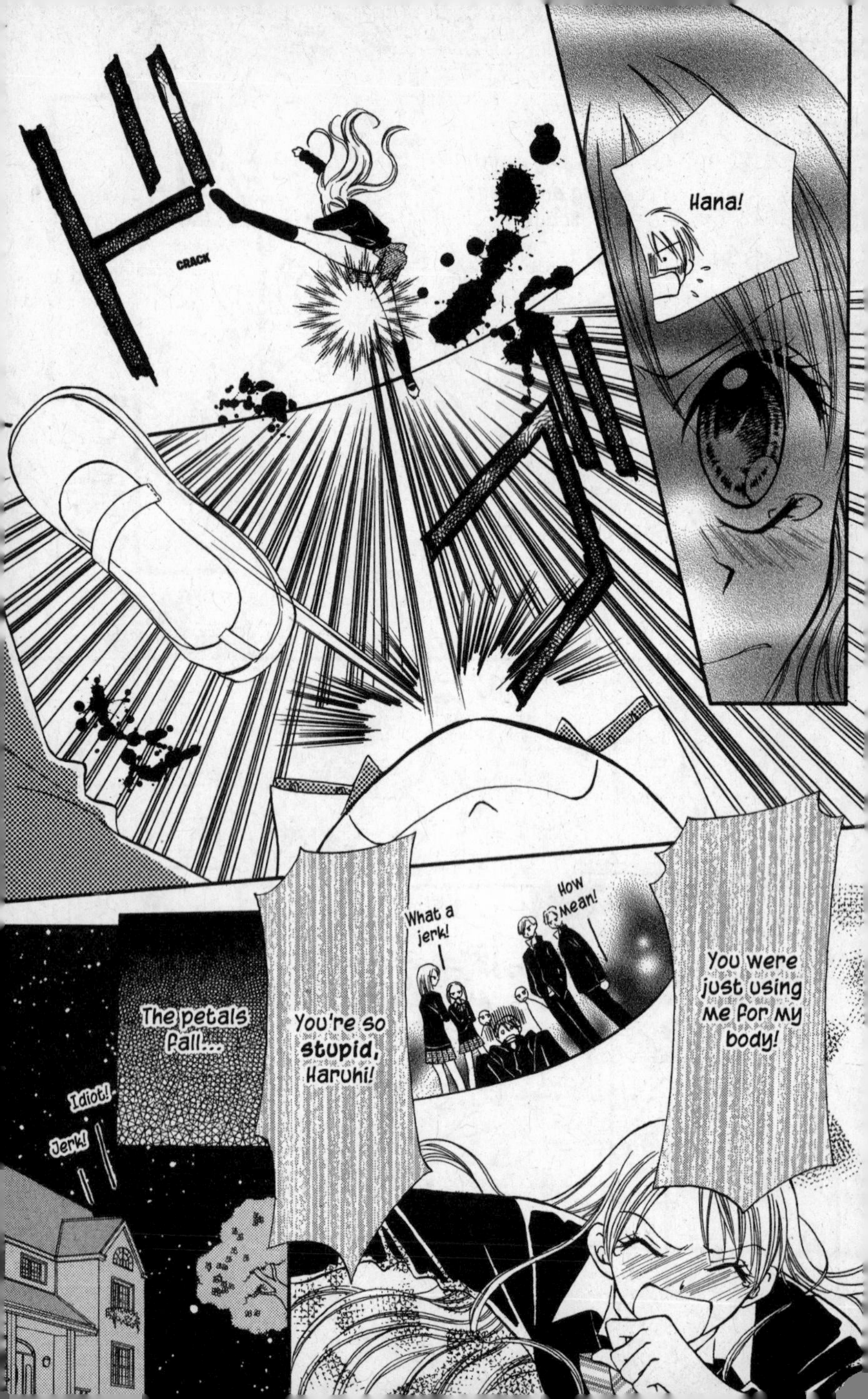
Hana!
CRACK
You were just using me for my body!
How mean!
What a jerk!
You're so stupid, Haruhi!
The petals fall...
Idiot!
Jerk!

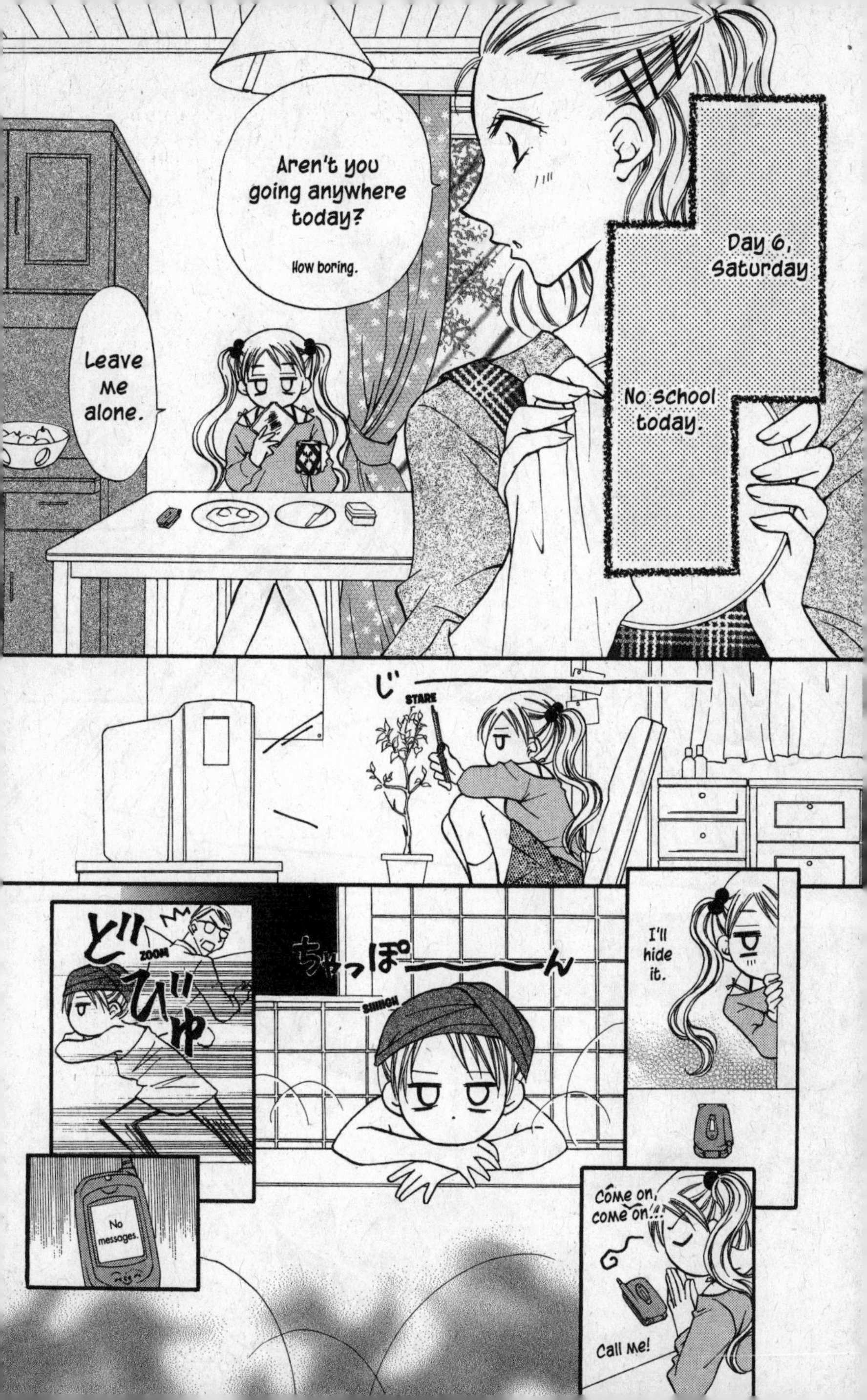
Day 6, Saturday
No school today.
Aren't you going anywhere today?
How boring.
Leave me alone.
じ——
STARE
I'll hide it.
Come on, come on!!
Call me!
ちゃっぽ——ん
どひゅ
ZOOM
No messages.

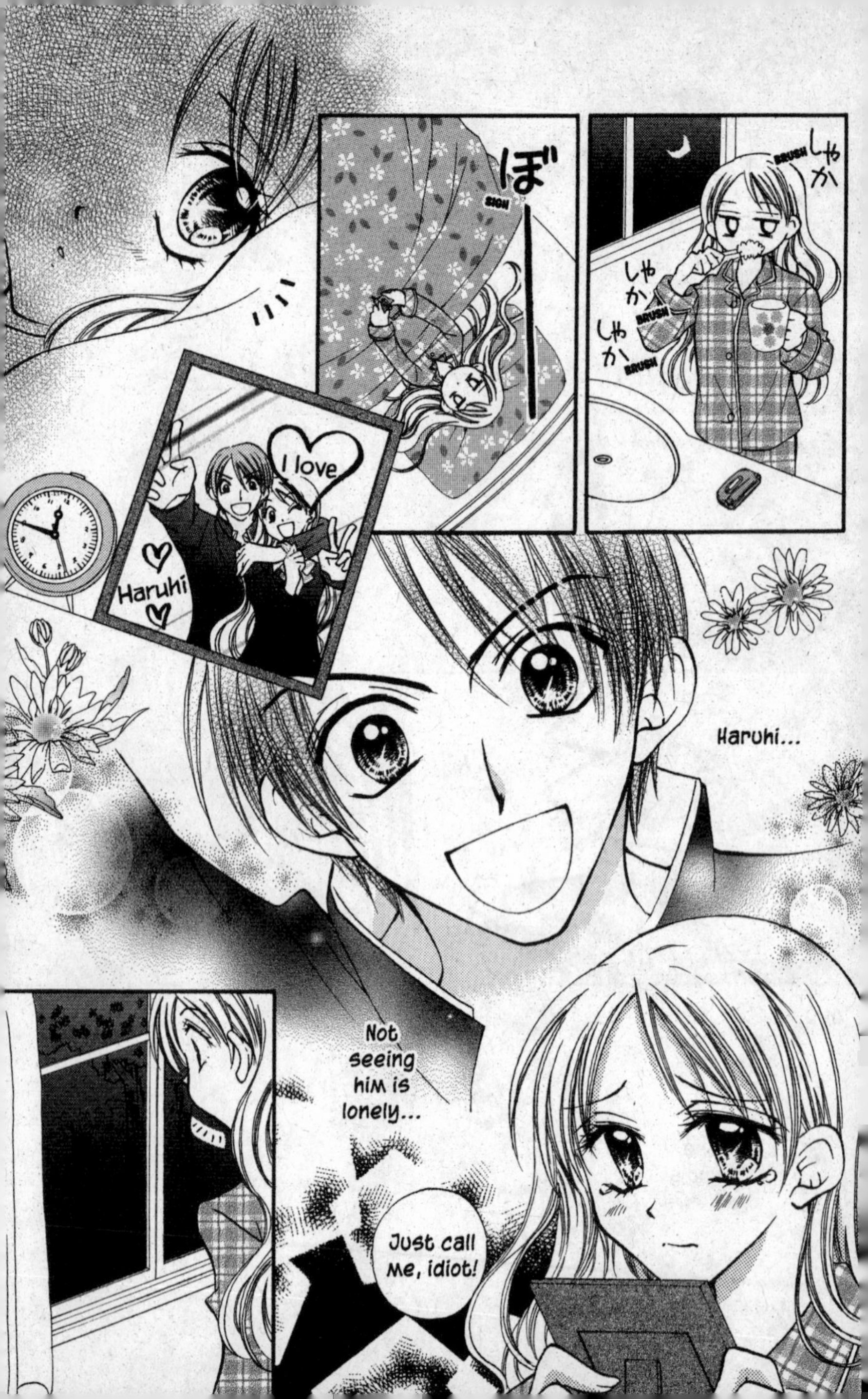
しゃか
BRUSH
しゃか
BRUSH
しゃか
BRUSH
ぼー
SIGH
I love
Haruhi
Haruhi...
Not seeing him is lonely...
Just call me, idiot!

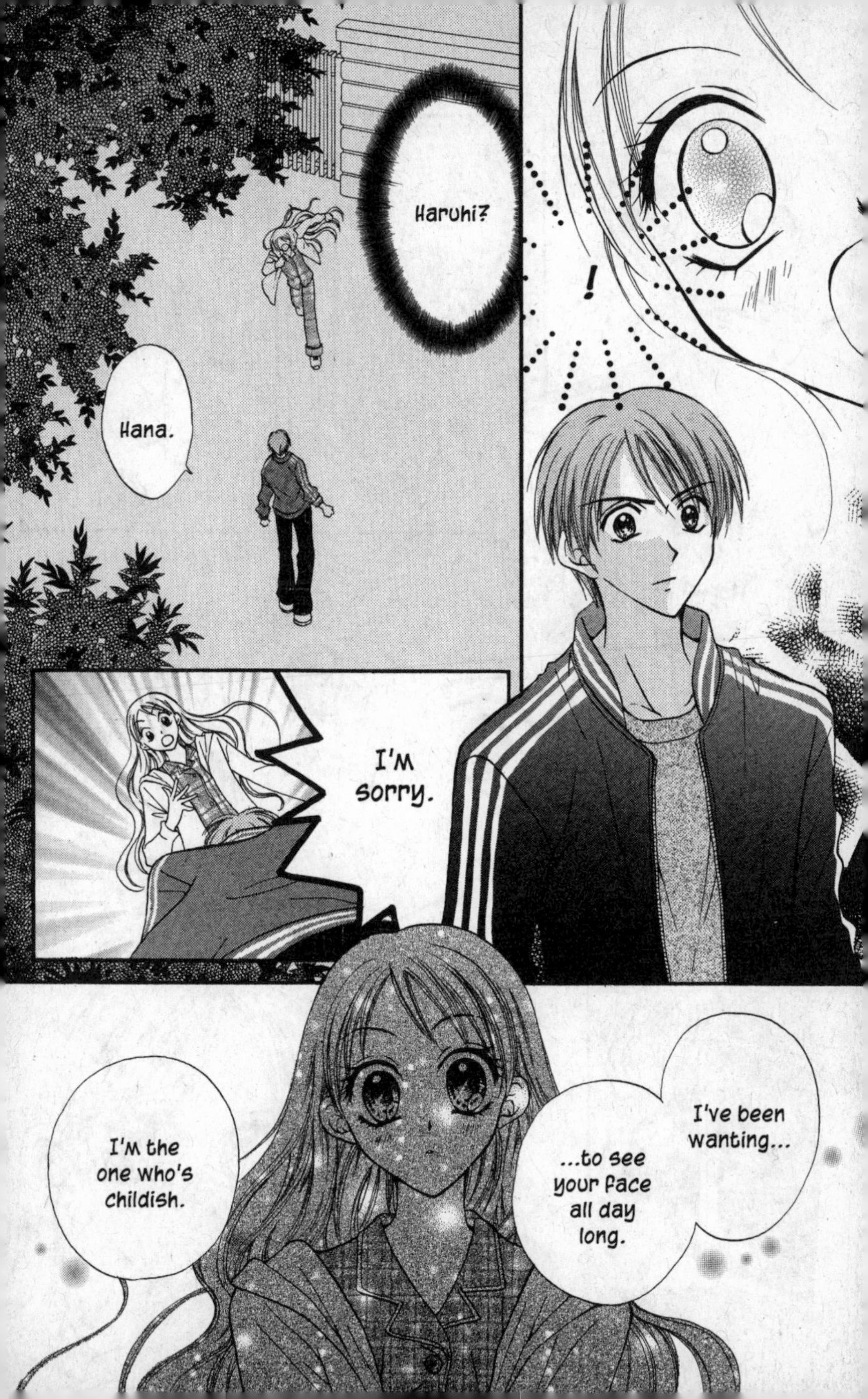
!
Haruhi?
Hana.
I'M sorry.
I've been wanting...
...to see your face all day long.
I'M the one who's childish.

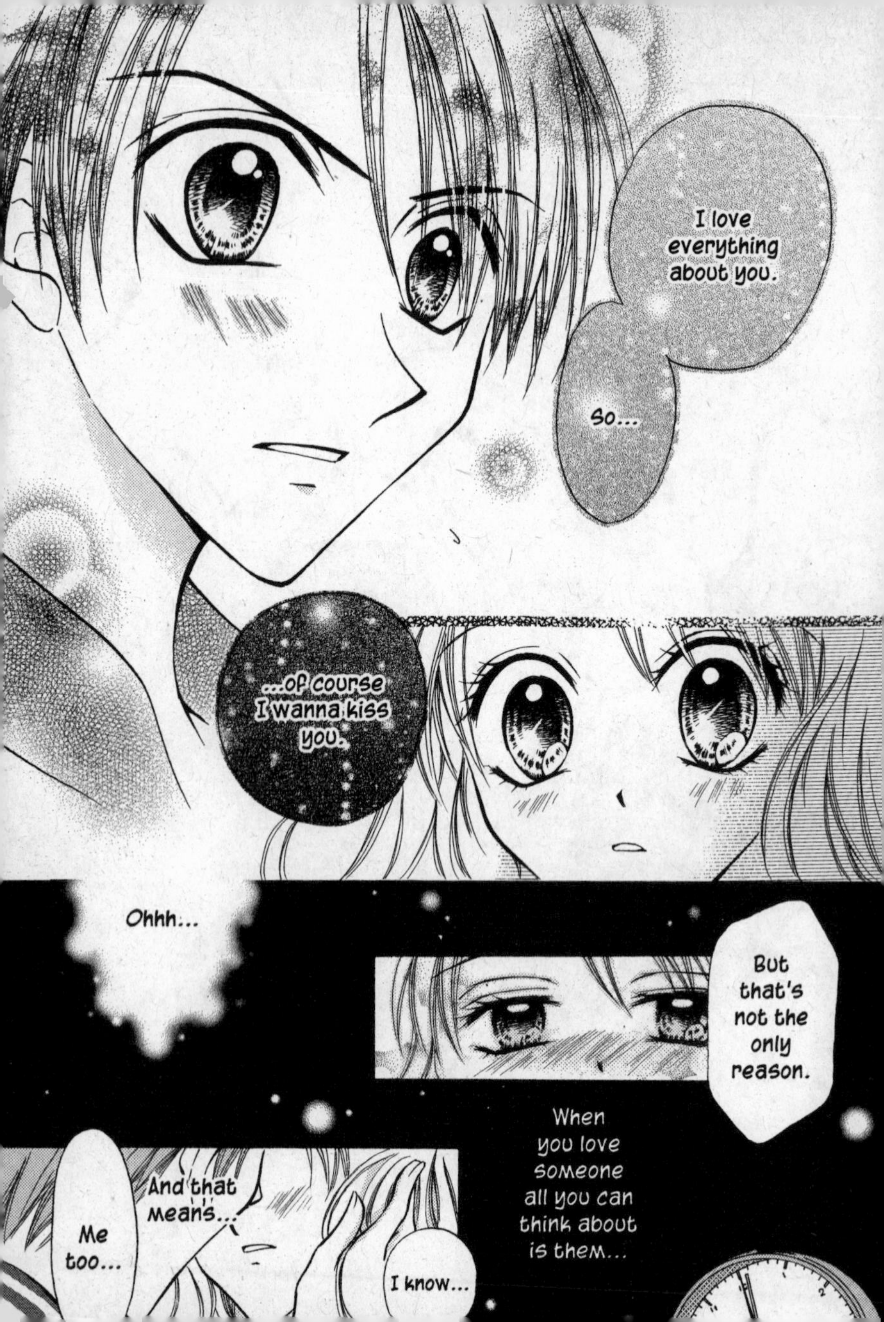
I love everything about you.
So...
...of course I wanna kiss you.
But that's not the only reason.
Ohhh...
When you love someone all you can think about is them...
I know...
And that means...
Me too...

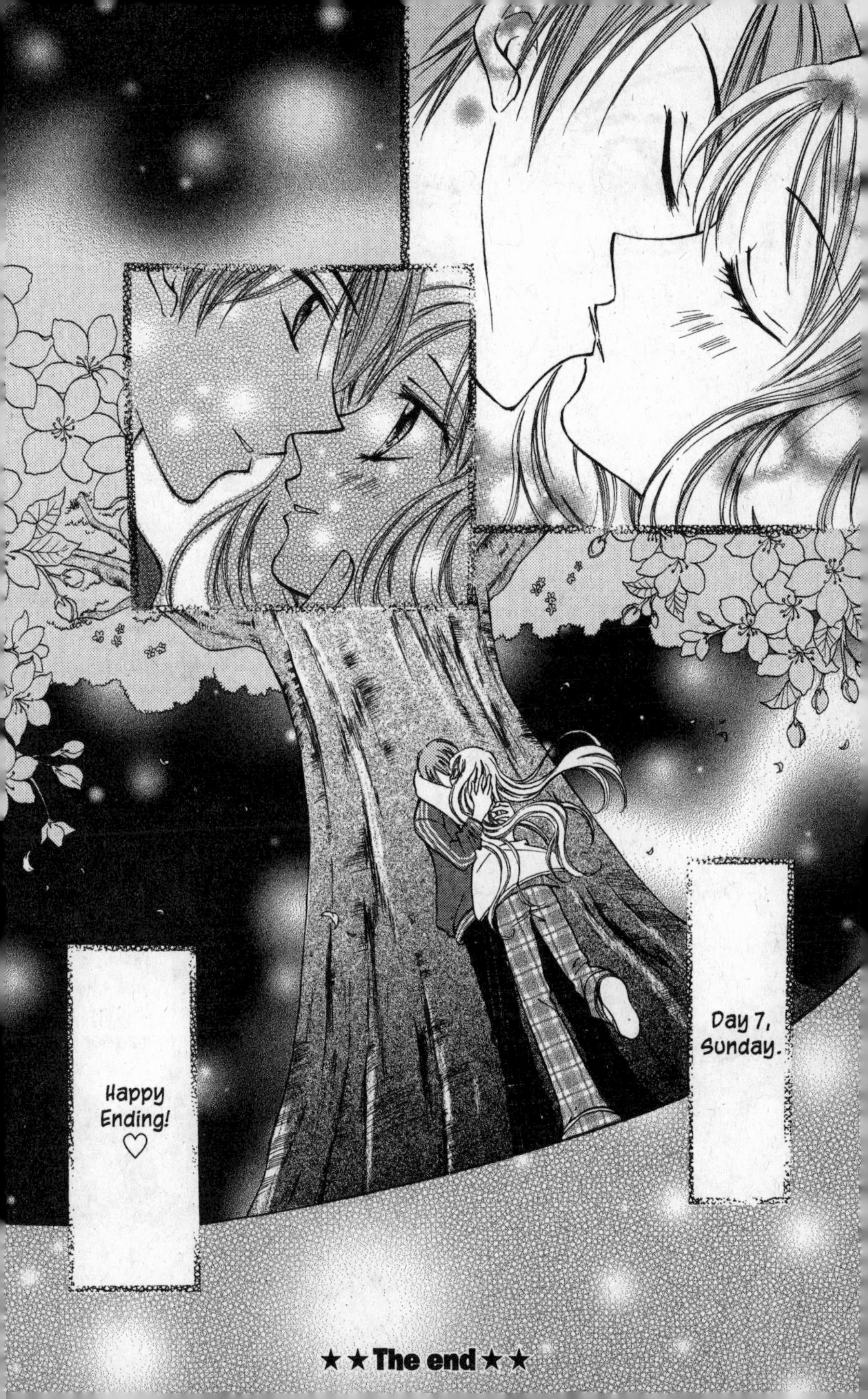
Day 7, Sunday.
Happy Ending! ♡
★★The end★★

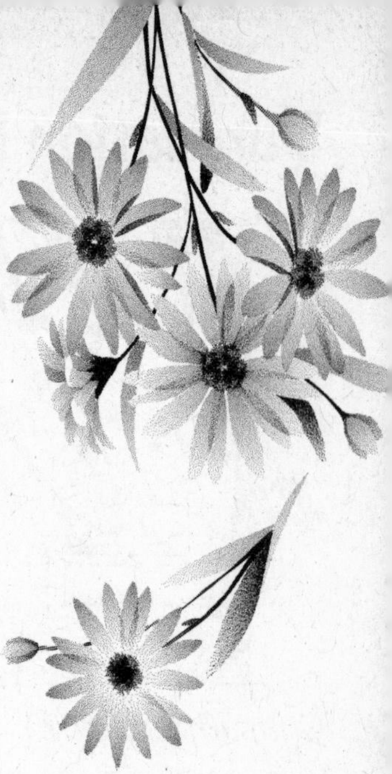

7 Days 'til the Kiss

I wrote this with the theme of "kiss" in mind. I've always wanted to draw a heroine with long hair, but it took a really long time to draw Hana's! This story was originally printed in the spring so there are a lot of cherry blossoms. After that I went to go see them in person!! I wanted to see them at night so I went to the local park, but there were no lights on so it was pitch black! ✱

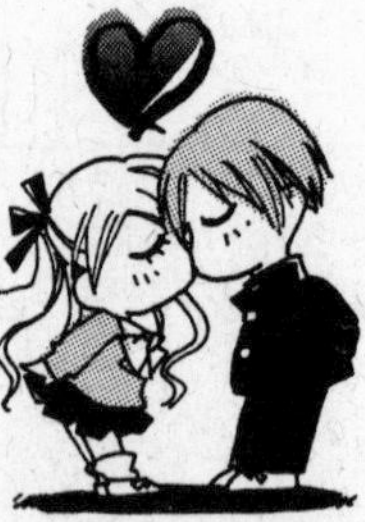

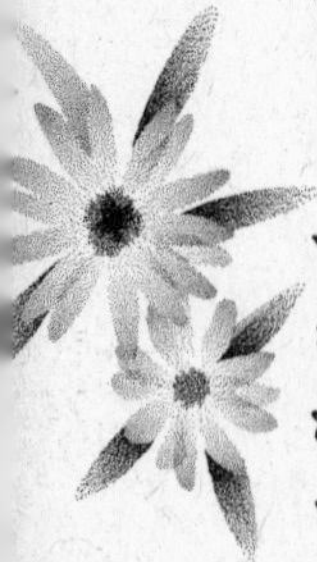

Thank-yous

✱ Maruyama-sama ✱

✱ Shobayashi-sama ✱

✱ Komiya-sama ✱

✱ Kishimoto-sama ✱

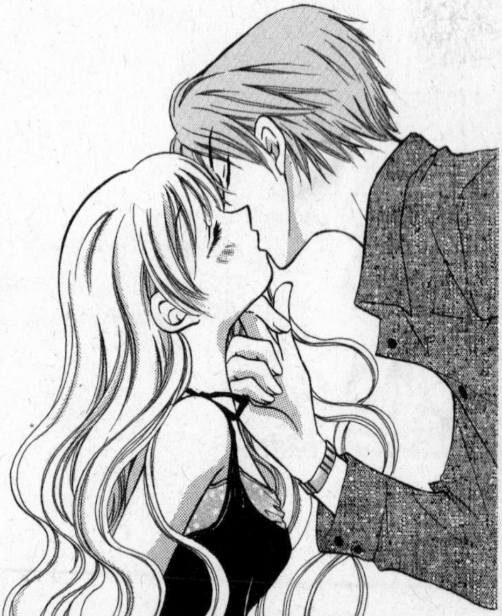

And thanks to all my readers!

See you next time!

Natsumi Ando

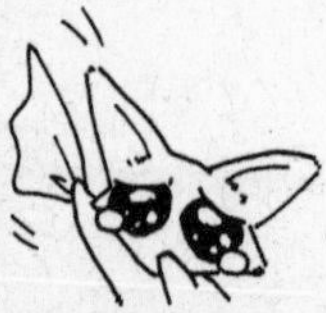

Translation Notes

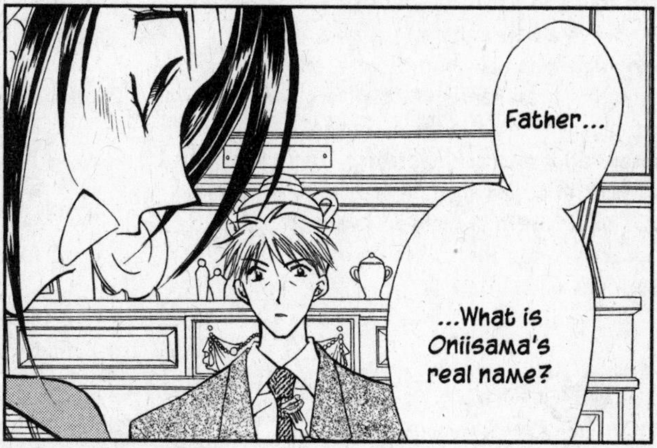
Father...
...What is Oniisama's real name?

Oniisama, page 23

Literally means "older brother," but has a higher degree of respect with the -sama honorific attached.

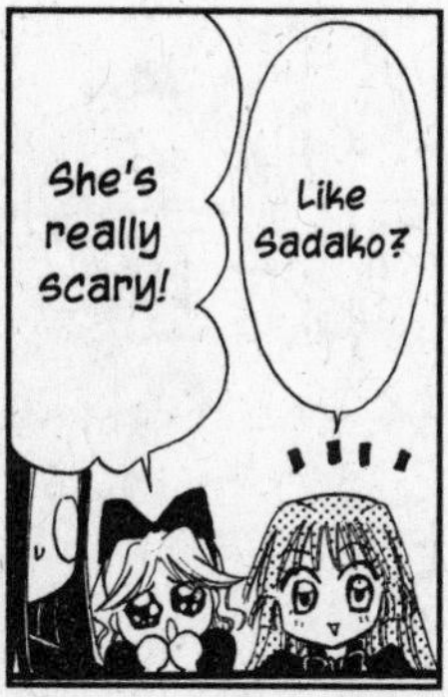
Like Sadako?
She's really scary!

Sadako, page 133

Sadako is the antagonist in Koji Suzaku's novel *Ring*, which was adapted to a movie in 1998.

KITCHEN PRINCESS

STORY BY MIYUKI KOBAYASHI
MANGA BY NATSUMI ANDO
CREATOR OF ZODIAC P.I.

HUNGRY HEART

Najika is a great cook and likes to make meals for the people she loves. But something is missing from her life. When she was a child, she met a boy who touched her heart—and now Najika is determined to find him. The only clue she has is a silver spoon that leads her to the prestigious Seika Academy.

Attending Seika will be a challenge. Every kid at the school has a special talent, and the girls in Najika's class think she doesn't deserve to be there. But Sora and Daichi, two popular brothers who barely speak to each other, recognize Najika's cooking for what it is—magical. Could one of the boys be Najika's mysterious prince?

Special extras in each volume! Read them all!

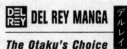

TOMARE!
[STOP!]

You are going the wrong way!

Manga is a completely different type of reading experience.

To start at the *beginning*, go to the *end*!

That's right! Authentic manga is read the traditional Japanese way—from right to left, exactly the *opposite* of how American books are read. It's easy to follow: Just go to the other end of the book, and read each page—and each panel—from right side to left side, starting at the top right. Now you're experiencing manga as it was meant to be.